S0-DTR-013

WOMEN IN CONTEXT

WOMEN IN CONTEXT

Two Hundred Years
of British Women Autobiographers
A Reference Guide and Reader

Barbara Penny Kanner
with the assistance of
Jane Decker, Penelope Moffet, Anne-Marie Poole,
Margaret Robe Summitt, and Rhona Zaid

G.K. Hall & Co.
An Imprint of Simon & Schuster Macmillan
New York

Prentice Hall Hall International
London Mexico City New Delhi Singapore Sydney Toronto

G. K. Hall & Co.
An Imprint of Simon & Schuster Macmillan
1633 Broadway
New York, NY 10019

Library of Congress Cataloging-in-Publication Data
Kanner, Barbara.
Women in context : two hundred years of British women autobiographers, a reference guide and reader / Barbara Penny Kanner.
p. cm.
Includes bibliographical references and indexes.
ISBN 0-8161-7346-X
1. Women—Great Britain—Biography—Bibliography. 2. Women—Great Britain—History—Sources—Bibliography. 3. Autobiography—Women authors—Bibliography. I. Title.
Z7963.B6K35 1997
[HQ1593.A3]
016.3054'0942—dc21 96-29645
CIP

Printed in the United States of America

Printing Number

1 2 3 4 5 6 7 8 9 10

Contents

Acknowledgments

I deeply appreciate the sponsorship and encouragement of *Women in Context* by the UCLA Center for the Study of Women, where I have held a faculty-level appointment as continuing research scholar throughout the life of this project. I must thank especially Lena Astin, Karen Rowe, Millie Loeb, Kate Norberg, Dawn Waring, and Sandra Harding for their support. I am also grateful to the faculty of the UCLA Department of History, particularly Dar Sardesi, Hans Rogger, Muriel Maclendon, Ron Mellor, and Peter Reill for the appointments I have received, both as visiting associate professor and as research scholar, intermittently throughout the term of project development.

The UCLA Research Library, with its remarkable collections, research facilities, and interlibrary loan department, has been very generous with its excellent technical support and with its continuing interest in serving the project's needs.

I acknowledge the invaluable network of support from Stanford University, as well as Stanford's Institute for Research on Women and Gender for its role in the research phase of the autobiographical work I undertook with my codirector, Susan Bell, on "British Women's Autobiographies, 1750–1950." Barbara Gelpi of the Stanford English Department, who was our closest adviser, has my gratitude and admiration.

The National Endowment for the Humanities made the early research possible with the award of a seed grant. Both "British Women's Autobiographies" and *Women in Context* were exceedingly expensive projects to develop.

Student assistants for library and archival work in Los Angeles, 1991–96, have earned my deep appreciation, not only for their proficiency but also for their wholehearted commitment to *Women in Context*: Margaret Astin, Jerry Boak, Neil Coleman, Patricia Hanley, Sandy Holguin, Maia Irell, Erica Stephenson, Jaimie Stephenson, and Kevin Thomas were the most steadily employed.

Among colleagues upon whom I relied for substantial consultation, I must name Nupur Chaudhuri, Leonore Davidoff, David Doughan, Joyce Duncan Falk, Deborah Gorham, Dorothy Helly, Maryanne Horowitz, Mitzi Myers, Peter Stansky, Margaret Strobel, Ernest Toy, and Martha Vogeler.

I am also grateful for the computer consultation and other technical assistance of Eric Splaver, Wayne Kaufman, and Patty Kelner. Others who contributed to the project in various ways include Dr. Russell Denea, Lee Fox, Bruce Hochman, Chris and Isabella Summitt, Dr. Mark Thompson, and, most of all, Ed Kanner.

The following list represents outside readers who, during the research phase of the project in the years 1987 to 1989, answered questionnaires, giving their impressions of the autobiographies covered in *Women in Context.* However, none of the outside readers participated in writing entries.

Adrienne Adam
Nancy Fix Anderson
Elizabeth Sanders Arbuckle
Mildred Ash
Patrice Bailey
Susan Groag Bell
Gladys Bender
Joyce Berkman
Barbara L. Berman
Linda Blackwell Billingsley
Patricia Bird
Harriet Blodgett
Pat Blumenthal
Elsa "Midge" Bowman
Lesley Bracker
Rachel Brown
Margaret Bruning
Doris Bryant
Jennifer L. Bryant
Jean Burdge
Selma Burkom
Barbara Cambron
Elizabeth Cervantes
Kate Chimenti
Beth Clewis
Beth Colvin
Mary Jean Corbett
Anne Coulter
Edith L. Crowe
Tracy Davis
Elizabeth Dickinson
Zelma Dorfman
Lish Dudley
Trudi Eitner
Joanne A. Ernst
Marjorie Erpelding
Margaret Gage
Lyn Gamble
Gerry Ganan
Michele Garside
Jessica Gerrard
Joanna Gillespie
Paula Gillett
Madeleine Gleason
Penny Gold
Margaret Gordon
Deborah Gorham
Mary Ann Grant
Beth Gray
Nan Hackett
Lucia Hammar
Kim Handler
Andrianne Harris
Ann Heinemann
Pamela Herr
Edythe Hickman
Margaret Hopkins
Paul Hopkins
Mamie Hubert
Leslie Hume
Maia Irell
Charlotte Irvine
Katherine Burger Johnson
Christie Junkerman
Rima Kay
Anne T. Keenan
Sue Klarreich
Christa Knebel
Julia Kringel
Martha G. Krow-Lucal
Joanne Lafler
Denise Larrabee

Andrea Leigh
Selma Lesser
Judy Liggett
Rose Lowenstein
Karen McAdams
Kathy McCann
Gay MacDonald
Sandra MacMahon
Kay Mahon
Linda Mann
Jane Marks
Linda Mather
Marcia Matz
Judith Maxwell
Laura Mayhall
Elaine Mew
Gertrude Miller
Ann Thomas Moore
Reed Moyer
Sue Moyer
Mary Murphy
Ardis Oglesby
Carol Osborner
Patricia Pate
Kate Pecarovich
Leah Peluffo
Karen Perlroth
Marie Powell
Jenny Presnell
Kathleen Prior
Elizabeth Proctor
Alice Ann Roberts
Sherri T. Roberts
Elizabeth Roden
Leigh Romero
Jacqueline Roose
Danielle Roth-Johnson
Elizabeth Rush
Joyce Sanders
Kathe Schoenberg
Leah Schoolnik
Marian Schuster
Jill Sellens
Susan Severin
Claire Sherman
Frieda Sherman
Marian Shuster
Raman Singh
Martha Skeeters
Nancy Spitters
Vera Steckler
Edna Steward
Karla Sundin
Victoria Tang
Joye Tatz
Sue Thomas
Ruth Trager
Viviana Tul
Marion Ury
Claudia Utley
Rosemary Van Arsdel
Sara Van Dyck
Kate Walker
Linda Watson
Elizabeth Webb
Joan Wight
Jo Anne Woodson
Linda World
Mary Yost

Guide to Abbreviations and Terminology

academic: any person teaching at the university level or holding a university position, such as a departmental chair. This term includes instructors, senior instructors, lecturers and tutors (British usage), dons, and professors.

ARP (Air Raid Precautions) committee: a borough council committee that helped locals arrange shelter during the Blitz of World War II

ATS (Auxiliary Territorial Service): a branch of the British Army overseas staffed entirely by women. Begun in WWI, it became a regular institution in peacetime. Although its system of ranks mirrored ranks within the men's army, duties were different; ATS provided the men directly involved in military action with support services, including radio and other communications, lodging and transportation arrangements, mechanical maintenance, and provisions supply management.

BBC (British Broadcasting Company [later, British Broadcasting Corporation]): a radio monopoly established under the auspices of the British government in 1922 but not subject to its day-to-day control. In the late 1930s it began making the world's first regular television broadcasts.

BEF: British Expeditionary Force

Black and Tans: British auxiliary policemen stationed in Ireland around 1920; so named for their khaki uniforms with black caps and armlets

board schools: grammar schools under the control of a government school board, designed to give a sound basic education to children from lower socioeconomic classes borough councillor: a member of the municipal council, usually a volunteer, in one of the local government divisions of London

C.B.: Companion of the Order of the Bath

C.B.E.: Companion of the Order of the British Empire

C.H.: Companion of Honour

council housing: housing for the poor overseen and subsidized by a municipal council

county councillor: a member of the council directing the administrative and legislative affairs of an urban county

C.R.L.: Canons Regular of the Lateran; a Roman Catholic order

d.: died; used preceding a death date (e.g., d.1945)

d.a.: died after; used when exact death date is unknown, preceding a death date (e.g., d.a.1945)

D.B.E.: Dame of the British Empire

D.C.L.: Doctor of Civil Law

Hon. D.C.L.: Honorary Doctor of Civil Law

D.D.: Doctor of Divinity

D.S.O.: Distinguished Service Order

estate agent: a person selling residential and commercial property

feminist: a woman who expresses feminist ideas in her text, whether she identifies herself as a feminist or not. For simplicity, this term has been used whenever the above conditions apply, without regard to considerations of when the term "feminist" actually came into active usage.

feminist activist: a woman actively involved in promoting the welfare, education, employment opportunities, or political empowerment of women

feudal dame: a woman holding effective rulership of the Isle of Sark, which is not part of Britain but an independent nation still operating under a medieval feudal system

F.R.A.S.: Fellow of the Royal Astronomical Society

F.R.C.M.: Fellow of the Royal College of Music

F.R.G.S.: Fellow of the Royal Geographical Society

front. port.: portrait of the author included as frontispiece in her autobiography

F.R.S.: Fellow of the Royal Society

F.S.A.: Fellow of the Society of Antiquaries

F.Z.S.: Fellow of the Zoological Society

G.B.E.: (Knight or Dame) Grand Cross of the British Empire

G.C.M.G.: (Knight or Dame) Grand Cross of the Order of St. Michael and St. George

G.C.V.O.: (Knight or Dame) Grand Cross of the (Royal) Victorian Order

Hon.; the Hon. (The Honourable): a title of courtesy given to sons of peers from the ranks of earl, viscount, and baron, or to daughters of peers from the ranks of viscount and baron

illus.: This term appears in an entry's first paragraph if an autobiography's contents include any sort of illustration, photographs, drawings, or portraits.

IRA: Irish Republican Army

J.P.: justice of the peace

K.C.B.: Knight Commander of the Bath

K.C.M.G.: Knight Commander of the Order of St. Michael and St. George

K.T.: Knight of the Thistle

Kt.: Knight

LL.D.: Doctor of Laws

Hon. LL.D.: Honorary Doctor of Laws

Lord; Lady: a title of courtesy (when followed by a first name rather than a surname) given to younger sons of peers from the ranks of duke and marquess or to daughters of peers from the ranks of duke, marquess, and earl

L.R.A.M.: Licentiate of the Royal Academy of Music

Memsahib: A form of address used in colonial India for a European woman married to a man in the Imperial service. Here used to indicate an author whose activities or whose husband's activities involved participation in some aspect of colonial administration.

M.P.: member of Parliament

NUWSS: National Union of Women's Suffrage Societies

O.B.E.: Officer of the Order of the British Empire

PEN: [The Society of] Poets, Playwrights, Editors, Essayists, and Novelists

P.M.: prime minister

Poor Law Guardian: a member of a government board extant in England that administered the poor laws until 1930

poor laws: British statutes governing the support of the poor. In the nineteenth century such laws characteristically tried to improve the moral character of the poor—promoting temperance, piety, frugality, and sexual restraint—at the same time that they alleviated their distress. Although these laws made some allowance for "out-of-doors" assistance, for much of the century workhouses were in force, which required the indigent to surrender family ties and to live and work in single-sex institutions in order to receive aid.

port.: used in the bibliographic paragraph to indicate that a portrait of the author appears in the autobiography

pseudonyms: If the author's autobiography was published under a pseudonym, the book will be listed under this name; her real name, if known, will appear within parentheses immediately following the pseudonym, e.g., FAKE, Jane (pseud.; Jane Real). If the author published her autobiography under her real name, but published other works under pseudonym(s), or used a different stage name, the real name is employed in the entry; the pseudonyms follow her name, within parentheses, e.g., REAL, Jane (Jane Fake, pseud.).

pupil-teacher: a grammar school position open to a girl of lower socioeconomic class with scholarly aptitude. From 14 to 18 years of age, a pupil-teacher could remain at her grammar school and teach, earning accreditation.

R.A.: Royal Academician

RAF: Royal Air Force

religionist: a woman who was not merely a member of a particular religion but someone whose faith centrally informed the progress of her life

RRC: The Royal Red Cross

s.l.: still living; used when death date is uncertain and author may still be alive, preceding a death date (e.g., 1898–s.l.1982)

suffragist: a woman who gave her public support, verbally or in writing, to the cause of gaining the vote for women

suffragist, militant: a woman who engaged in public action, such as marching or civil disobedience, in support of the vote for women

trade unionist: an associate of a trade union organized by workers in a common industry for the protection of their mutual interests

tutor: a person who schooled others privately and for pay in specific subjects; this is not someone who held the formal title of Tutor in the university system (*See also* academic)

U.D.: Urban Districtman

VAD (Voluntary Aid Detachment): an independent organization of women who had not been nurses before WWI, but received a few months of intensive training to perform army nursing during the war. They served as assistants to regular nurses who had joined the Army Nursing Corps with previous professional experience and schooling. VAD assignments, leaves, and transfers were under direct British Army control.

WAAC (Women's Army Auxiliary Corps): the WWII reincarnation of the Auxiliary Territorial Service, intended to increase Army "manpower" by filling support positions with women, freeing most male soldiers for military action.

WAAF (Women's Auxiliary Air Force): Like the WAAC, this organization provided female-staffed support services. When the Army Air Corps became established as the Air Force, an independent military branch, the WAAF became subsumed under Air Force direction.

WCTU (Women's Christian Temperance Union): A nondenominational group, the WCTU had extensive connections among religious and secular temperance groups in Britain. The most widespread of the temperance activist groups within the United States during the nineteenth and early twentieth centuries, the WCTU worked to educate adults and children about the dangers of drink, to turn people from alcohol to God, and to persuade legislators of the need for legal sanctions against alcohol. In the twentieth century, the WCTU was influential in the imposition of Prohibition in the United States.

WEA (Workers' Educational Association): a mixed group run by collaboration consisting of philanthropists, professional educators, and workers themselves. This association served privately just as public university extension courses serve today, making higher learning accessible to working people through night and weekend classes as well as through lectures by notable figures in the sciences, arts, and academia.

WFL (Women's Freedom League): founded by the Irishwoman Charlotte Despard in 1907; lasted fifty years. This strongly feminist group was a watchdog organization monitoring British legislative and judicial actions and an educational venture seeking to raise the public's consciousness through pamphlets on contemporary women's issues and legal decisions.

WSPU (Women's Social and Political Union): founded in 1903 by Emmeline Pankhurst, this organization utilized militant tactics—creating public uproars, destroying property, stone-throwing—to protest the continuing lack of suffrage for women, and to press the cause of women's voting rights. When arrested, its members frequently launched hunger strikes in prison, a tactic which prompted prison officials to force-feed the protesters.

How to Use This Book

Having limited space within which to encapsulate the autobiographies in this collection, I have designed a style that allows us reliably to convey each author's text and tone, her prioritization of the major subjects she discusses, her chronology, and her ideas and opinions, without interjecting our own judgments or interpretations in the descriptions of the individual narratives. Considering that *Women in Context* is a collection of the past, it should not be surprising that this design follows the principles of historical practice more closely than the traditional style of listing texts in bibliographies. This is, therefore, a work in bibliomethodology, rather than a standard bibliography. For each author, the format consists of a numbered entry organized into four paragraphs.

1. The first paragraph provides bibliographical information. It contains the author's name(s) and forms of address; birth and death dates (exact or approximate); book or article title; publication information, especially for the edition used for the entry, and also for the first edition if different from the one cited. The place of publication is London, unless otherwise indicated. Not every edition of each autobiography is given; other editions are not cited unless they differ significantly from the version of the book used for *Women in Context.* A major catalog reference is given to enable readers to request the autobiography through interlibrary loan. All entries are numbered and alphabetized by the authors' surnames for purposes of consistency. If an author is a member of the peerage and therefore is also known by another name, she is cross-referenced by her title in the alphabetical listings: e.g., "Brownlow, Emma Sophia, Countess Cust." is cross-referenced as "Cust, Countess. [*See* Brownlow, Emma Sophia]."

2. The second paragraph contains biographical information about the author, gathered mainly from the autobiography itself. In this paragraph can be found the author's place of birth or upbringing, names of her parents, number and names of famous siblings, and a list of any his-

torically significant friends not mentioned in the third paragraph. Information about the author's marital status, children, primary occupations, and social class are also included in this paragraph. When these data are not given by the author, we have done limited library research to uncover essential biographical details about the autobiographer. In a few cases of exceedingly obscure or reticent memorialists, we have been unable to provide much in the way of straightforward biographical data.

3. The third paragraph renders the content of the autobiography itself. Beginning with a statement of the author's overall theme and the timespan covered by the book, this section surveys, in an abbreviated style, the text as it flows according to the author's expression of her major concerns and her main topics of discussion within the changing context of her life over time. The amount of space the author gives to a subject is a primary basis for our considering the concern to be major. We have tried within this section to preserve the author's experiences and opinions in the terms she uses, and to avoid either inserting our own interpretations of her meanings and motivations or placing matters important to late twentieth-century studies over her own concerns. In this section of each entry, we have attempted to make the author's mental makeup transparent to readers.

4. The fourth paragraph places the author and her narrative into a larger sociohistorical context. For example, we may examine the connection between an author's expressed attitudes about race and social class and her attitudes toward issues about which she has only hinted. If an autobiography covers only a part of the author's life, the fourth paragraph may offer some additional biographical information to assist our readers' decisions about consulting her full text. When we believe it to be appropriate, we identify individuals the author designates as important to her but who she only mentions. Additional autobiographies by the author may also be mentioned here; 133 of our authors wrote multiple autobiographical narratives. These additional autobiographies have been numbered and indexed, although they are discussed very briefly. There are autobiographies that are mentioned but not numbered because they have not been annotated by our staff and are not included in the indices. In some cases, in this last paragraph we briefly compare or contrast the author's narrative with the works and life stories of other authors included in this guide.

To facilitate usage of this guide by readers seeking information about particular categories of women and related topics, we have created three indices.

The Author Index of Twenty-Year Cohorts arranges authors generationally in twenty-year divisions, listing the autobiographers by their dates of birth. Within each cohort, authors are listed alphabetically. Included for each author are her full name and titles, her life dates, all identification terms that apply to her, and her entry number, boldfaced.

Her nationality appears only if it is other than English. This index makes visible any temporal patterns that these narratives suggest, and facilitates comparative study of the various autobiographers.

The Identification Index lists vocations; activities; marital status; social class; political, religious, and ethical belief systems; and other designations the authors have assigned to themselves. In the identification index, subsumed under each term are the surnames of the authors, not their entry numbers.

The Subject Index contains an alphabetical list of key subject words and phrases that identify significant topics treated by authors in their texts. Each appropriate subject term is followed by the assigned entry numbers (as in the author index) of every autobiography that discusses the subject matter. Some of the topics that this index identifies may not appear in the third paragraph of the entry. This discrepancy between the subject index and the book's entries results simply from the thoroughness of the subject index, based on our exhaustive reading of each book, something which the entry's summary (the third paragraph) is not intended to duplicate.

Preface

Women in Context is an analytical, critical, and biographical guide to 1,040 published narrative autobiographies by 812 British women of all social classes, born in the British Isles and the extended British Empire from the early eighteenth to the early twentieth centuries.

This guide is intended as a resource for researchers of history, biography, women's and gender studies, literary criticism, and related fields. Students working in these areas, creative writers, artists, and other investigators of women's life narratives will also find this volume useful. Writers of fiction, plays, and film scenarios may discover material for storylines and characters in historical and contemporary settings. *Women in Context* is also intended to inform general readers seeking to improve their understanding of the past through the self-reported histories of women of various eras.

Women in Context is intended more as a guide for researchers than as a source of new theoretical conclusions. Its primary purpose is to acquaint scholarly readers from every discipline with a host of lesser-known personal narratives offering fresh historical, literary, or psychological insights. Because each entry is a secondary rendition of the author's primary text, the entries themselves are not presented for literary analysis. Further, because most of these autobiographies were written by inexperienced writers, many of them have too little textual sophistication for academic literary theorists to consider them literature meriting analysis.

The women autobiographers presented and compared in this study convey in detail a striking diversity of talents, interests, experiences, beliefs, opinions, involvements, and occupations. Directly and indirectly, the majority of these writers present images of the sociohistorical milieux in which they were immersed, and express themselves on spiritual, didactic, or literary themes. For example, authors' discussions of their origins reveal regional variations and local culture. In telling their family histories, they describe their formative social inheritance as well as the more private expectations they were supposed to fulfill. These authors' renditions of their employment and education frequently contradict previously held generalizations about social restrictions on women's paid work and other activities. In expressing their religious conversion experiences, they provide insights, directly or suggestively, into the influence of spirituality on the formation of their characters, values, and behavior. Self-reflections on gender identification tend to inform or otherwise coincide with choices in relationships and lifestyles and personal aspirations. Descriptions of impulses toward travel, exploration, emigration, and colonization often suggest new perspectives on outward-bound women during the last two centuries.

A limited number of female autobiographies have been repeatedly acknowledged in recent publications and are therefore well known. The authors of these much-cited memoirs usually fall into one of several classifications: royalty; wives and daughters of political and other leaders; members of eminent families; honored literary figures; legendary reformers; and women who were historically extraordinary. Another group, largely found in bibliographical lists of women's history monographs, are writers of childhood memoirs. Unacknowledged, however, are lesser-known or ordinary women narrators who kept personal records and published life stories in which they contextualized themselves within specific circumstances, experiences, and occupations—some still to be thoroughly researched. *Women in Context* illustrates that a very large number of women's autobiographies await discovery and evaluation both for sparking new questions and for testing previous generalizations.

Women in Context has been an ongoing project since 1991. It evolved from the research project "British Women's Autobiographies, 1750–1950" that I codirected with British studies historian Susan Groag Bell at Stanford University's Institute for Research on Women and Gender. Each of us came to the project with almost twenty years' experience of studying autobiography as a source for British women's history and culture. Our goal was to pool our personal archives and expand our list of autobiographies to about fifteen hundred in number, evaluate them for content, and design a computerized database as a ground for comparative analysis. We were awarded a seed grant from the National Endowment for the Humanities for 1987–1989. Stanford University administered the grant through the institute, where Susan Bell and I were appointed senior research associates and affiliated scholars.

As the number of autobiographers on our list grew, we devised a questionnaire and asked qualified volunteer readers to provide detailed answers and evaluations of some of the texts for our database. The questionnaire included inquiries into specific aspects of each author's life data, experiences, opinions, and activities. We entitled and copyrighted the questionnaire BELKAN. Susan Bell undertook administration of the BELKAN questionnaire at the institute, and I designed and continually expanded the database and directed research at UCLA. By 1989, more than two hundred questionnaires had been returned to us. At the end of this two-year study we embarked on separate research, each retaining copies of the completed questionnaires.

Susan Bell has continued her work on the questionnaire project. I undertook additional research in England and established the publication project, *Women in Context,* at UCLA. In time I came to believe that the original questionnaire format required readers to approach the autobiographies in a standardized way that did not take full account of the wide variety of individual voices represented. I therefore reconceived the project, employing a small staff to work with me in reading or rereading and annotating the autobiographies included in *Women in Context.* I now regard each author and her narrative as unique and individual, so that it is the character and content of each author's book that dictates the analysis of her text in the final version of this guide. But this is not to underestimate the contributions of the many volunteer readers who participated in the genesis of this book. The questionnaires were most useful to me for the readers' own personal reactions to and opinions of the particular book(s) that each evaluated.

As might be expected, this guide shows preference for authors whose consciousness and vision reach beyond exploring their inner thoughts and feelings to encompass the social, historical, cultural influences on their identities and perceptions. These life stories, therefore, invite interdisciplinary interpretation. You may, as I do, also find them inspirational.

Barbara Penny Kanner
Los Angeles, 1997

Introduction

Literary Theory, Feminist Response, and Autobiographical Authorship

"Now we think it an immense mistake to maintain that there is no sex in literature. Science has no sex: the mere knowing and reasoning faculties, if they act correctly, must go through the same process, and arrive at the same result. But in art and literature, which imply the action of the entire being, in which every fibre of the nature is engaged, in which every peculiar modification of the individual makes itself felt, woman has something specific to contribute."

—GEORGE ELIOT, 1854[1]

Any reader who surveys this collection of more than eight hundred individual women's self-narratives may be overwhelmed by the diversity of social class, occupational interest, family constellation, and strategies of writing. My fondest hopes are that this collection is large enough to confound any a priori theories of categorization that the reader may bring to the task of reading. Any such confusion is all to the good; my principles of inclusion for this collection aim to unite a body of work that challenges current autobiographical theory, emphasizes its provisional nature, and inspires scholars to reinvestigate the growing number of primary autobiographical documents being recuperated for the modern-day reader's study and appreciation.

To achieve this end, I have chosen to incorporate British women writers whose narratives meet current literary prescriptions for autobiography and those who for various reasons have yet to win academic notice.

Most of this second group are not accustomed to being literary writers at all. They are not women for whom the creation of a text is a practiced, familiar means of self-assertion or contemplation. They are instead farmers and shopkeepers, missionaries and governesses, domestic servants or public ones. Some lived in Britain, some in remote corners of the British empire, some in foreign nations. Some were born before America declared independence from England; others are still alive as this volume goes to print.

With such diversity, what then do they share? The most salient feature may be each woman's conviction that her life is worth the labor to record it. Even this one shared factor, however, is not subject to a simple interpretation. Autobiographical theory in the twentieth century has produced a number of divergent perspectives from which to interpret the impulse behind self-reflexive narrative. Accordingly, a brief overview of autobiographical study conducted over the last four decades can help readers to assess the present collection from a literary, psychological, historical, or feminist perspective.

Some forty years ago, the pioneering autobiographical critic Georges Gusdorf posited that the autobiographer's established sense of self-worth (which he held to be a necessary precondition for writing autobiography) should be described as the "conscious awareness of the singularity of each individual life."[2] It was Gusdorf's contention that autobiography should be seen as a process that moves from collective consciousness (a state that characterizes the very young infant) toward increasing individuation. Gusdorf associated the proliferation of autobiographical writings in the last few centuries with the Industrial Revolution and the resulting rise of capitalism and individual competition. As people increasingly came to consider the individual to be a legitimate focus of their curiosity, the literary result of this increasing interest in the individual was autobiography. Gusdorf observed that as a genre autobiography records the mark, or signature, of the individual in the form of language, much as the explorer's solitary ventures in the new world inscribed his individuality in the historical record.

Gusdorf's perspective was adopted and expanded by succeeding theorists, notably among them James Olney, who equated the autobiographer's creation of the text to an assertive re-creation of the self. For Olney, the act of writing the autobiography generates a "second self" produced through the labors of memory, so that the written text and the writer come to overlap. The truth of autobiography for Olney is not historical but rather the truth of the private interchange between the self who lives the life and the second self whom the first one brings into being through remembering.

Olney assumes a mutual reflexivity between writer and text, with the latter serving as a record of the individuality of the former. But scholars concerned with issues such as race, class, and gender point out that such a theory of autobiography must be qualified considerably in order to be workable: if each and every autobiographer were in fact motivated to write chiefly by a felt uniqueness, this impulse—by ignoring differences between people based upon sex, economic condition, or historical period—undermines the very factors that reveal the writer's contextual historical perspective. Olney himself appears sensibly reluctant to endorse this inference following from his line of reasoning; his practical considerations of autobiography instead exhibit a healthy appreciation of autobiography's power to clarify historical and cultural distinctions:

> autobiography—the story of a distinctive culture written in individual characters and from within—offers a privileged access to personal experience . . . that no other variety of writing can offer. . . . Autobiography renders in a peculiarly direct and faithful way the experience and vision of a people, which is the same experience and the same vision lying behind and informing all the literature of that people.[9]

Although they appear to conflict, autobiography's double identities, as both textual self-portrait and historical repository, are reconcilable. One theoretical means of reconciliation lies in Jacques Lacan's metaphor of the autobiographical text as a mirror, which effectively "splits" the image it is trying to communicate between the writer and the writer's intended audience. Through this split, meaning is shifted from the text of the autobiography onto each reader who, consulting his/her associative map, derives different meanings from the text. In studying children's psychological development, as did Freud, Lacan notes that human children pass through a "mirror stage" in which they discover that the strange mirror image outside themselves renders a likeness of their perceived self-image. However, the child will perceive that image—which looks perfect and complete—as false or artificial, for the image lacks the inner, invisible qualities and feelings that the child perceives to be its true self. Only people other than the child, who see both the child and the mirror image from the outside, will be able to trust the truthfulness the image conveys. Theorists who have further applied Lacanian thinking to autobiography, including Gregory Ulmer, Gerald Kennedy, and Willis Buck, cite another and separate reason why autobiography must fail to produce absolute truth: the words used by the author to create the image of the self are abstract units of language, arbitrary units of signification. As symbols whose nature is therefore separate from any grounding in reality, they will always ultimately fail to refer back to the real world.

The theoretical split in perception between the writer and the writer's audience simultaneously provides the outside viewer of the autobiography with a seemingly realistic image of the author, while providing the author with a jarring sense of falsity. Feminist critics identify a paradoxical difference, determined by gender, in the responses of autobiographers to the impact of the autobiography's apparently distorted reflection. Margo Culley writes:

> No woman, as we know, truly sees herself in a mirror; she sees herself through the imagined (or real) gaze of another. And to the extent that the autobiographical text can be thought of as a mirror, it is a mirror gazed at in public. Any woman can tell you of the difference (in degree at least) between viewing her image in the privacy of a bathroom or bedroom mirror and catching a glimpse of herself in a mirror in public, a store window or mirror placed strategically in a department store. For women, all mirrors in public are two-way mirrors behind which invisible security guards convict her of her failures or her crimes.[4]

Feminist critic Shari Benstock calls this moment of mirrored perception "a differentiation that is potentially frightening, a moment that cannot be recaptured through memory as such, a moment that hangs in a space that is neither dream nor fact, but both." She finds the most interesting aspect of this autobiographical moment to be the degree to which "self" and "self-image" do not coincide, but instead "exploit difference and change over sameness and identity." Benstock adds that

> such writing puts into question the whole notion of "genre" as outlined by the exclusionary methods of Gusdorf's rather narrow definition of the autobiographical. And it is not surprising that the question of "genre" often rides on the question of gender.[5]

Benstock asserts that autobiography fulfills a different goal for female writers than for male ones. Although the text as mirror image must always make its author conscious of gaps between past reality and subjective memory, for male authors the "whole thrust of such writings" is to conceal the temporal and "mnemonic" gaps they expose. In Benstock's view, men's autobiographies work diligently in their style to plaster over the apparent gaps and structural problems to present a smooth, seamless appearance that soothes the audience and bolsters the writer's self-regard. Just as Plato counseled his disciples to "be what you wish to seem," Benstock sees men as using autobiography to incarnate the ideal self they would like to be. Women, Benstock argues, have been culturally conditioned to be self-critical and are less easily beguiled by themselves than are men. Men work to repair the image while women study the exposed falsity to garner insight. Women focus not on autobiography's power to reinvent a public image but its power to reveal private predicaments to themselves.

Feminist perspectives on the writing of autobiography generally agree that difference in women's means of expression from that of men is the product of women's cultural circumstances. What most male critics have attributed to individual development, feminist critics assert to be inseparable from the individual's place, role, and treatment within her cultural surroundings. Surveying the historical implications of feminist criticism, Catharine Stimpson notes that it has not produced theory so much as evolved from a loose, constantly changing interaction of theory and politics. She suggests that fruitful feminist criticism empowers a woman to reinterpret a written text by placing her own subjectivity at the center of audience response. For feminist critics, Stimpson says, "the 'I' entered discourse and played upon the page." She adds that in the 1970s autobiography dominated feminist theory: "subjective writing was even a 'female' response to 'male' objectivity, that putative casting of a net of arid, abstract generalizations over the raw territories of life."[6] Feminist critics considered autobiography a shaped, interactive response of the female autobiographer to the external conditions defining her own existence.

It is the historical conditions contextualizing the woman writer that feminist theorist Sheila Rowbotham has examined and developed in her influential book, *Woman's Consciousness, Man's World.* Rowbotham imports some of French feminist Simone de Beauvoir's ideas from her provocative work *The Second Sex.* De Beauvoir elaborates on the different conditions of life and consciousness under which men and women in Western civilization exist because of their separate treatment and unequal acculturation. Rowbotham argues (in response to Gusdorf's hypotheses) that a woman writer will customarily be unable to experience herself as a unique entity because she cannot escape the awareness that society defines her as "woman"—a member of a group whose identity has long been crystallized and defined by the male hierarchical perspective that shapes society. Like Lacan, Rowbotham employs the metaphor of the mirror to describe the development of (woman's) consciousness. But she locates the mirror image not in the autobiographical text but in the panorama of cultural ideology into which the woman must look to discover who she is. Because of imposed cultural generalities, that mirror can never reflect a unique identity for the female onlooker; rather, it projects a categorized image of Woman, into which all female onlookers are challenged to fit.[7]

Feminism's notion of the power of cultural representations is equally applicable to all autobiographers. Western culture confronts the aspiring autobiographer with long-established and restrictive definitions of almost all its citizens. All autobiographers are grounded in their cultural specificity. The autobiographical text is always telling a provisional truth, mediating between self-concept and cultural image using both as reference points from which to orient itself.

Feminist criticism cautions against the very formation of dogmatic general theory by showing that contradictions must unavoidably arise from the autobiographer's circumstances of existence in a real society. This sense of openness to change, modification, fresh thought, and resistance to theory is precisely what makes *Women in Context* feminist. I hope to discourage hard and fast theories, which can insidiously coerce the scholar into preformed opinions and exclusionary prescriptions. Instead, I aim to provoke the readers' examination of these largely critically untrodden autobiographies.

During the long years that my staff and I have devoted to this anthology, we have striven consciously to attune ourselves to the messages of the authors rather than our preformed expectations. Always, we have tried to keep ourselves and our assumptions from bending either our field of inquiry or our readers' perceptions. We confine comments on a narrative to the final paragraph of each entry to illuminate—not upstage—each author's attitudes and understanding of her own condition. Only a minority of these autobiographers had the literary sophistication to use autobiography as an art form, yet all lived lives which, in their broad spectrum of experience, of concepts, ideals and goals, are of great comparative value in studying the broad face of their culture. The diversity represented includes the range of the British class structure (in all its vertical and horizontal complexity) and two hundred years of permutations to British culture. The diversity replicates, as no simplified categorical schema can, the complexities and contradictions of these women's historical context.

By listening to the multiple voices in these narratives with a principle of non-interference, we found that they began to transform themselves for us into a complex map displaying many different kinds of social geography, rich in new perspectives for scholars in diverse disciplines. Anthropologists will uncover unusual details here in the descriptions of women's living conditions in all reaches of the British empire. Social historians will profit from the many instances of women with uncommon vocations (among them theatrical producer, aviator, gold miner, and screenwriter) insufficiently documented elsewhere, for whom the professional woman herself serves as chronicler. Scholars studying women's involvement in scientific disciplines will be able to harvest information directly from the many personal narratives by women in nearly every scientific field. This collection of personal testimony shows that women were far more professionally involved than historians have generally suggested. Whatever the discipline or profession under consideration, women autobiographers document its contemporary state in their respective eras, their participation within it, and their broader sense of how professional women in traditional male fields were actually received. Academics who research mine-laying in World War I, nineteenth-century business administration, surgery, entomology, or a plethora of other vocations will find women working within that specific field.

Of equal interest are those narratives that testify to women's deep investment in volunteerism. Operating charity homes for soldiers, organizing air raid shelters during the blitz, or providing free maternity nursing to London's East End mothers, these woman engaged in a social activism that can't be easily documented through payroll or company records. *Women in Context* expands our knowledge of women's contributions to national development and social reform. Of course, most of the women in these texts also discuss their engagement in the personal sphere, providing details of their familial relationships and their attitudes toward gender divisions, both as adults and as children. In this arena, too, we have found that the life stories they record often violate our twentieth-century indoctrination concerning nineteenth-century gender roles, parental ties, sibling interactions, and sexual mores. The multiple voices of these women richly detail British life in the preceding two centuries. They clarify some matters scholars have only partly researched and add additional dimension to scholarly deduction in others. In the topical sections below, we relay broader inferences about relational, occupational, and migrational patterns within the autobiographies.

RELATIONAL TIES: KINSHIP, MARRIAGE AND FRIENDSHIP

Family Bonds

The single most salient topic in these narratives is that of family connections, with only one in two hundred of these autobiographers choosing not to mention their parents at all. One in eight, or 111 of the autobiographers, indicate that their strongest feelings of love, as well as their self-esteem, were brought forth by their fathers, and they frequently refer to the father by name even when the mother's name is omitted in the text. In a recently published study of fathers, Emory University psychologist John Snarey observes that fathers significantly influence their children's later success in life, and that their influence is greatest when their encouragement runs contrary to gender stereotype. "It is hard to find a daughter," notes Snarey, "whose career is unusually successful who didn't have a father who was very involved." Applying Snarey's present-day observations also to our authors' discussions of their fathers, the stock characterization of the Victorian father as the stern, distant paterfamilias should be held up to question. Home education shows up as a frequent theme in *Women in Context,* and nearly as frequently it is the father who is the home educator. Mary Irene Ravensdale and Lillah MacCarthy, for instance, give details of their fathers' loving intellectual tutelage. In addition, professional fathers often gave their daughters entree into fields that were resistant to women practitioners. Elizabeth

Chesser followed her physician father's footsteps into medical school and into an active career; she records his strong support for her ambition. Gertrude Bacon's father taught her scientific skills at home and took her aloft with him in his scientific balloon to view solar eclipses; she testifies to his inspiration in her becoming a balloonist and a life-long public aviation proponent.

Those women who cite negative relationships with their fathers were nevertheless profoundly affected by them, often implying that their choice to reject marriage was related to a failed father/daughter experience. Esylt Newbery, whose parson father administered "savage and cruel punishments," elected to remain single because every admirer eventually reminded her of him. When Eliza Lynn Linton's marriage failed, she unhesitatingly attributed the failure to the character traits of her father (also a clergyman): his pride and laziness, his abuse of his clerical position, his beating of the children and his neglect of their education. In both positive and negative aspects, the authors in *Women in Context* suggest that the strongest influence on the formation of their character, and the development of their lives, was a father to whom they looked for both caring attention and the nurture of their self-esteem, notwithstanding the role of their mother.

Writers in *Women in Context* discuss mothers as a topic less often than they do fathers, frequently neglecting to provide even their mothers' names. At least 300 autobiographers in this collection, or three of every eight, make no mention of their mothers' names whether or not their fathers' names are included. Certainly, some narrators may be reflecting their culture's long-standing dismissal of the significance of mothers, but others may be evading uncomfortable memories or revealing considerable ambivalence. Other authors, particularly those born into the middle or higher classes, reflect an emotional distance between their mothers and themselves that is the direct product of the intervention of intermediary caregivers, nannies and governesses. Of course, a few writers may have so cherished their mother's memory that they wanted to keep it private; their narrative omissions may suggest that the intimacy of the mother/child relationship is of an altogether different nature than the relatively public one between father and child, and that such an intimacy, formed in private, was meant to stay so.

The narratives of working-class women tend to discuss family relationships openly. Lilian Slater's working-class "Mam" shines in her text as a strong, positive figure. In working-class families—demographically a frequent site of paternal absence—the mother often held the family together, a cohesive power emphasized by Elizabeth Flint and Mary Hewins. Winifred Beechey recounts working with her mother to establish a shop, the family's means of escape from lower middle-class penury.

Although many middle- and upper-class writers in *Women in Context* address their personal experience of the mother/child relationship less openly, those who did tend to perceive their mothers as either saints or demons. Annie Besant's mother aroused her fierce loyalty and utter devotion, emotions which the theosophist Besant appears later to have transferred to her spiritual guide Madame Blavatsky. Ida Wylie shared this spirit of mother worship; after losing her mother in childhood, Wylie constructed a fantasy life around the lost parent and spent her adolescence seeking out a series of female mentors, tendencies her text analyzes in Freudian terms. Against this catalog of maternal saints stand the mothers of Anita Leslie, Elma Napier, and Lady Baden-Powell, all described by their daughters as self-absorbed and interfering, from whom the daughters resolutely distanced themselves. The autobiography of Angelica Garnett appears to be a biography of her mother, Vanessa Bell, so overshadowing is the place she occupies in her daughter's life; only gradually does the reader sense Garnett's emotional conflict to her mother's domineering love.

In parent-child relationships that involved strife, whether with the father or the mother, narratives in *Women in Context* show women frequently marrying hastily and fleeing from the family. Strife with stepparents shows up consistently, particularly in the lower classes, with numerous writers disclosing portraits of abusive stepfathers or stepmothers. Other women testify that as children they had been the targets of parental violence: Doris Bailey, a working-class author, recalls her alcoholic father's "uncertain temper," although she appears to take for granted his calm power to tyrannize over and to abuse both herself and her mother.

Brothers and sisters customarily occupy only a peripheral section of these autobiographies, but when writers do mention siblings more centrally, they often single them out as objects of personal devotion. Yet when sibling relations are turbulent, they tend to come to the fore in autobiographies, as in the narrative of Jessica Mitford. Underscoring culturally based gender inequities, writers frequently describe brothers as mentors and providers of support—emotional or financial—as do Isabella Gilmore, Harriet Martineau and Charlotte, Lady Wake. Older sisters, by contrast, might serve as mother substitutes; in her personal narrative, Virginia Woolf's elder sisters fill this role. And elder daughters in their texts relate their maternal role; Rose Gibbs mothered her younger siblings to the extent of taking the baby to school with her.

Marriage and Romance

Husbands (or paramours) tend to share the periphery of these women's narratives, when the autobiographers are not outright silent on the subject. The writers appear far less willing to discuss their intimate emotional relationships than the more practical aspects of their married existence. Some narratives discuss the woman's own career or her more tacit role as partner-behind-the-scenes in her husband's advancement. We find that the women very tangibly affected the success (or lack thereof) of their husbands' careers. Catherine Nicoll describes how she hosted a regular literary salon that brought her husband, eventual editor-in-chief of the *British Weekly,* the social connections within writing and publishing circles that his advancement required. Ishbel Gordon, Marchioness of Aberdeen, documents her life-long political partnership with her husband; she actively waged his battles in the Liberal Party as he rose to be governor-general of Canada and viceroy of Ireland. Gordon belongs to a small category of narrators who wrote joint autobiographies with their husbands. On the negative side, Constance Flower, Baroness Battersea, made her parliamentary member husband turn down an appointment as governor of New South Wales so that she could remain in England near her mother; Battersea's insistence effectively ended her husband's career.

When the women in *Women in Context* pursued independent vocations, they often record with gratitude the support of their husbands. One such woman is Eleanor Acland, who established herself as a Liberal politician and testifies to her husband's aid; another is Vera Brittain, whose new husband, academic George Catlin, in 1925 encouraged her to undertake what became her notable series of historical autobiographies. When husbands were unhelpful, our authors tended to complain volubly of this deficiency. Highly interesting is the written record of Doris Booth, gold miner and emigrant to New Guinea. In tart terms she comments on her husband's poor attitude toward the work and her own consequent intensification of effort; advancing from miner to mine operator, she also ran a hospital for native workers and made intensive study of New Guinea culture while her husband turned from his failure at mining to shopkeeping.

Novelist Enid Bagnold discusses seven decades of her life and achievements as a novelist and playwright without giving us a glimpse of her husband, while Ethel Mannin charts her progress from poet to novelist to noted editor in detail but leaves us to guess from a few mentions of her solitude that she has separated from her husband. Barbara Cartland has nothing to say about the effects, good or ill, of either of her two husbands on her writing career. Edith Summerskill, awarded a life peerage for her work in medicine and in government administration, feelingly praises her father's contribution to her medical and political career but makes no mention of her marital partner. After briefly discussing her husband's early military post, Lisa Sheridan drops any mention of him in the detailed account of her increasing success and fame as a photographer. Although in many working-class accounts of family life and economic struggle the husband may be absent altogether, the textual absence of the husband in narratives of other classes constitutes an unwritten story.

Coupled with this silence is the more profound one on intimate and manifestly sexual marital matters. One pattern of narration occurs so often in these narratives that it establishes a decorum of form: the woman records her life from childhood to adolescence (with romantic feelings openly described) to courtship and the wedding ceremony. Describing the process of being single to being married, autobiographers shift in focus (as it were) from romance to finance. The window open to the woman's erotic feelings is customarily closed by the text's recitation of the marriage ceremony. This generality is not uniform in its application; if bits and pieces of the marital picture do surface, it is usually to justify later marital strife or separation.

A harmonious relationship tends to remain concealed. Barbara Cartland is willing to document that her divorce from her first husband was occasioned by his infidelity, but is unwilling to document her happiness with her second husband. Many working-class wives record domestic violence, but domestic happiness as a topic is left unexplored. One possible factor in this reticence may be the close associations between married life and sexual intimacy, a discussion of which, in most of these historical narratives, appears socially taboo. It is evidently less acceptable to discuss marital sexuality than it is to discuss sexual relations external to the marriage in which one partner or the other may have engaged; illicit lovers receive more open mention than a woman's legally sanctioned bedpartner.

Roughly five percent of the families remembered in these narratives—a significant minority—experienced domestic violence. One eighteenth-century victim, Mary Farrer, devotes her entire text to exposing her husband's physical and psychological terrorism of her and to charting her repeated legal failures in trying to prosecute him. A century later, Minnie Tyrrell gives documentation of her working-class husband's alcoholism, infidelity, misappropriation of family funds, and cruelty toward her. After turning both her and their small children out into the streets to live, he was imprisoned for robbery, yet Tyrrell found divorce unobtainable. A woman nicknamed "Caddie," an Australian barmaid and domestic worker, records rescuing her children from her husband's abuse yet glosses lightly over her own beatings at his hands.

From the accounts of marital violence (both in autobiographers' marriages and the marriages of their parents) a dominant image emerges: violence is a working-class phenomenon with significant links to alcoholism, poverty, and class disempowerment. This impression is augmented by studies of domestic violence conducted both by contemporary observers and by present-day historians. In her 1878 essay on "Wife Torture," social reformer Frances Power Cobbe exposes working-class men's widespread indulgence in kicking, blinding, maiming, burning, strangling, and stabbing the women legally bound to them, using an arsenal of contemporary newspaper articles, criminal court statistics, and her first-hand witness to beaten wives' laments. Although Cobbe meticulously counts the thousands of court cases dealing with domestic abuse in the decade of the 1870s, she does not estimate how large a percentage of the working-class population her statistics entail. Present-day historian

Ellen Ross notes two factors providing a context for Cobbe's figures. First, Ross points out, only the most sensational of these cases ever made it to court, because working-class culture accustomed women to view less serious beatings as a normal, expected part of marriage. Second, when a man wrought exceptional violence against his spouse, her realistic fear of him prevented her from reporting the case; Ross estimates that only one out of a hundred incidents of violence against wives ever found its way into the statistical record. As a result, the historical record appears skewed to represent only those women willing to come forward or those crimes so atrocious that the police intervened, despite law enforcement policy that wife-beating was a husband's legitimate response to domestic provocation and thus a "minimum offence" to which public opinion ought to extend "a particular kind of indulgence."

While working-class domestic violence dominates the autobiographies in *Women in Context,* tacit omissions of personal marital matters create points of invisibility where abuse may be concealed; as with sexual intimacy in these accounts, the intimacy of domestic violence is also withheld from material intended for publication. Although these autobiographies can be suggestive, their patterns of concealment indicate that unpublished materials—personal letters and diaries—should be sought out to amend the incomplete picture in official records. Cobbe acknowledges that while court records give her a window on violence in the working class, she lacks concrete information about married relations in the higher classes. Instead, she estimates the occurrence of violence in middle-class families from indirect suggestions. Scholars in the twentieth century have little more information to work from concerning middle-class marital relations than did Cobbe in the nineteenth century.

Personal Friendship and Professional Affiliation

By choice, many women in this bibliography remained single. Although not all of them were financially independent, many did, in fact, develop professional careers. Some single women, such as Margaret Murray, Margaret Bondfield, Harriet Martineau, Frances Power Cobbe, and Catherine Spence, indicate that close female friendships compensated for the absence of marriage. Violet Trefusis discusses her friendship with Vita Sackville-West while omitting its erotic nature. In her own autobiography, however, Sackville-West discusses their friendship and its sexual elements openly.

Naturally, not all of the woman/woman relationships discussed were friendly. Women competing in the same profession often reveal conflicting feelings about the other, amity in uneasy alliance with jealousy. Beatrice Lillie records watching with ambivalent longing as her friend Gertrude Lawrence, taking Lillie's place on an American tour, achieved success and won rave reviews.

Clusters of these autobiographers acknowledge a key pioneer in their own field, from medicine (Scharlieb and Elizabeth Garrett Anderson both reverently naming Elizabeth Blackwell) to gardening (Muriel Marson and Marion Spring aspiring to live up to the landscape design genius of Gertrude Jekyll). Many diverse professions—golfing, aviation, international journalism, publishing, national politics, horsebreeding and entrepreneurship among them—are represented in this bibliography by practitioners whose differing views of their personal fields provide fascinating and illuminating contrast.

EDUCATION AND CAREER

Educational Opportunities

After the mid 1860s, truly academic secondary and higher educational institutions opened for women. Bolstered by the likes of education reformers Elizabeth Sewell and Elizabeth Wordsworth, who helped to win parliamentary support for their cause, the women's education movement continued to advance. Interestingly, this collection of narratives suggests that the best preparation for one of these new, scholastic institutions was a sound home education (often by the father). Increasingly, women who had performed well used their college education to teach, becoming college lecturers, tutors, or dons—as did academics Jane Harrison, Margaret Mary Leigh and Frances Ralph Gray. In fact, the educational progression from student to academic for many of these writers (among them Eleanor Lodge, history tutor at Lady Margaret Hall, Oxford and Eliza Marian Butler, chair of German at Newnham, Cambridge and at Manchester) occupies the center of their narratives.

Secular Careers

With increased commercialization, multiplication of marketplaces, and consumerism, women began entering the fields of science, economics and politics. In the sciences, many of our women writers tended to be observers, like naturalists Eliza Brightwen and Margaret Hutchinson, and teachers, like Francis Pitt. By the latter half of the nineteenth century, however, the women in *Women in Context* show an active scientific engagement, progressing from being self-taught amateurs (like agriculturalist Eleanor Ormerod and botanist Marianne North) to being formally educated scientific professionals and innovators, such as entomologist Evelyn Cheesman and astronomer Cecilia Gaposchkin, who in the 1930s emigrated to America to escape the career restrictions she found in Britain. Women in medicine also record their successful efforts to acquire formal education and to practice despite a professional atmosphere of male resistance.

Closed institutional doors did not prevent the lucky and ambitious from entering a wide range of new professions. Networking, mentorship, and nepotism were some of the ways women gained entrance. In the case of Beatrice Holmes, a male mentor helped her to establish herself as stockbroker and financier. Zoe Hart Dyke successfully turned a hobby of raising silkworms into a profitable enterprise. Through her husband and her father-in-law, Flora Eaton became vice president of one of Canada's largest retail empires. Numerous aviators formed a close-knit professional sisterhood as a bulwark of mutual encouragement: Amy Johnson, Gertrude Bacon, Beryl Markham, Jean Batten, Winifrid Brown, flying partners Pauline Gower and Dorothy Spicer, and solo balloonist Dolly Shepherd.

Women's presence in politics on any of several levels, from the local to the national, is evident from the eighteenth century onward. Often a woman might manage her husband's (or paramour's) public career from behind the scenes. Harriette Wilson, Catherine Cary, Mary Ann Clarke, and Margaret Coghlan all record waging political intrigue—or having it waged against them.. In eighteenth-century France, Lady Grace Elliot aided royalists to escape from the Reign of Terror. During the same period in Britain, women established themselves as political patrons, hostesses, lobbyists, pamphleteers, influence peddlers, and speechwriters; their activities markedly affected the structures of power in political, diplomatic, and royal circles.

However, roughly a century later, near the close of the nineteenth century, women's opportunity for more direct political engagement expanded further. Several of the writers represented in *Women in Context* document careers of great political influence, among them conservative Members of Parliament Katherine Stewart-Murray and Thelma Cazelet Keir, Labour M.P.s Edith Picton-Turbervill, Elizabeth Braddock, and Margaret Bondfield (also a cabinet minister), and socialist M.P.s Jenny Lee and Leah Manning. It was feasible for a determined woman to gain entrée to a political career through family relationships, a tactic displayed in the personal history of Thelma Cazalet Keir, with her ties to the family of statesman David Lloyd George. Eleanor Acland, as well, profited from her own family's tradition of supplying England with Liberal male M.P.s, her grandfather, father, and husband all filling this office. And established women politicians sometimes married men in their own field, leading to an effective partnership; such was the case for Labour M.P. Elizabeth Braddock who, together with her husband, Jack, (also a Labour Member of Parliament) combined forces in their political work. As Lady Mayoress of Leicester, Lady Isobell Barnett worked together in municipal government with her husband, a City Councilman, while socialist Jennie Lee, the youngest ever woman M.P., married another illustrious House of Commons member, Aneurin Bevan, with whom she waged joint efforts at legal reform.

However, the scope of political involvement for women in this bibliography was much broader than a tally of elected officials can indicate. It ranges from the service of social reformer Catherine Spence (first woman in Australia to run for elective office) on the national Advisory Board for the Education Department, through the work of Dame Enid Lyons as her Prime Minister husband's campaign manager, to the political militancy of South African Helen Joseph, anti-apartheid activist and close associate of the Mandelas. In India, the woman known as Mirabehn (formerly Madeleine Slade) forsook Western culture and converted to Buddhism in order to work for India's independence as the close personal aide of Mohandas Gandhi.

The arts have an especially strong showing in this bibliography. In England, it was difficult for women painters to master their craft due to restrictions placed on their access to the Royal Academy and its satellite schools. Until a very late date, for example, women were barred from fulfilling the requirements to attend life drawing classes and so had no opportunity to work from the nude figure. Still, a number of women artists represented here transcended these barriers. With a mother who was herself a Royal Academician and a family who championed her aspirations, Estella Canziani developed into an influential artist. Military painter Elizabeth Butler, wife of a colonial general, found that her artistic preoccupation with colonial subjects and regimental ritual coincided neatly with Britain's romance with its own imperialist ventures. As a direct result, her canvases became tremendously popular and remunerative.

Moreover, these women artists largely espoused feminist points of view. The strong-willed Henriette Corkran, for instance, a realistic painter with a private Royal Academy exhibition to her credit, vociferously challenged Sir Frederick Leighton's opinion that women's art should be pretty. As for Stella Bowen, a painter from the school that included Walter Sickert, her autobiography discusses the restrictions binding women painters that confined her, for practical monetary reasons, to painting portraits instead of rendering more vigorous and imaginative scenes. In another challenge to aesthetic and gender conventions, a colony of women artists in the 1920s established a congenial base in bohemian Paris, autobiographers Nina Hamnett and Emily Carr among them.

Electing to take training in the more egalitarian atmosphere of the Continent, sculptor Mary Bromet attained renown in her field, ultimately assuming the presidency of the Society of Women Artists in Britain. Sculptor Consuelo Sheridan, inflamed by her passionate youthful advocacy of Communism, traveled to Russia and sculpted the heads of Lenin and Trotsky, using the live leaders as models; she later worked in creative art circles in New York and Hollywood. Dame Barbara Hepworth, a major abstract sculptor who trained at the Royal College of Art, traveled to Florence to teach herself the sculpting of Carrara marble, and became—as did her husband—a leading light of the twentieth-century's Constructivist movement. Hepworth was also an established art critic, as was Moma Clarke, who served as English delegate to the women's arm of *l'Academie Goncourt,* theatrical reviewer for the London *Standard,* and foreign fashion correspondent for *The Times,* in addition to reviewing new pictorial art for *Leisure* magazine.

Professional singers are well represented in these accounts, among them opera singers Isobel Baillie and Dame Nellie Melba as well as popular singers Jose Collins and Cecile de Banke. A substantial number of other women gained fame as instrumentalists or composers. Pianist Alice Diehl studied in France and Germany in preparation for her concert career and performed internationally; the blind Eva Longbottom had a concert piano career and pioneered new methods of teaching blind musicians using Braille. Pianist and composer Adelina de Lara studied with Clara Schumann and Johannes Brahms before going on to write orchestral compositions; composer Ethel Smyth earned renown for her musical compositions, orchestral work, and operas. In a different musical arena was Maude Valerie White, who undertook music studies in Paris and at the Royal Academy of Music before venturing out as a freelance songwriter.

In theater the most widely practiced occupation was acting (as opposed to stage managing or producing), with well over twelve percent of the autobiographers in this collection having acted for pay. Before the middle of the nineteenth century, women for whom acting was a lifelong profession characteristically had parents for whom theater was the family business. Charlotte Charke's father was playwright Colley Cibber. Marie Bancroft and Adelaide Calvert were both child actors from theatrical families. However, as autobiographies begin to represent twentieth-century events, they show that commercial theater expanded and women, including job seekers from the working- and lower-middle classes, were recruited for small, temporary parts. Janet Hitchman, an orphaned working-class young woman who had made the rounds of many short-lived jobs, such as dispatch clerk, fabric saleswoman, and switchboard operator, tried her hand at acting because her husband's wages as a laborer needed supplement. Following WWII, former domestic worker Jean Rennie took advantage of her delicate facial features to become one of the many temporary actresses hired by the British film industry during its early period of expansion. Working-class Molly Weir accepted many short-term jobs as a bit player before getting a break that won her long-term triumph as a radio personality. Whatever their class origins, many women approached the acting profession seriously, undertaking lengthy formal study of their craft. Gertrude Benson, daughter of an infantry officer, records her extensive London training in playing boys' and character roles as she worked her way toward more prominent billing; Jessie Bond, a singer/actress in light opera, undertook years of voice lessons to qualify for roles in Gilbert and Sullivan operettas.

For some women from the upper classes, acting seemed a natural accompaniment to their status as "professional beauties." In this latter category falls diplomat's daughter "Mrs. Pat" Campbell, whose beauty, despite her inexperience, won her a place in a touring acting company. The same is true for Lady Diana Cooper, who despite no formal training won a career in early film (playing opposite the likes of John Barrymore) through a combination of looks, talent, and social connections.

Numerous authors in *Women in Context* acted only briefly before turning to other vocations, a common experiment recorded in autobiographies from the eighteenth through the twentieth centuries. These authors often comment on having spent a year or two struggling to prosper as an actress in the same tone that they might use to discuss secretarial jobs. Some stories, certainly, are more spicy: in the eighteenth century the colorful Mary Anne Clarke tried a spot of stage acting here and there as variety (one supposes) in her ongoing career as mistress to politically powerful men. A century later, Peggy Webling abandoned her performing career for writing, turning out novels, short stories, plays, and screenplays, one of which (adapted from her own script for stage) became the basis of Hollywood's first *Frankenstein* movies. Turning in a different career direction, Molly Weir ultimately found her niche in radio comedy.

Many times, too, professional acting careers encouraged women to delve into the wider aspects of theatrical direction, production, and other kinds of stage and property management. It is of interest that, of the authors in *Women in Context*, the earliest group of women with independent, profitable careers are those who managed their own theaters. Gladys Cooper, daughter of a theater critic, was lead performer and manager of the Playhouse Theatre for twelve years. Marie Bancroft, an esteemed actress, came into her own as a theatrical manager. Together with her husband, she shared management in the mid-nineteenth century of the most popular and lucrative stage in London. Ellen Terry, Eva Le Gallienne, Ethel Smyth, and a host of other women performers also found congenial and influential niches as producers and directors.

Where Vocation and Belief Intersect

Many of these accounts show that religious or spiritual conviction ultimately determined a woman's choice of vocation. The spectrum here is quite broad. At one end of it, women followed their Anglicanism or Catholicism into a religious sisterhood and a lifetime of missionary work or social service; at the other end, women who sought to find meaning in their rapidly changing world chose spiritualism and Theosophy, both as a philosophy and as a career. As the nineteenth century advanced, embracing science and dismissing the supernatural, some women who found science and Christianity to be in impossible contradiction turned to spiritualism to resolve the conflict. While Annie Besant, Alice A. Bailey, and Alice Dracott became followers of the Theosophical Madame Blavatsky, and Margaret Cousins and her husband practiced both Theosophy and vegetarianism, Emma Hardinge Britten and Georgiana Houghton gave their philosophical curiosity a more professional turn, developing careers out of spiritualist mediumship. World War I boosted the cultural fascination with spiritualism, with many people seeking to communicate with loved ones who had been killed in the war. Gladys Osborne Leonard was a professional psychic who staged such sèances; Eileen Garett also pursued this career for a time, but ultimately rejected it in order to study her clairvoyant gifts scientifically. For the Theosophical women who followed Blavatsky to India, their confrontation with India's political and social problems led them to work for Indian welfare, as with Annie Besant's endeavors in Indian politics and Margaret Cousins's work for Indian political independence.

Traditional religious vocations still held a foothold among women, and, with the late nineteenth century's focus on social and political issues, a woman's participation in a religious order was frequently a platform from which to fight for political and social reform. Anglican Deaconess Isabella Gilmore used her position to organize a collective battle against poverty in the slums of Battersea; Katherine Warburton, as a sister in an Anglican convent in East End London, founded clubs for girls and women, a school for poor boys, and refuges for the homeless. Rosamund Essex edited the Anglican *Church Times*; Anglicans Edith Picton-Turbervill and Maude Royden agitated for women's ordination. In the Catholic ranks was Frances Wynne, whose conversion led directly to her political championing of Welsh nationalist militants. Margaret Fletcher founded the Catholic Women's League and publisher Maisie Ward used her position and education in the socioeconomic theories of Catholic writers G. K. Chesterton and Hilaire Belloc to fight for Catholic labor reform. Sister Mary Frances Cusack devoted her life to political activism on behalf of Irish working girls and Irish tenants. She and Sister Mary Aloysius Doyle—as well as the anonymous author of the *Life of an Enclosed Nun*—give space in their personal narratives to an evaluation of the British Catholic-Protestant conflict from a Catholic perspective, while an anti-Catholic perspective is featured in the autobiographies of Charlotte Elizabeth Tonna, Eliza Smith Richardson, and Ellen Dando.

Working within religious societies or social reform organizations, women whose narratives appear in *Women in Context* set out to better the lot of others: educating them in ethical principles, easing their poverty, and changing their lives. Central among these religious societies were the sects of Nonconformist Christians who, in their rejection of Anglicanism, the state religion, gained the moral distance necessary to cast a conscious, critical eye on what they viewed as its lack of piety, complacent Anglican worldliness, and inequities of the social class system.

Of these sects, Quakerism receives substantial space in our text in many personal narratives by Quaker activists. Within this denomination that specified active female roles, many women felt they had been called to be itinerant preachers. They recorded their travels; Mary Alexander, Elizabeth Ashbridge, and Dorothy Ripley are representative examples. Many preachers traveled around the British Isles, some going farther afield to the United States and Canada. Because Quaker women ministers characteristically mention the names of female colleagues in their traveling networks, their autobiographies provide useful documentation of the scope of Quaker activities and of the extent of their religious community. In addition to working for spiritual renewal, Quakers have also traditionally been keenly involved in social activism; autobiographers who offer an excellent record of such activism include Priscilla Hanna Gurney and Hilda Deichmann. From a different vantage point, Mary Charlotte Sturge paints a vivid picture of the private Quaker milieu, while Sarah Greer—after a life of Quakerism—defected from the denomination and launched a personal anti-Quaker campaign.

Among other Nonconformist denominations, Methodists are the second most frequent to document their activities in *Women in Context.* As did the Quakers, Methodists perceived a cause and effect relationship between alcohol use and working-class problems of domestic violence, unemployment, and homelessness. Both denominations worked actively in the temperance movement, a field especially well-described by the Methodist Lucy Broad. Raised in Cornwall by a temperance advocate mother, not only Lucy but her three siblings became life-long ministers of the cause. Ellen Dando, from a different background, was converted from Catholicism to Methodism and became a Methodist lay preacher; her account closely documents the contemporary conditions under which women could attain that position and the duties that it entailed. Beatrice Hawker, on the other hand, was spiritually moved in the opposite direction, becoming a convert from her childhood Methodism to Roman Catholicism—not before living as a preacher in the Junior Free Church Council, which stationed itself outside pubs to challenge pubgoers to a conversion experience. As Sturge does for Quakerism, Hawker provides a window on the Methodist subculture of her era.

Other Protestant denominations are represented here: Christian Science, Congregationalism, the Plymouth Brethren, Presbyterianism, Baptism, and Unitarianism. Unitarian women echo Quakers in their attraction to social reform networks, as with Harriet Martineau and Georgiana Kirby, who was a resident of the politically idealistic Brook Farm in New England. The Jewish women in this present collection show particularly intense sociopolitical engagement, whether in philanthropy (Baroness Battersea and Helen Bentwich) or in social reform

(Lily Montagu). Even those Jewish women who converted to Christianity maintained Jewish traditions of social service, as with Henrietta Leslie and Naomi Jacob. Most of the Jewish autobiographers in *Women in Context* were also involved in the issue of Zionism, whether defending or questioning it.

Many writers here, however, while documenting their personal devotion to Christian endeavor, leave unspecified what denomination, if any, to which they adhered. Despite the diversity of their spiritual vocations, distinct patterns emerge: these women overwhelmingly engaged in philanthropic activities, reaching out without remuneration to alleviate the social problems of their time. Of the women whom we have identified as "religionists," only a handful accepted the confinement of their homes. The rest worked actively in the general community, raising money, tending the sick, teaching children, building homes for the homeless, running soup kitchens.

Social reform, however, was hardly the exclusive property of the religiously inspired. With increasing secularization, the meaning that religious belief had formerly lent to life could still be found in a belief in social betterment. For a significant percentage of the women in *Women in Context*, reform became a religion in itself. This eagerness to participate in social betterment embraced all of the social classes. In the aristocracy, social work and activism permitted women such as Lady Aberdeen and Lady Baden-Powell to fulfill a personal commitment to social improvement that also expressed their expected noblesse oblige. Lady Airlie did public service by helping to organize the Red Cross, while Lady Clodagh Anson used the influence her title gave her to improve conditions during WWI for prisoners and for the homeless. Middle-class humanitarianism significantly affected national conditions; Olive Mackirdy is an emblematic figure in the social movement to better conditions for poor working girls and women. She states that such commitment helped to cure her despair over the accidental death of her young husband. In the lower middle and working classes as well, women often found a calling in social service, frequently a highly personal one. The frequency of alcoholism in lower-class environments is reflected in the many women from these classes who worked as temperance activists, notable among them Letitia Youmans, the Canadian mother and housewife who founded Canada's Women's Christian Temperance Union. Such women might also take upon themselves the humanitarian vocation of charitable visitor, unconnected to any official organization. Both Fay Inchfawm in England and Bella Cooke as an émigré to New York undertook such a personal commitment.

These small, private stories of social involvement are matched by those of women who undertook broader political battles, among them suffragists and other feminist activists. Nearly ten percent of the women in this collection were involved in the suffrage movement, one out of three to a militant degree. It is startling to find so many women matter-of-factly recounting their time in jail, incarcerated for their public protests. Certainly the Pankhurst women devoted their lives and considerable talents in sacred fashion to this cause, and Sylvia Pankhurst's written history of the suffrage movement reads like the history of a world religion.

Beyond suffrage, women were to the fore in every large-scale social movement. The Quaker Doris Daglish spearheaded the pacifist movement at the onset of WWI (a movement also championed by other writers in *Women in Context*, among them Vera Brittain, Maude Onions, Ethel Mannin, and Emily Pankhurst). The battle against vivisection and animal abuse, initiated by the 1824 founding of the RSPCA, was characterized truthfully, if disparagingly, by its opponents as being fought by "a pack of women." Many of the autobiographers in *Women in Context* assert their commitment to animal activism, among them Sophia De Morgan, Dame Louisa Lumsden, and Isabel Fyvie Mayo (the last two authors serving as energetic editors of antivivisection publications). Known equally for her outspoken feminism, animal welfare activist Frances Power Cobbe successfully waged political battle for the passage of the 1876 parliamentary bill restricting the practice of vivisection. At an earlier time, women's abolitionist work was center-stage, an involvement extensively documented in the narratives of Fanny Kemble, Josephine Butler, Mary Howitt, Harriet Martineau, and numerous others. Countless women also committed their talents to the socialist movement, as writers (among them Vera Brittain, Ethel Mannin, and Beatrice Webb), activists (such as Theresa La Chard and Helen Joseph), public speakers (Muriel Lester, Frances Greville, and a host of others) and as elected public servants. The most powerful women in this last category are Labour M.P.s Leah Manning and Jennie Lee, who directly influenced British legislation.

Finally, a discussion of women's engagement in social action must certainly address the many women missionaries who voluntarily gave up the familiarity of home and nation to preach and teach in other cultures. However, missionary dispersion is so intimately bound to Britain's expansion through imperialism and colonization that we have reserved it to discuss as part of the phenomenon of British women's world-wide diaspora.

MIGRATION AND EMIGRATION

Urbanization

Because the chronological scope of this anthology coincides fairly closely with the onset of the Industrial Revolution and its developing social consequences, a pervasive topic in these narratives is migration, either of families or individuals, from rural environments to urban ones. Whether this relocation proved traumatic or stimulating, the narratives suggest, depended largely on the strength of a family's ties and the stability of its values. Such is the case for Margaret Penn, whose nurtured childhood with her parents and foster parents in a rural village sustained her emotionally through the cultural dislocation of her move to London and to the homes of other foster parents who looked down on her rural customs. Born to a coal miner's family in rural Cloucestershire, Winifred Foley's occupation as a domestic servant introduced her to many unfamiliar environments, from country houses to urban London, exposing her in the process to the dangers of sexual predation. Maintaining her self-respect, as she recounts, she avoided such snares and eventually developed a writing career. Not all migration was from country to town; abused by her father, Londoner Mary Saxby made good her escape by taking up the vagrant life in the countryside and working seasonally as a migrant harvester. She ultimately recovered from the trauma of her dislocation through the agency of a substitute family, her Methodist chapel.

If these accounts deal practically with the adjustment difficulties inherent in urban relocation, they also share a fascination with the unspoiled rural locales that were lost, both to the individual and to Britain itself, with the inexorable encroachment of progress. The wistful nostalgia that these narratives demonstrate toward authors' rural origins suggests that in reliving their lives through the act of writing them, these writers are sometimes less concerned with introspective personal exploration than with returning to a time and place that is otherwise unrecoverable. Their collective discourse valorizing Britain's earlier, agricultural ways reflects a fascinating opposition to Britain's industrial urbanization, and a chronological arrangement of these narratives (which can be seen in *Women in Context*'s Author Index by Twenty-Year Cohorts) shows that, as urbanization progressed, the number of autobiographies obsessed with the rural memories of childhood increased dramatically, with each one being painted in loving detail. Accordingly, because such accounts provide a cultural photograph of their era, they offer historians important evidence of past rural life and customs and of the strategies used by rural natives to preserve their culture. Peig Sayers is one remarkable example of a rural native who preserved her Irish Gaelic culture through the ongoing ritual of telling folk stories. Other women in this collection such as Alison Uttley and Mathena Blomefield recount folk beliefs and customs in order to recreate their vanished culture in their narratives. Flora Thompson's childhood reminiscences fully realize her ambition to reconstruct, detail by loving detail, the farm, village, and town life of rural Oxfordshire.

Urban natives included in *Women in Context* also seem to share the urge to celebrate rural simplicity. Many urban working-class writers (Kathleen Dayus and Jane Walsh among them) cite brief childhood holidays on farms as having profoundly affected their developing view of the world, awakening their sense of injustice at being confined to the ugliness of city life. In a more recent autobiography, the elderly Daisy Baker uses her narrative to lament the invasion of her quiet rural roads by weekend traffic from the city, juxtaposing Baker's donkey cart with the automobile, an emblem of future rural extinction. After WWI, some urban professional women took up farming as a respite from city living, as did Margaret Leigh, who abandoned an academic career at Oxford to pursue farming in Scotland. Dorothy Easton, an urban writer, also forsook intellectual labor for farm work; Justina Spencer-Knott, a city girl from England, committed herself to life in South Africa as a rural stockbreeder. In each instance, these narratives contrast the writers' expectations with their actual experiences, and in each instance the text highlights the profound reverence for the natural world that such a return to the soil provided for these women. Leigh expresses it the most clearly; she compares the urban dweller converted to farmer to a converted Catholic who, unlike his born-into-the-faith neighbor, can never take the true religion for granted.

Emigration

If some of our authors tried to recreate more innocent times by returning to the British countryside, others did so by emigrating. Many of the accounts in *Women in Context* are by women pioneers or homesteaders who participated in the growth of a newer nation. Critic Anna Jameson married a Canadian barrister and found herself in that new country at the age of twenty-nine; Nellie McClung left her Ontario home to take up homesteading in the western provinces. Suffolk native Susanna Moodie's marriage took her to Canada's northern provinces, while Georgiana Binnie-Clark was only a child when her innkeeper father, determined to start his life over, committed his family to homesteading in Manitoba. Each of these writers reflects on the maturation of a distinct Canadian national identity. Other autobiographers, securely established in Canada, choose to focus on more specific issues of Canadian society, as with Letitia Youmans, organizer of temperance reform.

Inevitably, as Canada itself matured and was caught up in the global twentieth century influences of world war and urban development, its women produced autobiographies demonstrating both a growing rural-urban rift and a waning sense of Canadian uniqueness. Flora Eaton, an Ontario native who married into her husband's family business and rose to be the president of Canada's largest retail manufacturer, writes a success story indistinguishable in its outlook from that of any other businesswoman, whether in Britain or in the far-flung empire. Her urban narrative stands in strong contrast to the one from Luta Munday, daughter of an English immigrant, whose marriage to a Royal Canadian Mounty took her into the world of frontier outposts among native Americans and the earlier mode of tribal living preserved unchanged.

Wherever women authors in *Women in Context* emigrated, they tended to write of their pioneer experiences in similar ways. Catherine Helen Spence, Agnes Hunt, and Mary Stawell homesteaded in Australia, Helen Wilson in New Zealand. Yet each woman, regardless of her regional residence, focused on her increasing engagement with her developing nation, her participation in creating social institutions, and her commitment to social reform. As a result, their collective narratives create a fertile field for comparative cultural study, whether of women emigrants of different social classes (from "Caddie" the Sydney barmaid to Mary Stawell, wife of Australia's attorney general), of their experiences in different colonies, or of female social reform work in various regions of the British Empire.

THE EMPIRE AND IMPERIALIST PERCEPTIONS

Racism at Home

Racial and cultural attitudes informed by hostility toward foreign cultures manifest themselves in many narratives in *Women in Context,* whether these views originate with the writer or with her culture at large. Nor arc such accounts always the product of the writer having lived in a foreign country; several of our collected authors complain about the treatment of people of color in the British Isles. Some Anglo-Indian writers recorded bringing their Indian ayahs (children's nursemaids) to Britain and spoke of the bigotry which these servants encountered. Julia Curtis abruptly took her family back to India rather than endure the racial prejudice the ayah was subjected to in England. In the 1930s, Beatrice Ali married a native of East Pakistan and lived with him in a non-white working-class borough of East London. In spite of her acquired cultural familiarity with non-Europeans, however, Ali's recorded assessments of Indian and Pakistani character are full of negative cultural stereotypes. Ironically, she does not seem to associate her own racial beliefs with the discrimination she and her Eurasian children faced, and about which she complains bitterly in her writing.

Racism Abroad

By far the greatest number of texts that deal with racism and cultural paranoia, however, do originate from writers in colonial locales. In this regard, many of the autobiographies in *Women in Context* exhibit a animosity and irritation toward the "natives" that, one strongly suspects, is the autobiographer's sense of cultural discomfort and homesickness using a handy outlet to vent itself. To cite one instance, the Irish Elizabeth Fenton felt exiled in India and uses her narrative to denigrate

India, its customs, and the character of its people. Her views were tainted by the death of her young husband by fever in the 1820s and other familial and economic frustrations; although her views are characteristic of colonial ideology about the white man's obligation to "civilize" nonwhites, she opines that the Indian character is such that any efforts to alter it are wasted. Other foreign residents, such as Isabel Burton and Ethel Knight Kelly, lived in many places, met peoples of many different cultures, and yet expressed dislike toward all of them in general.

Counterracism

Some of the authors in this collection demonstrate, in their writing, their own efforts to gain multicultural sensitivity; good examples are Margery Perham and Sylvia Leith-Ross in Africa, who discuss the British colonial presence from both British and native perspectives. Other women studied native cultures in the area to which they had emigrated and reflect their cultural respect in their narratives; gold miner Doris Booth became fascinated by New Guinea natives and their customs; she learned their language and discusses cannibalism with calm objectivity. Margaret, Lady Brooke, wife of the British Rajah of Sarawak, together with her husband divided her time between England and Malaysia; she mastered the Malay language and developed such a cultural intimacy with Malaysian women that her husband reprimanded her "excessive familiarity" with the natives. Another wife of a civil servant, the irrepressible Flora Annie Steel, established herself in India as teacher, amateur medic, objective arbiter of native disputes, and advocate for female Indian welfare in combat with the colonial administration. Anna Leonowens (possibly of Eurasian origins herself) gained fame for the relationship of mutual esteem which she established with the King of Siam and his many children; her reverence for all aspects of Siamese culture receives profound expression in her text. In China, the missionary Lucy Soothill deliberately assimilated to the culture, speaking Cantonese, wearing Chinese dress and hairstyle, and adopting Chinese perspectives in order to comment on Europeans and on Christianity. In the United States, sculptor Consuelo Sheridan traveled among the Blackfeet and Crow tribes, whose physical beauty leads her narrative into a discussion of cross-cultural concepts of beauty and an examination of the factors behind white prejudices against native Americans. The most extreme example of a woman embracing a foreign culture is that of Mary Jemison; taken captive as a child in the French and Indian Wars, she acculturated herself to Indian life and customs, married twice into Indian tribes, and completely adopted a native American identity. However, racial issues were only one of the cultural controversies affecting the women in this bibliography who chose to migrate with the expanding empire.

THE WOMEN'S DIASPORA: IMPERIAL MIGRATIONS

Imperial Ideology

As the British Empire expanded, the commonly circulated sociocultural beliefs of its home nation moved outwards as well. Numerous autobiographies in *Women in Context* that originated in areas of British colonial influence reflect the conflict then being enacted between British cultural concepts and non-white cultural realities; each women writer's viewpoint of this controversy is profoundly illustrative of her own inner assumptions. Whether living in Britain's far-flung colonies or merely visiting, these women show themselves as being drawn to comment both on imperial expansion and on the control exerted by colonial governments in terms of both native reactions to outside government and the British counterreaction. These personal narratives reveal the writers' evident awareness of the profound impact that British imperialism exerted on native social structures, religious practices, and natural habitat; however, such awareness does not always imply that these authors judged such impact to be bad. One representative example of a dyed-in-the-wool imperialist is Emily Bayley, who mourns in her book the demise of the East India Company's rule in India. Fascinated with Anglo-Indians, she sees the true natives of India only as potential servants, and judges them primarily on their domestic merits. In diametric opposition to such a racist outlook is the narrative of the nineteenth-century South African settler Mary Anne Broome, who became preoccupied with native cultural ceremonials and makes them the centerpiece of her autobiography.

Some perceptions of a writer such as Bayley are certainly determined by her historical period and milieu. In India, where British social institutions had been established long enough to ossify, women write of living in a cocoon that shielded them from interaction with—or even knowledge of—the native culture surrounding them. Bayley joins writers Lillian Luker Ashby and Augusta Becher in not only celebrating the lives and legends of other Anglo-Indian colonists but in lamenting the cultural isolation that their life in a foreign colony entailed. In many instances, political turmoil also influenced the writers' negative views of non-British peoples or culture; the 1857 Indian Mutiny is just one of the catalyzing events that both altered the British colonialists' outlook and persuaded them to change their policies toward the native peoples. Harriet Tytler (who records her presence at the siege of Delhi) contributes the most vivid account of the mutiny to this collection. Only Elizabeth Fenton's account documents settler life in India prior to the mutiny, and it, too, emphasizes the isolation and depression experienced by young Europeans toiling in India to contribute to Britain's colonial project.

Missionary Zeal

Another reaction to non-white culture was to try to change it. Some of these well-intentioned attempts include those of British social reformer Mary Carpenter who, upon hearing a London lecture on the abominable treatment of Hindu women, traveled to India to investigate the nation's social conditions. She tried to apply British models of education, morality, and femininity to the education of Indian women. Carpenter may have been a secular missionary, but for other women social reform goals overlapped with religious ones. A good example of this dual role is the missionary work of Mary Warburton Booth, who began as a reformer interested in women's issues and then experienced religious conversion. She traveled to India and mastered Urdu in order to give Bible lessons to *zenanas* (Indian women living in gender-secluded communities). Another missionary, Rose Greenfield, a member of the Society for Promoting Female Education in the East, chose to enter the houses of secluded women in order to teach them; Greenfield not only schooled herself in Urdu but wrote a book in that language about Biblical women figures.

The missionary motivation operated in close ideological parallel with the nation's imperial goals, in that both took for granted, on different levels, their benevolent enlightenment in relation to the benighted non-European, as well as their own resulting obligation to "improve" native culture and/or beliefs by means of westernization. Accordingly, missionaries figure importantly as a transcultural influence. The narratives collected here represent missionaries and what is known as missionary wives—women whose husbands felt religious callings and won official church appointments. Under the missionary banner, these wives followed their husbands into other countries and in the ongoing effort of conversion. However, in practical terms, missionary wives are indistinguishable from women who were missionaries in their own right, because both ultimately performed the same labors. Formally, they gave colonized people the rudiments of a Western education and sought to engineer their religious conversion. Informally, they tried to expose their subjects to the trappings of Western culture, befriended the women, and gave them a transcultural sounding board for their grievances, introduced practical concepts of Western medicine and hygiene, and exposed indigenous peoples to a unfamiliar set of ethical values. Emily Banks, fellow missionary to her husband in the Congo, became intensely involved with her native pupils and their welfare. Establishing a local school and learning the language and culture, she took sides with Congolese wives against the subjugation they experienced from their husbands, and with her husband fought the African slave trade and to protect Africans from colonial abuses.

The African Experience

Because of Britain's extensive colonial activities in Africa from Egypt to Cape Horn, the differing attitudes and adjustments of British women who settled on this continent serve as a representative microcosm of world-wide British outlooks. Interestingly, the autobiographies in *Women in Context* suggest that European women had greater scope for ambitious activities in Africa than they did in India. Unlike India's relative cultural homogeneity, the diversity of African tribal societies hindered the British creation of a powerful colonial government. In Africa the efforts of colonization were more of a struggle. British missionary women in Africa had full scope for their endeavors. Whatever their proselytizing goals, these women effectively prioritized literacy and health, establishing schools, hospitals, and other vital parts of the infrastructure of these developing colonial territories.

Other British women found that Africa released them from gendered restrictions on their activities, too. In this continent, women might undertake explorations on their own, accompanied only by native guides or porters for their luggage. In 1909 Marguerite Roby did exactly this, making a solo trek into the Congo (in order to see for herself the validity of reported Begian atrocities against the natives) aided by her bicycle, guide, and porters. Together with her military husband, Constance Larymore ventured on surveying expeditions in Nigeria, the first Englishwoman to enter its northern provinces. Beryl Markham, whose father emigrated to Africa when she was four, lived a life of intrepid freedom divided among race-horse training and daredevil aviation. Coming out to South Africa to take up a governess position, Sarah Heckford lingered, becoming a farmer, selling her produce from a traveling wagon, and operating as a trader during the Boer War.

In Africa, European women's attitudes concerning their new surroundings differed dramatically. As a newlywed, Sylvia Leith-Ross traveled to Nigeria with her husband; she eventually rose to be the nation's ministerial secretary of education and made a study of the race and gender problems in Nigeria's turbulent politics. Australian-born Mary Gaunt, on the other hand, valued Africa primarily for its settlement potential. Although she condemned the ecological impact of the British deforestation policy in Africa, she also belittled the capacities of the natives and celebrated the "discipline" used by the various colonial administrations to govern them. Perceiving the cultural taint of Africa in the behavior—both social and sexual—of European male immigrants, Gaunt addresses her book to white women, encouraging them to emigrate to Africa in large numbers in order to re-impose European morality on these men. She shares this sentiment with Mrs. Horace Tremlett, wife of a mining engineer, who experienced first-hand the male culture that had developed in a Nigerian tin prospecting camp. The urge for women to come to Africa as a civilizing influence has close, secular parallels to the missionary impulse. Often, women who ventured to Africa with the determination to impose their home culture rather than accepting the one they found in Africa discovered the continent to be *No Place for a White Woman,* as Mary Elizabeth Oake entitled her autobiography, or *The Land That Never Was,* Alyce Simpson's chosen title for her disillusioned account of her failed attempt at farming in Kenya. In the twentieth century, autobiographers in *Women in Context* record the dissolution of the colonial structures of government and the concomitant rise of racial strife. Some, like Barbara Carr, waxed bitter about the turbulent social changes. Anti-apartheid activist Helen Joseph celebrated a new multiracial society that seemed to be waiting in the future.

THE GREAT WAR

The Great Divide

The single most important event in our authors' accounts, one which marks a watershed change in the outlook of women's autobiographies, is World War I. Earlier personal narratives tend largely to present their author as a unique woman whose accomplishments and rare experiences are worthy of record. However, the cataclysmic effects of WWI on the fabric of British society produced autobiographers whose sense of themselves is much more modest. As with the urban migration that left behind images of rural tranquillity, the post–WWI period produced a spate of women's narratives sweet with pre-war nostalgia. Characteristic of these autobiographies is their identity as self-portraits not of extraordinary women who merit documentation but rather of typical women who had experienced an extraordinary time, the irretrievable past. Thus, a relatively larger proportion of mid-twentieth-century personal narratives stops with the end of childhood, attempting to crystallize the memories of a Victorian or an Edwardian childhood. Molly MacCarthy was an important member of the Bloomsbury group and married to literary critic Desmond MacCarthy, yet she chiefly relives the late Victorian era of her wonderful childhood and teen years. In another personal narrative that recalls Victorian Britain before the author's adolescence, Olive Haweis even chooses to publish anonymously, entitling her text merely *Four to Fourteen: by a Victorian Child.*

War Work

The war effort itself forms a center of meaning in many narratives from women. Women diverted their charitable and activist energy to the war effort. They ran air raid shelters, were wound dressers in London hospitals, took in refugees, operated canteens. More than one out of five of our authors from the 1860 and 1880 cohorts in *Women in Context* performed official WWI volunteer work, and this number does not include those women who took over factory or farm jobs previously held by men or whose elected political labors became, in effect, their war contributions. These writers record their belief that the war served as catalyst for subsequent social change in Britain. Katherine Furse, wartime director of the Women's Royal Naval Service, observed how war conditions obliterated the social restrictions under which young women had hitherto labored. Newspaper journalist Dorothy Lawrence neatly evaded gender barriers (and official channels) by disguising herself as a man in order to enlist; her account sensationally documents a soldier's life in the trenches. Peggy Hamilton, an upper-class young woman doing munitions work, recounted that girls of all social classes suddenly mixed; working together as nurses, driving ambulances, laboring in factories. Monica Salmond, daughter of a baron, as a volunteer nurse and X-ray technician on the European front lived and worked closely with women of every conceivable background. Frequently, these women aver that the war, by promoting social bonds between women, directly promoted feminist activism.

Other war experiences were unsettling or traumatic. Gilbert Stone, in his 1917 anthology *Women War Workers,* documented the varied experiences and trials such women encountered. In *Women in Context,* Mabel Lethbridge narrates vividly her injury in a munitions factory explosion. A wartime administrator of the Auxiliary Territorial Service, Helen Gwynne Vaughan recalls her frustration that women's roles in the military were haphazardly informal and unrecognized. Another journalist, Anne Gladys Lloyd, trapped in Belgium when the war erupted, carried on with her job despite being suspected of spying for the British.

The largest proportion of volunteers did nursing, with generous numbers in professional nursing and in the Voluntary Aid Detachment. While novelist Enid Bagnold's VAD nursing memoirs record primarily her antipathy to the shortages, personality conflicts, and death surrounding her, Olive Dent's more public record maintains good humor as it offers character sketches of fellow nurses, anecdotes of patients' good will, and comic accounts of ingenious substitutions for supplies and equipment. VAD nurses, unused to the medical consequences of war, produced stark pictures of what they saw in field hospitals, the most illuminating and also the most horrific being Lesley Smith's narrative of her four years nursing on the French front. Professional nurses such as Catherine Black render a less impassioned view of wartime conditions and battlefield wounds, but many volunteers, such as Lady Diana Cooper and Gertrude Kingston, with scanty experience seemed to have performed with determined fortitude. Maud Onions, an equally dedicated nurse, gained a deeply held pacifist conviction from the atrocities she beheld.

War Politics

Publications become propagandistic, and memoirs were no exception. Several of the selections in this anthology that were published during the 1914–18 period demonstrate such an aim, among them the anonymous *Recollections of a Royal Governess in Austria.* The young governess, identified only as May, ends her account with the murder of the Austrian empress in 1898, and up until then she provides lurid glimpses of Austrian, Hungarian, and Italian court life with political betrayals and machinations. In her *Memories of the Fatherland* governess Anne Topham, who had joined the Prussian Court in 1902, gives a close view of Kaiser Wilhelm during the war, mingling respect with a hard analysis of German vanity and political closed-mindedness. Edith Keen's *Seven Years at the Prussian Court* is outspokenly anti-German, lambasting Prince Leopold's wife-beating activities, the legal plight of married German women, and Germany's growing police surveillance.

Labour politician Mary Agnes Hamilton was shattered by the advent of WWI, whose barbarities outraged her humanist convictions; she worked in the organization of the national pacifist movement. Among the many women in the pacifist movement with her was writer and Quaker convert Doris Dalglish, whose work for the war ministry led her ultimately to oppose its efforts and to agitate for peace.

ISSUES OF FORM AND INTERPRETATION

Conjoined Narratives

Although a guillible acceptance of these autobiographies as totally factual can foster misconceptions, this documentary weakness caused by the authors'subjectivity is countered by the interconnectedness of many of these narratives. One connected narrative is by writers who established a vocation for themselves mainly in the writing of autobiographies; in this category falls Ethel Mannin, whose five autobiographies published from 1930 to 1971 chart her progress and transformations over a period of seventy years. Highly representative of this veritable vocation as professional autobiographer are Ursula Bloom and Naomi Jacob, who successfully turned their lives into their livelihood. In a fascinating self-reflexive loop, they lived double lives, living them and then reliving them as they wrote. With several autobiographical texts from one person, covering different time periods and written in different stages of her life, the identity of the autobiographical "I" can start to shift between the writer and the remembered self. At the same time, this variation of viewpoint in the same author can provide the same sort of multifaceted view of her life that an old-fashioned stereopticon produces from a flat photograph, converging the images produced by two lenses with different perspectives to convey a dramatic sense of three-dimensional reality.

Because a number of the autobiographers in *Women in Context* are linked by ties of family relationship and circumstance, they provide important individual viewpoints that counterbalance each other. Authors whose familial ties make their narratives accessible to such a reading include the sisters Violet Trefusis and Sonya Keppel, the Vanbrughs, the du Mauriers, the Martindales, and Lucy Littleton Cameron and Mary Martha Sherwood. Perhaps the most revealing familial links, however, are intergenerational, between mother and daughters, as with pairs Annabel Jackson and Anne Fremantle, and Helen and Myfanwy Thomas. Other intergenerational ties surface as well, such as those between aunt and niece: Marianne North and Katherine Furse, Janet Ross and Lina Waterfield, Constance Gordon-Cumming and Elma Napier, Virginia Woolf and Angelica Garnett. Worthy of special note, the women of the Haldane family evince the most complex interweave of multiple personal narratives, from Mary Elizabeth Haldane (1825–1925), to her daughter Elizabeth (1862–1937), to daughters-in-law Charlotte Franken Haldane (1904–1969) and Kathleen Louisa Trotter Haldane (1863–1961), and ultimately to Kathleen's daughter Naomi Haldane Mitchison (1897–1991). In addition to juxtaposing complementary views of individuals, family, or outside events, the study of such linked narratives can facilitate tracing social and attitudinal changes as new generations take the place of older ones.

Genre Considerations

I spoke earlier of at least one pattern of writing that our writers consistently tend to follow: the characteristic decorum of preserving privacy that can turn middle-class women's narratives into relatively impersonal documents. However, nearly every autobiography in this collection follows long-established patterns of personal narrative writing that suggest its author's previous exposure to older, widely read autobiographical models.

With the spiritual autobiographies that, beginning in the early eighteenth century, predominate in women's writing (a pattern visible in the Author Index), women established a pattern of expository writing that, as feminist critic Mary G. Mason has observed, creates identities for themselves in the process of searching for and finding their God. This pattern of literary self-discovery is particularly noticeable among the itinerant women preachers, Quaker and Methodist, who wrote their lives. Journeying from township to village to preach, they consistently discuss the pattern of their accumulating experiences in a way that equates their wandering lives with a journey toward God, a widely used Christian metaphor from Exodus that pious Britons would have been familiar with in Augustine's *Confessions,* John Bunyan's *Pilgrim's Progress,* and earlier Christian converts and preachers. It is interesting to note that these narratives predictably look forward to a surer life beyond this one, conveying a sense of anticipation that stands in marked contrast, for example, to those autobiographies written after WWI that look resolutely backward in time.

The sensational memoir, an example of eighteenth-century female personal writing that appears alongside the spiritual autobiography, is in many ways its opposite. Here, mutually interactive influences of factual memoir and fiction are fascinating. The several narratives in *Women in Context* from servant girls, for example, are clearly akin to Samuel Richardson's *Pamela,* although it is not clear whether the novel preceded these autobiographies or vice versa. These narratives show two other distinct motifs: the first-hand tale of court intrigue and covert diplomacy and the saga that might be called "the courtesan's progress" (or the progress of any significant social transgressor). With this latter memoir, its clear affiliation with Daniel Defoe's *Moll Flanders* draws attention to the fictive elements that appear to permeate both. Exemplifying this latter category of writing is the saga told by Mary Anne Talbot (male impersonator and sailor in the royal Navy). The narrative of Lady Grace Elliot—royal mistress, prison inmate, and loyalist in the French Revolution—mingles the "courtesan's progress" and a lurid account of court intrigue.

Also in the eighteenth century, narratives from women colonialists concerning their frontier experiences start to appear. While men's equivalent autobiographies tend to obsess over the business end of colonial struggles, women writers usually look widely about themselves, describing first-hand experiences with native culture. In general, men's accounts, it has been said, commonly discuss natives and their customs as distant-seeming curiosities. In *Women in Context,* women authors seem to create a picture of native culture for self-study, informally using the same techniques of recorded observation that would later be practiced as part of twentieth-century comparative anthropology.

By increasingly emphasizing introspection and personal maturation, nineteenth-century writings of women from the more privileged classes reflect their century's increased preoccupation with the individual as he or she develops. Such narratives function reliably to reflect the general population's familiarity with popular autobiographical works that were circulating widely during that time period: William Wordsworth's *Prelude,* the autobiographies of John Stuart Mill, Charles Darwin, and Edmund Gosse, and the fictionally treated *David Copperfield* by Charles Dickens and *Aurora Leigh* by Elizabeth Barrett Browning. In Harriet Martineau's autobiographical narrative, we see her enormously dilated treatment of her childhood period and its re-enactment of her childhood terrors as well as her childish passion for justice; in this described child, we clearly see the immature social reformer and economist who, because her book reproduces her childhood so realistically, seems to grow out of the text. At a later period, social reformer Olive Mackirdy and Dr. Louisa Martindale would demonstrate in their own autobiographies their familiarity with Martineau's text, would both record its impact on their own girlhood sensibilities, and would show the influence of Martineau's choice of autobiographical form. By directly citing previous female writers as inspiration, these autobiographies show that, as women in younger generations began to read the personal accounts of those women who had preceded them, they began to welcome these earlier female narratives into their personal conceptions of the form written autobiography should take.

As the nineteenth century progressed, narratives by women in *Women in Context* show an increasing divergence in tone and shape, depending upon the woman's social class. It appears that the spiritual autobiography, conveying the idea of life as a meaningful journey toward a better end, had taken on secular form for women of comfortable means while retaining its original spiritual connotations for those lower-class women whose economic situations necessitated a more narrow perspective. Whatever the reason, the sense of a providential destiny and a lifepath moving toward an appointed end continues with the authors in *Women in Context* to characterize working-class accounts only. Late in the nineteenth century also appear the memoirs of a new generation of "bad girls," (see the entries of Vita Sackville-West, Violet Bankes, and Diane de Bunsen) who use their autobiographies as public stages on which to act out their transgressions over again. The flavor of these late nineteenth- and early twentieth-century narratives differs from the eighteenth century's deliberately scandalous memoirs. The more modern ones seem to aim less to titillate readers than to shock them, with the writer affirming her uniqueness through written statements of defiance.

Ultimately, World War I appears to have undermined the collective production of these autobiographies, whose general focus can be seen to retreat chronologically and concentrate less on the living of life in the present time to its pre-war manifestations. This tactic appears to have helped women autobiographers claim citizenship in the earlier, more gracious era that the war destroyed. Much as do men's published self-narratives around the 1920s, women's accounts tend to cherish vanished friendships and ways of life, dwelling on past voices. Yet a reading of working-class narratives allows the opinion that they were not as vulnerable to the wistful temptation to look backward. By the 1920s, in fact, working-class autobiographies demonstrate a development of their own lively subgenre, as with Jean Rennie's *Every Other Sunday: The Autobiography of a Kitchen Maid.* They record a remarkable resiliency to hard knocks—war-induced or otherwise—and a hope founded in a growing sense of class pride. By the 1920s, then, one can posit a developing tree of women's autobiographical genres whose branches diverge from each other, continuing to manifest individual characteristics even as they mature. The collective record within this book suggests two hundred and fifty years' worth of an organic literary development. It is my goal that *Women in Context* will pilot a continuing quest for more knowledge about and imaginative association with British women of the past.

Notes

1. George Eliot, "Woman in France [1854]," in *Essays and Leaves from a Notebook* (New York: Harper and Bros., 1884), 172.
2. Georges Gusdorf, "Conditions and Limits of Autobiography," in *Autobiography: Essays Theoretical and Critical,* ed. James Olney (Princeton: Princeton University Press, 1980), 29.
3. James Olney, "Autobiography and the Cultural Moment," in *Autobiography: Essays Theoretical and Critical* ed. James Olney (Princeton: Princeton University Press, 1980), 13.
4. Margo Culley, "Introduction," in *American Women's Autobiography: Fea(s)ts of Memory* ed. Margo Culley (Madison: University of Wisconsin Press, 1992), 5–6.
5. Shari Benstock, "Authorizing the Autobiographical," in *The Private Self: Theory and Practice of Women's Autobiographical Writings* ed. Shari Benstock (Chapel Hill: University of North Carolina Press, 1988), 14–15.
6. Catharine Stimpson, "Feminist Criticism," in *Redrawing the Boundaries: The Transformation of English and American Studies* ed. Stephen Greenblatt and Giles Gunn (New York: Modern Language Association of America, 1992), 252.
7. Sheila Rowbotham, *Woman's Consciousness, Man's World* (Harmondsworth, England: Penguin, 1972; New York: Penguin, 1974), 10–25.

"When I was twelve years of age, I was sent away to a very genteel boarding school; indeed, too high for my fortune. . . . I soon left off praying and reading my Bible and was never happy but in reading romances, novels, plays, and other books of the devil's inspiring; and more than once attempted to write them myself."

—JOANNE TURNER, METHODIST COTTAGE PREACHER, 1732–1785

"I have been tempted to begin writing by George Eliot's *Life*—with that curious kind of self-compassion which one cannot get clear of. I wonder if I am a little envious of her?"

—MARGARET OLIPHANT, NOVELIST, 1828–1897

"In one of these [children's periodicals] was a series of descriptive articles on men who had been poor boys, and risen to be rich and great. Every month I hoped to find the story of some poor, ignorant *girl,* who beginning life as handicapped as I, had yet been able by her own efforts and the blessing of God upon them to live a life of usefulness, if not greatness. But I believe there was not a woman in the whole series."

—MARIANNE FARNINGHAM, WRITER AND TEACHER, 1834–1909

Women in Context: Two Hundred Years of British Women Autobiographers, A Reference Guide and Reader

---

1 ABDULLAH, Morag (née Murray). c.1897–?. *My Khyber Marriage: Experiences of a Scotswoman as the Wife of a Pathan Chieftain's Son.* G.G. Harrap, 1934. 272 pp.; front.; illus. NUC pre56 1:522.

Raised in Edinburgh, Scotland. Father: James Murray. Mother not named. 1 brother. Married c.1916, Syed Abdullah, Pathan chief's son. 1 daughter. Foreign resident (near Peshawar, in present-day Pakistan); religionist (Islamic convert); WWI volunteer. Middle class; Pathan upper class; married into foreign culture.

Scottish woman's enthusiastic embrace of Pathan culture in the highlands between Afghanistan and India, 1916–c.1923. Her brother's death in WWI; working as a volunteer flag seller to alleviate her grief, 1916. Meeting her future husband at a party for war volunteers. Courtship; overcoming their fathers' opposition to the marriage. Becoming a Muslim. Having marriage ceremony twice, once in a Muslim rite and once according to Western law. Birth of a daughter, 1917. In 1920, traveling by boat to Karachi, India; traveling inland to the Khyber Pass; entering the "Free Land of the Hills." Her growing appreciation for the simplicity of the Muslim faith. Being warmly welcomed by her husband's family; being given milk and rosewater baths for a week, in preparation for a third, very elaborate wedding. Games held in honor of the event; magnificent gifts of jewels, clothing, carpets given to the couple; author's noting a link between the gifts of good-luck amulets and Scottish Highlanders' belief in luck and omens. Moving with husband to another of the chieftain's forts. Discussing the social and cultural rules by which the seventy-eight clans of Pathan people live, in an 800-mile-long territory separating India from Afghanistan. Visiting a neighboring harem;

discovering that, contrary to what she had heard in the West, few Muslim men have more than one wife. Describing servants. Describing rivalries among Khyber clans; high value placed on bravery in battle; women's role as fighters if all the men are killed. Experiencing a raid while visiting the fort of a neighboring chieftain; arming herself with a rifle, but not having to use it. Successfully intervening on behalf of her husband's younger sister, who loved a chieftain's son not in favor with her father. Traveling with her husband and daughter to visit a rajah in India, 1922; being unimpressed by the rajah and by the empty lives led by the ranee and princesses. Describing Indian customs. Visiting the Simla hills; attending a hill fair; describing a marriage market. Noting Christianity's negative impact on Indian untouchables. Hearing that her mother was ill; returning to Scotland to see her; unfavorably comparing life in Edinburgh to life in Pathan country; asserting that Pathan and Indian women have greater independence than do women in the West.

Apparently able to make a major cultural shift without any difficulty, Abdullah seems to have embraced her new life—including the custom of women's wearing the veil and the segregation of the sexes in Islam—wholeheartedly. No doubt the author's transition to a new culture was eased by the wealth and status of her husband's family, but her apparent ability to change her way of living and thinking rather matter-of-factly is nonetheless remarkable, as demonstrated in this lively, dialogue-filled narrative.

ABERCONWAY, Baroness. [*See* McLaren, Christabel Mary Melville.]

ABERDEEN and TEMAIR, Marchioness of. [*See* Gordon, Ishbel Maria.]

ABINGER, Baroness of. [*See* Wootton, Barbara.]

2 ACKLAND, Valentine (Mary Kathleen McCrory Ackland). 1906–1969. *For Sylvia: An Honest Account*. Chatto & Windus/Hogarth Press, 1985. 135 pp.; foreword by Bea Howe. BLC 1982–1985 1:93.

Born in London. Father not named, dentist. Mother not named. 1 sister. Married 1925, Richard Turpin; divorced c.1927. Poetry books include *Whether a Dove or a Seagull* (1934, written with Sylvia Townsend Warner), *Country Conditions* (1936), *The Nature of the Moment* (1973). Knew Sylvia Townsend Warner, Nancy Cunard. Poet; short storyist; religionist (Roman Catholic convert); lesbian; cross-dresser; Communist. Upper middle class.

Confessions of the author's turbulent emotional development and sexual nonconformity, from childhood to middle age. Seeking the childhood origins of her alcoholism and religiosity. Her affluent father's having sent her to an expensive private school for young ladies that provided riding, swimming, and violin lessons. Mother's being High Church

Anglican, beset with religiosity and hypochondria. Author's being a sickly child, unfairly accused of hypochondria by her bullying older sister. Also being bullied by her nurse. After age 8, avidly reading books of religion and philosophy to satisfy her religious hunger; writing poetry on Christian themes. During adolescence, experimenting sexually with a homosexual boy and a woman. Starting a sexual affair with another woman; being made to feel horror and shame when her parents discovered it; becoming permanently estranged from her father. Attributing her adolescent lying and stealing to feelings of unworthiness. Recounting ongoing conflict between family pressure to marry and her homosexual desires. Describing how she began wearing male clothing, and the sense of liberation she derived. After 1923, living a Bohemian life in London. Trying heterosexual lifestyle by marrying, 1925; miscarriage of both her pregnancy and the marriage; divorcing, 1927. Giving herself the androgynous penname "Valentine." Converting to Catholicism, 1927, without resolving conflict between her faith and her homosexuality. Establishing her long-term relationship with Sylvia Townsend Warner, 1930; discussing their life together at Kingston Lacy, Dorset, 1930s–1940s. During WWII, working as a civil-defense clerk; her alcoholism's worsening. Beginning an affair with Elizabeth Wade White, 1947; separating from Warner. Returning to Warner, 1949; writing this memoir to tell the emotional truth about herself to her long-time companion.

Ackland fictionalizes names and possibly some details in this account of her developing sexual identity. Her life and relationship with Warner are also treated in Wendy Mulford's *This Narrow Place: Sylvia Townsend Warner and Valentine Ackland: Life, Letters and Politics 1930–1951* (1988), which provides biographical details omitted by Ackland's account, including her Communist Party membership, her sojourn in Spain with Warner during the Spanish Civil War, and her journalistic contributions to the *Daily Worker* and other leftist publications. The autobiography itself is a revealing psychological study of a poet, virtually unknown during her own time, who merits new critical examination both in the context of gay studies and as a writer whose work imaginatively explores contemporary social issues.

3 ACLAND, Lady Eleanor Margaret (née Cropper). 1878–1933. *Good-Bye for the Present: The Story of Two Childhoods*. Hodder & Stoughton, 1937. 318 pp.; intro. by G. M. Trevelyan; two parts, originally published separately. NUC pre56 3:50. (1st pub. 1935.)

Born at Cordale, Westmorland. Father: paper mill owner, landowner, Liberal M.P. Mother not named. 1 brother; 2 sisters. Married c.1905, Francis Acland, later baronet, Liberal M.P., Cabinet minister, landowner. 3 sons; 1 daughter. Wrote novel *Dark Side Out* (1921). Politician; politician's spouse; novelist. Upper class.

Twin memoirs of the author's Victorian upbringing and of the brief life of her daughter, covering 1878–90 and 1913–24. Vol. 1: Author's childhood to age 12. Until age 10, living in rural Westmorland; her family's being the local squires for two generations. Father, mother, and grandfather's being pious Anglicans; keeping the Sabbath so stringently they locked the toy cupboard on Sundays. Parents' having a loving relationship. Children's only grievance being their abusive "nurse Barley," whose version of events the parents always believed. Mother's nurturing author's literary bent through shared reading. Vividly recalling annual seaside holidays; adults' wearing body-concealing bathing costumes. Parents' exerting efforts to keep children in the dark about sex; author's believing that honesty of modern parents is superior, sparing children unnecessary repression and shame. Suspecting link between her parents' repressions and their religious earnestness. Being terrified by notions of sin and Hell; only belatedly accepting Christianity. Entire family's embracing Liberal Party politics, in accord with Christian charity toward the poor. Grandfather's and father's serving as Liberal M.P.s; mother's being a Poor Law Guardian; family's nevertheless preserving rigid class boundaries, requiring the children to remain aloof from villagers. Author, brother, and sister's being schooled by a governess in Latin and algebra. After brother left for school, these subjects' being dropped as unnecessary for a "purely feminine" classroom. Vol. 2: Author's marriage, 1905, being joyful and producing four children. Family's living in London townhouse, 1905–17, during husband's tenure in several cabinet posts; his resigning when Liberal Prime Minister Asquith was defeated, 1916. Family's living in Devonshire, 1917–23. Author's emulating her own mother in reading with the children. Taking pride in her husband's political career; working for him in three parliamentary elections; touring Devon to give her own political speeches. Remembering her mother's work for her father's political career, and her father's political goal to improve conditions for the common people. Family's moving to north Cornwall, 1923, which husband served as M.P. Author's joining local Women's Liberal Association; entertaining extensively; serving as a Girl Guide leader. Childhood of her daughter, Ellen: her goodness, intelligence, and capacity for inspiring love. Grieving over Ellen's untimely death, which shook author's faith. Explaining how she ultimately came to accept God's will, and to believe Ellen still lives.

In this double biography, Acland both memorializes her young daughter and contrasts the child's upbringing with her own, highlighting changes in child-rearing theories and in modes of class interaction. Acland states that she wrote this book to record what children saw and heard in Victorian days so that later generations could understand the influences that shaped their forebears, although she firmly asserts that she is unconcerned about autobiography as a literary genre. Acland's esteem for the political work of her grandfather, father, and husband are clearly expressed, yet she neglects any mention of her own political aspirations, which led her to campaign as Liberal candidate for Exeter. Instead, her book imaginatively focuses on what it is like to be the child of a politician during two different eras, and on how such an upbringing shapes the child's maturing character.

AIRLIE, Countess. [*See* OGILVIE, Mabell Frances Elizabeth.]

4 ALEXANDER, Mary. 1760–1809. *Some Account of the Life and Religious Experience of Mary Alexander, Late of Needham Market.* Ed. by William Alexander (author's brother). Philadelphia: Griggs & Dickinson, 1815. 184 pp.; ed.'s preface. NUC pre56 8:285.

Born at Needham Market, Suffolk. Father: Dykes Alexander, Quaker elder. Mother: Martha Biddle, Quaker minister. 3 brothers; 2 sisters. Single. Religionist (Quaker); preacher; clergywoman's daughter. Lower middle class.

Quaker minister's travels, preaching, and lifelong spiritual introspection, covering her childhood to 1809. In childhood, not thoroughly understanding Quakerism but esteeming adult Quakers for their goodness. Feeling called to the ministry, age 17. At age 23, receiving permission from Woodbridge Monthly Meeting to travel and preach with other Quakers; determining henceforth to forsake all "unprofitable reading" and stay with the Bible. Father's death, author's age 26; establishing residence in his house with her brother William. At age 29, hearing a voice calling her to preach the Gospel; seeking assurance of her readiness in prayer; preaching her first words at a Quaker meeting. Being recommended as a "minister in unity," age 31; describing her meetings and visits throughout East Anglia. Receiving permission, age 34, to travel and preach with another woman Quaker; recounting her travel and ministry with Ann Tuke through Cambridgeshire, Huntingdonshire, and Lincolnshire. Frequently preaching with her brothers and other Quaker friends. In York, visiting Quakers imprisoned for refusing to pay Anglican tithes. Brother William's marrying Ann Tuke, 1796. During next two years, author's continuing itinerant preaching but having impaired health; experiencing conflict between her commitment to the Lord's work and her doubt of her ability to fulfill it; working through crisis by more rigorous travel and ministry. Continued preaching around England and Scotland, 1800–05. Discussing England's crying need for spiritual regeneration. Extensive diary entries covering her preaching schedule throughout southeast England, 1800–02. Being hampered in her work by helping sister Ann depart for America, 1802. Resolving to extend her preaching northward to Scotland and the Isle of Man, 1804. Preaching amiably alongside Methodists, but encountering conflict with Glasgow Quakers, whom she felt served God from tradition rather than inner faith. Berating herself upon return from Scotland for failing to inspire others. Sister Ann's returning, 1805, but leaving quickly with William for York. Author's resolutely keeping to her preaching schedule, but confessing her loneliness and depression; asserting that her comfort is the spiritual good she has brought about. Visiting Ann and brother William in York.

Alexander's account, which ends abruptly, is completed by the author's brother William, who relates his sister's last preaching tour and her death from smallpox. In the preface, William also provides a biography of his sister's early life. Unlike many Quaker autobiographies, which commonly focus on spiritual metamorphosis, this one is rich in practical diary entries that give a concrete sense of women ministers' duties on their working journeys.

5 ALI, Beatrice (née Webster). c.1916–s.l.1975. *The Good Deeds of a Good Woman*. Ed. by Clive Murphy. Dennis Dobson, 1976. Ordinary Lives series. 121 pp. NUC 1973–1977 3:126.

Raised in Luton, Bedfordshire. Father: Alfred Webster, butcher. Mother not named, washerwoman. 1 brother; 2 sisters. Married 1936, Basit Ali, seaman, Pakistani; separated 1966. 2 sons. Domestic servant; prison inmate. Working class; married person of different race.

Working-class woman's employment, failed marriage, and imprisonment, with emphasis on racial and cultural tensions, covering her birth to 1975. Worst blow in her life's being desertion by her husband, 1966. In 1973, unmoved by news of his death, unlike her grief over her mother's death in 1947. Having moved into a Salvation Army hostel after desertion; her sons' being ashamed their mother lived in a charity hostel. Believing that her sons carried excess shame from facing racism. Recalling having married at age 18; husband's being a Pakistani seaman staying at the dockside hotel where she was a chambermaid. Considering this marriage to have been a "big mistake." Evaluating her childhood: remembering doing odd jobs in a Luton hospital; enjoying a stable school life, ages 5–14; remembering her father's character. Moving to London, age 19. Two years later, mother's becoming paralyzed and remaining helpless until her death ten years later. Her deserting husband's having robbed her of a large sum of money. Discussing racial and cultural prejudices against "coloureds." Discussing bearing her children, and the hardships of child-rearing during WWII. Being loyal to her husband despite his liaison with an underage girl; testifying on his behalf; his being imprisoned. His remaining lazy and jobless, angering author and sons. Author's working a series of kitchen jobs to support the family. Commenting on Queen Elizabeth's lack of concern for working class families. Husband's departing for East Pakistan, 1964; his returning two years later with another, pregnant wife. His setting fire to his shop for the insurance, then disappearing with his new bride, locking author out of the flat and renting it to other people. Homeless author's resorting to

Salvation Army hostel. Giving charity to her neighbors; realizing their need was as great as her own. Struggling to recover; working and renting a flat; collapsing from depression. Being given shock treatments, 1967. Suffering several burglaries of her flat; being unable to pay creditors from her income as a hotel worker; being evicted; returning to the Salvation Army hostel and later a convent hostel. Spending six weeks homeless. Being refused charity by "coloured" people; likening their "stinginess" to her husband's. Smashing windows of an employer who cheated her; being sent to Holloway prison, 1975, to await trial. Meeting lesbians in prison. Her case's being dismissed when she swore on the Koran she was innocent. Returning to the Salvation Army hostel; giving further anecdotes of her help to fellow boarders.

The author's words were transcribed from tape recordings made in 1975. Ali's speech is chatty, with frequent exclamations, rhetorical questions, and obscenities. Occasionally she expresses herself in her husband's native language. The editor appears to have led Ali to discuss certain topics, including her childhood and her sons, but she soon digresses. Despite its associative organization, Ali's account renders a vivid sense of life in East London between the world wars, and of the multiple forces of non-European immigration, unequal marital roles, social prejudice, crime, and economic hardship that often shaped working-class lives.

6 ALLAN, Maud. c.1879–1956. *My Life and Dancing*. Everett & Co., 1908. 128 pp.; front. port.; preface; illus. BLC to 1975 5:375.

Born in Toronto, Canada. Father: William Allan, physician. Mother: Isabel Maud Hutchinson, physician. Single. Dancer (modern). Upper middle class.

First three decades in the life of an innovative modern dancer, emphasizing her opinions on dance technique, choreography, and women's issues, c.1879–1908. Growing up in Canada attended by a nurse and governess. At age 7, family's moving to San Francisco via train. Reporting how she had to be rescued when Indians abducted her at a train stop. Camping out with her parents; finding in this the purest freedom imaginable. Being a daring child who climbed tall trees and could ride any horse. At an early age, resolving to be a professional pianist; parents' enrolling her at the San Francisco School of Music. While there, teaching a dance class to young children; being praised for her intuitive teaching. At age 12, seeing Sarah Bernhardt perform in San Francisco; her immediate yearning to rival Bernhardt. Beginning to think of dance as a career, but finding the movements of ballet somewhat unnatural. Praising her parents' emotional and financial support for her every ambition. Traveling alone to Berlin, age 16, to pursue piano study at Berlin's Royal High School of Music; remaining until age 21. Being visited periodically by her mother, who took her on Continental holidays.

On a trip to Florence, being inspired by Botticelli's art to think of dance as a way to turn music, painting, and sculpture into movement. Shunning mechanized movement and using music to make each movement a spontaneous inspiration. At age 21, traveling to Weimar to study with composer Ferruccio Busoni; remaining for one year (1901) but ultimately deciding to commit herself to dance training. Seeking help from composer and Greek scholar Marcel Remy, who introduced her to ancient Greek dance. Giving her first performance in Vienna, 1903; its excellent reception's winning her contracts for two successful dance tours of Europe. A proposed performance in Munich, 1907, being banned by the town council as "immoral" because of author's bare legs and sinuous movements. Giving her first London performance at the Palace Theatre, 1908; giving a command performance for Queen Alexandra. Her beliefs about women's unreadiness to receive the vote, their need for equal education, their faculty for intuitive rather than rational careers, and their rightful destiny as wives and mothers. Her new dance "The Vision of Salome," which created a sensation with audiences; explaining that she choreographed it by turning the Biblical story of Salome into movement.

Written at the height of Allan's early fame, this book shows the author flushed with success and eager to explain the high origins of her art. She went on to tour America, 1909–11, and continued to dance until 1923, performing for worldwide audiences and drawing critical attention for both the virtuosity and voluptuousness of her style. In April 1918, Oscar Wilde's play *Salome* was revived at London's Court Theatre, with Allan in the starring role; here she displayed her new "Dance of the Seven Veils," in which she discarded all of the veils, one by one. When writer Noel Pemberton Billing, one of England's more vocal champions of purity, publicly condemned Allan's performance as pornographic and added slurs about her morals, Allan sued him for libel. Until Billing's acquittal the same year, the public was entertained by a case whose prurience approached that of modern tabloids. Billing went on to form his own Purity Party, running candidates in by-elections. Allan danced for five more years before retiring.

7 ALLEN, Dorothy F. Halford. 1896–1959. *Sunlight and Shadow: An Autobiography*. Ed. by C. K. Allen (author's husband). Oxford University Press, 1960. 185 pp.; preface by ed.; illus.; app. BLC to 1975 5:443.

Born in Evesham, Worcestershire. Father: Edward Halford, customs and excise official. Mother: Jane Spurway. 2 brothers; 3 sisters. Married 1922, Carleton K. Allen, Oxford don. 1 daughter; 1 son. Knew John Masefield. Oxford hostess; academic's spouse; actress; child-care provider; WWII volunteer. Upper middle class.

Victorian upbringing, marriage to an Oxford academic, charity work, and WWII contributions of an Oxford faculty wife and university hostess, c.1898–1952. Her earliest memory of family's moving to London. Having a happy childhood despite stern parenting. Attending an Anglican church and its affiliated high school. During WWI, filling the usually male position of school attendance officer. Being drawn into Oxford social circles by attending dances there. Managing play centres for underprivileged children at Oxford and acting with the Oxfordshire Players. Marrying an Oxford don, 1922. Starting a local club for underprivileged youth. Husband's being invited to lecture in India; traveling with him. Having two children, 1927 and 1931; noting changes in parenting between Victorian and post-WWI eras. Family's moving into Rhodes House, Oxford's residence for Rhodes scholars, when husband was appointed its head, 1931. Entertaining scholars and notable visitors, including poet John Masefield, George Bernard Shaw, Mohandas Gandhi, and the British royal family. Accompanying her husband on a lecture tour of U.S. and Canada; giving first public speech of her own in New York. Their attending royal family's celebration of King George's coronation, 1937. WWII: sending her 12-year-old daughter to Canada; turning Rhodes House into a bomb shelter and evacuation center. Discussing patriotic acceptance by British populace of wartime shortages. American troops' being billeted at Oxford; author's managing Oxford's information centre, which helped orient them. Noting postwar changeover at Oxford from soldiers to students; resuming her duties as Rhodes House's official hostess. Contrasting England's continued postwar privations with the returning prosperity of America. Expressing pride in her husband and children's achievements: son's winning scholarships to both the Royal Academy and the Royal College of Music, husband's receiving knighthood. Author's receiving honorary M.A. from Oxford at time of husband's retirement, 1952.

Written during Allen's terminal illness, this account was edited by her husband in tribute to her memory. Although published by Oxford University Press as a document of university history, Allen intended her informal account to educate her grandsons about the dramatic cultural changes between her own childhood and theirs. Her reminiscences of Oxford, particularly of Rhodes House, chart its accommodations to turbulent times between 1925 and 1952, and give practical details of the diverse managerial and ambassadorial duties the author fulfilled as hostess to the international scholarly community.

8 ALLEN, Mary Sophia (Commandant O.B.E.). 1878–1964. *Lady in Blue*. S. Paul, 1936. 286 pp.; front.; illus. NUC pre56 9:408.

Born in Cheltenham, Gloucestershire. Parents not named. Single. Wrote *The Pioneer Policewoman* (1925). Suffragist, militant; political activist;

policewoman; aviator; organizer (labor); public speaker; WWI volunteer. Middle class.

Author's adult transition from suffragette law breaker to law enforcer, covering her career to age 58 and her activism in women's social concerns, c.1910–36. Being a sickly child; believing she would grow up to be a semi-invalid. Being dismissed from her parents' home for her vocal support of the suffrage cause; moving to London and joining the suffragettes. Recounting her 1910–14 suffragette activities in London: working with the Women's Social and Political Union; breaking windows in the Home Office; being imprisoned for this offense and forcibly fed. Praising the inspiration of Annie Kenney and Emmeline Pankhurst. In WWI, organizing women munitions workers. Evaluating general impact of the war. Volunteering for the newly created Women Police Volunteers; recognizing her passage from lawbreaker to defender of the law as the central paradox of her life. With other women, training in police skills and physical conditioning; patrolling the London streets together. Traveling to Ireland to help set up a women's police force. After the war, helping establish a women's force in Cologne, Germany, to patrol British occupation soldiers. Discussing the 1920s "White Slave Trade," in which young women were kidnapped for sexual purposes; working actively to help victims of this trade. Running unsuccessfully for Parliament as a Liberal candidate, 1923. Traveling to the U.S. and Canada to speak on establishing women's police units; while there, acquiring a private pilot's license. Discussing her participation in the first two International Women's Conferences; her continued work for women's causes.

The women's police force for which Allen volunteered was organized by Margaret Damer Dawson, who—like Allen—had been a suffragette. In *The Pioneer Policewoman,* Allen's history of this movement, she writes that "many of the women attracted by the idea of women police had been prominent workers for Woman's Suffrage in the militant days before the War. Their efforts had brought them into close touch with the police, teaching them how very unpleasant it is for an alleged woman culprit to be handled by men." In her active police work Allen gave special attention to the problems of women criminals—particularly drug addiction and prostitution—and their vulnerability to sexual exploitation. In this respect, Allen embodies a central feminist principle of her time: that women's public work could infuse traditionally "feminine" values into public matters.

9 ALLINSON, Francesca. 1902–?. *A Childhood.* Hogarth Press, 1937. 187 pp.; foreword; wood engravings by Enid Marx. NUC pre56 10:18.

Raised in London. Father not named, scientist, researcher, writer, lecturer. Mother: Sally. 1 brother. Single. Academic's daughter. Middle class.

Childhood memories of growing up in an intellectual household and searching for a comfortable gender identity and meaningful spiritual beliefs, c.1909–15. "Illness": Author's enjoying attention of her hired nurse while ill with measles; faking headaches. Wishing for more religious "structure" than her agnostic, freethinking parents could provide. Author's father's being remote and scholarly; her mother's being warm and loving, but too ready to sacrifice herself for her genius husband. Housekeeper's serving as sole disciplinarian of the children, for which author admired her. Frugal parents' not hiring additional servants. "Sunday": Recounting Sunday activities: lectures; walks; long intimate conversations on religious topics, including Judaism, with author's closest friend Thea, a Jewish schoolmate. Describing assorted Christmas festivities, which omitted Christmas's religious connotations. "Forest": In childhood, admiring her brother's physical strength; wanting to be a boy. Staying with brother at Uncle Robert's country home; exploring a Roman mine and haunted house with brother; being afraid of things hidden in forests and moorland. Confiding her frustrations at being female to her uncle; his holding up female role models who exemplified women's achievements and gifts. "Seaside": Describing seaside holidays with Aunt Scuttles, Uncle Timothy, and their children. While on holiday, developing a violent crush on a young woman singer; author's contrasting this romantic female figure with her mother, who was sobered by cares and responsibilities. Moving from infatuation to admiration, then to acquaintance and friendship with this singer. "Pity": Recounting the awakening of her conscience to social class inequities. Envying Thea's family's wealth; after author's father relinquished a research fellowship, mother's having to take in lodgers for a year to make ends meet. Author's professing love for beggars; hating it when father made her kiss a beggar; later giving a beggar all her savings, with which she had planned to buy books. Confessing her personal fears of poverty.

In her foreword, Allinson says that the childhood experiences and feelings she expresses in this book were shared by many of her contemporaries. It is likely that Virginia Woolf, who selected this memoir for publication by the Hogarth Press, was one of the contemporaries to whom Allinson alludes, since the marital relationship between Woolf's parents—as expressed in the fictionalized Ramsays in Woolf's novel *To the Lighthouse*—mirrors that of Allinson's parents. The narrative is organized topically rather than chronologically, omitting all dates and full names of family and friends. As a study of an early Edwardian family, this account gives a vivid depiction of the gender-divided parenting roles in a middle-class family, and also portrays a child's dawning awareness of contemporary social issues.

10 ALLISON, Susan Louisa (née Moir; Stratton Moir, pseud.). 1845–1937. *A Pioneer Gentlewoman in British Columbia: The*

Recollections of Susan Allison. Ed. by Margaret A. Ormsby. Vancouver: University of British Columbia Press, 1976. 210 pp.; ed.'s intro.; map; illus.; apps.; notes; index. NUC 1973–1977 3:581. (1st pub. in *Vancouver Sunday Province,* 1931.)

Born at Colombo, Ceylon. Father: Stratton Moir, British coffee planter. Mother: Susan Louisa Mildern. Stepfather: Thomas Glennie. 1 brother; 1 sister. Married 1868, John Fall Allison, son of English emigrants, gold miner, trader, d.1897. 14 children. Wrote long narrative poem *In-Cow-Mas-Ket* (1900), pub. under pseud. Stratton Moir. Emigrant (Canada); pioneer; poet. Middle class.

Frontier life of an emigrant to Canada and her cultural observations on native Indian tribes, 1860–94. Family's returning to England from Ceylon following father's death, 1849; their living in London at author's age 15. Hearing news of Fraser River gold fever; stepfather's deciding family should emigrate to British Columbia. Sailing to Victoria via Panama Canal; describing settlements near Victoria. Family's traveling by steamer up the Fraser River to Fort Hope. Describing the adjacent Indian village. Stepfather's building house in forest near Fort Hope; recounting their first few years there, including expansion of this frontier town and marriage of author's elder sister. Author's implying stepfather's failure to make the farm thrive, owing to inexperience and financial troubles. Stepfather's disappearance; moving with her ailing mother to New Westminster; author's being recommended by family friend William Charles, chief Hudson's Bay Company trader at Fort Hope, for a position as governess to his relatives in Victoria. After two years as a governess, author's receiving legacy, age 21, which freed her to rejoin friends in New Westminster; earning money by needlework to supplement her small income. Author and mother's returning to Fort Hope and opening a small school. Meeting her future husband; their marrying and moving to the Similkameen River wilderness. Describing her joy at their "wild, free life"; depicting character, customs, and legends of the Indians, as well as their own sightings of Sasquatch and "Ogopogo," the local lake monster. Family's moving to a new house in Princeton. Noting frontier men's negative attitudes toward her refinement; their doubting she could run a farm. Describing preparations of farm and buildings for winter. Her first child's being delivered by Indian midwife, c.1870. Discussing her many friends among Indians, who comprised most of the local population. Births of more children. Doctoring sick Indians; hiring Indians as child minders. With husband absent on business, renting a Hudson's Bay Company house in the town of Keremeos. Depicting character of Keremeos Indians. Moving to their second home at Lake Okanagan, 1873, to oversee their cattle; recording local Indian folklore. Visiting local Roman Catholic mission, which had established excellent relations with the Indians. Onset of Indian unrest in British Columbia, 1874, due to U.S. Army's pursuit of Nez Perce toward Canada.

Husband's business plans' changing; his returning to Princeton; author's joining him. Author's teaching eldest children at home. Family's losing home in fire, 1882; rebuilding. Discussing local visit of General William Tecumseh Sherman. Family's house being destroyed by flood of the Similkameen River, 1894.

Allison appends several additional essays to her autobiography, including an account of the Similkameen Indians, another on local frontiersmen, and a third comprising collected Indian legends. This is a rare account of a pioneer woman's life in British Columbia, and Allison is the only authority we have on the Similkameen Indians. Although she was just as inexperienced at frontier living as fellow Canadian emigrant Susanna Moodie (author of *Roughing It in the Bush; or, Forest Life in Canada*), Allison, unlike Moodie, found frontier life fulfilling. In the introduction and notes, editor Ormsby points out textual inaccuracies in names and dates, and provides information that the author omitted.

11 ALSOP, Christine R. Majolier. 1805–1879. *Memorials of Christine Majolier Alsop*. Ed. by Martha Braithwaite. Samuel Harris & Co., 1881. 248 pp.; front. port.; preface by ed.; app. NUC pre56 10:430.

Born in Congenies, Department du Gard, France. Father: Louis Antonine Majolier, English Society of Friends schoolmaster, surveyor. Mother: Marie Brun. 6 siblings. Married 1847, Robert Alsop, pharmaceutical chemist, English. Widow. Philanthropist; religionist (Quaker); teacher; governess; interpreter. Middle class.

Religious views and philanthropic activities of teacher and representative of English Society of Friends, from her childhood to old age. Family connection with Society of Friends in England. During author's childhood, her father's opening Friends' School at Congenies, despite English Society of Friends' refusing him financial aid. Father's working as a land surveyor under the Bonaparte administration; his refusing to enrich himself illegally. His and other Protestants' suspecting that their liberties would be endangered if the Catholic Bourbons returned to rule. At age 12, author's being sent to safety in England; living with the family of Quaker William Allen. Being homesick for life in the south of France. Journal extracts describing her religious reflections and activities during her adolescence in England: helping care for William Allen's children, teaching French, and studying at Susanna Corder's school for girls at Stoke Newington. Accompanying English Friends as interpreter on a visit to the south of France, Switzerland, and Germany; describing their visits to prisons. Returning to live at Nimes, France, because of ill health; refusing to be attended by any doctor disrespectful of her religious views. Finding an acceptable physician; living in his home and tutoring his daughter in Friends theology. History of French Protestantism. Accompanying American Friend Lindley Murray Hoag on his ministry in France. Discussing Quaker views embracing women in the ministry; author's becoming well-known through her ministering visits to Friends' meetings throughout continental Europe. Accepting request of a Canadian Indian chief's daughter, recently converted to Quakerism, to visit and speak in Canada. Author and her husband's moving to England. Receiving gifts from the British royal family, acknowledging her service to Britain through her religious visits. Remarking on cholera outbreak in London. Organizing sewing class for poor mothers in East End of London under Friends' committee; serving as committee treasurer. Supporting children's hospital; visiting inmates at almshouses. Outbreak of Franco-German War, 1848; helping prepare and taking three appeals to Christians in France with her husband. Journal extracts describing her work on behalf of the Friends in France. Death of her husband. Expressing gratitude for the many friends who supported her in her grief; finding strength in her religious beliefs.

Frequently interrupted by lengthy explanations provided by the editor, Alsop's account expresses her religious views with a methodical thoroughness rather than with open feeling. Although she avoids drawing a parallel between her life of active service and the Quaker belief in gender equality, her memoir demonstrates that her affiliation with the Society of Friends freed her to exert her energies unrestrictedly. Her account is useful for its contemporary 19th-century discussion of Quaker and French history, particularly the development of French Protestantism, and for its portrayal of political strategies used by Christian leaders during the Franco-German War.

12 ANDERSON, Doris Garland. c.1900–?. *Nigger Lover*. L. N. Fowler, c.1938. 282 pp.; author's foreword; foreword by Lady Cherry Poynter; preface; illus. BLC to 1975 7:516.

Born in England. Father not named, physician. Mother not named. 2 brothers; 1 sister. Married 1935, Garland Anderson, playwright, lecturer, American. Knew Canon Richard Sheppard, Sir John and Lady Simon. Secretary; charitable volunteer; traveler (U.S.); physician's daughter. Upper middle class; married person of different race.

Author's marriage to a black American writer and her observations on American and English race relations, covering 1931–38. First being introduced to Garland Anderson in London, 1931; his having risen from hotel bellboy to playwright in the U.S.; his being the son of a slave. His visiting London for production of his play *Appearances;* its being the first play by a black to be produced in New York and London with a mixed cast. Author's living in Chelsea among artists and political activists, working for Mrs. Appleby's homeless shelters; meeting Garland through her 1930s Labour Party socialism. Explaining his Christian philosophy, influenced by Christian Science, psychology, and metaphysics. His being well accepted by author's liberal friends; his career's being helped by

Lord and Lady Simon, the Bishop of London, and Queen Mary. Novelist John Galsworthy's inviting Garland to speak at the London PEN Club; Garland and author's socializing with Chelsea art circles. Growing closer to Garland while helping him in the writing of *Uncommon Sense: The Law of Life in Action;* serving as hostess at his lectures. Author's sister, an emigrant to Africa, writing an article about Garland for an African newspaper, but having to omit his race in order to get it published. Author's refuting public opinion that Garland is too exceptional to be representative of his race, or that his intelligence is due to his presumed white ancestry. Author's making arrangements for Garland's U.S. lecture tour, 1935. Parents' and siblings' supporting author's intended marriage. Traveling to U.S. as future husband's secretary; his giving lectures to predominantly white audiences. Recording her impressions of New York and Harlem; learning more about Garland's early history. Visiting British Columbia and Washington state. Getting married in Vancouver, Washington. Traveling to Seattle, Portland, and San Francisco. Staying in a "coloured" hotel in Los Angeles; husband's speaking on topic of prejudice to National Association for the Advancement of Colored People. Discussing black actors in Hollywood, cults, and pseudo-religions in 1930s Los Angeles, and jealousy among blacks toward those who succeed. Visiting Hawaii, noting its relative absence of racism. Garland's lecturing there; his comparing Negro progress in the U.S. to suffragist progress in England. Comparing racial attitudes in England and the U.S. Discussing American reactions to her marriage (mostly curious rather than hostile), stereotypes of black sexuality, bigotry faced by children of mixed marriages, and the 1936 American election. Wanting to travel through the American South with her husband, but accepting its present impossibility. Returning to London to nurse her sick mother; after her mother's recovery, rejoining Garland to live in New York.

In her preface, Anderson remarks that she is an Englishwoman of social standing who married a Negro and subsequently found, despite friends' gloomy predictions, that interracial couples could find acceptance. Her record of their harmonious, intellectually compatible marriage serves as a tacit rebuke to racial prejudice. Although optimistic that many mixed marriages can succeed, she notes the social hurdles which must be faced. She also discusses means of overcoming national prejudice, explaining that America's history of widespread slavery exacerbates American racism. Always cautious of their reception, Anderson and her husband steered clear of trouble by avoiding discriminatory laws and bigotry rather than defying them; consequently, they accepted their inability to travel together in the American South. As Anderson phrases it, "I believe in facing a situation if necessary but not in creating it."

13 ANDREW, Jane. 1815–d.a.1890. *Recorded Mercies: Being the Autobiography of Jane Andrew, Living at St. Ives, Liskeard, Cornwall;*

also, Reminiscences of Her Valued Friend, the Late Mrs. Daniel Smart of Cranbrook, Compiled by Her Younger Daughter, as an Affectionate Tribute to her Mother's Memory. E. Wilmshurst, c.1890. 51 pp. BLC to 1975 8:249.

Born at Egg Buckland, near Plymouth, Devonshire. Father not named, farmer. Mother not named. 5 brothers. Single. Religionist (Baptist convert); farmer. Rural farming class.

Author's farm childhood, Baptist conversion, and adult struggle to provide for herself and her younger brother, interpreted providentially, 1815–89. Mother's being the child of a wealthy shoe manufacturer and a convert from Anglicanism to the Baptist faith. Father's attending an Independent church; his quarreling with mother over whether children should be baptized by sprinkling or immersion. Father's coming from a Devonshire farming family. Parents' running a large Devonshire farm, Lame Barton; losing it due to economic depression after the Napoleonic wars, author's age 6. Family's acquiring smaller farm nearby; their living there twelve years. Family's moving to farm in Cornwall, 1836, and then to farm outside St. Ives, 1838. Author's discussing her piety (traveling eighteen miles to attend Baptist services) and family's poverty. After father's death, 1840, author's being afflicted by crippling illness. Promising her dying mother, 1843, that she would care for her younger brother, Robert; mother's worrying because eldest brother's inheritance left younger children with nothing. Author's asserting that on the night of her mother's death God promised to provide for the younger children. Eldest brother's announcing he was marrying; prospective mother-in-law's demanding he eject author and younger brother from his farm. Widowed friend's dreaming she should provide home for author; author and brother's living with her eight years until friend married a second husband, Daniel Smart. Author and brother's moving out; author's becoming bedridden from dropsy; depending upon her brother's support. Following physician's advice to seabathe at Plymouth; recovering her mobility and praising the Lord. Their being asked to emigrate to America with eldest brother; Robert's farm accident and consequent Baptist conversion; coming to believe that God intended them to stay in England. Author and Robert's renting a farm together; its survival's being assured by many providential sources of income: eldest brother's contributions from America, Christian lodgers they housed, timely donations from generous friends. Death of Mrs. Smart, author's greatest friend, 1867. Praising the kindness of Mrs. Smart's eldest daughter; reminiscing about Mrs. Smart. Thanking God for the prosperity He had ultimately brought to author and Robert.

Andrew's style is very simple and suggests a basic education. She often exclaims praises to God and quotes passages of Scripture, claiming that God speaks directly to her; the tone of the book is religious throughout.

Andrew says this book was written for the glory of God, but it was also written at the request of Mrs. Smart, a long-time friend of her mother and herself. The text, compiled by Mrs. Smart's eldest daughter, is divided into short chapters. This is a good source for Baptist chapel activity and farm life in rural Cornwall and Devonshire.

14 ANDREWS, Elizabeth (née Smith; O.B.E., J.P.). 1882–d.a.1960. *A Woman's Work Is Never Done: Recollections of Childhood and Upbringing in South Wales and a Lifetime of Service in the Labour Movement in Wales.* Ystrad Rhondda, Glamorgan: Cymric Democrat Publishing Society, n.d. 43 pp.; front. port.; foreword by James Griffiths; preface. NUC pre56 16:374.

Born at Hirwaun, near Aberdale, Breconshire, Wales. Father: Samuel Smith, coal miner. Mother: Charlotte. 4 brothers; 6 sisters. Married 1910, Thomas T. Andrews, Independent Labour Party (ILP) officer. Organizer (political); politician; magistrate; political activist; feminist activist; dressmaker. Rural laboring class.

Labour Party organizer's extensive activity among Welsh mining families, covering her birth to 1960. Father's coal mining and later death of lung disease. Author's studying Bible in Welsh; attending Welsh Wesleyan chapel, Sunday school, Band of Hope. Attending local board school, ages 4–13; parents' lacking the funds to send her to teacher training college as she wanted. Mothering her younger siblings. Miners' strikes. Family's moving to Mardy, Rhondda; father's being rescued from 1885 mine explosion there. Family's returning to Hirwaun. Describing politics among South Wales miners; their electing one of their own as Liberal-Labour M.P., 1885. Author's working as a dressmaker, ages 17–26. Marrying a socialist, age 28; describing husband's Independent Labour Party activities. Joining Co-operative Movement; helping form first Co-operative Women's Guilds in the Rhondda, 1910–19. Joining nonmilitant suffrage movement; noting the movement's history since Mary Wollstonecraft and the benefits women have gained by the vote. WWI: serving on pensions and disability retraining committees. Being the first woman elected to executive of Rhondda Labour Party, 1916. Organizing Labour women in Wales, 1919. Campaigning for miners' candidates in general and by-elections, 1918–20. With T. C. Morris, being given all of Wales to organize; preaching "new gospel" of socialism throughout. Devising visual aids to promote Labour social policy to housewives. Investigating health and working conditions among miners for Welsh Ministry of Health, 1920–32, but ministry's shelving her recommendations. In worsening conditions after 1926 general strike, Communists' making inroads on Labour power in the Rhondda; Labour Party's responses to Communists and Liberals in Wales. Labour women's groups' aiding miners locked out after the general strike. Citing work of Quaker and Salvation Army hostels in the Rhondda; discussing unemployment. Attending international labor conferences, 1927, 1931. Discussing growing maternity and child welfare services. History of fight for pensions since 1889. Serving on WWII Labour Party committees in Wales. Retiring from Labour organizing, 1948, to work in hospital management assisting nurses' training. Sitting as magistrate for thirty-two years; explaining how she dealt with offenders. Calling on women to acknowledge their debt to the Labour movement.

Writing at the outset of Britain's materialistic 1960s, Andrews calls up memories of the less self-focused and more idealistic nation she recalls from her 1948 retirement, when the triumphant post-WWII Labour government's sweeping reforms in industry, health, and welfare seemed to bring the fulfillment of her lifelong work. In closing her book by invoking women to sober historical reflections, Andrews challenges the complacency of their social security with a reminder of the hard political struggles that had been necessary to achieve it.

15 ANNESLEY, Lady Mabel Marguerite. 1881–1959. *As the Sight Is Bent: An Unfinished Autobiography*. Ed. by Constance Malleson. Museum Press, Ltd., 1964. 157 pp.; preface; port.; wood engravings by author; index. BLC 1968 2:200.

Born in rural Ulster, Ireland. Father: Hugh Annesley, 5th Earl of Annesley, Crimean War hero, M.P., J.P. Mother: Mabel Markham, d.1891. Stepmother: Priscilla Cecilia Moore. 1 brother; 2 half-sisters. Married 1904, Gerald Sowerby, R.N., flag-lieutenant to Prince Louis of Battenberg, d.1913. Widow. 1 son. Artist; military spouse; traveler (Middle East, Australia, New Zealand, South Africa). Aristocracy; married into upper class.

Privileged upbringing, brief marriage, and increasingly independent widowed life of an Anglo-Irish aristocrat, from the 1880s to 1959. Childhood memories: family's Irish estate, horseback riding, summers in London. After her mother's death, author's age 9, father's second marriage to family cousin. Author's education's being left to governesses. Disliking balls and parties; failing to become popular. At age 23, marrying a naval officer; giving birth to their son a year later. Accompanying her husband to his posting in Malta; painting landscapes of the island. Older brother's assuming family title upon death of father, 1908. WWI: death of author's husband and brother in quick succession. Author's resuming the surname Annesley; returning to manage family's Irish estate. Recounting the strife in Ireland, beginning 1921, over England's deferral of Irish Home Rule; expressing her loyalty to England and endorsing its continued military presence. Family's estate's being taken over by the new Earl, a distant cousin. Author's acquiring cottage to share with her lifetime friend, Kate Fisher; their touring Ireland together. Painting landscapes; studying wood engraving. Moving to her newly purchased cottage in Connemara; describing its countryside and wildlife. Traveling in Egypt and Greece, 1935; being reminded by British officers in Egypt of her parents' years in India; reminiscing about Queen Victoria and vanished Victorian graciousness. Excerpts from letters to Kate, discussing Egyptian culture, history, 1930s politics. Outbreak of WWII: author's returning to Irish family seat, which had been commandeered by the British army. Author's doing war work in Belfast. After her stepmother's death, wanting to leave war-torn Ireland. Touring South Africa, Australia, and New Zealand; describing social customs, indigenous architecture, and scenes she painted, c.1941–42. Returning to England briefly, 1945, then returning to New Zealand. Excerpts from letters to her granddaughter Margaret, 1949–59, on art, literature, and Margaret's own work as an artist. Author's returning to Ireland and renting a cottage in Suffolk, 1955–59.

Lady Margaret's autobiography charts the family adversities which obliged this shy, traditionally raised daughter of Victorian aristocrats to mature into a self-reliant adult. Decimated by WWI, her family lost its patriarch, its eldest son, and the author's military husband in short order, obliging the author to assume responsibility for keeping the family fortunes afloat. Her account manifests her growing sense of capability in governing her own destiny, practicing her art, and exploring foreign cultures; only in a few wistful memories of her parents and the Victorian era does the book allude to her sense of loss. Although the body of the autobiography is incomplete, the author's letters to her granddaughter fill in many gaps regarding her later life.

16 [Anonymous]. c.1840–d.a.1916. *Up and Down the World, by a Passionate Pilgrim*. Robert Jenkins, 1916. 261 pp.; preface by Zacchery Bowen (author's grandson); illus. NUC pre56 625:469.

Born in Scotland. Parents not named. Siblings. Married before 1857, husband not named, businessman. 1 daughter; 1 son. Foreign resident (Italy, Philippines, China). Upper middle class.

Author's childhood and education in Scotland and England and her travels in East Asia after marriage, covering 1840s–1878. Coming from a family of Scottish landowners; remembering visiting tenants' cottages in the Border country. Living with her wealthy father in Edinburgh most of the year. Discussing schism within the Church of Scotland and resulting Free Church of Scotland, early 1840s; father's causing family rift by joining the Free Church. Deploring elaborate Victorian mourning obligations; having been made to spend seven consecutive years wearing black for dead relatives. Condemning compulsory needlework for Victorian gentlewomen; asserting that neither their 18th-century grandmothers nor their 20th-century granddaughters would have submitted to it. Receiving an excellent secular education in Edinburgh, c.1850s. Contrasting her school experiences with those of her daughter and son, schooled in the 1870s. Attending lectures at the Philosophical Institution, age 16; relating that T. H. Huxley, the evolutionist, scandalized good Christian listeners. Loving to read John Ruskin's *Stones of Venice;* considering him the principal influence on her own writing. Remarking on modern women having much greater career options than she had, c.1850. After marriage, accompanying her husband to the Philippines, 1857. Labeling Philippine natives "Indians" and "blacks." Stereotyping Philippine natives as indolent and sensuous. Having her servants "capture" an aborigine for inspection by visiting scientists. Discussing Spanish church and government exploitation of islands. Being the first Englishwoman to enter the interior. Birth of her first child. Visiting China, 1859, at time of Peking massacres. Traveling with husband in official delegation to Japan, after Lord Elgin had opened it to the West. Their returning to Manila, 1860–61; returning to England with her two small children while husband remained in Manila. Living with her husband's parents in western England. Husband's returning to England for a rest year, 1864; their living in Paris. Moving to London when her husband returned to Manila. Abandoning her attempts to teach her own children; hiring a tutor. A friend's joining Robert Owen's socialist commune; author's resisting the temptation to join it herself. Collapsing emotionally over death of unnamed loved one, 1868. Traveling with her children in Italy; studying art and architecture; meeting John Ruskin; leaving before the 1870 upheaval. Returning to live in Middlesex. Revisiting Rome, 1878; arriving at the time of the election of Pope Leo XIII; visiting receptions being held for the visiting U.S. president, Ulysses Grant. Providing metaphorical description of taking an imaginary "astral journey" in 1916 over all the countries she had previously visited; describing how they had changed.

Although anonymous, the author evidently intends part of her readership to know her identity, as she cites by name such Scottish ancestors as George Bell, and discusses with considerable pride her reputation as an author. While her account has value as a travel record of English experiences in the Far East, the author proves to be a product of her time in the unquestioning assumption of her own racial superiority, which colors her attitudes about non-Europeans. The book's closing "astral journey" appears to be her adaptation of a remarkably similar passage in *Stones of Venice,* in which Ruskin invokes the reader's imaginary flight over the Mediterranean and southern Europe.

17 [Anonymous]. pre-1900–?. *Experiences of an Officer's Wife in Ireland.* Blackwood & Sons, 1921. 136 pp. ECB 1921–1925 A-K, p. 516.

Raised in Scotland. Parents, siblings not mentioned. Husband not named, British Army regimental officer. 1 daughter. Military spouse. Upper class.

Account of growing unrest in 1920s Ireland, by the wife of an officer in the occupying British Army, climaxing in I.R.A. attack on her husband and other officers and her participation in trial of the accused, covering 1920–21. Accompanying her husband to his military post in Dublin. Meeting hostile Irish while house-hunting in Dublin; expressing horror at the dirtiness of Dublin flat she inspected, and at landlady's keeping goats there. Noting the Irish people's holding a grudge against the British. Tram and cab drivers' refusing to take passengers to British strongholds. Author's failing to understand why the Irish don't like British soldiers; claiming British "Tommies" made friends in every other country in which they fought. Being bored for lack of amusements in Dublin. Encountering an atmosphere of fear at British dinner parties; author's avoiding venturing out at night. Playing golf and tennis at Dublin Castle. Claiming to have observed Sinn Fein spies at work. British soldiers and families' suffering constant strain of Irish hatred; later discovering that British government let wives stay in order to avoid the appearance of being afraid. Noting raids on I.R.A. strongholds by British troops. Praising Britain's notorious Black and Tan auxiliaries; saying that although she knew "little" of Black and Tan activities, they successfully put "the fear of God" in Irish rebels. Irish railways' refusing to carry Royal Irish Constabulary soldiers. Berating Irish indifference to the suffering of British soldiers in WWI. Castigating Roman Catholic church for assisting Sinn Fein propaganda, turning Belgian public opinion against British soldiers. Author and husband's sharing house in Dublin with other British officers; describing an early morning raid on their house, Nov. 21, 1920, by armed Sinn Fein gang, with "carnage" in the hallways resulting in murders of two officers and wounding of author's husband. Simultaneous attacks taking place across British Dublin. Assisting other wives and police investigators before retreating to England. Returning to Ireland to give testimony; identifying suspects in prison lineup; later returning to Dublin again for trial of murderers; describing the trial and her testimony. Returning to London.

Published at the height of the 1921 Irish Rebellion, the author's account functions as part of the British propaganda effort, emphasizing the suffering of British innocents at the hands of I.R.A. soldiers while omitting mention of any of the political abuses that led to the uprising. This writer is silent on the capitulation of Irish leaders to British deferral of Home Rule in 1920, and on the resulting wave of fury that swept the Irish populace. Her wonderment that British soldiers weren't popular in Ireland as they had been in WWI France is illuminating; she conveniently fails to distinguish being the presence of liberation forces and the presence of soldiers conducting a hated occupation. Her story does have documentary value she could not anticipate, in its vivid evocation of the disparity between the wealth of the occupying British and the poverty of the native Irish. Readers of this memoir will be helped by reading two complementary memoirs which convey a fuller picture of British and I.R.A. actions: Irish novelist Kate O'Brien's *Presentation Parlour,* which outlines Black and Tan atrocities against the native Irish, and Annie Mary Smithson's *Myself—and Others* (1944), which describes her own Sinn Fein activities during the 1920–21 unrest.

18 [Anonymous]. c.1867–?. *The Life of an Enclosed Nun by a Mother Superior.* A. C. Fifield, 1910. 124 pp.; front. port.; pub.'s note. BLC to 1975 228:263.

Raised in London. Father not named, physician. Mother not named. 4 sisters. Single. Religionist (Roman Catholic convert); nun. Upper middle class.

Author's convent schooling, conversion to Catholicism, and life as a nun and as a mother superior, covering 1883–1911. Family's having limited means; author's realizing she and siblings must all earn their own living. Eldest sister's studying nursing at London Hospital; second eldest's working as a nursery governess. To lighten costs for other sisters, mother's sending author, age 16, to a "very cheap" Belgian convent school to learn French in preparation for a teaching career. Author's being warned not to become "an idolater," but gradually overcoming her pro-English, Protestant prejudices. Her nominally Anglican family's being frankly agnostic and tolerant of other religions. At the convent, British children's being sent to Protestant Sunday services. Author's growing curious about Catholic services; being permitted by her mother to attend the nuns' Christmas midnight mass. Expressing her respect for the nuns' ascetic lives. Returning to England, age 19, and working as a governess in London, 1885–86. Growing increasingly dissatisfied with Protestant services; reading Catholic works; being instructed in Catholicism by an Irish priest. Formally converting to Catholicism, age 20; even her agnostic father's admitting that she was better and happier afterward. Wanting to become a nun; searching for an order that could supply her with a sense of vocation. Receiving a £1,000 legacy that enabled her to join a Catholic sodality. With her father's consent, being admitted as a novice into a Midlands convent, age 21. Describing the convent and its routine; her daily activities. After one year, making her full profession as a religious sister. Being appointed Sister Sacristan for two years. Experiencing one episode of feeling her life as a nun was useless; recovering with help from a priest who taught her new esteem for her vocation. Accepting the responsibilities of being elected. Extensively discussing her inner life, the rules of silence, and the convent's loving atmosphere. Leaving the convent's enclosure only three times in her later life: to move to new quarters in London, 1900, to visit Rome for a general assembly of her order, 1903, and to attend London Eucharistic Congress, 1908. Describing lay sisters and retreats by lay people at the convent. Assisting novices who doubt their vocation. Describing her familial affection for an old, invalid nun under her care.

The author indicates that she intended her 1911 memoir to refute rumors being circulated about the cruelty of penances imposed upon nuns in the convent. Her book also serves as a psychological self-portrait, explaining how she found greater spiritual freedom within the restrictions of her order than outside them. This contemporary treatment of nearly thirty years in a convent traces the impact on nuns of changing social conditions, including women's new opportunities in secular society and the increasing government resources being devoted to public welfare. Because of the latter, the Church's traditional role as provider of charity was being usurped, a factor reflected in the author's struggles with feelings of uselessness. At a time when political activism was claiming an increasing share of secular women's energies, this early-20th-century account helps to document why the religious life still held a legitimate appeal.

19 [Anonymous]. c.1866–?. *Memoirs of Martha: An Autobiography (Elicited and Edited by her Mistress)*. Arthur Barker, Ltd., 1933. 332 pp.; intro. by "Martha's Mistress." ECB 1931–1935 p.1164.

Father not named, sailor. Mother not named, maid. Orphan. At least 1 brother. Single. Domestic servant. Working class.

Restricted working-class childhood, work history, decision to emigrate, and resulting self-empowerment of a domestic servant, from c.1866–1909. Memories of her father's death at sea in the West Indies. Mother's working as housemaid for a titled lady. Attending the village school. Playing with her baby brother at the estate where her mother worked. Her mother's being carted away to the sanitorium to die from tuberculosis, author's age 9. Living with her uncle and aunt; losing her brother when he was sent to live with another relative; author's developing an independent spirit despite her overbearing aunt. Going to work as a kitchen maid, age 10, for her mother's former employer. Becoming nursemaid at a rectory in Sudbury, age 16; holding various nursemaid positions for the next two years. At age 20, deciding to emigrate to Australia; describing the two-month sea voyage. In Australia, being bewildered by another young woman's verbal explanation of prostitution; confessing that she was ignorant until late in life that sex existed. Being hired into the household of the Bishop of Brisbane. A year later, becoming housemaid to a family near Sydney. Going to Melbourne; working as a kitchen maid at Government House. Using a large jar to strike a fellow servant intent on stealing a kiss. Experiencing a change in household with appointment of a new governor; being promoted to under stillroom maid. Returning to England, 1890. Finding a job as a nursemaid for the child of a naval officer's wife who was bound for

China; stopping in Australia en route; staying there. Returning to Government House. Traveling to the U.S.; visiting San Francisco and Chicago; selling souvenirs at the World's Fair. Visiting Niagara Falls. Finding a child-care job with a family in New York. Returning to England, c.1899. Holding several temporary jobs. Working for a professor's family for almost ten years. Expressing her lifelong passion for travel, new experiences, and reading. Praising her present mistress's assiduousness in pulling details about her life from author.

In the introduction, Martha's mistress explains that the book is both hers and Martha's and that both wish to remain anonymous. After recording Martha's story as it was related, her employer has reorganized it into a coherent narrative that effectively conceals where Martha begins and her mistress ends. This memoir of an itinerant housemaid is strikingly similar to that of another adventurous traveling domestic servant in Australia during the same years, Agnes Stokes, who wrote *A Girl at Government House: An English Girl's Reminiscences "Below Stairs" in Colonial Australia*. Both authors fortuitously found that domestic skills were at a premium in late-19th-century Australia, ensuring their owners much greater income, opportunity, and mobility than if they had chosen to remain in England.

20 [Anonymous] (Bartram, Lady Alfred). c.1800–?. *Recollections of Seven Years at the Mauritius, by a Lady*. James Cawthorn, 1830. 208 pp.; preface. NUC pre56 38:99.

Born in the West Indies. Parents not named. 1 sister. Married, husband not named, of Scottish descent, d.1826. Widow. 2 daughters. Foreign resident (West Indies, Mauritius). Upper class.

Bereaved widow's memoir of transatlantic voyages and details of life on Mauritius, 1819–27. Parting emotionally from her father and sister in the West Indies; briefly staying in England with her husband. Their traveling to Bombay and Mauritius with their 2-year-old daughter, 1819, because her husband hoped to obtain a lucrative government position in Mauritius. Remarking that she had made three previous voyages between England and the West Indies. Author's being pregnant on 1820 voyage to Mauritius; giving birth to younger daughter the day she arrived. Family's staying with a relative of husband, who also worked for the Civil Service. Cholera's being epidemic at that time. Feeling homesick for England, but working through it by investigating local customs and wildlife. Noting the restrictiveness of female education on the island. Almost losing her older daughter to severe illness. Discussing tense relations between British settlers and natives, and the encouragement of native unrest by the recent events of the French Revolution. Reflecting on the practical need for the institution of divorce, the origins of racial prejudice, and the pros and cons of slavery. Waiting for her husband to receive a lucrative appointment, which never materialized.

Final illness and death of husband, 1826; recounting the great hardship of her bereavement. Discussing husband's life story: his being Jamaican born and of Scottish ancestry. Author's returning with children to London, two months after his death. Sailing out to the West Indies, c.1827, to rejoin her family, but contracting an illness that forced her to return to London.

Written shortly after her husband's demise, the author's account memorializes him for the benefit of her daughters, recording his relationship with them in their infancy. As a record from the pen of a colonial wife, this memoir helps illustrate the complex connections between one part of the British Empire and another by showing the connections within her own family. As the daughter of British emigrants to the West Indies, the author helped further her family's traditional role in Britain's expansion by marrying another colonial and settling with him on the far side of the world. The fact that events such as France's revolutionary struggles could have so great an impact on class relations in a place as remote as Mauritius also indicates the degree to which politics had already become global in the 1820s.

21 [Anonymous] (Broome, Mrs. Louis). c.1880–?. *The Sweepings of an Old Broom*. Favil Press, 1936. 202 pp. NUC pre56 703:62.

Born in St. John's Wood, London. Father not named, magazine journalist. Mother: Bessie James. Stepmother not named. 6 siblings. Married c.1900, Louis Broome, son of governor-general of Western Australia, miner, engineer. 1 daughter; 1 son. Foreign resident (Australia, U.S., Panama, China); restaurant manager. Middle class; married into upper class.

Author's London childhood, Australian marriage, and global peregrinations with her husband as he followed his engineering profession, 1880s–1920s. Mother's having fallen in love with author's father at age 17 and run away from school to marry him. Recounting his struggles to make a living in journalism, and the help he received from the *Belgravia*'s editor, novelist Mary Elizabeth Braddon. Family's moving frequently around London with fluctuations of income. Mother's dying from heart failure, author's age 10. Feeling she scarcely knew her mother, because the children had been sequestered in a nursery to be "seen and not heard"; vowing to lavish affection and intimacy on her own children. Father's remarrying soon after mother's death; author's being sent away to day school; boarding with her older married sister. In adolescence, being kept ignorant of sexuality by this prudish sister, who managed to conceal three pregnancies while author was living with her. Deciding to seek independence in Australia; aboard ship, meeting and flirting with the son of the governor of Western Australia. Marrying him despite her family's disapproval. Sharing a shack with him in the west Australian gold fields; contracting puerperal fever from having her first child under these primitive conditions, 1895. Author and husband's traveling to Seattle and Alaska to find engineering work for him; author's giving birth to her second child in Seattle, 1901. Their moving briefly to Detroit, Michigan, where husband worked in an electrical plant. Relocating to Panama when husband was hired as one of the engineers building the new Panama Canal. Family's health's suffering in the tropical climate: author's catching "Black Water Fever," which turned her hair white; husband's having nervous prostration; her son's becoming deathly ill with boils. Husband's undergoing the "Weir Mitchell" rest cure; his rebelling against its restrictions. Resolving for their health's sake to send the children to be raised by her brother-in-law in England; missing them greatly. Spending five years in Peking, China, with her husband during his tenure as representative of an engineering firm, 1910–15. Her son Jack's enlisting in the navy at the onset of WWI. Author's returning to London alone; running a Red Cross war depot and living in a hotel in Queensgate. At request of Red Cross, moving to Cairo to run a WWI canteen for Australian forces. Rejoining her husband in Panama after the war. With her children grown, indulging in travel: to the U.S., to India to visit her now-married daughter, to England, and to Switzerland. Traveling to Malta to visit her son in the Mediterranean fleet.

Broome's roving international life with her engineer husband is exemplary of the growing demand for technical professionals throughout the opening world economy in the early 20th century. Her account of conducting family life in Panama as the canal was being built is fascinating, and in its domestic aspects helps to flesh out better-known accounts of the canal's construction. The surge in business ties between Britain and formerly isolated nations such as China is also documented in Broome's book, much as the development of Anglo-Chinese religious ties is charted in Grace Stott's *Twenty-Six Years of Missionary Work in China* (1897). The incident of Broome's husband's taking the rest cure popularized by the American doctor Silas Weir Mitchell echoes the ordeal described in the 1899 story "The Yellow Wallpaper," by American writer Charlotte Perkins Gilman, who underwent the same treatment.

22 [Anonymous] (Felicité). c.1900–?. *My Deeds and Misdeeds*. William Blackwood, 1932. 303 pp.; foreword. ECB 1931–1935 13:1240.

Born in English North Country. Married c.1918, "Jimmy." 3 children. Military spouse; fashion model; saleswoman. Middle class.

Aspects of a young naval wife's experiences, including travel to foreign ports, occasional jobs, and amusing herself during her husband's absences, from c.1918–28. Portraying herself as charmingly flighty and changeable. Author and her married friend Elizabeth's being characteristic of attractive naval wives in dating a circle of Army men during their husbands' absences. Looking back to her marriage, 1918, and her fond memories of visiting Gibraltar while the Atlantic fleet was stationed there. Reminiscing about the fun of drinking Burgundy and gin at cocktail parties, and the adventure of spontaneously dating men she meets. Flirting with her husband's knowledge and with no intention of being unfaithful. Author's visiting her husband in Malta during his tour there; describing the island and attending social events with husband. Describing boarding houses and landladies both in Malta and in Edinburgh, where she lived as a new bride. Playing golf and socializing with other naval wives. While boarding in London during one of husband's absences, working briefly as a mannequin, then as a saleswoman. Noting logistical inconvenience to her of the sudden change of plans and itinerary for husband's ships; dangers for a woman traveling alone; recounting incident of a man trying to force his way into her hotel room. Discussing pranks she and husband have played on each other, as well as their mutual flirting with outsiders; explaining that neither one is upset because they genuinely love and trust each other. Staying at Malta during husband's absence; with female friend, pursuing her habit of dating outsiders. Discussing her children, whom she calls the "Three Bears"; describing how navy life has often obligated her to leave them with relatives. Discussing how naval husbands' absences make their wives ready prey for other officers; noting the many advances she has had to rebuff. Further discussing partygoing and drinking with husband. Adopting a sober tone to discuss family's financial straits; saying their situation is typical of Navy families; asserting that their means are enough if wives accept some financial sacrifices instead of demanding luxury. Writing down her memories to occupy her time during yet another of her husband's absences at sea. Friends' reactions to her writing this work. Describing desolation, special difficulties of military wives; looking forward to her husband's return. Overall, expressing gladness that she married.

Although this author's autobiography is rife with descriptions of her coy flirtations outside marriage, she represents her activities as characteristic of naval wives' accommodations to their isolation. This representation is problematic; while she may picture her own activities with considerable accuracy, the flirtatious recreation she describes seems more indicative of the cultural era about which she writes than of the navy in general. Married in 1918, she was young, attractive, and relatively footloose during the period of social and sexual experimentation that accompanied the 1920s, and in many ways her expressed attitudes toward revelry, alcohol, and flirtation seem to mirror those in an F. Scott Fitzgerald novel. For a more characteristic discussion of the lives of naval wives, readers may consult Joy Packer's autobiographies, *Pack and Follow: One Person's Adventures in Four Different Worlds* and *Grey Mistress*.

23 [Anonymous] (Greer, Sarah D.; née Peregrine). c.1811–?. *Quakerism; or, The Story of My Life, by a Lady, Who for Forty Years*

Was a Member of the Society of Friends. Dublin: S.B. Oldham, 1851. 400 pp.; preface. NUC pre56 217:281.

Born near Dublin, Ireland. Father: John Peregrine (possibly a pseud.), wealthy merchant, landed proprietor, Quaker elder. Mother not named, Irish. 5 siblings. Married c.1830, husband not named, English. 6 children. Religionist (Quaker; anti-Quaker; Anglican convert). Upper middle class.

Quaker upbringing, spiritual disillusionment, and exposé of Quaker Church's failings by an insider who converted to Anglicanism, 1811–51. Her parents' being better educated than most Quakers. At day school, author's being embarrassed at having to wear Quaker plain dress and say "thee" and "thou"; her Anglican-raised mother's allowing her to forego these customs. Noting preponderance of female preachers at Quaker meetings; being bored by meetings; becoming interested in Catholicism through influence of family's Irish Catholic servants. Having non-Quaker tutors at home in various subjects; local Quakers' objecting vociferously. Mother's bowing to the monthly meeting's demand that she replace non-Quaker servants with Quakers; author's satirically describing a women's monthly meeting. Recounting her father's prison reform activity; author's serving as his amanuensis in his letters to various judges. Attending a strict Quaker girls' boarding school as well as quarterly meetings with her father; much Quaker preaching's striking her as ranting and nonsensical; many Quakers being ignorant of the Bible. Discussing itinerant Quaker women preachers and the sect's failure to regulate them. Noting rudeness and hypocrisy of a visiting American Quaker minister, 1827; author's questioning Quakerism for its failings: sanctimoniousness, heterodoxy, spiritual pride, false humility, worldliness, and financial fraud. Typifying superficiality of Quakers' concerns by their anger toward her pious father for allowing his children to dress well. Comparing Quakerism and "Popery"; perceiving that both require subservience to priests and outward conformity. Noting destructive effects of mutual distrust between Quakers and other Christian prison and charity workers. Meeting future husband at London yearly meeting; their obtaining permission to marry from their respective monthly meetings; moving to Bristol after marriage. Discovering that Quakers in Bristol evade the sect's prohibition against paying tithes. Discussing Quakers' marriages to outsiders and opportunistic conversions to Quakerism by people hoping to marry into Quaker wealth. Author's distrusting women preachers; deriving satisfaction from attending Anglican services, where preachers were all men; being pleased to hear the name of Jesus spoken, as Quakers avoid saying it. Resisting Quakers' pressure on her to get her husband to serve as a minister; husband's leaving Quakers. After death of author's father, their moving to Devonshire with author's mother. Author's experimenting with Methodist, Independent

Quaker, and Anglican services there. With husband, returning to Ireland after the deaths of her mother and sister. Irish Quakers' ostracizing her because of her Anglican leanings and criticism of women's preaching; author's ultimately resigning and converting to Anglicanism. Depicting local Quakers as hypocrites, unconcerned about sexual misconduct at a nearby Quaker boys' school. Calling on her Quaker readers to read and follow the teachings in the Bible.

A rare attack on the Quakers, Greer's book represents the denomination as having fallen prey to the peccadilloes of human nature while retaining a rigorously pious façade. Although her representation of Quakerism is analogous to pictures of spiritual decline in the Catholic Church shortly before the Reformation, it is interesting that her critique of the Friends studies the denomination not in its decline but in the early 19th century, at the height of its public influence on child welfare, social progress, and the abolition of slavery. While much of the denunciation in Greer's story evidently originates in her personal resentments, her account of everyday Quaker life is meticulous and fleshes out the practical details, which conventional Quaker spiritual autobiographies usually omit. Her book is also a very useful source for varying 19th-century attitudes toward women as preachers.

24 [Anonymous] (Haweis, [Alethea] Olive). c.1873–?. *Four to Fourteen: By a Victorian Child*. Robert Hale, 1939. 157 pp.; foreword; front. port.; illus. NUC pre56 179:304.

Raised in London. Father not named. Mother not named, writer, artist. (Grandparents were probably Hugh Reginald Haweis, preacher and writer, and Mary Musgrave Joy, artist.) At least 2 brothers. Artist's daughter. Upper middle class.

Childhood memories to age 14 of upbringing shaped by mother's harsh discipline, together with family's social connections in London's artistic circles, covering 1873–1887. Loving her nursemaid, Ann, but fearing her zealously authoritarian mother. Mother's being a writer; her making school seem frightening by threatening to ship author off to school if she spoke "like a servant." Receiving plenty of religious instruction: from Aunt Mary, from Sunday school, and from her vicar grandfather. Family's moving to St. John's Wood Road. Kate Greenaway's illustrated books of children becoming popular in author's childhood, c.1880; mother's dressing author in elaborate Greenaway-inspired clothes, which author hated. Being sent to a school run by her aunts, despite nursemaid's belief she was too young. Remembering her aunts rolling bandages to aid British troops in siege at Khartoum. Mother's hiring a "Mademoiselle" to teach author French, only to fire her for stealing. Describing summer holidays in Devonshire and parents' travel abroad. Mother's abruptly dismissing author's nursemaid just when the young woman had been deserted and robbed by her former fiancé, then laughing at author's outrage. Author's suggesting that nursemaid was pregnant and declaring hatred for her mother's callousness. Remembering the London writers, actors, and artists in her parents' circle of friends, including poet Clifford Harrison, Herbert Beerbohm Tree, Mrs. John Wood, Edward Alma Tadema, and Edward Burne-Jones. Recalling other vivid scenes from childhood: mother's confinement of author to bread and water diet because her room was untidy; public grief over General "Chinese" (Charles) Gordon's death in Khartoum, 1885. Author's noting her own lack of progress in school. Her parents' making a lecture tour of America, c.1886. After their return, author's being taken to see Buffalo Bill's Wild West Show in London. Being allowed to live for a time with her kind vicar paternal grandfather; after his death, resigning herself to returning to her parents' house. Being introduced by her parents to their wide social circle, including artists Sir Frederic Leighton, G. F. Watts, women novelists Lady Jephson, Mrs. Humphry Ward, and Lady Dorothy Nevill. Remembering Queen Victoria's fifty-year Jubilee celebration, author's age 14.

Derived from the diary Haweis began writing at age 10, this autobiography combines these undated, day-to-day accounts with later, reconstructed memories of her early childhood. Names of the author and family members have been changed. Although Haweis edited these entries for publication in her adulthood, she maintains a child's viewpoint throughout, recording her childhood memories without the intervention of hindsight. Consequently, her account preserves, from a child's-eye view, many images of historical and social interest; this memoir touches on 19th-century methods of child-rearing, upper-class exploitation of servants, and the cultural atmosphere of 1880s London.

25 [Anonymous] (Miss M.E.). c.1856–s.l.1918. *Life as I Saw It.* Kegan Paul, Trench, Trubner, 1924. 216 pp.; preface. NUC pre56 332:584.

Raised in London. Father not named, magistrate. Mother not named. Brothers; at least 4 sisters. Single. Knew author Elizabeth Rundle Charles, author/preacher Hugh Reginald Haweis, publisher Charles Kegan Paul. Religionist (Roman Catholic convert); social reformer; philanthropist; temperance activist; short storyist. Upper middle class.

Formative childhood influences and wide-ranging adult social work of a reformer and Catholic convert, from the 1860s to 1914. Attempting to record significant childhood religious experiences, despite difficulty of differentiating between her psychological and spiritual development. Receiving her earliest Christian education from her sister's Nonconformist nursemaid, who also expressed strong socialist views. After being taken to a phrenologist who predicted her future character, author's believing in spiritualism; asserting her childhood home to have been haunted; saying physicians and clergymen often see manifestations of the spirit world. Learning to care for others by tending her younger sisters and minding parishioners' babies. Being confirmed, age 16. Family's moving to Devonshire; author's attending school and Anglican Church there. After her father's death, author's living briefly with friends in Switzerland, then moving to London. Working in a series of socially useful jobs: supervising playgrounds, helping young servants through the Metropolitan Association, doing temperance work and aiding children at Lambeth Mission. Working with her sister at Octavia Hill's school in Lambeth. Living alone in her Lambeth flat. Following her mother's death, acquiring a more permanent home in Lambeth. Publishing a book of stories. Having a growing interest in working-class welfare: attending socialist meetings; starting a lending library to provide books to boys toiling in factories. Assisting her Anglican curate brother in his parish duties; reading to infirmary patients; teaching Bible classes. Studying nursing on an informal basis so she could assist in poor parishes unable to afford medical care. Living at Anglican Sisterhood Mission House at Plymouth. Working with boys' and men's clubs and teaching a Bible class in Vauxhall. Deaths of her sister and curate brother. Searching for a fuller commitment to social service; visiting Roman Catholic convent in Brittany; ultimately converting to Catholicism. After returning to London, moving to rooms near Southwark's Catholic Church. Asserting that she witnessed miracles while on a pilgrimage to Lourdes. In London, extending her social work by visiting infirmaries and workhouses; managing a Boys' Club at Bethnal Green. Accepting a request to manage another Boys' Club in Wapping; starting its tradition of serving free dinners to hungry children. Through mental illness of one of her sisters, author's acquiring an interest in psychology and in caring for the insane. Making a summer retreat at a French convent near Dover to reflect on her life; with onset of WWI, discussing living and working in fear of bombing.

Full of information about Anglican and Roman Catholic home missionary activities, this spiritual autobiography traces its author's maturation even as it documents the vital social services performed in poorer, pre-WWI London by churches. By choosing to live in lower-class Lambeth, the author placed herself near the residence of the Archbishop of Canterbury and consequently near the central hub of the Anglican Church's charitable enterprises. After her Catholic conversion, she moved to other quarters where she would be similarly accessible to her new charitable commitments. This anonymous author typifies the commitment in more modern spiritual autobiographies to spiritual growth through meaningful social contribution.

26 [Anonymous] (Miss "May"). c.1865–?. *Recollections of a Royal Governess (in Austria).* Hutchinson, 1915. 328 pp.; front.; illus.; index. BLC to 1975 271:461.

Raised in Cornwall. Father not named. Mother: "Ver." At least 2 sisters. Single. Governess. Middle class.

Saga of eight years spent as a governess in various royal households, highlighting the impact of political events in Austrian and Polish royal and aristocratic circles, covering c.1891–98. Traveling by train via Vienna and Cracow to the Polish province of Galicia, to serve as governess to Wanda, daughter of Count Badini, the provincial governor. Extensive diary entries on her life with the Badinis: traveling with them to Russia, attending royal Hapsburg wedding in Vienna, accompanying them to horse races and shooting parties. Describing mixed Ruthenian and Polish ethnicity of local region. Bitter feelings existing among Polish Catholics toward Jews. As a Catholic herself, author's venturing alone into the Jewish ghetto to try to understand the hatred; pitying the Jews for being persecuted but also finding them repellent. Discussing other political tensions in the Austrian Empire; nearly being arrested as a suspected Nihilist because she dared to visit a theatre unaccompanied; being reprimanded by the count for transgressing customary female restrictions. Concluding her job with the Badinis by summering with them in 1894 at Abbazia, an Adriatic resort. Making a three-month retreat at a Catholic convent in Vienna, then traveling to Hungary to become governess to the children of Countess Karolyi. Describing the local peasants and gypsies. Taking excursions with the Karolyi family. Family's being persecuted by Emperor Franz Josef over political disagreements. In Hungary, becoming interested in seeing Rome through her friendship with Madame Merry del Val, wife of the Spanish ambassador to Rome. Leaving her governess post; traveling to Rome and staying at the Spanish Embassy. Diary extracts recording her audiences with Pope Leo XIII, 1894–95. While in Rome, finding a new position as governess to the daughters of an Italian marchesa. During this job, receiving appointment as English governess to the archduchess Elizabeth Marie, granddaughter of Franz Josef. Traveling to Laxenberg, Austria, to commence service to the 14-year-old archduchess. Excerpts from letters to her mother covering court intrigue, the assassination of Crown Prince Rudolph by order of the emperor, and gossip about royals. Visiting Rome again, as guests of the Merry del Vals; describing international aristocrats she met at the Spanish Embassy. Extensively discussing incidents of political intrigue in the Austro-Hungarian Empire, mingled with accounts of galas she attended with the royal family. Discussing political furor in the Catholic Church concerning the Vatican's rejection of the Borghese papers supposedly proving Anglican claims to the validity of Anglican clerical orders. The Anglican Church's seeking reunion with the Roman Church, but Vatican's resisting, c.1896; author's believing that Anglican and Roman churches should be spiritually united. Author's having troubles with the unruly young archduchess but fearing to discipline her due to her high rank. Under conditions of increasing tension between Germany and Austria, author's returning temporarily to Cornwall to tend her ailing mother. Returning to Austria. Political tension's beginning to affect her employer's family; Count Badini's dueling with German diplomat who insulted his Polish pride, involving himself in intrigues against the Germans, eventually being forced by the emperor to resign his office, 1897. After the 1898 murder of Empress Elizabeth, Franz Josef's wife, author's ending her service to the Austrian court; marriage of the archduchess soon after the author's departure. Remembering how her first young charge, the Polish Wanda Badini, had hated Austria and cursed Emperor Franz Josef; reflecting that the curse had come true with the events of WWI.

When the author published this account in 1915, her experiences in aristocratic households scattered through Poland and Franz Josef's empire were some 20 years old. Her decision to collate her old diaries and correspondence into an autobiography/political survey of the period was very likely provoked by WWI, with the public scrambling to learn more about the forces of the suddenly menacing Austro-Hungarian Empire. Although the author's retrospective commentary is colored by her hindsight about the war, it is more than balanced by her inclusion of day-to-day observations. This book holds a wealth of useful historical detail to complement more conventional public accounts of events adumbrating the first world war.

27 [Anonymous] (Menzies, Amy Charlotte; née Bewicke). c.1850–d.a.1917. *Memories Discreet and Indiscreet by a Woman of No Importance*. Herbert Jenkins, 1917. 352 pp.; front.; illus.; foreword; index. NUC pre56 376:470.

Born in Yorkshire, near Stockton-on-Tees. Father not named, country squire, attorney. Mother not named. 1 sister; 2 brothers. Married c.1876, Captain Stuart Menzies of the 92nd Gordon Highlanders. 1 son. Wrote *Further Recollections, As Others See Us* and *Life As We Live It*. Knew Queen Victoria, Her Highness Nawab Sultan Jahan Begum of Bhopal, the Empress Eugènie and her son the Prince Consort, Lord Kitchener, Lady Cornwallis-West, others. Military spouse; colonialist (India, Egypt); cultural historian; memsahib; society woman. Rural gentry.

An insider's view of British colonial life in India and Egypt, as well as personal memories of her late adolescence in England and early married life, covering 1870s–c.1917. Recalling parties her parents hosted for aristocratic guests. Author's being insubordinate toward her governess. Her sickly constitution. Local gossip. Her first engagement, based on her immature desire for marriage. Becoming engaged for the second time; marriage; her ignorance of sexual and economic aspects of marriage. Anecdotes of Violet Tweedale and Colonel Burnaby. Husband's departure for India; birth of their son; her voyage to India with infant; discomforts of life in India. Husband's lack of understanding and foresight in planning for family on the long inland journey. His departure for Afghan war, 1878; her return to England; death of their son in England, c.1881. Reuniting with husband in England; returning with him to India; his being wounded in Afghan battle. Further melancholy and discomfort in India; visiting regimental hospitals. Visiting Egypt with her brother, 1885; her preference for Egypt over India; arranging for husband to be transferred there. Anecdotes of military officers and war correspondents she knew in Egypt. Returning to England, c.1890. Preachers she knew. Her friendship with Charles Stuart Parnell. Many anecdotes of leading British officers and colonialists, including Kitchener, Rhodes, Lord Robert. Secondhand anecdotes of heroism in 1881 Boer War, Afghan war, Indian mutiny, Sudan campaign.

Although she protests "profound ignorance" of military matters, more than half of Menzies's book consists of anecdotes and intelligent comments about British military officers' service to the Empire. The tone is chatty, somewhat gossipy in this insider's view of the upper ranks of the British army and diplomatic service in the 1880s. After this book's success, Menzies wrote sequels: **28** *Further Indiscretions* (1918) deals mainly with her 1880s social life, repeating much society gossip and revealing her tolerance of upper-class infidelity so long as good manners prevailed, and also discusses WWI's effect on her social circle; **29** *Sir Stanley Maude and Other Memories* (1920) consists of anecdotes largely concerned with diplomacy in India and Russia c.1884–1920; **30** *Recollections and Reflections* (1922) is a revealing look at the unwritten code of upper-class manners and mores and postwar changes, told through more gossip; **31** *Joys of Life* (1927) recounts nostalgically Menzies's own childhood memories: her father's passionate temper, her mother's teaching her to regard marriage as a duty, her helping to supplement her husband's income by training and breeding horses, and her close personal friendship in India with the Begum of Bhopal, a native noblewoman.

32 [Anonymous] (Panton, Jane Ellen; née Frith). 1848–1923. *Leaves from a Life*. New York: Brentano's, 1908. 368 pp. NUC pre56 440:243.

Born in Bayswater, London. Father: William Powell Frith, artist. Mother: Isabelle Baker, charity worker. Stepmother not named. 9 siblings. Married 1869, James Panton, brewer. 5 children. Wrote *From Kitchen to Garret* (1890), novels *Jane Caldecott* (1882), *Having and Holding* (1890), *Leaves from a Garden*, others. Knew Queen Victoria, the Archbishop of Canterbury, and many artists and literary figures of her time. Gossip writer; columnist; novelist; artist's daughter; artist's model. Upper middle class.

Lively upbringing and adulthood of a famous artist's daughter among artistic and influential circles, with the beginnings of her writing career, c.1850–1900. Childhood memories of London: being wheeled in Regent's Park by nursemaids; teaching herself to read, age 2; loving to visit the zoo. Father's being her chief playmate. Discussing her father's distinguished painting career and lucrative commissions. On Sundays, being taken to visit his artist colleagues. Queen Victoria and other royal family members' visiting their house to have their portraits painted by author's father. Author's frequently accompanying father to his appointments; remembering playing on Buckingham Palace grounds while father painted the queen. Being taught only a bit of French and geography; noting that girls' schooling in those days was the worst imaginable. In 1850s, being immortalized by Augustus Egg as a child figure in his painting "The Gambler's Wife"; this being the first of many stints as artist's model. Briefly attending a despised boarding school in Bath; returning home and insisting upon educating herself thereafter. Calling post–Civil War America "perhaps the most detestable nation that has ever been called into existence" because of its capitalism and crumbling class barriers; expressing her love for the defeated American South, which she considered genteel. Alluding to marrying and having a son during the 1860s. Continuing to sit for artists; commenting knowledgeably on picture dealers and how to distinguish authentic paintings from copies. Meeting Charles Dickens while her father painted his portrait; discussing the scandal of Dickens's sending his wife away. Despite author's mother's championing Mrs. Dickens, her father's defending the novelist. Discussing effects of the rift on the novelist's children; recalling Dickens's 1870 funeral. Recalling sitting for a drawing by Gerald Du Maurier, later published in *Punch,* 1868. Commenting negatively on the antifeminism of Eliza Lynn Linton's "Girl of the Period" article in *The Saturday Review;* declaring its author must be a man as no woman could so betray her own sex. Opining that too much worthless writing is published nowadays. Beginning her own writing career, 1880–81. Ridiculing the prevailing spiritualist movement through a series of anecdotes; meeting and disliking Madame Blavatsky. Affirming her deep commitment to the Church of England, but stopping short of rigid orthodoxy and Romishness. Being her father's companion at many high-profile contemporary trials: divorces, celebrity scandals, even the political trial of Charles Stuart Parnell. Recalling her father's testimony in the famous Whistler-Ruskin libel trial. Remembering Oscar Wilde's trial; calling him "bad and disgusting" despite his genius. Providing a retrospective on people she had known and social changes of the preceding fifty years.

In this not-strictly-chronological account, Panton focuses on her early life and on the eclectic range of distinguished Victorians with whom she came in contact. Because of her broad acquaintance, and particularly because of the taste she and her father shared for the drama of the courtroom, Panton's is one of the most useful and observant of the memoirs documenting London life in the late 19th century. In **33** *Fresh Leaves and Green Pastures* (1909), Panton's focus is much more inward, contrasting her unhappy marriage to the happiness of her childhood. She describes her suicidal impulses, the redundant lives of young unmarried women in a rural England made desolate by the large-scale emigration of gentry to the cities, and family controversy over her husband's brewing business. She also satirizes the social pretensions of rural living. Panton wrote two anonymous "tattle" books: **34** *More Leaves from a Life* (1908) contains gossip about her friend Basil Hodges and Lady Arundell's adulterous affair with him, and **35** *Most of the Game* (1911) tells of her friend Phoebe Summers's adulterous affair with Franz von Macoczy.

36 [Anonymous] (Sturge, Mary Charlotte; née Carta). 1860–?. *Some Little Quakers in Their Nursery*. Clifton: J. Baker & Son, c.1929. 112 pp.; illus. NUC pre56 574:685.

Born in Bristol, Avon. Parents not named. 5 sisters; 4 brothers. Single. Religionist (Quaker). Middle class.

Retrospective evaluation of effects of Quaker upbringing and family beliefs on the author's developing psyche to age 19, covering 1860s–1880. Sensing that she and her siblings were raised differently from non-Quaker children. Seeing honor in their Quaker resistance to violence; noting that her Quaker great-uncle had endured prison for his refusal to fight in the Napoleonic Wars. Describing growing up in Bristol: its predominantly Quaker populace and values. Seeing melancholia as the inevitable result of the Quaker belief in universal human degradation; from age 4, consequently having feelings of unworthiness which her non-Quaker nursemaids failed to understand. One older sister's trying to cheer author with Berkelian notion of human perfectibility through effort. Detesting the Quaker plain dress in which her pious parents clothed her. Describing Quaker meetings from a child's perspective; her difficulty in concentrating on God; her frustration with adults' abstract religious thought. Recounting her childhood spiritual worries: fear of hell, uncertainty about heaven, incapacity for prayer. Death of her elder brother; worrying about what would happen to his soul, c. author's age 10. Because of her parents' strict seclusion of their children, being isolated from nature; longing for a sense of unity with all creation. Finally finding a kindred spirit upon reading Ralph Waldo Emerson, age 18. Family's objecting to her reading for pleasure rather than doing needlework. Attempting to analyze traumas of her earlier childhood: guilt and fears of punishment, anxiety about her developing body and its functions, learning difficulties which her parents treated like moral failures. Puzzling over words that Quakers were forbidden to use. Author and sisters' envying a young cousin whose family had left the Society of

Friends. Feeling self-consciousness and shame at being the sole Quaker in her day school. Encountering additional problems at a Quaker boarding school in the south of England; receiving punishment for playing pranks; becoming inattentive to lessons; finding school worship meetings arduous. Coming to appreciate her Quaker heritage as she grew older.

Open in its meditations on the cultural and familial aspects of Quakerism in the 19th century, this author's memoir records both the benefits and adversities to which her parents' Quaker piety and practice exposed her. With unusual candor the author confesses her own deficits. In its striving for objectivity, this largely good-humored discussion of Quaker influences upon Sturge's childhood character differs from the acrimonious retrospective on Quakerism presented in another anonymous autobiographer's book, *Quakerism; or, The Story of My Life, by a Lady, Who for Forty Years Was a Member of the Society of Friends.*

37 [Anonymous] (Vince, Sydney). 1888–?. *Me, Some Men, Some Women and Affairs, by "A Human Woman."* Birmingham: Cornish Brothers, 1930. 281 pp.; front. port. NUC pre56 638:246.

Raised in London. Father not named, politician. Mother not named. 2 brothers. Single. WWI factory inspector; foreign resident (U.S.). Upper middle class.

An incorrigible flirt's attention-seeking childhood and adolescence, and her later career and romantic adventures, 1890s–1919. Describing herself as gifted in the art of flirtation from birth; meditating on whether she is beautiful or merely pretty. Growing up spoiled, the sole girl among several boys. Rebelling against her nurse; flirting precociously with her father's adult male colleagues. Assuming all women are vain. Describing dressing in her mother's clothes to win praise, and dressing in her father's clothes to imitate Vesta Tilley, a popular male impersonator and singer. Her father's being an enthusiastic politican and enormously popular with the aristocracy; author's boasting of his many titled friends and visitors. As a child, reveling in attention from adults, ranging from father's political friends to anonymous policemen. Claiming that although her acquaintances Ellen Terry and Sir Henry Irving recognized her acting talent and supported her desire to go on stage, her parents opposed and prevented it. Alluding briefly to school attendance, with incidents of punishment, practical jokes, and attempts to make boys quarrel over her. Accompanying her parents on an extended visit to the U.S., c.1900; visiting Boston, New York, Chicago; traveling by train to San Francisco. Meeting novelist Jack London, author's age 15; claiming to have dressed in male clothing to visit Chinatown with him. Parents' sending her to a coeducational and multiracial school in southern California. Increasingly desiring male companionship and dreaming of a soulmate; wistfully describing weddings of American schoolmates. Venturing into California real estate speculation with the support of her permissive father. Through the chivalry of a male friend, being rescued from a sexual assault by a lustful, gibbering "dago." Her family's sheltering refugees from the 1906 San Francisco earthquake. Family's returning to England, c.1910; author's referring to an American friend's cousin as "my fiancé"; describing men's falling in love with her aboard ship. In England, being pressured by her unnamed godfather, a prominent Tory politician, to accept English suitors. Briefly joining the militant suffragettes; willingly chaining herself to the House of Commons and throwing things at M.P.s, but refusing to destroy property or hit men. Turning her attentions to doing charity work for her local Anglican church. Recounting a wide assortment of romantic overtures she rejected. Claiming that all women are materialists who lack a spiritual sense. Speaking at her godfather's Tory political meetings during his election campaign. Becoming a supporter of the Liberal Party through her endorsement of Irish Home Rule, thus incurring the wrath of her Tory father and godfather. Father's death, c.1913. Her American fiancé's arriving to comfort her. Rejecting advances from an Anglican vicar with whom author worked to reform public morals. Resisting proposal from her mother's lawyer, who demanded that she erase a debt against her father's estate by marrying him. After being a witness for the prosecution in a court case, author's suffering attempted rape by the defendant's attorney. Family's fortunes collapsing in WWI; author's resolving to become the family mainstay. Receiving an appointment in the Ministry of Munitions; as a factory inspector at Woolwich, supervising men and women munition workers; describing hazardous working conditions. Being appointed a factory inspector over male workers. Finding women officials to be untrustworthy; some of them accusing her of flirting to win promotions. Discussing wartime profiteering and its effects on factory production. Her fiancé's being sent into action in France. Having a psychic vision of fiancé's death in battle; its coming true. Discussing her physical collapse after war's end, 1919, and taking a rest cure in the south of England. Advising women at her hotel on how to deal with the men in their lives; being gossiped about for flirting.

This early-20th-century memoir offers one woman's rather limited perspective on what she takes to be her gender's wholesale characteristics: flirtatiousness and manipulativeness in pursuit of personal aggrandizement. Of particular interest here is what might be considered Vince's Lolita complex, given her many references to the satisfactions she drew from behaving seductively with her father's adult friends. It is difficult to know how much trust to have in Vince's many anecdotes of repelling male advances, because they do tend to diminish her credibility. This is regrettable, as her involvement in factory inspection for the British WWI munitions effort gives the latter part of her book a great deal of documentary value.

38 ANSELL, Evelyn. c.1830–?. *My Reminiscences of Colonial Life*. Royston: John Warren, 1882. 107 pp. BLC to 1975 9:140.

Born in Cambridge. 1 brother. Married 1852, in England. Colonialist (Australia, New Zealand); miner; teacher; school administrator. Middle class.

Record of colonial life (thirteen years in Australia and twelve in New Zealand), pinpointing the Australian "gold fever" years, covering 1852–77. Boarding ship at Gravesend with her husband in order to seek their fortunes in the Australian gold fields, 1852; sailing halfway around the world; fearing she may never see her "dear ones" again. Recounting shipboard experiences: constant seasickness, crossing the equator, being becalmed for days, fighting storms and sharks. Mutiny's breaking out among drunken sailors on New Year's Day, but quickly abating. Arriving in Williamstown after three months; reuniting with old friends who had emigrated earlier. Scarcity of houses; many locals' living in tents; enduring poor sanitation and dysentery. Author and husband's continuing on to Melbourne; living in a "matchbox house" in Richmond for some months. Living in "rough country"; encounters with snakes, tarantulas, centipedes. Describing "gold mania" which enticed Englishmen from every class to seek wealth in the gold fields: "noblemen's sons with diamond rings" digging with their hands, uneducated folk getting rich by selling goods and services to the miners. Author's sharing all of the hard physical work of settlement and mining. Capably dealing with problems, including venomous insects and natural disasters. Gold mania's creating new business opportunities: land speculation, house construction. Depicting the scene in Ballarat mining district. People's claims to their diggings being unstable; author's recounting mistake of abandoning a claim after working it briefly, only to have new owners find gold there. Enduring disappointment with bad luck at digs and husband's inadequacy as a gold-seeking pioneer; his turning to storekeeping instead. Describing local aboriginal culture, as well as local animal life and birds. With husband, leaving Ballarat diggings for Maryborough, one hundred miles distant. While husband tried his luck, author's returning to Melbourne in ill health. Visiting friends in New Zealand to recover her health, 1865; describing voyage, Maori natives, and Scottish settlers. Comparing New Zealand Maoris with Australian aborigines. Starting a school in New Zealand, but being advised by physicians to return to England. Describing her unaccompanied return voyage to England.

By graphically describing the hopes that Australian immigrants pinned on the discovery of gold, this autobiography provides exceptionally valuable testimony to the global journey, hardships, and cultural dislocation that British gold miners faced. Ansell's account eloquently testifies to the accommodations she and her husband made to disease, climate, and disappointment. Her itemizations of their hardships create a characteristic image of Australian immigrant existence, c.1860, and its transformations under the influence of global gold fever.

39 ANSON, Lady Clodagh De La Poer (née Beresford). 1879–?. *Book: Discreet Memoirs*. G. Bateman Blackshaw, 1931. 379 pp.; front. port.; illus. NUC pre56 17:537.

Born in London. Father: John Henry Beresford, 6th Marquis of Waterford, Ireland. Mother: Lady Blanche Somerset. 1 brother; 2 sisters. Married 1901, the Hon. Claud Anson, son of earl of Lichfield. 1 daughter; 2 sons. Philanthropist; WWI volunteer; charitable volunteer. Aristocracy.

Aristocratic social life, travels, and philanthropy motivated by increasing awareness of social injustice, covering author's childhood to c.1930. From childhood onward, author's younger sister being her best friend. Growing up in London; father's closing his Irish estate, Curraghmore, due to Fenian strife when author was age 2; not reopening it until author was age 6. Viewing Fenian grievances about landlord-tenant relations disapprovingly; insisting that English hunting parties help support the local Irish economy. Family's returning to Curraghmore, 1886; author's recounting its history. Father's being crippled in a riding accident. His leading the Irish Unionist Party (against Gladstone) in the House of Lords. Author's childhood's being uncommon, since both her parents were invalids. Recalling visits of Edward, Prince of Wales, to their London home; other aristocratic visitors. Mother's making charitable visits to an insane asylum; her employing an inmate as a servant. Praising her mother's generous personality. Author's living at Ramsgate one year and observing scandal caused by women cyclists; bicycling without her father's knowledge. Later, living with her grandparents at Badminton; extensively discussing her grandparents and social life there. Traveling to Egypt with her parents, 1892–94. During grave illnesses of both parents, father's anxiety about mother leading to his depression and suicide, 1895; through father's psychological treatment, author's having met Swedish psychotherapist Axel Munthe, who became a lifelong friend. Author's social debut, 1897; mother's death, one month later. Traveling to Italy with siblings and servants to recover. Upon returning to England, siblings' leasing houses together in Oxfordshire and London. Author's being presented at court, 1898. Visiting Italy a second time and staying with Dr. Munthe in Capri. Stating that the Boer War had a more devastating effect on her life than did WWI; noting many war deaths among her friends. Marrying a peer's son with a cattle-raising hobby, 1901; departing for husband's Texas ranch. Describing ranch life. Praising their friendly neighbors, but acquiring neighbors' prejudices against Mexicans and "negroes." Praising the local Indians and Scottish immigrants. Accompanying her husband to Mexico City; extensively criticizing the country and its people: finding Aztec natives "treacherous," Mexican attitudes toward death callous, native food inedible; thinking the country's "savagery" cried out for legal suppression. Their returning to Texas; author's describing shootings, murder cases in local courts, rodeos, and roundups. Returning to England. Births of a daughter and a son. Moving to Ireland. Describing society life in Ireland and relations with her extended family, 1904–14. Describing events in Ireland consequent to WWI: battle deaths of several close friends, the home war front effort, submarines along the Irish coast, dangers of crossing the Irish Sea to visit England. Vaguely referring to the "bad times" in Ireland (probably the 1916 Easter Rebellion). Author's relocating to London to do war work: volunteering in canteens and later founding her own; making night rounds to dispense meals and clothing to homeless people in the streets. Explaining how she coped with fraudulent requests for aid. Indignantly discussing police persecution of the poor, and the combined power and prejudice of magistrates that made them the bane of lower-class life. Discussing both London low life and the various missionary efforts to alleviate suffering: poorhouses, sailors' missions. Discussing changes in society due to modern conveniences; improved master-servant relations; women's independence; changes in middle-class social life and amusements; liberalization of marriage and divorce laws. Commenting favorably on the social freedom of the young.

Primarily caught up in aristocratic social life until WWI, Anson's involvement in wartime canteen work among the poor of England evidently increased her awareness of social class differences and the social prejudices of her own class, although she never openly reevaluates her own earlier prejudices. In **40** *Another Book* (1937), she expands on her aristocratic background, her marriage, and residence with her husband on a Texas ranch after 1901, and also notes her own and her sister's interest in Britain's ongoing women's suffrage movement. This sequel highlights her indictment of the legal system's mistreatment of prostitutes and of the misconduct of institutional charities. She treats her class background irreverently, although it did open doors for her as a charity worker.

41 ARBENINA, Stella Zoe (Baroness Meyendorff; née Whishaw). c.1890–?. *Through Terror to Freedom: the Dramatic Story of an Englishwoman's Life and Adventures in Russia before, during and after the Revolution*. Hutchinson, 1929. 288 pp.; front. port.; illus. NUC pre56 380:404. [cat. under Meyendorff.]

Born in Russia. Father: surname Whishaw, English. Mother: née Law, chaplain's daughter. 2 brothers. Married c.1910, Baron Paul Meyendorff, a Latvian (changed name to Arbenina in 1917 to cover family origins). 1 son; 2 daughters. Actress; foreign resident (U.S.S.R.); anti-Communist. Upper class; married into aristocracy.

Author's privileged life in Russia until the 1917 Revolution and her subsequent acting career, covering her birth to c.1925, focusing on 1914–21. Through her marriage, being one of Imperial Russia's aristocracy. Just before Russia's entry into WWI, author and friends' making a luxurious weeklong automobile tour of western Russia. Upon returning to St. Petersburg, discovering that the tsar had joined the war against Germany; Tsar's renaming St. Petersburg "Petrograd" to eliminate linguistic ties with Germany. Additional factors' conspiring to produce Russia's downfall: the tsarina's susceptibility to Rasputin, Rasputin's controlling the tsar's public policy, and war-induced peasant starvation. Russian women's volunteering for the war effort; author's training alongside the tsarina for Red Cross nursing. By 1916, frightened nobles' collaborating to assassinate Rasputin, but too late to halt the oncoming 1917 revolution. Shortages and starvation's being exacerbated by severe blizzards; mutinying soldiers' storming the family house in search of guns. Tsar's abdicating, March 1917, in favor of his brother, who also abdicated for fear of revolution. Socialists' rising to power under the dictator Kerensky; her husband's resigning from the military because it no longer served the tsar. Bloody struggles' worsening because of arrival of Vladimir Lenin, who raised forces to overthrow Kerensky. Author's daily war nursing; collapse of expected income from their estate; their need to earn income. Recalling her childhood desire to go on stage after having acted in informal family theatricals, age 10. Acting in amateur troupes. Studying operatic singing. War's ending her theatrical hobby, but not her singing lessons. Successfully auditioning for Stanislavsky's Moscow Art Theatre, 1917, but realizing she could not leave her family alone in Petrograd to face potential annihilation. Discussing the brutal defeat of Kerensky's Provisional Government by the Bolsheviks, and Lenin's paranoid extremism and resolve to destroy the privileged classes. Family's selling jewels to survive while author developed a professional acting career at Petrograd's Alexander Theatre. During persecution of Slavs, changing their surname to Arbenina to conceal Slavic origins. Her debut performance at Alexander Theatre, 1918. Recalling the massacre of the tsar and his household at Ekaterinburg. Touring with her company in Vologda, but having to flee political violence and return to Petrograd. Many residents' escaping; Alexander Theatre's bravely continuing to perform to nearly empty houses. Food shortages. Bolsheviks' confiscating all private property; author's family's taking shelter on father-in-law's country estate. Leaving her children there; returning to Petrograd. Beginning of wholesale executions of former royalists; author and husband's planning escape to Moscow, but husband's being preemptively arrested. Author's being arrested trying to persuade Bolsheviks to release him. Being reunited with her husband and other former nobles in prison; their being interrogated and starved, threatened with death unless they confessed to being counterrevolutionaries. Despite winning release, author's being frantic because Bolsheviks retained her husband; rushing to their flat to use valuables as bribes for his release, only to find the Bolsheviks had already stolen everything. Selling her rings (her last possessions) to win husband's freedom. Their escaping from Russia to Riga, Latvia, October 1918; feeling humiliation in having to accept Germans as their saviors. Discovering husband's family estate near Reval had been plundered; deciding to stay despite fighting in nearby Estonia. The Reval Theatre's courageously reopening in 1919; author's acting there through 1920. Latvian authorities' voluntarily ceding their lands to the peasants to preempt revolution. At Christmas 1919, receiving news from husband's family left stranded in Russia: death of her father-in-law from starvation, but her children's continued health. In October 1920, at last being reunited with her children. Taking her family to safety in Berlin; winning roles in stage and film productions, beginning 1921. In 1923, visiting her brother in London; noting city's excellent theatre opportunities and deciding to live there. Winning a role in *The Prisoner of Zenda;* its paving her way to prominence in the London theatre.

Although it was Arbenina's celebrity as an actress that induced her to record her experiences in the Bolshevik revolution, her documentation of Russian aristocratic society's extraordinary refusal to accept the imminence of political change lends rare insight into the process by which the old Russia was destroyed. In its descriptions of the breathtaking luxury of Arbenina's social circle's prewar years, Tsar Nicholas's naive reliance on the peasants' loyalty to him, and the author's own outrage over having peasant hands touch her family pearls, this account is redolent with the same assumptions about class and privilege that fueled Russia's problems. On an individual level the book is moving, as Arbenina vividly evokes the sufferings of her family and friends. From a more detached perspective, however, the reader can see in Arbenina and her kin a type of thinking that helps to explain Russia's peculiar vulnerability to class-fomented revolution.

42 ARGALL, Phyllis. 1910–?. *My Life with the Enemy*. New York: Macmillan, 1944. 290 pp. NUC pre56 20:117. (other ed.: 1945, entitled *Prisoner in Japan*.)

Born in Canada. Parents not named. Journalist; foreign correspondent; prisoner of war; missionary; foreign resident (Japan). Middle class.

WWII correspondent's early life, upbringing in East Asia, and residence in Japan, with focus on her imprisonment and interrogation by the Japanese military, covering her childhood to 1944. Although born in Canada, being raised by her aunt and uncle in London after death of her mother, author's age 4. Aunt and uncle's having lived in Japan, 1905, where uncle was a partner in a Kobe business firm. Describing WWI bombing raids in London. Moving with aunt and uncle back to Japan, 1916; doing missionary work there with her uncle. Living in Formosa, c.1930–35; heading mission school until forced to leave by Japanese government. Working as a news correspondent for *Japan News-Week, Atlantic Monthly,* and *Time* magazine, 1930s. Suffering arrest and imprisonment in Japan, 1941–44; extensively describing her trial, interrogation, and prison conditions. Being released, 1944, and returning to England.

In this memoir, committed to paper following her release, Argall scrutinizes the militarism and fanaticism of the Japanese in WWII. The book's centerpiece is her prison ordeal, provoked by her publication of articles which the Japanese viewed as threatening to their military plans. Of patent documentary value, Argall's account gives firsthand testimony to the ambience of political paranoia and imperialism in Japan which preceded and accompanied WWII.

ARGYLL, Duchess of. [*See* Campbell, Margaret.]

43 ARIA, Eliza (née Elizabeth Davis). 1866–1931. *My Sentimental Self.* Chapman & Hall Ltd., 1922. 251 pp.; foreword by Stephen McKenna; illus.; index. BLC to 1975 10:484.

Born in England. Father not named, artist, photographer. Mother: Bella. 9 siblings. Married David Aria; divorced. 1 daughter. Knew actor Sir Henry Irving, H. G. Wells, Oscar Wilde, Arnold Bennett, others. Journalist; publisher; editor; artist's daughter; religionist (Jewish). Upper middle class.

Victorian career woman's life as filtered through her consciousness as an Orthodox Jew, covering her first fifty-six years. In childhood, having an awkward relationship with her father, largely due to the restrictions of her strict Jewish upbringing. Her closest ties being with her sister Julia. Marrying briefly and unwisely; separating after birth of her child. Finding work as a journalist to support herself and her daughter. Rising to the position of fashion editor for *Hearth and Home*. Writing energetically, contributing freelance articles to *Woman, Jewish Society, Black and White,* other magazines and newspapers. Being publisher and editor of *The World of Dress*. Discussing her working relationships with fashionable people in the theatre and the arts, 1880s–1890s. Frequently noting instances of anti-Semitism she confronted in her acquaintances. Evaluating herself in terms of her love of life's luxuries and her need for intellectual contacts. Making sporadic comments on the "woman question" that rebuke male criticism; sympathy with militant suffragette activities. Discussing her association with Sir Henry Irving, both as publicist for the Lyceum Theatre and in charitable enterprises.

Aria's memoir functions to memorialize the circles in which she traveled and worked rather than herself as an individual. Consequently, her account merits attention as a picture of the day-to-day working relations between artists, actors, and the editors who gave media attention to their doings. Aria also painstakingly documents the stereotypical presumptions she encountered, as a Jew, in the supposedly civilized circles of the late-19th-century theatrical world. Much of her esteem for Henry Irving derives from his freedom from prejudice, and her sketch of the illustrious actor thus provides an unusual perspective on his character.

44 ASHBRIDGE, Elizabeth (née Sampson). 1713–1755. *Some Account of the Early Part of the Life of Elizabeth Ashbridge*. Philadelphia: Benjamin & Thomas Kite, 1807. 66 pp. BLC to 1975 12:315. (other ed.: Worster, Mass: American Antiquarian Society, 1970.)

Born in Middlewich, Cheshire. Father: Thomas Sampson, naval surgeon. Mother: Mary. 2 step-siblings. First husband not named; married c.1734, surname Sullivan, schoolteacher, died c.1740. Married 1746, Aaron Ashbridge, third husband. Religionist (Quaker convert); teacher; indentured servant; preacher; emigrant (America). Middle class.

Pious childhood, rebellious adolescence, American emigration, and providential conversion of an itinerant Quaker preacher, 1720s–1750s. Being raised and taught by her Anglican mother, with her father away at sea. Being a pious child. Running away at age 14 to marry; being widowed after five months; her father's never forgiving her. His refusing to let her live in the family home; author's taking refuge with Quaker relatives in Dublin. Being tricked into signing away her freedom as an indentured servant; escaping when she discovered the plot. Resolving to find her own fortunes in America. Taking ship passage, 1732; discovering plot of some Irish aboard ship to murder the English crew; earning enmity of Irish passengers by reporting the plot. Being tricked again into indentured servitude in New York. Suffering physical and mental hardships as a servant; because of her undeserved sufferings, beginning to have religious doubts. Flirting with Catholicism and atheism; also attempting suicide. After her term of servitude ended, earning her livelihood as a seamstress. Marrying a schoolmaster who was drawn to her by her gaiety; their living in Long Island. Author's also becoming a schoolteacher; with her husband, living and teaching in various places while still seeking a religion she could believe in. Being drawn to the Quakers, despite her aversion to women preachers; at last joining them. Her husband's declaring he would rather see her dead than Quaker; his verbally and physically ill-treating her. Attributing his short temper to his fondness for drink. When she prayed aloud for his conversion, his retaliating by enlisting in the British army and abandoning her; author's grieving that he later died in England from harsh corporal punishment for a military offense. Author's working as a schoolteacher and a Quaker minister in New England and New York; discharging her late husband's debts. Marrying Aaron Ashbridge, 1846, and heeding a call to return to Britain to preach, 1853.

In this account of an 18th-century life lived on both sides of the Atlantic, Ashbridge graphically depicts both contemporary perils, such as the semilegal kidnapping of British citizens to serve indentures in the colonies, and some of the era's spiritual preoccupations, including the itinerant revivalism that made Quakerism a force to be reckoned with. This memoir is partially a conventional conversion narrative that charts the author's finding of her spiritual way after worldly misdirection. It also preserves a number of pertinent details regarding education, social customs, and women's employment during America's colonial period.

45 ASHBY, Lillian Luker with Roger Whatley. 1876–d.a.1928. *My India: Recollections of Fifty Years*. Boston: Little, Brown & Co., 1937. 352 pp.; illus.; epilogue. NUC pre56 23:362.

Born in Monghyr, province of Bengal and Bihar, India. Father: Harman Luker, police inspector. Mother: Ellen Lewis. Maternal grandfather: Thomas Baker Lewis, Jr., indigo planter, elephant breeder. 4 siblings. Married c.1899, Robert J. Ashby, sergeant, telegraph master of military office in Dinapur, India, police inspector. 1 daughter; 1 son. Memsahib; civil servant's spouse (India); hotel administrator; restaurant manager; foreign resident (U.S.). Upper middle class.

Anglo-Indian's culturally isolated childhood and married life, subsequent employment, and her new cultural exposure from emigration to the U.S., 1876–1928. Being schooled at home by an English tutor. Having closer contact with the family's Indian servants and their children than with her distant parents; consequently learning Hindustani before English. Being doted upon by her grandparents, who lived nearby. Describing the regional Anglo-Indian lifestyle: riding elephants, hunting game, observing holidays full of reminders of England. Contrasting this life to the natives' lifestyle and customs in rural India. Telling anecdotes about the Indians, their beliefs, habits, and customs. Giving particulars of positive and negative interactions between natives and foreigners. At age 23, marrying a minor civil servant. Birth of her daughter. Husband's later work as a police inspector; living with him at his remote post, author's age 31, entirely surrounded by native Indian culture. From 1900–03, seeing only two European women. Birth of her son, 1904. Discussing dangers of police work, and her anxiety over her husband's safety in the local labor riots. Recording moments of significance among mostly uneventful years: seeing Halley's Comet in 1910, visiting the Taj Mahal in Agra. Spending her later years in Sakchi, an industrial city. Having strong, caring family relationships. Recording her children's departures for college, c.1920s, as well as their eventual departure from India. Author's winning her first job outside her home as a restaurant manager; later becoming a hotel administrator. Using her long-practiced skills in working with members of a foreign culture to motivate Indian natives to be responsible employees. Recalling the memorable occasion when she waited on Gandhi at the hotel. Leaving India for the first time, 1928, to visit her daughter's family in the U.S. Returning to India; later making the decision to relocate with her ailing husband to the milder climate of Santa Monica, California. Making "startling" discoveries about domestic life in America, such as how to use a broom; confessing that the excess of servants in India had prevented her from ever learning housework skills.

In remembering her life in India, Ashby shows an uncommon capacity both to appreciate native Indian culture and peoples and to endorse the virtues of British Imperial rule. Toward the end of the book, as she describes her resettling in America, she expresses some nostalgia as she realizes she has left behind not only a country but an entire colonial era. In this regard, her chosen title is significant, as the fifty-odd years of her account take her from residence in an active British colony to citizenship in a former one, much as these fifty years marked a significant movement for Britain away from its longstanding imperial identity.

46 ASHFORD, Mary Ann. 1787–d.a.1840. *Life of a Licensed Victualler's Daughter, Written by Herself.* Saunders & Otley, 1844. 91 pp. BLC to 1975 12:350.

Born in London. Father: Joseph Ashford, skinner, tanner. Mother not named. Siblings. Married 1817, husband not named, soldier, shoemaker, d.1829. Married 1830, husband not named, sergeant. Widow. 5 sons; 1 daughter. Domestic servant; cook; military spouse. Working class.

Vivid emotional reactions to childhood experiences, followed by adult occupational and financial difficulties, covering childhood to 1830s. Family history. Mother's being friends with a nursemaid, Mrs. Long; author's staying with Mrs. Long several days a week. Attending day school, then being a day scholar at Mrs. George's boarding school. Hating school because her fellow students ridiculed her as a charity student. Family troubles' beginning with father's illness and his resulting inability to work, 1799; his financial reverses. Mother's illness and death. Father's being consigned to hospital and soon dying; author's arranging his burial. Having to confront the grim fact of being an orphan and without other means of support. Taking post as a domestic servant for low wages. Encountering ordeal after ordeal; being unsophisticated and unable to comprehend her employers' refusal to help servants overcome their crises. Working for a Jewish family; describing favorable working conditions there as unusual. Working elsewhere as a cook. At age 30, marrying half-pay soldier after quick courtship. Her circumstances' improving due to husband's steady work as a shoemaker. With husband's death, return of her monetary hardships; being repeatedly frustrated in attempts to collect her husband's military pension. Commenting on the callous attitude of the army toward widows and children. Writing a letter of complaint to Queen Adelaide. Attempting to place her children in schools, but remembering her own childhood aversions to charity status. Courting with another military man; remarrying on promise that new husband would help rear children. Unexpectedly being barred from living in military quarters with him due to the presence of her children; being forced by army regulations to board the children out.

Ashford's narrative sharply re-creates the difficulties faced by orphans and widowed women of the lower classes before passage of some reforming parliamentary legislation later in the 19th century. She candidly assesses the callousness of prevailing employee-servant relations and articulately expresses her grievances with the army's official disregard for its female and minor dependents.

47 ASHWELL, Lena (née Pocock, O.B.E.). 1872–1957. *Myself a Player*. Michael Joseph, 1936. 287 pp.; illus.; app.; index. BLC to 1975 12:394.

Born aboard ship *Wellesley;* raised in Tynemouth, Northumberland. Father: Captain Pocock, naval officer, businessman. Mother not named. 4 sisters; 2 brothers. Married c.1896, Arthur Playfair, actor; divorced 1908. Married 1908, Henry Simpson, physician, d.1932. Widow. 1 adopted daughter. Wrote *Modern Troubadors* (1922), *Reflections on Shakespeare*. Actress; theatre manager; suffragist; theatrical writer; WWI volunteer; feminist; physician's spouse. Upper middle class.

Formative years, early stage training, and theatrical progress of a distinguished actress and theatrical producer, with testimony to the inequities of women's early-20th-century treatment under marital and property laws, 1870s–1930s. Her parents' being strictly observant Anglicans. Her father's embodying the positive Victorian ideals and values in his moral uprightness and concern for social justice. His grieving over death of author's mother, c.1878. Family's moving to Toronto, Canada, 1880; author's attending school there. Their returning to London, author's age 15. Attending boarding school in Switzerland; also developing her singing talent at the Lausanne Conservatoire. Studying voice at the Royal Academy of Music. Making her stage debut in *The Pharisee,* c.1892. Marrying an actor, 1896, but suffering marital unhappiness. Discussing her husband's intemperate drinking, their separation, and her reluctance to divorce from fear of scandal's effect on her career. Noting the rampant gender inequities of the divorce system. Adopting the daughter of her dead cousin; illustrating the public's propensity for scandal in the prevalent rumor that the girl was actually her illegitimate child. Needing to support herself, her daughter, and her sister. Touring the U.S. for monetary reasons, but suffering illness. After her divorce was final, 1908, quickly marrying a physician whom she had been seeing for some time.

Adoring her second husband; feeling they shared an equal marital partnership; commenting on her opening of Kingsway Theatre, 1907, and its financial ramifications. Comparing her career and marriage with the lives of careerless wives of one hundred years ago; believing these women also were strong partners who managed marriage as a joint business. Commenting on tax laws' injustice to married women; extensively discussing women's property rights. Commenting on the domestic arrangements of her lesbian friends and their status under prevailing property laws. Author's endorsing women's suffrage and participating in suffrage work and marches, c.1909–14. Joining Actresses' Franchise League. Becoming a practitioner of Eastern mysticism, c.1910; also believing in the future of socialism and attending Fabian meetings. Helping establish a regular club for young women in the arts. WWI: entertaining troops. Receiving O.B.E. for her war work, 1917. Founding the Women's Emergency Corps. Reflecting on the "nature of woman." Discussing her continuing commitment to concert tours. Commemorating her husband's death and the end of her own career as a performer.

In this account of one actress's successful career, Ashwell manages to touch significantly upon many of the issues that affected women in general from the 1890s to the 1930s. Although she downplays her business concerns, she was an entrepreneur as well as an actress; she started and managed her own theatre, and produced plays for WWI troops. She does not mention that from 1919–29 she ran the Lena Ashwell Players, presenting performances in less-affluent suburbs of industrial cities. After 1924, her players became a fixture at London's Century Theatre, where they provided high-quality plays at prices within the range of working-class purses. In addition, throughout her career as a producer, Ashwell made a point of providing opportunities for young actors.

48 ASQUITH, Lady Cynthia Mary Evelyn (née Charteris; Leonard Gray, pseud.). 1887–1960. *Haply I May Remember*. New York: Scribner & Sons, 1950. 237 pp.; preface; illus.; index. NUC pre56 23:668.

Born in Cheltenham, Gloucestershire. Father: Hugo Charteris, later 11th Earl of Wemyss and March, magistrate, M.P. Mother: Mary Wyndham. 2 sisters; 4 brothers. Married 1910, Herbert Asquith, son of Liberal prime minister, writer, d.1947. 2 sons. Under pseud. compiled story collections *The Ghost Book* (1926), *The Child at Home,* novel *Spring House* (1936). Knew Sir James Barrie, Marie Belloc Lowndes, Mary Vesey, Violet Asquith, George Wyndham, D. H. Lawrence. Society woman; children's author; biographer; anthologist. Aristocracy.

Privileged upbringing governed by traditional gender restrictions, marriage, and creative career of a prolific and versatile writer, covering 1887–1945, with an emphasis on the author's childhood. History of

Charteris ancestors. Father's being unpredictably moody, but children's being able to rely on mother's radiant temperament. Her first experience with tragedy being the death of her brother Colin, author's age 5. Family's moving to the south of France to recover. Author's disliking her nanny. Being schooled primarily by her governess, Miss Jourdain, with whom she was temporarily infatuated. Attending Cheltenham school one day a week for one term, age 15. Being a day pupil at boarding school for two incomplete terms, age 18. Being discouraged from trying to become a writer by her parents' determination to make her a society woman. Parents' hiring French maids to teach author French; visiting Paris to practice the language. Staying in Dresden eight months to learn music, art, and German. Yearning to attend Oxford, c.1905; father's rejecting this notion. Having a hard experience during her social debut, due to her shyness and inferiority complex. Marrying, 1910; having sons. Traveling with husband throughout Europe and Britain. WWI's effects on her family being tragic: two brothers' deaths, invalidism of her husband and a brother. Expressing her frustrated desire to write by keeping diaries during the war. Suddenly needing income because war injuries effectively ended her husband's career at the bar; after the Armistice, 1918, becoming private secretary to author J. M. Barrie. Discussing the beginnings of her writing career and the belated discovery of her individual literary voice. Discussing political changes and ideas; considering "woman's place" in the world; resisting female stereotypes and roles. Extensively discussing the inequities of class differences and the obliviousness of the well-off toward the plight of the poor. Delighting in teaching her children French; taking them on excursions. Struggling to maintain a balance between career and family.

Asquith's life remembrances connect her own careful upbringing to her later stewardship of her children, whose education she includes in her discussion of her concern over social injustices. At present, the extensive diaries of her WWI experiences, first published posthumously in 1968, are considered to be her major writings. In later years she turned to biography as her primary genre, recording the lives of several members of the royal family and of J. M. Barrie, her longtime employer and collaborator. Her sequel to this autobiography, **49** *Remember and Be Glad* (1952), consists mainly of sketches of people she knew from the Edwardian period.

50 ASQUITH, Margot, Duchess of Oxford and Asquith (née Emma Alice Margaret Tennant). 1864–1945. *The Autobiography of Margot Asquith*. Ed. by Mark Bonham Carter (author's step-grandson). Eyre & Spottiswoode, 1962. 342 pp.; intro. by ed.; illus.; index. NUC pre56 436:235. (1st pub. in 2 vols., 1920 and 1922.)

Born in Glen, Peebleshire, Scotland. Father: Sir Charles Tennant, businessman, manufacturer, Liberal M.P. Mother: Emma Winsloe. 4 sisters; 3 brothers. Married 1894, Rt. Hon. Herbert Asquith, Duke of Oxford and Asquith, Liberal Prime Minister, d.1928. At least 1 son, 1 daughter; 5 stepchildren. Wrote novel *Octavia* (1928). Knew King Edward VII, Queen Alexandra, King George V, Queen Mary, Lord Balfour, William Gladstone, David Lloyd George, Lord Kitchener, Lord Randolph Churchill, many others. Political hostess; society woman; novelist; anthologist; politician's spouse. Upper class; married into aristocracy.

Author's devotion to her husband's political career in England, following her youth in Scotland, covering her birth to 1918. Part 1: Living at the family's Scottish country estate. Regretting the scanty education she received owing to gendered educational traditions and the large number of children in the family needing schooling. Reminiscences of her sister Laura; Laura's early death. Discussing her love of riding to the hounds. Remembering the social whirl of coming out; receiving proposals of marriage. Living on her own in London; visiting mill workers in East London and learning how the less-privileged live. Being presented to Alexandra, the Princess of Wales. Discussing the popular enthusiasm for photographers' "beauties," 1880s–1890s, and the prevailing furor over many of them, including Lillie Langtry. Being sent to boarding school in Dresden. Discussing prime ministers of the 1880s–1890s: William Gladstone and Lord Salisbury. Discussing author's own literary social circle in London, known as the "Souls." Telling anecdotes of famous Victorians she was privileged to know: hearing Tennyson read his poetry; debating about hell and the soul with Gen. Booth of the Salvation Army. Meeting Henry Asquith, 1891, when he was still married. Breezily dismissing the furor over author's engagement to Asquith and subsequent marriage, 1894. Recording friends' reservations about the marriage, as well as difficulties arising from differences in Tennant and Asquith family temperaments and from her stepchildren. Part 2: Author's expressing her opposition to women's suffrage and women in authority, and endorsing the belief that women belong at home. Grieving over her father's death, 1906. Discussing behind-the-scenes machinations in the general election of 1906, when Henry was made chancellor of the exchequer for the victorious Labour government. His becoming prime minister upon the resignation of Campbell-Bannerman, 1908. Recounting her experiences as 10 Downing Street's official political hostess. Relating anecdotes on her familiarity with the royal family, including her invitation to Windsor Castle and the death of King Edward VII, 1910. Commenting on rarity of her husband and herself as Liberals in high society. Outbreak of WWI during her husband's tenure as prime minister. In 1916, Henry's being forced to resign in favor of Lloyd George over public unhappiness with his war record. Author's being accused of being pro-German. Armistice Day in London. Character sketch of President Woodrow Wilson. Recalling the general election of 1918: defeat of the Liberals and the resulting end of Henry's political career.

This abridged version of Asquith's autobiography, edited by her step-grandson, leaves out much information conveyed in the memoir's original form. In his introduction, Mark Bonham Carter helpfully puts Asquith's autobiography into historical context, but in shortening the book he deleted many details about her youth and early married life. Upon first publication, this book caused a stir, particularly for its revelations about the events of the munitions scandal that drove her husband out of office during WWI (details omitted from this edition). Asquith herself leaves out much significant information, focusing more on her sisters than on her brothers, and on her stepchildren than on her own children. She also glosses over the chronology of her relationship with Asquith, which began before his former wife's death. Asquith produced several other personal writings: **51** *Places and Persons* (1925) records travel impressions of Egypt, the U.S., Spain, and Italy; **52** *More Memories* (1933) expresses more detailed opinions about statesmen, literature, and social change; **53** her contribution to the essay collection she edited, *Myself When Young* (1938), discusses her youth and education in detail, with special emphasis on the limitations of her sex; and **54** *Off the Record* (1943) expresses her opinions on adult friendships, marriage, and family life.

55 ATHILL, Diana. 1918–?. *Instead of a Letter*. Garden City, NY: Doubleday, 1962. 192 pp. BLC to 1975 13:169.

Raised on father's East Anglia estate. Father not named, Army officer, landowner. Mother not named. 1 brother. Single. Publisher; journalist. Upper middle class.

Introspective study of the author's search for self-affirmation, highlighting her career as a publisher and her affirmation of human sexual intimacy, from her childhood to 1962. Author's growing up in family manor in East Anglia; associating its pastoral beauty with Milton's "Lycidas." Dominant relative's being author's live-in maternal grandmother, who as daughter of an Oxford don decided the author's destiny was to attend Oxford. Despite living on gracious estate, her father's having financial hardships which abruptly worsened, author's age 13; family's paring expenses. Author's being frightened by news that she would neither inherit their beautiful house nor have family income to rely on. Family's staying in manor while father lived and worked elsewhere. Discussing parents' unhappy marriage; mother's being repulsed by marital intimacy but enduring it; her quarreling frequently with father. Father's unease around his children. Children's realizing their mother was too embarrassed by sex to answer questions; their learning by observing farm animals and reading books in their grandfather's extensive library. At age

11, author's finding and devouring a hidden copy of Marie Stopes's *Planned Parenthood;* later following its instructions in her first sexual encounter. Author's adolescent fantasies' being fueled by Stopes's book; when a handsome tutor arrived to prep her brother for Oxford, author's age 15, Athill's deciding to become sexually involved with him. By age 13, author's having driven off seven governesses through her rebelliousness; grandmother's shipping her off to a girls' boarding school for four years to prepare for Oxford. Hating the school's regimentation and despising math, but discovering a love of writing. By her senior year, dropping Anglicanism and God's rules, mostly from the desire to enjoy an active sex life before any possible marriage. Also adopting socialism, pacifism, and agnosticism; scandalizing her conservative grandmother by standing as Labour candidate in her school's election. Attending Oxford, 1936; finding it restrictive also; putting pleasure before study and taking a third-class degree. Becoming engaged to her brother's tutor. His being stationed in Egypt with RAF; his falling in love with someone else and ceasing to write to author, 1938, crushing author's confidence in her own lovability. At onset of WWII, passively avoiding war work by taking jobs; working briefly in Bath and later at the BBC. Learning of tutor's war death. From loneliness, taking to promiscuity; finding herself pregnant; obtaining an abortion. Describing her anger at the counselor who tried to manipulate her decision by describing abortion as murder. Establishing an undemanding sexual relationship with publisher André Deutsch; their sharing political and aesthetic interests. With Deutsch, founding Allan Wingate Publishing House. For many years, sharing a flat with a female cousin and feeling social isolation as a middle-aged single woman among married couples, but finding her life peaceful. In later life, beginning to write fiction. Winning a £500 prize in a short story contest; experience's restoring her self-esteem and personal happiness. Father's death. Realizing that her inhibitions in close relationships had frustrated her lifelong wish to have a husband and child. Meditating on death.

In this frank and self-analytic autobiography, Athill's primary audience is herself as she attempts to render a personal answer to her dying grandmother's question: "What have I lived for?" Her reconstruction of her own development places sexual intimacy and its resulting bonds at the center of her life, yet she effected admirable achievements in other life areas while her stated goals went unmet. The frankness of her literary treatment marks a radical shift from the more public and euphemistic memoirs that characterized the late 19th and early 20th centuries. Accordingly, while the events in Athill's life may not characterize any particular social trend, her written treatment of these events and her chosen focus are early examples of 1960s trends toward publishing much more sexually candid material.

56 ATHLONE, Alice, Countess of (Princess of Great Britain; formerly Princess Alexander of Teck). 1883–1981. *For My Grandchildren: Some Reminiscences*. Evans Bros., 1966. 306 pp.; intro.; illus.; list of family names; family tree charts; index. NYPL to 1972 16:519.

Born at Windsor Castle, Berkshire. Father: Prince Leopold, Duke of Albany. Mother: Princess Helen of Waldeck. Paternal grandmother: Queen Victoria. 1 brother. Married 1904, His Serene Highness Prince Alexander of Teck, later Earl of Athlone. 2 sons; 1 daughter. Knew Alice, Grand Duchess of Hesse, Tsarina Alexandria of Russia, Queen Victoria, Helene of Nassau, Princess Helena Victoria. Princess. Royalty.

Orderly chronicle of eighty years in the British royal family by one of its members, vividly depicting family's historical crises and accommodations to progress, from the 1880s to the 1960s. Author's looking back eighty years, recalling the vanished luxuries of royal domesticity and royalty's automatic noblesse oblige. Believing that she was happier than young women today, despite difficulties of looking for a husband in royal circles. Being one of Queen Victoria's four living grandchildren, c.1960. Having been born at Windsor Castle; her mother's being German royalty. Going back in time to the national curiosity over whom her father would marry, and the governmental machinations to influence his selection; Queen Victoria's permanent dislike of Prime Minister Gladstone for his opposition to her matchmaking ideas. Father's being Queen Victoria's favorite son and serving as her confidential secretary. Although part of the British royal family, author's and mother's suffering financially after death of father, 1884, because his annuity was cut off. Mother's raising author and younger brother alone; teaching them Church of England catechism and serving as a role model for charity work. Author's spending her childhood at many royal estates: Claremont, Windsor, Balmoral, and Osborne. Despite financial troubles, mother's surrounding them with plenty of servants. Being schooled with her little brother by a governess who stressed history and relieved them of their self-conscious stuffiness. Later being sent to London for lessons in drawing, chemistry, and literature while brother attended Eton. Recalling occasions of visiting "Grandmama," Queen Victoria, at Windsor; describing her Diamond Jubilee, 1897. At age 17, being taken on a grand tour of Germany to see her mother's native land; thus being absent at the time of Victoria's death, 1901; describing the resulting turmoil over the succession. Marrying a German, Prince Alexander of Teck, 1904. Births of her three children, 1906–10; the last boy's dying before six months of age. Living with her husband at Claremont Castle and describing their early leisured lifestyle. Recounting events surrounding the death of her uncle, King Edward VII, and George V's coronation. During WWI, author's doing volunteer work at a London military canteen. In 1917 atmosphere of British hatred toward Germany, author and husband's changing their German surname to "Athlone." Accompanying her husband to South Africa during his appointed tenure as its governor-general, 1923–30; sponsoring a new orthopedic hospital while in South Africa; death of her remaining son, Rupert, there. After returning to England, author's involving herself intensively in charity work: for the National Children's Adoption Association, the Mothers' Deptford Fund, and the Royal School of Needlework. Author and her husband's serving as royal ambassadors to France, Siam, Sweden, the Bahamas, Holland, and Germany. Living in Canada, 1940–46, during husband's tenure as its governor-general; their returning to England, 1946, for him to accept the chancellorship of the University of London. Author's evaluating the drastic changes in royal duties between the eras of Queen Victoria and of Queen Elizabeth II. Offering advice and praise to her grandchildren.

More a private history than a book for public consumption, Princess Alice's account nevertheless richly documents the permutations the British royal family survived in moving from the Victorian age to modern times. As one with a personal acquaintance both with her grandmother, Queen Victoria, and with the present reigning monarch, Princess Alice is immensely knowledgeable in the intricacies of dynastic change and international politics. Because she writes for royal grandchildren whom she presumes will understand British history as well as she does, her unexplained references may sometimes require further research by the reader. She brings a noteworthy Victorian ethical sensibility to her commentary on both 19th-century and 20th-century events.

ATHOLL, Duchess of. [*See* Stewart-Murray, Katharine Marjory.]

57 BACON, Gertrude (F.R.A.S.). 1874–1949. *Memories of Land and Sky*. Methuen, 1928. 244 pp.; front. port.; illus.; index. NUC pre56 29:483.

Raised near Coldash, Berkshire. Father: Rev. John M. Bacon F.R.A.S., scientific lecturer, aeronaut. Mother: née Myers. Stepmother not named. 1 brother; 1 half-sister. Single. Wrote *All About Flying* and *Balloons, Airships and Flying Machines*. Public speaker; scientific writer; balloonist; biographer. Middle class.

Author's scientifically advantaged upbringing, participation in Britain's early aviation ventures, and public career as an aviation proponent, c.1876–1927. Describing 1880s village life and election politics in South Berkshire. Depicting local poverty and one local woman's work among workhouse inmates; father's also being a local philanthropist. His taking sole charge of his children's education, teaching them cutting-edge scientific methods. Advent of bicycling, c.1888; despite scandal of women cyclists, author's daring to ride her own bicycle, 1894. Her father's founding local men's club; his hosting celebrated scientific lecturers.

Father's being an early scientific aeronaut; author's sharing balloon voyages with him from 1898 on; their viewing solar eclipses in Norway, 1896; India, 1897; U.S., 1900. Most memorable trip's being a night flight, viewing a meteor shower; balloon's drifting ten hours unable to descend. On American trip, their visiting Yerkes Observatory in Chicago. Father's 1900 Benz auto's being among first motorcars in England. His conducting acoustic experiments in cathedrals and aloft in balloons. His taking author on field trips to see Cornish tin mine and London Underground before its opening; author's publishing technical articles on these experiences. Recounting early aviation history to 1910. Being first woman passenger to ascend in a motorized balloon, 1904; father's death, the same year. Ballooning with her brother in France, 1907, at time of Wright brothers' visit there. At Rheims Aviation Meeting, 1909, being the first Englishwoman to fly as a passenger in a biplane. Throughout 1910–11, author's speaking and writing on aviation; interviewing aviator S. F. Cody after his forty-mile cross-country flight. Describing cross-country air races in Europe, 1911, and newly developed English hydroplanes. Author's riding in seaplanes; describing experience of "looping the loop"; learning deep-sea diving. Explaining methods of effective public speaking: good slide presentations, charming the audience. Addressing audiences she found intimidating, from women prisoners to Borstal boys. Rejecting reputation of Victorian women for weakness; calling Florence Nightingale and explorer Mary Kingsley just as typically Victorian as any insipid heroine of a novel. During WWI, author's working with Red Cross; helping in prisoner exchanges in Holland. Zeppelin's bombing her home near the Greenwich Observatory, 1916. After 1918 Armistice, speaking on aviation to Australian troops in France. Discussing postwar advances in aviation and her first passenger flight to Paris, 1919.

Bacon's account highlights memories that show the family propensity for daring, especially in her father. In studying scientific phenomena and participating in flight firsthand under his aegis, Bacon joined one of a group of Victorian women whose personal achievements were made possible through the mentorship of their gifted fathers. John Bacon was invited into the Royal Astronomical Society in 1888; he also made successful experiments from a balloon in wireless telegraphy and published Britain's first accounts of aviation, *By Land and Sky* (1900) and *The Dominion of Air* (1902). As a result, Gertrude Bacon's work to further aviation also furthered the family enthusiasm which she was privileged to share. One of Gertrude Bacon's most important published works is her biography of her father, *The Record of an Aeronaut* (1907).

58 BADEN-POWELL, Dame Olave, Lady Robert (née Soames; G.B.E.). 1889–1977. *Window on My Heart*. As told to Mary Drewery. Hodder & Stoughton, 1973. 256 pp.; illus.; family tree chart; list of countries visited; index. BLC to 1975 264:192. [cat. under Powell.]

Born at Stubbing Court, near Chesterfield, Derbyshire. Father: Harold Soames, brewer. Mother: Katharine Hill, former governess and lady's companion. 1 brother; 1 sister. Married 1912, Lord Robert Baden-Powell, founder of Boy Scouts and Girl Guides, d.1941. Widow. 1 son; 2 daughters. Knew Violet Markham, Annie Besant. Organizer (Girl Guides); philanthropist; charitable volunteer. Rural gentry; married into aristocracy.

Progress of a Victorian woman from restricted youth to the pinnacle of worldwide Girl Guide leadership, highlighting her collaborative partnership with her husband, 1890s–1973. Being schooled by a governess until age 12; never being sent to school, although brother attended Eton. Family's moving frequently between various country homes. Describing her sheltered upbringing; noting that "the system" for young ladies prescribed home confinement until matrimony brought release. At age 17, coming out; hurling herself into social life to overcome sense of a wasted life; aching for a man to love. Wishing to train as a nurse; mother's considering both that and author's volunteer work with crippled children a waste of time. During family voyage to Jamaica, 1912, meeting military hero and scouting leader Robert Baden-Powell, thirty-two years her senior; admiring his purposeful life; secretly marrying him. Adjusting to husband's hectic schedule and elite social life. While pregnant, worrying over her aging husband's health. Gaining self-confidence; working publicly for her husband's scouting cause; becoming devoted to scouting; striking out independently by promoting the Girl Guides. Discussing WWI's adverse effect on recruiting young people. Doing YMCA work in France. Birth of her daughter. Enduring lengthy separations from her children; acknowledging they came third after her husband and the Guides. Author's mother's opposing her Guide work; seeing it as detrimental to her domestic duties. History of the Girl Guides: husband's founding group, 1909, because of boys' rejection of girls as fellow scouts. Guides' first leader's being Robert's sister Agnes, who stressed traditional female domestic roles; author's taking over as Girl Guides chief, 1918; introducing more modern goals. Helping found American Girl Scouts; prevailing over husband's desire to reserve the name "scouts" as boys' privilege. Husband's dismay at being granted a peerage, 1929; his fear this would alienate the boys he led. Author's traveling worldwide to promote girls' scouting; being elected World Chief Guide, 1930. After her mother's death, 1931, being distressed but not surprised to find she had been cut out of the will. Receiving Grand Cross of the British Empire, 1932. Promoting scouting in Africa; author and husband's moving to Kenya at beginning of WWII. Her ailing husband's death, 1941. Author's resuming speaking tours, trying to return breakaway scouting groups to the fold. Explaining her Girl Guide administrative activity. Having heart attack and diabetes; reluctantly following a slower schedule after 1963. Noting how scouts worldwide celebrated her eightieth birthday.

Although Lady Baden-Powell is not a self-declared feminist, her memoir dramatizes her successful struggles both on her own behalf and on behalf of girls in every nation to be useful, productive, and independent. She is the person responsible, as she implies, for developing the principles of the Girl Guides in their early years. Baden-Powell devotes much of her book to the mentorship of her husband, under which she blossomed, and to his active life of service on which her own was modeled. In 1964, she produced a biography of her husband, *Baden-Powell: The Two Lives of a Hero* in collaboration with William Hillcourt. Two useful biographies of Lady Baden-Powell herself are Eileen Wade's *The World Chief Guide* (1957) and *Baden Powell: A Family Album* (1986) by Heather Baden-Powell, the author's daughter.

59 BAGNOLD, Enid (Lady Roderick Jones). 1889–1981. *Enid Bagnold's Autobiography*. William Heinemann, 1969. 127 pp.; BLC to 1975 16:255.

Born at Rochester, Kent. Father: Arthur Henry Bagnold, major in the Royal Engineers. Mother: Ethel Alger. 1 brother. Married 1920, Sir Roderick Jones, chairman of Reuters. 1 daughter; 3 sons. Wrote seven novels, including *National Velvet* (1935), eight plays, one book of poetry. Novelist; playwright; poet; nurse (WWI). Upper middle class; married into upper class.

Formative years and career development of a noted creative writer, emphasizing the literary and theatrical circles in which she worked, 1889–1960s. Being spoiled as a child by mother, but military father's demanding obedience. Receiving a conservative upbringing until father received appointment in Jamaica, 1898. After moving there, author's imagination's being shocked into life by Jamaica's exotic beauty: "It was like a man idly staring at a field suddenly finding he had Picasso's eyes." In Jamaica, age 9, beginning to write short stories and poems. After returning to England, attending Prior's Field School run by Aldous Huxley's mother; her encouraging author's writing. Winning a poetry contest while there. Attending school in Paris for a year. Enduring "coming out" rituals, age 18; despising attending social functions. Publishing her first poem in *The New Age*. Living alone in London; studying art; living a bohemian existence as suffragette, artist, and life model. Making friends with theatrical designer Lovat Fraser and poet Katherine Mansfield. Barely supporting herself in journalism; realizing she must live with her parents to work on her fiction. Publishing her first short story just before WWI. During war, studying for VAD nursing certificate; working in the Royal Herbert Memorial Hospital for convalescing soldiers; keeping a journal of her nursing experiences published as *Diary without Dates;* being abruptly dismissed as a result of its publication. Becoming close to H. G. Wells; noting his opinions on beauty versus sense in women. Meeting and marrying Sir Roderick Jones, head of Reuters news agency, 1920; asserting marriage opened avenues of experience to her. Publishing *National Velvet,* 1935. Publishing an article on Hitler's Germany after visit there with her husband; Hitler's inviting them to Nazi rally on the strength of the article; author's husband's sensibly refusing. Author's extended literary circle, including George Bernard Shaw and Rudyard Kipling. Being invited to New York to have a play produced; making friends with actor Charles Laughton, who played the lead; establishing ties with Hollywood. Death of author's husband, 1962; meditating on old age and death, the arbitrariness of religious belief, and gender as determinant of one's feeling of belonging.

Bagnold's introspective account tends to shortchange her accomplishments. Although the author of fiction, poetry, and many well-received theatrical comedies, she is best known for the 1944 motion picture made from her children's book *National Velvet,* starring the young Elizabeth Taylor. This was also Bagnold's favorite novel; she remarks that it was her closest fictional approach to autiobiography. Early in her life she wrote another memoir, **60** *Diary without Dates* (1918), which got her dismissed from wartime nursing for reviewing its conditions with too much candor and too little patriotism. This book was published with a foreword by novelist Monica Dickens, whose own experience with being ejected from wartime nursing for writing an exposé of it parallels that of Bagnold. Dickens's memoir, *One Pair of Feet,* covers her experiences in WWII and, when read in tandem with Bagnold's WWI account, reveals how little the traditional nursing establishment had changed between the wars in its treatment of young women who volunteered their labor.

61 BAILEY, Alice Ann (née La Trobe-Bateman). 1880–1949. *The Unfinished Autobiography of Alice A. Bailey*. Lucis Press Ltd., 1951. 305 pp.; foreword by Foster Bailey (author's husband); intro.; apps. NUC pre56 30:476.

Born in Manchester. Father: Frederick Foster La Trobe-Bateman, engineer. Mother: Alice Hollinshead. 1 sister. Married 1907, Walter Evans, soldier, clergyman; divorced 1919. Married Foster Bailey. 3 daughters. Wrote *A Treatise on Cosmic Fire, The Soul and Its Mechanism,* many others. Knew Elise Sandes, Augusta Craig. Theosophist; religious/spiritual writer; vegetarian; foreign resident (U.S.). Upper class.

Author's progress from emotional rejection and Christian dogma to adult fulfillment within Eastern religion, 1880–1923. In author's infancy, family's moving to Montreal, Canada; author's sister's being born there. Author's attempting suicide, age 5, by hurling herself downstairs; later regarding this attempt to experience death as start of her spiritual quest.

Family's accompanying father to engineering job in Switzerland; returning to England for consumptive mother's death, author's age 6. Feeling she had no real home; father's resenting daughters, especially author, in belief they caused their mother's death. Father's taking job in Australia, leaving girls with their grandparents; his dying on voyage out, author's age 9. With sister, being raised by grandparents on Surrey estate; discipline's being left to governesses; its cruelty provoking two more suicide attempts in author, ages 11 and 15. Rich great aunt's becoming author's guardian after grandparents' deaths, author's age 13. Being sent to French Riviera to prevent consumption, age 15; receiving excellent classical education there from French governesses. At this time, having vision which changed her life: image of a turbaned man who urged her to serve "your Master." Later believing this to be spirit of an ascended Hindu adept; recounting later visions of Hindu significance, although declaring them compatible with Christian belief. Attending a London finishing school, age 18; being a zealous YMCA worker and Sunday school teacher. Being socially ignorant, age 20; later attributing it to Victorian practice of preserving naiveté of upper-class girls. Committing herself to evangelical work among British troops and in Elise Sandes Soldiers' Home; surmounting her fear of public speaking. Being sent to India to continue this work; returning home with broken health, 1906; starting to accept karma and reincarnation. Being plagued by doubt about Christian notions of hell and self-righteousness, 1906–15. Having resolved to stay single; nevertheless marrying lower-class soldier, 1907; hoping his evangelical Christian beliefs would revive her own. Their moving to Cincinnati, Ohio; attending Lane Theological Seminary there. Hating racial discrimination she witnessed in U.S.; also discussing how to eliminate anti-Semitism. Accompanying husband to new parish in California; depicting life as clergyman's wife: raising chickens, cooking, and cleaning on her own for the first time. Having three daughters; fearing her husband's physical abuse; youngest child's being born sickly after husband abused author during pregnancy. Separating from husband, 1915; supporting daughters by working in a sardine cannery. Her divorce's becoming final, 1919, at same time as author's meeting second husband, a Theosophist. Having her second important vision, 1920, of "The Tibetan," a spiritual master. From 1920s–40s, promoting Theosophy with husband via lectures and public classes in U.S. and Europe. Discussing her belief in karma and reincarnation, vegetarianism, and numerology. Becoming disillusioned with Theosophical Society. With husband, founding the Arcane School in New York, 1923.

This book served Bailey as a didactic tool as well as a personal record; she declares that she published it to show her audience how a "rabid, orthodox Christian worker could become a well-known occult teacher," as well as how her class consciousness and narrow-minded Christianity opened up to the world of higher spiritual values. Bailey's spiritual journey parallels that of Annie Besant, whom she apparently never knew. Both progressed from insecure childhoods, evangelical Christianity, and unhappy marriages to clergymen that ended in divorce, to a sense of spiritual liberation within Eastern religious teaching. Besant's *Autobiography* (1893) combines with Bailey's later account to provide eye-witness testimony to Eastern religion's spread during half a century.

62 BAILEY, Doris M. (née Clark). 1916–?. *Children of the Green: a True Story of Childhood in Bethnal Green, 1922–1937*. Stepney Books, 1981. 126 pp.; illus. BLC 1976–1982 2:493.

Raised in Bethnal Green, London. Father: Joe Clark, furniture polisher. Mother: Janey, factory worker, homemaker. 3 sisters. Married Eric Bailey. Sons mentioned. Clerk; teacher (Sunday school). Working class.

Growing up in working-class London culture, covering author's life to age 21. Going to school in Bethnal Green; school nurse's routinely searching students for head lice. Describing life in Cockney neighborhood. Father's growing vegetables and raising pigeons to eke out income. Daughters' fearing father's temper and heavy drinking; not daring to stand up to him; suspecting his anger at having no sons. Describing neighborhood stores and vendors, author's fondness for school, taking swimming lessons. Being ignorant when man exposed himself indecently to her; noting that modern children have better sex education than she did; being misinformed about sex by a neighborhood girl. Family's resorting to temporary shelter when without rent money; father's refusing to let them borrow or shop on credit. Babysitting to help family with money. Mother's being shattered by death of author's baby sister. Being sent to Sunday school so parents could have sex in privacy; author's later attending Victoria Park Baptist Chapel on her own initiative. Family's enlarging income by taking in boarders. Recalling local anger during general strike of 1926. Winning scholarship to attend school in Clapton; aspiring to become a teacher. Finding work, age 15, in printing and bookbinding shop; employer's trying to kiss and fondle her. Switching jobs; doing office work in a clothing factory. Attending Clapton School until age 16. Becoming a Sunday school teacher, age 17, just before moving with her family from Bethnal Green to Leytonstone, 1938.

This account of life in working-class London before WWII dramatizes the accommodations of a family determined to preserve its respectability in the face of financial privation. Bailey mentions her marriage only in passing, since it occurred after the time period on which the book focuses. Her autobiography offers enlightening contrasts to that of Elizabeth Ring, whose *Up the Cockneys!* (1975) records her experiences in another working-class London neighborhood during roughly the same years, although in a family scornful of the morality and work ethic which

Bailey's parents upheld. Together, these two remembrances suggest the range of working-class London's lifestyles.

63 BAILLIE, Dame Isobel Douglas. 1895–1983. *Never Sing Louder than Lovely*. Hutchinson, 1982. 208 pp.; prologue; illus.; apps.; discography; title index; composer index; postscript; index. BLC 1982–1985 2:434.

Born in Hawick, Roxburgh, Scotland. Father not named, baker. Mother: "Biddy" Douglas. 1 brother; 2 sisters. Married 1917, Henry Leonard Wrigley, singer, later cotton trader, died c.1958. Widow. 1 daughter. Singer (opera, concerts); traveler (world). Working class; married into middle class.

Modest origins, determined rise, and illustrious career of an international concert soprano, including sketches of colleagues and their work, 1895–1982. Family's Scottish origins: one grandfather's having been carpenter on Duke of Buccleugh's estate, other grandfather's hailing from the ancient Douglas clan. Father's being baker on the estate of the earl of Dalkeith; resolving to better himself by starting his own bakery in Newcastle, author's age 5. Family's moving to Manchester, opening another bakery. Father's dying suddenly, shattering family's finances; author's 14-year-old brother's managing the bakery. Attending government board school for poor children, age 9; its headmaster's discovering her singing voice. Attending high school in Manchester; working in a music shop. Starting to sing professionally. Clerking in Manchester town hall to pay for voice lessons. Discussing local singing engagements in her teens; through these meeting her future husband, another singer; beginning their lengthy courtship. Fiancé's being wounded in WWI; his abandoning his own singing career to promote Isobel's. After marriage, public's often mistaking husband for author's chauffeur. Their daughter's inheriting their singing talents. Author's studying voice in Italy. Discussing merits and faults of her own voice. Anecdotes of conductors, singers, and musicians on the Italian scene. Returning to England to make her London debut, 1923; winning immediate success; discussing her grueling concert schedule all over England; meeting challenge of learning to dress as if born to privilege. Visiting Los Angeles to sing at the Hollywood Bowl; discussing her working relationships with esteemed conductors, including Sir Malcolm Sargent, Sir Thomas Beecham, Adrian Boult, and Arturo Toscanini. Touring New Zealand performing opera pieces, 1939. Being chosen to perform series of new works by composer Dame Ethel Smyth. Further discussion of acquaintance with noted composers: Sir Edward Elgar, Ralph Vaughan Williams, Sergei Rachmaninov, and Sir Walford Davies. Analyzing her own performances of Handel's Messiah; explaining how it should be sung. Discussing correct vocal techniques. Discussing her broadcasting and recordings, WWII concerts, and postwar performances in Paris. Touring New Zealand and Malaya in

1948. During German tour, her career's being disrupted by injury from a car accident, c.1950. Teaching at Royal College of Music, 1952. Traveling to Washington, D.C.; making tours of South Africa, Kenya, and Rhodesia, 1953. Living in America, 1960–61. Touring India and Far East, 1970. Explaining why she retired certain pieces from her repertoire. Explaining why she prefers to sing opera in English. Performing new works with composers. Recalling talented singers she encouraged.

Baillie's record of her rise in the world of elite musical performance is much like Benjamin Franklin's well-known autobiography; both affirm frugal living, hard work, and faith in one's own talents. Baillie takes particular pride in the contrast between her father's early feudal servitude and her own distinguished career; her extensive advice to other up-and-coming singers clearly indicates her book's design as a model of how to achieve success. Along with being a practical manual for beginners, however, Baillie's account is generous in its depictions of the luminaries, especially composers, who reincarnated classical music as a 20th-century phenomenon. Regarded as one of the world's great oratorio singers, she was made a dame of the British Empire in 1976.

64 BAKER, Daisy Ellen (née Crockett). 1894–s.l.1974. *Travels in a Donkey Trap*. New York: St. Martin's Press, 1974. 160 pp.; illus. by Pamela Mara. BLC to 1975 16:504.

Born in rural England, probably Sussex or Surrey. Father not named, jockey, van driver. Mother not named, housekeeper. 1 brother. Married 1921, Bill Baker, WWI navy veteran, club porter, died c.1938. Widow. 1 daughter. Domestic servant. Working class.

Author's celebration of the freedom of movement given to her in old age by her donkey and cart, coupled with life memories, 1900–1970s. Author's living frugally on old-age pension, age 76; having "sudden brain wave" to get a donkey and cart for transportation in the Devon countryside. Like her father, an old-time jockey, being fond of horses; remembering his horse-drawn van. Father's naming author "Daisy" after the first race-winning horse he rode. Author's being photographed by local paper with her donkey "Darkie" as quaint example of the old ways. Describing her first ride with Darkie; observing countryside from her cart. Associating these cart trips with childhood family outings; recalling her fiancé, Fred, killed in WWI. In 1921, marrying Fred's brother Bill; their living in Chelsea; author's working at a London club. Country-bred author's missing rural scenes; their consequently moving fifteen miles outside London, 1931. Bill's death, 1938. Author's meditating on her donkey cart as return to simpler way of life. Driving Darkie to see the Devon coast; recalling nearly drowning, age 10, while seabathing with little brother near their Sussex home. Driving Darkie on highway among cars; comparing Darkie's slower pace to elderly author's own relations to the modern world. Memories of working as a housemaid for two bishop's daughters after her father's death, 1909; her mother's having to put little brother in London orphanage, but taking housekeeping job to be near him. Brother's death of diphtheria, age 12. Bishop's daughters' remedying author's ignorance of the Anglican catechism, preparing her for confirmation. Reverting to present memories of Devon: caring for her rabbits, goats, and family of rescued cats. Leaving the bishop's daughters for a maid's position in large Surrey household, age 17; describing her many labors. Remembering childhood sense of security; recalling singing in the Young Helpers' Choir at the local workhouse. On a cart trip with Darkie, rescuing another kitten. Like other elderly people, being confused by Britain's new decimal money, introduced in 1972. Associating thoughts of money with her third domestic job, 1911, where employers half starved her. Taking a fourth job near her mother in London; meeting Fred, a porter in the neighborhood, there. Meditating on the donkeys that carried Christ; buying hay for Darkie and gathering hedge trimmings for her goats. Thanking providence for the return of her lost dog. Returning to thoughts of childhood: discipline at home and school, her protectiveness of her little brother. Attending assorted Sunday schools in rural Surrey. Watching Darkie and her goats nibbling hedges during autumn; anticipating Christmas; remembering childhood Christmas celebrations. Providing food for rabbits and wild birds in December; gathering holly and ivy for Christmas. On Christmas eve, neighbor boy's visiting to see her donkey; Darkie's kneeling, as the ass kneeled at the manger of the Christ child. Meditating on her first year with Darkie and her consequent liberation from the loneliness of old age.

Citing Robert Louis Stevenson's *Travels with a Donkey* as her inspiration, Baker tells her life story in a series of associative meditations while driving in her donkey cart. In addition to drawing her journeys by cart into parallel with her life journey, she records unusually acute observations of the behavior patterns and personalities of wild and domestic animals. They predominate over humans in her book as they do in her remote Devon landscape, and Baker draws their lives also into implicit parallels with her own. This combination of naturalistic observation and autobiography evokes memories of Gavin Maxwell's meditations on his otters in *Ring of Bright Water* (1960), although Baker's book may actually be more effective at placing its author's own life within the context of nature, seasons, and the passage of time.

65 BALDERSON, Eileen, and Douglas Goodlad. 1916–s.l.1982. *Backstairs Life in a Country House*. David & Charles, 1982. 128 pp.; intro.; apps.; index. NUC 1987-74273b-697-365.

Born in Hull, Yorkshire. Parents not named. 8 siblings. Married Jack Balderson, domestic servant. Domestic servant; WWII enlistee. Working class.

Detailed account of domestic service in affluent English country homes, covering 1930–82. Being youngest of nine children; leaving school to start earning wages, age 14. After death of her mother, being close to her sister Hilda, an experienced domestic servant; author's first housemaid job's being at Rise Park, where Hilda worked. In 1931, Hull citizenry's being excited that local girl Amy Johnson was flying solo to Peking; Johnson's success's inspiring author's own ambitions to do well. Refuting notion that domestic servants are usually exploited; citing her fair wages and working conditions. Preferring small households where servants felt like family to large ones with regimented staffs. Describing upper-class pastimes she witnessed: fox hunts, cricket matches. Being proud; never asking for special privileges from employers. Meeting Jack, her eventual husband, while working at Rise Park. Having successive housemaid positions on estates in several counties, including a residence in Shropshire owned by British royals. Working at Grove Lodge in Windsor for Sir Colin Keppel, 1936; learned to ride a bicycle; disliking serving in Keppel's London house; preferring the country. Having romantic dreams stimulated by the cinema; courting with George, the Keppels' butler. Hilda's marrying another butler. Working in a Grosvenor Square house in London; being lonely; renewing acquaintance with old friend from Hull who came to work there. Remarking on privileges of her employers' pets, including their choice diet. Joining the WAAFs in WWII; serving as a batwoman because she was too short to qualify for transport duties. After the war, taking job at Middlethorpe Hall, near York; leaving because house was considered haunted. Taking new post in Leicestershire. Discussing house parties, guests, menus, and Hilda's recipes and cookery books.

Goodlad's contribution to the text is a brief final chapter sketching the author and her husband, about whom Balderson says little except that she met him while in service. Apparently conscious of some memoirs by servants which effectively offer their employers' private lives for public consumption, Balderson states that her purpose is not to gossip but to describe a servant's life and duties in upper-class homes. Her book, which describes more than a dozen of these households, is a valuable study of the structure of relationship and obligation between employer and servant in the present century.

66 BALDWIN, Monica. c.1897–c.1975. *I Leap Over the Wall: Contrasts and Impressions after Twenty-Eight Years in a Convent*. New York: Rinehart, 1950. 313 pp.; intro. NUC pre56 32:136. (1st pub.: Catholic Book Club, 1948.)

Born in England. Parents not named. Uncle: Stanley, Lord Baldwin, three times prime minister. 1 sister. Single. Religionist (Roman Catholic); nun; ex-nun; munitions worker; librarian; novelist. Upper middle class.

Introspective study of a nun's decision to leave the convent, contrasting her conventual and secular experiences, 1914–50. In 1941, leaving cloister she had first entered in 1914; having to adjust to wearing sheer women's garments instead of bulky habits. Being shocked at social changes; discussing convent rules and nuns' hostility toward permissive outside world. Exemplifying nuns' sheltered existence by how little they had heard of WWI; reflecting on WWII. Being horrified at sex and gritty realism in 1940s books; nostalgically remembering books she had read in the convent. Visiting various relatives; eventually realizing she must look for work. Considering munitions work, since she had only an "average" education by governess followed by finishing school. Knowing typing but no shorthand; having taught in the convent school but not really liking teaching. Reflecting on her other work experience: illuminating manuscripts, some casual nursing; ruefully acknowledging her only expertise lies in interpreting the works of St. Augustine. Through influence of cousin, getting position in the Women's Land Army; describing her experiences there. Learning to drink and smoke. Failing at a job as aircraft design trainee. Working as factory supervisor; this job's falling through also. Becoming assistant matron at munitions workers' hostel; later doing war work. Finally winning assistant librarian position at the Royal College of Medicine. Wanting to move to Cornwall; eventually realizing this ambition. Remembering her childhood sense of religious longing; having decided, when only 17, to become a nun. After eighteen years in the convent, realizing she must leave to keep her sanity. Commenting on nuns' youthful naiveté, preserved by their sheltered existence; saying of herself, "My outlook was still that of a 12-year-old schoolgirl."

Baldwin's story is like that of a traveler sleeping in a time capsule, disoriented by the galvanic cultural changes she finds when she awakes. Although her former life was in a religious order, her memories of it are not exclusively religious; instead, she depicts the convent as a repository of Edwardian values whose existence is an anachronism, and whose morality forms her standpoint for evaluating 1940s society. Like Rip Van Winkle's, the author's task was to become a naturalized citizen of the modern era and, as with many immigrants from foreign countries, she is often more observant of cultural details than natives of that culture would be. She went on to develop her writing talent, producing a successful novel, *The Called and the Chosen* (1957), on the life of a cloistered nun in medieval Europe, and *Goose in the Jungle,* a journal of travel and cultural observations about her two-year journey around the world, 1972–73.

67 BALFOUR, Lady Frances (née Campbell). 1858–1930. *Ne Obliviscaris. Dinna Forget.* Hodder & Stoughton, 1930. 2 vols. NUC pre56 32:255.

Born in London. Father: George Douglas Campbell, 8th Duke of Argyll, Lord Privy Seal, postmaster general, secretary of state for India, Whig peer. Mother: Lady Elizabeth Sutherland-Leveson-Gower, daughter of 2nd Duke of Sutherland. Stepmother: Amelia Claughton. 5 brothers; 6 sisters. Married 1879, Eustace Balfour, architect, d.1911. 2 sons; 3 daughters. Knew Dr. R. H. Story, Mary Gladstone, Lady Maud Cecil, Laura Tennant Lyttleton, Lady Pembroke, Arthur and Gerald Asquith, Lord and Lady Finlay, Betty Balfour. Wrote *Life of Lord Aberdeen, Life of Lord Balfour of Buleigh.* Suffragist; social reformer; biographer; feminist activist. Aristocracy.

Liberal but austere upbringing, socially conscious marriage, and active political commitments of an aristocratic suffragist and social reformer, 1860s–1920s. Being lame from untreated disease in hip joint, age 2. Gaining religious sensibility from attending Church of Scotland. Discussing her courtship and marriage, age 21; being temporarily swayed from liberalism by marrying into the Tory Balfour family. Growth of her social consciousness after her introduction to feminist causes, 1880s. Learning about mother's and grandmother's involvement with abolition of slavery; later using antislavery arguments to support women's equality. Through husband, her becoming involved with Pre-Raphaelite artists. Being persuaded to oppose Irish home rule; detesting the pro–home rule zeal of Charles Stuart Parnell; working on committee of Women's Liberal Unionist Association, an anti–home rule group. Briefly joining the Primrose League, founded in 1883 in memory of Tory Prime Minister Disraeli to disseminate Conservative views. Assisting Working Ladies Guild, which helped "decayed gentlewomen." Participating in march of the unemployed, 1885. Opposing disestablishment of the Church of Scotland, 1880s–1890s. Working on a committee for women's suffrage, 1887–1914; disapproving of militant suffragism. Joining Freedom Defence League. Traveling to Paris, 1888, 1891. Serving on Commission on Matrimonial and Divorce Laws, 1910–12, working toward marital law reform. Deaths of her mother, father, and husband in rapid succession. Publishing two biographies, of Lord Aberdeen and Lord Balfour. Discussing adverse effect on many Liberal members of Parliament of Irish Home Rule Act of 1920. Discussing her participation in the Victoria League. Describing women's role in politics, c.1923, as "ornaments." Concluding that racial and gender subjugation are against the laws of God.

As the daughter of a Scottish Whig peer who held high office in several administrations, the author grew up in political circles, and political issues continued to interest her greatly throughout her life. She knew several prime ministers well, including Lord Salisbury, her uncle by marriage. An early suffragist, for more than twenty years Balfour worked with Millicent Fawcett's National Union of Women's Suffrage Societies as an active supporter of women's rights. Her book offers a cogent perspective on the many important political battles of 1870–1910.

68 BANCROFT, Marie Effie, and Sir Squire George. 1840–1921 (Marie). *On and Off the Stage*. Richard Bentley & Son, 1888. 2 vols. Vol. 1: 443 pp.; illus; index. Vol. 2: 457 pp.; illus.; index. NUC pre56 33:468.

Born in Doncaster, Yorkshire. Father: Robert Pleydell Wilton, actor. Mother: Georgiana Jane Faulkner. 5 sisters. Married Squire George Bancroft. Actress (child, stage); theatre manager; singer (popular). Middle class.

Marie's portion of this jointly written autobiography, charting her acting career from childhood and highlighting the Bancrofts' collaboration as theatrical managers, 1840s–1880s. Vol. 1: Status of acting profession in her father's youth. Growing up in Manchester in theatrical family; at age 3, being recognized as a gifted child actress. Having no games or toys in childhood; recalling only work. Building a reputation in the provinces playing children's parts; winning immediate success in debut at London's Lyceum Theatre. Playing small roles, including boys' parts, at the Haymarket, Adelphi, and Strand theatres; acting in burlesque choruses; soon landing ingenue roles. Anecdotes of theatrical mishaps; explaining how she used personal emotions to shape roles. Squire's narrative of his early life; his first meeting Marie when both were performing at Strand Theatre. Describing Marie's first venture into managing at the Prince of Wales's Theatre, London; opening their first play there, 1865. Squire and Marie's sharing performing and managing responsibilities; for fifteen years, their having the most profitable theatre in London. Catalogue of their performances and plays; thriving by risking capital on new playwrights. Vol. 2: Extracts of correspondence from noted actors and actresses. Marie's acting in *The Merchant of Venice,* one of only four Bancroft productions that lost money. Ellen Terry's refusing the role of Peg Woffington in playwright Charles Reade's *Masks and Faces;* Marie's stepping in; making the role famous. Noting acting skills of London's beggars; their faking afflictions to solicit charity. Becoming friends with French playwright Victorien Sardou; being first in England to produce his plays. Buying and managing the coveted Haymarket Theatre, 1880. Retiring from management after twenty successful years, 1885; the Bancrofts' farewell season.

Prominent impresarios of the late-19th-century English stage, the Bancrofts distinguished themselves with their business acumen and understanding of the public taste. In reading this dual autobiography, the reader is struck by the overall sense it conveys of 19th-century theatre as a business venture and of their careers as dealing solidly with pounds, shillings, and pence. In a later work, **69** *The Bancrofts,*

Recollections of Sixty Years (1909), Marie's contribution remains substantially smaller than Squire's, but both volumes are valuable historical repositories that record the data of the Bancrofts' professional lives with fidelity to date, place, circumstance, and financial arrangements.

70 BANKES, Viola Florence Geraldine. c.1900–s.l.1965. *Why Not?* Jarrolds, 1934. 288 pp.; front.; illus. NUC pre56 34:12.

Born in Kingston Lacy, Dorset. Father: Walter Ralph Bankes, art collector. Mother: Henrietta Jenny Fraser. 1 brother; 1 sister. Married Norman Hall. Wrote *Shadow-Show*. Novelist. Upper class.

Author's affluent but loveless childhood, rebellious adolescence, and adult search for happiness through unconventional lifestyle, 1900–34. From infancy, author's being rejected by mother for being dark-skinned, by father for being a girl. Father's having three illegitimate sons by a mistress; his frustration that they could not be his heirs. Recalling parental rejoicing at birth of her younger brother. At author's age 4, mother's hiding father's death from children; their being shocked when nanny revealed it. Showing no resentment toward father's mistress, but perceiving the bequests in his will as "tactless": only £30,000 to his wife, £40,000 to his mistress. Resenting mother's detachment from author and siblings; this allowing nanny to maltreat them all, including the much-valued brother. Anecdotes of visitors whom family knew through father's art collecting, including Daisy, Princess of Pless, Kaiser Wilhelm, King Edward VII, and his mistress, Lily Langtry. Visiting their Dorset neighbor, Thomas Hardy; hearing him read *Jude the Obscure* in progress. Having a governess, but primarily schooling herself through reading decadent French novels and Oscar Wilde; remarking that these were her only education in sex. At age 19, publishing a novel, *Shadow-Show;* despite favorable reviews, mother's labeling it "the autobiography of an undesirable young woman." Making her debut: adoring dancing; flirting with occult practices learned from new society friends. Escaping her mother through study at the Sorbonne, age 19; traveling frenetically on the Continent; having a nervous collapse. Mother's berating her extended travels, demanding author marry, and adopt a conventional lifestyle. Defying her mother: avoiding marriage, befriending homosexuals, taking a bohemian London flat. Experimenting with marriage to an old family friend who was pagan like herself; citing their mutual admiration of Aleister Crowley. Author and husband's joining nudist camp outside London; living communally and eating health food. In France, being arrested for indecent exposure following nudist practices. Shocking the dean of St. Paul's by discussing nudism at a dinner party. Believing that the highest and lowest classes have the loosest morals, that father-daughter incest is natural, and that "coloured people" are sexually closer to nature than whites. Cultivating social acquaintance among London's black population. Connecting her own life to her reading of Oscar Wilde's *de Profundis,* which looks back without regret on a life of sin; like Wilde, valuing personal freedom more than the world's good reputation.

Produced in her thirties, early in her literary career, Bankes's memoir is dominated by her reading of other authors, especially Oscar Wilde, whom she invokes like guiding saints. In light of Wilde's legendary pronouncement that "life imitates art" and Bankes's pairing of her memoir with the one Wilde wrote in prison, it is noteworthy that Bankes evidently shaped her young life to reflect features in this decadent reading: the defiantly unconventional living arrangements, habits, and sexual experimentation. While Bankes says only that she "associated" with homosexuals, she adds cryptic commentary about her reading of books of sexual inversion, such as Radclyffe Hall's *Well of Loneliness,* that suggests her more direct involvement. As an unusual picture of London's counterculture during the 1920s–1930s, Bankes's memoir has much to offer. Although she wrote no more novels, in 1953 she produced a family memoir, *A Dorset Heritage: The Story of Kingston Lacy,* and later collaborated with Francis Bamford on *Vicious Circle: The Case of the Missing Irish Crown Jewels* (1965). Her reminiscences of her childhood were posthumously collected by Pamela Watkin in *A Kingston Lacy Childhood* (1986).

71 BANKS, Emily (née Tiptaft). c.1867–d.a.1928. *White Woman on the Congo.* Fleming H. Revell, 1943. 192 pp.; front. port.; foreword by Emory Ross; preface by Charles Sidney J. Banks (author's son). NUC pre56 34:32.

Parents not named. 2 sisters. Married 1887, Charles Blair Banks, missionary, d.1900. Widow. 3 sons; 2 daughters. Missionary/missionary's spouse (Africa); emigrant (U.S.). Middle class.

Account of missionary life in the Belgian Congo, together with the author's changing evaluations of native culture and conditions, c.1887–1928. Author's accompanying her new husband to Africa "to win the souls of the ignorant Blacks." His warning her of earlier experiences in the "treacherous" Congo; author's believing her faith would protect her. Their traveling upriver by steamer and hammock. Wanting to mother the natives; expressing horror at their lack of sanitation. Repeatedly noting natives' awe of her whiteness. Author's treating natives' wounds, helping husband fight the slave trade. Deciding to save a slave girl by buying her; discovering the girl feared her new owners planned to eat her. Starting a school for native children; learning the language and culture. Noting proudly that natives called her "White Mama." Becoming pregnant; missing support of other white women. After child's birth, 1888, author's becoming ill; commenting that the constant sight of sin, heathen rites, and cannibalism had done their worst. Returning to England; leaving her infant daughter with sister; returning to the Congo, 1890. Husband's defending author against a native who declared his intent to steal her. Natives' flattering the author and husband: asking them to stay forever and teach the wisdom of the "Book." Natives' declaring they believe the Gospel because it comes from the truth-speaking white man, but showing no sign of Christianizing their lives. Discussing Belgian atrocities in the Congo, 1890s, and husband's unsuccessful appeal to King Leopold to stop them. Author and husband's ending native practice of killing slaves to mourn a chief's death; husband's breaking up a witch doctor's ceremony, throwing away his charms. Their trying without success to protect natives from cruel whites. After birth of son, author's sister's visiting to take child back to England. Births of more children. Family's returning to England, 1898; author's discovering her son had been punished more harshly at the home for missionary children than "savages" would have done. Resolving to tell story in England of native tribes' cruel subjugation of wives. Death of her husband, 1900, at age 43; eulogizing him for bringing Christianity and civilization to Africa. Transplanting family to U.S., 1909; settling in Oregon. Recounting her grown son's missionary work among American Indian tribes, c.1920s. Revisiting Africa for the Leopoldville missionary conference, 1928. Closing with poem by her son celebrating his father's work.

Banks's memoir looks back to the colonialist ideals she and her husband first embraced in their zeal to bring religion to the benighted African "savages." Without saying so, however, Banks's narrative suggests that direct exposure to African culture and individuals brought about a significant shift in their thinking. Upon arriving in the Congo, the author clearly believed that she was dealing with people whose authority and intelligence were less than her own; later she shows amusement that they had flattered her into thinking so. Distressed at first by African standards of hygiene, she ultimately turned her anger toward the cultural treatment of African women, as well as the iniquities in whites' behavior toward the Africans they supposedly came to "enlighten." Although Banks remains firm in her commitment to the missionary cause, her goals in her narrative undergo change, from saving souls to saving individuals from the cultural injustices she had witnessed firsthand.

72 BARBER, Mary Ann Serrett. c.1801–1864. *Bread-Winning; Or, the Ledger and the Lute. An Autobiography*. William Macintosh, 1865. 125 pp.; preface by the Rev. John Garwood. BLC to 1975 18:338.

Born in England. Father not named, scholar, author. Mother not named. 1 sister. Single. Wrote *Childhood Duties; or, Precepts for Little Emma* (1842), *Nursery Tales for Little Listeners* (1855), others. Children's author; editor; essayist; philanthropist; teacher; governess. Middle class.

Author's journey from an unappreciated childhood to an adult career nurturing children's imaginations through her writings and philanthropy, c.1805–60. Mother's having mental disorder; her giving author to author's uncle for adoption, then reclaiming her, declaring separation hurt too much. Author's regretting having to go back. Uncle's informing her that she would eventually have to support herself; author's thinking of becoming a teacher. After mother's death, father's belittling her as too uneducated to be a teacher; author's getting her sole moral support from sympathetic sister. Being educated at home and at a country school. Taking a governess post, but suffering from loneliness. Hardship of her work's being aggravated by ongoing illnesses; refusing to console herself with Christian notions of bearing her burden meekly; borrowing money; going abroad for her health with sister. Feeding her intellectual curiosity through study. Discussing her sense of unfolding spiritual purpose in her life. After returning to England, author's moving to London; venturing into magazine writing. Envisioning writing as her future livelihood. Beginning to write children's books. Editing *Children's Nursery Magazine*. Contributing articles to *Church of England Magazine, Christian Ladies' Magazine,* others, 1847–64. Reaching out to children in Africa, India, and North America through her missionary writings; publishing stories in *The Coral Missionary Magazine*. Promoting interest of British children in missionary work through church missionary schools; also providing support for children in a London reformatory. Looking back on her life as being rich both in trials and ultimate fulfillments.

Barber's story is a secular conversion narrative that follows its protagonist from an existence of self-doubt to one of confidence and purpose; what she herself never received she ends up freely giving to others. During the account of her travels with her sister, she records a moment of insight concerning the worth of her own abilities that functions as her point of conversion to faith in herself and belief in her power to create a meaningful existence.

73 BARLOW, Amy. 1893–c.1960. *Seventh Child: The Autobiography of a Schoolmistress*. Gerald Duckworth & Co. Ltd., 1969. 144 pp.; illus. NUC 1968–1972 7:484.

Born in Friern Barnett Parish in Middlesex-Hertfordshire border. Father: surname Barlow, bank manager. Mother: née Davies. 5 sisters; 3 brothers. Single. Wrote *The Barlows in Essex, 1730–1924*. Teacher; genealogist; family historian. Middle class.

Progress of a girl in a large family whose circumstances paved her way into a teaching career, 1893–c.1945. Despite father's banking income, his choosing to give the children necessities but not luxuries. Loving her eldest sister, Katie, who mothered her, but competing for attention with her younger twin sisters. Father's being the primary parent; his taking author, age 4, to London for Queen Victoria's Diamond Jubilee. Mother's being Welsh both in ancestry and temperament: artistic and prone to nerves; seeming to "pass into a world of her own" while playing her piano. Author's attending private day schools and high schools until family's move to Brentwood; then attending local school at Highbury. After leaving school, realizing that with three younger sisters living at home, she must become independent. Narrowly losing competition for an Oxford scholarship. Recalling her admiration for schoolteacher Jo in the novel *Little Women;* accepting father's suggestion to study teaching at University College of Wales. Taking her degree; becoming temporary English mistress at a private school in Surrey. Teaching next at a girls' school in Lancashire; describing her misery from spartan accommodations and rigorous teaching duties; being compensated by friendships among colleagues and her new zest for field hockey. Receiving news of her father's death, 1914. Winning teaching post at Sedbergh Boys' Prep School; gaining new sense of freedom there. Discussing romances and marriages among siblings since her absence from home; reflecting on her own youthful romances; noting that she never married from fear of losing her freedom. Memories of students and close friends among male colleagues at her boys' school. Leaving to become form mistress in a county school in Bedgebury, Kent. Being furious at interruption of her career by hyperthyroidism; undergoing partial thyroidectomy in a nursing home. Returning to her school; teaching for sixteen more years. Using school holidays to explore Europe, Canada, and the U.S. During WWII, helping evacuate school to Wales. Resigning her post because of eye problems; taking a flat in Bournemouth and teaching part-time at Southbourne High School. Researching her own family history; writing *The Barlows in Essex, 1730–1924*. Eventually being compelled by arthritis to move into an orthopaedic nursing home; feeling old and ill before her time.

One interesting feature of this autobiography is its discussion of the vicissitudes faced by faculty, particularly female faculty, in English secondary schools during the early 20th century; Barlow's study of her position within a family of many girls also makes the precarious position of unmarried women at that time understandable. Had she been born thirty years earlier, or to a less open-minded father, she might have found herself one of England's redundant spinsters, having to tend the children of male relatives and depend upon their munificence. Instead, her father maintained at home those girls who needed his protection, while providing his most capable daughter with the opportunity to make her own way. Barlow's later meditations provoke consideration of the conflicting claims of marriage versus career.

74 BARNES, Annie. 1887–d.a.1958. *Tough Annie: From Suffragette to Stepney Councillor: Annie Barnes in Conversation with Kate Harding and Caroline Gibbs*. Stepney Books, 1980. 69 pp.; front. port.; intro. by Harding and Gibbs; illus. BLC 1976–1982 2:128.

Born in Stepney, Greater London. Father not named, shopkeeper. Mother not named. Stepmother not named. 11 siblings. Married 1919,

Albert Barnes, furniture designer, d.1958. Widow. Knew Sylvia Pankhurst. Suffragist, militant; political activist; social reformer; pupil-teacher. Working class.

Author's rise from limited circumstances to a local political career committed to women's suffrage and general social betterment, 1887–1958. Family's being poor in author's childhood; mother's finding way to help less-well-off neighbors. Attending Ben Jonson Board School for poor children; training as a pupil-teacher. Leaving school, age 16, to care for ailing mother and to raise younger siblings. After mother's death, 1910, author's discovering suffragette meetings in the East End; joining the East London Federation of Suffragettes; admiring its founder, Sylvia Pankhurst, for endorsing suffrage for working-class women as well as upper-class ones. Author's participating in less militant protests, due to demanding home responsibilities. Discussing suffragettes' imprisonment and forcible feeding during hunger strikes. Walking the streets selling copies of Sylvia Pankhurst's *Workers' Dreadnought,* 1914. With other suffragettes, joining the socialist Independent Labour Party at Sylvia's behest; later leaving the party when Sylvia turned Communist. At time of WWI, author's resolving never to marry; believing her father's disregard for his children was typical of men. Meeting her husband-to-be, 1918, finds him an exception. Father's remarrying immediately after author's marriage, 1919; his new wife's mistreating author's siblings. Author's husband's agreeing to remain childless so they could parent author's siblings; buying roomy house to hold them all. Getting to know Labour political activist George Lansbury; his inspiring her return to the Independent Labour Party, 1919. Giving political speeches; canvassing for candidates. Recounting Sylvia Pankhurst's continuing fight for universal suffrage, and her own shock at Pankhurst's choosing to have an illegitimate son. Organizing the first Women's Co-operative Guild in Stepney, 1929. Winning election as Stepney councillor; holding that position 1934–49. In her elected post, serving on the housing committee and working for slum clearance. Serving on Stepney's public health committee; encountering opposition from Catholics because she favored birth control. Joining the committee of the Charity Organisation Society, 1938; finding upper-class women on the committee unsympathetic to the needs of the poor; changing the name to the Family Welfare Organisation. Working for the Women's Voluntary Service during WWII. After being bombed out of their home, 1944, family's living temporarily at a settlement house, Toynbee Hall, where author met journalists, educators, and politicians. Husband's death, 1958. Elderly author's no longer being able to attend meetings, but still writing letters of advice and recommendation to Labour M.P.s.

A compilation of taped conversations, Barnes's account was edited for colloquialisms and repetitions. It is informative concerning East End

Labour Party activities and working-class participation in the suffrage movement. Noteworthy is Barnes's discussion of the factionalism between women of different social classes in the suffragette ranks, conflicts that foreshadow class-based divisions among present-day feminists.

75 BARNETT, Isobel Morag, Lady (née Marshall). 1918–s.l.1973. *My Life Line*. Hutchinson, 1956. 194 pp.; intro.; illus.; index. BLC 19:281.

Born in Aberdeen, Scotland. Father: Robert McNab Marshall, physician, M.B., Ch.B. Mother not named. 1 brother. Married 1941, Capt. Sir Geoffrey Barnett, d.1970. 1 son. Physician; broadcaster; politician (mayor); politician's spouse; public speaker; physician's daughter. Upper middle class; married into upper class.

Physician/broadcaster's attempts to balance career, home, and community involvement, spanning her 1920s childhood to 1956. Her physician father's being shy and scholarly, author's chief influence in deciding to be a doctor. Parents sending her to school, age 3; their believing she needed companions her own age. At 11, attending a girls' private day school; boarding at The Mount School, York, from age 13. Resolving to attend medical school despite little family support; her father's believing the work might be too difficult for a woman. After father's death, 1932, family's becoming comparatively poor. Attending school in Switzerland, then entering Glasgow University Medical School. Working in a Glasgow hospital. Marrying an Army captain, 1941; having a son a year later. Resenting controlling nanny's attempts to displace the child's affections; being torn between her career and her child. After family's move to Leicestershire, deciding to be a full-time mother, 1945. Husband's starting to serve on the Leicester City Council. Author's also being elected to council. When husband became lord mayor of Leicester, author's assuming duties of lady mayoress, c.1952. Recalling their formal roles at the coronation of Elizabeth II. Going to work for the BBC as program host on *What's My Line?;* also doing women's programming. Appearing in the film *Simon and Laura*. Taking public speaking tours to promote BBC programming. Regretting having gone into entertainment without further pursuing her medical career.

Lady Barnett uses her book to answer "what's my line?" for herself and for the show's audience. Along the way, her memories illuminate the family pressures—both lingering ideas about women's intellectual fragility and later maternal obligations—that created barriers to her long-term practice of medicine. The fatherly discouragement of ambition she describes also shows up in the books of reminiscences by Yorkshire animal physician James Herriot, who successfully dampened his daughter's enthusiasm for veterinary practice but later—after working with women veterinarians—expressed regrets. Lady Barnet's own regrets about leaving her medical career suggest how deeply affected she had been by tacit cultural repression on the issue of women's proper roles.

76 BARR, Amelia Edith (née Huddleston). 1831–1919. *All the Days of My Life: An Autobiography, the Red Leaves of a Human Heart*. D. Appleton, 1913. 527 pp.; illus.; app.; index. NUC pre56 36:346.

Born in Ulverston, Lancashire. Father: William Henry Huddleston, Methodist clergyman. Mother: Mary Singleton. 2 sisters. Married 1850, Robert Barr, entrepreneur, accountant, d.1867. Widow. 4 sons; 5 daughters. Knew editor Louis Klopsen, Henry Ward Beecher, Harriet Beecher Stowe, General William Booth. Novelist; emigrant (U.S.); journalist; feminist. Middle class.

Transition from life in England to life in various regions of the U.S., offering an immigrant's perspective on civil war tensions, 1831–1913. While in England, parents' enjoying happy relationship; family's moving to follow father's parish assignments in Lancashire, Yorkshire, and Cumberland. Attending private primary school; reacting negatively to being taught only hemming and sewing because she was a girl. Liking secondary school for its greater intellectual content. Family's settling in Whitehaven, Cumberland, 1844–52. After father's financial losses, author's age 16, teaching school in Norfolk for one year. Enrolling in the Normal School in Glasgow, age 18; planning to work in Methodist schools for the poor. Meeting her future husband. Marrying happily, age 19; in-laws disapproving of her as non-Calvinist. With husband, emigrating to U.S.; living in Chicago, 1853–56. Husband's starting several unsuccessful businesses; his declaring bankruptcy. Author's becoming pregnant soon afterward. Their starting over in Memphis, Tenn., 1856. Recounting sickness and terror of a regional cholera epidemic. Describing slaves who worked for her; starting to detest slavery. Noting current events: Mexico's sale of Texas to the U.S.; Lincoln's election to the presidency; the Emancipation Proclamation; disputes in border state Tennessee over Union/Confederacy loyalties. Family's relocating to Austin, 1856–66; enduring a diphtheria epidemic there. Living in Galveston, 1866–68. Discussing both the graciousness and defects of Southern women. Discussing "women's place"; her lifelong awareness of the injustice done to women. In Galveston, enduring third epidemic: yellow fever. Deaths of husband and two sons from the fever; six of her children's having died when young; author's clinging to her faith to survive suffering over their deaths. Striking out on her own; moving away; starting a school in Ridgeway, New Jersey; also running a boardinghouse. Settling permanently in New York City, 1868–97. Writing novels, poetry, serials, and articles for *The Christian Herald*. Feeling brokenhearted over the departure of her two surviving daughters through marriage; confessing her dependency on them. Recounting illnesses afflicting her later years, including brain inflammation in the 1880s and protracted nervous exhaustion.

Barr's introduction asserts that this book will correct errors about her that had previously appeared in the press. She notes that she intends this consciously feminist autobiography "mainly for the kindly race of women" and notes that "I have drank [*sic*] their cup of limitations to the dregs." More concerned with her personal struggles than her professional ones, she passes over important details of her prolific writing career. Barr authored more than sixty historical novels, the most praised being *Jan Vedder's Wife* (1885), set in the Shetland Islands, *The Bow of Orange Ribbon* (1886), a novel about pre-Revolutionary America, and *Friend Olivia* (1889), which addresses Cromwell's persecution of Quakers.

77 BARRAUD, Enid Mary. c.1908–?. *Set My Hand Upon the Plough.* Worcester: Littlebury, 1946. 91 pp.; illus. NUC pre56 36:438.

Born in London. Parents not named. 1 brother. Single. WWII volunteer; farm laborer; clerk. Lower middle class.

Author's agricultural war work, through which she acquired new self-confidence, 1939–46. Although a London child, author's having seen country life during WWI; having been sent to Surrey to escape bombing. Describing air battles between English and Germans, 1939; finding them more frightening than WWI Zeppelins. Working as an insurance clerk in London, 1939. At start of WWII, beinging accepted into the Women's Land Army. Expecting to be able to return to her old office job; being sacked one month later. Enjoying her agricultural work in Cambridgeshire; finding satisfaction despite earning 1 shilling per week instead of old salary of £5 per week. Keeping a diary. Describing characters of fellow workers. Organizing and running a village library. Doing unspecified "literary work." Death of a fellow worker; being emotionally moved by elegy at his funeral, although not considering herself a churchgoer.

Focusing mainly on her agricultural work during WWII, Barraud indicates pride in her growing competence at farming. "I shall never be able to face going back to town life," she writes. Useful in providing firsthand testimony to the conditions in the Women's Land Army, Barraud's book also marks her successful transition from urbanite to rural landswoman, a type of migration documented by a small but significant number of autobiographers, including Margaret Leigh, Dorothy Easton, and Kathleen Strange.

78 BARRETT, Elizabeth (Mrs. Robert Browning). 1806–1861. "Glimpses into My Own Life and Literary Character/Written by Elizabeth Barrett in the Year 1820 when Fourteen Years Old," pp. 3–28 in *Hitherto Unpublished Poems and Stories with an Inedited*

Autobiography, Vol. I. Boston: The Bibliophile Society, 1914. NUC pre56 79:673.

Born in County Durham. Father: Edward Moulton-Barrett, Jamaican landowner. Mother: Mary Graham-Clarke. 11 siblings. Married 1846, poet Robert Browning. 1 son. Wrote *The Seraphim* (1838), *Aurora Leigh* (1856), *Poems before Congress* (1860), others. Knew Margaret Fuller, Anna Jameson, Eliza Ogilvy, others. Poet; poet's spouse. Upper middle class.

Formative experiences of a major poet, covering her childhood from ages 3–14. Discussing her ideas about immortality. Providing justification for writing a personal narrative. Recalling father's giving her 10 shillings in a letter addressed to "the Poet Laureat [*sic*] of Hope End" for writing "some lines on virtue." Mother's encouraging author to celebrate family birthdays in verse. Sharing all her adventures with her "Dear Brother," who shared her interest in literature. Taking lessons with her brother and his tutor. Discussing her intellectual development and literary interests. Recognizing herself as a writer; publishing her first work, *The Battle of Marathon,* age 15; comparing her writings to those of published authors. Adoring literature, foreign languages (especially Greek), and metaphysics. Brother's departure for school; author's concern for his virtue; asserting that if her brother's morals lapsed it would destroy her.

Barrett's early picture of herself—energetic, optimistic and outgoing—provides a startling contrast to her later plight, age 40, as a psychosomatic invalid held virtual prisoner by her pathologically dominating father; it also illuminates the inner woman that Robert Browning discovered and rescued. In addition, this account cites many of the books that shaped Barrett's literary sensibilities in childhood and clearly shows her precocious intellectual drive and hopes. The reader can only empathize with the young writer who, upon proudly receiving a printed copy of her first work, raced home to compare the fruit of her genius with Alexander Pope's antiquated *Iliad,* only to realize that she had a long way to go to achieve his level of poetic excellence.

79 BARRINGTON, Charlotte Mary Leicester, Viscountess Barrington (née Stopford; formerly Mrs. Arden Birch). 1850–1935. *Through Eighty Years (1855–1935): The Reminiscences of Charlotte, Viscountess Barrington.* John Murray, 1936. 254 pp.; front.; note by author's son; illus.; index. NUC pre56 37:3.

Raised in London. Father: Major George Stopford, R.E. officer. Mother: née Burgoyne. 1 sister; 1 brother. Married Arden Birch, financier, d.1897. Married 1904, Walter Bulkeley Barrington, 9th Viscount Barrington, d.1933. Widow. 3 sons; 2 daughters; 7 stepchildren. Knew

Lady Jane Taylor, Sir Alfred Milner, Frederick Eckstein, Joseph Chamberlain, others. Philanthropist; traveler (South Africa, Egypt). Upper class; married into aristocracy.

Author's upbringing, marriages, travels, and extensive adult commitment to philanthropic work, covering her entire life. Family background. At age 5, being introduced to High Church Anglicanism; adoring it. After father's death, author's age 6, mother's devoting herself to her children, guiding their religious and social upbringing. Author's living with mother and maternal grandparents until age 21. Having a happy childhood: seaside and mountain holidays, well-liked governesses, a love for reading. After grandparents' deaths, mother's taking children to live in Hampton Court Palace; discussing palace's history and social life there. Making a successful marriage to Arden Birch; discussing their children and family life; grieving at his death, 1897. With her children, returning to live with mother at Hampton Court Palace. Raising her children; touring Germany and France to find good preparatory schools for her sons. On trip to South Africa, c.1899, becoming concerned with conflicts between the Boers and British; making several return visits during the Boer War. Collaborating on Mr. Fairbridge's scheme for child emigration to Australia; also working with Lady Jane Taylor's group to combat the teaching given in the Socialist Sunday schools. Keeping a schedule of regular hospital visiting. After seven years of widowhood, marrying Lord Barrington; declaring her devotion to him; their married happiness. Visiting South Africa with her new husband. Settling in his country estate in Berkshire, 1906. Their traveling extensively in Europe and Egypt, 1911–13. Discussing food shortages during WWI; author's working for the Soldiers' and Sailors' Families' Association, 1914–16. Raising funds for construction of disabled veterans' settlement houses in Shrivenham, Berkshire. Starting the first Boy Scout and Girl Guide troops in the local community; creating women's institutes for veterans' families. Noting postwar social difficulties: housing shortages and unemployment for returning men, women war workers' unwillingness to return to domestic work, the Miners Strike of 1921 and general strike of 1926. Citing effects on upper-class families of 1931 financial depression.

Lady Barrington's autobiography reflects both her appreciation for the graciousness of upper-class life and her empathy for the lower classes, the disabled, and the disenfranchised. The viscountess is exceptionally perceptive concerning social dilemmas; she discusses them in detail in her narrative and contemplates how to solve them. As a result, her account constitutes a clear and vivid picture of British class and economic issues in the mid-20th century, including changes wrought by the impact of war.

80 BARRY, Alice Frances. 1861–1951. *Armchair Reflections: Reminiscences of an Old Lady*. Brighton: Southern Publishing Co., c.1948. 165 pp.; foreword. BLC 20:60.

Raised in Clapham. Parents not named. 2 siblings. Single. Essayist. Middle class.

Thirty-eight topically distinct autobiographical essays, concentrating on changing social phenomena throughout author's lifetime, 1870s–1940s. 1) Memories of her pre-Victorian grandmother, and of attending school classes held in church buildings. 2) Memories of 1870s railway travel during visits to relatives in Berwick, Northumberland; accompanying her vicar uncle on parish visits there. 3) Vanished toys and games from the 1870s. 4) "Cap and apron," traditions of domestic service, 1870s. 5) Churchgoing, 1870s; regretting laxity of Anglican religious education compared to Catholic diligence, and disappearance of general Christian education for children. 6) Memories of the Crystal Palace. 7) Civilization's progress despite two world wars. 8) How the meaning of "time" changes as one ages. 9) Praising simplicity of modern dress. 10) Christmas festivities from her childhood. 11) The advent of radio broadcasts; condemning broadcasts of Dorothy Sayers's Christian plays because of their use of vulgar speech. 12) Author's adoption of the bicycling fad. 13) Her mother's garden parties. 14) Patterns in English surnames and given names. 15) Thoughts on children in general. 16) Gardens and gardening. 17) The craft of cooking. 18) Rationing in wartime. 19) Vanished custom of paying social calls. 20) English birds. 21) Memories of author's holiday at Clovelly. 22) Meditations on beauty. 23) Thoughts on the qualities of darkness; her lifetime fear of the dark. 24) Memories of a Belgian holiday in the 1920s. 25) Her love of dogs; dogs she has known. 26) The uses and meaning of windows. 27) On curtains and what they conceal. 28) All about parrots. 29) Meditations on keys. 30) Childhood memories of learning to drive a carriage. 31) A Swiss holiday, c.1890. 32) Analysis as a modern habit of mind. 33) Praise for elasticity of intellect. 34) Meditations on body and soul. 35) Thoughts on trees. 36) The significance of envelopes. 37) Clouds: in nature and in the mind. 38) Meditations on beds.

These short essays were collected and reprinted from the *Mid-Sussex Times* and the *British Weekly*. Many of them were written in the early 1940s as a diversion from WWII. In her writing, Barry functions as the observer of human society's response to the physical phenomena of its surroundings, animal, vegetable and mineral; common sights she records serve as the focus for her own experience and vision of the moral and philosophical conditions of past and present.

81 BATHGATE, Janet (née Greenfield). 1814–1898. *Aunt Janet's Legacy to Her Nieces: Recollections of Humble Life in Yarrow in the*

Beginning of the Century. Selkirk: George Lewis, 1895. 207 pp.; front. port.; preface; poems. NUC pre56 39:145.

Born in Sunderland, Scotland. Father: John Greenfield. Mother: Tibbie. 4 brothers; 1 sister. Married 1832, James Kemp, shepherd's son. Widow. Domestic servant; teacher; religionist (Presbyterian). Rural laboring class.

Modest upbringing, years of domestic service, marriage, and school-teaching experiences of a devout Presbyterian Scotswoman, c.1820–1854. Growing up in a rural, poor, pious Presbyterian family; being afraid to play with her doll on the Sabbath. Going into service, age 8, helping local farmer as cowherd and companion to his aging mother; taking different work as babysitter to a local family. Teaching herself to read. Becoming a domestic servant to Tibbie Hogg, aunt of Romantic poet James Hogg; working for other families. Teaching herself to write. After marriage of female friend into a wealthy Edinburgh family, friend's giving author a domestic job. Improving her learning by sitting in on lessons of her employer's children. Being wooed by local boy; rejecting him for being ungodly. Marrying James Kemp, a God-fearing, nondrinking man, 1832. Many hardships: her own infection with smallpox, her husband's lung disease and death, her impoverished widowhood. Writing poetry; being encouraged by her niece and nephew to publish her verses. Beginning a rural school for girls as fulfillment of her religious calling.

Adhering to the Calvinist tradition of spiritual autobiography, Bathgate frequently uses scriptural citation to place the trials of her life in a context of providential meaning. She makes her account novelistic, using both third-person narration and direct dialogue in Scots dialect, with the evident intent to hold the interest of the nieces for whom she created this historical record. As a result, her memoir, which preserves the rural cultural ambience of the author's Scottish, Regency-era surroundings, is of interest to late-20th-century readers as well.

82 BATTEN, Jean Gardner. 1909–s.l.1982. *My Life*. George Harrap, 1938. 304 pp.; foreword by the Marquess of Londonderry; illus.; list of flights, honors, trophies. NUC pre56 39:236.

Born in Rotorua, New Zealand. Father not named, dental surgeon. Mother not named. 2 brothers. Single. Aviator. Middle class.

Aviator's childhood and later flying exploits, c.1914 to the late 1930s. Father's having a dentistry practice in Rotorua; his leaving it to enlist in WWI. Family's moving to Auckland, 1914. Author's being tremendously impressed by the England-Australia air race, 1919; this sparking her interest in aviation. Being further inspired by Charles Kingsford Smith's flight, 1928. Deciding to be a pilot; facing father's opposition. Selling her piano to pay for flying lessons; being encouraged by her mother. Taking flying lessons in England, c.1933. Becoming first woman to make a solo flight from England to Australia and back, 1934–35. Flying to South America via Morocco and Africa; setting record for fastest time for Atlantic crossing from Africa to Brazil, 1935. Making solo flights between New Zealand and England. Being accompanied by her mother on flights to Spain, Marseilles, and Paris. Flying to Australia, Denmark, and Sweden. Becoming engaged in London, 1935; deciding her commitment to flying required her to remain single. Receiving honor from Royal Aero Club. Installing of a waxwork of author at Madame Tussaud's. Author's being received by Queen Mary. Being awarded gold medal of the Fédération Aéronatique Internationale, 1938.

In this self-portrait, Batten traces a career she clearly found absorbing and fulfilling. Essential for the study of aviation in the 1930s, this memoir places the author in the company of successful British women aviators such as Amy Johnson, whose solo flight record from London to Australia Batten triumphantly shaved by four days. After ceasing to fly competitively in 1938, Batten preserved her interest in aviation through sponsorship and public speaking engagements.

BATTERSEA, Baroness. [*See* FLOWER, Constance.]

83 BAX, Emily. 1882–1943. *Miss Bax of the Embassy*. Boston: Houghton Mifflin, 1939. 331 pp.; preface; illus.; app.; index. NUC pre56 40:332.

Born in Tooting, Greater London. Parents not named. 4 siblings. Single. Secretary; WWI volunteer; emigrant (U.S.). Middle class.

Clerical and diplomatic work of a confidential secretary to U.S. Embassy in London, covering 1900–18. Her father's early death. Attending girls' day school in Westminster; headmistress's suggesting she seek a career in secretarial work. Teaching herself typing and shorthand while working as an unpaid errand girl and secretary in the House of Lords. Finding work as a stenographer at American Embassy in London; being only English employee there, 1902–13. Discussing personality of her employer, John Ridgely Carter, second secretary of the embassy. U.S. Embassy's establishing Rhodes Scholarships by the terms of Cecil Rhodes's will, 1902. Reviewing contemporary diplomatic issues, including Anglo-American relations relative to Ireland and Irish-Americans. Confidentiality as a requirement of her position. Her youngest sister's joining staff of the military attaché, c.1908. Discussing militancy of the American women in the English suffrage campaign; author's support for suffrage despite her employers' opposition. Traveling to the U.S.; feeling renewed interest in her work. Outbreak of WWI. Praising the American Foreign Service for diplomatic conduct during the years of America's neutrality in the war. Leaving the London embassy to live in

New York as a private secretary, 1914; feeling like a deserter. Being unable to return home the next summer; British Embassy in Washington refusing to give her a passport; women being a low priority during WWI. After 1917, working as a YMCA volunteer in France. Becoming an American citizen.

This record of Bax's clerical career is also a behind-the-scenes study of Britain's diplomatic establishment in its day-to-day workings. Although concentrating on Bax's vocational experiences, it preserves both a portrait of private resistance to women's advancement within the governmental establishment and a record of the many passing problems in international relations that influenced Britain's decisions during WWI.

84 BAYLEY, Emily (Lady Clive; née Metcalfe) and Sir Thomas Metcalfe. 1830–d.a.1880 (Bayley). *The Golden Calm: An English Lady's Life in Moghul Delhi: Reminiscences by Emily, Lady Clive Bayley and by her father, Sir Thomas Metcalfe*. Exeter: Webb & Bower, 1980. Ed. by M. M. Kaye. 220 pp.; intro. by Lt. Col. John Mildmay Ricketts, M.C. (author's great-grandson); front. port.; index. BLC 1976–1982 4:306.

Born in Delhi, India. Father: Sir Thomas Metcalfe, British governor of Delhi, d.1853. Mother: Felicity Annie Browne. 1 brother; 2 sisters. Married 1850, Edward Clive Bayley, administrator in British India. 13 children. Colonialist (India); civil servant's spouse; memsahib. Upper class.

Memories of early life in Delhi and London and a lament for the passing of the East India Company's rule in India, covering 1830–80. Being educated by her mother in Delhi until age 6, then being sent to England to live with her grandmother. Undergoing ten surgeries on her neck, age 7, without anesthesia; being expected by her stern grandmother to endure pain. Attending day school to receive a "lady's education" in English, history, literature, piano, harp; one fellow student's being the future Empress Eugénie. At age 12, receiving news of death of her mother, whom she had not seen in seven years. Grieving, but remembering her mother as angelic, not real. Enjoying a secure economic situation in England; contrasting it with her family's extreme affluence in India. Perceiving servants in both countries as invariably kind and merry; later meeting wives of native Indian troops; wondering "how they could be so cheerful living on such a pittance." Making return voyage to India, age 17. Admiring her father greatly for his civilized, educated personality. Having no interest in native language or culture, but esteeming Moghul architecture. Suffering from the heat; needing to keep servants constantly employed working water coolers and fans. Closing her book, 1880, with nostalgia for the serene, happy place she perceived British-ruled India to have been before the Mutiny of 1857 and the destruction of the Moghul empire.

Written for the author's family as a memorial, especially of the role Bayley's father played in Anglo-Indian government and his murder by political intrigue, her memoir openly yearns for the "golden calm" before the 1857 Indian Mutiny. The author confines her commentary to the leisured life of Anglo-Indians and seems unaware of natives, native culture, and the grievances that provoked the mutiny she deplores; she also omits her family's fortuitous trip to England, 1854, which saved them from the slaughter inflicted by rebel Sepoys. While Bayley's attitude helps show why the British presence was so resented by the native Indian population, her statements are best supplemented by a reading of Frances Duberly's *Campaign Experiences in Rajpootana and Central India, during the Suppression of the Mutiny, 1857–58*. Although Duberley was also a colonialist, her observations of native conditions gradually led her to troubling reflections on the wisdom of British rule.

85 BECHER, Augusta Emily (née Prinsep). 1830–1909. *Personal Reminiscences in India and Europe (1830–1888)*. Constable & Co., 1930. Ed. by Hugh George Rawlinson. 230 pp.; front. port.; intro. and preface by ed.; apps.; genealogical tables. NUC pre56 42:111.

Born aboard ship "Duke of Lancaster." Father: Augustus Prinsep, East India Company official. Mother: Elizabeth Ommanney. Stepfather: Samuel Beechcroft, architect. 3 stepsiblings. Married 1849, Septimus Becher, army captain, d.1908. 4 daughters; 5 sons. Colonialist (India); military spouse; memsahib. Upper middle class.

Life and times in England, India, and Europe of seasoned traveler and Anglo-Indian wife, from her 1830s childhood to middle age. Father's having died ten days before author's birth. Prinsep family history; her long-established, extended Anglo-Indian family. Living with her mother in her maternal grandparents' London home. Being raised by her mother until age 6; after mother's remarriage, remaining with her grandparents. Traveling to France and Switzerland with her family. Studying French with a governess. Visiting her adored mother periodically; being resentful of her stepfather and his evident ill-treatment of mother. Attending primary school; later enjoying the intellectual stimulus of boarding school. Marrying Captain Septimus Becher, age 17; expressing her great love and admiration for him. Their living in India; author's admiring the beauty of India and describing remembered images of Benares. Relating customs and practices of Indian people. Socializing with other Europeans at Lahore. Memories of Calcutta: the cold weather, being served questionable dishes by servants. Dutifully caring for her children and empathizing with them, although her husband came first in her priorities. Aiding in the general colonial evacuation following 1857 Mutiny; afterward, author and husband's returning to Simla. Undergoing periodic bouts of heat-associated debilitation; taking holiday for her health with mother and stepfather in England; returning to India some months later. Living with her husband and growing family at Barrackpore. Visiting temple ruins in Chenee. With family, returning to England, 1868; eventually settling in Dresden, Germany. Discussing many aspects of European colonial society: etiquette, recreations, festivities, and child-rearing.

Produced from Becher's diary by a secondary editor, this consequently unfocused book gives detailed observations of Indian social life and customs and also describes the Mutiny of 1857. For Becher, life in India under the British Raj seems to have provided no examples of women who questioned their domestic roles, and the author—although remarkable for her endurance of near-continuous pregnancy, heat, disease, and the deaths of several children—shows herself content in a complete and voluntary subjugation to her husband. The editor notes that when she returned to England in 1868, "Mrs. Becher lost 'that scared expression' which so disturbed her relatives," and her apparent contentment reinforces her declarations throughout this memoir of being completely happy with her married lot.

86 BECKWITH, Lady Muriel Beatrice (née Gordon-Lennox). 1884–1961. *When I Remember*. Ivor Nicholson & Watson, 1936. 317 pp.; foreword by Lord Lonsdale; photos; index. NUC pre56 42:542.

Raised in Scotland. Father: Charles Henry Gordon-Lennox, the Duke of Richmond. Mother not named. 3 brothers; 3 sisters. Married Major William Beckwith. 1 daughter. Society woman. Aristocracy.

Author's youth in aristocratic British circles, within the context of her commentary on a changing world, covering 1901 to WWI. Growing up happily in the Scottish countryside; family's making frequent trips between London and Edinburgh. Author's earliest influence's being her dynamic governess. Acquiring early love of Scotland and Scottish music. Recalling her father's aristocratic hunting parties at Glenfiddich. Looking back on her childhood love for family servants; lamenting changes in master-servant relations in modern times. Family's moving to London, c.1901. Making her social debut; describing the rounds of parties and balls. Commenting on Britain's turn-of-the-century politics. Traveling to Canada and U.S.; finding superficiality and greed in New York; consequently having greater esteem for London. Considering North Americans both extravagant and hospitable; in contrast, seeing sense of humor as the essence of British character. Mourning disappearance of the "Grand Manner" after WWI; observing a growing sense of familiarity and intimacy between aristocracy and commoners. Discussing her family's ongoing ties with King Edward VII, Queen Alexandra, and the duke of Connaught.

In this portrait of upper-class life at the outset of the 20th century, Lady Muriel draws many conscious comparisons between cultural aspects of the Victorian and Edwardian periods. She is equally observant of details during her visits to the new world, and contemplates manifestations of American character in parallel with their British variants. The author manages simultaneously to spare her reader from lengthy lists of her prominent acquaintances and to provide the type of book social historians love to find, a thorough record of the cultural nuances of an era.

87 BEDDINGTON, Frances Ethel (née Mulock). c.1880–?. *All That I Have Met*. Cassell & Co., Ltd., 1929. 286 pp.; front.; illus.; index. NUC pre56 42:612.

Raised in England and India. Father: Frank Mulock, Indian civil service officer. Mother not named. Married Claude Beddington. Knew Enrico Caruso, Sir Edward Elgar, the Prince of Wales, George Wyndham. Society woman; horsewoman. Upper class.

Anecdotes from the author's upper-class and well-connected life, told from the perspective of her pride in being Irish, 1880s–c.1925. History of her Irish family: her cousin Dinah Mulock and her literary career; literary tendencies of family. Branding the failure of Gladstone's 1886 Home Rule Bill for Ireland as one of the world's great tragedies; recognizing Ireland's need for self-government. Profoundly admiring Ireland's homegrown intellectuals; remembering her awe at meeting Dublin native Oscar Wilde. Recalling childhood hardships, especially the evil nature of her nursery governess. Growing up in both England and India; becoming educated through travel. Attending the famous horse-racing season at Newmarket; discussing her love for her own horse, Old Times. Telling anecdote about the "Day of the Fallen Women," when author and other women tumbled while riding to the hounds on a foxhunt. Sitting for her portrait by John Singer Sargent. Deciding she preferred the company of men to that of women. In 1905, being present at the London debut of the marvelous Irish tenor, John McCormack. Conducting a correspondence with Irish compatriot W. B. Yeats. During WWI, playing piano as her contribution to canteen work. Discussing the famous performers who also volunteered, and the ties she developed with the theatre. Closing with her expressions of admiration for the Irish-born Lord Curzon, who helped to rebuild Britain's international position following WWI.

Beddington's lighthearted chattiness in this volume is deliberate; she remarks that she is following the advice of an American interviewer who claimed that "The public of to-day wants anecdotes. . . . They like plenty of conversations in a book of reminiscences." She does, however, refrain from salting her memoir with copious opinions, although the ones she includes, particularly on Irish Home Rule, seem well considered. Despite her anecdotal intentions, the author has produced a useful contemporary record of Irish contributions to British culture.

88 BEDELLS, Phyllis. 1893–1985. *My Dancing Days*. Phoenix House, 1954. 224 pp.; illus.; index. NUC pre56 42:641.

Born at Knowle, Avon. Father not named, church organist, founder of the Bristol Amateur Operatic Society. Mother: stage name Phyllis Stuart, stage performer. 1 brother. Married 1918, Lt. Ian Macbean. 1 son; 1 daughter. Dancer; teacher (dance). Middle class.

Author's early life and stage career, 1893–1935. Identifying both parents as musicians and stage performers; parents and their colleagues' fostering author's love of music. Author's playing theatre and writing plays as a child; having mother's enthusiastic encouragement. Being a day girl at the Convent of St. Agnes at Knowle; learning needlework; taking dance lessons. Dancing in mother's theatre company. Learning ballet and other dances at school in Nottingham. Receiving general education through home study. Performing in ballets, beginning at age 13. Being strongly influenced by Dame Adeline Genée; receiving lessons from Alexander Genée, Adeline's uncle; studying under Anna Pavlova. Author's citing her numerous productions, some of which she choreographed, others in which she received top billing. Worshipping actor Owen Nares. Having a series of courtships; becoming engaged to Lt. Ian Macbean; their marrying after his return from WWI. Author's wanting to start a family, but husband's insisting she wait, in order to continue her career; this conflict's straining their marriage. Births of their children, 1923 and 1924. From rigors of ballet, author's beginning to suffer chronic knee pain. Partially resting by teaching dance classes. Suffering a second injury, a torn calf muscle, effectively ending her performing career. Helping to form the Ballet Society, a national ballet corps; also codeveloping the Association for Operatic Dancing; traveling to Cape Town and Denmark with the association. Receiving a moving tribute from her peers and colleagues at her retirement from ballet, 1935.

This professional memoir helpfully itemizes the productions in which Bedells danced as well as other productions and plays of her era that she attended; with her critical eye, her judgement about which artists and productions to include in her memoir is formidable. This volume is a worthy companion to Ninette de Valois's *Come Dance with Me: A Memoir, 1898–1956;* collectively they contribute a multidimensional perspective on dance in England in the first half of the 20th century.

89 BEECHEY, Winifred (née Robinson). c.1911–s.l.1991. *The Rich Mrs. Robinson*. Oxford University Press, 1984. 145 pp.; illus. by Mary P. Taylor. BLC 1982–1985 3:158.

Raised in London and Vale of Aylesbury, near Bishopstone, Buckinghamshire. Father not named, WWI veteran, chair factory worker. Mother not named, dressmaker, shopkeeper. 1 sister; 1 brother; 1 other sibling. Shopkeeper; secretary. Lower middle class.

Memories of author's semirural upbringing and adolescence, emphasizing dedication of her mother, "the rich Mrs. Robinson," to improving the family's situation, c.1914–30. Having an impoverished childhood in rustic Buckinghamshire. Father's volunteering in WWI; his serving in distant Russia. Illustrating her parents' opposite attitudes toward money: father's certainty family would go broke, mother's confidence they would become rich. Describing character of mother and mother's four sisters. Attending village school near Bishopstone. Joining the Young Helpers' League to support Barnardo Orphan Homes. Father's returning home pensionless, 1919; his finding temporary work with a coal merchant, then working in a chair factory. Recounting mother's business efforts to support family; her success as a dressmaker and shopkeeper. Helping in mother's shop. Discussing averse postwar economic conditions for demobilized village men. Visiting London with mother and siblings. Author's believing her schooling would continue until told by her headmaster, at age 14, that her parents had decided she would not take the examination for a scholarship. Having to work; finding a secretarial job at the chair factory. Mother's difficult pregnancy; birth of another sibling, author's age 15. Growing family prosperity through parents' combined efforts and father's sale of his chair-bed invention; finally having enough money for father to buy a car. Old age of mother; mother's death, 1950s.

In a humorous tribute to her mother, the "rich Mrs. Robinson" of the book's title, Beechey novelistically re-creates her youthful admiration for her mother's successful efforts to raise the family out of poverty. Beechey also conveys the flavor of her childhood in this rural village, and her picture of post-WWI economic conditions and their manifold impact on her youth is memorable for its clarity. Beechey went on to write a further memoir, published in 1991, *The Reluctant Samaritan: Aspects of Growing Old*.

90 BELL, Mary Hayley. 1914–s.l.1995. *What Shall We Do Tomorrow? The Story of My Families*. Philadelphia: J.B. Lippincott, 1969. 235 pp.; illus. BLC to 1975 24:122. (1st pub. Cassell, 1968, as *What Shall We Do Tomorrow? An Autobiography*.)

Born in China; raised in Macao. Father: Hayley Bell, commissioner for Chinese Imperial Maritime Customs in Macao. Mother: Agnes MacGowan, American. 3 brothers; 2 sisters. Married 1941, John Mills, actor, director. 1 son; 2 daughters (child actresses Hayley and Juliet). Wrote novel *Avolena,* plays *The Two Harlequins, Men in Shadow, The Uninvited Guest,* others. Actress (stage); playwright; novelist; foreign resident (China). Middle class.

Author's foreign childhood within an Anglo-Chinese family and later work with her actor husband in London's theatrical milieu, 1922–68.

Growing up in Macao until age 12. Being influenced primarily by her father, who lived by the Buddhist philosophy; author's having been named for him. Mother's being a devout Presbyterian; mother's father's having been Christian missionary Dr. John MacGowan, author of a children's book on China, *Beside the Bamboo.* Both parents' coming from trader and missionary families, in China since the 19th century. Father's teaching author to read from Spenser's *Faerie Queene,* the poems of Tennyson, and Sir Walter Scott's novels. With siblings, being schooled in foreign languages, Macao history, and Roman Catholicism by a native Catholic tutor; sticking to her father's Buddhism and mother's Christian prayer. Mother's wanting author to have prep school education; father's consequently taking her to England, age 12. His introducing her to London theatre. Boarding at Sherborne School for Girls in Surrey; being expelled; attending Malvern Girls' College; remaining until age 16. Returning to China; meeting her husband-to-be, John Mills, touring in a stage production. At age 19, playing her first role in "The Barretts of Wimpole Street" in Shanghai. Deciding to move to England; auditioning; playing juvenile roles in Manchester and London; meeting John Mills again. Beginning to write plays, 1939. Traveling to New York to act on Broadway, c.1940. After return to London, marrying John Mills. Traveling with husband to film locations. Continuing her playwriting while raising three children. Writing the play *Journey North* to commemorate the death of her father, c. 1945. All three children's yearning to act; daughter Hayley's succeeding as a child actor in films; Juliet's also becoming famous actress. Writing her first novel, *Avolena;* realizing that seclusion aided her writing. Meditating on the death of her own mother, who had been possessive of her children; resolving not to emulate her. Buying a farm to live on outside London in Richmond.

Bell was an emigrant in multiple senses, coming to British culture as a virtual foreigner, and to the working world of London theatre from a life in the Orient among merchants and diplomats; her transition from early surroundings to adult ones marks a watershed in her book. As a result, it has two foci of interest, both her re-creation of the ambience of Portuguese-ruled Macao, and her firsthand study of the inception and growth of the illustrious Mills acting dynasty. In discussing this latter topic, she casts light on family dynamics of mentorship as well as their acting careers.

91 BENSON, Gertrude, Lady (née Samwell). 1860–1946. *Mainly Players: Bensonian Memories.* Thornton, Butterworth, Ltd., 1926. 313 pp.; front. port.; illus.; preface; intro. by A. Machen; index. NUC pre56 47:220.

Probably born in India. Father: Morshead Fetherstonhaugh Samwell, Madras Light Infantry officer. Mother not named. Married 1886, Francis R. Benson, actor, acting company manager, knighted 1916. 1

son. Actress (stage); theatrical producer; costume designer; choreographer; WWI volunteer. Upper middle class.

Military childhood in India, early London stage training, and later career landmarks of a noted Shakespearean actress, 1860s–c.1925. Father's death before author's birth; author's being cared for by a beloved Indian amah. Mother's suffering financial hardship; author's consequently making early choice of a stage career. Moving to London, training as an actress. Her first engagements: playing roles of boys and "second old women." Discussing family history and stage career of her future husband, Frank Benson. Being engaged by his theatrical company; describing rehearsals, responsibilities, daily life in company. Secret engagement to Frank; their marrying, 1886. From 1886, Frank's producing Stratford's annual Shakespearean festivals for thirty years; author's recalling her roles in Frank's *MacBeth, Timon of Athens,* and numerous other Shakespearean plays. Touring throughout Ireland and England. Playing Ophelia in *Hamlet;* researching her role in an insane asylum. Expounding her reasons for loving to play Shakespeare. With Frank, having produced thirty-five of Shakespeare's thirty-seven plays; regretting lessening demand for them in modern era. Telling anecdotes of her acquaintance with Oscar Wilde and Henry Irving. Appearing with Ellen Terry and Basil Rathbone. During WWI, women's having to play men's roles because of wholesale male enlistment; author's also designing costumes and doing choreography thanks to absence of male professionals. Frank's temporarily leaving the stage; doing war work in hospital in Salonica. Author's directing canteens in France under French Red Cross; working with hospitalized soldiers. Mourning the war death of her son. At close of WWI, author and husband's returning to England; touring in provincial English music halls.

From a career that began in the early 1880s, dominated by Henry Irving's Lyceum Theatre, Benson progressed to becoming one of her manager husband's principal Shakespearean stars, as well as collaborating with him in all business aspects of the annual Stratford festival. As the main summer attraction for international tourists to Britain, the festival contributed mightily to the British economy and was known as the "nursery" for the English stage. Benson and her husband were recognized by the crown for providing world-class training to young actors.

92 BENTINCK, Lady Norah Ida Emily (née Noel). 1881–1939. *My Wanderings and Memories*. T. Fisher Unwin, 1924. 272 pp.; front.; illus.; index. NUC pre56 47:341.

Born in Campden, Gloucester. Father: Charles Hubert Noel, 3rd Earl of Gainsborough. Mother: Mary Dease. 1 sister; 1 half-sister; 3 brothers. Married 1915, Captain Count Robert Bentinck, d.1932. 1 daughter; 1 son. Wrote *The Ex-Kaiser in Exile* (1921), novels *The Ring of Straw* (1925),

The Puzzled Wife (1926). Novelist; philanthropist; society woman; singer (concerts). Aristocracy.

Author's ancestry, social life, brief singing career, and abiding musical interest, 1896–1924. Proudly listing her distinguished English forebears back to 1066; admiring "good breeding" in manners as well as descent. From ages 15–17, attending convent day school; overcoming stuttering with voice and musical lessons, ages 17–19. Deaths of her half-sister and Queen Victoria, 1901; author's expressing her religious beliefs about eternal life. Entering Edwardian social life. Enjoying amateur public singing. Touring the world, 1911, as a soloist with the Sheffield Choir. At start of WWI, using earnings from concert singing to open Home for East-End Baby Boys at Exton; also providing food for hundreds of children during the docker's strike in Mile End Road. Attending most of the current London concerts and operas. Discussing the self-effacing qualities that she believes make "an admirable woman"; nevertheless believing that female monarchs were Britain's best rulers. Discussing her travel and attendance at musical performance in many places: the Oberammergau passion play, Egypt, the Near East, Paris, opera in Bayreuth and Prague. Marrying a military officer, 1915; having to smooth conflict due to her Catholic background and her husband's Protestant background. Discussing her children.

In her autobiography, Bentinck functions as an amateur historian as well as singer, telling a number of entertaining anecdotes about her ancestors in many eras. Concerning her own life, she limits extensive discussion primarily to the year she traveled with the Sheffield Choir. However, her memoir benefits from her musical training as well as her financial means, since she was able both to afford traveling to the major European musical venues of her era and to judge which performances and artists merited inclusion in this record. Her book vividly surveys classical musical performance in Europe during the ten years after WWI.

93 BENTLEY, Phyllis. 1894–1977. *O Dreams, O Destinations, an Autobiography*. Victor Gollancz Ltd., 1962. 272 pp.; illus. BLC to 1975 25:341.

Born in Halifax, Yorkshire. Father: Joseph Edwin Bentley, manufacturer. Mother: Eleanor Kettlewell. 3 brothers. Single. Wrote *The Spinner of Years* (1929), *Environment* (1935), others. Novelist; public speaker; feminist; literary critic; teacher. Upper middle class.

The integration of a novelist's childhood experiences with her adult writing career, both focused on her native Yorkshire and its problems with economic and cultural viability, 1894–1960. Recalling her affluent childhood home; being taught to honor her parents. Noting conflict between father's pleasure-loving character and mother's puritanical repressiveness. Learning to read and write from her brother Frank;

being favored over her brothers for being delicate and a girl. Father's business's eventually failing from heavy tariffs on imported British cloth; citing trade unions and American tariffs as the two main threats to Yorkshire's middle-class stability, c.1900. Father's finding textile job in Huddersfield; moving family there. Author's being sent to boarding school; suffering there from poor food and abusive bullying. Father and oldest brother's returning to Halifax to start new dyeing business. After pleading to change schools, author's attending an Ursuline convent; coming to detest Catholicism for its lurid art and perceived hypocrisy. Detesting being sent to a state high school in Halifax, but excelling academically. Describing student experiences at Cheltenham Ladies' College: academic work, part-time teaching, her feeling of aimlessness after leaving. Becoming interested in agnosticism and socialism. Returning to Cheltenham for a B.A. degree. At start of WWI, age 20, teaching Belgian refugees. Taking a teaching post in London; losing it as a result of inability to handle rebellious students. Returning home; supporting herself as a librarian. Starting her first novel, *Environment,* taking first aid and home nursing classes; doing YMCA work. Finding new wartime teaching post at Heath Grammar school. Adopting pacifism; declaring British women's liberation to be only benefit of the war. Paying to have her first book of stories, *The World's Bane,* published. Doing clerical work at Ministry of Munitions until war's end. Returning to Yorkshire; helping elect a woman to the Halifax Town Council. Reviewing books for the *Yorkshire Observer*. Having novels accepted by publishers. Discussing prosperity and garishness of the 1920s. Lecturing on her literary work. Father's health failing from trying to maintain a business during the 1926 general strike; his death. Joining local Halifax author's circle; getting to know fellow novelists Hugh Walpole and J. B. Priestly. Having further novels published. Noting her mother's business acumen; mother's working with author's brothers to keep business afloat; author's contributing by making business loan to her brothers. Rising steadily in her writing career; noting mother's harshness to her in times of difficulty; discussing problems of small businesses in recessionary times. Visiting with writer Vera Brittain, who offered to aid author's career. Marking the moment, age 40, when she heard first words of praise from her censorious mother. During WWII, lecturing in America. Attending the Writers Conference of Allied Nations in Hollywood, 1943. Writing scenario for the film *We of West Riding*. Her mother's final illness and death. Revering Sigmund Freud; wishing a woman psychoanalyst would illuminate the female psyche as Freud had done for the male. Discussing 20th-century literary focus on the working class, her own efforts to preserve cultural life in the West Riding, and a writer's obligation to illuminate human destiny.

While charting her own advances, Bentley has also written an economic history of 20th-century Yorkshire. The family business, in which all family members pulled an oar, was a barometer of prosperity or adversity which indelibly affected her creative consciousness; her memoir in fact suggests that her career was a product of the West Riding social landscape, the scene of all of her writing. Another factor influencing the social conscience appearing in her writing was her wartime work; as she notes, after WWI she was one of the million postwar "surplus women" whom the country consigned to oblivion. Her most acclaimed novels are *Carr* (1929), and *Inheritance* (1932), both set in Yorkshire's textile industry. From the 1940s–1960s she produced several critical studies of the Brönte sisters, also Yorkshire natives, as well as a book-length study of narrative, many writings for children, and contributions to numerous periodicals.

94 BENTWICH, Helen Caroline. 1892–1972. *If I Forget Thee: Some Chapters of Autobiography, 1912–1920.* Paul Elek Books, 1973. 170 pp.; intro.; letters; diary excerpts; illus. NUC 1973–1977 11:529.

Born in London. Father not named, senior partner in banking firm. Mother not named, manager of schools in East End. 1 sister; 4 brothers. Married 1915, Norman Bentwich, lawyer, civil servant, chief legal secretary in Palestine, writer. Jewish activist; Zionist; organizer (labor); socialist; social reformer; WWI volunteer; political activist; emigrant (Palestine). Upper class.

Social reformer's upbringing and early commitment to social causes, highlighting her Jewish identity and activism, c.1900–1920. In childhood, being disturbed by Jewish prayer in which men thank God they aren't women. Attending boarding school and Bedford College. Following social rather than religious Judaism; committing herself to philanthropy as part of social Judaism's tenets. During WWI, working with a VAD detachment; later working as peripatetic group leader for the Women's Land Army. Becoming a socialist; joining National Federation of Women Workers. Serving on County Council Educational Committee; noting that education for poor people is shamefully inadequate. Remarking that women in England should start crêches—cooperative child-tending societies—to have care for their babies while they join the Land Army. Emigrating to Palestine to join her husband; organizing Jewish women there in land work.

Both Bentwich and her husband were ardent Zionists instrumental in the 1948 founding of the nation of Israel. However, while Norman Bentwich is esteemed as a Zionist, pacifist, author of many histories, Jewish biographies, and political treatises, and one architect of the United Nations, Helen's contributions to his writings, to the Socialist party, and to British public education have been largely forgotten. She wrote several books, including *Mandate Memories, 1918–48,* which in some ways helps to flesh out this incomplete autobiography whose planned further volumes were forestalled by her death. Her independent works, written in the 1970s, focus on British regional history. For information on her later life, the reader may consult her husband's autobiography, *My 77 Years: An Account of My Life and Times, 1883–1960*.

95 BERTENSHAW, Mary. 1904–s.l.1991. *Sunrise to Sunset.* Ed. by Alan Yardley. Manchester: Printwise Publications, Ltd., 1991. 127 pp.; foreword by ed.; intro.; illus.

Born in Buxton, Derbyshire. Father: James, no surname given, doorman, lodging-house keeper. Mother: "Polly," fancy ironer, lodging-house keeper. 2 sisters; 1 brother. Married 1926, "Eddie." 2 sons; 1 daughter. Factory worker. Working class.

Coming of age in working-class Manchester, 1909–1927. Family's moving to Manchester, author's age 5. Attending a Catholic school. Adoring her father, who demanded obedience; recalling his spanking her for visiting a friend without permission; attending Osborne Theatre free because father worked there. Remembering cultural phenomena of the era: tram cars, magic lantern shows. Performing in a school musical; having her drawers fall down during performance. Recalling Friday night baths; mother's thriftiness in not wasting anything, including hot water. Neighbors' needing to pawn possessions on a regular basis to survive. Poor children's having country holidays provided by the Board of Guardians. Unemployment's and drunkenness's being standard neighborhood problems. Family's moving to great-aunt Betsy's lodging house; eventually inheriting house on her death, 1914. Memories of individual lodgers: Mick the traveling ventriloquist, Mrs. Blake who left without paying, Mary Ann the charwoman. Loving to go to silent films. Another lodger's having a child out of wedlock; author and parents' successfully reuniting Lettie with her upper-class parents. Author's childhood wish for siblings being granted by birth of her sister Evelyn. WWI: new regulations for lodging houses; parents' having to register all lodgers. Birth of another sister. At her Catholic school, staff's resenting author for avoiding church and "fraternizing" with Protestants. Family's moving to house in Red Bank; author's spending year in hospital from complications after a tonsillectomy. At age 14, going to work in a furniture factory, then in a rubber foundary. Noting her awakening interest in sexual matters. Father's suffering leg ulcers; author's wanting to comfort him but being unable to overcome reserve between them; author's never kissing father during his lifetime. Birth of her brother. Father's death; her questioning God as to why he was allowed to suffer and die at a young age. Working in a hat factory. Mother's starting a romance with Mick the ventriloquist; his abusing her; author's deciding to leave home. Meeting Eddie; becoming engaged; marrying after discovering she was pregnant. Both author and husband's having to work to make ends meet. Remaining close to her mother, sisters, and brother, although continuing to despise Mick.

Bertenshaw's book resurrects domestic life among Manchester's industrial workers. It is worth noting that although her memoir covers the period of WWI, the war never penetrated her youthful awareness. This omission augments indications in other working-class narratives of the priority that urgent family needs maintained, even in the face of public appeal for wartime volunteers. Bertenshaw's narrative also indicates that her childhood benefited from a combination of public and private charity: free tuition at her Catholic school as well as Board of Guardians outings. Bertenshaw's book coincides with the radio play which was first broadcast by B.B.C. Radio Manchester in 1980.

96 BESANT, Annie (née Wood). 1847–1933. *Annie Besant: An Autobiography*. T. Fisher Unwin, 1893. 368 pp.; front. port.; illus.; preface; astrological chart; index. NUC pre56 50:688.

Born in London. Father: William Persse Wood, physician, businessman, Anglo-Irish. Mother: Emily Mary Roche. 2 brothers. Married 1867, Rev. Frank Besant; separated 1873. 1 son; 1 daughter. Social reformer; feminist activist; Theosophist; birth control activist; religious/spiritual writer; physician's daughter. Upper middle class.

Spiritual journey of a heralded feminist, socialist, educator, and Theosophist from Christianity to atheism to Theosophy, 1847–91. Chart of the author's horoscope; advising readers to judge her character by astrological indications. Family's being penniless after father's death, author's age 5. Moving to Harrow; mother's taking in Harrow pupils as boarders; author's brother attending Harrow. From age 8, author's receiving free private schooling from well-off spinster Florence Marryat, a devout Christian; being introduced to books of Christian allegory; yearning to be a religious martyr. At age 18, becoming engaged to an Anglican vicar; imagining role of vicar's wife as chance for charitable self-sacrifice. Marrying, age 20; being shocked by reality of sex; resenting husband's attempted domination. Selling stories to the *Family Herald;* being immensely pleased with the money; discovering it was legally her husband's. Births of her son and daughter, 1869 and 1870; nursing her daughter through whooping cough; losing her own health; consequently doubting God's goodness. During next three years, losing her faith while having to profess belief as clergyman's wife. Husband's giving her ultimatum: take Communion or leave. Author's choosing to leave; taking daughter with her, 1873. Working as a housekeeper; planning to make a home for her mother; mother's death, 1874. Meeting atheist Charles Bradlaugh, 1874; joining Bradlaugh's National Secular Society. Explaining atheism as faith in humanity rather than in an imaginary God; noting atheism's moral dedication to human betterment. With Bradlaugh as mentor, launching a public speaking career; speaking on women's political status and atheism, 1874–75. Working for Bradlaugh's parliamentary campaign, 1874; lecturing and publishing

National Reformer with him. In 1877, their publishing an American birth control pamphlet; being tried for disseminating obscene material. Author's explaining to her readers Malthusian views of overpopulation's threat; need for reliable birth control. Losing custody of her daughter due to trial's notoriety. Studying for a science degree at London University, 1878; earning teaching certification in chemistry, botany, mathematics, physiology, and physics; teaching at the Hall of Science. Bradlaugh's being elected to Parliament, 1880; being ejected for refusing to take Anglican oath; finally being seated, 1884. Author's attending Fabian lecture by George Bernard Shaw, 1885; joining the Fabians and adopting socialism. Severe unemployment, 1885–87, provoking "Bloody Sunday" labor riots in Trafalgar Square; author's meeting investigative journalist W. T. Stead there; author and Stead's cofounding a weekly paper, *The Link,* to address abusive labor conditions, child labor, and prostitution. Author's creating the phrase "White Slavery" in her 1888 exposé of conditions for women workers in a match factory. Participating in matchgirls' strike against phosphorous poisoning; helping them organize a union, 1889. Writing review of Madame Blavatsky's *The Secret Doctrine,* 1889; believing book held great spiritual truths; going to meet Blavatsky; joining the Theosophical Society. Embracing her new spiritual beliefs; formally resigning from the atheistic National Secular Society, 1890. With deaths of Bradlaugh and Blavatsky, 1891, author's entering new phase of her life; effectively becoming British leader of the Theosophical Society.

Besant's earlier autobiography, **97** *Autobiographical Sketches* (1885), ends with her embrace of socialism. Written in midlife, both accounts stop short without charting Besant's later important work in India. By ending this second autobiography with her sense of triumph at finding the true faith, Theosophy, Besant avoids discussing the later scandals which nearly destroyed Theosophy and Besant's reputation. After Blavatsky's death, Besant began to receive spirit communications—letters in unknown handwriting suddenly dropping down from ceilings—which were later exposed as fraud. A former Anglican priest, C. W. Leadbetter, scorned by Blavatsky, rose after her death to hold equal influence with Besant among the British Theosophists; however, after Besant moved Theosophy's headquarters to India in 1893, Leadbetter was accused of molesting prepubescent Indian boys and his trial blackened the Theosophists' image. Besant fought the scandals through hard work. She made India her permanent home and gradually widened Theosophy's mission to embrace improvement of India's educational system and Indian home rule. In 1898 she founded the first of several interracial schools in India. She actively began her campaign for Indian home rule in 1913, launching two Indian newspapers covering Indian public affairs and incurring the wrath of the British colonial administration. She was jailed for six months by the British in 1919 for her political activism; immediately afterward she was elected president (and only non-Indian member) of the native Indian Congress, which had embraced her nationalistic ideals. Not until 1923 was she finally superceded as national leader by the figure of Mohandas Gandhi, himself an early Theosophical convert. A complete and succinct account of Besant's life is available in the 1986 biography of her by Rosemary Dinnage.

98 BETHAM-EDWARDS, Matilda Barbara. 1836–1919. *Reminiscences*. George Redway, 1892. 354 pp. BLC to 1975 92:183.

Born at Westerfield Hall, Ipswich, Suffolk. Father: Edward Edwards, farmer. Mother: Barbara Betham. 5 siblings. Single. Wrote novels *The White House by the Sea* (1857), *Kitty* (1869), *Love and Marriage* (1884); travel books *French Men, Women and Books* (1910), others. Knew George Eliot, Barbara Leigh Smith Bodichon, John Stuart Mill, others. Travel writer; novelist; antivivisectionist; foreign resident (France). Rural gentry.

Upbringing, intellectual life, and social observations of a prolific novelist and travel writer, 1836–92. Childhood memories of rural Suffolk: anecdotes and legends; attending school, age 4; describing local characters. Noting class snobbery of local Anglican church; most farmers' attending Nonconformist chapel. Acquiring early love of literature; reading Harriet Martineau's social reform works in childhood; regretting that in her family girls were not expected to be educated, but instead to wait on their brothers. Recalling local women farmers; calling female landownership "a capital argument on behalf of female suffrage." Discussing moral standards and education of Suffolk farmers. Attending day school, age 10; becoming skilled in French language and literature. Describing her life as a pupil-teacher, age 12, at a young ladies' school with low ethical and intellectual standards; becoming friends there with her first cousin, Amelia Blandford Edwards, later a famous Egyptologist. Writing her first novel, age 20. Living in Germany as governess to a baron's children, 1862. Living in "semi-Bohemian" Paris. Returning to Suffolk. Anglican clergy's supporting slavery during American Civil War; author's consequently distancing herself from Church of England. Moving to London. Admiring principles of atheism proponent Charles Bradlaugh. Attending meetings of International Working Man's Association, presided over by Karl Marx, 1867–71. Becoming friends with writer George Eliot. Seeing women's suffrage as a matter of "abstract justice," with little attraction for her. Discussing educator Emily Davies's plans for a women's university. Author's lacking enthusiasm for the idea; feeling academic education would have inhibited geniuses like the Brontës and George Eliot; also asserting the special value of women's ethical sensibilities; fearing their degradation by a scientific education that would force women students to practice vivisection. Traveling to Leipzig; gaining access to literary circles abroad through friendship with critic George Lewes. Visiting Goethe and his family at Weimar. Meeting Franz Liszt. Discussing her friendships with Catholic clergy. Closing with her own poem, "The Bridge of Years."

In tracing the origins of her social awareness and writing career, Betham-Edwards discusses a wide range of religious, cultural, and educational factors influencing her late-19th-century development. Because she subscribes to the Victorian idea of women's moral nature being superior to that of men, she acknowledges women's rights but is reluctant to see women inadvertently become more like men through higher education. Betham-Edwards's familiarity with vanished social and religious patterns in rural England lends considerable interest to her autobiography, as does her familiarity with the characters of George Eliot and her cousin Amelia Blandford Edwards. The latter, a well-known novelist, travel writer, and Egyptologist, is discussed at greater length in Betham-Edwards's second memoir, **99** *Mid-Victorian Memories* (1919), which also recalls other distinguished professional women with whom the author was acquainted. Betham-Edwards's writings on France and Algeria—**100** *A Winter with the Swallows* (1867), **101** *Anglo-French Reminiscences* (1900), **102** *Home Life in France* (1905), **103** *In French Africa* (1912), and **104** *Under the German Ban in Alsace and Lorraine* (1914)—express her anti-Catholic prejudice, indignation at Prussian oppression in occupied Alsace-Lorraine, and curiosity about Arab culture in Algeria. For her writings on France, the French government in 1891 conferred on Betham-Edwards the title *Officier de l'instruction publique de France*.

105 BIELENBERG, Christabel. 1909–s.l.1971. *The Past is Myself*. Chatto & Windus, 1970. 285 pp.; foreword; prologue; "Dramatis Personae." BLC to 1975 32:157. (other eds.: Corgi, 1968, 1970, 1984.)

Born in Totteridge, Hertfordshire. Father: Percy Collingwood, Irish, advertising director. Mother: Christabel Burton. Uncle: Lord Rothermere. 1 sister. Married 1934, Peter Bielenberg, German, attorney. 3 sons. Foreign resident (Germany); anti-Nazi activist. Upper class; married into foreign culture.

Perilous experiences of an Englishwoman with a German husband under the Nazi regime in Germany, 1932–45. Attending a Paris finishing school; making her social debut; being assured by her parents that she would have financial independence when she married. Moving to Hamburg, 1932; becoming a German citizen by marrying a young law student in Hamburg. Observing the rise of Nazism. Couple's moving to Berlin; participating in an underground anti-Hitler network, 1939. Author and husband's planning to emigrate to Ireland. Before being able to leave, husband's being drafted into the German army; author's fleeing to Denmark with their children, but soon returning to Germany. Moving to Rohrbach in the Black Forest. Details of German daily life during WWII. Lacking the courage to employ a Jewish fugitive as her housekeeper. Sheltering an American airman. Husband's participating in plot to assassinate Hitler, July 1944; husband's arrest and imprisonment; the hanging of his underground colleague, Adam von Trott zu Salz, a Rhodes scholar in the German Foreign Office. Death of husband's father. Author's going to Berlin to seek news of her imprisoned husband. Visiting husband in Ravensbruck concentration camp; receiving secret message providing her with answers he gave in his interrogation; voluntarily undergoing Gestapo interrogation to corroborate his story; winning her husband's release. Their moving to Ireland; author's depicting their new life there. Regaining her British citizenship in 1946.

Of the few accounts written by British citizens trapped within Germany during WWII, most are from prisoners of war; Bielenberg's book merits attention for her role as an ordinary—if naturalized—citizen who observed Germany's transformation during the rise of the Nazi Third Reich. Bielenberg's status as outsider facilitated her objectivity in this memoir; her British origins and democratic values also very likely played a part in the willingness of the author and her husband to join the anti-Nazi underground, something most of Germany's residents were either too patriotic or too fearful to do. Her depiction of the underground's agenda and operations gains breadth from comparative reading with Anita Leslie's *Train to Nowhere* (1948), which discusses the activities of the French Resistance working covertly within Nazi Germany. In 1968, Bielenberg's memoir was awarded the Richard Hillary Memorial Prize for its contributions to WWII history.

106 BINNIE-CLARK, Georgina. 1871–c.1947. *A Summer on the Canadian Prairie*. Edward Arnold, 1910. 311 pp.; front.; illus. NUC pre56 58:119.

Born in Dorset. Father: Arthur W. Binnie-Clark, innkeeper. Mother not named. 5 siblings. Single. Emigrant (Canada); pioneer; farmer; journalist; feminist activist; political activist. Middle class.

The struggles, stumbles, and eventual success of British emigrants in adjusting to farm life on the Canadian prairie, c.1905–07. Embarking from England with her sister Hilaria to meet their brother Lal in Canada. Being discouraged about her writing career in England; planning to settle in New York as a writer after visiting Canada. Arriving in Montreal; noting the leveling of social class in Canada among emigrants from different social strata; hoping that Canada's good climate and food would improve English emigrant children's health. Describing their difficult rail journey from Montreal to Winnipeg. Sisters' reuniting with Lal; discovering his plans to sell the homestead and acquire a dairy farm near Winnipeg. Sisters' being distressed by Lal's dislike of homesteading; reminding him of their father's commitment to homesteading plans; persuading Lal to show them the homestead. Discussing conditions of Canadian farm workers. Meeting Lal's lazy, incompetent partner. Sensing that Lal was lazy also; perceiving his homesickness for England; sisters' deciding to try to prevent loss of investment money their father had sent Lal. Despite trying conditions and hard work, author's enjoying the physical beauty of the prairie. Discussing homesteading; difficulties of getting a patent to their land. Receiving visits from Anglican parsons; describing life of a Protestant minister on the prairie. Hilaria's becoming disgusted with Lal; eventually leaving. Author's planning to extend homestead by buying nearby wheat farm. Discussing homesteaders' views on taxes for local schools. Enlisting help of mothers and emigrant teachers in campaign for local school. Condemning Lal's laziness; pointing out the greater prosperity of their diligent neighbors. Describing individual neighboring farmers from the British Isles and Hungary. Hilaria's returning after unsuccessfully seeking work in Winnipeg. Sisters' nursing Lal through illness. Author's buying a wheat farm near Fort Qu'Appelle, despite father's opposition and Lal and Hilaria's unwillingness to help her. Proposing to work the farm herself; purchasing mares and farm equipment. Lal and Hilaria's consenting to help her on the farm.

Binnie-Clark and her siblings helped claim the prize of landownership that their innkeeper father dreamed of back in England. Serving as a newcomer's guide to the ins and out of Canadian homesteading, her book paints the author and her siblings as rather amiable and ordinary young people who suffered due to their illusions and inexperience with rural life. This is a good source on emigration to Canada and Canadian settlement, with much observant commentary about frontier social adjustments and daily duties in the lives of homesteaders. In **107** *Wheat and Woman* (1914), the author traces the ways in which pioneer life and feminism became inextricably linked for her in turn-of-the-century Canada.

108 BLACK, Catherine. c.1883–?. *King's Nurse—Beggar's Nurse, by "Blackie."* Hurst & Blackett, c.1939. 256 pp.; illus. NUC pre56 59:414.

Born in Ramelton, County Donegal, Ireland. Father not named, linen draper. Mother not named. 3 brothers; 3 sisters. Single. Knew Eva Luckes, Ernest Morris, Sidney Holland (later Lord Knutsford), Edith Cavell. Nurse. Middle class.

Vocational decision, training, and diverse professional experiences of a longtime nurse, c.1895–1936. Recalling the contrast between her strict Calvinist father and lively mother. Noting mixed religious influences in her village; its Catholic priest and Presbyterian minister's being both friends and rivals. Being well-educated at a private school; making early decision to become a nurse. Family's opposing this because author was the eldest; their assuming she would care for younger siblings after leaving school. In 1900, nursing's just beginning to be honorable employment for educated women. Commenting on nursing profession before and after Florence Nightingale. Being turned down, age 18, for nurses' training by City of Dublin Hospital; being accepted by a hospital on the south coast of England. Working in an East End London hospital, 1901; describing appalling conditions in surgical theatre and wards. During WWI, nursing in France, 1916: treating shell-shocked officers and those with self-inflicted wounds; participating in general Allied retreat of March 1918. Returning to her East End hospital after the war; working through the 1920 typhoid epidemic. Being hired as personal nurse to King George V, 1928; tending him until his 1936 death; sketching his character, describing Princesses Margaret and Elizabeth. Commenting on nursing as a profession and the progress of medical discoveries. Traveling to Australia, 1936; seeing how nurses lived in the outback.

Black's chosen title rightly indicates the unusual scope of her nursing experiences in tending people from both the lowest and highest levels of Britain's class structure. Charming as are her observations of the Windsor family during the reign of the much-beloved King George V, her comments on 20th-century conditions of medical treatment for the poor in London's East End have greater value and suggest how lingering inequities in the British class structure permeate every physical aspect of existence.

109 BLACKBURN, Elizabeth Knibb. 1902–s.l.1980. *When I Was a Little Girl: A Bunch of Childhood Memories, 1907–1916*. Burnley: Brown, 1982. 73 pp.; front. port.; illus. by Frances Carlile; note to the reader. OCLC 12076175.

Raised in Blackburn, Lancashire. Father not named, mill worker. Mother not named, former teacher. Factory worker; trade unionist. Working class.

Formative experiences of a trade unionist, set amid general memories of life in pre-WWI northern England, 1907–16. Living among an extended family, including many cousins too old to play with. Mother's detesting housework; having been forced to give up teaching because of her marriage; living a disappointed life. Parents' attending adult school run by Society of Friends; author's attending Methodist Sunday school with her best friend, Polly. Attending coeducational Council School, age 6. Discussing her childhood reading, including the Bible; noting mother's worry over her indiscriminate secular reading. Recalling mother's teaching her about the birds and bees. Parents' being members of Workers' Educational Association. Leading a mock protest at school, 1912, over boys receiving a half-holiday which girls were denied: making "Votes for Women" signs and singing suffrage songs. Author's and mother's supporting the suffragettes. After start of WWI, receiving a certificate to leave school and go to work in the mill, age 13. Joining the union with Polly, 1916. Weaving war supplies at the mill. Attending a trade union meeting; being the only woman present. Attending a Quaker meeting; getting to know Quaker conscientious objectors. Discussing her love of poetry. Recalling holiday in Wales; constrasting its pastoral scenes with her customary industrial surroundings.

Blackburn wrote this booklet when she was past age 70. In it, she reconstructs her early life from a child's viewpoint and in a child's voice, using each chapter to recall a single year from 1907 to 1916. Blackburn apparently worked in the mill all her life and was active in improving labor conditions, and her commentary on how feminist and suffragist thinking penetrated even the consciousness of rural schoolchildren is one of this memoir's most interesting aspects. In a previously published work, *In and Out the Windows* (1980), the author discusses more extensively the particulars of mill workers' existence in her native Lancashire.

110 BLACKWELL, Elizabeth (M.D.). 1821–1910. *Pioneer Work in Opening the Medical Profession to Women. Autobiographical Sketches by Dr. Elizabeth Blackwell.* New York: Schocken Books, 1977. 264 pp.; preface by Dr. Mary Roth Walsh; intro.; letters; apps. NUC pre56 59:670. (1st pub. Longmans Green, 1895.)

Born in Bristol, Avon. Father: Samuel Blackwell, sugar refiner. Mother: Hannah Lane. 3 sisters; 5 brothers. Sisters-in-law: Antoinette Brown Blackwell, 1st American woman minister; Lucy Stone, women's rights leader. Single. 1 adopted daughter. Wrote *The Laws of Life* (1852). Knew Lady Noel Byron, Fanny Kemble, Bessie and Barbara Rayner Parkes, Leigh Smith, Florence Nightingale. Physician; academic; school founder; foreign resident (U.S.). Middle class.

Formative personal and professional experiences of the first woman to earn a medical degree in the U.S., covering 1821–1906. Growing up in Bristol. Her pious Protestant parents' having a happy marriage; ensuring their children felt loved. Until age 11, receiving a broad-ranging education from her governess. Moving to New York City with her family, 1832; attending primary school. Family's moving to Cincinnati, Ohio, author's age 17. Her father's death. Enrolling at Geneva Medical College in Geneva, New York, 1847; serving residency at Blockley Almshouse; graduating with honors from medical school, 1849. Moving to France; studying midwifery at La Maternité in Paris; losing sight in one eye; consequently giving up her goal of becoming a surgeon. Taking the "water cure" at Grafenberg, Germany. Studying at St. Bartholomew's Hospital, London, 1850. Pursuing self-study through reading, library research, informal visits to hospitals and clinics. Taking further medical courses in Liverpool and London. Returning to New York, 1851, to practice medicine. Rejecting marriage in favor of her career; adopting a daughter, author's age 33, to dispel her loneliness. Actively supporting the medical career of her younger sister, Emily. Establishing the New York Infirmary for Women and Children with Emily and Dr. Marie

Zakrzewska (author's student and protegée), 1857. Becoming the first woman listed in the Medical Registry of the United Kingdom, 1859. Discussing the American Civil War; expressing her abolitionist opinions. Serving as medical advisor to the Ladies Sanitary Aid Association, helping soldiers and recruiting nurses. Founding a medical school for women in the U.S.; establishing a three-year program and an examining board of independent physicians, 1868. Returning to England to live, 1869. Attending various denominational churches, but forming no strong affiliation. Joining Josephine Butler's movement to repeal the Contagious Diseases Act; denouncing the sexual double standard for promoting the spread of venereal disease. Assisting Sophia Jex-Blake in opening the first medical school for women in the United Kingdom, the London School of Medicine for Women, 1874. Revisiting the United States, 1906.

As her book's title forthrightly proclaims, Blackwell was a leader in opening the medical profession to women and uses her autobiography mainly to document her work in making a medical career a possibility for women in general. Many excerpts from Blackwell's correspondence with relatives and friends, as well as passages from her journal, contribute to the book's overall portrait of social prejudices barring her path, c.1900. In her preface to the 1977 edition, Dr. Mary Roth Walsh notes that, although other women practiced medicine in America before Blackwell, the latter was the first to earn a degree from a medical college.

111 BLACKWOOD, the Hon. Alicia. 1818–1913. *A Narrative of Personal Experiences and Impressions During a Residence on the Bosphorus Throughout the Crimean War.* Hatchard, 1881. 318 pp.; illus.; app. (notes and letters). NUC pre56 59:688.

Born in England. Father: George Frederick Augustus, Viscount Kilcoursie. Mother: Lady Sarah Coppin. 1 brother. Married Dr. Blackwood, Anglican minister, chaplain to British troops at Great Barrack Hospital, Scutari. Nephew: Lord Kilcoursie. Knew Florence Nightingale, Mary Seacole, Lady Stratford de Redcliffe. Nurse (Crimean War); clergyman's spouse. Aristocracy.

Record of humanitarian services in the Crimean War shared by a nurse and her clergyman husband, with her commentary on social conditions in a Moslem society, 1854–56. After news of the Battle of Inkerman, 1854, author and husband's deciding to serve in the Crimea. Husband's joining the army as military chaplain before departure. Describing their voyage to the Crimea and arrival in Scutari. Depicting miseries of patients in Great Barrack Hospital. Author's furnishing their married quarters; struggling to find good servants. Describing her husband's ministry at hospital; his converting many dying soldiers. Recounting Florence Nightingale's many good works at the hospital; author's being assigned by Nightingale to care for 250 soldiers' wives; extensively describing misery of these women, who suffered from disease, vermin, and insufficient medical attention. Expressing worries over British unpreparedness for Crimean War; blaming British officers for plight of soldiers' wives. Establishing shelter and dispensary for these wives; facilities' being plagued by insects and rats. Opening a school for soldiers' children. Praising Nightingale's advice and abilities. Visiting Turkish women; describing their subjugation; feeling that education and Christianity would gradually make them fight for their own equality. Observing procession of Sultan and his wives to a mosque. Purchasing a horse, "Sultan." Nurses' treating more casualties from Sebastopol and Redan. Author's helping establish a missionary school for the children of German Jews. Cofounding a lending library for soldiers. Receiving news of the fall of Sebastopol. Taking advantage of short holidays to see Therapia and the Black Sea. Assisting women of the Polish Legion at Scutari. Coping with cholera epidemic among German troops at Great Barrack Hospital. Depicting her husband's role in the deputation that won religious freedom from the Sultan for foreign troops; Sultan's also guaranteeing foreigners' right to purchase land; his promising to establish roads, railroads, a regulated Customs House, and a European-style bank. Recalling proclamation of peace, 1856. Bringing her horse, Sultan, back to England. In later years, returning with her husband to the Crimea; visiting old battlefields. Visiting Mary Seacole's shop near Balaklava. Returning to England; living in Yorkshire and Hertfordshire.

Blackwood writes that she was moved to create this autobiography from her diaries by the 1880 death of Sultan, the horse she adopted from the Crimea, who was her last reminder of these years. As a 19th-century Englishwoman with fairly advanced ideas, Blackwood got an eye-opening education in Moslem gender inequities through her Crimean war work. While her record of her nursing experiences is valuable, her first-hand commentary on Turkish society stands as one of the few from Englishwomen other than diplomatic wives, and goes far to illuminate the private attitudes of Turkish women to their traditional second-class status. This is one of the best overall sources on the nonmilitary aspects of the Crimean War.

112 BLOMEFIELD, Mathena. pre-1880–d.a.1944. *The Bulleymung Pit: The Story of a Norfolk Farmer's Child*. Faber & Faber, 1946. 157 pp.; front.; intro. by Lilias Rider Haggard; illus. by Mildred E. Eldridge. NUC pre56 61:495.

Born in West Norfolk. Parents not named, farmers. 2 brothers; 3 sisters. Married, husband not named. Children. Farm child; children's author. Rural farming class.

Vivid memories of Norfolk farm life in the author's Victorian childhood, c.1870s–1880s. Describing her childhood home and flower garden. Feeding dogs and rabbits, goat and ducks; asking father's permission to nurse the runt piglets back to health; tending her pet mice. Her chief companions' being animals; having no near neighbors and no siblings near her own age. Being partly crippled from early leg injury and unable to walk to school; being given reading lessons by her sister Rachel. Taking her Jew's harp with her everywhere. Imagining conversations between animals. Going hunting with the rabbit catcher. Recounting local belief that a neighborhood scold, "Slapcabbage Sal," practiced witchcraft. Family's attending weekly market day at the nearby town; taking Saturday baths; attending church services. Describing vanished home remedies. Children's collecting eggs; catching eels in pit ponds; helping with the annual threshing. Recounting many animal stories. Helping to rescue a foal from drowning. Being traumatized when her rescued piglets were slaughtered for meat. Receiving a tortoise in the mail, not knowing how to care for it; being bitten by a monkey at a tea party.

The "bulleymung" of the title refers to buckwheat, which Blomefield's great-grandparents grew on the family farm; the "pit" is Norfolk for pit pond. Part of Blomefield's ability to evoke the complex social milieu of her youth so vividly lies in her decision to return to a child's viewpoint in her writing, incorporating dialogue between her animals in a matter-of-fact way. The text, which often uses Norfolk dialect, is written in the third person; Blomefield refers to herself as "Nessel," her father's pet name for her. Her sequels, **113** *Nuts in the Rookery* (1946) and **114** *Bow-Net and Water Lilies* (1948), expand upon her childhood memories, recording Norfolk folktales about Spring-heeled Jack, her brief school attendance before her leg injury, Harvest Home teas, and rural Christmas customs.

115 BLOOM, Ursula (Sheila Burns, Mary Essex, Rachel Harvey, Deborah Mann, Sara Sloane, Lozania Prole, pseuds.). 1893–1984. *Without Make-Up*. Michael Joseph, 1938. 288 pp.; front. port. NYPL 1911–71 81:212.

Born in Chelmsford, Essex. Father: James Bloom, Anglican vicar, teacher, writer. Mother: Polly. 1 brother. Married 1916, Sir Arthur Denham-Cookes, d.1918. Married Gower Robinson, naval officer. 1 son. Wrote over 520 books, including *No Lady Buys a Cot,* a humorous WWII incident (1943); *Me—After the War,* advice to young women entering the postwar labor force (1944); *No Lady in the Cart* (1949); *Victorian Vinaigrette,* a commentary on the Victorian age, (1956); *Sixty Years of Home* (1960). Novelist; journalist; advice writer; clergyman's daughter; military spouse; dressmaker. Middle class; married into upper middle class.

Prolific novelist's childhood, writing endeavors, and troubled marriages, highlighting her family-induced fears about sex and intimacy, 1893–c.1930. Disliking her sickly brother. Family's moving to

Whitchurch, near Stratford-on-Avon. In childhood, being shy and self-conscious about being fat. Recalling her early attempts at writing; scheming to make a fortune as an author. Totally lacking formal education: at age 3 teaching herself to read; reading in her father's library; from age 9 learning about life from reading novels; receiving some lessons from her parents. Retrospectively wishing she had been born with a confident male outlook on life. Her family's enjoying friendships with sensational novelist Marie Corelli, actress Ellen Terry, and publisher George Grossmith. Author's clergyman father's indulging in passionate flirtations; author's becoming terrified of sex and its secretiveness from her father's self-justifying confessions. Spurning an older suitor. Describing virtuous character of her mother; feeling alienated from her father; discussing her "mother-fixation." Starting serious writing efforts in adolescence. Having become good-looking; being made miserable by unwanted attentions. Being conscripted as unwilling confidante to her father's *amours*, her mother's also demanding sympathy about her bad marriage. Escaping her parents via her writing; emulating literary style of Marjorie Bowen's novels. With mother, leaving father's home; her parents' separating legally. Suffering from gossip about the family scandal. Attending concert by pianist Margaret Cooper; taking Cooper's successful career as indirect inspiration for her own ambitions. Unsuccessfully attempting a stage career. Mother's breast cancer. Making and breaking two engagements. Moving with mother from St. Albans to Walton-on-the-Naze. During WWI, her mother's health's worsening, her brother's enlisting in the army, author's playing piano in a cinema many grueling hours daily. Legally forcing father to help support family. Becoming engaged to Denham Cooke; escaping family plight by marrying him without love. Loathing her first husband and in-laws; describing her punishing, irrational mother-in-law. Pregnancy. Discovering her husband's alcoholism. Mother's death. Learning that her father planned to marry his mistress; making full disclosure of father's conduct to the archbishop of Canterbury, resulting in father's suspension from Anglican orders; feeling shame afterward at having done this. Birth of her son. Attempting to earn her own money through dressmaking. Husband's worsening alcoholism and death in 1918 flu epidemic. Discussing her financially troubled widowhood. Resolving to support herself with a Fleet Street journalism career; teaching her son at home; writing her first novel. Discussing her interest in Theosophy, c. 1920, with its doctrine of eventual justice through reincarnation. Establishing relationship with Gower Robinson; reconciling with her father. Marrying Robinson; settling in London, 1928; this move's making her writing career much easier.

In this private memoir, Bloom avoids putting on the cheerful front that glosses over personal events in her other amazingly prolific autobiographical writings. Here, she delves with candid absorption into her parents' rift, her childhood fears, and the intensely ambiguous importance of sexuality in her life; she notes, for example, that her life "really began" when she was 11 years old at a Christmas party, because it was the first time that a man took notice of her. Bloom's efforts constitute a classically literary autobiography aimed at making developmental sense of the author's early memories, although the conflict between her father's promiscuity and his clerical orders forms an important secondary focus, one that helps illuminate the Anglican priesthood's troubles in an era of increasing secular permissiveness. Bloom's later volume, **116** *Life Is No Fairy Tale* (1976), covers the same years as *Without Make-Up,* but omits discussion of her writing in favor of close examination of her irresponsible father, her besotted first husband, and her demented in-laws; it includes photos of herself and family members. Her tone is breezier and more flippant in the remainder of her autobiographical writings, which include **117** *Mistress of None* (1933) and **118** *No Lady with a Pen* (1947), both about her writing career; **119** *The Log of No Lady* (1940), depicting her evacuation from London during WWII; and **120** *Time, Tide and I* (1942), surveying social changes in her lifetime. In **121** *No Lady in Bed* (1944), Bloom deals humorously with her own experiences with illness. Her volume **122** *The Changed Village* (1945) is effectively a social history of Whitchurch since her childhood, while **123** *No Lady Meets No Gentleman* (1947) studies courtship customs of the author's youth. Both **124** *The Elegant Edwardian* (1957), a portrait of her parents, and **125** *Youth at the Gate* (1959) also look closely at how WWI affected her generation.

126 BLOOMFIELD, Georgiana, Baroness Bloomfield (née Liddell). 1822–1905. *Reminiscences of Court and Diplomatic Life.* Kegan Paul, Trench, 1883. 2 vols. Vol. 1: 341 pp.; front.; preface. Vol. 2: 348 pp.; illus. NUC pre56 61:583.

Born in London. Father: Thomas Henry Liddell, 1st Baron Ravensworth. Mother: Maria Susannah Simpson. 15 siblings. Married 1845, the Hon. John Arthur Douglas Bloomfield, minister plenipotentiary to Russia, 2nd Baron Bloomfield. Knew Queen Victoria. Diplomat's spouse; foreign resident (Russia). Aristocracy.

Author's childhood and married life within British and Russian aristocratic circles, emphasizing the author's associations with royalty at both courts, 1822–1850s. Describing her large family of siblings; being distant from siblings married before her birth; having nephews older than herself. Recalling family's Portland Place residence. At age 4, attending children's ball at St. James's given by George IV. Being schooled by a governess. Playing boys' games with her brothers; cutting off her own hair to be like a boy. Enjoying rich fantasy life with fairies at Ravensworth, the family castle in County Durham. Death of her oldest brother Charles, the heir, 1832. At age 13, being only daughter left at home;

becoming her father's companion. At age 15, receiving Anglican confirmation by bishop of London in the Chapel Royal. Mother's example and character. After departure of her governess, becoming almost head of household, age 16. Attending Queen Victoria's coronation, 1838. Meeting poet William Wordsworth and ornithologist James Audubon during her youth. Being presented at Court, age 17; accepting post of maid of honour to Queen Victoria; living at Court three months each year. Extracts from mother's letters of advice to her at Windsor. Extracts from the author's diary and letters to 1844. Meeting her aristocratic husband-to-be; marrying in 1845; departing for his diplomatic post in St. Petersburg. Describing social life among the Russian aristocracy there. Mother's death, 1845. Returning to London to care for her husband's dying father, 1846. Returning to St. Petersburg; traveling in Russia and Finland. Extracts from her travel correspondence with her husband, 1848. Describing poverty of Russian villages. Extensively describing the Russian imperial court and its customs.

Extracts from Lady Bloomfield's diary and correspondence predominate after the early part of Vol. 1; the latter third of this volume consists almost entirely of lengthy diary entries covering several months at a time, with occasional, brief commentary on the people or events described. Vol. 2 is compiled entirely from diary entries. Lady Bloomfield's role as the daughter of a family with established diplomatic ties lends authority to her descriptions of the Russian Imperial Court, as well as to her innocent perceptions of the cruel contrast between imperial opulence and peasant poverty in Russia, fifty years before Russia's first socialist revolution. This is a fascinating memoir, both for its naive trust in eternal royal prerogatives and for its insider descriptions of rituals, politics, and personal attitudes in Russian and English royal courts of the early 19th century.

127 BLUNT, Fanny Janet Sandison, Lady. 1840–d.a.1901. *My Reminiscences*. John Murray, 1918. 316 pp.; intro. by Admiral Sir Rosslyn Wemyss; preface; illus.; index. NUC pre56 62:193.

Born in Therapia, near Constantinople, Turkey. Father not named, British Consul in Turkey. Mother not named. 4 sisters; 1 brother. Married 1858, Sir John Blunt, vice-consul at Uskub, Albania. 1 son. Wrote *The People of Turkey* (1878). Knew archaeologist Heinrich Schliemann, philanthropist Angela Burdett-Coutts. Diplomat's daughter; diplomat's spouse; foreign resident (Turkey, U.S.). Upper class.

Youth and married years spent in the Near East by a woman born and married into British diplomatic culture, 1840–1901. Growing up in Brussa, Turkey; describing her father's duties there as British consul general. Reading travel books to entertain herself. Author and siblings' taking lessons with children of American missionary at Brussa. Family's being stricken with cholera, author's age 10; death of one sister. Start of

Crimean War, author's age 14; living through a great earthquake in Brussa the next year. Attending balls in Brussa, 1850s; being in demand as one of the only English girls there. Living with her sister in Bitholia (Monastir), 1858; meeting and becoming engaged to the British consul to Albania; their discussing whether to be married by Turkish, Roman Catholic, or Greek Orthodox rites. After wedding, 1858, accompanying husband to his successive consular appointments; living with him in Uskub (Albania), 1858–60; in Macedonia, 1861–62; in Adrianople, 1862; and in Belgrade, 1865–71. Birth of her son, c.1870. Returning with husband to Macedonia, 1872–76; commenting on foreign intrigue in Bulgaria; massacre of the consuls at Salonika, 1876. Visiting Schliemann's Trojan excavation, 1876. Traveling to England, 1878; meeting Angela Burdett-Coutts, the philanthropist who had helped Turkish refugees in the Russo-Turkish War. Writing *The People of Turkey* the same year. In 1880, husband's being appointed consul general in Salonika; burning of the British Consulate at Salonika, 1888; author and family's finding temporary quarters. Visiting Egypt, 1895–95; outbreak of Sudanese War, 1896; her son's beginning a military career with the Connaught Rangers. Accompanying her husband on his appointment as consul in Boston, 1898–1900; his receiving knighthood, 1898. Explaining the extensive duties of a consular wife.

Blunt's observant presence in Turkey during both the Crimean War and the years in which Britain secured its colonial presence among Moslem states makes her autobiography absorbing reading. Formally a citizen of Britain, she grew up entirely outside its borders with an openness to Eastern culture that resonates throughout her book. Although the existence of a diplomat's wife is necessarily peripatetic, Blunt was in her element, fulfilling childhood fantasies of travel. Historians interested in Blunt's career as a diplomatic hostess will gain further insight by reading Anne MacDonell's *Reminiscences of a Diplomatic Life* (1913). An exact contemporary of Blunt, MacDonell followed her consular husband to posts all over the globe, and her easy adaptation to such a footloose existence mirrors Blunt's own ready accommodations.

128 BOLTON, Sybil and Glorney Bolton. c.1903–s.l.1978 (Sybil). *Two Lives Converge: The Dual Autobiography of Sybil and Glorney Bolton.* Blackie & Son, 1938. 246 pp.; front. port. NUC pre56 65:113.

Born in Basutoland, South Africa. Parents not named. Maternal grandfather: James Roberts, industrialist. Siblings. Married 1936, Glorney Bolton, journalist. 1 daughter. Journalist; short storyist; literary critic; secretary; environmentalist; traveler (Canada, U.S.). Upper middle class.

Sybil's portion of this shared autobiography, including her travels, development as a writer, and impressions of English, Canadian, and South African societies, c.1903–38. Living in Basutoland, South Africa. Family's moving to Milner Field, her maternal grandparents' home.

Recalling her grandfather's career as an industrialist. Family's moving to Edinburgh, then to Dublin; later settling in Yorkshire. Author's attending boarding school and convent school in Holland during WWI; recalling shortages due to the war. Describing changes in manners and hospitality after WWI. Working as private secretary to a girls' school. Relocating to Canada; working as a stenographer in Montreal; learning to ski. Visiting the U.S.; recalling her unfavorable first impression. Writing for the *Montreal Star,* reviewing books; being promoted to interviewer; interviewing Sylvia Pankhurst and the prime minister of Quebec Province. Traveling to Vancouver. Working as a liaison to foreign consulates. Becoming interested in environmentalism. Recalling the financial crash of 1929 and resulting social problems in Canada. Traveling to England by cargo boat, 1929; encountering her journalist husband-to-be; remaining unimpressed by the meeting. After returning to Montreal, covering Prime Minister Ramsay MacDonald's 1929 visit. Returning to England, 1932. Becoming reacquainted with writer Glorney Bolton; describing his liberal political views and friendship with Gandhi. Selling her first short story. Taking a cottage in Sussex. Visiting her father in Vienna. Marrying Glorney, 1936. Birth of their daughter, c.1937.

This book includes alternating chapters on the lives of Sybil and Glorney Bolton. Although light on dramatic incident, these chapters—covering the author's and her husband's journalistic development in very different venues, from Canadian dailies to *The Times of India*—offer a broad picture of journalistic philosophy, training, and practice in the early 20th century. Rather than being exceptional in their own right, Sybil and Glorney Bolton and their colorful journalistic and marital partnership are representative of a professional media trend in their era.

129 BOND, Alice (née Hurd). 1896–s.l.1980. *Life of a Yorkshire Girl.* Hull: Bradley Publications, 1981. 120 pp. BLC 1976–1982 6:111.

Born in Brantingham, East Riding, Yorkshire. Father: George Hurd, farmer. Mother: Elizabeth. 11 siblings. Married Edwin Bond, engineer, d.1970. Widow. 1 son. Farm child; teacher; photographer. Rural laboring class.

Vignettes of a Yorkshire youth, followed by familial and professional memories and experiences, c.1900–1980. Growing up in small cottage on the estate of a "big house," Brantingham Thorpe. Some family members' working and living at the manor house; this "relieving crowding" in the cottage. Author and siblings' walking many miles to school. Living in three different villages before age 6. Attending a village girls' school endowed by the lady of the manor; noting "the big house was a power for good"; pupils' writing on slates, learning basic literacy by rote; being caned for misbehavior. Vicar's proposing to adopt her, age 9; mother's refusing, although "sending one away" to receive greater advantages was a common practice. Working as a carrot weeder, age 12; noting that women received only half as much pay as men for field work; young women's often preferring domestic service, which provided free food, lodging, clothing, and training in housewifery. Large families' being viewed by parents as "insurance" against having nobody to care for them in old age. Author's describing children's chores: scrubbing the privy, selling human manure as "night soil," washing the clothes, cooking mash for the pigs. Author's father's farming from dawn to dusk; winning prizes and fame for his vegetables at fairs. At age 13, author's winning scholarship as an "intended teacher" to boarding school; describing differences between cooperative life at home and the competitive female community at school; feeling that her intellectual ambitions were never fully accepted at home. At age 19, author's entering Hull Municipal Training College, 1915. Winning her first teaching assignment in Driffeld. Receiving and rejecting three proposals of marriage. Her father's death, 1918. Taking a post closer to family home but enjoying living in her "own digs." Playing tennis at a club; meeting her future husband there, an engineer who shared her literary interests. Marriage; having to give up teaching because married women were not employable as teachers. Moving with husband to the West Riding, Yorkshire. Their being unable to afford a car; riding a motorcycle; author's having a nearly fatal accident. Finding work as a photographer by answering an advertisement. Having one child; returning to domesticity; discussing monetary struggles during the Depression years. Enjoying close ties with her in-laws in Cambridge. After death of her husband, 1970, resolving to see the world; starting her journeys at age 74. Despite widowhood and old age, being determined to maintain her independent life.

Reaching back in time to her rural Victorian upbringing, Bond is mindful of the idiosyncracies of habit, artifact, and attitude that mark this earlier era in her native Yorkshire, and she describes them with a meticulous attention social historians will appreciate. Also of interest is her book's depiction of her family's status as feudal retainers, a type of social arrangement that is nearly extinct. Bond's personal evolution holds the narrative together, as she progresses from 19th-century notions of women's place to 20th-century ideas of women's intelligence and initiative. This is one of the better sources on regional Yorkshire, especially in its survey of the interplay between rural and urban lifestyles.

130 BOND, Jessie (Charlotte). 1853–1942. *The Life and Reminiscences of Jessie Bond, The Old Savoyard. As Told by Herself to Ethel Macgeorge.* John Lane, The Bodley Head, 1930. 244 pp.; front. port.; preface; intro.; illus.; index. NUC pre56 65:425.

Born in Camden Town, Greater London. Father: John Bond, musician, piano maker. Mother not named. At least 2 brothers, 2 sisters. Married c.1870, F. A. Schotlaender, Liverpool Choral Society director; divorced c.1872. Married 1897, Lewis Ransome, civil engineer, died c.1928.

Widow. 1 child. Singer (popular); actress (stage). Lower middle class; married into middle class.

Career and personal reminiscences of light opera singer/actress, 1853–1930. Having a mother who loved theatre; recalling her own early desire to act. After family's moving to Liverpool, studying the piano. Acquiring an early aversion to domestic work. Joining the choral society in Liverpool; performing in musical entertainments, giving concerts. Studying voice; singing with a Benedictine church choir. Being nearly kidnapped by the director of the choral society; his persuading author to marry him and work for him permanently; abusing her after marriage. Childbirth; death of their 3-month-old child. Author's winning a divorce from her husband, c. 1872; returning to her parents' home; studying voice in London. Performing in London and provinces to favorable notices. Performing with D'Oyley Carte company in *H.M.S. Pinafore;* touring America. Starring in London in *The Pirates of Penzance, Iolanthe, The Gondoliers,* and *The Mikado*. Acting in *Patience,* 1870s; meeting Oscar Wilde, on whom the musical's principal character was based; finding him effeminate and affected. Meeting her husband-to-be as a stage admirer. Deciding to pursue acting instead of voice; regretting giving up serious music. Gilbert's supporting her acting ambitions, Sullivan's discouraging them. Giving a royal command performance of *The Gondoliers*. Noting rise of the suffrage movement; its causing disagreement among actresses. Marrying Lewis Ransome; his Quaker family accepting her despite initial objections to her profession. Having a happy marriage on the second try; husband's having great affection for her and sharing her musical tastes. Deaths of Gilbert and Sullivan. Her husband's death. Settling permanently at Worthing, the Sussex coastal town popular among theatrical retirees. In 1929 at age 76, producing a play at the Lyceum Theatre. Seeing artistic life as its own reward.

Ending this ghost-written autobiography on a note of active professional commitment despite her advanced age, Bond presents herself as not only a professional actress but as a sort of "new woman," in 1890s terminology, whose career came before any domestic responsibilities. Although Bond's memory may not match historical fact, since women had been carving out theatrical careers for themselves since the Restoration, it is of note that she consciously ties her endeavors to the 19th-century women's movement. One might wish that she would speak more directly about the suffrage movement, but Bond does show she is conscious of women's professional struggles and how this issue impacts on her own choice of vocation; it is also interesting that her second husband's family could still, in 1897, voice objections to her profession on religious grounds. Bond's enduring association with Gilbert and Sullivan and D'Oyley Carte, and her detailed accounts of many of their productions, make this a valuable resource for historians of popular culture.

131 BONDFIELD, Margaret Grace (Grace Dare, pseud.). 1873–1953. *A Life's Work*. Hutchinson, 1948. 368 pp.; preface; illus.; index. NUC pre56 65:473.

Born in Furnham, Somerset. Father: William Bondfield, foreman lace worker. Mother: Ann Taylor. 10 siblings. Single. Knew George Bernard Shaw, Beatrice and Sidney Webb, Mary Middleton, Margaret MacDonald, Amelia Hicks, others. Politician; member of Parliament; cabinet minister; trade unionist; feminist activist; suffragist. Working class.

Upbringing, career in English labor movements, and political life of England's first woman cabinet minister, 1873–1940. Growing up in a Nonconformist family with radical sympathies. Attending a private school founded by her female relatives; later attending another private school. After loss of her father's factory job, attending Chard Board School for poor children; discussing her inadequate education there. Working as a London shopgirl. Beginning her political career in trade union activities. Writing for the National Union of Shop Assistants under the pen name Grace Dare. Developing socialist views after seeing Yorkshire textile workers' appalling plight, 1910. Doing suffrage work, 1909–12; participating in the Independent Labour Party, Women's Labour League, and the Women's Co-operative Guild. First visiting U.S., 1910. Being hit hard by deaths of her Labour colleagues Mary Middleton and Margaret MacDonald; author's being sidelined by an emotional breakdown, 1911. Describing trade unionism during WWI. Being elected to parliamentary committee of the Trades Union Congress, 1918. Revisiting the U.S. as first woman delegate to American Federation of Labor, 1919. Traveling to the USSR, 1920, after Labour government formally recognized Soviet governing body. Death of fellow trade unionist Mary MacArthur, 1921. Serving as parliamentary secretary to Ministry of Labour, 1923. Being Labour M.P. for Northamptonshire, 1923–24, and Wallsend, 1926–31. Serving as minister of labour, 1929–31; being first woman to hold a cabinet position. Returning to the U.S., 1933; making further political visits to the U.S. after retirement. Commenting on her choice of career over marriage and her strong Christian commitment. Reflecting on 1930s politics.

In this detailed historical record of Bondfield's place in Britain's labor movements, information is arranged topically in businesslike paragraphs. As cabinet minister, Bondfield lost her support from the left after 1930, as she waxed increasingly conservative about treasury and unemployment policies. Her trade union organizational work continued until 1938, when she took on the roles of vice president of the National Council of Social Service and chair of the Women's Group on Public Welfare; she persevered in these obligations until age 76, four years before her death: As a loyal Labour Party operative during the turbulent post-WWI years in British government, Bondfield uses this book to contextualize her career rise against the many party turnovers, general elections, and labor strikes that darkened the economic landscape; her leadership of the labour ministry during Ramsey McDonald's second Labour government makes her autobiography one of the most immediate accounts of the period available.

132 BOOKER, Beryl Lee (née Cumming). c.1888–?. *Yesterday's Child: 1890–1909*. John Long, 1937. 263 pp.; illus.; index. NUC pre56 66:379.

Born at Blenheim Lodge, Oxfordshire. Father: Jack Cumming, army officer. Mother: Mary de la Rue. 1 brother; 1 sister. Married c.1910, her cousin Arthur Cotton, civil servant. 4 daughters. Society woman; foreign resident (South Africa, India). Upper middle class.

Author's 1890s childhood and Edwardian adolescence, against a rich backdrop of societal attitudes concerning gender roles and marriage, covering the author's first twenty years. Coming from military family: paternal grandfather and father's both having been cavalry officers. Adoring her father; being his favorite child. With her brother, living at a cousin's house during mother's last pregnancy; cousin's telling them making babies involved planting cake in sand and watering it with boiled milk; author's consequently acquiring dread of boiled milk. Wishing she were a boy; cutting her hair short; on special occasions, being allowed to wear brother's sailor suit. Parents' being unaware that cruel nanny terrorized the children; author's being starved and abused during summer holidays, 1895–96, when nanny had children to herself. Getting rid of her when family moved to London, 1896. Brother's being sent to boarding school; author's being tutored by governesses; envying her brother's formal schooling. Mother's sending author to a girl's boarding school in Broadstairs, c.1901. Describing its curriculum: academics, music, and deportment. Author's parents' preserving happy marriage by maintaining separate bedrooms and separate social lives; father's enjoying clubbing and sports, mother's running a fashionable "amateur" boutique, 1898–1902. Mother's taking author to Vienna to study piano, 1902. Father's losing his fortune; author's brother having to leave Eton in favor of a "cheap French school"; author's attending a cheaper girls' school in Eastbourne; noting dismissal of one lesbian teacher for propositioning students. Seriously considering her financial future: being barred from a career as pianist by spinal curvature; hoping to find a husband. Mother's promoting her in the marriage market; despairing over author's disregard for clothes and mania for dogs. Leaving school, age 17. Noting great changes in women's beliefs about marriage, from 1905 to the 1930s; women in 1905 seeing marriage as "the only gate to independence"; modern women seeing it as bar to their freedom. Attending dances and balls as part of business of finding a husband; making her debut, 1906; being presented at court. Accepting marriage proposal of her first cousin; implying she kept an eye open for other options. Seeking independence; going out alone to South Africa, 1907; experimenting with living on a farm. Returning to England, 1908; struggling to start an acting career; living miserably in a Kensington boardinghouse; deciding she could not advance without compromising her virtue. Marrying her cousin, 1910; noting that her marriage brought financial security: £500 yearly and a free house and carriage at his civil service post in India. Writing this memoir for her four daughters, ages 12 to 25; wanting them to know about the vastly different social circumstances of her youth.

Booker's rueful memoir of her youth contains illuminating descriptions of many turn-of-the-century social phenomena, from her parents' open marriage (presented as quite common among their social set) to her own open-eyed view of marriage as a career option. Of especial interest is her description of the covert abuse the children suffered from their nanny while the parents lived in ignorance, an assertion that mirrors and gives credence to similar statements in other women's autobiographies of the era. One is never quite sure where Booker's father's income came from, nor how he lost it; nor does she clarify under what circumstances her family was living on the estate of the Duke of Marlborough at the time of her birth. These gaps, however, do not impair the book's ability to convey many subtle nuances of British social convention and thought in the years before WWI.

133 BOOTH, Doris Regina (née Wilde). c.1900–?. *Mountains, Gold and Cannibals*. Cecil Palmer, 1929. 179 pp.; front.; intro. by C.W.C. Marr; illus.; glossary; index. NUC pre56 66:484.

Probably born in Australia. Parents, siblings not mentioned. Married Charles Booth, planter, miner. Planter's spouse; miner; foreign resident (New Guinea). Middle class.

Observations on culture and politics of native society in New Guinea, accompanied by personal travel and gold-mining adventures, 1924–27. Author and husband's deciding to mine in New Guinea goldfields, despite government's discouraging women from entering territory of hostile natives. Departing from Kokopo for Bulolo, 1924. Describing German mission station, a native funeral, and a native wedding. Husband's departing from station before author. Her arranging for native porters to carry their supplies; treating natives with medicines. Discussing cannibalism; viewing a human foot taken from cannibals. Supervising about 150 carriers; threatening them at gunpoint to avoid mutiny. Reuniting with her husband; their mining in Bulolo. Author's also managing a friend's mining claim. Striking gold on their claim, also on friend's; building a house in Bulolo. Author's training native boys to work the claim; having to bully them to establish her authority; sternly meting out punishment. Doing further prospecting in highlands near Edie. Treating a dysentery epidemic in Bulolo; operating a small hospital with up to fifty patients; mentioning her previous intern work at Brisbane General Hospital before marriage. Couple's deciding to leave New Guinea due to poor health; returning to Brisbane.

In this portrait of 1920s mining operations in New Guinea, Booth's primary interest seems to lie in depicting the natives and their customs. Although she expresses much concern for their health and sanitation, in fact the diseases for which she treated them were all introduced to New Guinea by European settlers. Photos in the book show her with the New Guinea natives she and her husband hired, panning for gold. Booth's reflections on the natives, mingling mistrust, impatience, motherliness, and intellectual superiority, offer the reader a close look at the complex attitudes of well-intentioned white colonials toward indigenous tribes in the early 20th century.

134 BOOTH, Mary Warburton. 1872–c.1947. *My Testimony*. Pickering & Inglis, 1947. 159 pp.; front. port.; illus.; foreword by Edith M. Brown; intro. by Elise Page. NUC pre56 66:511.

Born in England. Parents not named. Siblings. Single. Wrote a companion volume, *These Things I Have Seen,* about her missionary service among women and girls of India. Missionary/missionary's spouse (India); deaconess; religionist (Wesleyan); social reformer. Middle class.

A life of dedication to social reform programs in England and India, emphasizing interest in women's issues, set within a framework of Christian inspiration, 1870s–1944. Growing up in happy family; parents' deliberately refusing to give children religious instruction. At age 18, becoming fascinated with love and beauty radiating from a Christian friend; reading the Bible; deciding to become a Christian; giving up worldly pleasures. Attending Wesleyan class meetings with friend; wanting to be baptized. Deaths of her mother and sister. Deciding to commit herself to a life of service. Recounting her conversion experience. Reading interpretive aids to the Bible. Training to become a Mildmay deaconess; performing district visiting in the East End; starting a club for young men and Bible classes for men and women. Discussing lives of the poor and their social conditions; recounting conversion-inspired recoveries of alcoholics. Leaving East End for Mildmay, 1907; during deaconess training, feeling divinely called to serve in India. In India, living at Gorakhpur for the next thirty-six years. Studying Urdu and Hindi; taking language exams. Teaching Bible classes for Zenana women and English-speaking Indians; becoming frustrated over her lack of converts. Returning to Mildmay, 1914; not wishing to return to Gorakhpur, but praying and deciding to go. Anecdotes of conversion experiences among children and nominal Indian Christians. Author's describing her own experience of redemption. Praising the people of London, c.1940, for sending gifts to her mission while enduring WWII bombing. Converting many Hindu women. Being unworried about her mission's fate during wartime; trusting God to provide for their needs.

Booth's chosen title identifies her aim in this didactic book, which is to testify to her teaching mission in India as the product of God's hand in her life; the text includes many poems by Booth on Christian themes, as well as crudely hand-tinted photographs. Booth makes no mention of early educational efforts among Indian women, such as those of Theosophical Society; nonetheless her combined spiritual, educational, and social aims for these women extend earlier British missionary efforts and were directly instrumental in shaping the educational system India adopted as a free state. Printed in the year that India at last achieved independence from colonial rule, 1947, this memoir does not clearly indicate whether Booth lived long enough to experience this fulfillment of many of her hopes for Indian dignity.

135 BOSWELL-STONE, Lucia Catherine. 1806–1891. *Memories and Traditions*. Recorded with W. G. Boswell-Stone. Richard Clay & Sons, Ltd., 1895. 69 pp.; front port.; illus.; app. BLC to 1975 314:377.

Born in Dorchester, Dorset. Father: Edward Boswell, writer. Mother: Edith Feaver. Married 1831, Joseph Stone, county treasurer of Dorset. 1 son. Family historian; civil servant's spouse; spiritualist. Middle class.

Recollections of regional life in coastal Dorsetshire, 1806–c.1877. Dorchester history and families of longstanding, including her own; author's citing 1790s political events there from her aunt's diary; a naval midshipman's being hanged for forgery, c.1794, on the strength of her grandfather's testimony. Dorchester's having been the 18th-century site of "hang fairs"; people's traveling from neighboring counties to witness executions. Author's suffering loneliness as an only child; having recurrent nightmares of being pursued by death. Debating the merits of spiritualism to her readers. Attending day school in Dorchester; having her first psychic experience there by seeing her own double; seeing another apparition in a nearby town. Describing Anglican church services, c.1820, and women's contemporary home education stressing polite accomplishments and shortchanging academics. Recalling idiosyncracies of the local schoolmaster; his later dying mysteriously at sea, 1824. Neighbors holding frequent country balls; regretting being unable to dance well. Discussing living conditions of tenant farmers; their decreased prosperity after the end of the protective Corn Laws, 1831; their adjustment to having the vote under the Reform Bill of 1832. Recalling local Christmas rituals, foods, games, and pastimes.

Inheriting a lively regional historical interest from her father, author of *The Civil Division of the County of Dorset,* Boswell-Stone has written an account that effectively situates her own experiences of childhood there against the region's recent political and cultural history. As noteworthy as are her individual comments, whether on women's education during the Regency era, 18th-century judicial practices, or the spread of spiritualism, collectively they create a portrait of 18th-century and early-19th-century life that is particular to England's south coast.

136 BOTTOME, Phyllis. 1882–1963. *The Challenge*. Faber & Faber Ltd., 1952. 407 pp.; preface. NUC pre56 68:671.

Born in Rochester, Kent. Father: William Bottome, Anglican clergyman, American. Mother: Margaret Leathem. 2 sisters; 2 brothers. Married 1917, Alban Ernan Forbes Dennis. Wrote *Old Wine* (1926), *Private Worlds* (1934), *Heart of a Child,* many others. Novelist; traveler (U.S., Europe), clergyman's daughter. Middle class.

Study of the author's tense post-adolescent family life and the changes wrought by tuberculosis on her destiny, c.1900–1917. Beginnings of author's writing career, c. age 19, at same time as death of her sister Wilmett, mother's favorite; author's taking over Wilmett's dominant family position. Being diagnosed with tuberculosis; taking a sea cure as first of many therapeutic travels. Being anxious over exile from participation in the family; wryly noting mother's willingness for her to go; discussing mother's avoidance of her children's serious illnesses. Having already published one novel; resolving to continue her writing career despite tuberculosis. Memories of Elena, author's friend and traveling companion; recalling an earlier friendship with "K" and their breakup. One year after Wilmett's death, mother's being "frozen" in grief. Author's being unable to reach mother emotionally; moving in with Elena; visiting France and Italy with her. Staying in sanitorium at St. Moritz; discussing the town's daily life; befriending another female patient, Lislie. Moving into hotel at St. Moritz, age 21. Becoming friends with atheistic sanitorium physician; their sharing theological discussions. Being joyful at visit from her father; noting his anger and anxiety that she was not yet well. Spending summer in England; visiting Lislie's home and family; staying with Elena in Salisbury; feeling torn at leaving her family again for St. Moritz. Starting tentative romance with a fellow patient, Ernan. Joining Elena in Italy, c.1905; discussing pro-fascist Italians, her response to Italian art. Attending Easter confession; feeling finally absolved of guilt about Wilmett. Becoming engaged to Ernan. Traveling in Europe with mother and Ernan. Author and Ernan's consulting tuberculosis specialist in Davos, Switzerland; his predicting their complete recoveries. Reacting emotionally to deaths of fellow patients.

Spending another summer with family; noting resurgence of family ill feelings. Finishing her third novel. Discerning family conspiracy to prevent her marriage to Ernan; feeling trapped. Returning to Davos; suffering relapse. Staying several more years in Davos; visiting Lislie's home, but not her own. Separating from Ernan; both of them fearing commitment; realizing they had been raised to be cowards by weak, possessive mothers. Rejecting God because of Elena's death; lacking courage to keep living; investigating Alfred Adler's psychological methods for achieving wholeness. Befriending another writer who asked for her literary help; realizing writing was her Adlerian means to power. Spending winter in Rome with her friend Lislie, 1912. Closing her relationship with Ernan by destroying his photographs. Feeling herself a feminist but having ambivalent feelings toward suffragists; fearing their political aims might impair improved employment, higher education for women. Progressing in her family relations; loving her father more, identifying less with her mother. Experiencing setback after father's death; trying to remedy conflict between herself and mother; their spending winter in Rome together. Moving to London; writing short stories; starting lifelong friendships with Ezra Pound and dramatist Ivor Novello. Becoming reacquainted with Ernan in London. Describing London cultural life, c.1914. WWI: Ernan's joining the army; author's resenting her physical inability to help in volunteer war effort; working at Ministry of Information. Spending leaves with Ernan; reaching new level of understanding with him; deciding to marry. Describing wartime conditions of their marriage, 1917.

This volume is an extension of Bottome's self-styled autobiographical "fragment," **137** *Search for a Soul* (1947), in which the author uses her psychoanalytic understanding to study the complicated family personalities and relationships of her childhood: her oppressed clergyman father, her narcissistic, manipulative mother, and the author's own jealous hatred of her sister, Wilmett, who received all the family's love. Both volumes, however, trace Bottome's efforts to transcend self-pity and make a life for herself through her writings. In portraying the special psychological conditions of a tuberculosis sanitorium and the exaggerated sense of mortality that affects its residents, Bottome's book is evocative of Thomas Mann's *Magic Mountain,* although Bottome avoids Mann's choice to fictionalize her personal sanitorium experiences. Following the years covered in this book, she underwent intensive psychoanalysis with Alfred Adler. Bottome completed her life story with **138** *The Goal* (c.1973), which focuses on her work to educate the public about "individual psychology," Adler's chosen name for his discipline. In addition to her autobiographical works, Bottome's *Life of Adler* (1939), helps flesh out her personal understanding of the application of his theories.

139 BOURNE, Pamela (later Pamela Bourne Eriksson). 1908–?. *Out of the World.* Geoffrey Bles, 1935. 288 pp.; front.; illus. NUC pre56 161:400.

Parents not named. Single. Journalist; sailor; traveler (South Pacific Islands). Middle class.

Fast-paced nautical adventures of intrepid journalist-turned-ship's mate, accompanied by detailed recollections of exotic South Pacific locales visited, 1933–35. As journalist, receiving a pay raise from editor; celebrating by inviting her mother to join sea voyage from Cape Town to South Sea Islands, 1933, aboard the Norwegian ship *Thermopylae*. Volunteering to serve as ship's mate; eventually being accepted as part of crew. Sketches of the Norwegian crew. Reporters' beginning to follow her from port to port. Riding horses in Australia; visiting Australian ports. Sailing with her mother on a luxury cruise liner to Fiji. History of Fiji; describing natives and their customs; living on island for several months. Fijian folklore. Disapproving of missionaries' forcing their social and political customs on natives. Departing by freighter for Tonga. Perceiving that all missionaries exploited Tongans, and all except Mormons took money from them; discussing dearth of skilled jobs for educated Tongans. Meeting Tonga's queen. Making a difficult, roundabout voyage to New Zealand. Discussing Samoa's racial tensions over presence of half-castes. Living in Tahiti; marveling at promiscuity of the natives. Describing various tourists; going reef diving to escape the tourist hordes. Learning Swedish from her shipmates. Beginning to write about her experiences; disliking the result. Departing for New Zealand; taking walking tour of its South Island. Noting popularity of movie houses in the South Seas. Meeting rural inhabitants of New Zealand, spending Christmas with them. Touring back country on horseback; hiking out alone; visiting sheep station. Taking steamer voyage with mother up to Greenstone Valley. Mother's departure for England. Leaving Wallaroo; serving as ship's mate on return voyage. Relishing her life at sea and feeling "a horror of the land"; however, succumbing to the reality of life on land upon returning to Belfast.

Bourne's willingness to work as a crew member won her the respect of her fellow sailors, although she notes that scorn "is still the Anglo-Saxon attitude toward a woman who wants to be other things as well as a woman." Tracking her voyage through the South Seas culturally as well as physically, she creates a sociological study using the exotic practices she witnessed to make comparative commentary on European customs and thought. In later years Bourne married a Scandinavian mariner, and in 1958 she published a historical biography entitled *The Duchess: The Life and Death of the Herzogin Cecilie*.

140 BOWEN, Elizabeth Dorothea Cole (Mrs. Cameron). 1899–1973. *Bowen's Court and Seven Winters: Memories of a Dublin Childhood.*

Virago Press, 1984. 52 pp.; intro. by Hermione Lee. NUC pre56 70:285–86. (1st pub. The Cuala Press, 1942.)

Born in Dublin, Ireland. Father: Henry Bowen, barrister. Mother: Florence Colley. Married 1923, Alan Cameron, d.1952. Wrote *The Hotel* (1927), *The Death of the Heart* (1939), *The Demon Lover*. Novelist. Upper middle class.

Childhood until age 7 in a prominent turn-of-the-century Anglo-Irish family, emphasizing Irish cultural attitudes and history, 1899–1906. As a child, taking Dublin to be the model for all cities. Experiencing claustrophobic fears in unknown parts of the city. Not being allowed to learn to read until age 7; her great frustration. Family's attending Protestant services; author's growing to understand that Protestants were a minority; noting parents' detached attitude toward Roman Catholics. Her father's lapsing into mental illness; author and mother's staying near him during treatment in England. Bowen and Colley family histories and traditions; both families' having Irish Protestant obsession with owning land. Discussing Irish history, Anglo-Irish Dublin society. Discussing foreigners: continental Europeans being acceptable to the Irish, but the English (like her governess) being regarded as inferior. Anglo-Irish children's being raised to be obliging to adults and to each other; shyness being viewed as a deformity.

In this sensitive study of Anglo-Irish attitudes during her early childhood, Bowen brings back to life Ireland's principal city and people as they existed during the Edwardian period, in which a separation on many levels between the Protestant Anglo-Irish and Irish Catholics helped to determine the conditions of existence. With her father institutionalized, Bowen was left virtually an orphan by her mother's death in 1912; she embarked on an independent life through WWI nursing in Dublin, followed by postwar art studies in London, where she married Alan Cameron in 1923, at the same time as her stories were first published. Following her father's death, 1930, she inherited the family home in Dublin. Her many novels and plays tend to focus on the life experiences of women, and her last novels, *The Little Girls* (1964) and *Eva Trout* (1968), examine many psychological underpinnings of girlhood. In 1986, writer Patricia Craig produced a comprehensive biography of Bowen.

141 BOWEN, Stella. c.1893–c.1955. *Drawn from Life*. Collins, 1940. 253 pp.; intro. by Julia Loewe (author's daughter); illus. BLC to 1975 39:503.

Born in Adelaide, Australia. Parents not named. 1 brother. Single. 1 daughter. Knew Ford Madox Ford, Ezra and Dorothy Pound, Gertrude Stein, Alice B. Toklas, Edith Sitwell, Peggy Guggenheim, Ernest Hemingway, James Joyce, others. Artist (painter); art critic. Upper middle class.

Education and life struggles of a woman painter, focusing on her unmarried liaison with novelist and editor Ford Madox Ford, c.1900–1940. Being scantily educated by a governess; later attending a small private school. From age 17, studying art with teacher Rose MacPherson. Mother's death. Moving to England, age 20. Studying at Westminster School of Art in London under painter Walter Sickert. Describing England during WWI. Having a long-term relationship with Ford Madox Ford, 1919–30; discussing his neurotic personality and his other love affairs, especially with Caribbean novelist Jean Rhys. Author and Ford's sharing a Sussex cottage, 1919–22; birth of their daughter, 1920. Their living together in France, 1922–33. Author's describing her personal trauma caused by 1930 breakup with Ford; afterward, coming to value her independence. Vignettes from their social life among expatriates in Paris. Describing her practice of painting, primarily doing commissioned portraits in Sussex and France; being frustrated that she could not use more creative freedom. Suffering hardship during the 1930s Depression; art's being luxury item whose market disappeared. Returning to England, 1933; supporting herself for eighteen months as newspaper art critic. Raising her daughter; relying on servants for child care. Ford's death, 1939. Outbreak of WWII. Life in London, 1940; her fear of losing her new home to bombs.

Bowen's youthful memoir is fascinating on two fronts, both as a study of a woman's early-20th-century career struggles in the arts and as an eye-opening look from a victim's viewpoint at the man, Ford Madox Ford, who gave turn-of-the-century slogans about "free love" a bad name. Although Bowen passes lightly over the name of writer Violet Hunt, she was also—along with Bowen and Rhys—held sexually captive by the charms of Ford while he persuaded her that marriage was old-fashioned. While Bowen does not philosophize about the practical effects of changing sexual standards or gender roles, readers will be strongly tempted to apply her individual experiences to understanding these ongoing social phenomena.

142 BOX, Violette Muriel (née Baker; Baroness Gardiner). 1905–s.l.1990. *Odd Woman Out: An Autobiography by Muriel Box.* Leslie Frewin, 1974. 272 pp.; illus.; poems; list of plays, screenplays; index. NUC 1971–1977 15:184.

Born in Lime Grove, New Malden, Surrey. Father: Charles Stephen Baker, railroad clerk, gambler, violinist. Mother: Caroline Beatrice Doney Tyler. 1 brother; 1 sister. Married 1935, Sidney Box, writer, film entrepreneur. Married 1970, Gerald Baron Gardiner, barrister, member of the House of Lords. 1 daughter. Wrote many screenplays, plays, a biography of Gardiner, and a novel, *The Big Switch* (1964). Knew George Bernard Shaw, J. Arthur Rank, Lady Summerskill. Screenwriter; playwright; biographer; novelist; filmmaker; feminist; anti-nuclear activist. Middle class.

Author's family, educational background, and career progress as a screenwriter and film director, 1905–70. At age 7, developing romantic passion for musician friend of her father's, who served as her mentor. Describing family relations, including conflict with her mother; her parents' quarrels. Effectively filling parental role for her brother and sister. Attending Holy Cross convent school; studying dance, chorus, and acting. Attending Regent Street Polytechnic school. Recounting her stage apprenticeship; starting to work in film industry. Becoming increasingly socialist through influence of George Bernard Shaw. Enjoying long, productive marriage with Sidney Box; collaborating with him on plays and screenplays for all-female casts. Traveling to the U.S. after her film success. Taking holidays in Spain, France, Wales. Describing disruptions and influences of WWII. Censorship of her film, *The Truth About Women*. Publishing novel and screenplays on feminist, anti-nuclear, and socialist themes. Coming to terms with father's death. Mother's death at age 90. Discussing anti-Semitism in the Air Ministry. Marriage to Gerald Gardiner.

Box credits Virginia Woolf's *A Room of One's Own* with awakening her feminism, which serves as the genesis of the gritty women's roles that fill her plays and screenplays; she notes that Woolf effectively inspired her activism for women's equality. Box met her husband Sydney in 1935; eleven years later they shared an Academy Award for best screenplay for their collaboration on *The Seventh Veil*. In the 1950s she progressed from writing to directing, and in 1966 founded Femina Books, which she directed as a publisher dedicated to disseminating works with an interesting angle on women. From a historical perspective, perhaps her most noteworthy personal study is *The Trial of Marie Stopes* (1967), which places this early female family planner within the context of moral prejudices of her time.

143 BOYLE, Mary Louisa. 1810–1890. *Mary Boyle: Her Book (Reminiscences)*. Ed. by Sir Courtney Boyle, K.C.B. (author's nephew) and Lady Muriel S. Boyle. John Murray, 1901. 292 pp.; intro.; illus.; poetry; index. BLC to 1975 40:174.

Born in Cavendish Square, London. Father: Sir Courtney Boyle, vice admiral and commissioner at Sheerness Dockyard. Mother: Carolina Amelia Poyntz, lady of Queen Charlotte's bedchamber. 2 sisters; 3 brothers. Single. Wrote *The State Prisoner, a Tale of the French Regency* (1834), *The Bride of Melcha: A Dramatic Sketch* (1844), *My Portrait Gallery and Other Poems* (1849), *Tangled Weft: Two Stories* (1865), others. Knew Charles Dickens, Tennyson, Fanny Kemble, Benjamin and Mrs. Disraeli, others. Society woman; poet; novelist. Upper class.

Privileged Regency-era childhood and later life and friendships among England's literary and theatrical set, 1810–70. Relating her distinguished family history. Until age 8, living in family home at Sheerness. Enjoying supportive relations with her nanny, governess, and one brother. Recalling innocent flirtations while growing up. Having cousins who owned and managed Drury Lane Theatre; sharing her father's love of theatre. From author's age 8, family's living at Hampton Court while father lived in London; describing architecture of Hampton Court as royal residence. Her family's being friends with the playwright Sheridan family. Memories of relatives in the peerage; spending holidays at their Brighton estate. Attending Miss Poggi's boarding school; taking part in theatricals. Recalling elder sister's appointment as maid of honor to Queen Caroline, c.1820. Being taken on Continental tour, c. age 13; spending much time in Italy; meeting female sculptor Felicie de Vauveau and Caroline Bonaparte, sister of Napoleon. Death of William IV and coronation of Queen Victoria, author's age 27. Death of her father. Anecdotes of friends in the theatre world, including Charles Kean and Fanny Kemble. Discussing the 1848 French Revolution; its effect on Europe. Living in villa in Florence; establishing friendships with the Brownings, Walter Savage Landor, and other English residents in Italy. Returning to live in Devonshire. Doing amateur theatricals; thinking of becoming an actress; being encouraged by her friend Charles Dickens; never realizing her dream. Becoming close to Dickens's sister-in-law, Georgina Hogarth. Enjoying friendship with Benjamin Disraeli and family; also being friends with Sir Evelyn Denison, speaker of the House of Commons. Expressing her distrust of supporters of Prime Minister Gladstone, whom she believed were "undermining the constitution of England and imperilling the safety of the throne." Mourning the death of Dickens, 1870.

In Boyle's account of growing up within the circle of the royal Court, she documents the impact of contemporary political events on family life and her father's career, and she includes behind-the-scenes anecdotes regarding many of the influential figures in British 19th-century politics and literature. While she jests about her unrealized fame as an actress, she neglects to mention her serious vocation as a romantic novelist and her eleven published works in addition to this memoir. In the introduction, however, her nephew fulfills his function as editor by fleshing out the biographical details Boyle omitted.

144 BRADDOCK, Elizabeth (née Bamber) and Jack Braddock. *The Braddocks*. 1899–1970 (Elizabeth). Macdonald, 1963. 244 pp.; front. port.; illus.; apps.; index. BLC to 1975 40:309.

Born in Liverpool. Father: Hugh Bamber, bookbinder, newspaper worker. Mother: Mary Little, Warehouse Workers Union official. 1 sister. Married 1922, Jack Braddock, hide shipper, M.P. for Everton.

Politician; member of Parliament; social activist; WWII volunteer; Communist; anticommunist. Working class.

Inception and growth of an outspoken Northern English Labour M.P.'s political commitment and career, 1906–63. Recalling hunger among the unemployed in Liverpool during the winter of 1906–07; resolving, age 8, to devote herself to mending the gap between the haves and have-nots. Discussing her family's lean finances and interest in socialism; her parents' maintaining a strong moral sense. Attending socialist Sunday school until age 11; joining youth section of the Independent Labour Party. Leafletting with her mother; running errands for the Warehouse Workers Union. Witnessing "Bloody Sunday" police assault on 40,000 railway strikers, August 13, 1911. Attending National Council of Labour Colleges and the Workers' Education Association, where she "began to learn the political and economic history I had been denied in elementary school." Beginning to work, age 14, as a seed packet filler; working in drapery department of store until 1918; her mother's insisting author join union. While young, becoming interested in the suffragist movement. Joining the Communist party. Marrying Jack, author's age 23; his being sent to prison; author's being left in charge of his district of the Communist Party, including Lancashire, Cheshire, and North Wales; finding life with the Party "exciting, absorbing, and sometimes hilarious." Beginning to question Party policy from Moscow; realizing how little it helped economic problems in Britain; leaving the Party, 1924. Staying with families in tenement housing to investigate living conditions. Being elected to the city council. Jack's being reelected as city councilor despite being in prison for inciting a riot. Author's becoming full-time ambulance driver during WWII; training other drivers. Becoming Labour M.P. for Exchange Division, 1945: being first woman M.P. from Liverpool. Being very anti-Churchill; seeing his Conservative policies as reactionary and anti-worker. Serving as magistrate in juvenile court. Trying to begin urban redevelopment in Liverpool. Being suspended from House for misconduct. Serving on Port Sanitary and Hospitals Committee; describing unsanitary conditions in hospitals. Visiting Russia; recounting her disillusionment from seeing the Soviet Union. Addressing her constituents' problems; unsuccessfully trying to gain assistance for injured workers. Seeing Aneurin Bevan as "the influence which has done most to weaken the (Labour Party) movement since the thirties." Discussing the need for rank-and-file workers to combat Communists and Trotskyites in Great Britain, and thus preserve democracy.

Braddock's portion of this shared autobiography provides a graphic look at Liverpool's labor and economic problems during the industrial slowdown of the first decade of the century, clarifying the factors in the widespread acceptance of socialism, and outlining the influences that shaped her into a prominent advocate of the rights of the working class. She rises above her partisan political interest to provide an extremely useful account of the British Communist Party in the 1920s and of the inner workings of Parliament and the British legal system. Further augmented by her parliamentary husband's political evaluations, this book invites comparison with the political memoir produced by Labour M.P. Jennie Lee, *Tomorrow is Another Day* (1939). As wife of Labour M.P. Aneurin Bevan and a principal leader within the Labour Party in her own right, Lee's opinions diverge in important ways from those of Braddock; together, these two intelligent acounts provide a range of political opinion characterizing the era.

145 BRADLEY, Josephine. 1900–1961. *Dancing Through Life*. Hollis & Carter, 1947. 153 pp.; front. port.; preface; illus. NUC pre56 71:550.

Born in London. Parents not named. 7 siblings. Married 1927, Douglas Wellesley-Smith, WWI veteran, dance instructor, d.1931. Widow. Dancer; teacher (dance); broadcaster. Middle class.

Detailed observations on the history of ballroom dancing and author's dual roles as performer and teacher, covering c.1900–1945. Father's death, author's age 10. After death of author's sister from consumption, family's moving from smoky London to the Hertfordshire-Buckinghamshire border for author's health. Attending convent school; leaving school due to dress regulations; studying music at home. Playing piano for ballet class; leading class during holidays; having her gift for dancing recognized. Taking ballet lessons in London. Joining the Three Arts Club, a club for women in the arts, c.1917–18. Describing London night life. Adoring jazz and ballroom dance; deciding to give up ballet. Noting that after the 1918 Armistice, public interest in dance intensified. Describing 1920s jazz clubs, dancers, fashions for men and women dancers. Teaching dancing to blinded WWI veterans. Winning dance competitions with her American partner, G. K. Anderson, 1920; their remaining unbeaten through 1924; author's becoming world's foxtrot champion. Beginning her own dancing school. Judging dances at Queen's Hall Championship. Training six women dance champions of the 1920–1930s. Developing new dancing style, adapted to faster tempos and crowded dance floors. Traveling to Paris to learn the tango. Her membership on first committee representing the Ballroom Branch of the Imperial Society of Teachers of Dancing, 1924; standardizing dance techniques and soothing traditionalists opposed to "vulgar" dances. Conducting examinations to certify dance teachers. Courtship and marriage; dancing with her husband in Munich competition; being traumatized by his death from stroke, 1931. Making dance tour of America, 1932; training dance teachers in Copenhagen; making her comeback as professional dancer. Touring Holland, Norway, Denmark, and France, 1934–39. Giving up her studio at start of WWII; inaugurating the tradition of Grosvenor House tea dances. Living and touring in New Zealand and Australia, 1940–41; teaching dance at Presbyterian College in Melbourne. Traveling to South Africa, 1941; doing radio broadcasts there. Returning to England, 1942. Opening new dance studio in Kensington, 1945.

At the outset, Bradley announces that her didactic book is designed to promote community feeling among ballroom dance teachers and to show the general public that ballroom dancing is an art with both a scientific basis and benefits for health. However, her book serves two important additional functions, both as an historical record of ballroom dance during the 20th century and as a study of what was effectively a secular ministry for Bradley in the field of dance; the reader may well be struck by the parallels between Bradley's worldwide missionary efforts and those of earlier figures in service to Christianity. For a close look at the parallel growth of British ballet in the same years, dancer and choreographer Ninette de Valois's memoir, *Come Dance with Me* (1957), should be consulted.

146 BRAY, Anna Eliza (née Kempe). 1790–1883. *Autobiography of Anna Eliza Bray*. Chapman & Hall, 1884. Ed. by John A. Kempe (author's great-nephew). 356 pp.; front. port.; preface; intro. NUC pre56 73:275.

Born in Newington, Surrey. Father: John Kempe, landlord, bullion porter at the mint. Mother: Ann Arrow. 1 brother; 1 sister. Married 1818, Charles Alfred Stothard, artist, d.1821. Married Edward Atkyns Bray, vicar, d.1857. Widow. 1 daughter. Wrote *Warleigh: A Legend of Devon* (1834), *Courtenay of Walreddon: A Romance of the West* (1844), *Joan of Arc* (1874), *Life of Thomas Stothard, R.A.* (1851). Knew Robert Southey, George Stubbs, Mary Colling, John Murray. Novelist; biographer; historian. Middle class.

Romance novelist's upbringing, friendships among Romantic-era writers, and thoughts on the practice of writing, 1790s–1843. Family history; her grandfather Nicholas Kempe's noted 18th-century literary and artistic friends. Author's having been born amid a Christmas morning lightning storm, and dropped in the font at her baptism. In childhood, suffering an eye inflammation which permanently weakened one eye. Being kept home due to her mother's dread of disease; having a "very miscellaneous education at home" until age 10. Attending her godmother's school, ages 10–12; returning home permanently when her best friend died; mother's fearing further contagion. Participating in amateur theatricals at home; admiring actress Mrs. Siddons. Planning a stage career; abandoning it due to her nervous disposition. Becoming engaged to and marrying artist Charles Stothard, 1818, son of historical painter Thomas Stothard. Charles's having ambitions to copy Bayeux tapestry; author's accompanying Charles to Bayeux in Normandy for this purpose. Publishing her letters home to her mother; receiving favorable reviews; deciding on a writing career. Recalling furor over George IV's 1920 trial of Queen Caroline for allegedly poisoning her own daughter. Pregnant author's being shattered by husband's death in fall from a painting scaffold, 1821; giving birth to a daughter one month later; baby's death, age 7 months. In husband's honor, publishing a biography of her royal academician father-in-law. Wondering what constituted successful fiction, the works of Sir Walter Scott being her principal model. Being proud of her friendship with Robert Southey, then poet laureate; describing his character; his encouraging her career. Assessing novels of Daniel Defoe and Samuel Richardson; objecting to the questionable morality of writers Jean Jacques Rousseau and Madame de Staël. Discussing her courtship and marriage to Reverend Edward Bray. Confiding several inspirations of her novels; noting attack on her novel *The Protestant,* set in the time of Queen Mary, for its historically founded anti-Catholic sentiment. Befriending working-class poet Mary Colling; helping her get her poems published. Extended excerpts from her correspondence with Robert Southey; his death, 1843.

In this slightly scattered work, Bray sighs over herself as an impulsive person who takes on projects she regrets. As editor (and possibly anticipating curiosity over Bray's avoidance of customary upper-class charitable activities), her great-nephew amplifies this character portrait: "Mrs. Bray was too impulsive in her benevolence, too excitable in her sympathies, too credulous, too nervous, and indeed too variable in health for anything like useful visiting among the poor." Whatever the impulses of her nature, they served her well as a romantic novelist; although her works are forgotten today, during the whole of her writing career they sold respectably to a public still fond of Scott's romanticized histories and other works of the same ilk. She left autobiographical notes up to the year of her second husband's death, 1857, but the editor found them too fragmentary for publication; thus the account ends with the death of Southey, a date that seems to mark for Bray the close of the Romantic literary era in which she flourished. The editor's introduction provides a brief sketch of the last thirty years of her life.

147 BRIGHTWEN, Eliza (née Elder). 1830–1906. *Eliza Brightwen: The Life and Thoughts of a Naturalist.* T. Fisher Unwin, 1909. Ed. by W. H. Chesson. 215 pp.; front. port.; intro. & epilogue by Edmund Gosse; illus.; index. NUC pre56 75:568.

Born in Banff, Scotland. Father: George Elder. Mother: Margaret Elder. 5 siblings. Married c.1854, George Brightwen, senior clerk, d.1883. Widow. Wrote *Inmates of My House and Garden* (1895), *Glimpses Into Plant Life* (1897), *Quiet Hours with Nature* (1904), others. Knew writer Edmund Gosse. Naturalist; nature writer. Upper middle class.

Evolution of a naturalist, together with an extended journal of her later writing years, 1830s–c.1900. After her mother's death, author's age 7, being adopted by her uncle Alexander Elder, founder of Smith & Elder publishers; going to live in his country house in Streatham. Being "horribly shy"; loving nature. Discussing her isolated early life; having no companions her own age; recalling her uncle's kindness and aunt's harshness. Moving with them to Thornbury Park, near Stamford Hill, age 8. Learning about birds and insects on uncle's ten acres; seeking answers about animals in her uncle's library; praising his wisdom in letting her learn on her own. Receiving a pet donkey from another uncle. Feeling lonely, lacking female friendship. Briefly attending boarding school, age 12. Family's rarely attending church; youthful author's worrying about excessive accumulation of sin. Family's wintering in Paris, 1847–48; visiting Belgium before returning to England. Grieving over midshipman brother's shipboard death from cholera, 1849. Meeting George Brightwen through friends. Becoming engaged; feeling she would grow to love George; marrying him; being happy. Having seen marriage as a way to escape her aunt; nevertheless feeling sad to leave uncle. Appending a journal, recording her development and popularity as a writer of books about animal behavior and nature.

The writings in this book are in three sections: "Autobiography," "Thoughts," and "Journal"; only the autobiographical section on Brightwen's professional life has been annotated for this entry. Introduction and epilogue writer Edmund Gosse had been trained in natural history by his father Philip Gosse, one of the foremost paleontologists of the late 19th century; he uses his personal acquaintance with Brightwen and her writings to fill in gaps in her narrative, such as the omission of her husband's death. The journal section, tracing Brightwen's career as a self-taught naturalist and author, helps to place her within the natural history tradition and profits from comparative reading with naturalist Frances Pitt's memoir, *Country Years* (1961). Pitt's account records a youthful enthusiasm for nature and animals that mirrors that of Brightwen, although Pitt's 20th-century career provides illuminating professional and educational contrasts to that of Brightwen a century earlier.

148 BRITNIEVA, Mary. 1893–1964. *A Stranger in Your Midst*. Arthur Barker, 1936. 344 pp.; front. port.; preface by Arthur Barker. NUC pre56 76:671.

Born in St. Petersburg, Russia. Father: Charles H. Bucknall, English businessman. Mother not named, Russian. 3 brothers; 3 sisters. Married 1918, Alexander Britniev, Russian physician, d.1931. Widow. 1 son; 1 daughter (Lady Maria St. Just). Nurse (WWI); foreign resident (Russia); translator. Upper class.

Memories of a British subject who married a Russian and experienced persecution by the Soviets, and her subsequent life in England, covering 1914–35. During WWI, serving in Russia as Red Cross Sister of Mercy; meeting her future husband, a doctor. Recalling Bolshevik rise to power; noting political peril of British subjects in Russia. Author's family, other Britons being hounded by the Cheka (secret police); parents' and siblings' escaping to England, 1918. Husband's being forced to serve as Red Army doctor in the Russian Civil War. Births of their children. Describing onset of Russian famine; author's contracting tuberculosis; children's being ill from malnutrition. Author's departing for England with children; their recuperating while living with her parents, 1922–24. Describing English suspicions of Soviet emigrés like herself; resenting being treated like an outcast; recalling her very English nanny and English school she attended, although in Russia; thinking of herself as British. Corresponding with her husband; counseling him not to emigrate for fear of suspicion, her fears coming true with his arrest as accused spy; author's returning to Russia, securing his release. Returning alone to England, 1925. Discussing her children's schooling in London and their sense of English identity. Taking a summer holiday with her children in France, 1926. Wanting children to continue speaking Russian. Visiting husband in Russia, 1927–28. Returning alone again to England. Husband's finding work as a ship's doctor, visiting author periodically when his ship came to London. Struggling to raise children on her salary as translator; paying for daughter's ballet lessons and son's prep school. Learning of husband's second imprisonment following mass arrests of former intelligentsia, 1930; returning to Russia to help him, 1931; being shattered by news of his execution, 1931. Returning to England; tutoring students in foreign languages; working as a private nurse. Her daughter's entering the Ballets Russes de Monte-Carlo; her son's continuing his public school education. Living with emigré friends; doing odd jobs and private nursing. Visiting friend in Berlin. Visiting USSR with children, but realizing they must not stay there. Returning to England.

Similar ground is covered in **149** *One Woman's Story,* published earlier in the same year (1936). However, Britnieva adds information about her later years in England and her final visit to Russia. Withholding none of her emotional responses, Britnieva draws the reader intimately into her family's perils as official foreign nationals during the Russian Revolution. She provides invaluable details of life in the newly created USSR c.1918–31, charting the efforts of the populace to replace the culture the revolution had superceded against a background of coercion by the secret police. In her later years in England, Britnieva translated the memoirs of Diaghilev ballet set designer Alexander Benois, advised on the production of Russian plays, and taught Russian in Cambridge and London.

150 BRITTAIN, Vera Mary. 1893–1970. *Testament of Youth: An Autobiographical Study of the Years 1900–1925*. New York: Macmillan, 1980. 661 pp.; preface; foreword. BLC 1976–1982 7:51. (1st pub. Victor Gollancz, 1933; other ed.: Fontana, 1978.)

Born in Newcastle-under-Lyme, Staffordshire. Father: Thomas Brittain, paper manufacturer. Mother: Edith Bervon. 1 brother. Married 1925, George Catlin, professor. 1 son; 1 daughter. Wrote *The Dark Tide* (1923), others. Close friends with Winifred Holtby. Political activist; feminist; pacifist; public speaker; socialist; novelist; poet; nurse (WWI); WWII volunteer. Upper middle class.

Coming of age of a feminist and pacifist before, during, and after the cataclysm of WWI. Having an idyllic prewar childhood. At age 8, praying for the sick King Edward VII to recover; her prayer's evident success giving her a sentimental religious faith ultimately destroyed by WWI. At day school, older girls' forcing frightening sexual information on her. Being sent, age 13, to boarding school for fashionable young ladies. Yearning to enter Oxford; headmistress's encouraging her, but ill-preparing her for entrance exams. Other girls' finding her peculiar for loving studies. Entering Somerville College; discovering its poverty compared to men's colleges. Going through coming-out rituals; flirting with Roland Leighton, another Oxford student. After start of WWI, horde of male students' volunteering for war; academic life's being completely disrupted. Roland's enlisting, departing for France. Author's volunteering for wartime nursing; being posted at Devonshire Hospital; describing patients and treatment. Being shaken by Roland's battlefield death; growing angry at war's evils. At Roland's Catholic funeral service, fighting disbelief in God; writing her poem "May Morning" about his funeral. Transferring to hospital on Malta; nursing German P.O.W.s. Recognizing legitimacy of pacifists' aims. Returning to nursing in London. Fearing for her soldier brother; receiving news of his death; her consequent despair. Consciously rejecting duty to "God, King, and Country." After the armistice, Oxford's having an intellectual Renaissance; author's resuming her interrupted student career. Writing her poem, "The Lament of the Demobilised." Befriending feminist Winifred Holtby. Publishing "The Point of View of a Woman Student" in *Oxford Outlook;* its marking the serious start of her writing career. Realizing she could never tolerate unequal marriage; as postwar feminist, deciding that self-support and freedom from marriage were the only acceptable life. Lecturing to promote the League of Nations. Learning about problems of the poor; tending increasingly toward political rather than charitable solutions. Becoming active in the Society for Constructive Birth Control and the Six Point Group. Publishing her social history, *The Dark Tide*. Evaluating political situation between Germany and England, c.1924. Marriage.

Prominent in Brittain's retrospective is her unappeased resentment against the British governmental powers, which she indicts for having embroiled her generation in a pointless conflict. However, she makes no attempt to account for the origins of the well-nigh universal idealism with which her male friends went off to immolate themselves in the war, tacitly suggesting that she found this as natural as breathing. A valuable work that chronicles how war catalyzed a permanent change in the public outlook, Brittain's book has less to say about the origins of her feminism, making it seem not acquired but bred in the bone. She continues her autobiography in **151** *Thrice a Stranger* (1938), which documents her experiences in and reactions to American culture and society. Spanning the era of post-WWI optimism to pre-WWII pessimism, *Thrice* traces the author's increasing feminism and her interest in socialist principles. A more detailed picture of her role in Britain's WWII involvement is set out in *England's Hour: An Autobiography, 1939–1941* (1941). **152** *Testament of Friendship: The Story of Winifred Holtby* (1942) focuses on the author's close friendship with writer Holtby; Brittain charts the growth of mutual support and admiration between them as she takes over the task of finishing Holtby's literary work after Winifred's early death. In **153** *Testament of Experience: Autobiographical Story of the Years 1925–1950* (1957), Brittain situates her developing career and political work against the condition of pre- and post-WWII Western society. This volume in particular highlights her dedication to pacifism and social justice and depicts Brittain's emotional commitment to humane ideals as having reached full maturity.

154 BRITTEN, Emma Hardinge. 1823–1899. *Autobiography of Emma Hardinge Britten*. John Heywood, 1900. Ed. by Mrs. Margaret Wilkinson (author's sister). 275 pp.; front. port.; preface by J. J. Morse; "In Memoriam," by Will Phillips. NUC pre56 77:21.

Born in England. Father not named, sea captain. Mother not named. 1 brother; 1 sister. Married 1870, Dr. William Britten, American, d.1894. Widow. Wrote *History of Modern American Spiritualism; Nineteenth Century Miracles; Wildfire Club; Faiths, Facts, and Frauds of Religious History;* others. Published magazines *The Western Star* and *The Unseen Universe;* edited newspapers *The Two Worlds* and *Christian Spiritualist*. Knew Robert Dale Owen; mediums Dan Home, Judge Edmonds, Mrs. Fox and her daughters, Mrs. E. J. French. Spiritualist; clairvoyant/psychic; teacher (music); public speaker; religious/spiritual writer; publisher; editor. Middle class.

Spiritualist's upbringing, discovery of her psychic powers and widespread career in England and U.S., 1820s–1890s. Being born with the spiritual gifts peculiar to mediums; as a child, craving the solitude of churches and church ruins; seeing visions, hearing voices, uttering prophecies; servants' believing her visions and prophecies. Studying music. Experiencing profound despair upon death of her father, author's age 11; being sent out to support the family as a pupil-teacher of music. Feeling emotionally disturbed, entertaining thoughts of suicide; hearing her father's voice bidding her to return to school. Going to Paris to pursue music studies; abandoning opera training after losing voice from screaming in her sleep; mother's stopping her work as pianist and composer upon learning author had clairvoyant powers and could intuit what pieces her audience wanted to hear. Returning to England; beginning an acting career; continuing acting in Paris, London, and New York, age 19. Being introduced to New York spiritualists, 1856; her initial skepticism's being overcome by receiving messages from many dead friends and her dead brother. Convincing her mother of the reality of spiritualism. Describing table-rapping sessions; author's automatic writing. Taking training from the well-known public medium, Mrs. Kellogg. Sitting as "test" medium for all who required her services. Meeting other mediums from several nations. Quitting her stage career; fearing she would lose her femininity if she obeyed the spirits' commands to lecture on spiritualism. Editing the *Christian Spiritualist;* giving piano lessons. Overcoming her qualms about lecturing. Public speaking and composing music in trances. Giving talks in U.S. prisons and in Canada. Confronting hostility from audiences and local Christian clergy; being pursued by a mob in New York; resenting narrowmindedness of orthodox Christianity. Spirits' asking her to stop being a "test" medium, telling her they cannot communicate through her if she continues. Lecturing in East, Midwest, and South, 1859–60. Receiving unwanted attentions from romantically inclined impostor mediums. Lecturing in California and Nevada, 1863–64; donating $20,000 she earned to the Sanitary Fund for the Union Army; campaigning for Abraham Lincoln. Returning to England, 1866; having a vision of American Indian spirits invading England, destroying churches, entrusting the cross of St. Paul's to her "until the people of earth know better how to use it." Marriage to Mr. Britten in New York, 1870; their making many trips across the Atlantic. Leaving the American Spiritualist movement because of its association with "free love." Lecturing and debating in Australia and New Zealand with her husband, 1878. Returning to England, c.1881; mother's death. Residence in Manchester. Husband's death, 1894.

Charting not only Spiritualism's practice but the accompanying cultural phenomena of fraud, trickery, and opportunism, Britten lets her audience know that she has weathered them all and means to separate the real from the fraudulent for her readers' benefit. Consequently, her writing carries an aura of candor that disassociates her from American Spiritualism's historical ties to confidence tricksters. In addition to being a medium, Britten was a principal historian of the Spiritualist movement, and her autobiography stands beside her formal histories as one of the most engaging and informative documents of the 19th-century occult world.

155 BROAD, Lucy. c.1864–?. *A Woman's Wanderings the World Over.* Headley Bros., 1909. 189 pp.; front. port.; preface; illus. BBI 1:239.

Born at Clennick, Cornwall. Parents not named, farmers. 6 siblings. Single. Temperance activist; missionary; religionist (Methodist); traveler (world). Working class.

Author's warm Cornwall upbringing, dedication to temperance principles, and international missionary and temperance work for the Methodist Church, 1870s–1907. Father's drinking alcohol, but mother's abstaining because of her children; influencing all seven to be abstainers and non-smokers; three of them, including author, becoming temperance workers. Their moving frequently, but staying in the countryside; author's always loving long tramps and accessibility of nature. In Liskeard, Cornwall, family's joining local Methodist church; eldest brother's later becoming a Methodist preacher. Urged by mother, author and brother John's founding local branch of the temperance group Band of Hope; quickly attracting more than 150 members. Father's death; author's subsequently living with each of three brothers. Having "burning desire" to be of service to the world; leaning toward foreign missionary work despite mother's opposition. After mother's death, feeling free to pursue her goals. Setting out on travels, 1897, to preach temperance on the Continent; traveling with another woman but finding her too slow; in Nice, sending for her bicycle; deciding to ride through Italy; coping successfully with thieves, beggars, and bicycle crashes. Joining the Women's Christian Temperance Union, 1898; traveling to South Africa; in Durban, starting work for the Greyville Methodist Church. Admiring the natives' beauty, vitality, and natural way of life. Serving as WCTU president at Flower Mission for two years; starting YMCA temperance home for young women. In 1890, leaving to travel on foot through South Africa; visiting native reserves. Traveling by bicyle through Madagascar, 1901; visiting various branches of the London Missionary Society. Visiting Australia, 1904; speaking at missions and temperance meetings throughout the Continent. Taking her trusty bicycle to New Zealand, 1905; working for country's unsuccessful Prohibition campaign; calling New Zealand "the most progressive country in the world" with universal suffrage, old-age pensions, a government-run railway, and other public welfare amenities. Hiking through South Pacific islands, 1906; praising the native people; rejoicing that influence of Christian missionaries had changed their "dark" customs of slaughter. Serving as delegate to the WCTU world convention in Boston the same year. Leaving the U.S. for Asia, 1907; lecturing in Korea and Japan, admiring "women of culture and capacity" she found there. Returning to America for ten months; celebrating the virtues of American women; confidently asserting that women of the world will bring in a "Golden Age" by their example.

Broad enlivens her narrative with occasional descriptive passages from her travel diaries. Her many direct addresses to her reader are effectively mini-sermons on exotic cultures and other races, and they suggest how she must have sounded as a public speaker. Although not a declared feminist, Broad's unmistakable sense of women's moral superiority pervades every page; she also gives the reader a fulsome glimpse of her democratic political ideals in her eulogy on the socialist innovations in New Zealand. Her twin topics of missionary work and foreign cultures are both engaging, but despite her own admiring fascination with non-European peoples, this is one of those books in which the author's personality, in all its amiable eccentricity, comes to dominate the work. This volume serves as both a source on the global spread of temperance principles, 1890–1906, and a study of a woman's unconventional life and open multicultural attitudes which gives the lie to many established historical truisms.

156 BROMET, Mary (née Pownall). c.1870–1937. *Response*. Methuen & Co., 1935. 246 pp.; front.; illus. NUC pre56 77:488.

Born in Leigh, Lancashire. Father: surname Pownall. Mother not named. 1 brother; 2 sisters. Married 1902, Alfred Bromet, barrister. Artist (sculptor); foreign resident (France, Germany, Italy, Switzerland); organizer (artistic). Upper class.

Artist's upbringing, training, and impassioned career as a sculptor, emphasizing her parents', sister's, and husband's faith in and support of her talent, 1870s–1935. Being much loved by her parents; learning a benign attitude toward poor tramps from her father. Feeling drawn to art, age 5; being schooled by a governess. Later attending a girls' boarding school; in art class, making three-dimensional scenes in cardboard; criticizing other students' work. Being permitted to set up sculptural studio at home. Noting visits of lawyer Alfred Bromet to family; receiving kindly encouragement from him. Meeting sculptor John Cassidy in Manchester; practicing modeling under his supervision; studying anatomy from specimens and books. Friends' trying to discourage her, opining that sculpting was not "woman's work." Having a small statue exhibited at Manchester Art Gallery, 1890. Persuading reluctant parents to let her study in Frankfurt and Paris; being accompanied by her sister Lucy. Spending ten years in Europe; competing in art exhibitions; describing Continental artists and instructors of her acquaintance. Becoming increasingly close to her sister. Owing much inspiration to the works of Rodin. Being wooed by unspecified "great artist" who planned for her to become his mistress. Being grateful for continued support from parents; studying in Switzerland and Rome with Italian masters. On visit to England, accepting marriage proposal from Alfred. Returning to Rome; opening her own studio there. Discussing her artistic interest in classical mythology; serving as her own model for sculpting "The Harpy," part-bird and part-woman; receiving splendid notices for this work. Marrying Alfred in Switzerland, 1902; returning to England afterward. Opening a home studio; recounting her prolific production, particularly of sculpted portraits. Despite controversial reactions to "The Harpy" during exhibit at the Royal Academy, this particular sculpture's being chosen to represent British sculpture at the International Exhibition in Rome, 1911; purchase of "The Harpy" by Mary, Princess of Wales. Serving as president of the Society of Women Artists. Death of both her parents, 1913. Regretting both "wasted years" in her life and her inability to attain her ultimate goal: creating a great Renaissance-style fountain on a grand scale, entitled "Life is a Mystery." Having been much praised for her completed design of the fountain; feeling herself a failed artist for leaving these plans unfulfilled.

Photographs of Bromet's sculptures accompany her descriptions and illustrate the broad range of human emotion and physical type embodied in her art. As an account of the art education available throughout Europe in the late 19th century, her autobiography is excellent, although the reader might wish that she would say something about her social origins, the education of her brothers and sisters, and the family's general principles about women's education and work. The most enlightening feature of this work may be its display of Bromet's all-consuming dedication to her art, which took precedence over family and marital ties, apparently with the acquiescence of all concerned. Readers of Bromet's memoir will also want to peruse sculptor Kathleen Kennet's *Self-Portrait of an Artist* (1949); Kennet actually studied under Rodin, and her commentary on his technique affirms many of Bromet's judgements.

157 BROOKE, Gladys Palmer (Her Highness, the Dayang Muda of Sarawak). 1884–?. *Relations and Complications: Being the Recollections of H.H. The Dayang Muda of Sarawak*. John Lane, The Bodley Head Ltd., 1929. 253 pp.; front.; foreword by Rt. Hon. T. P. O'Connor, P.C., M.P.; illus.; index. NUC pre56 77:647.

Born in Reading, Berkshire. Father: Walter Palmer, biscuit manufacturer, M.P. Mother: Jean Craig Palmer, society woman. Married Bertram Brooke, the Tuan Muda of Sarawak, 2nd heir to the Raj, also aide de camp to governor of Queensland. 3 daughters; 1 son. Society woman; farmer; shopkeeper. Upper class; married into aristocracy.

Author's childhood and adult life among England and France's cultural elite, featuring her marital ties to the British rulers of Sarawak and emphasizing the incompatibility between her independent character and her husband's possessive one, 1884–1929. In childhood, becoming acquainted with countless personalities in her parents' artistic, political, and social circles; noting her mother's particular friendships with Oscar Wilde, John Ruskin, and George Meredith. Going abroad on many brief trips with her father. Meeting Isadora Duncan when the actress first arrived in England, c.1870; becoming her lifelong friend. Father's having been Liberal M.P. for Kennington; his turning Unionist and elected Unionist member for Salisbury. Meeting Margaret Brooke, Ranee of Sarawak and her future mother-in-law; learning history of Sarawak; meeting her husband-to-be, Lady Brooke's son Bertram; agreeing to marry him despite loving another man, Lucien Daudet; many years later, discovering that Lucien had asked for her hand but received her parents' refusal. Finding incompatibilities between herself and Bertram: his disliking artists she adored, his lacking passion for life. Marriage. Husband's being appointed aide to governor of Queensland; their moving to Australia; returning to England after author became ill. Recalling social interchanges with artists Sir Philip and Sir Edward Burne-Jones, the duc d'Orleans, and composer Ethel Smyth. Having growing fondness and respect for Rajah of Sarawak, her husband's father; when he was in England, learning his views on how to govern British Eastern possessions. Traveling to Egypt without her husband; being exposed there to the British "military type"; expressing her aversion to it. Her parents' sudden deaths. Birth of her third daughter. Accompanying her husband's parents to Sarawak; traveling up-country with the rajah; reflecting on his demonstrated benevolence toward subjects. Sharing discussion about institution of marriage: Rajah's asserting need to reform it; author's believing that marriage should be spontaneous, not rigid; her husband's disagreeing. Returning with family to England; being sorry to leave Sarawak; birth of her son, 1912. During WWI, author's performing volunteer war work; Bertram's traveling with army to the Suez Canal. Author's buying and running farm estate on border of Shropshire and Wales; husband's coming home on leave; his insisting unsuccessfully that she sell the farm. Author's resolving to make farm pay for itself. Rajah's successfully petitioning Colonial Office to release Bertram from war duties to help govern Sarawak. Author's sponsoring theatrical evenings at the farm with aid of long-time friend Ellen Terry. After the Armistice, author's setting up craftshop in London; producing silent film starring Terry. Seldom hearing from her husband; his suddenly returning to England after three years' absence; showing disdain for her work "in trade." To placate him, author's putting farm and shop up for sale; his suddenly making their children wards of the court under the Ranee's guardianship. Author's grimly perceiving that "the English law regarded a woman and a mother as the chattel of her man." Joining her husband and children in house he had selected in St. Leonards; feeling oppressed by its bleakness. Deciding to live in Nice with two younger cousins; hoping her children would join her for holidays. In France, getting to know Princess Daisy of Pless; trading stories about Sarawak and Germany. Summering with her children in Cornwall, 1925. Returning to France; becoming part of literary circle there, including writers Kay Boyle, Gertrude Stein, James Joyce, others. Meeting Lucien Daudet after a gap of twenty years. Converting to Catholicism; planning a visit to Rome and a special audience with the pope. Having learned in her life to take things as they come.

Sarawak is part of the present-day nation of Malaysia; it occupies the northern portion of the island of Borneo. During the late 19th century, the Brooke family enjoyed great esteem as the liberal rulers of this island domain, and were instrumental in improving its education and living standards by secular rather than missionary means. Lady Brooke's account suggests indeed that it was her esteem for the ranee and rajah, her prospective in-laws, that induced her to marry into the family, although how the enlightened, gifted, and humanitarian Brookes could raise such an oppressively sexist boor as their son Bertram will remain forever a mystery. Unhappily for Lady Brooke, her husband's use of punitive legal means to control her behavior highlights the drastic gap between women's confidence in their independence, c.1920, and the actual legal situation. Those interested in this account will also want to read *My Life in Sarawak* (1913) by the author's mother-in-law.

158 BROOKE, Margaret Alice Lilly, second Ranee of Sarawak (née De Windt). 1849–1936. *My Life in Sarawak*. Methuen, 1913. 320 pp.; front.; preface by Sir Frank Swettenham, G.C.M.G.; intro.; illus.; map; index. NUC pre56 77:660.

Probably born in Chateau d'Epinay-sur-Orge, France. Father: Clayton Jennings (later De Windt), captain, 15th Hussars. Mother: Lily Willes Johnson. 2 brothers. Married c.1872, Charles Brooke, Rajah of Sarawak. 3 sons; 1 daughter. Wrote novel *Impromptus*. Knew Oscar Wilde, Edward Burne-Jones, the Rev. Stopford Brooke, Marianne North, Henry James, Sarah Bernhardt. Ranee (wife of a rajah, ruler of an independent Asian state); society woman; travel writer; feminist; foreign resident (Malaysia). Middle class; married into aristocracy.

Author's girlhood and marriage to the British ruler of Sarawak, focusing on her supportive work within Malay society, 1850s–c.1900. Author's family's moving from France to rural Wiltshire; father's death soon after. In childhood, author's establishing habit of keeping diaries. Criticizing her education as a mid-Victorian girl; having learned music, dancing, and "two or three" European languages, but not "the important things in life." Visit to England by her mother's cousin Sir Charles Brooke, 1868, upon his becoming Rajah of Sarawak. Their marrying and traveling to Malaysia, c.1872; author's finding Sarawak breathtakingly beautiful. Taking initiative; hosting a reception for native women. Befriending Datu Isa, wife of her husband's chief minister. Admiring native women's dress; expressing surprise that this beauty evolved while rest of the country was "sunk in a state of barbarism" before the first rajah came. Displaying her newfound knowledge of Malay life and customs to her husband; visiting natives and treating their illnesses; being told excessive familiarity with natives was unseemly in a rajah's wife. Becoming increasingly devoted to Malay society; feeling absurdity of the color bar. Joining with Malay wives to protect a servant girl. Births of her first three children; receiving kindness from native Muslims after having a miscarriage. Suffering from malaria; returning to England; deaths of her children from illness during return voyage to England. Expressing anger that British government would not receive her husband as Rajah of Sarawak and refused to acknowledge him as ruler of his own country. Birth of another son in England. Condemning the prevailing English fashion of women's wearing plumes from egrets, a species near extinction. Returning with her husband to Sarawak; recounting his expedition against hostile Dyak tribe; acting to protect fort while husband was away. Receiving a visit to Sarawak from naturalist Marianne North; commencing an enduring friendship with her; disagreeing with North's view of natives as "savages" because they were headhunters. Birth of another son. Learning Malay; teaching native women to write. Occasionally returning to England; birth of son Harry there. Gradually spending increasing periods of time in England. Sarawak's becoming a British protectorate, 1888; Britain's officially recognizing author's husband as its ruler. Traveling with her son Bertram throughout the Malay islands.

The anomalous situation of the Brooke family in Sarawak dates from 1838, when Sir James Brooke, a British Army officer born in India, aided the Sultan of Borneo in eradicating Dayak rebel piracy on his north shore and received Sarawak in token of the sultan's gratitude. As rajah, Sir James was tremendously influential, introducing free trade and a new constitution, as well as making headhunting punishable by death. At his demise in 1868, he was succeeded by his nephew Charles Johnson, who changed his own surname to Brooke; this is the husband of the present author. Lady Margaret Brooke's memoir, which shows her work as a champion of human rights, omits mention of other of her notable actions, including her promotion of women's education both in Sarawak and England. In **159** *Good Morning and Good Night* (1934), Lady Brooke further expands upon daily life in Sarawak and describes her personal responsibilities as ranee. An admiring perspective on Brooke is provided by her future daughter-in-law, Gladys Brooke, who in *Relations and Complications* describes how Sarawak natives praised the ranee's efforts on their behalf.

160 BROOKE, Sylvia Leonora, third Ranee of Sarawak (née Brett). 1885–1971. *Queen of the Head-Hunters: The Autobiography of H.H. the Hon. Sylvia Lady Brooke, Ranee of Sarawak*. Sidgwick & Jackson, 1970. 194 pp.; preface; illus. BLC 42:148.

Born in London. Father: Reginald Baliol Brett, 2nd Viscount Esher, Conservative M.P., governor of Windsor Castle, secretary to Office of Works and Public Buildings. Mother: Eleanor Van de Weyer. 2 brothers; 1 sister. Married 1911, Charles Vyner de Windt Brooke, later 3rd Rajah of Sarawak, d.1963. Widow. 3 daughters. Wrote *The Street with Seven Houses* (1919), *A Star Fell* (1940), others. Knew Enrico Caruso, George Bernard Shaw, James Barrie, Beerbohm Tree, Noel Coward. Ranee (wife of a rajah, ruler of an independent Asian state); society woman; novelist; playwright; foreign resident (Malaysia). Aristocracy.

Author's aristocratic but lonely upbringing and later marriage into the British family that ruled Sarawak, emphasizing her marital separation as a result of her husband's obligations in Sarawak, 1890s–1970. Family history. Noting mother and father's absorption in one another; their consequently neglecting the children. Feeling alienated from parents and subservient to her brothers. Attempting suicide, age 12. Family's living alternately in London and on Windsor Castle estate; growing up playing with children of the royal family. Making her social debut; being a "flop" as debutante. Writing short stories, with encouragement from J. M. Barrie and George Bernard Shaw. Joining amateur orchestra sponsored by Margaret Brooke, Ranee of Sarawak. At age 17, being attracted to Lady Brooke's son Charles; her parents' objecting initially to his suit. Author and Charles's trying unsuccessfully to elope; parents' later relenting. Marriage, 1911. Pregnancy; birth of her first daughter. Accompanying husband and in-laws to Sarawak. Husband's arguing with his parents over their governing policy in Sarawak; returning with author to London. Husband's departing again for Sarawak by himself, leaving author in England. Discussing economic and political impact of WWI on Sarawak's alliances with European nations. Author's having series of difficult childbirths. Visiting Sarawak with her children. Writing plays and novels in London. Husband's acceding to title of rajah upon death of his father, 1917. Author's making yearly voyages to Sarawak. Traveling to South Africa for her health; flirting with another man. Describing court life in Sarawak; her husband's role as ruler. Depicting Sarawak tribal customs, child marriage, and promiscuity. Knowing of her husband's infidelities; tolerating them. Traveling by herself in east Asia; making lecture tour of the U.S., 1939. Recounting her husband's political difficulties in tense political atmosphere preceding WWII. Returning to England after start of war; setting up her own establishment apart from husband in London. Making farewell visit to Sarawak; recalling her husband's decision to cede country to the Crown, 1946. Their returning together to London. Living in Barbados for fifteen years. Celebrating their golden wedding in London. Husband's death; tributes to him.

Taken with the autobiographies by Gladys Brooke and Margaret Brooke, who also married into the ruling family of Sarawak, this memoir adds additional detail to the experience of Malaysia shared by these late-19th- and early-20th-century British women. Unlike her mother-in-law Margaret, who seemed inspired to devote herself to bettering conditions for Malay women, Sylvia presents herself as sympathetic to her husband's royal calling but understandably stressed by its overwhelming demands, particularly on the structure of her marriage. For an earlier account of her life, see **161** *Sylvia of Sarawak. An Autobiography by H.H. the Ranee of Sarawak* (1936), which focuses on Brooke's social obligations in Sarawak and her literary interests in England, covering her late Victorian childhood to the 1930s. Lady Brooke and her husband were the last British royal rulers of this island principality; Sarawak effectively ceased to be an independent nation when the 3rd rajah turned its governance over to England just after the close of WWII.

162 BROOKSBANK, Mary (née Soutar). 1897–1978. *No Sae Lang Syne: A Tale of This City*. Privately printed, n.d. 59 pp.; preface. OCLC #2454185.

Born at Shiprow, Aberdeen, Scotland. Father: surname Soutar, founder-member of Aberdeen Dockers' Union, dock laborer. Mother not named, domestic servant. 4 brothers. Married 1924, husband not named, dock worker, d.1943. Widow. Wrote *Sidlow Breezes*. Knew Margaret McCarthy Mackey, Annie Flynn, Annie Murray. Organizer (political); political activist; social reformer; Communist; poet; atheist. Working class.

Struggles of a committed social reformer, covering her early-20th-century childhood to 1978. Being born in one of Aberdeen's worst slums; describing her childhood poverty. Being educated at Catholic schools: Summer Street and Convent of the Sacred Heart. Family's moving to Dundee; author's attending St. Andrew's School there. Going to work in the mills, age 13. Discussing economic and political impact of WWI and 1920s union agitation and strikes. Joining the Communist Party, age 21; subscribing to need for revolution to overthrow capitalism. Leaving the mills, age 22; finding work as domestic servant. Coming under the influence of John Maclean, a socialist organizer. Working as a janitor and a waitress. Marrying, age 27. Looking back on Catholicism as having repressed her natural desires and ambitions; rebelling against Catholic Church for retarding social reform; becoming a militant atheist. Being imprisoned in Perth Prison for political activity. Working in the National Unemployment Workers' Committee movement. Speaking out against inadequate housing for workers. Being imprisoned for demonstrating against unemployment on Armistice Day. Being fired from series of jobs because of her labor activism; struggling to stay employed. Being arrested for participating in protests. Participating in the 1930s Hunger March. Founding Dundee Working Woman's Guild, c.1930. Chairing Old Age Pensioners Association, c.1955; fighting for higher pensions. Twice standing for Dundee Town Council. Discussing WWII and its effects on workers. Moving with husband to Foundry Lane; becoming involved with women's community in new neighborhood; expressing her enduring concern with women's issues. After her husband's death, 1943, bringing her parents to live with her. Her father's death, 1953. Beginning anthology of her own poetry. Commenting on 1960s politics, American involvement in Vietnam, and British troops' role in Ireland.

Brooksbank announces frankly that she intends her autobiography to demonstrate capitalism's failure to handle the social problems of the working class. Written as one individual's survey of troubling labor conditions over more than sixty years, the book's built-in historical perspective makes it a noteworthy resource. As the daughter of a dock worker, close to the shipping industry which traditionally has employed a significant percentage of Britain's laborers, Brooksbank observed firsthand the plight and uphill battle for rights of individual workers. Her book makes an informative companion to the memoirs of British labour leaders at the governmental level such as Elizabeth and Jack Braddock, whose joint autobiography, *The Braddocks* (1963), traces their shared work as Labour M.P.s to remedy the grievances of the laboring classes in the early 20th century.

163 BROOME, Mary Anne, Lady (née Stewart). 1831–1911. *A Year's Housekeeping in South Africa*. Macmillan, 1883. 335 pp.; illus. NUC pre56 78:277. (1st pub. 1877.)

Born in Jamaica. Father: Walter G. Stewart, island secretary of Jamaica. Mother not named. Married Col. Sir George R. Barker, K.C.B., d.1861. Married Sir Frederick Napier Broome, sheep farmer in New Zealand, colonial secretary of Natal, governor of Western Australia, d.1896. 1 son. Wrote *Station Amusements in New Zealand* (1870), *Colonial Memories* (1904), *Letters to Guy*. Colonialist (South Africa, Australia, New Zealand); miscellaneous writer. Upper class.

Author's memories of a year's sojourn in South Africa, featuring her reactions to native peoples and culture, covering 1875–76. Accompanying her husband to South Africa on his appointment as colonial secretary. Their arriving in Cape Town, 1875. History of Cape Town's colonization. With her husband, traveling through Durban and Maritzburg; depicting towns, native wildlife, and local tribes. Resenting dismissive attitude of established colonists toward recent arrivals. Witnessing building of first inland railway, New Year's 1876; imagining hardships of travel before it was built. Admiring native Kafir justice system: native disputes, magistrate arbitration, court of appeals, some individual cases. Being knowledgeable about Kafir religious and general education; criticizing treatment of Kafir servants by colonials. Describing native "kraals" or villages; clothing differences between natives and colonials, native medicine practices. Being interested by natives' belief in "witch-finders" and witches; female witches' being looked upon as men, engaging in warfare and hunting. History of the earlier reign of Chaka, King of the Zulus, c.1815. Depicting Christian missionary activities, including history of Edendale, the Wesleyan mission station; describing mission girls' school. Asserting that Britain's lower classes would make excellent prospective colonists. Depicting wide range of events in Natal: a bazaar to benefit the Natal Literary Society, a commando raid by a colonial captain. Enjoing receiving official visit from native Princess Mayikali. Being interested to learn that in Kafir weddings, the bride and groom wear western attire. Traveling to a native kraal; visiting with Mazimbulu, a local chieftain. Visiting camp of Natal Mounted Volunteers; also making trek into the bush; seeing vast number of animal skins and horns accumulated by colonial hunters.

In looking at the colonial environment of South Africa, Broome offers little in the way of politics but is led by her lively curiosity to record much fascinating detail on native social structure and customs. Readers accustomed to accounts of South Africa's racial and nationalist tensions during and after the Boer War will appreciate this picture from twenty-five years earlier of a tribal system before the great rush of Europeans to the gold and diamond fields, when tribesmen had not yet been subjected to extremes of colonial exploitation. Broome's intelligent appreciation for indigenous tribal customs is evident, particularly in her praise for the native system of justice; she suggests that if "civilized" people handled their affairs the same way, the Western legal system would be vastly improved for everyone but the lawyers. In later years Lady Broome earned recognition as a prolific writer and contributor to *Cornhill* magazine.

164 BROWN, Beatrice Curtis. c.1901–?. *Southwards from Swiss Cottage.* Home & Van Thal, 1947. 112 pp. NUC pre56 78:589.

Born in London. Parents not named. 2 brothers. Married c.1925, husband not named. Knew Mabel Lethbridge. Secretary; public speaker; social worker. Middle class.

Nostalgic and detailed memories of author's youth in West London, c.1905–1925. Growing up in St. John's Wood, London; describing neighborhood in detail; noting local houses were all built in the 1830s–1860s. Family home's being named "Swiss Cottage"; author's loving its small garden. During author's childhood, traffic's being horse-drawn; motorcars' just starting to appear. Shops near Swiss Cottage. Attending a girls' school; her younger brother's going to prep school. Recalling many childhood activities: theatricals, Christmas parties, dancing class, the Eton-Harrow match at Lord's cricket field. Start of WWI, author's age 13; recalling public response to war; being terrified of zeppelin raids; elder brother's fighting in France. Family's moving to Hampstead, then to Chelsea, author's age 18; describing new house and its riverbank locale. Leaving school this same year; doing clerical work to ensure against lack of the marital success she had expected as a debutante. Exploring London with coworker during lunch hours, age 19. In early 1920s, doing social work for English families of American soldiers;

discussing their living conditions; helping families emigrate to America. London social life, c.1920s; having trouble finding dates; feeling less sophisticated than girls who had been war workers. Preferring theatre-going, c.1919–25; describing individual London theatres and queuing system for tickets. Frequently seeing Mabel Lethbridge in front of theatres; describing her queue-stool business. Describing offices in Berkeley Square where she worked as secretary. On her own time, doing research in the British Museum and Public Record Office; investigating 18th-century political documents for her own interest. Walking in London's Parks; describing their individual "moods." Recalling her family's West Chelsea neighborhood in the 1920s: gathering places, elections, street-corner orators. Organizing local political rally. After marriage, moving from riverbank to early Victorian Chelsea; recalling shops on Kings Road. Returning to memories of St. John's Wood in her childhood.

Brown wrote this book in New York in 1940, apparently after emigrating, for she observes that her homesickness for London made her try to re-create it on paper. Like Joy Packer's *Pack and Follow* and Sylvia Leith-Ross's *Cocks in the Dawn,* this autobiography is a product of the author's nostalgia intensified by the circumstances of WWII; it gives the reader a full sense of scenes in West London as residents would have experienced them. Brown's book fits into a natural pairing with the 1910 *Recollections of What I Saw, What I Lived Through and What I Learned During More than Fifty Years of Social and Literary Experience* by Isabel Mayo, a native of London, who employs the same sort of total recall to portray her childhood neighborhood within London's ancient Roman walls.

165 BROWN, Jane. 1902–?. *I Had a Pitch on the Stones*. Nicholson & Watson, 1946. 226 pp.; foreword. NUC pre56 79:135.

Born in London. Parents not named. 1 sister. Married c.1920, Don Brown. 1 son; 1 daughter. Businesswoman; antique dealer; charwoman; civil defense worker (WWII). Middle class.

Author's accidental journey from a middle-class upbringing to a career as an open-air marketeer, 1902–40. Parents' being disappointed the author was born female. Studying the piano; having lessons with French governess; later attending St. Cecile's School. Training to become a dancing teacher; teaching dancing for several years. Family's owing its prosperity to father; his having made a fortune on the stock exchange. Recounting his financial reverses after WWI. At age 18, author's marrying Don Brown, an antique dealer in London's open-air markets. Recalling her first attempt at selling in London's Caledonian Market; recounting market's history. Author and husband's sharing full-time duties; managing their stall together. Recalling individual customers; problems with sneak thieves. Being short of funds, especially after births of her children; cleaning billiard halls to supplement family income; eventually having to accept public assistance. Trying to cope with husband's serious illness and many operations. Returning to selling in the Market; holding special sales in honor of King George V's Jubilee, 1935. Waiting on celebrity customers: Greta Garbo, Charles Laughton, Hermione Gingold, Gertrude Lawrence, and Douglas Fairbanks, Jr. Noting generosity of stallholders toward one another. Middle- and working-class children's being more polite as customers than children of wealthy parents. Prior to WWII, finding civil defense job. London's markets' closing during WWII as precaution against bombing. In his years of selling, husband's having become authority on antiques; author and husband's opening a small antique shop in London.

One of the few extended portrayals of London's trademark open-air markets, Brown's lively account does a commendable job of conveying their working atmosphere and day-to-day operations. The author seems resilient about the precipitous family losses that propelled her into these markets; and her book conveys the sense that in this colorful mercantile environment, patronized by people of every class, social distinctions between different sellers mean very little. Her picture of how sellers coped with the 1930s Depression helps place the markets in the context of Britain's overall economic picture.

166 BROWN, Jean Curtis. c.1900–?. *To Tell My Daughter*. Rodney Phillips, 1948. 116 pp.; foreword; illus. by Eleanor Moynihan. NUC pre56 79:136.

Raised near Liverpool. Father not named, Presbyterian minister, Scottish. Mother not named, Scottish. 1 sister. Married, husband not named. 1 daughter. Clergyman's daughter. Middle class.

Memories of author's childhood activities and attitudes, set against background of life in an observant Presbyterian home, c.1903–12. Growing up in industrial Merseyside. Father's being "an eminent and popular Presbyterian minister"; his being a Glasgow native; having had an extensive university education in Glasgow and Leipzig. In childhood, noticing they were poorer than their neighbors. Recalling her stern Presbyterian upbringing; being attracted to colorful imagery in Catholic services; not daring to tell her parents. Being much younger than her sister; having nobody to play with. Resenting being overdressed in restrictive clothing. Reading the Bible; her father's also letting her read anything in his large library: Andrew Lang's fairy books, *Alice in Wonderland, Water-Babies,* books of Italian paintings. Neither parent's spending much time with her; author's feeling herself on periphery of their lives. Spending time caring for her rabbits. Receiving adult affection from the Nicholsons, father's parishioners, who doted on author. Disliking being sent to girls' day school; recalling courses in posture training, calisthenics, and French. Recounting schoolgirl friendships there. Describing her father's involvement in Presbyterian church's self-government; her mother's daily routine of social calls, unflagging parish work for the church.

Having her tonsils and adenoids removed by operation at home; mother's doctoring her afterward. Taking holidays in Scotland; loving Scotland as her ancestral home. Going on holidays in continental Europe for father's health. Being sent to a larger boarding school in East Anglia, age 12; father's death the same year.

Brown indicates that her upbringing was neither restricted nor sheltered along Victorian lines, but neither was it as unsupervised as many "modern" childhoods. Her picture of early-20th-century organization in the Presbyterian Church is informative, and she provides unwitting commentary on the economic conditions of its clergy through her naive childhood wondering as to why, when her father was so well educated, her family was still so poor. Writing to educate her daughter about the terms and conditions of existence within a clergyman's family, Brown has also created a work of much interest to historians of Liverpool interested in its immigrant Scottish population.

167 BROWN, Lilian Mabel Alice Richmond, Lady (née Roussel; F.L.S., F.R.G.S., F.Z.S., F.R.A.I.). 1885–1946. *Unknown Tribes, Uncharted Seas*. New York: D. Appleton, 1925. 268 pp.; front. port.; illus.; preface; addendum; index. BLC to 1975 44:292. (1st pub. Duckworth, 1924.)

Born at Rohais, Isle of Guernsey. Father: Robert Roussel. Mother: not named. Married 1906, Sir Melville Richmond Brown, 3rd Baronet, d. 1944. No children. Travel writer; explorer; traveler (Panama). Upper class.

A year spent exploring natural history in Caribbean waters, c.1920–21. At age 35, residing on her husband's family estate in Hampshire; recuperating from a serious operation; deciding to travel in rebellion against forced inactivity. Joining her old friend Mitchell "Midge" Hedges, explorer and deep sea researcher, on his expedition to the Caribbean and Central America. Recounting their voyage to Jamaica; describing Caribbean scenery; hunting alligators with Midge. Describing plagues of mosquitos and hurricanes; observing underwater life while diving. Photographing fish; collecting coral and shells; studing turtles and manatees. Discussing West Indian native customs and dress. Writing article for London *Daily Mail* on shark attack in Kingston Bay. With Midge, sailing to Costa Rica and to Colón, Panama; describing the canal and Panamanian social life. Buying a yacht with Midge; sailing to San Blas Islands, off Panama's Atlantic coast; depicting San Blas Indians, native customs, villages, and dress; treating diseases and injuries of Indians; author and Midge's enhancing their prestige by demonstrating use of lighters, rod, reel, and guns. From there, sailing to the mainland; hunting iguana. Traveling inland to previously unvisited village of primitive Chucunaque tribe. Devising, with Midge, dramatic ceremony using ship's flares and author in white dress and costume jewelry to convince tribe of their divinity and potential wrath unless permitted to treat the sick. Treating disease-ridden Chucunaque. Collecting tribal fetishes. Describing tribal rites and customs. Returning to San Blas Islands; voyage through narrow reef channels; landing a great white shark. Taking their yacht through Panama Canal; exploring Panama's Pacific coastal islands. Midge's catching enormous sharks and sawfish; press reports of their catches and explorations. Author's narrowly escaping a shark's jaws; experiencing nightmarish memory flashbacks. Catching 415-pound shark, world record for a woman. Exploring and hunting in Bayano River valley. Returning to Panama City; departing for Liverpool, leaving Midge behind; their eventually reuniting in England. Excerpts from scientific reports on their collected specimens. Speculating on ethnography and racial ancestry of Central American Indians.

Although silent on her history before this Carribean adventure, Brown seems already to be an experienced sailor at the outset, a skill that very likely came from growing up on one of Britain's Channel Islands. Her memoir, drawn from her diaries, is virtually a geographical textbook on Panama's Indian tribes, the jungle's natural history, South America's coastal islands, and the region's marine wildlife. Brown and Hedges lived together solely as colleagues; she never finds it necessary to mention their domestic arrangements on the yacht or in the jungle, noting that in the jungle she underwent a metamorphosis: "I am not the same being—sex has disappeared from my thoughts." She invites comparison with Lady Dorothy Mills (author of the autobiography *A Different Drummer*), another explorer of South America, and with 19th-century Englishwomen travelers such as Isabella Bird Bishop, who also traveled in rebellion against forced idleness.

168 BROWN, Mary Solomon. 1847–1935. *Mrs. John Brown; an Account of her Social Work in Lancashire and South Africa, of her memories of Lancashire folk, and her friendship with Olive Schreiner*. John Murray, 1937. Ed. by Angela James & Nina Hills. 214 pp.; front. port.; list of author's published writings; foreword by Countess Buxton; preface by eds.; index. NUC pre56 79:258.

Born at Sea Point, near Cape Town, South Africa. Father: Henry Solomon. Mother: Julia Middleton. 10 siblings. Married 1869, John Brown, physician. 2 sons; 2 daughters. Knew Gen. William Booth, Keir Hardie. Philanthropist; temperance activist; political activist; social reformer; editor; Poor Law Guardian; suffragist; teacher (Sunday school). Middle class.

Social reformer's South African youth, emigration to the British Isles, and lifetime commitment to bettering conditions for poor people and for women, c.1850–1920. Loving her father greatly; pondering his early conversion from Judaism to Christianity. Attending dame school; later attending the first classes for women at Cape Town University; her father's refusing to let her study medicine but encouraging other studies. Meeting medical student John Brown; admiring his progressive views on freedom and education for women. Traveling to Scotland to meet future in-laws. Marrying; settling in Edinburgh. Births of her first two children; being shattered by death of her third child from disease. Admiring her husband's work with Lord Lister to promote asepsis. Becoming concerned about plight of Edinburgh's poor; describing Edinburgh slums. Teaching Sunday school; supporting temperance. Maintaining long-distance friendship with South African writer Olive Schreiner; helping Schreiner find publisher for *The Story of an African Farm*. Speaking on behalf of temperance; helping form branch of British Women's Temperance Association and Women's Co-operative Guild. Having a firm religious faith; receiving confirmation in the Church of England. Sympathizing with socialism's goals, if not methods. Attending workers' meetings during a coal strike. Helping to start shelter for "friendless" girls. Making temperance speaking tour of Canada and the U.S. with the British Association. Family's moving to Lancashire; author's winning election as first woman guardian of the poor in northeast Lancashire. Working for women's suffrage. Expressing her great attachment to South Africa; returning to live there; being emotionally traumatized by Boer War. Serving as Women's Christian Temperance Union superintendent for moral education; editing the WCTU magazine. Speaking out against white slave traffic in South Africa. Helping enroll one of the first biracial students at Grahamstown University. WWI: organizing war work; helping start League of Honour. Working steadily despite declining health; coping with death of her husband. Asserting that extending the franchise to women would be the best means to promote South Africa's moral welfare; commenting on social and economic ramifications of miscegenation in South Africa.

Brown served effectively as her husband's partner in their collaborative efforts to ameliorate social conditions, matching his work in disease control with her own socialist-oriented activism for the poor. As the daughter of a Jewish emigrant to South Africa, she is ethnically representative of South Africa's colonial history, during which many Jews from eastern Europe settled and throve in Cape Colony, the primary British protectorate. Her autobiography, covering fifty years of her work, surveys a broad range of social ills as they affected people in the British Isles and Empire.

169 BROWN, Winifred. 1899–1979. *Under Six Planets*. Peter Daires, 1955. 273 pp.; front. NUC pre56 79:441.

Born in Manchester. Father: Sawley Brown, grocery proprietor. Mother: Elsie Rowlinson. Married 1939, Ron Adams; divorced c.1941. 1 son. Feminist; aviator; sportswriter; nurse; WWI volunteer; traveler (Europe, Australia, New Zealand, Hawaii, Canada, South America). Middle class.

Tomboy childhood and thrill-seeking adult years revealing exploits of one of England's early woman aviators, 1905–1950s. Having a dashing father who drove fast motorcars. Sensing her father's disappointment that she was not a boy; cutting off all her hair, age 6. Believing conflict in her parents' marriage centered on herself: father's encouraging her to smoke and defy traditional definitions of femininity; mother's smothering her with overprotectiveness. Attending local academy; taking drawing and painting class at an art studio. Picking up soldiers, age 14, but surviving the experience still a virgin. During WWI, taking training in first aid and home nursing; being posted to Sedley Hall Hospital as a VAD. At age 17, being sexually assaulted by a soldier in the hospital. Becoming engaged to working-class trombone player; being uncomfortably aware of their class differences; fiancé's giving her premarital initiation into sex. Being terrified at thought of marriage and childbirth; breaking her engagement; entering relationships with other men. Taking tennis lessons. Being increasingly interested in thrill of aviation; overcoming restrictions of Lancashire Aero Club to become its first woman flying member, 1926; earning her license, 1927. Her proud father's buying her an airplane. Winning King's Cup Air Race, 1930; suddenly being deluged with publicity and fame. Traveling through Europe, Australia, New Zealand, Hawaii, Canada, and the Amazon to further her aviation career. Describing crashes and injuries. Playing golf in the British Open; touring with Manchester women's ice hockey team in France and Switzerland; sailing a yawl from North Wales to Spitsbergen, 1936. Her father's contracting mental illness; dying in hospital; leaving all his money to author, provoking mother's bitterness. Discussing women pioneer aviators. Marrying Ron Adams, 1939; their divorcing after son's 1940 birth. Mother's sudden death, 1949. At time of writing, author's feeling insecure as a single parent; wondering how to be both father and mother to her teenage son; feeling more like a father than a mother. Being told she would make a "damned fine husband" for some woman. Her son's praising her parenting.

As well as being a good short history of early aviation in Britain, Brown's autobiography centers on gender issues, and from beginning to end it draws her many deliberate transgressions against female gender role prescriptions into a coherent whole. Historians of gender studies will be strongly interested in the family constellation that Brown so vividly describes, with its limited domestic role for Brown's mother and the adventurous father whom Brown both wanted to please and sought to emulate. Brown derives the title of her book from the horoscope cast at her birth by her father's brother, a professional astrologer; the author gives a detailed account of the chart's various indications for her, including omens of great bravery and renown. In later life, she produced two further memoirs of her daredevil experiences, *No Distress Signals* and *Duffers on the Deep*.

BROWNING, Elizabeth Barrett. [*See* BARRETT, Elizabeth.]

BROWNLOW, Countess of. [*See* CUST, Emma Sophia.]

170 BRUDENELL, Adeline Louisa Marie, Countess of Cardigan, later Countess of Lancastre (née de Horsey). 1824–1915. *My Recollections*. New York: John Lane, 1909. 176 pp.; illus. NUC pre56 95:125.

Born in London. Father: Spencer Horsey de Horsey. Mother: Lady Louisa Maria Judith. 2 brothers. Married 1858, Earl of Cardigan, d.1868. Married 1873, Don Antonio Manuelo, Count of Lancastre, d.1898. Widow. Society woman. Upper class; married into aristocracy.

Colorful personal recollections, accompanied by tart analyses and comparisons of Victorian and modern societies, spanning 1820s to 1909. Growing up in affluent Berkeley Square, Mayfair. Adoring her mother; being schooled by French governesses and tutors in Latin, modern languages, music, and dancing. Depicting upper-class social events and intrigues; relating contemporary society gossip, c.1830s. Attending fashionable children's parties. Being presented at Court. Mother's death, 1843; keeping house for her father; discovering that he was secretly keeping a mistress. Enjoying country weekends at the estate of Lord and Lady Essex. Making and breaking a betrothal to a Spanish count, age 25. Becoming intimate with Lord Cardigan, a married man; citing his wife's infidelity as justification for their liaison; rebelling against father and brothers by continuing their romantic involvement. Setting up bachelor establishment for herself in Park Lane. Marrying Cardigan in Gibraltar, 1858, after his wife's death. Relating Cardigan's life story, including his leading the Charge of the Light Brigade in the Crimea. Declaring her wifely devotion and married happiness; being shattered by her husband's death, 1868. Receiving marriage proposals from Count Lindemann and Benjamin Disraeli (whom she rejected for bad breath). Describing assignation house of the 1850s, the "Parrot Club," where noblewomen could meet their lovers. Finally marrying Don Antonio Manuelo of Portugal, 1873. After his 1898 death, establishing contact with his spirit at a séance.

Full of juicy gossip, Lady Cardigan's memoir was bound to cause hard feelings among the Victorian aristocracy; her friend Maria Damer bought up and burned most of the first edition. Mixing rumor and innuendo equally with scandalous and surprising truths, Lady Cardigan takes great pleasure in tattling on her social circle, all the while condemning the present age for its lack of manners, by which, one assumes, she means the Victorians' compulsion to expose sexual irregularities instead of politely ignoring them. Lady Cardigan's memoir occupied much the same position in the Victorian years that similar memoirs do in our own era; she was one of the last of the Regency aristocracy, maintaining its social values to the end of her life and frowning on moralistic innovations. Her book is an illuminating look at aristocratic attitudes, unsullied by the mid-19th-century awakening of social conscience.

171 BRYHER (pseud.; Annie Winifred Ellerman). 1894–1983. *The Heart to Artemis: A Writer's Memoirs*. New York: Harcourt, Brace & World, 1962. 316 pp.; index. NUC 1963–1967 8:318. (other ed.: Collins, 1963.)

Born in Margate, Kent. Father: John Reeves Ellerman, industrialist, financier. Mother: Hannah Glover. 1 brother. Married 1921, Robert McAlmon, writer, American; divorced 1927. Married 1927, Kenneth Macpherson, filmmaker; divorced 1947. Wrote *Region of Lutany and Other Poems* (1914), 10 novels, *Amy Lowell: A Critical Appreciation* (1918), others. Poet; novelist; literary critic; travel writer. Upper middle class.

Introspective study of growth of the author's imagination from childhood to maturity, against a backdrop of her participation in international literary circles, 1894–1940. Father's being of German ancestry, although British; author's speculating on her personal heredity. Family's moving from London to Worthing, author's age 4. Teaching herself to read; from *Swiss Family Robinson* gaining love for books, lust for adventure. Running away from home several times adventuring for the unknown. Enjoying frequent travel necessitated by her father's career in North Atlantic shipping trade; his taking author, age 5, to see the 1900 Paris Exhibition; this awakening her lifelong wanderlust. Learning to read French from her father; at age 6, reading Colette. Father's taking family to Italy and French Riviera every winter, 1901–1909; their visiting Egypt, author's age 9; her fantasizing about explorations of Richard Burton; family's traveling to Spain and North Africa; author's being disappointed that Algiers was insufficiently "exotic." Discussing England's profound world influence through exporting English governesses. Learning to fence and ride horses after family moved to Eastbourne, author's age 13. Becoming interested in paleontology; traveling in Sicily and France; vicariously experiencing past events at historical sites. Taking painting lessons; speculating on course of her life if she had become a painter; deciding that social taboos force women into writing careers instead. Disliking girls' boarding school, 1910, but being pleased to be introduced to world literature; adoring mythologist Jesse Weston's accounts of King Arthur; preferring Arthurian aspirations to boring Victorian restrictions. After leaving school, feeling thwarted by social conventions; believing WWI finally freed women by making it necessary for them to work. Taking classes in Arabic and hieroglyphics; being barred by her parents from training as archaeologist. During WWI, escaping to the Scilly Islands; reading poetry of Amy Lowell and Hilda

Doolittle; publishing her first study of modern poetry in *The Saturday Review*. Meeting Hilda Doolittle ("H.D.") in London, 1918; moving in with her; joining her circle of friends, including Ezra Pound, Havelock Ellis, and W. B. Yeats. In her first book, *Development,* attacking boarding school system; starting a public controversy. Moving with H.D. to New York, 1921. Visiting California; befriending poet Marianne Moore and writer Robert McAlmon. Marrying McAlmon; his taking her to Paris; introducing her to Sylvia Beach, Ernest Hemingway, James Joyce, Gertrude Stein, Berenice Abbott, Man Ray, and André Gide. Watching her idol Stephane Mallarmé self-destruct on alcohol; deciding never to drink. Describing bar-hopping life of artists and writers in Paris, c.1920s. Settling in Vaud, Switzerland. Divorcing McAlmon, 1927; marrying film-maker Kenneth Macpherson. Visiting Vienna with H.D. and Kenneth; meeting Freud while there. With Kenneth, starting a film magazine *Close Up;* visiting Germany to see nation's new films. Being psychoanalyzed in Berlin, 1928–32, by Dr. Hans Sachs, becoming confirmed Freudian. Making last trip to Germany, 1933; Kenneth's making documentary films in which author, H.D., and Paul Robeson acted. Her father's death, 1933. Traveling to America, 1930s; discussing American art and literary scene. Becoming aware of Nazi influence during her 1930s residence in Switzerland; helping Jewish refugees. Her mother's death. Briefly living in Paris; working for French Ministry of Information, 1940. Moving with H.D. to London, 1940.

In her writing, Bryher consistently places her own life and thought against a background of European history and legend, as she would if portraying a fictional hero. One might call her book a portrait of the artist as a young woman, illuminating her interior growth. On the exterior level, readers will appreciate Bryher's memoir for its panoramic view of writers and their international culture in the 1920s, '30s, and '40s. In a later autobiography, **172** *The Days of Mars: A Memoir, 1940–1946* (1971), Bryher describes her experiences in WWII London, living with the poet H.D. (Hilda Doolittle). She portrays her affection for H.D. as both literary and intimate. Although devoted to the sexually unconventional works of such writers as Colette and Amy Lowell, Bryher's own works usually stop short of challenging gender conventions.

173 BUCHAN, Anna (O. Douglas, pseud.). 1877–1948. *Unforgettable, Unforgotten*. Hodder & Stoughton Ltd., 1945. 247 pp.; front. port.; intro.; illus.; index. BLC to 1975 86:273.

Born at Kirkaldy, Fife, Scotland. Father: Rev. John Buchan, Presbyterian pastor. Mother not named. 3 brothers (including novelist John Buchan, governor-general of Canada); 1 sister. Single. Wrote *Olivia in India* (1913), *The Proper Place* (1926), *The Day of Small Things* (1930), *Farewell to Priorsford* (1950), others. Novelist; WWI volunteer; charitable volunteer. Upper middle class.

Changes wrought by six decades in one close-knit Scottish family, covering the late Victorian era to WWII's end. Parents' providing a secure, happy childhood. Eldest brother John's having a passion for learning. Father's being unworldly; teaching children to revere learning; undergoing financial reverses during author's childhood. Mother's being patient and domestic. Recalling rowdy brothers' gentleness with the new baby, Violet. Spending childhood summers in the Scottish borders. Father's acquiring parish in Glasgow; family's moving there; author's attending two schools in Glasgow. Mother's teaching Bible class and starting a Women's Meeting; author's describing Women's Rural Institutes in Scotland. Violet's death's shattering the family, causing author's crippling shyness. Being sent to school in Edinburgh; boarding with family friends. Adoring new baby brother, Alistair. Leaving school; continuing her studies at home; loving drama; giving dramatic readings for her family. John's entering and thriving at Oxford. Author's visiting Oxford; attending theatre there. Hearing Richard Le Gallienne lecture; noting 1890s were exciting time for a girl to grow up. With mother's serious illness, author's assuming charge of household. Her brothers' adulthood's bringing family changes: parents and Alistair's moving to South Africa; brother Willie's entering the Indian Civil Service; John's becoming a successful publishing director and marrying; his bestowing a living allowance on author. Visiting Willie in India; commenting on physical environs of Calcutta, Anglo-Indian women, Indian people, social problems, and markets. After death of father, author's assuming sole care of her mother. Death of her brother Willie. Publishing her first novel, *Olivia in India*. During WWI, brother Alistair's dying at the front, author's doing volunteer work for the Soldiers and Sailors' Families Association. Each year visiting Alistair's grave in France. Developing her own writing career. John's being elected Scottish M.P.; later being appointed governor-general of Canada; author and mother's visiting him in Canada. Death of her mother, leaving author desolate. John's dying in an accident. WWII's vastly altering roles of women both at home and in the workplace.

Unlike the accounts rendered by women with more public preoccupations, Buchan's renditions of British social transformations over three reigns and two world wars gauge them from a family perspective. Her milestones are both the accomplishments and deaths of those she loves, whose presence in her thoughts overshadows historical events and self-reflections. Perhaps too unassuming to discuss how profoundly these losses have affected her, she tacitly testifies to her shyness. Nonetheless, because of her family's intimate involvement in Indian colonialism, Canadian government, and, in particular, Scottish culture, her sensitive account is a valuable document of British social history.

174 BUCHAN, Susan Charlotte, Baroness Tweedsmuir (née Grosvenor). 1882–1977. *The Lilac and the Rose*. Gerald Duckworth

Co., Ltd., 1952. 150 pp.; biblio.; front. port.; preface; illus.; genealogical table; index. NUC pre56 605:605.

Born in England. Father: the Hon. Norman Grosvenor, 3rd son of 1st Baron Ebury. Mother: Caroline Susan Stuart-Wortley. 1 sister. Married 1907, the Hon. John Buchan, later 2nd Baron Tweedsmuir, politician, governor-general of Canada, d.1940. 3 sons. Society woman; philanthropist; foreign resident (Italy, Canada). Aristocracy.

Youthful memories of upper-class life by a member of one of Britain's titled families, 1880s–1907. Describing her father's many talents and love of music; her mother's artistic interests and obsession with her illnesses. Learning how to read human nature from great-aunt Lily; being taught to paint by elderly aunt Mamie. Author's having a romantic nature; endlessly reading romance and adventure novels. Recalling meeting Rudyard Kipling, a favorite author. Family's living briefly in Italy; becoming friends there with novelists Mrs. Humphry Ward and Violet Jacob, also Violet, Lady Paget. Spending winter in Cairo with mother; shopping in bazaars; witnessing parades on camelback; staying with uncle during his tenure as general officer commanding British troops in Egypt. Family's returning to England. Visiting country houses of friends; author's describing their architecture and house parties, c.1900; discussing rural gentry's contributions to political and intellectual life of nation. Attending London balls and parties during same period; being confirmed at St. Paul's Cathedral; living outside London at Moor Park, the Grosvenors' family estate. Starting career in welfare work under Mrs. Humphry Ward; working for Charity Organisation Office in London; describing her duties; noting her mother's disapproval. Working for Adult Education. Waxing nostalgic about Moor Park; recalling graciousness of her late grandparents; calling her grandfather's 1893 death "the end of the old regime." Marrying John Buchan, 1907; encountering controversy with her mother-in-law over remaining Anglican while Buchan was Presbyterian. Recalling domestic servants of her youth; noting the lack of interest in that employment in the early 20th century.

Lady Tweedsmuir's book tends to establish her as a significant person not as an individual but for her place in the august Grosvenor family, holders of two peerage titles, whose many members and public contributions she discusses with equal interest. Lady Tweedsmuir evidently views herself as part of a family fabric permanently woven into the tapestry of British history. It is interesting to note that although her memoir closes with her marriage, when she was 25, it shows her to have been drawn to family members far older than herself; they seem to represent for her the more gracious era she missed by having been born too late. After her marriage, Lady Tweedsmuir's life path was shaped by the multiple careers of her husband. During WWI, he rose to become British director of information, earning fame as a historian for writing *Nelson's History of the War*. After serving as M.P. for the Scottish Universities until 1935, he was made governor-general of Canada and granted a peerage by George V, simultaneously becoming a best-selling author of spy thrillers. Lady Tweedsmuir covers the wide experiences of her married years in **175** *A Winter Bouquet* (1954), which contains amusing and reflective sketches of her husband and members of their literary circle. She concludes her autobiographical reminiscences in **176** *The Edwardian Lady* (1966), her attempt to analyze the phenomenon of Edwardianism within a larger historical context.

177 BURLEND, Rebecca (née Burton). 1793–1872. *A True Picture of Emigration*. Ed. by Milo Milton Quaife. Chicago: Lakeside Press/ R. R. Donnelley, 1936. 167 pp.; front. port.; preface by Edward Burlend (author's son); illus.; intro.; index. NUC pre56 85:446. (1st pub. anon., Berger, 1848.)

Born in Yorkshire, probably in Barwick-in-Elmet. Parents not named. Married c.1813, John Burlend, tenant farmer, d.1871. 14 children. Farmer; emigrant (U.S.). Rural laboring class.

Account of an emigrant's life, ages 38–53, homesteading in mid-19th-century Pike County, Illinois. Couple's deciding to emigrate to America, 1831, because of their poverty; author's describing her homesickness upon leaving. Describing voyage from Liverpool to New Orleans; traveling by flatboat up the Mississippi River to St. Louis. Arriving in Pike County; meeting local resident who had supplied their information on the region; discovering his claims of prosperity were false. Recounting legal details of homesteading; buying improvement rights from squatter. Extensively discussing county's climate, vegetation, and wildlife; family's making their own furniture, soap, and candles. Describing local methods of hunting, fence-building, cattle-raising. Harvesting wheat crop with only her 9-year-old son to help; injured husband's being unable to work. Recovering from chronic asthma in the drier climate. Buying cattle on credit; paying debt with help of their emigrant neighbor; selling maple sugar to repay him. Neighbors' helping to sow their corn crop. Losing part of crop to fire; author's harvesting remainder while pregnant with twins. Achieving greater prosperity; buying property and protecting it from speculators. Commenting on general lack of education among frontier settlers; discussing establishment of schools. Contrasting English and American Methodism; explaining her dissatisfaction with American Methodism. Death of an emigrant neighbor; being visited by his English brother; author's returning to England with the brother, 1846, to see her friends and family. Advising potential emigrants that it is no disgrace to leave overpopulated England for America.

Burlend dictated this account to her schoolmaster-poet son Edward while she was on her 1846 visit home to England. While Edward was careful to maintain the factual content of the memoir, the book's style, Latin and English epigrams, scientific observations, and philosophical comments are his embellishments. In the 1830s, when the author and her husband left for America, farmers throughout Britain were hungry; not only was there a general economic depression, but Corn Laws made it impossible for them to sell most of their grain, despite their hard work. Throughout her book, Burlend contrasts this British plight with the modest prosperity she and her husband established in America. It is indicative of British farmers' continuing hardships that her book was a bestseller upon publication.

178 BURNHAM, Dorothy. 1915–?. *Through Dooms of Love*. Chatto & Windus, 1969. 223 pp.; port. BLC to 1975 48:340.

Raised in Lewisham, Greater London. Father not named, unemployed WWI veteran. Mother: Beatrice Palmer. Stepmother not named. 1 sister; 1 brother; 5 half-siblings. Married c.1936, husband not named, actor. 2 sons. Domestic servant; factory worker. Working class.

Blighted childhood in a family compromised by unemployment and abusiveness, and its adverse effects on the author's emotional health in later life, c.1919–45. Return of her father, whom she had never seen, from WWI. Commenting on homes broken by stresses of WWI. Beginning school, age 4, around time of mother's death, c.1919. Living with fundamentalist Christian grandparents; being closest to her older sister. After her father remarried, his quarreling with author's grandfather, taking author to live with him. Stepmother's treating author callously, ignoring her welfare. Being in hospital for long period with pneumonia; recounting her experiences at children's convalescent homes on Kentish coast. Recalling her constant hunger. Depicting father's character and habitual unemployment. Household's being visited by relief officers. Father's trying to earn something extra by rag picking; having his welfare docked through the Means Test; author's defending to her readers government's practice of monitoring welfare recipients' incomes. In childhood, being molested by a stranger. Author's both pitying and despising her father and stepmother; perceiving their physical abuse of herself and siblings as means to take revenge on each other. Father's spoiling his surviving son. Discussing Salvation Army intervention and help in her family's life. Being punished at school; feeling something must be wrong with her; hating teachers who punished her for poverty. Fearing feelings of affection as well as sexuality. Leaving school, age 14, to become domestic servant. Taking art classes; being encouraged to sit for Royal Society of Arts scholarship; refusing from feelings of incompetence. Holding series of brief domestic jobs; hating the work; starting to work in factories. Having panic attacks, fearing contact with people; neurotically refusing a good job as an actress. Marrying professional actor; seeing her marriage as a "truly dreadful affair" due to her emotional problems. Becoming pregnant. Being abandoned by husband during WWII. Seeking treatment for her mental illness.

Although declaring this moody, literary account to be true as she remembers it, Burnham notes nevertheless that memory is selective. She uses variations on the "Mirror, mirror on the wall" rhyme to comment subjectively on remembered incidents, as well as consciously tying them to scenes from well-known fiction and mythology. Although she benefited from both government and private charitable systems during her upbringing, Burnham evinces a pull-yourself-up-by-the-bootstraps view of life and focuses not on general social welfare but on the individual psychological welfare and quirks of her family. Like a good novelist, also, she does not openly announce the nature of her mental illness, but lets her readers make the causative connections between the atmosphere of her childhood home and her later emotional symptoms. Burnham's book represents the serious use of autobiography by an amateur writer to render her psychological portrait.

179 BURROWS, ? (Mrs.). c.1840–?. "A Childhood in the Fens About 1850–1860," pp. 109–114 in *Life as We Have Known It: By Co-operative Working Women*. Ed. by Margaret Llewelyn Davies. New York: W. W. Norton & Co., 1975. 141 pp.; ed.'s note; intro. letter by Virginia Woolf. BLC to 1975 78:2. (1st pub. Hogarth Press, 1931.)

Probably born in Lincolnshire. Parents not named. Married surname Burrows. Farm laborer; factory worker. Working class.

Author's experiences as a child laborer, both in farm and factory work, 1840s–1850s. Having to leave school at age 8; commencing four years' work as a field hand. Working in a "gang" of child laborers. Describing working conditions in the fields: long hours, exposure to all kinds of weather. Wistfully recalling one occasion when a shepherd's wife permitted children to eat in her cottage. Migrating to Leeds to do factory work, c. age 18. Her ailing father's being unable to work; recalling her mother's sacrifices to keep family together. Remarking on use of opium in Crowland; noting its effects on users and the community in general.

Solicited for an anthology on working-class women's experiences, Burrows's account, with its unadorned language, paints a plain, clear picture of rural hardships that until the mid–20th century were the norm for farm workers. In her introductory letter to this volume, Virginia Woolf notes how foreign such a lifestyle seems to her. Woolf's comfortable middle-class existence segregated her from any knowledge of working-class hardships and limitations. This anthology was intended to remedy such ignorance in its middle-class readers, and in the late

20th century retains its informative usefulness for all readers who wish to familiarize themselves with women's lives in previous eras.

180 BURSTALL, Sara Annie. 1859–1939. *Retrospect and Prospect: Sixty Years of Women's Education*. Longmans, Green, 1933. 286 pp.; preface by Sir Michael Sadler; prologue; app. NUC pre56 86:421.

Born in Aberdeen, Scotland. Father: Henry A. Burstall, civil engineer, agent for English company. Mother: Annie Hepzibah King. 2 brothers. Single. Wrote *Education of Girls in America* (1894), *English High Schools for Girls* (1907), *Story of the Manchester High School* (c.1911), *The Old Testament, Its Growth and Message* (c.1923). Teacher; educator; academic; headmistress; feminist; women's rights advocate; justice of the peace; education issues writer; education activist; religious/spiritual writer. Middle class.

Author's mid-Victorian education and later work to improve women's education at all levels, 1859–1933. Growing up in Scotland. Describing Scottish folk customs; developing sense of English identity despite her Scottish childhood. Taking lessons from her father and governesses; teaching herself to read; attending a Scottish academy, c.1870. Family's moving to London, 1871, after father lost his commercial job. Describing female education in the 1870s. Attending Frances Mary Buss's North London Collegiate School for Girls, 1871–78; expressing her praise and admiration for Buss. Going on to Girton College, Cambridge, 1878–81; describing status of early women students there; feeling stymied in pursuing courses she desired; resenting women students' rigid curriculum. Recounting social restrictions on women students. After leaving Girton, teaching at Buss's school, 1882. Receiving her degree at University College, London, 1884. Not being a natural public speaker; describing her course of self-training. Explaining details of Buss's elaborate and rigid disciplinary system. Noting that working for Buss nurtured her sense of competence, as well as fostering other capable young women. Moving from her family's home to her own flat, 1888. Visiting U.S. to study American systems of education. Describing advances in English women's education during the 1890s. Buss's death, 1894; author's becoming deputy to the new headmistress, Sophie Bryant, 1895–98. Noting that the bicycling trend gave women independent means of travel and effectively ended chaperoning. Serving as headmistress to Manchester High School, 1898–1924; accommodating curriculum to students' desires; adding classes in housewifery and clerical work to encourage girls to stay in school longer. Recalling consequences of the Education Act of 1902. Speaking at numerous educational conferences; becoming active in local high school and college associations. Serving as president to the Association of Headmistresses of Public Secondary Schools, 1909–11. Being reluctant to participate in militant suffrage activity because of her public reputation; fearing she might harm her educational influence. Her school's being conscripted as a hospital during WWI; author's organizing women volunteers. Tracing her educational work until her retirement, 1924. Serving as justice of the peace for the Magistracy of Manchester, 1924. Being advisor to the Colonial Office on education in Africa and to the Girl Guide movement in Manchester, 1925. Moving to Derby, then London, 1931. Commenting on relations between secondary schools and universities, the need for flexible curricula, and public support of higher education.

Burstall establishes herself solidly in favor of the type of female educational reform that introduces girls to the strict disciplinary atmosphere and challenging courses customary in boys' public schools. Her position at Girton in the 1870s was much like the position of women students at America's private military colleges today, with Burstall and her classmates being taken less than seriously by the Cambridge establishment. After her experiences there, her work to promote women's educational equality became virtually a mission. This account constitutes a valuable compendium of the many issues pushing women's educational reform for fifty years after women first entered Britain's schools of higher education. Because Burstall effectively idolized her mentor, the controversial educator Frances Mary Buss, readers interested in studying Buss's impact on her students may want to look also at memoirs by two of her other pupils, Mary Vivian Hughes and Netta Syrett. Burstall's commitment to women's education after WWI extended her influence into parallel fields, such as the creation of educational systems for native peoples in British colonies. Her autobiography helps the reader to appreciate both the progress of female education in the early 20th century and the remarkable energy and commitment of women like Burstall who made it possible.

181 BURTON, Isabel, Lady (née Arundell). 1831–1896. *The Romance of Isabel Lady Burton, the Story of Her Life Told in Part by Herself and in Part by W. H. Wilkens*. Cambridge: Cambridge University Press, 1897. Ed. by W. H. Wilkens. 2 vols. Vol. 1: 374 pp.; front. port.; preface by ed.; illus.; letters. Vol. 2: 403 pp.; illus.; letters; index. NUC pre56 86:495.

Born in London. Father: Henry Raymond Arundell. Mother: Elizabeth Gerard. 9 brothers; 4 sisters. Married 1861, Sir Richard Burton, diplomat, explorer, author, d.1890. Widow. Wrote *The Life of Captain Sir Richard Burton* (1893), *The Passion Play at Oberammergau* (1900). Biographer; travel writer; society woman; diplomat's spouse; traveler (Europe, South America, Middle East, India). Upper class.

Extraordinary life and experiences of the woman who married Britain's foremost explorer, 1831–c.1895. Vol. 1: Being "spoiled" by her father; mother's indulging her stepbrother. Attending a Roman Catholic convent school; regretting having left school early, age 16. Loving to read books on the occult. Being attracted to Eastern culture and gypsies; visiting gypsy camps; making gypsy friends. Socializing in London; attending balls and operas; seeking her ideal image of a man. Studying in Boulogne; Richard Burton's coincidental stay there; meeting him; feeling awed by his gypsy-like quality. Returning to London determined not to marry anyone else. Envying his pilgrimage to Mecca in the guise of an Arab, 1853. Resolving to nurse in the Crimea; her help being declined by Florence Nightingale. Starting a club for underprivileged girls in London. Encountering Burton again in London; entering secret engagement with him; his leaving again for African exploration. Traveling on the Continent with her sister; dreaming about Richard; refusing marriage proposals from a wealthy American and a Russian general. Recounting Richard's African explorations; his returning to England in disfavor with the Royal Geographic Society. Introducing him to her mother; mother's detesting Burton's outspoken agnosticism; author's deciding to marry despite mother's objections. After marriage, Richard's presenting her at Court; author's hearing but dismissing rumors about his sexual practices abroad. Accompanying him on his consular appointment to West Africa, 1861; exploring with him in the Canary Islands. Richard's leaving to assume consulship in Santos, Brazil; author's later joining him. Enjoying European society in Rio de Janeiro; complaining about food, climate, native people, and cholera. Accompanying husband on explorations of Brazil's interior; witnessing slavery practices. Richard's suffering failing health; her engineering a consulship of Damascus for him; defending Richard's activities before the Royal Geographic Society. Accompanying him to Damascus via Alexandria; describing exotic sights. Vol. 2: Househunting in Damascus; collecting menagerie of Eastern animals. Entertaining the governor-general of Syria; learning to ride a camel. Visiting Palmyra; while there, wearing male attire; passing as Richard's son. Surviving cholera outbreak in Damascus. Depicting ongoing hostility between Moslems and Christians; visiting the Holy Land. Alluding to unspecified incident between Burton and two young Jewish boys; his being accused of anti-Semitism; governor-general's demanding Richard's diplomatic recall. Regretting leaving Syria with slur on her husband's name. Richard's accepting consulate at Trieste, 1872. Author's visiting England to facilitate publication of husband's books; noting that his *Inner Life of Syria* earned critical acclaim. Traveling to India; participating in Indian rituals and festivities. Visiting England; trying unsuccessfully to secure promotions for Richard. Entertaining British officers while husband was exploring the Guinea coast. Richard's health worsening; his beginning to translate *The Arabian Nights;* author's lamenting his refusal to drop explicit sexual passages. Burton's receiving a knighthood, 1886; accepting consulship at Tangiers. Disliking Morocco. Richard's death, 1890. Controversy over author's having called Roman Catholic priest to husband's deathbed.

Protecting Richard's papers and manuscripts. Burning his translation of *The Scented Garden,* primarily for its observations on primitive sexual customs, to protect Richard's reputation. Facing life as a widow. Living in London. Publishing a biography of Richard.

In calling her autobiography a romance, Lady Burton is harkening back to medieval concepts of romance as the exploits of brave knights in pursuit of daring deeds. At least at heart, Lady Burton was a bold adventurer whose ambitions were frustrated by being born a woman during the 19th century. Certainly, she found her husband to be romantically attractive in the adventurous sense and declares frankly that she lives his explorations in her own imagination. By marrying him, she circumvented Victorian gender restrictions and made herself able to share his exotic travels. Her claims to have "protected" her husband's papers after his death are problematic, for she burned much of his work, not merely *The Scented Garden,* and as editor of his collected works severely censored the whole, omitting every reference to his comparative studies of homosexuality that have made him, in the late 20th century, a figure of central interest to gay studies. To many scholars, in fact, Isabel Burton will live in infamy for her sanctimonious destruction of her husband's irreplaceable travel writings in the name of respectability. In a certain sense Lady Burton censors her autobiography as well, selectively remembering their marital partnership but omitting or obscuring details of the scandals that frequently engulfed him. Students of the Burtons will also want to look at Glenn Burne's 1985 biography of Sir Richard, which discusses his covert explorations and private psychology; another enlightening book that says much about the tensions in the Burtons' marriage is Sir Richard's own volume, *The Erotic Traveller.*

182 BUTLER, Eliza Marian. 1885–1959. *Paper Boats: An Autobiography.* Collins, 1959. 192 pp. BLC to 1975 49:231.

Born in Lancashire. Father: Theobald Fitzwalter Butler, coal and iron firm owner. Mother: Catherine Elizabeth Barraclough. 3 sisters; 3 brothers. Single. Wrote *The Saint-Simonian Religion in Germany* (1926), *The Tempestuous Prince* (1929), studies of poets Byron, Goethe, Rilke, and Heine, books on magic and myth. Academic; literary critic; mythologist; biographer. Upper middle class.

Childhood emphasis on education, secondary school and university careers, and later scholarly endeavors of an academic and expert on comparative myth and magic, 1885–1954. Father's being a self-made man; orphaned at 15, his rising from bank clerk to industrial magnate; attending Heidelberg University, and teaching himself four languages. His caring passionately about educating his many children. Author's feeling somewhat lost among so many siblings. After lessons with a governess, author's and sister's being sent to German boarding school, 1896–1901; feeling that English were superior to Germans. At age 15, being sent to boarding school in Paris, 1901–04; coming to understand the English were vastly inferior to the French. Attending school in Reifenstein, Germany, 1904–05; this school's preparing affluent girls to run large establishments and manage estates. Returning with sister to England, 1906; father's offering them either traditional domestic role or chance to be independent. Author's choosing independence; entering Cheltenham Training College; disliking school's ladylike atmosphere. One teacher's recommending her for a woman's college at Cambridge; father's enrolling her. Attending Newnham College, 1908–11; being fellow student of later classicist Jane Harrison; discussing teachers and curriculum. After graduating, teaching but hating it; deciding to write. Doing research at Bonn University, 1913, on dramatist Friedrich Hebbel. Returning to England during WWI; becoming substitute lecturer in German at Newnham College. Teaching French and German at George Watson's Ladies College in Edinburgh, 1915; being detained there by police under suspicion of being a German spy. Returning to Cambridge; again being detained for questioning, 1916. Studying Russian under Jane Harrison to prepare for wartime nursing in Russia. Serving in Odessa, Russia, 1916–17; at start of Bolshevik revolution, working her way slowly back to England. Researching and writing her first book, on Heine and the Saint-Simonians, in Leipzig and Berlin, 1923–24. Researching and writing biography of Prince Buckler-Muskau, 1926–29; being attacked by scholars for her book's discussion of prince's sexual aberrations; deciding she was fundamentally unfit for academic life. Considering her biography of William Brinsley Sheridan a failure. Traveling with female friend to India, 1934–35. Publishing her critique of German Hellenism; through this book, becoming friends with eccentric millionaire Baron Eduard von der Heydt; briefly living at his Monte Verità colony, 1937, in futile hopes of obtaining material on Rainer Maria Rilke; describing the colony's resident occultists, Theosophists, and spiritualists. Serving as chair of German at Manchester University and at Newnham. Writing biography of Rilke; collaborating on drama about his life. Discussing Nazism. Studying magic in relation to Faust myth and German culture, 1940, to try to understand the Third Reich. Interviewing Aleister Crowley, 1946; not taking him seriously. Writing novels based on her dreams and encounters with ghosts, 1950. Lecturing about and writing book on Byron and Goethe, 1949–54.

This account offers a wealth of detail on curricula, organizational structure, and women's position as faculty members within women's higher education in Britain during the early 20th century, as well as providing a rare, close picture of the women's academic community at Cambridge. Butler's later studies in myth, magic, and ritual practices in European culture brought her interests into close parallel with those of her colleague and long-time friend Jane Harrison, whose groundbreaking studies on ancient Greek mystery religions made her a household name. Harrison's own early autobiography, *Reminiscences of a Student Life* (1925), validates Butler's commentary on the women's colleges at Cambridge and adds further details about academic life there.

183 BUTLER, Elizabeth Southerden, Lady (née Thompson). 1850–1933. *An Autobiography*. Boston and New York: Houghton Mifflin, 1922. 336 pp.; front.; foreword by M.E. Francis; illus.; index. NUC pre56 87:342.

Born in Lausanne, Switzerland. Father not named. Mother not named, artist. 1 sister; 1 stepsister. Married 1877, Gen. William Butler, d.1910. Widow. 3 daughters; 2 sons. Artist (painter); military spouse; society woman. Upper middle class.

Artist's early studies and rise to fame with canvasses celebrating the British Empire's military exploits, 1850–1919. Acquiring early love of drawing historical subjects. Studying French, Italian, and painting. Enjoying her art studies; tending toward military art. Showing her first picture, "Horses in the Sunshine," at Women Artists' Exhibition. Studying art in Florence. Her painting, "Magnificat," earning praise from Italian judge in competition. Selling a painting; having another painting accepted by Royal Academy. Sketching the Cameron Highlanders. Interviewing Crimean soldiers before painting "Calling the Roll after an Engagement, Crimea," 1874; having canvas accepted by the Royal Academy; Queen Victoria's viewing it privately. Being admitted to privileged social circles in tribute to her work. Being elected member of the Royal Institute of Painters in Water Colour. Finishing "Quatre Bras"; feeling its superiority to "The Roll Call"; recalling its popularity with crowds. Describing her creation of many works, and her increasing celebrity with the public. Major William Butler's being fascinated with her work before meeting her; proposing on their first acquaintance. After marriage, living and painting in Ireland. Death of her first-born daughter. Husband's serving in Zulu War; author's creating painting commemorating the war. Accompanying husband to his appointment as adjutant-general at Plymouth; births of four more children there. Husband's entering Egyptian campaign; joining him there; describing beauty of the East; attending reception in a harem. Working on "Review of the Native Camel Corps at Cairo." Her husband's being given command of infantry brigade at Aldershot; his later being transferred to Dorset. After taking command of British troops in South Africa, his being attacked in the press for opposing idea of South African war. Returning with husband to Aldershot; painting Boer War themes. Her husband's retirement; their moving to Tipperary, Ireland. Death of husband and mother, 1910. Her son Patrick's serving with the Royal Irish; his being wounded at Battle of Ypres. Describing London during WWI. Discussing the 1916 Sinn Fein rebellion in Ireland.

Although Butler is interested in her own career, rather than in the status of women artists at large, she does relate one anecdote about an Italian judge's discomfiture at finding that a painting he liked had been created by a woman. Her descriptions of pre-painting research—she once went so far as to have herself charged on a battlefield by two young cavalrymen, to get an idea of what combat was like—graphically depict the nuts and bolts of an artist's labors. Butler enjoyed an unusual degree of celebrity for her paintings, whose large canvases, exciting subjects, and patriotic themes had a natural affinity to popular tastes. Although she is not well known today, perhaps the closest analogy to her reputation as a painter would be the contemporary reputation enjoyed by the poet Tennyson, author of "Charge of the Light Brigade" and "Ode on the Death of the Duke of Wellington," for both individuals seized on matters that galvanized the public imagination, augmenting and romanticizing them with their artistic vision. Butler's account will fascinate historians of women's involvement in art, for her untypical attraction to subjects usually painted by men seems to have minimized any gender barriers to her progress.

184 BUTLER, Josephine E. (née Grey). 1828–1906. *Josephine E. Butler. An Autobiographical Memoir*. Ed. by George W. & Lucy A. Johnson. J. W. Arrowsmith Ltd., 1928. 276 pp.; preface; intro. by the Right Hon. James Stuart, M.A., LL.D.; letters; illus.; index. NUC pre56 87:404. (1st pub. 1909.)

Born in Milfield Hill, Northumberland. Father: John Grey, farmer, estate manager, bank investor. Mother: Hannah Annett. 4 sisters; 3 brothers. Married 1852, George Butler, Church of England clergyman, teacher, schoolmaster, d.1890. Widow. 3 sons; 1 daughter. Wrote books and pamphlets including *The Education and Employment of Women* (1868), *Woman's Work and Woman's Culture* (1869), and *The Constitution Violated* (1871); also wrote many speeches, articles, and biographies. Knew Anne Jemima Clough, Catherine Booth, William Lloyd Garrison, Victor Hugo. Feminist activist; women's issues writer; pamphleteer; biographer; political activist; political writer; abolitionist; temperance worker; philanthropist. Rural gentry; married into middle class.

Anthology of the writings of a dynamic 19th-century social reformer, covering her religious and feminist views, social activism, and life from childhood to widowhood, 1828–1906. Discussing her family's genealogy as French Huguenots; their leaving France during the 18th-century persecution. Growing up in Northumberland; being strongly attached to the "border country." Being influenced by her father's social conscience and mother's Anglican piety; also acquiring humanitarian Quaker ideas; declaring her antislavery principles. In adolescence, turning to religion to assuage excess emotionality; acquiring early sense of solidarity among women. Being schooled by mother and a governess; progressing through secondary school and boarding school. Being horrified to learn about crimes against women, such as rape and government-sponsored prostitution; believing in women's equality as an inalienable right. Marrying an idealistic vicar, 1852; being emotionally and intellectually fulfilled in marriage. Living in Oxford, 1852–57; taking in male student boarders; disliking their denigrating conversation about women; rebelling openly against men's dominance of society. In Oxford's libraries and galleries, copying art and maps with husband; studying Italian. Their living in Cheltenham, 1857–64; again taking in student borders to augment income. Her antislavery principles. Being traumatized by her daughter's death from a fall, 1864; being further distressed by deaths of her niece and father a year later. Living with her husband in Liverpool, 1866–82; giving refuge to girls from Belgian houses of prostitution; creating "House of Rest" in Liverpool, for the city's homeless; sheltering battered and abused women. Becoming president of North of England Council for Promoting Higher Education of Women, 1867–73. From 1869, leading the Ladies' National Association (LNA) to repeal the Contagious Diseases Act; the act's branding prostitutes in the public eye, but letting male customers remain anonymous. Recounting public meetings of the LNA and conferences such as the Congress of the International Abolitionist Federation (to abolish government regulation of prostitution), 1877. Also working for the Good Templars (temperance) society. Traveling extensively in Britain and Europe to promote her causes. Husband's being appointed canon of Winchester; moving to Winchester, 1882. Gaining notoriety for her crusade against regulation of vice; her husband's career's suffering as a result. Husband's rheumatic fever and death, 1890; sister Harriet's death. Retiring to Wooler, North Milfield, c.1900–06.

The editors compiled this autobiographical memoir at the request of the Ladies' National Association for the Abolition of Government Regulation of Vice; it is a chronological selection of Butler's political writings, speeches, pamphlets, and letters. In 1896 Butler had published **185** *Personal Reminiscences of a Great Crusade;* this is included as a section of *Josephine E. Butler* and is the book's closest approach to a narrative autobiography, although confined to a discussion of her lifework to end licensing of brothels and to repeal the Contagious Diseases Act. Butler believed that women's role is to raise the moral standard for both sexes. She also believed strongly that prostitution was a social, rather than a moral, disease which arose from poverty and hopelessness and could be cured by restoring the prostitute's self-respect; her objection to the Contagious Diseases Act was that in regulating prostitution and publicly identifying the women involved, they became stigmatized permanently, losing all chance to regain decent lives. In 1885 she collaborated with like-minded investigative journalist W. T. Stead, editor of the *Pall Mall Gazette,* in exposing the underground sale of child prostitutes in Britain;

his resulting article, "The Maiden Tribute of Modern Babylon," produced an explosion in the public awareness, earning Stead jail time but also leading to the 1885 Criminal Amendment Act cracking down on white-slavery practices.

186 BUTTS, Mary Frances. 1892–1937. *The Crystal Cabinet: My Childhood at Salterns*. Methuen & Co., 1937. 279 pp.; front. port. sketch of author by Jean Cocteau. NUC pre56 87:625. (other ed.: Boston: Beacon Press, 1988.)

Born near Poole, Dorset. Father: Frederick John Butts, retired naval officer. Mother: Mary Jane Briggs. Stepfather: "Freddy" Hyde, retired army officer. 1 brother. Married 1918, John Rodker, poet, publisher; separated c.1920. Married 1930, Gabriel Aiken, cartoonist, separated 1934. Wrote *Ashe of Rings* (1925), *Armed with Madness* (1928), others. Novelist; historian. Middle class.

Intimate youthful memories and philosophical, social, and religious speculations, covering 1892–1912. Memories of the family home, "Salterns." Recalling her first thoughts about God, mercy, and punishment. Seeing animism, or the sense that everything is alive and aware, as natural attribute of childhood; observing that Shelley in his poetry addresses the living consciousness in nature. Feeling lingering presence of her half-brother, who died before her birth; her father's love for him. Attending day school. Father's allowing her to read whatever she pleased. Birth of another brother, 1902. Father's death, author's age 10; afterward, mother's burning those of father's books that she found scandalous; author's comparing her act to Knox and Calvin's burning witches; feeling "the old implicit respect for things of the mind" was gone from Salterns; contrasting Victorian prudery with modern acceptance. Mother's selling father's William Blake paintings and nonscandalous books to pay his death duties. Mother's remarrying, author's age 15; author's depicting conventional, brisk character of her new stepfather. Attending St. Andrews' School in Fife, Scotland, ages 15–18; describing school's policies, ideas, and spiritual coldness; having one excellent teacher there. Publishing her first article in the *Weekly Outlook*. Reacting to *Origin of the Species* by starting to doubt Christianity; doubting it further after reading *The Golden Bough* on comparative religion. Attending church less. Failing entrance examination for Cambridge. Attending Westfield College in Hampstead, part of London University; supporting women's fight to be admitted to higher education; being irked that nine out of ten women students only wanted to be married. At age 20, being an incipient socialist.

A study of the formative influences on the author's imagination and curiosity, this autobiography unfortunately stops before the beginnings of her adult writing career. She does not mention that her student days at Westfield College ended with expulsion over illegally attending a horse race, although this transgressive impulse tends to characterize her later life. She went to work for the London County Council and became part of a literary circle including Hilda Doolittle, Ezra Pound, and John Rodker, whom she married in 1918. Leaving him two years later, she settled in Paris with painter Cecil Maitland and became part of occult practitioner Aleister Crowley's set. She cultivated acquaintance among Djuna Barnes's sophisticated lesbian circle, slept with both men and women, and experimented with drugs. Her friend, publisher Sylvia Beach, brought out some of her works, which deal with occult practices and imagery that she had become familiar with through Crowley. In 1930 she returned to England, marrying cartoonist Gabriel Aiken and separating from him in 1934. Her works from the 1930s are primarily historical novels, although her later short stories were anthologized by the novelist and poet Bryher, who was also a member of Butts's literary circle. The 1987 biography of Butts by Hanscome and Smyers contains further details of her later career. Her literary work has recently experienced a revival, and this autobiography consequently received a reprint in 1988.

187 BYNG, Marie Evelyn, Viscountess Byng (née Moreton). 1870–1949. *Up the Stream of Time*. Toronto: MacMillan, 1946. 274 pp.; foreword; illus. NUC pre56 88:100.

Born in England. Father: Richard Moreton, businessman, assistant marshal of ceremonies to Queen Victoria, comptroller to Lord Lorne. Mother: Janie Ralli, Lady-in-waiting to Princess Louise and to Duchess of Albany, Greek. Married 1902, Julian Byng, Viscount Byng of Vimy, British Army field marshal, governor-general of Canada, metropolitan police commissioner, d.1935. Widow. Wrote novels *Barriers* (1912), *Anne of the Marshland* (1914). Knew Princess Alice (later Countess of Athlone), Jan Smuts, Lord Kitchener, King George, Duke of Windsor. Society woman; military spouse; novelist; WWI volunteer; foreign resident (South Africa, Canada). Upper class; married into aristocracy.

Author's carefully reconstructed memories of her family life in childhood and in marriage, covering 1870s–1945. Family ancestry. Being educated by governesses in English, Greek, and "all fine things." Mother's showing dissatisfaction with author's lack of beauty; wishing author were male; author's consequently feeling deeply inferior; at least feeling loved by her father. Mother's selecting author's friends; arranging her debut. Socializing with royalty and wealthy people. Marrying, 1902; author and husband's being strongly devoted to each other. Wanting children, but feeling awkward around them. Having a desire to write. Describing life with a military husband: having to move frequently, his many absences, his distinguished WWI service. During WWI, author's doing volunteer work. Recalling her many beautiful homes and gardens during her marriage. Wishing for a more private life. Enjoying her extended foreign residences in South Africa and Canada. Visiting California; being fascinated by Hollywood filmmaking. Meeting President Roosevelt. Husband's death; author's feeling a great void. Performing volunteer work in WWII. Recalling being stranded without money in Canada during WWII, due to her funds being frozen; receiving help from friends.

Nostalgic in impulse, this autobiography is declared by Lady Byng to have been written "to give brief sketches of days gone by." The writing of this wistful narrative seems to have served as the writer's positive self-therapy during WWII to fill the emptiness left by her husband's death, and she dedicates the book to the many Canadian friends who were her other source of wartime comfort. Her two novels, which closely follow the conventional model of romances, implicitly question society's restrictions on women.

188 BYRNE, Muriel St. Clare. 1895–1983. *Common or Garden Child: A Not-Unfaithful Record*. Faber & Faber, 1942. 187 pp. NUC pre56 88:160.

Born in England. Father not named, probably an architect. Mother not named. Single. Wrote *Elizabethan Life in Town and Country* (1925), *Somerville College, 1879–1921* (1922), others. Historian; playwright; editor. Upper middle class.

Nostalgic and imaginative recounting of personal memories, emphasizing gender issues, covering author's ages 4–14. Writing her first poems at age 4. Envying her male cousins for having better hoops than she did. Remembering her aunt and uncle in mourning after death of Queen Victoria, author's age 6. Being closest to her father; his teaching her male standards of conduct; learning to swear from him; sensing that men's possessions, standards, and values were superior to women's. Preferring to play with boys. Describing her private garden; comparing the interior of her family's house with that of family friends. Attending school; being fascinated with 1910-era short stories of dashing young men enjoying college life. Discussing her childhood fears, particularly of suffocation. Comparing her intellectual and athletic abilities with those of the more feminine Helen, her best friend and schoolmate. Acting in school theatricals, playing golf; loathing sewing and knitting. Recalling her childhood political bias towards conservatism; appreciating having family servants. Valuing the Edwardian ethos; its promoting building construction and business expansion. In her early teens, attending an all-girls school; learning to enjoy literature there, especially about male characters. Attending Tory political meetings, literary lectures. Grieving over her father's death; rebelling against staying at a girls' school; going to coeducational high school in a new city.

Byrne chooses a perspective and style suitable for rendering the viewpoint of a child. As fragmentary as it is, her memoir is strongly organized around her youthful questioning of gender constraints on roles and her imaginative experimentation with possible social roles for herself through identifying with male characters in fiction. Succinct and evocative, Byrne's memoir has a natural place in gender studies, and suggests some of the means by which clever girls in the 19th century could reject traditional roles for women and invent their own for serviceable use.

189 CADDIE. 1900–s.l.1950. *Caddie, A Sydney Barmaid: An Autobiography Written by Herself.* Ed. by Dymphna Cusack (author's employer). Constable, 1953. 274 pp.; intro. by ed.; postscript. NUC pre56 88:598. (other ed.: Melbourne: Sun Books, 1966.)

Born at Penrith, Australia. Parents not named. 1 brother. Married c.1918, John Marsh; divorced c.1935. 1 son; 1 daughter. Barmaid; bookie; domestic servant. Working class.

Pinched childhood circumstances, work history, and struggle against poverty of a Sydney barmaid, emphasizing the working-class plight during Australia's Great Depression, c.1905–1950. Becoming a barmaid, age 24, to support her family despite never having touched liquor herself. Being shocked to hear profanity for the first time. Her emigrant Scottish grandparents being higher class, but their daughter, Caddie's mother, having married a woodcutter. In childhood, author's protecting family from father's drunkenness by catering to his whims. Children's being teased because of their poverty, surviving on handouts from grandparents. After grandfather's financial ruin, father's finding work on a distant railway line; family's moving to her father's tent camp, living there for two years. At age 12, author's working in a boardinghouse. After mother's death in childbirth, author's keeping house for her father and brother; dreaming of escape to Sydney. Brother's dying during WWI; author's running away with girlfriend to Sydney; working as a café waitress. Both girls' becoming infatuated with a customer; author's dating and marrying him, age 18. Being relieved by news of her father's death. Husband's being dominated by his mother, who gradually persuaded him Caddie was too low for him. Husband's being shiftless, fired from every job. Caddie's taking and losing job as wet-nurse. Husband's abusing her and cheating on her with her best friend; scheming with his mother to take the children. At age 24, Caddie's fleeing with the children; seeking a place to live; landlords' discriminating against women with children. At last finding a "dump" of a boardinghouse to live in; hiring a babysitter; going to work in a teashop; later becoming a barmaid for higher pay. Describing bar, drunken customers, brawls, men's incontinence and vomiting. Discovering her neighbors were prostitutes;

leaving the boardinghouse. Being amazed that her bar sold liquor illegally on election day. Discovering babysitter's abuse of her children; firing her; nursing daughter through nearly fatal diphtheria. Commenting on friend's illegal abortion; friend's risking death rather than face public abuse over unwed motherhood. Lacking child care; boarding her children in a church home; taking a classier saloon job close to them. Experimenting with drinking but stopping: "Drink couldn't make me forget my worries." Being strictly practical in her workplace behavior to keep her job and promote tipping: shortening her skirt, encouraging customers to drink, listening without offering opinions, catering to her boss. Dating patron involved in underworld liquor racketeering. Starting a love affair with Peter, a Greek businessman; his leaving for Greece. Using money from Peter to start a grocery business which failed. Hiring on at a hotel bar for the sake of its free room and board; enduring her tyrannical landlady; noting the bar's illegal practices. Quitting, then working at another bar until she could no longer stand the rats. Like other Australians, being jobless during the Depression; finding occasional jobs in slum pubs. Being ashamed to go on the dole, but finding neighbors in the unemployment lines with her. Divorcing her husband; working at a hotel bar job; rooming with friends; suffering malnutrition and exhaustion. After recovery, finding a job; hiding her earnings from welfare officers; losing her welfare after neighbor reported her. Appealing to local M.P.; his demanding sexual favors in return for restoring her welfare. Running numbers for neighborhood bookie; becoming a bookie herself and discovering how profitable it was. After Peter's wife's death, his sending marriage proposal to author; Caddie's refusing from fear of her ex-husband's getting the children. Peter's returning to Australia, 1935; resuming their relationship briefly; his dying in a car crash. WWII; author's daughter's working for the government; son's qualifying as architect. Author's fearing her son's enlistment and possible death, but declaring she had found faith in herself at last.

In her foreword, the editor informs readers that she hired Caddie as a domestic servant in Sydney and encouraged her to write her life story; the editor's postscript adds details from Caddie's life after the war. Caddie's nickname derives from "Cadillac," and was given to her by the barkeep at her first job, who thought her too classy for her position. A fascinating study of Australia's working-class culture in the years surrounding the Great Depression, her autobiography was also published just as the Royal Commission on Liquor in New South Wales was exposing the mob-run liquor racket. It is a rare firsthand look at the illegal practices and payoffs that the racket entailed.

190 CALDWELL, Taylor (Janet Taylor Caldwell). 1900–1985. *On Growing Up Tough*. Old Greenwich, Connecticut: Devin-Adair, 1971. 159 pp. BLC to 1975 51:55.

Born in Manchester. Father: Arthur Francis Caldwell, journalist. Mother: Ann M. 1 brother. Married 1919, William Fairfax Combs. Married 1931, Marcus Reback. Married 1972, William E. Stancell. Married 1978, William Robert Prestie. 5 children. Wrote 35 best-selling historical novels. Novelist; foreign resident (U.S.). Middle class.

Seventeen essays illuminating the author's conservative mindset through her views on liberal social trends of the 1960s, using autobiographical incidents to exemplify her points, covering her life from 1905–71. 1) "Mrs. Buttons": Caldwell's epithet for her aunt in Manchester, who snipped buttons off clothing she donated to the poor. Father's working at the *Manchester Guardian,* mother's staying home, author's attending private Catholic school. Recalling father's advice to her, age 5: grow up as independent as possible. 2) "Irma Jones Never Came Back": emigrating with the family, age 6, to Buffalo, New York; seeing black and Jewish children hurt by liberal teacher's singling them out to teach tolerance. Lamenting America's polarization along race lines; blaming liberals; perceiving liberal conspiracy in the press. 3) "The Day When I Was Absolutely Perfect": recalling idiotic behavior produced by her childhood desire to be a saint; just like 20th-century liberals, author's deluding herself perfection was possible. 4) "Sharing": describing how social workers' interference infects public schools. At age 7, innocently recounting a parental spat; teacher's reacting by sending police to her house. 5) "The Purple Lodge": another school incident, showing that children aren't good, but born with fully developed human defects. 6) "The Child Lovers": how child-welfare workers at school influence children to exploit government sympathy with false complaints. 7) "Learning the Liberal Lingo": sarcastic commentary on using liberal buzzwords to preserve one's job. 8) "Onomatopoeia": using a cocktail party's setting to expose the fatuousness of small talk. 9) "Pioneering in Kentucky": her married life in Kentucky from age 19. Husband's going there to get rich as an oil driller; author's hoping to get money for college, having quit school at 15 to work. Hill folks' teaching her wilderness survival; author's working part-time as a stenographer. After husband's employer's bankruptcy, author's returning to Buffalo; being helped by Salvation Army to find a job and place to stay; observing that private charity, not public, put her back on her feet. Saving money for her husband to return; starting night college. 10) "What Happened to American Men?": blaming liberal government's welfare policies for the new weakness and lack of self-respect she sees in men. 11) "Women's Lib": believing that doing a man's work in the home is not liberation but a burden. Envying nonworking housewives; noting that women's economic and sexual liberation is really men's liberation from responsibility. 12) "T.L.C.—Keep Your Paws Off Me!" Discussing her hypochondria and exposure to the despicable condescension of doctors. 13) "Luv and the Law": citing legal cases to show the disastrous effects of liberal cosseting of criminals with disadvantaged backgrounds. 14) "Dolts and Love Cultists": expressing contempt for "the American insanity of loving everybody" and for "irresponsible" activists protesting on behalf of liberal causes. 15) "Plastic People": protesting synthetic foods and synthetic people. 16) "Why Not a S.P.U.V.V.?": suggesting the establishment of a Society for the Protection of Us Victims of Victims; arguing that most "victims" seek sympathy for personal advantage; discovering this during her "volunteer" (i.e., socially coerced) work in WWI. 17) "On Hippies": observing that 1960s hippies were like their grandparents in the 1930s, one element of society despising others who were hardworking and ambitious, passing irresponsibility on to their descendants. Believing the hippie movement to be covertly communist.

Provoked by the ultra-liberal sixties, Caldwell's reactionary essays fail as political writing but are good snapshots of her private formative experiences. Emigrating as a child from England to the U.S., she eventually achieved fame with her novels, most of them historical, including *The Eagles Gather* (1940), *Dear and Glorious Physician* (1959), and *Ceremony of the Innocent* (1976). Her romantic fictionalizations echoed her own private sensibilities; in a well-known interview from the 1970s, before her fourth marriage, she remarked to a reviewer that her career was less important to her than finding a man to love forever. She is the subject of two books by reincarnationist Jess Stearn, who was convinced that the historical and scientific knowledge demonstrated in her historical novels was proof of her earlier lives. Caldwell, however, repudiated reincarnation and remained a lifelong devout Catholic, giving novelistic treatment to her own Christian views in *Dialogues with the Devil* (1967) and *I, Judas* (1977).

191 CALVERT, Adelaide (Mrs. Charles). 1835–1921. *Sixty-Eight Years on the Stage*. Mills & Boon, Ltd., 1911. 271 pp.; front. port.; illus; facsimile letters. NUC pre56 91:225.

Born in England. Father: James Biddles, actor, comedian. Mother not named. Stepmother not named. 1 sister; 2 stepsisters. Married Charles Calvert, actor, theatre manager, producer. 6 children. Actress (child, stage); feminist; philanthropist. Upper middle class.

The stage career of a noted international actress, from childhood through old age, c.1842–1910. In childhood, learning to perform in musical theatre productions. Appearing in Southampton in her first principal role. Describing theatrical colleagues of the 1840s–1850s. Traveling to perform in America; appearing with the Boston Theatre Company. Marrying fellow actor Charles Calvert. Joining movement to improve living conditions of aged actors and actresses; fundraising for the cause. Appearing in the Prince's Theatre in Manchester, which her husband managed. Discussing child labor laws and attempts to change them, 1831–74. Letter extracts. Describing staging of Shakespearean plays and ceremonies at the opening of the Shakespeare Memorial Theatre in Stratford. Her husband's illness and death. Becoming friends with American actor Edwin Booth; touring with his company in the U.S. Visiting Utah; discussing Mormonism. Accompanying Lily Langtry on tour of the English provinces. Appearing in Herbert Beerbohm Tree's production of *Henry VIII,* 1890s. Noting changes in the public attitude toward theatre and the lessening of puritanical influences, c.1910; perceiving that being a wife and mother is no longer viewed as a bar to women's advancement in theatre. Remarking on English theatre's being more dignified in modern times than in the past century.

While cataloguing the achievements of herself and her husband, Calvert also clarifies many of the day-to-day details of British theatre in the 19th century. As a young actress she had playwright aspirations of her own, producing a melodrama, *Amy Laurence: The Freemason's Daughter* (1851), at a time when melodrama dominated theatrical production. Her descriptions of several early movements to improve actors' working conditions and benefits are noteworthy, as is her discussion of the connection between child actors and the new mid-Victorian child labor laws.

CAMBRIDGE, Alice. [*See* ATHLONE, Alice, Countess of.]

192 CAMERON, Agnes Dean. 1863–1912. *The New North: Being Some Account of a Woman's Journey through Canada to the Arctic.* New York & London: D. Appleton & Co., 1910. 398 pp.; front.; illus.; map. NUC pre56 91:555.

Born in Victoria, British Columbia, Canada. Parents, siblings not mentioned. Probably single. Explorer (Canada); teacher; school trustee. Middle or upper middle class.

Author's six-month exploration of the Canadian wilderness, 1908. Planning and saving for two years; considering Canada to be the last frontier; wanting to explore it south to north, rather than the usual east to west. After departing from Chicago in May, being outfitted by the Hudson's Bay Company in Winnipeg. Describing the region's geography, especially wheat production; attending a meeting of the Women's Canadian Club. Traveling on to Calgary and newly founded Edmonton, city of tent housing; traveling north by stagecoach to Alberta's Athabasca Landing. Admiring local Cree Indians. From there, starting 2,500-mile journey by river, lake, and portage to the Arctic Ocean; enjoying rough manners of fellow travelers and sleep under open sky. Describing running rapids, porting overland, and being eaten alive by mosquitos; relating legends about wildlife: bison, wolf, caribou, whale, moose. Discussing Hudson's Bay Company's fur trade and role in the settlement of Canada. History of settlements visited in her journey: Fort McMurray,

Fort Chepewyan, Fond du Lac, Smith's Landing, Fort Smith, Fort Resolution, Hay River Mission, Fort Providence, Fort Simpson, Fort Norman, Fort Good Hope, Fort Rae. Admiring the Indian way of life: communal property, respect for nature. Recounting trading habits of the Chippewa Indians. Praising the work of Europeans living in Canada: missionaries, Hudson's Bay Company employees and their families. Noting anthropological distinctions between Indians and Eskimos, their religions, social customs, family life, and second-class treatment of women. Critiquing relations between natives and the British government: treaties, trading, intermarriage between Europeans and natives. Explaining how natives conducted trading; speculating about origins of their customs of bigamy, child-rearing, and cannibalism during times of famine. On reaching the Arctic Ocean, describing practice of whaling. Returning from the Arctic; arriving back in civilization September 15, just before winter snow made the journey impossible for many months.

Cameron's wide-ranging geographic study of northern Canada is augmented by her record of tribal beliefs, such as the origins of humans from various totem animals. She consciously maintains a noncensorious attitude toward native cultures, although some paradox does arise in her discussion of white interactions with Canadian natives; despite exalting the work of the Hudson's Bay Company and European missionaries, she finds the resulting changes to Eskimo and Indian ways of life to be deplorable. Changes since 1908, however, have not been extensive because of northern Canada's inhospitable climate for extensive settlement, so that Cameron's account preserves contemporary relevance. Interest in her explorations has been revived through a 1986 University of Nebraska reprint of her book, edited by David Richeson.

193 CAMERON, Charlotte (O.B.E., F.R.G.S.). c.1880–1946. *Two Years in Southern Seas*. T. Fisher Unwin, 1923. 315 pp.; preface; front.; illus.; maps. NUC pre56 91:565.

Raised in London. Parents not named. Wrote *A Woman's Winter in Africa, a 26,000 Mile Journey* (1911) and *A Cheechako in Alaska and Yukon* (1920). Travel writer; traveler (Africa, U.S., Canada, New Zealand, Australia, South Pacific islands). Middle class.

One woman's South Pacific travelogue encouraging British colonization and reinforcing cultural stereotypes, covering c.1919–23. Memories of travel in Germany's African colonies, 1913; during WWI, having worked in the U.S. promoting the Allied cause. Embarking by ship from London to New York, c.1919; from New York, traveling by rail to El Paso, Texas. During visit to Ciudad Juarez, Mexico, feeling that Mexicans' faces seemed "vile, almost subhuman." Taking train through Arizona to San Francisco; from there, sailing to Honolulu. Describing Hawaii; noting that its Japanese residents outnumbered Americans;

fearing their threat in case of war; describing Hawaiian territorial government, surfing, and tourist sites. Making long voyage from Hawaii to Sydney; praising Australia's marvelous opportunities for settlement: "It is white working people that she needs in unlimited numbers." Admiring Sydney's Lever Bros. soap works and its use of native laborers. Establishing Sydney as her base for two years, speaking publicly on travel and ardently praising the virtues of British imperial expansion. Visiting New Guinea; sketching its colonial history; describing natives, funeral customs, conditions of native women, and the horrors of cannibalism. Meeting members of the Boyce Expedition after their tour of exploration. Visiting Yule Island's Sacred Heart Mission; approving of its Christianizing the natives, but believing that compulsory Western clothing was less healthy for natives in the heat than nakedness. Visiting Rabaul Island, under German rule; discussing German hatred of the British. Visiting Fiji; depicting its native customs, exports, missionary history, and inferior treatment of women. From Fiji, sailing to Samoa; noting beauty of Samoan natives, the new threat to coconut planters of the rhinocerus beetle, and Robert Louis Stevenson's residence in Samoa. Traveling via New Zealand to Tahiti; describing its beauty and destruction under German WWI bombardment. On island of Moorea, befriending a Scottish aviator and his English-Moorean wife. Making a separate trip to the Solomon Islands; describing their British protectorate government and local missionary activity. Discussing the conflict between agendas of planters and of Christian missionaries; fearing natives despite their Christian conversion. Admiring British empire builders in the remote Russell Islands. Returning to London; recommending long sea voyages to readers and emphasizing that Australia is "just like home" and ripe for colonization.

At its core, Cameron's book is profoundly committed to the colonial expansion of the British Empire, and the author—despite a knack for observation—belittles native culture for every one of its departures from civilized European behavior. She is particularly obsessed with cannibalism, which becomes her standard attribution to indicate a culture's desperate need for British moral intervention. Trying to filter accurate perceptions through Cameron's racism is also a problem, for her commentary figures nonwhite races as being inferior physically, mentally, and morally, despite whatever education and religion the beneficent Europeans may have given them. As a result, Cameron's account is less valuable for its observations than as a study in the complicated mental outlook of British colonialists in their confrontations with nature and primitive cultures, with their simultaneous impulses to uplift and subjugate. In this capacity, this travelogue is comparable to Anna Forbes's *Unbeaten Tracks in Islands of the Far East: Experiences of a Naturalist's Wife in the 1880s;* both books share a longing to impose familiar Western culture on exotic surroundings.

194 CAMERON, Clare (pseud.; née Winifred Wells; later Burke). 1896–s.l.1980. *Rustle of Spring: Simple Annals of a London Girl*. New York: George H. Doran, n.d. 284 pp. BLC to 1975 51:502.

Raised in Dagenham, Greater London. Father not named, dock worker. Mother: Julia. 1 brother. Poet; religionist (Buddhist convert); pacifist; clerk. Working class.

Growth and inception of an aspiring writer, and her hopes to escape the limits of working-class life, c.1900–1914. Father's being a laborer; family's living on his meager wages. Author's doing errands for her mother; talking butcher into selling them meat on credit. From young age, author's attending board school for poor children; taking needlework and composition lessons; father's making her learn piano. Father's supplementing his dock pay by repairing shoes. Author's shrinking from her relatives' crassness; illustrating this with Cockney vulgarisms from her aunt. Taking care of herself due to mother's frequent illnesses. At age 12, starting to kiss boys. Winning a secondary school scholarship; later winning a short story competition; loving to write. Spending her summer holiday in Clacton; contrasting its industrial pollution with clean country skies she later discovered. Having to quit school, age 15, to help support family. Mother's wanting author to be apprentice to a dressmaker; author's wanting to become a journalist. Working as a clerk in a newspaper office; feeling inadequate because she couldn't dress as nicely as her coworkers. Being given more responsibilities, higher pay. Wishing she were a man so she could do manual labor in the countryside; preferring country to city. Losing her job; finding another one at a publisher's. Taking private French lessons to better herself. Resenting the social difference between herself and fellow employees; quitting chapel in embarrassment over having to associate with the lower class; mother's accusing author of wanting to rise above her station. Author's sticking to her own cultural ambitions: reading literary works, becoming acquainted with grand opera. At beginning of WWI, age 18, having her first poems accepted for publication; beginning to date an artist from West London. Envisioning her future life as an unknown land to be discovered.

The governing issue in Cameron's memoir is her yearning to rise above both the poverty and the lack of aesthetic sensitivities that she believes are embodied in London's working class. Desperate to embrace the beauties of culture, she smarts at every instance of her parents' Philistine outlook and their attempts to define her ambitions for her. While not fully objective, Cameron's account is characteristic of a type of class rebellion, c.1870–1920, that made aesthetic standards its rallying point. Cameron went on to fulfill her ambitions as a poet, publishing many volumes of her poems through the next six decades. She also became a

Buddhist and a committed pacifist, and during WWII spoke widely on behalf of pacificism. Her final volume of poetry was published in 1980.

195 CAMERON, Lucy Lyttleton (née Butt). 1781–1858. *The Life of Mrs. Cameron: Partly an Autobiography*. Ed. by Charles Cameron (author's son). Darton & Co., c.1861. 572 pp.; front. port.; preface; illus.; letters; diary entries. NUC 91:595.

Born at Stanford, Worcestershire. Father: Dr. George Butt, county rector, chaplain to George III. Mother: Martha Sherwood. 1 sister (Mary Martha Butt Sherwood, author, missionary, social worker); 1 brother. Married 1805, Rev. R. C. Cameron. 12 children. Wrote *Margaret Whyte* and *The Two Lambs*. Teacher (Sunday school); children's author; clergyman's daughter; clergyman's spouse. Middle class.

Moral lessons drawn from the author's upbringing and youth, applied to her career as a writer of children's literature and advice to mothers, 1780s–1858. Early life with her father and mother, who instilled piety in her. Mentioning her childhood reading, including some books of questionable morals; advising her readers to guard children by controlling everything they read. Father's receiving new parish in Kidderminster, c.1787; family's relocating there. Mother's teaching author academics and Christian charity. Father's being called to London, 1788, as chaplain to George III during the king's mental illness. Author's brother's receiving excellent education at grammar school and Westminster public school. Believing her religious sense to be harmed by her schooling at Reading, ages 11–17. After schooling's end, author's returning home; her brother's studying toward Anglican orders at Oxford. In Reading, French immigrants' stirring over news of French Revolution. Relating British shock at the execution of Louis XVI, 1793. In her 20s, confronting mortality through family friend's death in childbirth and her father's fatal stroke, 1795; using her own religious acceptance as model for her readers. After father's death, family's moving to Bridgenorth; author's teaching Sunday school there with her sister. Discovering that society tolerates wicked people more than she suspected; asserting that despite men's greater depravity, women of pure minds should regard all men as their superiors "until sad experience in individual cases teaches them otherwise." Writing *Margaret Whyte*, age 27; starting to keep a regular journal. Riding circuit with her clergyman brother; meeting her husband-to-be, a fellow cleric, on these journeys, 1799. Expressing hostility toward Catholics, c.1800. Visiting London friends; regarding fashionable London's mania for opera and theatre as sinful and foolish. Following their return to Bridgenorth, author and sister's leaving their Sunday school and traveling to Bristol and Bath, visiting reformer Hannah More. Regretting that her father's death left her without domestic duties; describing a round of visiting throughout England.

After her sister's departure for India with her new husband, author's lamenting men's freedom to determine women's fate, but believing it wrong to challenge "divinely-ordained" distinctions of class, age, gender, and rank. Author and mother's living in Shropshire; later moving to Stockton-on-Teme. In 1805, marrying Rev. R. C. Cameron. Advising ladies to leave their anxieties with God for the comfort and happiness of their families.

Frequently quoting Scripture, Cameron uses her own life to provide didactic moral lessons for her intended readers, her children and grandchildren. Although writing her memoir as family history at the request of her son, the author died before finishing it. After the first 160 pages the text becomes increasingly her son's third-person narrative, incorporating extracts from her diary entries and letters. This book is a useful source for study of children's education, Anglican parish history, and women's beliefs concerning their own subordinate roles during the late 18th century.

196 CAMERON, Lady Mary (pseud). 1900–?. *Merrily I Go to Hell: Reminiscences of a Bishop's Daughter.* New York: Brentano's Publishers, 1931. 302 pp.; poem. NUC pre56 91:599.

Born outside Oxford. Father not named, Anglican bishop. Mother not named. 2 sisters; 7 brothers. Married Patrick Dennison, Irish rugby player. Actress (stage); nurse (WWI); secretary; traveler (South Africa, India, China, U.S.); clergyman's daughter. Middle class.

Youthful rebellion, WWI nursing ventures, and later touring career of a stage actress, 1900–1930. As a child, showing a strong individualistic streak. Receiving a classical education and strict discipline from her father at home. Studying in a High Anglican school sponsored by her father; hating its harsh discipline and compulsory sports. After start of WWI, envying her brothers' departure for France; engineering her own expulsion from school despite her father's fury. Serving as a VAD in France with British Red Cross; describing the Red Cross's wartime atmosphere. Meeting Patrick Dennison; impulsively marrying him after a week's acquaintance; being shattered by his death in battle soon afterward. Working as a secretary in the Air Ministry; also acting in military camp theatres throughout England. Touring South Africa and India with her theatrical troupe. Socializing in English Bombay society; scandalizing its members by staying out all night with a man. Traveling to Madras, Rangoon, and Singapore. Enjoying practical jokes and freedom of manner among her acting troupe; being disappointed by people's disapproval of her on her return to England. Going on tour with theatrical company in America; leaving it after successful pursuit by an ardent suitor. Rooming with a female friend in New York. Taking a job with another theatre company; touring the U.S. Making acquaintances among the bootleggers in America; noting her own increasing alcohol consumption.

Reminiscing about life on the road. Discussing her inability to return the love of the men who loved her, and her yearning for "grand passion" rather than marriage.

Born into a traditionally patriarchal family whose father's authority was bolstered by his religious and classical education, the author remembers herself as having always been the "odd woman out." However, Cameron's rebellion against her father seems to owe less to her individualism than to generational conflict; while her father's athletic and Christian child-raising principles seem to come straight from the mid-Victorian precepts of Charles Kingsley and Thomas Arnold of Rugby, the author's own appetites are for modern liberation. In discussing her own experiences, ranging from WWI nursing camps to America's Prohibition days in the 1920s, the author's discussions of historical detail are less important than the glimpses we see of her mind frame. Like a character from F. Scott Fitzgerald, the author is using her freedom to conduct a seemingly aimless search for something to fill an inner need she can't quite name. As a result, her book manages to convey the mental outlook of an era.

197 CAMPBELL, Beatrice, Baroness Glenavy (née Elvery). c.1888–d.a.1955. *Today We Will Only Gossip*. Constable, 1964. 206 pp.; illus.; ports.; index. BLC to 1975 52:104.

Born in Dublin suburbs, Ireland. Father: William Elvery, shopkeeper. Mother: née Teresa Moss. 3 sisters; 2 brothers. Married 1912, Charles Henry Gordon Campbell, later 2nd Baron Glenavy, cabinet secretary, later governor of the Bank of Ireland, d.1963. 2 sons (including Patrick Campbell, a prominent journalist); 1 daughter. Artist (painter); teacher (art); artist's model. Lower middle class; married into aristocracy.

Fond recollections of noted individuals in the arts, interspersed with personal memories and artistic endeavors, covering author's childhood to c.1955. Until age 6, growing up in the Dublin suburbs. Noting the strong class barriers, c.1890; being scorned by schoolmates because her father ran a shop. Mother's being from large family whose men were scientists and theologians; father's being a gifted cellist. Family's moving briefly to Carrickmines, then to Fox Rock, Dublin, author's age 8. Author's starting to read enthusiastically; loving literature and art. Studying at Dublin Metropolitan School of Art. While there, befriending the young W. B. Yeats; modeling for painter and writer William Orpen; reading Orpen's *Stories of Old Ireland and Myself*. Spending summer holiday in Paris; wanting to study painting there, but father's refusing. Going to London to study at the South Kensington School of Art, age 16. Working in stained glass, sculpture, and illustration, c.1906. Making and breaking an engagement to a young architect. Studying at the Slade Art School in London. Making friends with writers Katherine Mansfield and her husband John Middleton Murry; through them meeting

Campbell, whom she married in 1912. Also making friends with Frieda and D. H. Lawrence, as well as translator Samuel Koteliansky; evaluating their characters and talents. Births of a son and daughter, 1913 and 1914; author and husband's bringing Irish nanny over to London to care for them. During WWI, author's husband's serving in the Ministry of Munitions. Hearing news of the Easter Rebellion, 1916; although living in England, empathizing with the native Irish demand for home rule. Her mother's Dublin home's being burned by irregular soliders opposing the Cosgrave government, 1922. Birth of another son, 1924. Author's writing a play, 1928, after reading George Grossmith's *Diary of a Nobody*. Reading D. H. Lawrence's last novel, *Lady Chatterley's Lover;* praising its authenticity of voice. With her husband, visiting Italy, 1932, and other parts of Europe, 1936. Returning to Ireland to teach drawing and painting at the Royal Hibernian Academy, 1938. Discussing Irish neutrality during WWII. Death of her daughter in an air raid, 1944. Reading Samuel Becket's "Endgame." The death of Koteliansky, 1945, coming to symbolize for her the end of her youthful aspirations and friendships, of which he was a part.

In Lady Glenavy's memories, her literary circle of friends looms large, setting the character and flavor of her young existence. Her own book is full of notations from her reading of her friends' writings, and every mention of her meeting a new writer is followed by commentary on that person's work. As a secondary member of Ireland's literary set during its 20th-century revival, Lady Glenavy is more important as an observer than a participant, making her account a useful source on the circles surrounding D. H. Lawrence and John Middleton Murry and on the changes in Ireland's literary output as a response to war and political ferment, c.1910–40.

198 CAMPBELL, Beatrice Stella (née Tanner; Mrs. Patrick Campbell; later Cornwallis-West). 1865–1940. *My Life and Some Letters*. New York: Benjamin Blom, 1969. 451 pp.; front. port.; illus.; letters; index. NUC 1968–1972 15:327. (1st pub. Hutchinson, 1922.)

Born in London. Father: John Tanner, diplomat. Mother: Maria Romanini. 3 brothers; 2 sisters. Married 1884, Patrick Campbell, actor, d.1900; married 1914, George Cornwallis-West. 1 son; 1 daughter. Knew G. B. Shaw, Oscar Wilde, W. B. Yeats, Sarah Bernhardt, others. Actress (stage); theatrical producer; traveler (Europe, U.S.). Upper middle class.

Youth and career progress of a celebrated stage actress, against a backdrop of the British and American theatrical world, c.1870s–1917. Her Italian mother's adoring art and music. Her diplomat father's losing his money, departing permanently for Texas to seek his fortune in oil. Mother's sending author to Guildhall Music School for two years; author's meeting and eloping with Patrick Campbell. Being introduced to acting through an amateur stint. After ailing husband's departure for Australia's dry climate, author's getting her first professional acting job at Liverpool's Alexander Theatre. Noting hardships for traveling actors. Performing in experimental outdoor performances of *As You Like It* and *Midsummer Night's Dream* at Wilton, 1891; losing her singing voice due to open-air performances. Debuting at London's Shaftesbury Theatre; performing at the Adelphi; receiving letters of congratulation from Oscar Wilde, Herbert Beerbohm Tree, and Squire Bancroft. Learning of her father's death in Texas, 1893. Husband's prospecting unsuccessfully for gold in South Africa; his returning to England an invalid. Author's touring Germany in *Hamlet, Macbeth,* and *The Second Mrs. Tanqueray;* Shakespearean acting's being frustrating, with failures being reckoned to the actor, successes to the playwright. Performing in Maeterlinck's *Pelléas and Mélisande*. Meeting and describing Sarah Bernhardt. Death of her husband in the Boer War, 1900. London theatre attendance (and earnings) suffering because of the Boer War and Queen Victoria's death, 1901; author's deciding to tour the U.S. with Liebler and Company; resolving to earn enough to erase her debts. Performing in Chicago and New York. Discussing the education of her children: Beo's serving in the royal Navy, Stella's studying acting in Germany. Author's sharing the stage with Sarah Bernhardt in London, 1906. Touring, producing, and acting in many American productions, 1904–08. Leaving the stage after becoming incapacitated by a taxi accident; becoming close friends with playwrights George Bernard Shaw and Sir James Barrie. Marrying George Cornwallis-West, 1914. Outbreak of WWI; death of her son in France three years later.

Entering the acting profession at age 23 with a superb voice but no training, "Mrs. Pat" nevertheless rose by virtue of a natural gift for acting and reached the first crown of her career in Pinero Jones's 1893 *The Second Mrs. Tanqueray,* written as a vehicle for her. According to Margot Peters's authoritative 1984 biography of Campbell, she was one of the first British actors to work with Stanislavsky's system of emotional fidelity to the role. Her negative critiques of others' compromises in performance could occasion backstage conflict. In 1898, for example, Campbell was not happy with starring in Maeterlinck's *Pelléas and Mélisande* until she herself had artistic control of its production, direction, dress design, and music; her zeal was later rewarded when Sarah Bernhardt, profoundly impressed by the production, invited Campbell into partnership to restage the play in its original French. Campbell's career was notable for her starring roles in the new British "problem plays" inspired by the works of Ibsen, in which playwrights such as Pinero Jones and George Bernard Shaw used female protagonists to dramatize contemporary conflicts about women's social, sexual, and vocational roles; in fact, Shaw wrote the role of Eliza Doolittle for Campbell, then 37 years old. As someone whose counsel was sought by other eminent actors and playwrights, her well-judged memories contribute invaluably to the history of British theatre during its period of fin de siècle vitality. For more insight into her character, her book is usefully complemented by a reading of *Bernard Shaw and Mrs. Patrick Campbell, their Correspondence,* collected by Shaw in 1952.

199 CAMPBELL, Margaret, duchess of Argyll (née Whigham). c.1912–s.l.1975. *Forget Not: The Autobiography of Margaret, Duchess of Argyll.* W. H. Allen, 1975. 248 pp.; illus.; index. NUC 1973–1977 6:390.

Born at Newton Mearns, Renfrewshire, Scotland. Father: George Hay Whigham, civil engineer, chartered accountant, synthetic fabrics magnate. Mother: Helen Hannay. Married 1933, Charles Sweeney, principal of the Federated Trust & Finance Corp., American; marriage annulled 1947. Married 1951, Ian Campbell, 11th Duke of Argyll; divorced 1963. 1 son; 1 daughter. Society woman; WWII volunteer; foreign resident (U.S.). Upper class; married into aristocracy.

A Scottish society woman's upbringing, romances, and life among the international jetset, highlighting the glaring tabloid notoriety of her divorce from her second husband, 1912–75. Discussing how her 1963 divorce from the duke of Argyll had traumatized her; having lost the case because enemies influenced the divorce courts against her. Moving backward in time to relate her whole life. Her parents' histories, her happy childhood in New York while her British father was president of the Cuban Railroad. Parents' taking her to London to select a nanny, whom author loved and kept until age 25. Family's summering in Britain each year after 1919; their returning to England, 1926, in fear of cultural changes affecting America. Being shipped off to English boarding school; attributing her poor performance to the school's crushing her individuality. Blossoming intellectually when allowed to leave; studying under a governess. Making her elite social debut; discussing events at Ascot, the Embassy Club, and other social venues; being crowned Debutante of the Year, 1933, by England's newspapers. Enjoying a series of brief, broken engagements with sons of the peerage, then marrying Charles Sweeney, 1933. Converting to Roman Catholicism, her husband's religion, but declaring she would never accept papal infallibility or pray to a saint. Carrying on with married social life despite a series of illnesses and miscarriages; noting: "Charlie and I were known as the ideal married couple for many years." In aristocratic circles, being affected personally by the death of King George, 1937, same year as the birth of their daughter. Regretting the Wallis Warfield Simpson scandal; remarking that the king could have just kept seeing her instead of rushing into marriage. During WWII, giving birth to their son; author and husband's evacuating the children to Wales while they remained in London. Author's volunteering with the American Red Cross as entertainment officer, arranging for stars to entertain the troups. Discovering her husband's philandering, and realizing how long it had been going on; due to her emotional state, suffering a catastrophic fall down an elevator shaft. At end of WWII, divorcing Charlie and traveling to New York to console herself. Working briefly as reporter for *Women's Illustrated*. Using her new single freedom to pursue a series of romances; noting that although slightly crippled from her fall, her father's addition of conveniences to her London flat made life as effortless as before. Meeting Ian, Duke of Argyll, at a social event; marrying him despite friends' warnings about his violent nature, 1951. Declaring their marriage to have been shaky from the start. Having their first brutal fight during a Bahamas vacation. Husband's needing money to restore Inverary Castle; author's suggesting opening the castle to the public, with disastrous results. Author and duke's quarreling over every possible topic and principle; his taking pleasure in hurting her, especially after drinking heavily. Author's feeling alone after her mother's death, 1955. Duke's demanding she defer to his wishes; prohibiting her from joining the Inverary Town Council; becoming enraged at her for doing other philanthropic work. Husband's persuading her private secretary to sue her for libel and slander; resulting libel trial's being sensationalized in the tabloids. Duke's being preyed upon by his unethical physician, who provoked marital conflict and tried to have the author certified insane. Keeping her chin up; managing her daughter's wedding, 1958, in the midst of the media furor. Taking a last trip with her husband to Australia, 1959, but realizing reconciliation was hopeless; husband's stealing her diaries and private letters to use against her in a divorce case. Losing the libel trial; unsuccessfully contesting husband's divorce suit; ultimately paying £8,000 in damages. Preventing husband from publishing newspaper articles attacking her. Traveling in Asia, Africa, and Latin America. In Portugal, 1961, meeting "Bill," a married businessman; beginning a love affair with him; author and Bill's hiding from the paparazzi because of public interest in the ongoing Argyll divorce. Suing a magazine to prevent its publishing an interview with the duke exposing intimate marital details; this suit's establishing a legal precedent leading to Parliament's "Argyll law" on marital disclosure. Continuing her philanthropy, ensuring the survival of an animal sanctuary and of the financially needy Argyll and Sutherland Highlanders. Adopting two working-class boys, but having their family life destroyed by media hounding. Traveling to Washington, D.C., to visit Washington hostess Pearl Mesta; recounting her friendship there with J. Paul Getty. Death of the duke in 1973; calling him a sad, dejected man. Stating her intention, c.1974, to move to America to recover the privacy and happiness she enjoyed there when young.

Although this book could easily have been written by a betrayed aristocratic wife of the 18th century, it escapes being standard melodrama because the Duchess of Argyll fought back with some success, recovering her reputation. She tries to give her own side of a much-publicized story, maintaining a frank and conversational manner as she attempts to analyze the complexity of her relationship with the duke.

200 CAMPBELL, Margaret (Gabrielle Margaret Vere Campbell; Marjorie Bowen, pseud.). 1886–1952. *The Debate Continues, by Margaret Campbell, Being the Autobiography of Marjorie Bowen.* Heinemann, 1939. 298 pp.; foreword. BLC to 1975 52:126.

Born on Hayling Island, Hampshire. Father: Vere Campbell. Mother: Josephine Elizabeth Ellis, would-be playwright. 2 sisters. Married 1912, Zefferino Emilio Costanza, d.1916. Married 1917, Arthur L. Long. 4 children. Novelist; biographer; playwright; children's author. Middle class.

Emotionally repressed childhood and search for marital happiness of a prolific writer, c.1890–1935. Mother's family history. Recalling family's poverty in her childhood and parents' unhappy marriage. Their moving frequently around London and nearby Kent. Mother's being the family disciplinarian; author's also suffering tyranny from the children's nurse. After father deserted them, author's age 5, mother and nurse's blaming all problems on the author, while showering affection on her baby sister. Mother's becoming exasperated trying to teach author to read, punishing her abusively and abandoning attempt. Author's studying sciences and languages on her own; being shipped off to live with her grandmother in Hampstead; coming to detest women because female relatives treated her so much worse than male ones did. Paradoxically, being chiefly influenced by her mother, who was charming, sophisticated, and moved in theatrical circles; the more mother rejected her, the more desperately Margaret tried to please mother. Wanting to earn money to help mother escape poverty. Training herself in drawing; attending London's Slade Art School. Working small research jobs at British Museum while writing a novel at night. Attending Paris art school; sensing mother was glad to get rid of her. Yearning to marry and have children to find love among a new family. Gaining confidence from success of her first novel, *The Viper of Milan,* age 17; believing herself a born storyteller; happily signing contract for more books. Mother's being jealous of author's success; author's financing family trips to Rome and Holland; supporting the family but growing to feel enslaved. Father's death. Before meeting her husband-to-be at a Bloomsbury party, having resigned herself to singleness. Marrying, 1912, in order to escape to the beauty and freedom of her husband's native Sicily. Once there, submitting to the cultural subordination of women, but feeling oppressed by husband's violent temper. Hating barbarity of Sicilian customs; turning vegetarian from seeing animals butchered at street markets; buying market animals to free them. During pregnancy, 1914, fearing outcome of childbirth under Sicilian ideas of sanitation. While in Sicily, persevering in writing; selling short stories to help their desperate financial need. During second pregnancy, returning to England; attempting poultry farming in Kent. Grieving over death of her young daughter. Son's birth, 1916. Rejoining her husband in Italy, leaving son in England; husband's failing from terminal illness. Describing months of nursing husband in Tuscany. Author's finding new love with husband's physician; planning to marry after husband's death. Returning to England to fetch her son, but her physician lover's dying also. Author's seeking stability through remarriage to an Englishman. Mother's death. Author's retrospectively believing that her life had been sacrificed to her children, and that her dreams of a loving home died with her Italian physician.

In this introspective account, Campbell frequently shifts her narrative viewpoint from first to third person, noting in her foreword that this device aids her detachment. One would never suspect from the life disappointment that this book expresses that Campbell was so successful a writer, nor that despite her emotional trials she wrote steadily for forty years, producing more than 150 historical and mystery novels, including *The Viper of Milan* (1906) and *William, by the Grace of God* (1916), as well as several serious histories and a biography, *This Shining Woman: Mary Wollstonecraft* (1937). In fact, she made her literary pseudonym "Marjorie Bowen" such a goldmine for publishers that they hired two male novelists, Joseph Sheering and George Preedy, to keep up with the demand; Sheering and Preedy continued to publish novels as "Marjorie Bowen" after Campbell's 1952 death. The author also contributed an autobiographical essay, **201** "Margaret Campbell (Marjorie Bowen)," to *Myself When Young: By Famous Women of Today* (1938).

202 CANDLER, Ann (née More). 1740–1814. *Poetical Attempts by Ann Candler, a Suffolk Cottager, with a Short Narrative of Her Life*. Ipswich: John Raw, 1803. 68 pp.; list of subscribers; poems. BLC to 1975 52:505.

Born in Yoxford, Suffolk. Father: William More, glove maker. Mother: née Holder. Married c.1762, husband not named, soldier; separated c.1781. 5 sons; 4 daughters. Workhouse inmate; poet. Working class.

Autobiographical memoir in the form of a letter to her patroness, bound with the author's poems and recounting her marital and financial tribulations, 1762–1801. Her present circumstances, c.1801: living in a workhouse in Sproughton, having lost three children in infancy, not knowing the whereabouts of two others. Two daughters' being married; a third's being a domestic servant. Having lost sight of her husband years ago; assuming he's in the army, if living. After being married one year, husband's secretly enlisting in the Guards at Ipswich; pregnant author's going to fetch him back; reluctantly letting him enter the militia instead.

Husband's impoverishing the family by drinking; life being easier after birth of author's fourth child due to receipt of her aunt's legacy. Writing poem as letter of thanks to visiting minister for his charity, c.1771; his becoming patron of her writings. With six children, author's learning that her husband had reenlisted in the Guards and abandoned her. Placing four of her children in a workhouse (Tattingstone House of Industry), keeping eldest and youngest with her; later regretting she had not entered the workhouse to keep family together. Accepting charity from friends. After husband's return, author's being persuaded to move family to London; once family was settled, his abandoning them again; his using emergency army duty in the Gordon riots, 1780, as excuse to live with the Guards. Impoverished author's suffering abuse from husband when he infrequently appeared; deciding to leave him and return to Sproughton; her uncle's providing funds to make return possible. Entering workhouse upon return. Losing twin sons, born in workhouse, during infancy. After three years, husband's reappearing; author's refusing to live with him until he had funds. When they did lodge together, husband's lapsing into drunkenness. Author's leaving him for good, 1781; returning to workhouse for next twenty years. Praising her lady patrons for their goodness to her.

Biographical details in this letter are fleshed out by the editor's introductory notes, which supply information about the financial troubles of the author's father, the family's move to Ipswich, her mother's death, the author's self-education, and her marriage at age 22. In a postscript, the editor also records a suggestion from Candler's lady patrons that if she could earn enough by publishing her poetry, she might be able to rent a furnished room near her married daughter. Many of Candler's poems are autobiographical, concentrating on subjects including the death of her twin sons and her situation in the workhouse. The dramatization of the author's social plight gives illuminating details about both the circumstances of enlisted soldiers' families during the 18th century and the conditions and terms of existence within workhouses.

203 CANZIANI, Estella (Louisa Michaela). 1887–1964. *Round About Three Palace Green*. Methuen, 1939. 403 pp.; front.; preface; illus.; apps.; index. BLC to 1975 53:144.

Born in London. Father: Francesco Enrico Canziani, civil engineer, Italian. Mother: Louisa Starr, Royal Academy painter, American. Single. Wrote *Costumes, Traditions, and Songs of Savoy* (c.1911), *Piedmont* (c.1913), *Through the Appenines and the Lands of the Abruzzi* (c.1918). Artist (painter); teacher (art); social historian; religionist (Quaker convert); artist's daughter; WWI volunteer; travel writer; traveler (Europe, Morocco). Upper middle class.

Memories of growing up in London's art circles and establishing her own painting career, 1890s–1930s. Family's living in London, author's age 3.

Having been born partially deaf. Parents' being part of the Italian colony in Clerkenwell and Soho; noting distinction between Italian and English cultural ideas. Recalling sketching expeditions with both parents; being closest to her father; describing his engineering career. Mother's being a Royal Academy artist with many awards; father's Italian parents having opposed his marriage to so dominant a woman. Mother's being outspoken about social disadvantages of her fellow women; using feminist subjects in her painting; also writing articles on dress reform and the servant problem; endorsing Ruskin's precepts of morality in art. In childhood, author's accompanying her father to Italy to meet his parents; family's also visiting politicians Lord and Lady Aberdeen in Scotland. Recalling her parents' friendships with Sarah Heckford, Dr. Marie Stopes, and artist Frederick Leighton. Author's beginning her art career by illustrating Walter De La Mare's poems; gaining interest of British museum patrons who watched her sketch; also being noticed by Mr. Horsley of the Royal Academy. Family's making annual visits to Italy; describing Italian peasant life and folklore. Attending a private religious school in London; doubting its teachings; later converting to Quakerism. Having her first Royal Academy exhibition, age 17; winning admission to the Royal Academy School. Mother's death, 1909. After leaving school, author's holding several exhibitions at Walker's Gallery. Painting *Peace Baby* and *The Piper of Dreams.* Traveling to Abruzzi with father, 1913, and to Morocco, 1914. Lecturing on Italian folklore. WWI: working with Belgian refugees and in Women's Land Service Corps, doing paintings of ghastly war wounds. Teaching drawing and painting at Lily Montagu's West-Central Working Girls' Club for Jewish girls. Father's death, 1931.

This memoir by the artist daughter of a well-known portrait painter portrays the character of Canziani's mother as vividly as the author's own. The book gives an informative picture of the cultural accommodations negotiated between her feminist mother and her patriarchally raised Italian father, as well as providing a wealth of casual detail from her mother's career and her own on the acceptance of women artists within London's elite painting establishment in the early 20th century.

204 CAPPE, Catharine (née Harrison). 1744–1821. *Memories of The Life of the Late Mrs. Catharine Cappe, Written by Herself.* Boston: Wells & Lilly, 1824. 408 pp.; apps. NUC pre56 94:519.

Born at Long Preston, Craven, Yorkshire. Father: Rev. Jeremiah Harrison, Church of England clergyman. Mother: née Winn. 1 brother. Married 1788, Newcome Cappe, minister, died c.1800. Widow. 3 stepdaughters; 3 stepsons. Wrote *Observations on Charity Schools, Female Friendly Societies, and Other Subjects Connected with the Views of the Ladies Committee* (1805). Social reformer; clergyman's daughter; clergyman's spouse; religionist (Anglican); religionist (evangelical); teacher (Sunday school); religious/spiritual writer. Middle class.

Author's devout Yorkshire upbringing, marriage to a clergyman, and later social reform work, c.1750–1812. Recalling her mother's cheerfulness and good looks; author's own looks being scarred from childhood smallpox. Family's moving to Catterick when father obtained parish living there; her father's being open-minded about Methodist and Quaker dissenters, although an Anglican cleric himself. Knowing she was her father's favorite, despite his reluctance to say so or to support "the development of the female mind." Being sent to day school in York to learn dancing and needlework; later attending boarding school there; being persecuted by fellow students for her lack of wealth. After leaving school, living with aunts in York; their dissuading her from harming her feminine brain with "excessive" reading. Worrying over her father's failing health and brother's misbehavior; mother's preferring brother and rejecting author's concerns. Being grief stricken by her father's death, 1763. Befriending Rev. Lindsey, her father's successor in Catterick parish. Moving with her mother to Bedale; starting a Sunday school for poor children there. Lindsey's opening a chapel and questioning tenets of Church of England; his being formally accused by detractors. Rev. Cappe's defending Lindsey from charges; his being author's future husband. Lindsey and wife's moving to London to open a room for public worship; author's visiting them; following their lead in seceding from Trinitarian worship. In York, organizing the Female Benefit Club for miners' wives and daughters; attending Mr. Cappe's chapel there and socializing with him. His being a widower with a son older than the author; author's admiring his character and wanting to marry him. After marriage, 1788, Mr. Cappe's suffering two partially paralyzing strokes; his continuing preaching with help from a parish assistant. Husband's death, c.1800; author's finding strength in religious faith; furthering her social reform causes. Working to enlarge Female Benefit Club. Training lower-class girls for employment as domestics; believing domestic service to be the best option for these girls, who have no "little trades" open to them. Establishing District Committees of Ladies to help poor women throughout the country. Noting difference between knowing the gospel and living by its tenets.

Cappe's exhortations to readers to be vigilant lest they fall into "whirlpools of vice and folly" sets the moral tone for her book, which paints a many-faceted contemporary portrait of 18th-century English social customs, religious trends, and gender roles. Her account suggests the degree to which traditional Anglican clergy were affected by the surrounding evangelical zeal of Nonconformists, and provides a quietly ironic contrast between the limited expectations she faced as a girl and the breadth and strength of her later philanthropic work. She began a writing career the year she married, her first work being an abridgement of an advice manual by Jonas Hanway. Her later writings include articles for religious periodicals, discussions of charity schools, and a life of her husband published as a preface to his sermons.

205 CARBERY, Mary (née Toulmin). 1867–?. *Happy World: the Story of a Victorian Childhood.* Longmans, Green, 1941. 273 pp.; front. ports.; foreword. NUC pre56 95:2.

Born in Hertfordshire. Father: Harry Toulmin. Mother: Emma Wroughton. 7 sisters; 2 brothers. Married, husband not named. Wrote novels *Children of the Dawn, The Germans in Cork, The Farm by Lough Gur.* Novelist. Upper middle class.

Memories from childhood to age 14 illustrating the advantages of a Victorian upbringing, 1867–1891. Father's early life; his rejecting the family sea-trading business in favor of an army career. Mother's childhood and courtship with father; his giving up his army career at insistence of his bride's father. Newly married parents' living in home of paternal grandmother, who dominated them. Author's birth. Family's moving to nearby house, "The Pré." Author's hearing being permanently damaged by nursemaid's boxing her ear. Birth of her brother Harry. Being taken to visit houses of country gentry. Running away to see the world, age 4, but being led home by kindly servants. The Pré's being the "happy world" of her childhood; after paternal grandfather's death, mother's refusing to move back into grandmother's home; grandmother's having to move away instead. Discussing character of her parents and nanny; recalling nanny's medicines and tactful disciplines. Trying to teach herself to read, age 4. Being taken to her first hunting meet. Birth of sister Florence. Father's introducing her to custom of prison visiting. Learning reading and arithmetic, age 5, from sister's governess. Visiting the poor with her mother; describing cottagers' rural dialect and work with sheep and cattle. Births of another brother and sister. Mother's taking her to London to visit maternal grandmother. At age 7, staying with London cousins from a banking family; learning about money from them. Being homesick for Hertfordshire. Recalling a visit to her Hampshire grandfather, where she had met Lewis Carroll. Asking her mother what makes men masculine and women feminine; after receiving answer, being unhappy she was not a boy. Nanny's history as Benjamin Disraeli's childhood nurse; author's staying with nanny's family when grandfather died. Nanny's leaving due to illness; pregnant mother's hiring harsh German governess to replace her. Death of little brother Eddie, on same day as birth of new brother. Beginning to make friends with other adolescents. Having a succession of new governesses; mother's refusing daughters' request for a tutor to give them "a proper boy's education." Author's Anglican confirmation. Discussing religion, politics, poetry with her London cousins; meeting poets Matthew Arnold and Wilfred Blunt at their house. Fearing death during a serious bout of peritonitis. Upon recovery, deciding to polish her childhood memories for publication.

In her autobiography, Carbery has revised an account of her life written in childhood, very likely a diary, and she adopts a child's point of view throughout her narrative. It is interesting that her childhood memories often contradict 20th-century generalities about the Victorians. For example, although the author's constantly pregnant mother produced the large family Victorians are known for, she also violated expected family duties by putting her husband's domineering mother in a nursing home rather than accepting her into the family. Rather than recording a life of notable individuality, Carbery's book effectively resurrects the features of a comfortable household in the mid-Victorian years, replete with charity visits and Victorian sages whom the child was privileged to meet.

CARDIGAN, Countess of. [*See* BRUDENELL, Adeline Louisa Marie.]

206 CARPENTER, Mary. 1807–1877. *Six Months in India*. Longmans, Green, 1868. 2 vols. Vol. 1: 299 pp.; front.; preface; illus. Vol. 2: 255 pp.; front.; illus.; apps. NUC pre56 96:316.

Born in Devonshire. Parents not named. 1 brother. Single. Wrote *Our Convicts, The Last Days of Rammohun Roy, Morning and Evening Meditations*. Social reformer; education activist; juvenile crime specialist; reform school founder; religious/spiritual writer; biographer; traveler (India). Middle class.

Origins and progress of a social reformer's brief stay in India, concentrating on the changes wrought by British social work on India's educational and economic systems, 1866–68. Vol. 1: Doing social work with neglected and criminal children in Bristol. Hearing a lecture by a young Brahmin on the subordinate and ignorant condition of Hindu women, 1860; deciding to travel to India to investigate social conditions, 1866. Discussing English racial ideas about lower-caste Indians, including the supposed limits of their capacity for "improvement." Arriving in Bombay; being granted authority to visit and inspect hospitals and insane asylums. Attending a trial; visiting a prison; describing conditions there. Discussing the caste system. Visiting schools; giving detailed descriptions of each. Visiting a lunatic asylum. Discussing female education both with English residents and Indians. Objecting to native men's wearing nothing but loincloths. Lack of trained women officials. Discussing the inferior social position of Hindu widows; polygamy. Visiting reformatory and mission schools. Inspecting schools; touring orphanages. Trying to raise support for a female teacher-training school. Native officials' objecting to English-style women's education. Traveling to Calcutta. Meeting reformer Baboo Keshub Chunder Sen. Life story of Rajah Rammohun Roy. Beginning a small school for Indian boys. Lecturing on teacher-training school plans; encountering opposition from Indians who fear education will make wives disobedient. British officials' lacking any interest in prison reform. Helping found the National Social Science Association of India. Vol. 2: Visiting girls' schools in Bombay. Trying to start new girls' schools. Noting progress toward Christian conversion of Bombay's educated Indians. Discussing history of the Bombay Mechanics' Institute and Bengal Social Science Association. Believing that Indian servants are a bad moral influence on English children raised in India.

After returning to England, Carpenter gained fame as a social reformer for her writings and work with juvenile delinquents; she also founded the Red Lodge Girls' Reformatory. Her Indian memoir has much to say on cultural factors impeding the development of women's education in India, as well as providing a discussion, without the usual missionary focus, of India's economic development under British influence. Despite her emphasis on practical education, Carpenter's Christian perspective leads to her condemnation of native beliefs and customs; this disapproval of non-Western values highlights the assumptions of even the most well-intentioned British citizens doing social work in India. Carpenter's 1868 account, covering only six months, gains historical perspective from comparative reading with *The Life and Times of Mrs. Sherwood (1775–1851)*. Mary Martha Sherwood spent the years 1805–16 in India teaching in native schools and wrote on many of the same cultural problems addressed by Carpenter.

207 CARR, Alice (née Strettell). 1850–s.l.1915. *Mrs. J. Comyns Carr's Reminiscences*. Ed. by Eve Adam. Hutchinson & Co., Ltd., c.1926. 328 pp.; illus.; index. NUC pre56 96:386.

Raised in Genoa, Italy. Father: Reverend A. B. Strettell, Anglican chaplain. Mother not named. 1 sister (Alma, author of *The Bard of the Dimbovitza*); 1 brother. Married 1873, Joseph Comyns Carr, journalist, drama critic, art gallery director, playwright, dramatist. 1 daughter; 2 sons. Wrote *North Italian Folk, La Fortunina*. Knew Sir Edward Burne-Jones, James McNeil Whistler, George du Maurier, John Singer Sargent, Sarah Bernhardt, Herbert Beerbohm Tree, James Barrie, Henry James, George Meredith, Edward Alma Tadema, others. Costume designer; clergyman's daughter; foreign resident (Italy); miscellaneous writer. Middle class; married into upper middle class.

Memories of forty years backstage in London's theatre world, highlighting its illustrious figures both on and off stage, 1873–1915. Brief memories of author's Italian childhood. Rendering sketches of life in London's bohemian art and theatre circles of the 1880s–1920s, and of New York City's Broadway of the same period. Noting that by 1870, people of the theatre were becoming more socially acceptable to the upper middle classes in England. Discussing her husband's tenure as director of the Grosvenor Art Gallery and his cofounding, with Charles Halle, of the

New Art Gallery; his having written a play, *King Arthur,* as a star vehicle for his close friend, actor Henry Irving. Author's remembering Ellen Terry as the most gracious star for whom she designed costumes. With her husband, buying Charles Dickens's notebook of dramatic readings at auction; their prizing it above all other possessions. Extensively discussing personalities of artists, writers, and theatre people of her acquaintance.

More than a history of her own life, this book presents Carr as the recorder of a dynamic era in theatrical history whose course and personalities she was privileged to know firsthand. We learn almost nothing about her training in costume design, but an immense amount about her social interactions with such folk as Ellen Terry and Sir Henry Irving and other artistic friends who, as an appreciative audience, supported the Lyceum Theatre. By stressing so many social interchanges, Carr's book is a welcome supplement to the numerous theatrical memoirs of this period and its cultural milieu in general.

208 CARR, Barbara (née Lennon). 1920–?. *Cherries on My Plate*. Cape Town: Howard Timmins, 1965. 220 pp. NUC 1963–1967 9:532.

Born at Dagshai, India. Father not named, prison and lunatic asylum administrator. Mother not named. 1 brother. Married c.1945, Norman Carr, lieutenant in the King's African Rifles, later game warden. 2 daughters; 1 son. Wrote *Not for Me the Wilds*. Military spouse; colonialist (Africa); secretary; nurse; journalist. Middle class.

Author's adult life in southern Africa, emphasizing her colonialist views of its native peoples and culture, covering 1940–65. Father's family history. Parents' travels to India and Asia before and during her infancy. During childhood, living on Jersey and the Isle of Wight; family's later living in Africa, author's ages 11–14. Being schooled by parents, then sent to boarding school in England, ages 14–19. Traveling from England to join father in Nyasaland, 1940; keeping house for him. Describing father's household, his menagerie of native animals, his doctoring the natives. His managing both the local prison and insane asylum; author's describing his methods of treatment and reform. Relating story concerning a native servant; her father's taking him to Johannesburg to see his reactions to a modern city; servant's marveling at the achievements of the white man. Mother's arriving from England after several years. At age 20, author's leaving home; working for the government secretariat; discussing slowness of native employees there; coworker's insisting that natives aren't capable of initiative. Author's wondering why official policy forbids whites to speak to natives in their own language; believing natives might understand their tasks better that way. Contracting amoebic dysentery; noting British women's enduring African climate for the sake of their husbands' jobs. Visiting the leper colony at her father's prison; witnessing a prison escape; watching prison hangings. Meeting and marrying an English military officer; honeymooning on Lake Nyasa before his departure for North Africa. Author's working as a military decoder in Zomba; later joining her husband in Kenya. Their living on the farm of a fellow officer and his wife; author's sympathizing with wife's hatred for local tribes, the Masai and Kikuyu; noting that British policies favor the "murderous" natives and forsake the whites who made Kenya a thriving land; describing her belief in an international conspiracy to spread lies about colonialism and colonialists. Returning to Nyasaland on husband's home leave. Pregnancy and childbirth; having another daughter three years later. Working successive jobs in northern Rhodesia as a railway agent, newspaper reporter, and court reporter. Despite needing the income, expressing her wish to be with her children rather than working. Feeling discomfort in social contact with Africans. Author's being hospitalized in Johannesburg with hyperthyroid disease; family's moving to be near her. After recovery, working as her doctor's clerk and nurse. Learning shorthand; working secretarial jobs for various Johannesburg firms. Death of her father. Charting several family moves between Rhodesia and South Africa. Visiting new nations of Rhodesia and Malawi; noting native people's distrust of elected native officials in newly independent nations. Being disturbed by social disintegration wrought by independence in Malawi. Evaluating white flight from Rhodesia to South Africa. With her husband, operating a roadhouse in Johannesburg; deciding to live there permanently.

Affirming her commitment to the British Empire and its colonial mission, Carr asserts that the British government betrayed the hardworking white man in Kenya and Rhodesia by turning power over to natives, whom she said "did nothing before the advent of the white man but sit and stare at the horizon or wallow in the bestiality of cannibalism." This is the most fully articulated of her negative views of the natives, although at odds with her more parental attitude toward native fellow workers, whom she seems to regard as children. Her ambivalence toward the native Africans who surround her is an excellent example of those white colonial attitudes that led to South African apartheid. A contrasting view of South Africa's racial tensions is accessible in *Side by Side: The Autobiography of Helen Joseph* (1986), which charts the white author's struggles for black equality in South Africa during the 1950s–1960s.

209 CARR, Emily. 1871–1945. *Growing Pains: the Autobiography of Emily Carr*. Toronto: Oxford University Press, 1946. 381 pp.; front.; illus.; foreword by Ira Dilworth. BLC to 1975 54:354.

Born in Victoria, British Columbia, Canada. Father: Richard H. Carr, merchant. Mother: Emily Saunders. 4 brothers; 3 sisters. Single. Wrote *Hundreds and Thousands: The Journals of Emily Carr* (1966) and *Pause: A Sketch Book* (1953). Artist (painter); teacher (art); boardinghouse owner. Middle class.

Artist's Canadian childhood and international peregrinations in service to her art studies and professional career, 1870s–1940s. Growing up in Victoria; family's being ruled by father's iron hand. Father's being devastated by mother's death. Author's becoming his companion; helping him in the garden; taking drawing lessons from him; his death. Eldest sister's taking charge of family; giving herself airs as only child born in England; punishing author harshly. Author's going to live with guardians in San Francisco; studying art at the Mark Hopkins School; moving into a boardinghouse; describing San Francisco boardinghouses, c.1890s. After returning to Victoria, starting a children's art class. Rebelling against orthodox religion; spending a summer in a mission house in a local Indian community. Deciding to study art in England; living in a London boardinghouse; describing its socially pretentious boarders and drunken landlady. Studying at Westminster School of Art, 1899. Resenting the unfamiliar British attitude of "men first." Rejecting a suitor's marriage proposal in favor of continuing her art studies. Adding night art classes to her curriculum. Moving to St. Ives, Cornwall, to join its art colony. Returning to Canada; being dismissed from a teaching job at Ladies' Art Club of Vancouver for taking her work too seriously. Sketching in an Indian village at Sitka; becoming interested in American Indian art. Going to Paris; studying art at the Académie Colarossi there. Disliking large cities; enjoying the countryside in Brittany. Returning to Canada; opening a studio in Victoria; making pottery and raising sheepdogs for additional income, but being forced to take in boarders. Meeting established Canadian artists in Toronto. Visiting friends in New York and showing her work to New York artists; her work's being selected for a collective New York show. Discussing relative merits of representational and abstract art. In New York, writing *Klee Wyck,* about her life among Indians; receiving critical acclaim for book.

Canada's best-known woman painter impressionistically records her memories, primarily emphasizing essential differences between English and Canadian social expectations in the late 19th and early 20th centuries, although a minor but intriguing focus of her book might be called an analytic survey of the world's boardinghouses. In **210** *The Book of Small* (1942), Carr describes her childhood in Victoria, B.C., and the city's development from the 1870s to c.1940. After 1940, Carr's health problems influenced her to adopt writing in favor of painting. *Klee Wyck* was the first of several books she wrote on quasi-autobiographical topics, including *The House of All Sorts* (1944) on her own experiences running a boardinghouse, this memoir, and two posthumously printed works, *The Heart of a Peacock* and *Pause: A Sketch Book* on her stay in a British sanitorium. She also published a cultural study of British Columbian Indian tribes in *Klee Wyck* (1941).

211 CARSWELL, Catherine Roxburgh (née MacFarlane). 1879–1946. *Lying Awake: An Unfinished Autobiography and Other Posthumous Papers*. Ed. by John Carswell (author's son). Secker & Warburg, 1950. 231 pp.; front. port.; intro. by ed.; illus.; poems; letters. NUC pre56 97:78.

Born in Glasgow, Scotland. Father: George Gray MacFarlane, commission agent for shipping company. Mother: Mary Anne Lewis. 2 brothers; 1 sister. Married 1903, Herbert Jackson. Married 1917, Donald Carswell, journalist. 1 daughter; 1 son. Wrote novels *Open the Door!* (1920) and *The Camomile* (1923), biography of D. H. Lawrence *The Savage Pilgrimage* (1932), edited anthologies *A National Gallery* and *The English in Love*. Biographer; novelist; editor; literary critic. Middle class.

Topically arranged chapters meditating on incidents from the author's entire lifespan, 1880s–1940s. Part I, Ch. I: "The Clock." Considering old age: her body, her invisibility to others because of loss of beauty, her belated appreciation of humble homes. Her mother in old age, and her mother's family history. Ch. II: "Glasgow." Describing the city's slums; in her youth, accompanying parents on charity work. Parents' being 19th-century Christian philanthropists; author's critiquing their charity from her own socialist perspective. To impress her with the evils of drink, father's having taken her to a pub to witness a drunken orgy. Mother's fervently desiring to convert all Jews to Christianity; at age 12; author's being persuaded to teach English to poor Jewish immigrants. Noting that the family's children never inherited their parents' missionary spirit. Describing her family home and attendance at the Free Presbyterian church; relating its history of social reform. Ch. III: "In My Father's House." Despite father's pious Philistinism, author's and siblings' having enthusiasm for arts. Recalling her father's shipping office; money's being mysterious to her in childhood. Believing that her family's piety brought them prosperity; at age 13, seeing father suffer financial reverses despite his faith. Analyzing her family's Calvinism; its providing a sense of preparedness that helped her cope with WWII. Ch. IV: "Mount Quharrie." Depicting summer farm her father leased in the highlands, 1880s. Author's first visiting the farm, age 7; family's enjoying simple lifestyle there. Ch. V: "Holidays." Summer seaside holidays. Visiting Loch Katrine during father's tenure as Glasgow town councillor; hearing local proverbs, playing with rural children. Being naively ignorant of sexuality despite understanding anatomy. Ch. VI: "Town and Country." contrasting her urban Camden Town home with her other residence on Hampstead Heath. Part II, Ch. VII: "The Zov: The Dream." Meditations on freedom and her love of animals. Ch. VIII: "Frank: The Boards." Memories of visits to her grandparents on the south English coast, age 4, and to her Uncle Frank in Italy. Ch. IX: "Florence: The Bank." History of her mother's family in Italy. Ch. X: "Music: The Arts."

Memories of early piano and voice lessons. Revering music above the other arts. Ch. XI: "Letters and Women." Disliking confessional writing from women; examining the sources of her own prudery. Ch. XII: "Men and Women." Noting that the best autobiographies by married people conceal details about their marriages; noting "marriage is at once too important and too inessential" for written discussion. Ch. XIII: "Age and Youth." Meditating on age in general, age's bodily effect on women, and the course of her own aging in particular. Ch. XIV: "Intimations of Mortality, and of Senility." Memories of significant old people in her life. Part III: "Fragments." Meditations on religion, love, and beauty. Poems and letters from 1926–46.

Carswell's collected writings are bound together with a collection of her brief observations and aphorisms, compiled by her son. A close friend of D. H. Lawrence for twenty years, she omits mention of him in her personal meditations; readers seeking information on their friendship can consult the opening section of his biography by Carswell. Her discussion of the connections between the Calvinism of her childhood and the missionary duties it required of her family illustrates the sociological complexities of religion, social mores, and class obligations in late-19th-century Scotland.

212 CARTLAND, Mary Barbara (née Hamilton). 1901–s.l.1995. *The Isthmus Years*. Hutchinson, 1943. 196 pp.; front. port.; index. NUC pre56 97:256.

Born in England. Father: Bertram Cartland, businessman. Mother: Polly Scobell. 2 brothers. Married 1927, Alexander McCorquodale, son of printing magnate; divorced 1933. Married 1936, Hugh McCorquodale (husband's cousin), d.1963. 1 daughter; 2 sons. Wrote over 300 novels, as well as advice books on sex and marriage. Novelist; advice writer; journalist. Upper class.

Prolific novelist's personal relation to what she considered Britain's stupidity, apathy, and ignorance in the interwar years, 1919–40. During WWI, accusations of German complicity tainting even Prime Minister Asquith's family. In her teens, regarding the war as a bore. Despite being of good family, her mother's lacking the money to join high society; wanting to launch her daughter socially; author's using her mother's ambitions to persuade her to move to London. Discussing her social debut and private awareness of not being beautiful. Having received forty-nine proposals by the time of her 1927 marriage; attributing them to men's postwar desperation to be married. Discussing employment problems for women after WWI; noting huge number of widows. Observing loss of refinements in British society due to influx of Americans. Discussing 1920s trend of nightclubs and party life; author's teetotalism's saving her from debauchery. Beginning to contribute to the *Daily Express* gossip column; through her job becoming friends with politicians Lord Beaverbrook and Lord Birkenhead, actress Lady Diana Cooper, and Noel Coward. Writing her first novel as a new genre: the insider's view of high society. Recording novelist Winifred Graham's comments on the new strength of the modern girl. Mother's opening a knit shop in London; author's running a hat shop while writing more society novels. Being presented at Court, 1925. Making friends with dramatist Michael Arlen; discussing 1920s theatre. Commenting on spreading knowledge of birth control, despite official silence about it; also noting silence in 1920s on topics of prostitution and venereal disease. After marriage, 1927, moving to a new London home. Writing prolifically; using her earnings to visit far-flung places. Writing social columns for the *Evening Standard,* the *Tatler,* and the *Sunday Chronicle.* Birth of her daughter. Meeting unproductively with working women, 1935; asserting that women are secretive and avoid speaking frankly. Discussing Britain's economic woes in the worldwide Depression. Alluding to her bitterly contested divorce, 1930s. Continuing to compose novels without interruption; dictating more than 8,000 words daily to her stenographers. Commenting on 1930s popularity of spiritualism; discussing feminism, but opposing it on the grounds of women's maternal obligations. Believes wealth unnecessary to happiness; regarding the pinched days of her youth as her happiest. Marrying again, 1936; seeing Egypt for the first time on a visit to her husband in Khartoum; writing a novel set in Egypt, 1938. Writing her twentieth novel as WWII began, 1939. On holiday in Canada, 1940, receiving news of both brothers' battlefield deaths. Closing, c.1943, by affirming her British identity and appealing to British readers for an all-out war effort.

Popularly heralded as Britain's "Queen of Romance," Cartland has, in the 1990s, become known for a majestically feminine persona whose fame transcends her prolific writing career. Formerly the British version of Hedda Hopper, writing gossip columns for four publications and enjoying access to every important social function, she gained a new role in the 1980s (through the 8th earl of Spencer's second marriage to her daughter Raine) as the celebrated literary grandmother of Princess Diana. During this recent burst of interest in her career, PBS made a film biography of her with her cooperation, letting the public see the famous pink chaise on which Cartland reclines to dictate her novels to her four secretaries. Her novels dwell on love, celebrating home, passion, and marital faithfulness, although she avoids these topics when discussing her own life, keeping her focus resolutely on her public career. Her remarkably complete memoir records names, places, and dates for everything she wrote, as well as being a virtual compendium of the social trends and ongoing political issues in the years between the two world wars. Cartland also wrote several other volumes of autobiography: *The Years of Opportunity* (1948), a narrative of her WWII experiences, *I Search for Rainbows* (1967), and *I Seek the Miraculous* (1978).

213 CARY, Catherine E. c.1770–d.a.1825. *Memoirs of Miss C. E. Cary*. 2nd ed. T. Traveller, 1825. 3 vols. Vol. 1: 394 pp.; preface. Vol. 2: 244 pp. Vol. 3: 145 pp.; political documents; errata. NUC pre56 97:408.

Born in England. Father not named, allegedly a Roman Catholic duke. Mother not named. Married c.1817, husband not named. Knew Queen Caroline, Lord Palmerston, Lady Anne Hamilton, the Marquis of Hertford, others. Lady-in-waiting. Aristocracy.

Improbable and intentionally vague account of early life author claims for herself, with a defense of her supposed actions in the Court intrigue surrounding Queen Caroline, c.1770–1825. Vol. 1: Withholding the hard facts of her birth: place, date, parents' or guardians' names. Mother's having been secretly married by Roman Catholic rite to an unnamed duke; retiring to an unnamed county seat to give birth to author. Mother's letting duke believe author was stillborn, but giving her to Roman Catholic family to raise. After mother's death, author's being overseen by a girlhood friend of her mother, the Catholic "Madame D." When still young, being taken to an unspecified foreign convent by Madame D., who posed as author's mother. Being educated in French, while being fed on bread and water by priests hoping to "bend her temper." Successfully persuading the kind priest who catechized her to help her escape; taking with her stolen papers from Madame D. After escape, returning to England. Unable to find her former guardians, taking refuge with a Protestant duke in a hostile Catholic region. Guardians' discovering her whereabouts, attempting to make her mistrust and leave the Duke; author's discovering guardians are secretly planning to marry her off; their abducting her when she resisted. Author's regretting leaving the convent. Pawning Madame D.'s gold jewelry to survive. Joining the aristocratic social life in London and Brighton by unspecified means. Vol. 2: By 1816, leading an expensively genteel life; being arrested for debt as part of a plot by a man trying to compel her to marry him. Being imprisoned for unspecified forgery; while incarcerated, being forced into marriage at knifepoint by an unnamed visitor; considering suicide. Once out of prison, beginning to correspond with cabinet minister Lord Palmerston; being rumored to be his mistress. When Queen Caroline was accused by George IV of poisoning Princess Charlotte, author's publicly declaring her confidence in the queen's innocence; immediately being arrested at the instigation of "a treacherous friend." Vol. 3: In White Cross Prison, being identified as "Miss Cary," a notorious prostitute; lamenting this blow to her family's good name. Suspecting guards are trying to kill her with cold, starvation, and terror. Being falsely blackmailed by another villainous woman. Discovering, 1825, that she has been imprisoned because of accusations that she forged a letter to Queen Caroline. Telling the story of the Queen Caroline scandal: testifying to her innocence and offering "proof" of the real facts. Author's having known the queen through an unnamed mutual acquaintance. In 1820, having been induced by self-proclaimed "friends" of the queen to write a dictated letter of unspecified nature; in apparent gratitude, queen's sending a messenger to her, "Mr. Knight," with a false offer of friendship; queen's also appointing author second lady-in-waiting, under Lady Anne Hamilton. Being forced to copy secret documents as part of her duties; refusing to sell the originals to unnamed persons, who forged copies anyway, then punished author's refusal by identifying her with Miss Cary, the prostitute. Stating that the original documents included letters implicating the queen as poisoner. Author's being persecuted, arrested, and imprisoned; then "rescued" and harbored by Lady Anne, the first lady-in-waiting. Author's escaping Lady Anne; taking refuge in Windsor Castle. Meanwhile, George IV's becoming king, 1821; Queen Caroline's being denied admission to the coronation and dying soon afterward. Author's knowing too much; Lady Anne's having her incarcerated in White Cross Prison, hoping she would die there. Author's printing extracts from Lady Anne's letters to her, documenting these claims. Pleading for public faith in her testimony.

Cary's cryptic account makes hard reading for a 20th-century audience. The facts of the intrigue surrounding Queen Caroline begin earlier, with George IV's secret 1785 marriage to Mrs. Fitzherbert, politically unacceptable as queen. In heavy debt from gambling, George repudiated his marriage in exchange for a £161,000 parliamentary grant to pay his creditors. After he amassed further debts, Parliament refused to pay them until he married Princess Caroline of Brunswick, 1895, but George soon abandoned her, returning to Mrs. Fitzherbert and plotting with his courtiers to rid himself of Caroline. Caroline fought back with her own courtiers for twenty-five years, during which Caroline tried to have herself declared coregent with her husband during George III's periods of madness, and George's courtiers repeatedly framed her for supposed infidelity, poisoning her own daughter, and espionage against British interests. At George III's death, 1821, George IV exerted every effort to keep Caroline from being declared his consort, including having a henchman bar her from the coronation and, possibly, having her poisoned. Cary's work is effectively a roman à clef designed to lure contemporary readers familiar with the Queen Caroline affair into trying to identify each of her veiled characters. As with many 18th-century memoirs both fictional and factual, Cary's is so full of improbable events that the book's authorship should be questioned. On the one hand it covers historical occurrences; in fact one of its characters, Mr. Knight, can be confidently identified as Sir William Knighton, keeper of George IV's privy purse, who pretended to ally himself with Caroline in order to undo her. On the other hand, Cary the supposed aristocrat is unable to write a convincing life story for herself, leaving glaring inconsistencies and being unable to explain which figures are on which side in the royal controversy, or how a moneyless girl fleeing abductors might have found her way into relationships with so many dukes, lords, and other notable figures. The most reasonable estimate is that "Miss Cary" is an unidentified adherent of the queen—probably a servant, with only vague ideas of aristocratic doings—who watched, rather than participated, in the events she described. However, even though she may not wholly understand the events she records, hers is one of the few firsthand records of the Regency era's covert power struggles.

214 CAVE, Ann Estella Penfold, Viscountess Cave (née Mathews). c.1875–1938. *Odds and Ends of My Life*. John Murray, 1929. 215 pp.; front.; preface; illus. NUC pre56 100:412.

Born in London. Father: William Mathews. Mother not named. 2 sisters; 1 brother. Married 1885, George Cave, Viscount Cave, M.P., home secretary, lord of appeals. Essayist; antique collector; society woman. Upper class; married into aristocracy.

Society woman's collected essays recalling childhood and married life and commentary on various arts that make life more gracious, c.1875–1920s. Childhood memories: family's rural home, nannies who discouraged imagination in author and siblings. After father's death, children's Aunt Elizabeth's becoming their guardian. Author's sister marrying a vicar in the West Country; author's marrying a London barrister. Recalling her sister's daughters and their childhood literary efforts; author's raising them after her sister's death. Commenting on her long-time cook and servants as family retainers. Discussing principles of household furnishings: color, style, and ambience; discussing psychology of what women wear; critiquing dress styles of historical figures; noting that women of all classes try to emulate dress style of aristocrats. Her husband's early political career. Discussing British professional art painting and her own amateur art. Discussing the history of British gardening, and personal gardens she has planned; recommending medicinal herbs to grow. Discussing dreams as possible signs of past lives. Counseling readers to let young people decide their own futures.

Gathering previously written essays with separate points of focus, Lady Cave's book contains close but brief studies of the physical surroundings of upper-class life in the late 19th and early 20th centuries. The author, whose interest in personal and household adornment dominates her book, is both knowledgeable on the history of British domestic arts and observant of subtle details in her art and costume descriptions. Her essay on gardening is perhaps her most interesting, tying famous British gardens to their designers' historical eras and design principles. This book is a useful source for historians researching British civilization's material culture and artifacts.

215 CHAMBERLAIN, Ena (Penny Cooper). 1918–s.l.1994. *29 Inman Road*. Virago, 1990. 250 pp.; illus. BNB 1990 2:1075.

Born in London. Father: Joe Chamberlain, laundry owner. Mother: Emma Peggs. 3 sisters; 1 brother. Married 1941, W. H. Hammersley; divorced. Married 1945, Peter Croft, film producer; divorced. Married 1972, Alfred Frank Cooper, civil servant. 2 daughters; 1 son. Civil servant; family historian; teacher; short storyist; journalist. Lower middle class.

Journalist's preserved memories of her struggling family and urban childhood in 1920s London. Describing father's small laundry business. Recalling village-like environs of Inman Road; mother's strong Cockney identity and closeness to her two daughters. Lacking central heat; children's bathing in front of the kitchen range. Contracting tuberculosis; during bedrest, amusing herself by writing short stories. Remembering large family gatherings. Describing Inman's neighbors' mutual hospitality; resident "witch" who put curses on bill collectors. Family's being disrupted when sister Elsie decided to emigrate to Canada. Daily neighborhood scenes: the carter, the eel man, the rag and bone man, daylight drunkards, and evictions. Funerals' inspiring great display of finery and neighborliness. From youth, author's liking Shakespeare and acting Shakespearean scenes with friends. Being fond of school. After several bouts of tuberculosis, being sent to recover in the Lake Country. Remembering Empire Day, the only time when separately taught boys and girls celebrated together. Describing bulkiness of girls' winter attire, 1920s. Attending Anglican England Sunday school; sharing the Inman neighbors' suspicions of Roman Catholicism. Describing local workhouse and inhabitants, Anchor Mission, and work of local missionaries. Passing Junior County Exam for admission to Christ's Hospital boarding school, but losing it after revealing her tuberculosis. Attending Mayfield school. After father's death from stroke, family's selling laundry business; buying a new house in Worcester Park. Author's feeling torn about leaving Inman Road: seeing this as the event dividing her childhood from her adolescence.

Chamberlain effectively resurrects the sights, sounds, and smells of her local London neighborhood in the 1920s, augmenting her portrait with commentary on the problems of money, family discord, and alcoholism that restricted life for much of its population. Although often wittily expressed, the author's memories show nostalgia in returning to the modest circumstances she left behind. During WWII Chamberlain served as a member of the Women's Royal Naval Service, and she later contributed articles and stories to *Homes and Gardens, Woman and Home,* and other publications. She also worked as a schoolteacher from 1970–79.

216 CHARKE, Charlotte (née Cibber). 1713–1760. *A Narrative of the Life of Mrs. Charlotte Charke, Daughter of Colley Cibber.* Gainesville, FL: Scholars' Facsimiles & Reprints, 1969. 281 pp.; front. port.; illus.; intro. by Leonard R. N. Ashley; index. NUC pre56 104:47. (1st pub. W. Reeve, 1755; other ed.: Constable, 1929.)

Born at Twickenham, Greater London. Father: Colley Cibber, well-known actor, theatre manager, playwright. Mother: Katherine Shore, actress. 3 brothers; 6 sisters. Married c.1729, Richard Charke, theatrical musician; deserted by husband (d.1738). Married 1745, John Sacheverell, d.1745. Widow. 1 daughter. Wrote the farce *The Art of Management* (1735) and novels *The Mercer* (c.1755), *The History of Henry Dumont, Esq.; and Miss Charlotte Evelyn* (1756) and *The Lovers' Treat* (1758). Knew Henry Fielding, David Garrick. Actress (stage); playwright; novelist; cross-dresser. Middle class.

Maturation, rebellion, and ultimately self-destructive escapades of an actress, cross-dresser, and famous playwright's daughter, charting her periods of poverty and prosperity, 1713–1755. Parents' courtship and marriage. Author's being resented by her elder siblings as a late-born intruder; their envying parents' love for her. From childhood, loving to cross-dress, especially in her father's clothes. Making father furious by riding a donkey in the streets of Hampton. At age 8, attending a London boarding school; being tutored in Latin, Italian, geography, music, and dance. Moving with mother to Hillingdon. Learning to shoot game, age 14; later submitting to mother's prohibition against hunting. Refusing to learn housewifery, despite repeated family efforts. Learning to perform medical treatments from Dr. Hales, a physician and relative; trying to dispense medicines to neighbors at Hillingdon; their trusting her advice utterly. Learning the arts of gardening and horse grooming; confessing her pretensions at both medicine and gardening. Wishing she could prove her courage by having house burglars to drive away. Marrying a man who was both extravagant and unkind; leaving him after birth of their daughter. Debuting on the London stage, age 17; discussing her success-induced extravagance. Acting in first production of Lillo's *The London Merchant,* 1731, with her brother Theophilus's company; acting at Drury Lane in many "breeches parts" or male dress. Cross-dressing offstage. Writing farce *The Art of Management* to pillory Drury Lane's manager. Receiving high pay for acting in Fielding's *Pasquin.* Angering her father by impersonating him in her role as Fopling Fribbler in Fielding's *The Battle of the Poets;* antagonizing most of London's theatre managers; losing her father's support; ending her acting career. Boarding in poverty with her sister; itemizing failures of her businesses: grocery shop, a puppet show in London and Tunbridge Wells. Suffering series of adversities: husband's mistresses, mother's death, husband's death in Jamaica. Attempting a stage comeback. Being arrested and imprisoned for debt while dressed as a man. Remarrying secretly; second husband's death. In poverty, receiving aid from London prostitutes; hiding from bailiffs. While in male dress, courting an heiress as part of a fraud conspiracy. Her playwright father's refusing to assist her financially; describing her miserable existence seeking work among itinerant players. In male guise, working briefly as "Mr. Brown," houseboy to Lord Anglesea; later selling meat in Newgate Market. Borrowing money from her uncle; using her male persona to be hired as a pub waiter. After a series of miserable touring engagements, achieving success as Macheath in *The Beggar's Opera,* 1744–45. Recording her wanderings with a "Mrs. Brown," a female companion who passed for author's wife; their collaborating in a pastry cook business which failed. Managing theatre company at Bath. Noting her daughter's making a foolish choice of husband, just as author had. Writing this narrative to inform reader of her penitence over all her outrageous behavior.

After her 1730s friction with her father, Charke was alienated from most of her family, although her brother, Theophilus Cibber, employed her occasionally as an actress and once found her a position as a secretary and companion to a lord—a post she lost when the aristocrat decided it was improper to employ a woman for such work. When Charke adopted her male guise full-time, she fell into further disgrace with her family; when her father died, two years after this autobiography was published, she received no part of his estate. Although this swashbuckling account of her life bears signs of her own reading of picaresque 18th-century fiction—especially that of Fielding—Charke's historical identity is undisputed. Accordingly, her early taste for masculine dress and manly roles on and off stage make her book of vital interest to historians of gender and gay studies, who will find it one of the most complete early accounts of a "passing woman."

217 CHARLES, Mrs. Rundle (Elizabeth). 1827–1896. *Our Seven Homes: Autobiographical Reminiscences of Mrs. Rundle Charles, Author of "The Schönberg-Cotta Family."* John Murray, 1896. 236 pp.; front. port.; preface by Mary Davidson; illus.; note; list of author's publications; index. NUC pre56 104:87.

Born at The Bank, Tavistock, Devonshire. Father: John Rundle, M.P., owner of lime kiln, banker, philanthropist. Mother not named. Married 1851, Andrew Paton Charles, factory manager. Widow. Wrote *Tales and Sketches of Christian Life in Different Lands and Ages, Against the Stream, Diary of Mrs. Kitty Trevelyan*. Widow. Religious/spiritual writer; religionist

(Plymouth Brethren); short storyist; teacher; philanthropist; abolitionist. Upper middle class.

Record of the author's journey from her affluent Devon childhood to her London writing career and widowhood, 1830s–1889. Recalling games with her father; practicing the pianoforte. Family business interests: lime kilns, brewery, iron foundry. Memories of her aunt Elizabeth's founding of village schools. Recalling her father's liberal politics, village popularity, and philanthropy. Mother's being author's model of capable household management. With female cousins, enjoying relatively liberal schooling by governesses. Being taken by father to see London and Plymouth parliamentary sessions. Acquiring early interest in problems in Ireland; being puzzled by mystical concepts at Church of England services. Moving to her grandfather's country estate; studying with tutors; enjoying access to a local baronet's library. Reading Harriet Martineau's "Political Economy" stories. In her teens, publishing her first story, written to please her father; enjoying great friendship with father as she matured; praising his teetotalism. Starting to redefine her relationship with God, reexamining Catholicism and other Christian sects; recalling the strict beliefs of a cousin who belonged to the Plymouth Brethren; eventually embracing ecumenical Christianity. Marriage; moving to Hampstead Heath with her husband, 1851; teaching poor children near his factory. After her parents' business failure, their coming to live with author's family. Giving Bible lessons at Servants' School. Commenting on the Oxford Movement; John Henry Newman. Writing *Chronicles of the Schönberg-Cotta Family,* a story of Martin Luther. Father's death, 1864. Her books' becoming popular in America; author's endorsing abolitionist cause in American Civil War. Following her husband's illness and death, moving with her mother to a London flat. Overcoming loneliness through charity work in a factory neighborhood. Moving with her mother to Hampstead; death of her mother, 1889.

Charles's spiritual convictions formed the basis of her social welfare work, which, arising from her adult exposure to urban poverty, attempted to ameliorate the social problems and class barriers confronting the poor. Her account of her own precocious writing career is too modest; her early efforts won praise from both Froude and Tennyson. At age 35, she achieved fame with the huge popularity of *Chronicles of the Schönberg-Cotta Family* (1862), which turns the life story of Martin Luther into the form of a novel. Although her fiction's primary purpose was didactic, it is enlivened by her experimentation with a wide range of narrative techniques.

218 CHARLTON, Barbara (née Tasburgh). 1815–1898. *The Recollections of a Northumbrian Lady, 1815–1866, Being the Memoirs of Barbara Charlton (née Tasburgh) Wife of William Henry Charlton of*

Hesleyside, Northumberland. Jonathan Cape, 1949. 288 pp.; front. port.; preface; intro. by L. E. O. Charlton (author's grandson); illus. NUC pre56 104:199.

Born in Hampstead, Greater London. Father: Michael Anne Tasburgh, Yorkshire squire. Mother: Augusta Roselia Tasburgh. 1 brother; 2 sisters. Married 1839, William Henry Charlton, Esq., involved in establishing Border Counties Railway. 5 sons; 3 daughters. Society woman. Upper class.

Details of Catholic author's traditional upbringing and married life to middle age during the early Victorian years. Growing up in a Catholic family. Having two older sisters; being mother's favorite, despite father's viewing additional daughters as superfluous. Mother's being unfailingly kind; father's wielding stern, repressive child-raising methods. At age 6, family's moving to France; author's being schooled at a strict French Catholic convent. Family's returning to England due to 1830 French Revolution. Although author remained close to mother, father's estranging himself from family through increasing eccentricity. Participating in upper-class social life, but father's insisting she learn to cook, sew, and do her own hair in case of absence of servants. Attending Queen Victoria's coronation, 1838; at last minute, father's foiling her plans to be presented at Court. Noting Catholic Church's attempts to influence English law during Oxford movement, c.1840s–1850s. Becoming engaged to a wealthy Catholic suitor; noting she did it because it was expected, not from love. Both families' supporting the match but quarreling over proposed allowances to young couple; author's asserting that Catholics, barred from politics until 1830, had focused instead on money; both families' being obsessed with money; author and husband's eloping to avoid controversy, 1839. Moving in with husband's parents; author's being victimized by her mother-in-law's mental illness and judgementalism; husband's growing increasingly like his mother. Author and husband's moving abroad. Suffering periodic depressions and grief over deaths of children and other family members; centering her life around her family. Spending Holy Week in Rome each year. With advancing age, feeling that her value decreased with each passing year.

The writer's grandson fills in details missing from this account, which ends abruptly because of the author's death. Charlton's book is interesting for its study of a Catholic family's historical accommodations to British strictures on Catholic political participation. However, the author herself would have thought this a minor issue; writing at age 77, Charlton shows a sensibility alive to domestic matters but uninterested in contemporary world events. Editor L. E. O. Charlton has put his grandmother's experiences into context by inserting a section into each chapter regarding the relevant history and politics of the era.

219 CHEESMAN, (Lucy) Evelyn (O.B.E.). 1881–1969. *Things Worth While*. Hutchinson, 1957. 330 pp.; front. port.; foreword; maps. BLC to 1975 60:100.

Born in Westwell, Kent. Father: Robert Cheesman, shopkeeper. Mother not named. 1 sister; 2 brothers. Single. Wrote *Everyday Doings of Insects* (1924), *Hunting Insects in the South Seas* (1932), *Six-Legged Snakes in New Guinea* (1949), others. Entomologist; scientist; traveler (South Pacific); scientific writer. Middle class.

Author's early interest in nature and development of career as field entomologist in South Pacific islands, 1881–1955. Commenting on her childhood reading; being taught at home by mother; attending school in Ashford. Loving nature and exploring the Sussex downs; having many pets despite aggravations to her asthma. Attending school in Germany, ages 13–14; in England, working briefly as a governess in the Midlands. Teaching herself animal anatomy, c.1906. Twice applying to veterinary college, 1912; being refused due to her gender. Finding a job as a veterinary nurse. Father's death, 1915. During WWI, author's filling clerical civil service position at Neutral and Enemy Trade Index. Having to quit with severe lung congestion; being delighted to receive request, 1919, to head the Insect House at Zoological Society's gardens in Regent's Park. Studying entomology intensively for two years at Royal College of Science; rebuilding the zoo's insect collection. Accepting invitation to join research expedition to Panama's Pearl Islands and Galapagos Islands, 1923–25; extensively describing journey, terrain, and wildlife. Expedition's continuing across Pacific; author's collecting insects in Marquesas Islands and Tuamotu Atolls; leaving group to do solo fieldwork in Society Islands and Tahiti. Returning to London; changing her affiliations from the Zoological Society to the British Museum of Natural History. Classifying her collection of 500 Pacific islands insects. Receiving a grant for further field research in the New Hebrides Islands, 1928–30; native guides treating her powers of observation as supernatural. Discussing cannibalism, native taboos, and Christian missionary efforts at reform. Cutting her stay short due to malaria; returning to England; undergoing surgery effectively relieving her asthma. Making a solo expedition to Papua New Guinea, 1933–34; her resulting plant collection's being destroyed due to official negligence. Recording her South Pacific expeditions, 1935–39, that garnered 20,000 insects for the Adelaide Museum. WWII: author's doing war work in Liverpool, 1939; later working with the London Censorship Office; being a plane-spotter for an East End factory. Lecturing in England on military operations in Pacific islands. Her mother's death, c.1944. Continuing her natural history expeditions in Pacific islands.

Had Cheesman lived in a later time, she would certainly have had a veterinary career; paradoxically, the 19th-century gender bias that frustrated her plans ensured her access to a more distinguished line of work. Colored by her love of animals and nature, Cheesman's account of her early life—although she says it is not an autobiography—foreshadows her mature career; the latter portion is a conscientious and orderly depiction of the island ecosystems Darwin had stimulated interest in seventy years earlier. In a further autobiographical account, **220** *Time Well Spent* (1960), Cheesman catalogues her day-to-day experiences as an insect collector in the South Pacific, with many anthropological observations on South Seas natives. At Cheesman's death, the London *Times* obituary noted the simplicity of her life, her professional defiance of cultural expectations of women, and her many contributions to the study of entomology.

221 CHESSER, Elizabeth Sloan, M.D. 1878–1940. "Elizabeth Sloan Chesser, M.D.," pp. 75–96 in *Myself When Young: By Famous Women of Today*. Frederick Muller, 1938. Ed. by Margot Asquith (Emma Alice Margaret Asquith, the Countess of Oxford and Asquith). 422 pp.; port. BLC to 1975 12:477. (1st pub. Thornton Butterworth, 1925.)

Raised in Glasgow. Father: surname Sloan, physician. Mother: née MacFarlane. 5 brothers; 4 sisters. Married 1902, husband surname Chesser. 2 sons. Wrote books on sex education, birth control, child development, and women's health and hygiene. Physician; scientific writer; women's issues author; feminist activist; social activist; birth control activist; physician's daughter. Upper middle class.

Progressive upbringing, medical training, and wide-ranging career experiences of an early woman physician and feminist activist, 1880s–1917. Despite poor school performance, yearning to be a physician; receiving father's encouragement. Father's having advanced ideas, opposing stays and corsets for his daughters as unhealthy. Author's favoring comfortable clothing; riding bicycles with father despite local prejudice against women cyclists. Secretly indulging in cigarette smoking and makeup. Enrolling at medical school, age 17. Enjoying her medical studies at Queen Margaret College; cultivating frivolous exterior to hide her studiousness. Writing a column on her college for a Glasgow evening paper. Wanting to have both professional success and marriage; discussing her society's double standard toward women's sexual conduct. Graduating from medical school; learning midwifery; assisting births in tenement houses; gaining concern for the welfare of the poor. Marrying in 1902; honeymooning in China and Japan; rendering her impressions of Japan and the Japanese. Writing articles on the Far East for the *Glasgow Herald*. With husband, renting a house in Gloucestershire. Meeting Lady Maud Perry, actress Mrs. Patrick Campbell, and Gladys Holman Hunt through work for the suffragist and feminist movement. Speaking publicly on behalf of suffrage and prison reform. Helping to establish Child Welfare Centres in Gloucester and Churcham; being forced to resign from her Gloucester Child Welfare position because of advocating birth control. Writing on the health aspects of convents. During WWI, husband's serving in France; author's performing volunteer medical work in Gloucestershire; widening her experience as a medical officer in hostels and in a women's war hospital. Traveling to France, 1917, to inspect WAAC facilities; writing articles to encourage women recruits.

Chesser's story of following her father's lead into a male-dominated profession is characteristic of women pioneers in many fields, although it is interesting to note the ways in which she struck out on her own, being drawn by the women's suffrage movement into an active working relationship with women from diverse vocations. She continued her advocacy of birth control despite the religious and traditionalist fury it provoked, making a name for herself among women in both England and America for breaking the taboo against writing openly about female physiological maturation, pregnancy, and sex. For historians of the birth control movement, Chesser's factual account is usefully paired with the brief autobiographical essay "Dr. Marie Stopes" in the 1950 collection *If I Had My Time Again: An Anthology Contributed by Twenty Distinguished Men and Women*. This is a good source on turn-of-the-century social attitudes toward feminine achievement, sex education, and sexual conduct.

222 CHICHESTER, Sheila Craven. 1905–s.l.1969. *Two Lives Two Worlds: An Autobiography*. Hodder & Stoughton, 1969. 160 pp.; foreword; photos; index. BLC to 1975 60:490.

Born in Belle Eau Park, Nottingham. Father: Gerald Craven, landowner. Mother not named. 1 sister. Married 1937, Francis Chichester, aviator, sailor, publisher. 1 son; 1 stepson. Wrote *Shopping and Fashion Guide of London*. Businesswoman; publisher; vegetarian. Upper class.

Author's progress from a conventional childhood to an adventurous married life and collaborative publishing career with her husband, highlighting her devotion to Eastern medicine and spirituality, c.1910–1969. During childhood, pretending unawareness of father's suicide to spare her mother's feelings. Having contact with royalty through her maternal great-grandmother, former supervisor of Queen Victoria's royal nursery. Being educated at a strict private boarding school; receiving certification in domestic arts. Studying fashion drawing at a school in Paris. Wanting to work, but being prevented by her mother. After age 21, no longer being chaperoned; having several affairs. Catching chicken pox in adulthood; having a nervous breakdown; meeting a healer who restored her to health through prayer, meditation, and constructive thought. After mother's illness and death, author's blaming doctors for not saving her; acquiring permanent distrust of orthodox medicine. Traveling to India, Abyssinia, Portugal. Meeting her future husband while in Europe; marrying, age 32. Living in New Zealand with husband and asthmatic stepson; author's feeling fated to have sick people attached to her. Their returning to England because of author's loneliness. Husband's piling up business debts. During WWII, husband's making author refuse paid work with the Women's Royal Air Force; her doing YMCA work instead. Caring for her sick sister. Studying natural childbirth; describing the natural birth of her son as the most wonderful experience of her life, c.1946. Becoming vegetarian, but incurring conflict with husband who loved to hunt. Learning to sail and entering women's regattas. After husband's diagnosis with cancer, author's requesting friends of many religions to pray for him; utilizing laying-on of hands to heal him; noting his successful recovery. Because of husband's illness and absences on sailing trips, author's becoming active director of Francis Chichester Ltd., Map and Guide business; also publishing *Shopping and Fashion Guide of London* (entitled *London Women* at the time, and still in print in 1969). Accompanying her husband on further sailing voyages. His receiving a knighthood, 1967. Summing up her adventurous life as the outcome of her love for simplicity in clothing, food, possessions, and lifestyle.

Lady Chichester's marriage to a world-renowned pilot opened her life up to adventure; Sir Francis was not only the father figure of British yachtmanship, he had been the second person to fly solo to Australia, 1929, and the first to sail solo around the world, 1960, in his ketch, the Gypsy Moth. In addition to providing an unusual firsthand record of world travel by sailboat, Lady Chichester's book looks closely at the nuts and bolts of the publishing business in the 1960s. Of particular interest is her commentary on the natural childbirth movement, founded by England's Dr. Grantly Dick-Read in the 1930s; the author, as was typical of her, was one of the first to experiment with this new technique.

223 CHILD-VILLIERS, Margaret Elizabeth, Countess of Jersey (née Leigh). 1849–1945. *Fifty-One Years of Victorian Life*. John Murray, 1922. 392 pp.; front. port.; illus.; index. NUC pre56 279:693.

Born at Stoneleigh Abbey, North Warwickshire. Mother: Lady Caroline Grosvenor. Father: William Henry Leigh, 2nd Baron Leigh. 2 sisters; 5 brothers. Married 1872, George Villiers, later 7th Earl of Jersey, lord-in-waiting to queen, governor of New South Wales. 4 daughters; 1 son. Society woman; diplomat's spouse; traveler (world). Aristocracy.

Aristocratic woman's supportive upbringing, married life in governmental circles, and emigration to Australia, highlighting her experiences as a diplomat's wife and her views of other cultures, 1850s–1904. Earliest memories: being taken to see the Crystal Palace, age 2; learning to knit for soldiers in the Crimean War. Recalling her English governess as a character model; her mother's successful use of praise instead of punishment to guide her children. Recalling Queen Victoria's visit to her parents, 1858, and ex-Confederacy president Jefferson Davis's visit in 1868. Making her social debut, age 19. Becoming engaged; being welcomed by her fiancé's aristocratic family; marrying, 1872; moving to Oxfordshire estate of husband's parents. Birth of a son. Describing rural upper-class life: garden parties, cricket games, lawn tennis matches. Entertaining American ambassador James Russell Lowell, poet Robert Browning, and educator Thomas Hughes. Husband's being appointed Lord Lieutenant of Oxfordshire, 1887. Traveling in Greece and India; in Madras, studying Hindu religion with Brahmin teachers; discussing schisms within Hinduism, its affinities with Christianity and Jainism; also visiting with Col. Olcott, Theosophical Society organizer. Sailing to Egypt; visiting Alexandria and Cairo; traveling overland to Jerusalem, Jericho, Beirut, and Damascus. After returning to England, husband's accepting appointment as governor-general of New South Wales, 1890. Leaving England for Australia. Describing Australia's convict settlements and husband's public duties, commenting on Australian trade unions and economic conditions; frequently entertaining visiting heads of state. Accompanying her husband on diplomatic travel to Tonga and Samoa, Hong Kong, China, Japan, and North America. Returning via Egypt; dining there with Lord Kitchener. After death of Queen Victoria, 1901, author's founding the Victoria League; serving as its president and charting its growth.

Lady Jersey's active work for her statesman husband furthered good will in Australia and internationally, as well as garnering firsthand experiences for her memoir. At the time of her husband's Australian appointment, New South Wales was still the destination for many of England's convicts, and Lady Jersey's close study of prisoners' conditions, treatment, and employment opportunities after release is a strong feature of her book. Although she tends to regard South Pacific customs as defects that good missionary efforts can cure, her beneficent attitude toward a wide range of peoples lends worth to her social commentary. This account is a useful adjunct to the more privately focused memoirs of missionaries and settlers in the late-19th-century South Seas.

224 CHOLMONDELEY, Mary. 1859–1925. *Under One Roof: A Family Record*. John Murray, 1918. 166 pp.; front.; intro.; "Extracts in Verse." NUC pre56 107:630.

Born at Hodnet, Shropshire. Father: Richard Hugh Cholmondeley, clergyman. Mother: Emily Beaumont. 4 brothers; 3 sisters. Single. Niece: novelist Stella Benson. Wrote novels *The Danvers Jewels* (1887), *Red Pottage* (1899), others. Novelist; clergyman's daughter. Middle class.

Loving memories of the author's sister, interspersed with stories about their shared youthful activities, covering author's childhood and adolescence. Family history. Father's love of flowers, literature, playing the piano and tennis; his reading aloud to the children (theology and novels of Scott, Dickens, Thackeray, Edgeworth, Austen, and Stevenson). His raising daughters unaided due to wife's invalidism. Mother's austerity and personal sacrifices; her dislike for art, fascination with the physical sciences. Mother's reading to the children from German storybooks, writing and "producing" plays for them. Remembering an influential nursemaid, "Ninny." Author's illness with asthma as a child. Her attachment to her youngest sister, Hester. Grieving over Hester's death at age 22. Hester's leaving behind a voluminous diary containing material on family life. Extracts from Hester's poetry and literary essays, written in her teenage years.

This family record was written to memorialize the author's sister Hester, using material from Hester's diary. The main focus is on family life and family members, particularly Hester, rather than on the author herself. Rather than recording lives of individual character, Cholmondeley stresses the vanished character of an era, providing an intimate view of middle-class family life in the late 19th century.

225 CHORLEY, Katharine Campbell, Baroness Chorley (née Hopkinson). 1897–1986. *Manchester Made Them*. Faber & Faber Ltd., 1950. 288 pp.; index. BLC to 1975 61:311.

Born in Alderly Edge, near Manchester. Father: Edward Hopkinson, engineer. Mother: Minnie Campbell. 1 brother. Married 1925, Robert Samuel Chorley, later 1st Baron Chorley. Wrote *Armies and the Art of Revolution; Hills and Highways; Arthur Hugh Clough: The Uncommitted Mind*. Miscellaneous writer; editor; political activist. Middle class; married into aristocracy.

Childhood and adolescence in Manchester within an affluent bourgeois family, c.1900–1919. Family history. Her family home, Ferns. Cherishing time with her father; describing his Liberal politics; his standing as candidate for Parliament from Lancashire. Father's being friends with Gladstone, who visited Ferns. Mother's doing social work in working-class neighborhoods; both parents' being hostile to the "idle rich." Discussing living conditions of Manchester's poor. Discussing differences between Catholic and Protestant tenets. Noting rules of Victorian decorum, including men's and women's expectations of each other. Commenting on bourgeois life in Manchester: men's status as "money-lords," idle, dependent women as emblems of men's success. Trying to improve her education by attending university extension lectures. Attending school in Folkestone. Thinking about attending Cambridge University; parents' discouraging her; never seriously studying to take Newnham College's entrance exams because convinced she would fail. Supporting social reform issues and social reformers who work with the poor. Working for Liberal Party candidate John Murry, her cousin by marriage. Her brother's serving in WWI. Her father's death. Noting changes in attitudes toward sex, before and after WWI.

Perceiving upper class's use of its familiarity with arts and culture to assure itself of superiority to the lower classes.

In Lady Chorley's account, her middle-class childhood home with its simultaneous gender inequities and active social ethics becomes a microcosm of the era's English bourgeois culture. She describes the awakening of her social conscience through her parents, both of whom demonstrate the charitable ethic and socialist-inspired concern for the problems of northern England's industrial working class that typified Liberal politics, c.1900. However, she also complains of the idleness that bourgeois ideals impose upon female members of an affluent family in order to demonstrate their freedom from the necessity to work. In this regard, the urban middle class belatedly adopted a practice already rebelled against by women from more genteel families; echoes of this complaint can be found in the writings of women from Florence Nightingale to Charlotte Brontë, going back to the 1860s. In her eyewitness study, the author subjects the cultural gender prescriptions of her youth to a careful and knowing feminist evaluation. After WWI the author worked as a secretary, in 1924 marrying a lawyer who served as London University law professor and member of the king's household staff before receiving a barony in 1945. Lady Chorley continued her work for working class welfare, which included a critical study of populist poet Arthur Hugh Clough. An active outdoorswoman, she also edited a mountaineering journal.

226 CHRISTIE, Dame Agatha (née Mary Clarissa Agatha Miller; Mary Westmacott, pseud.). 1890–1976. *An Autobiography*. Collins Sons & Co., 1989. 560 pp.; preface; illus.; index. NUC 1978 3:861. (other eds.: 1977, 1978.)

Born in Torquay, Devonshire. Father: Frederick Alva Miller. Mother: Clara Boehmer. 1 sister; 1 brother. Married 1914, Archibald Christie, businessman; divorced 1928. Married 1930, Sir Max Mallowan, archaeologist. 1 daughter. Wrote over 60 novels, 30 collections of short stories (mostly on crime themes), a book about an archaeological dig, *Come, Tell Me How You Live* (1946), and (under Mary Westmacott) *Unfinished Portrait* (1934). Knew many contemporary British writers and archaeologists. Novelist; short storyist. Upper class.

Lucid images from the childhood and private life of England's premiere mystery writer, c.1895–1970s. Rating her childhood as happy. Being less influenced by her simple, generous father than her "startlingly original" mother. In her own childhood, mother's having been sent to live with an aunt; ultimately marrying her aunt's stepson. Mother's adoring educational and religious experiments; trying to keep author from learning to read until age 8. Mother's flirting with Catholicism, Unitarianism, Theosophy, and Zoroastrianism before joining the Church of England, in which she had author christened. Author's own beliefs' coming from "Nursie," a Bible Christian; recalling reading with Nursie. Taking family holidays in France and Brittany. After father's death, author's turning more to mother. In adulthood, regretting her lack of formal education, although having attended several finishing schools. Depicting youthful social events: a debutante party in Cairo, a house party at Goodwood. Traveling to Italy by herself. Writing her first story. Courting with Archie; their becoming engaged. In WWI, doing volunteer hospital work. Moving to London at WWI's end. Giving birth to her only child. Traveling extensively with her husband. Her mother's death's bringing upheaval to her life. Divorcing Archie. Concentrating on her daughter's education. Recalling her travels to the Canary Islands and to the Middle East on the Orient Express. Marrying a second time; author and husband's taking honeymoon in the Mediterranean. Her best-selling novels' bringing her fame. Writing novels of a different sort under a pseudonym, Mary Westmacott. Outbreak of WWII; husband Max's departure for Egypt. Their home, Greenway, being conscripted by the British Admiralty for wartime use. Reflecting on her daughter Rosalind's having a baby; its implications for her own life.

As Virginia Woolf did in writing her autobiography *Moments of Being*, Christie began this memoir to distract herself from a more onerous ongoing project. Also in the fashion of Woolf, Christie illuminates individual memories rather than telling a continuous story, and uses her early memories as vehicles for reflecting upon her identity. "We may never know the whole man," she writes, "though sometimes, in quick flashes, we know the true man." Interestingly, although she evidently chooses incidents to oblige her readers' curiosity about her, she omits mention of the widely publicized incident following her second husband's confession of infidelity to her, c.1970: she disappeared from her home; her car, containing all her clothes, was found in a ditch; ultimately she was discovered at a hotel, registered under the name of her husband's mistress (an event recounted but not explained in the unsigned preface). However, Christie's writing method, designed to pull the truth of her life from discreet but insightful flashes, makes the omission, although tantalizing, fairly unimportant.

227 CLARKE, Mary Anne (née Thompson). 1776–1852. *The Rival Princes; or, a Faithful Narrative of Facts Relating to Mrs. M.A. Clarke's Political Acquaintance with Colonel Wardle, Major Dodd, etc.* C. Chapple, 1810. 2 vols. Vol. I: 216 pp.; front. port.; preface. Vol. II: 307 pp. BLC to 1975 63:358.

Born in London. Father: surname Thompson. Mother not named. Stepfather: surname Farquhar. 1 brother. Married 1794, surname Clarke, in the stonemason trade. 3 children. Mistress; political conspirator; actress (stage). Probably middle class.

Vengeful, self-justifying account by the ex-mistress of the duke of York, defending her involvement in political plot against the duke, 1808–10.

Vol. I: Clarke's describing her earlier extravagant life as mistress of the duke of York, commander-in-chief of the British Army, c.1803–08. The duke's ultimately rejecting her; author's living in poverty with her children near London. In 1808, being contacted by Col. Wardle; his offering to relieve author's poverty in return for information about both York's misuse of public funds and his feud with his brother, the duke of Kent. Wardle's speaking on behalf of Major Dodd, Kent's private secretary; author's being offered £5,000 plus £400 a year from the duke of Kent for her evidence. After author agreed, Wardle's successfully starting parliamentary investigation into the duke of York's abuses, January 1809. Kent's making sensational confession before Parliament concerning the brothers' mutual hatred, February 1809. Dodd's possession of her papers becoming widely known; author's hiding away secretly. Trying unsuccessfully to collect the promised funds; Wardle's neatly evading her. Author's angrily condemining Wardle's character: his treachery, his mistress, his ignorance of military science. Condemning Dodd's character as well; Dodd's disclaiming any political acquaintance with the author. Vol. II: Writing her memoirs; noting attempts by the duke of York's agent to suppress this memoir; as a result, author's deciding not to publish. Having money extorted from her by one of Wardle's associates, an "American spy" who threatened to publish the memoir anyway. Author's testifying before Parliament, February 1809; Wardle's attempting to distance himself from her. Author's deciding ultimately to publish her book in order to finance her children's education. Wardle's losing a case brought by one of author's creditors, and being forced to pay the bill for author's furniture. His accusing author of perjury; her countering with a printed accusation against Wardle. Clarke's being tried for libel and acquitted. Persisting in attacks on the characters of Wardle, Dodd, and Phillips; making veiled accusations of their plotting treason against King George III.

Clarke's preface declares her intent to clear her name of all suspicion of perjury and conspiracy, although the "rival princes" of her chosen title suggest her book's appropriation of themes from 17th-century dramas set among ruthless, scheming princes in Renaissance Italy. Presenting her own motives and conduct in the best possible light, Clarke sanctimoniously blackens the character of Wardle and his associates. Her treatment, however, provides insights into the strategies and particulars of Regency political intrigue. Clarke's case and its notoriety ensured her inclusion in the *Dictionary of National Biography,* which states that her extravagance and resulting need for money while she was York's mistress led her to accept bribes from military officers seeking advancement. Wardle used this information to bring charges for wrong use of military patronage against York, but the charges were not proven. A later publication by Clarke, "A Letter to the Right Hon. William Fitzgerald," brought new libel charges against her, and in 1813 she was sentenced to nine months in prison. She moved to Paris in 1815, and died in Boulogne in 1852. More biographical information about Clarke can be found in *Authentic Memoirs of Mrs. Mary Anne Clarke,* by her friend, Elizabeth Taylor.

228 CLARKE, Moma E. c.1882–?. *Light and Shade in France.* John Murray, 1939. 236 pp.; front.; illus.; index. NUC pre56 111:338.

Born in rural England. Married c.1910, husband not named. Journalist; theatrical writer; art critic; fashion writer; travel writer; foreign resident (France). Upper middle class.

Memories of a British journalist's education and later career in France, emphasizing her fascination with French culture, c.1900–1939. First coming to Paris, c.1900, to study at the Sorbonne; describing the city, her *pension,* her landlady, and other foreign students. Taking Paris excursions with landlady; picnicking by the Seine; shortchanging her studies. Describing city travel before the advent of the Metro, surveying Parisian holidays and women's chic, uncomfortable clothing styles. Years later, being present for the Allied Army's parade through Paris after the Armistice. After marriage, c.1910, writing for a Parisian English-language literary review. Visiting middle-class French people's homes; noting that despite Frenchwomen's complaints of legal injustice for women, they nevertheless observed strict social conventions. Through her journalism, becoming friends with novelist Anatole France and sculptor Auguste Rodin. For twenty years, collaborating with the Comité Femina Vie Heureuse, the women writers' academy attached to the *Académie Goncourt;* having been made its English delegate in 1914, when the Northcliffe Prize for literature was instituted. Describing peculiarities in French children's education. Writing theatre reviews for London *Standard.* Describing Parisian actors and theatre before and after WWI. Discussing her French friends, including writers Cécile Sorel and Colette. Becoming Paris fashion correspondent for London *Times,* 1913; depicting the world of Paris couture: designers Lanvin, Chanel, and Schiaparelli. Describing Paris in 1914: King George V's visit, society dinners, war conditions. At this time, author's living in the village of Auteuil; working on women's committee to aid French dependents of British military personnel. Recounting disruption of social customs in postwar Paris. Early in her marriage, author's discovering the benefits of having the maid do housework rather than herself; discussing individual French servants and the freedom that having servants provides. Visiting friends in the provinces; traveling with her husband. Describing peasant life and changes in French social classes after WWI. Returning to England, c.1930; continuing to think about Paris; recalling people she had known there, the city's gradual modernization, and the passing of its artisans. France's returning to stability, 1939. Expressing great faith in the future of this ancient, enduring civilization.

As a Gallophile's memoirs of her beloved chosen country, Clarke's book preserves the character of urban Parisian culture during her thirty-year stay and is augmented by her humorous evaluations of a broad range of cultural phenomena, from gender roles to Paris fashions. Hers is also one of the few accounts describing WWI conditions in Paris for an English-speaking readership, although her book, published on the eve of WWII, discusses the rebuilding of post-WWI France without anticipating a second conflagration. All of her books dwelt on the topic of France; her first one, *Paris Waits* (1914), supports France in its expectations of Allied help during its postwar recovery. She followed this with two travel guides to France, *Cameos of French Life* (1924) and *Paris* (1929). Clarke's last published book is a French historical novel, *A Stranger Within the Gates* (1942).

229 CLEEVE, Marion (pseud.). pre-1880–d.a.1930. *Fire Kindleth Fire, the Professional Autobiography of Marion Cleeve, Ex-headmistress of the Snellham Municipal Secondary School for Girls*. Blackie & Son, 1930. 212 pp.; foreword. BLC to 1975 64:49.

Probably born in England. Parents not named. Educator; headmistress; teacher. Middle class.

Detailed views of myriad aspects of British education for working-class girls, emphasizing and outlining needed changes, c.1900–1930. Discussing poverty of Snellham's community. Becoming headmistress of Snellham Municipal Secondary School for Girls; confessing that she initially wasted time on self-congratulation. Struggling to overcome the nervousness of students toward her class differences from them; learning to make herself approachable. Describing the school's curriculum. Teaching Latin; giving students hands-on botany instruction through vegetable cultivation. Noting that both teaching Scripture and providing a good example instill moral principles in students. Trying to find ways to increase students' appreciation of art, music, and literature. Describing working relations with the school's five form mistresses. Noting her administrative concerns as headmistress, including staff management and devices for winning support from local government. Commenting on headmistress's responsibility for students' emotional needs. Helping organize the girls' Literary and Debating Society; describing its literary evenings. Declaring that scolding students undercuts the important task of winning their affection. Reflecting that narrow ideas of duty seldom accord with the genuine service needed from a teacher. Earning a reputation with the school board for getting her own way.

In her foreword, the author states that all names, including the school's and her own, are fictitious, and she chooses generalities in recording her experiences there. Following her stated intent to advise readers on how to run a girls' school effectively, Cleeve confines her discussion to administrative and pedagogical matters; however, she traces her own decision to become a teacher to a spiritual sense of duty. Although the school she describes is municipally sponsored, the author's frequent citations of Catholic authors may provide a key to her own religious orientation and outlook on her students' spiritual requirements. This is an excellent source from a practicing educator on the goals and procedures of British girls' schools at the beginning of the 20th century.

230 COBBE, Frances Power. 1822–1904. *Life of Frances Power Cobbe, by Herself.* Boston & New York: Houghton, Mifflin, 1894. 2 vols. Vol. 1: 330 pp.; front. port.; preface; letters. Vol. 2: 318 pp.; illus.; letters; index. NUC pre56 113:319.

Born in Dublin, Ireland. Father: Charles Cobbe, army officer, landowner. Mother: Frances Conway. 4 brothers. Single. Wrote *The Workhouse as an Hospital* (1861), *Why Women Desire the Franchise* (1869), *Wife Torture* (1878), others. Social reformer; essayist; antivivisectionist; animal welfare activist; journalist; editor; pamphleteer; public speaker; feminist activist; suffragist. Upper class.

Anglo-Irish childhood, limited mid-Victorian female education, and extensive writing and social reform career of an outspoken feminist, moralist, and antivivisectionist, 1830s–1870s. Vol. 1: Remarking that if a woman has money, her life is best fulfilled without marriage. Recounting her family's place in Dublin history. Being adored as family's only daughter. Being sent to a boarding school for young ladies, age 14; using it to illustrate the defects of girls' education, c.1840: excessive cost, pretentiousness, a curriculum that stressed feminine "accomplishments" over academic subjects. Author's telling 1890s female readers to thank her generation for winning them full educational rights. After leaving school, age 16, finally learning math, literature, and history from a Dublin parson. Author's parents' following Arminianism; author's losing her own early religious devotion; becoming agnostic, age 17. Father's ejecting her from the house as an unbeliever; author's living with brother in Donegal until recovering her faith through "reason"; being allowed back home. Deciding her personal creed was Theism. Death of her mother, author's age 20. Discussing aspects of her 1855 *Essay on the Theory of Intuitive Morals;* considering it her magnum opus; its being attacked for exhibiting unfeminine stoical ideas. Discussing Irish living conditions, c.1840s–1850s: starvation and mass emigrations from the potato famine. Father's death, 1857. Leaving the family home; taking an extended journey through Europe and the Middle East. After return to England, working for Mary Carpenter's reformatory for children in Bristol; describing the city's working and living conditions for the poor. Volunteering in a workhouse; describing its conditions, c.1850s; earning her first £14 selling "Workhouse Sketches" to *Macmillan's Magazine;* raising funds for workhouses. Making extended stay in Italy for her health,

1857–79; visiting charity hospitals there. Having bad medical treatment in Italy; becoming permanently distrustful of doctors. Vol. 2: More Italian memories. Establishing friendship with Italian residents Robert Browning and Elizabeth Barrett; meeting Harriet Beecher Stowe there. Returning to London. Publishing antivivisection writings, "Darwinism in Science and Society." Writing for *Echo* and the *Evening Standard,* 1870s. Being friends with noted philosophers: remarking John Stuart Mill's support for women in medical schools, Matthew Arnold's interracial friendships, Thomas Carlyle's work to end vivisection. Discussing opposition to vivisection of Cardinal Manning, Lord Hallam Tennyson, Wilkie Collins, and Lord Shaftesbury. Becoming secretary of the antivivisectionist Victoria Street Society. History of animal protective legislation, including the 1824 founding of the Society for Prevention of Cruelty to Animals. Citing causes of cruelty to animals, including Judeo-Christian ideas of human dominance. Starting the *Zoöphilist,* an antivivisection forum; also publishing the *Modern Rack.* Discussing the passage of the 1870 act restricting vivisection; its partial success. Death of her brother Thomas; adopting his children as her own. Explaining history of women's suffrage; tracing origins of her own suffragism; collaborating with Millicent Garrett Fawcett; working for the vote through her published writings. Investigating cases of cruelty to wives by husbands; helping win legislation to protect wives from spousal abuse. Investigating women's health issues; writing "Little Health of Ladies." Retiring to Wales.

When Cobbe retired to Wales, she went with her long-time companion Mary Lloyd, although her autobiography, in conformity with 19th-century decorum, preserves silence on the subjects of both her homosexuality and her living arrangements. An energetic and prolific writer, she made her pen the weapon of choice in a war for the rights of women, the reform of British law to protect the helpless against exploitation, and the improvement of domestic relations, especially among the working classes. Cobbe continued her wide-ranging and influential reform work until 1884, when the receipt of an inheritance enabled her retirement. Cobbe's evaluations of social ills and their causes, coupled with the far-ranging scope of her reform career, makes her autobiography a case study in the Victorians' sociological understanding as well as a primary resource for study of Victorian England's diverse reform movements.

231 COGHLAN, Margaret (née Moncrieffe). c.1763–? *Memoirs of Mrs. Coghlan, Daughter of the Late Major Moncrieffe: Written By Herself with Introduction and Notes*. New York: T. H. Morrell, 1864. 158 pp.; intro. and notes by publisher. NUC pre56 114:176. (1st pub. 1794; other ed.: Arno Press, 1971.)

Born in Dublin, Ireland. Father: Major Moncrieffe, British Army officer. Mother: Margaret Jephson. 1 brother; 1 half-sibling. Married 1777, surname Coghlan. 2 daughters; 2 sons. Knew General Gage, Frederick Jay,

Lord Thomas Clinton, the Comte d'Artois. Adventuress; prison inmate; prisoner of war. Middle class.

From childhood onward, author's transatlantic wanderings from one adventure to another, emphasizing her financial accommodations with a series of lovers, 1760–1794. Death-torn family history; author's mother's marrying at age 14, dying at 20. Author's and brother's spending infancy in family friend's home; at ages 3 and 5, being sent to separate boarding schools. Father's returning to Dublin, author's age 8, with new wife; taking children to live in America, 1772. After death of stepmother, father's receiving legacy; marrying six months later; second wife's dying in childbirth. Father's fighting in the Revolutionary War; sending children to live with their uncle, a member of new U.S. Congress. Author's running away to a family of British sympathizers. In 1777, narrowly escaping being massacred by treacherous Indians attached to the British Army. Being held hostage during Revolutionary War by George Washington's command; falling in love with one captor, an American colonel; his making sure she was returned to her father. Father's absolutely opposing their romance. Enduring forced marriage, age 14, to Mr. Coghlan of the British Army. Once married, Coghlan's selling his commission; taking author back to Britain. Author's escaping his attempted imprisonment of her; receiving shelter from her childhood caretaker, General Gage; his sending her to a French convent. Being helped by a sympathetic male friend to escape the convent; when Gen. Gage found her back in England, his sending her to board with a London family. Confronting father's expectation that she support herself; resolving to go on stage. After debuting at Drury Lane, finding wealthy benefactor; his fathering her child, supporting them both for four years. Having a daughter from a brief affair with Lord Hervey. Having two children by a Captain B. Becoming mistress to Mr. Giffard, but accumulating debts that caused her to move to France. Embarking on various romantic liaisons in Paris, including one with an improvident Mr. Beckett; his fleeing due to debts; his creditors' imprisoning author while seven months pregnant. Receiving financial assistance from other men, including the Comte d'Artois and an Irish nobleman. Returning to England; being caught and imprisoned for old debts; giving birth in prison. Suing her husband for financial support. After death of her father, trying unsuccessfully to win part of his estate and part of her paternal grandfather's estate. Being accepted by her mother's sisters. Being imprisoned again; being released. Making a final plea to the rich, especially the Crown, to assist those in poverty and be tolerant of young people's extravagant ways.

Despite bearing a passing resemblance to Defoe's *Moll Flanders,* this classically picaresque 18th-century memoir seems to be genuine, naming real names and providing precise details of troop movements during America's Revolutionary War. Apart from that, the author uses her relationships as kept mistress to a series of men to insist that no matter what a man's nature is—cruel or kindly, well intentioned or not—a woman in such relationships, unprotected by marriage or male relatives, will inevitably suffer due to men's greater legal advantages. While Coghlan undercuts her credibility by pleading victimhood in her debt situation, she also shows the clear beginnings of a feminist sensibility that takes her memoir out of the ordinary.

232 COLE, Dame Margaret Isabel (née Postgate). 1893–1980. *Growing Up into Revolution*. Longmans, Green, & Co., 1949. 224 pp.; preface; illus.; index. NUC pre56 114:615.

Born in Cambridge. Father: John Percival Postgate, professor of Latin. Mother: Edith Allen, mathematician, classicist. 4 brothers; 1 sister. Married 1918, George Douglas Howard Cole, economist, historian, Oxford professor, political organizer, detective writer. 2 daughters; 1 son. Wrote *Beatrice Webb* (1945), *Makers of the Labour Movement* (1948), others. Political activist; political writer; academic; short storyist; biographer; socialist; feminist; social reformer; academic's daughter; academic's spouse; teacher; crime writer. Middle class.

Dual biography of the author and her economist husband, both influential Fabian activists and reformers, 1890s–1940s. Studying Latin with her father and trying to meet his standards; recalling mother's character and academic career. Memories of family holidays, Anglican services, and boarding school. Moving from Cambridge to Liverpool with family; attending Roedean school. Attending Girton College on scholarship; noting freedom of college life. Being introduced to English socialism and feminism; abandoning Christianity and working for women's rights. After graduation, moving to London; teaching at St. Paul's Girls School. Doing volunteer work for the Fabian Research Department of the Guild Socialist Movement; becoming colleague of Beatrice and Sidney Webb. Marrying fellow socialist and economist G. D. H. Cole, 1918. Births of two daughters. Continuing Fabian work: entertaining Ford Madox Ford, assisting union strikes; collaborating with husband on writing projects. Husband's accepting doctoral fellowship to Oxford, 1925. At Oxford, becoming friends with classics professor Gilbert Murray, later president of both the League of Nations and United Nations General Council; discussing postwar role of Woodrow Wilson and League of Nations. Teaching through Workers' Education Association. After husband's becoming advisor to Ramsey McDonald's Economic Council, author's founding Society for Socialist Inquiry and Propaganda; discussing rise of Nazism in Germany and reaction of British socialists. Visiting socialist writer H. G. Wells. Traveling through Soviet Union on lecture tour, 1932; lecturing in Egypt, 1939. When WWI began, continuing to work for the New Fabian Research Bureau. Traveling to New York to visit her daughter. Discussing changes in social classes and living conditions in

England, 1890s–1940s. Seeing 20th century as the century of the common man.

Although Cole would in 1971 produce a full biography of her husband, this memoir effectively constitutes a dual biography of them both, situating their shared socialist activism against a panoramic backdrop of early 20th-century England's economic and class struggles. As a source of information about British socialists as well as their agenda, this thorough study complements Fabian cofounder Beatrice Webb's two volumes of autobiography, *My Apprenticeship* (1926) and *Our Partnership* (1943), by extending observations of the socialist movement beyond WWII. Cole and her husband were active partners in every aspect of their lives; in addition to their commitment to social reform, they coauthored more than thirty detective stories before his death in 1949. Cole was created D.B.E. in 1970, honoring her contributions to English social welfare.

233 COLEMAN, Ann Raney. 1810–1897. *Victorian Lady on the Texas Frontier: The Journal of Ann Raney Coleman*. Ed. by C. Richard King. Norman, OK: University of Oklahoma Press, 1971. 206 pp.; front. port.; ed.'s intro.; afterword; biblio.; index. NUC 1968–1972 19:493.

Born in Whitehaven, Cumberland. Father: John Raney, bank partner, businessman, teacher. Mother not named. 2 brothers; 1 sister. Married 1833, John Thomas, farmer, plantation owner, American, died c.1846. Married c.1847, John Coleman, storekeeper; divorced 1855. 2 sons; 1 daughter. Emigrant (U.S.); teacher; governess; domestic servant. Middle class.

Recollections of childhood, emigration, and the Texas frontier, covering 1832–90. In author's childhood, father's losing an inherited fortune and mismanaging a company into failure. After declaring bankruptcy, 1829, father's seeking a fresh start in Texas. At age 22, author's sailing with mother and sister to join father in Texas. Recounting perils of sea voyage: persistent suitors; their ship's being attacked and plundered by pirates. Reuniting with father in Texas. Shortly after arrival, seeing the Battle of Velasco; molding bullets and making bullet patches for Texan soldiers. Living independently of her parents at Sterling McNeel's plantation. Parents' deaths from fever. Marrying a nearby planter; having misgivings about his character. Discussing her sister's bad marriages. Birth of author's first son, age 24. Discussing her relations with slaves and local Indians; husband's selling her favorite slave. Seeing ghost of plantation's former owner. During civilian retreat from advancing Mexican army, 1836, husband's abusing author; his selling the plantation without her knowledge. Moving to Louisiana; births of second son and daughter; sons' deaths. Moving to another plantation; refusing husband's demand that she sign a mortgage on the property to finance building a house. Husband's death. Marrying a New Orleans shopkeeper, 1847; his selling all her property, including slaves; absconding with the money. Recounting her life in New Orleans as a housekeeper. After Coleman's return, accepting him again as her husband. Traveling alone to England; trying unsuccessfully to recover father's property in Texas through the courts. Finally standing up to Coleman's abusiveness; divorcing him, 1855. Moving to Texas to live with her married daughter; teaching school, helping raise her grandchildren. Noting the independent work of Texas women in U.S. Civil War. After the war, holding a series of jobs: governess, schoolteacher, housekeeper. Unsuccessfully seeking pension from Texas governor and legislature on basis of her war service, 1882; being refused on grounds that she had been married twice. Daughter's death, 1890.

Details from Coleman's early life in England come from the journal she kept at the behest of an early fiancé, Henry Marks. The editor also provides explanatory footnotes. Coleman's presence as an Englishwoman during Texas's struggles for nationhood as well as the American Civil War is well documented in her book, which is a rare record of women's active and covert participation in the two wars. Students of women's history as well as of the American frontier will find in this book a wealth of information. A typescript copy of the complete manuscript is in the Archive Department of the Texas State Library in Austin, Texas.

234 COLERIDGE, Sara. 1802–1852. *Memoirs and Letters of Sara Coleridge*. New York: Harper & Bros., 1874. Ed. by Edith Coleridge (author's daughter). 528 pp.; front. port.; preface and biographical sketch by ed.; letters. BLC to 1975 65:492.

Born at Greta Hall, near Keswick, Cumberland. Father: Samuel Taylor Coleridge, poet and philosopher. Mother: Sarah Fricker. 2 brothers. Married 1829, cousin Henry Nelson Coleridge, father's literary executor. 1 daughter; other children. Wrote *Pretty Lessons in Verse for Good Children* (1834), *Phantasmion* (1837); annotated and edited her father's writings; translated Dobritzhofer's *An Account of the Abipones* (1822). Knew William Wordsworth and his family, Thomas De Quincey, Robert Southey. Poet; translator; poet's daughter; editor. Middle class.

Ambivalent relationship of famous poet's daughter with her father in childhood, 1802–c.1811. Being sickly; consequently never living with her father more than a few weeks at a time. Father's calling her his "meek little Sara," but doting on his son Hartley as the replica of his visionary self. At age 5, moving with family to Bristol; living at Greta Hall. Paying visits to nearby aunts and to writer Thomas de Quincey. Clinging to her mother; on an extended visit with father to William and Dorothy Wordsworth at Grasmere Lake, father's trying to gain her love with fairy stories and other attentions. Recalling political conversations between father, Wordsworth, De Quincey, and Southey; these adults' having unusual ideas about attire; dictating what author and other children present should wear. Fearing the dark from "nervous sensitiveness and morbid imaginativeness"; father's comforting her.

Most of this volume is comprised of Coleridge's letters; her narrative autobiography, supplemented by her daughter's preface and biographical sketch, fills less than fifty pages. It was the author's stated intention to include her youth, wedded life, and widowhood in this memoir, but she died before completing the book. She pauses after giving the historical events of her life to age 9 to ask several very Wordsworthian questions: "But can I in any degree retrace what being I was then?—what relation my then being held to my maturer self? Can I draw any useful reflection from my childish experience, or found any useful maxim upon it? What *was* I?" Of her father's literary circle, she seems to have been closest to Southey, whom she calls "my Uncle Southey." This book portrays the family side of Samuel Taylor Coleridge as a father and storyteller and also shows a vivid picture of the intellectual and social interchanges in his legendary circle of Romantic writers.

235 COLLIER, A. c.1809–c.1881. *A Biblewoman's Story: Being the Autobiography of Mrs. Collier, of Birmingham.* Ed. by Eliza Nightingale. T. Woolmer, 1885. 2nd. ed. 125 pp.; intro. by ed.; app. BLC to 1975 66:114.

Born in England. Parents not named. Married, husband not named. 1 son. Religionist (Wesleyan Methodist); charitable volunteer; landlady; laundry worker; physically handicapped woman. Working class.

Dramatic personal memories, focusing on author's voluntary career as a Wesleyan Biblewoman and counselor on conversion as well as on her financial and health problems, covering c.1831–75. At age 22, living in a country village; reading a tract that convinced her of her own sinfulness. Moving to Birmingham, 1847; being kept by partial deafness from attending worship for two years. Later attending Wesleyan Chapel; hearing the Rev. Joseph Wood; converting to Methodist beliefs of sin and salvation. One month after her conversion, husband's losing his reason and being confined to an insane asylum. When permitted to see him, being told she must take him home or he would die. Praying for him; his converting during a brief lucid period. Husband's relapsing and being removed to Worcester, then to Fairford. Author's successfully converting her son to Methodism before his early death. Bringing husband home during another period of sanity. Author's taking in washing to support herself. Caring for a friend's orphan son. Husband's sudden disappearance and reappearance; author's fearing he might murder her. Author's taking in lodgers, who left abruptly after meeting husband. Husband's final disappearance. Distributing tracts; converting people and organizing Cottage meetings in Birmingham. Bringing children to Sunday school; bringing parents to religious commitment through their children. Having difficulties collecting rent from lodgers. Suffering theft of her laundry mangle, the main means of supporting herself. Going hungry but receiving friends' charity. Taking in two factory girls who were abused by their parents. Converting Roman Catholics to Methodism. Leading Bible classes; by 1869 having five hundred subscribers to her tracts. Expanding her washing business. Later, suffering reduction of income due to her failing health. Having a leg amputated; contracting cancer, 1875. Living with a Wesleyan family she had formerly aided.

Frequently quoting Scripture and hymns, Collier mingles factual detail with an account of her inner changes in this spiritual autobiography of a 19th-century Methodist lay preacher. The book provides a wealth of information on the organization, writings, and spread of Methodism during the author's lifetime. The editor, who lived with the author for three years and may have been a member of a family that received Collier's assistance, revised the text after Collier's death at age 76.

236 COLLIER, Constance (Mrs. Julian L'Estrange). 1878–1955. *Harlequinade: The Story of My Life*. John Lane, 1929. 294 pp.; front. port.; preface by Noel Coward; intro.; illus.; index. NUC pre56 115:476.

Born at Windsor, Berkshire. Father: surname Hardie, actor. Mother not named, dancer, pantomime player. Married Julian L'Estrange, actor, d.1918. Knew Ellen Terry, Maurice Maeterlinck, Noel Coward, Lillian Gish, others. Actress (child, stage, film); playwright; theatrical producer; philanthropist; traveler (Europe, Ireland, U.S.). Lower middle class.

Actress's theatrical upbringing and later career in a range of venues from provincial pantomime to Hollywood films, 1880s–1920s. In childhood, actress mother's being devoted to author; taking her to pantomimes, providing her with ballet lessons. Trying to attend school while accompanying her mother on theatrical tours. Family's suffering financial hardships from father's heavy drinking; his recovering through religious experience. Author's dutifully attending Anglican services, but disliking imposed religion. Performing in her first play, age 4. Disliking her boarding school's strict discipline; being "rescued" from school by her mother. Through theatrical exposure, growing to love Shakespeare. Beginning acting in comedy choruses despite father's growing dislike of the theatre; his wanting her to become a nurse. Performing at the Gaiety Theatre. Auditioning unsuccessfully for the Lyceum Theatre with Bram Stoker, the manager. Appearing in H. V. Esmond's play, *When We Were Twenty-One*. Performing at His Majesty's Theatre owned by Herbert Beerbohm Tree. Establishing friendships with writers Somerset Maugham and Sidney Colvin, also the Beerbohm family. Meeting and marrying a fellow actor. Recounting a series of performances in England and Ireland; giving a command performance for the Kaiser in Berlin. Performing in the Stratford Shakespeare Festival. Having marital problems because her career was more successful than her husband's. Their accepting roles in American productions; socializing with colleagues; author's impressions of America. British theatres' closing after start of WWI. Grieving over the death of her mother. Founding the Arts Fund. Performing in *Peter Ibbetson,* a musical play for which she wrote the libretto. After husband's joining the Canadian Air Force, accepting an offer to go to Hollywood. Meeting Charlie Chaplin, D. W. Griffith, Lillian Gish, John Barrymore. Death of her husband in the worldwide influenza epidemic, 1918. Accepting a motion picture contract. Contracting diabetes; noting she was the first patient to be treated with insulin. Establishing friendship with dramatists Ivor Novello and Noel Coward; Coward's persuading her to write her memoirs. Describing changes in the theatre between Victorian times and the late 1920s.

Never a major theatrical star, Collier was nevertheless well-known to her fellow actors, and she knew many of the most eminent figures of the theatrical world as it moved into the era of film. This chatty memoir includes many anecdotes about well-known artists and producers in England, New York, and early Hollywood. Collier wrote several plays, worked as a producer, and late in life served as an acting coach for Katherine Hepburn.

237 COLLINS, Jose (Josephine Charlotte Cooney). 1887–1958. *The Maid of the Mountains: Her Story.* Hutchinson, 1932. 287 pp.; illus.; index. NUC pre56 115:663.

Born in Salford, near Manchester. Father not named. Mother: Lottie Collins, music-hall performer, actress. Stepfathers: Mr. Cooney, d.1902; James W. Tate. 2 sisters. Married Leslie Chatfield; divorced 1917. Married Lord Robert Innes Ker. Actress (child, music hall, stage, film); singer (popular). Lower middle class; married into aristocracy.

Rise and fall of a music-hall dancer's daughter in her own international stage career, 1890s–1930s. Being of Jewish and Spanish ancestry. Stepfather's being Catholic; having all of his stepdaughters rebaptized as Catholics. Actress mother's being frequently absent on tour; her earning fame for her naughty, original performance of the song and dance number "Ta-ra-ra-boom-de-ay," 1891. Mother's sending author and sisters to convent school; resolving to foil author's long-time desire to go on stage. Mother's relenting; allowing author to bill herself as "Lottie Collins's daughter." At age 10, appearing with mother in *The Little Dressmaker.* Cooney's death, 1902; mother's quickly marrying again. Mother's death, 1910. Author's marrying Leslie Chatfield; divorce, 1917. Her second marriage, to Lord Robert Innes Ker. Stage roles. Touring in America with Lee Schubert in *Vera Violetta.* Appearing in grand opera *The Merry Countess.* Dancing and singing in the Ziegfeld Follies. Enjoying her greatest success in title role of *The Maid of the Mountains,* 1932. Friendships with Charlie Chaplin and Noel Coward. Having a brief film career. Going on a South American stage tour. Suffering professional failures and financial reversals, 1936; her illness and money woes' making newspaper headlines. Cataloguing her regrets.

Distinguished from the customary run of actors' memoirs by its record of the unsuccessful end of her career, despite her hard work, Collins's account looks at the volatility and instability of the theatrical business. It also looks at the increasing social mobility actors enjoyed in the 20th century through the marital histories of the author as well as her mother; both married well, despite having no pretentions to respectability except talent. Collins's book shows the range of theatrical production types in the first two decades of the century, and suggests how easily actors could move from one to another.

238 COLLYER, Margaret. c.1874–c.1935. *Life of an Artist*. Philip Allan, 1935. 389 pp.; illus. NUC pre56 116:92.

Born in England. Father: W. J. Collyer. Mother not named. 1 brother; sisters. Single. Artist (painter); foreign resident (Kenya); horse breeder; stock farmer. Upper class.

Transition of a woman painter from genteel British art circles to her personal liberation in frontier Kenya, 1880s–1934. Her family's showing apathy toward childhood interest in art; discouraging her desire for a professional art career. At age 18, studying art in Germany for one year. Returning to England; living with her grandmother. Loving horses and dogs; painting them as subjects. Through a chance meeting with old family friends, being introduced to the president of the Royal Academy; his encouraging her career. Living with friends while studying in Pelham Street School of Art; working toward a scholarship for the Royal Academy. Painting *The Dancing Fawn* as her entrance exam; being accepted at the Royal Academy. Describing the technique and process of her painting. Winning a medal for drawing. Memories of her early patron, Flora Smith. Discussing how she lived on her own; giving advice to young artists. Recounting her experiences with animal subjects. Painting *The Deserters* and *Horse Fair*. Exhibiting in London, 1893–1910, but being insecure about the extent of her talent. During WWI, doing VAD nursing in an Allied Field Hospital; being sickened by the maiming and slaughter caused by the war. Visiting her sister in Africa, 1915. Describing Kenya's native peoples, culture, and rituals. Helping in sister's horse trading business. Falling in love with the beauty of Africa and its wildlife. Deciding to live (rather than paint) her art. Living independently in a primitive area of Kenya. Lacking modern equipment; living in a tent for years before her house was built. Kikuyu tribe workers' serving as author's protectors. Braving all circumstances because of her pleasure in the African landscape. Hunting. Learning to speak Swahili. Celebrating her artistic instincts through her lifestyle, although lacking time to paint. Warding off loneliness; mourning her dogs' deaths in fights with wild animals. Experiencing drought, famine, fire, and earthquake. Having her bleakest year, 1925, with locust plague and sister's absence in England. Having trouble growing cereals; preferring stock farming to agriculture; raising cattle. Discussing influx of Europeans for land, 1917–27; unemployed English ex-soldiers being encouraged to settle in Kenya and farm. Receiving visit from Prince of Wales when he visited district settlers. Year of depression and drought, 1933; return of rains, greenness, as sign of optimism for the future.

Collyer's autobiography anthologizes a number of topics of historical interest, among them women's growing inclusion in the Royal Academy, settler society in Kenya, and the profound freedom from gender role expectations that this frontier society provided. The author's optimistic narration is best characterized by her tendency, when any of her thoughts lead to unpleasant associations, to break them off by writing "the less said the better." When fire struck her ranch, Collyer lost many original papers; she does not elaborate on the nature of these papers, but their destruction was a blow not only to her, but to the record of early women settlers' lives in East Africa.

239 COLVILLE, Lady Cynthia (née Milnes; D.B.E.). 1884–1968. *Crowded Life*. Evans Bros., 1963. 215 pp.; illus.; index. BLC to 1975 67:23.

Raised in Yorkshire. Father: Robert Offley Ashburton Crew-Milnes, Earl of Crewe, Baron Houghton. Mother: Sibyl Graham. Stepmother: Lady Peggy Primrose. 2 sisters; 1 brother. Married 1908, the Hon. George Charles Colville. 3 sons. Lady-in-waiting; political appointee; justice of the peace; philanthropist; society woman. Aristocracy.

Author's aristocratic upbringing in a family dedicated to public service and later extensive adult philanthropic work, 1880s–1953. Mother's death, author's age 3; author's being sent to live with her eccentric uncle Crewe. Author and her sister Celia's being shaken, whipped, and nearly drowned by their new governess; author's nevertheless remembering her as "a very conscientious and thorough teacher." Enjoying riding horses and keeping bees at her uncle's. At author's age 10, father's being appointed lord lieutenant of Ireland by Prime Minister Gladstone; his supporting the 1894 Home Rule Bill. Recounting her father's lifetime political positions: member of the House of Lords, secretary of state for both India and the colonies, lord of the privy seal, and secretary of state for war, 1931. Author's staying at her uncle's, receiving a "finishing" governess at age 15. Father's marrying an 18-year-old aristocrat, 1899; author's worrying about problems arising from her age similarity to her stepmother. Father's letting her be schooled away from home; author's studying piano in Dresden and later at the Royal College of Music. Making her social debut, 1902. Noting changing face of aristocratic social life and diminishing role of servants. Marriage, 1908. Births of her three sons. Believing it would be interesting to school them herself; their later attending Harrow. Author's doing volunteer work during WWI. Her work with the Lend-a-Hand Club; founding the Personal Service Association; working with the Charity Organisation Society; doing social work in Shoreditch. Serving as woman of the bedchamber to Queen Mary, 1923; describing the royal household and the queen's character. Serving as justice of the peace in London, 1929. Serving at East London Juvenile Court. Expressing opinions on women's lack of fortitude and endurance; young women's lack of moral scruples; prostitution as a social issue. Serving on departmental committee to inquire into the workings of the Midwives' Acts, 1931. Traveling to Jerusalem, the Mediterranean, Canada, New Zealand, Australia, and India. Being created dame of the British Empire, 1953.

Although writing a personal autobiography, Lady Cynthia contextualizes her own social compassion and work against a backdrop of her family's historical prominence as British public servants, attributing her humanitarianism to her inheritance of the family character. Although many 20th-century memoirs from the women in Britain's titled set suggest a lessening of the traditional obligation to engage in charitable works, Lady Cynthia's book shows that this was far from universal. At the time she began charity work in Shoreditch, its infant mortality was the highest of any London borough; it improved dramatically when Lady Cynthia became the honorary secretary of a new infant welfare centre for Shoreditch, serving in this office for twenty years while balancing other public service commitments.

240 COMPTON, Fay (pseud.; Virginia Compton Mackenzie). 1894–1978. *Rosemary: Some Remembrances.* Alston Rivers, 1926. 265 pp.; intro. by Compton Mackenzie (author's brother); illus. NUC pre56 118:279.

Born in London. Father: Edward Compton, stage name; surname Mackenzie, actor. Mother: Virginia Bateman (stage name), actress. 2 sisters; 2 brothers (including novelist Compton Mackenzie). Married Harry Pelissier, theatre owner, died n.d. Married Lauri de Freece, producer. Married Leon Quartermaine, actor. Married Ralph Champion Shotter; divorced 1946. 1 son. Knew Faith Compton Mackenzie (her sister-in-law). Actress (stage, film); traveler (Europe, East Asia, South America); WWI volunteer. Upper class.

Actress's education, travels, and career, with focus on her love of theatrical performance and her encounters with cultural attitudes toward women traveling alone, c.1900–26. After father's long absences on acting tours, his coming home to family rejoicing. Author's believing she enjoyed happiest of childhoods. Family's living in London, but having country houses in Hampshire and Cornwall. Mother's providing the discipline. Attending a convent kindergarten and day school, then a large boarding school in Surrey. Loving to act; playing a dormouse in *Alice in Wonderland.* Traveling to Italy for her mother's health; learning from mother how to protect her chastity while traveling. Attending finishing school in Paris; running away from school. Joining Harry Pelissier's Follies Company; marrying him seven weeks later; honeymooning in South Africa. Birth of her son. During WWI, doing volunteer work in a Belgian nuns' hospital; later doing Red Cross war work in Denmark, Finland, and Russia. Being forced by husband's death to support herself; initially failing to find stage work; later appearing in many plays and in films. Earning success as the star of *Mary Rose,* in a role written for her by J. M. Barrie; meeting and marrying Leon Quartermaine. Her father's death. Recalling playing Ophelia in *Hamlet* opposite John Barrymore. Discussing her opinions on acting technique and her decisions on how to play individual roles. Traveling in Spain and Latin America; hiring a duenna at each hotel as escort; believing a woman traveling alone must always preserve her reputation for chastity.

Relying upon her boarding-school diary, Compton renders a lively self-portrait somewhat altered from the original, as in her omission of her second marriage to Lauri de Freece. Once described by the *New York Times* as "Sir James M. Barrie's favorite actress," in her long and active career Compton appeared in six Barrie plays, including the title role in *Peter Pan*. She was also featured in many other stage productions, and in seventeen films.

241 CONQUEST, Joan (Mrs. Leonard Cooke). 1883–1941. *Strange Beds: Life Story of Love, Thrills and Adventure*. Jarrolds, 1937. 320 pp.; front. port.; illus. NUC pre56 120:213.

Born in England. Father not named, civil engineer. Mother not named. 2 sisters; 1 brother. Married, husband not named. Wrote *Desert Love, The Hawk of Egypt, Zarah the Cruel, Forbidden,* many other novels. Novelist; traveler (world); nurse (WWI); charitable volunteer. Upper middle class.

World travel and cultural impressions and opinions, as recorded by noted novelist, covering her childhood through the pre-WWII years. Loving her beautiful mother; early death of her father. Attending convent school in Paris; having further schooling in Paris and Italy. After onset of WWI, training to be a nurse; being assigned to a hospital in France; later working for the Russian Red Cross in Petersburg; describing Russian customs, food. Traveling to India and Egypt. Marrying after a quick courtship; honeymooning in South Africa. Successfully publishing her first novel, *Desert Love*. Traveling to Egypt and Asia; visiting the Taj Mahal and the Great Wall of China. Discussing Chinese and Japanese social customs. Helping to start Porridge Kitchen for poor Chinese. Visiting the Forbidden City. Working with the poor in England. Touring in Spain and Morocco. Traveling across the U.S. by bus; discussing American Indians; U.S. history, customs; perceiving high sexual energy on the Pacific coast. Visiting Mexico, Peru, Uruguay, Brazil; describing South American peoples, customs. Noting mental and moral endurance and self-control needed for traveling.

An autobiographical narrative that doubles as a travelogue, Conquest's memoir mirrors the openness of its author to exotic travel, transcultural erotic customs, and social work at home and abroad. Although passing fleetingly over such private details as her marriage, Conquest excels at conveying the observations culled from her worldwide travel. When read in tandem with earlier travel accounts by British colonialists and missionaries, Conquest's evident multicultural sensitivity dramatizes the 20th-century progress of British attitudes toward non-European peoples.

242 COOK, Dorothy Violet Medhurst. 1906–?. *I Married a Soldier*. Bala, North Wales: Dragon Books, 1973. 259 pp. NUC 1973–1977 26:29.

Born in London. Parents not named. 1 sister. Married 1928, Christopher Thomas Medhurst Cook, soldier, x-ray technician. 3 sons. Military spouse; foreign resident (India). Lower middle class.

Detailed portrait of domestic military life in Britain and India, 1924–59. At age 18, meeting her soldier husband-to-be; their marrying four years later in Christ Church, Streatham, 1928. Living on his meager military pay, 22 1/2 shillings weekly. His being posted to Lichfield, Staffordshire; author's briefly remaining in their Brixton flat; being let go from her firm, due to its policy against employing married women. Joining husband in married quarters in Lichfield barracks. Discovering her pregnancy. Taking Anglican instruction; being confirmed by the bishop of Lichfield. Suffering difficult childbirth, 1929; hemorrhaging severely. Birth of second son, 1932. Family's moving many times in search of a more suitable place to live. Husband's being posted to Bombay, India; their moving; author's being intensely homesick; adopting dogs and a cat to remind her of England. Third son's birth, 1937. Author's worrying over children's eating unsanitary food; resenting Anglo-Indian cultural obligations to hire an ayah/nursemaid; wanting to care for children herself. Family illnesses, including malaria. During WWII, author's working for the Indian Red Cross; also starting a library for hospital patients. Family's leaving India for Liverpool, 1946. Describing postwar married life in England. Author's joining Army Guild of St. Helena; noting problems caused by army's prohibition of socialization between enlisted wives and officers' wives. Husband's retirement, 1959.

Cook's account is an excellent study of the domestic aspects of British army life for families in its lower ranks. With money and frequent household moves constantly at issue, Cook unconsciously shows by her own example the coping strategies that families of ordinary soldiers have traditionally exhibited in the face of the military's almost official discouragement of married life on posts for soldiers. This book serves best as a companion piece to any of the personal accounts from British officers' wives, such as Viscountess Byng's *Up the Streams of Time* (1946); the domestic obsessions that occupy Cook's mind—even in the exotic surroundings of India—contrast strongly with the interests expressed by better-off military wives in the culture and people around them. In this capacity, Cook's memoir suggests that inequities of pay and structured conditions of life have caused the army to mirror the differing class attitudes of British society at large.

243 COOKE, Bella (née Beeton). 1821–1908. *Rifted Clouds; or, the Life Story of Bella Cooke, a Record of Loving Kindness and Tender Mercies.* Ed. by the Rev. Joseph Pullman. New York: Palmer & Hughes, 1886. 3rd ed. 448 pp.; front. port.; prefatory notes by John Stephenson, Henry Dickinson, & S. A. Lankford Palmer; diary entries; correspondence; testimonials; illus.; index. NUC pre56 121:322.

Born in Hull, Yorkshire. Father: John Beeton, soldier. Mother: Elizabeth Smawfield. 2 sisters; 6 brothers. Married 1840, Joseph Cooke, lead mine owner, Methodist teacher, d.1849. Widow. 5 daughters. Charitable volunteer; religionist (Methodist); seamstress; physically handicapped woman; teacher (Sunday school); foreign resident (U.S.). Lower middle class.

Author's journey from her Yorkshire childhood to her American old age, charting her spiritual progress and good works in the face of adversity, 1820s–1880s. Mother's Methodist family's having known John and Charles Wesley; mother's being expelled from the church for marrying a non-Methodist. Family's moving to Sheffield, author's age 6. Attending local Methodist schools and both Methodist and Anglican Sunday schools. Having a Methodist conversion experience, age 13; later being briefly drawn to Quakerism. Teaching Sunday school and distributing tracts. Being bled with leeches as treatment for "inflammation of the brain." Marrying a Sheffield mine owner and Methodist teacher, author's age 19. Emigrating to New York with husband, 1847, following husband's business losses; objecting to traveling in steerage among poor, heretical "Romanists"; death of one daughter on the voyage. Living with sister in New York while husband sought work; being dismayed at another pregnancy. Interpreting her depression following childbirth and attendant money worries as a weakness of her faith. Finding work for her husband through her New York prayer meeting; family's moving up the Hudson River to escape the city. Husband's dying in the cholera epidemic, 1849. Author's working as a seamstress; easing family's poverty with charity from neighbors. Death of another daughter. During a near-fatal illness, having a vision of Jesus; being told to serve him; beginning volunteer work at Bellevue Hospital. Being hospitalized with an unspecified progressive disease; its limiting her activities severely after 1855. Missing her married daughters. Providing diary entries and extracts from friends' journals tracing her charitable works through 1884.

In this didactic account, Cooke offers her own life as a repository of incidents revealing the hidden hand of Providence. This late example of a classic spiritual autobiography shows the genre's applicability to an enormous range of experience. Although bedridden for much of her later life, Cooke was able to coordinate extensive charitable activities. Cooke's account is a document of a British immigrant's difficulties in 19th-century America.

244 COOKSON, Catherine Ann (Catherine Marchant, pseud.). 1906–s.l.1992. *Our Kate: Her Personal Story*. Macdonald, 1969. 238 pp. NUC 1973–1977 26:58. (other eds.: 1973, with new foreword by author; Corgi, 1974; Futura Press, 1990; Warner Books, 1990.)

Born in Tyne Dock, South Shields, Durham. Father not named, a "gentleman" never known to author. Mother: Catherine Fawcett, domestic servant. Stepfather: David McDermott. Illegitimate child. Married 1940, Thomas Henry Cookson, grammar school master. Wrote dozens of novels, story collections, and children's books. Novelist; children's author; short storyist; broadcaster; public speaker; teacher (art); domestic servant. Working class.

Illegitimate daughter's impoverished youth, difficult relationship with mother, self-education, and adult treatment for emotional and other illnesses, 1906–68. Depicting Tyne Dock and its different social classes. Mother's early life and employment as barmaid; mother's seduction by a "gentleman" lover; author's birth. From age 3, wandering the streets alone. Attending Simonside Protestant School, age 4. Family's moving to East Jarrow; author's growing up there, ages 5–22. Discussing mother's drinking problem, servitude to author's grandmother and step-grandfather, and sexual harassment by her half-brother Jack. Describing their East Jarrow neighborhood, neighbors, and life of poverty. Author's being shaken to discover her illegitimacy. Fetching beer when mother pleaded; feeling both hatred and pity for her. Step-grandfather's insisting author attend Catholic school, where she bullied other children. Witnessing drunken rows between step-grandfather and Uncle Jack; getting injured trying to separate them. Rebuffing neighbors' pity for her being a bastard. Making her first confession; concealing her illegitimacy from the priest; fearing afterward she had made her confession falsely. Attending Tyne Dock school; teachers' awakening her love of poetry. Discussing poor people's scorn for those who rise above their social class. Resisting going to pawnshop for mother. Family's taking in homeless children and other lodgers; one lodger's trying to molest author. Uncle Jack's dying in WWI. Author's resolving not to spoil her own life with drink. At age 14, finding work as a kitchen maid. Beginning a home business teaching decorative cloth painting, but suffering slow lead poisoning from the paint. Beginning to write stories. Working as a laundry checker in Harton Institution Workhouse, ages 16 to 21. Being afflicted with vascular problems after age 18. Longing to be a writer; educating herself at the library. Living in Hastings; working as a workhouse laundry manageress. Operating a boardinghouse with mother after step-grandfather's death, 1931; meeting her future husband; having conflicts with mother over continued drinking; mother's eventually departing. Marrying at age 34. Having three miscarriages, 1941–43; priest's telling her to let her husband use birth control; author's losing faith in some aspects of Catholicism. Undergoing voluntary psychiatric treatment; having electroshock therapy. Leaving the Catholic Church. Overcoming her suicidal impulses; writing; joining Hastings Writers' Circle. Publishing her first novel. Giving BBC broadcasts based on her life. Mother's recovering from alcoholism, 1953; living with mother for three happy years until mother's death. During hospitalization, 1956, author's discovering she had a rare vascular disease (haemmorhagic telangiectasia) inherited from her father. Feeling able to discuss her illegitimacy with others for the first time. Having a continuing sense of her mother's presence.

The "Our Kate" of the title is not the author but her mother, with whose life and struggles Cookson herself eventually identified. In her book, the author implies that being illegitimate helped her empathize with her mother's experiences with alcoholism, because both women were forced to endure a fear of disclosure and a sense of social shame brought on by circumstances beyond their control. In her own words, Cookson dedicates this book "to all bastards," explaining that she wrote it as personal therapy for an emotional breakdown resulting from her illegitimacy, 1945. She gained fame as a best-selling author of family sagas; many were autobiographical, including her seven novels featuring the protagonist Mary Ann, who ultimately succeeds in saving her alcoholic father from self-destruction. In 1968 Cookson won the Winifred Holtby Award for best regional novel from the Royal Society of Literature.

245 COOPER, Lady Diana Olivia Winifred Maud, Viscountess Norwich (née Manners). 1892–1986. *The Rainbow Comes and Goes.* Rupert Hart-Davis, 1958. 256 pp.; illus.; index. NUC 1958–1962 10:410.

Born in London. Father: Henry, 8th Duke of Rutland, secretary to Lord Salisbury, M.P. Mother: Violet Lindsay Manners, artist. 2 sisters; 2 brothers. Married 1919, Sir Alfred Duff Cooper, 1st Viscount Norwich, foreign office clerk before WWI, later first lord of the admiralty, minister for Far Eastern affairs, ambassador to France. 1 son. Knew Enid

Bagnold, Clare Sheridan, Winston and Clementine Churchill, Ellen Terry, Hilaire Belloc, George Moore, Lady Cunard, the Asquith family, Max Beaverbrook, others. Actress (film, pantomime); society woman; nurse (WWI). Aristocracy.

Aristocratic daughter's transition from genteel but limited family circumstances to a film career, as solution to her financial necessities, 1890s–1920s. Childhood memories of her family's London home and country estates; her maternal grandfather, John, Duke of Belvoir; family's living under constant shadow of financial ruin. In infancy, author's receiving galvanic electric treatments for health problems; consequently being indulged by family. Not being given any structured education; learning by self-directed reading. Assessing her mother's character, artistic sense, and beauty; feeling herself unattractive next to mother. Father's inheriting title when author was age 14. Adolescent years: her fashion creations for family friends; traveling to Italy; advent of automobile, telephone, and gramophone. Being inexperienced and gauche; developing socially through participation in a peer group, the "Coterie." Before her debut, socializing at Oxford with male students. Being presented at court, 1911. Discussing eligible young men in her social circle. During WWI, working as a nurse at Guy's Hospital and later at Rutland Hospital; noting deaths of friends in war; corresponding with her husband-to-be during his military service abroad. Winning her reluctant parents' permission to marry a nontitled man of limited means. Marriage, 1919; discussing her early married happiness. Thinking of ways to make a fortune; embarking on a film career. Being offered leading roles in two silent films. Being chosen for leading role in a New York production of Max Reinhardt's pantomime *The Miracle,* 1923. After several years of marriage with no pregnancy, fearing barrenness.

As one of the earliest young women to fulfill dreams of rising to Hollywood stardom, Lady Diana may seem too privileged to be writing a Cinderella story, but—as this early memoir demonstrates—impoverishment of old titled families has become a familiar 20th-century phenomenon in Britain. In a further volume of autobiography, **246** *The Light of Common Day* (1959), Lady Diana focuses on her acting career, the birth of her son, and her life with her husband between the world wars. Her third installment, **247** *Trumpets from the Steep* (1960), includes extensive correspondence and journal entries recording the author's volunteer war work and global travel experiences. The friend of many well-known contemporary artists and writers, Lady Diana was also the inspiration for the character of Julia Stitch in Evelyn Waugh's novel *Scoop*.

248 COOPER, Gladys Constance (Mrs. Herbert Buckmaster; Lady Pearson). 1888–1971. *Gladys Cooper*. Hutchison, 1931. 287 pp.; foreword; illus.; letters; index. NUC pre56 121:576.

Born in Lewisham, Greater London. Father: Charles Frederick William Cooper, drama critic, editor of *The Epicure*. Mother: Mabel Barnett. 2 sisters; 2 half-brothers; 2 half-sisters. Married 1908, Herbert Buckmaster, WWI cavalry officer; divorced 1921. Married 1927, Sir Neville Pearson, Baronet, publisher; divorced 1936. Married 1937, Philip Merivale, actor, d.1946. 1 son; 2 daughters. Actress (stage, film); theatre manager; philanthropist; journalist. Upper class.

Inception and growth of author's international acting career, from childhood in a drama critic's family to Broadway fame, 1890s–1931. Loving but fearing her intellectual father; adoring her mother; seeing her parents' happy marriage as an ideal. Being close to her sisters; mothering her younger deaf sister, Grace. Hating her French governess; refusing to learn French; later disliking convent school also. Beginning her acting career at London's Gaiety Theatre, working for manager George Edwards and actor Charles Hawtrey. Meeting an unemployed stage admirer; father's forbidding the marriage; author's eloping, 1907. After onset of WWI, entertaining troops at a concert party; husband's departing for the front. Winning a libel suit against the *London Voice,* 1915, for rumors implicating author as another man's mistress. Including letters from her husband, showing increasing estrangement; divorce. Author's winning custody of her children. Describing scroll kept in her dressing room, signed by famous friends: King George V, the Prince of Wales, Rudolph Valentino. Relocating to New York; performing at the Royalty Theatre; co-managing the Playhouse Theatre with Frank Curzon, 1922–33. Developing working friendships with actors Gerald du Maurier and Sybil Thorndike, writers Noel Coward, Ivor Novello, Sir James Barrie, and Somerset Maugham. Happily marrying again, 1927. Writing for *My Day* and the *Royal Magazine*. Supporting Fresh Air Fund charity for disadvantaged city children and St. Dunstais Home for war-blinded servicemen. Enjoying fox hunting, sports, fixing up old houses.

Readers in search of historical scandal will be disappointed with Cooper's book; her admitted need to be liked colors her views of colleagues, whom she recalls only in terms of their virtues. However, because she emigrated to work in America, her book provides a close study of the fully developed international scope of theatre, with the same writers and actors working on both sides of the Atlantic. Largely confining her discussion to her public life, Cooper's omission of personal information is remedied in *Gladys Cooper* (1979), by her grandson, actor Sheridan Morley. After marrying her third husband, British actor Philip Merivale, Cooper lived in the U.S., enjoying frequent movie roles, and earned an Academy Award nomination as best supporting actress for her role in *Rebecca,* based on Daphne du Maurier's novel. She returned to England in 1966, twenty years after Merivale's death.

249 COOPER, Margaret. 1888–?. *Myself and My Piano*. John Ouseley, 1909. 85 pp.; front. port.; foreword by Harold Simpson; illus. NUC pre56 121:692.

Probably born in England. Parents not named. Musician (pianist, violinist); songwriter; singer (concerts); antisuffragist. Middle class.

Emotionally supportive upbringing, musical training, and rising success of a pianist and songwriter, 1880s–1909. Thanking her beloved father for making possible her musical education and career. Starting to play piano, age 5; parents' taking her to concerts for encouragement. Being both a delicate and naughty child; going through one governess after another. Parents' finally sending her to day school in Paddington; author's misbehaving there, but blossoming as a pianist. Attending college in Westbourne Park, age 10; winning six academic prizes, but forfeiting two on account of "bad conduct." Taking singing lessons from Henry Wood, husband of popular novelist Mrs. Wood. After four years at Westbourne, being sent abroad for lessons in French, German, and violin and piano technique. Returning to England, 1894; successfully applying to the Royal Academy of Music for further piano studies. Recalling her first London appearance as a singer. Being appointed accompanist to the academy's Medal Examinations, 1897. Academy students' needing three certificates for graduation; author's earning hers in singing, piano, and violin; being made a licentiate of the academy. Having trouble with accompanists; deciding to accompany herself. Singing mainly popular and concert songs; becoming well known. Appearing at the Chappell Ballard concerts, 1901 and 1904. Wanting to make the public see the value of "Songs at the Piano" as sung by women. Singing for King Edward VII, the king and queen of Spain, and Sir Herbert Beerbohm Tree. Discovering the public wanted humorous songs; singing songs that lampooned the suffrage movement. Soon afterward, receiving letters from suffragettes saying she should be ashamed of denigrating votes for women; author's commenting she herself would vote for women's spending time with their children. Singing other songs that made fun of women's intelligence; believing listeners should simply enjoy songs without taking lyrics too seriously. Concluding with a discussion of her singing style and her many imitators.

While Cooper states that she undertook this work at the behest of admirers, not really understanding why anyone would find her own "dull" life interesting, she seems frankly dazzled by her own early successes. Barely 21 years of age when she wrote it, she shows herself, through her commentary, to be too busy with her profession to have thought about the social and feminist issues around her. This autobiography, dedicated to her "dear father" for his patience and love, is an excellent study in the positive father-daughter relationships that nurtured so many successful women. She continued her career for several decades; as late as 1958, she recorded a series of Scottish and Irish ballads for commercial release.

250 CORFIELD, The Hon. Mary Hay (née Burns; O.B.E.). 1871–1965. *Some Memories of a Scotswoman*. Elliot Stock, 1934. 134 pp.; front.; preface; intro. by George A. Birmingham; illus. BLC to 1975 70:23.

Born in Scotland. Father: Sir John Burns, later 1st Baron Inverclyde, industrialist. Mother: Emily Arbuthnot. 2 brothers; 2 sisters. Married Claud Corfield. 1 daughter. Wrote *Claud Corfield* and *Beauty*. Biographer; charitable volunteer. Aristocracy.

Biographical memories of a prominent Scottish family, set within detailed presentation of Scotland and upper-class Scottish society, covering author's childhood to 1930s. Expressing pride in Scotland and Scottish tradition. History of father's family as industrialists who built Glasgow. Discussing her grandfather, Sir George Burns, founder of Cunard Shipping Line; his admiration for the Mercantile Marine forces leading to innovations in civilian shipping. Recalling watching launching of ships on the Clyde. Depicting parents' extensive social life and father's friendships with African explorers David Livingstone and Henry Stanley, politicians Lord and Lady Aberdeen, and Prime Minister Gladstone. Family's moving from Castle Wemyss to Glasgow, author's age 8. Describing Scottish turns-of-phrase, customs, sense of humor. Being taken on charity visits with mother; learning to love the sea from yachting with father. Sailing to visit the Isle of Skye and Iona; recounting their histories and legends of western Scotland. Recounting folklore of Highland clans and Prince Charles Edward Stuart. Discussing numerous historical topics: the 1692 Glencoe Massacre; the Pageant of Braemar; Scottish soldiers and war memorials. Expressing her love for the Highland moors.

Mainly a compilation of articles written at various times, this book also incorporates some chapters from the author's book *Beauty* alongside newer material. Effectively a family biography that pays as much attention to her forebears as herself, Corfield's memoir vividly brings to life Scotland's 19th-century industrial era and the captains of industry who planned and guided its future. In her autobiography, Corfield leaves her own adult life undiscussed, but later she developed an active career in politics and philanthropy, serving as a county alderman for Berkshire, a mayor of Wokingham, and a member of the House of Laity, as well as becoming life vice president of the Mothers' Union.

251 CORKE, Helen. 1882–1978. *In Our Infancy: An Autobiography Part I: 1882–1912*. Cambridge University Press, 1975. 236 pp.; preface; foreword; illus.; app. NUC 1973–1977 26:195.

Born in Hastings, Sussex. Father: Alfred E. Corke, grocer. Mother: Louisa Gallop, Hastings harbor-master's daughter. 2 brothers. Single. Wrote *The Class Books of World History* (four volumes, 1927–30), novel *Neutral Ground* (1933), *Toward Economic Freedom* (1936), poems *Songs of*

Autumn (1960), others. Historian; biographer; poet; novelist; teacher; vegetarian. Lower middle class.

Author's intellectual growth from a book-rich childhood to her adult inclusion in D. H. Lawrence's chosen circle of friends, from birth to age 30. Parents' loving books and reading constantly; nature of this influence on her life. Parents' having modest income but great expectations based on faith in "the Liberal gospel of success." In author's infancy, family's moving to Tunbridge Wells. At first, being educated at home. Learning about religion from a children's book on the imminent horrors of judgement; rejecting this image of God and searching for a kinder one. Attending day school, ages 7–10; learning to notice differences between rich pupils and poor ones like herself. Learning nothing from having to share class with pupils unable to read; being promoted to a higher level through a routine government inspection of schools. Family's moving to rural Horley, then to South Norwood, author's age 11. Attending board school for poor children there. Discussing her favorite childhood books; beginning to develop a fantasy life from her reading. Family's being impoverished by father's business failure; father's losing self-esteem from failing to live up to the gospel of success. Author's needing income; having no money for further schooling, but seeing pupil-teaching as a dead end. Writing stories that didn't sell. Receiving sex information from mother; wondering why a woman would ever want to marry; resolving to remain single despite financial need. Deciding to accept a position as pupil-teacher at her former South Norwood school. Contrasting herself and her cousin Evelyn, who yearned to marry and have children. Discussing adverse effects of school regimentation; inspectors' visits; her sense of inadequacy as a teacher. Age 19, rebelling against mother, who thought author read too much. Looking for a kinder God in Buddhism; becoming vegetarian. Teaching at Dering Place Mixed School in Croydon. Studying violin under concert violinist "H.B.M."; falling in love with him; mother's objecting because he was married; author's resisting his attempted seduction. Discussing difference between sexual mores of early and late 20th century. Meeting D. H. Lawrence, 1908, while Lawrence was teaching at Davidson Road School. Cousin Agnes's dying in childbirth; author's being moved by her early death to seize enjoyment in her own life. Secretly meeting "H.B.M." for a five-day love affair on the Isle of Wight; his committing suicide afterward. Suffering profound depression and considering suicide herself; writing account of their last days together, the basis of her later novel *Neutral Ground* (1933). Reading and writing poetry with D. H. Lawrence; their forming a three-person friendship by including Lawrence's friend Jessie Chambers (called "Muriel" by all three, after one of Lawrence's characters). Lawrence's expressing unreciprocated sexual desire for Corke; both women's rejecting his advances. Discussing Lawrence's false portrait of Jessie in *Sons and Lovers*. As his mother lay dying, Lawrence's impulsively marrying an old school friend. Corke's recounting her last meeting with Lawrence. Accompanying Jessie to Germany; their receiving news that Lawrence had eloped from England with another man's wife, 1912.

The other man's wife with whom Lawrence eloped was Frieda von Richthofen, cousin of WWI's infamous Red Baron and married to Ernest Weekley, a professor at Nottingham University; she divorced him and married Lawrence in 1914. Just as Frieda later became an inseparable part of Lawrence's creative life, so too did the circle of friends described in Corke's autobiography form a creative circle that inspired their own works. This autobiography won the Whitebread award for 1975; in »it, the youthful personality of D. H. Lawrence emerges vividly in its impulsiveness, intense devotion to his mother, and early literary ambitions. Although Corke's book is a helpful source for understanding D. H. Lawrence and his circle, her earlier biographies of the group (*D. H. Lawrence's "Princess": A Memoir of Jessie Chambers* [1951] and *D. H. Lawrence: The Croydon Years* [1964]) yield even greater detail. Corke served as headmistress at a school in Kelvedon, Essex, 1919–28, taught at Aylett's Foundation in Essex, and wrote several history textbooks. She died in Kelvedon, Essex, after finishing another volume of autobiography, still unpublished, covering the later years of her life.

252 CORKRAN, Henriette. c.1850–1911. *Celebrities and I*. Hutchinson, 1902. 362 pp.; preface. NUC pre56 122:669.

Born in Paris, France. Father not named, poet, Irish. Mother not named, Irish. 1 sister; 1 brother. Single. Knew Thackeray, Disraeli, Samuel Butler, others. Artist (painter). Upper class.

French upbringing and British art training of an Irish portrait painter, against a backdrop of her connections to prominent European artists and writers, c.1850–1900. Although having Irish parents, growing up in Paris where her mother conducted a salon; father's residing mainly in London. Author's and sister's being educated by a governess. Finding mother austere and humorless, but having her imagination profoundly stimulated by mother's spiritualism. Growing up believing in Theosophy and phrenology. After accompanying mother to a medium, needing medical treatment for nightmares and sleepwalking. In Paris, developing precocious interest in music, art, and theatre. Seeing work from many artists, including Velasquez, Rubens, and Michelangelo; learning to evaluate it. Seeing both the French actress Déjazet and American actress Charlotte Cushman; comparing their techniques. In adolescence, c.1870s, accompanying family on visit to relatives in Dublin; meeting Sir William and Lady Wilde, parents of Oscar; noting Lady Wilde's outspoken schemes for dress reform. In Ireland, rejecting a marriage proposal from a "Mr. A," too famous for author to identify. Family's traveling onward to Scotland, then returning to Paris. Author's taking art classes in Paris; later attending London's Slade Art School. Finding studies monotonous; unsuccessfully writing short stories in emulation of her sister Alice's published work. Exhibiting her works at the Royal Academy. Working as a portrait painter; comparing her technique with that of Raphael and Millais. Meeting John Ruskin; discussing art with him. Meeting Lord Frederick Leighton, president of the Royal Academy; his chiding her ambitions to paint with realism, saying women's work should be "pretty." Gazing in a crystal ball; receiving a message to go to Italy. While there, meeting Theosophists Madame Blavatsky and Annie Besant and antivivisectionists Anna Kingsford and Edward Maitland; this becoming a turning point in the author's spiritual beliefs.

Partly a portrait gallery, partly a self-portrait, Corkran's book focuses outward on others as much as on herself, producing an exceptional picture of cosmopolitan late-19th-century circles in London and Paris. Mentioned only briefly, Corkran's sister Alice was an art historian as well as an important 19th-century children's writer who produced books of history and anthropology for young readers as well as girls' fiction with a quietly feminist perspective. Their father, unnamed in this memoir, was probably the Dublin-born poet B. A. Bruen Corkran. Henriette herself continues her story in a sequel, **253** *Oddities, Others and I* (1904), which frequently incorporates whimsical conversation about love and marriage. Corkran declares that she always desired to be a serious artist and never expected to marry, but remained wed to a more demanding suitor—her art. In 1905, Corkran published a further memoir of her family, *Lucie and I*.

254 COURTNEIDGE, Cicely (C.B.E.). 1893–1980. *Cicely*. Hutchinson, 1953. 224 pp.; front. port.; illus.; index. NUC pre56 125:211. (1st pub. 1927.)

Born in Sydney, New South Wales, Australia. Father: Robert Courtneidge, actor, theatrical producer. Mother not named. 1 brother; 1 sister. Married 1916, Jack Hulbert, actor, theatrical producer. 1 daughter. Actress (stage, music hall, film, radio); theatrical director; WWII volunteer; traveler (Europe, South Africa, Australia, New Zealand, U.S.). Upper middle class.

Memories of actress's upbringing, stage career, and ventures into film and broadcasting, 1890s–1950s. Being born into a theatrical family; growing up in Manchester. Doing poorly in school; being sent to finishing school in Switzerland. Making her first stage appearance in one of her father's productions. Meeting her husband-to-be through roles in the same play. Accompanying her mother to South Africa for mother's health; suffering greatly when mother died. Marrying shortly before WWI; husband's departing for war, leaving her in England. Looking for roles outside her father's company, c.1917; appearing in a music hall comedy; playing boys' roles. Starting her own touring music hall company. Discussing financial and emotional rewards of theatrical life. Her daughter's birth. Appearing in Little Revues. Touring in America; visiting an Indian reservation; noting effects of Prohibition on life in U.S. Meeting Al Capone in a speakeasy. Discussing how theatrical people guard their marriages during forced separations: never listening to gossip, working together when possible. Recalling early days of British film industry. Making her first film, *The Ghost Train;* missing the stage while working in films. During a stage performance, learning of her father's death; demonstrating "show must go on" attitude. WWII: touring in Italy, broadcasting on the BBC. Joining Victory Variety Programme on radio, 1946. Playing in New York to poor notices. Touring in Australia and New Zealand. Anecdotes of working with dramatist Ivor Novello. Being created companion of British Empire for her contributions to British troops' WWII morale. Describing changes during her fifty years on the stage.

In this celebration of a half-century in the theatre, Courtneidge creates a good addition to the many professional accounts of 20th-century working life on stage and in film. Unlike other actors who have chosen in their autobiographies to omit private matters in favor of career details, Courtneidge candidly shows how the itinerant theatrical life makes special demands of marriage and family affections; in fact, her discussion of marriage between two professional actors anticipates later sociological interest in the profession. Her experiences in Britain's infant film industry also constitute a repository of data for film historians.

255 COURTNEY, Janet (née Hogarth; O.B.E.). 1865–1954. *Recollected in Tranquility*. William Heinemann, 1926. 279 pp.; front.; preface; illus.; index. NUC pre56 125:214.

Born in Barton-upon-Humber, Lincolnshire. Father: George Hogarth, Anglican clergyman. Mother: Jane Elizabeth Uppleby. 13 siblings. Married 1912, William Courtney, editor of the *Fortnightly Review,* later Oxford lecturer, d.1928. Wrote *Freethinkers of the Nineteenth Century* (1920), *The Making of an Editor: W.L. Courtney, 1850–1928* (1930), *The Adventurous Thirties: A Chapter in the Women's Movement* (1933), others. Teacher; bank administrator; historian; biographer; book club manager; editor; feminist; suffragist; WWI volunteer; clerk; academic's spouse. Upper middle class.

Author's mid-Victorian upbringing, early Oxford education, many-faceted work history, and pointed commentary on women's acceptance in the workplace, 1860s–1920. Describing Barton, a small village river port rich in naval history. Catching diphtheria in an epidemic, 1870s; three siblings's dying from it. Recalling piety of Barton's citizens and her vicar father's popularity with them; questioning town's zealous practices such as persecuting women bearing children out of wedlock. With few job opportunities, local women's sharing their husbands' active interest in politics. Describing Barton's farming society, assorted churches, and secular schools. Author's father's endorsing education, but fearing higher education for women lest new scientific theories, c.1840s–1870s, undermine women's faith. Discussing father's devotional exercises; problems caused when meddlesome parishioners branded them excessive. Noting that, unlike her father, most country vicars chose the profession for reasons of financial security. Memories of Lincolnshire's political conservatism, 1870s. Leaving to attend Lady Margaret Hall, Oxford. Studying philosophy; enjoying intellectual climate, but contrasting women's limited curriculum with men's broad one; noting strictly gender-based social roles. Describing daily life for women at Oxford (students, female faculty, and relatives of male faculty) c.1870s. Being hired to teach at Chelten ham Ladies' College; recalling its principal, the feminist Dorothea Beale, and her wide-ranging reforms of women's education. Teaching in Girls' Public Day School in London; recalling reaction against high schools' training women for careers. Questioning elite public schools for boys; citing advantages of coeducational system. Accepting a clerical appointment in office of secretary of Royal Commission on Labour; discussing women's civil service disadvantages, 1890s; women's being consigned to "menial" clerical work without hope of advancement; bureaucrats' defending practice with the usual reasons, including men's being the breadwinners, women's always leaving to marry. Winning an administrative job with the Bank of England's women's department. Reading submissions for the editor of the *Fortnightly Review*, whom she later married. Managing bookshop and book club for the *Times;* discussing problems with censorship in club's selection process; noting book club's importance in competing against the monopoly of circulating libraries. Working on the staff of *Encyclopedia Britannica;* describing firm's structure and elaborate research methods. Marrying William; afterward, deciding to continue working; discussing common objections to married women in the work force. During WWI, heading a committee to deal with distress among working women. Praising passage of Sex Disqualification Removal Act of 1919; hoping women will take full advantage of advances begun with suffrage and expanded through their entrance into the WWI workplace.

In the early portion of Courtney's autobiography, her rendering of rural England validates several novelistic treatments of the 1870s, including the picture of clerical practicality in Anthony Trollope's *Barchester Towers* and the depiction of conservative rural politics in George Eliot's *Middlemarch*. Courtney, however, effectively left this era behind when she decided to study at Oxford. One of the university's first women students, she presents a finely drawn picture of female student life that adds needed historical depth to Virginia Woolf's later representation of it in *A Room of One's Own*. Courtney's perspective on women's employment is also valuable, documenting fifty years of rapid change in women's education and workplace opportunities.

256 COUSINS, Margaret E. (née Gillespie) and James Henry Cousins. 1878–1954 (Margaret). *We Two Together*. Hamish Hamilton, 1950. 784 pp.; illus.; biblio. of the Cousinses' books; index. NUC pre56 125:283.

Born at Boyle, County Roscommon, Ireland. Father: surname Gillespie, government official. Mother not named. 11 siblings. Married 1903, James Henry Cousins, vegetarian, Theosophical activist. Knew Annie Besant, Christabel Pankhurst, Mohandas Gandhi. Theosophist; suffragist, militant; feminist activist; animal welfare activist; antivivisectionist; suffragist, academic; vegetarian. Middle class.

Author's contributions to a jointly authored memoir charting her work for suffrage and feminist causes in Britain and India, and her shared Theosophical activism with her husband, 1880s–1943. Being the eldest child; adopting her parents' ardent nationalistic Irish politics. Recalling influence of evangelical Protestantism in her childhood. Attending government-run coeducational schools. Initially acquiring a feminist consciousness from resentment over her younger brothers' receiving preferential treatment. At age 21, meeting her husband-to-be; his influencing her to lose faith in conventional religion. Finishing her studies at the Royal Irish Academy of Music; earning a bachelor's degree in music. After marriage, 1903, adopting her husband's vegetarianism. Being shocked by realities of sex, but later believing reincarnation will let humans evolve more attractive means of procreation. Reading Madame Blavatsky's *Secret Doctrine* and books on vegetarianism by Anna Kingford; their permanently changing her spiritual outlook. Conducting psychic experiments with husband. Becoming secretary of the Irish Vegetarian Society, 1905. Meeting Anna Kingford at the National Council of Women in Manchester, 1906; being influenced by Kingford's feminism as well as spirituality. Working for the WSPU, 1907, and for the antivivisection movement. Organizing the Irish Women's Franchise League, 1908; hosting Christabel Pankhurst there. Being imprisoned for militant suffragism in London, 1910, and in Dublin, where she went on hunger strike, 1912. Founding the Church of the New Ideal, a church for women, in Liverpool, 1914. Claiming husband received a psychic message from Annie Besant, asking them to join her in India, 1915. Living in India, 1915–25, while husband traveled and lectured; working for women's suffrage; teaching English; working with Annie Besant in Indian Women's Association, 1916–22. Touring and lecturing in Europe, 1920s. Returning to India to work for Indian independence; organizing first All-Asia Women's Conference, 1930. With husband, touring the U.S., living in New York, 1931–32; teaching at Columbia University; founding New York Vegetarian Society. Visiting Gandhi in Indian jail, 1932; spending a year in the same jail after participating in a free-speech demonstration; afterward teaching Western music at the University of Madras. Supporting Margaret Sanger's birth control movement. Visiting the Himalayas, 1939; starting a child welfare and maternity centre there. Giving up writing due to poor health, 1943.

Cousins calls this book a "duography," in which she and her husband maintain independent perspectives mirroring the largely independent lives they led; a picture of the principles governing their work emerges from reading the whole. A storehouse of information on many historical topics, this book provides background on the suffrage movement in Ireland and India in addition to rare information on the spread of the vegetarian movement and its close relationship to the spread of Theosophy. Heavily cited by Besant's biographer Rosemary Dinnage, the Cousinses' book is an invaluable extension of Annie Besant's 1893 *Autobiography* and documents Besant's Indian work through the 1920s. However, the book's original intent was didactic; it was printed by a Theosophical publishing house in India to showcase the Cousinses as successful converts from Western decay to Eastern regeneration, in the same way that Augustine's *Confessions* became a staple of Christian inspirational reading to model the Christian conversion process.

257 COX, Adelaide. c.1865–?. *Hotchpotch*. Salvationist Publishing and Supplies, 1937. 94 pp.; front.; foreword by General Evangeline Booth; illus. BLC to 1975 71:419.

Probably born in England. Father not named, pastor, North London Mission church. Mother not named. 1 sister; 1 brother. Single. Salvation Army worker; missionary; philanthropist; clergyman's daughter. Middle class.

Religious life and work of Salvation Army missionary in England and France, c.1880–90. While attending an Oxford prayer meeting with father, undergoing a conversion experience; committing herself to life of service. Working with Miss Macpherson's Flower Mission and the Church of England Zenana Mission in London's East End. At her father's North London church, starting services for working-class men. Meeting members of the Christian Mission, later to be called the Salvation Army; with her sister as chaperone, going to the East End to meet its founder, General William Booth. Booth's proposing she accompany his daughter Catherine to found a Salvation Army mission in Paris. After Paris, their being sent to Switzerland to win more French-speaking converts. Winning support of feminist activist Josephine Butler who was in Switzerland to work for the abolition of brothels. Salvation Army's being persecuted in Geneva; author's describing trial of Catherine Booth. Author's being recalled to France, 1885; serving as Salvation Army's divisional officer, 1885–88; afterward serving in Nîmes. From 1888 onward, heading an East End receiving home for "fallen women" (usually prostitutes); recounting stories of rescued women. Serving on Hackney Board of Guardians and as chair of the Committee of the London County Council Hospital at Mile End. Serving as a Poor Law Guardian. Launching Community Homes for the Aged in London. Receiving commander of the British Empire honor in Queen's Birthday Honours List.

A dedicated Salvation Army worker, Cox concentrates on the social problems she helped to alleviate—poverty, disease, and social maladjustment—and urges readers, as she did, to heed "God's call to service." A contemporary of the Welshwoman Rosina Davies, who recorded her Salvation Army work in her 1942 memoir, Cox rose in the organization more easily than Davies, perhaps from her direct work with the army's founders. In charting the mission to expand the Salvation Army beyond the shores of Britain, Cox's book is an essential addition to primary Salvation Army documents such as General Booth's *In Darkest England* and charts the individual efforts of Salvation Army workers within Booth's world-famous enterprise to ameliorate society's ills through a combination of religion and public service.

258 CRAVEN, Lady Elizabeth, Baroness Craven (née Berkeley; afterward Margravine of Anspach). 1750–1828. *The Beautiful Lady Craven; the Original Memoirs of Elizabeth, Baroness Craven, afterward Margravine of Anspach and Bayreuth and Princess Berkeley of the HRE.* Ed. by A.M. Broadley & Lewis Melville (pseud.). John Lane, 1914. 2 vols. Vol. 1: 141 pp.; front. port.; ed.'s note; intro.; illus. Vol. 2: 306 pp.; front port.; illus.; apps.; poetry of Lady Craven; biblio.; genealogical tables; index. NUC pre56 126:516.

Born in England. Father: Augustus, 4th Earl of Berkeley. Mother: Elizabeth Drax; later, Lady Nugent. 2 brothers; 1 sister; 2 half-sisters. Married 1767, William Craven, later Baron Craven, died n.d. Married 1791, Margrave of Anspach, d.1806. Widow. 3 sons; 4 daughters. Playwright; traveler (Europe). Aristocracy.

An aristocrat's upbringing, social contacts, and two marriages within European Court society, set within the context of 18th-century history, 1750s–c.1810. Vol. 1: Her father's being generous, with a gentle disposition; his death, author's age 3. Being cared for by a Swiss nurse, since mother disliked small children. Memories of her stepfather, Lord Nugent. From infancy, visiting Paris with mother; studying French with a governess. In London, spending time away from home with female relatives; their teaching her housewifery to make her capable of instructing servants. Sisters' receiving visits from eligible suitors; author's trying unsuccessfully to dissuade her older sister from an elopement; afterward, author's being made to share her mother's bed to deter any future elopements. Being presented to Queen Caroline. At Court, winning the affections of Mr. Craven, heir to a barony; his arranging his finances to be able to marry her. Births of her first two daughters. Her early feelings of gratitude toward her husband developing into love. Memories of titled London neighbors, including classical scholar Lady Denbigh; socializing in London with Horace Walpole, Dr. Johnson, David Garrick, and Sir Joshua Reynolds; refraining from their political talk in her youthful belief that politics were outside women's domain. After birth of her son, taking attitude of resignation toward husband's abandoning her for a mistress. Signing a separation settlement with husband, but privately doubting his compliance. Taking refuge with a friend in Paris; husband's forbidding daughters to write to her there. Noting Marie Antoinette's popularity with the people, c.1780; explaining origins of her dispute with the Duc d'Orleans. Forming an alliance with the French Duc D'Harcourt; being suspected of adultery by Marie Antoinette. Discussing her social activities among the French aristocracy; traveling in Italy, Austria, and Poland and being received by their royal families and Courts. Traveling to St. Petersburg and staying with the Empress Katherine; spending time among diplomatic circles in Constantinople. Visiting her children in England; resolving to take her son with her, since Lord Craven prevented their correspondence. Visiting the Prussian province of Anspach; meeting the margrave and his wife, the margravine; contrasting margravine's icy character with the margrave's geniality. In Anspach, forming society for encouragement of arts and sciences; collaborating with margrave on plan to build an orphanage. Writing two short plays for Court theatre; margrave's producing them. Discussing margrave's covert affair with a French actress, and actress's jealousy of author's influence. Vol. 2: Coauthoring Court play *Le Seducteur*. Accompanying margrave incognito to Italy; enjoying luxuries of Italian Court; continuing with him to Berlin and the Prussian Court. Resisting her brother's attempt to force her return to her husband; using a false name for son's enrollment at Harrow in order to prevent husband's finding him. Deaths of margravine and of Lord Craven in close succession; author's wedding the margrave, 1792. Honeymooning in Spain; while passing through Paris, feeling deep grief at King Louis XVI's murder by the "barbarian" revolutionary hordes. Returning to England, but her four eldest children's refusing to see her; Queen Charlotte's also refusing to receive her as margravine. Being vilified by English newspapers for sexual misconduct. Reconciling with her eldest daughter just before daughter's early death. Entertaining at Brandenburgh House, the margrave's London residence; recalling the brilliant wit of Dr. Johnson and bluestocking Elizabeth Montagu; joining literary circles. Writing her memoirs at suggestion of Louis XVIII of France, to preserve a record of aristocratic life before the Revolution. After 1806 death of margrave, rumors' appearing in English newspapers of her remarriage to various men. Staying in England until her son was established as chamberlain to the Princess of Wales; retiring to Naples.

Serving as a vast compendium of behind-the-scenes actions in European history of the late 18th century, Lady Craven's text provides vital details on dynastic secrets, covert decisions, and crucial relationships between European rulers. She seems to have known everyone in Britain and continental Europe who affected public policy—including mistresses and lovers who governed indirectly. Unlike her deliberate genteel vagueness about her private concerns, her insider descriptions of London's literary circles and of French society and royal intrigue before the Revolution are so explicit as to earn the gratitude of historians. Lady Craven's offering stands among the best contemporary memoirs of the period.

259 CRESSWELL, Louisa Mary (Mrs. Gerard). c.1840–?. *Eighteen Years on the Sandringham Estate, by "The Lady Farmer."* Temple, c.1887. 235 pp. ECB 1881–89, p. 173.

Born in England. Parents not named. 1 brother. Married c.1860, first name Gerard, rural gentry, farmer, died c.1864. Widow. 1 daughter; 1 son. Knew the Prince of Wales (later King Edward VII), Constance Gordon-Cumming (a relative of her husband's). Farm manager; farmer. Rural gentry.

Lively presentation of long-term land dispute with the Prince of Wales, accompanied by author's rendition of her tenant-farming experiences, c.1860–81. Describing life of rural gentry in author's youth, c.1860. Marrying an impoverished younger son of gentry; couple's deciding to earn their living by tenant farming; their managing a small farm at Sedgeford, Norfolk. Author's hiring servants for indoor work; helping her husband farm, but finding the servants were incompetent. Their renting the estate at Sandringham, Norfolk; after improving it, estate's being bought by the Prince of Wales. Recalling Prince's visit, 1863. Author and husband's building their new house on estate. Following husband's death, c.1864, author's deciding to manage the farm herself, despite opposition from friends. Willingly absorbing herself in a solitary life of farm work; describing working with and supervising her laborers. Winning lawsuit brought by a corrupt former steward; relating blow-by-blow description of the trial. Objecting to Prince's desire for a "battue" system of game hunting, in which animals are driven en masse to a place convenient for the shooters; informing the Prince that resulting expenses from destruction of crops were not covered by his fees. Prince's gamekeepers and agents' usurping her authority; Prince's believing their misrepresentations about her. Author's taking legal action to collect damages and clear herself; partially recovering the Prince's goodwill. Commenting on traditional hunting as less cruel to animals than traps or vivisection, although stating need for more humane treatment of children and animals. Publishing book on how to improve farm conditions. Depicting her long-established farm routine, learned from self-education in farm management. Receiving visit from Constance Gordon-

Cumming, the explorer and game hunter. Discussing detrimental effects of schooling on farm laborers; fearing it will render country boys unfit for farm work; questioning having a single standard of education for town and country. Recalling social events at Sandringham church; prince's parties and balls; objecting to his extending hospitality to all classes. Condemning trade unionism; noting its detrimental effects on farm labor. After resumption of hunting controversy with Prince's agent, author's eventually conceding and leaving Sandringham, 1881; discovering the Prince rewarded those who contributed to her expulsion. Traveling in the American West.

The motivation behind Cresswell's book appears to be her desire to vindicate herself in her longstanding property rights dispute with the Prince of Wales, later King Edward VII. This is an excellent source on 19th-century rural class relations, game management, farm labor disputes, and some Victorian attitudes toward hunting and cruelty to animals. It also shows the relations and uneasy accommodations between the royal family and their tenants, a relationship that is one of the last remnants of the feudal system and has grown increasingly difficult under conditions of Britain's democratization.

260 CRESTON, Dormer (pseud.; Dorothy J. Baynes). c.1900–?. *Enter a Child (Reminiscences of the Author's Childhood)*. Macmillan, 1939. 230 pp.; illus. BLC to 1975 72:386.

Born in London. Parents not named. Wrote (under pseud.) *David Cecil, The Regent and His Daughter,* others. Biographer. Upper middle class.

Introspective study of the author's emotional deprivation in childhood, covering her first ten years. Living almost entirely within her sensations and emotions until age 5; parents' using excessive discipline in effort to cure her nervousness. Sensing her father's remoteness and impatience; loving her mother, but being kept at arm's distance by mother's obsessive demands for ladylike behavior; mother's always deferring to father's disciplinary wishes. Laboring over a handmade gift for father's birthday; being shattered by his failure to acknowledge it; never forgetting the emotional injury. Disliking all her studies with governesses. Being warmly loved only by her nanny; after nanny's departure, entirely lacking affection; thinking about suicide. Lavishing her love on toys. Being socially crippled by shyness and harsh self-judgement. Spending summer holidays with relatives at Hilldrop country house; contrasting this warm experience with the emotional frost of London home life; starting to enjoy an improved self-image because of relatives' fondness for her. Falling in love with an adult visitor. Becoming more focused and patient.

In this candid account, Creston effectively re-creates the despair she felt from the emotional isolation of her upbringing. While her focus remains personal, historians may well generalize Creston's experiences to the child-raising principles of the era in which she was born. Her parents clearly enjoyed the financial means to use governesses, nannies, and separate house nurseries, factors which in themselves were often barriers to the child-parent bond and are frequently mentioned in other memoirs of the Victorian and Edwardian periods as visible signs of a family's failure to cohere. Although it stops short at her tenth year, Creston's book includes both a partial bibliography of her biographical works and testimonials from other authors to her merits as a writer.

261 CRISP, Dorothy. c.1910–?. *A Life for England.* Dorothy Crisp & Co., Ltd., 1946. 311 pp.; front ports. NUC pre56 127:303.

Born in Yorkshire. Parents not named. Married John Becker. At least 1 child. Wrote *England—Mightier Yet, Commonsense of Christianity, England's Purpose,* others. Political writer; religious/spiritual writer; political activist; publisher. Middle class.

Growth of a conservative polemicist from childhood through her mature writing career, set within the context of her lifelong strategies for promoting the British Empire, c.1915–1945. Recalling her father as domineering, her mother as overprotective; author's consequently being a solitary child. Attending Anglo-Catholic convent school; becoming infatuated with the Bible; learning portions by heart. Becoming curious about the women's suffrage movement, age 5. Loving to read; "soaking" herself in English poetry. Thinking of her life in successive stages: childhood, theological worship, poetry, young adulthood, and history/political philosophy. Starting to attend the County Conservative Club, c. age 17; speaking on conservative issues at meetings. Studying history and political philosophy at Oxford. Writing a first novel; its being rejected by publishers. Being outraged at pronouncement that socialism and Christianity are alike; writing article rebutting this for *National Review.* Disliking President Woodrow Wilson, the League of Nations, and all pacifist activities. Traveling to Vienna; writing articles about Vienna for *Yorkshire Evening Post.* Making friends with historian and parliamentarian John Buchan; citing his encouragement of her political writing. Drawing up a conservative manifesto; submitting it to members of the Under Forty Movement. Working with the Indian Empire Society to oppose Indian Home Rule. Exulting in the crash of the Labour government, 1931; demanding that the Conservative Party be outspokenly anti-socialist; regretting that political opinion in England was divided by social class. Denigrating the pro-pacifist stance of Canon Sheppard and other clergy. Publishing editorials on the need for Britain to impose a "Pax Britannica," created by manifesting total, unquestioned authority and military might. Writing articles to defeat growing pacifist menace, including "Christ is No Pacifist." Publishing *England—Mightier Yet.* In WWII, criticizing Chamberlain's policies of appeasement; working for the Ministry of Information under John Buchan, its director. Describing Labour M.P. Aneurin Bevan; his identity as the Conservative Party's nemesis. Writing more books of conservative polemic. Adamantly opposing dividing the British Empire by granting colonies home rule; traveling through Ireland, both north and south; deriding the Free State of Ireland created by the 1926 Home Rule Bill. Opposing American WWII presence in outposts of the British Empire. Unsuccessfully standing for M.P. as independent candidate from Acton. Starting her own publishing company. Moving to Kent to await birth of her first child, 1945. Joining the Committee of British Housewives League. Planning to write *The Inevitability of British World Leadership*.

If Crisp only showed a sense of humor, the reader might suspect her of having written this memoir as a caricature of British imperial hubris as the Empire withered before 20th-century eyes. Unfortunately, the merits of her thinking are obscured in this autobiography by the author's use of heavily derisive remarks to dismiss every opponent or idea that threatened her. Writing at the conclusion of WWII, she persists in clutching an image etched in Victorian nostalgia—and naiveté—about the future of British expansion and rule. Despite the valuable commentary in this book on British policy of the 1920s–1940s, its partisan nature requires balance from other sources, ideally from *Tomorrow is a New Day*, the 1939 political memoir by Jennie Lee, wife of Aneurin Bevan and an influential Labour M.P. in her own right.

262 CROSLAND, Camilla Dufour (née Toulmin). 1812–1895. *Landmarks of a Literary Life, 1820–1892*. New York: Scribner's, 1893. 298 pp.; front. port.; preface; index. NUC pre56 128:59.

Born in London. Father: William Toulmin, solicitor. Mother: née Wright. 4 brothers. Married 1848, Newton Crosland. Wrote *Light in the Valley: My Experiences of Spiritualism* (1857) and novels *Lydia: A Woman's Book* (1852) and *Mrs. Blake: A Story of Twenty Years* (1862). Novelist; poet; religious/spiritual writer; editor; feminist. Middle class.

Literary and artistic friendships, social life, and cultural observations of a prolific writer, 1814–92. Remembering parents' discussing the Battle of Waterloo, author's age 3. Depicting life of London's "cultivated" middle class, 1810–20; noting that males were legally empowered to be laws unto themselves; little girls' submitting even to the tyranny of younger brothers. Informing her readers, c.1892, what "hot ploughshares" women had walked over to win their rights. After father's death, author's age 8, mother's being impoverished; author's realizing she would not receive the classical education father had promised her. Wondering how to support herself; explaining that paid employment, even as governess, lowered middle-class women in society's eyes. Realizing she might write books; resolving to educate herself by reading at the British Museum,

1838; soon abandoning her rigorous self-appointed study. Having a family friendship with the Chambers brothers, Edinburgh publishers; beginning her career by submitting work to their periodical; contributing verses and stories to *Chambers's Journal* for over fifty years. Submitting work regularly to poetry annuals; becoming assistant editor of one of them, *Friendship's Offering;* later serving as editor of *Ladies' Companion*. Memories of many writers and artists, including music critic Henry Fothergill Chorley, sculptor John Graham Lough, and author Grace Aguilar. Publishing stories in the *Illuminated Magazine*. Discussing American literary friends and acquaintances, including Nathaniel Hawthorne and Harriet Beecher Stowe. Discussing the mid-century craze for spiritualism; never "but once" visiting a medium, but discussing prominent people who practiced spiritualism regularly. Traveling to Florence, Italy, to visit Robert and Elizabeth Barrett Browning, 1857–1858. Closing with the death and public funeral of Tennyson, 1892; this effectively signalling the close of a literary era.

Further information on Crosland's life is available in her husband's autobiography, *Rambles Round My Life,* 1898. In her own memoir, all discussions of the women artists and writers she knew are grounded in her understanding of the gender inequities built into 19th-century British law. Repeatedly, Crosland points out that, although many men are naturally chivalrous and defer to women from simple good breeding, the unequal legal power they enjoy tends to produce male tyranny. Although written in the 1890s, this is evidently her longstanding opinion; as a result, it is difficult to say whether John Stuart Mill's nearly identical assessment of gender power relations in *The Subjection of Women* (1869) is Crosland's source or merely her validation. Crosland's struggles to make writing into a viable livelihood resonate with the plight of Isabel Mayo in her 1910 memoir, *Recollections of What I Saw, What I Lived Through and What I Learned During More than Fifty Years of Social and Literary Experience*. Collectively, these two accounts constitute a survey of women's employment over a seventy-year span.

263 CROWLEY, Ann. 1766–1826. *Some Account of the Religious Experience of Ann Crowley*. Lindfield: W. Eade, 1842. 50 pp. NUC pre56 128:257.

Born in Shillingford, Oxfordshire. Parents not named. 7 sisters. Single. Preacher; religionist (Quaker). Lower middle class.

Itinerant preacher's childhood conversion and extensive adult travels in service to her Quaker vocation, c.1770–1826. In childhood, being caught between need for God's love and enjoyment of worldly things. Experiencing a visitation from God, age 16. At age 17, losing her father to death from an apoplectic fit; losing three sisters to marriage soon after; death of another sister, author's age 25; author's realizing she must rely on the consolations of God to overcome her bereavements.

After sister's death, 1791, receiving help from English, French, and American Quaker friends; being moved by their teaching to accompany their preaching travels. Doubting whether to accept their invitation to preach; commencing by speaking at local Quaker meetings. Attending half-yearly Quaker meeting in Newtown, Wales, 1794; en route, attending thirty local meetings. Attending sister's funeral in London, February 1795; mother's death from stroke soon after. Making visits to Quakers in Worcestershire, Warwickshire, and Herefordshire. Obtaining permission from her monthly meeting to travel and preach as a Quaker minister, 1796. Agreeing to support her sisters; moving with them to Uxbridge. Sharing travels with another woman preacher; speaking at more than fifty Quaker meetings in central England. Death of a married sister, c.1796; remaining sisters' taking charge of the widower and children; author's informing readers that her lot was not to share in caring for them, but to spread the Lord's word. Author's accompanying a woman Quaker from Pennsylvania to nearly four hundred meetings throughout England, Scotland, and Wales, 1799. Traveling with another Quaker woman preacher to 115 meetings in southern England, 1801; making another tour of London and Middlesex meetings. Visiting meetings in Surrey and Sussex, 1804. Making a tour of northern England, 1804–06, again sharing preaching duties. Continuing her itinerant ministry despite her own ill health and that of her sisters at home; declaring that God had made her willing to preach, leaving natural ties behind. Death of yet another sister, Rebecca, 1814. Author's feeble state preventing travel after 1821; remaining at home; illness's increasing her desire for contemplation and prayer.

Each of the many scriptural citations that Crowley incorporates in her work is tied to an account of her official journeys, and she addresses the facts of her personal life solely in the context of their effect on her work. Her spiritual autobiography takes the form of a traditional conversion narrative, showing her redemption through divine visitation and her providential guidance in her vocation thereafter. Itinerant preachers of both the Quaker and Methodist denominations wrote in this genre; there are so many of these memoirs that they seem to have served both as didactic models for converts and testimonials of the writers' true vocation for other denomination members. Crowley's writings were published by her friends and edited anonymously; the editor describes Crowley's death and adds an account of the death of her sister, Rebecca Crowley.

264 CULLING, Eve Victoria Helen (née Sarell). c.1895–?. *Arms and the Woman: A Canteen Worker with the French*. John Murray, 1932. Written in collaboration with John Bennion Booth. 228 pp.; front. port.; foreword by Laurence Binyon; illus.; app. NUC pre56 129:174.

Father not named, possibly French. Mother not named. 1 sister. Married, husband not named. 1 son. Knew suffragettes Eva Moore and Emmeline Pethick-Lawrence, actress Evelyn D'Alroy, *Daily Telegraph* editor Malcolm Watson, poet Laurence Binyon, Lady Angela Forbes, and the Vicomtesse de la Panousse, head of the French Red Cross Comité Britannique in London. WWI volunteer; Red Cross administrator; philanthropist. Upper class.

Well-documented memories of the French Red Cross's WWI activities and the author's role as relief worker, covering 1914–21. Describing what upper-class life was like in England and Europe before WWI. Knowing a few suffragettes, but having nothing to do with the suffrage movement. Visiting her sister in Ireland when WWI started, 1914; upon return to England, joining the Women's Emergency Corps. Evaluating the Women's Auxiliary Army Corps police. Joining the French Red Cross because it needed volunteers more urgently than did the British Red Cross. Beginning her Red Cross work in a canteen in France; all hotel charges coming out of volunteer's own pockets. Her canteen's being visited regularly by the French president; author's dreading his visits because enemy bombing usually followed. Taking a London hiatus, 1915; visiting British hospitals. Noting the difficulties of raising money in England for French-sponsored canteens. Discussing French soldiers' mistrust of women volunteer workers due to cultural differences. Returning to France; working at a Canadian hospital in Paris. In Revigny, working with French troops, 1916–17; being with the first Red Cross unit to reach that side of the front. Noting how reports of German atrocities were minimized to control morale. Discussing ongoing monetary problems in the French Red Cross: their demanding money from volunteers, their refusing to provide more aid to units. Contrasting laxity of French army discipline with British army's tight rules. Describing the "Marraine system" under which Frenchwomen sponsored individual soldiers, sending them food and clothing. Discussing receiving notes of gratitude from French soldiers for her canteen's work. Describing daily routine at the Revigny canteen: two shifts, frequent bombing, constant precautions against espionage. American troops' joining the French ones, 1917; being disliked for their vulgarity, loudness, and drunkenness. Turning her canteen over to other Englishwomen. Before leaving France, paying a visit to the battle-ruined city of Verdun. Italian and Franco-Belgian hostilities' causing difficulty for canteen workers after the war. Visiting sites of German devastation. Opening a canteen in Alsace, 1919; relating tales of German atrocities heard there. Accepting France's invitation to serve its army in Syria; establishing canteen there. Receiving the Croix du Guerre for her wartime relief work. In the Near East, traveling extensively; contracting paratyphoid disease in Port Said; this effectively ending her relief work.

In light of Culling's distinction as one of the few British citizens awarded the French Croix du Guerre, the publisher John Murray appears to have sought her out, because of her name recognition with the public, to produce a woman's war story. Her book is at once a detailed and impartial account of the French Red Cross and its English connections during WWI, and one of the few available in English. In his survey of the French war effort, *For Dauntless France,* historian Lawrence Binyon notes that at the outset of WWI many British women approached the Comité Britannique seeking to serve France; those, like Culling, who lacked specific training were assigned to establish canteens. Required to pay for their transportation and their keep, these volunteers also had to prove themselves to a French military which had traditionally resisted accepting women, even as nurses. Culling evidently passed muster, as her receipt of France's highest honor testifies. Her book gains considerable depth from comparative reading with accounts from women serving in other WWI assistance organizations, among them Lesley Smith's *Four Years Out of My Life* and Vera Brittain's *Testament of Youth*.

265 CUNARD, Nancy. 1896–1965. *These Were the Hours: Memories of My Hours Press*. Ed. by Hugh Ford. Carbondale, IL: Southern Illinois University Press, 1969. 216 pp.; foreword by ed. NUC 1968–1972 22:126.

Born in Leicestershire. Father: Sir Bache Cunard. Mother: Lady Maud Emerald. Single. Wrote *Outlaws* (1921), *Sublunary* (1923), *Parallax* (1925), *Grand Man*. Publisher; poet; novelist. Upper class.

Professional experiences of an English publisher of avant-garde writers in France, 1928–34. Purchasing the Hours Press, outside Paris, and Three Mountains Press, 1928; providing history of private presses in France. Moving from England into a house at La Chapelle-Reanville. Publishing George Moore's *Peronnik the Fool* and Louis Aragon's French translation of Lewis Carroll's *The Hunting of the Snark*. Explaining the system of authors' royalties. Becoming friends with Arthur Symons, the expatriate English author. Discussing her growing interest in the writings of the Harlem Renaissance and various avant-garde cultural trends (including surrealism). Discussing French surrealist movement and its leaders. Moving her press to Paris. Establishing friendships with English writers Robert Graves and Laura Riding; publishing Graves's *Ten Poems More* and Riding's *Twenty Poems Less* and *Four Unpublished Letters to Catherine*. Meeting with Samuel Beckett; choosing Beckett's poem "Whoroscope" as winner of the Hours Press poetry contest. Meeting James Joyce and Ezra Pound; acquiring Pound's *A Draft of XXX Cantos* for her firm. Publishing the poems of Roy Campbell and Harold Acton, as well as Havelock Ellis's *The Revaluation of Obscenity* (1931). Closing the Hours Press, 1931; briefly returning to publishing with the *Negro Anthology* (1934). Speculating about why Ezra Pound and Roy Campbell supported fascism. Commenting on political events before WWII. Returning to Reanville in 1945; finding her house had been destroyed by the German army; trying to unearth fragments of manuscripts and letters from her days as a publisher there.

Obviously proud of her publishing house's treasury of so many gifted writers, Cunard discusses how she provided them with an avenue to public recognition. Although she played a significant role in the avant-garde life in Paris, she confines her book to the story of the Hours Press, so that it becomes almost as much the firm's biography as her own. Although her familiarity with key participants in contemporary art and literary movements in Europe and the U.S. makes a fascinating read, for more complete biographical information about Cunard herself, readers may consult Anne Chishol's *Nancy Cunard* (1979) and *Nancy Cunard: Brave Poet, Indomitable Rebel, 1896–1965* (1968), ed. by Hugh C. Ford.

266 CURTIS, Julia. c.1870–d.a.1920. *Mists and Monsoons*. London & Glasgow: Blackie & Son, 1935. 166 pp.; front.; illus. NUC pre56 130:99.

Born on the west coast of Scotland. Father not named, tenant farmer. Mother not named. 1 brother; 3 sisters. Married c.1892, John Percival Curtis, Anglo-Indian planter. 2 children. Planter's spouse; colonialist (India). Rural farming class; married into upper middle class.

Affectionate memories of the author's Scottish childhood and adult life in India as a coffee planter's wife, 1870s–c.1920. Part I: Describing scenery, rural poverty, and churchgoing life of her childhood community. Father's valuing learning; his encouraging family reading. Mother's history. Elder brother's attending school; sisters' having a governess, then attending convent school in Aird. Spending summer holidays with maternal grandmother in the Outer Hebrides; describing older ways of life preserved on the islands; being present when Mrs. Kennedy Frazer visited to collect folksongs. Describing Communion Sundays at her family's Free Presbyterian Church. Commenting on local people's efforts to preserve Gaelic language and Highland customs, despite official sanctions in favor of English. Father's subletting farm to tenants due to monetary losses. Recalling her brother's departure for India; at age 20, author's going to India to join him. Part II: Arriving at brother's coffee plantation in southwest India; describing monsoons, long journeys over muddy roads. Meeting her husband-to-be, John Curtis, owner of the neighboring estate. Assuming management of her brother's estate; struggling to keep the kitchen clean; firing servants who knew nothing of sanitation. Learning about mistresses and illegitimate half-caste children of Anglo-Indian planters; pitying the lot of these half-castes. Describing plantation activities during coffee-picking season. Acquiring her own ayah to nurse her through a bout with malaria. Brother's marrying an Anglo-Indian woman who took over the author's duties. Author's refusing a proposal from John Curtis and sailing for England; discovering he was onboard, accepting his second proposal and marrying in England. Their returning to India, living happily in Mistypur for next twenty-five years. Discussing social relations with the native aristocracy. Birth of her first child. Weathering a cholera epidemic; sympathizing with the felt need of some European mothers to send their children home while remaining in India themselves. Family's returning to England, but finding it cold and inhospitable; encountering local prejudice over employing an Indian ayah. Returning to India, but revisiting England often to see her sons and relatives. Their final return to England; author's commenting on the tragedy of never seeing India again, and her nostalgia for two places, which had kept her moving between them.

Because Curtis disguises place names in this personal saga of a life divided between two regions of the world, the reader may sense that the author's experiences are meant to apply to the emigrant experience in general. While many accounts exist of military life in India, colonialists connected to the British army or colonial government seem to have been more insulated from the surrounding native culture than was Curtis, whose own reactions to half-caste children were unconventionally compassionate. Her description of more than twenty-five years of plantation life in India renders a colorful portrait of Britain's colonial agriculture and its attractions to younger sons like her brother, who emigrated to seek fortunes in order to compensate for their lack of inheritance under British laws of primogeniture. For useful comparison, readers may consult Justina Spencer-Knott's *Fools Rush In* (1949), containing the account of her colonial farming experiences in Africa.

267 CURZON, Lady Mary Irene, Baroness Ravensdale. 1896–1966. *In Many Rhythms: An Autobiography*. Weidenfeld & Nicholson, 1953. 328 pp.; front. port.; illus.; index. NUC pre56 482:477.

Born in London. Father: George Nathaniel Curzon, 1st Marquess and 1st Earl Curzon of Kedleston, M.P., Viceroy of India. Mother: Mary Victoria Leiter, American. 2 sisters. Single. Society woman; social activist; feminist; WWII volunteer; foreign resident (India); traveler (Europe, Persia, Far East, U.S., Canada, Russia). Aristocracy.

Family distinctions, privileged upbringing, and later adult philanthropic activities of an eminent British politician's daughter, c.1900–1950s. Family's living in India during father's tenure as viceroy. Returning to England; living in Walmer Castle. After death of author's mother, father's taking charge of improving his daughters' minds. Author's being sent to study music in Germany. Making her social debut, just before start of WWI. During the war, Belgian royal family's taking refuge in her home. Her father's heading the Foreign Office; his death during WWI. After the war, author's traveling extensively throughout

India, Ceylon, China, and Japan. Touring Canada; visiting Indian reservations there. In Hollywood, meeting Charlie Chaplin; dining with William Randolph Hearst and actress Marion Davies. After return to England, chairing the Union of Women Voters; confessing her discomfort in the position. Chairing Highway Clubs and committee on British Women's Symphony Orchestra. Meeting Arturo Toscanini, other composers. Visiting Russia, c.1930; discussing Russian peasants, working class, and communism. Recounting her sister Cynthia's election to Parliament; memories of Cynthia's husband, Oswald Mosely, and his fascist sentiments. Death of her sister Cynthia; assuming partial responsibility for Cynthia's children. Attending Nazi Congress in Nuremberg, meeting Hitler; commenting on the power of his oratory. After start of WWII, helping organize evacuation of children; working in air-raid shelters. Discussing Japan's entry into the war, 1941. Starting old people's home in Birminghamshire. Touring South Africa, 1948; discussing South African colonial politics.

Born into a family with a long tradition of public service and awed by the many offices filled by her distinguished father, Lady Ravensdale evidently regarded herself as the family misfit who failed to inherit its general zeal. Nevertheless, she threw herself into the charity work expected of women of leisure, although she comments that those charities were "served poorly" by her efforts. As her account progresses, the reader gradually sees how her interests in society and the art world are at odds with the philanthropic duties she resolutely pursues, perhaps in anxious competition with her sister Cynthia, the natural inheritor of their father's political talents. A fascinating study in family relations, Lady Ravensdale's book also helps document the British aristocracy's work in Britain's troubled diplomatic relations during the first half of the 20th century. Another memoir by Curzon, **268** "Parental Vagaries" in the 1932 anthology *Little Innocents,* focuses on her childhood, and is notable for its portrait of her father, who grilled his daughters and their governesses on academic subjects at the dinner table.

269 [Anonymous] (Cusack, Margaret Anna; a.k.a. Sister Mary Frances Clare, M. F. Cusack). 1829–1899. *Five Years in a Protestant Sisterhood and Ten Years in a Catholic Convent: An Autobiography.* Longmans, Green, 1869. 324 pp.; preface; notes. NUC pre56 174:396.

Born in Dublin, Ireland. Father: Samuel Cusack, physician. Mother: Sarah Stoney. 1 brother. Single. Wrote *An Illustrated History of Ireland* (1868), *The Life of the Blessed Virgin* (1884), *Life Inside the Church of Rome* (1889), others. Knew Margaret Goodman. Religionist (Roman Catholic convert; Anglican convert; Methodist convert); nun (Anglican sister); nun (Roman Catholic); social reformer; teacher; historian; religious/spiritual writer. Middle class.

Author's life as an Anglican sister, her conversion to Catholicism, and her later life as a Catholic nun, focused on c.1851–69. Her Anglican parents' being zealously anti–High Church and anti-Catholic. After mother's death, author's wearing deep mourning for years; comparing it to her nun's habit. After the end of her schooling, educating herself in religion; reading works of Dr. Pusey and other High Church clergy; acquiring High Church views. Suffering serious depression, ages 18–20; resolving to heal herself through a life of service; deciding to remain single and become a Protestant Sister of Mercy. Entering an Anglican sisterhood in London despite family opposition. Discussing her wish to help the poor. Developing esteem for her first superior; being distressed when the sisterhood was broken up by departure of superior to the Crimean War. Discussing autocratic behavior of her second superior; declaring abuses of authority were inevitable, given the anomalous position of a quasi-Catholic sisterhood within the Protestant church. At that time, being ignorant of true Catholicism. Being furious when a student in the sisterhood's boys' college was flogged. Leaving the sisterhood and returning home; being subjected to Nonconformist attempts to convert her. Returning briefly to the Anglican sisterhood; after her cold reception, privately beginning comparative study of the Catholic Prayer Book and the Anglican Articles of Faith; consulting both Anglican and Catholic priests. Resolving to convert to Catholicism; weathering her family's rejection. Describing her warm reception into the Catholic convent at Helston, c.1856. Reexamining her vocation; beginning work among friendless girls in collaboration with Irish Catholic sisters, the Poor Clares, 1860. Teaching in convent schools. Transferring to the Poor Clare convent in Kenmare, County Kerry, 1861. Reading the autobiography of Sister Margaret Goodman. Commenting on women's intellectual and spiritual condition; disputing the commonly held notion that women cannot live together without quarreling.

A fuller view of Cusack's life is available through reading all three of her autobiographical volumes. This earliest one, containing commentary on the organizational abuses within established churches in the 19th century, closes before Cusack was attacked by the Irish priesthood for her social activism. Known as the "Nun of Kenmare" for her famine relief work there, 1878–80, she left in 1881 to escape community controversy. In 1884, after founding the Sisters of Peace in Ireland, she went to the U.S. to organize a convent helping immigrant Irish girls, writing her second volume, *The Nun of Kenmare,* after she was forced to abandon the project. Her later defection from the Catholic Church forms the subject of her last book, described below. The informative 1970 biography of Cusack by Irene Ffrench Eager is also entitled *The Nun of Kenmare*.

270 CUSACK, Margaret Anna (a.k.a. Sister Mary Frances Clare, M. F. Cusack). 1829–1899. *The Story of My Life by Sister Mary Frances.*

Hodder & Stoughton, 1891. 403 pp.; preface; port. BLC to 1975 74:430.

Biographical: See *Five Years in a Protestant Sisterhood and Ten Years in a Catholic Convent*.

Childhood in a broken family, life in Anglican sisterhood, and the author's later tenure as a Roman Catholic nun, highlighting her struggles against Catholic hierarchy, c.1830–90. Describing mixed religious influences in her childhood: mother's nominal Protestantism, father's fervent Anglicanism, great-aunt's Plymouth Brethrenism. Moving back and forth between her parents' and great-aunt's households in childhood. After parents' separation, mother's taking her from Ireland to Exeter. Death of her father. Describing resistance from mother and great-aunt to author's intended marriage. Author's suffering a two-year breakdown after her fiancé's death; recovering by joining Anglican sisterhood. Leaving sisterhood to become a Catholic nun. Explaining her independent attitude toward the church and her superiors; incurring archbishop's censure; suing a priest for libel. Beginning her writing career. At Kenmare, Ireland, collecting, controlling, and distributing a large relief fund for Irish famine victims, 1879. Being suspected by British authorities of heading the secret "Ladies' Land League." Gaining worldwide fame as the "Nun of Kenmare." Arguing with superiors over her activities. Leaving Kenmare to found Sisters of Peace convent at Knock, Ireland. Relocating to New York; trying to open a convent school to aid immigrant Irish girls, but encountering opposition from local powers, 1885–88. Writing for the *New York Sun*. Recounting further efforts by higher clergy to stop her political activities. Making a desperate decision to leave the Catholic Church, 1888. Writing book *The Nun of Kenmare* (1889), which she later expanded into *The Story of My Life;* its being censored by the Catholic clergy. Returning to England; converting to Methodism; writing and lecturing on evils of the Catholic Church.

Writing in a spirit of self-justification, Cusack retrospectively condemns general injustices within the Catholic Church. With a sense of independence fostered by her success as an author and a control of her money alien to convent principles of poverty, Cusack inevitably ran into conflict with the Catholic Church's principle of absolute authority over its members. In her written record of confrontations with ecclesiastical dictates, her sense of injustice tends to hide the drive for recognition that is implicit in her choice to record her good works for publication. Cusack's multivolume saga helps to characterize the Catholic Church's distance from democratic principles of self-direction and to show how this causes problems for the church in trying to retain members in its religious orders as the 20th century progresses.

271 CUST, Emma Sophia, Countess of Brownlow (née Edgcumbe). 1791–1872. *Slight Reminiscences of a Septuagenarian from 1802 to 1815*. John Murray, 1867. 199 pp.; preface. NUC pre56 80:58.

Born near Richmond, Greater London. Father not named, career diplomat. Mother not named, world traveler. 1 sister; 3 brothers. Married 1828, Henry Cust, Lord Brownlow. 6 stepchildren. Society woman; foreign resident (France). Aristocracy.

Recollections of personal and political events in England and France during the Napoleonic period, covering 1798–1815. Author's earliest memory: witnessing the flogging of British naval mutineers in Plymouth Sound, 1798. Traveling with her mother to Spain, 1802; visiting Frankfurt; recording her unpleasant impressions of Frankfurt's Jewish quarter. In Louisberg, visiting the princess royal and the Duchess of Wurtemburg. Being filled with horror, admiration, and awe at her first sight of the Emperor Napoleon in Paris, c.1803. Returning home to Ham Common; attending Christmas ball given by Queen Charlotte. England's declaring war on France, 1803. Author's studying at home with a governess, 1804–05; recalling fainting at news of Nelson's Trafalgar victory. Attending trial of Lord Melville, 1806. After mother's death, 1806, father's selling their villa at Ham Common; family's moving to Mount Edgcumbe. Recalling visit of Princess Charlotte to her family, 1807, and father's disillusionment with the princess. Author's meeting her future husband, 1809. Witnessing George III's jubilee. Her sister's marriage, 1812. Author and brother George's visiting London with their uncle, Lord Castlereagh; accompanying uncle to negotiations with Napoleon in Paris, 1813. Recalling a side tour to Holland. Describing the political situation in Paris, April 1814. Viewing the aftermath at Belleville battlefield. Visiting opera with Castlereagh and the duke of Wellington; noting the French public's reaction to the sight of Wellington. Attending dinner parties of the conquerors and the conquered. Traveling to Malmaison with Lady Castlereagh to visit Empress Josephine; learning of Josephine's death. Returning to England. After Napoleon's escape from Elba and defeat at Waterloo, accompanying the Castlereaghs to France again, 1815; noting intensified English presence in Paris. Providing readers with an account of a Russian army review on the plains of Vertus, complete with diagrams. Also witnessing reviews of the English army. Recalling French bitterness at being forced to return foreign art treasures Napoleon's forces had taken. Visiting studio of Napoleon's officially appointed painter, Jacques Louis David. Being present during the court-martial of Marshal Ney. Returning to England after the peace treaty.

Lady Brownlow discusses people and events of the Napoleonic period far more extensively than she does her own life. She vividly and usefully depicts places she visited and key personalities on both sides in the twenty years of diplomatic and military struggle between England and post-Revolutionary France. In **272** *The Eve of Victorianism: Reminiscences of the Years 1802 to 1834* (1940), Lady Brownlow continues her established pattern of charting her life against a fabric of the political events in England and France. This second autobiography, a jumble of twelve-month summaries, diary entries, and narrative reminiscences, contains a wealth of anecdotes from aristocratic and upper-class society and may be more useful for research on the author's own life than her earlier volume.

273 DALGLISH, Doris N. 1894–1954. *We Have Been Glad.* Macmillan & Co., Ltd., 1938. 231 pp.; poems. NUC pre56 131:516.

Born in Wandsworth Common, London suburbs. Father not named, Presbyterian deacon in Tooting. Mother not named. Great-grandfather: William Campbell, hotel proprietor. Single. Wrote *Presbyterian Pirate, a Portrait of Stevenson* (1937), *The People Called Quakers* (1938). Teacher; political writer; religious/spiritual writer; religionist (Quaker); pacifist; civil servant; journalist; poet; biographer; WWI volunteer. Middle class.

Growth, education, and meditations of a woman intellectual, Quaker convert, and pacifist, from childhood to the 1930s. Giving brief family history; being strongly influenced by her Scottish mother and grandmother; identifying with her Scottish heritage. Having no formal religious training in childhood. Detesting school she was sent to, age 7, which lacked books, maps, and other educational materials; coming intellectually alive at Clapham High School, which taught new concepts; its environment's stimulating her literary imagination. Family's visiting Scotland, author's age 10. In adolescence, becoming interested in Quakerism and Catholicism; eventually converting to Quakerism. Attending Oxford, 1913–17; observing the tawdry "prunes and custard" life of women's college residents as described by Virginia Woolf; wanting to avoid controversy of defending the intellectual life for women against charges of its indecency. Experiencing romantic feelings for women friends; referring to herself as a "spinster" and believing that marriage means intellectual death for a woman. Judging that intellectual women have developed mentally rather than biologically, remaining sexually immature. At Oxford, searching for a creed to meet her need for religious structure; trying Anglicanism. Outbreak of WWI; discussing its effects on Oxford thought; doing volunteer work in a Westminster canteen. Teaching in Devon, 1917–18. Disliking teaching; writing for magazine competitions and publishing poetry in the *Oxford Magazine.* Clerking briefly in the Treasury Department; maturing politically during the war. Judging the Armistice and the Treaty of Versailles to be immoral; stating that "negative pacifism," or simply opposing war, accomplishes nothing. Praising Woodrow Wilson's visit to England promoting the League of Nations. Becoming active in the Worker's Educational Association, 1918, and in the Labour Party. Working to promote socialism and the extension of general education. Continuing to search for a fulfilling religion; studying Catholicism; noting its disagreement with socialist ideals. Admiring a married female friend for having bloomed intellectually despite marriage. Converting to Quakerism; explaining its creed of pacifism and social activism; attending Quaker Meetings at Wandsworth. Disliking work; wanting to "drift"; speculating that female intellect and imagination may be too weak to succeed at literary re-creation of experience. Finding work at the Old Age Pension Office. Continuing to contribute writing to various periodicals. Opposing the Spanish Civil War; decrying possibility of a new world war. Mulling over the reasons for pacifism's failure, and the difficulties for the lost generation to avoid extremes and disillusionment.

Dalglish's gentle, retiring character is conveyed in the oblique manner in which she refers to herself—often in the third person—and in her expressed yearning to escape from the workaday world. Her heroes and heroines are writers, and she states that she pines for a life of sheer intellectualism, although she is unduly beset by cultural notions that women are incapable of sustained intellectual work. In keeping with her Quaker principles, she worked actively for social betterment through socialist and pacifist means, and she is a notable figure in the post-WWI pacifist movement.

274 DANDO, Ellen D. c.1890–d.a.1935. *Out of Romanism.* Marshall, Morgan & Scott, 1938. 119 pp.; front. ports.; foreword by R. Wearmouth; preface; "In Memoriam." BLC to 1975 76:169. (other ed.: Grand Rapids, MI: Zondervan Publishing House, 1946.)

Born in Newcastle-upon-Tyne, Northumberland. Father not named, deputy overman in coal mines. Mother, stepmother not named. 2 siblings. Married the Rev. David John Dando, teacher, Methodist minister. Preacher; religionist (Methodist convert); missionary; WWII volunteer; clergyman's spouse; domestic servant. Lower middle class.

Author's progress from passive Catholic faith in childhood to the active, working Methodism of her adulthood, from the 1890s to WWII. Growing up in a mining village in County Durham. Father's converting to Catholicism to marry author's Catholic mother; mother's exerting profound religious influence in the home. Author's making regular confessions, ages 7–17. Being forbidden even to enter a Protestant church. Being awed by her first communion, since the doctrine of transubstantiation asserts that the bread and wine literally become Christ's body and blood. Catholicism's feeding human craving for color and pageantry. After death of her mother, being comforted by Catholic belief in efficacy of prayer for the dead; her father's turning to drink and marrying a much younger woman who disliked the children. Author's finding work as a mother's helper for Rev. Thomas

Middlemast, a Methodist preacher; reading the Bible for the first time; discovering Methodism encourages the believer to interpret for herself; becoming unhappy that Catholics were required to believe what priests tell them. Angering her family priest by deciding to leave the Catholic Church; converting to Methodism. Attending Primitive Methodist services that stressed gender equality among believers; also attending Christian Endeavour meetings. Deciding to be a Methodist lay preacher; discussing women's increasing presence as Methodist lay preachers. Doing missionary work in London's East End; conducting Sunday prayer meetings; recounting the many economic and social problems the City Mission worked to solve. Marrying another evangelist; discussing the spiritual debate between marriage and celibacy. Husband's being appointed to the Methodist ministry; author's working as his assistant; their shared sense of vocation giving them joy. Calling Methodism the dynamic part of Christianity's 2,000-year-old faith. Author's volunteering to conduct chapel in Blackfriars despite dangers from WWII bombing.

Although Dando was not an overt feminist, her entrance into the ranks of the Methodist Church's women lay preachers provided scope for her energies and independent mind that early-20th-century Catholicism could not supply. Dando's account forms an illuminating contrast to Maude Petre's *My Way of Faith* (1937); Petre also rejected blind faith in priestly edicts, but she chose to stay in the Catholic Church, changing it from within in her role as a Catholic modernist theologian.

275 DARE, Phyllis. 1890–1975. *From School to Stage.* Collier, 1907. 147 pp.; front. port.; preface; illus. NUC pre56 133:164.

Born in London. Parents not named, apparently workers in the theatre. 1 brother and 1 sister, also child actors. Single. Actress (child, pantomime). Middle class.

A child actress's vocational rise, covering the 1890s–1907. Feeling timid about writing her life story, but doing so because of public curiosity about her youthful acting career. Discussing her early enthusiasm for acting; gradually overcoming stage fright when allowed onstage by her parents. Winning her first London role, age 9; defending acting as honorable for children, especially those who have to support needy parents. Becoming well known through a London role, age 10; having to answer fan letters. Being schooled at home by a governess, while intensively studying singing and dancing. Her first leading role's being in the pantomime, age 10; praising pantomime theatre, touring companies, and provincial audiences for supporting and encouraging actors in learning their craft. Sharing stage with actor George Alexander, 1901; acting with her brother and sister. Balancing demands of her schooling with ongoing roles. Studying at a Brussels finishing school, but being suddenly called home to fill the starring role in the long-running play, *The Belle of*

Mayfair. Receiving tremendous first-night ovation; adjusting to being stared at as a public personality. Suffering from unspecified rumors about herself; commenting on damage done by malicious gossip to actors' livelihoods. Excerpts from letters seeking advice on how to start a stage career; author's giving recommendations. Playing a role (involving much bare skin) that sparked a marriage proposal from an infatuated fan. Discussing the physical rigors of the acting life, theatrical superstitions, and the grief when theatrical colleagues pass away.

Making her first attempt to write at the age of 17, Dare is noticeably diffident about her talents. Full of praise for audiences and theatre life, she covers every aspect of her professional career but says little about her family. She was assisted in writing her story by Bernard Parsons, possibly an editor. Her book benefits from comparison with the autobiography of Peggy Webling, another child actress of the same period. In *Peggy: The Story of One Score Years and Ten* (1924), Webling writes from an adult perspective, recalling her childhood acting years in the light of her later worldly experiences.

276 DAVIES, Catherine. 1773–d.a.1816. *Eleven Years' Residence in the Family of Murat, King of Naples.* How & Parsons, 1841. 92 pp.; preface; app. NUC pre56 134:348.

Born at Beaumaris, Island of Anglesea, Wales. Parents not named; stepmother implied. 32 siblings and half-siblings. Single. Governess. Middle class.

Author's impoverished Welsh childhood, dependent spinster years, and perilous life as governess to relatives of Napoleon, with a vivid account of intrigues within the French empire, covering 1773–c.1816. Her childhood in Wales. Author and siblings' all being forced by father's financial distress to leave home young. At age 15, author's moving in with a merchant's family in Liverpool. At age 29, in 1802, moving to London to live with her married sister; later during this year taking job in Paris as companion to a young English girl and being stranded in France when its borders closed at outbreak of Napoleonic Wars. A friend's recommending author for position as governess to children of Madame Murat, second sister of Napoleon. Living in Paris with Murat family and another English paid companion, 1802–08. In 1808, the Murats' being crowned king and queen of Naples by Napoleon; author's accompanying family to Naples. Discussing uncovering of conspiracy to murder the entire royal family. Prince and Princess of Wales's paying formal visit to Naples, 1814. Political intrigue's eventually forcing Murat to escape from Naples; remaining family members and author's taking refuge in the fortress of Gaeta. Witnessing naval battle between Neapolitan and British ships. Fort's being seized by the British, who abducted Murat family and author as political prisoners. Murats' begging for author's release; her being threatened by British as a spy, but sent back to

Naples. Being robbed and beaten as she traveled alone to Paris, 1814; upon reaching London, suffering additional blow of learning her parents had died. Returning to her home on the Isle of Anglesea.

Like other accounts of service to royal families (Anne Topham's *Chronicles of the Prussian Court* and Anna Leonowens's *The English Governess at the Siamese Court),* Davies's memoirs dwell more on the personalities and circumstances of her employer's lives than they do on her own. The book's main appeal lies in its dramatic presentation of political intrigue; it offers an insider's view of a French Empire royal family during the ongoing uncertainties of the Napoleonic Wars.

277 DAVIES, Celia (née Gardner). 1902–?. *Clean Clothes on Sunday.* Lavenham: T. Dalton Ltd., 1974. 188 pp.; foreword; illus. NUC 1973–1977 28:302.

Born in Woodford Green, Essex. Father: Soames Freeman Gardner, hay merchant, president of British Hay Trades Association. Mother: Ethel Grace Marshall. 2 sisters; 1 brother. Married John Davies. 2 sons. WWI volunteer. Upper middle class.

Childhood and early youth amid affluent family surroundings, 1902–1920s. Her maternal grandfather's having frittered away his inherited fortune. By contrast, her paternal grandfather's founding a mercantile empire in hay trading; her father's inheriting it. Author's being a sickly, tiresome child; growing up good only because she was disciplined by her beloved "Nannie." Having a series of incompetent governesses; consequently not taking lessons seriously. Sex's being unmentionable in the household; Nannie's telling fairytales about author's mother's pregnancy. Describing the vanished pastimes and holiday customs of her Edwardian upbringing. Most traffic's being horsedrawn; automobiles' being "still a rich man's whim." Family's traveling by horse and carriage to visit grandparents in the countryside. Her social conscience's awakening when she first saw poor children. Describing the filthy living conditions and diet of the poor at that time, and her childish bewilderment at extreme class inequities. Describing sights and sounds within London's city walls near the family business. Family's moving to new estate in Hoddeson, author's age 7. Disliking primary school; being allowed to leave after two terms. Discussing village life and neighbors in Hoddeson. Hay trade's flourishing until 1916; father's reluctance to acknowledge that the motorcar would ultimately destroy his business. Author's recounting history of the White Chapel Hay Market. Peaceful life's being disrupted by WWI, author's age 12. Family's billeting soldiers; attending charity entertainments for Belgian fund. Giving a sample of anti-German propaganda. Family's enduring Zeppelin raids and rationing. Assessing cultural and social changes, Edwardian era to 1918. Remembering the 1920s as the dawn of both the welfare state and liberal political thinking. Father's facing the reality of the automobile, 1926, and retiring. Author's weighing losses, such as her father's, caused by progress, against gains such as women's greater cultural voice. Realizing the future will bring still more unanticipated changes; welcoming them.

Recalling the first twenty years of the present century from the vantage point of old age, Davies looks closely at the calm acceptance in those years of the extreme disparity between poverty and affluence. Demonstrating a sound historical overview, Davies evidently regards herself as having been part of a distinguished era but embraces modernity optimistically. Her memoir provides both a vivid rendering of Edwardian domestic life and an investigative study of its social disruption by WWI. This book has been used as a social history text.

278 DAVIES, Dame Clara Novello (née Davies). 1861–1943. *The Life I Have Loved.* William Heinemann, 1940. 323 pp.; foreword by Ivor Novello (author's son); illus. NUC pre56 424:188.

Born in Cardiff, Wales. Father: Jacob Davies, iron miner, founder of Blue Ribbon Choir. Mother: Margaret Evans. 1 brother. Married 1883, David Davies, local government official. 1 daughter; 1 son, composer Ivor Novello. Choir conductor; teacher (music); composer. Middle class.

Welsh childhood, musical influences, and rewarding adult career of a women's choir organizer and composer, from the 1860s–1932. Author's having strong sense of Welsh identity; reciting family's long Welsh history. Father's having passion for fine music; his naming author for then-famous soprano Clara Novello. Father's being her greatest lifelong influence. Speaking Welsh at home. Being sent to a seminary in Cardiff, age 5; learning English there. From youth, intending to marry future husband David Davies, who sang in her father's choir. At age 12, being sent to private school; having to leave because of father's business failure. Resolving to support herself by teaching music, a career she followed for sixty-six years. Attempting a solo piano career, but lacking virtuoso technique. Wanting to tour as a singer; her parents' forbidding it. Becoming accompanist for her father's temperance choir, age 22. Mother's suffering grave illness during author's courtship with Davies. Their marriage, 1883, being followed by mother's death. Author's husband's winning post on local Government Board. After her first baby's death from birth injuries, author's resolving never to have children and to focus on her work. Founding and conducting the Royal Welsh Ladies' Choir; beginning to compose original works for them. Inadvertently becoming pregnant again; rejoicing at birth of her son, Ivor, 1893. Taking baby with her to 1893 Chicago World's Fair, where her choir won the world vocal competition. Choir's giving command performance for Queen Victoria; making exhibition tour of the U.S.; performing at the 1900 Paris Exhibition. Her son Ivor's being the choir's accompanist, ages 12–17; author's remaining close to him throughout his adult musical career. During WWI, author's sponsoring recreational orchestra for soldiers and finding sponsors to donate free musical instruments. After WWI, author's beginning new career in Hollywood as vocal coach. Helping to inaugurate the Women's League of Peace, c.1920s, and serving as conference delegate to the World Women's Party. Death of author's husband, age 80, in 1932.

Davies's book was prepared for publication by her son, Ivor Novello, songwriter and dramatist, whose composition "Keep the Home Fires Burning" was a patriotic theme song of WWI. In a sense Davies's memoir is a generational biography, which seeks out the origins of the family's musical gifts and charts their maturation from Clara's father, through herself, to her son, Ivor. Despite her mid-19th-century birth, Davies's career seems to have been unmarred by gender barriers, reflecting the general acceptance of careers for women in the performing arts long before their acceptance in other fields.

270 DAVIES, Rosina. c.1865–d.a.1942. *The Story of My Life*. Llandyssul, Wales: Gomerian Press, 1942. 2nd ed. 293 pp.; front. port.; foreword by H. Elvet Lewis; list of patrons. BLC to 1975 78:22.

Born at Treherbert in the Rhondda, Wales. Father: surname Davies, hauling-contractor. Mother: Hannah Jones. 4 sisters; 2 brothers. Single. Salvation Army worker; preacher; temperance activist. Lower middle class.

Welsh upbringing, conversion experience, and life's spiritual work of a Salvation Army preacher, from the 1860s to c.1940. Discussing the close-knit mining families in her village and her parents' histories. Speaking Welsh at home. After suffering heart damage from scarlet fever, being schooled at home in letters and religion by her parents. Parents' belonging to the Carmel Welsh Independent Church; author's singing in its Band of Hope choir. Describing the decline in village religious life caused by increased business prosperity. Attending Salvation Army meetings against her parents' will; converting to its nondenominational evangelism; eventually gaining her parents' consent. Preaching in Welsh at Salvation Army revival meetings in Maesteg Valley, age 14; receiving mixed public reactions because of her youth and gender. Asserting that Christianity's denominations are unimportant. Conducting a week's mission at Porthcawl, creating a sensation as "a girl preaching and singing the gospel"; praying for the men who spat on her and threw stones. Being received into the Church of England, but under an interdenominational Salvation Army committee. Making many preaching and missionary tours of Wales while still in her teens; depending on local hospitality for her livelihood. Joining delegation of Welsh ministers to Salvation Army Mission in London, 1883. Believing that her mission required her to remain single, because a married woman's sacred duty is the care of her home. Author's friends in the ministry defeating resolution against women preaching the Gospel. While staying with friends in London, 1884, educating herself through attending a men's debating society. Continuing her annual mission tours of Wales, 1881–c.1902; citing contemporary records of the hundreds of services she gave and countless converts she made. Taking voice training in London, although dedicating her voice to the Lord, not the stage. Depicting the rites at an old friend's Jewish wedding, 1890. Author's missionary efforts' being impeded by a series of grave illnesses. In early 1890s, beginning to use her sermons politically to denounce social injustice to workers. Touring Welsh congregations in America, 1893, and meeting with Mormon elders in Salt Lake City. Diary excerpts covering her extensive U.S. travels. After returning to England, resuming her Welsh mission tours. Following death of her sister, author's adopting sister's seven children. Author's also providing home for her ailing father; his death, 1902. Beginning mission tours in England, for which she accepted partial payment; having never accepted pay for her Welsh work. Preaching at canteens and factories during WWI. Working in the South Wales Women's Temperance Union, c.1918–30, to promote the temperance political campaign. Discussing her heavy debts, c.1926–42, and business assistance from her friends; disliking having to accept charity. Making her third American tour, 1930. Believing women's only true emancipation comes through Christian service.

Largely composed of diary entries, Davies's memoir takes on the coloration of her Christian worldview. As a traditional conversion narrative, her account consistently attributes providential design to the events in her life. However, Davies's memories are so focused on her personal successes that her account also strongly reflects the 19th-century ideal of the self-made man or woman popularized in Samuel Smiles's book *Self Help*. Her book provides a useful glimpse of the ways in which late-19th- and early-20th-century evangelism found common cause with the socialist workers' movements active at this time.

280 DAVIS, Elizabeth Cadwaladyr. 1789–1860. *The Autobiography of Elizabeth Davis, a Balaclava Nurse, Daughter of Dafydd Cadwaladyr.* Ed. by Jane Williams (Ysgafell). Hurst & Blackett, 1857. 2 vols. Vol. 1: 308 pp.; front. port.; ed.'s preface; intro. Vol. 2: 298 pp.; apps.; ed.'s postscript. NUC pre56 134:590.

Born at Pen Rhiw farm near Bala, north Wales. Father: Dafydd Cadwaladyr, itinerant Welsh Calvinistic Methodist minister. Mother: Judith Erasmus. 15 siblings. Single. Domestic servant; nurse (Crimean War); teacher (Sunday school); clergyman's daughter; traveler (world); kidnap victim. Rural laboring class.

Improbable memoirs of a Welsh domestic servant, world traveler, and self-professed Crimean nurse, from her birth to 1857. Vol. 1: Father's prominence as a Methodist preacher. Mother's death, author's age 5.

Father's taking children to Anglican as well as Methodist services. Being schooled entirely in Welsh. Growing up physically robust; loving exercise and dancing. To escape an elder sister's tyranny, author's running away, age 9, to home of Rev. Mr. Lloyd in another Welsh village; being taught English there in exchange for domestic work. At age 14, running away again to cousins in Liverpool. Foiling a robbery by chasing down and beating the thief. Changing her name to Davis, the anglicized version of her father's first name. Finding domestic work in Liverpool with a baronet. Chasing down another thief; his being hanged due to her evidence at trial. Accompanying baronet's household to Scotland. Rejecting two marriage proposals. Traveling with her employers to France and Europe; catching another thief who stole their luggage; cross-dressing as a soldier to attend a ball with the family maid, age 19. Visiting Waterloo battlefield five days after battle, June 1815. Returning to England; father's forbidding her to accompany baronet's family to India. Escaping one suitor by his death at sea; escaping another by running away to London; finding more domestic jobs there. Escaping a third suitor by signing on as nursemaid to family of Capt. Smith, Nov. 1820, and sailing for the West Indies. Describing the captain's family, their arrival on island of St. Vincent, debauchery of West Indian colonists. Author's witnessing pursuit of a snake that had twelve feet, six wings, and a shark's head. Author's visiting a slave plantation at Demerara; teaching black children at the mission school. Mrs. Smith's threatening to have her flogged for unspecified reasons; author's retaliating by letting children rampage. Leaving the Smiths' service; being hired by the family of another ship's captain, Mr. Foreman, and sailing with them for Australia. Ship's nearly perishing in a storm from lightning-induced fire; author's quickly putting fire out by lowering the wet sails over it. Arriving in Hobart; noting eagerness of the women emigré passengers to marry; author's refusing more marriage proposals. Author's voyaging to India and China, learning to ride elephants and camels, meeting her hated eldest sister; sister's not recognizing her. Returning to Australia. Accompanying the Foremans to India. Witnessing a suttee in Bombay, Indian mothers drowning their babies in the Ganges, and the ritual of people throwing themselves beneath the wheels of a juggernaut. Befriending missionaries in India, c.1825. Captain Foreman's ship's being purchased by a Portuguese merchant, Mr. Barbosa; under his command, sailing for Singapore. Riding elephants; seeing an elephant kill a lion. Sailing to Canton. Visiting the Chinese emperor's harem and council room. Sailing for Sydney; on board ship, teaching adult and Sunday school to Sydney convicts. Voyaging to Rio de Janeiro; while there, seeing a friend murdered; discussing the murderer's execution on a rack. Being kidnapped by an infatuated Barbosa; escaping on foot to Rio; arriving just in time to board the Foremans' outward-bound ship. Vol. 2: Voyage to South Africa. Refusing more marriage proposals. Voyages to India, China, Australia, the Mediterranean, Rio. Acting in ship theatricals. Returning to England, 1835. Losing £1,000 of savings in bad investments. Serving as housekeeper to a London lawyer. Meeting the great actor Charles Kemble; his recognizing her acting talents; author's refusing his offer of a position in his acting company because actors were "ragged wretches." Her employer's death; being cheated out of a legacy from him by his heirs. Applying for a position as nurse during the Crimean War, 1854. Arriving in Scutari; applying to go to front; being rejected by Florence Nightingale. Accusing Nightingale of mismanagement, tyranny, selfishness. Arriving at Balaclava hospital after Nightingale disowned her. Appealing to Lord Raglan to protect all nurses who had come without Nightingale's approval. Boasting of her single-handed improvements at Balaclava hospital. Expressing her continuing resentment of Nightingale's interference. Being forced by illness to return to England, 1856.

Vanity and imagination commingle in Davis's memoir, which contains both startling claims and resentments of perceived injustices in equal measure. Nightingale in particular earns Davis's displeasure; the author depicts the army's nursing administrator as selfish and domineering. Although other sources describe Nightingale as a difficult woman, Davis has assuredly embellished her account here, as she does in many places, to make a good story. Even Davis's admiring editor, Jane Williams, who took down this oral account, politely expresses reservations about some of Davis's assertions. Yet Davis appears to have been an extraordinary woman for her time: full of initiative, physically strong, and fearless. The reader can't know which of the author's adventures are real and which are cobbled together from her imagination, but this memoir paints a vivid, if romanticized, panorama of the British empire in the first half of the 19th century.

281 DAYUS, Kathleen. 1903–s.l.1991. *Her People.* Virago, 1982. 194 pp.; intro. by John Rudd; illus. BLC 1982–1985 7:279.

Born in Birmingham, Midlands. Father: Sam, jewel and metal worker. Mother: Polly. 3 brothers; 2 sisters; 7 other siblings died in infancy. Married 1921, Charlie Flood, sawdust jobber, d.1931. Married 1946, Joe Dayus, bookmaker. 2 sons; 3 daughters. Wrote *The People of Lavender Court*, a social study. Social historian; factory worker; workshop owner. Working class.

Author's childhood poverty, factory employment, marriage, and destitute widowhood, c.1903–39. Describing poverty, scanty food, and overcrowding among workers in Birmingham's metal foundries, c.1903–11. Community's completely lacking privacy; despite ignorance of sex, children's seeing sexual activity daily by having to sleep in parents' bedrooms. Author's dreading her large, cruel, and spiteful mother. Mother's being illiterate; father's barely being able to read a newspaper. Seven children's dying in infancy before author's birth. Shoplifting's being customary practice; author's stealing from butcher when she was hungry. Most children's having lice; all children being expected to work for their own support. Getting a taste of rural living when mother took children to work picking hops on a farm; while there, brother's being caught stealing a pig to have a pet. Author's encountering a child molester, age 11. Leaving school, age 14, to work in WWI munitions factory. Finding another job making army trouser buttons and a later one making jewelry boxes. Marrying, 1921; having to quit work because of pregnancy. Husband's being chronically unemployed; his buying sawdust from mills to sell to pubs and butchers. Being ignorant until after fifth child that pregnancy could be prevented. Eldest son's death in an accident, age 7; second oldest boy's having to care for the new baby. Author's applying for parish relief; being prevented from working by enforcement of relief eligibility. Husband's dying of drink and depression, 1931. Widowed and impoverished at age 28, author's deciding to put her children in a Barnardo orphans' home. Opening her own enameling shop. When WWII began, being enabled by business prosperity to rescue her children from the orphanage, 1939. Her mother and sister's dying in an air raid, which destroyed their Birmingham house. Concluding with a summary of her life since WWII.

Although all of Dayus's autobiographies cover the same material, each makes a close examination of a different period in her life. In *Her People* the author's emphasis is on the social conditions of her working-class Birmingham upbringing, conditions that the editor's introduction places in useful historical context. Dayus uses dialogue to reproduce the dialect of her family and neighbors and makes enlightening commentary on rural farm life from the perspective of her urban childhood experience. Of her sequels, **282** *Where There's Life* (1985) discusses her working and family life through middle age, 1914–45; **283** *All My Days* (1988) fleshes out memories of childhood and adolescence with information on her later emotional ties with her children and second husband; **284** *The Best of Times* (1991) emphasizes reunions in her later life with childhood friends, and the changes in their shared perceptions through the passage of time.

285 DE BANKE, Cecile. 1889–1965. *Hand over Hand: An Autobiography.* Hutchinson, 1957. 263 pp.; foreword by Richard Church; illus.; index. NUC 1942–1962 38:263.

Born in London. Father not named, pub owner, later "turf accountant." Mother not named. Single. Actress (stage); singer (popular); teacher (elocution). Lower middle class.

Urban childhood, musical training, and early career of a talented popular singer, with her experiences of class-based social exclusion, 1890s–1925. Being raised in urban London; remembering affectionate aunts and a series of "slattern" nursemaids. Expressing pride in her own

Cockney heritage. Living briefly with aunt in rural Loughton; developing fear of woods after becoming lost in nearby Epping Forest. Family's moving to Buckhurst Hill in Essex; father's giving up pub management to become turf accountant; his alternating fortunes. Remembering the access her father's job gave her to horses; riding all over Essex. Attending dame school; acquiring love of reading. Going to the races with her father. Attending riding school, where she met her lifelong friends, the Harriman family; their introducing her to music. Her parents' being fond of pleasure and indifferent to religion; author's being confirmed in Anglican church without their knowledge. Having her first romance with Launce, the Harrimans' son. Enrolling at the Brighton School of Music. Giving her first singing concert in London. Through the Harrimans, socializing in professional circles; being snubbed as daughter of "the racing set." Suffering emotionally when Launce chose to marry a girl with better class connections, at same time as her father's financial failure. Catching tuberculosis; traveling with the Harrimans in Norway to recover. In London, supporting herself by teaching elocution in a girls' school. Creditors' seizing her parents' goods. Resolving to pursue her singing career despite lack of parental aid. Winning her first role at the Olympia Theatre. Touring with theatrical company all over England and Ireland as the director's assistant. Describing hardships of life on the road, including shabby boarding houses, drunken landladies, and untended illnesses; enduring them out of need to support herself and mother. Winning position as understudy in London play; touring in the lead role. Outbreak of WWI; remarking that theatre prospered during the war because audiences were desperate for entertainment. Suffering permanent damage to her singing voice through bronchitis; turning her efforts to acting. Joining extended theatrical tour to South Africa. Returning to England to visit in 1922, and again in 1925 at the time of both parents' deaths.

In this quiet study of her origins and later theatrical success, De Banke attributes her personal resolve and energy to qualities inherited from her Cockney ancestors. Her personal history provides an informative look at the many nuances of class-based perception that governed social interaction in early-20th-century Britain. For a memoir of De Banke's South African experiences, which also examines closely her stage career and teaching experiences, see **286** *Bright Weft: An Autobiography Covering the Period 1915–1929* (1958). In **287** *American Plaid* (1961), De Banke vividly portrays vignettes of American life. As an irreverent Englishwoman, she observes and appraises the socioeconomic factors that influence American living conditions and beliefs.

288 De BUNSEN, MARY. c.1910–s.l.1954. *Mount Up with Wings.* Hutchinson, 1960. 224 pp.; preface; illus.; index. BLC to 1975 78:501.

Born in Madrid, Spain. Father: the Rt. Hon. Sir Maurice de Bunsen, Bart., G.C.M.G., G.C.V.O., C.B., British ambassador to Spain. Mother not named. 3 sisters. Single. Aviator; secretary; journalist; physically handicapped woman. Upper class.

Origins and unfolding of a woman aviator's career, from her physically impaired childhood through her adult reclamation of health, 1910–54. Being born the fourth daughter in the family; suffering from a congenital heart defect; father's being disappointed she was not a son. During father's Viennese ambassadorship, author's being stricken with polio, age 4. Undergoing four operations for polio; wearing a surgical boot throughout childhood. Attending a day school, age 11, which gave her advanced intellectual preparation for boarding school. Mother's disliking brainy people and preferring charming ones; father's frowning on intellect in women. Attending a boarding school with the same upper-class standards as boys' public schools, stressing athletics and good marriages rather than good education. Acknowledging women's financial need for prudent marriages, but remarking "with a lame leg and horn-rimmed spectacles, I stood no chance whatever." Her two oldest sisters' marrying well; author's favorite brother-in-law's encouraging her interest in aviation. Author's sampling different vocations: taking courses at Royal Academy of Dramatic Art, auditioning successfully for the London Bach Choir, learning to fly at age 20. Making her first solo flight, 1930. Asserting flying to be safer and more suitable for young ladies than horseback riding; flying enthusiastically for 17 years despite her borderline medical status. Taking secretarial courses, age 21, in order to work as a secretary at Heston Airport, 1931–36; handling the airport's public relations and writing its newsletter. Being poorly paid; being deferential to male pilots, lest her piloting accomplishments damage their male egos. Only feeling comfortable discussing flying with male pilots more accomplished than herself. Traveling to Germany, 1935 and 1939, to earn gliding certificate. On her 1939 trip, discussing uneasy European political situation with young German flying students; leaving Germany just three weeks before outbreak of WWII. During the early war years, driving for both the London Auxiliary Fire Service and Ambulance Service. Flying in the Air Transport Auxiliary, 1941, and serving as ferry pilot; discussing the war death of pilot Amy Johnson and the wartime public prejudice against women pilots. Asserting that Englishwomen feel less emancipated than women of other nationalities; stating that despite having accumulated considerable savings, only when her health failed, c.1947, did her new status as invalid make her feel free to travel. Buying a yacht and sailing to China, 1952; making later voyages to Australia and South Africa. Undergoing major cardiac surgery in America, 1954, to repair her congenital heart defect.

As a young woman of uncommon intellect but unprepossessing physical appearance, De Bunsen was totally unsuited to the traditional gender expectations that her well-heeled family imposed upon her. Further handicapped by physical weakness from a malformed cardiac valve, De Bunsen faced double hurdles in life: her choice of an aviation career and the later cardiac surgery to give her access to normal health. It was the latter that inspired her to review her life and career as a woman in a male-dominated society and profession. Bracketing this autobiography at the beginning with her birth defect, and at its conclusion with that defect's successful surgical repair, De Bunsen conceptually ties her physical handicap to the social one she successfully overcame as a woman pilot in a hitherto male domain.

289 DEICHMANN, Hilda Elizabeth, Baroness (née Von Bunsen). 1848–d.a.1925. *Impressions and Memories by the Baroness Deichmann.* John Murray, 1926. 302 pp.; foreword; illus.; index. NUC pre56 137:150.

Born at the Prussian Legation, London. Father: Ernest Bunsen, Prussian Army cadet. Mother: Elizabeth Gurney. 3 brothers; 1 sister. Married 1873, Hugo von Krause, d.1874. Married 1877, Adolf Wilhelm Deichmann, d.1907. Widow. 1 son; 2 daughters. Wrote *Notes on St. John and the Revelations, Carmen Silva,* and *Hereafter* (1901). Knew Queen Elizabeth of Romania, Lady Troubridge, the Quaker families Fox and Gurney, Dean Liddell of Christ Church College, Oxford, and his daughter Alice. Spiritualist; religious/spiritual writer. Aristocracy.

Multicultural upbringing, education, and close German aristocratic ties of an upper-class Victorian woman, 1849–1925. Recounting her family's English and German origins. Family's moving to Regents Park in author's infancy. Having an extensive array of tutors and governesses. Her father's believing in evolution; mother's disagreeing, reading Bible daily to her children. Attending the Anglican church despite mother's Quaker beliefs. Family's spending summers in Switzerland, winters in Germany. At author's age 10, family's visiting Cannes to see author's grandfather, Baron Bunsen; recounting grandfather's career in the diplomatic corps at Rome. Author's being frustrated in her desire to attend college, unheard-of for girls at that time. Making extensive visits to Europe, age 17, with family members. Giving histories of both her German grandparents and her Quaker English grandparents, the Gurneys. Recalling a brief stay with a maiden aunt, Sarah Gurney; receiving Quaker instruction from her and being obliged to keep a spiritual diary. Discussing her mother's aunt, social reformer Elizabeth Fry (née Gurney), and her work to improve prisons. Making her debut at English Court, 1872. Marrying a German suitor, 1873; their buying a house in Kensington. Husband's dying in a riding accident just three weeks after her son's birth, 1874. Author's moving to Germany and living on husband's ancestral estate to raise her son. Marrying Baron Deichmann, 1877, after three years of widowhood. His being a horse-fancier and holding Conservative political opinions; his preventing them from acquiring an automobile long after cars became available. Death of her second husband, 1907. In 1911, buying and moving into her childhood home at Regents Park; regretting that her parents' deaths in 1903 made it impossible for them to return to their beloved home. Suffering torn loyalties in WWI, with three of her children married to natives of Germany. Discussing further German marriages in the family: her daughter's wedding in 1919, her son Wilhelm's marriage to Princess Lieven in 1921. Wilhelm's acquiring a stepdaughter who did farmwork with local peasants as part of her agricultural studies; author's being perturbed at first by this mingling of social classes, but coming to accept it as a "modern" idea. Author's believing in spiritualism and studying Theosophy; writing books on Christian and spiritualist themes. Living with her sister in Chelsea at the time of writing these memoirs, 1925.

Much like a private version of the British royal family, Deichmann's family was an intricate network of intermarried German and English citizens, whose loyalties to country and to family became deeply conflicted by WWI. The baroness's memoir is reflective both of upper-class lifestyles and of the transitional period between what she calls "Victorian" and "modern" ideas. She locates her own attitudes about class and women's roles within the Victorian code, yet expresses admiration for women who step outside these expectations.

290 De LARA, Adelina (stage name; née Tilbury; a.k.a. Adelina Preston). 1872–d.a.1954. *Finale.* Written in collaboration with Clare H-Abrahall. Burke, 1955. 222 pp.; foreword by Myra Hess; front. port.; illus.; list of recordings by author. NUC pre56 137:450.

Born at Carlisle, Cumberland. Father: George Matthew Tilbury, engraver, illuminator. Mother: Anna de Lara, of Spanish-Jewish background. 2 half-brothers; 2 half-sisters. Married 1896, Thomas Kingston, actor, d.1911. Widow. 2 sons. Musician (pianist); composer. Middle class.

Upbringing and career experiences of a noted pianist, including author's association with the Schumann-Brahms circle in Germany, 1870s–1954. Author's exotic foreign ancestry. Being the only child of a second marriage for both mother and father; having several half-siblings. Author's musical father's having fallen in love with her mother's fine singing voice. Family's being poor but highly musical. Author's never entering school; receiving lessons from parents in reading, drawing, Italian, and piano. Family's moving to Staffordshire, author's age 6; author's giving her first public concerts at that time. Taking mother's maiden name as stage name. Traveling all over England as a child prodigy pianist; giving recitals at the Liverpool waxworks for £4 a week; at age 9, being her family's main financial support. Suffering catastrophe of her parents' deaths and suicide of her half-sister Helen, 1883, when author was only 11. Living and making concert tours with her remaining half-sister, Penelope. Their being adopted by their maternal aunt. Because of her talent and loss of her parents, author's winning the interest of pianist Fanny Davies, who prepared author to audition for Clara Schumann. Winning a musical scholarship; studying with Clara Schumann in Frankfurt; also taking lessons from Schumann's friend Johannes Brahms; learning from Brahms how to play his original compositions. Describing Brahms's esteem for Clara Schumann, as well as Clara Schumann's character and technique for playing the works of her husband, Robert Schumann. Discussing her acquaintance with Antonin Dvorák and Edvard Grieg. Author's listing her own musical compositions, including orchestral works. Returning to London, 1891; making her concert debut. Receiving many romantic offers through her public career; eventually marrying actor Thomas Kingston, 1896, although fearing that he would insist she abandon her career. Having two sons in quick succession; continuing her career with husband's approval; converting to Catholicism "in gratitude for his goodness to me." Marital strains arising from husband's touring Australia without her, from her own infatuation with a ship's officer, and from a strange hermaphrodite houseguest who declared his love for the author. Separating from her husband. Discussing her friendships with composer Ethel Smyth and pianist Myra Hess. Retiring from concerts, 1951, and being awarded an O.B.E. Giving her farewell concert at London Musical Club, of which she was president, 1954.

Career and personal life are evenly balanced in De Lara's memoirs, although it is interesting that, despite the help she received from other professional women to make possible her own career, she is silent on the subject of women's status either on stage or in society. As with other women in the performing arts during the 19th century, De Lara had professional opportunities not available to women in more mundane fields.

291 De MORGAN, Sophia (née Frend). 1809–1892. *Three Score Years and Ten: Reminiscences of the Late Sophia Elizabeth De Morgan.* Richard Bentley & Son, 1895. Ed. by Mary A. De Morgan (author's daughter). 259 pp.; front. port.; intro.; index. BLC to 1975 80:216.

Born in London. Father: William Frend, Church of England clergyman, scholar, insurance actuary. Mother: Sarah Blackburne. 1 sister. Married 1837, Augustus De Morgan, professor, died c.1873. Widow. 7 children. Social reformer; educator; suffragist; antivivisectionist; animal welfare activist; clergyman's daughter. Middle class.

Formative childhood influences and life dedicated to public service of an ardent Victorian reformer; discussing many aspects of social injustice needing correction, 1809–86. Being born at the Rock Insurance company office where her father was an actuary. His religious history; as an earnest social reformer, father's establishing friendships with John Quincy Adams, Thomas Malthus, Charles Lamb. Family's living in Blackfriars, outside London. Father's abandoning Church of England to explore unconventional religious beliefs; author's describing the resulting home atmosphere of both Eastern and Western spiritual speculation. When young, author's doing volunteer work in invalid asylum for young women; discussing the history of lunatic asylums and treatment, c.1792–1820s. Through her father, author's meeting Quaker scientist and reformer William Allen and attending his chemistry lectures at Guy's Hospital. Discussing her father's philosophical correspondence with London University math professor Augustus De Morgan, 1835–36, leading to author's marriage to De Morgan. Discussing the first working-class cooperatives, which enabled laborers to profit directly from sale of their products. Noting that most social and political reformers rejected religious dogma; author's adopting personal Unitarian beliefs. Being introduced to women's rights issues and socialism through a speech by Scottish-American Frances Wright; becoming interested in communism and the writings of Robert Owen. Marrying De Morgan, 1837. Noting the need to improve the treatment of criminals and the prison system; praising the work of Elizabeth Fry. Strongly endorsing higher education for women; helping establish the Bedford College for Women, 1849. Joining the suffrage movement; persuading husband to give lectures at Bedford College in support of suffrage. Participating in the workhouse reform movement. Discussing the abolition movement in the U.S. and her meeting with Harriet Beecher Stowe, who had just published *Uncle Tom's Cabin,* 1852. Noting her friendship with Thomas Carlyle. Death of her husband, 1873. Expounding the principles of antivivisection; working in the antivivisection movement under Lord Shaftesbury's leadership. Dedicating herself to usefulness as long as she might live.

Recounting the many rich friendships and working relationships that the author and her father established with key social reformers of the 19th century, De Morgan's memoir aids in documenting their work, their collaboration, and their ongoing thinking. De Morgan's use of autobiography to affirm her ethical beliefs is an excellent example of the 19th-century spiritual autobiographies that were rooted not in religion but in the creed of social usefulness.

292 DENT, Olive. c.1891–?. *A V.A.D. in France.* Grant Richards, 1917. 349 pp.; illus. NUC pre56 139:477.

Born in England. Parents not named. Single. Nurse (WWI). Middle class.

Cheerful presentation of WWI volunteer nursing activities, emphasizing the domestic details of hospital work, covering 1914–17. Recalling shock of hearing England had declared war, 1914; author's resolving to help soldiers by nursing; already having a college nursing degree and ambulance experience. Joining Voluntary Aid Detachment; describing activities in English hospitals. Being sent to the French battlefront, 1915. With 100 VAD nurses, traveling to field hospital in Boulogne. Describing the tent hospital, her duties there, and daily improvisations due to lack of equipment. Receiving and caring for convoys of new cases. Keeping soldiers cheerful; comforting the dying. Describing nursing conditions during winter blizzards; focusing on routine and camaraderie with other nurses to keep going. Describing how nurses kept house and cooked in their personal quarters. Explaining procedures for sending soldiers on home leave; explaining duties of troop-train nurses. Increasingly appreciating the soldiers' good humor; recounting their troop slang and anglicized French. Thanking her Red Cross volunteer readers in England for their knitting and needlework for soldiers; exhorting them to keep up the war effort. Emotionally describing funeral of a fellow VAD Recounting heroism of ordinary soldiers in WWI; claiming a place for them in history. Providing samples of their correspondence and that of the nurses. Recalling surge in numbers of incoming wounded during a major offensive, July 1916. Being granted two weeks' home leave, November 1916. Being on night duty during a major freeze, winter 1917; describing her routine and the dying soldiers. Depicting the hospital kitchen and its limited menus. Recounting conversations between nurses on the purifying, ennobling aspects of war. Soldiers' rejoicing at being sent home when her camp hospital was evacuated to let the arriving American forces take control of it.

Published in 1917 during a troublesome period in Britain's war morale, Dent's memoir conveys an optimistic tone throughout. It was clearly published to reassure English audiences of the homey atmosphere in hospital camps and of the soldiers' continued courage. When Dent does discuss suffering and death, she puts them in a heroic, ennobling context that omits the appalling particulars of wounds and disease. Such is not the case in the memoir of VAD nurse Lesley Smith, whose *Four Years Out of Life* (1931) confronts the atrocities rather than concealing them, offering the realistic viewpoint necessary to counter the propagandistic optimism of Dent's version.

293 DESMOND, Florence (stage name; née Dawson). 1905–1993. *Florence Desmond by Herself.* George Harrap, 1953. 303 pp.; preface; photos; index. NUC pre56 140:510.

Born in Islington, Greater London. Father not named, bootmaker. Mother not named. 1 brother. Married 1935, Tom Campbell Black, pilot, d.1936. Married 1937, Charles Hughesdon, pilot. 1 adopted son.

Knew pilot Beryl Markham. Actress (child, comic, film, music hall, stage); dancer. Lower middle class.

London childhood, early stage training, transatlantic career, and marital details of a gifted actress of stage and screen, c.1910–46. Her childhood confidante's being "Nannie" (Ann Ware, family's live-in cook). Being inspired by frequent theatre attendance in childhood to go on stage. Taking dancing lessons and piano lessons, age 9; beginning regular stage roles, age 10; deciding on her stage name. At age 13, attending Dame Alice Owen's school in Islington but receiving a sketchy education there. Acting in pantomime, variety acts, and comedy reviews; being coached in voice and singing for three years by Euphan McLaren, in return for a percentage of her earnings. Father's death from brain tumor, author's age 19. Assuming responsibilities of supporting family; selling her father's shop; sending her brother to boarding school; embarking on her London career with a chorus part in a West End theatre. Winning lucky break, 1925, when producer C. B. Cochran gave her starring roles in his musical stage productions. Recounting her many musical roles, as well as the stage tour of New York with Noel Coward that made her famous, 1928, when she substituted for the ailing Beatrice Lillie. In New York during Prohibition, working in nightclubs and speakeasies. Winning a film contract; listing her numerous film roles, 1930s; her film career's being interrupted when movie producer Archie Selwyn sued her for breach of contract. Meeting private pilot Tom Black, who fell in love with author's comedy impersonation of female WWI pilot Amy Johnson. Their courtship's receiving widespread media attention. After their marriage, 1935, author's having premonition of disaster, fulfilled by Tom's death in an airplane accident, September 1936. Returning to London. Marrying another pilot, 1937; his worrying that if European war broke out he would be conscripted by the R.A.F.; his persuading her to leave London and move to Paris. Author's suffering miscarriage, 1939; afterward becoming obsessed with desire for a child; adopting a 7-month-old boy despite husband's displeasure. Having another miscarriage. Their moving to a farm in Essex, 1940. Author's periodically touring to entertain WWII troups, 1941–44; discussing her technique for doing impersonations. Discussing the death of "Nannie," her sole link with her childhood. Author and husband's moving permanently to a farm in Dunsborough, 1946.

Desmond states in her preface that she was moved to write a retrospective of her life by the death of "Nannie," to whom she had remained close. Desmond's memoir surveys both the London and New York acting venues during the 1920s and 1930s, and provides a glimpse of the fevered pace of film productions during Hollywood's early decades. Because Desmond's two marriages to pilots introduced her to the field of early aviation, her book is also informative on various personalities in early aviation circles.

294 DeSTEIGER, Isabelle. 1836–1927. *Memorabilia: Reminiscences of a Woman Artist and Writer.* Rider & Co., 1927. 310 pp.; front. port.; preface by Arthur Edward Waite; illus. NUC pre56 566:447.

Born in Liverpool. Father: Joshua Lace, solicitor, law firm partner. Mother: née Cameron. 7 siblings. Married Rudolf Adolf von Steiger von Riggesberg, merchant. Widow. Wrote *On a Gold Basis, Super Humanity;* translator, ed. of *The Cloud upon the Sanctuary.* Artist (painter); religious/spiritual writer; journalist; Theosophist; spiritualist; antivivisectionist; translator; society woman. Upper middle class.

Childhood interests, artistic education, and independent creative life of an unconventionally minded artist, emphasizing her experiences in both artistic and spiritualist circles, 1830s–1927. Family history. Acquiring an early interest in art and music. Being religiously inclined in childhood. Discussing her school attendance; noting that managing a school was the only form of self support available for "redundant" women. Her independent destiny's being determined by the deaths of her mother and father in close succession. Studying at the Art Academy, c.1850; blaming the growth of evangelicalism for the mid-19th-century decline in art and literature; noting her own lack of enthusiasm for Christianity and her esteem for the doctrine of reincarnation. Briefly discussing her social debut and marriage. Developing her oil-painting techniques by copying masterworks; being particularly influenced by Edward Alma Tadema. Discussing the moral and religious hypocrisy of mid-Victorian society; believing (c.1925) that occultism would be the next spiritual belief to dominate Western civilization. Feeling strangely free after the death of her husband, c.1870. Studying at the Slade School of Art in London; living in Chelsea; becoming friends with Oscar Wilde and his mother, the Irish poet Speranza Wilde. Noting her growing political commitment; endorsing higher education for women; ironically contrasting the living conditions of rich and poor, c.1870; joining philanthropic committees. Holding a one-woman exhibition of her paintings. Comparing cultural concerns in 1870s London to those of the 1920s; remarking that religious skepticism dominates all 20th-century activities, including art. Becoming involved in spiritualist investigations. Memories of Madame Blavatsky and Annie Besant. Undergoing a past-life regression under hypnosis. Studying Theosophy and Buddhism. Contributing articles to the Theosophist journal, *The Light.* Disliking women socialists for their materialism; wanting to find the common ground between Christianity and Eastern religion. Discussing developments in her painting style. Working for Lord Shaftesbury's movement to outlaw vivisection, 1874–76. Discussing the 1880s Theosophists and their gradual alteration of the society. Discussing her cessation of painting in later life due to its physical demands, and her avoidance of a second marriage; reconciling herself to spending her last years "far from art and human affection." Viewing the soulless state of the cynical modern world as a "debacle"; stressing the necessity of spiritual studies to the human spirit.

Although born the year before Queen Victoria came to the throne, DeSteiger enjoyed an unusually liberated life, which she owed to a combination of factors: childhood freedom from religious indoctrination, freedom from parental control after her parents' early deaths, and freedom to follow her intellectual inclinations due to her inheritance. Her account helps illuminate interactions between aesthetic and social concerns in late-19th-century Britain, offering both eyewitness testimony and a 20th-century retrospective on many contemporary movements, including spiritualism, socialism, antivivisection, and the crusade for women's higher education.

295 De VALOIS, Ninette (née Edris Stannus). 1898–s.l.1956. *Come Dance with Me: A Memoir, 1898–1956.* Hamish Hamilton, 1957. 234 pp.; photos; index. BLC to 1975 81:519.

Born in Baltiboys, County Wicklow, Ireland. Father: Captain Stannus, army officer. Mother not named. 1 sister; 2 brothers. Married 1935, husband not named. Knew economist John Maynard Keynes, Russian ballerina Lydia Lopokova, W. B. Yeats. Dancer; teacher (dance); theatrical producer. Middle class.

Ballerina's childhood and upbringing, followed by detailed account of her career as a performer, teacher, and producer, 1898–1956. Seeing celebrations of her younger brother's birth as first-born son; wishing to be special also. Wishing she had her elder sister's beauty. Having a governess at home because she was too shy to attend school; her gentle, understanding father's giving her encouragement. Finding her talent by attending dancing class, age 11. Studying dance at the Lila Field Academy; touring as a dancer in her early teens. Teaching dance to children during WWI. Learning of father's war death, 1917. Spending most of her income taking dance training with Italian choreographer Enrico Ceccheti. Winning her first role at the Covent Garden Opera House, 1919, with the visiting Russian Ballet. Discussing London's wild enthusiasm for the Russian Ballet and her roles with the company. Also dancing roles in music halls. Founding Roland Gardens, a private ballet school, in Kensington, 1926. Being invited to choreograph at the Festival Theatre in Cambridge; also teaching at the Old Vic with Madame Lillian Baylis; becoming a regular Sadler Wells staff member. Producing dance works at Dublin's Abbey Theatre; discussing her association with W. B. Yeats. Marrying, 1935. Touring with Sadler's Wells Theatre Ballet, 1940; witnessing bombardment of Holland while on tour. Making tours of Eastern and Western Europe and America after WWII. Visiting the Metropolitan Opera Ballet in New York; summing up her impressions of the U.S. Visiting the Moscow Ballet, 1956.

De Valois's focused account of her life in the world of dance charts ballet's dynamic growth as a performing art in early-20th-century Britain. While other memorialists, notably artist Charles Ricketts in his *Self-Portrait* (1939), have recorded the sensational impact on London audiences of the visiting Russian Ballet and its breathtaking choreography and virtuosity, De Valois shows this excitement from a performer's-eye view. Her memoir is invaluable in contextualizing the establishment of dance in Britain's pantheon of national arts.

296 DEVENISH, Dorothy. 1912–?. *A Wiltshire Home, a Study of Little Durnford.* B. Batsford, Ltd., 1948. 115 pp.; intro. by Edith Olivier; illus. NUC pre56 141:591.

Raised on her grandfather's estate, Little Durnford, Wiltshire. Parents not named. Married, husband not named. Farmer. Rural gentry.

Topical vignettes of English country life and the author's youthful participation in it, emphasizing relationships and obligations between the various social classes, from 1912 to WWII, with glances at postwar years. Brief family history: forbears' livelihood as farmers; grandfather's increasing affluence; his buying the manor house at Little Durnford, Wiltshire, where author's father, maiden aunt Alice, and later the author grew up. Remembering her grandfather as a distant figure, preoccupied with banking matters. Aunt Alice's being a "Lady Bountiful" to the village people, unlike author's stern and managerial mother, who left villagers alone unless they pleaded for her aid. Parents' running the manor in an easygoing way. Briefly depicting her family members. Describing the servants, their personalities and status with respect to each other. Depicting the relations between her privileged family and village people who performed services for them: author's nanny, gardeners and gamekeeper, parson, and family butler, from whom author learned much about people and social relationships. Remembering the environment and activities of country life: the architecture, furnishings, and extensive gardens of the manor house, its working farms, and local hunting. Author's explaining social class distinctions: upper-class attitudes and responsibilities toward servants and village dependents, the need for a charitable upper class before the institution of government public aid, and the servants' proprietary attitude toward "their" employers, expecting them to behave as befits the gentry. Different classes' consequently being prevented from mingling at social functions.

In this meticulous picture of rural living in the years between the two world wars, Devenish shows how people of various classes implicitly understood and respected the complexities of rural social structure which contributed to their mutual well-being. Her book conveys the reassuring sense of place and identity that was imparted to her by growing up in the country, as well as her symbolic, even spiritual, connection to all who work the land for their livelihood. Devenish's intended audience is evidently the members of the "New Order" generations arising after WWII, who lacked awareness and appreciation of the fading way of life that had preceded their own. The volume's photographs successfully assist the reader in visualizing the scenes of the day.

297 DICKENS, Mary (Mamie). 1838–1896. *My Father as I Recall Him.* New York: Haskell House, 1974. 128 pp.; front. port.; illus. NUC pre56 143:62.

Born in England. Father: Charles Dickens, novelist. Mother: Catherine Hogarth. 9 siblings. Single. Novelist's daughter. Upper middle class.

Family biography by the daughter of novelist Charles Dickens, from her 1840s childhood at the height of his renown to 1870. Charles Dickens's reverence for his home and home life. Father's taking author and her brother Plorn seabathing at Broadstairs during summers. After Plorn emigrated to Australia, father's using tearful memories of parting with him to feel pathos while writing Paul Dombey's death in *Dombey and Son*. Discussing her sister Katie and mother's young sister Georgina, who lived with them. Father's being unfailingly patient with his children, and extremely punctual and tidy in his work habits. His helping in the sick room during the final illness of author's aunt, Mary Hogarth, and sobbing at her death. Author's describing family homes, first at Devonshire Terrace and later at Gad's Hill; sharing the former's nursery with her sister. Father's giving memorable parties at Gad's Hill; author's remembering their one-of-a-kind celebrations at Christmas and Twelfth Night. While convalescing from a fever in her father's study, author's observing him making facial contortions in the mirror as an aid to creating his characters; remembering his periods of feverish writing and his genius at inventing characters. His sorrowing over the death of fellow novelist W. M. Thackeray, 1863. Father's loving sports and animals; his providing the family with many pet dogs and birds. Recalling his legendary reading tour of America, 1867–68; discussing the deleterious health effects of his overwork and twelve years of public readings (1858–70). Family's moving to London, 1870, where he gave his last readings; author's observing his unusual weariness. His dying from a sudden stroke while working on another novel, 1870. Excerpts from tributes to him by his friends. Remembering his burial in Westminster Abbey.

Not an autobiography in the usual sense, Dickens's book remembers her great novelist father from a daughter's perspective as a private rather than a public figure. Extensively quoted in other biographies of the novelist, this account, while evocative of Charles Dickens as the quintessential Victorian family man, is lovingly protective rather than objective, omitting many controversial events in her father's life. For instance, although she discusses the family turmoil over her father's railway accident in 1865, she fails to mention that rescuers found him to be traveling with his young mistress, actress Ellen Tiernan, an incident that caused a flurry of scandal. Richly rewarding as a window on the private Charles Dickens, this account should be read alongside the recent biography by Peter Ackroyd, *Charles Dickens* (1993), which has been hailed as definitive.

298 DICKENS, Monica. 1915–1992. *One Pair of Feet.* New York, Harper & Bros., 1942. 310 pp. BLC to 1975 82:451.

Born in London. Father: Henry Charles Dickens, lawyer. Mother: Fanny Runge. Great-grandfather: novelist Charles Dickens. Siblings. Married Roy Stratton, naval officer, author. 2 daughters. Wrote *The Winds of Heaven* (1955), many others. Social issues writer; crime writer; journalist; nursing student; children's author; domestic servant. Middle class.

One woman's discoveries about both the possibilities and limitations of nursing as a female profession, from her experiences as a WWII nursing student, 1939–42. Jobs' opening to women with the advent of WWII. Becoming interested in nursing; enduring rigors of entrance interview for Redwood Nursing School at Queen Adelaide Hospital. Describing dormitory life, routine duties, and diet, as well as the nursing hierarchy there. Disparaging some of the nursing supervisors; discussing the friendships and animosities she made among fellow nursing students. Anecdotes of patients. Having trouble with her feet from long hours of hard work. Signing up for lectures designed to qualify nurses for state registration despite prevalent negative attitudes toward these lectures; many students' having failed the registration exam repeatedly. Some nurses' complaining regularly about their restricted life and lack of other career options. Author's being transferred to men's surgical ward, establishing bonds there with other students. Recalling their emergency nursing for victims of a factory explosion. Feeling imprisoned in the hospital; cherishing moments of escape. Describing hospital's preparations for Christmas; nurses' trying to humanize conditions for patients, while being governed by a harsh, dehumanizing bureaucracy. Single-handedly dealing with patients' crises during night duty. Overhearing denigrating comments about nurses while attending an officer's luncheon party; becoming defensive about her vocation; author's satisfaction being partially restored by helping to save a patient's life. Hospital's having an influx of VAD nurses during the early war years; nurses' welcoming their help, but sisters' belittling their inexperience. Enjoying assisting in surgery and working in the maternity ward. Many nurses' desiring to escape through marriage; marriages and resulting births rising dramatically during wartime. Describing nursing under wartime conditions of blackout, supply shortage, and bombardment. Preparing for preliminary nursing exam; describing the nerve-racking oral exam. Assessing fulfilling and tiresome aspects of nursing. Publishing an unflattering story about nursing life in the periodical *Hyacinth;* being warned by matron never to write about the subject again. Describing her feelings of anger at this censorship, and her strong desire to write a book. Giving matron notice of her resignation while still smarting from the authoritarian warning.

In her early writing years, Dickens made a career out of autobiography, publishing several volumes of her assorted experiences which had, in her own words, been "exaggerated a bit." In the volume preceding this one, **299** *One Pair of Hands* (1939), Dickens regales readers with an account of her twenty jobs—in two years—as a cook-general in affluent London households. In another book, *My Turn to Make the Tea* (1951), she recounts her experiences as a cub reporter for the *Hertfordshire Express.* For twenty years she also contributed a column to *Woman's Own.* After marriage to an American, she settled in the U.S. and began to write on sociological topics, notably child abuse. While her early books are useful in showing the galvanizing effects of the early 20th century on women's employment, Dickens reflects on the panorama of her upbringing and career in her 1978 autobiography, *An Open Book.* This retrospective exercise in memory vividly re-creates her growing childhood awareness that her family worshipped its progenitor, the novelist Charles Dickens. She contextualizes the development of her creativity within family circumstances, and also uses her own nanny-and-nursery upbringing to comment on 20th-century shifts in child-raising theory. As she traces the progress of her family and career beyond WWII, Dickens creates a study of one family's adaptations in moving from Victorian to modern cultural practices.

300 DIEHL, Alice Georgina (née Mangold). 1844–1912. *The True Story of My Life.* John Lane, 1908. 347 pp.; illus. NUC 143:366.

Born in Aveley, Essex. Father: Carl Mangold, musician, piano teacher. Mother: Eliza Vidal, music teacher. 1 brother; 2 sisters. Married Louis Diehl, violinist, composer. Several daughters; 2 sons. Wrote *The Story of Philosophy,* nearly 50 novels, including *Eve Lester, The Hollywood Mystery,* others. Musician (pianist, violinist); novelist; journalist; short storyist; teacher (music). Upper middle class.

Childhood, musical studies, and career permutations of a pianist, music teacher, and professional writer, 1844–69. Being born into a musical family. Being proud of her father's German heritage; music's being innate to Germans. In childhood, pitying the poverty of tenant farmers on her grandfather's estate. Teaching herself to read; writing her first poems. After father's financial reverses, mother's eking out family income by teaching music. Unexplained illness's permanently impairing health of author's sister; mother's fearing its hereditary nature. Author's showing same symptoms; parents' forbidding her to write in order to shield her health. Remembering a visit to her godmother as the turning point in her life; its disclosing music to her as her profession. Going to

Germany; studying music with the pianist Henselt; reestablishing links with her father's German relatives. Going on to Paris, 1861; studying piano there; meeting Chopin's pupils; giving her first piano concert. Author's rating performance in the 1860s as lacking creativity. Returning to England; making her English concert debut. Feeling drawn to violinist Louis Diehl at their first meeting; marrying him despite mother's anger. Health problems plaguing her: purulent tonsillitis, difficult childbirth, debilitation. Spending winter in Nice for her health; depicting balls and musical soirées there; meeting violinist Sivori, Paganini's only pupil. Health and monetary problems' contributing to episodes of strife with husband. Noting the beginnings of the Music College Movement; becoming a piano teacher at North London Collegiate School. Beginning to write short stories; publishing *The Story of Philosophy*. Ill health's forcing her to resign her teaching post; continuing to write articles for musical periodicals. Evaluating how to educate her children, visiting Newnham and Girton Colleges with her daughters in mind. One son's death, the other's emigration to America and eventual disappearance. Remarking on the dwindling supply of private music students because of the Music College Movement. Explaining her process for writing novels. Expressing her belief in the importance of facing life confidently.

Contemporary reviews of this, Diehl's second autobiography, found it almost too confiding, notably in her spare-no-details approach to depicting her marital tumult. For readers in the 1990s, however, the fact that Diehl was entranced by the lofty Continental musical circles in which she studied guarantees her account's value, as well as qualifying her to discuss mid-19th-century trends in musical education. Although in this memoir she comments merely that she found later success in writing professionally, in her earlier autobiography, **301** *Musical Memories* (1897), she notes that she left music as a profession to take up writing on the advice of *Times* music critic James W. Davison, who felt her greater talents lay in writing.

302 DIXON, Ella Hepworth (pseud. Margaret Wynman). 1857–1932. *"As I Knew Them": Sketches of People I Have Met on the Way.* Hutchinson, c.1930. 287 pp.; foreword; illus.; index. NUC pre56 145:104.

Born in London. Father: William Hepworth Dixon, journalist, editor of *The Athenaeum.* Mother: Marion MacMahon. 7 siblings. Single. Wrote novel *The Story of a Modern Woman* (1894), story collection *One Doubtful Hour,* play *The Toy-Shop of the Heart.* Knew Robert Browning, Alice Meynell, Henrik Ibsen, H. G. Wells, others. Novelist; journalist; short storyist; playwright; WWI volunteer; artist (painter); editor; feminist. Middle class.

Author's development as a writer and feminist, with portraits of artists, writers, and editors she knew, covering her childhood to c.1920. Family history. Her father's being a noted editor and historian, but his frowning on intellectual women; mother's being a suffragist who attended all of Ibsen's feminist plays. Parents' hosting a circle of artists and writers. Author's never having a woman teacher; father's deciding she should attend a school in Germany taught by a male professor, c.1870s. Family's living briefly in Regent's Park, and establishing friendship with the artistic De Morgan family. Father's death, 1879. Making her expected social debut. Beginning to write for publication, 1880s: contributing articles to newspapers and a short story to *Woman's World,* edited by Oscar Wilde. Beginning to paint portraits. Speaking out on women's suffrage; being labeled a "New Woman" by critic Edmund Gosse. Visiting New York in the 1890s and noting conditions for American women. In 1894, publishing a feminist novel, *The Story of a Modern Woman.* Being part of the Yellow Book circle of artists and writers, including Wilde, Aubrey Beardsley, and W. B. Yeats. Editing *The Englishwoman,* 1895–1900, a periodical that also served as a women's employment bureau. During WWI, being taken by her friend, Sir Claude Phillips, to study art collections in London and Florence; working as a portrait painter. Sewing shirts for the Red Cross as her part of the war effort. Continuing her freelance journalism, writing newspaper opinion pieces on social relations. Wryly evaluating the editors and the quality of various publications for which she wrote.

Although this "collection of portraits" focuses on other people, a portrait of the author also emerges. As a woman wed to a career rather than a husband, Dixon was, in the 1890s, part of a group of women beginning to be noticed by the media under the label "New Women." In her fiction and journalism, Dixon examines this identity—the negative impact of fin-de-siècle derision directed at the women's movement, and modernity's alterations of men's and women's expectations. Although she omits mention of it, Dixon also served in later life as vice president of the Femina Vie Heureuse and Northcliffe Prizes for Literature.

303 DOBRIN, Nancy (née Machin). 1914–s.l.1980. *Happiness: A Twinge of Conscience Is a Glimpse of God.* Regency Press, 1980. 175 pp.; cover port.; illus. BLC 1976–1982 13:35.

Raised in northeast England. Father not named, ship riveter. Mother not named. 2 brothers; 1 sister. Married c.1951, Paul Dobrin, Viennese Jewish refugee, died. Married c.1966, "Frank." 1 daughter; 1 son. Factory worker; physically handicapped woman; charitable volunteer. Working class.

Physically limited childhood, economic hardships, marriages, and personal losses of a working-class woman and mother, 1914–80. Being born with club feet; spending her first five years in hospital, having thirteen corrective surgeries. Being unable to walk until age 5; envying her healthy younger brother. Attending primary school and Sunday school; also being introduced to spiritualism by her mother. Father's being an epileptic and out of work; town's having no available jobs. Author's discussing tensions of Protestant-Catholic relations in the town, and the local Labour candidacy of Harold Macmillan, afterward Prime Minister. Remembering hearing Labour M.P. Ellen Wilkinson speak there. Leaving school, age 14, because family could not afford high school; doing housework for mother. At age 17, earning twopence a week caring for another family's children; lacking money to buy her necessary orthopaedic shoes. Traveling to London, age 22, to search for a job; finding work in a biscuit factory. Family's moving to London, 1936. Author's working in a laundry; being largely unaffected by WWII; returning to her hometown a few years later. Working a series of jobs: in a penicillin plant, as a bread cart driver, in a research laboratory, and in a knitwear factory. Suffering from asthma attacks and loneliness; feeling suicidal; escaping by reading at the public library and taking literature classes at the Worker's Education Society. Meeting a Viennese Jewish refugee there; marrying him, age 37. Giving birth, ages 38 and 39, to a daughter and son. Husband's death. Spending twelve years raising her children alone; breaking a marital engagement after discovering the man was married. Opening a café to earn money toward buying a house, but banks' refusing to grant mortgage to a widow. Increasing her income by renting flats to college students. At age 52, marrying Frank, former husband of a dead friend; sending her son to boarding school because Frank disliked children. Enjoying improved financial circumstances, but suffering problems with Frank's hypochondria and jealousy. Author's daughter's becoming rebellious: bringing men to her room, possibly taking drugs, writing suicidal plans in her diary. Daughter's committing suicide, age 19; author's afterward being moved to volunteer at the Good Samaritans' suicide prevention hotline. Assuaging her grief by turning again to spiritualism; being guided by friends in the knowledge of yoga, spirituality, and astrology.

Dobrin's book opens with her work at the suicide hotline and narrates her life as a flashback. She tells her readers that writing this memoir is her means of recovering from her daughter's suicide. Dobrin effectively makes her autobiography into an offering of understanding to her dead daughter, showing empathy with the girl's struggles in growing up through relating the story of her own hardships. This account also illustrates the depressed economic conditions that afflicted Britain's working class during the years between WWI and WWII, the influence of the Labour Party among workers, and the directions that Britain's spiritualist movement began taking after the 1970s.

304 DOYLE, Mary Aloysius (Sister). c.1821–d.a.1855. *Memories of the Crimea.* Burns & Oates, 1904. 96 pp.; preface by J. Fahey; app. NUC pre56 148:302.

Born in Ireland; resided in Carlow, Ireland. Parents not named. Single. Nun (Roman Catholic) in the Convent of Mercy; nurse (Crimean War); missionary (Turkey). Social class unspecified.

Animated memories of the author's Crimean War nursing experiences, emphasizing religious conflicts between Catholics and Protestants in the war zone, 1854–55. Being one of two nuns chosen for a two-year mission to the Crimea. Traveling with two other Sisters of Mercy from Ireland to Turkey; staying at convents in France en route. Hearing they were not wanted at Scutari, the site of Florence Nightingale's headquarters; taking refuge with French Sisters of Charity in Turkey until obtaining permission to enter Scutari; their eventual arrival in Scutari, 1854. Describing provisional wartime nursing techniques. Florence Nightingale's relying upon nuns' emergency nursing during cholera epidemic. Recounting deaths of two nuns. Receiving anonymous letters from Protestants objecting to Catholic nuns nursing soldiers. After nuns promised not to proselytize non-Catholic soldiers, appearance of ultra-Protestant pamphlets ridiculing the nuns for transferring allegiance from the pope to Nightingale. Nightingale's holding friendly conversations with the nuns, in which she made light of Catholic-Protestant conflict. Author's Crimean diary being eaten by rats at Balaklava. The nuns' making a return voyage to Ireland. Belatedly receiving the Royal Red Cross from Queen Victoria for her nursing work, 1897.

In this documentary narrative of her Crimean experiences, Doyle focuses on the collective efforts of the nuns rather than on herself. Because Florence Nightingale used a wide range of auxiliary nursing help, Doyle's experience as a religious sister differs significantly from that of nurses serving in other capacities. Accordingly, Doyle's account gains breadth from comparative reading with Protestant Alicia Blackwood's *A Narrative of Personal Experiences and Impressions During a Residence on the Bosphorus Throughout the Crimean War* (1881), and with informal volunteer Mary Seacole's *Wonderful Adventures of Mrs. Seacole in Many Lands* (1857). Doyle's appendix includes wartime correspondence between herself and other Sisters of Mercy.

305 DRACOTT, Alice Elizabeth. c.1890–d.a.1930. *The Voice of Mystic India.* Rider & Co., c.1930. 142 pp.; foreword; illus. NUC pre56 148:346.

Probably born in England. Parents not named. Siblings. Married, husband not named. 2 daughters. Wrote *Simla Village Tales.* Spiritualist; publisher; cultural historian; foreign resident (India); vegetarian. Upper middle class.

An Englishwoman's life and spiritual searches in India, reconciling Eastern and Western spiritual beliefs, covering author's first four decades. In childhood, interpreting dreams with her siblings. Deciding to write about her psychic experiences despite possibility readers will think her deranged. Living in Simla, India, during her father's lifetime. Since childhood, hearing voices that warn her of mishaps and dangers. Having a dream that accurately foresaw her father's death; managing his weekly newspaper in India after he died. Author and sister's witnessing their dead father watching them through a window. Moving to Benares. Beginning to attend Buddhist services; accommodating her acquired Hindu theology to her basic Christian beliefs, although retaining her Christian belief that wisdom must be acquired throughout a lifetime, not by sudden enlightenment. Discussing Madame Blavatsky's Theosophical text *The Secret Doctrine* and its congruence with Hinduism. Being influenced spiritually by Indian surroundings. Mentioning that her friend, London newspaper publisher W. T. Stead, died in the 1912 *Titanic* disaster despite her inner voice's insisting he escaped; suspecting a few of her inner voice's messages to be wish fulfillment. Deaths of many loved ones in quick succession: her brother-in-law, sister, and mother; believing that death did not really change them. Explaining that just as Christ remained "master" after his death, all people in the next world maintain the character they had in this one. Asserting that keeping a vegetarian diet opened her up to psychic impressions. Believing that the West was just discovering psychic truths the East had always known; also believing that every individual's psychic flowering is realized through the thought of the Creator.

Dracott's matter-of-fact account does not present her psychic experiences as being out of the ordinary. Instead, these experiences serve to instigate her search for a reality not accounted for by the strict domain of Christian belief. Like Madeleine Slade, who converted to Buddhism in the service of Mohandas Gandhi, Dracott found necessary insights in Eastern religions. A comparative reading of Dracott's book together with Slade's autobiography, *The Spiritual Journey* (1960), offers a useful study of factors that increased Western receptivity to Eastern religious paradigms during the early 20th century.

306 DUBERLY, Frances Isabella (née Locke). 1829–1903. *Campaigning Experiences in Rajpootana and Central India, during the Suppression of the Mutiny* 1857–58. Smith, Elder, 1859. 254 pp.; preface; maps; app. NUC pre56 149:560.

No birthplace given; author was English. Parents not named. Married Henry Duberly, British military officer. Wrote *A Journal Kept during the Russian War.* Military spouse; colonialist (India); memsahib. Upper middle class.

Eyewitness account of frustrating regimental march in India pursuing sepoy rebels during the 1857 Mutiny, covering 1856–58. Traveling with her husband's regiment in the Crimea; returning briefly to England before departing with his regiment for Bombay, 1857. After arrival, husband's buying horses from "price-gouging" native dealers; author's training her own riding horse. Attending a native wedding; admiring the costumes but finding the music "disagreeable," the dancing "graceless." British authorities' executing two mutinous sepoys from the Native Infantry; noting British anxiety over being outnumbered by Native Infantry. Citing British distaste at being banqueted by local wealthy Parsees while native troups and populace were dying in the violence. At the banquet, author's assessing Anglo-Indian women as discourteous snobs. Quoting native refugees from the Lucknow uprising who called for vengeance against the sepoy rebels; praising British swiftness in seeking to punish the mutineers. Author's sailing with regiment to Mandavee; their beginning expedition inland from the bay of Cutch toward Gwalior, author's riding with husband. Visiting a ranee's court at Bhooj; praising her political knowledge. Regiment's marching to British station at Deesa, then crossing the mountains. Shifting their baggage to camels, discarding a portion to lighten their load. Author's observing wildlife and opium cultivation during the trek. Describing administration of lashes to "unwilling and loitering" native servants. Regiment's making night march to Boondee, then to besieged town of Kotah. Deploring military command's failure to order troops to crush retreating rebels at Kotah. Author's witnessing plundering of Kotah by "loyal" native troops and their consequent punishment by the British. Regiment's being ordered to march in pursuit of rebels. Their running low on provisions; marching in heat of 120 degrees Fahrenheit; feeling frustration at being always one step behind the fleeing rebels. Soldiers' dropping dead of heatstroke. Troops' preparing once more for siege, only to find city of Chandaree deserted; author's blaming native servants' acting as spies for giving rebels advance notice. Troops' battling some rebels in Antree Pass, then joining other British forces to recapture the fort at Gwalior; local Maharajah and Maharani's thanking British for rescue. Maharani's being curious about author as sole woman riding with fighting troops and summoning her to an interview; Maharajah's promising to give author, as well as male troops, decoration for valor. Regiment's being ordered to Sepree; marching during heavy rains, then being ordered back to Kotah. Their obeying series of conflicting marching orders from distant commanders; exhausted troops' failing to cut off rebels at flooded river. Recounting a rebel Rajah's atrocities, but implying he was provoked by the greed and duplicity of the East India Company. Regiment's routing the rebels at Dum-Dum in surprise attack. Author's decrying rebel atrocities there, but assuming care of some children left behind by the rebels; losing her confidence in the moral rightness of British military actions. Queen Victoria's promising amnesty to all rebels not guilty of cruelty; rebels' greeting this news with derision. British command's discovering that rebel strategy had been precisely to separate and exhaust British forces through fruitless pursuit. Author's breaking off her account, 1858, after spending a year on the march and covering more than 1,800 miles on horseback.

Duberly painstakingly documents a march hampered by bad weather, defective intelligence, conflicting orders, and an elusive enemy. Her early enthusiasm for British punishment of "loitering servants" and rebellious sepoys waned when she confronted the troublesome realities of colonial rule, including the sufferings of the Indian populace under British exploitation—conditions that provoked the violence of the mutiny. At the close of her account, Duberly writes, "It seems to me that all this Indian warfare is unsatisfactory work, and although it may be true that in this rebellion severity is mercy, yet there have been cases of ruthless slaughter [of natives] of which the less said, the better." As a woman's firsthand account of the Mutiny, Duberly's account merits comparison with *An Englishwoman in India: The Memoirs of Harriet Tytler 1828–1858* (1986), but Tytler was a noncombatant hostage, whereas Duberly witnessed events from the viewpoint of the fighting forces themselves.

307 DUDLEY, Mary (néc Stokes). 1750–1823. *The Life of Mary Dudley, Including an Account of Her Religious Engagements and Extracts from Her Letters, with an Appendix Containing Some Account of the Illness and Death of Her Daughter Hannah Dudley.* Philadelphia: Benjamin & Thomas Kite, 1825. Ed. by Elizabeth Dudley (author's daughter). 327 pp.; intro. by ed.; app. NUC pre56 150:333.

Born at Bristol. Father: Joseph Stokes. Mother: Mary. Married 1777, Robert Dudley, d.1807. Widow. 5 sons; 2 daughters; 3 stepsons. Wrote pamphlet *Extempore Discourse.* Knew John Wesley. Religionist (Methodist convert, Quaker convert); preacher. Middle class.

Author's conversion from Anglicanism to Methodism to Quakerism, and her subsequent journeys as an itinerant Quaker missionary, covering her childhood to 1822. Parents' belonging to the Church of England. Author's loving "vain amusements" although acquiring some sensible, serious-minded friends, ages 17–18. Author's being shocked out of her vanity, age 20, by her grandmother's death; becoming aware of life's brevity; undergoing conversion experience. Attending meetings of Methodists and other dissenting sects, looking for communion with God; joining Methodists shortly before discovering the Society of Friends. Adhering to Quaker principles; being ridiculed by friends for adopting plain dress. Extracts from her poems, ages 20–21. Turning down John Wesley's invitation to become a class leader because of her doubt over Methodist tenets. Formally joining the Quakers, 1773, after her father's death. Overcoming mother's disapproval of her Quakerism. Marrying, age 27, and moving to Clonmel, Ireland, 1777. Her vanity at being made overseer of Clonmel's Quaker meeting causing return of her worldly temptations; overcoming them through prayer. Beginning her Quaker ministry, age 36, preaching with a female colleague in Limerick. Their traveling and preaching together through Holland, Germany, and France, 1788; author's leaving behind her husband and seven children to serve the Lord. Preaching to Anabaptist and Moravian congregations in Europe. Extensive diary extracts of her missionary journeys through Ireland, 1788–92; the Channel Islands, northern England, and Scotland, 1792; England and Ireland, 1792–96. Continuing her missionary activities in England and Ireland, 1796–1807. Deaths of her husband and son, 1807. After death of her daughter Hannah, 1809, moving with remaining children to London. Undertaking further religious mission travel in England, 1809–22.

After its first seventy-five pages, the text consists entirely of letters and diary extracts strung together by the editor's biographical commentary. As a collage rather than a unified autobiography, this book lacks the retrospective viewpoint of a traditional conversion narrative, which makes meaning out of life experiences. Because of its richness as a day-to-day journal, however, Dudley's book has considerable value in documenting the 18th- and 19th-century growth of Quaker missionary activities.

308 DUFF-GORDON, Lucy Christiana, Lady (née Sutherland). c.1863–d.a.1932. *Discretions and Indiscretions.* Jarrolds, 1932. 288 pp.; front. port.; illus. NUC pre56 150:480.

Born in London. Father: Douglas Sutherland, engineer, distant relative of the duke of Sutherland. Mother: née Saunders. Stepfather: David Kennedy. 1 sister (novelist Elinor Glyn). Married c.1881, James Stuart Wallace; divorced. Married 1900, Sir Cosmo Duff-Gordon, 5th baronet, d.1931. Widow. 1 daughter. Knew Ellen Terry, Sarah Bernhardt, Gertrude Atherton, Margot Asquith, King Alphonso of Spain, Isadora Duncan. Costume designer; entrepreneur; fashion writer; businesswoman. Upper class.

Migratory childhood, marital adventures, and transatlantic career of a legendary fashion designer, with self-justifying account of her notorious escape from the sinking *Titanic,* c.1865–1932. Father's death at author's age 2; mother's taking author and younger sister to live on their maternal grandparents' ranch in Canada. Growing up a tomboy, but having traditional female education, including much sewing; loving to design and make dolls' clothes. Mother's remarrying a Scotsman; family's returning to Scotland. Their moving to Jersey in author's adolescence; author's recalling her younger self as "chic," a term she herself introduced into English usage. Attending the youthful Lillie Langtry's wedding on Jersey, 1881. Breaking three engagements before marrying an unsuitable man twenty years her senior, age 18; their moving to London. Finding herself pregnant; husband's running away with a pantomime dancer. Enduring the scandal of divorce. Becoming friends with actresses Ellen Terry and Sarah Bernhardt. Turning to dressmaking out of financial need; opening couturier shop, "Lucile"; designing her first theatre costumes. Moving her business to more prestigious quarters in Hanover Square; being successful because she approached dress design as a fine art. Marrying Sir Cosmo Duff-Gordon, her business partner and love of her life, 1900; contrasting romance in women's lives in 1900 vs. 1932; declaring herself one of the generation who fought for the modern girl's sexual and professional freedom. Being among the first women of her social class to run a business; enduring resulting loss of caste that barred her presentation at Court, despite her husband's baronetcy. Introducing many fashion innovations, including the modern brassiere, which replaced corsets; using runway models. Gossiping about society infidelities. Being acquainted with the Pankhursts, but dismissing the suffrage movement as "a huge joke." Being couturier to many aristocrats, 1907; her daughter's marrying a viscount the same year. Traveling to New York, 1909, to open a new branch of her shop, Lucile; noting rich Americans' predilection for expensive clothes. Introducing models to New York and doing fashion journalism; becoming the toast of New York. Traveling between her fashion houses in New York and London. Sailing with her husband on the *Titanic,* 1912; their deviously bribing to escape disaster in a lifeboat meant for forty-two people. Facing public fury because hundreds perished without a lifeboat; husband's never emotionally recovering from the scandal that dogged them. Opening a branch of Lucile in Paris, just before WWI. Florenz Ziegfeld's hiring her New York branch to costume his dancers; Mary Pickford's also being a client. Selling her U.S. branches—"one of the great mistakes of my life"—in 1920 because she perceived public apathy about fashion. Financial hardships' forcing her to sell Lucile; doing freelance fashion writing for London papers. Envying the unclouded success of her sister, Elinor Glyn, who worked as a Hollywood screenwriter for Clara Bow. Death of her beloved husband, 1931; attributing their happiness to her maintaining a career. Commenting on changes in society and fashion, c.1890–c.1932.

Whimsical when discussing her "indiscretions," Duff-Gordon waxes fervent in defending her late husband's role in the *Titanic* disaster. The couple earned unenviable fame for commandeering a lifeboat and six rowers for themselves and their servants, with Sir Cosmo slipping each crewman a £5 note, apparently for preferential rescue. For Duff-Gordon, the resulting notoriety effectively blighted what had been a golden career. Her many connections among the international social elite, theatre notables, and Hollywood personalities during the early years of the film industry make her book a fund of useful detail on these circles.

309 DUGDALE, Blanche E. C. (née Balfour). 1880–d.a.1940. *Family Homespun.* John Murray, 1940. 196 pp.; front. port.; illus.; index. NUC pre56 150:594.

Born in Scotland. Father: Eustace Balfour, architect. Mother: Lady Frances Campbell. 2 brothers; 2 sisters. Maternal grandfather: George Campbell, 8th Duke of Argyll. Married 1912, Edgar Dugdale, J.P., Captain of Leicestershire Yeomanry. 1 son; 1 daughter. Wrote *The Life of Arthur James Balfour.* Biographer. Upper class.

Memories of childhood and young adulthood in a family of privilege and power, accompanied by characterizations of illustrious individual family members, from the 1880s to c.1900. Family's spending Christmases at grandfather's ducal estate, Inveraray Castle; noting Campbell family's Church of Scotland affiliation and passion for ecclesiastical matters. Describing Campbell aunts and uncles; one aunt's being Queen Victoria's daughter Princess Louise, who had married author's eldest Campbell uncle in 1871. Discussing distinguished naval career of her favorite uncle George. Growing up at Whittingehame, the Balfour family estate in East Lothian, Scotland. Childhood memories of her uncle Arthur Balfour, noted politician, diplomat, scholar, and first earl; receiving early schooling in politics by discussing the Irish question with him. Memories of Balfour relatives and of visiting another uncle, the marquis of Salisbury, at his London residence, Hatfield; commenting on Hatfield's historical significance. Describing London life, 1880s–1890s. Being invited to Kensington Palace by her aunt Louise; giving her childhood impressions of visiting with Queen Victoria, 1887. Being presented at Court, 1898. Commenting on the power and influence large families like hers wield in shaping individual members. In London, making her first friend outside the family, Olive McLeod; their becoming friends for life. Making the acquaintance of noted Greek translator S. H. Butcher; visiting him in Edinburgh and in Killarney; being enchanted with Ireland and sad to leave. Seeing the first motorcars at Whittingehame, c.1900, as a sign of the advent of the future.

Dugdale's memoir is that of an ordinary woman surrounded by relatives who possess an extraordinary breadth of intelligence, accomplishment, and power; these relatives collectively controlled the course of British politics. Prominent among them is the uncle whose biography she wrote, Arthur James Balfour, who had a Litt. D. from Cambridge and honorary doctorates from nearly every British university. At various times, as Dugdale recounts, he was Disraeli's secret agent in Germany, leader of the House of Commons, lord of the Treasury, a League of Nations representative, and chancellor of Cambridge University. Although writing in the late 1930s, Dugdale ends her account with the close of the 19th century and Queen Victoria's death, as if her ties to her distinguished family had lent her youth a lustre she is moved to preserve.

310 Du MAURIER, Angela. 1904–?. *It's Only the Sister.* Peter Davies, 1951. 265 pp.; front. port.; illus. NUC pre56 151:393.

Born in London. Father: Sir Gerald du Maurier, actor, stage manager. Mother: Muriel Beaumont. Grandfather: George du Maurier, novelist. 2 sisters (including novelist Daphne Du Maurier Browning). Single. Knew Gladys Cooper, Sir Herbert and Viola Tree, George Alexander, John Barrymore, Sir Laurence Olivier. Wrote novels *Reveille, Lawrence Vane, The Perplexed Heart,* others. Novelist; charitable volunteer; WWII volunteer; animal welfare activist; actress (stage). Upper middle class.

Memories of a typical childhood and adolescence in an untypically talented family, as well as author's widely assorted vocations and pursuits in adulthood, c.1910–50. Never having felt jealous at being called either the daughter of Sir Gerald or the sister of Daphne du Maurier; having been just as spoiled and loved by her parents as was Daphne. Discussing father's background and acting career, as well as mother's bit parts. Growing up surrounded by theatre folk, including actress Gladys Cooper and actors George Alexander and Beerbohm Tree. Being sent to day school; narrowly escaping expulsion for telling other girls where babies come from; sexual ignorance for girls being compulsory in her childhood. Outbreak of WWI: father's training for the Brigade of Guards; 10-year-old author's being terrified of air raids. Melodramatically contemplating suicide, age 14, over her unrequited crush on a WWI soldier. Attending finishing school and music school in Paris; asserting that boarding schools' reputation for harboring lesbian relationships is false, with intense female friendships being simple hero worship. At age 19, most boarding school girls' viewing marriage as their immediate goal. Attending school in Wimbledon; loving tennis and grand opera. Discussing her active adolescent social life and her parents' waiting up nights for her. Praising her father's role as friend and teacher; reading plays for him and helping him practice roles. Playing Wendy in *Peter Pan* on London stage to a poor critical reception; discussing her lack of discipline as an actress. Discussing youthful traumas, including being jilted by a visiting Japanese prince and struggling with a tendency to overspend. Becoming honorary RSPCA secretary for the Actors Orphanage Committee, 1927. Volunteering for office work during the 1929 general election; suffering spinal damage in an auto accident the same year. Marriage of her sister Daphne, 1932; commenting on Daphne's career as novelist; being mistaken for her. Working as a VAD in children's clinics, c.1933. Discussing family changes caused by the death of her father, 1934. Author's first book's being published in 1939, at outbreak of WWII. Excerpts from her correspondence with Daphne during the war.

Joining WWII home guard, 1943. Discussing modest progress in her writing career. After the war, becoming a welfare worker for the Women's Land Army.

Quite an independent spirit in her own right, the author renders a vivid picture of what it was like to grow up a du Maurier. She pays tribute to the positive and nurturing factors of her family environment, frequently backtracking in her chronology to associate elements in her adult character with anecdotes from earlier life. The eclectic variety of paid and volunteer positions in which the author worked also provides a glimpse of Britain's social needs from the 1920s through the 1940s. Letters from her sister Daphne and from her actor father are interspersed throughout the text.

311 Du MAURIER, Dame Daphne. 1907–1989. *Growing Pains: The Shaping of a Writer.* Victor Gollancz, 1977. 173 pp.; front. port.; author's note; illus. NUC 1973–1977 31:550.

Born in Regent's Park, London. Father: Sir Gerald du Maurier, actor, stage manager. Mother: Muriel Beaumont, actress. Grandfather: George du Maurier, novelist. 2 sisters. Married 1932, Frederick Arthur Montague "Tommy" Browning, Grenadier Guard, d.1965. 1 son; 2 daughters. Wrote *Rebecca* (1938), *My Cousin Rachel* (1951), others. Knew Sir James Barrie, Sir Arthur Quiller-Couch. Novelist; biographer; playwright; short storyist. Upper middle class.

Inception and growth of the author's identity as an imaginative novelist, from childhood through early adulthood, c.1910–32. Recalling infancy in the household nursery with her sisters and nanny; being taken to visit London sites. Writing her first book, age 4; always wanting the books she read to continue past the last page; playing "continuing games" about books with her sisters. Identifying with books' male heroes and playing male roles in games; believing her childhood identification with men led to her writing novels with male narrators. Being closer to her actor father than to her more conventional mother; also identifying with her 19th-century novelist grandfather (whom she never met), author of *Trilby.* Attending day school with her older sister for one year. Being stunned at her first menstruation, since her mother had withheld information and deflected her curious questions. Discussing her intense and reclusive adolescent reading; envying her sister Angela's popularity. Starting a platonic love affair with her older, married first cousin Geoffrey. Katherine Mansfield's becoming her literary ideal. Attending finishing school in Paris, age 18. Her imagination's being stimulated by a family holiday to the Lake District. Being expected to debut socially and marry well; wanting instead to be independent; beginning to write seriously, age 20. Family's having made its first visit to Cornwall, 1926; author's wanting to live there. Parents' purchasing a summer cottage in

Fowey, Cornwall; author's successfully pleading to live there alone. Writing short stories in London and Cornwall. Depicting Cornish customs and history; sailing near its coast. Becoming friends with the nearby family of novelist Arthur Quiller-Couch. Family's endeavoring to end the romance between author and Geoffrey. Remembering her first sight of the abandoned Menabilly estate in Cornwall, the inspiration for Manderley in *Rebecca.* Publishing her first stories in 1929. Having series of romances on European holidays. Writing her first novel, *The Loving Spirit,* based on Cornish history. Continuing with a second novel. Her future husband's reading *The Loving Spirit* and being curious about its author; his arranging a romantic meeting with her. Their marrying speedily; author's viewing marriage as an exploration of what it means to love.

Each of the seemingly insignificant memories and incidents that comprise du Maurier's narrative takes on greater meaning as she traces how her literary imagination developed. Based on her 1920–32 diaries, her introspective narrative repeatedly glances backward in her experiences to find the origins for later developments in her fiction. Her later autobiographical book of essays, **312** *The Rebecca Notebook and Other Memories* (1981), re-creates her childhood impressions of her father as well as documenting the background and creation of her most famous novel, *Rebecca.*

313 DYKE, Millicent Zoe Hart, Lady (née Bond). c.1900–1975. *So Spins the Silkworm.* Rockliff, 1949. 165 pp.; front. port.; illus.; app.; index. BLC to 1975 90:360.

Raised in Dorsetshire. Father: Mayston Bond, physician. Mother not named. 1 brother; 2 sisters. Married 1922, Sir Oliver Hart Dyke, baronet; divorced 1944. 2 sons; 1 daughter. Farmer; businesswoman; entrepreneur; broadcaster; clerk; physician's daughter. Upper class.

Professional and personal memories of a sericulturist, accompanied by detailed history of silk industry, spanning the first half of the 20th century. Becoming interested as a child in how silkworms were raised. Attending St. Paul's day school in London; taking lessons from its resident musician, composer Gustav Holst. Attending boarding school in France; teachers' humorously encouraging her silkworm hobby. Returning to England after onset of WWI. Working briefly as a clerk for an insurance firm, 1914. Marrying a baronet, age 22. At age 34, visiting Milan to study its silk cultivation and industry. Beginning to raise silkworms at husband's estate at Lullingstone Castle, Kent. Advertising in newspapers and periodicals, seeking public help in finding a source of mulberry leaves to feed to the worms. Turning her silk farm into a viable business; describing hiring silk spinners and buying looms and other machinery. Selling her first silk fabric. Preparing for an official visit from Queen Mary to author's farm. Noting the media attention that her silkworm-raising had brought; responding in print to frequently asked media questions. Being appointed by King George and Queen Mary to weave the silk for their coronation robes, 1937. Exhibiting her wares at fairs throughout Scotland and England. Lecturing and making radio and television broadcasts on sericulture. WWII: troops' being stationed on her farm grounds; war's adversely affecting her business. Traveling to Cyprus to study its silk industry, 1945. Forming her own private company. Noting the varied success of British government's efforts to encourage the silk industry. Providing a detailed picture of all aspects of silk cultivation and history.

Lady Hart Dyke traces her progress and innovations in the silk industry with the focus of a true enthusiast. Her memoir demonstrates both her knowledge of the field and her business acumen, and shows how effectively she developed her childhood hobby into a lucrative and thriving vocation. The author's experience with patronage from the king and queen is characteristic of the manner in which the royal family does business with merchants who provide everything from wine to wool socks, and her book provides an interesting picture of this particularly British custom.

314 EASTON, Dorothy (née Messiter). 1889–?. *You Asked Me Why.* Selwyn & Blount, 1936. 285 pp. NUC pre56 154:336.

Born in England. Father: surname Messiter. Mother not named. 1 sister. Married Jonathan Easton. 1 son. Wrote *The Golden Bird and Other Sketches* (1920), *Tantalus* (1923), *Bid Time Return* (1934), gardening book *Gay Gardening* (1932). Novelist; farmer; businesswoman; horticulture writer; short storyist; gardener. Middle class.

Personal and occupational reminiscences of urban writer turned farmer, covering her young adulthood. Being a solitary child; her family's thinking her "odd." Meeting her future husband; exchanging books with him. Finding that her perception of human unworthiness shaded her opinions. Reading, gardening, playing the piano. Going to London. Her mother's unconventionality and Tory politics; her ambivalence toward author's writing career. Her parents and friends' objecting to author's romantic liaison with Jonathan, who had few financial prospects. Author's secretly marrying Jonathan. Her first unsuccessful housekeeping attempts; trying to manage on a budget. Making peace between her parents and her husband. Taking a vacation in Sussex. Commenting on simultaneously glamorous and oppressive aspects of London. Moving to the country; noting energizing nature of work there. Learning to grow plants. Going to London to await birth of her child. Describing her difficult labor. Adjusting to taking care of her son. Building a house with a gift from her godfather. Growing flowers for sale at Covent Garden, London; experiencing fluctuations in flower prices. Endless hard work's taking its toll on the romantic side of her marriage. Her feelings of having lost herself amid mundane duties. Keeping a diary. Finishing her second novel. Growing fruit for sale. Learning secret of endurance from working as a grower. Becoming convinced that women's hard farm work should be recognized and applauded.

Easton's novelistic third-person memoir arose in response to her young son's questions about his parents' history, and celebrates the dedication they demonstrated in making a success of living off the land. Although many urban Britons ventured into farming by emigrating to agricultural parts of the Empire, such as Canada or New Zealand, Easton is one of a significant group of women in the early 20th century who participated in a reverse migration from the city to the country within England, seeking to reestablish the symbiosis with nature that had been declining since the industrial revolution. Several noteworthy memoirs were produced within this group that make useful reading alongside Easton's, among them Margaret Mary Leigh's *Highland Homespun* and Justine Spencer-Knott's *Fools Rush In*.

315 EATON, Flora, Lady (née McCrea). 1881–1970. *Memory's Wall: The Autobiography of Flora McCrea Eaton.* Toronto: Clarke, Irwin, 1956. 214 pp.; front. port.; foreword by the Rt. Hon. Arthur Meighen; illus.; index. NUC 1953–1957 7:116.

Born in Omemee, Ontario, Canada. Father: John McCrea, cabinetmaker. Mother: Jane McNeilly, member of Ladies' Aid and Women's Missionary Society. 7 siblings. Married 1901, Sir John Craig Eaton, department store owner, d.1922. Widow. 4 sons; 1 daughter; 1 adopted daughter. Businesswoman; entrepreneur; philanthropist. Lower middle class; married into upper middle class (Canadian).

Author's transition from modest family circumstances to wealth through marrying into one of Canada's richest families and later becoming vice president of its retail empire, c.1881–1955. Her parents' emigration from Northern Ireland to Canada. Author's happy, close childhood home. Mother's dividing household tasks among the children. Father's furniture workshop. Describing her siblings' characters; parental discipline. Description of Omemee and winter leisure amusements. Learning about retail business from her storekeeper uncles. Fire's destroying the family's house. Attending school; recalling difficulty of having her elder sister as her teacher. Author's caring for sick relatives during diphtheria epidemic in her last year of high school. Training as a nurse in a Toronto hospital; meeting her future husband, a patient there; speculating about what attracted a wealthy young man to an unsophisticated country girl. Analyzing their successful marriage. Adjusting to having servants and living a life of luxury. Describing Toronto social life and its seasonal entertainments. Son's birth, 1903. Husband's acquiring a private railway car and yacht. Learning retail business from her father-in-law; explaining importance to frontier settlers of his mail-order division; opening of Winnipeg branch store and future expansion throughout Canada. Author's taking singing lessons, giving private concerts for friends. Husband's inheriting presidency of Eaton's. In 1907, visiting London; encountering superior attitude of English "society" toward wealthy colonials like herself; visiting Paris and Ireland. Second son's birth, 1909; moving to Ardwold, a spacious semi–country estate in Canada; social evenings there. Outbreak of WWI: Eaton Company's equipping the Eaton Machine Gun Battery. Author's receiving title of lady when husband was knighted for war service; doing volunteer work for the Patriotic Fund. Living in the wilderness for a month with a woman friend. Her daughter's birth. Husband's death upon returning from a family holiday in Switzerland, 1922. Her direct involvement with company management, expansion, labor relations; her experience as a director and company vice president. Traveling through Canada with her sons; their formal education in England. Going to Cannes for her health; adopting a daughter there. Buying a villa in Florence, Italy, for winter residence. Being presented at Court in London; later presenting her children there. Selling her country estate; managing Eaton Hall and adjoining farm. During WWII, author's bringing British children to live on the farm; her later turning the house over to the navy for use as a convalescent home. Describing her many philanthropic activities, charity volunteer service, honorary degrees; her support for the arts. Recalling Christmas celebrations at Eaton Hall. Deaths of her close friends and relatives.

Although Eaton's memoir is one of personal accomplishment, the reader can discern that without her husband's untimely death, the author's entrepreneurial talent and business acumen might never have emerged. Like many women pioneers in other specialties, such as medicine or aviation, Eaton had previous ties to men in her field—both her husband and her cabinetmaker father—who provided her with education, experience, and eventually with a crucial chance to show what she could do. Her rise as a woman entrepreneur was also significantly eased by her birth family's emigration to Canada, away from the relatively inflexible class barriers of the British Isles. Historians of entrepreneurship in North America will find a treasure trove in this book.

316 ECHLIN, Elizabeth Gladys. c.1901–?. *Keep Off—Death! Being the Chronicle of Elizabeth G. Echlin.* William Hodge, 1939. 336 pp.; poems. NUC pre56 155:31.

Born near London. Father not named, businessman. Mother not named. 2 brothers; 1 sister. Single. Wrote *The Thief and Other Poems* (1923), *From Nietzsche down to Hitler;* translated *La Vie de Clemenceau.* Poet; translator; civil servant; clerk; tutor; foreign resident (Italy); physically handicapped woman. Lower middle class.

Introspective and associative memoir of a writer, centered around the impact of chronic tuberculosis on her life, 1905–39. Recounting family history. Contracting tuberculosis at age 4; beginning an ongoing series of sanitorium confinements; defining her life in terms of a battle against her disease. After father's loss of income, her mother's taking in boarders to support the family. Author's remembering the strength of her family's love for her. Tubercular relapses' constantly interrupting the progress of her childhood education; compensating by teaching herself French and Italian. From ages 9–11, living in Florence, Italy, for its warm climate. Yearning to live a normal life. In adolescence, finding her first job as a clerk in London. Receiving a marriage proposal, but deciding to remain single. Finding new work with the Labour Exchange; tutoring pupils in French and Italian. Her poems' being published in *Country Life*. Wanting to be self-supporting through her writing; working on novels; later destroying at least one of them. Having a tubercular relapse following her mother's death, walking as a recuperative exercise, avoiding doctors as much as possible. Making a firm commitment, despite her illness, to retaining independence.

Echlin made something of a career out of her moody and self-reflective autobiographies, of which three appeared in short order. Although this first one ends before the outbreak of WWII, her second volume, **317** *Live Unafraid* (1944), gains increased contemporary focus from its dramatic backdrop of London during the WWII German bombing campaign, and consistently juxtaposes the London populace's struggles with air raids to the author's own battles with the ravages of her body. In her final autobiographical volume, **318** *Vertigo: A Further Chronicle* (1946), the background of wartime London retreats behind her retrospective meditations on important friendships, lessons learned during medical confinements, and the implied analogy between her current vertigo and the social dislocation suffered by Londoners under the German bombardment.

319 EDWARDS, Kate Mary. (née Papworth) and William Henry Edwards. c.1880–d.a.1965. *Fenland Chronicle: Recollections of William Henry and Kate Mary Edwards.* Ed. by Sybil Marshall (author's daughter). 280 pp.; foreword by ed.; illus. by Ewart Oakeshott; "Dad's Book," pp. 3–157; "Mam's Book," pp. 161–280. Cambridge University Press, 1967. BLC to 1975 212:328. [cat. under Marshall, Sybil.]

Born near Lotting Fen, Norfolk. Father: John Papworth, higgler (trader and barterer). Mother: Mary. 1 brother; 1 sister. Married c.1902, William Henry Edwards, farmer, drainage officer. 1 son; 2 daughters. Farmer; paid companion. Rural laboring class.

Nostalgic reminiscences of the life of a fen woman from childhood to middle age, as edited by her daughter. Her christening the day of

Queen Victoria's Jubilee, 1887. Nursery and children's play rhymes; schoolyard games that led to youthful romances. Encounters with her future husband, ten years her senior; thinking him "very nearly a god." Remembering local superstitions about how children were physically marked in the womb by their mothers' fears and unfulfilled cravings. Commenting on midwives and medical men. Difficulties of lives in the fens: too much water in winter, not enough in summer. Her parents' fierce quarrels; her mother's nearly leaving the family when author was very small. Mother's publicly whipping a man who falsely claimed to be having an affair with her. Beginning to attend school, age 4; difficulties of reaching the school three miles away; a teacher's forcing author to do chores for her every day rather than attend lessons. Many accidental drownings of neighborhood children in the waterways and dipping holes. Recalling special fen and traditional holiday celebrations. Attending Ramsey fair each summer. Commenting on the responsibilities of fen wives: washing, cleaning, cooking, sewing, raising large families. Mother's protecting author from going into domestic service until age 16, when the family desperately needed money; at 18, author's working as a companion to a wealthy older woman. Commenting that many local girls entered service at age 11 and were treated as "little slaves" by their employers. Courtship with William; marriage to him at age 22. Child-rearing. Local belief in omens. Discussing mourning and burial customs in the fens. Her husband's generosity with neighbors; his work on the family farm; his mean-spirited mother's taking advantage of him. Memories of her mother; mother's terminal illness. Difficulties of farming and getting products to market; decline of their business; author's and husband's illnesses. Leaving the fens after WWII.

Life in the fens (wetlands that have to be drained for farming) offers particular difficulties for those, like William Henry and Kate Mary Edwards, who cultivate crops. Sybil Marshall collected her parents' recollections of fen life and divided them into two sections; the section by her mother is annotated here. The contributions of both narrators re-create the simplicity of rural life in late Victorian England, its drawbacks as well as its advantages. Combined, these dialect-filled narrations provide an unadorned view of a people, locality, and way of life often passed over by social historians and novelists. For another rendition of life in the fens of Norfolk, readers may consult the account of Mrs. Burrows, "A Childhood in the Fens About 1850–1860," pp. 109–114 in *Life as We Have Known It: By Co-operative Working Women.*

ELLERMAN, Annie (see BRYHER).

320 ELLIOT, Mary Caroline, Countess of Minto (née Grey; dame of justice of the Order of St. John of Jerusalem). 1867–1937. "Mary, Countess of Minto, C.I.," pp. 215–258 in *Myself When Young: By Famous Women of Today.* Ed. by Margot Asquith. Frederick Muller,

1938. 422 pp.; port. BLC to 1975 12:477. (1st pub. Thornton Butterworth, 1925.)

Born at Windsor Castle, Berkshire. Father: General the Hon. Charles Grey, private secretary to Prince Albert and later to Queen Victoria. Mother: née Farquhar. 3 sisters; 1 brother. Married 1883, Gilbert John Elliot, Viscount Melgund, later 4th earl of Minto and governor-general of Canada. 2 sons; 3 daughters. Philanthropist; politician's spouse; foreign resident (Canada); lady-in-waiting. Aristocracy.

Childhood and youth at Windsor Castle, marriage, and philanthropic service as wife of Canada's governor-general, 1870s–1930s. Living at Windsor Castle to age 11. Excerpts from father's letters on political issues. Father's death, 1870. Author's taking lessons in a schoolroom that had been a 16th-century prison. Disliking starched petticoats; wishing she were a boy; playing boys' games when allowed. Excerpts from her grandparents' letters; influence of her grandfather, Lord Grey, on the 1832 Reform Bill. Living with her mother at St. James Palace; studying with a German governess; taking dancing and singing classes. Social life and royal balls. Mother's permissiveness toward author's courtship. Author's marriage; living in Canada after marriage during husband's service as military secretary to Lord Lansdowne, 1883–85. Husband's refusing a great career opportunity to go to Egypt in order to stay with her; his serving as chief of staff under General Middleton in the Riel Rebellion, 1885. Birth of their first daughter. Their returning to England to live at Minto Castle, near Selkirk, Scotland; births of more children. Remarking on the bicycling craze; accompanying her husband on a bicycle tour of Switzerland and Italy, 1897. Returning to Canada upon husband's appointment as governor-general, 1898; inheriting the philanthropic role left her by Lady Aberdeen, wife of her husband's predecessor, benefiting Canadian women through work with nurses, hospitals, schools, and institutions. Meeting Theodore Roosevelt, then governor of New York. Husband's making popular decision to send Canadian troops to the Boer War. Traveling with husband and staff to the Yukon, 1900; finding corruption and misrule in Dawson; visiting a gold mine; visiting an Indian reservation. Her recreations: white-water rafting, camping, canoeing, skiing, sledding, skating. Raising money to establish small hospitals in Northwest Territories settlements. Brief mention of residence in India, 1905–11, while husband was viceroy; founding the Minto Nursing Association in India to provide nurses for Europeans of all classes. Author and husband's returning to England, 1911. Becoming vice president of the Territorial Army Nursing Service. Serving as lady-in-waiting to Queen Mary for twenty-six years.

Lady Minto's memoir charts the philanthropic role that the wife of one of Britain's senior government officials overseeing the Empire was expected to fill. Born into the Earl Grey family, which enjoyed a long-established position of service to the Crown, she cemented that role by marriage into another aristocratic family with a history of governmental service. It is of note that when her husband stepped down from the governor-generalship of Canada in 1904, her brother Henry George, 4th Earl Grey, assumed the office in his stead. Like Ishbel Gordon, Lady Aberdeen, who was her immediate predecessor as consort to the governor-general, Lady Minto performed duties as good-will ambassador in addition to her philanthropy. This book is a useful follow-up to Lady Aberdeen's own chronicle, *We Twa: Reminiscences of Lord and Lady Aberdeen;* together the two books span thirty years of Canadian history. For information about Lady Minto's life in India, readers may consult her book *India, Minto & Morley* (1934).

321 ELLIOTT, Grace Dalrymple, Lady. 1765–1823. *The Journal of My Life During the French Revolution.* The Rodale Press, 1955. 153 pp.; preface by anon. ed.; illus. NUC pre56 158:366. (1st pub. 1859.)

Born in Scotland. Father: Hew Dalrymple, barrister, attorney general to the Grenadas. Mother not named. 2 sisters; 1 brother. Married c.1780, Sir John Elliott; divorced. Liaison with Prince of Wales (later William IV). 1 daughter. Society woman; Loyalist (French Revolution); prison inmate; foreign resident (France). Upper class.

Testimony of a British aristocrat and confirmed royalist living in France to the atrocities of the mob during the early years of the French Revolution, 1789–c.1794. Outbreak of the Revolution; fighting and confusion in Paris; Paris mob's thrusting a severed head into author's carriage as she was driven through the streets. Describing contention between the duke of Orleans and the king; author's defending the duke. Expressing loathing for the Revolution and those who caused it. Noting fall of the Bastille and excesses of the Paris mob. Expressing affection for Queen Marie Antoinette. Traveling to Brussels, 1790, where political turmoil was also rife; discussing religious pretext for rioting and excesses in Brussels. Returning to Paris. Rendering her favorable opinion of Louis XVI. Royal family's attempting to escape, 1791, only to be returned to Paris in shackles. Describing attack on the Tuileries. Hiding Swiss soldiers in her house. Daringly helping Marquis De Chansenets to escape from Paris; proclaiming her steadfast royalist loyalties. Declaring her fury that the mob dared to bring the king to trial; recalling her despair when the duke of Orleans defected to the anti-royalist cause. King's execution's unleashing Reign of Terror, 1793. Author's being arrested as a conspirator. Describing degrading treatment of high-ranking women by officials. Her release and rearrest; interrogation by Comité de Salut Publique; release, re-arrest. Being sent to Recollects, where prisoners could eat only if they could pay for the putrid food available. Meeting Dr. Germ, an English fellow prisoner; noting his atheism and resulting despair in times of trial; by contrast, author's being sustained by religion. Revolutionaries' confiscating her money. Suffering with fever and a throat ailment. Prison warden's forcing author to take a glass of wine with an executioner. Extolling the bravery of the queen as she faced execution. Author's shock that the duke of Orleans was executed despite his support for the Revolution. Being removed to prison at Nantes. Remarking on executions of lower-class people who expressed displeasure with the new system. Forming friendships with prisoners of all social classes, including Madame Beauharnais, later Madame Bonaparte. Emotionally depicting the devastation caused to families by endless executions. Finally winning release after 18 months.

At the royal command of George III, Elliott produced her emotional memoir of the French Revolution for dissemination among Britain's upper circles. Presumably, it circulated privately for many years before its first imprint in 1859. Clearly intended as a horrifying depiction of the atrocities associated with revolution, it humanizes France's upper classes but leaves the lower ones as a faceless mob, with the exception of those who opposed the new regime and thus shared Elliott's sentiments and imprisonment. King George was still smarting from the loss of his American colonies by revolution when the French debacle took place, and the class overthrow in Paris was creating terrifying murmurs of unrest within England. Consequently, Elliott's experiences as revolutionary victim and her heartfelt royalism made her account ideal reading material, from the royal viewpoint, to caution the English against following a similar political path. After her release Elliott returned to England and in 1814 she renewed her liaison with the Prince of Wales, the father of her daughter.

322 ENGLAND, Daisy. 1910–s.l.1981. *Daisy Daisy.* Regency Press, 1981. 102 pp.; preface by John Burnett; illus. BLC 1976–1982 11:352.

Raised in London and in a remote Midlands village. Father not named, WWI soldier. Mother not named, domestic servant. 2 sisters. Domestic servant. Working class.

Memories of childhood poverty and rejection by both parents, set amidst details of rural working-class life in the Midlands, covering 1910–24. Being raised by her aunt in London, 1910–18, then returning to her mother's village, 1918. Sisters' scorn of her "inferior urban qualities." Mother's hope that postwar life would favor family happiness and understanding; this having prompted her to reunite the family. Describing the village. Attending school. Feeling homesick for London. Her growing awareness of rural attitudes and customs; lack of sanitation and health care. Father's return from WWI; his drinking himself into rages. Mother's favoritism toward author's elder sister. Contrasting her maternal grandparents, who provided author's family with food, and her paternal grandmother, a surly laundress. Implying that one sibling was not her father's child. Childhood games and amusements. Father's fitful work habits; family poverty; father's abandonment of family. Mother's rejecting author and younger sister; author's collecting charity for herself from local gentry; mother's departure for London, leaving author and younger sister to the workhouse, author's age 10. Living in the workhouse for six months. Attending Anglican school. Living with a foster family in Oxford. Enjoying Girl Guide activities. Being turned down for a scholarship because of her family situation. Visiting her mother; mother's bringing author and younger sister to live with her at her Wesleyan employer's home. At age 14, being removed from school by Poor Law Guardian and placed in domestic service. Her new house and mistress; earning £12 per year.

Although England spent her early childhood in London during the WWI bombardment, she has nothing to say about these traumas; the reader infers that they pale in comparison to family disruptions she faced from a combination of parental rejection, poverty, and the alcoholism endemic among the working classes. Although she does not address the issue directly, her parents' troubles were very likely exacerbated by the unemployment that faced workers when the war's boom economy subsided; in the industrial Midlands in particular, the factories that had made armaments went through an adverse period of readjustment. England draws contrasts between poor people's lives in rural areas before and after WWI, and comments favorably on improvements brought by the welfare state.

323 ESSEX, Rosamund. 1900–1985. *Woman in a Man's World.* Sheldon Press, 1977. 178 pp.; intro.; illus. NUC 1978 5:669.

Born in Bournemouth, Hampshire. Father: Herbert Essex, Church of England chaplain. Mother not named. 1 brother. Single. 1 adopted son. Wrote *Parish Practicalities,* children's book *Into the Forest,* and, with Sidney Dark, *The War Against God.* Religionist (Anglican); journalist; editor; religious/spiritual writer; children's author; preacher; secretary; clergyman's daughter. Middle class.

Author's upbringing, religious conversion mediated by her father, and subsequent life of innovative service to the Church of England, with observations on the interrelationship of religion, society, and politics, from c.1905–1977. Father's believing she had good character but no brains; his overall kindness. Author's learning classical languages; loving Greek plays and Latin poetry. Father's conversion experience at age 40; new importance of religion in the household; his becoming a chaplain. WWI: her brother's death. Attending St. Hilda's College, 1919. Studying political science. Discussing conventions circumscribing social lives of women. Experiencing doubts about God; gradually returning to faith. Training as a secretary in London. Working as a secretary for Viscountess

Rhondda. Helping to prepare articles for the periodical *Time and Tide.* Working with Society for the Propagation of the Gospel. Entering Franciscan Order as a postulant, but leaving the convent due to pettiness and intellectual tyranny of certain nuns and the mother superior. Continuing attendance at High Church. Writing for *Church Times;* memories of editor Sydney Dark. Encountering prejudice from some other journalists about her work in religious journalism. Writing about poverty and unemployment issues. Discussing distrust of the poor toward the established Church of England. Participating in a protest march about unemployment. Deciding to adopt a child, 1939; discussing single-parent adoptions. Collaborating on a book about atheism with Sydney Dark; discussing how her belief in God was reinforced through this work. Her promotion to assistant editor, then editor of *Church Times;* being the first woman to hold the top post. Wanting to change the paper's abrasive viewpoint. Receiving angry letters from readers, some of whom saw her as a Conservative, some as a Communist. Wishing to protect orthodoxy of the Church of England. Working with Hungarian and Greek refugees for Inter-Church Aid and Refugee Service, beginning in 1956. Resigning from *Church Times,* 1960. Continuing to work for Inter-Church Aid. On her travels, meeting protestors against totalitarian regimes; acclaiming their valor. Learning to preach; being the first woman to preach in Eton College chapel. Traveling in India for Christian Aid, 1970; discussing Indian customs and conditions. Contributing to *Church Times* as a freelance writer. Discussing difficulties in retaining religious faith in a modern and permissive world.

Essex's book incarnates the conversion narrative in modern form. While it testifies to her development of an articulate faith, it also documents the means by which she helped ensure the viability of the Church of England in its 20th-century transition from an older world of rigid social barriers and inequities to a modern one of multiculturalism, class mobility, and international calls on the church's aid. As well as telling her own story, Essex contextualizes the problems of an established church within the framework of its public image and social changes, not the least of which being new and vital roles for women.

324 EVANS, Dame Joan (D.B.E.). 1893–1977. *Prelude and Fugue: An Autobiography.* Museum Press, Ltd., 1964. 161 pp.; front. port.; preface; illus.; biblio. of author's publications. NUC 1967 16:507.

Born at Nash Mills, Hertfordshire. Father: Sir John Evans, paper mill manager, antiquarian, numismatist, amateur archaeologist, historian. Mother: Maria Millington Lathbury, academic. Several half-siblings, including archaeologist Sir Arthur Evans. Single. Wrote *Magical Jewels of the Middle Ages and Renaissance* (1922), *Life in Medieval France* (1925), *Time and Chance: The Story of Arthur Evans and his Forebears* (1943), others;

translated *Saint Joan of Orleans* (1926), others. Art historian; historian; biographer; translator; academic; antiquarian; academic's daughter; librarian. Upper middle class.

Victorian upbringing within a family devoted to archaeology, and the author's adult achievements as an antiquarian and historian, 1890s–1944. In childhood, reading about early-19th-century England; musing over its resistance to women's attending Oxford. Acquiring an early reverence for beautiful ornament. Loving dolls despite her parents' belief that children should be denied toys to make them face the real world. Memories of her father: his raising his first family after first wife's death; his work in geology and archaeology; his collections. Her mother's having studied at Oxford; her lecturing on Greek archaeology; her dismay at having children; her cool relationship with author. Warm memories of her nanny. Attending Watford school; learning catechism at home; studying heraldry with her father. Father's death, 1908. Writing a book about English jewelry, 1911–14. Visiting Italy; her growing interest in medieval art. Visiting Greece with her mother. Attending St. Hugh's College, Oxford, 1914; studying classical archaeology. Outbreak of WWI. Working as a librarian at St. Hugh's, 1916–22. Noting her half-brother Arthur's appointment as keeper of Ashmolean Museum. Researching history at the Bodleian Library. Serving as secretary of New Tory Association and the Arts Club. Receiving a traveling fellowship to Sweden, 1922. Conducting research in France and Italy. Publishing *Pattern, a Study of Ornament in Western Europe from 1180–1900* (1931) and *Monastic Life at Cluny, 910–1107*. Visiting Egypt and Greece, 1935. Death of her brother Arthur, who had become a noted archaeologist, in 1941. Researching her family history. Death of her mother, 1944. Discussing the growth of societies in which men and women enjoyed equality; how a person's values change with age.

Evans's record of her experiences at Oxford documents the character of women's education there during and after WWI; due to the large-scale absence of male students, women students actually enjoyed increased respect, which ameliorated what Virginia Woolf had termed the "prunes and custard" existence at women's colleges during the prewar years. This memoir situates Evans within a framework of her distinguished family's collective achievements in history and archaeology, and she focuses on these influences when recounting her early education, although her mother is characterized, perhaps unwittingly, in stereotypical terms as a woman whose intellectual interests supplanted rather than supplemented her womanly role as mother. As an adult, Evans remained distant from her mother, who evinced apathy toward her daughter's scholarship. Others recognized Evans's abilities, however; she was awarded the *Legion d'Honneur* and made a dame of the British Empire.

325 EVEREST, Elsie Eroica. c.1870–d.a.1922. *Finding a Soul: A Spiritual Autobiography.* Longmans, Green, 1922. 130 pp.; preface by the Rev. Vincent Scully, C.R.L., D.S.O. NUC pre56 164:196.

Raised in London. Father not named, geologist. Mother not named, invalid. 1 sister; 1 brother. Single. Religionist (Roman Catholic convert); secretary. Middle class.

Account of the author's conversion from atheism to Catholicism, which she claimed was due to Beethoven's music and a convent education, also involving difficulties with her atheist father, c.1870–1922. Being continually exposed to her father's devotion to Beethoven's music. Father's naming her for the Eroica Symphony; his teaching her music. Author's senses becoming encoded with Beethoven melodies. Father's training the children to defend their atheism; at age 5, author's pouring a bottle of ink over a Bible to obliterate its "lies." Author and siblings' preaching atheism at their kindergarten and forming their own atheistic society. Maternal grandmother's making the children pray with her when they visited; author's shocking her by running naked around her supper table. Maternal grandfather's death; children's pretending to be religious at funeral. Author's nearly drowning during a swimming lesson when her father refused to come to her aid because he wanted her to be as physically capable as her brother. Father's idiosyncratic ideas about diet and dress. Reading scientific books in his library; questioning a wholly mechanistic view of creation. Her inability to express her profound misery after mother's death. Deciding to commit suicide, age 12; chemist's refusing to sell her poison. Attending an Anglican boarding school, age 15; being pressed to make a profession of faith; deciding to try playing the role of a Christian. Attending every available Protestant church. Her amazement at father's deciding to send her to a convent school in Belgium for further musical education. Initially rejecting the school's Catholic customs; growing curious and then enthusiastic. Learning to play Beethoven's music correctly; discovering he was Catholic. Father's opposing her studying Catholicism. During holiday in England, age 18, experiencing spiritual conversion and being baptized without father's knowledge. Returning to school in Belgium; visiting an Adoration convent. Upon learning of her conversion, father's demanding that author return home; his disowning her and casting her out upon her return to London. Living in poverty while seeking work as a typist. Pawning her typewriter. Experiencing crippling illness and near-blindness from neglect of her health; recovery. Father's death; her regret that she was not present when he asked for her. Imagining his soul, after death, ascending stairs from Purgatory to Heaven.

Everest was one of many late-19th-century children who found that the new scientific paradigms of the world's origins were no satisfactory replacement for spiritual faith, and her case typifies the spiritual hunger experienced by educated people who sought a larger meaning in human existence than science could provide. Interestingly, Everest's account suggests that her father also needed religion, however much he repudiated it, for he turned science itself into a faith, in which Christianity became the dreaded heresy and his daughter the despised heretic. In discovering her fulfillment in a pious devotion generated by Beethoven's music, Everest demonstrates one way in which educated people overcame science's mid-19th-century challenge to Christianity by finding alternative personal sources of belief.

326 EVERETT, Katherine (née Herbert). 1872–d.a.1951. *Bricks and Flowers: Memoirs of Katherine Everett.* Constable, 1949. 252 pp.; front.; illus.; family genealogy. BLC to 1975 104:149.

Born in Killarney, Ireland. Father: surname Herbert, landlord. Mother not named. 1 brother; 1 sister. Married Herbert Everett, artist; separated 1914. 2 sons. Wrote *Walk with Me* (1951). House builder; artist; paid companion; WWI volunteer; feminist; traveler (Europe, Canada, U.S., Australia). Upper middle class.

Privileged youth, productive adult career, and socially conscious observations of an amateur artist and professional house designer, from 1880s through WWII. Being afraid of her mother, whose invalidism and morphine dependence terrorized the household. Author's devotion to her nursemaid. Lack of amenities, even for the rich, in Irish houses of author's youth. Her early love for art. Visiting her Aunt Aurelia in London; aunt's involvement in philanthropy: raising money for Soldiers' Homes and doing temperance work. Staying with Aurelia in Switzerland. Back in London, attending the South Kensington Art School and the Slade School of Fine Arts. Traveling with Aurelia in Canada and New York. Marrying; taking honeymoon cruise to Australia. Attempting to rescue Aurelia from a financial crisis. Author and husband's renting a house in Dorset; caring for their infant son. Needing to express her creativity; finding an outlet by building a house for her family near Broadstone. Beginning to design and build houses professionally. Separating from her husband, 1914. With onset of WWI, working as a VAD nurse; describing patients and her inability to become inured to their suffering. Working briefly as a gardener-companion, then moving to Dublin to live with a wealthy relative, Lady Ardilaun. Describing oppressive political occupation of Ireland after the 1916 Rebellion, with IRA terrorism and policing by the British Black and Tans. Recounting stories of Irish people's anger over continued suppression. Running errands all over Ireland for Lady Ardilaun; with the lady's death, moving to Cannes; disliking France; taking a house near Florence, Italy. Depicting Florentine servants, opera, and cuisine. Working as a nurse in an Italian hospital; distinguishing between English and Italian theories of medicine. During a tour of Annecy, France, with her son, feeling drawn to the locale; ultimately moving there to continue her work building and restoring houses. Loving gardening and its promotion of "unity with the earth." Recalling significant acquaintances dead and living: Oscar Wilde in his post-prison French exile, writer George Moore and his vanities, Emmeline Pankhurst and her suffrage obsessions, Beatrice Webb and her socialism. In WWII, barely escaping death in bombing; experiencing serenity in believing that death was at hand. Being weary of war. Feeling grateful for her love of beauty and optimism. Believing that all religious faiths are fundamentally one; looking forward with hope, if not certainty, to a life after death.

Because Everett's creative energies drew her away from her Anglo-Irish origins to art studies in England, her memoir provides two chronologically separate pictures of the Anglo-Irish existence: one from her 1880s girlhood and another from the years following the 1916 Catholic Rebellion. Through these cultural portraits she charts the declining security felt by British loyalists in Ireland and the effects of increasing Catholic resistance. Everett herself ultimately loosened her ties to Ireland, joining Continental circles. Like many memorialists of her generation, including Vera Brittain and Doris Dalglish, Everett charts the growth of an independent female career and spiritual individuation in the face of increasing political disillusionment following WWI.

327 EYLES, Margaret Leonora (née Pitcairn). 1889–1960. *The Ram Escapes: The Story of a Victorian Childhood.* Peter Nevill, 1953. 200 pp. NUC pre56 165:14.

Born at Tunstall, Staffordshire. Father: Sir A. Tennant Pitcairn, owner of pottery works. Mother not named. Stepmother: mother's sister. 1 sister; 1 brother. Married A. W. Eyles; divorced. Married 1928, David Leslie Murray, editor of *Times Literary Supplement.* 1 son; 2 daughters. Wrote *Hidden Lives* (1922), *Careers for Women* (1930), *Commonsense about Sex* (1933), *Death of a Dog* (1936), *Unmarried but Happy* (1947), others. Novelist; advice writer; women's issues author; crime writer; emigrant (Australia). Middle class.

Memories of a developing writer's subjugated childhood, and her determined escape to self-supported independence, 1889–c.1910. Growing up on a Sussex farm, 1889–98. Parents' incompatibility: father's being sensual while mother was sweetly ethereal. Being schooled at home by mother; later attending day school. Father's cruelty; his once hurling author across the room and breaking her arm; her forced servitude to him in later childhood; his continually worsening finances; his alcoholism. Author's seeing her sister as being more daring than herself. Religious atmosphere's pervading the family as a result of father's life-threatening heart disease. Attending secondary school and reading voraciously. Mother's death; author's grief and emotional breakdown. Father's marrying his deceased wife's sister; Church of England's consequently refusing communion to father and aunt/stepmother. Doing housework after mother's death; enjoying sewing. Aunt/stepmother's petty cruelty: her telling author her menstruation was caused by her bad character. Aunt/stepmother's surreptitious use of cosmetics. Author's giving charity to the poor before she herself became poor. Father's death. Leaving home to reside in rooms in London, 1902–05. Using bicycle as transportation in London; lacking decent clothes while job hunting. Author's being approached by procurers seeking virgins for a brothel; her innocence about sexuality. Finding a job in London answering direct mail. Emigrating to Australia to find work in her late teens. Mentioning writing books in her twenties. Briefly alluding to her fourteen years of marriage to Eyles, a drunkard.

Eyles's account stops short of her return to England and her later, satisfactory marriage to a literary reviewer. Her own published writings were both prolific and diverse, ranging from novels through crime mysteries to candid advice for other career women; all of her works nevertheless reflect her vivid memories of her traumatic upbringing and her earnest personal battle to secure dignity and independence as a woman. She openly attacks the cultural and sexual exploitation of women in her best-known books, including *The Woman in the Little House* (1922), *Careers for Women* (1930), and *Commonsense about Sex* (1933). Another autobiographical work by Eyles, *For My Enemy Daughter* (1941), is addressed to a daughter living in fascist Italy during WWII, and also resurrects her childhood traumas for personal reflection.

328 FAGAN, Elizabeth (née Kirby). c.1877–?. *From the Wings, by "the Stage Cat."* Collins, 1922. 239 pp.; front.; illus.; indices. NUC pre56 165:472.

Born in England, possibly near Birmingham, West Midlands. Parents not named. Married c.1900, husband not named. 1 son; 1 daughter. Knew Geneviève Ward, Mrs. Patrick Campbell, Herbert Beerbohm Tree, Christabel Pankhurst, Hubert Henry Davies, others. Actress (stage, music hall); suffragist; WWI volunteer. Middle class.

Lively discussion of the English theatrical landscape and its luminaries, highlighting author's personal and professional experiences, c.1895–1914. Mother's death and author's consequent need to earn her own living. Through a family friend, editor of the *Birmingham Post,* being introduced to actress Geneviève Ward; becoming Ward's pupil; their lifelong friendship. Ward's introducing her to manager George Alexander, actresses Madge Kendal and Ellen Terry. First taking a walk-on part. Being introduced to Frank Benson; acting in Benson's Shakespeare company; touring England and Ireland with company. Discussing actors, Benson's character, daily touring life, romances among the players. Leaving Benson's company; touring with another company. Acting in musical comedy under George Edwardes's management; her successful fight to be reinstated when Edwardes dismissed her for marrying, c.1900. Joining company of Mrs. Patrick Campbell; memories of Sir Herbert Beerbohm Tree, other actors and managers. Queen Victoria's death, 1901. Discussing state ceremonies, including Victoria's funeral, as staged events. Various acting engagements. Interruption of stage career by author's domestic life; traveling abroad. Resuming acting in comedy with Eva Moore. Discussing dangers of laughing inappropriately on stage. Meeting Yvette Guilbert; being introduced by her to suffrage movement through the Actresses' Franchise League. Attempting public speaking on behalf of suffrage; her acquaintance with Christabel Pankhurst. Rehearsing under playwright Granville-Barker. Her friendship with playwright Hubert Henry Davies. Anecdotes of Tree, George Bernard Shaw, and other theatre people. Evaluating amateur productions such as the 1912 Oberammergau Passion Play. Touring one year in U.S.; finding America hospitable, but money-mad and seemingly callous about human life. Performing in New York, Boston, Pittsburgh, and Chicago. Author's fear and objections to being waited on by blacks; relating anecdote of a black steward who chloroformed a white woman. Her WWI service on committee for a War Hospital. Making a visit to Annie Besant's Theosophical Society headquarters at Adyar, Madras, in India. Discussing irresistible attractions of matinée idols for young girls; how actors play love scenes. Temptations in stage life for young actresses. Author's dislike of theatre lifestyle for young men, whom she believes are more likely than girls to confuse simulated emotion with real feelings. Commenting on matinée idols' swollen egos.

One of many memoirs of the English fin de siècle stage, Fagan's book is a worthy record from a minor player of the doings of the major ones. Fagan also preserves an account of early-20th-century social factors that had a significant impact among British theatrical folk, including women's suffrage and the actors' exposure through touring to American racial issues. Whereas the remembrances of principal stars of the period tend to focus on their own careers, Fagan's account "from the wings" devotes relatively more space to a portrait of the theatrical milieu at large.

329 FAIRBROTHER, Sydney (pseud.; Emilie Tapping). 1872–1941. *Through an Old Stage Door.* Frederick Muller, Ltd., 1939. 256 pp.; front. port.; illus.; intro. by Stephen Gwynn; appreciation by Sydney Carroll; index; family tree. NUC pre56 165:642.

Born in London. Father: John Parselle, actor. Mother: Florence Cowell, actress. Stepfather: A. B. Tapping, actor. Married Percy Warr-Buckler, actor, d. at 23. Married Trevor Lowe, actor; divorced. 1 son. Knew George Bernard Shaw, Sir Henry Irving, John Gielgud, others. Actress (child, stage, film); businesswoman. Middle class.

The first five decades of a life on the stage, recalled by an international actress and daughter of a theatrical family, 1870s–1920s. Traveling with her actress mother; discussing her theatrical roles as a child under the stage name "Little Emile Ebsworth." Having little interest in school; often being truant. After mother's departing for India, author's age 8, attending a convent school in Blackpool; becoming interested in Catholic religious observances. Attending a boarding school in High Barnet; later attending a school in Germany. Going on mother's American tour; author's discussing her early stage performances with the Kendal company, 1890, and with her first touring company. Discussing her stepfather's theatrical company, Cartwright and Tapping, and plays they produced. Secretly marrying actor Percy Warr-Buckler. Living in theatrical boarding houses. Birth of her son. Illness and death of her husband; reminiscing on her former happy home life with him. Performing in *Star of India* and Barrie's *Little Minister;* commenting on character of audiences in 1890s. Touring in melodrama *Little Jim.* Touring U.S. in *Punchinello.* Discussing actors' living conditions in New York. Memories of Sir Herbert Beerbohm Tree. Traveling to Russia on a fact-finding mission for Mr. Barker, an American industrialist; her business dealings with Russian engineering executives; touring Russia. Marriage to Trevor Lowe. Outbreak of WWI; performing at Haymarket during air raids. Author's foray into motion pictures; working with London film company. Acting in silent films *The Mother* and *Confetti.* Memories of Henry Irving, George Bernard Shaw, Ellen Terry, John Gielgud. Commenting on music hall life; differences between modern and older plays; changes in melodrama.

Fairbrother concentrates on her own developing career in this account from the busy British theatrical milieu as it entered the 20th century. As a child born into a 19th-century stage family, Fairbrother's career mirrored the historical changes in the acting profession itself as she progressed from child actor to stage ingenue to star of the silent screen. Sparing of anecdotes about other stage personalities, Fairbrother confines her observations to a discussion of theatrical life in late Victorian and Edwardian times and the growth of the then-infant film industry.

330 FAITHFULL, Lillian M[ary]. 1865–1952. *In the House of My Pilgrimage.* Chatto & Windus, 1925. 287 pp.; front. port.; intro.; illus.; index. NUC 166:67.

Born in Hertfordshire. Father: Francis G. Faithfull, secretary in war office, Merchant Taylors' Company clerk. Mother not named. 5 sisters; 3 brothers. Single. Wrote *You and I* (1927). Teacher; school administrator; educator; academic; secretary. Middle class.

Personal memories and professional accomplishments of a well-known educational innovator, c.1870–1920. Her father's influence on her; his sense of humor. Mother's giving her religious instruction at home and devising novel aids to memorization. Taking classes at the Grange (boys' prep school) by special permission of her uncle, the headmaster; her later opposition to coeducation. Attending local University Extension lectures, 1880. Attending Somerville College, Oxford, 1883. Remembering 1880s Oxford notables. Seeing higher education as a deterrent to early marriage, because it offers women more alternatives. Taking a secretarial post. Teaching at Oxford High School. Describing high school's positive role in securing women's university education. Accepting a lectureship in English Literature at Holloway College. Becoming vice principal of King's College, London; experiencing economic deprivations. Remembering the decision to make King's College coeducational. Accepting post as Cheltenham College principal; enforcing strict but fair discipline. Discussing difficulties experienced by women seeking intellectual camaraderie with other women. Outbreak of WWI: training English girls in defense work at Cheltenham; receiving evacuated children; strength of women students throughout the war. Commenting on dramatic changes, 1870–1920, in arts, science, education. Noting generations' changing tastes in literature. Discussing differences between boys and girls in their ability to learn; teachers' need for self-discipline, good training, and native intuition; importance of avoiding talking down to young people. In retirement, finding her life empty; having trouble adjusting to being unneeded.

In keeping with her decisive approach to teaching, the opinions Faithfull expresses in her book are authoritarian; she calmly asserts the rightness of her own views about the type of teaching girls need and what motivates them academically. If her severe disciplinary measures (typified by her statement that she "disapproves of coddling") reflected her time, they were also intended to toughen women up to succeed in a male-dominated world. Although she makes few references to the women's movement, she uses her book to underscore the need for better women's education at both high school and university levels. In 1940, Faithfull published another autobiography, *The Evening Crowns the Day*.

331 FANE, Lady Augusta Fanny (née Cornwallis). 1858–1950. *Chit Chat, Book of Reminiscences*. Thornton Butterworth, 1926. 288 pp.; front. port.; foreword by Charles McNeill; illus.; index. NUC pre56 166:420.

Born in England. Father: John Edward Cornwallis, 2nd Earl of Stradbroke. Mother: née Musgrave, widow of Col. Bonham. 3 half-siblings; 2 brothers; 4 sisters. Married 1880, Cecil Francis William Fane; marriage dissolved 1904. 2 sons. Knew Lord and Lady Randolph Churchill, Lord Dudley, Lord and Lady Lonsdale, painter James McNeil

Whistler, the countess of Warwick, H.R.H. the duke of Cambridge, others. Society woman; horsewoman. Aristocracy.

Author's moneyed upbringing, leisured lifestyle, and social contacts among London's 1870s artistic circles, highlighting her portraits of significant members of this circle and her own enthusiasm for horses and riding, 1860s–1926. Father's fighting against Napoleon before her birth; his raising greyhounds; his interest in politics. Mother's instituting the Coal Club and Lending Library in Wangford. Author's childhood summers in Cromer. Her nanny; commenting on servants and their duties. Taking piano and dance lessons. Traveling to Paris with her governess, age 16. Death of her youngest sister. Being presented to Queen Victoria. Discussing the discomforts of women's fashions. Attending Ascot races with her sister, 1878. Attending balls and garden parties; social events with Prince and Princess of Wales. Describing Rotten Row in the 1870s as a venue for riding. Receiving rich American visitors in England. Recalling career of the courtesan, "Skittles"; regretting the passing of the discretion with which men used to keep their mistresses. Forming a stage company with her husband; acting in various plays. Taking tea with Oscar Wilde and Frank Miles in the 1870s; being acquainted also with Wilde's public nemesis, James McNeil Whistler. Feeling women friends are more loyal than men. Discussing the history of hunting; going hunting in Leicestershire. Seeing women as better hunters and riders than men. History of Melton Mowbray, in connection with hunting. Visiting her sister in Canada, 1896; also visiting New York. Observing differences between American and British women. Returning to Canada to visit her son, 1906. Describing hunting in Canada and New Jersey, scenery and history of Western Canada, New York horse shows. Noting differences in New York since 1896. Her third trip to America, 1908. Visiting with Alexander Graham Bell; discussing his invention of the telephone. Traveling to Switzerland with her son. Discussing fashion of bicycling. Outbreak of WWI: son's enlistment in army; organizing over 50 concerts for WWI soldiers; finding air raids thrilling. Going to Buckingham Palace on Armistice Day. Commenting favorably on emancipation of women from lives of hopeless apathy.

Lady Augusta's heyday was the 1870s, when as a young woman she was on socially intimate terms with many members of the Aesthetic movement in London. Hers is one of the few memoirs, along with that of Sarah Bernhardt, that records taking tea with the young Oscar Wilde in his frugal London flat as he worked to create a personality cult around himself. Lady Augusta's passion for horses also makes her account an informative read about fox hunting and horse shows on both sides of the Atlantic, as well as providing a vivid picture of the international character of the upper class participating in these events.

332 FANSHAWE, Elizabeth (née Mansfield). 1912–s.l.1983. *Penkhull Memories.* Stafford: Staffordshire County Library, 1983. 22 pp. BLC 1982–1985 18:501.

Born in Penkhull, Staffordshire. Father: H. Mansfield, railroad fireman. Mother not named. 5 siblings. Married Ken Fanshawe, d.1977. Widow. Businesswoman; hotel proprietor; WWII volunteer; clerk; entrepreneur. Working class.

Nostalgic recollections of country family life and author's later work as a businesswoman, covering her childhood to 1983. Family history and father's life story; author's close bond with father; details of his account books. Meeting members of royal family with father. Being a sickly child. Taking Sunday lessons at Cross Street chapel; attending Infants School, Penkhull School, Hanley High School. Family Christmas customs, holidays. Amusements and playmates of her childhood. Being publicly ridiculed by teachers for not dressing well enough. Becoming rebellious toward her parents. Quitting school to work as a sales clerk in a shoe shop. Traveling throughout England, Rhodesia, Italy, Austria, Malta; her faith in travel as a great educator. Foot-fitting in a London shoe store. Opening and running a shoe store in Salisbury, Rhodesia, 1935–38. WWII: working in Women's Land Army, Wales; traveling in Europe. Running family hotels in Austria and a hotel for 8th Army nursing sisters. Being deeply affected by her father's death, 1959. Returning to Penkhull after husband's death, 1977.

Although Fanshawe rose above her working-class origins to become a successful entrepreneur, she devotes most of this short account to memories of her childhood and her father. Descriptions of his character and habits are interspersed with the minutiae of rural village life in the pre-WWI years, depicting modes of transportation, customs, and individual villagers. Without saying so, she makes her father into the embodiment of all the values and simpler ways that at the time of her writing had vanished. Of interest to students of rural Britain, Fanshawe's brief memoir may have been solicited as part of an effort to preserve Staffordshire history.

333 FARJEON, Eleanor (Nellie). 1881–1965. *Portrait of a Family.* New York: Frederick A. Stokes Co., 1935. 456 pp.; foreword; letters; poems. NUC pre56 166:666. (other ed.: as *A Nursery in the Nineties,* Oxford University Press, 1980.)

Born in London. Father: Benjamin Leopold Farjeon, novelist, journalist, playwright, printer. Mother: Margaret Jane Jefferson, American. 4 brothers. Single. Wrote plays, poems, lyrics, short stories, novels, children's books *The Cardboard Angel, Martin Pippin, Ladyscope,* others. Knew Henry Irving, Ellen Terry, Olive Routledge, Georgie Catling, William Terriss. Novelist; children's author; playwright; poet; songwriter; short storyist. Middle class.

Portraits of author's parents and their celebrated friends, interspersed with the minutiae of everyday life in an intellectual, middle-class milieu, covering author's childhood to 1904. Family history and biographical sketches of extended Jewish family. Parents' early lives: father's breaking away from Judaism and filial duties to go prospecting in Australia's gold fields, age 16. Author's being devoted to father despite fearing him slightly. Father's being unable to pass up a bargain and buying prodigal quantities of clothes and books; his idolizing Charles Dickens and half-consciously emulating him in both his journalism and novel writing. Mother's encouraging the children's role-playing; author's being devoted to siblings' game of "Tar," for which she invented many personalities for herself. Despite living in London, never having to attend either religious services or school; being raised agnostic and enjoying a permissive existence; having lessons at home from nannies and governesses. Reading voraciously; starting to write poetry and prose at age 5. Being given wonderful gifts and toys; receiving money from her grandfather. Parents' encouraging her to attend plays, operas, concerts. Author's enjoying close ties with her brothers. On holidays, siblings' indulging in cricket, croquet, golf, piano, dance lessons, singing, parties at family home. Pets: rabbit, dog, mouse, sparrow. Lacking self-confidence, except in writing; suffering from painful shyness and insecurity; believing that the intense family intimacy delayed her maturation; never experiencing her sexuality until 30 years of age; suffering constant headaches and nervousness in adolescence. At age 18, writing the libretto for her brother Herbert's opera. Discussing the fatal stabbing of well-known actor William Terriss. Observing her father's thriving writing career and Herbert's burgeoning one; worrying lest she was adopted and had not inherited their talent. Remembering Queen Victoria's Diamond Jubilee, 1897; seeing the 1901 death of Queen Victoria as the literal and figurative end of the 19th century. Reflections on her relative John Wilkes Booth and the assassination of Abraham Lincoln. Memories of Edwardian times. Her father's carriage accident and death.

Farjeon's record of growing up a London child in the 1890s portrays the lifestyle of a moderately affluent family before the modern abandonment of servants, nurseries, and nannies. In other ways, however, she characterizes her family by their bohemian and liberal-minded notions, especially her father, whose death she uses to mark the end of her childhood. In 1913 she fell in love with a young soldier who died in WWI; thereafter she avoided marriage. Farjeon collaborated with her brother Herbert in the successful play *Kings and Queens* in 1932 and was herself a distinguished children's writer, winning both the Carnegie Medal and the Hans Christian Andersen Award for *The Little Bookroom* (1955). The Children's Book Circle also makes an annual award in her name. In 1986 her niece Annabel Farjeon produced a retrospective biography of her.

334 FARNINGHAM, Marianne (pseud.; Mary Anne Hearne). 1834–1909. *A Working Woman's Life.* James Clarke & Co., 1906. 281 pp.; front. port.; foreword; illus.; poems; addendum. NUC pre56 237:269.

Born at Farningham, Kent. Father: Joseph Hearne, postmaster, tradesman. Mother: Rebecca Bowers. 2 sisters; 2 brothers. Single. Wrote *Girlhood, Harvest Gleanings, Our Queen,* and *Women and Their Work.* Religious/spiritual writer; biographer; journalist; editor; teacher; headmistress; teacher (Sunday school); religionist (Nonconformist); public speaker. Middle class.

Progress of a Christian writer and educator from her gender-restricted Victorian girlhood through a notable adult career, covering the 1830s to c.1905. Remembering her Baptist grandfather's preaching; her grandmother's writing poetry. Attending Sunday school and dame school; the Anglican Church's National Schools' barring Nonconformist children from attending. Studying at home; cherishing her mother despite mother's determination to turn her from love of reading to diligent housework. Attending Nonconformist school; author and schoolmates' escaping the gloom and hellfire of their religious schooling through merry games. Deaths of her little brother and mother; family's grief; with mother's passing, author's having to leave school and assume housekeeping duties, age 12. Reading Sunday school monthlies to console herself; being angered that the stories encouraged boys to excel but ignored girls; wondering if girls like herself had ever achieved success. Recalling when Rev. Jonathan Whittemore became pastor of the Baptist Church at Eynsford. Going to Bristol to teach at a Quaker school; admiring the determination of its girl students. Nursing her younger sister through terminal illness and death; feeling spiritually enriched by the experience. Being introduced to *The Christian World* through Rev. Whittemore, its editor; writing for the periodical under the pseudonym Marianne Farningham. Whittemore's wife's encouraging her to publish her first book, *Lays and Lyrics of the Blessed Life.* Being lonely at a new teaching job in Gravesend; taking post as headmistress in a Northampton school. Recounting the founding of *The Sunday School Times* and the *Home Educator.* Beginning her lifework as biographer of Grace Darling, David Livingstone, and Queen Victoria; conducting research at the British Museum. Her father's moving to Northampton to join her. With his death, feeling she had become free to travel; touring England, Palestine, and Egypt. Becoming editor of *The Sunday School Times.* Being introduced to the art of Italy by taking a rest holiday there. Meeting Frances Power Cobbe; commenting on her notable activist career. Retiring from teaching; taking up public speaking on behalf of the Girls' Guild of Free Churches. Commemorating the 50th anniversary of *The Christian World.* Discussing the appeal of her writings to the working class and the pros and cons of journalism. Noting the 1901 death of Queen Victoria as the passing of an age. Evaluating the changes in children's education, 1840–1900. Believing marriage had not been God's plan for her. Discussing changes in scientific, religious, and social beliefs, 1850–1900, and the value of sorrow in the soul's self-discipline and growth.

Historian Deborah Gorham uses Farningham's autobiography in *The Victorian Girl and the Feminine Ideal* (1982) to characterize some of the obstacles faced by intelligent girls ambitious for a career in the early 19th century. In her memoir Farningham discusses how, despite her dreams, she was pressured to immerse herself in needlework because she was female and to abandon school for domesticity because she was the eldest. Farningham's well-intentioned mother is a useful example of how women themselves often guarded the traditional social barriers most difficult for their daughters to surmount.

335 FARRER, Mary (née Goldsmith). c.1760–?. *The Appeal of an Injured Wife against a Cruel Husband.* Privately printed, 1788. 66 pp.; indenture signed by Henry Farrer and Mary Goldsmith. NUC pre56 167:293.

Probably born in Surrey. Parents not named. 1 brother; 3 sisters. Married 1781, Henry Farrer, captain in Royal Navy. Military spouse; abused wife; milliner; laundry worker. Lower middle class; married into upper middle class.

Author's physical and psychological abuse at the hands of her adulterous husband, and the outrageous conduct of her husband's paramour, 1781–88. Husband's destitute condition at the time of their marriage. Their moving from Surrey to London. Author's unsuccessful attempt to supplement family income with millinery and working as a laundress; becoming ill with rheumatism. Husband's departure for Scotland, then East India. Her discovery that his credit was no good. Residing with her relative, Mr. Norman; leaving him after he attempted to seduce her. Husband's return to England; hearing of his premarital amours; suspecting him of continuing to see other women. Living with him in Kensington; his also keeping chambers elsewhere. Author's moving in with her sister. Gaining proof of husband's affairs. Confronting him with one of his mistresses, Mrs. Parks. Discovering his relationship with Lady Strathmore. Husband's moving author to Kent to keep their marriage secret; his insisting she live under the alias of Smith. His attempts to rape author's sisters; his indignation at author's protests. His threats to cut author off financially. Returning to London; being physically abused and threatened with death by husband; returning to the country. Submitting habitually to his demands. Her belief that Lady Strathmore wanted to marry her husband, if only they could dispose of author. Not believing husband planned to kill her, but thinking he would find her death convenient. Producing her marriage certificate to refute husband's assertion that he and author were never legally married. Husband's forcing her to sign an indenture (using her maiden name) giving up all claim on him as husband and banishing herself 100 miles from London, in exchange for £100. Lady Strathmore's husband's forcing author's husband away. Author's belief that Lady Strathmore will try to get a divorce so she can marry author's husband. Publishing this book to publicly forbid the unhallowed banns.

Farrer dedicated this book to Lady Strathmore, her husband's paramour. However, she turns the customary flattery of 18th-century dedications on its head, writing with irony intended to infuriate the "patron" whose seduction of Farrer's husband constitutes her "sponsorship" of the book. While its content shows fully the helpless legal situation of women in abusive marriages before late-19th-century ameliorations of divorce and marital property laws, the fact that Farrer published this account to influence her husband's actions shows her politic use of the means available to her in the 18th century to seek retribution.

336 FAWCETT, Dame Millicent Garrett. 1847–1929. *What I Remember.* T. Fisher Unwin Ltd., 1925. 272 pp.; front. port.; illus.; index. NUC pre56 168:107. (other ed.: Hyperion, 1976.)

Born at Aldeburgh, Suffolk. Father: Newson Garrett, merchant, owner of trading vessels. Mother: Louisa Dunnell. 5 sisters (including physician Elizabeth Garrett); 3 brothers. Married 1867, Henry Fawcett, postmaster general, Cambridge professor, M.P., d.1884. Widow. 1 daughter. Wrote *Political Economy for Beginners* (1870), novel *Janet Doncaster* (1875), biography *Life of Queen Victoria* (1895), *Women's Victory and After* (1918), others. Suffrage leader; political activist; political writer; organizer of societies (social reform); novelist; biographer; magistrate; academic's spouse. Upper middle class.

Eminent suffragist's work for women's causes and wider social reform, 1847–1919. Childhood memories of her father: his character and love of sailing, his malting factory at Snape. Being taken to visit London in her father's carriage. Recalling her comfortable Victorian childhood: servants, neighbors, spending winters at Snape and summers at Aldeburgh. Her evangelically religious mother's displeasure with father's lack of religious zeal. Being sent, ages 12–15, to a school taught by Louise Browning, aunt of poet Robert Browning. Recalling her elder sisters' friendship with feminist Emily Davies and endorsement of Davies's nonviolent activism. Attending London sermons of Anglican theologian F. D. Maurice. Being close to her cousin, suffragist Rhoda Garrett; recounting Rhoda's extensive activism. Father's financial reverses' forcing author to leave school and study on her own at home; recalling her physician sister Elizabeth's concurrent battle to be included in the British Medical Register. Attending one of John Stuart Mill's election meetings; his support for women's enfranchisement deepening her own interest in the suffragist cause. Meeting and marrying Henry, a radical M.P., 1867; his ardent Liberal politics; his enthusiasm for social activities and sports despite being blind. Dining in London with Mill, historian George Grote, and social economist Herbert Spencer; their collectively debating women's suffrage. Pressing charges against a pickpocket who stole her purse; being appalled at his receiving an excessive seven-year sentence; its producing a lifelong effect on her thinking about the legal system. Developing increasing political awareness through reading to her blind husband and serving as his amanuensis. Discussing intricacies of social life at Cambridge: controversies between heads of colleges, snobbishness toward people of inferior university rank. Anecdotes of Professor Sedgewick, founder of Newnham College, and of playwright Ivan Turgenev, lecturing at Cambridge. Beginning her activism and writing for the suffrage movement. Being presented at Court. Husband's being appointed to head the post office; his consequently helping to expand employment opportunities for women. Creating National Union of Women's Suffrage Societies. Her husband's illness and death, 1884. Preparing booklet logically defending women's suffrage for widespread dissemination. Suspending her suffrage work during the Boer War; visiting concentration camps in South Africa. After the war, participating in Women's Social and Political Union. Memories of the roles played by Annie Kenney and Emmeline Pankhurst in the suffrage movement. Debating antisuffragist Mrs. Humphry Ward. Meeting with Prime Minister Lloyd George to seek his support for suffrage, 1910; movement's obtaining support of Sir James Barrie and George Bernard Shaw. WWI: describing the expanding role of British women in carrying out war work. Attending Paris peace conference with suffragists from many countries. Commenting on the impact of contemporary events on the suffrage issue; her work on the Married Women's Property Bill; history of the Society for Promoting the Employment of Women; reasons for the political victory of the suffrage movement in 1918.

This is a detailed source on the English militant and more moderate, constitutionalist suffrage movements, as well as an exploration of the failures and excesses of the criminal justice system; Fawcett's interest in law led her to become a magistrate, an occupation her memoir mentions only briefly. Her work in suffrage spanned fifty years, beginning with her participation in the first women's suffrage committee in 1867; in 1897 she became president of the NUWSS, and held that post until 1918. She also worked for social purity and protection of young girls through the Vigilance Society. Fawcett was highly prominent as a political figure; in addition to her work on women's issues, she frequently visited Ireland to speak publicly against Home Rule. She was made a dame of the British Empire in 1925, the year this autobiography was published. For further information, readers may consult the biography by Ray Strachey, *Millicent Garrett Fawcett* (1931).

337 FENTON, Elizabeth Sinclair (née Knox; former Mrs. Campbell). c.1800–1875. *The Journal of Mrs. Fenton: A Narrative of Her Life in India, the Isle of France (Mauritius) and Tasmania during the Years 1826–1830.* Ed. by Sir Henry Lawrence. Edward Arnold, 1901. 396 pp.; preface by ed. NUC pre56 169:500.

Born in Ireland, possibly Kilderry. Father: John Russel Knox, rector of Lifford and afterward of Innismagrath, County Leitrim. Mother not named. 1 sister; 1 brother. Married Niel Campbell, colonial military official, d.1827. Married 1828, Captain Thomas Fenton, colonial military official. 1 daughter. Colonialist (India); farmer; clergyman's daughter; military spouse; memsahib. Middle class.

Domestic life and cultural observations of a colonial wife and Irishwoman transplanted to India, covering 1826–30. Sailing to India with her military husband, 1826. First glimpses of India: homes and customs of colonial society, Indian servants, customs and dress of affluent natives. Wistfully recalling scenes from her native Ireland. Noting many Christian Hindus in India; questioning the merit of using church money to convert Hindus when their own religion seemed to suit them. Traveling through Calcutta and Chinsurah to their new home at Rajemahl, residence of the Rajah of Bengal. When ill, preferring to employ an Irish woman as nurse rather than a native. Remembering first meeting Captain Fenton, her future second husband, in Dinapore. Contrasting ostentatious consumption of colonial living to modest and religious native lifestyle. Husband Campbell's last illness and death; her anguish at loss of her husband; choosing to stay in Calcutta despite illness and homesickness. Arrival of Captain Fenton in Calcutta; their quick courtship and marriage. Returning to Chinsurah with her new husband. Commenting on India's being overrated by outsiders; rating contemporary life in England well above life in India; decrying loneliness from living in a foreign land. Accompanying husband to the Isle of France (Mauritius), 1828. Birth of her beloved daughter, 1829. Relocating to Tasmania in order to farm, but staying in town of Hobarton while husband looked for land. Describing laborers' living conditions in Hobarton, c.1830. Being unfavorably impressed by house that her husband bought in Fenton Forest. Husband's resigning his military commission; his attempts at farming; her domestic duties as a farmer's wife.

Working within an epistolary format, Fenton seems torn between her hostility toward the "barbarous" and overrated "East" and her need to be there for the sake of two husbands. She does not satisfactorily explain why, despite intense homesickness, she remained after Campbell's death. But although her grief over losing him and feeling marooned in India seems to color her every opinion, she is both observant and fair in her observations. Her account provides much cultural information about the lives of both natives and Europeans in India and Tasmania, creating a historically useful portrait of colonial life in the early 19th century.

338 FERGUSON, Margaret. 1904–?. *Bid Time Return.* Robert Hale Ltd., 1941. 256 pp.; front. port.; foreword by Sir Frederick O'Connor; biblio.; illus. NUC pre56 169:657.

Born in Tabriz, Persia. Father not named, manager of Imperial Bank of Persia. Mother not named. 1 sister; 1 brother. Wrote *The Sign of the Ram* (1945), *Sugar and Spice* (1952), others. Foreign resident (Persia); novelist; traveler (India). Upper class.

Remembrances of coming of age in the Middle East, set within a larger discussion of early-20th-century Persian and European emigré society, 1904–22. Describing southern Persia: culture, customs, clothing, food, religion. Her childhood house, garden, playmates; riding a donkey. Visiting England for the first time; disliking London; visiting her great-aunt in Edinburgh. Returning to Persia. Journeying with a caravan; camaraderie of travelers; threat of tribal wars. Remembering family Christmases. Arrival of German consul; friendship with him. Memories of the commander of the American military force. Studying with her mother. Recalling domestic servants. Socializing with officers of the Central India Horse Company and their families. Sailing to England. Attending boarding school; intensely disliking school and rules. Outbreak of WWI: returning to Persia. Tribal uprising against the British; family's being evacuated from Shiraz without any of their possessions; being set upon by Persian nationalists. German consul's plan to incite Tangistanis to hold one of author's family hostage; mother's electing to place family under Tangistani protection. Staying in Murree, India. Discussing alienation experienced by Europeanized Indians. Socializing with English officers. Her joy at returning home to Shiraz. Organizing entertainment for troops. Arrival of Indian troops at Shiraz. Mutiny at Khanizinian; witnessing executions of mutineers. Suffering with plague. Celebrating Christmas after the Armistice. Her father's suffering a heart attack. Realizing, with father's resignation of post, that she would lose her semi-celebrity status in Persia. Family's moving to England; author's attending school in Liverpool; her fierce indictment of schoolgirls' cruelty. Father's banking appointment to Baghdad; parents' deciding to leave her in England, author's age 17. Traveling in England. Spending a summer in Switzerland. Visiting Baghdad; her first impressions of its inhabitants, society, social events. Spending a winter in Delhi. Returning to England. Commenting on her youthful belief in reincarnation and mysticism; having quasi out-of-body experiences. Recalling her yearly pilgrimage to holy mountain caves considered the dwelling place of Shiva.

Ferguson's account of her youth in the kingdom of Persia during the early 20th century points up the contrasts between its ancient Islamic traditions and tribal enmities, and the cosmopolitan internationalism of its wealthy modern cities. Born in Persia, Ferguson was at heart a native Persian whose fond depictions of her country's ambience stand in opposition to her cool assessment of England and its boarding school culture, which might be enjoyable if only, as she remarked, her fellow students could be eliminated. Ferguson seems never to have acclimated fully to England, which ultimately became her home as a young woman and rising novelist; as an adult, she continued to return periodically to the East. Several of her novels are set in Persia; the best known of them, *Sign of the Ram,* was made into a motion picture by Columbia Studios in 1947.

339 FFOULKES, Maude M.C. 1871–1949. *My Own Past.* Cassell & Co., 1915. 350 pp.; front. port.; illus. NUC pre56 171:369.

Born in Brighton, Sussex. Father: William Craven, civil engineer. Mother: Mary. Stepfather: surname Waterhouse, spice merchant. Married 1894, Charles Ffoulkes; separated 1895. Wrote with the ex-Crown Princess of Saxony *My Own Story,* with Lord Rossmore *Things I Can Tell* (1912), with Countess Marie Larish *My Past* (1913), others. Ghostwriter; biographer; journalist; secretary; actress (stage, pantomime). Middle class.

Dismal childhood, transitory ventures into acting and marriage, and ultimately successful authorial career of a self-starting ghostwriter to the elite, 1876–1914. Family history. Father's death at author's age 5. Mother's lacking affection for author, who was acutely lonely; seeing herself as unlovable. Attending day school; later attending and disliking boarding school. Mother's remarriage. Hating her stepfather; describing his bullying nature, womanizing, profligacy. Attending finishing school in Brussels, age 16. Becoming secretary to writer Douglas Sladen in London; commenting on London society. Winning part at Drury Lane Theatre; describing the life of a novice actress and family's opposition to her acting. Appearing in pantomimes. Suffering a thwarted romance with Edward, due to his mother's disapproval of her being a chorus girl; marrying Charles Ffoulkes on the rebound, 1894. Staying with her husband's family at Oxford; being bored with her life. Separating from her husband, 1895. Writing for *Printseller.* Publishing her first book, *Famous Beauties of Two Reigns.* Meeting the countess of Cardigan; collaborating with her on *My Recollections.* Meeting ex-crown princess of Saxony in Italy; collaborating with her on *My Own Story.* Collaborating with Lord Rossmore on *Things I Can Tell.* Her strong friendship with publisher Eveleigh Nash; his requesting her to write the story of Crown Prince Rudolph at Meyling. Collaborating with Countess Marie Larish. Speculating that houses absorb the tragedies of their occupants. Collaborating with Dowager Maharanee of Cooch Behar. Author's experiences with Indian royalty. Suffering a severe bout of depression; yearning to escape the solitude and seeming pointlessness of her life; suicide attempt and resulting long illness, 1914. With recovery, rediscovering satisfaction in continuing her life.

As its imitative title suggests, Ffoulkes's memoir wittily follows the pattern of the autobiographies she coauthored for famous and titled people and sets out a lofty catalogue of her literary accomplishments. Although a late-Victorian child, Ffoulkes makes no attempt to evoke particulars of her era, instead concentrating on her individual formative experiences. Nonetheless, her profession as biographic facilitator to the famous brought her into close contact with many prominent individuals from the pre-WWI years whose personalities she depicts in this volume. Her later memoir, **340** *All This Happened to Me* (1937), covers the period from WWI to 1936 and preserves further anecdotes of her acquaintance with luminaries of British and Continental society.

341 FIELDS, Dame Gracie (stage name; née Grace Stansfield) 1898–1979. *Sing as We Go: The Autobiography of Gracie Fields.* Frederick Muller, 1960. 203 pp.; front. port.; illus.; index. BLC to 1975 108:256.

Born in Rochdale, Lancashire. Father: Fred Stansfield, sailor, engineer on cargo ship, worker at Robinson's Engineering Works. Mother: Sarah Jane Bamford. 2 sisters; 1 brother. Married 1923, Archie Pitt, her theatrical manager; divorced 1940. Married Monty Banks, her theatrical manager, Italian, d.1950. Married 1952, Boris Alperovici, film director. Actress (child, stage, film, radio, comic, pantomime); singer (popular). Working class.

Child performer's progress to becoming one of England's premiere music hall attractions, covering her birth to 1960. Living in poverty in childhood. Describing parents' hard-working lives. Her admiration for her mother. Mother's history: having been an orphan raised by a strict aunt; working in a cotton mill at age 10; later working as charwoman, washerwoman, scrubwoman. Author's interest in performing. Acting in a traveling troupe, beginning at age 10. Having a scanty education outside of theatre. Performing in revues and pantomimes. Meeting and marriage to first husband, 1923; his managing her career. Acting in radio and films. Having surgery (possibly a hysterectomy) in 1939. Divorcing her first husband, 1940. Marriage to second husband; his role as manager in her career. Resenting her first two husbands' making decisions for her. Buying a house on Capri as an act of independence. Her romantic, ardent love for her third husband. After becoming wealthy, making financial donations to her family and spending much time with them. Receiving honors and decorations; being presented at Court. Remaining away from England during WWII; consequently being called a traitor. Her mystification at her personal success. Being semiretired after 1950.

"Our Gracie" both records the events of her life and attempts to justify her absence from England during WWII. Writing for a general readership, she frames her accomplishments both for her readers' appreciation and her own. When she was made a dame of the British Empire in 1979 (the year of her death), she received warm tributes honoring her considerable contribution to English popular culture—despite having spent most of the last forty years away from both acting and England. The title of this book is also the title of her popular 1934 film; the height of Fields's popularity came in the 1930s, when she was a highly paid star of English comedy films.

FINGALL, Countess of. [See PLUNKETT, Elizabeth Mary Margaret.]

342 FINN, Elizabeth Anne (née McCaul). 1825–1921. *Reminiscences of Mrs. Finn.* Marshall, Morgan & Scott, 1929. 256 pp.; front. port.; foreword by Marchioness of Aberdeen and Temair; illus.; end note by her daughter. NUC pre50 179.22.

Born in Warsaw, Poland. Father: Alexander McCaul, Anglican clergyman, Irish. Mother: née Crosthwaite. 5 sisters; 3 brothers. Married 1846, James Finn, British consul for Jerusalem and Palestine, d.1872. Widow. 3 daughters; 2 sons. Wrote *Home in the Holy Land and Its Sequel, a Month on the Mount of Olives, Palestine Peasantry,* others. Religious/spiritual writer; historian; social reformer; organizer (cultural, agricultural); philanthropist; foreign resident (Jerusalem); clergyman's daughter. Upper class.

Multinational upbringing, social and labor activism, and lifelong interest in Jewish culture of an Anglican cleric's daughter and British consul's wife in Jerusalem, 1820s–1863. Her early childhood in Poland; her father's admiration for Jewish culture and character; his desire to aid (and convert) the Jews. Author's studying Hebrew with a rabbi, age 3. Studying the English Bible; learning German and Yiddish; her parents' not allowing her to learn Polish. Following the 1830 Polish revolution, moving with her family to Breslau, then Berlin; continuing to study Hebrew. Family's relocating near relatives in Dublin for one year; moving to London, author's age 6. Father's history: his education, his interest in Hebrew literature, his advocating building hospital and Anglican church in Jerusalem, his becoming principal of a Hebrew missionary-training college. Recalling watching the red light in the sky produced by the burning Houses of Parliament, 1834. Hearing cannons salute Queen Victoria's coronation, 1837. Author's being taught basics by her mother, and Hebrew, Greek, Latin, and Euclid by her father. Author's teaching her siblings, beginning age 15. Meeting James Finn, 1841; his being appointed consul for Jerusalem, late 1845; marriage to him, January, 1846. Traveling with husband to Jerusalem; building new Anglican church there, 1847. Describing differences among the Ashkenazi and

Sephardic Jews; Christians and Muslims in Jerusalem; conflicts between various religions. Accompanying her husband on consular tours of his district: Jerusalem, half of Lebanon, much of Palestine. Death of her infant daughter. Birth of her first son, 1847. Author's employing poor Jewish community members who visited the consulate seeking work. Her husband's extended district travels; his settling many disturbances; their receiving visitors from many countries. Founding Jerusalem Literary Society with her husband, 1849. Providing water to Jewish community during a drought. Effects of the Crimean War on Palestine, 1853–55. When the Russian government stopped remittances from Russian Jews to Palestine's hungry Jewish populace, 1854, author and husband's providing emergency bread. Creating an agricultural project to employ two hundred Jewish men. Being allowed by a new, more liberal Pasha to visit a Muslim temple sanctuary usually closed to non-Muslims. Jewish schools' being founded by Miss Cooper, Lord Montefiore, the Rothschilds, Dr. Frankel of Vienna; their educating girls as well as boys despite regional rabbis' displeasure. Assuming custody of her nurse's children upon nurse's death; rabbis' later compelling children's father to remove the children from the Finns. Designing further projects for Jewish workers; contributing to rebuilding of Holy City. Observing Russians' secret buying-up of land; arrival of a Russian consul-general, 1858; a new Pasha's anti-British and anti-Jewish attitude. Death of another baby daughter. Noting increase of crime in Jerusalem. Visit of Prince Alfred to Jerusalem. Increasing turmoil in Jerusalem and Lebanon, 1860. Her husband's continuing serious illness. Writing a semi-fictionalized account of her years in Jerusalem. Being visited by the Prince of Wales. Pasha's continuing attempts to undercut British influence in the Ottoman Empire. Word's spreading of her husband's appointment to another consulate; Jewish groups' sending several requests to Queen Victoria, requesting that their benefactor not be removed. Returning to London, 1863.

Throughout her memoir, Finn documents the political permutations in mid-19th-century Jerusalem and Palestine. She relates shifts in power chronologically to policy, particularly before and after the Crimean War, describing how a succession of Ottoman Empire–appointed Pashas governed much of life in Jerusalem and beyond in conjunction with representatives of the various European powers. In a brief epilogue, her (unnamed) daughter describes Finn's life in England with her husband until his 1872 death, her service as translator for the patriarch of the Ancient Syrian Church in 1875, her aid in raising money for the Palestine Exploration Fund, and her role in founding the Society for Relief of Distressed Jews to assist Russian Jews during the 1880s.

343 FITZ-CLARENCE, Wilhelmina, Countess of Munster (née Kennedy-Erskine). 1830–1906. *My Memories and Miscellanies.*

Eveleigh Nash, 1904. 288 pp.; foreword; illus. NUC pre56 401:658. [cat. under FitzClarence.]

Born in Montrose, Scotland. Father: the Hon. John Kennedy-Erskine, son of 12th Earl of Cassilis. Mother: Lady Augusta Fitzclarence. Stepfather: Lord Frederick Gordon. Maternal grandfather: King William IV. 1 sister. Married 1855, her first cousin, William George Fitz-Clarence, 2nd Earl of Munster, d.1901. 5 children. Society woman; social historian. Aristocracy.

Author's childhood within Britain's royal circle, youthful education by grand tour, and adult observations of aristocratic life under Queen Victoria, 1830s–1870s. Memories of her childhood home, Railshead, in England. Anecdotes of her maternal grandfather, King William IV; his kindness to her. Her grandmother Dorothy Jordon, the king's mistress. Customs of Windsor Castle. Her father's death. Her mother's remarriage. Death of William IV. Going to live at Kensington Palace. Attending wedding of Victoria and Albert, 1840. Visiting Queen Adelaide at Marlborough House. Going to Dresden with her family; studying German. Visiting Prague and Italy. Memories of Naples: fashions, customs, beggars. Climbing Mount Vesuvius. Recalling the Court of Louis Philippe of France. Perceiving the importance of keeping a journal. Remembering the Paris revolt of 1848, its political and social ramifications. History of the Hanoverian line; Court lore and customs. Anecdotes about Queen Victoria's first years at Court. Marriage; gambling in Hamburg on her honeymoon. Believing in the importance of good manners. Speculating on the decline of the English language due to slang and misuse of words. Outlining the mutual obligations of domestic servants and their masters. Her friendship with Fanny Murray Vicars, head of the Brighton Home for Female Penitents. Relating ghost stories, including a personal encounter with an apparition. Describing social customs and observances among the aristocracy.

Although Lady Munster dwells on pastimes and social events, her charting of the British royal existence amid its early-19th-century familial and political ties to the Continent makes her book a valuable historical repository. As well as recording gossip (such as the scandal over the relationship between her maternal grandparents), the author preserves minutiae of Court customs, dynastic frictions, and details of the British aristocracy's perspective concerning ongoing events. Another useful memoir by a British royal insider is Princess Alice of Athlone's *For My Grandchildren: Some Reminiscences* (1966). A granddaughter of Queen Victoria, she charts the royal family's lives from the 1880s into the early 20th century, effectively complementing Lady Munster's account by discussing later royal developments.

344 FLETCHER, Margaret. 1862–1943. *O, Call Back Yesterday.* Oxford: Basil Blackwell, 1939. 213 pp.; foreword. NUC pre56 175:261.

Born in Oxford. Father not named, Oxford professor, Anglican vicar. Mother not named. 8 siblings. Single. Wrote *Christian Feminism* (1915), *Catholic Women: The Ideals They Stand For* (1918), *The Christian Family* (1920). Religionist (Roman Catholic convert); journalist; WWI volunteer; publisher; founder of Catholic Women's League; clergyman's daughter. Middle class.

Anglican upbringing, formative Catholic and feminist experiences, and later social activism of a Roman Catholic reformer, 1870s–1920s. Having her tonsils removed without anesthetic; Victorian medical practices. Receiving her first Anglican religious instruction from her father; receiving art lessons from her mother, who was a talented copyist. Town and gown memories of Oxford life; changes in Oxford students between mid–19th century and 1938. At age 10, attending lectures given by John Ruskin at his School of Art. Noting the opening of Oxford women's colleges, 1875. Attending Oxford High School. Her father's being an early feminist, writing sermon, "Women's Equality in Christ." Author's becoming feminist also; reading feminist books which opened her eyes to child pornography and prostitution. Memories of Josephine Butler's political activism. Discussing antireligious propaganda novels of the 1890s and the concurrent doctrinal disintegration of the Church of England. Attending Bloomsbury's Slade Art School, age 17; winning admission to the Royal Academy of Art two years later. Campaigning unsuccessfully to obtain scholarships for women art students; being irate that in England, women were barred from taking life-drawing classes. Studying art in Paris instead; noting women art students' more egalitarian treatment there. After return to England, gaining interest in Roman Catholicism by reading St. John of the Cross. Converting and being accepted as Catholic by her Anglican family. English Catholics' lacking organizations; author's helping launch *The Crucible,* a newsletter forum for Catholic women feminists. Commenting on suffrage militancy. Starting Catholic Women's League, 1906; incorporating Fabian ideas for social reform into league platform. Discussing controversy between CWL and birth control advocates. During WWI, CWL's doing war work and staffing rescue houses in France. Serving as CWL president; working with CWL in postwar Austria, Czechoslovakia, and Poland. Publishing *The Catholic Woman's Outlook,* beginning 1916. Discussing social effects of child labor.

When Fletcher entered the Catholic Church in 1897, it was imbued with reforming energy derived from the mid-19th-century Oxford movement under which many Anglicans, following the lead of Henry Cardinal

Manning, experienced conversion to the older faith. Manning had expressed a need for Catholics to be active social reformers in terms of their being "downright" and "masculine," but the group of laywomen who formed the English Catholic Women's League were instead feminists with a socialist slant, who devoted the new league's efforts to implementing the progressive social ideas outlined in Leo XIII's papal encyclical of 1891. Within the church, Fletcher committed her life to helping women overcome class and gender barriers. She wrote on social as well as religious topics, producing a manual, "Prostitution, the Moral Bearings of the Problem," which candidly discussed venereal disease. After retiring as CWL's president in 1923 she increased the feminist focus of her work, throughout WWII addressing transatlantic audiences on the theme of every man and woman having an equal right to justice.

345 FLINT, Elizabeth. 1910–?. *Hot Bread and Chips.* Museum Press, 1963. 183 pp.; illus. by Margaret Fowler. BLC to 1975 110:250.

Born in London's East End. Father: Sam Flint, vegetable jobber. Mother not named. 2 brothers; 2 sisters. Married Charlie Binner, dairy farmer. Domestic servant; farmer. Working class.

Author's first ten years of life amid the social surroundings of London's East End, 1910–20. Recalling her childhood home, living conditions, chores. Her mother's dissatisfaction with life, sternness with children. Describing East End street sights. Helping a neighbor with cleaning; being taught to read by her; author's mother's resenting their relationship. Family Christmases: food, finery, customs, shopping. Attending Hampstead Heath Day. WWI: parents' reacting against "Kaiser Bill." Marriage of her brother Ted. Spending time with Ted and his wife. Ted's induction into the army. Recalling patriotic propagandizing during war. Visiting Southend; war's casting a pall over amusements. Her fear of Zeppelins. Ted's death in France; family's reaction, father's special distress; mother's revealing that Ted was not his son. Describing food shortages, other privations of war. A neighbor's death; describing mourning and funeral customs. Her sister Dolly's liaison with Tony Kistler; her mother's objections, harsh treatment of Dolly. Her sister Mabel's joining the Salvation Army. Family's dependence on wages earned by older siblings. Contrasting her friend Ada's middle-class surroundings with her own environment. Attending church, for the first time, with Ada. Speculating on difference between wickedness and sinfulness. Mother's veiled criticism of author's interest in reading. Dolly's becoming pregnant although unmarried and leaving the family home; this signaling end of childhood for author.

Despite its brevity, Flint's early memoir vividly documents London's working-class existence in the period surrounding WWI, addressing the many social issues—scarcity of money, limited education, wartime conditions, and generational illegitimacy—that affected her family, as well as rendering a multifaceted sketch of East End culture. This account helps illustrate the response of England's urban working class to WWI, a war in which England relied entirely on volunteerism. As happened in Flint's own family, while young working-class men went off to war, their sisters and mothers were significantly less likely than were higher-class women to volunteer on the home front, owing to the obligations of economic necessity. Continuing her story in **346** *Kipper Stew* (1964), Flint relates her experiences as a dairy farmer from 1926 to the mid-1940s.

347 FLOWER, Constance, Baroness Battersea (née Rothschild). 1843–1931. *Reminiscences.* Macmillan, 1922. 470 pp.; preface; illus.; genealogical tables; index. NUC pre56 39:248.

Born in England. Father: Nathan Meyer Rothschild. Mother: Louisa Montefiore. 1 sister. Married 1877, Cyril Flower, barrister, M.P., later Baron Battersea, d.1907. Wrote, with her sister (as C. and A. de Rothschild), *The History and Literature of the Israelites* (c.1870). Philanthropist; society woman; political activist; Jewish activist; politician's spouse; political hostess; historian. Upper class; married into aristocracy.

Evolving commitment to philanthropy and social causes, rooted in upper-class Jewish background and education, covering author's 1850s childhood to 1901. Being schooled by private instructors. Visiting European branches of family with her parents and sister. Her social circle of influential, wealthy, upper-class people. Women's role as hostesses in their country homes and as organizers of social life, often with political intent. Perceiving great houses as center of English society and political life. Her husband's parliamentary career. Author's insisting that her husband refuse appointment as governor of New South Wales to avoid a separation from her mother; this effectively ending his career; his consequently becoming a leisured gentleman. Her devotion to husband's interests in architecture, gardening, arts, music, friends, sports. From 1837, Disraeli's being a close family friend; author's sharing Disraeli's deep interest in removing civil and political disabilities of Jews; supporting bill making Jews eligible to hold seats in House of Commons. Seeing her own Jewish identity as ancestral rather than religious. Reflecting Jewish heritage by choosing special causes: assisting Jewish factory girls, promoting literacy, supporting Benevolent Jewish Ladies Aid Society and Jewish Free School work. Also supporting Temperance League; visiting women prisoners; providing concerts and libraries for poor and working classes in general. Serving as president of National Union of Women Workers, 1901. Seeing philanthropy as a privilege of the rich.

Like the influential Montefiore family, to whom they were related by a series of intermarriages, the Rothschilds during the 19th century were committed to the cause of Zionism. As a Rothschild daughter, Lady Battersea inherited and furthered this aim while also performing the active philanthropy that was the trademark of Victorian upper-class women. The picture of her family's close ties to Benjamin Disraeli is telling; despite Disraeli's youthful Anglican conversion, he still thought of himself as Jewish, as did the Rothschilds. Lady Battersea's remark about viewing her own Jewish identity in ethnic rather than religious terms helps show that this modern attitude had already gained currency by the early 19th century.

348 FOAKES, Grace (née Pratt). 1901–?. *Between High Walls: A London Childhood.* Shepheard-Walwyn, 1972. 83 pp.; intro. by Lady Henriques, C.B.E.; prologue; illus. by Dinah Dryhurst; poem. NUC 1973–1977 37:139.

Born in London's East End. Father not named, wharf worker, subsequently unemployed. Mother not named. 4 surviving siblings (out of 13). Married 1929, Reuben Foakes, tugboat worker. 2 daughters; 1 adopted son; 1 adopted daughter. Domestic servant; shopkeeper; waitress. Working class.

Hunger and poverty of author's East London childhood and young adulthood, c.1901–30. Her father's aloofness; author's not learning to love him until late in life; his often working both nights and days at the wharf; his making sure author knew how to do laundry and use the sewing machine. Her mother's having a new baby every year, to the children's surprise; endemic disease; resulting deaths of nine of author's siblings. Author's awareness of family's poverty; because vermin infested their tenement flat, father's tearing down pictures author put on the walls. Longing for grass to play on; stealing a flower for her mother. Her love of cats. Attending a board school and a Wesleyan Sunday school. With her Sunday school, taking a fortnight's rural holiday that exposed her to another way of life. Father's losing his job for pilfering tea, 1912; his pawning household possessions, stealing food; author's religious objections to eating this food; giving in to hunger; feeling she had failed as a Christian. Describing children's accidents, illnesses; their ignorance of human sexuality. Leaving school, age 14; working as a waitress. Running the household while her mother was bedridden with cancer; stealing money from her father, who hoarded most of his earnings. Courtship with a friendly neighbor; marriage to him six weeks before her mother's death. Father's remarriage to a Salvationist; author's brothers and sisters' moving to home of author and her new husband. Author's first pregnancy; her shock at learning the facts of childbirth. When their house was burglarized, author's becoming determined to leave East London. Appealing personally to the London County Council to be allowed into a new estate at Dagenham, Essex; housing officer's making exception for her that violated normal restrictions. Hating to leave intimate friends, but realizing her child could have a better life only by leaving.

Foakes's book resurrects the physical surroundings of the East End in the Edwardian period, exposing their unclean, neglected condition, as well as confronting the untreated disease, uncontrolled births, and poverty-induced crime. Foakes was in one of the early generations of East End dwellers to benefit from combined private and governmental efforts to provide education, resulting in her awareness of the wider opportunities available beyond the surroundings of her birth. Her sequel, **349** *My Part of the River* (1974), is a collection of short essays on her childhood, with further emphasis on the degradation of a life of poverty and toil. **350** *My Life with Reuben* (1975) tells of her happy marriage, caring for her own children and those of relatives, her husband's suffering with strikes, lockouts, and injuries at work, her struggle to keep the family together during WWII, her dry-goods shop, moving to the countryside at war's end, and writing *Between High Walls*.

351 FOLEY, Alice. 1891–1974. *A Bolton Childhood*. Manchester: Manchester University, 1973. 92 pp.; postscript. BLC to 1975 111:35.

Born in Bolton, Lancashire. Father: casual laborer. Mother: Meg Mort, laundress. 2 sisters; 3 brothers. Single. Trade unionist; socialist; cotton-mill worker; clerk; justice of the peace. Working class.

Trade unionist's working-class upbringing and later immersion in labor organizing work, 1891–1919. Paternal grandparents' having moved from Ireland to Lancashire during the 1849 potato famine. Maternal grandparents' work as weavers. Mother's illiteracy; her supporting family with her washtub; her having six children she never really wanted. Father's sporadic jobs, unpredictable temper, physical abusiveness, drunkenness, gambling, disappearances; his also declaiming Shakespeare, reading Dickens and George Eliot aloud to the family. Mother's inability to love or understand author's father. Author's great love for her mother and fear that she would leave the family. Father's Catholicism; author's attending Roman Catholic primary school; mother's lack of religious feeling. Discussing problems encountered by children of marriages between those of different religious orientations. Father's Irish political activism and membership in Sinn Fein. Author's going to work as "tenter" in a cotton mill, age 13. Attending evening classes, but receiving her real education from her elder sister, who was a textile trade union official, a suffragette, and a member of the Labour Church. Being appointed by trade union to visit sick workers, age 21. Monotony of mill work; union work's being more to her liking. Becoming a clerk in the Bolton Weavers office, age 25. Attending Labour church and socialist Sunday school after father's death. Her diminishing faith in Christianity and rising acceptance of socialist ideas. Recalling visit of Mohandas Gaṇdhi to her union office. Enjoying attending theatre and visiting art galleries. Her interest in the works of

Robert Blatchford, Shaw, Galsworthy, Keats, Longfellow, Shelley. Attending extramural classes at Manchester University through the Workers' Educational Association. Believing in importance for lower classes of trade unionism and self-education.

The extensive interlacing network between many avenues of working-class activism—socialism, Fenianism, and trade unionism—shows up graphically in Foley's rendering of industrial northern England at the beginning of the 20th century. The unsigned postscript to the book indicates that Foley received an honorary M.A. in 1962 for her work with the WEA and with the Manchester University Joint Committee for Adult Education. She also served as secretary of the Bolton district Weavers and Winders Association from 1949–61, was awarded the M.B.E. in 1951, was president of the Bolton United Trades Council, 1956–57, and served as a justice of the peace for more than forty years, beginning in 1931.

352 FOLEY, Winifred (née Mason). 1914–s.l.1992. *In and Out of the Forest.* Cheltenham, Gloucestershire: Thornhill Press, 1992. 155 pp.; port. BLC 1982–1984 9:287. (1st pub. Century, 1984.)

Born in Brierley, Forest of Dean, Gloucestershire. Father: Charles Mason, coal miner. Mother: Margaret. 2 brothers; 3 sisters. Married 1938, Sydney John Foley, sawmill worker. 3 sons; 1 daughter. Wrote play *Abide with Me.* Domestic servant; playwright; scriptwriter; conscientious objector; pacifist; public speaker; news agent; waitress; charwoman. Rural laboring class.

Memories of growing up in the Forest of Dean and encountering limited work opportunities (coal mining for boys, domestic service for girls), c.1920–1980s. Contrasting the beauty of the Severn-Wye confluence and the cramped lives of miners such as author's father. Recalling mine strikes of post-WWI recession. Economic necessity's forcing her Aunt Lois to leave her child and miner husband and return to domestic service outside the forest. At strike's end, author's father's being banned from the pit as a strike leader; continuing poverty of author's family. Recalling a parsimonious preacher who became a prosperous sawmill owner and lecher; other interesting neighbors. Becoming a domestic servant, age 14, in Gloucestershire. Later working in a London boarding house; being pestered by male boarders; one female boarder's being a prostitute, another a nightclub hostess. Working as a waitress in an Italian café. Seeking work as a film extra, 1931; receiving unwanted sexual advances from potential employer; abandoning the idea of working in films. Marriage to Syd, 1938; their initial sexual prudery but companionability; their agreeing on pacifist ideas. Author and husband's managing a newsagent's and tobacconist's shop together. Outbreak of WWII; their moving to the Forest of Dean. Birth of their son. Author and husband's registering as conscientious objectors; his being ordered to work in sawmills. Moving back and forth from Gloucestershire to London during the war; enduring the London bombing raids; author's concern for husband's malnourishment. Their second son's birth. Syd's continuing to work in sawmills after the war. Expressing gratitude for generous rations and price controls at war's end. Birth of another son and a daughter. Returning permanently to the Forest of Dean, 1956. Publication of her first autobiographical work, *A Child in the Forest,* 1974; its being a best-seller and broadcast on radio and television; buying and refurbishing a cottage with her earnings. Describing her new neighbors. During a bad freeze in 1982, recalling the rough winter of 1947, when author worked as a charwoman in London. Fans' unexpectedly turning up on her doorstep; receiving invitations to appear on radio and television programs; speaking to women's groups about her writings. Taking excursions to other parts of Gloucestershire and the Cotswolds after husband's retirement, c.1982; remembering her siblings' stays in sanitoria as children. Adapting *A Child in the Forest* into a play, at a producer's request. Revisiting sites of her first domestic service jobs in Gloucestershire. Her close relationships with her children; her identification with her grandchildren and their imaginings. Thoughts on the deleterious effects of television, on modern immorality, on the loss of simplicity in people's lives. At age 78, after minor strokes, wondering about the nature of existence and the possibility of an afterlife; still enjoying her garden and her life with Syd, who has recovered from a heart attack.

The first book published under this title was a supplement to Foley's more detailed earlier writings. The 1992 edition, entirely rewritten, contains less about her early life as a domestic servant and more about the hardships of life during the 1930s, her marriage during WWII, and her pacifism and social liberalism. Foley frequently uses dialogue to re-create local dialects. Like Flora Thompson's *Lark Rise to Candleford,* Foley's works are important to the study of rural English social history. In an earlier autobiography, **353** *A Child in the Forest* (1974), Foley describes her transition from rural to urban life, moving from her Forest of Dean childhood to domestic service with a London Jewish family, a shift that influenced the development of her political opinions. With **354** *No Pipe Dreams for Father: Scenes from a Forest of Dean Childhood* (1977), Foley further describes her early years, covering her life from ages 3 to 14, and in **355** *Back to the Forest* (1981) she tells of her married life during WWII, her move back to her rural home village after the war, and the beginning of her autobiographical writing.

356 FORBES, Lady Angela Selina Blanca (née St. Clair-Erskine). 1876–d.a.1929. *Memories and Base Details.* New York: George H.

Doran, 1922. 321 pp.; front. port.; foreword; poems; illus. NUC pre56 177:401.

Born in London. Father: Francis Robert St. Clair-Erksine, 4th Earl of Rosslyn, horse dealer, mine owner. Mother: Blanche Adeliza Fitz Roy. 2 sisters; 2 brothers; 2 half-sisters. Married 1896, Lt. Col. James Forbes, 9th Lancers, Warwickshire Yeomanry; divorced c.1910. 2 daughters. Wrote novel *The Broken Commandment,* others. Novelist; society woman; WWI volunteer; editor; philanthropist; antisuffragist. Aristocracy.

Society woman's transformation into WWI volunteer and philanthropist, 1880s–c.1920. Being the youngest offspring of her father's second marriage; feeling isolated agewise from her siblings. Being named for her godmother, social reformer Angela Burdett-Coutts. Her father's being her principle influence: his kindheartedness, his imperiousness, his strict guidance of her education. Father's being close to progressive economist Moreton Frewen; supporting reform for miner's working conditions. Father's ruling the family, mother's giving in gracefully. Author's being overly sheltered, forbidden even to cross the street without her nurse. Father's teaching the children deportment, Latin, and botany; providing German governesses the author hated; author's commenting that parents are often ignorant of how governesses abuse their children. Family's moving to Burleigh Park, where father bred and raced horses. Beginning to write poems in her adolescence. Father's illness; his quest for a cure; his death's shattering the author, age 14. Making her social debut, c.1892; being presented at Court. At age 18, casually accepting a marriage proposal from an Army officer whose only shared interest was horses; privately believing the marriage would fail. Their having two daughters while living in Grosvenor Square; husband's expressing unhappiness at not having a son. Feeling relieved that his military duties abroad ensured long separations; devoting herself to riding and hunting. Traveling to America alone; attending horse races; envying American women's freedom to divorce. Obtaining a Scottish divorce due to more liberal Scottish divorce laws; husband's contesting divorce because author refused to surrender daughter to him. His cutting off her allowance, declaring Scottish divorce invalid because he was English. Her documenting his Scottish lineage to win divorce. After divorce, educating herself in politics and history. Supporting family by editing a natural history magazine and writing fiction; her first novel, *The Broken Commandment,* being banned by libraries as scandalous. Publishing two more novels. In WWI, assisting in hospital in France; opening the first British Soldiers' Buffet in France; Red Cross's deciding to sponsor her buffet work. Returning to England; volunteering at Westminster Hospital. Returning to France; creating a canteen for British soldiers at Boulogne; receiving support from the Salvation Army but antagonism from the YMCA. Experiencing the first German gas attack in France; witnessing the arrival of the First Aid Nursing Yeomanry, the first women's contingent in France. Recounting rescue work done by English VADs. Returning to England; creating a training program for disabled soldiers in England. Author's strongly antisemitic feelings: stating that, if she were prime minister, she would form a firm alliance with France, fight alien labor, and squash the Jewish invasion. Describing uneasy relations between France and England after WWI.

The focus in Lady Angela's memoir highlights the contrast between the unhappy and monotonous life she led as an idle society wife and the increasingly aware, empowered life of social purpose which she built after her divorce. Taking account of herself, she discovered her writing ability, improved her education, and became a dynamic wartime organizer. The second part of the book contains detailed anecdotes of WWI military and civilian life in France. Her 1932 sequel, **357** *Fore and Aft,* is written under her maiden name St. Clair-Erskine, to which Lady Angela officially reverted in 1929. This later book discusses her travels since WWI, evaluates her early writing efforts, and comments dryly on negative social changes in post-WWI Europe and her experiences in starting a dress shop for aristocrats and actresses.

358 FORTESCUE, Winifred, Lady (née Beech). 1881–1951. *There's Rosemary . . . There's Rue.* Boston: Houghton Mifflin, 1941. 428 pp.; front. port.; index. NUC pre56 178:467–468. (1st pub. W. Blackwood, 1939.)

Born in Great Bealings, Suffolk. Father: Howard Beech, rector of Great Bealings. Mother not named. 2 brothers; 1 sister. Married 1914, Sir John Fortescue, historian, librarian at Windsor Castle, d.1933. Widow. Journalist; actress (stage); WWI volunteer; dress designer; entrepreneur; businesswoman; foreign resident (France); clergyman's daughter. Middle class; married into upper class.

Nurturing childhood, diverse career ventures, and happy marital partnership of a creative fashion designer and the wife of England's premiere military historian, 1880s–1933. Growing up in her father's rectory; adoring her father; attending his Easter services and harvest festivals. Father's popularity as pastor; mother's kindness and concern for the poor. Author's studying at home; having growing interest in decorating and writing. Going to London to study acting. Winning a walk-on role in Sir Herbert Beerbohm Tree's acting company; having a speaking part in Graham Robertson's *Pinkie and the Fairies,* 1900, which also starred Ellen Terry. Touring Wales and Ireland in an early play by George Bernard Shaw; discussing internal organization of theatrical companies. Through Terry's influence, appearing at the Lyceum Theatre in London. Recalling the career of Mrs. Patrick Campbell, London's crowning actress. Author's brother's becoming infatuated with Campbell, proposing, and eventually marrying her. Meeting her future husband, then librarian at Windsor Castle; visiting him there; establishing a courtship.

His having toured India as aid to King Edward VII. Marrying, 1914, and relocating to Hampstead. Outbreak of WWI: working at crêche for unwanted babies and in YMCA canteen; walking with blind soldiers. Husband's writing *Interim History of the War.* Meeting ex-Prime Minister Lord Rosebery; becoming close to widowed Queen Alexandra and frequenting Windsor Castle; anecdotes of Princess Victoria. Discussing her friend Sir Edward Elgar and his musical career. Accepting request from influential women friends to serve as honorary secretary to the Women's Municipal Party. Opening a dress design business at Hampstead; presenting fashion shows of her designs; showing dresses in America; closing business for the sake of her health. Writing for *Punch* and *The Evening News;* inaugurating a women's fashion page for the *Morning Post.* Her husband's receiving a knighthood, 1926, at same time as close deaths of author's parents. Family's moving to a country house; author's husband's finishing writing *History of the British Army,* despite continuing series of illnesses. Author's attending husband in his final illness; his death, 1933.

Lady Fortescue is quick to note that the linchpin of her life is her relationship with her revered historian husband, twenty-two years her senior, whose most noted work was his 1925 biography of the duke of Wellington. In many ways Fortescue helped to further her husband's researches, making her own considerable successes in acting, dress designing, and journalism seem peripheral to the supportive intimacy of their marriage. A closer look at Fortescue's life in the 1930s is provided by **359** *Perfume from Provence* (1937), a humorous account of the author's daily life in that region.

360 FRANKAU, Pamela (Sydney Dill, pseud.). 1908–1967. *Pen to Paper, a Novelist's Notebook.* New York: Doubleday, 1962. 237 pp. BLC to 1975 115:23. (1st pub. 1961.)

Born in England. Father: Gilbert Frankau, novelist. Mother: Dorothea Drummond-Black. 1 sister. Married 1945, Marshall Dill; divorced. 1 son. Wrote novels *Marriage of Harlequin* (1927), *Jezebel* (1937), *A Wreath for the Enemy* (1954), others. Novelist; short storyist; journalist; broadcaster; playwright. Upper middle class.

Growth and development of a novelist's career, covering her childhood to 1961. Loving to write as a child; aspiring to emulate Rebecca West; winning a bronze medal, age 8, for a piece she published in *Little Folks* magazine. Attending boarding school; writing fiction. Working for Amalgamated Press, age 18; publishing her first novel (the fourth she had written). Making friends with playwright John van Druten and with her literary idol, Rebecca West; being uninterested in people outside the literary world. Having only nebulous ideas about God, early 1930s, and tending toward atheism; developing growing spirituality as time progressed. Converting to Roman Catholicism, 1942. Defining herself culturally and religiously as a "half-Jewish lady of the Catholic religion." Discussing subjects open to exploration by Catholic writers. Working as inspector of army education during WWII; also broadcasting her own BBC talk show. Writing for women's magazines in Massachusetts and later in California, 1946–49. After returning to England, serving as reviewer for the Book Review Society, 1950. Expressing her strong sense of social justice and dislike of censorship. Living in Martha's Vineyard, Massachusetts, 1950–c.1954. Writing a play for her friend Tyrone Power based on Senator Joseph McCarthy's investigations of Communism in the U.S. Discussing potentially corruptive influences on writers and the perniciousness of television. Relocating to New York, 1958–61. Seeing British and Americans as being as unlike as cats and dogs; viewing herself as having become part cat, part dog after prolonged stays in the U.S.

Frankau examines her life from the perspective of her writing, discussing those incidents and relationships that contributed meaningfully to the unfolding of her creativity. Although the writing of fiction was the family profession, with both her father and her sister Ursula also being novelists, Frankau's comments on her father are brief; Gilbert Frankau's books are characterized by extreme conservatism and larger-than-life heroes, whereas his daughter Winifred was an openly questing writer whose work explored multiple spiritual and social possibilities. Frankau also discusses some of the challenges facing the British literary community from 1930–1960. In an earlier autobiographical work, **361** *I Find Four People* (1935), she introspectively describes her childhood and adolescence.

362 FREEMAN, Anne (née Mason). 1797–1826. *A Memoir of the Life and Ministry of Anne Freeman, a Faithful Servant of Jesus Christ, Written by Herself. And an Account of Her Death by Her Husband, Henry Freeman.* Ed. by Henry Freeman (author's husband). Darton & Harvey, 1828. 195 pp.; preface; ed.'s memoir of his wife; diary extracts; letters. NUC pre56 184:45.

Born at Horathorne, Devonshire. Father: William Mason, farmer. Mother: Grace. 12 siblings. Married 1824, Henry Freeman, street preacher. Religionist (Methodist convert, Quaker convert); preacher. Rural farming class.

Nonconformist religious seeker's sampling of various sects, from childhood to age 20. Part I: Being taught to pray and say the Anglican catechism by her farmer parents; this being all that local people, including the parish minister, thought necessary to be religious. Local folks' seeming religious but not being truly converted. Seeking her own spiritual salvation, but being forbidden to read religious tracts lest she become melancholy. Briefly attending Methodist revival meetings, age 14, but being deterred by hearing evil reports about Methodism. Being apprenticed to a dressmaker, age 14; falling prey to consumption a few months later and consequently contemplating death. Being moved to take confirmation in the Church of England, but still being in a state of sin. Moving with her family to Sutcombe parish, Northcott, age 17. Continuing to express her religious yearnings; family's reprimanding her for being "righteous overmuch." With her sister, joining the Methodists, age 18; stating that the resulting banishment from her father's house confirmed her in her faith. The two sisters' being allowed home again after a few days. Beginning to attend meetings of Arminian Bible Christians (Bryanites), age 20; feeling herself "filled with the Spirit"; family conflict's ceasing when they also sensed the Spirit within her. Commencing her Methodist public preaching, age 20. Part II: Visiting her future husband during his imprisonment for street preaching, age 26. Entertaining thoughts of marriage and praying about it. In 1824, reading the journal of George Fox, 17th-century founder of the Quakers; becoming attracted to the Society of Friends; joining them. Traveling and doing public preaching in England. Her marriage. Undertaking a preaching tour of Ireland with her husband. Returning to England, age 28. Her unspecified final illness.

Only the first ten pages of this book are straight narrative autobiography; the second part, documenting Freeman's life from 1817 onward, consists of diary entries and letters. Although her conversion account follows conventional patterns, particularly in its hortatory tone and providential view of her progress toward salvation, it is valuable for Freeman's description of her early-19th-century experiences with the two Nonconformist denominations noted for their egalitarian gender roles and their vital dependence on the evangelism of itinerant women preachers.

363 FREMANTLE, Anne (née Huth Jackson). 1910–s.l.1992. *Three-Cornered Heart.* New York: Viking, 1971. 316 pp.; illus.; index. BLC to 1975 116:68.

Born in Tresserve, Savoie, France. Father: Frederick Huth Jackson, privy councillor, sheriff of London, director of Bank of England. Mother: Clara Annabel Caroline Grant Duff, writer. 1 brother; 2 sisters. Married 1930, Christopher Fremantle, artist, Oxford graduate. 3 sons. Wrote *Poems* (1931), *George Eliot* (1933), *Come to Dust* (1941), *The Age of Belief: The Medieval Philosophers* (1955), *By Grace of Love* (1957), *The Island of Cats* (1964), others. Novelist; biographer; poet; historian; anthologist; broadcaster; journalist; religionist (Roman Catholic convert); traveler (Southeast Asia); emigrant (U.S.). Upper class.

Detailed family memories, including extensive history of author's mother, followed by author's spiritual, political, and literary maturation under her mother's influence, 1909–60. Being born in a castle in France; family's moving to London in author's infancy. Father's remaining distant from his children, especially after his heart trouble began, 1913. Family's moving to Sussex upon father's inheriting Possingworth estate there. Praising her father's distinction as banker; his refusing both a peerage and baronetage. Spending summers at Possingworth, 1914–18; gathering wild plants on estate for food to eke out WWI rations. Speaking only French and German until age 11; parents' forcing the children to speak English because of WWI. Parents' hosting Belgian war refugees on the estate. Author's dearly loving rituals of religion in any form. Attending Anglican services because her father was patron of two Anglicans living in Sussex. Unconventional mother's practicing Eastern-influenced religion at home, venerating a bronze Buddha and burning joss sticks, encouraging author's childhood exchange of letters with Gandhi. Being exposed to death by observing dead game animals on the estate; meditating on death and war. Recalling a visit from Irish revivalist and family friend Lady Gregory, "Aunt Augusta," in mourning after her son's war death. Author's mother's being a committed pacifist and International Labour Party member. Under mother's influence, author's believing that only politics, war, and religion were worth discussing; turning to literature to cope with her fear of war. Mother's detesting "German baiting" during WWI; cofounding the postwar Fellowship of Reconciliation; being a pro-Nazi sympathizer in the 1930s. Author's father's death, 1931; learning more about father from the *Times* obituary than she had ever known during his lifetime. From monetary need, mother's selling the English houses and moving the family back to author's birthplace in France. Author's learning Catholic theology; adoring French life; author and sisters' being horrified when mother sent them to boarding school in Kent. Mother's having kept them ignorant of the facts of life, telling them only that no one but the "lower classes" enjoyed sex. Innocently writing her mother about a schoolmate who "loved" another girl; mother's consequently removing her daughters and sending them to Cheltenham Ladies College. Recalling telling her mother much later that she enjoyed sex; mother's replying, "Darling, how like a housemaid." Traveling with her mother in Europe, c. age 16; flirting and evading marriage proposals. Returning to England. Wanting to become Catholic; horrified mother's sending her to a psychiatrist. Friend's introducing her to Catholic intellectual Hillaire Belloc; author's later turning story of the Belloc family into a novel. Coming out, age 17; meeting her future husband at a hunt ball; planning eventual marriage. Staying with Lady Gregory in Ireland to write an essay on J. M. Synge; being introduced to W. B. Yeats. Raising money for her mother's Planned Parenthood Association. Securing mother's consent to attend Oxford by winning a scholarship. Discussing second-class citizenship of Oxford women and their general desire for degrees as economic insurance against spinsterhood. Announcing her engagement to her fiancé's family; ironically contrasting their Low Church conservatism with her own family's pluralist spiritualism and socialist principles. Marriage, 1930. First publishing fiction, 1931, under a pseudonym disguising her "bourgeois" name. Unsuccessfully running as a Labour candidate in the 1935 election. Traveling as a *Times* correspondent to Italy and to the USSR. Touring the U.S. to lecture on behalf of the English Speaking Union. Mother's making sojourn to India and back, c.1939; mother's death. Author's working for the British embassy in Washington, D.C., during WWII. Converting to Catholicism, 1943. Becoming an American citizen after WWII. Traveling to Saigon, 1960; her views on the Vietnam War.

The separate first part of Fremantle's book is a portrait of her mother, Clara Annabel Jackson, and a powerful maternal presence can be felt throughout the rest of the narrative. As an unconventional thinker in both religion and politics, Fremantle's mother backed her iconoclastic principles up with social commitments whose influence shows in her daughter's own life. Fremantle's memoir forms a companion piece to her mother's autobiography, *A Victorian Childhood.* Fremantle's approach to her own life is detached and evaluative, an effect of her third-person narration. Her account of life in a moneyed and eccentric family shows its accommodations to sixty years' worth of turbulent political and social transition.

364 FUDGE, Dorothy. 1901–s.l.1980. *Sands of Time: The Autobiography of Dorothy Fudge.* Ed. by Frank Alcock. Dorset: Wimborne Town Council (Word and Action), 1981. 39 pp.; illus. BLC 1976–1982 17:94.

Born in Sherborne, Dorsetshire. Father: Francis Park, worker on Sherborne Castle estate, hospital worker in WWI. Mother: Eliza Gillingham. 4 brothers; 1 sister. Married 1929, Horace Fudge, d.1976. Widow. 1 adopted son. Domestic servant; nurse (children's); factory worker. Rural laboring class.

Modest upbringing, work history, and eventual marriage of a diligent and conscientious domestic worker, 1901–1929, with glances at her later, fulfilling married life. Meticulously describing her childhood home: its furnishings, allocation of one bedroom to boys and one to girls, its lack of indoor plumbing. Attending infants' grammar school, ages 3–9; subsequently attending Sherbourne Abbey Boys and Girls' school. Noting the townspeople's rigid class consciousness. Family's being pious; attending church twice every Sunday. Fondly remembering her father; his winning prizes with home-grown vegetables, his wielding the family authority. At age 13, leaving school for a job as nursemaid with an army major's family; with onset of WWI, being evacuated with them to a tiny, remote nursing home. Contracting diphtheria; spending two months in a hospital. Being hired by the major's neighbors for a new post as parlor maid. Being confirmed in the Church of England, age 15; employer's buying her confirmation dress and veil. After five years, finding another job as house-parlor maid at a vicarage, 1918; helping with children and housework. Meeting a sailor; employer's allowing her to entertain him at home. Author's beginning to enjoy poetry; receiving complimentary tickets to concerts; attending parties. With help of a Sherborne woman, finding a job as undernurse for children at Hucknall. Finding routine boring; leaving job. Returning home. Working as a parlor maid at Sherborne High School for Girls for three years. Looking after her ailing mother. Working in a glove factory. Finding a new parlor maid position, with Col. and Mrs. Adams; their considerate treatment of her. Forming a lifelong friendship with their cook; attending church with her; falling in love with Horace Fudge, the organ blower. Detailing her courtship with Horace. Marriage, 1929. Their staying childless for six years; adopting her brother's son after her sister-in-law's death. Her generally happy married life for forty-seven years. Her husband's death. Remaining active in old age.

Despite her many changes of job resulting from her stated determination "to better herself," Fudge spent her entire life within a stone's throw of Sherborne, Dorset. Her autobiography, under the aegis of a local Dorset town council, appears to have been solicited for a local historical project. Its depiction of her childhood home, c.1900, provides an unusual depth of sociological detail. While there are many urban memoirs addressing their authors' experiences with WWI conditions, Fudge's account is unusual in showing the impact that the war had in distant rural areas; she also takes pains to show the extensive network of mutual obligation that governed her family's interactions and helped to compensate for limited economic resources. This brief memoir is a fund of useful detail for historians of rural Britain in the 20th century.

365 FURSE, Dame Katharine (née Symonds; G.B.E.; R.R.C.). 1875–1952. *Hearts and Pomegranates: The Story of Forty-Five Years, 1875 to 1920.* Peter Davies, 1940. 407 pp.; foreword; front. port.; illus.; index. NUC pre56 188:199.

Born in Clifton, Avon. Father: John Addington Symonds, academic, classicist, historian. Mother: Janet Catherine North. Aunt: botanist and painter Marianne North. 3 sisters. Married 1900, Charles Wellington Furse, A.R.A., artist, d.1904. Widow. 2 sons. WWI administrator; nurse (WWI); Red Cross worker; academic's daughter; organizer (youth). Upper middle class.

Childhood influences, marriage, and WWI professional activities of a gifted administrator, covering her birth to 1940. Parents' characters, courtship, marriage. Author's closeness to her sister Charlotte and their mother. Living in Switzerland, c.1880–82, to control her father's tuberculosis; his moodiness from being effectively exiled from England; his many literary friends including children's poet Edward Lear. Author's making many visits to her aunt, noted naturalist Marianne North; mother's later editing North's autobiography; author's sharing love of botany felt by mother and aunt. Being schooled at home in classics, literature, and science by her parents and governesses. Death of her eldest sister. Commenting on the unusual life she led as a child, permeated by the intellectual atmosphere surrounding her father; seeing ages 12–15 as the most glorious time of her life. Family's spending each spring in Venice; its influence on her growing attraction to Catholicism. Her enthusiasm for winter sports, including the newly introduced downhill skiing. Mother's friendship with Anne Thackeray Ritchie, daughter of the novelist Thackeray. Family's being guests of noted journalist Janet Duff Gordon Ross at her Italian castle. Being in awe of her distinguished father, who taught her history from texts he had written himself; author, youngest of four daughters, sensing he had wanted a son. Parents' loyalty to each other. Discussing a biography of her father; before its publication, her mother's suppressing its mention of his written studies of homosexuality. Discussing the precision of her father's literary style, as well as his collaboration on sexual studies with Havelock Ellis and Walt Whitman. Because of this, author's being familiar from childhood with technical terms relating to sex and physiology; noting the consequent peculiarity of her family by Victorian cultural standards; having early morbid fears of sexual predation. At age 17, deciding to pursue schooling in Lausanne. Father's death, 1893. Informally attending lectures at King's College, Cambridge, while training as a masseuse. Staying with literary critic Leslie Stephen and his family, including daughter Virginia Woolf, during the winter 1893–94. Deciding to follow the family vocation of academia; applying to Newnham College, Cambridge, but being rejected. Describing her personal heroes from history, including Joan of Arc and Josephine Butler, all of them feminist icons. During an 1897–98 London residence, suffering renewed sexual fears and terror of walking alone in the streets. Deciding to train as a nurse. Meeting and marrying Charles Furse, an artist and invalid; wanting to mother and support her genius husband in imitation of her parents' marriage. Dividing their residence between Europe and England; realizing she disliked English conventions and restrictions. Birth of their first son, 1901. Considering herself a "most unnatural" mother; hating breast-feeding. Becoming pregnant again despite using "rather primitive" contraception. Suffering depression over her husband's death three days after second son's birth, 1904; his dying from tuberculosis, just like her father; her struggling to cope with the duties of parenting. Emerging from her emotional problems through Red Cross volunteer work, 1912–13. Her mother's death, 1913. Outbreak of WWI: working as a VAD nurse in France. Receiving the Royal Red Cross from King George V, 1916. Conducting prisoners' wives to Switzerland. Despite opposition from army command, launching an Officers' Training Corps for women. Receiving further honors for her war work. Resigning from VAD in protest over wasteful conditions. Becoming director of the Women's Royal Naval Service, 1917; lamenting that the War Office dismantled the service completely after WWI.

Marching in the Peace Procession, 1918. Undergoing psychoanalysis with Carl Jung in Zurich; being reassured by Jung's assertion that it was a healthy woman's "duty" to perform public service, helping people recover sanity after the war. Helping to found the World Association of Girl Guides and Girl Scouts, 1930–40.

Furse's memoir is one of an interrelated set of autobiographies by distinguished women of her family, among them Margaret Symonds's *Out of the Past* (1925) and *Recollections of a Happy Life, Being the Autobiography of Marianne North* (1892). Raised primarily on the Continent because of her father's need for a sunny, dry climate, she and her sisters received the benefits of his frustrated career as an Oxford professor and were educated far more rigorously and—as she notes—more candidly than the vast majority of young women, even those at England's major universities. Nonetheless, her mother and aunt were even more influential in Furse's life, and were among the capable, feminist heroes she admired. Although she omits mention of it, in 1917 she was made a dame of the British Empire in appreciation of her service to Britain's naval forces in time of war.

366 GADSBY, Elsie (née Goodwin). 1912–?. *Black Diamonds, Yellow Apples: A Working-Class Derbyshire Childhood between the Wars.* Ilkeston: Scollins & Titford, 1978. 61 pp.; illus. by author. BLC 1976–1982 17:183.

Born in Derbyshire. Father: not named, collier. Mother not named. 2 brothers; 1 sister. Married surname Gadsby. Miner's daughter; mill worker. Working class.

Nostalgic family memories, covering author's childhood to adolescence. Death of her parents' first daughter. Father's gentle disposition and idealism; his work as a "daytler," lowest-paid collier, clearing the muck at the pit; his hoping for an inheritance. Mother's being strong, "big and bonny," the voice of authority. Author's dreaming of having a sewing machine to make things for her mother; never getting it. Making many drawings. Playing mainly with boys: looking like one, being accepted as one. Having a bath once a week. Suffering a bout with diphtheria. Daily life: family and gender roles, celebrations, deaths and funerals, generally austere diet, discipline and punishment of children. Birth of a new brother; feeling jealousy. Miners' being allowed one ton of coal a month: one shilling for the coal and four shillings for cartage. Vividly recalling her mam's shoveling the delivered coal into the house. Closeness of family members despite privations.

This brief, simply written autobiography provides a clear image of a few years in one working-class family's life in a rural English mining district. Gadsby's memories were dramatized for BBC radio, as were the reminiscences of Gloucestershire-born Winifred Foley, author of *A Child in the*

Forest and other memoirs. Gadsby's portrait of a mining family's life, restricted to a child's perspective, offers a rosier picture of working-class conditions than does Foley's.

367 GALLOWAY, Margaret Agnes. c.1885–?. *I Lived in Paradise.* Winnipeg: Bulman Bros., 1941. 257 pp.; foreword; front.; illus. NUC pre56 189:637.

Born in Manitoba, Canada. Father: Roper Galloway, born in Scotland, general-store owner in Canada. Mother: Margaret Erb, Canadian. 1 sister. Married, husband not named. 1 son; daughters. Pioneer (Canada). Middle class.

Documentation of late-19th-century family's pioneer life in western Canada. Narrating history of "Paradise" (pseudonym for her hometown near Winnipeg); nationalities of inhabitants; early homesteaders; turbulence caused there by the Riel Rebellion and Fenian Raids; their farming area's enjoying greater stability than mining or mill districts. Describing Windsor House, her family's home. Learning her ancestry by studying family albums with her parents. Describing regional foods, hobbies, and folkcrafts, 1880s–1890s. Having Indian neighbors; one local chief's telling her stories of his tribal youth in Minnesota. Depicting the natural surroundings and wildlife; emphasizing the value to humans of companionship from animals. Thinking affectionately of Scotland because of her Scottish father; his having emigrated in 1873 and set up a dry-goods store. Her mother's being from Paris, Ontario; her having Scottish ancestry also; her meeting author's father by working as a milliner in his store. Noting the store's varied merchandise, medicines, and furs. Describing men's and women's clothing styles, c.1880s. Observing that 1940s children seek passive entertainment from movies, while her own generation had entertained themselves with books and games. Her favorite books' being *Uncle Tom's Cabin* and the novels of James Fenimore Cooper. Learning to swim and ice-skate; riding bicycles and horses in the countryside with her friends. Attending Sunday school and church picnics. Describing Christmas celebrations and local courting customs. In 1892, a huge fire's burning much of the town, including her father's store. Depicting weather characteristic of the plains: local hailstorms and a cyclone. Re-creating through memory the vanished way of life of her childhood.

Rich in a sense of family tradition, Galloway's account illustrates some of the means (such as the carefully kept family album) that immigrant families used to overcome their regional dislocation and reestablish continuity with their old-world heritage. Equally strong in her writing is her tangible fidelity to a previous era, more rural and—in her own estimation—more worthy than the milieu in which she writes. Her book is a valuable resource for its discussion of the settling of western Canada and its author's painstaking re-creation of customs and culture.

368 GALWAY, Marie Carola, Lady (née Blennerhassett; C.B.E.). 1876–1963. *The Past Revisited: People and Happenings Recalled.* Harvill Press, 1953. 236 pp.; illus. NUC pre56 190:180.

Born in London. Father: Sir Rowland Blennerhassett, Liberal Unionist M.P. Mother: Countess Charlotte Leyden, scholar. 2 brothers. Married 1894, Baron Raphael d'Erlanger, biologist, d.1897. Married 1913, Sir Henry Lionel Galway, K.C.M.G., D.S.O., d.1949. Children. Society woman; philanthropist; Red Cross worker. Upper class.

Philanthropist's extensive involvement with charitable activities and organizations, following a conventional upper-class upbringing, covering her childhood to the WWI era. Father's interest in Austrian politics; his work as a Liberal Unionist M.P. Mother's scholarly work; her having written a book on Madame de Staël. Author's childhood household; having math, French, and German lessons with governesses. Moving to Bavaria, 1880s, to live with her maternal grandmother, Countess Leyden. Attending school in Bavaria; attending convent school in France. Courtship and marriage in Paris, 1894. Early death of her husband, 1897; her great shock and grief. Returning to London with their children, 1898. Her love of the stage; meeting Sarah Bernhardt and Eleanora Duse. Friendships with other famous people. Her interest in aviation; wanting to meet Wilbur Wright. Friendships with Gertrude Bell and Mrs. Humphry Ward. Traveling in Spain, Italy, and Constantinople. In London, dispensing charity to Boer War veterans' wives and children. Her reformist thoughts on applications of the Poor Law. Working with the Mothercraft Training Society, an organization teaching postnatal care. Serving as chair of the Model Training Centre for Welfare of Babies. With Lady Kenmare, working with nurses under Queen Victoria's Jubilee Nurses in Ireland. Traveling to Africa, then Australia; her Red Cross work in South Australia.

Although largely a portrait gallery of family, friends, and acquaintances, Lady Galway's memoir gives considerable space to an account of the author's varied charitable activities. Lady Galway's viewpoint is outward looking; she avoids dwelling on her emotional reactions to the events in her life. Nevertheless, the details of her activism create a picture of a woman with a social commitment characteristic of enlightened upper-class people of her time.

369 GAMBLE, Rose (née Naylor). c.1920–?. *Chelsea Child.* British Broadcasting Corp., 1979. 204 pp. BLC 1976–1982 9:92.

Born in London. Father not named, seaman, unemployed. Mother not named, factory worker. 2 brothers; 2 sisters. Saleswoman; WWII volunteer. Working class.

Personal and occupational memories, emphasizing the ups and downs of daily life in Cockney culture, spanning author's childhood to WWII.

Recalling her childhood neighborhood in Chelsea; traders, street merchants. Her parents' backgrounds and early married life; mother's having had fourteen pregnancies, but only five children's surviving. Father's old-fashioned discipline; rows resulting from his drinking and long-term unemployment. Mother's resorting to Poor Law Guardians for support. Author's enjoying her first schooling, age 3. Father's forcing children to pawn items; their having to eat discarded food; their stealing tar blocks from road crews. Author's having a bout of appendicitis; being christened during her hospital stay; being the only child in her family to enter the Church of England. Being hospitalized for meningitis. Urban renewal's forcing family to relocate to a flat in the new Guinness buildings. Author's interest in reading; winning book prizes at school; father's pawning her books. Father's educating children through walking tours of London; visiting libraries and museums. Attending Sunday school; writing a prize-winning essay. Winning a scholarship to a private school; feeling out of place, disliking snobs. Keeping her "school pronunciation" separate from her "home pronunciation"; feeling she is living "three lives": one at home, one with neighborhood children, and one at school. Wanting her parents to stay away from school on visiting day. Going to work with her sisters in a shop selling art objects. Absorbing the shop's aesthetic values; learning to speak easily with the cultivated patrons. Her growing awareness of fascists and communists and of Jewish refugees, late 1930s. WWII: working in Wales in the Women's Land Army. Discussing the profound changes wrought by the war.

Using her family as her focus, Gamble liberally employs Cockney dialect in her vivid re-creation of working-class life. The book's intensity suggests that the author remained nostalgic about her childhood environment, the main source of her evident strength of character, even after her pursuit of education gained her entrance into the middle class.

370 GANDY, Ida (née Hony). c.1884–?. *A Wiltshire Childhood.* George Allen & Unwin, 1929. 219 pp.; front.; illus. by Marjorie Whittington. NUC pre56 190:303.

Raised in Wiltshire. Father: Charles Hony, vicar. Mother: Annie Lewin. 2 brothers; 4 sisters. Married, husband not named, physician. Sons. Wrote *Round About the Little Steeple.* Family historian; clergyman's daughter; physician's spouse. Middle class.

Memories of a late-19th-century rural education and social life, covering author's ages 8–16. Father's teaching Latin to author and siblings. Family's raising bees. Author's learning to ring the church bells; reading the Bible to elderly people in father's parish. Visiting a gypsy tribe with her father. Memories of her nurse. Playing with her siblings at the canal: ice-skating, boating. With siblings, playing tennis, taking dance lessons, watching shepherds at work. Preferring playing outside to attending tea parties. Mother's abandoning governess system, sending children to a day school. Mother's encouraging daughters to be more sociable and attend formal functions. Author's describing neighboring villages she toured with a friend. Father's taking a smaller parish nearby; family's move. Portraying more aspects of country lifestyles.

Arranged topically in vignettes, Gandy's reminiscences constitute a wistful re-creation of a child's carefree existence in a now-vanished, gentler era. Rather than indulging in personal feelings, the author constructs images of the past that stir the reader's imagination. She also wrote **371** *Staying with the Aunts* (1963), a humorous account both of her eccentric aunts and of her family roots.

372 GAPOSCHKIN, Cecilia Helena (née Payne). 1900–1979. *Cecilia Payne-Gaposchkin: An Autobiography and Other Recollections.* Ed. by Katherine Haramundanis (author's daughter). Cambridge University Press, 1984. 269 pp.; illus.; intros. by Jesse L. Greenstein, Peggy A. Kidwell, and Betty Grierson Leaf; biblio. of works by author; "postlude"; index. CBI 1984 p.1082.

Born at Holywell Lodge, Wendover, Buckinghamshire. Father: Edward John Payne. Mother: Emma Leonora Helena Pertz, Prussian. 1 sister; 1 brother. Married 1934, Sergei Gaposchkin, Russian astronomer. 2 sons; 1 daughter. Wrote *Stellar Atmospheres* (1925), *Stars in the Making* (1953), *Stars and Clusters* (1979), others. Knew many leading astronomers of all nations. Scientist; astronomer; scientific writer; academic; emigrant (U.S.). Middle class.

In-depth discussion of scientific advances in astronomy and author's role as an academic researcher, emphasizing the difficulties faced by women in academia, accompanied by reflections on science, spirituality, and personal experiences, covering 1900–79. Ancestry and family history; each family generation having been dominated by prominent women. Her childhood fascination with nature. Feeling envious of her privileged younger brother. Memories of her father, his musical gifts; his sudden death when she was age 4. Attending dame school. Her handicap of left-handedness; developing ambidexterity. Receiving incomplete sex education from her mother; later completing it through botanical study. Analyzing the strengths and weaknesses of education she received at ages 6–12. Family's moving to London for brother's education; author's missing the country. Attending a large Church of England school, ages 12–17; this school's emphasis on religion; its principal's mistrust of science. Author's fascination with learning the chemical elements; tending to substitute science for God. Influence of her first woman mentor, science teacher Dorothy Dalglish. Studying botany. Outbreak of WWI. Learning more advanced science, despite school's attempt to train her as a classical scholar; school's expelling her, seemingly ruining her prospects for a Cambridge scholarship. At age 17, attending St. Paul's Girls' School. Being admitted to Newnham College, Cambridge, age 19;

leaving the study of botany for physics. Discussing lectures of Neils Bohr and prominent physicist Ernest Rutherford; Rutherford's scorn for women students. Deciding to study advanced physics with astronomy on the side. Her attempts to answer advanced problems in astronomy. Living in Cambridge, Massachusetts, after 1923; her difficulties in adjusting to U.S. culture. Offering a detailed discussion of the development of astrophysics; her research into stellar atmospheres under Harvard Observatory's director, Harlow Shapley. Eventually experiencing professional conflict with Shapley. Receiving the first Ph.D. in astronomy to be granted at either Harvard or Radcliffe. Working as editor of Harvard Observatory publications for twenty years. Becoming a U.S. citizen, 1931. In 1932, visiting astronomers in the USSR; discovering political repression there; in Germany, meeting her future husband, Russian astronomer Sergei Gaposchkin. Helping him emigrate; their marriage, 1934. Their joint studies of novae and variable stars. During WWII, their forming a debating society on international politics at Harvard. Becoming the first woman professor at Harvard, 1956. Shapley's retirement, 1959. Author's serving as chair of the Astronomy Department until 1966; being Harvard's first woman department chair. With her husband, extensively studying variable stars in the Magellanic Clouds. Discussing at length the difference her gender has made in her academic career; science and popular myth; her spiritual and philosophical development. Receiving prestigious awards; having a minor planetoid named after her in 1977.

The text shows the author's consciousness of herself as a trailblazing woman scientist and a significant contributor to 20th-century astronomy. A pioneer in applying atomic and spectroscopic physics to astronomy, Gaposchkin knew many leading astronomers from many nations. She comments in detail on her situation in academic science at a time when women had few opportunities for professional advancement, especially in England; she moved to the U.S. because of the greater opportunities there. She discusses the technical details of her research enthusiastically and at length. The prefaces by her colleagues place her work within its historical context; her daughter's preface is a memoir of her mother, with additional details on their travels together and on Gaposchkin's life after 1950.

373 GARNETT, Angelica. 1918–s.l.1992. *Deceived with Kindness: A Bloomsbury Childhood.* San Diego: Harcourt Brace Jovanovich, 1985. 181 pp.; prologue; illus.; index. BLC 1982–1985 9:595. (1st pub. Chatto & Windus, 1984.)

Born in Charleston, Sussex. Natural father: Duncan Grant, artist. Mother: Vanessa Bell, artist. Legal father: Clive Bell (Vanessa's husband), art critic. 2 half-brothers. Married 1942, David Garnett, artist, d.1981. 4 daughters. Wrote *Mosaics* (1967). Artist (painter); artist's daughter. Upper middle class.

Introspective study of relationships and emotional nuances between members of the author's famous "Bloomsbury" family from before her birth to the death of her biological father, Duncan Grant, c.1900–78. In 1975, living an isolated life in London after leaving her husband; frequently visiting Duncan at Charleston, the family home in Sussex, but resenting his preserving a polite distance toward her. Also feeling crippled by resentment of her dead mother, Vanessa. With Duncan's death, 1978, deciding to conquer family memories by writing them down. Vanessa's having been the oldest child of literary critic Leslie Stephen's second marriage; from age 15, having to manage household and younger siblings—including mentally unstable Virginia—after their mother died. Two years later, after death of her beloved half-sister, Stella, Vanessa's temporarily falling in love with Stella's widowed husband, Jack. Later, Vanessa's meeting Clive Bell, friend of her brother Thoby; suddenly agreeing to marry Clive after Thoby's death from typhoid, 1908; Angelica's believing both romances helped Vanessa establish links with dead loved ones; also believing Vanessa's happy marriage was soon undercut by jealous Virginia, who flirted with Clive, 1908–14; Clive's not having an affair with Virginia, but having other mistresses; his ceasing sexual relations with Vanessa after 1910. Vanessa's seeking happiness thereafter in two obsessions: her painting and her children. Vanessa's also having extramarital affairs, first with art critic Roger Fry, then with younger artist Duncan Grant. Duncan's being a Strachey cousin, born into the Bloomsbury enclave; Angelica's calling him "homosexual with bisexual tendencies"; his bringing young male lovers—including "Bunny" Garnett, later Angelica's husband—to Charleston to live with Vanessa and Clive *en ménage.* Vanessa's deciding to have a child by Duncan; birth of Angelica, 1919. Vanessa and Clive's acknowledging but never discussing Angelica's real parentage; its being known to everyone but Angelica. Angelica's growing up both at Charleston and in Bloomsbury section of London, petted by a crowd of famous adults: Duncan, Leonard and Virginia Woolf, Roger Fry, Maynard Keynes, Lytton Strachey. Being constantly exposed to unconventional sexual behavior: homosexual affairs between adults, Duncan's working naked, Aunt Virginia's demands for unwelcome bouts of kissing. Each Christmas, family's visiting Clive's kindly, Victorian parents in Wiltshire; Angelica's loving them; Vanessa and Duncan's privately ridiculing their conventionality. Asking to be sent to boarding school, age 10; anticipating independence there, but instead being coddled in deference to her famous family; Vanessa and headmistress's conspiring to omit classes Angelica found difficult. At school, gaining a close girlfriend, "Beetle," but friend's reacting aversely to seeing the Bells's eccentric living arrangements; Beetle's telling Angelica she was probably Duncan's illegitimate daughter; Angelica's declaring she instantly felt the truth of this. Until age 15, author's growing up in household *ménage*, either observing Duncan and Vanessa painting in their studio, 1920s–1930s, or roaming unchaperoned. Clive's being distant as a parent; Duncan's being friendly to Angelica but remote; Vanessa's smothering her. Angelica's favorite adults being Roger Fry, who taught her art, and Leonard Woolf, who demanded she fulfill obligations like an adult. Family's spending extensive holidays on the Continent, letting adolescent author wander in sexually provocative environments. Finding stability in the influence of her best-loved brother Julian, 1935; his being ten years her elder; author's listening to Julian and his friends discuss the looming European war, in awe of their brilliance. After Julian's accepting an academic post in China, author's feeling the direction had gone out of her life. Julian's returning briefly, 1938, then leaving to volunteer for Spain's civil war. The adults' collectively deciding Angelica's future was to go on stage; her taking acting lessons at the London Theatre Studio. Being frustrated by further coddling because of her family; turning to ballet training. Just before her first performance, receiving notification of Julian's death; returning to Sussex to comfort Vanessa. In her grief, Vanessa's telling Angelica that Duncan was her real father. Exulting privately, Angelica's being afraid to discuss it with Duncan; never succeeding in establishing a daughterly relationship with him. Although desperately needing a father figure, feeling she had none—unrelated Clive was responsible but reserved toward her, and Duncan was irresponsible. Beginning a courtship with David "Bunny" Garnett while at the London Theatre Studio, 1936. Bunny's living at Charleston when Angelica was born; his taking her as a child to visit his wife in Huntingdonshire; his being over 40 and still married while pursuing Angelica, age 17. Author's remembering how she had imitated Vanessa's pattern of using sex with one person to establish ties to another: Bunny Garnett had been Duncan's lover, and she needed Duncan's fathering. After death of Bunny's wife, his distressing Vanessa and Duncan by marrying Angelica, 1942. Angelica's writing that she saw the marriage as her chance to show independence; her and Bunny's leaving immediately for Northumberland; rusticating there for twelve years. In 1944, during Angelica's second pregnancy, Vanessa's being diagnosed with breast cancer; illness's reestablishing ties between author and her mother, but author's continuing to resent her, in belief that Vanessa's strong personality had conditioned her to be dominated by an older husband. Author's becoming obsessed by mothering four daughters; never developing a public life. Continuing to take extensive holidays with Vanessa and Duncan as they aged; during each one, Angelica's resuming her dependent behavior pattern. Vanessa's dying suddenly, 1961; author's feeling crushed that she had never been able to show her love for her mother. Returning to Charleston for the funeral; staying on with Duncan afterward; suddenly becoming aware that, with her mother's death, she was at last on her own. Finding the courage to leave the domineering Bunny; discovering she too had breast cancer; realizing that in her body as well as her character, she had a potent identification with her mother.

Although Garnett's prologue is self-absorbed, once she turns to the task of resurrecting her memories of the Bell family circle she is more successful than others of this family's historians at rendering not only the characters of individuals but the character and flavor of their relationships. Her memoir of the Bloomsbury group has a sense of immediacy and authentic testimony that no later study, however well-researched, can match. Considering the resentments toward family members which she is at pains to articulate, Garnett takes equal pains to be fair to them, and even her anecdotes of being overshadowed by Vanessa show her unstinting esteem. The most problematic portrait she draws is that of Virginia Woolf, which shows the novelist as unstable and predatorily jealous; the 1972 biography of Woolf by Angelica's brother Quentin helps flesh out this picture with greater detachment. Produced as personal therapy, Garnett's book benefits from comparative reading with scholarly biographies of the Bloomsbury group, such as Frances Spalding's *Vanessa Bell* (1983), which Garnett herself recommends.

374 GARRETT, Eileen Jeanette (née Lyttle). 1893–1970. *My Life as a Search for the Meaning of Mediumship*. New York: Arno Press, 1973. 225 pp. NUC pre56 191:607. (1st pub. New York: Oquaga Press, 1939.)

Born in County Meath, Ireland. Father: Anthony Vancho, Spanish. Mother: Anna. Orphaned after both parents committed suicide, c.1896. Married c.1909, Clive; divorced c.1915. Married c.1915, husband not named, WWI soldier, died c.1915. Married c.1918, husband not named, WWI veteran; divorced c.1930. 3 sons; 1 daughter. Clairvoyant/psychic; spiritualist; restaurant owner. Rural farming class.

Clairvoyant's psychic gifts and related difficulties in childhood and married life, and her rejection of practicing mediumship in favor of the scientific testing of her abilities and their meaning, covering her birth to 1939. Her early childhood on an Irish farm with her strict Protestant uncle and aunt. Aunt's coldness toward author; author's withdrawing into herself to shut out aunt's nagging voice. Her childhood visions of a "little old lady" and of three children who warn her not to believe much of what adults say; her aunt and uncle's accusing her of lying about her visions. Starting school, age 4. Seeing people's auras; learning she cannot speak of her visionary powers with others. Moving to Dublin; attending a National School there, age 8. Having an accurate premonition of another aunt's death; caretaker aunt's again accusing author of lying; in revenge, drowning aunt's brood of ducklings; seeing their souls rise from their bodies and deciding she had not killed them, only changed their form. Later forming a strong aversion to killing, hunting, and cruelty to animals. At age 10, receiving reassurance about her gifts from a gypsy psychic. Attending a Dublin boarding school; leaving after strict discipline weakened her health. Briefly attending a girls school. Uncle's death; her subsequent vision of him. Seeing a lack of spirituality in her Anglican confirmation, age 12; ultimately rejecting both Catholicism and Protestantism as empty forms. Acquiring a 24-year-old medical student as a suitor; his giving her information about sex. Aunt's informing her that author's parents had eloped and that they had committed suicide when she was age 3. Moving to a cousin's home in London, age 16. Impulsively marrying cousin's friend to escape boarding school. Husband's infidelity; his insistence on her having psychiatric treatment for her visions. Author's pregnancies; births and deaths of two sons; seeing their spirits leave their bodies; searching for further meaning in this; discovering the power to leave her own body. Visiting Ireland; attempting and abandoning acting there. Returning to London. Birth and death of her third son. Her expanding psychic sensitivity; husband and psychiatrist's defining it as insanity. Daughter's birth. Author's divorce during WWI. Opening a restaurant; enjoying her new freedom. Leaving the restaurant business; opening a hostel for wounded WWI officers; marriage to one of them; after his departure for the front, having a vision of his death before receiving word of it. Learning to control unbidden visions through auto-suggestion. Marrying another veteran. Her postwar Labour Party work. Meeting Edward Carpenter; his reassuring her about her psychic experiences. Discovering her powers of healing, psychometry, clairvoyance, and clairaudience. Visiting London séances; her disgust at their banality. While in trance states, discovering her "controls," Uvani and Abdul Latif; becoming a trance medium at British College of Psychic Science. Husband's objecting to her spiritualist interests; their divorce. Undergoing scientific experiments in the U.S., testing her powers of clairvoyance, trance, and psychometry, 1931–33. Reassessing trance mediumship; refuting spiritualists' explanations for her powers; analyzing unconscious interaction between medium and sitter. Deciding to use her psychic powers in scientific experiments only. Returning to England, 1934. Testing trance state in hypnosis experiments. Extensively analyzing her psychic capacities and how she developed them; believing that all humans possess psychic powers to some degree. Feeling reluctant to continue as a professional medium. Ultimately finding spiritualism too limiting; redefining her understanding of death.

Garrett's autobiography is a convincing portrayal of a woman who apparently possessed real psychic abilities. Although her chapters vary greatly in both length and development, suggesting her status as an amateur writer, Garrett's tone carries great conviction. Her search for the meaning inherent in these powers led her beyond spiritualism into scientific testing, to conclusions very unlike the mediumistic beliefs of an earlier generation. For an informative contrast, the reader may consult either *The Autobiography of Emma Hardinge Britten* or Georgina Houghton's *Evenings at Home in Spiritual Séance.*

375 GAUNT, Mary Eliza Bakewell. 1872–1942. *Alone in West Africa.* T. Werner Laurie, c.1912. 404 pp.; front. port.; illus.; index. NUC pre56 192:575.

Born in Australia. Father not named, emigrant to Australia during gold rush, gold commissioner on the Buckland River. Mother not named. 5 brothers; 1 sister. Married, husband not named, physician, died soon after marriage. Widow. Wrote 16 adventure novels, books on her travels in China and Jamaica, and *George Washington and the Men Who Made the American Revolution* (1929). Novelist; foreign resident (Africa); travel writer; miscellaneous writer. Middle class.

Novelist's research trip to Africa, with background on her youth in Australia, covering her birth to age 40. Family history: maternal grandfather as colonizer of Van Dieman's land; father as emigrant gold prospector to Australia, c.1862. Reading about Africa in childhood. Envying her brothers' freedom to earn money and travel; seeing marriage as her only option. Marriage; living with her husband in Warrnambool. Husband's death; author's determination to make her own living. Traveling to London; living in poverty as a writer. Researching and writing a novel about West Africa to raise money to go there. Traveling to Africa on friends' donations and publisher's advance to research further books. Living in Gambia at Government House, Bathurst. Being surprised by the beauty of Africa. Discussing Gambia's value to the British Empire. Visiting Sierra Leone and Liberia; meeting Liberian president and his wife. Her antipathy to interracial marriage and to blacks' adopting Western dress and manners; hoping white men will always rule Africa with a "strong hand." Doubting the value of missionary efforts; declaring "one white child was worth a thousand problematical souls of negroes." Feeling the burden of being looked after by solicitous men whose attentions she didn't really need. Visiting Guinea and the Gold Coast. Learning to be severe with native porters; traveling alone with them; being one of the few white women to enter certain areas. Believing in fresh air as vital to Europeans' survival in Africa. Visiting Accra; mentioning human sacrifice practiced by blacks there, 1911. Learning about porters' belief in taboos. Taking a canoe trip up the Volta; fearing "half-civilized" black workers at river stations; advising other adventurous white women against traveling up the river. Describing the isolation of some British colonials. In German colony at Togo, praising German administration and discipline of blacks; seeing the German methods with blacks as superior to those of the English. Visiting a sleeping sickness camp. Discussing marriage and motherhood among Keta tribeswomen. Risking her life crossing heavy surf at mouth of Volta. Visiting Ashanti gold fields; expressing the opinion that deforestation makes the climate more unhealthful. Recalling the days when her father was gold commissioner on the Buckland River. Visiting sites of a 1900 rebellion against the British. Describing West Africa's natural wealth and colonial civil service system. Encouraging women to go to Africa.

Before her husband's death Gaunt had taken a university degree and sold a novel, although she does not discuss this in her autobiography. As an Australian who had lived on the frontier, her perspective on African colonial life differs greatly from that of most Englishwomen. She tries to dispel prejudices against Africa's climate and to encourage Englishwomen to settle there, hinting that their presence is necessary for the moral restraint of Englishmen far from home. Nevertheless, as she confesses, she has "strong feelings on the question of colour" and consistently belittles the native Africans' capacity for learning and "civilization"; neither does she evince respect for Europeans trying to teach them. Gaunt also wrote books about her travels in China and Russia (**376** *A Broken Journey,* 1919) and Jamaica (*Where the Twain Meet,* 1922).

377 GAWTHORPE, Mary Eleanor. 1881–c.1960. *Up Hill to Holloway.* Penobscot, Maine: Traversity Press, 1962. 254 pp.; front. port.; maps. NUC 1963–1967 19:276.

Born in Leeds, Yorkshire. Father: John Gawthorpe, leather factory worker. Mother: Annie Eliza Mountain. 3 sisters; 1 brother. Single. Political activist; suffragist, militant; prison inmate; teacher; pupil-teacher; journalist; factory worker; politician; public speaker; foreign resident (U.S.). Working class.

Lively, informative presentation of suffrage activism, focusing on author's prison experiences and occupational endeavors, set in a framework of the social problems afflicting the lower classes, covering 1880s–1907. Grandparents' frugality, working-class lives; how her parents' ambitions were sacrificed to economic necessity. At age 5, attending St. Michael's church school, Leeds, where father was superintendent of Infants' Sunday School. Mother's nurturing of children. Attending girls' school, age 7. Father's brief infidelity to mother; his ceasing regular churchgoing. Deaths of two of her sisters in general family illness; author's hospitalization with typhoid. Discord between parents caused by father's bouts of drunkenness; author's siding with her mother. Describing leather factory where father worked. Assisting father in his part-time Conservative election work; his thwarted intellectual abilities. Extensive discussion of attending St. Michael's National School, Buslingthorpe. Teaching at St. Michael's church school in Leeds as a pupil-teacher, starting at age 13, due to father's influence. Author's positive relationship with her mother. Mother's character; her growing reluctance to sleep with father; her giving in to his demands. Discussing church and Sunday school; author's resistance to church membership in adolescence; eventually dropping church altogether. Continuing as a pupil-teacher to age 17. Realizing her duty to contribute to mother's support would keep her from attending teachers' training college; hinting that father habitually shirks his share. Employment, age 19, as assistant mistress at St. Luke's Boys' School, Beeston Hill. Moving to Beeston Hill, 1902, taking most of family with her. Self-education through reading magazines and secondhand books. Courtship with her first love; deciding not to marry. Taking courses at Leeds School of Music; taking an elocution course. Attending the Technical School of the Leeds Institute of Science, Art, and Literature, 1903–05. Receiving a teaching certificate, 1904. Earning £60 a year. Taking exams toward L.L.A. degree, 1904. Attending "Labour Church" services. Writing a woman's page for the weekly *Labour News*. Speaking on Labour, child care, and punishment of criminals. Working on Children's Relief Committee; this leading her to see the need for votes for women. Her activities in Leeds Arts Club; memories of Alfred Orage and Holbrook Jackson. Traveling to Edinburgh and Glasgow to assist suffrage movement. Her friendship with Ethel Annakin Snowden, author of *The Woman Socialist* (1906). Noting tensions between suffrage and Labour activists. Writing to the imprisoned Christabel Pankhurst to express support; meeting the Pankhursts; resigning her teaching post to work on suffrage campaign full-time. Her increased Labour activities in Leeds: speaking; organizing meetings; campaigning as Labour candidate in 1907 Cockermouth by-election. Her Women's Social and Political Union activities in Bramley. Traveling to London; participating in House of Commons suffrage protest; her arrest and imprisonment in Holloway, along with Christabel Pankhurst and Emmeline Pethick-Lawrence, for five weeks, 1906. Mother's tears over her imprisonment; father's pride in her suffrage activity. Friendships with suffrage leaders, including Mabel Tuke. Attending a banquet in honor of the released prisoners, presided over by Millicent Garrett Fawcett. Perceiving that the suffrage struggle has only begun.

Gawthorpe's idiosyncratic style suggests self-education; her tone is chatty and expansive. The book's chronology is loose, as she discusses in passing events following her first suffragette imprisonment. The author contributes much detailed information on Church of England schools, on the "Labour Church" (later the Socialist Institute) and Labour Party activities in Leeds, and on her active and passionate commitment in the early days of the suffrage movement. After 1916, Gawthorpe lived in the U.S.

378 GAY, Maisie (stage name; née Munro-Noble). 1883–1945. *Laughing through Life.* Hurst & Blackett, 1931. 284 pp.; front. port.; intro.; illus. NUC pre56 193:155.

Born in London. Parents not named. 1 brother; 1 sister. Single. Actress (comic, music hall). Middle class.

Tart observations and nostalgic anecdotes about the English theatrical world and author's experiences within it, spanning her childhood to 1930. Being an unwanted child, raised by her godmother. Until old enough for school, growing up entirely among adults. Being allowed to visit her parents only on Sundays; parents' raising younger siblings despite having farmed out the author. "Godma's" teaching her elocution, deportment, and spelling. From early childhood, author's sensing the powerful public impact of her own singing voice. After godmother's death, one of her nieces' paying to send author to a coeducational school in Germany, age 11; author's gaining social confidence there, and studying piano. After returning to England, attending Frances Mary Buss's North London Collegiate School for Girls, ages 12–15. Being too poor to train toward her goal of becoming an opera singer. Looking for work without thinking she might go on stage; through a chance encounter with an actress on an omnibus, landing her first chorus part in *The Cherry Girl,* 1890s; signing a contract. Taking the stage name of Maisie Gay. Gaining a reputation for being able to play any comic part; moving up to the London stage. Touring the provinces in *The Quaker Girl.* Performing at the Gaiety Theatre, London, in *Our Miss Gibbs.* Taking *The Quaker Girl* to New York. Offering her impressions of the U.S., where social opinions of actors were lower, theatre expenses and salaries higher, than in England. Memories of Prohibition. Back in London, beginning her association with Charlot Revues. Wanting to act in serious roles but not having the desirable glamorous "look." Her friendship with Gertrude Lawrence. Noel Coward's writing songs for her. Charlot's taking his top stars to America without her; Beatrice Lillie's earning fame by taking over author's "March with Me" song. Switching to musical comedy. Dealing with bad reviews. Her first incursion into vaudeville. Her reputation for off-color humor in her songs. Performing for troops during the 1926 general strike. Recalling her disastrous tour of Australia. Wishing press would not invade and expose actors' private lives. Discussing theatre lore: how to make an audience laugh, the art of costume and makeup, study of gesture and voice. Author's being short and dumpy; seeing beauty as a handicap to actresses who rely on it at the expense of emotion and ability. Providing nitty-gritty business details of producing shows. Discussing the infant film industry in England. Performing in sound films. Never broadcasting on the BBC because of its decency laws and censorship rules.

As a comedienne famous for her character roles, Gay exemplifies the busy working actress and uses her memoir as a guided tour of personalities, working conditions, and techniques of performance in comic theatre on both sides of the Atlantic. Although charting her own rise, she is particularly observant of cultural details in the places she visits, creating a memorable picture of New York and Prohibition during the 1920s as well as of the rise of "variety" or vaudeville. Gay's book is fascinating both as social history and as a study of the acting profession in the early 20th century.

379 GELL, Edith Mary (née Brodrick). 1860–d.a.1920. *Under Three Reigns, 1860–1920.* Kegan Paul, Trench, Trubner & Co., Ltd., 1927. 307 pp.; front.; intro.; illus.; index. NUC pre56 194:77.

Born in England. Father: the Hon. William Brodrick, later 8th Viscount Midleton. Mother: the Hon. Augusta Mary Fremantle. 2 sisters; 1 brother. Paternal grandfather: the 1st Baron Cottesloe. Married 1889, Philip Lyttleton Gell. Wrote *The Cloud of Witness, The Happy Warrior, The Empire's Honour.* Novelist; philanthropist; Oxford hostess; suffragist. Aristocracy.

Personal experiences and opinions of an aristocratic Oxford hostess, covering author's first six decades. Recalling the strict discipline of her childhood home. Her father's succession to the family title; family's moving to Peper Harrow. Her contact with wage-earners and their families on the estate and in the village. Attending Sunday Anglican church services; social class implications of church attendance. Visiting neighbor Alfred, Lord Tennyson. Attending ambulance (first aid) classes. During her adolescence, living in London; recalling her social debut and presentation at court. Commenting on changes in coming-out customs after the death of Queen Victoria. Her employment as "Lady of the House" (hostess) for the warden at Oxford. Religious life at Oxford. Remembering Matthew Arnold's visits. Commenting on Home Rule for Ireland advocates versus the Liberal Unionist League branch at Oxford; political meetings; politicians Jesse Collings and Lord Randolph Churchill. Her interest in women's education at Oxford. Marriage to Philip Lyttleton Gell, 1889. Her friendships with Benjamin Jowett, master of Balliol; William Stubbs, Bishop of Oxford; and Cosmo Gordon Lang, Archbishop of York. Recalling the establishment of Ladies' Oxford House for working-class women. Death of Queen Victoria; coronation of King Edward VII. Working on Women's Committee to save church endowments in Wales. Outbreak of WWI: describing national morale during the war; food rationing; establishment of factories for war work; women's entrance into the war-work market; activities of Soldiers and Sailors' Family Association. Growth of night-school classes for working people and their families. Victory of Women's Suffrage Movement, 1918; perceiving a need to politicize women voters.

A faint air of superiority suffuses the writing as Gell depicts the relationship between her personal experiences and the larger framework of late-Victorian life among the liberal and well-educated upper classes. She speaks of the "high level of probity in the second half of Victoria's reign" and of Victoria herself as "a wise old Queen who was justified in making immorality unfashionable" so that her "weaker" subjects might benefit—and, Gell implies, such "weaker" subjects were mainly to be found among the lower classes. Despite her evident biases, Gell provides considerable information about scholarly and political life at Oxford, and evaluates important contemporary events in England.

380 GIBBS, Rose. 1892–d.a.1967. *In Service. Rose Gibbs Remembers.* Cambridge: Ellison's Editions, 1981. 18 pp.; illus. BLC 1976–1982 18:62.

Born in East End of London. Father not named, soldier. Mother not named, domestic servant. 1 brother; 1 sister. Married 1915, Harry, d.1967. Widow. Domestic servant. Working class.

Memories of a deprived and difficult childhood, followed by demanding duties of life in domestic service, focused on 1890s–1915. Remembering, as a small child, having watched her father's regiment departing for the Boer War. His military history: having joined up while an adolescent, then deserted; his later reenlisting under the alias "George Hall"; his regiment's being posted to Egypt for eight years; his remaining in reserve for twenty-one years more, during which time he was sent to South Africa. Memories of Queen Victoria; her funeral. Recalling privations in her childhood home: existing on bread and black treacle; mother's trying to support three small children on army pay of 12 shillings per week. Her baby brother's accident on a train; his losing a foot; family's inability to afford to instigate a lawsuit. Father's being wounded; his being "invalided out" of the army with a pension of 8 shillings per week; his inability to find and hold work. Author's attending council school until age 13. Helping her mother raise the younger children; teacher's permitting author to bring her baby brother to school with her. Headmistress's giving author free tickets to a soup kitchen. Finding pleasure in attending church and singing. Entering domestic service, age 13. Working for a young couple for 10 shillings per month; having almost no time off. Finding a job in a large house looking after eight adults: cleaning, polishing, waiting table; working very long hours for four years. Taking a temporary job as third laundry maid in a London mansion; being given a recommendation by her employer, Lady Lovelace, to help her secure a job on a huge estate at Box Hill, Dorking, with the Dowager Countess of Harrowby. Life on estate: good food for servants, beautiful surroundings. Wanting to take a leave to visit London and see Harry, her long-time beau; employer's refusing request; author's choosing to leave; this marking the end of her being in service on a "really big" job. Saving money for four years to marry. Marriage, 1915. Recalling fifty-two years of happy married life. Husband's death when he and author were both age 75.

Without frills or fanfare, Gibbs recalls how the strained financial circumstances of her childhood led her to enter domestic service, which gave her room, board, and protection. She also portrays some of the poor working conditions she experienced and describes some difficult employers. Her memories are not self-pitying as she details her perspective on the domestic service market in terms of employers' expectations and servants' reactions.

381 GIELGUD, Kate Terry (née Lewis). 1868–1958. *Kate Terry Gielgud: An Autobiography.* Max Reinhardt, 1953. 239 pp.; front. port.; foreword by Sir John Gielgud; illus.; index. NUC pre56 199:129.

Born in Kensington, London. Father: James Lewis, silk mercer to Queen Victoria. Mother: Kate Terry, actress. Aunt: Ellen Terry, actress. 3 sisters. Married 1893, Frank Gielgud. 4 sons (including actor John Gielgud); 1 daughter. Society woman; WWI volunteer. Upper class.

Personal reminiscences and mild-mannered observations on the creature comforts of upper-class life in the late 19th and early 20th centuries, spanning author's childhood to the aftermath of WWI. Family history. Her love for her father; her mother's strictness and religiosity. Lewis Carroll's visiting the family. Studying at home with a governess. Describing family's lifestyle and activities. Seeing her aunt, Ellen Terry, perform at the Crystal Palace; theatrical careers of Ellen and her sister Marion. Terry family's long involvement in the theatre; state of the theatre, its elitist tendencies, c.1880s. Author's social debut. Attending performances at the Lyceum Theatre; memories of Henry Irving. Meeting Sarah Bernhardt. Being content as an "amenable daughter." Discussing the sheltered nature of her home life in youth. Going on grand tour with her parents. Courtship and marriage, 1893. Her father's sudden death. Joining the Sesame Club, an arts society. Her sister Mabel's theatrical career. Taking her son John to the theatre; his strong interest in it. Rise of suffragist movement and the Anti-Suffrage League; author's wishing to sidestep the whole issue. WWI: her husband's enlisting as a special constable; author's doing volunteer war work; going to visit her wounded son Lewis in France. Her son John's early stage career. Feeling a strong bond with her children.

This bland account seems to assert the image of the "typical" affluent Victorian to be fact, rather than an idealization of how people of means lived during Gielgud's era. The author's lack of opinions on any political or controversial issue is significant; she retreats behind a sheltering curtain of upper-class privilege, emerging only to perform some war volunteer work. The primary value of Gielgud's memoir lies in its insider's look at the Terry family's celebrated thespians and at the late-19th-century theatre milieu.

382 GILBERT, Ann (née Taylor). 1782–1866. *Autobiography and Other Memorials of Mrs. Gilbert (Formerly Ann Taylor).* Ed. by Josiah Gilbert (author's son). Kegan Paul, Trench & Co., 1888. 488 pp.; preface & intro. note by ed.; illus.; app. (author's poems); index. NUC pre56 199:375–376. (1st pub. Henry S. King & Co., 1874; other ed.: C. K. Paul & Co., 1878.)

Born in Islington, Greater London. Father: Isaac Taylor, engraver, publisher, Congregationalist minister. Mother: Ann Martin, invalid, amateur poet. 10 siblings (including Jane, author of "Twinkle, Twinkle, Little Star" and popular children's hymnals). Married 1813, Joseph Gilbert, classics tutor, Congregationalist minister. Children. With her sister Jane, wrote many volumes of children's verse. Poet; children's author; artist (engraver, illustrator); clergyman's spouse; academic's spouse; clergyman's daughter. Middle class.

Author's premarriage memories of the life shared by herself and her sister, from their home education and religious identity through their collaborative ventures as writers and engravers, 1780s–1813. Her grandfather's being Isaac Taylor, the 18th-century engraver, art publisher, and literary host. Author's father's following his father's profession, but also entering the Nonconformist ministry after Christian conversion. Mother's having learned from her strict Methodist father to abnegate her own will. Despite meeting author's father at a poetry reading, and courting by exchanging poems, mother's serving as father's drudge for years until resolving to claim her place as his intellectual companion. Births of author and her sister Jane in London, 1782–83; family's moving to rural Suffolk, 1786. Author's giving advice on child-rearing: mothers should not humor children, should take some holidays without their children, and should use these private times to take stock of themselves. Author's strongly defending "old maids"; condemning most fathers' habitual belittlement of spinsterhood; asserting that unmarried daughters have usually foregone marriage for unselfish reasons, and are vital to their parents' care in old age. Author and sister's receiving home lessons from their parents, not being isolated in a nursery. Father's instructing them in astronomy and biology; his regular Sunday services' being strict but not gloomy. Mother's reading aloud daily at meals; children's reading freely in the household library. Author and sister's collectively inventing a fantasy world; this nurturing their later writing talents. In childhood, sisters' loving to scribble verses; also reading a range of poetry: Isaac Watt's pious verses, Swift's satires, Wordsworth's innovations. Author's admiring Jane's adult poetic talent and learning; wishing she herself had read more. Describing rural fairs and women's cottage industry of spinning. At age 12, fantasizing ways to improve the lives of local poor families; retrospectively condemning her schemes as grandiose. Family's returning to London, 1787; births of brothers Isaac and Martin, 1787–88. Witnessing royal procession celebrating George III's recovery of a sound mind, 1789. Father's briefly prospering in his engraving business, but being forced to stop work by rheumatic fever, 1892; stress and financial worries also affecting mother's mental health. Family's regarding this in religious terms as their time of trials; also suffering from the English persecution of Nonconformists, 1794, from paranoia over the role of Huguenots in the French Revolution. Noting decision of another Nonconformist family to escape the persecution by emigrating to America. Family's moving to Colchester, 1795. Father's income's being cut off by wartime closing of the foreign market for engraving; his earning money by teaching engraving; author and Jane's also learning to engrave. Their father's paying them room, board, and wages; his believing this training would fit them to be self-supporting in later life, as well as keeping them at home with him. Author's first publication: an election song, 1796. With female friends, author and Jane's forming the literary "Umbelliferous Society," 1798. Winning a prize for solving a magazine puzzle, 1798–99; this success's encouraging sisters to become children's writers; author's believing Providence gave them this vocational guidance. Sisters' making engravings to illustrate books of children's verse; being hired as full-time engravers by the same publisher. Their being asked to supply publisher with verses and greatly desiring to earn money this way, but father's opposing their becoming authors, although later relenting. During his opposition, author's writing for pay under a pseudonym. Noting pervasive fear of French invasion, 1803. Author and Jane's collaborating on *Original Poems for Infant Minds,* 1804; author's noting their introductions to other writers, including Anna Letitia Barbauld. After financial failure of their publisher, sisters' searching for another publisher while supporting themselves through reviews of other writers, including Maria Edgeworth. Father's resigning from his parish, 1810; his acquiring a new parish after family's move to the Epping Forest, 1811. Sisters' accompanying their brother Isaac to Devonshire, 1812. Author's ending her narrative with her marriage to Joseph Gilbert, who sought her acquaintance in admiration of her poetry, 1813.

Although proclaiming with pride that her sister Jane's poetry was appreciated on four continents, Gilbert's commentary on her own accomplishments is restrained by her avoidance of self-flattery; readers can judge her works for themselves, however, for many of Gilbert's letters and verses are contained in the memoir by her brother, which is bound together with Gilbert's autobiography. Gilbert and her sister are noteworthy for their collaborative authorship, as well as for their father's training them to assume the family business as if they were sons, accepting their need to be self-supporting rather than pushing marriage on them. In paralleling the prevailing social derision of spinsterhood to the illogical paranoia that motivates religious persecution, Gilbert writes an unusually percipient account of her era that helps to flesh out details of late-18th- and early-19th-century cultural history.

383 GILBERT, Anne Hartley. 1821–1904. *The Stage Reminiscences of Mrs. Gilbert.* Ed. by Charlotte M. Martin. New York: Charles Scribner's Sons, 1901. 248 pp.; intro.; front. port.; illus. BLC to 1975 124:411.

Born in Rochdale, Lancashire. Parents not named. Grandfather: James Hartley, printer. 1 brother; 1 sister. Married 1846, G. H. Gilbert, dancer, d.1899. Widow. 2 sons. Actress (music hall, stage); dancer (ballet, music hall); emigrant (U.S.). Middle class.

Personal and theatrical memories in England and the U.S., as well as observations on 19th-century American society and the Civil War, spanning 1820s–1900. Living with her strict Methodist family on a farm. Father's seeking his fortune in London; his taking mother and brother, leaving author and sister with grandparents in Rochdale. Author's formal dance training at Her Majesty's Ballet School in Haymarket; her working hard and moving steadily up the ranks. Marriage, age 25, to another dancer. Touring rural communities with her husband. Their emigrating to U.S., 1849; settling in Wisconsin; birth of their son, 1850; continuing their stage acts; performing in variety shows, ballets, and farces; living on $16 a week. Touring the Midwest with her husband. Husband's injury; his becoming a prompter and stage manager. Moving to Cincinnati. Death of her young son. Onset of the American Civil War. Performing all over the U.S., including on Broadway, c.1864. Having her first big stage hit, *Pocahontas.* Seeing Edwin Booth in *Macbeth,* John Wilkes Booth in *Romeo and Juliet;* her opinions after John Wilkes assassinated President Lincoln. Acting in a foursome, which included actress Ada Rehan. Going on tour with the company of her acting manager, Mr. Daly, in England, France, and Germany, c.1880–90. Daly's close relationship with author; his influence, his methods of training actors. Shock at Daly's death, 1899; profound grief over the death of her husband the same year.

Enhanced by many anecdotes, Gilbert's memoir provides insights into the personal lives and careers of various English and American 19th-century actors and actresses who performed throughout the U.S. Her acquaintance with the Booth brothers allows Gilbert to provide a thought-provoking sidelight on Abraham Lincoln's assassin. Her discussions of Daly's methods of teaching and style of theatre managing give insight into changes in drama, performance, and audiences in the late 19th century.

384 GILCHRIST, Anne (née Burrows). 1828–1885. *Anne Gilchrist, Her Life and Writings.* Ed. by Herbert Harlakenden Gilchrist (author's son). T. Fisher Unwin, 1887. 368 pp.; preface by William Michael Rossetti; illus. NUC pre56 199:554.

Born in London. Father: John P. Burrows, lawyer. Mother: Henrietta Carwardine. 1 sister; 1 brother. Married 1851, Alexander Gilchrist, writer, d.1861. Widow. 2 sons; 2 daughters. Wrote *Magnet Shores* (1861); biography *Mary Lamb* (1883); published essays and letters "A Confession of Faith," "An Englishwoman's Estimate of Walt Whitman," "Three Glimpses of a New England Village." Biographer; essayist; miscellaneous writer. Upper middle class.

Author's childhood, literary friendships, and completion of her late husband's unfinished work, leading to her friendship with American Transcendentalists, covering her entire life. Family history. Her childhood education in an evangelical seminary. Marriage, 1851; taking a wedding trip through Cumberland. Births of her children. Family's moving to Chelsea, 1856. Her friendship and correspondence with Thomas and Jane Carlyle. Her husband's work on the life of William Blake. Beginning her own writing career. Family's bout with scarlet fever; husband's death, 1861. Author's taking over the writing of his biography of William Blake; corresponding about Blake with other writers and artists, including Dante and William Rossetti and Ford Madox Brown, 1862. Moving to Brookbank. Publishing the biography, 1863, and taking up her own writings about Walt Whitman, 1870. Visiting America, 1876–79; meeting Whitman, Henry D. Thoreau, Ralph Waldo Emerson, and Henry Wadsworth Longfellow.

Extracts from Anne Gilchrist's letters have been added to her chronological memoir. Although the editor attempts to enlighten readers about the value of his mother's literary contributions, his unconditional admiration and great love for her render the reliability of his qualitative evaluation uncertain. However, this autobiography is valuable both for the rendition of Gilchrist's life story and for the equal emphasis she places on the lives, letters, and activities of her important literary associates in England and the U.S. during the last half of the 19th century.

385 GILL, Maud (Maud Bevan, pseud.). c.1893–?. *See the Players.* Birmingham: George Ronald, 1948. 288 pp.; front. port.; foreword by Cedric Hardwicke; illus. index. BLC to 1975 125:79. (1st pub. Hutchinson, 1938.)

Born in London. Father: Edward Gill. Mother not named. 1 sister. Married Ernest Stuart Vinden, actor. 1 son. Actress (music hall, stage, film); stage manager; theatrical producer; journalist; teacher; teacher (dance); dancer (music hall); playwright. Middle class.

Lighthearted personal and professional memories of stage and screen actress, covering her childhood to the eve of WWII. Her early interest in stage performing. Doing well at school; headmistress's persuading her to be a student teacher; author's finding this monotonous. Studying dance as a hobby. Performing with her sister Mabel in her first professional appearance as an actress/dancer, age 18. Entering her profession with the Victorian attitude that teaching, nursing, and acting are the only female professions that do not deprive men of jobs. Perceiving the advantages of the stage as a profession; appreciating its egalitarian aspects. Touring in Berlin. Touring with a Shakespearean company; her opposition to staging Shakespeare in modern dress. Her interest in women's suffrage. Performing in melodramas. Touring with a company throughout the British Isles; encountering moralistic hostility to actors in Wales. Naming her favorite stage roles. Writing articles for *Punch* and *London Opinion.* Marriage to actor Ernest Stuart Vinden when they had only £15 between them and the promise of a year's steady work together in the same company; their happy marriage. Birth of a son, c.1914. Earning extra money by teaching ballet, writing short articles, and sewing at night. Enjoying her composition of doggerel verse and comic plays. Recalling theatre cats; her own dogs' performing on stage; her anger at the indignities to which animal "actors" were subjected. Outbreak of WWI: her husband's entering military service. Working as a stage manager; her excellent relations with her crew. Meeting George Moore, George Bernard Shaw, John Galsworthy, and Dame Ethel Smyth during her stage-managing career. Her husband's illness; his inability to return to the stage. Taking an opportunity to work as a film actress, appearing in film *Under the Greenwood Tree.*

Self-effacing wit is the hallmark of this book. Sprinkled with anecdotes about the theatre's public and players, the text shows the author's professional generosity in celebrating the achievements of her colleagues; she also expresses gratitude for her own career opportunities. Although Gill shows reverence for stage traditions, her support for progressive, egalitarian causes and concepts reflects her liberal and independent mindset. She wrote this autobiography in response to an invitation from the Birmingham Playgoers' Society to lecture on the drama.

386 GILMORE, Isabella (née Morris). 1842–1923. *Deaconess Gilmore: Memories Collected by Deaconess Elizabeth Robinson.* Ed. by Elizabeth Robinson. Society for Promoting Christian Knowledge, 1924. 55 pp.; front. port.; prefatory note by the dean of Wells; address by the Lord Archbishop of Canterbury at the memorial service for Isabella Gilmore; illus. NUC pre56 498:447.

Born at Woodford Hall, near Epping Forest, Essex. Father: William Morris, man of wealth. Mother: Emma Shelton. 2 sisters; 5 brothers (including well-known poet, artist, socialist William Morris). Married c.1860, Lt. Arthur Hamilton Gilmore of the Royal Navy, d.1882. Widow. Deaconess; religionist (Anglican); nurse. Middle class.

Exploration of responsibilities and activities of an Anglican deaconess and observations on contemporary social issues, principally those affecting the poor, covering 1886–96. Learning of Rochester Deaconess Institution, 1886, while happily employed as a nursing sister in Guy's Hospital; Matron Victoria Jones's suggesting that author be interviewed by Bishop Thorold. Bishop's asking author to become head deaconess for the diocese; author's having reservations about the proposal, but ultimately accepting it. Being interviewed and accepted by council. Commenting on the difficulty for women of her time to undertake such work; remembering her mother's disapproval of even her nursing work. Finding a house in Clapham for the institution. Her brother William's decorating the chapel for her; its opening, 1887. Her parish work in Battersea. Having difficulty recruiting deaconesses. Describing poverty in the slums of Battersea. Baptizing children. Discussing the independent work of deaconesses. Departure of Bishop Thorold for Winchester. Her mother's death, 1894; using her inheritance to found another chapel. Her brother William's plans to remodel the new chapel being cut short by his death, 1896.

The editor has added biographical chapters at the beginning and end of Gilmore's narrative and interpolates praise from the author's colleagues as well as excerpts from Gilmore's letters. This supplemental material describes the author's early years, education until age 17, marriage at 18, and widowhood at age 40, after which she entered Guy's Hospital as a lady pupil. The preface gives background on the deaconess movement of the Church of England. Gilmore tells many anecdotes in dialogue, and provides many significant details regarding the Anglican deaconess movement. Her narrative concludes in 1896, but the editor also supplies extracts from a paper Gilmore read at the 1904 Conference on the Organization of Women's Work in the Church of God, and some details about her later life. Gilmore resigned as head deaconess in 1906, and from 1913 until her death she lived with her nieces.

387 GLEICHEN, Helena, princess of Hohenlohe Lagenburg. 1873–1947. *Contracts and Contrasts.* John Murray, 1940. 344 pp.; front. port.; intro.; illus.; index. BLC to 1975 126:193.

Born in England. Parents: Prince and Princess Victor of Hohenlohe. 1 brother; several sisters. Single. Artist (painter); WWI worker; x-ray technician. Royalty.

Childhood and diverse adult experiences of a privileged royal in her career as an animal portrait artist and her WWI role as a medical technician, 1870s–1939. Gleichen family ancestry. Her volatile father's having played a strong role in her development. Painter Alma-Tadema's being a family friend. Author's disliking lessons. Her fascination with horses. At age 16, traveling with her parents to Corfu and Constantinople; socializing in diplomatic circles there. Being presented to Queen Victoria, c.1890. Winning an art scholarship. Being profoundly affected by her father's death. With family, spending time in Rome; visiting her uncle, an Italian cardinal; studying animal painting. Causing a scandal by living alone in her own cottage, 1892. Mourning the death of her pet terrier; recovering via a holiday in Paris and Berlin. Socializing with assorted members of European royalty. Taking another cottage near Hampshire. Continuing her animal painting. Affectionately recalling many of her horses; expressing her love for dogs; noting character and even telepathic abilities of special dogs she had known. WWI: driving ambulances, working in a French hospital; studying radiography in a Parisian military hospital and London. Working with the French Red Cross at St. Pol, and with the British Red Cross in Udine, Italy. Extracts of her letters to her family describing her Italian wartime experiences. Explaining methods of radiography; recounting attitudes of the wounded. Describing struggles to procure supplies; having a confrontation with rural gunmen. Gaining skill with x-ray equipment; resenting insubordination of British hospital employees. Assessing the Italian character. Describing the use of poison gas in battles and attack on Gorizia. Hospital's being visited by the Italian king. Painting works commemorating war themes. Revisiting Gorizia, 1916; taking Duke of Connaught there under dangerous conditions of Austrian bombardment. Trying to arrange medals for her hardworking medical assistants. Continuing her radiographic work in postwar France; later returning to England and her art. Holding solo exhibitions of her work. Feeling irreparable loss at death of her only sister, 1922. Discussing a sculptor friend whom she helped reinstate in the Royal Academy; giving her views on sculpture as an art form. Buying a house in Herefordshire. Advent of WWII, 1939. Feeling that only young people can be of significant use, that ultimately experience counts for nothing.

The chief interest of Princess Helena's memoir lies in the extraordinary diversity of her life experience, as her book's title indicates. Like many other distinguished women, she pays tribute to her father as the source of her willingness to rely on self-direction and to ignore social sanction. She acknowledges that, like other women, her contributions to the war effort gained her entrée to a world of experience usually reserved for men. If her family's wealth freed her from the economic constraints that often limited female ambition, her own artistic success came entirely from her own efforts. In addition to recording her unusual wartime technical experiences, this volume re-creates both the aesthetic and social facets of the early-20th-century London art scene.

GLENAVY, Baroness. [*See* CAMPBELL, Beatrice (née Elvery).]

388 GLENCROSS, Emily. 1914–?. *Breakfast at Windsor: Memories of a Salford Childhood 1914–1928.* Manchester: Neil Richardson, 1983. 56 pp.; illus. BLC 1982–1985 10:212.

Born in Salford, Greater Manchester. Father: John Drinkwater, deliveryman. Mother not named, factory worker, charwoman. 2 sisters; brothers. Married, husband not named. Working class.

Alternating lively and poignant memories of working-class life, covering author's first thirteen years. Discussing prevalence of drunkenness in lower-class homes; her father's habitual drinking's causing a chronic shortage of household money. Nursing mothers' receiving free dinners at John Street School; her mother's being "no doubt grateful" for these meals. Her mother's returning to factory work, at author's age 2. Being tended by her loving grandparents. WWI: food shortages, rationing. At age 9, her elder sister's having to shoulder child-care and housework; author's being "petted" by her mother's sisters, leading to her sister's jealousy. Starting school. Hardships faced by poor schoolchildren: no shoes, myriad illnesses. Loving her Methodist Sunday school and church activities. Attending Sunday religious services at Windsor Institute, a charitable institution organizing excursions and other services for the poor. Family Christmases; parents' buying a small present for each child at Woolworth's "if Dad was not drinking his money away." Describing generally impoverished conditions affecting community, 1923. Spending one Christmas at a Holiday Home in the country through auspices of Windsor Institute, at author's age 12. Discovering cooking and laundry classes in the school curriculum. Enjoying domestic work. Helping her mother with spring cleaning. Attending the cinema. Receiving new clothes for Whitsunday, the only day her father took the family out. Her love of school, reading, and learning; her excitement at discovering poetry. Many neighborhood children's being out of school with infectious diseases. Family's interest in sporting activities at the boys' school. Father's death in a horse-drawn lorry accident, 1927; author's later finding newspaper report of inquest in which mother declared father was "in good health and a teetotaller." Mother's taking an office cleaning job; author's assuming increased share of household tasks. Her pride in earning the Housewifery Certificate, age 13.

In re-creating the everyday world of her childhood, Glencross stresses the unity within her extended family and her resulting sense of well-being and belonging, despite the adversities faced by her family. However, balanced against her account of the rigors of labor and privation widely experienced by the working class is her record of the marked countering effect exerted by various benevolent institutions, which supplemented scanty larders, educated children, and provided them with a sense of structure and purpose. Glencross's enthusiasm for the broader outlook such intervention gave her is testimony to more positive working-class attitudes toward middle-class charity.

389 GLOVER, Elizabeth Rosetta, Lady (née Scott). c.1855–1927. *Memories of Four Continents: Recollections Grave and Gay of Events in Social and Diplomatic Life.* Seeley, Service, 1923. 318 pp.; front. port.; preface; illus.; note on Glover ancestry; index. BLC to 1975 126:294.

Born in Ireland. Father: James William Butler Scott, landowner. Mother not named. 1 sister. Married c.1875, Sir John Hawley Glover, British diplomat, administrator of Lagos, Nigeria, governor of Newfoundland, d.1885. Widow. 1 daughter. Wrote *The Life of Sir John Hawley Glover, G.C.M.G., R.N.* and *Lest We Forget.* Diplomat's spouse; foreign resident (Newfoundland, Antigua, Germany); biographer; women's issues author; traveler (Egypt, U.S., India, Burma, Ceylon). Upper class.

Personal and travel memories, interspersed among observations on colonial diplomatic society, spanning author's childhood to 1914. Family history. Mother's illness. As a wealthy Irish landlord, father's being endangered by Fenian attacks. Commenting on the impoverishment of country squires due to taxation. Mother's death at author's age 5. Author's wanting to learn foreign languages; father's hiring a German governess. Discussing tenant-landlord relations. Author's tour of Europe with her father. Courtship; father's opposition to author's marriage. Residing with her husband at St. John's, Newfoundland, 1875–81. Commenting on the British Empire as "one big family"; seeing England's greatness as lying in her empire. Describing social life at Government House; officers and diplomats. History of Newfoundland and its dependencies. Visiting New York; her impressions of American life. Husband's being appointed governor of St. Kitt; residing with him in Leeward Islands, 1881–83. Social life in Antigua. Discussing race relations; author's finding "full-blooded negroes" better servants than those of mixed race. Returning to England for husband's health. Visit to Queen Victoria. Residing in Hamburg during husband's spa cure; meeting English aristocrats, including the Prince of Wales. Discussing German army and militarism. Husband's being appointed to embassy in Paris; their living there briefly. Returning to London. Husband's death, 1885. Traveling in Italy for two winters. Settling down in London; writing husband's biography. Seeing Cecil Rhodes, Sir Richard Burton, and her husband as "three great African pioneers." Her social life in London. Friendship with Gladstone. Organizing a relief concert for British troops in Boer War; writing *Lest We Forget* on war widows and orphans. Traveling to India, 1901; describing Durbar festivities in Gwalior and Delhi. Traveling to Burma and Ceylon; returning via Egypt.

Describing London social life on eve of WWI. Irish unrest, 1914. Her admiration and love for the British Empire; her opinion that British rulers must correct injustices by learning the languages, cultures, and geography of British territories.

Glover's style is informal and anecdotal, with many digressions. At times her tone is nostalgic; at others, it expresses intense pride in the Empire. This book is primarily concerned with the author's travels and social life. It is a significant source on attitudes toward British rule in the Empire, especially in Africa.

390 GODDEN, Margaret Rumer. 1907–s.l.1993. *A Time to Dance, No Time to Weep.* Macmillan, 1987. 243 pp.; prologue; illus.; epilogue. NUC pre56 203:123.

Born in Eastbourne, Sussex. Father: Arthur Leigh Godden, steamship agent in India. Mother: Katherine Hingley. 3 sisters (including novelist and artist Jon Godden). Married 1934, Laurence Sinclair Foster, stockbroker in Calcutta; divorced 1948. Married 1949, James Haynes-Dixon. 1 son; 2 daughters. Wrote 22 novels, including *The River* (1946); seven books of nonfiction, including two written with sister Jon: *Two under the Indian Sun* (1966) and *Shiva's Pigeons* (1972), about their life in India; five books of poetry; and 22 children's books. Novelist; poet; teacher (dance); children's author; screenwriter; foreign resident (India); cultural historian. Middle class.

Novelist's childhood and maturation in England and India, focusing on her shifts between cultures, closeness to her sister, and early literary career, covering her life to age 40. Ancestry and family history. Parents' courtship; mother's suppressed desire for cultural and social life in India. Author's birth. Her lifelong closeness to her elder sister Jon. Her childhood years in India; describing life in remote towns on riverbanks, especially Narayangunj jute station in Bengal. Entire family's being treated for rabies, author's age 4. Home education by Aunt Mary. Writing poetry. Sisters' returning to England, 1915; living with their strict maiden aunts in London for 18 months. Living in India, 1916–20. Sisters' returning to England, ages 13 and 15, to attend Anglican convent school; encountering injustice at school; this increasing their mutual loyalty; mother's removing them when she discovered how thin, sick, and miserable they were. Attending five schools during the next two years. Living in Eastbourne; keeping a secret journal. Touring France at age 18; author's later novel about this holiday; Jon's romance with a hotel guest who proved to be an international jewel thief. In England, attending Moira School; other girls' cruelty to her sister Rose. Author's early efforts to publish her poetry; school principal's encouraging her to learn economy in language use. Her emotionally charged, platonic friendship with a schoolmate. Her love for her pets. Mother and daughters' returning to father in India, cutting off Jon's budding artistic career without considering it, because "in our family we did not have women professionals." Reading books about the British colonial presence in India; deciding it was beneficial. Returning to England, age 20; earning a teaching certificate in ballroom dancing. Returning to India to open dance schools in Darjeeling and Calcutta, against her parents' wishes. Experiencing native prejudice against her as an independent woman and for teaching half-caste pupils. Her marriage to Lawrence Sinclair Foster in 1934 after discovering she was pregnant; discussing abortion with him, but deciding to marry and have the child. Quarrels with her husband; birth and death of a premature son. Publication of her first novel, *Chinese Puzzle,* on the day of her daughter's birth. Working on more novels. Receiving favorable reviews from writer Gladys Bronwyn Stern; their later becoming close friends. Her friendship with publisher Peter Llewellyn Davies. Describing her double life as wife and novelist in India. Birth of her second daughter, 1938. Success of her novel *Black Narcissus,* 1939. Her sister Jon's novels. Living with her children in Alipore. WWII: husband's losing his job; his joining the army. Living with her daughters in Kashmir, 1942, and on Srinagar houseboat. Another pregnancy; having a miscarriage. Feeling her husband had lost interest in their family. Succumbing to paratyphoid, pneumonia, and jaundice; staying in a mission hospital. Economizing; living in a remote Kashmir mountain home off and on for five years; describing peasants' poverty and thievery. Daughters' schooling with a nearby Dutch family. Taking in a female artist; artist's arousing family hatred; a servant's trying to poison the artist; government's forcing family to vacate over the scandal. Being asked by Women's Voluntary Service Office to tour Bengal to refute charges that British women in India were not helping the war effort. Returning to England, 1944, carrying manuscript of her novel *The River.* Divorcing her first husband, 1948. Discussing her children and grandchildren.

Organizing her memoir topically rather than chronologically and employing many impressionistic descriptions, Godden depicts her life as a young writer, with special emphasis on her return journeys to England from India in 1920 and 1944. She describes the first journey as signaling the end of childhood and the second as closing the years of young adulthood. A popular novelist whose books have been reprinted frequently, Godden has often used material from her life in her fiction. She adapted several of her novels into film scripts.

391 GOODMAN, Margaret. c.1830–?. *Experiences of an English Sister of Mercy.* Smith, Elder, 1862. 234 pp. NUC pre56 206:351.

Probably born in England. Parents not named. Single. Nun (Anglican sister); nurse; nurse (Crimean War); teacher; school administrator; philanthropist. Middle class.

Stirring, if grisly, personal and professional memories and experiences, emphasizing trials of wartime nursing, 1852–55. Joining Sisters of Mercy at Devonport, 1852. Working in a slum area. Criticizing the excessive self-mortification of the sisters; her superiors' lack of sympathy for sick and dying sisters. Overseeing a school in Plymouth. Due to poor health, author's seeking and winning appointment to teach school inland in Asherne, Devonshire, 1854. Being summoned to Constantinople to care for the sick and wounded in the Crimean War, 1854; suffering intensely on the sea voyage. The sisters' being warned not to attempt to convert their patients. Serving with Florence Nightingale: hospital work at Scutari and Balaclava. Describing troop movements, battles, soldiers' equipage. Recounting pathetic stories of wounded men; encountering loathsome conditions in the hospitals. Returning to England from Balaclava, 1855.

Goodman's narrative vividly describes one woman's active participation in wartime nursing in the Crimea. Her percipient quotations from "The Charge of the Light Brigade" use Tennyson's own ironic perceptions of the war to contrast its reputed glory with its devastating reality. Initially motivated by spiritual commitment, Goodman ultimately left her order in 1858 in frustration over the way the sisters were regulated. Her observations on numerous details concerning Anglican sisterhoods are confirmed in the autobiographical writings of another Anglican sister, Margaret Frances Cusack.

392 GORDON, Helen. c.1885–?. *The Prisoner: An Experience of Forcible Feeding, by a Suffragette.* Letchworth: Garden City Press Ltd., 1912. 75 pp.; preface. NUC pre56 332:120.

Born in England. Probably married (to Liddle). Suffragist, militant; feminist; prison inmate. Middle class.

Militant suffragette's dramatization of the mental and physical aspects of serving a monthlong prison term in 1909. Describing her reasons for her belief in suffrage for women; her membership in the Women's Social and Political Union; WSPU tactics. Being incarcerated in Strangeways Prison, Manchester. Describing the immense weariness felt by political prisoners. Providing details of the inequities of the judicial system. Experiencing desperate loneliness in incarceration; bleakness of the physical surroundings; torment of attempting to fast. Finding desolation in the accustomed routine, but feeling terror at any break in this routine. Speculating on the effect of prison experience on a young girl. Rendering a history of men's attitudes toward women. Analyzing men's and women's roles in the creative process of evolution; seeing evolution and revolution as going hand in hand. Her growing physical weakness. Vivid description of rigors and horrors of force-feeding; feeling humiliation and anger. Speculating on the crimes of her fellow prisoners.

Medicines she is forced to take. Discussing the psychological ramifications of solitary confinement.

Making no attempt to disguise her outrage, Gordon re-creates the crude realities of solitary confinement and force-feeding within the context of her personal prison experience. She describes herself as "naturally unrebellious," but the text obliquely provides an image of the writer as courageous, independent, and passionately devoted to justice. Gordon's speculations about the historical development of men's and women's roles in society further suggest the depth of her intellect. Her brief work provides many telling details about one aspect of women's struggle to gain equal rights in England.

393 GORDON, Ishbel Maria, Marchioness of Aberdeen and Temair (née Marjoribanks) and John Campbell Gordon, first Marquis of Aberdeen and Temair. 1857–1939 (Ishbel). *We Twa: Reminiscences of Lord and Lady Aberdeen.* W. Collins, 1925. 2 vols. Vol. 1. 358 pp., preface; illus.; index. Vol. 2: 353 pp.; illus.; index. NUC pre56 1:649.

Born in London, raised in Scotland. Father: Dudley Coutts Marjoribanks, Lord Tweedmouth. Mother: Isabella Hogg. 4 brothers; 1 sister. Married 1877, John Campbell Gordon, 7th Earl of Aberdeen, Liberal politician, governor-general of Canada, viceroy of Ireland. 3 sons; 2 daughters. Wrote *Through Canada with a Kodak* (1892), *The Canadian Journal of Lady Aberdeen, 1893–1898* (1960), others. Philanthropist; political hostess; political activist; travel writer; foreign resident (Canada); feminist; organizer of societies (philanthropic). Aristocracy.

Lady Aberdeen's sections of this joint autobiography, covering 1860–1925, focus on her service to Liberal Party women's philanthropies in the British Isles and Canada. Vol. 1: Family history; being very conscious, as a child, of her noble ancestry. Home education with a Swiss governess; taking informal classes with a French tutor. Organizing a Presbyterian Sunday school, 1874. Being presented at Court, 1875. Attending parties. Courtship with John Gordon; being swayed by her mother's recommendation of him, and by his treating her not as a child but as a rational being. Marriage, 1877; her jewels' being stolen on their honeymoon in Egypt. Moving with her husband to Deeside, Scotland, then to Dollis Hill, near Willesden. Giving parties on behalf of Prime Minister William Gladstone, beginning in 1879. Births of her children. Her political activity in the Liberal Party. Being chairwoman of the Women's Liberal Federation, 1889. Traveling to Ireland, 1893. Organizing Irish industry exhibit for 1893 Chicago World's Fair. Visiting Jane Addams, Francis E. Willard, Oliver Wendell Holmes, Julia Ward Howe. Author's strong sense of Scottish national identity. Vol. 2:

Living in Canada; founding National Council of Women of Canada, of which she was president in 1893. Her involvement with Women's Liberal Federation of England, Scottish Women's Liberal Federation, and International Council of Women, 1893–1924. Living in Ireland. Organizing Red Cross activities in Scotland and Ireland. Her great grief at death of her son Archie, 1909. Her husband's receiving title Marquis of Aberdeen and Temair, 1915. Traveling to U.S. and helping to reorganize the National Council of Women of the U.S.A., 1915.

The detailed chronology of philanthropic activities presented here is one-half of the total intertwined work of Lady Aberdeen and her husband; her educated prose sets forth in an orderly manner the facts of her life and partnership with him. Through her travels in Britain and North America, Lady Aberdeen made contact with many kinds of philanthropists and social reformers. She is conscious of being a public figure in Canada and Britain and comments on her reputation as such. Through diary entries and friends' memoirs, **394** *More Cracks with We Twa* (1929) continues the details of Lady Aberdeen's philanthropic activities, including her support for women's home industry and for the work of missionaries in India. She also gives details of her residence in the British Columbia forest, discusses her life in Toronto while her husband was governor-general of Canada, and describes her life in Ireland during his tenure as viceroy. **395** *Musings of a Scottish Granny* (1936) focuses on Aberdeen's adult life and marriage, giving an inside view of British politics.

396 GORDON, Jane (pseud.; Peggy Graves; née Leigh). c.1905–?. *Married to Charles*. William Heinemann, 1950. 283 pp.; front. port.; illus. BLC to 1975 129:17.

Father: Rowley Leigh, poet. Mother: née Gordon, American. 1 brother. Married 1929, Charles Graves, journalist, novelist. Fashion writer; nurse (WWII); WWII volunteer; fashion model; nurse (children's); traveler (Europe, Middle East, U.S.). Upper class.

Wryly humorous memories of shared marital experiences, both in international journalism and in the London blitz of WWII, spanning 1924–45. At age 19, being sole bridesmaid for Rudyard Kipling's daughter; as a joke, allowing herself to be interviewed about the wedding by Charles Graves, news editor of the *Sunday Express;* her father's negative reaction to the article. Volunteering as a VAD nurse five days a week in a children's hospital; feeling volunteers were not taken seriously in the nursing profession. Her courtship with Charles; her parents' sending her to Egypt one winter, hoping she would forget him. Author's deciding she must earn her own living in order to marry; finding work as a model in a famous London dress house. Charles's publishing her fashion articles in the *Daily Express* under pseudonym of Jane Gordon; this leading to her career as a weekly fashion writer for several periodicals, including the *New York Times*. Marriage, age 25. Charles's family history, career in journalism, and travel writing. Author's writing on fashion and beauty for the *News-Chronicle*. Journalistic social life: café society, debutantes, and charity balls. Author and Charles's friendship with Marlene Dietrich; her close friendships with Beatrice Lillie and Merle Oberon. Taking jaunts to Europe and North Africa. Covering fashion openings in Paris, 1938. Their American travels, 1938–39. Learning of outbreak of WWII while covering Paris fashion shows. Assisting setup of First Aid Post and Gas Decontamination Centre at her former hospital in London. Charles's working as a war correspondent in France, 1939. Author's being dropped from the *Daily Telegraph* staff; writing for *Britannia and Eve*. Continuing her volunteer nursing. Her whimsical view of London life during the blitz. Sending her elderly parents to safety in America; father's dying there two years later. As part of citizen brigade, author's and Charles's wearing tin hats while walking to their posts during raids; her treating casualties at the hospital with water supplies cut off; learning that her best role in the war was keeping the nurses' spirits up; inspecting underground shelters for poor sanitation, vermin, bad drains. Their house's catching fire during an air raid. Undergoing surgery during bombing; returning to nursing soon after. Charles's writing a novel about Royal Air Force fighters. Her volunteering in a day nursery for toddlers: finding the ten-hour days, toilet training, and delousing exhausting for both staff and children; quitting job when she lost too much weight. Dreaming of food; everyone's being plagued by illness. German raids' being stepped up; author's singing humorous war songs to keep herself from panicking. Many friends' being killed in the bombing. Finding Americans' smugness at living in comfort and safety tiresome. Charles's publishing contract's not being renewed; author's fears of debts, high taxes, high cost of food. After liberation of Brussels, going to Belgium with Charles. Describing the destruction in Germany. Visiting hospitals, sick civilians; seeing V-2 bombs being shot down. Returning to England. Germany's surrender; author's lack of personal elation at war's end. Reunion of author and Charles with her brother in New York; indulging herself with candy, cosmetics, and clothes. Her good fortune in being married to Charles.

Conveying the effects of the WWII blitz of London with many small details, Gordon's book provides an in-depth view of London civilian life under the German bombardment. Laced with humor and full of dialogue and anecdote, this autobiography illustrates the therapeutic effects of humor as Gordon finds ways to distance herself from the terrifying memory of the blitzkrieg, a long-running drama that for three months "played out every night, including Sundays, from dusk to dawn, [with] plenty of matinées as well."

397 GORDON, Winifred (F.R.G.S.). c.1870–d.a.1930. *Echoes and Realities*. Hutchinson, 1934. 288 pp.; front. port.; foreword by Lord Robert Baden-Powell; prelude; illus.; index. NUC pre56 207:182.

Born in Scotland. Parents not named. 8 brothers; 4 sisters. Married Sir William Evans Gordon, musician. 1 son; 1 daughter. Wrote *A Woman in the Balkans, Roumania Yesterday and To-Day, A Wayfarer's Wallet, A Book of Days*. Travel writer; traveler (Asia, Europe, Africa, U.S.); Red Cross worker. Upper class.

Personal memories and celebrated friendships in the aristocracy and the arts, accompanied by observations made during author's world travels, covering her childhood to 1930. Her childhood in Grosvenor Crescent, Edinburgh. Recollecting trauma of her brother's death when his nurse fell asleep and smothered him at author's age 5. Father's losing his fortune in Scottish bank crash; family's selling some belongings and moving to London, author's age 7. Home education by governess; author's increasing interest in geography. Attending a French boarding school, age 16; disliking school but loving music, piano, and singing. Playing piano for composer Charles François Gounod; singing for Franz Liszt; meeting Sarah Bernhardt. Meeting her future husband in Edinburgh. Marriage; their travels and social life in Austria. Births and deaths of her two children. Finding a country home in England. Being presented to Queen Victoria. Recalling her friendship with Lady Dorothy Nevill. Meeting Oscar Wilde. Painting; publishing a few songs. Meeting George Meredith; her enthusiasm for his novels. Being in Switzerland when WWI broke out; joining Sir Roper Parkington as a member of the Montenegrin Red Cross. Discussing effects of WWI on the Balkans. After publication of *A Woman in the Balkans,* lecturing on the Balkans to recruits in Kitchener's army for the Allied Forces. Lunching with Queen Marie of Rumania; corresponding with her. Helping found the Rumanian Red Cross. Her dislike of collaborating with women in context of Red Cross work; finding women petty. Giving informal talks at St. Dustan's Home for blinded sailors and soldiers. Traveling to Korea, Japan, Turkey, Poland, Spain, Russia, Norway, Sweden, Africa, Italy, Egypt, and the U.S. Offering her opinion that black people in the U.S. are different from blacks elsewhere. Meeting Henry Savage Landor and Theodore Roosevelt, among other English and American notables. Going to Paris for an unspecified operation, 1930; believing that her illness was due to poisoned tinned foods and insect bites in East Africa. Undergoing nine operations. Observing that society life in London is more "united and varied than in France"; her opinion that French women are more socially restricted than English women. Being given hope for recovery from her illness.

Gordon uses many French phrases, literary allusions, and quotations. Most of the book consists of anecdotes about people she knew, yet she often makes rather vague references to individuals and incidents in her life; the chronology of events and the identity of the people discussed is sometimes unclear. Her discussion of her marriage and family is limited; for example, she only alludes to her son's death, which she acknowledges brought her great pain. The chief value of Gordon's work lies in its description of her activities on behalf of the Red Cross in the Balkans during WWI.

398 GORDON-CUMMING, Constance Frederica. 1837–1924. *Memories*. William Blackwood & Sons, 1904. 487 pp.; illus; app.; index. NUC pre56 207:184.

Born in Altyre, Scotland. Father: Sir William Gordon-Cumming, chief of Clan Comyn. Mother: Eliza Maria Campbell. Stepmother: Jane Mackintosh. 4 brothers; 5 sisters. Single. Wrote *A Lady's Cruise in a French Man-of-War* (1882), *Wanderings in China* (1886), *Two Happy Years in Ceylon* (1892), *The Inventor of the Numeral Type for China* (1898), others. Traveler (Asia, India, South Pacific, U.S.); travel writer; artist (painter); biographer; journalist. Upper class.

Detailed exposition of Scottish history and 19th-century personal and travel experiences, particularly in Japan and China, spanning author's childhood to her old age. Discussing Scotland's past, from medieval times to the 19th century. Recalling family celebrations and being lonely when her parents went to London and abroad each year. Death of her mother; its devastating effect on her father. Remembering Altyre. Her interest in sketching and drawing. Her father's remarriage. Attending school in London. Visiting the Great Exhibition of 1851. Discussing rules of correct decorum for young ladies, c.1850s. Outbreak of the Crimean War; death of her brother-in-law in the war. Deaths of her father, two sisters, and two brothers in rapid succession. Taking a voyage to Malta and Alexandria. Traveling to India; describing Calcutta, Umballa, Simla. Visiting Ceylon; describing native customs, clothing, and religion; European colonists' attitudes toward natives. Touring Fiji; discussing Fijian history. Describing various Christian religious sects in the South Sea Islands; political ramifications of islanders' having come into contact with Europeans. Visiting Japan; discussing Japanese politics, customs, dress, religion, folklore. Her fascination with Buddhism. Describing political pressures experienced by Eastern and Western religion. Climbing Mt. Fujiyama; learning about the devastating Japanese earthquakes and their social and physical ramifications. Visiting the U.S. Her interest in William Hill Murray, inventor of numeral type for China; his helping the blind and illiterate; his starting a school for blind women. Traveling throughout southern China. Returning to live with her sister in Perthshire, England.

One of the best-known 19th-century British women world travelers, Gordon-Cumming presents a formal yet friendly account of herself as she leisurely wends her way through nearly 600 years of Scottish history and then describes her travels. She does not style herself a feminist, but shows by example that a determined woman can achieve stature and respect through her intellectual contributions to society. She provides a valuable, detailed commentary on Buddhism and Christianity and the effect of political influences on these faiths.

399 GOULD, Cecily Audrey (née Brent-Good). 1914–s.l.1972. *Gossip: The Biography of a Yacht.* Gentry Books, 1972. 171 pp.; prologue; illus.; maps; epilogue. BLC to 1975 129:385.

Born in Freshwater, Isle of Wight. Father: Col. Cecil Brent-Good. Mother: Irene Saxby. 2 sisters; 1 brother. Married 1948, Sir Basil Gould. 1 son. Sailor; WWII volunteer. Upper class.

Author's lifelong interest in sailing, inspired by her father, from her childhood to c.1964. Father's life story; his love of sailing; his buying *Gossip,* the family yacht, in 1920. Mother's never really relishing sailing, but gamely adapting herself to life onboard. Author's being unlike others in the family; feeling herself a "changeling" because of her red hair, freckles, and love of books. Father's teaching daughters sailing; his being a gentle master. Her first cruise, age 8; her duties on board; her seasickness. Family's move from Isle of Wight to Yarmouth. Author's first boat of her own: a dinghy with a bath-towel sail; exploring the Yar River in dinghy with her sister Bess. Having a nanny and a governess. Family cruise to Scandinavia, 1927–28. Father's expectations that daughters do onboard tasks author considers more suitable for men than girls. Attending boarding school in England, age 14. Father's Baltic cruise, 1929. Family's racing for Schneider Trophy, 1929, 1931. Cruising to Channel Islands and then to Holland, 1932–39. Racing yachts with Bess, 1934; winning the Yarmouth One Design Challenge Cup, 1939. Author's WWII volunteer service as a VAD in England and Ceylon. Sisters' marriages. Making *Gossip* seaworthy again after the war. Author's marriage, 1948. Birth of her son, 1949. *Gossip*'s being used as a houseboat for her sister Lucia's children, 1952. Sailing to Brittany, 1953; father's surviving falling overboard, age 76, during a 1955 trip. His selling *Gossip,* 1964. Father's being 91 years old in 1972 and still racing sailboats.

This book provides an intimate, detailed portrait of the author's father, implying her affection for him and his eccentricities. Gould shows that her father's passion for sailing brought her and her sisters greater responsibilities and physical labors than were usually expected of girls, resulting in increased abilities in which they took pride. While focusing her memoir around the image of the family yacht, Gould also conveys a great deal of information about her own life and thought within a rather unconventional upper-class family.

400 GOWER, Pauline. 1910–1947. *Women with Wings*. John Long, 1938. 223 pp.; front. port.; foreword by Amy Johnson; prologue, epilogue by Dorothy Spicer; illus. NUC pre56 208:648.

Raised in Croydon, Greater London. Father: Sir Robert Gower, M.P. Mother: Dorothy McClellan-Wills. 1 sister. Single. Wrote *Piffling Poems for Pilots*. Aviator; teacher (music). Upper class.

Memories of two pioneer women aviators, covering their adventures in aviation, 1931–36. Author and Dorothy Spicer's deciding to work together as pilot and engineer. Hearing people make remarks that women shouldn't work with airplanes. Saving money to pay for flight training: Spicer's working as a saleswoman, Gower's teaching violin. During training, sometimes getting lost when flying. Their borrowing a plane from Amy Johnson to attend an International League of Aviators meeting in Paris; losing their bearings on the return flight to London. Gower's earning a Class B license, 1931; making many cross-country flights to improve her navigational skills; being given a plane by her father for her 21st birthday. Their camping out in summer in Berkshire, earning money from giving joyrides and providing air taxi service. Encountering prejudice against women aviators. Their attending All Women's Aviation Meeting, 1931. Plane's being sabotaged by a male pilot who wanted to monopolize the joyride business in Northampton. Buying a three-seater plane; participating in four air-circus tours, barnstorming England, Scotland, and Wales. Perceiving the potential contributions of women pilots in future wars; supporting aviation as a career for women. Mentioning deaths of parachutists and pilots in air circuses. Spicer and Gower's starting an air show in Hunstanton. Spicer's earning engineering licenses never before held by a woman; earning her Class B license, 1933. Author's having aircraft wireless and telephone operator's licenses, earning navigator's certificate, 1935. Author's head-on collision with another plane, followed by hospitalization, 1936. Both women's putting their careers on hold when author could no longer work as Spicer's full-time partner.

Gower's spirited book commemorates the partnership between Dorothy Spicer and herself, as both aviators contributed material to the memoir and Gower wrote it on behalf of both. Through frequent use of dialogue, anecdotes, and even diary entries the author paints a lively picture of their unconventional and daredevil experiences; she also holds forth enthusiastically on the importance of women's contributions to aviation. Gower and Spicer established the first female-partnered air travel business in Britain. Gower's other claim to fame is that she gave rides to more passengers than any other woman aviator of her time.

401 GRAHAM, Marjorie (stage name; née Hunter). 1904–1974. *Love, Dears!* Ed. by Clive Murphy. Dennis Dobson, 1980. Ordinary Lives series. 96 pp.; app. BLC 1976–1982 18:474.

Born in Edinburgh, Scotland. Father: Norman Hunter, ex-yeoman. Mother not named, dressmaker. Married 1930, John Rodger, insurance company manager; separated c.1939. Married 1963, Harry Vernon Davison, 2nd major of the Argyll and Southern Highlanders, died n.d. Widow. Chorus girl; actress (stage); waitress; singer (popular); WWII volunteer; domestic servant. Lower middle class.

Author's occupational experiences and descent into alcoholism, interspersed with oblique observations on contemporary society and gender roles, covering her childhood to 1973. Attending a private school in Edinburgh. Family's moving to town of Alloa. Being a willful child; not being tamed by parents' spankings. Taking piano lessons; feeling she had "acting in the blood." Her childhood boyfriends. Opining that children should not be told about sex until puberty. Attending Dollar Academy in Alloa. Father's alcoholism; his early death. Taking stage name of Marjorie Graham; acting with Jose Collins in *The Maid of the Mountains*. Producer Seymour Hicks's using "casting couch" for chorus girls who wanted better parts. Working as a film extra, soubrette, and waitress. Being raped by a date. Becoming pregnant by a married man, 1925; opting for abortion; her lifelong self-recriminations over this decision; experiencing severe depression. Traveling with her mother to Czechoslovakia; singing in a hotel in Marienbad. Her depression's lifting when she signed a guaranteed contract. Her first marriage. Escalating drinking of author and husband; their decreased sex life; his infidelity. His embezzling £13,000 from his company and confessing it to her; her forgiving him; his abandoning her and cleaning out their bank account. Author's heavy drinking. Her mother's pushing her to find a job; author's finding kitchen work in a dance hall. WWII: describing conditions in London. Working as a housekeeper to Cicely Courtneidge. Working with the Civil Defence Corps and the American Red Cross. Doing domestic work at American clubs; observing how G.I.s treat women. Death of her mother, 1953; author's desolation. Working as a washroom attendant at the Metropole cinema. Meeting Major Harry Vernon Davison; his being married at the time; eventually marrying him; his death soon after. Resuming her affair with the married man by whom she had become pregnant in her youth. Being awarded old age and widow's pensions by army. Being jailed for being drunk and disorderly conduct, c.1970. Declaring that drinking gives her happiness.

Based on transcribed interviews, this autobiography presents the tragedy that was Graham's life in an ironically breezy, conversational style. Her mode of self-expression suggests a limited education. Graham died before the interviews were completed; Murphy, the editor, has extensively rearranged the material. The book reads like a gripping fictional dramatization of some of the reasons people descend into alcoholism.

402 GRAHAM, Winifred (Mrs. Theodore Cory). 1873–1950. *That Reminds Me*. Skeffington & Son, 1945. 168 pp.; front. port.; illus.; index. NUC pre56 124:54. [cat. under Cory, Winifred.]

Born in London. Father: Robert Graham. Mother: Alice Hackblock, amateur actress. 1 sister. Married 1906, Theodore Cory, South Wales coal shipping businessman. Wrote more than seventy novels, including *What Next, The River of Thought, Christopher Carroll*. Novelist; short storyist; public speaker; religious/spiritual writer; spiritualist; journalist; religionist (anti-Mormon). Upper class.

Selected survey of author's experiences and religious explorations, covering her childhood to the beginning of WWII. Home study with governesses. Her early passion for writing; being encouraged by her parents; her special relationship with her father. Publishing her first short story, age 16; becoming a contributor to *Strand* magazine and *Evening Standard*. Her social debut. Joining Women Writers' Club. Courtship and marriage, 1906. Her happy domestic life; author and husband's deciding not to have children because "the world is too full of suffering already." Meeting Harry de Windt, 1906; joining his anti-Mormon crusade. Writing a miniature volume for library of the queen's dollhouse. Her Anglican religious views. Successful publication of her anti-Mormon novels *Ezra the Mormon* and *The Love Story of a Mormon*. Attending World Conference on Mormonism in Pittsburgh as anti-Mormon speaker. Discussing Mormon practices in the U.S. Death of her father, 1922. Her interest in spiritualism, hypnotism, and supernatural phenomena; her friendship with spiritualist Desmond Shaw. Receiving messages from her father through automatic writing; publishing these in *My Letters from Heaven* and *More Letters from Heaven*. Incorporating paranormal ideas into her novels. Her friendships with Desmond and Mary MacCarthy, Ella Wheeler Wilcox, Lady Seagrave. Her attempts to conciliate Christian and spiritualist practices. WWII: her husband's campaigning for National Prayer Day.

Having resolved never to write an autobiography, Graham tells her readers that she began this one when instructed to do so by a "voice" she heard during church. Organized only by association (as the title implies), this memoir moves from anecdotes of the famous to the author's iconoclastic spiritual opinions and back again. In representing herself not as a woman writer but as a writer whose gender is irrelevant to her craft, Graham makes plain her own comfort with female excellence. In **403** *Observations Casual and Intimate, Being the Second Volume of That Reminds Me* (1947), Graham covers her young adulthood to the end of WWII, continuing to focus on spiritual thoughts and ideas, with references to titled and/or literary friends. **404** *I Introduce, Being the*

Companion Volume of That Reminds Me, and Observations: The Trinity of an Autobiography (1948), offers some of the same information contained in the two preceding volumes, and covers Graham's childhood to middle age. Chatty and intimate, the book's focus remains on religious and spiritualist ideas and practices, which the author intersperses with opinions on English literature, history, and society.

405 GRANT, Anne (née MacVicar). 1755–1838. *Memoirs of an American Lady: With Sketches of Manners and Scenes in America as They Existed Previous to the Revolution*. New York: Dodd, Mead & Co., 1903. 2 vols. Vol. 1: 306 pp.; front. port.; preface by J. G. W. (James Grant Wilson); illus. Vol. 2: 233 pp.; illus.; app. NUC pre56 210:317. (1st pub. Longman, Hurst, Rees, Orme, 1808.)

Born in Glasgow, Scotland. Father: Duncan MacVicar, officer in 77th infantry, Highland Regiment, later a farmer. Mother: Catherine Mackenzie. Married 1779, Rev. James Grant, clergyman in Laggan parish, military chaplain, d.1801. Widow. 12 children. Wrote *Original Poems with Some Translations from the Gaelic* (1803), *Letters from the Mountains* (1806), *Popular Models and Impressive Warnings for the Sons and Daughters of Industry* (1815). Social historian; colonial American; poet; essayist; clergyman's spouse. Middle class.

Memories of pre- and post-Revolutionary life in colonial America, set within a finely detailed history of America up to the first decade of the 19th century. Vol. 1: Encapsulating history of Albany Settlement from before author's birth: its early Dutch settlers; customs and culture of tribes of Five Nations: Mohawks, Oneidas, Onondagas, Cayugas, and Senecas. Describing settlement living conditions, c.1710; colonial women's duties: religious instruction, planting; Albany's architecture. Black slavery; author's personal opposition to slavery; Indians' dislike of black slaves. Discussing French and British trading operations, their rivalry; traders' cheating Indians. Discussing earliest colonists' motives for leaving Europe. Influence of the severe climate on agriculture. Indians' logical arguments for resisting Christian conversion, preferring their own way of life; their lack of resistance to smallpox. Influence of Dutch clergy, who opposed theatrical presentations, on community. Vol. 2: Recounting details of Indian affairs. Father's being stationed as military chaplain at Oswego; at author's age 3, her mother's receiving permission to join her husband; their being the first European females to advance so far into the wilderness. Family's moving to Albany Settlement; their solitary living conditions there. Memories of Sir Jeffrey Amherst, commander-in-chief at Albany. Outbreak of the French and Indian war: describing French role and the strategies of Chief Pontiac. Father's moving family to Vermont, 1765; his ill health and resulting need to return to Scotland. Family's journey down the Hudson River. Noting some British colonists' dissatisfaction with their mother country.

Commenting on Mohawks' assisting colonial army; colonial governments at Ontario, Schenectady, and Fort Hendrick; British troop mutiny, 1765; waste of British national resources on war; history of Vermont; William Penn's establishment of Philadelphia, Pennsylvania; rise of American nation as a cultural phenomenon. Poorer social classes' being attracted to American expansion; their finding opportunities for work and enterprise there.

Formal and at times flowery, Grant's narrative appears to be guided by two aims: to create a record of her personal memories of colonial life and to provide an account of American history in the second half of the 18th century. The attitude she expresses toward American Indians emphasizes their humanity and dignity, and she displays cautious optimism regarding the fate of the new nation. "Memoir of the Life of Mrs. Grant" in **406** *Memoir and Correspondence of Mrs. Grant of Laggan* (1844) presents other details of the author's first half-century and includes her extensive and often highly self-revelatory correspondence.

407 GRANT, Clara Ellen. 1867–?. *Farthing Bundles*. Published privately, 1931. 178 pp.; preface. NUC pre56 210:331.

Born in Wiltshire. Father not named, house-painting business owner. Mother not named. Several brothers. Single. Social reformer; teacher; pupil-teacher. Lower middle class.

Professional recollections of an East End Board School teacher, framed by her traditionalist views of society and morality, spanning her childhood to old age. Life in rural Wiltshire. Moving to Frome; its history, churches. Describing Victorian customs, mores, and attitudes toward children. Attending Church of England National School. Becoming a pupil-teacher at age 13. Comparing head teachers of her youth to those of modern times. Attending Salisbury Training College: recalling austerities, activities, and obligations. Teaching in Wiltshire church school. Discussing social problems of 1880s London. Describing changes in educational system for primary children, including the Montessori method. History of Wapping; poverty of people in the district: prices vs. family budgets. East End culture, customs, attitudes toward extended families and old people, work fund. Details of her work with thrift clubs. Believing children capable of illuminating thoughts. Her opposition to birth control and to married women's working as teachers. Outbreak of WWI. Discussing the impact of early cinema. Enumerating ways to ameliorate East End social problems. Relating poor language skills to economic deprivation; seeing the importance of motivating students. Outlining ramifications of religion in school; perceiving a need for religion in human life. Describing East Enders' ideas about religion and philanthropy. Reviewing history and observances of the Church of England. Her belief that the Church of England and the free churches should reunite ecumenically. Discussing tenets and shortcomings of Roman Catholicism.

Grant's opinions on education and the many social problems affecting London's East End, colored by her rather rigid Victorian morality, emphasize mental and moral improvement over social reform. She offers a valuable catalogue of the day-to-day necessities of East End life, but does not seem to understand the connections between such forces as the cycle of poverty, the subordination of women and children, and overpopulation.

408 GRANT, Elizabeth. 1797–1885. *Memoirs of a Highland Lady: Elizabeth Grant of Rothiemurchus*. Edinburgh: Canongate, 1988. Ed. by Andrew Tod. 2 vols. Vol. 1: 349 pp.; preface; intro. by ed. Vol. 2: 345 pp.; index. NUC pre56 550:659. (1st pub. R. & R. Clark, 1897.)

Born in Edinburgh, Scotland. Father: Sir John Peter Grant, landowner, lawyer, M.P. Mother: Jane Ironside. 2 brothers; 2 sisters. Married 1829, Col. Henry Smith. 1 son; 1 daughter. Wrote *Irish Journals of the Highland Lady*. Society woman; journalist; secretary; diarist; foreign resident (India). Upper class.

Intimate personal and familial memories, accompanied by observations on contemporary attitudes, society, and travel, spanning author's childhood to 1845. Vol. 1: Family history. Growing up in London. Father's deciding to practice law. Experiencing sibling rivalry. Nursemaid's negativism toward author's brother; governess's failure to discipline children; children's rebellion against both. Parents' neglect of children's delicate health; their inadequate food and clothing in winter. Father's severe discipline of children: their being starved up to 30 hours when they refused to eat particular foods. Author's having been shy and misunderstood by parents, who called her wicked and evil. Author and siblings' inadequate education; author's regret that she did not discipline herself to study. Visiting Oxford; discussing the disruptive effect of young Percy Bysshe Shelley on the university, 1810–11. Having music and dance tutors. Mentioning illegitimate children of her grandfather and great-uncle; illegitimate births among family servants. Father's being elected M.P. for Great Grimsby; his selling property to pay costs of the campaign. Family's returning to their estate in Scotland, 1812. Moving to Edinburgh, 1814, so father could resume his law career. Vol. 2: Author's preoccupation with balls and beaux; her being separated from her younger sister so as not to infect her with "nonsense." A family ball's being disrupted by a mob's protesting father's pro–Corn Law position. Mother's prohibiting author's romance with a man "beneath her station." Flirting heartlessly to disappoint beaux and mother. Working as private secretary for her father. Family's traveling to Holland, Belgium, and France, 1819. Mother's improvident spending. Brother's academic education vs. prescribed female education in social graces; her own plan of self-education through reading. Father's retirement from Parliament, appointment to judgeship in Bombay; family's moving to India, 1827. Discussing gradations of Anglo-Indian society. Being wooed by Col. Smith; her mother's opposition to her marriage. Her honeymoon voyage to England via Ceylon and Mauritius, 1830. Living in Dublin and at her husband's Irish estate. Birth of her daughter.

Intended for her family alone Grant's memoirs include many anecdotes of friends and acquaintances. The 1988 edition, based on the original manuscript, is the most complete and includes the editor's footnotes. A selection from this book was first published in 1897, edited by the author's granddaughter, Jane Maria Strachey. Grant also wrote articles for *Fraser's* magazine, work she does not discuss in this book.

409 GRANT, Joan (née Marshall). 1907–s.l.1993. *Far Memory: The Autobiography of Joan Grant*. Columbus, Ohio: Ariel Press, 1985. 286 pp. BLC to 1975 130:415. (1st pub. as *Time Out of Mind*, Arthur Barker, 1956.)

Born in London. Father: Jack Marshall, entomologist. Mother: Blanche, amateur psychic. 2 half-sisters. Married 1927, Leslie Grant, barrister, photographer. 1 daughter. Wrote *Winged Pharaoh* (1937), *Redskin Morning and Other Stories* (1946), *So Moses Was Born* (1952), others. Clairvoyant/psychic; religious/spiritual writer; novelist; short storyist; traveler (Europe, Middle East, South America). Middle class.

Intriguing presentation of recollections of past lives, set within personal and travel experiences, covering 1907–37. Her mother's psychic abilities: her correctly predicting a roof's falling in and the sinking of the *Titanic*. Even as a child, author's feeling she had lived previous lives; learning not to talk about them. WWI: traveling to America with her family on the *Lusitania*. Her reactions to New York; finding Americans lively; meeting occultist Aleister Crowley and considering him "a kind of human toad." Mother's having a premonition that the *Lusitania* would sink on their scheduled voyage back to England; her forcing father to arrange an earlier return for them; fulfillment of her prediction about the later voyage, 1915. Author's attending a boarding school in Berkshire; finding her fellow students and the headmistress cruel. Her mother's transferring her to a day school. At age 10, having dreams about helping men who have died in battle to understand that they are dead; later finding out the deaths she had dreamed of were real. Studying mathematics with a tutor to prepare for entering Cambridge; tutor's encouraging author's interest in the paranormal; their unsuccessful attempt to exorcise a ghost from a room they both felt was haunted.

Popularity of spiritualism at the time; subsequent séances at the house with real and fake mediums; author and tutor's burning their planchette and foreswearing séances. Mother's disaffection with tutor; tutor's dismissal; author's refusing to study with any other tutor, thus giving up the chance of attending Cambridge, age 16. Father's extensive research on mosquitoes; author's assisting him with fieldwork and in the laboratory. Meeting H. G. Wells; his encouraging her to write. Breaking off an engagement to a man who asked her to stop talking about dreams and ghosts. Meeting Esmond; their having dreamed about each other for two years before meeting; their engagement. Her accurate precognition about his fatal accident. Recovering from grief at the home of Daisy, a woman she later recognizes as having been her mother in a former life. Impulsively deciding to marry Leslie, author's age 20. Going to Argentina with Leslie to meet his father; traveling on to Brazil with money author won in a poker game; observing society women with their lovers in Sao Paulo. Returning to England. Having more encounters with ghosts and malign, unseen entities. Wanting to learn more about the nature of her experiences with the supernatural. Author and friends' wanting to start a flower-arranging business; their being forbidden to do so by their husbands. Becoming pregnant; birth of her daughter, 1930. Author's discovering her psychometric abilities; Leslie's writing down her revelations. Leslie's having difficulty finding work as a barrister; his working as a photographer on an archaeological dig in Iraq; author's joining him there and participating in the dig, 1935. Visiting Egypt; feeling she had been there before. Developing the faculty of remembering her previous personalities. In a trance state, recalling her life in Egypt as Sekeeta, a priestess and future pharaoh; giving intimate, exact details of Egyptian existence and surroundings; with Leslie, confirming these through historical documentation. Midway through her work on Sekeeta, discovering another life in Italy in the 16th century; later recording this in *Life as Carola*. Leslie's fears that people would find author's claim to have been a pharaoh laughable; author's explaining that she and Sekeeta are not one and the same, but "two beads on the same necklace" of spirit. *Winged Pharaoh*'s acceptance by publisher Arthur Barker, 1937. Being able to give the first copy of the book to Daisy, whom she believes is a reincarnation of Sekeeta's mother, before Daisy's death.

Grant's enthusiasm for presenting evidence of past existences combines with her storytelling ability to give her autobiography an intensely personal flavor. At all times she favors corroborating her statements through historical documentation rather than depending on mere emotional response; she reserves strong displays of emotion for events that occur in her present life. She structures the expression of her ideas in a rational and thought-provoking framework.

410 GRAY, Frances Ralph (O.B.E.) c.1861–1935. *And Gladly Wolde He Lerne and Gladly Teche: A Book about Learning and Teaching.* Marston, 1931. 284 pp.; front. port.; index. NUC pre56 211:240.

Born in Roscrea, Ireland. Father: James Gray. Mother not named. 1 sister. Single. Knew Henry and Eleanor Sidgwick, Anne Jemima Clough, Lady Airlie. Academic; teacher; headmistress; feminist; WWI volunteer; justice of the peace; philanthropist. Middle class.

Literate, informed memories of professional educator, accompanied by observations about education for women, spanning author's childhood to 1931. Her home education and day-school attendance until age 12. Receiving Bible instruction from her mother. Attending Plymouth High School; having trouble being understood because of her Irish idioms. Attending Newnham College, later Sidgwick Hall, at Cambridge. Being appointed classical lecturer at Westfield College, University of London. Her students' becoming interested in women's suffrage. Attending Queen Victoria's Diamond Jubilee with her father, 1887. In addition to her duties at Westfield, where she taught for ten years, teaching English literature at a select boarding school for young ladies for two terms. Performing school inspections in North England for the Association of University Women Teachers, 1888. At Manchester education conference, delivering paper on overwork at girls' schools. Serving as headmistress at St. Katharine's Junior School at St. Andrew's; later serving as headmistress of St. Paul's Girls' School, 1904–27, in London. Asking for higher-than-normal salaries for her teachers. Seeing the main goal of St. Paul's as the education of future homemakers. Discussing discipline, honor societies, parents' roles, children's imagination, and use of workshops. Perceiving the importance of religion in schools, but not forcing girls to attend church if their parents asked for exemptions. Effect of WWI on St. Paul's: food shortage, fear of air raids. Assisting in founding Baby Weighing Centre and an association for teaching Belgian children, 1916. Receiving Commission of Peace, 1920. Discussing how a wider range of occupations was becoming available for women. Her interest in legislation affecting the welfare of children; visiting juvenile courts in London and the U.S. Her love for her profession. Stating principles she feels all teachers should follow.

Gray is highly educated and writes in an analytical style, showing knowledge of Latin and Greek. Her tone is straightforward, expressing definite opinions on school discipline and curricula. The book's order is mostly chronological, and the author occasionally alternates between first-person and third-person narration. Gray is among the educational pioneers who advanced female schooling and professional teacher training; she was a leader in the movement to promote higher education and careers for women. Made a justice of the peace in 1920, Gray was honored with the O.B.E. in 1926.

411 GREENFIELD, M. Rose. c.1850–?. *Five Years in Ludhiana; or, Work Amongst Our Indian Sisters*. S. W. Partridge, 1886. 128 pp.; front.; intro. NUC pre56 217:94.

Born in England. Parents not named. Single. Missionary (India); religionist (Evangelical); teacher; educator; foreign resident (India). Middle class.

Portrayal of late-19th-century Indian society, emphasizing women's roles, from the perspective of a Christian missionary, 1875–85. Joining the Mission of the Society for Promoting Female Education in the East, in Ludhiana, Punjab, India. After learning Urdu, teaching women in three private homes, 1876. Opening a small school for native girls in Maliganj, financially supported by author's Sunday school in England. Severe illness's forcing author to leave the mission to recover in the hills, 1878. Returning to England for ten months, 1879; returning to Ludhiana. Describing Ludhiana's ethnic makeup and languages; assessing the characters of Afghanis, Kashmiris, and Punjabis. Discussing how social customs of non-Christian religions negatively affect women: polygamy, child marriage, abominable treatment of widows, female infanticide. Teaching classes to female converts; visiting students in their own homes; describing how such *zenana* work spread with the growth of the mission school. Encountering Muslim and Hindu opposition to women's baptism; gradual acceptance of the missionaries over nine years. Using her small medical knowledge to treat various illnesses of women and children at the mission dispensary; discussing superstitions that led to disease. Touring nearby villages, 1880, accompanied by American missionaries; undertaking a more extensive tour, 1883–84, preaching and dispensing medicine. Society's beginning five village schools with native teachers; curriculum of these schools; author's being the "Lady Visitor" of the largest school. Anecdotes about pupils and native teachers. Evangelizing women at native fairs. Describing "saint worship" among the Muslims; seeing it as being as degenerate as that of Roman Catholics. Perceiving a need for books to be translated into Urdu; writing books in Urdu about the women of the Bible, Christian motherhood, and other topics for her pupils.

Greenfield addresses a readership of English Christians, seeking their aid and prayers for the society's mission in India. Her tone is Christian and evangelical, and her style reveals her knowledge of Indian languages. While Greenfield criticizes much about Indian religious and cultural customs, her book shows her keen empathy for the sufferings and hopes of Indian women.

412 GREENWOOD, Mary. c.1845–1923. *Passing Strange: A True Record of Experiences in Life and Christian Work. By One of the People*

Designated by the Apostle Paul, "Helps." John F. Shaw & Co., 1899. 96 pp.; front.; preface; illus.; app. BLC to 1975 132:65.

Born in England. Parents, stepfather not named. Single. Religionist (Quaker); missionary; preacher; philanthropist. Middle class.

Appraisal of a life of religious and philanthropic service, accompanied by personal memories and observations on Victorian society, covering author's childhood to 1895. Father's death at author's age 2. Mother's remarriage, author's age 3, to a man who would not assume responsibility for author; her being adopted by her father's childless brother and his wife. Feeling her uncle was kind and generous, but also recalling the puritanical religious environment of her new home with her Quaker relatives; austerities of daily life due to religion; their belief in "crucifying the flesh" to make her oblivious to the needs of the body; author's not being given gloves in winter or care when she contracted scarlet fever. Daily reading of scripture; Sabbath worship. Attending day school. Feeling her narrow life was unendurable; running away from home; being recovered by her governess. Attending boarding school for five years. Her aunt's death, 1860. Assuming domestic duties of home for uncle; her great devotion to him. Her strong desire to participate in philanthropic endeavors; managing a mothers' clothing club; unofficially adopting several poor girls. Wanting to preach. Recalling that a woman was the first missionary in the New Testament. Her uncle's death, 1885. Becoming ill with a nervous disorder as the result of her difficult financial situation. Recovering; going on an evangelical mission to the Channel Islands. Being invited by manufacturers to give "gospel addresses" in factories at mealtimes. Engaging in further travels for religious preaching and Bible-reading missions, 1885–91. Describing the influence on author of the works of Quaker minister Elizabeth Fry. Her missionary work in South Wales and Kent, 1893–94. Continuing to travel and preach; describing tent meetings. Suffering a serious illness, 1894. Her undiminished faith in God's ability to provide. Testimonials to her life's work and accomplishments.

Written informally and enlivened by occasional glints of humor, Greenwood's account provides details about her lifelong efforts to help others, particularly by bringing them the message of the Gospel. Despite her clearly expressed aversion to the religiously inspired rigors forced upon her in childhood by her Quaker relatives, Greenwood seems to have found her vocation within the Society of Friends. She conveys an image of herself as a dedicated and untiring worker, an image that is reinforced by the testimonials to her work, which conclude the book.

413 GREGORY, Isabella Augusta, Lady (née Persse). 1852–1932. *Seventy Years: Being the Autobiography of Lady Gregory*. Vol. 13 of the Coole ed. of Lady Gregory's works. Gerrards Cross, Buckinghamshire: Colin Smythe, 1974. Ed. by Colin Smythe. 583

pp.; front. port.; ed.'s foreword; illus.; index. NUC 1973–1977 44:115.

Born at Roxborough, Connacht, County Galway, Ireland. Father: Dudley Persse, landowner. Mother: Frances Barry. 8 brothers; 4 sisters; 1 stepbrother; 1 stepsister. Married 1880, Sir William Gregory, d.1892. Widow. 1 son. Wrote 27 plays, *Our Irish Theatre* (1913), *Lady Gregory's Journals* (1946), others; translated Molière, translated and adapted Irish folktales and legends; edited *The Autobiography of Sir William Gregory* (1894). Knew William Butler Yeats, John Millington Synge, Wilfrid Blunt, Sean O'Casey, many others. Theatre founder; playwright; translator; charitable volunteer; anthologist; Irish nationalist; traveler (Italy, India, Spain). Upper class.

Cultural and political activities of a major Irish theatre and literary figure, from her birth to 1917. Being educated at home by governesses. Recalling father's hunting parties and aristocratic friends. Family prayers and church attendance (Protestant); her Christian education by mother. First learning of Irish folk customs at a servants' ball. Reading poetry; studying Shakespeare; teaching herself German. Doing charity work in local villages; noting Catholic-Protestant tensions. Taking her elder brother to Cannes for his health, author's age 20; taking annual Italian holidays for a few years. Father's death, 1878. Meeting Sir William Gregory in Cannes; visiting his estate at Coole; comparing Coole and Roxborough. Death of her invalid brother. Marriage, 1880; honeymooning in Rome, Athens, and Constantinople. Living in Egypt during husband's diplomatic service, 1881; meeting poet and diplomat Wilfrid Blunt; Blunt's role in the invasion of Egypt. Having her interest in politics sparked by Egypt's revolutionary unrest and General Gordon's planned march into the Sudan; being disillusioned by the death of Gordon at Khartoum and Gladstone's attempts to shirk blame. Traveling to India, 1886. Resolving to work only indirectly for Irish independence. Providing a detailed discussion of the Charles Stuart Parnell scandal and Gladstone's Home Rule Bill; her letter-writing campaign against passing the bill in its current form, 1886–88. In London, undertaking Anglican charity parish work with children. Traveling in Spain, 1887. Recalling her husband's friends at the Athenaeum Club: A. W. Kinglake ("Eothen"), Sir Frederic Burton, Sir Henry Layard, Henry James, Sir Alfred Lyall, Robert Browning. Her husband's death, 1892. Editing his autobiography for publication. Corresponding with imprisoned Wilfrid Blunt. Following Parnell's death, growth of her interest in Irish culture. Strengthening of her friendship with William Butler Yeats and George Russell; founding the Irish National Theatre with them; recalling the theatre's first productions. Learning Irish. Meetings of the Irish Literary Society. Remembering reactions of Irish nationalists to the queen's visit to Ireland and to the Boer War. Collecting folklore; translating and editing Irish epics; publishing three volumes to good reception. Her son's marriage, 1907. Beginning to write plays; their production at the Abbey Theatre. Being closely identified with the Abbey in theatre history. Death of John Millington Synge, 1909. Corresponding with Theodore Roosevelt; his approval of her attending controversial production of Synge's *Playboy of the Western World*. Recording Irish views of WWI's effect on the Irish; author's anger at the war. Giving details of Ireland's 1916 Easter Rebellion; Yeats's criticism of the execution of the rebel leaders. Her son's death in WWI.

This final version of Lady Gregory's autobiography was discovered only in 1972, in the Berg collection of the New York Public Library. Largely composed of diary extracts and letters, it is arranged topically rather than chronologically. Using the third person, Lady Gregory employs fairytale language to address the first chapter to her grandchildren; thereafter her treatment is tailored to an adult readership. Her narrative is a major source of information on the Irish literary revival and Irish political affairs at the end of the 19th century.

414 GRENFELL, Joyce Phipps. 1910–1979. *Joyce Grenfell Requests the Pleasure*. New York: St. Martin's, 1976. 295 pp.; illus.; index. BLC 1976–1982 19:284. (other ed.: Bath: Chivers Press, 1979.)

Born in London. Father: Paul Phipps. Mother: Nora Langhorne, American. Stepfather: Maurice "Lefty" Flynn, football hero, film actor. 1 brother. Married 1929, Reggie Grenfell. Actress (stage, comic); songwriter; comedy writer; journalist; WWII volunteer; foreign resident (U.S.); charitable volunteer; broadcaster. Middle class.

Witty personal and show business recollections, with wry observations on contemporary theatre and society, covering author's childhood to the 1960s. Maternal family history in Richmond, Virginia; mother's being raised by a black nanny. Mother's spoiling her own children. Father's being half-British, Oxford-educated, left-wing. Family's living in U.S. during WWI. Attending English school in France; being removed because school was "too High Church." Forming secret societies in childhood; her friendship with her wealthy Astor cousins. From age 12, yearning to be an actress. Attending Clear View School in suburban London; acting in amateur and school plays. Attending Royal Academy of Dramatic Art. Meeting her future husband, 1927; losing interest in stage acting. Courtship; marriage, 1929. Resigning herself to her childlessness; feeling that childlessness helps couples to be more devoted to each other. Being shocked by her mother's second marriage; seeing her stepfather as "the villain who broke up the family." Writing radio criticism for the *Observer*. Writing songs and radio monologues; creating comic characters; acting in stage revues. Raising funds for the Conservative Party in Tunbridge Wells, 1926; later coming to distrust party politics. Her social service with Infant Welfare Centre in Slough

Trading Estate and Women's Institute. Her WWII volunteer work: giving charity concerts at the National Gallery; her hospital and canteen work; traveling to North Africa, Italy, and India to entertain troops; receiving an O.B.E. for her war service. Her postwar radio broadcasting; acting in films; appearing on a television quiz show, "Face the Music." Acting in a Noel Coward revue. Describing her ideas for characters, monologues, and comic songs. Opening of *Joyce Grenfell Requests the Pleasure* in London, 1953. Serving on Pilkington Committee on Broadcasting, 1960–62, and on the BBC Advisory Council, 1960s.

With trademark humor and cheekiness, Grenfell focuses on her inventiveness as a comic performer. Her energetic involvement in the rising British radio and television business of the 1930s–1950s lends her account a wealth of historical detail. She briefly passes over unpleasant memories, apparently preferring to emphasize the good times and the friendships with which she was blessed.

415 GRETTON, Mary Sturge. 1884–1962. *Re-Cognitions*. Oxford: Hall the Printer, 1951 (privately printed). 158 pp.; note; index. NUC pre56 218:97.

Raised in Bewdley, Worcestershire. Father: Marshall Sturge. Mother: Anne Burke. 1 brother; 2 sisters. Married Richard H. Gretton, J.P. Widow. 1 son. Wrote *Three Centuries in North Oxfordshire* (1902), *Some English Rural Problems* (1922), *The Writings and Life of George Meredith* (1926), others. Social historian; biographer; journalist; social reformer; magistrate; philanthropist. Middle class.

Informed, focused commentary on English history and world politics, as well as celebrated friendships within these arenas, accompanied by personal and professional memories, spanning author's childhood to post-WWII. Family's Quaker ancestry. Parents' having married in the West Indies. Author's education at The Mount School in York, a Quaker boarding school for girls; being secretary of the school debating society. Visiting writer George MacDonald in Italy. Attending lectures at Mason College. Working with a relief committee; arranging a picture exhibition with a men's university settlement at Oxford; participating in West Ham Free Picture Exhibition. Living in Oxfordshire. Occasionally writing for an Oxford magazine. Living in London, 1911–12. Being appointed to Oxfordshire Agricultural Wages Board by Lord Ernle, 1918–21. Husband's training for WWI; his being declared too old to fight. Observing widespread interest in social reform during the 1920s. Visiting Italy, 1924. Working on the Industry and Property Commission. Discussing the historical books she's written. Serving as justice in Oxford, 1921–34. Serving on First Instance Courts for twenty-five years. Husband's death. Moving to Burford to escape London bombing, 1940. Moving to Penrith for her son's health.

Sheltering her great-nephews during WWII. Her involvement in the Oxford Discharged Prisoners' Aid Society. Not understanding the "fuss" about women's suffrage.

Gretton comments extensively on English history and world politics. The book focuses more on well-known political figures and writers than on the author. Since Gretton writes about people whom she did not know personally, it is sometimes hard to distinguish her personal experience from historical commentary. The book is in chronological order but is not a record of day-to-day occurrences, as Gretton sets her life story in a wider historical context.

416 GREVILLE, Beatrice Violet, Baroness Greville (née Graham). 1842–1932. *Vignettes of Memory*. Hutchinson & Co. Ltd., 1927. 288 pp.; front. port.; illus. NUC pre56 218:126.

Born in Leicestershire. Father: James Graham, 4th Duke of Montrose. Mother: Caroline Agnes Beresford. 1 brother; 1 sister. Married 1863, Algernon William Folke Greville, 2nd Baron, Irish M.P. 2 sons; 2 daughters. Society woman; horsewoman; philanthropist; playwright; journalist; editor; WWI volunteer. Aristocracy.

Memories of aristocratic milieu and commentary on societal change, from author's Victorian childhood to the end of the Jazz Age. Paternal family history. Living in Scotland; loving horses, hounds, and hunting; having no playmates; her love of theatricals. Studying with a private tutor in London; studying music. Describing her pastimes with siblings. Visiting Compiègne with her family; meeting Napoleon III; her father's friendship with him. Attending social events in London; riding in Hyde Park. Marrying Lord Greville, 1863, despite her father's objection to her choosing an Irishman. Her first impressions of Ireland; riding horses; staying at Curraghmore, Lord Waterford's estate. Entertaining. Describing Irish entertainments, foods, and hospitality. Viewing the Irish poor as untidy and feckless, but happy. Returning to London. Her friendships with Anthony Trollope, the Rothschild family, James Whistler, Disraeli, Sir Richard Burton, Sarah Bernhardt. Meeting Oscar Wilde, Tennyson, and George Eliot. Doing charitable work: starting a maternity home; organizing a branch of the Soldiers' Family Association. Equating poverty with poor people's lack of values. Writing for society journal *The World*; temporarily editing another society newspaper. Being seized by "dramatic fever"; her friendships with the Bancrofts and Mrs. Patrick Campbell; taking acting lessons. Having her one-act play, *Old Friends,* produced. Outbreak of WWI: being temporarily detained in Germany; working for Soldiers and Sailors' Family Association; corresponding with three men in the Merchant Service. Visiting India; having a hunting accident there. Spending summers with her mother in Newmarket; going hunting; describing Newmarket society. Discussing responsibilities of marriage and treatment of children in

Victorian times. Seeing the present generation as lazy. Noting changes in attitudes toward women and society, 1860–1920s; present-day neglect of the Bible, common acceptance of Darwinism.

Seeming to combine stream-of-consciousness with an imperfect memory, Lady Greville drifts from topic to topic. Much of the book is comprised of lengthy descriptions of endless rounds of parties, teas, and balls and her lifelong passions for hunting and riding. Still, she provides a catalogue of the minutiae of quotidian Victorian life experienced by her social class, particularly from her youth in Scotland, along with historical reflections on important people and places.

417 GREVILLE, Frances Evelyn, Countess Brooke, Countess of Warwick (née Maynard; "Daisy"). 1861–1938. *Life's Ebb and Flow*. Hutchinson, 1929. 287 pp.; front. port.; foreword; illus.; epilogue; family tree chart; index. NUC pre56 649:413.

Born in London. Father: Col. the Hon. Charles Henry Maynard. Mother: Blanche Fitzroy. Stepfather: 4th Earl of Rosslyn. 1 sister; 3 stepsisters; 2 stepbrothers. Married 1881, Francis Guy Greville, Earl Brooke, later 5th Earl of Warwick. 2 sons; 2 daughters. Knew Queen Victoria, Prince Edward (later King Edward VII), Arthur Balfour, Cecil Rhodes, William Astor, Thomas Edison, Theodore Roosevelt. Philanthropist; socialist; public speaker; society woman; political hostess; educator; animal welfare activist; politician. Aristocracy.

Leisurely personal and philanthropic reminiscences, contained within occasionally tart observations on aristocratic British society, spanning author's childhood to 1929. Family history. Death of author's father when she was age 3. Mother's remarriage; author's closeness with her stepfather; grieving over his death. Being educated by governesses at Easton Lodge. Family religious observances; finding formal worship distasteful. Disliking commoners' deferential obeisances. Being conscious of her beauty at age 18; commenting ironically on the to-do of her "coming out." Dining with Queen Victoria to be "inspected" as a possible wife for Prince Leopold; Leopold's confiding to her that he loved someone else; his freeing her to marry Lord Brooke, his equerry. Marriage to Lord Brooke, 1881. Her friendships with Lord and Lady Churchill, Lady Georgina Curzon, many other titled people. Feeling that social conventions waste the talents of many aristocratic English women on frivolous engagements and entertaining. Feeling most at home in the country. Moving to Warwick Castle, 1895. Commenting on her "Lady Bountiful" style of charity to the servants on her estate. Being criticized by Robert Blatchford in a newspaper article for a luxurious ball she held during a time of great poverty; suddenly realizing the gap between rich and poor. Converting to socialism. Later addressing a socialist meeting in Warwick town. Recalling her work on the Warwick Board of Guardians and her other philanthropic pursuits. Her growing passion against injustice. Renouncing hunting and confessing shame at her former participation. Founding a nature sanctuary. Corresponding with W. T. Stead, reformer and editor of the *Pall Mall Gazette*. Traveling to New York to lecture. Supporting farm laborers' rights. Unsuccessfully trying to preach socialism to Edward VII. Her interest in French art; her friendship with Auguste Rodin. Comparing the social mores of past and present generations. Working with crippled children and underprivileged schoolchildren. Starting Essex Needlework School and a rural secondary school, 1897. Discussing English rural education. Founding an agricultural college for women at Studley. Helping to employ Salvation Army men. Creating a scandal by going alone to the 1903 International Socialist Congress in Amsterdam. Arranging a meeting between French statesman Georges Clemenceau and Sir John French before WWI. Writing the history of the Greville family's Warwick Castle. Her unsuccessful socialist bid for Parliament, 1924. Divesting herself of property and income to donate Easton Lodge for a Labour college, 1929. Realizing that the Labour leaders she most admired may have "no use for fine ladies like me." Commenting on contradictory elements in her rebellious personality.

Informal and conversational, Lady Warwick's first autobiography is given a scrapbook flavor by its anecdotal organization. She exhibits independence and intelligence and is quick to criticize frivolous lifestyles within her own social class. **418** *Afterthoughts* (1931) continues her personal experiences, particularly emphasizing actors and activities in the political sphere, covering her childhood to 1931. In **419** *Discretions* (1931) she presents enlarged observations on the dramatic changes in society from the late Victorian era to the time of publication. The author continues in her informal style in all three works, expressing her social conscience while also dropping many royal and titled names. The countess's life was one of philanthropic achievement, and she expended great effort to acquaint the upper classes with the problems of the lower echelons of society.

420 GRIEVE, Mary. c.1907–s.l.1962. *Millions Made My Story*. Victor Gollancz, 1964. 224 pp. NYPL to 1971 325:88.

Born in Glasgow, Scotland. Parents not named. 1 brother; 1 sister. Wrote *Without Alphonse*. Single. Journalist; editor; publisher; novelist; feminist. Middle class.

Behind-the-scenes look at journalism and the publishing industry, accompanied by detailed memories of a pathbreaking journalist and editor, covering her childhood to c.1962. Father's disapproving of author's desire for a career. Mother's dominating the family. Author's being a sickly, delicate child. Attending Church of Scotland. Trying to begin a journalism career in 1920s: working for a London weekly for six months; being discouraged by Glasgow newspaper editors who did not want to hire women. Regretting having returned to live with her parents instead of pursuing journalism in London, age 19. Working on a hospital magazine, *The Nursing Mirror*. Joining the editorial board of *Mother*, a new monthly magazine, 1936. Selling advertisements for a Scottish magazine. Editing *The Scottish Nurse* monthly. Working as a reporter for *The Bulletin*. Doing society reporting in the Highlands. Starting a new magazine, *The School Echo;* its failure. Writing *Without Alphonse,* a fictitious journal of a Frenchwoman touring Scotland. Launching *Woman,* 1937; its becoming Britain's highest-circulating women's monthly, 1940–62; serving as its editor. Author's personal commitment to socialism, but her struggle to keep *Woman* free of politics; being reticent about mentioning contraception in magazine in deference to its Irish Catholic readership. Her relationship with her staff. Influence of WWII on women's magazines. Believing she provides valuable information for working women who must also run households. Living with a female friend and coworker at Long Marston, beginning in 1949. Reporting on the royal family. Working for the Council of Industrial Design. Retiring from editing *Woman,* age 55.

Writing in an informal style, Grieve provides vivid and detailed descriptions of "women's" journalism, her personal difficulties in the profession, and her contributions to the field. Her portrayal of how she strove to bring useful information to her readership despite the publishing world's circumscribed view of women's issues also clearly depicts the prejudices about women current in the 1940s and 1950s.

421 GRIFFITHS, Winifred. 1895–?. "Winifred Griffiths, Shop Assistant," pp. 115–124 in *Useful Toil: Autobiographies of Working People from the 1820s to the 1920s*. Ed. by John Burnett. Harmondsworth, Middlesex: Penguin Books, 1984. 364 pp.; intro. by ed.; illus. BLC 1982–1985 25:97. (1st pub. Allen Lane, 1974.)

Born near Basingstoke, Hampshire. Father not named, paper-mill worker, Methodist lay preacher. Mother not named. Married c.1917, James Griffiths, Welsh miner, party agent for Labour Party, M.P. Domestic servant; shop assistant; political activist; socialist. Working class.

Political and occupational reminiscences of a socialist shop assistant, covering the WWI years. While working as a domestic servant, being converted to socialist ideas from reading a magazine article promoting equal distribution of goods and services. Outbreak of WWI: increased employment opportunities for women; author's working in grocery department at Co-operative Stores; describing the difficult working conditions there. Being further educated in socialism by a coworker; corresponding with a socialist friend of his, her future husband, James Griffiths. Visiting Wales: being moved by plight of miners, mining families; describing Swansea as "scarred" by industry; meeting and becoming unofficially engaged to James. Returning to Basingstoke; taking a job with Walkers Stores. Continuing to correspond with James; their mutual opposition to the war and belief in socialism; viewing the war as a class struggle rather than an ideological one. Missing James; moving to Wales and finding a job in a Co-operative Store not far from his mining village; coping with the store's inefficient management. Earning a pittance; struggling to save money to marry; eating less food; wishing she could afford fruit. Visiting James twice a month; their involvement in socialist meetings. Their marriage.

Griffiths focuses on the importance of socialism in her own life. To learn about socialism, she claimed, was to be awakened from a dream; these extracts from her autobiography, *One Woman's Story* (1979), demonstrate her wide-awake sensitivity to the social inequities of her time.

422 GROSVENOR, Loelia, Duchess of Westminster (née Ponsonby). 1902–1987. *Grace and Favour: the Memories of Loelia, Duchess of Westminster*. Weidenfeld & Nicolson, 1961. 244 pp.; foreword by Noel Coward; illus.; index. NUC 1941–1962 148:68.

Born in London. Father: Sir Frederic Ponsonby, later 1st Baron Sysonby. Mother: Victoria Kennard. 1 brother. Married 1930, Hugh Richard Grosvenor, 2nd Duke of Westminster; formally separated 1935, divorced 1947. Society woman. Aristocracy.

Aspects of a privileged but unhappy life, interspersed with observations on social changes in England, spanning author's childhood to the end of her marriage, 1935. Genealogy of the Ponsonby family since the Norman Conquest. Her father's being the godson of Empress Frederick of Prussia; family's residing in St. James Palace where father served as secretary to King Edward VII; author's evaluating Edward's capabilities. Describing her parents' busy social life in royal circles and consequent emotional distance from herself. Author's believing intimacy to be unnecessary to the success of turn-of-the-century upper-class marriages; noting the widespread acceptability of platonic male friends among married women. Also evaluating Edwardian servants; author and her brother's having endured the typical upper-class children's segregation in the company of servants for years; their being without recourse under a series of cruel, dictatorial governesses to whom author's mother surrendered her authority. At age 12, having a family trip to Holland cut short by the start of WWI. Remembering the arrival in England of Russian and Belgian refugees; father's managing the wartime household for the new king, George V, while author's mother did volunteer work in France. Author's being shipped away to a series of boarding schools during WWI; mother's continuing to keep her at emotional arm's distance. Making her expected social debut. Aristocracy's resuming busy social whirl after WWI's end; author's commenting on many aspects of this elite existence, including weekend country retreats, wages paid to servants, trends in women's fashions, and the changes produced by the motorcar. With adulthood, author's gaining closer relationship with her mother, who became an ally. Being presented at Court, age 18. Depicting the 1920s: its social activities, memorable hostesses, and new freedom in women's clothing. Recalling a luncheon party at which H. G. Wells and Sir Oswald Moseley were present, and occasions when fellow guests included novelists Michael Arlen and Evelyn Waugh. Describing the popular appeal, c.1920s, of the new breed of women pilots, and the upheaval of the 1926 general strike. Depicting scenes from her Continental travels, 1920s: traveling gypsy fortune-tellers, the sun-drenched Spanish landscape, the brutality of bullfighting. At age 26, author's meeting the 52-year-old Duke of Westminster, who was looking for a third wife; being dazzled by his worldliness and country estate. Events of their engagement: traveling aboard his yacht, arguments between duke and author's mother. Their marrying at a Registry Office, 1930, with Winston Churchill as the duke's best man. Sailing via yacht to the south of France for their honeymoon; living a peripatetic existence. Soon discovering her husband's tyrannical temperament; feeling obligated to obey him. Describing his irritating eccentricities: parsimony toward her own expenses, a preference for commoners instead of aristocrats as friends. Becoming interested in the new League of Nations; resenting her husband's jealousy toward her independent activities. Describing their luxurious lifestyle; author's finding activities to preserve distance from the duke. Visiting Cairo and meeting archaeologist Howard Carter during his excavation of the tombs at Luxor. Entertaining Charlie Chaplin and Randolph Churchill as houseguests. Formally separating from the duke, 1935; moving to a country estate in Surrey and visiting New York to mark the start of her new life.

Although the duchess is candid about the shortcomings of her former husband, her comments often sound wistful. She waited until 25 years after their separation to write about it, apparently out of respect for the feelings of the duke and his fourth wife, Anne; indeed, she granted her husband a divorce in 1947 so he could marry again. Looking back so many years to her heydey, the author makes the 1920s seem the golden age of the British aristocracy, although her descriptions of their privileged pastimes must stand against her analysis of the inadequate family bonds that the upper-class lifestyle generated. In describing habits, attitudes, and expectations, she is sometimes unintentionally funny, as when she elaborates on the emotional trauma she suffered over the duke's changing their cocktail hour; nevertheless her book constitutes a vivid firsthand picture of the British upper class in the 1920s–1930s.

423 GURNEY, Priscilla Hannah. 1757–1828. *Memoir of the Life and Religious Experience of Priscilla Hannah Gurney*. Ed. by Sarah Allen.

Bristol: J. Chilcott, 1841. 156 pp.; ed.'s preface; author's preface; intro. NUC pre56 223:502. (1st pub. 1834.)

Born in Norwich, Norfolk. Father not named. Mother: Christiana Barclay. Paternal grandfather: Joseph Gurney. 1 sister; 1 brother. Single. Religionist (Quaker); preacher. Middle class.

Author's personal religious odyssey from her Quaker upbringing to the Church of England and back again, and her ultimate vocation within the Quaker ministry, c.1763–1824. Being the granddaughter of Quaker preacher Joseph Gurney. First learning about Christ's promise of eternal life from her mother, author's age 6, when her father died. Believing that she was visited by "the Spirit of the Lord" before age 7, and that her relationship with God was stronger than other people's. At age 8, receiving religious instruction from her mother; resolving to pray for others; discussing how children come to learn disinterested love. Having a vivid imagination, but learning to restrain it within Quaker concepts of truth. With her sister, having several governesses; sisters' studying works such as *Pilgrim's Progress* and *Christian Magazine*. Mother's marrying again; author's stepfather's being a family cousin, but not Quaker. Family's moving near London and children's maternal grandparents. Because of stepfather's religion, author's being cautioned by Quakers against sliding into the Anglican Church, and advised to read her Quaker grandfather's *Apology* defending his beliefs; this strengthening author in her Quaker faith. Mother's receiving a third marriage proposal from another non-Quaker, causing so much conflict with Quaker friends that family moved to Bath. Author's imagination's being stirred by Bath's many secular amusements, age 14; regaining piety through reading William Penn's *No Cross, No Crown*. Because of mother's guilt over providing poor marital examples, author and sister's resolving never to marry non-Quakers. Recounting a series of confusing spiritual signs in her life, including an Anglican friend whose well-meaning parents kept trying to convert her; eventually being won over by a book that argued each soul's need for water baptism and Holy Communion, rites absent from Quaker practices. After deciding to join the Church of England, resisting the opposition of her uncle, Quaker writer David Barclay. Receiving Anglican baptism, age 15, but starting to notice unspiritual aspects of the Anglican Church, such as the costly rental of church pews and the poor's having nowhere to sit. Assuring her readers that the Spirit dwells in all Christian churches, but that God prevented her seeing it to ensure her continued search. Falling ill from her spiritual dissatisfaction; only later realizing God was directing her. Her illness's arousing concern in Quaker friends; author's staying in homes in Devon, Norwich, and London; in London, a Quaker preacher's instructing her to read *Barclay's Apology* by her uncle, which reawakened her Quaker faith. After six months of solitude, resisting rejoining the Quakers from conviction of her own worthlessness. During a visit to London relatives, buying laudanum to commit suicide; when her maid surrendered the laudanum to her aunt, author's acknowledging the power of God. Overcoming her sense of unworthiness by dreaming that at the Last Judgement God elected to save her. Author's Quaker uncle's urging her to marry a young Quaker whom she already liked; his proposing, but author's refusing from strong sense that God opposed the marriage; sensing residual sin within herself and falling ill again; many Quaker friends' coming to her aid. Accompanying several young Quaker women to Minehead, where they opened a boardinghouse for Quakers; author's beginning to teach there. At age 30, author's believing in a sign calling her to the Quaker ministry. Joining Quaker Martha Haworth in a preaching tour of the western counties; receiving a sign they must also preach in Guernsey and Jersey. Traveling and preaching with Ann Dymond for seven years; also preaching many times and places with others in the itinerant Quaker ministry. Mourning the 1809 death of her Uncle David, who had revived her faith. Death of many Quaker colleagues, 1810–22. In 1824, author herself's suffering from pulmonary disease, which forced her to cut back her arduous work, but never losing faith.

More concerned about documenting her spiritual journey than her travels throughout England to preach, Gurney gives a slightly different focus to her autobiography than is found in most Quaker narratives of the period. While other Quaker memoirs help clarify details of the Quakers' evangelism throughout England in the late 18th and early 19th centuries, Gurney's account stresses Quakerism's cultural aspects and social consciousness. Her own family of distinguished Quakers serves as an example of this ethos. Gurney's grandfather and her uncle David Barclay were prominent Quakers, and she was also cousin to prison reform advocate Elizabeth Gurney Fry and her brother John Joseph Gurney, who were known for their leadership in the antislavery cause.

424 GWYNNE-VAUGHAN, Dame Helen Charlotte (G.B.E.). 1879–1967. *Service with the Army*. Hutchinson, 1942. 168 pp.; apps.; index. NUC pre56 224:311.

Born in England. Parents not named. 1 sister. Married, husband not named, d.1915. Widow. Military officer; WWI administrator; academic; microbiologist; feminist; politician; philanthropist; scientist. Upper middle class.

Recollections of a professional military officer, emphasizing development of Queen Mary's Women's Army Auxiliary Corps (WAAC) and Women's Royal Air Force (WRAF), 1910–41. Author's heading Department of Botany at Birkbeck College, 1910–17; performing microbiology research. Onset of WWI; husband's death, 1915. Seeking WWI service position; being asked to serve with WAAC in France. Wondering whether the auxiliary service is "womanly." WAAC personnel's being intended to fill functions vacated by soldiers in combat. Describing status, pay, and discipline of WAAC. Encountering prejudice against military employment of women. Supervising all WAAC units in France, under Alexandra Mary Watson; describing women's work in canteens and on docks; trying to get the ban lifted on women serving in the same theatre of war as their husbands. Recalling the 1918 retreat. Disbanding of WAAC, 1921. Being offered the opportunity to serve as head of WRAF; her refusal. Returning to her position at Birkbeck College, 1920. Becoming a professor at the University of London. Serving on the executive committee of the Girl Guides, at Lady Baden-Powell's invitation. Running unsuccessfully for North Camberwell seat in Parliament three times, 1922–24. Accepting command of WRAF; serving as chair of Women's Legion and Emergency Service between wars. Development of Auxiliary Territorial Service (ATS); her dismay that initial design made it civilian; receiving complaints from women who applied for officer positions and were told that clerical and cooking jobs were open; hearing public objections to titled lady officers as "social butterflies." Teaching in ATS officers' school while working at the university full-time; being appointed director and chief controller of ATS, 1939. Struggling for recognition of women personnel as military professionals; retiring in protest. Her happiness at war secretary's 1941 decision that ATS is part of Crown Armed Forces under the Army Act and that ATS officers may now be commissioned and receive increased pay. Author's retirement, 1941.

Reflecting on the tension between the professional and feminine roles of military women, Gwynne-Vaughan recalls her own groundbreaking career. Her emphatic and outspoken narrative creates an image of her as independent and strong-minded in the face of considerable opposition. She does not mention that her retirement was forced upon her due to disagreements with senior officers.

425 HALDANE, Charlotte (née Franken). 1894–1969. *Truth Will Out*. New York: Vanguard Press, 1950. 339 pp.; app.; index. NUC pre56 226:534. (1st pub. Weidenfeld & Nicolson, 1949.)

Born at Sydenham, South London. Father not named, businessman, German. Mother not named. 1 sister. Married 1918, husband not named; divorced c.1926. Married c.1926, J. B. S. Haldane, Cambridge professor, leftist, Darwinian geneticist; divorced 1945. 1 son. Wrote *The Galley Slaves of Love* (1957), other novels, biography *Marcel Proust* (1951), two plays. Knew Malcolm Lowry, Anna Pavlova, Clara Novello Davies, others. Journalist; foreign correspondent; Communist; Soviet sympathizer; anti-Communist; political activist; broadcaster; novelist; playwright; biographer; translator. Middle class.

Life story of Communist Party member who renounced party membership in the late 1940s, covering her birth to middle age. Parents' characters. Her early awareness of anti-Semitism. Detesting all things German (including her governess) in childhood; her passionate love of England. Attending public school in England. Living in Antwerp after age 11; receiving a bilingual French and German education there. Her feminist desire for independence in youth. Attending a London business school. Working as ballerina Anna Pavlova's secretary. Her first marriage; birth of her son; suffering economic hardship after husband's severe injuries in WWI. Her employment as a gossip columnist and feature writer for the *Daily Express*. Meeting Haldane, then a biochemistry student at Cambridge; their love affair; divorcing her first husband to marry Haldane. Discussing her belief that heredity determines behavior. Translating German professor J. Lange's *Crime as Destiny*. Writing novels. Traveling to Moscow with her husband, 1928. Discussing Soviet society; her interest in Soviet doctrine. Returning to London. Her support for anti-Nazi causes. Visiting Spain with her husband, 1930s; discussing Spanish politics. Her son's joining the Communist International Brigade in Spain. Author's joining the Communist Party, 1937; becoming Communist Party secretary for Dependents' Aid Committee. Traveling to Spain as an interpreter for Paul Robeson; traveling to China. Returning; wanting to divorce Haldane; finding the party forbids it. Serving as an air raid warden. Traveling to Moscow as a war correspondent, 1941; her disillusionment with Communist rule; questioning her own ideology. Providing an analysis of Russian and Chinese society. In England, renouncing communism and breaking with the Communist Party; being barred by Communist faction in Fleet Street from practicing journalism; finding employment in BBC. Obtaining a divorce from Haldane. Analysis of her break with communism. Discussing communism in Britain and the Soviet Union; psychological factors of people's commitment to communism; Soviet persecution of intellectuals, particularly geneticists.

A rich source of information on communist organizations and the development of Stalinist ideology, Haldane's book is also a journey of self-discovery. She has written of her passion for music in **426** *Music, My Love!* (1936), in which she discusses her choral training under Clara Novello Davies, her work as a translator for Anna Pavlova, and her leftist political opinions as they apply to the operas of Wagner and Mozart and to Soviet opera. With **427** *Russian Newsreel: An Eye Witness Account of the Soviet Union at War* (1943), Haldane describes her service as a WWII war correspondent, 1938–41, with a major focus on her 1941 visit to the Soviet Union. In this book, written before her renunciation of communism, Haldane portrays the USSR in an entirely positive light, with many details of Soviet daily life in wartime. Her tone is humorous and breezy, but she waxes poetic when describing Moscow.

428 HALDANE, Elizabeth. 1862–1937. *From One Century to Another: The Reminiscences of Elizabeth S. Haldane*. Alexander Maclehose &

Sons, 1937. 322 pp.; front. port.; intro.; illus.; index. NUC pre56 226:534.

Born in Edinburgh, Scotland. Father: Robert Haldane. Mother: Mary Elizabeth Burdon-Sanderson. 4 brothers. Single. Wrote *The British Nurse in Peace and War* (1912), *George Eliot and her Times* (1927), *Mrs. Gaskell and her Friends* (1930); translated works of Hegel and Descartes. Knew Beatrice and Sidney Webb, Margaret Llewelyn Davies. Philanthropist; social reformer; political hostess; feminist; suffragist; political activist; biographer; translator; social historian. Upper class.

Achievements of a lifelong social reformer set against a backdrop of sociopolitical change, covering author's mid-Victorian childhood to the 1930s. Recalling childhood daily routine; family's two homes in town and country. Mother's inability to use her own money before the 1870 passage of the Married Women's Property Act. Discussing Gladstone's government: the Irish Question, 1868. At age 10, author's learning from her nurse about working-class struggles and the social conditions of Edinburgh's poor; reading Dickens's social novels. Attending a finishing school. Political ramifications of Presbyterianism in Scotland, 1870s; its influence in her life. Recalling the movement for higher education for women. Her interest in Fabian socialism; her acquaintance with the Webbs and George Bernard Shaw. Visiting London; recalling the popularity of the "aesthetic movement" and its cultural impact, 1870s. Visiting London hospital patients. Her friendship with the Carnegies and John Morley. Describing Anglo-Catholic movement at Oxford University. Discussing Country Franchise Bill, 1885, and Social Union movement in Scotland. Her interest in adult education in Scotland. Describing Scottish working-class attitudes toward the wealthy. Supporting the women's suffrage movement. Praising the work of General Booth's Salvation Army. Attending labor demonstrations in Hyde Park. Her brother's election to Parliament. Gladstone's policies, advances for working people, 1890s. Visiting Germany and America. Working for the Liberal Party in 1900 elections. Receiving an honorary doctor of law degree from St. Andrew's. Serving as London hostess for her parliamentary brother. Her interest in the work of the Poor Law Commission. Writing a memoir of her uncle John Burdon Sanderson. Serving on the Royal Commission on Civil Service; visiting the War Office in her official capacity. Describing frictions within the women's movement, 1912. Assessing the impact of WWI on British families, women, and society, 1920s.

In this far-ranging look at the most significant issues affecting the British Isles during the late 19th and early 20th centuries, Haldane occasionally indulges in nostalgia. Written on the eve of WWII, her realistic appraisal of modernity, warts and all, leads her to defend the more positive aspects of Victorianism, especially its spiritual concerns.

429 HALDANE, Louisa Kathleen (née Trotter). 1863–1961. *Friends and Kindred*. Faber & Faber, 1961. 248 pp.; illus.; family tree; index. NUC 1942–1962 60:134.

Born in London. Father: Coutts Trotter. Mother: Harriet Keatinge, Irish. Married 1890, John Haldane, scientist, physiology professor. 1 son; 1 daughter (writer Naomi Mitchison). Society woman; Oxford hostess; academic's spouse; feminist. Upper class.

Personal and familial memories, interspersed with opinionated observations on everyday upper-class British life, focused on the Victorian and Edwardian eras. Author's closeness with her father; effect of his hypochondria on mother. Her possible Jewish ancestry through her mother. Describing her Scottish childhood in Edinburgh. Traveling on the Continent with her parents. Her interest in Roman Catholicism; feeling a need to confess. Her parents' friends' being interested in the Evangelical movement. Memories of her governesses; later being educated by tutors. Father's nervous breakdown; mother's nervous collapse; author's taking care of family business details, ages 16–20. Meeting Annie Dundas, Elizabeth Hamilton; their work with the Edinburgh Association for the University Education of Women. Criticizing the lack of opportunities open to women. Discussing activities acceptable for "ladies" in Edinburgh, c.1880s. Changing her name to Kathleen. Refusing her husband twice before accepting his proposal. Being married in a Presbyterian rather than Episcopalian service because of her dislike of the Episcopalian custom of giving the bride away. Living in Oxford with her husband; describing his academic career and Oxford life; finding Oxford parties dull. Discussing Prime Minister Gladstone's policies and tariff reform. Helping found the Imperialists' Club. Being decorated by King Edward for her work for Empire and colonial students. Outlining the political situation in Africa before the Boer War. Her memories of Cecil Rhodes. Her pro-Boer position. Attending Queen Victoria's Jubilees and funeral; recalling coronations of King Edward and King George.

Haldane states that she wrote this book for the edification of her daughter and granddaughter, and she includes considerable detail about the personal and historical events encompassed by her long life. However, she is disappointingly reticent on the subject of her personal relationships with her children, who include novelist and autobiographer Naomi Mitchison, author of *Small Talk* (1973).

430 HALDANE, Mary Elizabeth (née Burdon-Sanderson). 1825–1925. *Mary Elizabeth Haldane: A Record of a Hundred Years (1825–1925)*. Ed. by Elizabeth Haldane (author's daughter). Hodder & Stoughton, 1925. 174 pp.; front. port.; intro. by Cosmo Ebor, Archbishop of York; intro. note by ed.; note by her eldest son;

illus.; letters and impressions; poem by Naomi Mitchison (author's granddaughter). NUC pre56 226:544.

Born in Rotherfield, Sussex. Father: Richard Burdon, colliery manager. Mother: Elizabeth Sanderson. 2 brothers; 1 sister. Married 1853, surname Haldane. Widow. 5 sons; 1 daughter; 5 stepchildren. Society woman; feminist. Upper middle class.

A brisk walk through personal memories, emphasizing the minutiae of early-19th-century society, spanning author's childhood to adolescence. Family history. Father's preparing for a clerical position in the Church of England. Family's settling near Tunbridge Wells; moving to Northumberland, 1826, after father received inheritance. Being educated at home by parents and governess; being severely disciplined by governess, who used religion to gain power over the children. Religious education's inculcating a sense of sin in author. Feeling insignificant in the family because of being a girl. Discussing the severe discipline in Yorkshire schools. Father's management of Wallsend Colliery; his activities as a justice of the peace. Moving to estate at Jesmond, Northumberland. Author's first seeing trains and aerial balloons. Remembering village fairs. Father's being baptized into the Plymouth Brethren sect. Living in Newcastle. Parents' withdrawing from their children into religious life.

Only the first eighty pages of this book are narrative autobiography. Haldane's tone is melancholy as she recalls the events of a largely isolated and unhappy childhood and herself as a sensitive and perceptive child who keenly felt her parents' emotional distance from her. The author conveys her innate love of children in her discussion of the joys of raising a large family according to her own ideas, rather than according to practices fashionable in her time.

431 HALE, Cicely. 1884–1981. *A Good Long Time (The Autobiography of a Nonagenarian)*. Barry Rose, 1975. 126 pp.; foreword by Robin Bosanquet; illus.; index. NUC 1973–1977 45:538. (1st pub. Regency Press, 1973.)

Born in London. Father: Charles Hale, physician. Mother: Bertha Poole. 2 brothers; 2 sisters. Single. Feminist; suffragist; midwife; journalist; nurse; social worker; secretary; WWI volunteer; physician's daughter. Upper middle class.

Nostalgic personal and professional reminiscences, set against the backdrop of a rapidly changing society and two world wars, covering 1880s–1960s. Suffering a long illness. Being a timid child. Describing her family home and servants; mother's strong influence on family. Studying with a governess; later attending school. Her social debut; being an awkward, unsuccessful debutante. Describing aristocratic women's fashions, c.1903. Remembering popular plays, actors, and actresses of the Edwardian theatre. Training as a secretary. Joining the Women's Social and Political Union; working as an assistant in the Information Department. Memories of Christabel Pankhurst: her necessary ruthlessness. Providing political background to suffragist actions, 1912; describing force-feeding. Young people's inheriting advances made by the suffrage movement. WWI: training as a midwife; working in Wartime Babies' Home and Infant Welfare clinic. Working as a health visitor in a slum district; recalling its people and living conditions. Sharing a London flat with her friend, Ann; taking holidays abroad with Ann. Writing for *Woman's Own* magazine. WWII: being evacuated from London. Ann's death; its effect on author. Writing an advice book on baby care. Becoming secretary to Girl Guides Association; her experiences as a guide camp nurse. Changes in society, education, manners, customs, inventions, from her youth to modern times.

Hale's autobiography traces her varied professional career and her political involvement in the women's movement. Her self-portrait shows a woman seemingly well equipped to meet the challenges of a changing society; her matter-of-factness about her considerable contributions underscores her apparent integrity and dedication to various causes. The book achieves two purposes: to record a life of service and to acquaint a younger generation with the social contributions of those living in an earlier age.

432 HAM, Elizabeth. 1783–d.a.1852. *Elizabeth Ham, by Herself: 1783–1820*. Ed. by Eric Gillett. Faber & Faber Ltd., 1945. 230 pp.; intro. by ed. NUC pre56 228:164.

Born in North Perrott, Somerset. Father not named, brewer, malter. Mother not named. 7 siblings. Single. Wrote *The Infants' Grammar* (1820), anonymously published poem *Elgiva or the Monks* (1824), *The Ford Family in Ireland* (1845). Children's author; governess; teacher; poet; biographer. Middle class.

Personal memories and historical observations, covering author's first four decades. Attending a school run by her aunt, dame school, and day school. Suffering with measles. Falling into a coal fire. Being sent by her parents to live with a cousin in Haslebury. Visiting her parents; mother's harshness toward her, favoritism toward her sister Anne. Author's negativism about her looks. Returning briefly to live at home, then boarding with her former governess. Father and uncle's enlisting in yeomanry. Recalling King George III's visit to family farm and brewery. Author's bout with scarlet fever; her constant craving for sympathy; convalescing with friends in Exeter. Describing the reaction in Weymouth to threat of a French invasion. Attending wedding and naval balls in Guernsey; visiting Bath with her father. Visiting her brother in Carlow; traveling through Ireland with her parents while her father sought cheap grain for the brewery. Family's living in Connaught; father's opening several malt-houses. Author's attending military balls; being secretly courted by a military officer, Mr. Jackson; his exposure as an unfaithful cad; her lifelong passion for him. Father's financial problems; author's writing to the lord lieutenant of Ireland for assistance. Dublin social activities. Her friend Anne Burrowes's preference for author's sister Mary; author's feeling deserted. Breaking up of the family home in Ireland, due to financial reverses. Visiting Weymouth, then visiting her brother in Guernsey. Living with her family in Coker. Briefly living with her aunt at Axbridge. Her unrequited infatuation with a married man; suffering depression. Her interest in Quakerism; thinking it is like Unitarianism; attending Unitarian services. Working as a governess; feeling lonely, disliking her profession. Being proposed to, then abandoned by, Mr. Edwards. Starting a school; its lack of success. Writing *The Infants' Grammar*. Trying governessing again. Noting popular entertainments, fairs, c.1790s. Describing contemporary opinions of King George III. Noting changes in women's education between 1790s and 1830s. Irish folk beliefs, customs, political insurgency, c.1805. Author's opinion that low moral standards in the Irish upper classes are due to overindulgence and absence of the need to work.

Although Ham's writing has the formality conventional in her time, she sounds as if she is seeking to win her readers' sympathies; she admits that her need for sympathy colored all her relationships with people. Her account mingles copious details of her own life with reports of important historical events (and people's reactions to them). As a result, the book is a rich source of information not only about Ham's own attitudes toward love, marriage, and patriotism, but about her contemporaries' attitudes toward these matters as well.

433 HAMILTON, Cicely Mary (stage name; née Hammill). 1875–1952. *Life Errant*. J. M. Dent, 1935. 300 pp.; front. port.; foreword; illus. NUC pre56 228:427.

Born in London. Father not named, army officer. Mother not named, Irish. 2 brothers; 1 sister. Single. Wrote play *Diana of Dobson's*, novels *William an Englishman* (1919), *Theodore Savage* (1922), social commentary *Marriage as a Trade* (1909), *How the Vote Was Won* (1909), *Modern Germanies* (1930), others. Actress (stage); suffragist; feminist; novelist; playwright; journalist; social historian; pupil-teacher; WWI volunteer. Middle class.

Forthright, informed account of personal and professional experiences, emphasizing feminist and philanthropic causes and author's role in these, spanning her childhood to c.1930. Father's long absences; mother's "farming out" her children to foster families; author's final separation from her mother, age 10, leading to grief, anxiety, and childhood suicide attempts. Being raised in a foster family until father's return from army campaign. Attending Malvern boarding school. Her early interest in acting. Studying in Germany. Working as a pupil-teacher; loathing it; going to London to seek acting work. Taking a stage name so as not to disgrace the Hammill family. Describing life in touring theatre companies. Providing a feminist analysis of marriage based on her disruptive family life as a child; supporting the birth control movement. Her first play's receiving critical acclaim. Becoming active in the suffrage movement as a member of the Women's Social and Political Union, Women's Freedom League, and the Women Writers' Suffrage League. Her friendship with suffrage leaders; infighting among them. Her WWI hospital work in Scotland and France. Acting in Lena Ashwell's troupe for soldiers in France, Germany, and England during and after WWI. Describing how the profound psychological impact of WWI and its aftermath led her to writing novels on war themes. Attending a conference of the Women's International Suffrage Alliance in Geneva, 1920. Working with the Save the Children Fund. Writing articles for *Time and Tide*. Her activity in the Open Door Council for women's job equality. Opposing the methods of militant suffrage leaders. Expressing her views on why civilized nations go to war and on fascist politics. Her faith in God. Her independence and lack of regret at never marrying. Opposing compulsory marriages. Criticizing mass psychology. Commenting on the state of English society; finding attitudes among the younger generation have changed, mostly for the worse, since the Victorian era.

Hamilton's educated style shows her familiarity with French and German phrases and with literature. Reticent about sharing in any depth her painful early childhood experiences, which may have contributed to many of her adult beliefs, she focuses instead on her development as a strong feminist and an independent thinker. One example of her appraisal of political issues can be found in her comment that the crises of the WWI period made women's suffrage seem an unimportant matter—a popular perception that cleared the way for women over age 30 to be granted the right to vote in 1918.

434 HAMILTON, Mary Agnes (née Adamson). 1882–1966. *Remembering My Good Friends*. Jonathan Cape, 1944. 320 pp.; index. NUC pre56 228:534.

Raised in Manchester, Aberdeen, and Glasgow. Father: Robert Adamson, professor of logic and mathematics. Mother: Margaret Duncan. 2 brothers; 3 sisters. Wrote novel *Dead Yesterday* (c.1917) and biographies of Mary Macarthur and Beatrice and Sidney Webb. Knew John Maynard Keynes, Bertrand Russell, Alfred North Whitehead, Eleanor Mildred Sidgwick, Helena Swanwick, Margaret Bondfield, Felix Frankfurter, Lady Ottoline and Philip Morrell, Henry James, Marie

Belloc Lowndes, others. Politician; member of Parliament; journalist; novelist; biographer; pacifist; academic's daughter. Middle class.

Politician and journalist's analysis of her intellectual development and her working relationships with political and academic figures, covering 1874–1944, with an emphasis on the years between WWI and WWII. Describing her parents' early lives; their marriage. Father's giving author her earliest lessons. Attending an Aberdeen primary school; walking to school with her father. Attending Glasgow Board Secondary School. Father's coaching her in logic to qualify for Cambridge; his intellectual creed. Attending Newnham College, Cambridge. Father's death; mother's insisting that children complete their university educations. Author's admiration for Eleanor Mildred Sidgwick. Her developing a humanist outlook; its being shattered by WWI. Her pacifist activism. Writing for the *Economist* and *Common Sense*. Her acquaintance with the Bloomsbury intellectual circle; perceiving it as having an atmosphere of self-satisfied superiority; her feeling that Virginia Woolf dissected her as a specimen of the "ordinary" person. Her activities with the International Labour Party. Describing the 1918 elections and the political mood in Britain during the 1920s. Discussing the character of Prime Minister Ramsay MacDonald. Writing for the *Review of Reviews*. Being elected to Labour party seat for Blackburn, Lancashire, 1929. Being League of Nations delegate, 1931; describing the failings of President Woodrow Wilson. Traveling in Italy (1926), Germany and Austria (1928–32), Greece (1933), France (1939), the U.S. (1923, 1932, 1942). Serving on the BBC Board of Directors, 1932–36. Rejecting humanism without God. Death of her mother, 1935.

Filled with detailed sketches of friends and associates, Hamilton's autobiography is interesting for its discussion of the political opinions of her fellow women members of Parliament. Chronological in organization, it is exhaustively thorough in its meticulous re-creation of the early-20th-century era of Labour politics. In her subsequent autobiography, *Up-Hill All the Way: A Third Cheer for Democracy* (1953), covering 1930s–1953, Hamilton continues a detailed discussion of her political activities and philosophy. Her work poses thoughtful and intelligent questions regarding social and economic problems, and offers possible solutions.

435 HAMILTON, Peggy. 1895–?. *Three Years or the Duration: The Memoirs of a Munition Worker, 1914–1918*. Peter Owen, 1978. 125 pp.; illus. NUC 1979 5:977.

Born in St. Albans, Hertfordshire. Father: George Tarlton Wills, son of wealthy shipping businessman. Mother: Minnie Louisa Smith. 2 brothers; 1 sister. Munitions factory worker; WWI volunteer. Upper class.

Upper-class young woman's factory work during WWI, with discussion of her prewar home life and wartime labor conditions, 1914–18. Luxurious circumstances of her early home life: eight servants, fourteen acres of gardens, swimming pool, and tennis court. WWI expediencies: boys entering the military as young as 13, women and girls—regardless of class—volunteering to nurse, drive ambulances, etc. The billeting of troops and convalescing soldiers from overseas in house of author's parents. Public outcry about the shortage of munitions for soldiers at the front, 1915. Suffragette-led campaign to recruit women for factory work; movement of women from unskilled to skilled work in the munitions factory; their training to become machinists and toolmakers. Author's signing on for factory work; moving into a rented room. Encountering general prejudice against women doing skilled work; women's higher wartime wages (highest was £3 a week for a 72-hour week) remaining half that of men's. 1915 founding of a Health of Munitions Workers Committee, to advise on health, safety, and hours. Author's work at Old Fuse Factory of Woolwich Arsenal and at the Government Rolling Mills at Southampton: her training in the toolroom; terrible hours, wages, and conditions; accidents; practical jokes' easing the strain. Her guilt over manufacturing weapons of destruction and her simultaneous belief in the ideal of the "war to end all wars." Relating stories about her friends and family. Recalling wartime social conditions; massive layoffs as the end of the war neared.

Throughout this autobiography Hamilton maintains an optimistic tone as she describes her transition from a luxurious home to a rented room and a war-related job that demanded she spend long hours performing boring, repetitive tasks. She acknowledges that for her this was a temporary change in lifestyle, while for others such limited circumstances were permanent. Through her personal experiences, Hamilton seems to attain greater compassion and social understanding, coming to acknowledge that the prewar period "was a golden age for those in a comfortable position, but in the big cities there was poverty, unemployment, and hardship in plenty" both before and after the war.

436 HAMMOND, Joan. 1912–s.l.1966. *A Voice, A Life*. Victor Gollancz, 1970. 264 pp.; illus.; app.; index. BLC to 1975 139:30.

Born in Christchurch, New Zealand; raised in Sydney, Australia. Father not named, electrical businessman. Mother not named. 3 brothers. Singer (opera); journalist; sportswriter; WWII volunteer. Middle class.

Opera singer's early life in Australia, her training and career, 1912–66. Parents' emigration from England to New Zealand; author's birth; moving to Sydney, Australia, as an infant. Attending Morven Garden School for boarding students, age 7. Taking violin and singing lessons. Playing many sports at school; winning Junior Golf Tournament. Bicycle accident's causing a severe, permanent injury to her left arm. Attending Presbyterian Ladies' College at Plymble; attending New South Wales

Conservatorium of Music, 1928, to study violin and voice. Realizing she could never play violin professionally because of her arm injury. Auditioning for the opera. Touring with Williamson Imperial Grand Opera Company, 1932; earning £3 per week. Father's insisting that author contribute financially to the family, 1933; working as a golf reporter for three newspapers: Sydney *Observer,* the *Mail,* and the *Telegraph.* Being the best woman golfer in Australia, but finding the choice between golf and opera easy because "singing was my whole world." Believing singing opera helped her overcome her shyness. Impressing Lady Hore-Ruthven (later Lady Gowrie) at a recital; winning her financial backing. Studying voice in Vienna, 1936; her debut there as Nidda in *I Pagliacci.* Singing at the coronation of George VI; being in London at the outbreak of WWII. Fearing war would destroy her career. Being rejected by Women's Auxiliary Air Force because of her bad arm. Securing a contract to sing in Milan at La Scala, 1940, but being expelled from Italy. Returning to London; living there during the 1940 blitz. Obtaining gas masks for herself and her dog; her voice pupil's being killed; poor people's living in underground stations. Her first recording, 1940. Working as an ambulance volunteer. Performing many concert and opera tours worldwide; giving benefit concerts and prison concerts. Having her operatic career ended by poor health, 1966.

Hammond states that for many years she lived in a cocoon, "cramped by the exigencies of my profession," and thus she had no regrets about cutting her career short. She implies nothing of her marital status except to say that now, in retirement, halcyon days are spent on "our" yacht, which suggests that she may have married in middle age. She mentions feeling shy or vocally insecure at times, feelings which she remedied by working hard on her singing technique.

437 HAMNETT, Nina. 1890–1956. *Laughing Torso: Reminiscences of Nina Hamnett.* Constable, 1932. 326 pp.; front.; illus.; index. NUC pre56 139:47. (other ed.: Virago, 1984.)

Born in Tenby, South Wales. Father: Col. George Hamnett, army officer. Mother: Mary Archdeacon. 1 brother; 1 sister. Married 1914, Edgar De Bergen, artist; separated c.1915. Illustrated Osbert Sitwell's *The People's Album of London Statues,* Seymour Leslie's *The Silent Queen.* Knew Amedeo Modigliani, Marie Beerbohm, Constantin Brancusi, Jean Cocteau, Marie Wassilieff, Aleister Crowley, James Joyce, Ford Madox Ford, others. Artist (painter, illustrator); artist's model; teacher (art); art critic. Middle class.

Artistic training, early career, and bohemian life in Paris and London, covering author's birth to 1932. Her childhood misbehavior; wishing she were a boy; disliking her father. Residence at Tenby, Saltash, and Belfast. Attending a young ladies' academy and the Royal School, Bath. Attending Portsmouth School of Art, 1903; attending Dublin School of

Art, 1905. Father's financial failure, resulting in author's need to earn a living. Attending Royal Academy lectures in London; breaking Victorian conventions of dress; privately using her own nude body as a model because women were barred from attending life-drawing classes. Attending London School of Art. Visiting Russia, 1909. Having a hysterical paralysis of her hands due to her father's ridicule of her painting; recovering. Describing bohemian life in London; meeting occultist Aleister Crowley. Recalling a friend's suicide. Giving painting lessons. Having her first exhibition. Receiving lessons in sculpture from Henri Gaudier-Brzeska, 1913. Working at Roger Fry's Omega Workshops. First visiting Paris, age 22; losing her virginity; adopting bohemian dress. Meeting Amedeo Modigliani; her friendship with Marie Wassilieff. Dancing nude before friends in cafés. Outbreak of WWI. Marriage; feeling bored with her husband; his imprisonment for being an unregistered alien; never seeing him again after his departure for France. Drawing the Sitwells and other poets. Teaching art at Westminster Technical Institute, 1919. Returning to Paris and her artist friends. Living in the south of France with a Polish artist; visiting Spain. Smoking hashish with Crowley and his hangers-on. Discussing her other friends: Ford Madox Ford, Jean Cocteau, Constantin Brancusi, Erik Satie, James Joyce, Francis Poulenc. Exhibiting paintings in London and Paris; having difficulty selling pictures. Attending art students' balls; being involved in Left Bank life. Visiting the French Riviera and Brittany. Drawing prostitutes. Describing expatriates, drinking cronies, artists, and literati. Living off occasional sales of her paintings. Returning to London for an exhibition of her work.

Full of drinking, pub crawling, and unconventional behavior, *Laughing Torso* consists largely of short, disconnected, repetitive anecdotes of Hamnett's friends and acquaintances. A flat narrative tone, simple sentences, and non sequiturs convey the impression that Hamnett lived from one minute to the next, seldom reflecting very deeply on her life and work. The book is probably most interesting for its anecdotes of the artists and writers of 1920s Paris. In the same year (1932) Hamnett published a childhood memoir, **438** "What I Wore in the Nineties," in Alan Pryce-Jones's anthology *Little Innocents*. In this, she comments ironically on late Victorian fashion and on her early desire to wear boys' clothing. With **439** *Is She a Lady? A Problem in Autobiography* (1955), Hamnett provides further anecdotes of pub crawls, parties, amusing people, her travels, and her drawings and paintings, 1926–48. Although she claims to have been serious about her art, this does not come through very clearly. Instead, she seems impelled to record other people's odd behavior and her own prodigious drinking. The book's title, in this context, may have been intended as a joke.

440 HANBURY, Charlotte. 1830–1900. *Charlotte Hanbury: An Autobiography*. Ed. by Mrs. Albert Head (author's niece). Marshall

Brothers, 1901. 236 pp.; front. port.; intro. by ed.; preface; illus. NUC pre56 229:304.

Raised in rural England. Father not named. Mother: Elizabeth Allen. 2 brothers. Single. Philanthropist; social reformer; religionist (Quaker, anti-Catholic). Middle class.

Personal, familial, and philanthropic memories, emphasizing Christian duty and brotherhood, spanning author's childhood to 1900. Family history. Grandfather's devotion to the antislavery cause; his friendship with Queen Victoria's father. Author's great admiration for her parents and her closeness to her brother Cornelius. Her parents' and family circle's connection to programs to teach literacy to Syrian women. Mother's working with Elizabeth Fry's prison-visiting programs. Memories of Fry as a famed Quaker leader; her effect on author. Receiving education from governess and older brother's tutor. Making a commitment to Quaker service, age 12. Her early interest in prison reform. Attending various Friends meetings. Author and brother's working with Ragged Schools, beginning 1845; opening their own Ragged School, 1850. Taking a therapeutic water cure in Wales; vowing to abstain from alcohol. Traveling in Italy, France, Germany, and Switzerland; climbing the Matterhorn with her cousins. Petitioning the German government for better treatment of certain prisoners; winning their release. Expressing sympathy for London's working poor. Traveling to Germany with her brother, 1860; their nursing work with fever victims. Moving to Blackdown Hills, bordering Devon and Somerset; evangelizing rural people. Recalling noteworthy friends: education writer Mary Anne Schimmelpennick, Marquis and Marchioness of Cholmondeley, Rev. Dwight L. Moody. Returning to Europe; visiting a French convent; expressing her anti-Catholic attitude. Voyage to Tangier, Morocco, to spread the Gospel and relieve prison conditions. Describing aspects of Moroccan society. Learning she has breast cancer; drawing closer to God. Testimonials: letters from friends.

Hanbury dictated this autobiography to her niece during the last three months of her life, and her niece then connected parts of the story from her own memory and from Hanbury's diaries. Written in an accessible style suffused with sentimentality, this book principally focuses on Hanbury's devotion to Quakerism and public service. Through her own and her family's connections to various philanthropic and social reform causes, Hanbury conveys a great deal about some of the major social movements of the late 19th century.

441 HARDY, Emma Lavinia (née Gifford). 1840–1912. *Some Recollections*. Ed. by Evelyn Hardy and Robert Gittings. Oxford University Press, 1961. 91 pp.; front. port.; intro.; illus.; poems by Thomas Hardy; app. BLC to 1975 140:26.

Born at Plymouth, Devonshire. Father: solicitor. Mother not named. 3 brothers; 1 sister. Married 1874, Thomas Hardy, novelist. Wrote *Spaces* (1912), *The Maid on the Shore, Poems and Religious Effusions* (1966). Novelist; poet. Middle class.

Personal recollections of growing up in England's rural West country, covering author's childhood to marriage. Being a quiet, unassuming child. Describing the intellectual environment in her family's Plymouth home. Her father's drunkenness and subsequent temperance pledge; teetotalling in their home; his love of literature; his difficult nature. Attending school, summer regattas, church; going to the weekly Plymouth Market with her mother. Family's moving to Cornwall; their country way of life there. Her sister's stint as a governess. Author's encounters with fortunetellers. Sister's marriage to Rev. Cadell Holder of St. Juliot; author's visiting them and helping in the parish; describing local customs, persons, and witchcraft. First meeting Thomas Hardy (then an architect); corresponding with him; marrying him, 1874. Commenting on popular authors of the 1860s: Dickens, Thackeray, Trollope, Bulwer-Lytton, Scott, Harriet Beecher Stowe. Perceiving differences between working-class people in Devon and Cornwall. Her steadfast belief in Christianity and the importance of the Christian ideal.

In this autobiography, written in 1911 but not published until 1961, Hardy writes in a style of understated elegance. Her tone is at once light—in summoning pleasant memories of her youth in Devon and Cornwall—and somber, as if presaging the turn her life will soon take with husband Thomas Hardy, although she omits mention of her later estrangement from her husband. Thomas Hardy's annotations and emendations to this autobiography distract from and occasionally change the author's intent. However, the image of Emma Hardy as a woman worthy of consideration in her own right still comes through clearly.

442 HARDY, Violet, Lady (née Leigh). 1875–1972. *As It Was*. Christopher Johnson, 1958. 195 pp.; foreword by Lord Dunsany; prologue; illus. NUC 1958–1962 19:240.

Born in London. Father: Sir Edward Chandos Leigh, counsel to speaker of House of Commons. Mother: Katherine Rigby. 2 brothers; 1 sister. Married 1900, Sir Bertram Hardy, 3rd baronet, d.1953. Widow. 2 sons. Wrote play *Riding for a Fall* (1918). Society woman; philanthropist; actress (stage); playwright. Upper class.

Memories of a gracious, upper-class life, lived against a backdrop of dramatic change in British society, covering author's childhood to the 1950s. Family ancestry; extinction of family dukedom. Her famous relatives, including actress Fanny Kemble and poet Rowland Leigh. Seeing her father as the ideal parent; discussing his accomplishments and career as parliamentary counsel. Describing family life in London. Mother's character, appearance, and independent income. Attending Queen Victoria's Jubilee. Author's brothers; their Harrow schooling. Traveling in Italy; visiting Byron's home in Venice; her grandfather Leigh's having had a close friendship with Byron at Harrow. Attending the Church of England but having few spiritual thoughts. Speculating that, by ending Hanoverian rule, Victoria's reign prevented an English revolution. Studying music and art with governesses. Her brothers' teaching her to smoke. Her sister's death, c.1889; its effect on author. Attending a plenitude of balls and parties. Marriage, 1900. Discussing her husband's character; his passion for hunting. Traveling with him to the Far East. During WWI, husband's serving in the Staffordshire Yeomanry; deaths of both of author's brothers. Changes in women's fashion, especially bathing costumes, from Victorian to modern times. Her ambivalent views on women's emancipation; dress, sports, cycling, ownership of property. Customs at society events. Her acting in Noel Coward's *Vortex*. Writing and presenting a play for charity, 1918. Assisting at Hyde Park Canteen during the general strike, 1926. Contrasting girls' education in the Victorian era and the 1950s. Perceiving a need to teach modern children morality, Christian behavior, and pride in their nation. Her opinion that Victorian attitudes limited women. Author's views on marriage and divorce. Seeing a connection between the atomic bomb and modern rootlessness.

Chatty and intimate in tone, Hardy's work compares various aspects of Victorian and modern times. The author seeks to penetrate the superficial changes in society, treating substantive issues such as women's emancipation and presenting forthright opinions about those changes.

443 HARRISON, Jane Ellen. 1850–1928. *Reminiscences of a Student's Life*. Hogarth Press, 1925. 90 pp.; photos. BLC to 1975 140:441.

Born in Yorkshire. Father: Charles Harrison. Mother: Elizabeth Hawksley. Stepmother not named. 11 siblings. Single. Wrote *Prolegomena to the Study of Greek Religion; Themis; Hymn of the Kouretes; Epilegomena*. Knew anthropologist Arthur Evans, novelists Samuel Butler, George Eliot. Classicist; academic; anthropologist; mythologist; public speaker; teacher; teacher (Sunday school); justice of the peace. Upper class.

Educational experiences and personal opinions on art and education of an esteemed classicist, from her Victorian childhood to the 1920s. Author's childhood fascination with Russia. Her religious upbringing; her stepmother's semirevivalist leanings and exhortations to author to give her whole heart to God. Father's dread of Catholics and foreigners, resulting in the hiring of a string of kind but ignorant English governesses. Describing the "ingenious uselessness" of Victorian education for girls; their daily practice at making "exquisite hems and seams."

Author's teaching Sunday school. Attending Cheltenham College; its students being forbidden to buy books because these contained "undigested knowledge"; contrasting this with the wider intellectual readings women later enjoyed at Cambridge. Meeting Ivan Turgenev and George Eliot at Cambridge. Lecturing on Greek Art; noting its contemporary popularity. Working for the council of the Girls' Public Day School. Associating with Cambridge academics: Henry Sidgwick, Frederick Myers, Edmund Gurney. Lecturing on classical art in London. Studying archaeology in Germany and Greece. Exploring Knossos in Crete with Arthur Evans. Traveling to Russia to study Kertsch antiquities. Serving as a justice of the peace. Her conservative prejudices; her Yorkshire dislike of pretentiousness. Noting Victorian ideas and puritan temperament regarding child-rearing. Disliking rigid systems for forming children's minds; perceiving home study as preferable to school attendance for girls. Disagreeing with Freud's views on the psychology of art. Seeing the relationship of art and ritual to religion; ritual's bridging the gap between art and life. Thinking marriage can hinder women's friendships and learning; reaffirming her decision to remain single. Her personal contentment in old age; the need for the old to remain intellectually active.

Wry humor accentuates Harrison's retrospective of her long life of academic and literary achievement and her resounding indictment of the prudery and fatuousness of girls' education in her own time. Her experiences seem to have left her free of intellectual snobbery, and her narrative documents her welcoming acceptance at public lectures of all who approached her out of love for learning and culture, regardless of their social class. Further details on her ideas about the barriers between women and academic success can be found in *Jane Ellen Harrison: A Portrait from Letters* by Jessie Stewart (1959).

444 HARRISON, Rosina with Leigh Crutchley. 1899–s.l.1970s. *Rose: My Life in Service*. New York: The Viking Press, 1975. 237 pp.; foreword; illus.; index. BLC 1976–1982 20:332.

Born in Aldfield, near Ripon, Yorkshire. Father not named, stonemason, church sexton, and caretaker. Mother not named, laundrymaid. 3 siblings. Single. Domestic servant. Working class.

Reminiscences of a life of domestic service, emphasizing details of author's employment by Lady Astor and her personal experiences with the Astor family, covering her childhood to 1970s. Author's having a desire to travel when she grew up, but having no great ambitions to rise above her social class; family's awareness of its place in society. Her love of school; attending school until age 16. Taking French lessons during her apprenticeship as a dressmaker. Being trained as a lady's maid, the highest level of servant. Her first job as a lady's maid to Lady Irene Tufton's daughter, Miss Patricia, in London, author's age 18. Taking the train to London for the first time. Describing her duties: chaperoning, tidying up, mending and ironing clothes, making underlinen, packing and managing luggage. Tufton family's move to Appleby Castle after the London season. Informal setting of the servants' hall because male servants were away in the military during WWI. Receiving wages of £24/year from the Tuftons; working for them four years. Father's death, 1924; moving home. Working for Lady Cranborne in Mayfair, London, 1925. Feeling pride in making Lady Cranborne's clothes. Traveling with her employer every weekend. Taking a new job in Cliveden, 1928, as junior lady's maid to Miss Wissie, Lady Astor's daughter, at £60/year. Her fondness for Mr. Lee, the Astors' butler. Working for the Astors in various capacities for thirty-five years. Being promoted to lady's maid to American-born Lady Astor, the first woman elected to Parliament. Eventual friendship between author and Lady Astor despite their class difference. Describing the Astors' large staff; social life among the servants. Frequently traveling with the Astors; having foreign beaus. Saving money and sending some to her mother; purchasing a bungalow by the sea for her mother. Lady Astor's interest in the welfare of author's mother; her sending occasional provisions to her at holiday times. Author's four trips to America on her own. Traveling with Mr. Lee at Lady Astor's expense. Her relationship with the Astor children. Author's version of the history of WWII. Involvement of Lady Astor's son in the Profumo diplomatic and sex scandal; author's hiding this from the now very ill woman. Lady Astor's death. Author's retirement to her mother's bungalow. Her continued contact with the Astor children.

Passages of dialogue with Lady Astor animate Harrison's work, even as she acknowledges that her lack of facility with words prevents her from being more analytical. She focuses on her life of service to Lady Astor and on the fulfillment of her dreams of traveling. The last quarter of the book, basically a biography of Lady Astor and her social life, is illustrated with many photos of Harrison's employer and her circle.

445 HASLETT, Dame Caroline Harriet. 1895–1957. "Caroline Haslett, C.B.E.," pp. 97–116 in *Myself When Young: By Famous Women of Today*. Ed. by Margot Asquith [Emma Alice Margaret Asquith, the Countess of Oxford and Asquith]. Frederick Muller, 1938. 422 pp.; foreword by ed.; ports.; index. BLC to 1975 12:477.

Raised in Haywards Heath, Sussex. Father: Robert Haslett, railroad engineer. Mother: Caroline Sarah Holmes, women's clubs and institutes organizer. 1 brother; 2 sisters. Single. Knew Mrs. Crompton Llewellyn Davies, Harry Llewellyn Davies, drama critic Arthur Bingham Walkley, Emmeline Pankhurst, engineer Sir Charles Parsons, Lilian Baylis, and aviator Amy Johnson. Engineer (electrical); suffragist; editor; feminist activist. Rural laboring class.

Electrical engineer's working-class upbringing, training under sponsorship of social reformer Mrs. Crompton Llewellyn Davies, and career, 1890s–1938. Experiencing Christian conversion, age 12. Preaching her first sermon at age 16. Her voracious reading. Her childhood illnesses. Feeling frustrated with the ladylike subjects she was taught in school. Meeting Mrs. Crompton Llewellyn Davies; her encouraging author by facilitating her training at a commercial college for a business career. Staying as a guest at the Llewellyn Davies's three homes. Living in London; finding employment in Mr. Llewellyn Davies's engineering firm. Justifying her suffrage activities to her father on Christian grounds. Working as a Sunday school superintendent, age 19. Recalling WWI bombing. Finding employment with a boiler-works firm in Annan, Scotland. Attempting to found a tennis club for girls. Being appointed as the first secretary to the Women's Engineering Society, 1919; editing its journal, *Woman Engineer;* describing her friends and colleagues in the society. Founding the Housecraft School to train young people in the use of electrical equipment. Founding, 1924, and directing (until 1956) the Electrical Association for Women; editing its journal, *Electrical Age*. Attending international conferences and expositions. Receiving support from the Duke and Duchess of York. Describing her activities with the Industrial Welfare Society. Serving on the board of directors of public companies. Her activities in Pioneer and Forum women's clubs. Her leisure activities: fishing, golf, swimming, tennis, boating, skating. Admiring women aviators. Supporting full employment of women. Her belief in the social value of women's work.

Writing in a conversational style, Haslett expresses gratitude for all the gifts and support she has received. She includes many anecdotes and highlights of her career, and ends with philosophical reflections on her work's significance. In the journal *Electrical Age* and other publications, Haslett encouraged the application of electrical devices to domestic work in order to give women more time for civic activities. After WWII she served on the British Electricity Authority, and she was awarded the D.B.E. in 1947.

446 HATHAWAY, Sybil Mary, Dame de Sark (née Collings; D.B.C.). c.1884–d.a.1957. *Dame of Sark: An Autobiography*. William Heinemann, 1961. 211 pp.; front. port.; illus.; map. BLC to 1975 141:469.

Born at Hirzel House, Isle of Guernsey, Channel Islands. Father: William Frederick Collings, 20th Seigneur de Sark. Mother: Sophie Moffatt, Scots-Canadian. 1 sister. Married c.1901, Dudley Beaumont, British Army officer, d.1918. Married Bob Hathaway, American. 3 sons; 3 daughters. Feudal dame; WWI volunteer; military spouse. Aristocracy.

Hathaway's upbringing and her rule of the Island of Sark as a modern-day feudal dame, covering her birth to old age. History of Sark and other Channel Islands; her family's inheritance of feudal lordship over Sark as allies of the British crown; Sark's being the world's last bastion of feudalism—not part of Britain, but an independent country still operating under a medieval feudal system; Sark's Norman heritage, medieval laws, and customs. Description of the island. Speaking English, modern French, and old Norman French in her childhood. Her lameness since infancy. Her violent temper. Relating legends and folklore of Sark. Father's teaching her to ride horseback and shoot. Her governesses. Attending exclusive Sacré Coeur convent school in Tours, France, age 14; her rebellious attitude; returning home. Believing that her lame leg put romance and marriage out of the question; resolving to be indispensable to her father. Her lifelong fear of the sea. Courtship with Dudley Beaumont, a military officer, age 17; defying her father's opposition to the proposed marriage; her removal to Guernsey; marriage in London. Her husband's Irish background. Yearly births of children; living in the Forest of Dean, Gloucestershire. Receiving a new car, "one of the first in England," 1903. Her mother's fatal illness. Returning to Sark. Author's WWI nursing work in England. Her husband's death after the war; her return to Sark to bear her last child. Expenses of widowhood. Moving to Cologne, Germany; doing YMCA work there. Acting in the Rhine Army Dramatic Company. Describing German inflation and civil unrest. Traveling to India; returning to live in Sark; becoming Dame of Sark upon father's death. Managing the island and its commercial dairy interests. Vacationing in New York, 1929; meeting her future second husband; husband's adjustment to his duties as Seigneur of Sark. Traveling to Burma and to the U.S., 1938. German occupation of Sark during WWII; her example of courage and steadiness to Sark residents. Death of her eldest son in the war. British commando raids on Sark; increased hardships and harsh German orders; deportation to Germany of civilians, including author's husband; her hiding grain and potatoes to feed her subjects. Reuniting with her husband after the war. Traveling to the U.S., 1946. Duke of Edinburgh's arrival in Sark to dedicate the rebuilt harbor. Her friendship with actor David Niven, who came to Sark to make a motion picture. Her second husband's death, 1954. Queen Elizabeth II's visit to Sark, 1957.

Hathaway's account of her life as Dame of Sark shows that being a feudal ruler in the modern world is not all romance—a reality exemplified by her detailed account of her resistance during the German occupation. She gives extensive information on Sark's history and her family ties to the island. In peacetime, her position allowed her to travel and to lecture. Well aware of her unique position, despite her independent temperament Hathaway expresses a strong commitment to tradition and duty.

447 HAWKER, Beatrice. 1910–?. *Look Back in Love*. Longmans Green, 1958. 149 pp.; illus. by Rosemary Haughton. BLC to 1975 142:254.

Born in Somerset. Father not named, steward, secretary. Mother: Emily. Married, husband not named, Methodist preacher converted to Catholicism. Preacher; religionist (Methodist; Roman Catholic convert); clergyman's spouse. Working class.

Background and upbringing of Methodist preacher, her affection for family and community and her eventual Catholic conversion, covering her childhood to 1958. Grandfather's conversion to Methodism; his religious activities; his death. Parents' characters: mother's discipline and involvement with charity work; father's youth, irregular employment, positive response to Methodist faith. Methodism in family and community. Author's closeness to her father. Nursing her parents during their illnesses; their deaths during author's adolescence. Moving to Baltonsborough to live with her aunts; discussing Methodist culture there. Her career as a Methodist woman preacher. Joining Junior Free Church Council, preaching outside pubs, age 22. Describing her extended family. Beginning to search for the truth of God as well as the love of God; her conversion to Catholicism; considering herself a rather heterodox Methodist before her conversion. Her continued friendliness with Nonconformist clergy after her conversion.

Intimately familiar with both Protestant and Catholic theology, Hawker writes quite freely about her affection for Methodism (toward which her "look back in love" is directed), occasionally nimbly introducing a Catholic perspective. Her central focus is on preachers and members of the Church. Interestingly, she avoids detailed discussion of her conversion to Catholicism and barely mentions her marriage.

448 HEAD, Alice Maud. 1886–1981. *It Could Never Have Happened*. William Heinemann, 1939. 251 pp.; front. port.; illus. NUC pre56 237:89.

Born in Notting Hill Gate, London. Father: F. D. Head, building contractor. Mother not named, former school teacher. 1 sister; 1 brother. Single. Knew William Randolph Hearst. Journalist; editor; secretary; publisher; traveler (U.S.). Middle class.

Personal, professional, and travel memories of women's magazine editor, set within detailed description of literary circles, spanning 1890s to 1939. Her early love of reading. Her Baptist father's influence. Attending Frances Mary Buss's North London Collegiate School for Girls: rigid discipline and school activities' making her acutely nervous. Contrasting the present atmosphere of the school with its earlier days. Deciding to become a journalist in order to escape going to Cambridge. Taking a secretarial course as the first step toward journalism. Attending Congregational Church. Working as a typist in the office of *Country Life* magazine; becoming secretary to the editor; moving on to a position with the parent firm under George Riddell; Riddell's making her the editor of the monthly magazine *Woman at Home,* 1909–14. Her friendship with *Woman at Home* founder Annie S. Swan and with Labour leader Mary MacArthur. WWI: air raids, living conditions in London. Being assistant editor of *Nash's* magazine, owned by William Randolph Hearst. Memories of Hearst; describing the difference between the real Hearst and his public persona. Helping to launch the English edition of *Good Housekeeping,* 1920. Becoming managing director of publishing firm. Her firm belief in astrology; consulting fortune-tellers. Traveling annually to America to see Hearst. Visiting Los Angeles and San Simeon; meeting Marian Davies, as well as other film stars and literary figures. Being agent for Hearst's purchase of St. Donat's Castle. Working, as editor, with novelists Marie Corelli, Michael Arlen, Robert Hichens, Rebecca West, Somerset Maugham, James Hilton, A. J. Cronin. Her code of business conduct. Offering advice to people seeking business success. Touring Italy with Hearst.

Head presents informally written, thoughtful portraits of the publishing industry and of contemporary luminaries. She is particularly insightful in her portrayal of the elusive William Randolph Hearst, who by including her in his parties and other social gatherings gave her a bird's-eye view of the opulent and eccentric lifestyle of a famous American publisher.

449 HECKFORD, Sarah. 1839–1903. *A Lady Trader in the Transvaal.* Sampson Low, Marston, Searle & Rivington, 1882. 412 pp.; preface. NUC pre56 237:612.

Born in Dublin, Ireland. Parents not named; author was orphaned in 1849. Married 1867, Dr. Heckford, physician, d.1871. Widow. Trader (farm produce); farmer; governess; emigrant (South Africa); physician's spouse. Middle class.

Irish emigrant's account of her employment in South Africa and her experiences in the Boer War, 1878–c.1882. Arriving in Durban, South Africa, 1878. Traveling 450 miles to the village of Rustenberg. Describing South African scenery; her travels in Orange Free State. Finding employment as an English governess for an Afrikaner family in the Transvaal; describing her teaching methods. Accepting her employer's offer to sell her half his farm. Working on the farm in summers, traveling to trade produce in winter. Her thoughts on the demoralizing effects of the country on English servants. Contracting a serious fever. Traveling with "Mr. Egerton" toward Pretoria to sell her farm produce. Trading with Boer women. Deciding to side with the English if war with the Boers came. Believing the English had the right to annex the

Transvaal, but that they unjustly punished Afrikaners and Boers who had remained loyal to them. Fearing a Boer attack. Author's internment in the besieged camp of Pretoria. Recalling military skirmishes around Pretoria. Author's views on the future of the Boers and Afrikaners.

Heckford states in her preface that she has substituted fictitious names for the real names of persons and farms. The scope of this narrative does not cover the whole of her extraordinary career, which she commenced in 1866 as a cholera nurse in Wapping (where she met her husband). Later, she carried on her husband's work of establishing the first East End children's hospital in London. After two years as a *zenana* missionary and medical advisor in India to the Begum of Bhopal (1877–79), Heckford decided to emigrate to South Africa. She wrote this book while in Pretoria under siege. Her narrative is level-headed and chronological, and makes a plea for better treatment by the English of loyal Boers and Afrikaners.

450 HELPS, Mary Alice (née Tapson). c.1860–1922. *Memories by the Late Mary Alice Helps*. Ed. by E. A. Helps (author's husband). Duckworth & Co., 1924. 159 pp. NUC pre56 239:654.

Born in London. Father: Alfred Tapson, physician. Mother not named. 9 sisters. Married 1884, Edmund A. Helps, inspector of schools. 1 son. Headmistress; teacher; philanthropist; editor. Middle class.

Wistful, literate journey through personal and professional memories, accompanied by observations on contemporary rural society and philanthropic activities, covering author's childhood to 1922. Being a bright, inquisitive child. Home education in a strict home environment. Studying drawing. Performing theatricals with her sisters. Acting in a skit on women's emancipation performed for Ruskin. Discussions with friends about marriages of famous people (Browning, Tennyson, Gladstone) and about "free love." Disliking being idle. Studying for and passing her senior Cambridge examination. Being permitted by her father to teach school. Working as assistant mistress of a girls' public day school. Becoming headmistress of a school in Norwich; her devotion to the students. Describing school responsibilities and activities. Meeting her future husband; courtship and marriage, 1884. Suffering from ill health; going to live in the country. Her philanthropic activities among poorer villagers. Anecdotes about neighbors and cottagers. Describing the joys of raising her son; anecdotes from his childhood and adolescence. Editing a volume of the artistic recollections of Mr. Horsely, R.A., a family friend, and a selection of Wordsworth's poems. Her final bout with pneumonia, 1922.

Literary citations introduce each chapter of Helps's account. During her final illness she transformed her diary entries from the previous twelve years into this narrative autobiography, which re-creates a life devoted to family, students, and the greater community.

451 HENWOOD, Loveday. 1788–1844. *Extracts from the Memoir and Letters of the Late Loveday Henwood*. Falmouth: J. Trathan, 1845. 116 pp. NUC pre56 241:372. (other ed.: C. Gilpin, 1847.)

Born in Cornwall. Parents not named. 1 brother. Single. Religionist (Methodist, Quaker convert); dressmaker; teacher. Lower middle class.

Spiritual autobiography of a Quaker convert, covering her childhood to approaching death. Mother's great spiritual influence on author. Attending boarding school; reacting to the irreligious family with whom she lodged. Being apprenticed to a dressmaker; experiencing the temptations of fashion; setting up her own dressmaking business and employing apprentices. Joining Methodists; getting to know Quakers. Teaching girls' day school at a Wesleyan meeting house. Smoking tobacco to cure her toothache; being unable to give it up; fearing God's judgment. Attending Quaker meetings. Her ten-year engagement to a local Methodist preacher; author's having her aged mother to support; consequent conflict's making her unwell. Her ambivalence about marrying; deciding that the "with my body I thee worship" passage of the marriage vows was idolatry; breaking the engagement because married women have less time to devote to God. Her growing inner spiritual darkness; leaning toward Quakers; joining them. Abandoning the dressmaking business because it catered to vanity. Suffering from serious illness; receiving divine visitations; hearing voices quote Scripture; her frequent bouts of weeping. Attending quarterly Quaker conferences; meeting international Quaker figures. Experiencing chronic pain and sickness; consuming brandy as self-medication. Relying increasingly on religion in making decisions. Her accelerating illness. Journal extracts and diary entries. Editor's description of author's last days.

Morality is the linchpin for Henwood as she uses the story of her spiritual journey to reaffirm her dedication to God. Interestingly, the conflicts between the sacred and secular sides of her nature are never resolved; her text reveals how the essential moral inconsistencies in her character managed to coexist with a genuine religious commitment.

452 HEPWORTH, Dame (Jocelyn) Barbara (C.B.E.). 1903–1975. *A Pictorial Autobiography*. New York: Praeger, c.1970. 128 pp.; illus. NUC 1968–1972 40:134.

Born at Wakefield, Yorkshire. Father: Herbert Raikes Hepworth, engineer. Mother: Gertrude Johnson. 2 sisters; 1 brother. Married c.1925, John Skeaping, sculptor; separated c.1930. Married c.1931 Ben Nicholson, painter; divorced 1951. 2 sons; 2 daughters. Wrote *Unit One: Barbara Hepworth* (1961), *J.P. Hodin, European Critic* (1965), *Michael*

Tippett (1965). Artist (sculptor); art critic; organizer of societies (artistic); theatrical set designer. Middle class.

Aesthetic development, education, and career of major 20th-century abstract sculptor affiliated with Constructivist movement, 1903–68. Her parents and family background. Early memories of West Riding landscape as a major influence on her vision as a sculptor. Attending Wakefield Girls' High School to 1918. Studying for nine months at Leeds School of Art; meeting sculptor Henry Moore at Leeds; attending Royal College of Art, London, ages 16–19. Living in Florence, Italy; her first marriage; residing for two years in the British School in Rome. Learning to carve Carrara marble. Having her first private exhibition with her husband; her first London show, 1928. Birth of her son; breakup of her marriage due to husband's desire to be free. Author's affiliation with Moore, art critic Sir Herbert Read, and other artists in Hampstead circle. First meeting her future husband, Ben Nicholson, 1931; having a 1932 exhibition with him. Visiting studios of Jean Arp and Pablo Picasso in France. Discussing the importance of light in relation to form. Giving interviews, receiving major reviews of her work. Pregnancy; unexpected birth of triplets. Returning to carving, 1934; finding a new, entirely formal direction for her work. Due to war fears, moving with Nicholson to St. Ives, Cornwall, c.1939. Her children's education. Discussing the formation of the Penwith Society of Arts among artists living in Cornwall. Writing on sculpture for art magazines. Being invited to observe a surgery in a hospital, 1947; making a series of paintings of surgeons at work. Acquiring Trewyn Studio in St. Ives; artistic inspiration of St. Ives. Dissolution of her second marriage. Designing the set for *Electra* at London's Old Vic, 1951. Having her first retrospective exhibition, 1954. Making carvings in hardwoods inspired by Greek themes. Being awarded honor of C.B.E., 1958. Winning Grand Prix at 1959 São Paolo Biennial Exhibition of Modern Art. Creating larger forms for outdoor settings. Her friendship with United Nations Secretary-General Dag Hammarskjold, 1960; dedicating a memorial sculpture to him at the U.N., 1964. Receiving honorary D. Litt. degrees. Commenting on her dedication to her family and to her art; perceiving an artist's work as an affirmation of life; discussing the meaning of form in sculpture.

Photographs of Hepworth's life and work predominate over text in this book; from Section 3 onward, photo captions are the main source of biographical information. Hepworth provides more detail about the meaning of her abstract sculptures and her fascination with form than about her personal feelings and relationships, but her position at the center of Britain's art world nevertheless lends significance to those stories she does tell. Her style is educated; her tone is often abstract and meditative.

453 HERBERT, Dorothea. 1770–1829. *Retrospections of Dorothea Herbert*, 1770–1789. Gerald Howe, 1929. 216 pp.; front.; intro.; genealogical chart; index. BLC to 1975 145:435.

Born in County Kilkenny, Ireland. Father: Nicholas Herbert, clergyman. Mother: Martha Cuffe, economist, factotum to her mother, Lady Desart. 3 brothers; 4 sisters. Single. Family historian; clergyman's daughter. Upper class.

Youthful hopes, illusions, and escapades within 18th-century upper-class Irish society, covering author's first nineteen years. Family history; visiting Desart county seat. Parish clerk's teaching author to write. Accompanying her mother to Bristol for mother's health; experiencing travel anxieties on the turbulent sea voyage. Studying dancing, music, and drawing. Her social debut. Discussing women's fashions, c.1780. Anecdotes of eccentric friends and relatives. Describing arcane beauty treatments. Performing plays at home with her siblings. Listing causes and consequences of parish rebellions of 1781–82; family house's being invaded by Irish dragoons in search of horses. Establishment of the Bank of Ireland and founding of the Order of St. Patrick, 1783. Memories of the signing of the peace treaty to end the American Revolution. Participating in pastimes at Castle Blunden: nutting, boating, dancing. Her fear of illness. Attending weddings; describing wedding finery. Going on excursions to Ross and Inisfallen Islands. A fever epidemic in Ireland and its consequences, 1789. Being courted by beaux. Meeting John Roe; being courted by him; visiting Rockwell, his estate; describing their engagement as his becoming "sole arbiter of my destiny."

Herbert devotes considerable detail to the frivolous pursuits of her early years, but her accompanying reports about political as well as social events bring Anglo-Irish society to life. In *Retrospections of Dorothea Herbert,* 1789–1806 (1830), she recounts, often melodramatically, the further details of her love affair with John Roe and his subsequent betrayal of her, and also offers glimpses of both her domestic existence and contemporary events.

454 HEWETT, Ellen (née Baker). 1843–d.a.1910. *Looking Back; or, Personal Reminiscences by the Widow of a New Zealand Pioneer Settler.* St. Albans: The Campfield Press, 1914. 102 pp.; preface; front. port.; illus.; app. NUC pre56 244:303.

Born in Liverpool. Father: surname Baker. Mother not named. 1 sister; 1 brother; 1 half-sister. Married 1859, James Duff Hewett, member of Wellington Provincial Council. Widow. 3 sons; 1 daughter. Colonialist (New Zealand); farmer; philanthropist; missionary (New Zealand). Middle class.

Recollections of a New Zealand colonist, covering her mid-Victorian childhood to 1910. Her childhood interest in New Zealand Maoris. Family's emigrating from Liverpool to New Zealand for her father's health, author's age 11; their arduous three-month sea voyage. Finding primitive conditions in the settlements. Family's home and garden in Nelson; author's delight in native birds. Mother's difficult adjustment to semi-outdoor life. Meeting James Duff Hewett; courtship; marriage, author's age 15. Arriving at her husband's farm. Describing the Maori war; destruction of their family home by fire. Visiting family in several New Zealand locales. Losing another home to fire. Husband's nomination as candidate for Wanganui to the Wellington Provincial Council; his contacts with important New Zealand statesmen. Renewed Maori uprisings; their evacuation due to feared attack. Her favorable assessment of Maori neighbors; their culture and customs. Having a mystical religious experience; author's consequent religious questions. Her father's death; husband's assassination by Hau Hau Maori sect. Seeking spiritualist answers; husband's appearing in a dream to declare his happiness in the spirit world. Living with her mother in Nelson; an epidemic's causing many deaths there; author's thankfulness that her small daughter was spared. Government's awarding author 400 acres and a widow's pension. Returning to England for children's education; entering missionary work; returning to New Zealand 16 years later. Performing Gospel-Temperance work among the Maoris. Her children's having become well-to-do settlers.

This account of Hewett's life as an emigrant farmer, wife, and widow is told plainly; it derives its central interest from the background of ongoing conflict and adjustment between the native Maoris and the colonial government. Hewett's increasing reliance on Christian faith as a refuge from adversity is reflected in her attitude toward the Maoris, which moves from early acceptance of their customs to her later work evangelizing them.

455 HEWINS, Mary Elizabeth. 1914–1986. *Mary, after the Queen: Memories of a Working Girl*. Ed. by Angela Hewins (author's daughter-in-law). Oxford: Oxford University Press, 1984. 122 pp.; front. port.; foreword by Paul Thompson; ed.'s preface and afterword; illus. BLC 1985 11:425. (other ed.: Oxford University Press, 1994, in omnibus edition with George Hewins's *The Dillen*, as *A Stratford Story*.)

Born in Stratford-upon-Avon, Warwickshire. Father: George Hewins, Stratford Church School caretaker, bricklayer. Mother: Emma Bayliss, domestic servant. 7 siblings. Single. 1 son. Factory worker; brewery employee; WWII volunteer. Working class.

Portrait of one English working-class family, from WWI to c.1950. Author's family life; being the youngest of eight siblings; at age 4, being crowded in council housing. WWI: memories of troop trains, father's being badly wounded. Family's hiding from bill collectors and truancy officers. Helping her father at his job cleaning a church school. Two of her sisters' entering domestic service, another's cooking in a pub. Her eldest brother's serving in the WWI Flying Corps; his middle-class pretensions. Author's envy of one sister's board school education. Parents' quarreling; father's drunkenness, jealousy of mother. Author's refusing to go into service; laboring at Stratford Aluminium Factory and at a brewery with her sister; spending her pay on cigarettes. Flirting, buying clothes. Brother's holding gambling parties, with father's keeping lookout for police. Mother's borrowing money from children and keeping it. Author's married sister and in-laws' moving in with family. Father's infidelity. Another sister's death from tuberculosis. Author's discovering herself pregnant; failing to make herself abort, being abandoned by her boyfriend. Being fired from her brewing job; going on the dole. Having her baby, Brian; failing to collect child support. WWII: volunteering for war work; toiling in a canning factory; describing the dreadful conditions there. Her love of mechanical work. Quitting her job to care for her ailing mother. Recalling evacuees and Italian POWs in Stratford. Feeling sympathy for German POWs, who remind her of Brian's father; never getting over him; learning that he survived the war. Visiting London with her mother and son to witness the victory parade.

Told in her own words as transcribed from taped interviews, Hewins's wryly humorous story contains a wealth of dialogue in working-class speech. Her account lends a lively and entertaining air to even the distressing details of her family's poverty. This book has been chosen as a set text by several British examination boards and was dramatized by the Royal Shakespeare Company at Stratford in 1985.

456 HEWITT, Kathleen (née Douglas). c.1895–s.l.1945. *The Only Paradise: An Autobiography*. Jarrolds, c.1945. 157 pp.; front. port.; index. BLC to 1975 147:203.

Born in Darjeeling, India. Father not named, Anglican missionary in India, later vicar. Mother not named, Zenana Missionary Society worker, boarding house manager. Stepmother not named. At least 1 brother; 1 sister. Married c.1912, husband not named, artist; divorced c.1925. Married c.1927, husband not named, engineer; divorced c.1936. 1 son; 1 daughter. Wrote novels *Strange Salvation*, *The Mice Are Not Amused*, others; wrote two plays. Knew Nina Hamnett and Henrietta Leslie. Novelist; playwright; clergyman's daughter; foreign resident (India, South Africa, West Africa); actress (stage); saleswoman; secretary; shopkeeper. Middle class.

Author's experiences in India, England, and South Africa, and her diverse jobs, covering her birth to 1945. Mother's missionary activities in India. Family's moving in author's infancy to a rectory in Essex; moving to another rectory at author's age 8. Memories of Queen Victoria's Diamond Jubilee, 1897. Home schooling by father; learning foreign languages from governesses. Bicycle as the family's only means of transportation. Mother's role as advisor/midwife to parish women. At author's age 9, moving with her mother to London; mother's overwork, poverty, and illness running boarding houses. Author's unpopularity at St. Paul's Girls' School; transferring to a Lancashire boarding school. Writing plays at age 15. Her mother's death. Returning to father's rectory; his sending her to University Tutorial College, London, to study medicine. Describing boarding school life in London: poverty; attending plays and suffragette meetings. Courtships. Writing a play. Father's remarriage. Having a romantic affair with a cocaine-addicted, married artist; escaping him; returning to teach at her old boarding school; losing this job because of ex-lover's harassment; having a nervous breakdown, age 17. Writing a novel. Rejections of her early work. Father's ignorance of her writing talents; his sending her to a commercial art school to learn fashion design. Traveling to Belgium; escaping from a woman who tried to lure her into prostitution. Looking for work; refusing London employer's sexual advances, losing job. Continuing her job hunt; pawning jewelry to buy food; suffering scurvy from malnutrition; pride's preventing her from going home. Drifting from one cheap lodging to another. Holding jobs as an artist's model and fashion sketch artist. Marrying an artist; birth of her son; husband's WWI service. Having more jobs as lingerie maker, film extra, telephone solicitor, chorus girl, canvasser for commercial dentistry racket. Daughter's birth; breakup of her marriage; moving to Brighton. Finding still more jobs: dogseller, touring actress, secretary at unwed mothers' hostel. Escaping with children and new beau to South Africa; resolving to keep writing fiction; raising produce for market; eventually divorcing her first husband. Feeling white women should not allow the slightest familiarity with blacks, "but they behave well enough if treated fairly." Becoming associate editor of the *Critic*, a Durban weekly. Returning to England; reconciling with her father; opening a dress shop in Reading. Making plans to marry an engineer and move with him to the Gold Coast. Her sustained writing efforts. Production in London of her play on interracial marriage. Returning to London. Publication and success of her novels. Socializing with famous writers. Father's death. Her second divorce. Discussing women's authorial viewpoint; perceiving people as being divided less by education and gender than by economic realities.

The polished diction of Hewitt's memoir belies the frank opinions it contains on London working-class life and race relations in Africa. The extreme diversity of Hewitt's life experiences seem to have offered her much raw material to use in writing her novels.

457 HICKS, Kathleen Nugent (née Savage). pre-1890–?. *From Rock to Tower: Memories with Reflections*. McDonald & Co., 1947. 284 pp.; foreword by L. S. Amery; intro.; epilogue by Canon J. A. Douglas; app. NUC pre56 245:108.

Born in England. Father: Canon Francis Forbes Savage, Anglican vicar. Mother: née Marley. 2 brothers. Married 1909, Nugent Hicks, Bishop of Lincoln, d.1942. Widow. Clergyman's spouse; clergyman's daughter; organizer (religious); WWI volunteer; religionist (Anglican). Upper middle class.

Experiences of an Anglican bishop's wife, covering her childhood to 1947, together with commentary on Christian themes and clerical responsibilities. Part 1: Author's childhood memories of Cornwall; her pranks and tomboyishness; her hatred of dolls. Family history. Memories of her father's church; commenting on the responsibilities and burdens of a vicar. Her love of reading and music. Attending a finishing school. Living in Austria. Having a dream warning her against suicide after her suitor killed himself. Visiting Italy. Lacking a clear vision of what to do with her life. Testing her vocation in an Anglican sisterhood; leaving the sisterhood after being told to wait another year before her Novitiate. Her brother's training to be a clergyman. Author's engagement and marriage to Nugent Hicks, 1909. Husband's Oxford background; his daily life as a cleric. Taking their "real" honeymoon in the Holy Land three years after marriage, 1912. WWI: brother's death; author's VAD nursing work in a London hospital. Her activities in the Cheshunt Girls' Diocesan Association. Describing the parish duties of a rector's wife. Moving with her husband to Brighton parish, c.1924. Husband's accepting the Bishopric of Gibraltar, 1927; their traveling frequently around the Mediterranean; visiting the Balkans. Husband's appointment as Bishop of Lincoln, 1933. Diocese life: church bazaars, socials. Husband's illness; accompanying him to Switzerland for treatment, 1938, then to Barbados. Her numbness at his death, 1942. Hearing parish gossip hinting she had interfered in his work; condemning such gossip as un-Christian jealousy. Finding she benefits from self-examination in writing her autobiography. Reflecting on the life she led with her husband. Part 2: Interpolating husband's thoughts on spiritual matters with her own. Discussing why he (and she, by implication) was neither Roman Catholic nor Nonconformist. Her views on marriage, prayer, suffering, friendship, spiritualism. Believing in her eternal bond with her husband.

Writing associatively and utilizing a rough chronology, Hicks combines her autobiography with a detailed look at her husband's career and views, moving from plain narration to profound introspection. She portrays the importance of Christian duty and responsibility in her own life and in the life of the greater community, expresses frustration against petty jealousies, and asserts the claims of Anglican Catholicism as opposed to Roman Catholicism. In some ways this book fills in gaps in Maurice Headlam's biography of Hicks's husband, *Bishop and Friend*.

458 HIEMSTRA, Mary (née Pinder). 1897–?. *Gully Farm*. Toronto: McClelland & Stewart, 1955. 311 pp.; front.; illus. NUC pre56 245:180.

Born in Yorkshire. Father: Walter Pinder, farmer, emigrant to Saskatchewan. Mother: Sarah Gomersall. 1 brother; 3 sisters. Married after time discussed; 1 son mentioned. Farmer; pioneer; emigrant (Canada). Rural laboring class.

Childhood memories of homesteading family life on Canadian farm, 1902–10. Author's early childhood in Yorkshire. Family's emigrating to Canada with the Barr Colony despite opposition from mother and other relatives. Tearfully parting from Yorkshire family members. Recalling the ocean voyage, followed by a train journey to Saskatoon; living there in a tent city. Quarrels among emigrants; death of one neighbor in childbirth. Father's buying a horse team; their traveling by wagon train; encountering dangers and rough conditions on the journey. Settling on new land; entire region's being turned into wheat farming country; father's later regret that all the trees were cut down. Author's disappointment that the family must build a house from scratch; feeling homesick; father's shifting her focus to Canada's natural beauty. Their bachelor neighbors; lack of eligible women on the frontier. Father's plowing; family's building a house. Women settlers' common desire to return to England. Confronting crises and responsibilities of frontier life. Father's dreams of the future. Author's mothering her younger siblings when her father is away and her mother is working in the fields. Winter hardships; Christmas celebrations; pastimes with other children. Food shortages. Mother's renewed yearning for England; her arguing with father, but deciding for the children's sake to stay in Canada. Author's helping her father plow; his holding an additional job on the railroad. Surviving another hard winter; author's feeling increasingly capable at farm work. Father's building a new house and barn; his giving mother a piano as a sign of permanency. Parents' deaths forty years later.

The primary focus of this vivid, novelistic memoir is on the relationship between Hiemstra's parents, which the author portrays as characterized by a conflict between her father's optimism and her mother's pessimism. Throughout the book Hiemstra stresses the different attitudes of men and women toward homesteading and examines the tensions arising from the emigrants' general unpreparedness for life on the frontier.

459 HITCHMAN, Janet (née Elsie May Fields). 1916–1980. *The King of the Barbareens*. Putnam, 1960. 254 pp. BLC to 1975 149:134.

Born at Oulton Broad, Norfolk. Father: Frederick Burrows. Mother: Margaret Mary Ames, née Mayhew, seamstress. Illegitimate child. Orphan. 1 sister; 1 stepsister. Married c.1940, husband not named; separated c.1946. 1 daughter. Wrote *They Carried the Sword* (1966). Scriptwriter; broadcaster; domestic servant; shop assistant; factory worker; actress (stage); stage manager. Working class.

Orphan's upbringing in foster homes and orphanage and her assorted adult jobs, covering 1916–c.1945. Her childhood memories of Yarmouth. Feeling unrelieved curiosity about her parentage. Her early life with an elderly couple she called "Gran and Granfa"; thinking they were her real grandparents. Having a series of foster parents. Staying in hospitals and a sanatorium for a series of illnesses: mastoid infection, rheumatic fever, and whooping cough. A 12-year-old boy's initiating sexual play with her; author's being punished for it; her sexual ignorance. Returning to school far behind the other children; their tormenting her. Living with a new, elderly foster mother, who encouraged author's desire for knowledge and culture; author's stealing 10 shillings from her. Attending a Primitive Methodist Sunday school. Living at Gimingham Hall Farm, another orphanage; many residents' being retarded, suicidal, epileptic, or kleptomaniac. Moving in with another new foster mother; feeling hated by the woman and her husband. Her growing dislike of men. Encountering a man who made lewd suggestions to her. Being glad to attend Thomas Anguish Hospital School of Housecraft for Girls in Norwich, but being unable to control her violent temper; attacking a schoolmate. Discussing menstruation and the taboos against talking about it; remembering the shock of her menarche. Living at Barnardo Children's Home in Essex, age 13; loathing it, being defiant; gradually gaining a new positive outlook toward this home. Noting lesbian feelings among some pupils and teachers. Because of her aversion to training for domestic service, being asked to leave the school before she was ready to take the school certificate, thus ending her dream of becoming a librarian. Attending All Souls' School in London, age 16, then attending Clark's College at Finchley. Living in a London working girls' hostel. Working as a parcels dispatch clerk, fabric salesclerk, switchboard operator, and in other service and factory jobs. Vowing never to marry. Being sexually harassed by an employer. Her dreams of being an actress. WWII: being refused a London Town Council job because she couldn't prove her father's British citizenship. Getting married, c.1940. Because of opportunities created by the war, being able to realize her dream of acting; performing at the Coliseum Theatre in Oldham; becoming a stage manager there. Having a daughter, born c.1944; becoming alienated from her husband. Having spent 13 years doing some form of domestic service; still loathing such work. Wishing she had not been institutionally raised, but instead raised by her mother, even in a slum. Being strongly influenced by religion; wishing she could feel it more; becoming a Quaker.

Since the time she read *Jane Eyre,* Hitchman declares, she has identified with that heroine and hence calls herself Janet. Her tone—sometimes acerbic, sometimes humorous—embellishes her wide-ranging criticism of the institutions that raised her, criticism that seems intended to be constructive. In its depiction of life at a Barnardo Children's Home, this autobiography bears comparison with that of G. V. Holmes, *The Likes of Us*. Hitchman says that her life has been easier since she accepted that she is not nice or likeable, but odd and peculiar. Noticeably reticent about her marriage, Hitchman has also apparently concealed the real names of people who played significant roles in her life. She wrote and broadcast autobiographical sketches about herself for the BBC, *Days from a Norfolk Childhood.*

460 HOARE, Nellie (née Barter). 1898–s.l.1982. *A Winton Story*. Bournemouth: Bournemouth Local Studies Publications, Vol. 666, 1982. 46 pp.; front.; foreword by Nora and Jack Parsons; family tree chart; map; illus.; epilogue. BLC 1982–1985 11:535.

Born in Winton, Hampshire. Father: Harry Charles Barter, road laborer. Mother: Frances Head. 5 brothers; 3 sisters. Married c.1918, Arthur Hoare. Widow. 1 daughter; 1 son. Domestic servant; brewery employee; delivery woman; laundry worker. Working class.

Memories of a working-class life in a rural English township, covering author's childhood to the 1980s. Remembering her grandparents and siblings; her jealousy of her younger brother. Describing household daily life: diet, kitchen and laundry facilities, clothing, amusements. Attending St. John's Girls' School and Sunday school. Describing herself as a "grizzler" (whiner) in childhood. Jobs held by her elder siblings. Her closeness with her brother Reg. Taking a job in a laundry at age 14; finding the work made her feel faint; working as a daily maid. During WWI, working as a milk deliverer and a bottlewasher in a brewery; discussing wartime food, shortages, prices; death of her brother Len in battle. Mother's becoming an invalid; her death. Author's courtship and marriage to a friend of one of her brothers, c.1918. Husband's making furniture for their house. Her father's death. Describing the characters of her children. Her husband's illness and death. Commenting on the difficulties of coping as a widow with two small children. Describing her children's games and amusements. During WWII, selling her sewing machine to buy shoes for her children. Her sons' helping by working jobs after they left school. Author's working in a part-time job. Discussing her seven grandchildren and two great-grandchildren. Expressing satisfaction with her life.

These reminiscences were written, Hoare states, at the request of her granddaughter; inspired by some of the Bournemouth Teachers' Centre Local Studies Group pamphlets, the author decided to add to the record of local history by chronicling her own life. Born when Queen Victoria still lived, witness to two world wars, Hoare has made a contribution to the cumulative record of her area with this simply written, chronologically ordered memoir.

461 HOLBROOK, Ann Catherine (née Jackson). 1780–1837. *The Dramatist; or, Memoirs of the Stage, with the Life of the Authoress, Prefixed and Interspersed with a Variety of Anecdotes, Humorous and Pathetic*. Birmingham: Martin & Hunter, 1809. 68 pp.; preface. BLC to 1975 150:354.

Raised in Norwich, Norfolk. Father: Thomas Jackson, stage comedian. Married c.1798, surname Holbrook, actor. Children. Actress (stage). Middle class.

Personal and professional experiences, set within a passionate and vivid formal protest against the vicissitudes of English provincial theatre life, spanning c.1781–c.1807. Author's upbringing within the theatrical profession. Describing her father: his career, friendships with George Alexander Stevens and Samuel Foote, Esq., companionship with aristocrats who appreciated his performances. Deaths of her parents in close succession. At age 17, on father's death, becoming the ward of his theatre manager; manager's not fulfilling his promise to care for her, refusing her a place in the company. Going to London in search of an acting job. Touring in a theatre company in Sussex. Meeting Mr. Holbrook. Marriage. Their leaving one acting company; having their contract with another company broken. Theatre fire's leaving them unemployed. Her difficult pregnancy. Suffering another broken contract; their resulting heated quarrel with the new theatre manager; husband's fearing for his family's financial security. Their joining Theatre Royal, Windsor; staying with the company eleven months, then joining Mr. McCready's company; experiencing extreme financial hardship with both companies. Abandoning the theatrical profession after devoting nine years to it. Appealing to Parliament on behalf of actors. Discussing the decline of the English theatre due to crushing of talent, nepotism, and inadequate pay for actors. Calling for a tribunal to examine prospective actors to make them adhere to what the playwrights intend them to say. Discussing the difficulties for actresses raising children; dangers of appearing licentious.

Only the first twenty-five pages of this formally written work are autobiography; the rest is an impassioned plea to Parliament for justice for actors and the theatrical profession. Holbrook's book constitutes a valuable source of detail on the English stage, particularly in the provinces, and on the situation of actors in the early 19th century. She also published an earlier book, *Memoirs of an Actress* (1807).

462 HOLMAN-HUNT, Diana. c.1910–?. *My Grandmothers and I.* Hamish Hamilton, 1960. 208 pp.; foreword; illus. BLC to 1975 155:471.

Raised on maternal grandmother's estate in rural England. Father: Hilary Lushington Holman-Hunt, military captain in India. Mother: Norah Freeman. Grandfather: Pre-Raphaelite artist William Holman-Hunt. Married, surname Cuthbert. Wrote biography *My Grandfather: His Wives and Loves* (1968). Artist's grandchild; secretary; biographer. Upper middle class.

Memories of author's grandmothers, eliciting atmosphere of Pre-Raphaelite artistic circles, covering author's childhood and adolescence. Ancestry and family history. Her childhood residence at maternal grandparents' country estate; having infrequent contact with her parents. Her grandmother's imperious manner. Taking piano lessons; going horseback riding; her toys. Recalling her grandmother's servants. Home education by maternal grandparents. Visiting her eccentric paternal grandmother Holman-Hunt in London; describing the exotic interior of her house; anecdotes of grandmother's late husband and his artist friends. Disliking her grandmother's miserliness and being made to wear very unconventional clothes. Suffering from appendicitis; having an appendectomy. Returning to the estate of her maternal grandmother. Author's curiosity about a servant girl's pregnancy; not receiving information about sex from her grandparents. Her friendship with a fisherman living on the estate. Paying another visit to her grandmother Holman-Hunt; disliking visiting art galleries with her to see grandfather's paintings; describing her grandmother's visitors. Discussing her paternal grandfather's having married his wife's sister after his first wife's death in Italy; this marriage's only later being made legal in England with passage of the Deceased Wife's Sister's Bill. After maternal grandmother's death, attending boarding school, age 15; asking father to remove her from school; living with him at the Holman-Hunt house in London. Living in Italy and Prussia, then returning to live in her grandmother Holman-Hunt's house; finding employment as a secretary, age 17. Her grandmother's death in a traffic accident. Returning to maternal grandfather's estate.

The author writes in a novelistic style, revealing information through dialogue, characterization, and scene-setting. Her tone is highly comic and ironic. The book contains much anecdotal and personal information about Pre-Raphaelite artists, conveyed through the author's conversations with her father's mother.

463 HOLMES, Alice A. 1821–d.a.1888. *Lost Vision*. New York: De Vinne Press, 1888. 95 pp.; preface; poems. NUC pre56 252:40.

Born in Winfarthing, Norfolk. Father: Will Holmes, tradesman. Mother not named. 8 siblings. Single. Wrote *Poems by Alice Holmes, Arcadian Leaves* (1849), *Stray Leaves* (1868). Emigrant (U.S.); poet; teacher (music); physically handicapped woman. Lower middle class.

Author's affliction with blindness in childhood, and her reeducation and self-support through writing poetry and teaching music, 1821–88. Her birth; family's moving to Shelfanger; birth of her sister, 1823. At age 4, detesting caring for her baby sister. Inducing her brother to teach her his school lessons. Attending dame school, age 5. Her tomboyish love of outdoor play. Father's deciding to sell his business and emigrate to U.S. despite family opposition, 1830. Outbreak of smallpox on the voyage; author's illness and resulting eye inflammation, causing permanent blindness. Another sister's birth in Staten Island, New York. Family's moving to Jersey City. Parents' taking author to eye specialists, who gave pessimistic diagnoses. Briefly attending a select school for young children and Sunday school. Yearning for something to do; persuading her mother to let her knit; excelling at it. After another eye inflammation, age 16, attending New York Institution for the Blind, 1838–44; studying under blind hymn-writer Frances J. Crosby; learning Braille; studying grammar, arithmetic, and music. Her father's death, 1847; author's resolving to support herself. Her friendship with poet Jean Bruce; Bruce's encouraging author to write and publish poetry. Publishing her first book of poems, 1849. Starting an annual musical/literary entertainment in Jersey City, 1851. Living with her mother; being the only child left at home. Being profoundly affected by her mother's death, 1865. Resuming her musical studies. Teaching piano to earn an income. Suffering from declining health, 1876–80; having a hernia operation. Visiting her brother in California, 1883. Losing her income due to illness. Dictating the poems of this present volume to her sister Mary, her long-time amanuensis.

Holmes's autobiographical narrative occupies fifty-three pages of this book, which also contains a substantial sampling of her poetry. Although she states that she wrote the memoir at the request of friends, she also asserts her desire to awaken public awareness to the needs of the blind. She addresses many poems to friends (including former teacher Frances Crosby), to family members, piano pupils, and her physician; other poems commemorate significant occasions in her life. Each narrative chapter also concludes with a poem, and the book ends with two extracts from New York newspapers giving biographical information about the author.

464 HOLMES, Beatrice Gordon. 1884–d.a.1943. *In Love with Life: A Pioneer Career Woman's Story*. Hollis & Carter, 1944. 207 pp.; front. port. NUC pre56 252:89.

Born in London. Father not named, physician. Mother: Maria Thérèse Coqui. 3 brothers, including her twin. Single. Knew Lilian Baylis. Businesswoman; entrepreneur; stockbroker; philanthropist; feminist; pupil-teacher; clerk; organizer of societies (vocational); news agent. Middle class.

Woman stockbroker's education, employment, and eventual independent career, covering her childhood to 1943. Implying that her father was a tyrant; recalling his being an "unenergetic" ear and throat specialist; family's living frugally on his earnings. Author's being a tomboy; her self-consciousness about her big hands and large mouth. Her unfounded fears of being abandoned by her parents. Mother's family history and South African childhood. Acquiring a feminist attitude through her mother and through a nursemaid who had been a pupil of woman doctor Elizabeth Garrett Anderson. Family's moving to Kew, 1885, then back to City Road, 1888. Home education to age 11, then attending day school. Attending North London Collegiate School for Girls and hating it; disliking pupil-teaching. Taking a shorthand and typing course at a business school; taking a typing job; feeling taken for granted as the family breadwinner. Performing clerical work for a Danish egg exporter; quitting when no raise was forthcoming. Organizing the Association of Shorthand Writers and Typists (later Association of Women Clerks and Secretaries). Mother's emotional and financial dependence on author, c.1907. Author's voracious reading. Selling suffragette papers in the streets. Being employed by a Canadian business firm in London; keeping her employer's business alive during WWI. Parlaying her knowledge of business into a career in finance; working in bond sales and deals; feeling the novelty of being a woman financier. Appreciating her independence as a single woman. Her love of music, films, and painting; her interest in fashion; working in the mental health field. Helping to raise money to found a mental hospital, 1918. Expressing thoughts on male homosexuality garnered during her mental health work. Starting her own brokerage firm, 1921. Her numerous travels: Europe, Scandinavia, Middle East, U.S., and Canada. Testifying before the Bodkin Committee regarding regulation of outside brokerage houses, 1936. Her mother's death. Her brother's death in a Monte Carlo motor rally. Recalling the WWII London blitz.

Expressing her opinions forcefully, Holmes fills her autobiography with details of her business career, along with advice to young women who are family breadwinners. She states that she wrote this book at the urging of a friend in order to record the events of what she characterizes as her "glamourous life" and to combat her depression over the onset of WWII.

465 HOLMES, G. V. c.1908–?. *The Likes of Us*. Frederick Muller, 1948. 192 pp.; intro. NUC pre56 252:79.

Born in England. Parents not named; apparently unknown to author. Single. Orphan. Telephone operator. Working class.

An orphan's regulated childhood and adolescence in a Barnardo Children's Home, from ages 2–16. Arriving at the home. Her first distinct memory's being winning two volumes of a *Children's Encyclopaedia* as a prize, age 3. Describing the orphanage: 1,400 girls up to age 16, living in groups of 15–20 in separate cottages, each cottage presided over by a "Mother." Author's pride in her cottage and its mother; each household's role as a substitute family; the presence of Negro or Chinese children lending prestige to a cottage. The girls' duties; Sunday Christian services; clothing and laundry provisions; health care. Taking cover during WWI air raids. Recalling school holidays and excursions; performing in an Albert Hall pageant. Being unjustly punished by the headmistress, age 9. Children's awareness that most people, including administrators, liked orphans as little girls, not adolescents; their attempting to appear "little and young" as long as possible. Visits to the home by Dr. Barnardo and by Stepney councillors. Censorship of the girls' letters. Closeness within cottages, but rivalry between them. Superior attitude of girls living in home toward those boarding outside with foster families. Becoming aware of sexuality from excursions in public; the girls' sensitivity to being asked if they were "love children." Changes at the home: more office staff, younger workers, a Mothers' Council. Author's failing a scholarship exam for County High School. Some older girls' preparing to enter domestic service. Resenting inspectors' unannounced visits to the home. Girls' being discouraged about inquiring about the circumstances behind their living in an orphanage. Author's being caned by the headmistress; headmistress's prophesying that author would ultimately fail in the outside world; author's consequent fear of leaving the home. Girls' receiving injections in a medical experiment. Author's being promoted to school prefect. Conferring with the home's governors on her future, age 14. Working a telephone switchboard; mending bicycles as occupational training. Being selected to attend secondary education classes preparing girls for the professions; her gratefulness for this opportunity, which made her able to attend college. Having adjustment difficulties, as an "institution child," upon entering the working world and adult life.

In a loosely chronological narrative written in simple, conversational English, Holmes expresses a generally positive view of her experiences in a Barnardo Children's Home. Her book contains a wealth of detail about orphanage life, its social order, and the attitudes that institution children faced. She closes her account with her advent into the outside world, but gives no hint of which college she might have attended or what vocational field she ultimately entered.

466 HOMEWOOD, Isabel Georgina. 1844–1933. *Recollections of an Octogenarian.* John Murray, 1932. 287 pp.; intro. by G. K. Chesterton. NUC pre56 253:225.

Born in London. Father not named, barrister with East India Company. Mother: surname Walker. Stepmother not named. 4 sisters; 1 brother. Married 1867, William Homewood, landowner. Widow. Foreign resident (New Zealand); farmer; midwife; WWI volunteer; traveler (world); cyclist. Upper middle class.

Memories of an unconventional woman traveler and cyclist, covering her first eighty years. Going on her first hunt with her father, despite hunting's being considered inappropriate for young girls. Studying with her mother; taking music lessons from a tutor; remembering her German governess. Death of her mother. Father's remarriage; author's friction with her stepmother. Discussing women's fashions, c.1850s. Marriage, 1867, to William Homewood. Traveling with him to New Zealand; their embarking on a farming venture; becoming freeholders; her love of farm life's freedom; socializing with neighbors. Her views on Maori culture. Returning to England for her health; living with her in-laws. Joining a musical society and an archery club. Her husband's death. Traveling in Europe; returning to New Zealand. Accompanying her father to Tasmania; memories of the city of Hobart. Traveling through Egypt and the Holy Land. Her father's requesting that she take no more "wild travels" in his lifetime. Becoming an avid cyclist; cycling in England, France, Italy, Scandinavia. Visiting Poland, Hungary, Russia; noting consequences of the Russo-Japanese War. Training to be a midwife; other students and nurses' disliking her for being a "lady of means." Working for tariff reform in England. Visiting the U.S.; discussing living conditions there, c.1910. Visiting Canada. Her last visit to New Zealand. WWI: helping in canteens; joining needlework parties. Continuing to cycle until her 80th year, logging more miles than any other woman cyclist.

Homewood's style resembles conversation so closely that it includes gaps and memory lapses. She records a remarkable life of global peregrinations, although she omits most intimate details, and she expresses great impatience with the Victorian imposition of "ladydom" on middle-class and upper-class women. One of her chief reasons for writing appears to be her desire to refute fallacies about aging and to condemn injustices inflicted on the aged.

467 HOPWOOD, D. Caroline (née Skene). c.1725–c.1800. *An Account of the Life and Religious Experiences of D. Caroline Hopwood of Leeds,*

Deceased. Leeds: E. Baines, 1801. 64 pp.; intro.; poems. NUC pre56 254:453.

Born in England. Father: army lieutenant. Mother: née Law. 1 brother; 1 sister. Married c.1760, husband not named, tradesman. 2 daughters. Religionist (Quaker convert); teacher; domestic servant. Lower middle class.

Restless, self-critical spiritual introspections, with observations on external religious practices, covering author's childhood to 1790. Family history. Her jealousy of her elder sister, her mother's favorite. Her sense of conviction of her personal sinfulness, age 7. Father's death, author's age 8; her praying for his salvation; her resulting dread of death. Her curiosity about why Anglican clergymen were not inspired, like the Apostle Paul. Reading Scripture often and praying. Her adolescent lapse into religious indifference; going to assemblies, dancing. Sudden, unexplained advent of reduced economic circumstances; believing that God sent her this trial to end her social frivolity. Needing money; finding work as a housekeeper; affluent employers' being ignorant of true religion, having a bad influence on her. Marriage, c.1760. Feeling an increasing sense of sin; withdrawing from the Church of England; being unwilling to take Communion; seeking another denomination but being dissatisfied by discussions with Presbyterians. Attending Methodist meetings, 1768. Arguing with Methodist ministers who insist deliverance from sinful nature in this life is not attainable. Hearing an inner voice calling her to God; deciding that receiving Communion hindered her spiritual progress. To supplement family income, opening a small school; teaching drawing, pastry-making, and needlework; mourning in her spirit over her sins; being forsaken by her Methodist friends, who saw her as having "lost her grace" and being obstinate in her opinions on religion. Becoming interested in Quakerism: rejoicing in its principles. Adopting Quaker speech and dress. Some students' parents' objecting to her new religion and removing their children from her school. Opposing the "continuance of war" (probably the American Revolution) and slavery; refusing to use articles made by slave labor. Author's warning her readers against sin. Suffering severe fever and pain; being cured through prayer. Becoming a member of the Society of Friends; speaking in meeting after her recovery. Being reproved and told she was not called to the ministry. Discussing her complete submission to God's will, 1781. Finding Quaker worship overly formal, lacking in feeling; seeing Methodist enthusiasm as lacking discernment. Her spiritual darkness, 1782; renewal of her sense of sin; ceasing to attend meetings; waiting for a sign from God that she should attend again. Quakers' labeling her "deluded" and increasingly shunning her upon her return. Author's observations on her experience of suffering. Feeling distanced from God; the eventual return of her sense of grace.

This detailed self-searching, written for Hopwood's children, depicts the author as serious, moral, and effusive. Toward the end of her narrative she frequently addresses the reader with Christian exhortations, and her style is formulaic, often echoing or quoting Scripture. Her obsessive search for spiritual perfection and her radical quietism were regarded as delusional, even by the Quakers. Her book is a worthwhile source on the 18th-century practice of both Methodism and Quakerism, especially for the contrasts she draws between these denominations.

468 HOUGHTON, Georgina. 1814–1887. *Evenings at Home in Spiritual Séance, Prefaced and Welded Together by a Species of Autobiography*. Trubner, 1881. 352 pp.; preface. NUC pre56 256:116.

Born in Palma, Grand Canary (Mallorca). Father: George Houghton, merchant. Mother: Mary Warrand. 4 brothers; 2 sisters. Single. Spiritualist; clairvoyant/psychic; journalist. Middle class.

Experiences of a spiritualist medium, framing her analysis of spiritualism in Christian terms, 1859–81. Being introduced by her cousin Mrs. Pearson to some of spiritualism's practitioners, 1859; entering into conversation with the spirit of her youngest sister, Zilla, who died in 1851; also thinking of her brother who died in 1826. Author's believing that mediumistic communication is by the grace of God for the winning of souls; testing the spirits to see if they are of God. Being the seventh child in her family; believing this enhances her psychic abilities. Being visited by a spirit who gives the author the power to draw "spirit flowers"; sharing drawings with another psychic. Holding séances with neighbors and her brother-in-law. Her first experience of a spirit (Zilla) speaking through her, 1862; her mother's asking for descriptions of the world beyond, but getting none through author. Contacting spirits of Shakespeare and Prince Albert. Father's injury and death, 1863. Mother's illness; author's receiving communications from archangels, who tell her they will give her all the medical advice necessary for her mother; saving at least £100 on medical bills. Mother's attending all of author's séances. Explaining the significance of the crystal ball, planchette, and other mediumistic tools. Writing for *Christian Spiritualist* and *Spiritual Times*. Consulting spirits about family's plan to move to avoid the nuisance of a new railway line near their garden. Singing in a church choir while practicing professionally as a medium. Working with famous mediums: Georgiana Weldon, Mrs. Guppy, Emma Hardinge, others. Having many visions and premonitions, such as of her mother's death; on her deathbed, mother's urging author to forswear spiritualism. Author's regarding spiritualism and Christianity as being compatible; believing that Roman Catholic saints were actually mediums. Her brother's death in a shipwreck; her after-the-fact vision of it. Her acquaintance with the American healer Dr. Newton.

In this first volume of a planned two-volume work, Houghton documents her practice of spiritualism, using frequent biblical allusions to reinforce her attempt to reconcile spiritualism with Christian belief. The second volume never appeared. This book's wealth of detail on mediumistic props and beliefs and other contemporary mediums make it a rare source on the phenomenon of 19th-century spiritualist practice.

469 HOUSLANDER, [Frances] Caryll. 1901–1954. *A Rocking-Horse Catholic*. New York: Sheed & Ward, 1955. 148 pp.; front. port.; epilogue. NUC pre56 256:241.

Born in Bath, Somerset. Father: Willmott Houslander, country squire's son. Mother: Gertrude Provis, former tennis player. 1 sister. Single. Wrote *The Flowering Tree* (poems), *This War Is the Passion* (1944; later titled *The Comforting of Christ*), *The Dry Wood* (1947), *The Stations of the Cross* (1954), others. Religionist (Roman Catholic); religious/spiritual writer, artist (graphic), teacher, poet. Middle class.

Early years of Catholic author, artist, and visionary, 1901–c.1923. Living in Bath until age 5; recalling her friendships with eccentric family servants. Being sensitive to adult teasing. Moving to Brighton. Her Catholic baptism; discussing influences leading her mother to raise the children as Catholics. Finding a lifelong confidant in lawyer George Spencer Bower, an agnostic with Catholic leanings; his influence on her remaining Catholic. Moving to Clifton, Bristol. Mother's making resentful author say lengthy prayers. Author's second Communion's miraculously curing her neurotic illness. Reflecting on the psychological suffering of the saints. Shock of her parents' separation, author's age 9; beginnings of her rebelliousness against authority. Being sent with her sister to a French convent school near Birmingham; feeling transformed by the nuns' love of God and the beauty of their simple life. During WWI, having her first vision of Christ in man: envisioning a German nun at the convent as an outcast crowned with thorns. Nuns' discovering her artistic aptitude. Leaving convent school, age 14, while suffering from a mysterious pain in her side; undergoing surgery for a diseased appendix. Disliking Protestant, Catholic, and council schools she attended; enrolling in an English convent school and disliking its snobbery. On the night of Tsar Nicholas II's assassination, seeing a vision of him as the martyred Christ; her resulting fascination with Russia. Attending St. John's Wood Art School, age 20. Attending Protestant, Jewish, and Buddhist services. Holding a series of short-lived jobs while living alone; her own poverty's giving her a greater awareness of the poor. Her friendship with Frank Sheed and Maisie Ward of the Catholic Evidence Guild. Having a third vision: looking at crowds and seeing Christ in everyone.

One can agree with Maisie Ward (author of *Caryll Houslander: That Divine Eccentric,* 1962) that Houslander's autobiography is a singularly perfect little work of art, but one that needs sorting out and amplifying. Houslander telescopes and omits many events; for instance, she does not discuss her love affair c.1918–20 with British master spy Sidney Reilly. Her own unconventional experience and behavior and her profound love of God helped her develop an extraordinary sensitivity and compassion for others that inspired her as a writer, artist, and, later, as a teacher and counselor to neurotic children.

470 HOWARD, Catharine Mary, Lady Henry (née Neave). c.1773–1849. *Reminiscences for My Children*. Carlisle: printed for the author by Charles Thurnam, 1836. 4 vols.: 216 pp., 254 pp., 307 pp., 176 pp. NUC pre56 256:546.

Born at Dagnam Park, Romford, Essex. Father not named, in 1780 governor of the Bank of England, later (1792) 1st Baronet Neave. At least 2 brothers; 2 sisters. Married 1793, "Mr. H. H.," Lord Henry Charles Howard, West York militia captain, later (1842) 13th Duke of Norfolk. 3 sons; 3 daughters. Society woman; married into aristocracy. Upper class.

Domestic life and historical testimony of an upper-class mother, covering 1793–1831. Vol. 1: Being at first too lenient raising her children; gaining greater firmness. Opposing contemporary practices of cold water plunges for children and making them walk too young; feeling wet nurses should not eat meat or cheese. Her own five children: their characters; their toys and games; her strict truthfulness with them. Describing local historical manors and churches. Howard family history; description of Naworth Castle, family seat in Warwickshire. Extended narrative of Napoleon's Russian Campaign. Marriages of her daughters. Her eldest son's becoming an M.P. after passage of the 1830 Relief Bill. Living in Germany and Holland, 1829–31. Vol. 2: Traveling to France, 1814. Being among the first English travelers there after the Revolution; her impressions of post-revolutionary France and Napoleon. Back in England, discussing society life among the aristocracy. Her father-in-law's inheriting a dukedom. Vol. 3: Family visits to author's mother at Dagnam Park, 1819. Recollecting author's marriage, 1793; her honeymoon through England; presentation to Queen Charlotte. Moving with her husband to Dublin, 1799; discussing the Rebellion and other Irish issues. Vol. 4: Living in Dublin, 1799–1800. Anecdotes of the Irish Rebellion. Returning to Liverpool, 1800. First being inspired to write her memoirs during the time of her children's infancy. Hoping to resume diary entries from the time of her second journey to the Continent.

Volumes 1 and 2 of Howard's chatty work are partly in diary form, partly in retrospective narrative. Volumes 3 and 4 are entirely in the form of diary entries. The jumbled order of the material arises from Howard's beginning with her children's early education, c.1800, skipping forward to their adulthood and back to her own youth until her account again reaches 1800, the time when she began keeping a diary. Despite her vagaries of chronology, Howard's eyewitness testimony to the turbulent events of her era gives her book considerable historical interest.

471 HOWITT, Mary (née Botham). 1799–1889. *An Autobiography*. Ed. by Margaret Howitt (author's daughter). Wm. Isbister Ltd., 1889. 2 vols. Vol. I: 326 pp.; front. port.; illus.; letters. Vol. II: front. port.; illus; letters; index to both vols. NUC pre56 257:286. (other ed.: New York: AMS Press, 1973.)

Born in Staffordshire. Father: Samuel Botham, land surveyor. Mother: Ann Wood. 1 brother; 2 sisters. Married 1821, William Howitt, writer, social commentator, poet, d.1879. Widow. 4 sons; 2 daughters. Wrote with William Howitt *The Desolation of Eyam and Other Poems* (1827); wrote *Seven Temptations,* others. Editor; poet; short storyist; translator; social reformer; abolitionist; religionist (Roman Catholic convert); philanthropist, feminist activist. Middle class.

Quaker upbringing, literary friendships, and lifelong social reform concerns of a mid-Victorian writer, extensively discussing prevailing social ills, and tracing the author's spiritual journey to Catholicism, 1805–1884. Vol. 1: Paternal family history. Author's feeling great isolation as a child. Her parents' devotion to Quakerism; author's disliking attending Friends' meetings. Being taught religion by her parents; their consigning children's general education to God. Mother's withdrawing from her children. Author's studying with a governess, later attending day school; imperfection of her education. Author and sister's teaching poor children at father's insistence; her automatic submissiveness to her father. Friendship with William Howitt; marriage, 1821. Collaborating with her husband on literary endeavors; jointly editing *Howitt's Journal of Literary and Popular Progress;* enjoying her partnership with husband. Her interest in the ideas of social reformer Robert Owen. Supporting the idea of affordable periodicals and serials for the self-improvement of the working class. Her support for the Reform Bill, 1832. Retaining her Quaker social conscience while rejecting formalized faith. Perceiving the need to educate poor children in England. Working with the Nottingham Provident Society, visiting the poor; speculating on the acceptability of this task for a woman philanthropist, 1835. Publishing *Birds and Flowers,* 1837. Dedicating her talents to "good purpose." Taking her children to Germany so they might receive a superior education. Her daughter Anna Mary's artistic talent. Learning about German Catholicism, culture, and history. Vol. 2: Author and husband's returning to live at Upper Clapton. Editing the *Drawing-Room Scrap-Book* journal. Learning Danish and translating the stories of Hans Christian Andersen; her friendship with him. Friendship with Dante Gabriel and Christina Rossetti, as well as others of the Pre-Raphaelite brotherhood. Deaths of her three sons, 1835–55; her continued and renewed grief.

Writing for Dickens's journal, *Household Words*. Her friendship with Tennyson. Her interest in American antislavery issues. Participating in the Committee for the Ladies' Address to Their American Sisters on Slavery. Describing the popular contemporary interest in spiritualism. Gradually changing her negative attitude toward Catholicism through study and investigation of the faith; adopting a positive view of Catholic "purists." Illness and death of her husband, 1879. Further ruminations on Catholic doctrine and tenets; deciding to convert. Her daughter Anna's death during a visit to author, 1884. Finding solace through the Catholic Church.

In this autobiography, Howitt portrays herself as sacrificing none of the responsibilities of marriage and motherhood even as she devotes much of her time to literary and spiritual quests as well as to social reform. An early campaigner for women's rights, she co-petitioned Parliament with Elizabeth Barrett Browning, Anna Jameson, and Mrs. Gaskell for support of the Married Women's Property Bill in 1856, but she does not discuss her feminist activism in this autobiography. Of interest for the particulars of Howitt's first decade is **472** *My Own Story, Autobiography of a Child* (1856), in which she re-creates the warmth and tranquility of English rural life in a pre-industrial world. Her anecdotes reflect 18th- and 19th-century views of morality and illustrate the problems confronted by people from various social strata.

473 HUGGINS, Molly, Lady (née Green). 1907–s.l.1964. *Too Much to Tell*. Heinemann, 1967. 328 pp.; photos; index. BLC to 1975 154:423.

Born in Singapore, Malaya. Father: Carlo Green, Malayan civil service worker, Anglo-Italian. Mother: née Smith. 2 brothers; 1 sister. Married 1929, John Huggins, British high commissioner for Malay States, later governor of Jamaica; divorced 1958. 3 daughters. Philanthropist; public speaker; politician; spouse of imperial governor; foreign resident (Malaya, Trinidad, U.S.); organizer of societies (social reform); social reformer; animal welfare activist. Middle class.

Memories and observations of an international philanthropist, from her childhood to c.1964. Her birth in Singapore; at age 3, being taken to Scotland to be raised by her maternal grandparents and three maiden aunts. Attending a private girls' school in Brighton, from age 13. Attending a secretarial school, c.1926; subsequently working as a secretary to a chiropractor. Returning to Malaya with her family, 1927; discussing her father's civil service career. Marriage to John Huggins, 1929. Giving birth to her children. Moving to Trinidad with her husband, 1938, during his acting governorship. Moving to Washington, D.C., 1942; her acquaintance with Eleanor Roosevelt and with Dwight and Mamie Eisenhower. Husband's receiving a knighthood, 1943; his being appointed to the governorship of Jamaica. Describing Jamaican social activities. Her organizing the Jamaican Federation of Women to help women be self-sufficient; helping to feed the poor; visiting schools, slums, and hospitals. Discussing Jamaican politics: the new constitution, universal adult suffrage, problems facing the new West Indian Federation. Returning to England, 1950. Taking four lecture tours of the U.S., 1948–57. Her unsuccessful candidacy for Parliament, 1955. Having an extramarital affair; death of her lover in an accident, 1955; visiting a psychic to contact his spirit. Touring Africa as the deputy chairman of the Conservative Commonwealth Council, 1956. Her husband's initiating a divorce, 1958; news of the divorce's hitting the international press. Author's traveling for healing and pleasure to the West Indies, Cyprus, Far East, Egypt, 1959–63. Founding the Metropolitan Coloured People's Housing Association in London, 1964. Her many activities promoting racial integration; her interest in the social welfare of women and birth control. Working with the Royal Society for the Prevention of Cruelty to Animals.

In her lifetime Huggins was called the Jamaican Eleanor Roosevelt for her efforts to combat racial prejudice in Jamaica. Although her writing is expository and unsentimental, giving little information about the characters of her many acquaintances, it is pervaded by optimism, energy, and a sense that she cannot fail. Huggins evidently saw her life as remarkable and wanted to make the historical record of it accessible to the public.

474 HUGHES, Alice. c.1852–d.a.1920. *My Father and I*. Thornton Butterworth, 1923. 288 pp.; front. port.; illus.; app. NUC pre56 259:76.

Raised in Kensington, London. Father: Edward Hughes, portrait painter. Mother: Mary Pewtner. Stepmother: née Margetts. 5 siblings. Single. Photographer; feminist; artist's daughter. Upper middle class.

Progress, trials, and practical techniques of a photographer's career, beginning with her childhhod and set within observations on women's professional roles, covering 1850s–1920s. Attending boarding school, age 5. Mother's death at author's age 7. Father's second marriage at author's age 9; stepmother's giving author the responsibility of looking after her younger siblings. Attending school in Brussels. Her father's career as a portrait painter. Becoming his companion after her stepmother's death; beginning her photography career by photographing his portraits. Studying at Polytechnic School of Photography. Father's having a small studio built for her; receiving royal clientele from him. Photographing Queen Alexandra in mourning; photographing Edward VII's coronation. Having trouble managing her money; making bad investments. Feeling frustrated at not being taken seriously as a professional. Having problems finding female trainees. Being influenced by the rise of the feminist movement. Discussing photographic subjects and techniques. Photographing only women and children, English and American, from different social classes. Becoming better known than her father; making prints of his works. Having financial difficulties. Father's death. Selling all her negatives, copyrights, and plant to a business with which she entered into a restrictive contract; going to Berlin with her sister to escape terms of the contract, 1914; photographing German royalty. Leading a confining life in Berlin with her sister. Her ignorance of the impending war. Returning to London; arranging a revised contract giving her greater freedom to photograph on her own; photographing admirals and servicemen. Her sister's death, 1920. Author's acute loneliness; her regret at having been too absorbed in her work to marry. Concluding that women in general still want marriage and family despite their new freedom to choose careers.

Ahead of her time in her choice of photography as a career, Hughes describes her achievements and also delineates the backgrounds and historical importance of her many eminent clients. Not adhering to a strict chronology, she shifts between her career and her father's, interspersing some personal opinions and insights. Plates of her father's work and her own photography enhance the account.

475 HUGHES, Katherine Price (née Barrett; C.B.E.). 1853–d.a.1944. *The Story of My Life*. Edgar C. Barton, 1945. 139 pp.; front. port. BLC to 1975 155:13.

Born in Bloomsbury, London. Father not named, magistrate, governor of Richmond College. Mother not named. 8 siblings. Married 1873, Hugh Price Hughes, Methodist minister, d.1902. Widow. 2 sons; 2 daughters. Philanthropist; teacher (Sunday school); feminist; suffragist; social reformer; WWI volunteer; temperance activist; clergyman's spouse; school founder; organizer (religious). Middle class.

Personal, professional, and travel memories, set within a framework of social reform and feminist views and activities, spanning 1850s–1944. Living in London and Leeds. Childhood traumas: her younger sister's death in infancy; drowning of family cat by a servant. Attending Anglican day school. Having her first serious thoughts about religion, age 12. Being a poor student. At age 15, meeting Hugh Price Hughes, her Bible class teacher and future husband. Attending Laleham School in London. Hearing lectures by Octavia Hill and Elizabeth Malleson, among others. Her awareness of the injustice of only men being able to attend college. Hearing a lecture by Elizabeth Garrett Anderson and Millicent Garrett Fawcett on higher learning for women. Opening a school at Upper Clapton; teaching Sunday school at a Clapton chapel. Courtship; marriage, age 18; honeymoon in Switzerland. Suffering a bout with typhoid fever. Opening a school for girls who needed help and protection in southwest London. Husband's helping to form a Methodist mission;

author's starting a sisterhood there. Visiting Italy and America, 1891; her impressions of the American South; commenting on Frances E. Willard and the Women's Christian Temperance Union. Author's perception that American women were satisfied with the social and sexual status quo, unlike British women. Her husband's death, 1902. Author's helping girls to escape from white slave markets. Opening a home for poor English girls in Walthamstow and an Open Door Shelter for Girls and Women in Drury. Running a mission in Chalton Street. Serving on the London Public Morality Committee, and on the executive committees of the British Women's Temperance Society and the Women's Liberal Association. Women's winning the right to sit on the Methodist conference, 1911. Supporting Millicent Garrett Fawcett's work for constitutional women's suffrage. WWI: author's relief work with wounded soldiers. Her great happiness that her daughter was able to attend college. Visiting India, 1922. Her daughter's death, 1933. Receiving the C.B.E., 1938.

Hughes's account encompasses many of the dramatic social changes of the years between the mid-Victorian era and the late modern age, and gives insight into her feelings as a child and adult. In her straightforward fashion she provides detailed accounts of social and religious reform activities and her role in these. Curiously, for one whose evaluations are often insightful, on her 1891 visit to the U.S. she found little evidence of feminist activism, and she inaccurately portrays American women as being more quietist than their British sisters. Still, she does provide rich detail about many aspects of social reform activity in her lifetime. After 1914, the text becomes more of a series of impressions than a sustained narrative.

476 HUGHES, Mary Vivian (née Thomas). 1866–1956. *A London Child of the Seventies*. Oxford: Oxford University Press, 1934. 173 pp.; preface; photos. BLC to 1975 155:17. (other ed.: included in *A London Family, 1870–1900: A Trilogy*. New York and Oxford: Oxford University Press, 1947.)

Born in Epping Forest, Essex. Father: Tom Thomas, stockbroker. Mother: Mary Vivian. 4 brothers. Married 1897, Arthur Hughes, math teacher, schoolmaster, barrister, d.1918. Widow. 1 daughter; 3 sons. Wrote *About England* (1927), *The City Saints* (1932), *Vivians* (1935), others. Teacher; historian; religious/spiritual writer; teacher supervisor; school inspector. Middle class.

Childhood in a home rich with love but sometimes poor in money, 1866–79. Author's loving toy soldiers, ninepins, and marbles. Father's fortunes' fluctuating from great affluence to poverty. Parents' easygoing attitude: children's never having a nursemaid or anyone else to supervise them; their being allowed to read at will in their parents' library. Reading Dickens and George Eliot, Scott, Byron, and Coleridge.

Describing her brothers' characters. Playing in Hyde Park and Epping Forest. Loving cricket and cooking. Attending St. Paul's Cathedral; family's strict keeping of the Sabbath. Mother's great influence on author; mother's expecting author to cater to her brothers. Father's stating "boys should go everywhere and know everything" while "a girl should stay at home and know nothing." Longing for her brothers' privileges; being included in their games. Believing her home education was better than her brothers' at school; mother's teaching her the Bible, French poetry, English history, geography, science, and Latin. Being sent to a school for "young ladies," age 12. Visiting her mother's relatives in Cornwall. Making an informal family magazine with her brothers. Memories of the last Christmas before father's 1879 death.

Apparently seeking to entertain her sons as well as general readers, Hughes wrote her autobiographies in an informal, chatty tone, employing dialogue throughout. Two major themes are her desire to share her brothers' adventures and the contrasts she finds between city life and country holidays. Her discussion of domestic life and activities is very detailed. With **477** *A London Girl of the Eighties* (1936), Hughes describes her education and offers reflections on the educational system of her time, covering her early adult life to 1890. This book is particularly valuable for its portrayal of women's educator Frances Mary Buss and of life at her North London Collegiate School. Hughes qualifies her negative reaction to Buss and the school by pointing out that she entered at age 16 and was thus more mature than most pupils. She analyzes in detail the British educational system of the 1880s and particularly the education of women. Following these, **478** *A London Home in the Nineties* (1937) discusses her supervision of teacher training at Bedford College, her marriage, her children, and her 1893 trip to the U.S.; **479** *A London Family between the Wars* (1940) discusses her widowhood, her work as a school inspector and examiner, the books she wrote for money and for pleasure, and her life alone after her sons were grown.

480 HUNT, Dame Agnes Gwendolyn. 1867–1948. *This Is My Life*. New York: Arno Press, 1980. 237 pp.; foreword by Morris Bishop; front. port.; illus. NUC pre56 260:604. (1st pub. as *Reminiscences,* 1942.)

Raised in Baschurch, Shropshire. Father: Rowland Hunt, d.1879. Mother: Marianne Humfrey. 4 brothers; 6 sisters. Single. Nurse; midwife; hospital founder; physically handicapped woman. Upper middle class.

Physically handicapped woman's fulfilling a sense of mission through her work as a nurse and hospital founder, 1870s–c.1930. Mother's having 11 children despite disliking them. Mother's severe discipline; her allowing nursemaids and older siblings to beat the younger children. Author's being trained in stoicism; her consequent fear of complaining to her mother about a painful blister on her heel; blister's leading to blood poisoning and crippling, age 10. Sudden death of her father, 1879. Moving to mother's family home in Leicestershire, 1882. Mother's hearing a lecture on Australia and deciding to move the family there, 1883; their assorted misadventures in the bush and outback. Author's attending convent school. Family's returning to London, 1887. Visiting New Zealand; visiting her brother in San Francisco. Becoming a nursing pupil at London hospitals, 1887. Noting the rarity of an upper-middle-class daughter's earning her own money; crediting her mother with instilling an independent attitude in her daughters by forcing each to choose a profession. Author's being trained as a nurse at Salop Infirmary and in Hammersmith, 1889–91; becoming certified as a midwife; receiving an appointment to Queen's Hospital, Isle of Wight. Mother's deciding that author should set up a convalescent home at Baschurch so that mother could live near her, 1900. Tending wounded soldiers there during WWI. Death of her mother, 1917. Beginning a job training center for crippled patients, 1927. Believing that she had been put on earth especially to help other cripples.

This autobiography begins breezily but the tone turns serious as Hunt recounts her substantial contributions to orthopaedic nursing at Baschurch. She attempts to make light of the many hardships and pains she suffered, not least the insensitivity of her indomitable mother. Without minimizing her handicap, Hunt shows how she accommodated it; she came to believe her injury freed her from conventional Victorian codes and allowed her to seek a profession.

481 HUNT, Violet. 1866–1942. *I Have This to Say: The Story of My Flurried Years*. Hurst & Blackett, 1926. 306 pp.; front. port.; foreword; illus.; apps. NUC pre56 261:56.

Born in Whitby, Yorkshire. Father: Alfred Hunt, painter. Mother: Margaret Raine, novelist (Margaret Hunt, pseud.). 2 sisters. Single. Novelist; journalist; suffragist; spiritualist; foreign resident (Germany). Upper class.

Romantic adventures and intimate views of life and literature, from the end of the Edwardian era to the beginning of WWI. Joining the suffrage movement; collecting funds for it; approving of militant methods. Believing she received quasi-metaphysical messages on the wireless. Writing for the *English Review*. Visiting with H. G. Wells. Her memories of Thomas Hardy and Henry James. Touring France. Introducing Christabel Pankhurst to Mrs. Humphry Ward. Socializing with Hugh Walpole and Ezra Pound. Her romantic liaison with novelist Joseph Leopold Hueffer (pseudonym for Ford Hermann Hueffer, later Ford Madox Ford); describing his personal history and career. Going into "exile" in Germany with Hueffer; his threatening to become naturalized in Germany in order to obtain a divorce from his English wife on grounds of desertion. Commenting on the political selfishness of Germany; the German military mind; German socialism. Receiving letters from D. H. Lawrence; visiting with George Bernard Shaw. Experiencing financial difficulties; Hueffer's not permitting her to engage in journalism. Reflecting on the importance of money in the world; her personal lack of interest in money. Visiting with Joseph Conrad. Finishing *The Governess,* a novel begun by her mother. Experiencing friction with her sisters due to author's "scandalous" romantic entanglement with a married man. Outbreak of WWI: Hueffer's participating in the British military. Her opinion that those who speak of suicide generally do not commit it. Discussing how loving kindness cannot exist between men and women who are romantically involved; seeing marriage as tyranny tempered by divorce. Providing details of the libel suit Hueffer's wife brought against her to correct the erroneous announcement of the author's marriage to Hueffer.

In this somewhat eccentric autobiography by a noted English eccentric, Hunt focuses on her relationship with novelist Ford Madox Ford. She also includes anecdotes about her encounters with other important literary figures, but leaves out most of the information memoirs generally contain about an autobiographer's family life and personal development. Hunt alludes to her support of the suffragist movement, but supplies scant information about her own participation. Her writing is sometimes flowery and verbose, complicated by a seemingly purposeful vagueness, and sometimes she uses modern colloquialisms, which seem out of place. A glimpse of Hunt as an old woman still fixated on her frustrated desire to have married Ford can be found in *Looking Glass*, the autobiography of Marguerite Steen.

482 HUNTER, Eileen. 1908–s.l.1965. *The Profound Attachment*. André Deutsch, 1969. 221 pp. BLC to 1975 156:59.

Born in London. Father: Edward Hunter, founder of the Anglo Engraving Company. Mother: Mabel. 3 sisters. Married 1932, George, antique dealer; divorced c.1939. Married 1941, Milorad Petrovitch, Serbian psychiatrist. 1 son. Businesswoman; interior designer; fabrics designer; fashion model; entrepreneur; journalist; actress (film); shop assistant. Upper middle class.

Candid analysis of a father-daughter attachment and conflicts, set within context of personal and professional experiences, covering author's childhood to 1965. Giving a detailed family history: parents' backgrounds, personalities, troubled marriage. Impact of WWI. Father's disappointment at having only daughters. Author's feeling her father preferred her younger sisters. Her silent "profound attachment" to him. Author's "cast" in her eye being inherited from her father. Observing friction between her parents; mother's cultural pretensions and disdain for father's family's being "in trade." Contrasting prewar British attitudes and increased postwar optimistic idealism. Having her illusions of romance destroyed by her mother's instruction about sex. Attending boarding school; experiencing homesickness. Attempting to enlighten a confused fellow student about sex; this ending in public humiliation for author; her resulting long-term self-consciousness about sex. To gain father's attention, trying to be fashionable and sophisticated. Attending finishing school in Paris, age 17. Attending acting school, age 18; finding brief work as a film extra. Attending wild parties. Writing for weekly *Weldon's Journal*. Modeling for a French dress designer; working as a dress-shop assistant; her parents' disapproval. Drawing dress designs, age 21. Having a complete rupture with her father on asking him to increase her annual dress allowance. Marriage; her intensely dependent love for George, her first husband. Her budding career as an interior decorator; George's pushing her professionally, encouraging her to seek her father's financial backing. Founding Eileen Hunter Fabrics company. Divorce, c.1939. Her subsequent marriage to a Serbian psychiatrist. Both husbands' helping to strengthen her relationship with her father. WWII: accommodating friends during air raids. Mother's death, 1942; author's helping father raise a memorial to her. Birth of author's son, 1945. Moving next door to father; his happy relationship with his grandson. Father's death, 1965. Recalling the strength of his personality.

The detailed, careful descriptions of furnished interiors in Hunter's narrative manifest the aesthetic taste she employed in her career as a fabric designer. When she presented her early designs to her father and he found them pleasing, it broke the ice in their relationship for the first time. From then on he did all that he could to help her. Hunter's book is structured to hinge on this reconciliation.

483 HURST, Margery (née Berney). 1914–s.l.1967. *No Glass Slipper*. New York: Crown, 1967. 176 pp.; front. port.; foreword by Commander Edward Whitehead; photos. BLC to 1975 156:185.

Born in Southampton, Hampshire. Father: Sam Berney, managing director of a film company, public works builder. Mother not named. 3 sisters. Married 1940, surname Baines, army major; he deserted her 1945. Married 1948, Eric Hurst, barrister. 2 daughters. Businesswoman; military officer; entrepreneur; philanthropist. Upper middle class.

Entrepreneur's education, marriages, army service, and founding of a successful secretarial agency, together with her evaluation of women in business and society, from her childhood to 1967. Her violent temper in childhood; learning self-discipline. Attending boarding school at Hampstead; later studying acting at the Royal Academy of Dramatic Art. Her opinions on dating and sex education. Her first marriage, 1940. WWII: undergoing officer training; serving as an officer in the Auxiliary Territorial Service. Deciding to get pregnant during WWII because pregnant women received preferential medical treatment; husband's deserting her. Needing to support herself; hiring a nanny for her child, opening a typing agency in west London, c.1946. Agency's prospering, becoming Brook Street Secretarial Bureau. Her second marriage, 1948; another pregnancy. Experiencing severe depression from overwork; taking drug and electroshock therapy. Doing philanthropic work with delinquent girls for the London City Council. Expanding her secretarial bureau to Australia and America. Founding the Society for International Secretaries. Commenting on the loneliness of single urban women, unwanted pregnancy, and abortion. Author's self-assessment as a woman entrepreneur in a man's world.

Upon being asked to write this book, Hurst at first refused out of a concern for her family's privacy and from a lack of self-confidence as a writer. She takes an intimate tone and speaks from experience on many aspects of her role as a successful businesswoman and mentor to young women employees. Her strong opinions and forceful personality come to the fore as she describes her career and her personal strengths and weaknesses.

484 HUTCHINSON, Margaret Massey. 1904–s.l.1994. *A Childhood in Edwardian Sussex: The Making of a Naturalist.* Hindhead, Surrey: Saiga Publishing Ltd., 1981. 150 pp.; front. port.; illus. BLC 1982–1985 12:169.

Born at Haslemere, Sussex. Father: Herbert Hutchinson, owner of brick and tile works. Mother: Mary H. Massey, farm caretaker. 6 brothers; 2 sisters. Single. Wrote *Children as Naturalists* (1947), *Making and Keeping a Box Garden, Making and Keeping a Vegetable Garden, Exploring a Park.* Naturalist; teacher; nature writer; educator. Middle class.

Family life and childhood pastimes in rural Sussex, recollected by a gifted naturalist and teacher, mainly focused on her first nine years. Describing her childhood home and farm. Family history; assorted family members' having a naturalist bent. Her Quaker upbringing. Father's love of culture; his informal practice of architecture, painting, and carving. Bird watching, studying bird books with her favorite brother; her early interest in natural history. Her inability to read until age 8; home study with father to age 12; his use of Froebel and Montessori teaching methods. Helping with farm work; memories of contemporary farm tools, pets, farm animals; her preferring animals in their wild state as she grew older. Exploring nearby woods. After age 12, attending Sidcot School as a day girl. Recalling family rambles and holidays. Describing the natural setting of Haslemere; visiting her paternal grandfather, Jonathan Hutchinson, F.R.S., founder of a museum in Haslemere that inspired her early nature studies. Visits to extended family; aunt and uncle's Gertrude Jekyll–style gardening. Family's moving to Somerset, author's age 17; her attending teacher training college. Eventually founding and heading her own school, c.1940. Using her knowledge of wild foods to supplement WWII war rations; going berrying in the English woods.

An innovator in methods of teaching nature study to children, when Hutchinson founded her own school she developed methods for motivating her pupils to direct their own studies in natural history. This account, centered on her youth, is meditative and rambling, ordered by location rather than chronology.

485 HUTTON, Isabel Galloway, Lady, M.D. (née Emslie). 1887–d.a.1946. *Memories of a Doctor in War and Peace*. Heinemann, 1960. 348 pp.; front. port.; preface; index. NUC 1942–1962 66:373.

Born in Edinburgh, Scotland. Father: James Emslie. Mother not named. 3 brothers. Married 1921, Maj.-Gen. Thomas Hutton, knighted 1944. Wrote *The Hygiene of Marriage, The Women's Change of Life*. Physician; health issues writer; hospital administrator; foreign resident (India); WWI volunteer; philanthropist; broadcaster. Upper middle class.

International experiences of a woman physician in war and peace, spanning 1905–46. Her parents' giving her a sense of mission to help those less fortunate; her feminist mother's encouraging author to become a doctor. Enrolling in medical school, age 17. Vivid details of her experiences—curriculum, exams, dissections, surgery—as a medical student and intern at Minto House, Women's Medical School in Edinburgh, the Royal Infirmary, and Edinburgh University. Discussing social restrictions on women medical students and physicians: segregation from male students; marriage being absolutely forbidden. Her indignation that moral disapproval of female sexuality made the medical field hostile to women's particular medical needs and concerns. Describing difficulties women with medical degrees faced in finding appointments. Beginning work as a pathologist at Larbert Asylum, c.1901; her six-month appointment to the Royal Sick Children's Hospital, Edinburgh; appointment to the Royal Mental Hospital. WWI: volunteering for overseas work; being assigned to Scottish Women's Hospital in Troyes, France, and in Serbia: treating wounded soldiers; enduring extreme weather; the high death rate; conducting battlefield surgeries. Volunteering as doctor-in-charge at Lady Muriel Paget's Mission for Children in Sebastopol. Her psychiatric studies in Vienna, 1920. Returning to her post at the Royal Mental Hospital in Edinburgh. Marriage to an army major, 1921; resulting dismissal from her hospital appointment. Moving to Harley Street, London. Her brief psychiatric research work for Maudsley Hospital laboratory; her job as an "honorary psychiatrist" (without appointment) for Maudsley outpatients; subsequently working as an honorary consultant psychiatrist at the British Hospital for Mental and Nervous Disorders, 1925. Setting up an antimalarial mission in Albania. In London, doing committee work for the Council of the Medical Women's Federation.

Heading the Ellen Terry Home for blind and defective children, 1926. Residing in India during her husband's tenure as commander of the Western Independent District, 1938–46. Her brief career in Indian radio as a cultural commentator; her appointment as head of the Indian Red Cross Welfare Service; her friendship with the Nehru family. Returning to London, 1946, to find their house had been destroyed in the WWII blitz.

Writing formally, Hutton provides great detail about her experiences as a woman in medical school and about her career in medicine. Her book testifies to her devotion to her work and to her pride in her accomplishments in a field so prejudiced against women. She appears to have been equally devoted to her husband. Excerpts from Hutton's diary are included in this autobiography. In her earlier work, **486** *With a Woman's Unit in Serbia, Salonika and Sebastopol* (1928), Hutton focuses on her volunteer work in war-torn eastern Europe, presenting her opinions on the war's immediate and long-term effects on local military and civilian populations.

487 HUXLEY, Elspeth Joscelin (née Grant). 1907–?. *The Flame Trees of Thika: Memories of an African Childhood.* Chatto & Windus, 1959. 288 pp.; front. NUC pre56 262:274.

Born in London. Father: Maj. Josceline Grant. Mother: Eleanor Lillian Grosvenor. Married 1931, Gervas Huxley. 1 son. Wrote *White Man's Country: Lord Delamere and the Making of Kenya* (1935), other books on Kenya history and East Africa, detective novels with African settings, *Atlantic Ordeal: The Story of Mary Cornish* (1941), others. Novelist; historian; colonialist (Kenya). Middle class.

Emigrant child's memories of family and colonial life on a Kenya farm with her parents, 1913–14. Family's arrival in Kenya. Father's plans to make a fortune raising sisal and coffee. Their friendships with other British colonists. Discussing difficulties women colonists faced in preserving class distinctions. Being educated by her mother. Mother's belief in the civilizing mission of Europeans. Forming friendships with Africans. Describing the tribal customs of Masai and Kikuyu; British-Dutch rivalry in Africa. Keeping a wild duiker (small antelope) and a chameleon as pets. Doctoring sick wild animals. Outbreak of WWI; parents' contributions to the war effort. Living with a neighbor family. Departing for England with her mother. Father's departure for WWI service. Commenting on natives' attitudes toward nature, author's horror at safari hunting, anti-missionary attitudes of some British colonists.

Novelistic scene-setting and dialogue are characteristic of this book. Huxley gives little specific biographical information about her family, focusing instead on invoking the Africa she knew as a child and recounting anecdotes of colonial life. Her second autobiography, *On the Edge of the Rift* (1962), continues the story of her youth in Africa, while her third, *Love Among the Daughters,* is a trenchant look at the author's American university education in the 1920s.

488 INCHFAWN, Fay (pseud.?; Mrs. Atkinson Ward). 1881–?. *The Adventures of a Homely Woman*. Ward, Lock, 1925. 314 pp.; front. port. NUC pre56 265:486.

Raised in rural England. Parents not named. Married c.1914, John, journalist, shopkeeper. 1 daughter. Children's author; poet; charitable volunteer. Lower middle class.

Housewife-author's balancing of career and domestic life, with accounts of her charitable work and commentary on housewives' situation, 1914–25. Praising housewives and the work they do; also noting the importance of imagination to women. Describing housework she performed during WWI. Being grateful for small gifts from neighbors and her mother-in-law. Husband's recognizing her writing talent; their collaborating on a book of children's verse. Publishing a book of light domestic verse, a genre favored by her editors. Husband's leaving his hack writing job; their moving to a West Country town where he kept a small shop. Describing characters of husband's relatives. Author's consoling a pregnant teenager with a message of God's mercy for the repentant sinner. Closeness to and kindnesses from neighbors; their helping her to care for her child; their aiding her in putting out a fire in her kitchen. Speaking at meetings of lower-class church women and mothers; visiting local servant women, Jewish residents, sick and dying people. Memories of her own long illness and dependence on others: being visited by condescending workers from the Nursing Association and Salvation Army; becoming bedridden and receiving care from husband and neighbors. Commenting on her Christian faith, how to comfort the dying, her passing the age of 40, women's need for patient forbearance as social reforms slowly improved their living conditions.

Inchfawn's informally written book is cheerful and optimistic, full of praise for homey, ordinary things like children's games, cats, cooking, and gardens. The author uses the word "homely" to mean homebody. She clearly wants her book to be morally useful, using many of the incidents in her own life to illustrate wider principles for her readers.

489 ISAACS, Eva Violet, Marchioness of Reading (née Mond). 1895–s.l.1960. *For the Record: The Memoirs of Eva, Marchioness of Reading*. Hutchinson & Co., Ltd., 1973. 240 pp.; foreword by Alex L. Easterman; illus.; apps.; index. NUC 1973–1977 96:217.

Born in Mayfair, London. Father: Sir Alfred Moritz Mond, 1st Baronet, later 1st Baron Melchett, industrialist, politician. Mother: Violet Goetze,

Anglican. 2 sisters; 1 brother (Henry, 2nd Baron Melchett). Married 1914, Gerald Rufus Isaacs, later 2nd Marquis of Reading, barrister, activist, d.1960. Widow. 1 son; 2 daughters. Knew David Lloyd George, Zionists Chaim Weizmann and Lieb Jaffe. Social reformer; political activist; Jewish activist; feminist; Zionist. Upper class; married into aristocracy.

Detailed behind-the-scenes glimpses of stellar events in 20th-century British history, highlighting the WWII years and the Palestinian situation, accompanied by author's varied philanthropic endeavors, covering her childhood to post-1960. Family history; descriptions of her grandparents and parents. Her nannies and governesses. Her early love of music (especially Wagner). Attending boarding and finishing schools. Traveling to Munich, 1913. Courtship with Gerald Isaacs, beginning in 1912; engagement and marriage, 1914. WWI years: husband's assignments; author's pregnancies. In the postwar years, setting up housekeeping; child-rearing; her interest in child welfare and day nurseries. Visiting India, 1922 and 1924. Beginnings of her Zionism: her friendship with Chaim Weizmann; her first visit to Palestine, 1928; discussing British policy in regard to Palestine, particularly the work of Ramsay MacDonald and Lord Passfield. Her husband's involvement on the Shaw Commission, 1929. Traveling to Poland with Lieb Jaffe to urge emigration to Palestine. Author's initiation into Judaism. Describing the house at Migdal (Palestine) built by Lord Melchett, which became author's own after his death (visitors included George Bernard Shaw and David Ben Gurion). Describing significant political events of the 1930s: 20th Zionist Congress in Zurich; Royal Commission to Palestine; coronation of George VI; Children's Refugee Movement. WWII years: her son Michael's service in the military; husband's work in the Pioneer Corps; author's service in the Red Cross and VADs; her work as an advisor to the minister of health; her work as chair of the Needlework Guild. Postwar years: author's activism in the World Jewish Congress, as president of the National Council of Women, and as a board member of the International Council for Women; author's receiving an honorary fellowship from Hebrew University (Tel Aviv); husband's obtaining a post in the Foreign Office. Husband's death, 1960; author's life without him.

Lady Reading provides an insider's view of many of the important political events of 20th-century Britain, filling in details topically rather than chronologically. She uses a great many quotations when writing about the war years and the political situation between Britain and Palestine, and the appendices provide texts of important speeches, interviews, and letters. Some parts of the book are so detailed that unless the reader is knowledgeable about the British-Palestinian issue, the material can be difficult to follow and understand.

490 JACKSON, Clara Annabel Caroline (née Grant Duff). 1870–1943. *A Victorian Childhood*. Methuen, 1932. 197 pp.; front. port.; illus.; index. NUC pre56 274:549.

Born in London. Father: Mountstuart Elphinstone Grant Duff, Liberal member of Parliament, afterward governor of Madras. Mother: Julia Webster. 4 brothers; 3 sisters. Married 1895, Frederick Huth Jackson, privy councillor, Sheriff of London, director of the Bank of England. 2 daughters; 2 sons. Society woman; foreign resident (India); feminist. Upper class.

Lively personal experiences and memories of growing up in England and India, including observations on Indian society and culture, spanning author's first eighteen years, with references to later events. Family's history, Scottish background. Father's social entertaining; his saying "vanish vanish" whenever his children entered his study, but author's becoming close to him through her love for Matthew Arnold's poetry. Her positive relationship with her mother. Recalling the close ties between children and loyal family servants. Her strong sense of Scottish identity. Her rebelliousness against authority in childhood. Living at the estates of Hampden House, Knebworth, and York House, Twickenham. Having the measles; regretting the burning of her toys, a custom of the time after a child had had an infectious illness. Recalling her nurses. Being educated at home by governesses; disliking most of them. Learning to read; her love of poetry. Becoming very religious, age 7. Writing poetry, age 9. Offering detailed comments on dress and fashion. Having psychic experiences in childhood. Fearing her brothers' games. Traveling to India, age 10, with her parents but without her brothers; feeling relief at the separation from the boys. Living, ages 10–13, at Government Houses in Madras. Feeling intense love "undisturbed by faintest lust" at that time for a Captain Gordon in India; secretly continuing a passionate, platonic relationship with him; later feeling this early love experience freed her to make a more mature alliance with her husband. Having pets in India. Riding and hunting. Attending church; admiring Indian religions and Greek philosophy. Parents' horror at their discovery of author's attachment to Captain Gordon; author's shock at being removed from India to attend school in England. Attending Cheltenham Ladies' College, ages 13–18; her initial negative reaction to the school; her later happiness there. Flirting with young Englishmen. Reading about white slave traffic; writing an impassioned poem on the subject; dating her development of feminist attitudes from an incident of a publisher's burning her poem because of his shocked disapproval at a young lady's knowing about such things. Her father's financial worries. Leaving school, 1888. Referring to her marriage, 1895; needing a year to recover from the horror of her first childbirth; raising her four children; expressing regret at not having had a career.

Jackson provides a detailed, sometimes sensuous, account of her life in England and India. Her tone is frank and slightly confessional; at age 60, she wrote this book for her grandchildren. The book's primary interest lies in its detailed description of an upper-class child's life in both England and India. The daughter of politically ambitious parents, Jackson was largely raised by servants, and her education was sketchy until she was sent off to boarding school as an adolescent. Although Jackson does not refer overtly to political events of her childhood, she does offer occasional shrewd assessments, as when she opines that the British damaged their prestige in India by sending there men who "were not gentlemen, and were rude to the natives." Other aspects of Jackson's life story are described in her daughter Anne Fremantle's autobiography, *Three-Cornered Heart,* which portrays Jackson as an unconventional mother who never lost her veneration for Eastern religion, and who encouraged her daughter's childhood exchange of letters with Gandhi.

491 JACOB, Naomi Ellington (Ellington Gray, pseud.). 1884–1964. *Me—A Chronicle About Other People*. Bath: Cedric Chivers, Ltd., 1972. 294 pp.; preface; illus.; index. NUC pre56 275:205. (1st pub. Hutchinson, 1933.)

Born in Ripon, Yorkshire. Father: Samuel Jacob, lecturer in history, German. Mother: Nana (also, Nina), Collinson, novelist, journalist, Poor Law Guardian. 1 sister. Single. Wrote novels *The Beloved Physician* (1930), *The Man Who Found Himself*, many others, biography *Our Marie* (1936), a book about animal rights, *Honour Come Back* (1952), plays. Knew Ursula Bloom, Marie Lloyd, Angela du Maurier, Seymour Hicks, Ellaline Terriss. Novelist; journalist; biographer; playwright; suffragist, militant; pupil-teacher; actress (stage, film); animal welfare activist; secretary; academic's daughter; foreign resident (Italy); WWI volunteer; socialist; factory manager. Upper middle class.

Author's childhood and varied career as a teacher, actress, secretary, and writer, from her earliest years to 1933. Her childhood nanny, pets, and amusements: reading, gardening, and attending theatre, horse races, and prize fights. Her Anglican upbringing; parents' Toryism. Father's absence after author's age 11. Her love and admiration for her mother; considering her the "greatest influence in my life"; making a series of moves with her. Her mother's being "intolerant of nothing except cruelty"; mother's work as a Poor Law Guardian and an animal welfare activist. Author's maintaining contact with her childhood nurse, Annie, into her adult life. Learning at home and at a primary school at Whitby; hating the school. Attending Higher Grade School at Leeds, then Middlesborough High School. Running away from boarding school. Her general dislike of school. Her interest in, and ultimate conversion to, Roman Catholicism. Her mother's pursuing a journalism career in America, leaving author alone and poor in England, age 15. Feeling "complete and absolute misery" while training as a pupil-teacher in Middlesborough; working as a pupil-teacher at St. Hilda's School in Marlborough. As a young woman, working with the Women's Social and Political Union in the suffrage movement; Christabel Pankhurst's discouraging her from going to prison for the cause because Pankhurst thought she'd "make a joke of it all, and play the fool." Enjoying employment as a secretary/companion to music hall actress Marguerite Broadfoote; touring with her. Her various WWI jobs: messenger, secretary, clerk, promoter in employment and emergency services; holding jobs in the toy industry; working as a munitions factory supervisor until 1919. Contracting tuberculosis; staying in sanatoria. Her early stage career: various roles, touring companies, acting colleagues; her horror at cruelty to performing animals; working as a film actress. Preferring to assume a masculine appearance, with short hair and trousers. Writing her first novel, *Jacob Usher*. Writing two one-act plays, one of which was produced by the Scottish National Players. Becoming involved in local socialist politics. Suffering repeated bouts of tuberculosis, which forced her out of politics, out of the theatre, and into Italy. Living in a private home in Logo di Gardi, Italy, c.1931.

Jacob says that she wrote this autobiography to immortalize the "really important things and people" in her life, but she also acknowledges that the book is not an "accurate chronicle, because I have never really been accurate about anything." Her tone is intimate but evasive and her style is conversational; she often directly addresses the reader, sometimes using Yorkshire dialect. She is outspoken on many topics and especially angry about cruelty to animals and children. The narrative is disorganized; the reader will learn more about Jacob's friends and enemies than about the author's own life. Subsequent books in the "Me" series cover much the same ground: **492** *Me—Again* (1937), **493** *More About Me* (1946), and **494** *Me—Looking Back* (1950). *Me—and the Swans* and *Me—and the Stags* deal with her female and male friendships; **495** *Me and the Mediterranean* (1945) covers her travels to entertain WWII troops; **496** *Robert, Nana and—Me* (1952) deals with her family history. Her last book is *Me—Thinking Things Over* (1964). A biography *Naomi Jacob: The Seven Ages of 'Me'*, by James Norbury, was published in 1965.

497 JAMES, Norah Cordner. 1894–?. *I Lived in a Democracy*. Longmans, Green, 1939. 327 pp. NUC pre56 276:621.

Born in London. Father: John James, consulting mining civil engineer. Mother: Marie, former singer. 4 brothers; 1 sister. Single. Wrote *Sleeveless Errand* (1929), *To the Valiant* (1930), *Sacrifice* (1934), others. Novelist; journalist; publisher's assistant; trade unionist; socialist; WWI volunteer. Middle class.

Fast-paced personal and professional recollections of life in bohemian London, spanning author's Victorian childhood to the beginning of

WWII. Having a succession of governesses in early childhood; briefly attending boarding school; returning home and attending day school. Grieving at her brother Denis's death from tuberculosis, 1906. Birth of a sister, 1907; author's feelings of jealousy toward the baby. Her mother's unsociability. Father's harshness; author's outrage at his caning her; his increasingly bad temper; his hatred for the women's suffrage movement. Author's losing her religious faith but being confirmed anyway. Writing poetry. Undergoing surgery for appendicitis; experiencing post-surgical complications. Attending Slade Art School for one year in late adolescence; studying painting and drawing. Outbreak of WWI. Working as a volunteer on a farm for one summer. Later working for the Ministry of Pensions; disliking the work. Approving of women's suffrage. Her interest in socialism. Her political views' clashing with her father's. Feeling increasingly oppressed in the family home; taking her own flat. Joining the 1917 Club, a social club where she met Labour party leader James Ramsay Macdonald and others. Working as a representative for trade unions; attending a trade union congress in Edinburgh; her support for the Labour party. Being hospitalized for a nervous breakdown. Commenting on the political and social conditions leading to the General Strike of 1926; marching in a trade union demonstration. Her friendships with Douglas and Margaret Cole and Sinclair Lewis. Working for publisher Jonathan Cape; making up copy for Cape's house magazine, *Now and Then*. Publishing *Sleeveless Errand,* 1929, about the hedonism of the postwar 1920s generation in England; its being seized by authorities as obscene. Enduring a series of serious illnesses. Visiting America; noting differences between life in England and the U.S. Visiting Germany; indulging in Berlin nightlife; noting the narrowness of the Nazi creed. Traveling in Sweden and France. Describing the political situation in England and Europe, 1938. Being fitted for a gas mask in London. Taking flying lessons.

An eminently readable style and conversational tone propel the reader through this unconventional, rebellious author's various stages of intellectual development. She offers few details about the social and political conditions that brought about the two world wars and the Great Depression—a surprising lack in the work of a socialist trade unionist. James conveys a general emotional detachment from the causes she supports.

498 JAMES, Winifred Lewellin (Mrs. Henry de Jan). 1876–1941. *Out of the Shadows*. Chapman & Hall, 1924. 280 pp.; illus.; map. NUC pre56 276:694.

Born in Victoria, Australia. 11 siblings. Married c.1916, Henry De Jan. Wrote *The Mulberry Tree* (1913), *A Woman in the Wilderness* (1915), *London Is My Lute* (1930), others. Novelist; travel writer; foreign resident (Panama). Middle class.

Intimate portrait of personal and travel experiences, set within general observations on British, American, and Panamanian societies, covering the WWI years. Traveling to Panama with Dr. William James, possibly her brother, 1915. Describing daily life there: terrain, illnesses, white people living in the jungle, the banana industry. Her opinion that the Negro has not arrived at the stage of his evolution that readies him for freedom. Organizing and successfully holding a Red Cross bazaar to benefit black Panamanians, despite encountering race prejudice. Suffering from fever in Panama; traveling to London to convalesce, 1916. Visiting Scotland; returning to London. Reflecting on her extremely strong pro-British feelings. Memories of growing up in Australia. Her unhappiness that the U.S. had not entered the war and at having lost her British citizenship by marrying a foreigner; not being allowed to serve as a volunteer in France as a consequence of losing her British citizenship. Describing zeppelin raids. Opposing women's driving buses in London; believing men should take those jobs due to women's delicate health. Decrying her own ruined health. Visiting Edinburgh; having her portrait painted. Visiting an Economy Exhibition for wartime austerities. Returning to Panama via Virginia. Assessing Americans: seeing their love of money as a unifying characteristic. Visiting Toronto. Meeting ballerina Anna Pavlova in Panama. Returning to the U.S. Describing Dr. James's joy at finally being permitted to serve the U.S. in the war.

This portrait of one woman's feelings about the importance of serving her country during WWI also provides a detailed picture of everyday life in Panama, England, and the U.S. James expresses many patriotic feelings, frequently quotes the Bible, and employs an often ironic tone as she explicates her fiercely pro-British sentiments. Her negative views about the abilities of women and black people, while far from progressive, are not unusual for her time.

499 JAMESON, Anna Brownell (née Murphy). 1794–1860. *Winter Studies and Summer Rambles in Canada*. Ed. by Paul A. W. Wallace. Toronto: McClelland & Stewart, 1923. 443 pp.; ed.'s intro.; front. port.; illus. NUC pre56 277:38. (1st pub. Toronto: Saunders & Ottley, 1838.)

Born in Dublin, Ireland. Father: Dennis Brownell Murphy, miniature painter, Irish. Mother not named, English. 4 sisters. Married 1825, Robert Jameson, London barrister, later chancellor, afterward Speaker of the House of Assembly in Upper Canada; separated 1837, d.1854. Wrote novel *A Lady's Diary* (1825), essays *Characteristics of Women* (1832), pamphlet *Relative Position of Mothers and Governesses* (1846), art criticism *Sacred and Legendary Art* (4 vols., 1848–60), others. Knew Fanny Kemble, Elizabeth Barrett Browning, Jane Welsh Carlyle, Barbara Bodichon, Lady Noel Byron. Essayist; traveler (Canada); novelist; art critic; publisher; cultural historian; pamphleteer; feminist; governess. Upper middle class.

Highly detailed view of the Canadian frontier, emphasizing author's experience of various aspects of Canadian society and American Indian culture, 1836–37. Traveling in winter through New York state up the Hudson to Toronto. Observations about Toronto: its geography and history, winter social activities, shops and businesses, servants, class system, political factions, dearth of honest men, and cultural life. Being introduced to the Chippewa Indians through an Indian agent; wanting to know all Indian tribes better. Visiting the Canadian Parliament. Commenting on the work of Methodist missionaries among the Missassagua Indians, and on rural clergy's inadequate pay. Canada's role as a refuge for escaped U.S. slaves; free blacks' protesting against escaped slaves' extradition. Observing public drunkenness in Niagara Falls; negative impact of American industrialization there. Describing Buffalo, New York. Traveling through Ontario en route to Toronto; discussing deforestation, the present condition of the Mohawk tribe, and expectations and resources of Englishwomen emigrants to Canada. Visiting Colonel Talbot's extensive wilderness lands and settlements. Comparing frontier settlers and members of the English working class. Noting the poor condition of rural schools. Canadian history; negative impact of the War of 1812 on both the U.S. and Canada. Discussing the need for Indian hunting tribes to learn agriculture; author's belief that Indian tribes cannot become civilized in Western terms; Indian-white relations; Moravian missionaries to the Delaware tribe. Voyage to Detroit, Michigan; author's severe illness; attending various churches. Discussing Chief Pontiac's role in the French and Indian War. Voyage to Mackinaw Island; visiting her friends the Schoolcrafts; Mrs. Schoolcraft's Chippewa ancestors; providing a detailed discussion of Chippewa culture. Meeting more Chippewas at Sault Ste. Marie; being adopted into the Chippewa tribe. Describing a tribal council with missionaries and U.S. and Canadian representatives to discuss Queen Victoria's accession, 1837. Defending women's social position in Indian tribes. Returning to Toronto.

The editor has omitted Jameson's journal entries concerning books she read during the winter of 1836–37, and possibly other personal material as well. Jameson's style is often romantic and poetically descriptive. This book is an important contribution to the literature of the Canadian frontier and is valuable to scholars of Canadian Indians; as an adopted daughter of the Chippewa tribe, Jameson describes their culture first-hand. She also comments at length on both white and Indian women and emigration to Canada. This author bears comparison to Susanna Moodie as an interpreter of Canadian identity. Prior to her marriage, Jameson had worked as a governess for fifteen years; her marriage was a troubled one, and after the visit to Canada described in this memoir, she and her husband separated permanently. In her later life she published articles and pamphlets dealing explicitly with feminist issues and, with Bessie Rayner Parkes and Barbara Leigh Smith Bodichon, founded the early feminist *English Woman's Journal*. A valuable biography of Jameson is *Love and Work Enough: The Life of Anna Jameson* (1967), by Clara Thomas.

500 JAMESON, Margaret Storm (William Lamb, James Hill, pseuds.). 1891–1986. *Journey from the North*. Collins & Harvill Press, 1969. 2 vols.: Vol. 1: 415 pp.; biblio. of author's works; front. port.; illus. Vol. 2: 384 pp.; biblio.; front.; illus. NUC 1968–1972 46:383.

Born in Whitby, Yorkshire. Father: William Storm Jameson, sea captain. Mother: Hannah Margaret Gallilee. 1 brother; 2 sisters. Married 1913, Charles Douglas Clarke; divorced 1925. Married 1926, Guy Chapman, historian. 1 son. Wrote *The Pot Boils* (1919), *The Triumph of Time* (1932), *The Green Man* (1952), many others, literary criticism *The Novel in Contemporary Life* (1938), others. Novelist; editor; publisher's agent; playwright; short storyist; literary critic; political activist; pacifist; feminist; academic; scriptwriter. Middle class.

Introspective reflections of a celebrated novelist on life, art, religion, international politics, and her prolific career in letters, from the end of Victorian times to the beginnings of the space age. As a small child, sailing with her mother and sea-captain father. Attending her first school; her love of reading. Her mother's paradoxical loving devotion and sternness toward her children. Great dissension in her parents' marriage: her mother's extravagance, her father's "cult of shabbiness." Her mother's dislike of animals; her giving away author's pet rabbit. Author's feelings of inferiority; not getting on well with other children; her inability to trust. Attending school in Scarborough. Taking Cambridge examinations. Attending Leeds University on scholarship. Memories of her first romantic attachments. Serving as secretary to Women's Representative Council. Marriage, 1913; miseries of her married life; her hatred of domesticity. Birth of her son; his becoming the center of her life. Going to work for an advertising agency; feeling unhappy with her job. Writing her first novels. Becoming sub-editor of the *New Commonwealth*. Becoming interested in the plight of European children affected by WWI. Her friendships with Rose Macaulay and Walter de la Mare. Doing research on birth control for Margaret Sanger. Discovering the existence of her husband's mistress. Working as an English representative of publisher Alfred Knopf. Her love affair with Guy Chapman; divorcing her husband. Traveling to New York on business; her intense feelings of remorse about leaving her son with her mother. Her great passion for France. Despite receiving critical acclaim, feeling dissatisfied with her novels. Attending a Labour conference in Whitby. Her loathing of war; oscillating between pacifism and support of the League of Nations; writing polemics against war and fascism. Her mother's death; continuing to feel her mother's presence in a quasi-supernatural way. Reasons for her agnosticism. Vol. 2: Serving as president of PEN. Writing more novels. Her feelings of fulfillment as a writer during the war years. Giving her reasons for deserting pacifism during WWII. Her husband's temporary appointment to Pittsburgh University; her teaching creative writing there. Her initial feelings of alienation in America; remarking on American excesses. Visiting New York and Texas. Returning to England; taking a flat in Leeds. Writing a play for the BBC. Publishing *The Green Man* to critical acclaim. Her friendship with Bertrand Russell. Investigating causes of jailed writers. Her love of travel; preferring it to writing. Her feelings of guilt at not having balanced motherhood and her career more successfully.

In this extremely literate and intellectual self-portrait Jameson ranges from melancholy to tart humor. Her apparently well-developed streak of misanthropy, which dates from her childhood frictions with her mother, seems to have been nourished in later life by the duplicitousness she ascribes to the human race. The second volume is less introspective and is mainly focused on the author's ongoing commentary on the domestic and international sufferings caused by WWII; she also discusses her personal ambivalence about pacifism. Expressing feelings of guilt about what she sees as her inadequacy as a mother, Jameson claims that women cannot simultaneously pursue careers and motherhood, but she is quick to note that it is society that limits women's flexibility in this regard. Jameson also wrote an earlier autobiography, *No Time Like the Present* (1933).

501 JEKYLL, Gertrude. 1843–1932. *Children and Gardens*. Woodbridge, Suffolk: Antique Collectors Club, 1982. 189 pp.; illus. by author; drawings by Kate Greenaway. NUC pre56 279:94. (1st pub. Country Life, 1908.)

Born in London. Father: Capt. Edward Jekyll. Mother: Julia Hammersley. 4 brothers; 1 sister. Single. Wrote *Garden Ornament*, *Colour Schemes for the Flower Garden*, others. Knew John Ruskin, others. Landscape designer; garden designer; artist (illustrator); horticulture writer; children's author. Upper middle class.

Personal memories of a professional gardener, together with practical garden-planning advice, covering 1843–1908. Her childhood memories of London parks and gardens. Moving to the country, age 5. Her love of outdoor activities and solitary rambles; feeling more like a boy than a girl. Remembering nannies and governesses; sisters' home life after brothers departed for school. Her interest in wildflowers; learning to identify them. Family wealth's enabling her to have her own garden and playhouse. Presenting plans for a child's garden and playhouse; recipes using produce from the child's garden. Suggesting that girls consult "the mathematical brother who understands Euclid" in making scale drawings of their gardens. Listing types of plants appropriate for children's gardens; explaining weeding, seeding, and tools. Simplifying botanical terms for children. Remembering her childhood summer holidays on the Isle of Wight; disliking the bathing machines there. Offering advice on finding and cooking edible wild mushrooms. Her home beside the Thames, age 24. Her friendship with Ellen Willmott, "the greatest of living women gardeners." Her Munstead Wood house, designed for her by Sir Edwin Lutyens, 1896. Having "adventures on the lawn" with hedgehogs, a tortoise, bats, and an owl. Enjoying going barefoot in gardens and on the beach. Instructions on playing with sand, fire, and water in the garden. Discussing pet cats as garden enhancements; the characters of her cats.

Addressing an audience of parents, Jekyll gives advice on gardening practices for children and other novice gardeners. Scientific data are presented accurately yet without pedantry. From beginning to end, Jekyll's charming stroll through gardens and gardening is replete with glimpses into her own life and character; she emerges as a woman of imagination and enthusiasm. Color drawings by the author and Kate Greenaway enhance the presentation. Jekyll was asked to write this book by her mentor, architect Sir Edwin Lutyens, with whom she worked professionally. She designed many of the gardens for his houses and became well known for the "wild" gardens she created. More information about Jekyll's life is contained in *Miss Jekyll: Portrait of a Great Gardener* (1966), by Betty Massingham.

502 JEMISON, Mary. 1743–1833. *A Narrative of the Life of Mrs. Mary Jemison, who was taken by the Indians...carefully taken from her own words, Nov. 29, 1823*. Ed. by James Everett Seaver. Syracuse, New York: Syracuse University Press, 1990. 167 pp.; front. port.; foreword by George H. J. Abrams; preface by ed.; intro.; app. NUC pre56 279:165. (1st pub. 1824; other ed.: New York: Putnam's, 1898.)

Born on ship *William and Mary* as family was emigrating from Londonderry, Ireland, to Pennsylvania. Father: Thomas Jemison, farmer. Mother: Jane Erwin. 4 brothers; 1 sister. After Indian captivity, married Sheninjee, a Delaware, died in the Cherokee wars. Married c.1761, Hiokatoo, a Seneca, died c.1813. Widow. 5 daughters; 3 sons. American Indian captive; colonial American. Rural farming class; as a Seneca, held high rank; married into foreign culture.

Oral history of an American Indian captive who adopted tribal life, covering c.1743–1823. Her parents' characters; family's emigration from

Ireland to America; their settling near present-day Carlisle, Pennsylvania. Recalling Indian attacks on whites during the French and Indian War, c.1752; death of her uncle at Fort Necessity; increased Indian violence after Washington's surrender. Being educated at home by her parents. Family's being attacked by French and Shawnees, 1755; all but her two eldest brothers being captured, murdered, and scalped; Indians' sparing author and another child captive. Being marched overland; traveling with the Shawnee down the Ohio River; her adoption into the Seneca tribe; describing tribal domestic life. Encountering other white captives. Marriage to Sheninjee, a Delaware Indian; her daughter's birth and death; her son's birth; naming him Thomas Jemison. Adapting to Indian culture; remembering the English language but losing the ability to read it. Describing the evils wrought on Indians by liquor and Christian missionary efforts. Walking 500–600 miles to join other members of her Indian family in western New York; seeing their white captives, pleading for the life of one young man. A successful Indian attack on Fort Niagara; her desire to avoid seeing Indians' torture of white prisoners. Receiving news of her husband's death in the Cherokee Wars; deciding to stay with the Indians. Her second marriage, which lasted fifty years, to Hiokatoo, a Seneca; having four more daughters and two sons with him; giving them all English names. Remembering the peaceful period between the French and Indian War and the American Revolution, 1761–76. Describing Seneca customs; their alliance with the British during the Revolutionary War; their attacks on Americans, 1776. American General Sullivan's invasion of New York, 1779, driving the Seneca to seek refuge with the British at Fort Niagara; author's seeing this as one of the darkest periods in Seneca history. The Senecas' returning to their devastated lands. Author's husking corn for two runaway slaves on their farm; living with them for two or three years; their departure; acquiring their land through a deed from the Chiefs of the Six Nations. Describing the life of Ebenezer Allen, a Tory who lived among the Seneca. After the Revolutionary War, author's being given permission by the Seneca to return to her own people; choosing to stay with the Seneca, fearing her white relatives would despise her Indian children. Her son John's separate murders of two of his brothers, occasioned by liquor and jealousy; John's being murdered by two other Indians; author's grief. Her second husband's death in 1811, at age 103; his life story. Her self-proclaimed cousin's cheating her out of some of her land; author's forcing him to leave. Becoming a naturalized U.S. citizen, 1817; having her title to her land ratified. Reviewing her life to 1823; expressing her pride in her daughters and their growing families.

Seaver's interview with Jemison in 1823 resulted in this book, transcribed in first-person narration, in which the editor's narrative voice overrides Jemison's and obscures her words. Seaver's hand is particularly evident in effusive, hortatory speeches delivered by Indians; however, he is careful to point out Jemison's own reluctance to cast any shadow on the characters of her descendants. Although Jemison seems to have fully adapted to Indian life, she gave her children English names, a choice she does not discuss in this memoir. The appendices to the 1898 and 1990 editions contain different material: the former gives various accounts of Jemison and her descendants, while the latter discusses Seneca customs and warfare.

503 JERMY, Louise. 1877–?. *The Memories of a Working Woman.* Norwich: Goose & Son, 1934. 188 pp.; foreword by R. H. Mottlam. BLC to 1975 165:8.

Born in Howe, Hampshire. Father not named, fish shop owner. Mother: Selina, manor house servant to Lord and Lady Mount Temple. Stepmother: Mary. Second stepmother not named. 1 brother; 1 sister; 2 half-brothers; 1 half sister. Married 1911, John Jermy, d.1922. Widow. 2 sons. Domestic servant; laundry worker; dressmaker. Working class.

Frank and intensely painful recollections of childhood, accompanied by subsequent occupational endeavors, covering up to the 1920s. Her birth on the Broadlands estate of Lord and Lady Mount Temple; her parents' being tenants there. Death of her mother, at author's age 18 months. Living with her maternal grandmother; closeness to her. Being told by her father that she was "different" from others; having the gift of second sight. Being quick to anger and arrogance; consequently being given the derogatory nickname "Lady Louisa." Growing up at Broadlands: describing customs, festivals, summer pastimes. Suffering from erysipelas, a disfiguring facial ailment. Father's remarriage and family's move to London. Attending British and Foreign Society School (Nonconformist). Looking different from other children: having cropped hair like a boy. While still a child, working a difficult mangle at home and fetching heavy bundles of soiled clothes to help the family income, at her stepmother's orders and father's insistence. Being beaten by her stepmother with a broom handle, poker, and other objects; father's incapacity or ignorance preventing his intervention. Having a bout with tubercular hip disease as a result of overwork; being partially crippled by age 13; staying in a hospital; praying to die. Author's closeness to her sister, with whom she fought "like a boy"; sister's taking author's side in family disputes. Going to live with her paternal grandfather. Knitting socks to sell for extra money. Walking on crutches. Returning to her family home. Being apprenticed to a dressmaker; showing talent for that work. Stepmother's continuing physical abuse of author, leading to author's rehospitalization. Suffering fainting spells. Her first dressmaking job; stepmother's insistence that author find better work; deciding to go into domestic service. Finding physical hardship in dealing with heavy work. Taking a position with a family in

Birmingham; their helping her toward self-education and a religious outlook. Her ultimate rapprochement with her stepmother. Taking a position as a cook in London. Her ten-year courtship with John Jermy. Working for the Klein family in London. Leaving her post to nurse her ill stepmother until her death. Marriage, 1921, to John. Living on the estate in Wroxham where John worked. Father's disapproving of her marriage. Births of her two sons. Husband's dying from pneumonia while the boys were small. Father's third marriage. Her pride in raising her sons without accepting charity. Becoming a laundress at the Broadlands estate. Assessing life as "the luck of the draw."

Frankly re-creating the trauma she experienced from physical and emotional abuse during her childhood, Jermy also describes her eventual recovery of self-worth and dignity through work. She provides a richly detailed picture of the economic and domestic problems of the working class during the late 19th and early 20th centuries.

504 JEUNE, Susan Mary Elizabeth, Baroness St. Helier (née Stewart-Mackenzie, C.B.E.). c.1845–1931. *Memories of Fifty Years*. Edward Arnold, 1910. 358 pp.; front. port.; illus.; index. NUC pre56 514:518. (1st pub. 1909.)

Born in Ross and Cromarty, Scotland. Father: Keith William Stewart-Mackenzie, aide-de-camp in 90th Regiment. Mother: Hannah Hope-Vere. 3 siblings. Married 1871, Col. John Constantine Stanley, Grenadier Guards, died n.d. Married 1881, the Rt. Hon. Sir Francis Jeune, later 1st Baron Jeune, Member of the Privy Council, d.1905. 1 daughter; at least 1 son. Wrote *Lesser Questions* (1895), *The Modern Marriage Contract* (1898). Women's issues writer; education writer; feminist; journalist; philanthropist. Middle class; married into aristocracy.

Entertaining reminiscences of socializing with aristocratic, political, literary, and other luminaries, emphasizing changes from c.1837–87. History of the Mackenzie clan. Discussing the political ramifications of the religious disruption of the Presbyterian Church, 1843; her parents' following the Free Church. Author's moving to Brahan Castle, age 15; spending the happiest years of her youth as a companion-secretary to her grandmother. Recalling family friendships with Prime Minister William Gladstone, Sir Edwin Henry Landseer, Sir Walter Scott. Describing highland traditions and superstitions; changes between her youth and modern times. Living in London, 1860s; meeting celebrated individuals at dinner parties: Charles Dickens, Bulwer-Lytton, Sir John Tenniel, Benjamin Disraeli. Marriage; her first husband's military career. Remembering the political situation in France, 1871. Accompanying her husband to the U.S. for his investigation of Emma Mine. Giving her impressions of New York; living conditions in various parts of the U.S.; Mormonism in Utah; San Francisco society, 1870s.

Returning to London. Relating anecdotes about her friends Thomas Carlyle, Alfred, Lord Tennyson, and E. M. Forster. Discussing the democratization of English politics through the Reform Bill; the importance of the 1870 Education Act. Alluding to her second marriage (without explaining what became of her first husband); conservative politics of author's second husband. Her friendships with James McNeill Whistler, Sir Henry Irving, Ellen Terry, others. Serving on a committee of a large girls' college. Her memories of Cecil Rhodes, his argumentative nature. Admiring the genius of Lord Randolph Churchill; extracts of his letters to author. Noting the improved social position of women, particularly as a result of the Married Women's Property Act, 1870. Her memories of the suffragette movement. Her Irish travels, 1880s: encounters with Irish character and humor. Discussing parliamentary debate about Home Rule for Ireland. Recalling Queen Victoria's 1887 Jubilee; seeing demonstrations of national pride as important.

Although Lady St. Helier's informal style and accessible tone are inviting, she omits much from her life story, particularly regarding the period between the apparent death of her first husband and her remarriage. Others have referred to the author as a philanthropist and writer, but she herself appears reticent to discuss her charitable and literary activities. Her work is principally a running commentary on the dramatic changes in society during the second half of the 19th century.

505 JOHNSON, Amy. 1904–1941. "Amy Johnson, C.B.E.," pp. 131–156 in *Myself When Young: By Famous Women of Today*. Ed. by Margot Asquith [Emma Alice Margaret Asquith, the Countess of Oxford and Asquith]. Frederick Muller, 1938. 422 pp.; port. BLC to 1975 12:477.

Born in Hull, Yorkshire. Father not named, fish merchant. Mother not named. 1 sister. Married 1930, James Mollison, pilot; divorced 1938. Aviator; secretary. Middle class.

Brief, romantic exploration of internal and external factors influencing career decision of an aviator, covering her childhood to age 23. Not appreciating, as a young child, her mother's household drudgery on her behalf. How her early love of fairy tales and music affected her outlook on life. Recalling romps with her father and younger sister. Attending private schools; not being satisfied by the limited curriculum; playing pranks to pass the time. Attending a coeducational secondary school in Hull, ages 12–19; rapidly developing an interest in the opposite sex; participating in all the boys' athletic sports; particularly loving gymnastics; continuing to rebel against school authority. Recalling WWI rationing; the terror of the air raids. Suffering a tooth injury, c.1917, which resulted in a speech impediment; no longer being popular with the boys; becoming more solitary. Trying repeatedly to run away from home. Attending the cinema; being entranced by a news item featuring an airplane. Wanting to see the world, not become a housewife. Attending Sheffield University; having ambitions to play the violin professionally; injuring her hand and abandoning that dream. Not being dedicated to her studies; attending classes as little as possible; leaving the university after three years. Attending a business college; working as a secretary for an accountant; hating it. Suffering a nervous breakdown. Working as a secretary for an advertising agency. Moving to London; working in shops; working for three years in a solicitor's office; learning about the law and finding it fascinating. Moving to a room near an airfield; envying the pilots; wishing she could fly. Taking her first flying lessons, age 23. Believing her desire for adventure to be inherited: her grandfather's having run away from home as a small boy, her father's having been one of the first to participate in the Klondike gold rush; seeing it as natural that she would set long-distance flight records. Expecting to undertake many new career challenges in the years ahead.

Best known for being the first woman to fly solo from England to Australia, after accomplishing that feat in 1930 Johnson set other long-distance flying records. She writes in a simple and humorous style, providing insights into her temperament, her frustrating search for a vocation, and her attraction to aviation. Her essay ends with a statement of her optimism about pursuing many new challenges in the years ahead, a not unusual sentiment which retrospectively seems poignant, for Johnson died in WWII as a pilot in the Air Transport Auxiliary.

506 JOHNSON, Pamela Hansford (later Lady Charles Snow; Nap Lombard, pseud.). 1912–1981. *Important to Me: Personalia.* Macmillan, 1974. 254 pp.; intro. NUC 1973–1977 57:525.

Born in London. Father: Reginald Kenneth Johnson, railway administrator on the Gold Coast. Mother: Amy Clotilda Howson, actress. 1 sister. Married 1936, Gordon Neil Stewart; divorced 1948. Married 1950, Lord Charles Percy Snow, writer, playwright, d.1980. 2 sons; 1 daughter. Wrote 27 novels, a critical study of Marcel Proust, essays, short stories, poems, and plays (some in collaboration with C. P. Snow). Knew Edith Sitwell, Aldous Huxley, A. L. Rowse, Yevgeny Yevtushenko, Ivy Compton-Burnett. Novelist; literary critic; playwright; short storyist; poet; clerk; social issues writer. Middle class.

Literary critic's analysis of her opinions, friendships, and career, 1912–c.1974. As a child, experiencing a conflict between her emotional Calvinism and her attraction to the Anglican Church. Being hospitalized with nasal diphtheria, age 9. Her father's life and character; his love of Africa; his death, author's age 11; family's consequent loss of prosperity. Mother's family history; her having acted in the D'Oyly Carte Opera Company before marriage; author's closeness to her after her father's death. Attending Congregational church after age 15. Due to family's straitened circumstances, author's leaving secondary school and giving up her dream of a university education, age 16. Undergoing secretarial training. Finding employment as a bank clerk; living in semi-poverty. Moving to Chelsea, 1934; writing novels and poetry. Her courtship with Dylan Thomas; their becoming briefly engaged. Having her first novel called "lewd"; her fear of prosecution for obscenity. Marriage to Gordon Neil Stewart, 1936; finding it a strain to have her mother live with them. Membership in the Chelsea Labour Party and Left Book Club; having a strong emotional attachment to the Spanish Republican cause. Describing London during WWII; births of her son and daughter during the war. Partly ascribing the breakup of her first marriage, 1946, to her mother's jealousy. Writing book criticism for the BBC; her self-education as a literary critic. Her second marriage, to C. P. Snow, 1950. Birth of their son, 1952. Her mother's sudden death, 1954. Traveling with Snow on his university lecture tour of the U.S. and to the USSR, 1960; commenting on the American presidential contest between John F. Kennedy and Richard Nixon. Analyzing the causes of her periodic bouts with depression. Visiting Auschwitz with Snow and their son, 1967. Attending the Moors Trial in Chester, 1967; writing columns for the Sunday *Telegraph;* writing a book on crime, *On Iniquity*. Discussing aspects of feminism with which she agrees and disagrees. Feeling that casual sex cheapens love, but believing premarital sex to be permissible after a certain age. Criticizing liberalism's dogma of collective guilt and its tolerance of violence and pornography. Discussing her ideas on education, especially for gifted children. Assessing the literary styles of various novelists. Criticizing the ugliness of modern urban life. Discussing children's duties to their parents. Commenting on her own aging.

In this highly literate memoir, Johnson offers many insights into English writers and literature and also records many opinions about feminism, social welfare, family relations, art, and politics. This book is not straight autobiography; the chapters are arranged topically rather than chronologically. For more information on Johnson, see the study by Ishrat Lindblad, *Pamela Hansford Johnson* (Boston: Twayne, 1982).

507 JOHNSTON, Elizabeth Lichtenstein. 1764–1848. *Recollections of a Georgia Loyalist.* Ed. by Rev. Arthur Wentworth Eaton. Spartanburg, South Carolina: The Reprint Co., 1972. 224 pp.; intro. by Hon. William Johnston Almon, M.D. (author's grandson); preface; front. port.; illus. NUC pre56 282:625. (1st pub. Bankside Press, 1901.)

Born at Little Ogeechee, near Savannah, Georgia, U.S. Father: John Lichtenstein, Russian, emigrant to U.S. Mother: Catherine Delegal, of French Huguenot descent. Stepmother not named. 2 stepbrothers. Married 1779, Capt. William Martin Johnston, physician, captain in the New York Volunteers or Third Loyal American Regiment. 5 sons; 5

daughters. Colonial American; Loyalist (American Revolution); military spouse; foreign resident (Canada, West Indies). Middle class.

Vivid account of the American Revolutionary period by a Tory daughter and wife, including her postwar residence in Canada, Britain, and the West Indies, covering 1764–1837. Author's ancestry and family history. Moving to Yamacraw, a Savannah suburb, in her childhood. Her father's command of a government scout boat, relieving remote families under danger from Indian attack; his plantation on Skidaway Island. Author's being educated at home by her parents. Spending a summer in Philadelphia with her mother. Attending school in Savannah. Her mother's death, c.1774. Outbreak of the Revolutionary War; violence against Tories; father's narrow escape from rebel army soldiers; his departure for Nova Scotia, 1776; at age 12, author's petitioning for possession of his property. Father's entering the Loyalist army in New York; his subsequent service in Georgia; his reunion with author. Living with her future husband's family in Savannah; his joining his regiment in South Carolina. The bombardment of Savannah; vividly describing the women's shelters; evacuation of the city; the rebels' withdrawal. Marriage, age 15; briefly living in Long Island and in Portsmouth, Virginia, with her husband. Returning to Savannah; birth of her son. The surrender of Georgia; evacuating to Charleston, South Carolina; birth of her daughter Catharine; their removal to St. Augustine, Florida. In 1784, traveling to Scotland; family's reduced circumstances. Leaving her eldest son and daughter in Edinburgh with relatives. Living in Kingston, Jamaica; births of five more children, 1787–92. Author's assessment of the deplorable state of religion and morals in Jamaica; giving her children a religious education at home. Returning to Scotland for her health, 1796. Son Andrew's dissipated life in Edinburgh; his death, 1805. Returning to Jamaica with her daughters. Daughter Catharine's delirium and coma in a yellow fever epidemic. Moving to Halifax, Nova Scotia, 1806; children's marriages. Husband's death in Jamaica, 1807. Discussing her children's families and domestic life; teaching her grandchildren. Death of her father, 1813. Deaths of her daughters Catharine and Eliza, 1819. A cataract's obscuring her vision; having successful eye surgery in Edinburgh. Death of her son John's wife in a fire due to her meekness and passivity; John's death from consumption. Living with son Lewis and his 14 children. Meditating on death. Letters (1773–84) between author and her husband; other family correspondence.

Written from a partisan Tory perspective, Johnson's eyewitness testimony to the American Revolutionary War serves as a balance to celebratory accounts by depicting domestic conditions and perils for noncombatant family members of British soldiers. A rich repository of detail on 18th-century family life, Johnson's memoir, because of the author's moral commentary on American and Jamaican customs, also exemplifies how British travelers' religious beliefs shaped their reactions to unfamiliar new world cultures.

508 JOHNSTON, Ellen. c.1831–?. *Autobiography, Poems and Songs of Ellen Johnston, the "Factory Girl"*. Glasgow: William Love, 1867. 232 pp.; index; testimonial by Rev. George Gilfillan; list of subscribers; poems; songs; app. NUC pre56 282:625.

Born in the Muir Wynd, Hamilton, Scotland. Father: James Johnston, stonemason. Mother: Mary Bilsland. Stepfather not named, mill worker. Single. 1 daughter. Factory worker; poet. Working class.

Working-class poet's struggle for literary self-expression despite family and job problems, 1830s–67. Father's emigration to the U.S. in her infancy. Her childhood at Bridgeton, near Glasgow. Receiving news of her father's supposed death. Mother's remarriage at author's age 8. Stepfather's moving family to London, putting author to work in a London factory against her will, age 11. Author's running away, but being caught by her uncle and beaten by her mother. Running away four more times. Having only nine months' formal education; her pride in having educated herself through reading Sir Walter Scott's novels. Courtship and pregnancy, c.1852; being deserted by her sweetheart; placing her daughter under her mother's care. Supporting her family by writing poetry for the Glasgow *Examiner* and other weekly newspapers; returning to mill work. Receiving news that her father is alive in America, c.1859; his remorse at discovering that his wife has remarried and his daughter is toiling in factories; his suicide. Mother's death, 1861. Author's moving between Glasgow, Belfast, Dundee, and Manchester, briefly doing mill work in each. Being fired from a Dundee factory; jealous coworkers' blackballing her after she successfully challenged her dismissal. Writing poems for the *Penny Post*; editor's assisting her by publishing them.

Serving as an introduction to a collection of the author's poems, Johnston's twelve-page autobiography is written in a romantic, effusive, somewhat self-dramatizing tone. She attempts to vindicate herself against coworkers and employers who accused her of being "rude, forward, and presumptuous." Still working in a Dundee factory at the time this book was published, Johnston avers that she has suffered in silence the many wrongs done to her there.

509 JOHNSTON, Margaret. c.1895–?. *Some Adventures with a School.* Jarrolds, 1934. 160 pp.; front.; foreword by Ethel Mannin; illus. BLC to 1975 167:175.

Born in Scotland. Parents not mentioned. 1 sister. Single. 1 adopted daughter. Knew A. S. Neill. Teacher; educator; school founder. Middle class.

Thought-provoking combination of author's educational theories, innovations, and teaching experiences, covering 1924–34. Her frustration after spending ten years teaching history in the secondary school system; finding the school discipline system ineffective; commenting on the rigid exam system dictated by traditional schools. Quitting her job, 1924. Founding her own boarding school; establishing a homelike atmosphere. Adopting a baby to teach her pupils responsibility. Accepting pupils of all ages from infancy to age 19. British government's prohibition against employing foreigners as teachers. Mixing lessons with play; finding it difficult to explain her teaching philosophy to the students' parents. Experimenting with various forms of discipline. Discussing sex with the children; emphasizing parents' responsibilities for sex education. Author's opinions on the advisability of children's keeping pets to learn responsibility. Believing that manners shouldn't be overemphasized. Children's helping with gardening. Successfully mixing students of varied religious backgrounds. Not believing in forcing children to eat what they dislike. Thinking children should be allowed the freedom to be creative without constraints. All of the students' working on original plays to present to the parents. Discussing parental control of children and its effects. Having her happiest times when the school is full of children.

Johnston's book sets forth her radical theories of childhood education, their implementation at her school, and their results. Although she was a disciple of A. S. Neill, she does not discuss him in this book. Her style shows a high level of education and is both analytical and expository, using many anecdotes to illustrate her theories. Johnston frequently asks rhetorical questions in a tone suggesting that she wants readers to find her opinions reasonable.

510 JONES, Doris Arthur (Mrs. William Hobart Houghton Thorne). 1888–?. *What a Life!* Jarrolds Publishers, 1932. 292 pp.; front. port.; preface by Somerset Maugham; illus.; index. NUC pre56 283:523.

Born in London. Father: Henry Arthur Jones, playwright. Mother: Jenny. 3 brothers; 3 sisters. Married 1904, William Thorne, lawyer; divorced 1923. 1 daughter. Wrote *The Life and Letters of Henry Arthur Jones* (1930). Biographer; theatrical reviewer; WWI volunteer; foreign resident (Morocco, Cyprus, Greece); civil servant's spouse; political hostess. Upper middle class.

Memories of a drama critic and civil servant's wife at home and abroad, along with literary and theatrical anecdotes, covering author's childhood to 1932. Receiving cruel treatment from her nanny; her resulting terrors and nightmares. Considering her playwright father the greatest influence on her life. Becoming close to American dramatist William Gillette, her father's friend; memories of actress Ellen Terry. Being impressed by famous people and collecting their autographs throughout her life. Attending Queen's College; liking history and geography; leaving school, age 15. Entering into secret engagement and marriage to

William Thorne, author's age 16; her father's violent disapproval when he learned of the marriage. Living in Paris with her husband; his finding work in London. Reconciling with her father. Memories of Henry Irving, Sarah Bernhardt, Mrs. Patrick Campbell. Attending theatre with her father; his theatrical career. Husband's appointment to a judgeship in Morocco, 1908; describing Moroccan social life; finding it difficult to tolerate native servants. Discussing Moorish history and traditions. Birth of her daughter, 1910. Husband's appointment as a judge in Cyprus; their entertaining Greek and Turkish dignitaries there, 1911–16. Sending her daughter back to England to live with author's sister. Describing the disadvantages of being in colonial service. During WWI, Cyprus's exemption from many privations; author's arranging concerts for British soldiers. Her husband's transfers to Egypt and Greece; her visiting a leper colony and a lunatic asylum in Egypt. Experiencing ill health; returning to Cyprus; visiting England. Her continuing ill health; her displeasure at having to live abroad. Friction with her husband; deciding to divorce him; remaining friends with him. Returning to her parents' house in London. Her mother's death; author's trying to help her father recover from his resulting depression while struggling with her own grief. Working on a school Care Committee. Meeting Joseph Conrad, P. G. Wodehouse, Vachel Lindsay; memories of her father's theatrical friends: Noel Coward, James Barrie, George Arliss. Her father's death; author's depression; her seeking psychiatric help. For a few weeks, working as a drama critic for a newspaper. G. B. Shaw's assisting her in writing her father's biography, which won critical acclaim. Alluding to financial reverses compounded by her gambling. Believing that one should say what one thinks of people only behind their backs. Her ex-husband's death, author's age 43; with the loss of alimony, having no income; writing this book because she needed money.

Although it obeys no particular thematic order, Jones's book intersperses her experiences in exotic locales with anecdotes concerning famous friends of her playwright father, Henry Arthur Jones. In line with her comment about not giving frank opinions about people to their faces, she consistently belittles (behind their figurative backs) the cultures to which her marriage gave her access. The contrast between Jones's attitudes toward British and non-British peoples points to a type of colonial arrogance that was not unusual in the early 20th century.

511 JONES, Emily Elizabeth Constance. 1848–1922. *As I Remember: An Autobiographical Ramble*. A. & C. Black, 1922. 96 pp.; front. port.; preface by Rev. William R. Inge; illus.; index. NUC pre56 283:565.

Raised in Langstone, Llangarron, Wales. Father not named. Mother: née Oakley. 9 siblings. Single. Wrote *An Introduction to General Logic* (1892), *A Primer of Ethics* (1909), *Girton College* (1913), others.

Academic; headmistress; librarian; educator; textbook writer. Middle class.

Personal growth and professional contributions of women's educator, covering 1848–1916. Her large, loving family. Being the eldest child, the only one "who started in life with an inexplicable love of books and hunger for knowledge." Mother's reading fairy stories, Bible stories, and history to the children. Learning letters and spelling from her maternal grandmother. Receiving lessons from an English governess, age 10; being forbidden to read novels, but nevertheless reading them voraciously. Father's moving the family to Stellenbosch, South Africa, at author's age 13; being educated in German literature and French by a German governess. Socializing with educated Dutch families. Returning to England, age 17. Attending the Miss Robinsons' school at Alston Court, Cheltenham, for one year; broadening her intellectual interests; Charles Dickens's giving recitations at the school; author's belonging to the school essay club. Taking country drives with her Aunt Charlotte Collins; appreciating architecture after visiting Tintern Abbey and other notable structures. Taking the entrance exam for Girton College; with her aunt's financial support, attending Girton in 1875. Remembering Emily Davies, Girton's founder. Her further education in philosophy. Being assigned by her mentors, Henry Sidgwick and James Ward, to translate the second half of Hermann Lotze's *Mikrokosmus*. After graduation, returning to live with her aunt. Death of her aunt, 1884; joining the Society for Psychical Research; overcoming her fear of ghosts. Being invited to lecture at Girton; her residence there for the next thirty-two years. Praising Girton's sense of community and its "disciplined freedom." Serving as lecturer and librarian, 1890–93, as vice-mistress, 1896–1903, and ultimately as headmistress of Girton, 1903–16; describing her administrative duties. Teaching classes in logic. Writing logic primers. Treasuring memories of what her academic students were achieving in the world. Leaving Cambridge, 1916.

In a straightforward narrative that focuses on her intellectual development, Jones conveys her love of knowledge and her gratification at having instilled that love in her students. In the process she provides mini-portraits of notable educators of the late 19th century, including Emily Davies, Henry Sidgwick, and James Ward. She also offers a telling picture of what life was like in the early years of Girton, which was founded as a small college for women at Hitchin in 1869 and was transferred to Cambridge in 1873.

512 JOPLING, Louise (née Goode; Mrs. Jopling-Rowe). 1843–1933. *Twenty Years of My Life, 1867 to 1887*. John Lane, The Bodley Head, 1925. 343 pp.; illus.; index. NUC pre56 284:527.

Born in England. Parents not named. 2 brothers; 3 sisters. Married 1861, Frank Romer, civil service employee, secretary to member of

Parliament; separated; d.1871. Married 1872, Joe Jopling, artist, died. Married 1888, George Rowe. 2 sons; 2 daughters. Artist (painter); teacher (art); civil servant's spouse; feminist. Middle class.

Lively account of a lifelong commitment to independence, featuring author's professional accomplishments as an artist and observations on women's role in contemporary society, covering 1867–88. Marriage to Frank Romer, author's age 16. Moving to France for her first husband's civil service employment. Studying painting; working on her painting at home. Contrasting the English perspective on the social unacceptability of married women's working with the European view that women can carry on career and domestic duties simultaneously. Taking classes in life drawing. Births of her first two children. Returning to England. Exhibiting her painting *Pretty Polly;* its sale. Wanting to attend the Royal Academy; Royal Academy's not permitting women artists to paint or draw from nude models. Attending Leigh's School of Art. Grieving over the death of her son, 1869. Meeting artists Mrs. E. M. Ward and the Misses Mutrie at the Royal Academy. Painting *Hilda* and *The Mendicant;* selling her work. Birth of a daughter. Her husband's gambling; his deserting her; her being left with immense responsibilities. Providing the financial details of her artistic career; her husband's threatening to seize her paintings as his property. Considering divorce; obtaining a judicial separation from her husband to avoid complications of child custody questions; her worries about her lack of economic rights as a married woman in the days before the Married Women's Property Act. Enjoying her independence and her extensive social activities. Her husband's death in America, 1871; author's not wanting to remarry; death of her daughter the same year. Corresponding with watercolorist Joe Jopling; accepting his marriage proposal, 1872. Painting a huge canvas, *5 o'clock Tea*. Meeting Oscar Wilde; anecdotes of his visiting her home in England; their encounters in Paris; his discussing his work with her. Counting as friends many playwrights and artists, including painter Sir John Millais. Birth of another son. Continually sending paintings to the Royal Academy, 1870s. Her second husband's death. Being courted by George Rowe; marriage, 1888. Teaching art. Lobbying the Society of Portrait Painters to grant voting rights to women members.

Jopling's record of her development as a painter sets her firmly within the late Victorian art world and illustrates the strategies necessary for the woman artist to acquire an education, a reputation, and a profitable career in this milieu. Johnson and her female colleagues may have enjoyed more acceptance in this traditionally male profession than women in less creative fields, but gender discrimination still prevailed. In addition to the Royal Academy's prudery-based refusal to let women take life-drawing classes, male artists were slow to think of women as their peers.

513 JOSEPH, Helen (née Fennell). 1905–1992. *Side by Side: the Autobiography of Helen Joseph*. New York: William Morrow, 1986.

249 pp.; illus.; index. CBI 1987 p.1945. (1st pub. Zed Books, 1986.)

Born in Sussex. Father: Samuel Fennell, served in WWI. Mother not named. 1 brother. Married c.1931, Billie Joseph, dentist; separated c.1945; divorced 1951. 2 stepchildren. Wrote *If This Be Treason* (1963), *Tomorrow's Sun* (1965) about South African political conditions. Knew Nelson and Winnie Mandela, Bishop Desmond Tutu. Anti-apartheid activist; political activist; social reformer; prison inmate; political writer; foreign resident (India, South Africa); teacher. Middle class.

White anti-apartheid activist's education in England and her labor and political activities, with focus on the South African racial justice movements of the 1950s and 1960s, covering 1905–85. Life in England to age 22: recalling WWI London air raids, her convent school education, her Anglican confirmation. Attending King's College, University of London, 1923. Teaching at a girls' school in India, 1928–30. Moving to Durban, South Africa; teaching in a boys' prep school. Marriage, c.1931; instability of her marriage; author and husband's drifting apart, finding other companionship. During WWII, author's serving in the Women's Auxiliary Air Force. Earning a sociology degree at Witwaterstrand University; directing community centers for coloured people. Becoming secretary-director of the Medical Aid Society of the Transvaal Clothing Industry. Her labor union activity in the Transvaal; friendships with union leaders. Remembering the 1952 civil disobedience campaign of the African National Congress. Author's assisting in forming the South African Congress of Democrats, a white organization for universal adult franchise. Speaking at the 1955 Women's International Democratic Federation conference. Joining the white women's protest against taking the vote from coloureds, 1955. Organizing the Federation of South African Women; mass women's demonstrations, protests against extending the pass system to women. Her friendship with women's leader Lilian Ngoyi. Organizing black children's protests against second-class education. Her arrest for treason; trials of author, Nelson Mandela, and other opposition leaders, 1956–61; her acquittal. Issuance of a political banning order severely restricting her activities and associations, 1956–62; government's banning other political justice movements. Author's questioning her own commitment to nonviolence; endorsing tactical sabotage. Visiting banished people, seeking to aid their families. Organizing informal women's clubs. Being placed under house arrest, 1962–72; being the first to be so punished. Giving up political activity; feeling the stress of constant surveillance, threats, and harassment; enduring reprisals for publishing books about the South African political situation through English publishers; losing her job. Taking a theology degree by correspondence. Being hospitalized, undergoing surgery for breast cancer, 1971; public pressure's causing the suspension of her restriction order. Describing cases of other banned persons. Her informal political activity; her national university lecture tour. Renouncing her British citizenship for fear that she might be deported. Describing the 1970s escalation of political repression. Being briefly imprisoned after visiting banished Winnie Mandela, 1977; her friendship with both Mandelas. Professing socialism. Her second banning, 1980–82. Describing the resurgence of women's organizations and conferences, 1980. Author's returning to a deeper Christian faith and to public speaking, age 77. Commenting on the formation of the United Democratic Front. Discussing the necessity of political force by anti-apartheid groups, her white guilt, 1985 political and racial conditions.

This book constitutes a major source on anti-apartheid movements in South Africa, 1950–85. Joseph was a central figure in these movements, particularly as they involved women. She writes in a very straightforward and educated style in this memoir, which is full of details about her own life and those of political figures with whom she worked. The book is dedicated to Nelson and Winnie Mandela. In 1990, South African President F. W. de Klerk at last lifted the restrictions on Joseph—a release she somewhat resented, as it implied she was no longer considered a threat to the government.

514 JOWITT, Jane. 1770–?. *Memoirs of J. J., the Poor Poetess, Aged 74 Years...Written by Herself*. Sheffield: J. Pearce, 1844. 54 pp. BLC 1983 169:61.

Born in Dublin, Ireland. Father not named, Irish barrister. Mother not named, English. Stepmother not named, actress. 1 sister. Maternal grandfather: English surgeon. Married, husband not named, soldier. Married again, husband not named. Widow. Poet; domestic servant. Middle class.

Sensitive portrayal of author's overcoming her personal trials, accompanied by an account of her occupational and professional endeavors, covering her childhood to middle age. Father's philandering with an actress. Her mother's jealousy and unhappiness; her confinement to bed after the birth of author's younger sister. Father's telling mother that if she died, he would marry the actress; mother's increased illness and death. Author's having been taught to read and write by her mother; her doting grandmother's placing her in a boarding school run by Mrs. Knowles, aunt of playwright Richard Brinsley Sheridan. Father's marriage to the actress; his taking her to London, where she found it difficult to find roles; negative reports in the press about the scandalous circumstances of the marriage. Back in Dublin, author's experiencing the social stigma of being seen as a "player's daughter"; nonetheless working hard at her studies and moving to the head of her class. Death of her grandmother. Continuing at Mrs. Knowles' school; being happy there. Having no contact with her father for three years; his return to Dublin, author's age 12; his bringing author home to be a "sort of waiting maid to an actress." Stepmother's venting her violent temper on author. Her father's imprisonment for debt. Visiting her grandmother's trustee; his placing her in a boarding school. Author's coming of age and receiving the inheritance left her by her grandmother; taking a house and garden at the seaside; renting rooms to lodgers in summer; fending off improper advances from some of the gentlemen. Running low on funds; going to Liverpool to seek employment as an "upper servant"; finding her Irishness an impediment to employment. Going to London and Dover. Being courted by a young Irish soldier; marriage; living in Dover seven years; taking in needlework for officers' wives. Going to the Bermudas when her husband was posted there; working as a cook for a general's wife. Returning to England. Her husband's illness and death. Author's earning income by writing letters for people. Beginning to write poetry; selling her verses. Regularly attending church. Marriage to an older man; his using her money to support his alcoholism; his death from drinking. Writing memorial poetry on commission; expanding into commissioned poems on marriage and friendship; having a talent for touching people's sentimental tastes. Living off her literary efforts.

Matter-of-factly, with no sign of self-pity, Jowitt describes her difficult life. The account of her personal battle for respectability, particularly in overcoming the stigma of being related to an unrespectable actress, reveals some of the attitudes of her era toward social class and position.

515 KAYE-SMITH, Sheila. 1887–1956. *Three Ways Home: An Experiment in Autobiography*. New York: Harper & Bros., 1937. 258 pp. NUC pre56 291:119. (other ed.: Cassell, 1937.)

Born in Hastings, Sussex. Father: Dr. Edward Kaye-Smith, physician. Mother: née de la Condamine. 1 sister. Married 1924, Rev. T. Penrose Fry, Church of England, Roman Catholic convert. Wrote 31 novels, including *The Tramping Methodist* (1908), *Sussex Gorse* (1916), *Shepherds in Sackcloth* (1930), poetry, plays, and *Talking of Jane Austen* (1943)—literary criticism with Gladys Bronwyn Stern. Novelist; literary critic; poet; playwright; religious/spiritual writer; religionist (Roman Catholic convert); physician's daughter; clergyman's spouse. Upper middle class.

Exploration of author's imaginative life and spiritual quest, set within personal, familial, and professional experiences, spanning her late Victorian childhood to 1929. Her mother's Huguenot family history; her snobbishness; its effect on author. As a child, author's verbally composing (but not writing down) forty to fifty novels; at age 15, deciding "to lay down my tongue and take up my pen." Writing six novelettes a year. Using her Sussex background as material for thirteen later novels about Sussex and

Devonshire. Her early High Church leanings; her parents' opposition; her spiritual searching. Disliking school. Having her first publishing acceptance, of her novel *The Tramping Methodist,* at age 21. Deciding to write under her own name instead of a male pseudonym; briefly teaching at her old school as an "auxiliary teacher" to earn money to pay for having her manuscripts typed; her naiveté about publishing. Being taken for a suffragette by local people because of her "emancipated" novel; not objecting to the label until she was accused of burning down the Borough Member's house in Hastings, almost certainly destroyed by militant suffragists; her father's clearing her name. Her uneasy reaction to the war fervor of WWI. Her literary friendships. Marrying an Anglican clergyman, 1924. Their inclination toward Anglo-Catholicism; author's writing *Anglo-Catholicism* (1925). Her belief that England's peculiar ecclesiastical history has made the English neurotic on the subject of religion. Author's giving lectures promoting Anglo-Catholicism. Couple's feeling discouraged in their church work; defying bishop's directive against working with ultramontane Anglo-Catholics. Her recognizing Anglo-Catholicism's anomalous position relative to the Church of England and the Church of Rome. With husband, formally converting to Roman Catholicism, 1929; their resulting peace and happiness.

In an educated and literary style, Kaye-Smith expresses her self-awareness through her description of her inner spiritual journey. Interweaving her personal roles in religious and literary spheres, she offers much information about Anglo-Catholicism and Roman Catholicism in England. Following this first memoir, Kaye-Smith wrote more autobiographical works, focused around the themes of food (*Kitchen Fugue,* 1945) and reading (*All the Books of My Life,* 1956). A critical biography about her by Dorothea Walker was published in 1980.

516 KEELAN, Alice Jeannetta. c.1890–?. *In the Land of Dohori*. Sydney: Angus & Robertson, 1929. 302 pp.; illus.; app. NUC pre56 291:409.

Probably born in Australia. Parents not named. 1 sister. Married c.1919, Jack F. Keelan, WWI veteran, magistrate in Papua, New Guinea. Colonialist (New Guinea). Middle class.

Travel and personal experiences, as well as observations on native Papuan society, covering 1919–29. Using *Dohori,* a New Guinea exhortation to be patient, as a metaphor for her stay in Papua. Her fiancé's being stationed in New Guinea; author's traveling to meet him; their marriage. Describing Rigo, their first home. Her views of native servants: finding they lacked a sense of cleanliness, but preferring "to train an intelligent native rather than the average white girl." Deriving much amusement as a distant spectator of native court cases. Discussing native life, customs, superstitions. Growing to love Papua, but believing its beauty and charm cloak harshness and cruelty. Her husband's falling ill from the climate, becoming unable to work; their returning to Australia for his medical treatment. His new posting to Samarai, on the southeast tip of New Guinea; author and husband's chilly reception by a suspicious official; their resolving to be unobtrusive. Author's suffering an attack of dengue fever. Living in an island house; one servant's being "either a betel nut addict or a clod"; author's having to tend house alone, taking care of servants and husband when all became ill. Husband's being transferred to manage a government plantation at Kemp Welch River; her weariness at changing homes; moving to a farm near Port Moresby. Both author and husband's suffering a recurrence of fever; having difficulty finding treatment due to their isolation from the European community. Husband's having difficulties arbitrating with natives; his losing a court case against them, resulting in his loss of prestige. Giving up the plantation; their heading south to retire. Living in a damp, uncomfortable shack while waiting for a European-style house to be built; being shocked to find that construction would not begin for a year. Their deciding to leave New Guinea, but regretting having to abandon the natural beauty of the countryside.

Although Keelan was evidently moved by the lush physical beauty of New Guinea, she was unhappy with the physical conditions of life there. She tends to complain frequently about her native servants' shortcomings, yet professes that she has always "been keenly interested in the natives, and anxious to understand them and their points of view on matters in general." It is implicit in the narrative that cultural differences exacerbated Keelan's overall discomfort during the time she lived in New Guinea.

517 KEEN, Edith. c.1875–?. *Seven Years at the Prussian Court*. Eveleigh Nash, 1916. 315 pp.; front. port.; illus. NUC pre56 291:441. (other ed.: New York: John Lane, 1917.)

Probably born in England. Parents not named. 1 brother. Single. Governess; paid companion; foreign resident (Germany). Middle class.

Author's service as a royal governess at the Prussian Court, with unfavorable comments on Prussian nobility and the Kaiser in particular, covering 1909–16. Having worked previously for the Duchess of Northumberland. Wishing to travel; answering a London newspaper advertisement for a "dresser for a German lady," resulting in her first meeting Princess Friedrich Leopold of Prussia, who was in London incognito. Traveling to Berlin; meeting the princess's daughter, Princess Margarethe, in whose service Keen had really been engaged. Living with the family at the Klein Glieniche castle. Everybody's extreme dislike for the Prince and Princess Leopold, who knew of the widespread antipathy and consequently employed detectives to spy on the servants. Author's fondness for Princess Margarethe. Observing the harshness of Princess Leopold's behavior toward her daughter: restricting her movements, censoring her letters. Author's disbelieving rumors of an imminent Anglo-German war. Negatively characterizing the prince and princess: their violent tempers and quarrels, their paranoid suspiciousness, the prince's wife-beating. Relating stories about the Kaiser: his extravagance, rudeness, horror of feminism; author's wishing Christabel Pankhurst was there to reply to him. Noting the Kaiser's poor opinion of servants. Author's returning to England for several months after Princess Margarethe's marriage, 1912, then returning to the Prussian Court. Coming into possession of Princess Leopold's letters; wondering whether the princess was acting as a spy during her incognito visits to England; accompanying the princess on these visits; observing her relishing freedom away from her husband. Attending a gathering of German royalties in England, 1913; speculating that the Kaiser had arranged it; returning to Klein Glieniche at Princess Leopold's request. Author's attending socialist meetings there; the prince and princess's being terrified of socialism. Outbreak of WWI. Author's papers and letters' being searched; her being prevented from returning home when Germany and England declared hostilities. Being placed under military supervision; developing neuritis from the strain of internment. Being given electroshock treatment by a Berlin doctor. Receiving a letter from her seriously ill father; resolving to return to England. Belatedly receiving a passport allowing her to depart. Having her luggage, along with that of all the other English leaving Berlin, seized; giving up her gold but saving her jewels; returning to England.

Before marriage, Princess Leopold, for whom Keen worked, had been Duchess Luise Sophie Charlotte of Oldenburg. The Leopold family had extensive interconnections with the British royal family; Prince Leopold's sister Louise had married Queen Victoria's son Prince Arthur, thereby becoming Duchess of Connaught, while Prince Leopold's grandmother was Princess Victoria, Queen Victoria's oldest daughter. In this memoir, Keen is lavish with Court gossip and depicts the Anglo-Prussian tensions that would later surface during WWI. She writes warmly of Princess Margarethe, but evidently disliked the princess's parents. Although Keen defends those in Germany whom she loved against accusations of wartime aggression, she writes, "I feel that personal friendship between English people and Germans has become impossible. I prefer to think of my German friends as I think of the dead." Princess Leopold later wrote her own version of events in *Behind the Scenes at the Prussian Court* (1939), which is a useful complement to Keen's book.

518 KEIR, Thelma Cazalet. c.1900–1989. *From the Wings*. The Bodley Head, 1967. 208 pp.; front. port; illus.; index. NUC 1968–1972 49:498.

Raised in Grosvenor Square, London. Father not named. Mother: née Heron-Maxwell, suffragist. 3 brothers. Married 1939, David Keir, journalist. Edited *Homage to P. G. Wodehouse*. Politician; member of Parliament; feminist. Upper middle class.

Political formation and career of one of the first women Members of Parliament, from birth through middle age. Being shy and nervous around her father; adoring her mother, her first political heroine. Lacking a formal academic education; having French and German governesses. Forming feminist opinions, desiring a political career, by age 10. Finding a role model in her brother Victor (later a Conservative M.P.). Her closeness to David Lloyd George through friendship with his daughter Megan; being his "honorary daughter" and family confidante; analysis of Lloyd George's character and opinions. Enjoying the political mentorship of feminist Flora Drummond. Her friendship with P. G. Wodehouse's family. Serving on the Shipbourne Parish Council; winning election to the Malling District Council; serving on the London County Council. Her election as M.P., 1931. Making observations on the career of Prime Minister Stanley Baldwin. Playing tennis and golf. Marriage. Encounters with Winston Churchill; his painting her portrait. Highlights of her fourteen and a half years as an M.P. Her political protégés Sir Arnold Robertson and David Eccles. Traveling on wartime fact-finding missions and later to postwar Germany. Estimating that her speech on equal pay for men and women brought down the Baldwin government. Her work in passing the 1944 Butler Act, providing uniform schooling for both sexes. Describing the clubbish atmosphere in the House of Commons; women M.P.s being excluded. After her parliamentary career ended in 1945, organizing and running a commercial flower garden, raising blooms to be sold at market. Being chair of the Equal Pay Campaign Committee, 1947. Becoming a governor of the BBC, 1956. Confirming her faith in Christian Science, her parents' religion.

Focusing on the working relationships she developed during her public career, Keir gives intimate portraits of major political figures she knew well. Her book offers an inside look at British politics, exposing the workings of the House of Commons, in which women politicians were striving to be included in the first half of the century. The description of the author's political work for legislation ensuring equal rights for women makes absorbing reading.

519 KELLY, Ethel Knight (née Mollison). c.1879–?. *Twelve Milestones: Being the Peregrinations of Ethel Knight Kelly*. Brentano's, 1929. 240 pp.; preface; front. port.; illus.; index. NUC pre56 292:482.

Born in New Brunswick, Canada. Father: surname Mollison, cotton merchant. Mother not named. Married c.1896, husband not named, died n.d. Married 1902, Thomas Herbert Kelly, militia officer, amateur musician. 2 sons; 2 daughters. Wrote *Frivolous Peeps at India* (c.1910), *Why the*

Sphinx Smiles, *Zara*. Travel writer; journalist; short storyist; playwright; foreign resident (India); actress (stage); WWI volunteer; society woman. Upper middle class.

Personal and professional experiences of a multitalented woman, set within the social activities and concerns of upper-class British, Continental, and colonial society, spanning author's childhood to 1924. Family history. Father's being disappointed that author was female. Author's great fondness for her gregarious mother; her feelings of awe for her grandmother. Having Homer, Shakespeare, the Bible, German folklore, and Scottish ghost stories "crammed" into her head by her father before she was age 5. Attending school; wishing she had a private governess instead because her fellow students teased her; at age 14, receiving private lessons in painting, dancing, and French. At age 15, reviewing books for *James Hanney's Review*. Publishing a story in the *Scottish American;* winning a prize for a piece in *Short Stories,* a New York publication. Writing a three-act comedy, *A Mischievous Miss;* its being "gossipy and in bad taste," but produced in St. John, with the author in the title role. Her parents' sending her to Boston to attend Cowell's Art School. Marrying before her 17th birthday; her husband's untimely death. Resuming acting; defending the morality of actors; asserting morality to be personal, not professional. Touring the U.S. with a theatrical company. Having her play *Swords and Tea* produced in Montreal, 1902. Suffering from career-related nervous exhaustion; traveling to Australia for her health. Meeting Thomas Kelly in Sydney; her second marriage, 1902. Daily life, socializing in Sydney. Accompanying her husband on his appointment to India. Births of her children. Describing colonial life, socializing with fellow Europeans; author's sarcastic comments on Indian peoples, Hindu culture, and religion. Writing *Frivolous Peeps at India,* c.1910. Traveling to Paris with a maharajah; noting her husband's respect for all cultured people. Returning to England. Socializing with titled and other socially prominent people; attending races at Ascot. Taking an extended holiday in Europe. Returning to Australia; fundraising for the Red Cross during WWI; describing Australia's participation in the war effort. Returning to acting in England. Visiting South Africa. Traveling to Belgian battlefields, 1919. Traveling to Holland, France, and Italy with her children. Writing for the magazine *Smith's Weekly*. Visiting Egypt, 1923; history of its archaeological finds. Her intensive travel within England, 1924. Author and husband's deciding to live in Florence; details of their pampered life there.

Writing with zest and vigor, Kelly relates a life of extraordinary energy and eclectic variety. Her frequent use of dialogue makes her work both friendly and accessible. While the author often demonstrates cultural or class prejudice as she describes people and locales, her expressed opinions have documentary value for their characterization of upper-class social assumptions in the early years of this century.

520 KEMBLE, Frances Ann (Fanny Kemble, stage name). 1809–1893. *Records of a Girlhood*. New York: Henry Holt & Co., 1879. 605 pp.; index. NUC pre56 292:667.

Born in London. Father: Charles Kemble, actor, theatre manager-proprietor. Mother: Maria Theresa de Camp, actress. 2 brothers; 1 sister (opera singer Adelaide). Married 1834, Pierce Butler, American, Philadelphia businessman and Southern plantation owner; divorced 1848. 2 daughters. Wrote correspondence collection *Further Records* (1890), others. Knew Henry Ward Beecher, Margaret Fuller, Giuseppe Garibaldi, Bret Harte, Henry Wadsworth Longfellow, Washington Irving. Actress (stage); playwright; abolitionist; diarist; poet; foreign resident (U.S.). Upper middle class.

Author's youthful stage career and personal experiences within the early-19th-century theatrical milieu, covering her life to 1834. Father's being very indulgent of her. Mother's fortitude and stage career. Memories of her aunt Sarah Siddons, the 18th-century actress known as "the Tragic Muse." Attending school in Boulogne; disliking it; disliking aspects of London. Being rebellious; being shipped off to school in Paris as punishment. Acting in school plays. Returning to England, age 15. Suffering smallpox; its permanently damaging her complexion. Considering alternatives to becoming an actress. Writing verse drama. Pondering the difficulties of women's achieving success in the theatre, especially if they aspire to be playwrights. Memories of writer Anna Jameson and phrenologist George Combe. Her friendship with Lord Byron; recalling his poetic genius, his vices. Details of her parents' acting engagements. Author's triumphant debut in *Romeo and Juliet*, 1829; adjusting to having a large income and luxuries. Her love of riding. Friendship with Sir Walter Scott, an admirer of her acting. Excerpts from her journal concerning her social activities and professional engagements, 1831–33. Touring in the English provinces. Her father's closing his Covent Garden Theatre; performing there with him for the last time. Touring in stage plays in the U.S. with her father; keeping a diary of details of the visit and the living conditions, amenities, and social customs in New York, c.1833. Commenting on the American attitude toward Negroes, c.1830s. Discussing the Kemble family's history of supporting the antislavery trade movement in England. Finding American slavery intolerable. Meeting her future husband on a second tour with her father; Butler's elaborate courtship. His introducing her to Philadelphia society, convincing her to marry him and reside there; his not revealing to her his Southern slavery connection.

Kemble mingles personal information with glimpses of 18th- and 19th-century literary and theatrical luminaries. Partially reconstructing her autobiography from old correspondence and journal entries, she relies on the literary device of contrasting remembered youth and present old age. In this first autobiographical work she does not discuss the abolitionist activities for which she ultimately became best known. The history of her antislavery writing began with her 1837–39 creation of the *Journal of a Residence on a Georgian Plantation* (1863), which is generally considered her finest autobiographical writing. Her discovery that her husband owned over 650 slaves in Georgia distressed her, and she focused this distress into opposition to the system she experienced firsthand. Conflict with her husband over ideology, marital roles, and American slavery laws led to his divorcing her in 1848. She could not publish the *Journal* until her children were free of their father's custody. President Lincoln's agents pressed for publication of the *Journal* in the belief that it could help deter England from supporting the South in the American Civil War.

521 KENDAL, Dame Margaret (née Margaret Shafto Robertson; Margaret Brunton Grimston; Madge Kendal, stage name). 1849–1935. *Dame Madge Kendal by Herself.* Ed. by Rudolf de Cordova. John Murray, 1933. 314 pp.; front. port.; intro.; illus.; index. NUC pre56 293:110.

Born in Cleesthorpe, Lincolnshire. Father: William Robertson, actor. Mother: Margharetta Elisabetta Marinus, actress. 21 siblings (including dramatist Thomas William Robertson, actors E. Shafto Robertson and Fanny Robertson). Married 1869, William H. Grimston (stage surname Kendal), actor, d.1917. Widow. 5 children. Actress (stage). Middle class.

Leisurely personal and professional recollections of a theatrical leading lady, accompanied by candid views of life in the theatre, covering author's childhood to old age. Family history. Her close relationship with her father, who educated her at home and managed her career and finances prior to her marriage. Idolizing her mother. Making her stage debut at age 5. Appearing as the child Eva in *Uncle Tom's Cabin.* Performing in Hull and Liverpool. Beginning to dislike the press. Her friendships with Ellen Terry, Mrs. Charles Dickens, W. S. Gilbert. Recalling the Prince of Wales's Theatre under the Bancrofts' management. Becoming a theatrical star, age 17. Marriage, age 20; her husband's family history; his theatrical career. Finding her marriage emotionally fulfilling. Comparing real-life and stage emotions; believing most younger performers' acting styles to be insincere. Author's great devotion to her eldest daughter, Margaret; Margaret's disastrous marriage, which was annulled; her unexplained early death; author's great grief. Her mother's failing health and death; author's mourning her also. Discussing changes in props, from Victorian to modern theatres. Her husband's becoming comanager of St. James's Theatre; author's appearing with him in *Impulse*. Discussing the need for performers to observe life outside the theatre. Being the first woman actress to read a paper on drama at the Congress of the National Association for the Promotion of Social Science. Seeing playgoers as being responsible for moral degeneration in the English theatre. Appearing in a command performance for Queen Victoria. Touring in America; explaining differences in how actors are viewed in England and the U.S. Becoming the first woman member of the Savage Club. Growing interested in the case of John Merrick, the "Elephant Man"; helping him attend the theatre; helping raise money for his housing and care; corresponding with him. Her sense of great loss at her husband's death, 1917. Being made a Dame of the British Empire, 1926. Analyzing changing attitudes toward divorce; her strong opposition to divorce. Entreating actors and actresses to retain the high standards of the past.

Although Kendal demonstrates little interest in feminism or women's issues, the narrative of her ascending career is a woman's success story in itself, one enriched by her assessments of the popular plays and players of her time. Like most women of her era, Kendal did not control her own earnings; before her marriage her father managed her finances, and after her marriage her husband (noted for his business acumen) paid the bills, gave her an allowance, and established a fund for her retirement. The book's editor, a friend of the author, respected Kendal's wishes by leaving out many personal details of her life, particularly concerning her apparent estrangement from her surviving children. Kendal's earlier memoir, **522** *Dramatic Opinions* (1890), gives details of her career before marriage and includes many observations about acting and the theatrical profession.

523 KENNEY, Annie. 1879–1953. *Memories of a Militant*. Edward Arnold, 1924. 308 pp.; front. port.; foreword; illus. NUC pre56 293:378.

Born in Springhead, Lancashire. Father: Nelson Horatio Kenney, cotton mill worker. Mother: Ann Wood, cotton mill worker. 10 siblings. Married 1920, James Taylor, civil servant. 1 son. Suffragist, militant; mill worker; organizer (political); public speaker; prison inmate; Theosophist. Rural laboring class.

Recollections of the growth of the militant suffrage movement, together with the early work experiences of a champion of women's rights, covering 1880s–1924. Author's childhood schooling. Working half-time in a factory while attending school, age 10. Leaving school to work full-time in a cotton mill, age 13. Moving to the village of Hey, age 17. Having religious doubts, but nonetheless being confirmed. Becoming interested in the Labour movement through Robert Blatchford's *Clarion* articles, author's age 20. First meeting Christabel Pankhurst at Oldham Trades

Council, age 26. Author's organizing a suffrage meeting among women factory workers; serving on trade union's local committee. Frequently visiting the Pankhursts' home; leaving her work at the mill; becoming involved with the Women's Social and Political Union (WSPU) full-time. Delivering her first public speeches. Being ejected from a Manchester Liberal rally and imprisoned three days for creating a commotion over women's suffrage. Drawing inspiration to continue her agitation from Christabel Pankhurst's committed, determined character. Being ejected after raising the suffrage question at a London Liberal rally. Adopting Pankhurst's policy of pressuring cabinet ministers into publicly addressing the suffrage issue. Moving to London with Sylvia Pankhurst to begin a suffrage campaign, 1907. Commenting on how the movement aroused hope among East End women that suffrage would eliminate housework and poverty; author's realizing that these dreams could be fulfilled only in the distant future. Meeting and befriending W. T. Stead, newspaper editor and women's advocate. Meeting the Pethick-Lawrences; praising their contributions to the suffrage cause. Meeting militant suffragist Lady Constance Lytton. Demonstrating with her sister Jessie; consequently being arrested again and sent to Holloway Prison for two months. Traveling to Scotland to oppose Asquith's candidacy as prime minister. Enduring a third imprisonment after joining a protest in the lobby of Parliament. Recalling the first meeting of the Women's Parliament, 1907. Undertaking a speaking tour of Germany with Emmeline Pethick-Lawrence. Author's joining the Theosophical movement; Christabel Pankhurst's persuading her to abandon it. Suffrage movement's splitting over the Pankhursts' autocratic rule and extremism; Kenney's supporting Pankhurst. Author's undergoing her fourth imprisonment. Asquith's rejection of the Conciliation Bill that supported women's suffrage. Suffragists' increased militancy and consequent arrest of all the suffrage leaders except Christabel Pankhurst, 1912. Author's being put in charge of the WSPU administration while Christabel evaded arrest by going to France; author's visiting Pankhurst weekly. The Pethick-Lawrences' being expelled from the WSPU by the Pankhursts for having questioned the militant protest policy of destroying property and politically harassing suffrage opponents. Failure of another reform bill to extend the franchise, prompting arson protests; passage of the "Cat and Mouse Act," toughening punishment for suffrage militancy. Author's being newly arrested and imprisoned, 1913; upon release, testing new act's release policy; being rearrested; undertaking a hunger strike. Speaking at political meetings in disguise. WWI: the Pankhursts' calling for suffragettes to support the war effort. Author's traveling to the U.S. to assist the suffrage movement there; commenting on the plight of intelligent half-breed Indians; her opinion that "American women are not as free as British women"; stating that America projects a dream of prosperity but its poor are the most miserable. Returning to

England. The vote's being granted to women over age 30, 1918. Christabel Pankhurst's political campaign for a seat in Parliament; her defeat. Parting amicably from Pankhurst; praising her. Commenting on the concerns of women voters and what the suffrage movement had accomplished.

Invaluable for its documentation of the British militant women's suffrage movement, Kenney's account records the blow-by-blow campaign to win the vote. Kenney's temperament appears to have been romantic yet fearless, a combination that meshed well with the dauntless characters of the movement's organizers. A rare example of a working-class woman who rose to a position of prominence within the WSPU, Kenney does not directly address issues of social class in her memoir, but she does include much information about her experience as a mill worker and trade unionist and how that helped her to organize women politically. After her marriage, Kenney rejoined the Theosophical movement.

524 KENT, Madeleine. c.1900–?. *I Married a German*. George Allen & Unwin, 1938. 349 pp. NUC pre56 293:485.

Born in England. Parents not named. Married 1931, Hans, schoolteacher, member of German Social Democratic Party. Foreign resident (Germany); anti-Nazi activist; teacher; public speaker; broadcaster; nursemaid. Middle class.

In-depth look at post-WWI German society, including well-informed observations on dramatic political changes in Germany, spanning c.1926–38. Author's first visit to Germany, 1926; meeting cultured, idealistic Germans; her sympathy for Germany's position as the underdog since WWI. Working for three months as an *au pair* for a German manufacturer, 1928. Commenting on the success of the Nazi party in the 1930 election. In London, becoming engaged to Hans, a German citizen fifteen years her senior; his laughingly dismissing the importance of Hitler. In marriage registry office, being told that marrying a German would deprive her of British citizenship; shrugging it off; preferring to be a "citizen of the world" rather than a patriot. Lecturing at evening institutes in London. Fighting to have journalist recorded as her occupation on her new German passport; being told that in Germany no married woman has a profession. Moving to Dresden with her husband; her father's grief at her leaving England. Discussing class, social, economic, and religious tensions in Germany; the brotherliness of the working class; the noise of the socialist settlement where they lived. Taking a holiday; finding German country life coarse, even among families with money. Lecturing in Dresden on English letters. Recounting a neighbor's complaint that German wives are slaves and doormats. Giving her impressions of the Hitler Youth movement. Describing struggles between democracy and fascism; 1932 elections; Nazis' bombing leftist businesses; escalation of

Nazi terror. Seeking out a cosmopolitan circle of friends. Lecturing on English authors; referring briefly to English weaknesses; witnesses' later declaring that she had attacked England in these lectures; this saving her from being sent to a concentration camp. Broadcasting literary lectures in English on German radio. Describing Nazi schemes to deprive people of freedom, 1933; the passive solidarity of social democrats and Communists. Being unofficially spied upon by their neighbors. Lutheran pastors' nonresistance to Hitler. Writing letters to British authorities about German atrocities; having the letters seized by police spies; being watched by German officials. Losing friends to prison and exile. Her husband's being denounced by his sister; author's literary lectures being canceled; losing more casual friends. Realizing she would suffer from her husband's socialist ideals; husband's suspension from his teaching post. Moving to an isolated farm; their house's being searched repeatedly; landlord's threatening them by killing their cat, then bringing suit against them for slander when the author called him and his wife savages. Author's being acquitted on the basis of the "pro-German" statements in her lectures. Executions of members of leading families, 1934–36. Traveling to Prague. Returning to Germany; discussing Nüremberg laws against Jewish people; Dresden under Nazi rule. Author's giving English lessons to the daughters of a prominent Jewish doctor. Her husband's working for a travel bureau; author's leading tour groups. Author and husband's deciding to depart for England to escape the violent fate they saw coming.

In an educated, analytical style, Kent reflects on the social, cultural, political, and economic events in Germany that culminated in the Nazi takeover, and assesses the changes to the German character during this tumultuous period. Although not overtly anti-German, she often describes the national character negatively as she records how living in Germany stripped away her illusions about German idealism. Safe in England, she concludes her book by reflecting on humanity's future and its need to cherish civilization and internationalism.

525 KEPPEL, Sonia Rosemary (the Hon. Mrs. Roland Cubitt). 1900–1986. *Edwardian Daughter*. Hamish Hamilton, 1958. 212 pp.; front port.; foreword; index. BLC to 1975 173:144.

Born in London. Father: the Hon. George Keppel, Lord Advocate of Scotland, Mayor of Tower of London, 3rd son of the 7th Duke of Albemarle. Mother: Alice Frederica Edmonstone, daughter of 4th Baronet Edmonstone. 1 sister (Violet Trefusis). Married 1920, the Hon. Roland Cubitt, WWI military officer, eldest son of 2nd Baron Ashcombe; divorced. 1 son; 1 daughter. Wrote novel *Sister of the Sun* (1925), biographies *The Sovereign Lady: A Life of Elizabeth–Third Lady Holland* (1974), *Three Brothers at Havana in 1762* (1981). Novelist; biographer; WWI volunteer. Aristocracy.

Memories of growing up among the circumstances and people of the Edwardian upper class, spanning the author's first twenty years. Adoring her mother; admiring the beauty of her mother and her "pretty sister Violet"; her own physical plainness in contrast. Author's accidental fall and resulting lifelong disability. Suffering from asthma throughout her youth. Memories of the London family home in Bedford Square; being educated at home. Describing her godmother and other cherished adults. Recalling London at Christmas time; spending holidays with other families in England and abroad. Author's great appreciation for toys and beautiful clothes. Her family's social interactions with King Edward VII until his death in 1910. Accompanying her mother on a world tour, 1910. Attending school in Germany; spending a holiday with her mother at St. Moritz. Her parents' active social life; anecdotes of their friends: Duchess of Rutland, Sir Fritz and Lady Ponsonby, others. Trying to write a novel, age 14. Outbreak of WWI. Author's mother's helping to run a field hospital at Etaples; her father's volunteering to rejoin the army. Onset of the zeppelin raids. Her mother's giving luncheons for politicians, soldiers, and diplomats, 1915, while continuing to work in English and French hospitals. Author's helping at Lady Limerick's Canteen for soldiers; doing volunteer work as a pantry-maid at Russian Hospital for officers. Bad feelings existing between soldiers at the front and munitions workers; people at home undergoing food shortages and rationing. Her godmother's turning her house into a convalescent home for soldiers. Fondly recalling household servants, particularly the family butler; admiring her mother's ability to do without the services of her personal maid during the war. Corresponding with her cousin, Edward Keppel; falling in love with him; his death in the war. Her social debut. Enjoying dressing fashionably; persuading her mother to let her wear stylish gowns. Being "chaperoned" to a concert by General Curzon, who attempted to kiss her in the carriage; furiously fighting him off. Being presented at Court. Meeting and becoming engaged to Rolie Cubitt. Mother's ordering author's trousseau and arranging the wedding. Receiving luxurious gifts from both families. Commenting on chivalry toward women in the Edwardian age, on Victorian/Edwardian practices of child-rearing and discipline, and on the manners and morals of Victorian and Edwardian society.

Enlivened by touches of humor, Keppel's informal account summons a vanished era and the individuals who peopled it. Her evident admiration for her parents, especially her mother (who is painted in all the colors of beauty and goodness), stands out in this book. While Keppel recognizes that WWI affected her less keenly than it did others, she also sees the war as the dividing line between her girlhood and adulthood as well as the event that brought a gracious era to a close. For intimate details of Keppel's childhood, see **526** "The Tail," in *Little Innocents: Childhood Reminiscences,* ed. by Alan Pryce-Jones (1932).

527 KERSWELL, Kate L. 1871–?. *Romance and Reality of Missionary Life in Northern Rhodesia*. W. A. Hammond, n.d. 96 pp.; front. port.; illus. NUC pre56 294:438.

Born in England. Married J. A. Kerswell, Methodist minister. 1 daughter. Religionist (Methodist); missionary (Africa); preacher; clergyman's spouse. Middle class.

African experiences of a Methodist missionary couple, set amid author's observations about native societies in Rhodesia, covering 1908–12. Author and husband's deciding to evangelize in Africa; his taking a three-month medical course to prepare. Their journeying by train, then by native carriers to Nambala in northern Rhodesia. Their living at Nambala mission, learning Chila language. Mission's establishing a boys' school. Author's teaching a sewing class for women. Observing native men's ill-treatment of women. Being visited by other preachers in the missionary network. Famine's striking the region, 1909. Traveling by hammock to Broken Hill while sick and pregnant; birth of her daughter. Author and husband's stressing useful labor and literacy, and the need for missionaries to be pragmatic as well as spiritual. Their doing evangelistic and medical work at Nambala among the Baila tribe. Opposing African marriage and dowry customs because they were unfair to women; saving unwanted native babies from infanticide. Their founding the Kampilu mission station among the Batonga tribe, 1910; evangelizing there. Repeatedly criticizing native workers for their laziness and lack of initiative. Calling "grotesque" the native religious belief that some men transform into lions at will, yet wanting to show Batonga that the mysterious Being they feared was the same God served by Christians. Author and husband's being less concerned with converting Africans than with giving them a work ethic. After nearly five years in Africa, returning to England at the close of their missionary tour.

Both she and her husband were official Methodist missionaries with a strong sense of vocation, something that occasionally brought them into conflict with native porters and other servants over the issue of perceived native "laziness." Despite this perception (a common one among British citizens living in non-European cultures), Kerswell and her husband seem remarkable in that their concern for the natives' practical needs for literacy, food, and health care was apparently considerably greater than their desire to convert them.

528 KEYNES, Florence Ada (née Brown). 1861–1958. *Gathering Up the Threads: A Study in Family Biography*. Cambridge: W. Heffer & Sons, Ltd., 1950. 120 pp.; illus.; apps. NUC pre56 295:50.

Born in Manchester. Father: John Brown, Congregational minister. Mother: Ada Haydon Ford. 3 brothers; 2 sisters. Married 1882, John

Neville Keynes, Cambridge professor, registrar. 2 sons; 1 daughter. Wrote *By-Ways of Cambridge History* (1947). Social historian; politician (mayor); feminist; charitable volunteer; academic's spouse; clergyman's daughter. Upper middle class.

Four-generation biography of the first woman mayor of Cambridge and her immediate family, set against the backdrop of Cambridge history, spanning author's mid-Victorian childhood to the onset of WWII. Her mother's family history. Extracts from letters between family members. Her father's family and personal history; his career as a clergyman. Recalling her childhood in Bedford; Bedford's history and commerce; memories of the vicarage. Her mother's beginning a home school, taking in some students at a reduced rate since "love of education rather than financial profit" was her goal. Author's studying with tutors at this school; studying German in Germany. Her mother's determination that all her daughters would have the best education available to them. Author's attending Newnham College, the first women's college at Cambridge. Meeting her future husband at Cambridge; his family history. Marriage, 1882. Births of her three children; their early years; feeling bereft when all three were away at school. Recalling 1880s Cambridge: university traditions, circles of poets. Discussing changes in child education theories, 1890s. Visiting Germany. Her eldest son Maynard's foreign service work in India. WWI: her younger son Geoffrey's military service in France. Author's being nominated to the town council; helping to change the law that stated only householders could be on the council, since married women by definition could not be householders. Discussing the importance of the Sex Disqualification Act for women and of pro-women and children legislation enacted after WWI. Working on health care issues; serving as secretary of the Charity Organisation Society. Being the first woman to become an alderman, 1931, and later mayor, 1932, of Cambridge; outlining the mayoral duties. Serving for eleven years as chair of the Public Service and Magistrates Committee of the National Council of Women; serving as president of the National Council of Women of Great Britain for two years. Noting the history of Cambridge, from medieval times to the late 1930s.

The eldest of Keynes's two sons is the economist John Maynard Keynes, who wrote his first economic treatise while serving in the India office as royal commissioner on Indian finance. Her younger son is the art critic Geoffrey Keynes. Keynes was justly proud of her family, and interconnectedness between family members underpins this experiment in biographical and autobiographical form. Using a narrative method reminiscent of a family tree, Keynes organizes her book along generational lines, fusing the recorded lives of her forebears, her children, her husband, and herself into an organic whole. Accordingly, she tacitly displays her own life as the outcome of a familial process, and also shows the inseparability of her own noteworthy career from the fabric of Cambridge history. Although she neither employs feminist terms nor discusses women's suffrage, her support of pro-women's legislation and women's higher education demonstrates her feminist position and her contribution to women's advancement.

529 KEYNES, Margaret Elizabeth (née Darwin). 1890–1974. *A House by the River: Newnham Grange to Darwin College*. Ed. by Geoffrey Keynes (author's husband). Cambridge: Darwin College, 1976. 259 pp.; front. port.; preface; ed.'s note; illus.; maps; postscript; index. BLC 1976–1982 25:183.

Born in Newnham Grange, Cambridgeshire. Father: George Howard Darwin, scientist. Mother: Maud Du Puy. Grandfather: Charles Darwin, naturalist. 2 brothers; 1 sister (artist Gwen Raverat). Married 1917, Geoffrey Keynes, art critic. 2 sons. Educator; civil servant; WWI volunteer; nurse (WWI); secretary. Upper middle class.

Detailed presentation of family history, celebrated ancestors, and the founding of Darwin College, set amid author's personal memories, covering 1890s–1963. Family history. Memories of childhood excursions; her pet Muscovy ducks and Ralph the Rook; cycling with her family. Her mother's having been the first woman cyclist in Cambridge. Family's visiting the 1900 Paris Exhibition. Author's visiting Rome with her brother, 1912, while parents attended the International Geodetic Association conference. Feeling great love and admiration for her father. Studying history at Somerville College at Oxford, 1912. Father's falling ill; author's coming home to care for him; his death. Working as honorary secretary of the Cambridge Juvenile Employment Exchange, 1913. Being a part-time secretary for the Boys' Employment Registry. WWI: being trained as a volunteer nurse at Saint Chad's home for wounded soldiers, 1915; sketches of her patients. Remembering Belgian refugees in Cambridge. Meeting German naturalist Ernst Haeckel, 1916, at a Cambridge scientific conference that had been founded by her father. Working at a paid civil service job in London: decoding German messages. Becoming engaged to Geoffrey Keynes, the younger son of the Cambridge registrar, 1916; marriage, 1917. Their living in Blackheath, and later London; memories of family cooks and housekeepers. Author's mother's living with them; strength of her mother's character; her strong-willed nature. Her mother's death, 1947; its effect on author. The last Darwins at Newnham Grange: her brother Charles and his wife; his death, 1962. Founding of Darwin College, 1963.

In this engaging account Keynes recounts the history and notable achievements of members of her family. Her father, George Darwin, was the son of naturalist Charles Darwin as well as being a distinguished scientist in his own right; her husband (the editor of this memoir) was the critic Geoffrey Keynes. Keynes's recollections of her own life focus on her professional activities rather than on her intimate feelings. In the latter half of the book she includes more directly autobiographical material; in the first half she relies for family details on her sister Gwen Darwin Raverat's autobiography, *Period Piece* (1952).

530 KING, Dorothy Elizabeth "Viva" Leonora Ursula. 1893–s.l.1960s. *The Weeping and the Laughter*. Macdonald & Jane's, 1976. 248 pp.; preface; illus.; index. BLC 1976–1982 25:273.

Born in Mendoza, Argentina. Father: surname Booth, landed gentry. Mother: née Thomas. Maternal great-grandfather: Capt. Frederick Marryat, novelist. 2 brothers. Married 1926, Willie King, pianist, d.1963. Widow. Knew artists Nina Hamnett, Donald McGill, Nancy Cunard, Ivy Compton-Burnett. Governess; art dealer; costume designer; WWI volunteer. Upper middle class.

Frank personal memories of unconventional family life, with recollections of artistic and bohemian circles in England and Paris, spanning 1890s–1960s. Parents' family history. Her father's intense sexuality and sexual history. Resenting her mother's giving physical affection only to her sons; mother's wasting away from "an issue of blood" which she wouldn't discuss. Family's returning to Yorkshire, England, after eight years in Argentina. Mother's attempting to divorce father by proving his physical cruelty. With author in tow, mother's confronting and shaming father's mistress. Father's leaving the family; his living in Paris. Mother's being left sole caretaker of family. Author's being schooled at home by her mother, then attending convent schools in Bruges, Belgium, and Sussex. Being frightened by a schoolmate's telling her that if she did not menstruate before reaching age 10, she would become consumptive. Visiting her father in Paris; becoming interested in art through his knowledgeability and the talents of his famous artist friends; trying to avoid exciting her father sexually; fearing that he desired sexual relations with her. Working as a nursery-governess in Yorkshire. WWI: working in her mother's boarding house and doing volunteer work with the Red Cross. A woman friend's setting her up for a liaison with a military officer, author's age 24; staying with him at a Brighton hotel; painfully losing her virginity. Deaths of her parents: author's relief at her father's death, 1921; grieving at her mother's death, 1922. Receiving a large inheritance. Forming friendships within a bohemian circle in Paris: painter Augustus John, writer Clive Bell, others. Being briefly engaged to musicologist Cecil Gray. Marrying Willie King, a pianist; meeting his parents; their disapproving of the young couple's bohemian lifestyle; her father-in-law's becoming infatuated with her. Husband's domineering character; his alcoholism. Their money problems; solving them with an inheritance after her father-in-law's death. Her love-hate relationship with actress Olga "Oggie" Lynn, a lesbian who attracted heterosexual women; designing costumes for her stage productions. Designing costumes for other people; winning renown for her work. Dealing in art and antiques. Recalling WWII and the London Blitz. Her husband's death, 1963. Being deceived, seduced, and robbed by a con man. Recovering from a heart attack. Her disapproval of the permissiveness of the 1960s.

King's interest in art began before WWI, when she was in touch with her father's bohemian world in Paris; photos of her in this milieu establish the connection, which later led her to professional work as a costume designer and art dealer. Her preoccupation with sexuality is evident in her frank discussion of the sexual history of her own and her parents' generations, and in her portrayal of her father's erotic desires and their disastrous effect on her own developing sexuality. Her restless search for a vocation in adulthood was evidently a consequence of her rootlessness as a child.

531 KINGSTON, Gertrude. 1866–1937. *Curtsey While You're Thinking*. Williams & Norgate, 1937. 307 pp.; front. port.; preface; illus.; index. NUC pre56 297:51.

Born in England. 2 sisters; 1 brother. Married Capt. George Silver, Imperial soldier, d.1899. Widow. Actress (stage); suffragist; playwright; WWI volunteer; nurse (WWI); philanthropist. Middle class.

Spirited personal, professional, and travel memories, along with sharp and tender observations on English art and society, covering author's childhood to the mid-1930s. In childhood, traveling with her mother to a German spa for mother's asthma; having a chance meeting with composer Richard Wagner. Suffering from insomnia and emotional fatigue as a child. Describing her conventional Victorian upbringing. Studying drawing, elocution, and French with tutors; disliking the idea of school life. Her great love of art. Accompanying her sister Jackie to lectures at Bedford College at London University, age 13. Having her love of theatre awakened by seeing Sarah Bernhardt perform. Oscar Wilde's introducing author and her mother to Lily Langtry. Author's performing in W. S. Gilbert's *Broken Hearts* at age 15. Acting in private entertainments. Collaborating on plays with George Moore. Attending art schools in Berlin and Paris; describing the ostentatious conduct of female English art students abroad. Discussing the futility of the Boer War. Upon accepting Capt. Silver's proposal, deciding to act professionally to supplement their income. Marriage; her husband's career in India and East Africa; his sudden death, 1899. Ellen Terry's trying to dissuade her from going on the stage because of the difficulties of theatrical life for an unknown actress. At Terry's suggestion, going to Margate to study with Sarah Thorne at the Theatre Royal; performing in melodramas; hating the public's hunger for cruelty in these. Receiving favorable notices from American but not English critics. Acting in many George Bernard Shaw plays. Strongly supporting suffragists, but having a personal dislike of militancy, 1912. WWI: working as a volunteer nurse; traveling to New York to enlist American sympathy for England. Returning to the stage to supplement her income. Philanthropically opening a cheap kitchen for the working class in Bethnal Green; being forced by other café owners to close the kitchen because they feared the competition. Commenting on social philanthropy. Publishing articles in *Nineteenth Century* on state censorship of the stage. Having a premonition of her sister's death, c.1927; believing she is still visited by her sister's spirit. Her interest in parapsychology and post-WWI spiritualism; using the Ouija board to recall spirits of war casualties.

Recollecting an exciting life in the arts, Kingston portrays herself as one whose personality combines the supposedly opposing forces of personal rebelliousness and Victorian conformity. She apologizes in her text for writing it, declaring that autobiography should be left to those who really make history. Nevertheless, her account is not only biographically valuable, but also useful for social and theatrical research regarding the diversity of Victorian women's experience.

532 KIRBY, Georgiana Bruce. 1818–1887. *Years of Experience: An Autobiographical Narrative*. New York: AMS Press, 1971. 315 pp.; illus. BLC to 1975 175:71. (1st pub. G. P. Putnam & Sons, 1887.)

Born in Bristol, Avon. Father: Francis Bruce, sea captain. Mother: née Stradwick. Stepfather not named. 1 sister; stepbrothers. Married 1852 Richard Kirby, tannery owner. 5 children. Social reformer; emigrant (Canada, U.S.); teacher; governess; abolitionist. Middle class.

Personal experiences, professional endeavors, and observations on transcendentalism and American society by a teacher and social reformer, covering author's childhood to young adulthood. Father's death before author's birth. Her mother's remarriage; stepfather's spending the family fortune. Author's attending the village school. Her inclination toward nonconformity. Longing for her mother's affection; being disliked by her sister; sister's convincing her that she was ugly. Attending a boarding school. Having to leave school to help with the housework; later returning to school for one more year. Studying Anglican catechism; questioning accepted theology. Working as a governess in London, age 14; traveling to Canada with her London employers; being given farm duties to perform; teaching in a school founded by her employers. Describing the social customs and hard lives of Canadian settlers. Returning to England with her employers, then deciding to journey alone to the U.S. to seek work, age 19, because she felt "England was the very best place in the world for a rich person, and the very worst for a poor one." Obtaining a governess position in Boston. Her opinion that the class system was more rigid in the U.S. than in England. Feeling that men are interested in women only for their bodies. Making friends with the servants in her employers' home; coming to feel great respect for the American laboring class. Being affected by the religious and political ferment in New England; hearing talks by Ralph Waldo Emerson, William Ellery Channing, William Lloyd Garrison. Her interest in Unitarianism. Becoming a member of the newly formed Brook Farm Association, age 23; living there two years; attending the school; describing the communal lifestyle. Her memories of Nathaniel Hawthorne, Emerson, and other notables. Discussing children's education at Brook Farm. Corresponding with author Margaret Fuller. Working with Elizabeth Furnham on prison reform at the New York State women's prison at Sing Sing; describing the poor conditions at the prison. Teaching at Monticello Seminary in Illinois, then accepting a teaching position in Missouri. Her relationship with slaves; her increasing abolitionist tendencies. Discussing the discrepancy between how religion is taught and how it is often lived. Teaching the children of railroad navvies in Massachusetts; going on to teach public school in Pennsylvania. Attending an antislavery convention in New York; commenting on the Abolitionists Society. Moving to California, age 32; her observations on California "gold fever."

Kirby's account of her emigration to America reveals an apparently well-developed sense of independence and a genuine longing for egalitarianism. From her life at Brook Farm, her work in prison reform, and her contribution to the abolitionist cause, she stresses the social, rather than the theological, responsibility of religion. In addition, she is able to offer an insightful assessment of the characters of 19th-century literary and philosophical luminaries. After she arrived in California in 1850, the year her book ends, Kirby sought teaching work but found that her radical views offended some of the local community in Santa Cruz. Turned away from teaching, she found work helping fellow reformer Eliza Farnham run a ranch, and both women became notorious because they wore pants while working. In 1852 Kirby married a prosperous tanner, Richard Kirby, with whom she had five children.

533 KIRBY, Mary (Mrs. Gregg). 1817–1893. *Leaflets from My Life: A Narrative Autobiography*. Simpkin & Marshall, 1887. 244 pp. NUC pre56 217:340. (other ed.: Leicester: J. & T. Spencer, 1887.)

Born in Leicester, Leicestershire. Father: John Kirby. Mother not named. 1 brother; 3 sisters. Married 1860, Henry Gregg, rector of Brooksby, d.1881. Widow. Wrote, with her sister Elizabeth, *Things in the Forest* (1869), *Aunt Martha's Corner Cupboard* (1875), *The Sea and Its*

Wonders (1884), others. Children's author; short storyist; clergyman's spouse. Middle class.

Charming, detailed personal and familial memories of rural English life, author's writing career, and observations on varied aspects of society, covering her childhood to 1881. Her father's generosity and goodness; his keeping the children well supplied with books and teaching them to love libraries. Author's closeness with her mother. Attending day school; not enjoying the multiplication tables; recalling one teacher's telling exciting stories. Increasing precariousness of mother's health, author's age 18; mother's death; author's desolation at being abandoned. Assuming housekeeping duties with her sister Sarah, with the assistance of inexperienced servants. Her love for learning; attending lectures by Sheridan Knowles on drama, Mr. Jukes on geology, others; describing the role of the Mechanics' Institute, a local organization that provided lectures and entertainments for the public, 1840. Going on excursions to London with her father and siblings; recalling an uncle's work with the London Orphan Asylum. Learning about the deplorable conditions for London shop girls and for seamstresses in small workrooms. Noting the popularity of mesmerism; meeting practitioners. Father's depression and illness; his undergoing several operations; his death, 1848. Author's sorrow and anxiety about the future; author and sister Elizabeth's planning to write books together. Adapting materials from the classics for young readers. Their writing children's novels and short stories; publication of their books in London. Meeting Henry Gregg; feeling the "mysterious influence" of love every time they see each other. Their courtship and marriage, 1860. Residing in Brooksby parish with Henry. Husband's death, 1881.

Promising that her narrative is "faithfully drawn and uncoloured by the hand of fiction," Kirby produces a re-creation of rural 19th-century life that moves associatively from topic to topic. Her artful descriptions of everyday events in Leicester combine with her commentary on the issues and attitudes of her time to provide a rich portrait of her time and place.

534 KNIGHT, (Ellis) Cornelia. 1757–1837. *Autobiography of Miss Knight, Lady Companion to Princess Charlotte*. Ed. by Roger Fulford. William Kimber & Co., Ltd., 1960. 222 pp.; front. port.; intro. by ed.; illus.; apps. BLC to 1975 176:228. (1st pub. W. H. Allen, 1861.)

Born in England. Father: Sir Joseph Knight, rear admiral. Mother, stepmother not named. 2 half-sisters. Single. Wrote *Dinarbas* (1790), *Flaminius* (1792), *Sir Guy de Lusignan* (1833); *Translations from the German in Prose and Verse* (1812). Lady-in-waiting; translator; political writer; poet; novelist. Upper class.

Personal reminiscences and political and historical observations on contemporary English and Continental societies, spanning author's childhood to age 60. Family history; commenting on her paternal ancestors' attachment to the royalist cause under Charles I. Memories of her mother's generous nature. Author's attending primary school in Switzerland, age 5. Her mother's friendships with Thomas Gainsborough and Sir Joshua Reynolds; memories of Samuel Johnson and his ideas on social order and justice. Death of her father. Traveling in France and Italy with her mother, 1776 and 1785; noting aristocratic Italian fashions and social customs. Discussing the Italian common people's horror at the French Revolution; occupation of Rome by French troops, 1798. Living in Naples; evacuating due to the political situation; living in Palermo, 1799. Her mother's death. Advance of the French army. Author's moving to Vienna, 1800; meeting Haydn. Returning to England. Being appointed to Queen Charlotte's suite at Windsor. Diary extracts about social activities and the king's madness. Discussing the proposed regency and its political ramifications, 1812. Entering the service of Princess Charlotte (the queen's daughter) at Warwick House. Meeting the Prince and Princess of Wales; dining with Grand Duchess Catherine of Russia. Discussing personal conflicts within the royal household; Princess Charlotte's reluctance to marry the Prince of Orange; author's expressing her loyalty to Princess Charlotte, 1814. Commenting on England's peace with America at Ghent, 1815; popular discontent over the Corn Bill. Princess Charlotte's death, 1817; author's leaving to tour through France and Italy.

Knight's style is elegant and formal; she frequently cites French verse and prose. She reveals herself mainly through her observations about her travels. Apparently her central aim in writing was to record her experiences as lady companion to Princess Charlotte and the personal, as well as political, problems faced by the British royal family in the first two decades of the 19th century. She provides a conservative and articulate analysis of her world. Her memoir bears comparison with Charlotte Papendiek's *Court and Private Life in the Time of Queen Charlotte* (1887) and Catherine Cary's *Memoirs of Miss C.E. Cary* (1825).

535 KNIGHT, Doris (née Eades). 1917–s.l.1974. *Millfields Memories*. Centerprise Publishing Project, 1976. 38 pp. BLC 1976–1982 25:411.

Born near Hackney, Greater London. Father: surname Eades. Mother not named, saleswoman, charwoman. Stepfather: "Charlie," butcher. 2 brothers; 1 sister; 1 half-sister. Married 1939, Ted Knight. 2 sons; 2 daughters. Dressmaker. Working class.

Candid assessment of the author's early life within the confines of economic and familial problems, covering her childhood to the onset of

WWII. Friction between her parents; their separations; mother's always accepting father back. Home birth of author's younger brother; his death from pneumonia; her grief. Attending a local infants school, age 5; getting in trouble for talking too much. During one of her father's departures, living with her maternal grandparents in London; moving to Islington; attending school there and fearing rough students in the district. Her mother's illness; author's staying with her mother's sister; recalling her uncle as the "meanest man I ever met"; disliking her cousin, their son. Father's returning to the family home; their move to Southend; mother's taking in boarders for income. Anecdotes about boarders and maids. Birth of her sister. Father's abandoning family; author's writing a poem about this; continuing to write poetry on emotional issues. Their discovering that father had left with another woman. Author's admiration for her mother. Mother's taking the children to her sister-in-law's in London; living with this aunt, her husband, two sons, and paternal grandfather above a cobbler's shop; remembering the bad smell and cramped living quarters. Mother's finding some housecleaning work through her brother-in-law; having almost no income; her shame in applying for public assistance. Describing the scant items granted through assistance: sugar, tea, stale bread, a little rice. Author and her brother's attending school; describing the school system of advancement based upon exams. Joining children's clubs. Their returning to live with her mother's parents when the aunt and uncle moved. Death of her sister from measles, author's age 12; author's illness due to grief; spending three months in a convalescent home. Deciding to attend trade school to learn dressmaking. Her mother's taking an additional job to pay for author's extra lessons in French and drama. Finishing school, age 16; beginning to earn income. Family's move to a separate home with the financial aid of author and her brother. Mother's taking in boarders; her remarriage to a boarder; author's dislike for her stepfather. Working in a West End design house making dresses for royalty, age 19. Going to a holiday camp; meeting her future husband there; their four-year courtship. Marriage, 1939. WWII: her husband's being called up to serve in the army. Author's continued closeness with her mother.

Recalling the events of her life with apparent pleasure, despite the many adversities she and her family endured, Knight focuses on her mother's strength in preserving family unity, a strength that served as both example and objective for the independent-minded author. Despite her frequently blunt assessment of people and situations, Knight also uses her own poetry to express tender and reflective emotions. Her detailed descriptions paint a compelling portrait of working-class life in London in the early 20th century.

536 KNIGHT, Dame Laura (née Johnson; D.B.E.; Academician of the Royal Academy of Fine Arts). 1877–1970. *The Magic of a Line: The*

Autobiography of Laura Knight, D.B.E., R.A. William Kimber, 1965. 348 pp.; illus.; index. BLC to 1975 176:252.

Born at Long Eaton, Derbyshire. Father: Charles Johnson. Mother: Charlotte Bates Johnson, artist, art teacher. 2 sisters. Married 1903, Harold Knight, R.A., artist, died c.1962. Widow. Knew dancers Enrico Cecchetti and Anna Pavlova, impresario Sergei Diaghilev, poets W. H. Davies and Conrad Aiken, circus performers Joe and Ally Bert. Artist (painter); teacher (art). Middle class; married into upper middle class.

Artist's upbringing and her career in painting varied subject matter in Britain, the U.S., and Europe, 1877–1965. Her father's death shortly after author's birth. Childhood memories of her family life, growing up in Nottingham. Attending boarding school in France, 1889. Deaths of her mother and one sister; living independently with her surviving sister, commencing in 1893; discussing how this influenced her art. Moving with her sister to Staithes, c.1898; being mentored artistically by Charles H. Mackie; teaching art. Meeting Harold Knight, her future husband. Marriage, 1903. Living in Staithes and Cornwall, with extended stays in Holland, until c.1918. Moving with her husband to London, c.1919; author's working there on her artistic studies of backstage ballet and theatre, 1920s–1930s; becoming close to W. H. Davies, "the poet tramp." Between ballet seasons and theatrical presentations, author's traveling with and doing studies of Bertram Mills's circus. Visiting the U.S. in 1922 as a judge at an international art exhibition. Visiting again in 1926, with her husband, to draw and paint portraits of the "darkies" in the wards of Johns Hopkins Hospital. Her election as an associate of the Royal Academy of Fine Arts, 1927; receiving title of Dame Commander of the Civil Division of the British Empire, 1929; her recognition by the Royal Academy as an academician, 1939; her continuing association with Royal Academy activities. Painting gypsies camped at Iver, late 1930s. During WWII, painting portraits, landscapes, and posters for the British War Office; being sent to Nüremberg as a trial sketcher, 1946. With husband, after 1946, painting in London during the winters and spending summers in their studios at Colwall. Believing her 1953 drawings for the records at the Old Vic Theatre are her best work. Ending her memoir with general reflections on her life as an artist.

In a primarily conversational style, frequently using dialogue, Knight tells the stories behind her paintings. Occasionally her writing is poetic and elegant as she describes a setting of artistic significance. She uses vivid yet unaffected language, suggesting a higher level of education than she records in this autobiography. For the most part she describes events unsentimentally, but in the last two chapters she expresses warmth and humor toward family and friends. In an earlier autobiography, **537** *Oil Paint and Grease Paint* (1936), she discusses her artistic career, the subject matter of her paintings, and her social life.

538 KYNOCH, Anne (née Nichol). 1913–?. *The King's Seat.* Letchworth: Wayfair Publishers, 1966. 192 pp. OCLC #1713182.

Born in Scotland. Father: Sandy Nichol, shepherd. Mother not named. 3 brothers; 2 sisters. Married Robert Kynoch, physician, died c.1945. Widow. Nurse; milkmaid; domestic servant; physician's spouse. Rural laboring class.

Cathartic recounting of author's early memories of her life in Highland crofts, her beloved dead brother, and her cruel father, focused on her first fifteen years but including events to about age 32. Recalling the Highland landscape of her youth; life there with her mother and siblings. Author's love of reading; her affection for her teacher. At Christmas, becoming aware of her Catholic, impoverished family's difference from other families; unlike her Protestant classmates, receiving no Christmas presents from her teacher. Her closeness to her younger sister and elder brother. Recalling solitary games and pastimes on the moor. Author's strong sense of her Scottish identity. Death of her beloved brother from lung disease caused by his exposure to WWI gas; her anger at her mother for not allowing her to sit up with him the night he died. Associating "the king's seat," a grassy knoll on the moor, with her brother and with meditation and solitude. Offering a philosophic statement on heroism in ancient and modern warfare. Rebelling against her alcoholic, brutish father when he returned from working as a shepherd in the Falkland Islands; describing his cruelty to animals. Author's attending Catholic school; finding the methods of instruction there restrictive; returning to her old school. Family's unity in opposition to father. Author's ignorance of sex; her shock and horror at menarche. Mother's illness and death. Author's being determined not to go into domestic service. Leaving school; wanting to protect her younger sister from her father, but needing to find work; moving in with her brother and sister-in-law, but having fights with them. Finding work as a milkmaid, domestic servant, and probationary nurse. Becoming a qualified nurse and entering the nursing profession. Meeting a young doctor, her future husband. Briefly discussing their happy marriage and residence in Hull. Husband's death in WWII bombing; author's feeling consumed by grief and hatred; her withdrawing from the world. Returning to the king's seat on the Grampian moors to seek peace.

Kynoch uses dialogue, Scots dialect, and novelistic scene-setting. She does not say how she acquired the education necessary to write this book, but she does say that she loved to read, especially poetry. The setting is especially important, for the Highland moors gave Kynoch a sense of freedom and peace, and her text repeatedly returns to memories of this beloved landscape. She freely expresses her passionate hatreds and loyalties, which seem ultimately to have brought her more suffering than benefit.

539 LA CHARD, Therese (née Meier). 1874–?. *A Sailor Hat in the House of the Lord: The Autobiography of a Rebellious Victorian*. George Allen & Unwin, Ltd., 1967. 179 pp.; front. port. BLC to 1975 181:412.

Born in London. Father: Gottlieb Meier, merchant. Mother: Therese. Stepmother: Frieda. 2 stepbrothers. Single (but took Louis La Chard's name). Wrote *New Clothes for Old* (c.1917). Teacher; governess; socialist; political activist; ghostwriter; miscellaneous writer. Middle class.

Personal reminiscences set within framework of dramatic societal changes from author's late Victorian childhood to the onset of WWII. Reflecting on her father's early life in Bremen, Germany; taking holidays with him; studying music, a special interest of his. At age 8, first meeting her German stepmother. Experiencing austerity in family home after births of stepbrothers. Attending Bromley Public High School. Father's refusing to permit author to take university scholarship; his subsequent coolness toward her. Author's deciding to study in Bremen; attending teachers' day college there. Accepting job as governess in Warwickshire; returning to England. Losing governess post; teaching in church grammar school; moving to her own flat. Renewing her interest in Christianity and Christian teaching. Being transferred to teaching post in Chislehurst; attending teachers' training college in Chelsea. Reacting to outbreak of Boer War, 1898. Becoming disillusioned with Church of England concurrent with her increasing socialism; separating from Anglican church. Befriending Peter Kropotkin, Russian refugee and liberal anarchist. Meeting English socialist Fred Weeks. Becoming head of village school in Anstead Brook. Meeting Louis La Chard; her marriage (not formalized) to him; his departing to work in Nigeria; author's learning of his illness there; her assuming he had died. Author's moving to London and beginning her literary efforts. Preferring the socialist movement over the women's suffrage movement; participating in London political and social life. Teaching at Stockwell Training College. Responding to the outbreak of WWI. Death of her father. Learning about and meeting La Chard's legal wife; sharp emotional effect on author. Publishing bestseller *New Clothes for Old*. Joining Labour Party. Managing several London elementary schools successively and helping to establish Day Continuation Schools in London. Ghostwriting autobiography of Harry Gosling, Minister of Transport. Meeting Louis La Chard again in London; renewing her friendship with him; his departing permanently for medical post in the West Indies.

Author's traveling to Germany, 1933; encountering Hitler supporters; revisiting Germany, 1938, for family reunion.

La Chard's work testifies to the profound social changes which occurred between the time of her late 19th-century childhood and the period of rising Nazi power preceding World War II; in this regard her close German ties through her father's family have made her a firsthand witness. Hers is an intensely personal autobiography that both documents the difficulties of a self-supporting single woman during this changing era and reflects her emotional reactions to her personal troubles and those of society. Having first embraced Christianity and the women's movement only to reject these in favor of socialism, La Chard evidently dedicated her life to the causes—and the people—in which she believed.

540 LAKEMAN, Mary. 1911–?. *Early Tide: A Mevagissey Childhood.* William Kimber, 1978. 208 pp.; foreword; illus. BLC 1976–1982 26:350.

Born in Mevagissey, Cornwall. Father not named, fisherman. Mother: née Pollard. 7 siblings. Single. Knew Ann Treneer. Pupil; fisherman's daughter. Working class.

Finely detailed recollections of Cornwall in the author's youth, interspersed with personal memories and activities, covering her entire life but focusing on 1911–30. Describing working-class character of Mevagissey in her childhood; community's dependence upon and love for the sea. Family's living in poverty before WWI. Detailed description of her father's earning his livelihood by fishing, the family boat (the *Ibis*), the seasons for catching fish and how to clean them, maritime industries in the town. Mevagissey people's maintaining closeness of community and family life. Recalling marriages, illegitimate children in other families, weddings, and funerals. Being raised as a Wesleyan; Nonconformist Christian denominations' prevailing over Anglicanism in Cornwall. Describing house she lived in from birth to age 6. Remembering town's response to WWI. Explaining treatments her mother and local doctor used for various family illnesses. Author's lying to doctor when he asked if she was saved: "I was already an unbeliever." Discussing family neighbors. Death of her maternal grandfather; sketch of his life story. Entering school at age 4; hating its severity; her younger sister's rebelling against school for the same reason. Attending board school, age 7; describing its teachers and curriculum; despising her treatment there so much that she adopted as heroes Robert Owen and A. S. Neill, socialist leaders who were champions of the oppressed. Liking middle school better; having a favorite teacher. Family's greater prosperity after WWI, enabling father to buy a new house. Paternal grandfather's coming to live with family; his death. Character of local shops and shopkeepers. Attending Wesleyan Methodist Chapel; disliking evangelists who probed her soul. Receiving scholarship to St. Austell County School, age 12; discussing her schoolmates, teachers, and reading; St. Austell teachers and students' feeling that pupils from Mevagissey were inferior. Author's maturing mentally; her reading the Bible and English literature; loving hymns but deciding that religion and morality were separate. Recalling picnics, sailing trips, Christmas celebrations. Leaving home, age 18, with no knowledge of social class barriers; undergoing shock from her transition to the outside world. Father's death, 1930s. Her elder sister Edith's death, 1971. Noting the changes brought to Mevagissey by tourism.

In this nostalgic account, Lakeman attempts to re-create as fully as possible the essence of the traditional Cornish life of her youth. Her writing style is informal but her descriptions are meticulous; she discusses events, places, and people in a loose chronology, making reference to the Mevagissey of the 1970s but in general limiting her account to the period 1910–30.

541 LANCHESTER, Elsa. 1902–1986. *Charles Laughton and I*. New York: Harcourt, Brace, 1938. 269 pp.; front. port.; intro. by Charles Laughton; prefatory note. NUC pre56 313:594.

Raised in Clapham Common, Greater London. Father not named, accountant. Mother not named. 1 brother. Married 1928, Charles Laughton, actor. Knew author H. G. Wells, actors Fredric March, Jeanette MacDonald, Norma Shearer, producer Irving Thalberg. Actress (stage, film); teacher (dance); organizer (theatrical). Middle class.

Impressions from the professional life of an actress and producer working within theatrical and film circles in England and the U.S., highlighting career of her husband, covering author's childhood to 1936. Noting that Clapham was a "veritable breeding ground" for theatrical people. Family's moving constantly in author's childhood. Failing at local council school; being allowed to attend private boys' school with her brother for seven years. Attending Isadora Duncan's dance school in Paris, age 12; feeling silly there; being relieved to return to boys' school in England at outbreak of WWI. Taking classical dance in London; teaching techniques she had learned from Duncan to neighbor children. Giving dance classes at Margaret Morris's school in Chelsea, age 15; these classes' evolving into "The Children's Theatre." Operating a late-night play production club, "The Cave of Harmony," for two years. Securing her first stage roles; meeting Charles Laughton; marrying him with no thought of giving up her career. His career's "rocketing ahead," in contrast to her own. Their traveling to New York to produce a play; this trip's opening the door to Charles's film career. Their buying country cottage in England; returning hastily to U.S. and taking up residence in Hollywood. Author's perceiving Los Angeles and Hollywood to be "rather like a film set." Supporting husband's rise to stardom in films such as *Henry VIII;* becoming determined to revive her own career. Charles's winning an Oscar for his role as Henry; her own part in the film's securing her a contract with Metro-Goldwyn-Mayer. Lamenting the typecasting of actresses. Her film roles for MGM and Universal, including *The Bride of Frankenstein* (1935). Recalling her feelings of inferiority when she contrasted her looks with the glamour of Hollywood beauties. Returning to England while Laughton shot *Mutiny on the Bounty;* their readjusting to domestic life after the film was finished, c.1935–36. Their privately enjoying gardening and art collecting. Her appreciating their household servants, who were forced to cope with actors' irregular lives. Undergoing plastic surgery to repair facial scar from auto accident; worrying about possible disfigurement's effect on her career. Acting with Laughton in film *Rembrandt;* knowing that others believed her famous husband, not her talent, had secured the role for her; her resulting stress. Undergoing strain of premieres and publicity. Playing Peter Pan opposite her husband, who played Hook in J. M. Barrie's play; touring with company to toughen herself as an actress. Author and husband's starting production company partnership together; her analyzing closely the practical, moneymaking details of theatre and filmmaking.

Welcoming her readers behind the scenes, Lanchester describes how stars were really made in the 1930s. The author, who helped shape the movies of Hollywood's golden period, portrays herself as one whose interests centered on the very practical details of her husband's career and her own. Although this 1938 book is far from comprehensive, since both Laughton and Lanchester's careers continued for decades afterwards, it does offer a wealth of anecdotes about the inner workings of the film industry.

542 LANSBURY, Violet. c.1903–?. *An Englishwoman in the USSR,* Putnam, 1940. 325 pp. NUC pre56 315:509.

Born in England. Father: George Lansbury, founder and editor of the *Daily Herald,* Labour Party leader. Mother: Bessie. Siblings. Married 1926 Igor Mikhailovich Reusner, academic. 3 sons. Communist sympathizer; foreign resident (USSR); socialist; secretary; translator; editor; academic's spouse. Middle class.

Passionate rendition of pro-Soviet commitment and travel of leftist secretary and translator, including her family's political background, from her childhood to 1935. Her parents' political commitments; her father's editing a liberal newspaper and having considerable influence in the Labour Party; his being at heart a political agitator and idealist. Author's beginning her own political involvement with the Soviets; working as shorthand-typist and translator for the first Russian Trade Delegation in London, 1920. Working in the Soviet Embassy in London, 1920–25; sharing London flat with a socialist colleague. Moving to the USSR in 1925; her first impressions of the USSR. Attending university in

Sverdslosk, Siberia. Her parents' visiting her, 1926; her father's having previously visited Lenin and Stalin. Meeting Alexandra Kollontai. Author's believing Russian priest who tells her there is no religious persecution in the USSR. Working in office translating Young Pioneers' letters from Russian to English for British dissemination. Marrying a Soviet academic. Defending the USSR's economic, social, and foreign policy against those who have "lied" about it. Adopting a 12-year-old foster son. Pregnancy; giving birth in Moscow hospital; praising postnatal accommodations and child-care arrangements made by Soviet employers. Working as shorthand-typist in offices of the Communist International. Working as translator in a publishing house. Serving as interpreter to the British Delegation of Workers, 1932; discovering the Delegation's tour guide is a subversive. Returning to translation work at the publishing house. After second pregnancy, going into rest home. Returning to England, 1935, leaving her two sons to be educated in Moscow.

Writing in an educated, argumentative style, Lansbury ardently defends the Soviet political system. She appears willing to supply excuses for the system's inefficiencies and explains her acceptance of punishments for "subversives" as deriving from her desire to believe only good of the Soviets. Her father was acquainted personally with Lenin and Stalin in connection with his Labour Party leadership.

543 LARYMORE, Constance (née Belcher). c.1875–?. *A Resident's Wife in Nigeria*. New York: E. P. Dutton, 1908. 306 pp.; preface; front. port.; illus.; index. NUC pre56 317:67. (other ed.: Routledge, 1911.)

Probably born in Fasque, New Brunswick, Canada. Father: Rev. Andrew Holmes Belcher, Anglican vicar. Mother not named. Married 1897, Capt. Henry Douglas Larymore, British military officer in India, Sierra Leone, and Nigeria. Military spouse; colonialist (Nigeria, India). Middle class.

Cheerful observations on Nigerian culture and the imperatives of frequent travel by a military wife accompanying her husband's expeditions, 1902–06. Memories of life with husband on Indian military stations, c.1898–1901; their dislike of seven months' stay in Sierra Leone, 1901–02. Their departing for Nigeria, 1902; her being first Englishwoman to enter northern Nigeria. Their station at Lokoja; surveying the northern Nigeria-Lagos boundary together. Describing scenery, villages, native customs. Dishonest interpreter's inspiring author and husband to learn the natives' language. Returning to Lokoja; deaths of her dog and pony. Traveling upriver; visiting emir's harem at Bida and Hausa tribe. Her friendship with a consumptive native. Author and husband's apprehending slave traders on a survey march, 1903. Husband's being transferred to Nassarawa Province. Discussing the tragic death of Captain Moloney in 1902. Their returning to England; husband's receiving the Hausa Scholarship at Cambridge, 1903. Their residing in Scotland; returning to Nigeria, September, 1903; author's being first white woman to visit Kano. Their residing in Katagum; returning to Lokoja. Exploring further inland, 1904. Author's botanizing. Describing the graceful ease of Kabba women. Discussing Mary Kingsley's observations of West Africa. Husband's reporting an attack on a small British military patrol. Returning to England in the company of two Arab merchants, whom they dressed as Englishmen to make them less conspicuous. Returning to Nigeria, late 1904; husband's headquarters at Bussa; his inquiring into thefts, native witchcraft, and deaths of two British officers who were putting down an uprising. Moving to Bida, Nupe Province, then making final return to England, 1906. Author's giving household hints and advice to Englishwomen who may be posted in West Africa: caring for household goods, managing native servants, gardening, riding astride, not bringing pets, how to keep camp on the march, necessary goods, garments a woman should bring (including corsets, to keep up morale).

Larymore relates many informal anecdotes of Nigerian life. She displays an extensive knowledge of botany, often identifying plants by their Latin names. Her concern about the details of every aspect of home life in Africa is evident in her devoting the second half of the book to advice to Englishwomen obliged to relocate there; she warns of the natives' limited ability to carry out the demands of domestic service for English families.

544 LAWRENCE, Dorothy. c.1895–?. *Sapper Dorothy Lawrence: The Only Englishwoman Soldier, Late Royal Engineers, 51st Division, 179th Tunnelling Company, B.E.F.* John Lane, 1919. 191 pp.; front. port.; author's note; illus. NUC pre56 319:425.

Born in England. Parents not named. Orphan. Journalist; mine layer; soldier; cross-dresser; male impersonator. Lower middle class.

Young reporter's adventures at the WWI French front while impersonating a British soldier, 1915. Arrival at French base camp in Creil. Noting the attitudes of French soldiers and peasants; observing effects of war. Being assigned by English newspaper to cover French front; male reporters' having been forbidden access to the front. Obtaining uniform from Tommies in Paris; disguising herself as "Private Denis Smith." Traveling to Amiens on forged papers. Seeing homeless fugitives as another grim result of war. Describing physical layout of front lines, life in the trenches, and the sounds made by falling shells. Explaining system of laying mines. Observing how vital young soldiers at the front gradually, insidiously lost their spirits and health. Author's suffering fainting fits after ten days and nights of incessant fire. Working as a sapper, laying mines. Being discovered, denounced to British headquarters as a woman and possible spy; being arrested; journeying through France under armed guard. Being questioned at Third Army headquarters; proving she was a journalist; being allowed to travel to St. Omer. Returning to England; meeting Mrs. Pankhurst aboard ship. Enduring additional questioning at Folkestone.

In a readable and entertaining style, enhanced by a hint of "cheeky" humor, Lawrence presents a cavalcade of remarkable adventures that read like fiction. However, she assures the reader of the veracity of the events. Although the author limits her self-focus to her public roles as reporter and soldier, her ethical beliefs and personal empathy are evident in her asides about the abuses of war and the sufferings of war's victims.

545 LAWRENCE, Gertrude. 1898–1952. *A Star Danced.* New York: Doubleday, Doran, 1945. 238 pp.; illus. BLC to 1975 186:110.

Born in Clapham, Greater London. Father: surname Klasen, of Danish descent, actor under stage name Arthur Lawrence. Mother: Alice. Stepfather not named. Married c.1917, Frank Howley, director; divorced. Married 1940, Richard Aldrich, banker, American. 3 daughters. Knew Noel Coward, Douglas Fairbanks, Jr., Beatrice Lillie, Phyllis Dare. Actress (stage, film); nightclub entertainer. Lower middle class.

Light, witty account of author's rise to acting fame, interwoven with details of her service as WWII troop entertainer, 1898–1945. Childhood residence in Clapham; father as actor; his drinking; parents' divorce, 1899. Fond memories of stepfather. Earning money during her childhood by singing funny songs. Mother's sharing reminiscences of author's father's career; these anecdotes launching author's fascination with acting. Family's poverty; frequent moves. Author's stage debut, age 10. Maternal grandparents' encouraging her career. Attending dancing school in London; beginning her lifelong friendship with Noel Coward, a fellow pupil. At age 13, running away from home to live with her father; touring with him; becoming self-supporting. Landing a part in André Charlot's Revue during WWI. Understudying Beatrice Lillie; taking over Lillie's act as male impersonator when Lillie was injured. Reconciliation with her mother. Performing in nightclubs. Author's courtships. Marriage; birth of daughter; breakup with husband; retaining custody of baby. First U.S. tour with Charlot, 1924; tremendous success in U.S. Acting with Lillie in London and on second U.S. tour, 1925–29. Acting in *Oh, Kay!* and *Candle-Light.* Noel Coward's writing *Private Lives* for her; starring in it. Conflict between her desire to marry an American stockbroker and her desire to continue her career. Success of *Private Lives* in U.S. Her stage and film acting. British government's seizing all her property for unpaid income taxes on her American earnings. Her success in play *Susan and God.* Marrying a second time.

Returning to London, 1940, after six years in U.S.; touring with ENSA to entertain troops in England and Scotland. Contrast between British audiences of WWI and WWII. D-Day; entertaining troops in Normandy, 1944–45.

Lawrence stastes that her autobiography was prompted, by her gratitude to her American audiences. Details of her theatrical career during various stages—childhood, adolescence, and adulthood—dominate the text. She expresses delight in having had opportunities to show audiences her comic as well as dramatic talents, and in having had so many friends. Although she gives details of some roles and performances, she does not include an account of her parts in *Lady in the Dark* and *The King and I*.

546 LAYTON, Lizzie. 1855–d.a.1914. "Memories of Seventy Years," pp. 1–55 in *Life as We Have Known It by Co-operative Working Women*. Ed. by Margaret Llewelyn Davies. New York: W. W. Norton & Co., 1975. 141 pp.; ed.'s note; intro. letter by Virginia Woolf. BLC to 1975 78:2. (1st pub. Hogarth Press, 1931.)

Born in London. Father not named, government employee. Mother not named. 13 siblings. Married, husband not named, railway carriage cleaner. 2 sons. Knew Margaret Bondfield, Mary Macarthur, Margaret Llewellyn Davies. Nurse (maternity); midwife; trade unionist; philanthropist; organizer (philanthropic); domestic servant. Lower middle class.

Personal and vocational memories and political observations of multifaceted working woman, from her childhood to the beginning of WWI. Mother's continual pregnancies; their effect on author's view of maternity and women's role in the home. Description of family home in Bethnal Green; its unsanitary living conditions. Neighborhood epidemics of smallpox and cholera. Her father's industriousness and kindness. Author's observing sweatshop conditions in matchbox-making at friend's family home; charity of Sisters of Mercy toward workers; author's increasing awareness of mistreatment of workers. Her joyful first holiday in the country. Entering domestic service, age 10. Attending Ragged School at night. Babysitting at general shop where customers pawned household goods. Being confirmed in the Anglican Church. Memories of her godfather's cruel treatment of his pupils. Working as a housemaid in Hampstead and in Kentish Town, where she learned to read during children's lessons. Observing her employer's maternity care. Being dismissed from post for refusing to give up her day off. Courtships and marriage. Giving birth; her forceps delivery without anesthetic; one son's death in infancy. Her growing interest in social problems involving free education and trade union movement. Joining Women's Co-operative Guild; serving as president of Child's Hill Guild branch. Training and working as a midwife.

Making successful efforts to purchase a house; putting mortgage in her name despite husband's objection. Participating in campaign for the National Care of Maternity; representing the Guild to government ministers on behalf of unmarried mothers' right to public relief. Serving as Guild's national vice president. Organizing a Guild clothing club. Attending Co-operative guildswomen's conferences in Europe.

This articulate account reflects Layton's dissatisfaction with and bitterness about the austere living conditions of her youth, as well as her determination to create a better life for herself and other working-class women. Like many other poor women, she found it necessary to work after marriage; she also continued her political and social service. Layton concludes that education is workers' best equipment for economic betterment.

547 LE BLOND, Mrs. Aubrey (née Elizabeth Alice Frances Hawkins-Whitshed). 1861-1934. *Day In, Day Out*. John Lane, the Bodley Head, 1928. 264 pp.; foreword by E. F. Benson; apps.; index. NUC pre56 321:649.

Raised in Greystones, County Wicklow, Ireland. Father: Sir St. Vincent Bentinck Hawkins-Whitshed. Mother: Alice Handcock. Married 1879, Col. Fred Burnaby, military man, d.1885. Married 1886, J. F. Main, physician, d.1892. Married 1900, Aubrey Le Blond, Oriental porcelain collector. 1 son. Wrote *The High Alps in Winter* (1883), *True Tales of Mountain Adventure, The Old Gardens of Italy,* and *Cities and Sights of Spain.* Knew Margot Tennant, Lord Curzon, Ethel Smyth, Henry Edwards Huntington, others. Explorer; mountaineer; travel writer; philanthropist; military spouse; foreign resident (Switzerland); organizer of societies (cultural, women's clubs). Upper class.

Renowned woman mountain climber's narrative of Alpine exploration, with accounts of East Asian, European, and American travel; early upbringing, covering her childhood to c.1928. Father's death, c.1872. Author's receiving inadequate education. Making her London social debut. Marrying Burnaby, twenty years her senior; his military career and service as a *Times* correspondent with General Charles Gordon. Husband's campaigning for Conservative parliamentary seat in Birmingham. Author's pregnancy; birth of son. Becoming ill; traveling to Switzerland for her health, 1881; exploring Swiss Alps; ascending Mont Blanc twice and climbing other peaks, despite her family's disapproval. Publishing *The High Alps in Winter,* 1883. Husband's death in battle of Abou Klea, 1885. Marrying for the second time, 1886; residing at St. Moritz; her enthusiasm for competitive winter sports and mountaineering. Becoming an authority on snow photography. Organizing St. Moritz aid fund. Climbing mountains in Norway. Being widowed again, 1892. Third marriage, to Aubrey Le Blond, 1900. Their traveling to

China, Japan, and Russia, 1912. Their fleeing homeward from Germany on eve of WWI. Her volunteer hospital work in France during war. Visiting Ypres, 1919, and Morocco, c.1920. Traveling to U.S., 1922; her enthusiasm for Hollywood. Visiting Henry Huntington's famous estate and library in San Marino, California. Participating in founding of the Anglo-French Luncheon Club.

This autobiography includes much correspondence from the author's husband, family, and close friends, but Le Blond does not allow the correspondence to carry the thread of the narrative. The book's organization is loosely chronological, anecdotal, and associative, and its tone is modest; the author does not play up the fact that she was considered the greatest female alpinist of her day. Le Blond was instrumental in founding the Ladies' Alpine Club in London, of which she was president from 1907 until her death.

548 LE BRETON, Anna Letitia (née Aikin). 1808–1885. *Memories of Seventy Years, by One of a Literary Family*. Griffith & Farren, 1883. Ed. by Mrs. Herbert Martin (author's daughter). 198 pp.; preface; memoir of Gilbert Wakefield by Mary E. Martin; index. NUC pre56 322:31.

Born in London. Father: Charles Rochemont Aikin, publisher, educator, author. Mother not named. Great-aunt: Anna Letitia Barbauld. 3 sisters. Married Phillip Henry Le Breton, publisher. At least 1 daughter. Wrote *Memoir of Mrs. Barbauld* (1874). Knew Joanna Baillie, Anna Jameson, John Flaxman, Fanny Kemble. Biographer; publisher's assistant; society woman. Upper middle class.

Detailed presentation of family history, with particular attention to celebrated ancestors, relatives, and family friends, as well as author's personal experiences from her childhood to 1883. Maternal and paternal family history. Tracing her delicate health to lack of drainage and sanitation in family's house. Her longing to live in the country. Learning to read from her great-aunt, poet Anna Letitia Barbauld; great-aunt's friendship with Maria Edgeworth. Recalling family friend Joanna Baillie, father's relatives in Stoke Newington. Studying at home with her father and his eldest brother. Her upbringing's being a Victorian anomaly, as she lived entirely in her parents' quarters and not in a separate nursery. Disliking population density of London; longing for countryside. Wishing she had made better use of her home's intellectual environment. Celebrations following Waterloo victory. Recalling her relatives' meetings with celebrated writers: Harriet Martineau, Charles Lamb, Robert Southey, Samuel Coleridge, William Wordsworth, Mary Shelley. Taking summer holidays in England and Wales. Attending Society of Arts events with her uncle. Mother's and sister's deaths resulting from inadequate sanitation provisions in their house; author's leaving London after Mrs. Barbauld's death. Returning to Hampstead. Helping husband prepare memoirs of her great-aunts Lucy Aikin and Barbauld.

Formally written and primarily containing recollections of generational ties and stories about the author's family members and their circle of illustrious friends, Le Breton's narrative focuses more on her family's collective relationships than on herself. Still, the account shows its author possessed considerable esteem for intellectual accomplishments, particularly those of her notable great-aunt Barbauld. While providing considerable insight into Barbauld's character, Le Breton demonstrates how her own character was strongly influenced by that of her great-aunt.

549 LEE, Jennie. 1904–1988. *Tomorrow Is a New Day*. The Cresset Press, 1939. 264 pp. BLC to 1975 187:267. (other eds.: Farrar & Rhinehart, 1942; Harmondworth, Middlesex: Penguin, 1948.)

Born in Lochgelly, Fifeshire, Scotland. Father: James Lee, collier. Mother: Euphemia Greig Lee, hotelier, homemaker. 3 brothers. Married 1934 Aneurin Bevan, M.P. Wrote *Our Ally Russia* (1941). Politician; member of Parliament; feminist; socialist; teacher; public speaker; journalist; political writer; politician's spouse. Working class.

Working-class upbringing and resulting leftist political development of a Socialist member of Parliament, birth to age 35. Her childhood interest in religion. Being greatly influenced by father's socialist political convictions and teachings. Her parents and her grandfather Lee's opposing WWI, as did many Independent Labour Party members. Family homes' customarily serving as meeting places for union leaders; author's becoming aware when very young of the social and political factors impoverishing the lives of Scottish coal miners. Gaining her education in Fife schools and at Edinburgh University; having a nervous breakdown after cramming to pass university admission tests; serving up stinging criticism on the mindless rote learning required to secure a university degree. Her loss of religious faith after childhood leading her to agnosticism. Her brother's emigrating, like many other Scots and Irish people, because of economic hardships in the 1920s. Her father's being blacklisted after siding with his union in General Strike of 1926; his resulting inability to find work; his collecting strike funds in Ireland as official of Fife Miners' Union. Author's earning her family's bread by teaching. Being offered the chance to run as Independent Labour Party candidate from North Lanark in the 1929 Parliamentary election; death of the incumbent, precipitating a by-election in which she was voted into the seat; at age 24, becoming the youngest woman M.P. ever. Two years later, with the worldwide depression, the Labour government's being voted out; author's losing her parliamentary seat. Taking up new roles, touring on the lecture circuit in the U.S., Canada, Spain, and Russia. Deciding to support the Independent Labour Party after it split from the Labour Party, 1932. Having taken an LL.B. in 1927, planning to practice law; encountering sexist prejudice against her becoming a barrister. Marrying Bevan, Socialist M.P. and party leader. Second nervous breakdown, 1935. Expressing her personal and political alarm over Hitler's rise to power. Taking up free-lance journalism, late 1930s. Supporting the loyalist cause in the Spanish Civil War; advocating support of loyalists by the British government.

Lee's political and social chronicle of her life during the pre-WWII years is as passionate in tone as her politics; she declares, "Politics, for me, means the fight against poverty . . . for those who were the underdogs, mere workbeasts laboring for the greater glory and profit of a caste-ridden plutocracy." Reviewed in 1939 by periodicals on both sides of the Atlantic as a book embodying the spirit of British socialism, this memoir is nevertheless incomplete as a chronicle of its author's life, for Lee went on to gain parliamentary reelection—together with her husband—in 1945. This first autobiography largely omits particulars concerning her famous, controversial husband, their marriage, or her other intimate relationships. A sequel, **550** *This Great Journey* (1963), continues the story of Lee's life through WWII, describing her husband's and her own wartime political activities. **551** *My Life with Nye* (1980) is comparatively more forthcoming about Lee's intimate involvements, her married life and her feminist opinions in relation to her work, yet it focuses mainly on her husband's career, for she wrote the book as an apologia for Bevan (whose nickname was Nye), "to bury the vicious nonsense written about Nye during his lifetime."

552 LEFEBURE, Molly. c.1920–s.l.1994. *Evidence for the Crown: Experiences of a Pathologist's Secretary*. William Heinemann, 1954. 235 pp.; foreword by Dr. Keith Simpson; illus. NUC pre56 323:381.

Born in London. Father: Charles Lefebure. Mother: Elizabeth Cox. Married John Edward Gerrish, oil company executive. 2 children. Wrote *Murder with a Difference* (1957), *Samuel Taylor Coleridge: A Bondage of Opium* (1974), others. Secretary; forensic investigator; literary critic; journalist; crime writer. Middle class.

Experiences of a secretary to one of London's chief specialists in forensic pathology during WWII, 1939–c.1946. Taking secretarial courses; studying journalism at London University. Working as journalist for chain of East London daily newspapers, 1939–40. Forensic specialist Dr. Keith Simpson's asking her to become his secretary. Her wanting to observe postmortems; working with Dr. Simpson in London's public mortuaries. Serving as secretary to the Southwark mortuary keeper; for him, performing frequent investigative work on "murders, suicides, manslaughters, infanticides, accidents, criminal abortions, and unexplained deaths" during WWII. Seeing ten to twenty-eight dead bodies daily; in five years observing more than 7,000 autopsies. Giving details of autopsy procedure. At social functions, being jarred by other people's reactions to her work, but putting her job ahead of her social life. Describing the art of public executions. Attending wartime meetings of the Medico-Legal Society. Witnessing bombing of London by V-2s. Habitually keeping a diary; periodically burning it. Winning fourth place in a novel-writing contest, 1945. Leaving secretarial job to marry a WWII veteran who had been in India. Declaring herself to have been "undermined" by domesticity, although happy: "Murders are infinitely less exhausting than motherhood."

Although she states that some of her friends considered her forensic work unfeminine, Lefebure took an entirely matter-of-fact approach to it and saw her job as nothing terribly unusual or demanding. She went on to yet another career as a scholarly literary writer.

553 LE GALLIENNE, Eva. 1899–1991. *At 33.* Longmans, Green, 1938. 262 pp.; illus.; app.; Civic Repertory Record. BLC to 1975 188:19. (1st pub. 1934.)

Born in London. Father: Richard Le Gallienne, poet. Mother: Julie Norregaard, Danish journalist; charwoman, milliner after divorcing husband. 1 stepsister. Single. Wrote *Flossie and Bossie* (1949), *The Mystic in the Theatre: Eleanora Duse* (1966). Knew actors James Welch, the William Favershams, Constance Collier, Eleanora Duse. Actress (stage); theatrical producer; theatrical director; translator; foreign resident (U.S.); biographer; children's author; poet's daughter. Upper middle class.

Richly detailed discussion of career in acting, producing, and directing by one of the most prominent theatrical actresses of the 20th century, from her childhood to c.1934. Being brought up in a matriarchal household with strong, independent women. Growing up surrounded by literary and theatrical friends. Her unconventional, multinational, and multilingual upbringing in England, France, Denmark, and the U.S., giving her self-esteem and confidence far beyond other girls of her era. Attending College Sévigné, as well as Trees Academy (which later became the Royal Academy of Dramatic Art). Making her acting debut, age 15, in Constance Collier's company. Winning her first Broadway role, 1915; playing starring roles on Broadway, 1920s. Producing plays. Founding the Civic Repertory Theater, one of the first repertory theatres in U.S., 1926; learning valuable managing lessons in developing this theatre. Also founding a free acting school associated with her theatre. Having directed thirty-two plays by age 32. Her lifelong connections to theatrical friends and mentors. Providing extensive discussion of the technical side of play production and of her philosophy of acting.

Extremely well known as an actress, Le Gallienne was able to use this memoir to disseminate her concerns about the destiny of the theatre in America and the negative aspects of unionism in the theatre. However, the book's primary focus is on the philosophy of acting and lessons learned in the development of a repertory company. In **554** *With a Quiet Heart* (1953), a more formal presentation of her career, Le Gallienne stresses memorable performances, translations, and union difficulties. These books omit the author's personal life, including her notoriety in 1930 for her intimacy with a younger actress who divorced her husband; the press identified the two women as lesbians and the scandal almost ruined Le Gallienne's career. A useful biography of this author is Robert A. Schanke's *Shattered Applause: The Lives of Eva Le Gallienne* (1992).

555 LEHMANN, Liza (Elizabeth; Mrs. Herbert Bedford). 1862–1918. *The Life of Liza Lehmann: By Herself*. New York: DaCapo Press, 1980. 232 pp.; front. port.; illus.; afterword; index. NUC pre56 324:375. (1st pub. T. F. Unwin, 1919.)

Born in London. Father: Rudolf Lehmann, artist. Mother: "A. L." Chambers, artist. 3 sisters. Married 1894, Herbert Bedford, member of the City of London Corporation, journalist. 2 sons. Wrote *Practical Hints for Students of Singing*. Composer; singer (concerts); teacher (music); textbook writer. Upper middle class.

Personal and professional experiences of a distinguished composer, together with her observations on contemporary musical artists, from author's childhood through WWI. Father's being a native of Germany. Family's spending summers in Italy; having friendships with Liszt and Robert Browning. Parents' giving musical soirées in London. Author's studying with German governesses. Attending day school for a year. Her mother's great love of music; her urging author to become a singer. Traveling to Continent to study languages, art, music. Studying voice with Jenny Lind. Singing for Verdi in Genoa. Visiting Clara Schumann in Frankfurt; meeting Brahms in Schumann's home. Making her singing debut at Popular Concerts and Novello Oratorio concerts in England. Marrying Herbert Bedford, 1894. Illness's causing permanent throat damage, ending her singing career; developing a serious, compensatory interest in composing. Publishing successful composition "In a Persian Garden," 1896, and subsequent musical compositions based on the poetry of Tennyson and Yonge. Births of her two sons. Composing light opera based on *The Vicar of Wakefield*. Touring with company performing her works throughout U.S. and Canada, 1909. Becoming president of Society of Women Musicians, 1911. Publishing *Practical Hints for Students of Singing*. Relating assorted superstitions of musicians and singers. Describing her perceptions of cultural differences between Europe and the U.S. Teaching at Guildhall School of Music. WWI: her husband's entry into London Anti-Aircraft Corps; one son's joining Royal Military Academy; his death from pneumonia. Author's returning to composing.

Although Lehmann centers her memoir around the development of her personal art, her book is also dense with witty anecdotes about celebrated Victorian musical artists. The author has chosen to include many pages of laudatory press notices, which at times tend to detract from her other purposes. However, the book remains an excellent source of information on musical and artistic trends from mid-Victorian through Edwardian times.

556 LEHMANN, Rosamond. 1901–1990. *The Swan in the Evening: Fragments of an Inner Life*. Collins, 1967. 156 pp. NYPL to 1971 428:557. (other ed.: Virago, 1982.)

Born in Bourne End, Buckinghamshire. Father: Rudolph C. Lehmann, editor of *Punch*, poet, athlete. Mother: Alice Davis, American. 2 sisters; 1 brother. Married 1922, Leslie Runciman; divorced. Married 1928, the Hon. Wogan Philipps, artist; divorced 1942. 1 son; 1 daughter. Wrote *Dusty Answer,* six other novels, a book of short stories, and a play. Novelist; playwright; short storyist; spiritualist; clairvoyant/psychic. Upper middle class.

Childhood, marriages, and psychological development of novelist, including a description of how the death of her beloved daughter turned the author's main focus to spiritualism, 1901–81. Author's childhood memories of family and place. First experiencing rules in kindergarten. Being punished unjustly by nanny and French governess. Reading and writing poetry in childhood; at age 8, planning to be "a great poetess." Meditating on death and religion. Suffering vague night terrors. Undergoing a painful tonsillectomy. Family's going boating on the Thames; taking summer holidays on Isle of Wight. Receiving a university education. Marrying an atheist, age 21. At age 26, writing her first novel, *Dusty Answer,* an account of a young woman's sexual awakening and rejection of dependence on men; novel's eliciting a torrent of letters to the author from women. During writing of novel, author's longing for divorce. Discussing the craft and psychological motivations of fiction writing. Following her divorce, marrying an artist, also an atheist. Birth of her daughter, Sally, 1934; Sally's childhood and young adulthood; author's sadness after Sally's marriage and departure for Java; Sally's death from polio, 1958. Author's suffering nervous exhaustion and eruption of psychic dreams; her attempting to communicate with Sally beyond the grave. Writing an account of her mystical experience for the spiritualist journal *Light,* 1962; enduring dismayed reactions of conventional friends and family to her spiritualist interests. Serving as a vice president of the College of Psychic Studies. Exploring her growing interest in Jungian psychology and Christian mysticism. Addressing meditations on death and spiritualism to her granddaughter Anna.

The first section of this book covers Lehmann's childhood memories; the second concerns her early adulthood; section three deals with the life of her daughter Sally; the epilogue is a letter to her granddaughter Anna. Lehmann passes over the specifics of her university education at Girton College, Cambridge and barely mentions her marriages, as if both subjects had little relevance for her all-absorbing topic, the awakening of her spiritualist awareness. This book is of considerable interest in demonstrating how one woman's life events led her to the field of psychic studies.

557 LEIGH, Margaret Mary. 1894–s.l.1952. *Highland Homespun*. Phoenix House, 1948. 296 pp.; front.; foreword. NUC pre56 324:658. (1st pub. G. Bell & Sons, 1936.)

Born in England. Single. Wrote *Driftwood Tangle*. Academic; historian; farmer. Middle class.

Former Oxford lecturer's portrait of her life as a Scottish tenant farmer, emphasizing differences between rural and urban living, covering c.1930–36. Deciding to leave Oxford to farm in Scottish Highlands. Recalling her Oxford studies and work as university lecturer; her reasons for abandoning city life. Expressing her spiritual passion for nature. Describing farm tasks: plowing, caring for cows. Explaining advantages and disadvantages of keeping a bull. Characters of her neighbors. Coping with difficulties in being accepted as intellectual, outsider, woman farmer. Disliking materialism. Doing spring planting and sowing; reflecting on amount of work done by women. Likening differences between born and "converted" countrymen to differences between born and converted Catholics. Describing peasants and class distinctions. Understanding futility of living in the country without having a stake in it. Describing pastimes of West Highland people; their attitudes toward work and time; the atmosphere and activities of haymaking. Having succession of Oxford women students as helpers. Farm wives' being faced by special problems. Discussing various crops and autumn harvesting. Author's preferring country life to formal social life. Experiencing problems with her potato crop. Discussing decline of industry and reversion to agriculture in West Cornwall. Noting details of craft of weaving; Scottish tweeds. Disliking modern machinery but accepting it for its practicality. Reflecting on the insignificance of human effort compared to the eternity of nature.

Leigh's memoir supplies a vivid picture of the ordinary and extraordinary aspects of farming and country life. Her discussions of God, nature, and the growing materialism of urban living are self-revelatory. She demonstrates a thorough knowledge of farming and of the history and politics of agricultural society in Britain. Her sequel, **558** *Harvest of the Moor* (1938), elaborates on a farm in Cornwall where she crofted after leaving the farm described here. By 1940 she had moved back to the Scottish Highlands, and she discusses her WWII farm life in **559** *Spade Among the Rushes* (1949).

560 LEIGHTON, Clare. 1900–s.l.1941. *Tempestuous Petticoat: The Story of an Invincible Edwardian*. New York: Rinehart & Company, Inc., 1947. NUC pre56 323:687. (other ed.: Victor Gollancz, 1948.)

Raised in Berkshire. Father: Robert Leighton, writer, historian. Mother: Marie Connor, newspaper serial writer, novelist. 3 brothers. Married Noel, no surname given. Wrote *The Farmer's Year, Wood Engraving and Woodcuts, The Musical Box,* others. Artist; social historian; art critic; horticulture writer; novelist's daughter. Upper middle class.

Vivid memories of an unconventional home, set against the backdrop of a changing English society, covering the Edwardian era to the end of WWI. Her parents' writing habits; family life in St. John's Wood, London. Edward VII's being author's childhood idol. Her mother's unorthodox leanings: supporting women's suffrage, encouraging male admirers, displaying vanity, exhibiting snobbishness, and airing revisionist opinions on education. Edwardian street life: Punch and Judy shows, knife grinders, barrel organs. Family's visiting East Anglia each spring. Women's fashions, c.1908. Maternal grandmother's objecting to author's father's Unitarian family; mother's bullying author's father to convert to Roman Catholicism. Author's suffering from lack of communication with her mother; feeling awed by mother's literary accomplishments. Her aunt Sarah's expressing egalitarian social views; their influence on author in later life. Studying music. Attending dame school. Yearning to become a great painter. During WWI, family's suffering from financial stress. Death of brother Roland; its traumatic effect on mother. Mother's holding strong views on need for class distinctions, for lower classes not to rise above their station.

Leighton's style is eminently readable as she recalls the life of her authoritarian mother, but the mood of her book is subdued, and the author refrains from commenting on the maternal portrait she paints. Despite the nostalgic and humorous descriptions of various colorful relatives, the author's mother holds center stage while Leighton offers only glimpses of herself and of her own opinions. In an earlier book, **561** *Four Hedges: A Gardener's Chronicle* (1935), Leighton taps a lighter vein in endeavoring to prove the therapeutic value of gardening and the human need to work the soil.

562 LEITH-ROSS, Sylvia (née Ruxton). 1883–1980. *Stepping-Stones: Memoirs of Colonial Nigeria*. Ed. by Michael Crowder. Peter Owen, 1983. 191 pp.; preface; ed.'s intro. & note; illus.; maps; postscript; notes. BLC 1982–1985 7:83.

Raised in Pau, France. Father: Adm. Fitzherbert Ruxton. Mother: Sylvia Howland Grinnell, American. 1 sister; 1 brother. Married 1907 Arthur Leith-Ross, military man, colonial administrator, Scots-Canadian, d.1908. Widow. Wrote *Fulani Grammar* (c.1925), *African Women* (1939), *African Conversation Piece* (1944), *Beyond the Niger* (1951). Colonial administrator (Nigeria); linguist; cultural historian; WWI volunteer. Upper middle class.

Intermittent episodes of residence in Nigeria as linguist, amateur anthropologist, and colonial administrator, 1907–60. Residing as newlywed in Nigeria, 1907–08. Her husband; his military career. Her father's naval campaigns off the African coast; his having died when she was 12; his relatives in India and China. West African culture; appreciating local foods. Europeans' maintaining formal social customs in Africa. Enjoying tennis, polo, shooting, and fishing. Hiring a Fulani maidservant, a freed slave. Husband's death from fever. Returning to France; studying at the Ecole des Langues Orientales in Paris. Second Nigerian residence, 1910–13. Studying the Fulani language; traveling upriver. Living with her brother, who served in the Royal Niger Company, and his French wife, 1925. Publishing *Fulani Grammar*. Serving as secretary to the Lagos Board of Education, 1926; feeling useless in this bureaucratic position. Fourth Nigerian residence, 1934–37. Receiving Leverhulme Research Fellowship to study languages, 1934. Investigating causes of Aba Riots, or Women's War (a native women's protest against direct taxation). Studying Ibo women. Fifth residence, 1941–43. Assisting wartime colonial administration. Sixth residence, 1951–55. Author's unsuccessfully attempting to open finishing school for potential wives of educated Africans. Seventh Nigerian residence, 1956–60. Diary entries. Classifying pottery for a museum. Her personal belief in British civilizing mission in Nigeria and her admiration of British colonists for upholding social conventions. Seeing enforced idleness as cause of petty behavior among colonial wives. Discussing Nigerians' capacity for self-government; Nigeria's wartime economy; native Africans' beginning to question white superiority; church relations and strained race relations in 1950s.

In this book, which was edited posthumously, Leith-Ross reflects on and analyzes aspects of native and colonial society, particularly as they directly affected women of both cultures. This is an excellent source on British colonial Nigeria and its development into an independent nation. In an earlier book, **563** *Cocks in the Dawn* (1944), Leith-Ross describes her sixty-year love affair with France, focusing on her education there and her volunteer work with the Red Cross in France during both world wars.

564 LEJEUNE, Caroline Alice. 1897–1973. *Thank You for Having Me*. Hutchinson, 1964. 256 pp.; front.; foreword; index. NYPL to 1971 429:347.

Born in Manchester. Father not named, German emigré. Mother: née MacLaren, Scottish. 4 sisters; 3 brothers. Married c.1927, Rolfe Thompson. 1 son (E. Anthony, writer and broadcaster under name of Anthony Lejeune). Wrote novel *Equal Thanks*, and nonfiction books, including *Chestnuts in Her Cap* and *Cinema* (1931). Knew Alfred Hitchcock, Alexander Korda, Leslie Howard, Lord and Lady Astor. Film critic; journalist; playwright; screenwriter. Middle class.

Detailed recollections of youth and later education of film critic in days of both silent and early sound films, with discussion of major British studios and directors, covering author's childhood to age 63. Father's death before author's second birthday. Being raised by her mother. Attending grammar school at Lady Barn House; high school at Wittington Girls' School; winning school tennis trophies. Deciding to become a journalist while still a teenager. Disliking school, but loving to read. Attending Somerville College, Oxford, and Manchester University; receiving and rejecting a graduate scholarship. Working as film critic for the Manchester *Guardian*, beginning 1922; moving to the London *Observer*, c.1928. Describing silent, Swedish, and German films. Contributing to the *New York Times*, the *New Yorker*, and *Good Housekeeping*. Affinity for grand opera and tennis playing. Courtship and marriage; birth of son. Her friendships with Alfred Hitchcock, Leslie Howard, others. Liking the intimacy and informality of television. WWII's forcing British films to "pursue a purpose and develop a character." Founding her own amateur production company; describing plays produced. Writing plays for television; describing production techniques, camera moves. Author's feeling the impact of aging. Her shock at being "dropped" from *Observer* staff at age 63. Accepting honorary doctorate of literature degree from University of Durham.

Lejeune documents how she became interested in writing at an early age and pursued it as a lifelong occupation. Her narrative pays particular attention to the technical details of film and television production, and offers a comparison of the two media.

565 LEONARD, Gladys Osborne. 1882–1926. *My Life in Two Worlds*. Cassell & Co., 1931. 300 pp.; front. port.; foreword by Sir Oliver Lodge. NUC pre56 327:105.

Born in England. Parents not named. 2 brothers; 1 sister. Married Freddie Leonard, actor. Spiritualist; clairvoyant/psychic; vegetarian. Middle class.

Vivid and detailed account of personal and professional experiences in the world of psychic phenomena, spanning author's childhood to 1926.

Youthful love of reading. Having been raised in a rural area. At age 8, being greatly affected by death of a family friend. Attending High Church Anglican services during mother's illness. Remembering her childhood as a time of great personal distress. Experiencing waking visions. Family's living on false promise of an inheritance; discovery that there was no inheritance; resulting suicides of aunt and uncle. Father's becoming mentally unbalanced; author, mother, and three siblings' leaving father. Living in north country town. Secretly attending spiritualist services; experiences with a medium; mother's forbidding her to continue attending sessions. Training to be an opera singer. Having a bout with diphtheria, causing permanent loss of her voice. Having a clairvoyant vision of mother after mother's death. Marriage. Husband's sympathy toward spiritualism; sitting at séances with members of his acting troupe. Conducting experiments in parapsychological practices, some of them terrifying. Being possessed by spirit of an American Indian; receiving healing powers. Setting herself up as a professional medium, 1914. Communicating with spirits of soldiers killed in WWI and with her dead father. Her association with the Society for Psychical Research. While under anaesthesia for teeth extraction, becoming the vehicle for spirits of departed doctors, who commanded the doctor and dentist to give her more anesthesia. Describing her out-of-body experiences; having visions of people just before they died; visiting the "other world" where suicides and bad people go. Various psychic phenomena; her experiences with these. Admitting to one occasion when she was deluded, thinking she heard a spirit's shuffling feet but discovering it was the sound of steam escaping from a hot water bottle. Author and husband's becoming vegetarians based on her vision of slaughtered animals.

Offering a history of her own psychic experiences, Leonard works from her detailed knowledge of mediumistic techniques to advise readers on seeking a medium and on developing their own psychic abilities. Interestingly, she usually announces the discovery of a new power in herself soon after reading about it in other sources. Her one account of self-delusion suggests that she may have been more prone to it than she realized.

566 LEONOWENS, Anna (pseud.; Ann Harriett Edwards). 1831–1914. *The English Governess at the Siamese Court*. New York: Roy Publishers, 1954. 267 pp.; intro. by Leigh Williams; illus. NYPL to 1971 430:343. (1st pub. Boston: Fields, Osgood, 1870.)

Born in Ahmednugger, India. Father: Sgt. Thomas Edwards. Mother: Mary Anne Glasscock, possibly Eurasian. Stepfather: Patrick Donoughey, army officer. Married 1849, Thomas Leon Owens, clerk, d.1859. Widow. 2 children. Governess; teacher; foreign resident (Siam). Middle class.

Entertaining, highly informative record of personal and professional experiences, emphasizing author's tempestuous friendship with King

Mongcut of Siam, covering 1862–67. Arriving in Siam. Feeling discouraged because accommodations were not ready for her. First impressions of Court ladies (harem), her future students. Siamese history, culture, Court amusements. First impressions of king; beginning of their stormy friendship. Her balanced view of pagan beliefs. Friction with king over his reneged-on promise to give her separate lodgings outside Royal Palace. Teaching royal family; translating French documents for king. Reflecting on harem as institution; her liking for members of harem, desire to protect them; anecdote of concubine imprisoned for asking favor of king. Slavery in Siamese society. Favorably comparing Eastern religions, particularly Buddhism, with Christianity. Discussing Buddhism, other religious issues with king. Author indicting certain Siamese superstitions. King's character, administration, diplomacy. Clashes with him stemming from cultural, gender-role differences; her grudging respect and affection for him. Deciding to take leave of absence; king's initial anger. Sadness of royal family at her departure. Traveling through Cambodia.

Leonowens's now legendary friendship with the king of Siam (the basis for the play *The King and I*) forms the centerpiece of her work; her knowledge of Siamese history and of contemporary issues serves to enhance this portrait of that personal relationship. Although conscious of observing the Victorian proprieties, the author manifests a spirited independence and forthrightness which apparently endeared her to Siam's royal family and to its curmudgeonly, yet sagacious, ruler. Leonowens's book somewhat romanticizes and sensationalizes her experiences; her fabrications about such matters as her ancestry, her education, and how her husband died have been exploded in recent biographies of the king and of Leonowens's son.

567 LESLIE, Anita. 1914–1985. *The Gilt and the Gingerbread: An Autobiography*. Hutchinson, 1981. 195 pp.; illus.; index. BLC 1976–1982 27:214.

Born in London. Father: Shane Leslie, Grenadier Guards officer, writer. Mother: Marjorie Ide, American. 2 brothers. Married 1936, Paul Rodzianko, horse trainer, Russian; separated 1940. Married "Bill," retired navy man. 1 son. Wrote *The Fabulous Leonard Jerome, Jennie: The Life of Lady Randolph Churchill, Edwardians in Love, Madame Tussaud, Waxworker Extraordinary,* travel book *Love in a Nutshell,* others. Knew Lady Randolph Churchill and her son Winston Churchill. Biographer; travel writer; WWII volunteer. Upper class.

Ironic and witty portrait of author's social life and of societal changes, covering her birth to c.1939. Ancestry and family history. Living in U.S. as a small child. Father's WWI service; family's move to Ireland when he inherited Castle Leslie near Glaslough, Ulster. Resenting her controlling mother. Family's being visited by author's great-aunt, Lady Randolph Churchill. Moving to London due to Irish civil war, early 1920s. Their household servants. Recognizing social changes and problems people faced due to unemployment. Family entertainments. Attending convent school and lycée in Paris, 1923. Returning to England; attending day school in London. Political and social ramifications of the Division of Ulster into the Six Counties. Her distaste for hunting parties on her father's estate. Traveling with her mother to Algiers and the Sahara. Returning to London, then attending Paris finishing school. Commenting on homosexuality in English public schools. Author's London social debut; social life at aristocratic homes; presentation at Court. Dancing in C. B. Cochran's production of *Nymph Errant.* Admiring other girls' rebellious behavior. Her impressions of Edward VIII and Mrs. Simpson. Her first marriage; regretting decision to marry; family's cutting off her allowance. Outbreak of WWII: London blitz; volunteering for duty with Mechanized Transport Corps in Kenya. Women's WWII employment; social changes resulting from the war. Her views on the upper class: frivolous pursuits and lack of compassion being characteristic; men being considered more important than women; expectations for upper-class single women. Discussing marriage as an institution. Cultural differences between England and Ireland.

Expressing a witty, ironic view of life, Leslie sprinkles amusing anecdotes throughout this book. However, her account seems permeated by a veiled feeling of personal unhappiness and by resentment of her parents' coldness. She often takes the upper class to task, describing its values as superficial and trivial and bemoaning its lack of compassion for hardships endured by the greater portion of society. In another autobiographical book, **568** *Train to Nowhere* (1948), Leslie discusses her work as a WWII ambulance driver with the French army, including her experience with the British Auxiliary Territorial Service's unequal treatment of women, her journalism work in Beirut, and detailed accounts of Allied battles, the French Resistance, and the liberation of a Nazi concentration camp. Her friendly relationship with Winston Churchill figures in her understanding of the war.

569 LESLIE, Henrietta (pseud.; Gladys Henrietta Schutze, née Raphael). 1884–?. *More Ha'pence Than Kicks: Being Some Things Remembered.* Macdonald, c.1943. 254 pp.; front. port.; illus. BLC to 1975 190:161.

Born in Marylebone, London. Father: Arthur Raphael, businessman. Mother: Marianna Florette "Moll" Moses. Married 1902, Louis Mendl, grain trader; apparently divorced c.1912. Married c.1913, Harry Schutze, microbiologist, Australian. Wrote *Memories of People and Places,* over twenty novels, and *Where East Is West: Life in Bulgaria.* Knew Christabel Pankhurst, Olive Schreiner, John Galsworthy, Canon Richard

Sheppard, Vernon Lee, Florence White. Journalist; novelist; travel writer; suffragist, militant; social reformer; pacifist; charitable volunteer; feminist. Upper middle class.

Writer's youth and career in politics, suffrage and social reform, covering her birth to middle age. Being born into a world of prosperous Jewry from which anti-Semitism had receded. Recalling strict Jewish observances of her maternal grandfather's family; her indignation at Jewish customs she found degrading to women. Being confined to wheelchair after hip injury; her eventual recovery. Father's being dismissed from family firm after gambling losses; his death soon after. Mother's reduced income, emotional withdrawal from author; mother's studying painting in Paris. Author's foreign governesses. Making her social debut; being presented at Court. Having difficulty adjusting to first marriage. Domestic expectations of newlywed wives. Traveling to Romania with husband. Membership in Women's Social and Political Union; suffrage demonstrations; assisting with Christabel Pankhurst's militant activities. Suffrage movement's educational value for women. Leaving her first husband for good. Marriage to Dr. Schutze, c.1913. Her pacifism in response to WWI. Writing novels and plays. Commenting on critical disrespect given to women artists. Reporting for the Labour Party's *Weekly Herald*. Friendship with Canon Sheppard; joining the Church of England, but feeling an overpowering urge to proclaim her Jewish origin during the 1930s. Love of ballet. Novel writing as a profession. Charity work for the Save the Children Fund. Membership in PEN, the international writers' organization. Traveling to America, 1939. Outbreak of WWII: considering the war's impact on the future for herself and for civilization generally. Returning to England.

Leslie writes anecdotally and episodically, using much dialogue; her tone is generally upbeat and amusing. This is a good source on upper-middle-class Jewish life in England and on the suffrage movement. Leslie was active in politics, charity work, and journalism; her comments on sex roles reveal her discomfort with both traditional feminine domesticity and suffrage militancy. She followed this book with **570** *Harlequin Set: Holidays in Many Lands* (c.1945), about her travels in Europe, and with **571** *Go As You Please: Memories of People and Places* (1946), about overcoming her childhood hip injury, modes of transportation she used during her life, and traveling with her second husband.

572 LESLIE, Mary (née Martin). 1879–d.a.1967. *Through Changing Scenes*. Youlgrave, Bakewell, Derbyshire: Hub Publications, Ltd., 1975. 90 pp.; front. port.; preface by Robin Gregory; illus. BLC 1976–1982 27:216. (1st pub. 1972.)

Born in Hull, Yorkshire. Father: Rev. Canon Martin, vicar. Mother: Mary Lunn. 6 brothers; 3 sisters. Married 1913, Norman Leslie, Australian, bank manager, Shell Oil Company executive. 4 sons; 1

daughter. Health administrator; midwife; feminist; foreign resident (China); clergyman's daughter; philanthropist. Middle class.

Vivid personal, professional, and travel experiences, interspersed with insightful observations on social problems, spanning author's childhood to 1913. Family history. Father's appointment to vicarage of Stockton-on-Tees. Being brought up with strict economy and discipline. Needy people in parish. External social problems being the focus of interest in clergyman's home. Changes in home comforts over the last 100 years; working conditions for small factories and workshops. Factory owners' flouting laws regarding workers. Poverty resulting from workers' large families and employers' iniquity toward workers. Social ramifications of alcohol abuse among lower classes. Changes in women's attitudes toward learning. Attending school; her schoolmates. Attending Queen Victoria High School. Attending Queen Victoria's Diamond Jubilee. Stockton's architecture, farmers, market day, shopkeepers. Accompanying her father on walking tours in England and Europe. Attending Durham University. Studying at Royal Sanitary Institute. Working for Stockton Public Health Office. Infant mortality statistics, 1902–67. Conducting house-to-house inspections; unsanitary conditions of poor people's homes. Training as midwife. Appointment as inspector of midwives in Public Health Department, Oxford. Working with Oxford Voluntary Health Society. Social life at Oxford. Engagement to Norman; traveling to India and Burma; arriving in Canton. Wedding day preparations. Husband's appointment as branch manager in Tientsin.

Primarily focusing on her Victorian childhood and on her work as a public health inspector—an untypical occupation for a "respectable" lady—Leslie unsentimentally catalogues social problems without assessing any undue blame to poor people themselves. Her chatty, sometimes humorous anecdotes enliven the work, and her character and strong social conscience emerge clearly. In **573** *Changes and Chances* (1981), Leslie tells more about her travel experiences and philanthropic activities in China from 1913–35, interspersing her personal memories with keen observations about China's postwar changes.

574 LESTER, Muriel. 1883–1968. *It Occurred to Me*. Harper Brothers, 1937. 281 pp.; apps. NUC 328:461. (other ed.: Student Christian Movement Press, 1939.)

Born in London. Father: surname Lester, businessman. Mother: Rachel. 4 siblings; 2 stepsisters. Single. Knew Gandhi, Jane Addams. Philanthropist; missionary; religionist (Christian Scientist); teacher (Sunday school); socialist; pacifist; public speaker; WWI volunteer; organizer (religious). Upper middle class.

Professional experiences of a public-spirited woman, set within a personal, spiritual, and social metamorphosis, spanning her childhood to 1935.

Paternal family history. Attending Presbyterian and Church of England services. Early curiosity about East End dwellers; being told these people were at fault for their own problems. Closeness with her father. Attending preparatory school, St. Andrews. Her attitude toward poor people dramatically changed by reading Tolstoy's *The Kingdom of Heaven Is Within You*. Attending a party at girls' club in East End; learning East-End etiquette. Family's taking a holiday on French and Italian Riviera. Keeping house for her brother. Traveling to Palestine. Being introduced to Christian Science. Teaching boys at Loughton Union Church. Her increasing concern about the contrast between rich and poor. Wanting to acquaint the affluent with problems of the poor. Setting up teetotalling public house for teaching Bible studies. Outbreak of WWI: starting women's adult school, opening Kingsley Hall Fellowship Centre, embracing Christian Socialism and pacifism. Women suffrage leaders' helping in East End during war. Author's speaking on behalf of socialist candidates. Helping establish International Fellowship of Reconciliation. Creating Rachel Cottage, a meditation chapel, on her family property with the emotional and financial support of her father. Supporting "voluntary poverty" movement. Forming the Brethren of the Common Table. Chairing Maternity and Child Welfare Committee. Creating London's first Children's House. Going to India, meeting Gandhi. Discussing Indian customs, superstitions, clothing; European discrimination against native peoples. Arranging Gandhi's visit to England. Opening temporary school and clubs for men and women. Visiting America to lecture about London's East End. Friendship with Jane Addams. Financing world tour by lecturing in America. Visiting cooperatives and Christian commune in Japan. Visiting the Soviet Union. Working with National Preaching Mission in Montana. Political situation in Ireland; the Black and Tans. General Strike, 1926.

Through her well-balanced mixture of personal feelings and objective reporting, Lester brings to life the problems of poor people, pointing up the similarities of difficulties endured by the lower classes everywhere. Largely unsentimental, she includes generally poignant anecdotes which nonetheless offer glimpses of her humor and irreverence. Her memoir presents her highly personal metamorphosis into a crusader for the causes of social justice and reform. In the process she also conveys a great deal of information about major social issues of the early 20th century.

575 LETHBRIDGE, Mabel. 1900–?. *Fortune Grass*. Geoffrey Bles, 1934. 238 pp. NUC pre56 328:574.

Raised in Ireland. Father not named, WWI soldier. Mother: Florence. Maternal grandmother: Countess Sergardi, Italian. 2 brothers; 3 sisters. Married 1922, Noel K.; separated 1924. 1 daughter. Munitions factory worker; estate agent; entrepreneur; domestic servant; disabled woman; transient. Lower middle class.

Author's early education, loss of leg in factory explosion, and struggle to regain independence, covering her childhood to 1926. Traveling with family to Mombasa, Kenya, to visit father, 1907. Traveling from there to Italy to visit maternal grandmother, then returning to England; author's illness. Family's move to Ballinhassig, Ireland, 1909. Receiving lessons from village schoolmaster. Attending convent school in Cork. Residence in Peake, 1912–15. Mother's illness, 1913. Being expelled from Irish boarding school after complaining about school to mother. Attending London day school for one year. Working eight months as London hospital nurse, 1917. Working at London munitions factory without mother's knowledge; dangerous working conditions. Being severely injured in factory explosion and losing her left leg, 1917. Undergoing operations, hospitalization, slow recovery. Experiencing difficulty in getting workers' compensation. Obtaining a job as a lady's maid. Mother's objection to author's working as domestic servant. Running away from mother. Her homelessness in London; friendships with homeless women. Life in WAAC shelter. Friendship and love affair with "Daddy," an older man, c.1919. Their faking job references, securing jobs as cook and butler at a hunting lodge. Aborting their unborn child at his insistence. Being briefly married to her lover's nephew; husband's drunkenness, instability, cruelty, and violence. Living in London again. Birth of her daughter. Separating from husband. Hiring out chairs to queues of theatregoers. Overcoming threats to chair rental business by gangs. Ex-husband's departure for Ceylon. Opening estate agent's office, 1926.

Lethbridge writes in an informal style; her tone is straightforward, devoid of self-pity. She avoids giving many details of her early childhood, but does discuss her munitions factory work and her encounters with the London underworld. In her sequel, **576** *Against the Tide* (1936), Lethbridge recounts her struggles to support herself and her daughter: hiding from her ex-husband when he threatened to kidnap their daughter, undergoing bankruptcy and repaying her debts, enduring suicidal feelings at the time of her mother's death, and eventually recovering her financial independence by becoming an estate agent.

577 LEWIS, Agnes (née Smith). c.1843–1926. *In the Shadow of Sinai: A Story of Travel and Research from 1895 to 1897*. Cambridge: Macmillan & Bowes, 1898. 261 pp.; front.; intro.; illus. NUC pre56 330:348.

Raised in Scotland. Parents not named. 1 (twin) sister (scholar Margaret Dunlop Smith Gibson). Married 1887, Rev. Samuel Savage Lewis, of Corpus Christi College, Cambridge, d.1891. Widow. Wrote *How the Codex Was Found: A Narrative of Two Visits to Sinai from Mrs. Lewis's Journals, 1892–1893* (ed. by Margaret Gibson), others; edited and translated *Some Pages of the Four Gospels Retranscribed from the Sinaitic*

Palimpsest, A Palestinian Syriac Lectionary, Select Narratives of Holy Women, others. Biblical scholar; translator; traveler (Greece, Egypt). Middle class.

Biblical scholar's travels with her twin sister and their major discoveries and analyses of ancient manuscripts, 1883–97. Traveling with sister to Greece, 1883. Unsuccessful attempt to visit Convent of St. Catherine, Mt. Sinai, 1886. Marriage, 1887; traveling with husband; his death, 1891. Sisters' decision to travel to Sinai and seek Syriac manuscript at convent, 1892. Learning Syriac through prior knowledge of Hebrew and Arabic. Learning to photograph manuscript pages. Traveling to convent in Sinai; sisters' discovery of an early and important codex of ancient Syriac Gospels in convent library, 1892. Returning to England. Their second journey to Egypt, 1893, accompanied by Cambridge scholars. Publishing their discovery at Cambridge, 1894. Third journey to Egypt, 1895: traveling by camel caravan, sleeping in tents. Bedouin tribes' customs and attitudes. At convent, further deciphering palimpsest; discovering previously unrecorded words in John 4:27. Traveling to Syria and Lebanon. Returning to England; publication of revisions to transcription. Fourth journey to Egypt, 1896; traveling on horseback to Jerusalem; buying a manuscript there; returning to England. A textual expert's identifying the manuscript as a fragment of original Hebrew Ecclesiasticus. Author's suffering from illness with rheumatism. Two visits to Egypt, 1897: buying another manuscript in Cairo. Returning to England.

The author's education is apparent in her style, which includes Greek quotations and also shows touches of light humor. Her own photographs illustrate the text. The story of Lewis's travel and historic discovery is inherently interesting, and her satisfaction in her research is evident. This is an important contribution to the field of biblical textual scholarship.

578 LEWIS, Edith Nicholl (née Bradley; E. N. Ellison). c.1850–?. *As Youth Sees It: Personal Reflections of Great Victorians*. Boston: The Meador Press, 1935. 187 pp. BLC to 1975 191:189.

Born in England. Father: George Granville Bradley, headmaster of Marlborough, head of University College, Oxford. Mother not named. 1 sister; 1 brother. Married, husband not named. Society woman; historian; philanthropist; academic's daughter; editor; horsewoman. Upper middle class.

Reminiscences of leisurely, comfortable Victorian youth, spanning author's childhood to the 1880s. Father's appointment to Marlborough; his religious views. Riding with him; her skill as a horsewoman. Family's receiving distinguished guests: Alfred, Lord Tennyson, William Gladstone. Studying music and German in Wiesbaden. Duties at Oxford as daughter of a college head. Memories of Charles Lewis Dodgson (Lewis Carroll), George Eliot, and Mary (Mrs. Humphry) Ward. With her uncle and sister, founding and reviving the *Miscellany* magazine for distribution among friends. Mother's contribution to founding Oxford Day School. Praising Octavia Hill's reform policies; working with charitable society based on Hill's guidelines. Memories of American society woman Mrs. Huntington Wolcott; staying in her home near Boston; her influence on author. Differences between English, American customs of behavior for young men and women. Assessing distortion in historical perceptions of Victorian women; her belief that middle-class women were able to receive fine educations. Changing fashions for men and women, 1850s–1880s.

In an informal, occasionally witty style Lewis records her memories, providing little intimate information and focusing instead on exploding myths about Victorianism. Although she chooses to ignore class differences, she does substantiate her overall view that there are many historical misperceptions surrounding the Victorian era and women's role in it. Her memories about some of that age's scholarly and literary luminaries often include glimpses into their characters and idiosyncrasies.

579 LILLIE, Beatrice, Baroness Peel. 1898–1989. *Every Other Inch a Lady*. Garden City, NY: Doubleday, 1972. 360 pp.; illus.; aided & abetted by John Philip; written with James Brough. BLC to 1975 192:268.

Born in Toronto, Canada. Father: John Lillie, served in India under Lord Kitchener, Irish. Mother: Lucy Ann Shaw, English. 1 sister. Married Sir Robert Peel, 5th baronet, later 1st Baron Peel. 1 son. Knew André Charlot, Fay Compton, Gertrude Lawrence, Noel Coward, Ivor Novello, Fanny Brice. Actress (stage, music hall, radio, comic); broadcaster; cross-dresser. Middle class; married into aristocracy.

Spirited recollections of a celebrated and varied theatrical career, interspersed with observations on a changing society, covering author's childhood to 1972. Prophecies of doctor and parents at her birth concerning her success. Telling fibs as a child to get what she wanted. Singing to earn nickels and dimes to buy admission to movies. Attending boarding school and public school; being unhappy and naughty in school. Witnessing incident of indecent exposure. Her mother's ambitions for daughters. Attending different churches due to mother's social ambitions. Being enrolled in acting lessons by her mother. Touring Ontario in a stage act with mother and sister. Moving to England. Attempting a career as a serious singer. Being discovered by André Charlot; acting in his vaudeville revue. Performing as male impersonator. Dressing in male clothing in London. Frantic gaiety of London night life during WWI. Courtship and marriage. Husband's gambling and overspending; quarreling with him. Her friendship with understudy Gertrude Lawrence. Pregnancy and child-rearing; her unhappiness that her career separated her from her son. Her strong belief that a mother should raise her own children. Leading separate life from husband; her emotional distance from him; learning about his mistress. Success of her New York revue, 1923, and of London revue, 1926. Residence in and impressions of Hollywood. Husband's death, 1930s. Author's desire not to marry again. Evading censorship of her radio performances. Undergoing gynecological operation. Entertaining in WWII troop hospitals. Death of son in WWII. Giving a command performance for the Queen. Being told by P. L. Travers that she was the inspiration for *Mary Poppins*.

Lillie's droll sense of humor seems to allow her to avoid explaining much about difficult relationships in her life; for instance, she tells little about her marriage, obscuring the reasons she and her husband drifted apart. She describes her memory as "notoriously erratic," which may be her tongue-in-cheek euphemism for some selective and artful misrepresentation.

580 LINTON, Alice. 1908–s.l.1970s. *Not Expecting Miracles*. Centreprise Trust Ltd., 1982. 79 pp.; intro. by Jean Milloy and Rebecca O'Rourke; illus. BLC 1982–1985 15:86.

Born in Hoxton, Greater London. Father not named, carman for a furniture business. Mother not named, uniform ironer, worker in upholstery factory. Stepfather: Jim. 3 brothers; 1 sister. Married 1928, John Linton. 1 daughter. Factory worker; laundry worker; nurse. Working class.

Assessment of author's childhood in poverty, her schooling, and her employment prior to marriage, 1908–28, with observations on 1970s working-class conditions. Mother's childhood and family; author's childhood fear of mother. Father's youth and family history. "Cot death" (crib death) of author's baby brother. WWI food shortages. Mother's work ironing uniforms. Father's unwillingness to share food and money with wife and children. Air raids. Eating free soup at a Ragged Mission. Parents' spanking author and her siblings. Attending Anglican parochial school. Author's closeness to her brother Albert; their being unattended after school. Childhood games and pastimes. Being sensitive about wearing secondhand clothes. Her attachment to Sunday school teachers. Feeling love and envy for the middle class. Author's rheumatic fever and resulting long hospital stay. Enjoying sea holiday provided through the school's Country Holiday Fund. Joining Girl Guides; attending a girls' private boarding school in Berkshire as part of a Girl Guide activity. Leaving school at age 14. Picking hops to earn extra money. Working in upholstering factory where mother worked. Working in a laundry. Neighborhood characters. Criticizing urban renewal's destroying her community. Father's illness and death from consumption. Going cycling with her future husband. Their saving money to pay for wedding. Mother's remarriage; stepfather's turning mother against author and her fiancé. Author having motorbike accident, causing postponement of her wedding. Marriage. Quarrels between parents-in-law.

Linton's plain writing reveals neither introspection nor a high degree of education, but the author does reflect on the lives of the people she knew in her youth, contrasting them with those of the same class in the 1970s. In 1960 Linton realized her ambition of becoming a nurse, but she does not discuss this in her autobiography.

581 LINTON, Eliza (née Lynn). 1822–1898. *The Autobiography of Christopher Kirkland.* Richard Bentley, 1885. 3 vols. Vol. 1: 297 pp.; preface. Vol. 2: 302 pp. Vol. 3: 320 pp. NUC pre56 335:108.

Born at Keswick, Cumberland. Father: James Lynn, vicar of Crosthwaite. Mother: Charlotte Alicia Goodenough. 11 siblings. Married 1858, William James Linton, engraver; separated 1864. Wrote essay "The Girl of the Period" (1868), many novels and nonfiction essays. Knew George Henry Lewes, George Eliot, Charles Dickens, Samuel Laurence, Mary Anne Schimmelpenninck, Elizabeth and Agnes Strickland. Journalist; antifeminist; novelist; essayist; clergyman's daughter; bisexual. Middle class.

Thinly veiled autobiography using male persona "Christopher Kirkland" and switching genders of some other major figures, tracing Linton's life, career, and erotic relationships from birth to middle age. Vol. 1: Society in the Lake District. Family background. Father's abuse of his clerical position; his beating his children and neglecting their education; his pride and indolence. Author's self-education through reading; her intellectual deficiencies; siblings' wasted potential. Author's loss of Christian faith, developing deist and ultimately agnostic views. Her erotic attachment to a young married woman. Writing and publishing poetry; departing for London, age 23. Publishing first novel; working for two years on the *Morning Chronicle* staff (Linton was the first Englishwoman journalist to draw a fixed salary). Her involvement in intellectual circle advocating free love; opinions of Lewes, Eliot, Laurence, Thornton Hunt; Walter Savage Landor's fatherly friendship with author; her writing for Charles Dickens's *Household Words;* author's dislike of John Forster. Vol. 2: Close, intense relationship with fashionable feminist aristocrat Lady Monson; pain of their breakup. Life in Paris as a newspaper correspondent, 1853. Returning to England; author's changed views on marriage and divorce laws. Love affair with a Roman Catholic; refusing to convert; their breakup. Vol. 3: Author's views on feminism and feminist issues, women's education, property, child custody; distaste for feminists themselves; scorn for women entering professions. Courtship and marriage, 1858. Separating from spouse. Extended meditations on religion, philosophy, and science. Jews in London society; Jewish attitudes toward Christianity. Author's attachment to a young aspiring woman writer; close relationship with another young woman and with a young man; their conversations about death. Reassessing character, faith, morals, loneliness, old age, losses.

Christopher Kirkland is best read with the aid of a biography of Linton, such as Nancy Fix Anderson's *Woman Against Women in Victorian England* (1987). Through a male persona, Linton reveals her strong male identification and at the same time gives a heterosexual character to her unadmitted lesbian attachments. She felt it imperative to publish her autobiography as a male author. Her biographer argues this was important as a revelation of her ambivalence about being a woman. The author's posthumously published **582** *My Literary Life* (1899) relates anecdotes of literary figures that she knew, her moral disapproval of Thornton Hunt, G. H. Lewes, and George Eliot, and her relationship to Walter Savage Landor, who served as a substitute father for her.

583 LISLE, Mary. c.1795–d.a.1856. *"Long, Long Ago": An Autobiography*. J. & C. Mozley, 1856. 325 pp. NUC pre56 335:494.

Born in Devonshire. Father not named, Anglican vicar. Mother not named. 2 sisters; 1 brother. Uncle: Gen. William Lisle, officer in India. Married c.1835, Mr. Wootton, minister, died n.d. Widow. Clergyman's daughter; clergyman's spouse. Middle class.

Novelistic, romantic account of childhood through early adult life at country vicarage, detailing family history and author's courtships, c.1795–1835. Arriving at Mitchelmore rectory. Parents' characters. Visit of mother's sister and her husband; aunt's shocking death by fire; her husband's severe grief; his death seven years later. Author's fear of death. Grandmother's death, 1802. New Court, the Lisle family seat. Life stories of illustrious Lisle ancestors and other relatives. Locals' fear of Napoleon's invasion, popular songs expressing English patriotism, 1803. Father's sending children to his Staffordshire farm for safety. False news of invasion. Putting on home theatricals. Author's cousin's death from typhus, due to improper care; family's grief. Part II: early romances of author and her sisters. One sister's unhappy marriage. Author's courtship and thwarted elopement with a lord's son who lacked a title; author's flight (alone) back to Mitchelmore. Meeting the lord's son years later. Father's death, 1834. Marriage to old Mr. Wootton, her father's colleague, c.1835.

At the beginning of her book Lisle tells her readers that, in order to avoid appearing egotistical, she will "narrate such circumstances as personally I had but little to do with," but in reality almost everything she describes concerns her personally. Her primary audience seems to be those already familiar with the scenes she happily recalls: she says she expects only a small circle of friends to read this memoir. Each chapter opens with an epigram and relates in detail many stories and legends. Lisle's novelistic scene-setting, dialogue, and social observations are strongly reminiscent of Jane Austen.

584 LLOYD, Anna. 1837–1925. *A Memoir. With Extracts from her Letters*. Ed. by Edyth M. Lloyd. The Cayme Press, 1928. 233 pp.; illus.; genealogical table. BLC to 1975 195:215.

Born in Wood Green, London. Father: Samuel Lloyd, businessman. Mother: Mary, Quaker minister. 8 siblings. Single. Philanthropist; feminist; Poor Law Guardian; clergywoman's daughter; charitable volunteer. Middle class.

Thoughtful presentation of author's overcoming internal conflicts between family and greater philanthropic concerns, accompanied by her pioneering experiences in higher education for women and other women's causes, covering her childhood to 1892. Growing up in a quiet, restrained Quaker household. Everyday life and diet. Home education by governess. Importance to family of Sabbath meetings. Quaker men's and women's clothing, c.1850s. Harriet Beecher Stowe's visit to the family, 1853. Mother's work as minister. Family discussions on religious topics. Author's desire to expand her sphere of knowledge. Meeting Emily Davies; deciding to enter college on Davies's suggestion. Davies and periodicals writer Anna D. Richardson's plan to open women's college in connection with Cambridge. Author's strong dedication to learning. Family's disapproval of her aspirations as "worldly"; her earning criticism for not being available to family in times of crisis. Entering Hitchin College: discussing its careful design, its personnel. Author's views on the need to run a women's college with the same intellectual emphases as a men's college. Davies's praise of author's usefulness in new college. Her contentment at Hitchin despite her academic difficulties; wishing more Englishwomen could have this opportunity. Women's early campaigns to be elected to school boards. Supporting women's right to higher education without expressing uniform support of all women's issues. Leaving Hitchin upon sister's request that author return to family duties. Living and traveling with family members as needed. Adopting painting as a pastime. Her charitable activities. Her election to the Board of Guardians of the Poor in West Bromwich, 1887, as the only female member. Pleading circumstances of poor girls in lying-in ward. Noting particular role of women Poor Law Guardians.

In this informative memoir, Lloyd provides details concerning the pioneering achievements of Hitchin College and its significance for women's opportunities in higher education in England. Despite her personal conflicts with her strict Quaker family resulting from their disapproval of her decision to follow "worldly" pursuits, she took an independent path. Only the first thirty-nine pages of the book are narrative autobiography; the balance consists of Lloyd's letters, directly quoted by the editor.

585 LLOYD, Anne Gladys. 1889–?. *An Englishwoman's Adventures in the German Lines*. C. Arthur Pearson, 1914. 128 pp.; port.; map. BLC to 1975 195:232.

Born in England. Parents not named. Single. Journalist; interpreter. Middle class.

Journalist's experiences in and escape from German invasion of Belgium, 1914. Being caught in the Belgian countryside near Liège on summer holiday at outbreak of WWI. Belgians' confusion during German invasion. Author's saving the village from burning and the villagers from being shot. Most of the villagers' fleeing; author and a few others' remaining. Interpreting German for Belgians. Germans' plundering the village, threatening villagers. Villagers' maintaining morale by telling stories of how near and brave the French military forces were. Author's being questioned, arrested, and searched; confessing to being a journalist. Eating diary she had concealed in her hair. Reflecting on the war from German women's point of view. Being transported to Cologne. Being freed. Describing her journey toward home through France.

Lloyd begins *in medias res*, writing in an entertaining style with much action and frequent dialogue; her chapters, paragraphs, and sentences are short, as is the length of this memoir. This book was published as a one-shilling popular paperback.

586 LODGE, Eleanor Constance. 1869–1936. *Terms and Vacations*. Oxford University Press, 1938. Ed. by Janet Spens (author's friend). 250 pp.; front. port.; illus.; ed.'s note; preface by Oliver Lodge (author's brother); tributes from contributors; epilogue. NUC pre56 338:47.

Born in Staffordshire. Father not named, businessman. Mother not named. 7 brothers. Single. Wrote *The English Rule in Gascony* (1926). Educator; academic; historian; feminist; WWI volunteer; governess. Upper middle class.

Professional and personal recollections, particularly of pioneer efforts in higher education for women, covering author's Victorian childhood to 1935 retirement. Uneasy relationship with father. Being extremely shy. Studying at home with mother and with cousins at Scrivelsby Rectory in Lincolnshire. Attending lady's school. Studying with private woman tutor in Oxford after her father's sudden death. Living in Oxford with her brother. Suffering severe illness; staying in a nursing home; convalescing in Germany. Serving as governess for her brother's children. Developing interest in psychical research; attending séances. Beginning student career at Oxford, 1890. Outlining importance of university education and social experience for women. Taking holidays on Continent. Tutoring at Lady Margaret Hall; becoming first woman history tutor at this women's college; being appointed vice-principal. Her love of teaching. Enjoying camaraderie between female faculty and students. Her interest in elementary education. Beginning Oxford National Education Association. Conducting medieval historical research in London, Bordeaux, and Spain. Publishing "Villenage in Gascony" in the *English Historical Review*. Her friendship with Janet Spens. Doing volunteer work during WWI: helping Belgian refugees in Oxford; doing farm work at a camp in Cotswolds. Traveling in France at war's end; memories of French, English soldiers, devastation in France; working in canteen for French Red Cross and as hospital worker. Campaigning for full membership of women at Oxford. Accepting post as lecturer at Westfield College. Being first woman to receive D.Litt. from Oxford. Becoming principal of Westfield College. Retiring from Westfield, 1935. Stressing importance of university education for women.

Employing a direct style and a somewhat dispassionate tone, Lodge describes her impressive achievements as a teacher and scholar and her pioneering efforts in higher education for women. Although she does not align herself formally with any feminist causes, her unwavering belief in women's right to education has gained her a place of honor in the estimation of feminist historians.

LONDONDERRY, Marchioness of. [*See* VANE-TEMPEST-STEWART, Edith Helen.]

587 LONGBOTTOM, Eva H.(annah), LRAM. 1892–?. *Silver Bells of Memory: A Brief Account of My Life, Views and Interests*. Bristol: Rankin Bros., 1933. 371 pp.; preface by H. P. Leonard; illus.; apps. NUC pre56 340:192.

Born in Halifax, West Yorkshire. Father: surname Longbottom, cabinetmaker. Mother not named. Maternal grandfather: organist, headmaster of St. Mary's Church School. Maternal grandmother: Eliza Hood, headmistress of girls' department, St. Mary's Church School. Single. Singer (concerts); musician (pianist); teacher (music); composer; physically handicapped woman; short storyist; columnist; songwriter. Middle class.

Animated, literate account of author's overcoming the handicap of blindness from birth to pursue a highly successful and diverse musical career, covering 1890s–1928. Always fearing the dark and being alone. Appreciating the lifelong companionship and loving assistance of parents. Early love of music. Family's moving to Liverpool to increase educational opportunities for author. Performing at Band of Hope (musical youth group) concerts. Author's mother as her teacher and fully committed protector. Receiving perpetual parental encouragement in every undertaking. Attending school for the blind. Studying piano with a blind teacher. Mother's learning braille so she could teach it to author. Composing songs and hymns, age 10. Studying at Royal Normal College and Academy of Music. Winning singing prizes, age 12. Publishing poetry, age 15. Starting to give piano concerts, age 16; also giving recitations at the concerts. Meeting Ralph Vaughan Williams and Caruso. Touring in English provinces. Studying with Mme. Blanche Marchesi, 1911. Outlining her opinions on why society should take an interest in education for the blind. Remembering the crucial advent of musical scores in braille (c.1914). Perceiving differences between male and female music teachers. Wanting advanced diploma from Royal Academy and Royal College of Music. Giving lessons in voice and piano. Describing her own methods for teaching sighted children: using books in braille while her pupils use books in print. Developing oratorio work especially designed for sightless people who could not follow a conductor. Her interest in Pelman Institute's work with memory. Her father's death. Studying Theosophy to help overcome her fear of death; discussing how death relates to music. Returning to Bristol with her mother, 1923. Mother's selling family jewelry to buy author a wireless set; author's gratitude for mother's sacrifice. Publishing article "Radio and the Psychology of Blindness," 1924. Writing stories and songs for broadcasting. Writing children's column for Bristol newspaper, 1928. Composing "The Brownie Suite" for junior pianists. Discussing theories on dreams and the sightless, including Freudian theory. Experiencing contentment in her life.

Longbottom presents herself as an exceptionally talented musician, teacher, and performer who coped with terror over her blindness all of her life. Besides her good fortune at having parents who were totally committed to caring for and supporting her, she had the advantage of pursuing a musical career at a time when public interest and support in her fields of endeavor, and expansion of opportunities for blind musicians, were moving forward rapidly.

588 LONSDALE, Sophia. 1854–1930. *Recollections of Sophia Lonsdale*. Ed. by Violet Martineau. John Murray, 1936. 320 pp.; front port.; preface by ed.; letters; poems; index. NYPL to 1971 444:288.

Born in London. Father: John Lonsdale, curate, canon of Lichfield. Mother: Sarah Jardine. 3 sisters; 1 brother. Single. Philanthropist; Poor Law Guardian; educator; clergyman's daughter; organizer of societies (philanthropic); social reformer. Middle class.

Reminiscences of author's London-based philanthropic activities and colleagues, 1884–1907. Living in parish of St. Martin-in-the-Fields; social life; importance to her of her fox terrier, Nipper. Undertaking philanthropies; becoming a rent collector from the poor for South London Dwellings Company; opening a place of entertainment for low-income working class people; working with Octavia Hill. Author's collaboration with Emma Cons. Visiting headquarters of London Charity Organisation Society. Starting Charity Organisation Society office in Lichfield. Studying administration of the Poor Law. Serving on Board of Guardians for the Poor. Effecting changes on the board: granting privacy to unmarried pregnant women; sending workhouse children to district schools. Serving on Poor Law Conference Committee. Founding Lichfield High School for Girls. Involvement in rescue work; serving on Committee of Little Home. Commenting on Lichfield's severe social problems; its slums.

Lonsdale's memoir recalls her entry into philanthropic work under the powerful influence of social reformer Emma Cons. Dedicated and untiring, one who preferred to support efficacious measures rather than to seek personal popularity, Lonsdale helped to effect dramatic changes during her tenure as a Poor Law Guardian. She was the first woman to fill that post in Lichfield.

589 LOWNDES, Marie Adelaide Julie Elizabeth Renee (née Belloc). 1868–1947. *Where Love and Friendship Dwelt.* Macmillan, 1943. 243 pp.; front.; foreword; illus. NUC pre56 343:497.

Born in London. Father: Louis Belloc, invalid. Mother: Elizabeth (Bessie) Rayner Parkes, early feminist leader, editor of *The Englishwoman's Journal.* Paternal grandfather: French painter Hilaire Belloc. 1 brother (Hilaire Belloc, poet, historian). Married 1896 Frederic Lowndes, London *Times* staff writer. 1 son; 2 daughters. Wrote novels *The Heart of Penelope, Barbara Rebell, What Really Happened,* others. Knew Elizabeth Rundle Charles, Gerald du Maurier, William T. Stead, Margot Asquith, Alice Meynell, Lady Dorothy Nevill, Maude Stanley, Lord Grey of Fallodon. Novelist; journalist; biographer; translator. Upper class.

Author's adolescence in France and beginnings of her writing career, with considerable family history, covering c.1881–96. Attending Sussex convent school. Family's return to France, 1885; mother's intense nostalgia for her married life after 1872 death of author's father. Socializing with French families who had known author's grandmother, translator and Byron biographer Louise Swanton Belloc; friendships with French political and literary figures. French politics, courtship customs; failed negotiations with a suitor's family. Family history and genealogy; author's strong Catholic faith. First meeting her legal guardian, Anatole Dunoyer. Writing a biography of Charlotte, Princess Palatine. Living in London, age 20; visiting authors Mrs. Humphry Ward, Eliza Lynn Linton, and Elizabeth Rundle Charles; their discouraging her from a career as a writer; author's deciding that she would always encourage would-be writers. Publisher W. T. Stead's employing her to write a guide to the 1889 Paris Exhibition; writing trade articles; translating the de Goncourt brothers' diaries into English. Her friendships with Edmond de Goncourt, Anatole France, poet Paul Verlaine, novelists Alphonse Daudet and Emile Zola. Visiting her aging French relations; interviewing French artists and writers; attending salons of Madame Juliette Adam, 1890s. Discussing French women writers, political activists, artists, and actresses. Her engagement, 1895; mother's lack of interest in her forthcoming marriage; her financial assistance to the Belloc family.

Lowndes calls this book "only a fragmentary story of nine years"; it is more about others than about herself, yet reflects her affection for art, literature, politics, and French history. The book contains many portraits of French writers. Her first autobiographical book, **590** *"I, Too, Have Lived in Arcadia": A Record of Love and of Childhood* (1942), is primarily a biography of her mother, discussing her mother's brief and happy marriage, Lowndes's childhood in France, family history, the destruction of the Belloc estate in the Franco-Prussian War, and French and English culture. Lowndes addresses her literary friendships further in her third and fourth autobiographical books: **591** *The Merry Wives of Westminster* (1946) deals with her marriage and career as a London journalist and novelist, with particular focus on women novelists and socialites; **592** *A Passing World* (1948) focuses on her fears of pre-WWI German belligerence, the war's effects on her novels' themes and on her political friends.

593 LUCK, Lucy M. 1848–1922. "A Little of My Life." Ed. by J.C. Squire, *London Mercury*, 13(76):354–373, Nov. 1925–April 1926. (Excerpt pub. as "Lucy Luck, Straw Plait Worker," pp. 67–77 in *Useful Toil: Autobiographies of Working People from the 1820s to the 1920s*, Allen Lane, 1974.)

Born at Tring, Hertfordshire. Father not named, bricklayer. Mother not named, manual laborer. 1 brother; 1 sister. Married 1867, Will L., farmworker. 3 daughters; 1 son. Milliner; weaver; millworker; factory worker; domestic servant. Rural laboring class.

Poignant memories, emphasizing personal and general hardships afflicting the working class, covering author's childhood to middle age. Father's brutality toward family, drunkenness, desertion of family before author's ninth birthday. Family's receiving aid from the parish. Mother's forced relinquishment of custody of her children; author and siblings' being sent to workhouse; author's growing up working at domestic jobs, in silk mills and in factories. Author's being placed with a drunken family. Death of sister, who left author a doll, author's sole toy. Working in tavern, age 13. Mother's death; author's subsequently being placed with another abusive family; witnessing wife beating; husband's attempting to rape author. Life in a public house where straw hats were made; author's determination to teach herself the art of straw plaiting, hatmaking. Courtship with Will; marriage. Childbearing; death of youngest daughter; son's birth near Luton. Moving to London, c.1870. Continuing to work as a straw plaiter in London; children's working at job alongside their mother. Expressing pride in her children.

Without minimizing her repellent and uncomfortable circumstances, Luck writes a straightforward, sobering account of a life of poverty and potential degradation. She emphasizes her commitment to maintaining personal respectability and to sustaining herself economically and as a capable role model for her children.

594 LUCY, Mary Elizabeth. 1803–1889. *Mistress of Charlecote: The Memoirs of Mary Elizabeth Lucy*. Victor Gollancz, 1983. 184 pp.; intro. by Alice Fairfax-Lucy; illus.; afterword; chronology. BLC 1982–1985 15:264.

Born in County Flint, North Wales. Father: Sir John Williams, baronet. Mother: Margaret, no surname given. 3 brothers; 4 sisters. Married 1823 George Lucy, M.P., d.1845. Widow. 8 children. Family historian. Upper class.

Warm and intimate personal and familial memories, set amid general observations on rural upper-class Welsh and English life, covering author's childhood to 1880s. Being educated by governesses and her mother. Justifying her idealization of mother. Music and drawing being favorite studies. Teaching reading to servants. Friendship with Mrs. Hester Thrale Piozzi; studying music with Hester's husband. Father's forcefulness; author's having to comply with his every wish. Associating with the "Ladies of Llangolen," Lady Eleanor Butler and Miss Sarah Ponsonby, cultured writers famous for their lifestyle in rural Welsh retreat. Meeting, disliking future husband; submitting to her father's wish for her to marry; hoping she will grow to love husband. Living in London. Social season at Lucy estate, Charlecote, in Warwickshire. Attending Church of England services. Impact on author of her parents' deaths. Traveling on the Continent, 1840. Her grief and desolation after five of her children die in close succession. Husband's art collecting. Managing Charlecote after husband's death. Burglary at Charlecote; her testimony at robbers' trial. Contemporary treatments for childbirth, injuries, diseases. Marriages of her surviving children. Doting on her grandchildren.

Written in a formal style, Lucy's memoir becomes intimate and chatty as the author vividly depicts the emotional and physical details of rural upper-class life in 19th-century Wales and England. She states that she wrote this autobiography to share her rich memories and experiences with her grandchildren. Although she downplays her grief at the loss of five children, her parents, and her husband, Lucy's sadness can nevertheless be felt in this painstaking re-creation of a vanished world.

595 LUMSDEN, Dame Louisa Innes, 1840–1935. *Yellow Leaves: Memories of a Long Life*. W. Blackwood & Sons, 1933. 200 pp.; front. port.; illus.; apps. NUC pre56 345:516. (other ed: Berkeley: University of California, 1955.)

Born in Aberdeen, Scotland. Father: Clements Lumsden, advocate, writer. Mother: Jane Forbes. 3 sisters; 2 brothers. Single. Educator; academic; feminist; suffragist; poet; antivivisectionist; animal welfare activist; editor. Upper class.

Scottish upbringing, Cambridge education, and career of a dedicated women's educator, highlighting her critique of cultural attitudes toward both animals and the rights of women, from c. 1845 to the 1920s. Family history. Being lonely yet spoiled child. Scottish customs, celebrations. Popularity of fox hunting; people's blindness to its cruelty. Attending school in Belgium and London; London school rigid. Spending winters in Aberdeen. Pondering the religious revival of late 1850s. Reacting to father's death. History of Aberdeen: local industry, folklore. Feeling drawn to incipient "votes for women" movement. Attending college for women at Hitchin, Cambridge. Deciding to sit for Classical Tripos. Recalling how women students helped each other. Working as a classical tutor at Girton, Cambridge. Receiving praise for her poetry from John Addington Symonds. Working to create public school for girls in Scotland. Founding St. Leonard's School. Working for University Hall, St. Andrew. Resigning post at St. Leonard's due to ill health. Visiting Canada and the U.S.: impressions of colleges, prisons, and other public U.S. institutions. Meeting Louisa May Alcott. Returning to Scotland. Serving on two school boards in Aberdeen. Resigning her academic post; traveling in Europe and the Middle East. Becoming president of Aberdeen Suffrage Society; factions within suffrage movement; author's personal objections to militants' tactics. Working with Scottish Society for Prevention of Vivisection, editing its publication. WWI: new opportunities for women in workplace. Differences in how she viewed her life and times when young, middle-aged, and old.

Lumsden uses an unadorned style and a somewhat businesslike tone to record the history of higher education for women and of public education for girls in Scotland, chronicling her own contributions in both arenas. Her autobiography is a rewarding journey through one woman's focused perspective on 19th-century women's issues.

596 LUTTON, Anne. 1791–1881. *Memorials of a Consecrated Life: Compiled from the Autobiography, Letters and Diaries of Anne Lutton*. Ed. by J. H. Westcott (author's friend). T. Woolmer, 1882. 523 pp.; illus. NUC pre56 346:596.

Born in County Down, Ireland. Father: Ralph Lutton, classical scholar, linguist. Mother: Anne Lutton. 9 brothers; 3 sisters. Single. Wrote *Poems on Moral and Religious Subjects* (1829). Poet; religious/spiritual writer; physically handicapped woman. Middle class.

Personal and familial memories and experiences, particularly concerning serious religious questions, focusing on author's childhood to young adulthood. Father's study of Methodism; author's Anglican and Methodist Christian education. Briefly attending dame school, having a sketchy education. Commenting on the plain education of girls in Northern Ireland, c.1800. Learning to write from her older brother; attending the Moravian Academy. Her love of literature; reading novels in secret against parents' wishes. Reproaching herself for disobeying parents and for acquiring "false tastes and morbid sensitiveness" through novel reading. Wanting to be a writer; experimenting with genres. Seeking out father's literary criticism. Moving to the countryside; her love of nature. Beginning in 1813, teaching herself Latin, Greek, myriad ancient and modern languages. Learning to play the flute. Her passionate desire to investigate metaphysics and moral and religious truth. Drawing up resolutions to avoid sin; inducing her family and friends to witness and sign them. Condemning "evil speaking." Considering some questions regarding God's existence. Praying, dedicating herself to God. Leading Methodist women's meetings in Ireland; her associating with both Church of England and Wesleyans. Bearing burden of becoming blind in 1854.

Written in a lively yet formal style, Lutton's work demonstrates her considerable learning. Occasionally effusive, she often quotes Scripture and maintains a high moral tone throughout. The memoir was written in 1834, but letters and diary excerpts cover Lutton's life up to 1863. The editor interpolates biographical commentary up to 1881, the year of Lutton's death.

597 LUTYENS, Lady Emily (née Lytton). 1874–1964. *Candles in the Sun*. Philadelphia & New York: Lippincott, 1957. 196 pp.; foreword; illus.; app.; index. NYPL to 1971 449:115. (1st pub. Rupert Hart-Davis, 1957.)

Born in England. Parents not named. Grandfather: Baron Lytton Bulwer-Lytton. 1 brother; 1 sister. Married 1897 Sir Edwin Landseer Lutyens, architect. 1 son; 4 daughters. Wrote *A Blessed Girl*. Theosophist; religious/spiritual writer; journalist; public speaker; feminist; suffragist; political activist; vegetarian; organizer of societies (political, religious); editor; traveler (India). Aristocracy.

Detailed description of personal spiritual quest experienced in context of the goals, activities, and growth of the English and worldwide Theosophical societies, 1910–36. Joining Theosophical Society. Lack of companionship in her marriage. Becoming ardent suffrage supporter. Discussing tenets and founding members of Theosophy and Theosophical Society in England. Becoming president of the central London Lodge. Lecturing on Theosophy. Wanting to develop her own psychic powers. Meeting Krishnamurti; recalling details of his life. Her friendship with Theosophy leaders Annie Besant and C. W. Leadbeter. Being admitted into Besant's "special group." Studying with Krishnamurti at Taormina, Italy. Seeing religion and love as intertwined. Writing for the Theosophist publication *Herald of the Star*. Husband's resenting her work. Inaugurating Indian Home Rule League in England. History of Liberal Catholic church, its combining Theosophy and traditional Christianity. WWI: Going to Bombay; attending Theosophical convention at Benares. Wintering in Sydney: her simple, spiritual life there. Observing Wesak, Buddhist festival in India. Having quasi-metaphysical experiences. Publishing *The Call of the Mother*, embodying Eastern and Western spiritual ideas. Describing Annie Besant's Happy Valley Foundation in Ojai, California. Friction among Krishnamurti's supporters. Author's resigning from Theosophical Society over dispute with Krishnamurti. Visiting India again; loathing Anglo-Indian life. Her disillusionment with Krishnamurti's beliefs. Seeking solace in a Catholic convent, but not converting. Her continuing friendship with Krishnamurti, but not as a disciple.

Using an informal style, Lady Emily sets out the details of her profound spiritual quest. Her narrative projects an image of a strong-minded and highly intelligent woman whose basic belief in the inevitable intertwining of love and religion remains intact, despite her disillusionment and disappointment with Theosophy and Krishnamurti. In the process, the author also vividly describes some of the early days of the influential religious movement, which synthesized both Eastern and Western spiritual ideas.

598 LUTYENS, Mary. 1908–?. *To Be Young*. Rupert Hart Davis, 1959. 192 pp.; illus. NYPL to 1971 449:115.

Born in London. Father: Sir Edwin Lutyens, architect. Mother: Lady Emily Lutyens, writer, suffragist, Theosophist. Married Anthony Sewell. 3 sisters; 1 brother. Foreign resident (India, Australia); Theosophist; vegetarian. Upper class.

Personal and travel memories of childhood and adolescence, emphasizing encounters with love and spirituality, covering author's first seventeen years. Growing up with Theosophist mother. Rift between parents upon mother's imposing vegetarian cuisine on household. Author's vivid imagination. Family Christmases with relatives Lord and Lady Lytton. Her father's lack of interest in his daughters' schooling; author's attributing this to the dominant male attitude that only boys need a thorough education. Understanding Theosophist philosophy. Her love for Nitya, an Indian boy. Traveling through Europe with her mother,

Nitya, and Krishnamurti. Trip to India with both parents; living at Theosophical Society headquarters in Adyar. Her disgust at British occupation of India. Wanting to join Theosophists so she could be close to Nitya. Living in Sydney, Australia, to prepare for initiation into Theosophist Society. Her first experience with boredom; realizing her own lack of spirituality. Death of Nitya; its effect on her.

Lutyens's chronological narrative is remarkable for its outspoken hostility to the British Raj in the 1920s as well as for its picture of her interracial romance with an Indian boy. It is also noteworthy for its demonstration of Lutyens's astounding memory and for her apparently objective analysis of her remarkable and unorthodox family. For a different take on her parents' life together, see *Candles in the Sun* by her mother, Lady Emily Lutyens.

599 Lynch, Patricia Nora. 1898–1972. *A Storyteller's Childhood*. New York: W. W. Norton, 1962. 343 pp. NUC pre56 347:286.

Raised in Fair Hill, County Cork, Ireland. Father: Tim Lynch, traveler. Mother: née Tighe, lacemaker. 1 brother. Poet; short storyist. Middle class.

Stories of author's childhood in Ireland mixed with account of a new life in England covering up to c. age 15. Attending kindergarten at convent school. Mother's practice of reciting poetry to her. Grandfather's tutoring "lads going up to the university" in classical languages and teaching Irish to those who wanted the old language. At age 6, author's boarding with Hennessey family near Cork, while rest of family joins father in America. Description of Hennessey cabin and its rural setting. Author's being teased for not knowing country ways. Learning folk stories from Mrs. Hennessey. Local Irish people's interest in emigrating to America. Receiving news of father's death in Egypt, c.1905. Return of author's family. Going with her mother to London to meet a friend who brought father's papers and money from Egypt. Feeling self-conscious over her country ways. Attending St. Winifred's convent school in London. Reading fairy stories and popular magazines. Leaving London upon arrival of father's legacy; family's settling in Rottingdean, Kent. Her brother's career as chartered accountant. Author attending Rottingdean convent school. Boarding with Martin family in Ashford; attending Ashford village school. Winning prizes in children's magazine storywriting competition. Having poems printed in local paper. Reading voraciously in London libraries. Living with her aunt and uncle, at author's age 14. Mother's departure for Egypt to take title to father's lands. Author's travel to Bruges, Belgium, en route to join mother. Becoming ill and unable to continue the journey; boarding with a family in Bruges; taking lessons from Madame. Receiving money from her mother in Egypt; deciding to go to college and become a teacher or a civil servant.

Lynch sees herself as part of the Irish storytelling tradition. Her style is poetic and conversational, full of the flavor of rural Irish speech, which she re-creates with frequent dialogue. She is vague about her family background, particularly her father's travels.

600 LYONS, Dame Enid Muriel (née Burnell). 1897–1981. *So We Take Comfort*. William Heinemann, 1965. 283 pp.; front. port.; illus.; intro.; index. BLC to 1975 203:450.

Born in Duck River, Tasmania, Australia. Father: William Charles Burnell, sawyer. Mother not named, shopkeeper. 2 sisters; 1 brother. Married 1915, Joe A. Lyons, treasurer and minister of education, Tasmania, later prime minister of Australia, d.1939. Widow. 6 sons; 6 daughters. Politician's spouse; teacher. Rural laboring class; married into upper class.

Author's personal history from childhood through adult life and detailed accounts of Australian society and politics of the 1920s and 1930s. Mother's family history; hardships of her earlier life. Father's character. Parents' incompatibility. Workers at sawmill where father was employed. Attending local school, beginning age 6. Her mother's Labour Party activism. Author's first meeting with Lyons, her future husband. Keeping shop and household and running post office for ailing mother, age 13. Her intellectual vanity's being countered by her mother's insistence that she learn housework. Attending Teachers' Training College in Hobart, age 14; working as junior teacher after certification. Engagement at 17 to Lyons. His family, background, early political career. Public disapproval of engagement due to her extreme youth and his Catholicism. Her conversion to Roman Catholicism from Methodism before marriage. Husband's politicking. Her self-consciousness as politician's wife. Her twelve pregnancies and childbirths; her subsequent illnesses. Living in Devonport and Hobart. Speechmaking for husband, aimed at audience of women like herself. Death of infant son. Engaging children's nursemaid. Nursing husband after his automobile accident. Enjoying housework and domesticity. Facing angry mobs during husband's 1931 campaign. His election as prime minister. Her difficulty taking on speechmaking and campaigning for her husband in addition to her domestic duties. Disastrous effects of economic depression in Sydney. Traveling alone on speaking tour, often facing hostile crowds, to oppose Western Australia secession. Traveling to London, Rome, Ireland, the U.S., and Canada. Husband's advisory role in Edward VIII abdication crisis. His pre-WWII diplomacy. His exhaustion and death.

Despite her protestations in support of the primacy of women's domestic role, this book demonstrates that Dame Enid found both energy and time to campaign for her husband and to fulfill the duties of a prime minister's wife. Her chronological narrative contains many detailed observations on Australian society and politics in the 1920s and 1930s.

601 LYTTON, Lady Constance (Jane Warton, pseud.). 1869–1923. *Prisons and Prisoners: Some Personal Experiences*. Virago Press, 1988. 337 pp.; intro. by Midge MacKenzie; illus. NUC 1988–90 microfiche #0180. (1st pub. William Heinemann, 1914.)

Born in Vienna. Father: Robert, 1st Earl of Lytton, viceroy of India, diplomat. Mother: Edith Villiers, lady-in-waiting to Queen Victoria. 2 sisters; 2 brothers. Single. Feminist; suffragist, militant; philanthropist; vegetarian; prison inmate. Aristocracy.

Personal experiences of a militant suffragist, set amid insightful observations on social and political aspects of English society, spanning 1906–12. Recalling her childhood in Vienna, Paris, Lisbon, and India. Mother's strong influence on author. Author's chronic invalidism and heart condition. Her youthful interest in music and journalism. Her passion for animals leading to her vegetarianism. Receiving a small inheritance from her godmother; using it to alleviate social problems of poor rural dwellers. Attending Church of England. Her hatred of industrialization; interest in rural traditions, especially folk song and dance. Working with Esperance Club for working girls; meeting Emmeline Pethick-Lawrence, Annie Kenney, Olive Schreiner. Author's "conversion" to suffrage cause. Her concern for women of all social classes. Subscribing to *Votes for Women* newspaper. Joining the Pankhursts' Women's Social and Political Union and the Women's Freedom League. Being arrested for militant unlawful protest as suffragette. Desiring no special treatment. Feeling sympathy with all other prisoners. Her views regarding upper-class women's ignorance as weakest link in the suffrage chain. Petitioning the Home Secretary on behalf of suffrage cause. Her partial hunger strike. Being force-fed; vivid descriptions of this abuse. Being arrested under name "Jane Warton"; disguising herself. Poor health resulting from prison treatment. Violence and brutality against delegation protesting shelving of Conciliation Bill, 1910. Determining to break the law again for the suffrage cause. Belief in need for political extremism.

Bolstered by her personal account of imprisonment and abusive treatment, Lytton's narrative is a stirring demand for positive recognition of suffragettes who were imprisoned and forcibly fed. Remarkably egalitarian not only in her support of the movement but in her interest in the social problems of women of all classes, Lytton offers a firsthand, detailed account of the votes-for-women battle.

602 MACARTNEY, Catherine Theodora, Lady (née Borland). 1877–1949. *An English Lady in Chinese Turkestan*. Hong Kong & Oxford: Oxford University Press, 1985. 236 pp.; intro. by Peter

Hopkirk; illus.; map; index. NUC pre56 348:388. (other ed.: Ernest Benn, 1931.)

Born in Castle Douglas, Scotland. Father: James Borland. Mother not named. Siblings. Married 1898, Sir George Macartney, civil servant, Anglo-Chinese, d.1945. 2 sons; 1 daughter. Civil servant's spouse (extended empire); foreign resident (China); traveler (Asia). Middle class; married into upper class.

Travels of civil servant's wife in Turkestan with husband, and comments on her loneliness and cultural dislocation, 1898–c.1918. Personal and family life. Traveling through Russia and Kashgar, Turkestan, sometimes by horse and camel. European servants; wanting to have native servants only in kitchen; training them. Her aversion to native servants; believing they will all have lice. Gardening. Husband's friendship with a Dutch Roman Catholic priest. Happiness in domestic arrangements; five English servants, garden, pets. Native dress and customs. Housekeeping difficulties; boredom, and feelings of uselessness and loneliness in Chingi Bagh (the British Residence). Living there with family, 1898–1908. Birth of a son and daughter, 1903 and 1905. Never getting to know Kashgari women. Reflecting on husband's positive attitude toward British empire. Returning with family to England, 1908. Birth of second son, 1911. Returning to Chingi Bagh, c.1912. Chinese revolution, 1912. Returning to England, 1914. Education of children by English governess. Journey across Europe during WWI via Russia, Finland, and Norway. Husband's solo return to Chingi Bagh post, 1918; author's inability to accompany him, due to change in civil service regulations. Residence after 1919 on Isle of Jersey.

This is a source on British civil administration in central Asia and on cross-cultural issues with a background of Macartney's adjustments to foreign residence and preserving her English identity. The account of her 1908 journey back to England is in diary form. The editor furnishes supplementary information on her husband's early life, including his Chinese mother, and mentions a biography of him, *Macartney at Kashgar* (Methuen, 1973).

603 MACBRIDE, Maud Gonne. 1865–1953. *A Servant of the Queen: Her Own Story*. Dublin: Golden Eagle/Standard House, 1938. 319 pp.; front. port.; foreword; preface; illus. NUC pre56 348:554. (other ed.: Woodbridge, Suffolk: The Boydell Press, 1983; Chicago, Illinois: The University of Chicago Press, 1994.)

Born in Tongham, Surrey. Father: Col. Thomas Gonne, English of Irish descent. Mother: Edith Frith Cook. 1 sister; 1 illegitimate half-sister. Married 1903, Maj. John MacBride, Irish nationalist; separated 1905. 2 daughters by French patriot Lucien Millevoie before marriage; 1 son by

MacBride. Knew W. B. Yeats, journalist W. T. Stead, politicians Charles Stuart Parnell, Michael Davitt. Irish nationalist; political activist; organizer of societies (political); politician; editor; publisher; intelligence agent; actress (stage); public speaker; prison inmate; political conspirator. Upper middle class.

Romantic, passionate militancy of a well-known Irish independence agitator, covering late 1860s–1901. Moving to Ireland from England. Mother's death at author's age 4. Family history; various homes in Ireland. Love of all animals. Visiting America as a young child; traveling to Rome with father. Frequent moves in rural Ireland. Absence of early schooling; ineffectiveness of later tutelage. English and French governesses' giving author most of her education. Living with great-aunt in London, and in Italy c.1876–81. Traveling to Hamburg c.1880, to France for lung cure, and to Constantinople. Meeting a Bonapartist and General Boulanger in France; smuggling documents into Russia for the Boulangist Party. Meeting W. T. Stead in Russia; her discomfort with his "sex obsession." Father's death, c.1883. Residence again in London with uncle; rebelling against him for supporting English hegemony in Ireland. Discovery and support of her illegitimate half-sister. Uncle's lying to author and sister Kathleen by telling them he had used up their father's legacy; author's deciding to support herself. Brief stage career; illness; an aunt's revealing that her father's legacy was still available; having enough money to live on. Witnessing Irish tenants' evictions, 1885. Her anti-British alliance with Lucien Millevoie, French Bonapartist. Irish politicians' views on Irish freedom. Being barred from joining Celtic Literary Society because of her gender. Standing for by-election at Barrow-in-Furness, Lancashire, against Liberal Party; winning the election. Personally reinstating Land League tenants. Becoming a legendary figure to the rural Irish. Refusing an English M.P.'s marriage proposals. Helping free Irish political prisoners. Escaping arrest for her anti-British political activity by lecturing in America, 1897. Supporting Charles Stuart Parnell. Acting in Yeats's play *The Countess Kathleen,* written for her, 1902. Supporting openly militant IRA activities. Converting to Roman Catholicism for both religious and political reasons. Campaigning against Boer War enlistment of Irish in British army. In Paris, plotting with French agents to sabotage British transport ships. Her Boer War imprisonment by the English as a suspected German spy. Editing newspaper *L'Irlande Libre;* founding women's political society *Inghinidhe na hEireann* (Daughters of Ireland), 1900. Courtship and marriage. Husband's execution by the English for his part in the 1916 Easter Rebellion. Justifying Irish terrorism. Her fearlessness; her lack of deep introspection.

MacBride's awareness of herself as a legendary Irish figure is reflected in the romantic image she paints of herself. The *Queen* of the title is the legendary Cathleen ni Houlihan—with whom MacBride identifies—and not Queen Victoria. This volume ends shortly after the death of MacBride's husband, from whom she had separated in 1905 (a subject not discussed in the book); her foreword mentions that she had begun a second volume. Maud Gonne MacBride is well known as a literary inspiration for Yeats, who was passionately devoted to her and saw her as a romantic symbol of Ireland.

604 MACCARTHY, Mary (née Warre-Cornish). 1882–1953. *A Nineteenth-Century Childhood*. Hamish Hamilton, 1948. 100 pp.; intro. by John Betjeman; author's note; illus. NUC pre56 349:73–4. (1st pub. Heineman, 1924; other ed: Constable, 1985.)

Born in England. Father: Francis Warre-Cornish, vice-provost, librarian at Eton. Mother: Blanche Ritchie, novelist. 4 sisters; 3 brothers. Married 1906, Desmond MacCarthy, literary and drama critic, member of Bloomsbury group. 2 sons; 1 daughter. Wrote *Fighting Fitzgerald*. Biographer; novelist. Upper middle class.

Lyrical reminiscences of author's late-Victorian family, covering 1880s–1901. Family history. Her closeness to her parents. Finding inspiration in observing her mother's writing talents. Her father's appointment to Eton; moving to Cloisters. Studying at home. Attending Anglican boarding school; love of High Church worship. Preparing for Holy Week at school. Spending Easter holidays with family; pastimes of music, poetry, playing charades. Earning swimming and fencing privileges at Eton (after hours). Feeling curiosity about Eton boys. Experiencing Eton Sundays as oppressively quiet; not being allowed to play. Attending school in Germany. Her passion for literature; visits to literary aunt, Anne Thackeray Ritchie. Deciding to have a career; consulting the *Englishwoman's Year Book* to find a profession. Family's London socializing. Attending Queen Victoria's funeral. Author's views on the state of the arts in Victorian era. Modesty of Victorian parents in discussing sexual matters with children. Commenting on social conventions for Victorian young men and women.

This charming and literate account of MacCarthy's late-Victorian childhood and girlhood is neither a nostalgic wade through memories nor an excuse for a self-serving "who's who" of social connections. Rather, it is mainly an unsentimental portrait of her era, its customs and expectations, and her place in it. She expresses great love and admiration for her parents, especially her mother, who tacitly emerges as a vibrant, intelligent woman and a source of inspiration for the author.

605 MACDONALD Bosville, Alice Edith, Lady (née Middleton). 1861–d.a.1929. *All the Days of My Life*. John Murray, 1929. 169 pp.; front.; illus. NUC pre56 350:28.

Born in Edinburgh, Scotland. Father: John Middleton, 1st colonel of 19th Lanarkshire Volunteer Regiment. Mother: Edith Anne Piercy Henderson. 10 siblings. Married 1886, Alexander Wentworth MacDonald Bosville, Highland chief, church organist. 1 son; 1 daughter. Singer (concerts); Scottish chieftain's wife; organizer (musical). Upper class.

Good-humored personal and familial memories, including reflections on Scottish history and lore and social changes in the modern world, covering 1860s–c.1929. Childhood memories of western Scotland. Moving to Perthshire, 1866; becoming acquainted with children of local aristocracy. Meeting renowned scholar and translator Benjamin Jowett of Balliol College, Oxford. Childhood passion for reading; borrowing books from brothers, who attended public schools. Having a Swiss governess; learning French. Death of brother Harry from consumption. Father's character; his increasing invalidism. Maternal grandmother's character. Traveling with her family in Europe. Her closeness with her sister Amy. Being educated at home to placate father, who opposed girls' schooling. Visiting London during the season; living there after presentation at Court. Death of father, 1880. Singing lessons and debut as singer. Courtship, engagement, and wedding; honeymoon and trip to Italy; husband's refusal to speak with foreigners in their own language, leaving all conversation to author. Living in Thorpe, Yorkshire. Appearing in amateur theatricals. Author's educating her young son. Organizing musical festivals at Bridlington. Her son's coming-of-age party, 1908. Husband's family history; author and husband's successful action in getting the Court of Session to recognize his grandfather's Scottish domicile; husband's regaining right to resume the name of MacDonald and position as chief of Clan MacDonald of the Isles, 1910. Author's selling valuable china, buying estate on Isle of Skye that once belonged to the MacDonalds. Husband's receiving a deputation of MacDonalds from entire island of Skye, 1911; his presiding over Skye Gathering in Glasgow, 1912. Outbreak of WWI. Son's marriage. General comments about changes in technology and social customs during author's lifetime.

Writing anecdotally, associatively, and, except for a few digressions, chronologically, Lady MacDonald Bosville describes the pleasant and amusing events of her life. The chapters are short and narrowly focused; the sentence construction is simple, not literary, suggesting moderate educational achievement. The author somewhat facetiously declares that she wrote this book "as the direct result of a marital command"; her husband gave her some blank manuscript books and directed her to record her life in them.

606 MACDONELL, Anne, Lady (née Lumb). 1850–d.a.1923. *Reminiscences of Diplomatic Life, Being Stray Memories of Personalities and Incidents Connected with Several European Courts and Also with*

Life in South America Fifty Years Ago. Adam & Charles Black, 1913. 292 pp.; front. port.; preface; illus.; index. NUC pre56 350:227.

Born in Buenos Aires, Argentina. Father: Edward Lumb. Mother: Elizabeth Yates. 15 siblings. Married 1870, the Rt. Hon. Hugh G. Macdonell, Secretary of British Legation, knighted 1903. 3 sons. Foreign resident (South America, Spain, Denmark, Portugal); society woman; diplomat's spouse. Upper class.

Personal and travel memories, set amid life in European and South American diplomatic circles, covering 1850s–1902. Family history. Closeness with only surviving brother, Charles. Life in rural Argentina: Indians, flora, *gauchos*, Argentine customs; social life in Buenos Aires. Being educated by governesses. Returning to England, 1866. Meeting future husband. Marriage, 1870. Returning to Argentina. Yellow fever epidemic. Father's death; its effect on author. Husband's posting to Madrid, 1872; living with him there. Spanish life, politics, housekeeping. Children's illness; author's returning with them to England. Socializing with diplomats. Husband's appointment to Berlin and Rome; society life in these cities. Husband's promotion to Rio de Janeiro; family's move to Brazil. Court life of the family of Emperor Pedro II. Rural Brazilian life. Suffering with malaria; returning to England. Husband's posting to Copenhagen; Danish Court life. Posting to Lisbon; living there, 1892–1902. Anecdotes of Anglo-Portuguese history; customs, culture of Lisbon; the Portuguese royal family.

Lady Macdonell announces that she is sure the domestic details of her life will not interest the reader; instead of relating much about personal matters, she dwells on the externals of her life, stringing together anecdotal memories of travel, history, and personal encounters with royalty. Sometimes she misuses words and misquotes English literature.

607 MACK, Marjorie (Marjorie Mack Dixon). 1887–s.l.1982. *The Educated Pin*. Faber & Faber, 1944. 190 pp. NUC pre56 145:130. [cat. under Dixon.]

Born in Norfolk. Father: John Mack, former Army officer, amateur photographer. Mother: Henrietta Ellen Packard. 1 sister. Married 1918, Harold Dixon, farmer. 2 sons. Wrote *Velveteen Jacket, The Red Centaur, Nonesuch Hall,* others. Knew Eleanor Roosevelt, Dorothy Strachey. Novelist; socialist; diarist. Middle class.

Schoolgirl's intense imaginative life and her growing desire for political and economic independence in opposition to parents, 1890s–c.1905. Parents' being forced to live abroad and rigidly economize before author's birth in order to pay off their debts, c.1879–85. Family residence at Paston Hall. History of Paston and North families. Her lifelong closeness to elder sister; their inventing imaginary playmates, including a brother. Exotic pets: mice, baby alligators. Home education by governess; making a playmate of a common black pin on which author projected all her desire to learn. Life with sister at Allenswood School, Wimbledon, where all pupils were required to speak French; studying English literature under Dorothy Strachey; being ostracized by other pupils and teachers due to family's straitened finances; becoming friends with fellow student Eleanor Roosevelt. Mother's later opposition to author's learning Greek. Love of poetry. Under the influence of French headmistress, questioning Christian doctrine. Keeping a voluminous diary. After her sister's marriage, spending more time alone. Rejecting the life her parents offered her at Paston Hall. Embracing Fabian Socialism, which her father hated. Deciding to earn her own living so she could attend Newnham College, Cambridge; her parents' bitter opposition to her visiting an employment agency.

Distancing herself from the self she portrays by alternating first-person and third-person narration, Mack nevertheless writes intimately of her imaginary playmates and of her intense desire for education. An introspective tone, focused on a fantasy life centered around her sister, predominates. She states that she wrote this book for "Genta," an imaginary granddaughter whom she invented for her sister Susannah.

608 MACKAY, Helen (Gansevoort; Edwards). 1876–1966. *Journal of Small Things*. New York: Duffield & Co., 1917. 284 pp. NUC pre56 351:663.

Born in England. Parents not named. Married, husband not named. Wrote *Accidentals, Stories for Pictures, London One November*, others. Novelist; short storyist; nurse (WWI); foreign resident (France). Middle class.

Glimpses of collective and individual suffering and losses, accompanied by observations on war's consequences, covering 1914–17. Life in prewar French chateau and small town. Attending Mass. Having nightmares, premonitions of violence. Parisians' attitude toward prospect of war. WWI: profound reactions of French women to sending loved ones off to war. Author's feelings about English involvement. Her surprise and sorrow at convalescents' willingness to return to front. Being surrounded by death and dying. Uncertainty about how to address relatives of fallen soldiers. Working as volunteer nurse. Feeling that youth of whole world is being destroyed. Crudeness of tending the wounded; refusing to romanticize war's "glories." Anecdotes of wounded; their dealing with lifetime afflictions. French religious observances. Incongruity of arrival of Easter, 1916. Praising the efficiency of nursing nuns and the beauty of their faith in God. Author's dissatisfaction with patriotic displays. Her precognitive dreams of war, now made reality.

With delicacy and power Mackay describes a war-torn world. In her lyrical yet grim diary entries she recalls the "small things," the forgotten things, in a series of vignettes that show the folly, devastation, and horror of war. While her account is not fully a narrative autobiography, it is highly self-revelatory in its eloquent illustrations of the author's aversion to war and its far-reaching consequences.

609 MACKENZIE, Faith Compton (née Stone). 1882–1960. *As Much as I Dare: The Autobiography of Faith Compton Mackenzie*. Collins, 1938. 286 pp.; front. port.; illus. NUC pre56 352:188.

Born on Isle of Thanet, Kent. Father: Edward Stone, Eton master. Mother: Lily Vidal. 9 siblings. Married Compton Mackenzie, former consul-general in Greece, novelist, playwright. 1 son. Wrote novels *The Four Winds of Love*, *The East Wind*, biography *Christina of Sweden*, short story collection *Mandolinata*. Knew Romaine Brooks, Norman Douglas, D. H. Lawrence, Noel Coward, Rebecca West, Clara Novello Davies, others. Novelist; biographer; short storyist; music critic; actress (stage); WWI volunteer. Upper middle class.

Memories of rural and urban personal and professional experiences and life in Italy, from author's late-Victorian childhood to early WWI. Mother's family history; mother's claim to having seen fairies and specters as a small child; mother's interest in spiritualism. Author's pastimes with other children. Her father's beginning a boys' school; having Desmond MacCarthy as one of his pupils. Attending Quaker school and then others in London and Suffolk. Her mother's being treated for chronic illnesses; effect of her nervous illness on household. Mother's conversion to Roman Catholicism; father's tolerating conversion. Author's attending high school in London. Studying music. Mother's death, 1898. Deciding on stage career. Touring in America and England. Describing living conditions for performers. Meeting Compton Mackenzie, marrying him; his father's disapproval. Husband's producing play, *The Gentleman in Grey;* his bout with scarlet fever; his passion for forlorn hopes and lost causes; his desire to become a clergyman; his launching a Sunday school; his resuming his stage career. Taking holiday in Capri; lifelong love of her home there. Outbreak of WWI: working with British Ladies' Red Cross Sewing Bee on Capri; doing volunteer work in England. Her father's death.

Mackenzie's endeavor to present the image of her general happiness as a child and young adult carries a suggestion of unacknowledged sadness. Although she was a talented musician and a moderately successful actress, she abandoned her career—and with it much of her independence—upon marriage. She was steadfastly loyal to her mercurial husband, and much of the book is Compton Mackenzie's biography rather than Faith's autobiography. In **610** *More Than I Should* (1940), she writes of their residence on Capri and smaller islands closer to home, her founding the *Gramophone* magazine and writing about recorded music, and her husband's trial for publishing classified information in his memoirs. In **611** *Always Afternoon* (1943), she lovingly re-creates scenes from her childhood and travels, yet refers throughout to her parents by their first names without identifying their relationship to her, thus creating a curiously impersonal tone. She also discusses Capri as a popular British playground and describes the scandal attending her husband's publication of *The Windsor Tapestry,* an unauthorized biography of the Duke of Windsor (Edward VIII).

612 MACKIRDY, Olive Christian (née Malvery). c.1880–1914. *A Year and a Day*. Hutchinson, 1912. 333 pp.; front. port.; illus. NUC pre56 352:437.

Probably born in India. Parents not named. Married Archibald Mackirdy, died c.1910. Widow. 1 son; 2 daughters. Wrote *The Soul Market, The Fool's Devotion, Thirteen Nights,* others. Knew Hilda Martindale. Philanthropist; novelist; journalist; social reformer; public speaker; social issues writer; temperance activist; Salvation Army worker; actress (stage). Middle class.

Detailed, frequently poignant personal memories and philanthropic experiences, set within an insightful voyage of religious discovery and observation, covering 1910–12. Brief reference to early career as an actress and singer before becoming a writer and lecturer. Her husband's accidental death; being left alone, with two small children and a third about to be born. Being devastated, having her faith seriously disturbed by husband's death; seeking to communicate with him through spiritualist mediums; finding these a sham; condemning spiritualism. Developing an aversion to physicians based on their treatment of her husband and her childbirth experiences. Immersing herself in philanthropic activities for poor, working women. Opening a London shelter for women and girls. Publishing *The Soul Market;* its inspiring the building of many missions. Establishing Club for Working Girls in Hoxton; case histories of some of its members. Her condemnation of free love as diabolical and of socialism because she perceived it as treating women solely as breeders. Supporting Salvation Army's campaign to raise the age of sexual consent from 16 to 18; her belief that such reform would purify and restore public morals; her valuing moral reform above suffrage. Writing for the *Christian Globe;* using it as a platform to arouse public opinion against sweated labor. Visiting factories to inspect working conditions; visiting schools and colleges where she brought together buyers and sellers, employers and workers. Her opinion on establishing a minimum wage; supporting compensation for motherhood. Praising enlightened factory and manufacturing conditions and industrial philanthropy of specific companies. Touring England and Wales as a lecturer on temperance and working conditions; giving singing recitals. Visiting Copenhagen and America. Perceiving goat farming as a worthwhile occupation for women. Attacking the medical profession again; her belief that women doctors might be beneficial; her admiration for Christian Scientists' health care practices. Discussing the Mackirdy House in London, a Salvation Army shelter she founded.

Beginning *in medias res,* Mackirdy evidently assumes that her readers will already be well acquainted with the events of her life. She interweaves personal feelings and issues with her views on prevailing social problems, particularly those affecting women. She consistently refers to traditional moral and Christian values as the means to bring about social justice.

613 MACKWORTH, Margaret Haig, Viscountess Rhondda (née Thomas). 1883–1958. *This Was My World.* Macmillan & Co., Ltd., 1933. 305 pp.; front. port.; illus.; intro. BLC to 1975 206:229.

Born in Llanwern, Wales. Father: David Alfred Thomas, 1st Baron and 1st Viscount Rhondda, Liberal M.P., colliery owner, businessman. Mother: Dame Sybil Margaret Haig. Married 1908, Sir Humphrey Mackworth, 7th Baronet; divorced 1923. Publisher; businesswoman; feminist activist; suffragist, militant; journalist; editor; secretary. Aristocracy.

Articulate record of personal and professional memories, emphasizing the maturation of an aristocratic businesswoman and feminist activist under the tutelage of her enlightened father, 1880s to early 1920s. Societal changes for women between Victorian and Neo-Georgian eras. Author's generally happy childhood. Attending St. Leonard's School; taking interest in father's political career. Contemplating one of her own. Unconventionality in mother's family; its effect on author. Developing youthful social conscience. Her increasing religious doubts. Social debut; participating in typical philanthropic and social activities of her class. Frustration at not being significantly occupied. Attending Somerville College, Oxford. Marriage to a baronet's son met at Oxford. Husband's family history. Feeling happiness in newfound status as a wife. Changing her politics from Liberal to Conservative to please her husband. Joining Women's Social and Political Union, 1908; shedding meekness. Working as secretary to her father. Details of father's business interests. Assessing difficulties women encounter in business world; men's jealousy, resentment, feelings of threat. Discovering the WSPU, the militant suffrage movement. Public speaking with Annie Kenney and Emmeline Pankhurst. Educating herself in feminism and political science. Writing for feminist causes in *Votes for Women* and local papers. As part of suffrage tactics, setting fire to letter boxes; being arrested, hunger and thirst strike in prison. WWI: working in Ministry of National Service; her patriotism, disinclination for pacifism. Working as father's full-time assistant while learning his business. Traveling to America with her father, 1915; returning on *Lusitania:* details of its sinking and rescue; fellow rescuees.

Discussing dramatic changes in the post-WWI world. Death of father, 1918. Becoming rich and titled. Forming the Six Point Group, an equal rights society; joining with the National Union of Women Teachers and the Open Door Council. Discussing the need to change minds as well as laws. Founding the feminist journal *Time and Tide*. Describing the incomparable joy of finding something immensely valuable to do. Ending her autobiography before her 1923 divorce.

Although Lady Rhondda's work is short on details regarding her pivotal role in inter-war feminism, it offers extremely valuable insights on the militant suffrage movement and on the cause of women's rights. She acknowledges that her social class and position aided her in her career, and that women who lack such advantages face great difficulties in attaining success both in commercial enterprise and politics.

614 MACMANUS, Emily E. P., C.B.E. 1886–1978. *Matron of Guy's*. Andrew Melrose, 1956. 228 pp.; front. port.; illus.; index. BLC to 1975 206:369.

Born in Wadsworth. Father: Leonard MacManus, physician. Mother: Julia Boyd. 2 brothers; 1 sister. Single. Hospital administrator; nurse; nurse (WWI); midwife; physician's daughter; foreign resident (Egypt). Middle class.

Personal memories set within a catalogue of professional recollections and observations on changes in nursing profession in England, covering 1880s–1950s. Family history. Aunts' training as nurses; effect of this on author's career choice. Accompanying father on medical rounds to poor areas; describing living conditions, diseases that afflicted poor. Her interest in social problems, local politics. Beginning nursing education at Guy's Hospital, 1904. History of Guy's and its founder, Thomas Guy. Describing courses, ward work, night duty. Anecdotes of patients. Being promoted to head-nurse, sister's deputy, 1910. Taking midwifery training at East End Mothers' Home. Comparing nursing service in early- and mid-20th century. Being interested in taking a temporary assignment abroad. Nursing at Kasr-el-Aini Hospital in Cairo. Egyptian nurses, culture, pastimes. Working as junior sister at Guy's. WWI: working with VADs; nursing in wartime France; French patients. Recalling grimness and privations of postwar England. Being promoted to assistant matron at Guy's. Working with Medical Research Council regarding influence of diet on children's health. Being appointed matron to Bristol Royal Infirmary. Promotion to matron of Guy's, 1927. Emphasizing importance of caring and concern, as well as technical skills, for nurses. Serving as delegate to International Council of Nurses in Canada. Investigating nursing conditions in the U.S. WWII: nursing in various hospitals; food privations and their effect on patients. Visiting health centers in West Indies and South America. Experiencing happiness in retirement.

In an informal but rather dry style, MacManus recalls her career achievements. She reserves her excellent descriptive skills for places and events, providing minimal personal information and revealing little or no emotion, even when re-creating the grim situations of war. Apparently the author cherishes an idea of professional objectivity; her style reflects little response to patients as suffering individuals.

615 MALLESON, Lady Constance (née Annesley; Colette O'Niel, stage name). 1895–1975. *After Ten Years: A Personal Record.* Jonathan Cape, 1931. 320 pp.; front. port.; map; index. BLC to 1975 209:101.

Born in County Down, Ireland. Father: Hugh Annesley, 5th Earl of Annesley, lt. col. of Scots Guards, representative peer for Ireland. Mother: Priscilla Moore. 1 sister; 1 stepsister; 1 stepbrother. Married 1915, Miles Malleson, actor; divorced 1923. Actress (stage); political activist, pacifist, playwright, traveler (Europe, South Africa). Aristocracy.

Personal and professional experiences and observations on daily life in upper-class Edwardian society, covering author's first thirty-five years. Father's moodiness; her sister Clare as his favorite. Protestant upbringing. The social seasons in London, summers in Newcastle. Her father's death; her feeling freed by it. Disliking school. Studying in Germany. Her interest in theatre; studying acting in France. Being presented at Court. Traveling to Norway, Denmark, and Germany. Studying at Royal Academy of Dramatic Art in London. Adopting the stage name Colette O'Niel; performing as an actress. Meeting Miles Malleson; their marriage, 1915. Working at information bureau of the No-Conscription Fellowship; meeting Bertrand Russell in connection with conscientious objectors. Involvement with WWI pacifist movement. Losing her religious faith and evangelical inclinations. Attending conference for establishing Workers and Soldiers' Council. Husband's refusal to return to the army; his appearance before a tribunal. Author's appearing in film version of *Hindle Wakes*. Performing in *The Trojan Women*. Touring with theatrical company. Appearing in Oscar Wilde's *A Woman of No Importance*. Getting divorced, 1923. Living with her mother. Visiting Switzerland. Living in Ireland, touring there. Writing play *The Way;* unsuccessfully staging it. Traveling, touring in South Africa: Cape Town, Johannesburg; political, racial problems; native customs, peoples; questionability of European presence there.

Lady Constance exhibits a talent for vivid description of places and people and she provides explicit details about many noted Edwardians, especially in the literary, theatrical, and political arenas, yet she offers comparatively restricted information about herself. Although she comments on serious topics of the day, including social and political problems, she gives limited substantive attention to these issues or to the theatrical profession.

616 MALLESON, Elizabeth (née Whitehead). 1828–1916. *Elizabeth Malleson: 1828–1916: Autobiographical Notes and Letters.* Ed. by Hope Malleson (author's daughter). Privately published, 1926. 239 pp.; front. port.; memoir by ed.; illus. BLC to 1975 209:101.

Born in Chelsea, London. Father: Henry Whitehead, solicitor. Mother: Frances Maguire. 10 siblings. Married 1857, Frank Malleson. 3 daughters; 1 son. Wrote *Notes on the Early Training of Children* (1885). Educator; feminist; teacher; social reformer; publisher; journalist; education issues writer. Middle class.

Personal and professional memories and experiences, emphasizing educational, philanthropic activities, set within detailed observations on Victorian/Edwardian English society, spanning author's childhood to WWI years. Powerful influence of maternal grandmother. Attending Misses Woods' Unitarian school. Training as a teacher at Birkbeck School, c.1852. Founding Portman Hall School with Barbara Leigh Smith Bodichon, 1854; Bodichon's progressive theories. Author's ill health; ending teaching. Marriage, 1857; enjoying "complete individual freedom while working side by side" with husband. Her children's education. Taking interest in F. D. Maurice's Working Men's College. Raising funds, from John Stuart Mill, George Eliot, Harriet Martineau, and others, in inaugurating College for Working Women, 1864. School admission's being open to all sects; college's having no fixed curriculum. Joining women's suffrage movement; canvassing for feminist J. S. Mill in his political campaign, 1865. Participating in London National Society for Women's Suffrage. Working toward repeal of the Contagious Disease Acts; supporting legislating of Married Women's Property Acts. Founding the *English Woman's Journal* with Bodichon, Bessie Parkes Belloc, and Anna Jameson. Participating in the Ladies' London Emancipation Society. Crusading for better midwifery in rural areas. Founding the Rural Nurses' Association, 1891. Initiating the Gloucestershire branch of the National Vigilance Association, 1913, at age 85.

Malleson's account was edited by her daughter, Hope, and privately printed ten years after the author's death. Beginning with a memoir by Hope, Malleson's story is told through a compilation of her narrative, diary entries, and letters, with the editor providing extensive information about family history. From these various sources a portrait of Malleson emerges as a seemingly far-sighted and egalitarian individual committed to the alleviation of women's social problems and advance of working-class education.

617 MANNIN, Ethel. 1900–1984. *Confessions and Impressions*. Jarrolds Publishers, 1930. 282 pp.; front. port.; index. BLC to 1975 210:138. (other ed.: Penguin Books, 1937.)

Born in Clapham, Greater London. Father: Robert Mannin, civil servant, letter sorter. Mother: Edith Gray. 1 brother; 1 sister. Married 1919, J. A. Porteus, Scottish; separated 1921. Married 1938, Reginald Reynolds, writer, d.1958. Widow. 1 daughter. Wrote *Children of the Earth* (1930), *Bread and Roses* (1944), *Mission to Beirut* (1973), many others. Novelist; travel writer; short storyist; socialist; pacifist; vegetarian; editor; advertising writer; secretary. Middle class.

Lively combination of introspection and social commentary, set against England and Europe's turbulent changes during the first three decades of the 20th century. Feeling she inherited her zest for life from her family. Her father's whimsicality; her mother's pragmatism. Beginning writing, age 7. Winning prize for essay against cruelty to animals. Being a solitary, sensitive, shy child. Briefly attending a private school; being sent, age 7, to a council school; leaving school at age 14. Considering England's educational system to be unfit for intelligent young people. Her youthful "conversion" to vegetarianism and agnosticism, age 16, based on doubts about Christian doctrine and her attraction to socialist ideology. Beginning a lifelong obsession with death; ultimately reconciling socialist creed with Christianity. Writing poetry. Winning a half-fee scholarship to a secretarial school. Working as a stenographer and editorial assistant. Helping edit *Higham's Magazine* and the *Pelican;* publishing her own stories, articles, and verses in the latter, age 17. Absorbing knowledge from an anarchist artist friend, "J. S." Writing advertising. Marriage, age 19, to a Scotsman 13 years her senior. Childbirth; being casual in her child-rearing practices. Demise of the *Pelican;* continuing to write profusely. Writing novelettes for income. Austerity of living conditions with husband. Visiting U.S.; New York City being "freedom" for her despite its being "sad and mad and bad"; summing up U.S. as a "country without a soul." Continuing journey to Canada. Returning to England. Implied separation from husband and a series of love affairs, but stating that "there is a great deal too much fuss made of sexual relations." Coping with a lover's suicide. Religion's being "for the defeated, or those who lack courage." Considering the need for a new social order. Decrying existing civilization as "anti-life," a corrupter of ingenuity and natural intelligence that will ultimately destroy humanity. Sketches and portraits: Paul Robeson, George Lansbury, Ellen Wilkinson, Charles Laughton, Radclyffe Hall, others.

Mannin vividly describes her unconventional and impulsive life and expresses delight in her ability to elude anyone else's neat categorizations or labels. In another autobiography on her early years and milieu,

618 *Young in the Twenties* (1971), Mannin recalls the "Indian summer" between the world wars and her own "indiscreet" youth in the Jazz Age; in **619** *Privileged Spectator,* c.1939, she describes her increasing maturity, reaffirming her leftist politics and pacifism in light of Europe's descent into the Great Depression and the eventual horrors of WWII.

620 MANNIN, Ethel. 1900–1984. *Brief Voices: A Writer's Story.* Hutchinson, 1959. 280 pp.; biblio.; note; index. BLC to 1975 210:137.

Biographical: See *Confessions and Impressions.*

Maturing political and philosophical reflections, emphasizing religious curiosity, accompanied by personal, professional, and travel experiences, covering 1938–1950s. Her admiration for Emma Goldman; writing a novel, *Red Rose,* based on Goldman's life. Converting to pacifism; working for pacifist causes. Refusing to support WWII through volunteer work. Noting other people's imprisonment for pacifism. Publishing *Bread and Roses*. Her romantic feelings about Ireland; writing a novel set there. Experiencing a spiritual crisis, attending Mass; studying the Augustinian system of morals; not being able to make the leap of faith to Catholicism. Being sent to Germany at war's end by *Daily Mail;* finding incredible devastation. Addressing public meetings in England on conditions in postwar Germany. Her father's death, 1949; its profound effect on her. Visiting India with her daughter: her initial dislike of Hinduism, then a growing interest in Buddhism. Her love for cats; writing a book about them. Visiting Burma, receiving help from U Chan Htoon, head of Buddha Sasana Council; making friends; becoming a vegetarian. Traveling to Sweden to conduct research on Folk High Schools. Finishing novel *The Blue-Eyed Boy*. Extending help to an unhappily-married young woman and her two children; buying the woman a house. Nursing her mother through a severe bout with pneumonia. Her second husband's journey to Australia to lecture to Quakers; her feelings of terrible sadness at his departure; his death of a stroke in Australia. Memories of his life and achievements; his religious belief in the afterlife. Her continuing interest in political causes; identifying with Direct Action Committee Against Nuclear War. Discussing the ethical evils of censorship. Noting similarities among all political parties in power. Her view that writers need to be aware of their political and social surroundings and be good storytellers. Her concern for the Christian principle of redemption. Presenting a detailed discussion of the laws of karma, yet not subscribing to any religious belief; feeling closest to Buddhism. Discussing the theory of oblivion, finality of death for those with no belief in an afterlife. Lamenting the violence, ugliness, and joylessness of "children of atomic age." Reacting to political changes between 1900 and the present.

Mannin's book demonstrates her ever-increasing political awareness and the ongoing evolution of her ideas about religion. Written in her middle years in a provocative and sophisticated style, the book is a celebration of life. It also represents her attempt to deal with the loss of her husband, Reginald Reynolds, by increasing her social and political reform activities, particularly her support of pacifism. Her **621** *Connemara Journal* (1947), documents her stay in a rural Irish cottage, 1945–46, her meditations in that setting on humankind's historical and moral development, and her own obsession with death. In **622** *Stories from My Life* (1971), she elaborates on the years 1962–71, and includes further anecdotes about travel and people she has met. **623** *Sunset over Dartmoor* (1977) is a discussion of the author's decision to retire to Devon, which inevitably extends to a reevaluation of life, death, and God.

624 MANNING, Dame Elizabeth Leah (née Perrett). 1886–1977. *A Life for Education: An Autobiography*. Victor Gollancz Ltd., 1970. 263 pp.; illus.; index. BLC to 1975 210:148.

Born in England. Father: Charles William Perrett, timber merchant. Mother: Harriet Tappin. 1 brother; other siblings. Married 1914, William Manning, Cambridge professor, died c.1945. Widow. Wrote *What I Saw in Spain*. Politician; member of Parliament; justice of the peace; political activist; teacher; socialist; factory manager; birth control activist; WWI volunteer; WWII volunteer; organizer (political); pacifist; philanthropist. Upper middle class.

Catalogue of professional and philanthropic activities, interspersed with occasional personal memories, spanning author's childhood to 1950. Family history. Huguenot emigration to England. Accompanying her parents to Canada. Returning to England. Incident that helped form her social conscience: playing with a group of poor children, having her boots stolen, lying about it to protect herself and the other children. Attending academy for young ladies. Reading *The Socialist Church;* its influence on her. Attending Cambridge. Her interest in the Fabian Society. Taking first teaching assignment in school for the disadvantaged; recalling student who died of malnutrition. Starting evening play center. Marriage, 1914. WWI: serving as VAD nurse. Her trade union activities. Serving on General Strike Committee, 1926. Becoming one of the first women justices of the peace. Organizing women workers at Cambridge University. Visiting Berlin, attending political meetings. Having a bout with tuberculosis; convalescing. Teaching in Open Air school. Serving as chair of National Union of Teachers. Becoming Labour M.P., c.1930. Working as joint secretary to Parliamentary Department. Friendships with M.P.s Oliver Baldwin and Margaret Bondfield. Becoming assistant education officer. Being joint secretary of Coordinating Committee against War and Fascism. Working with

Spanish Medical Aid Committee in Spain; evacuating children in Bilbao before and during Spanish Civil War. Opening Leah Manning Home for refugee children. WWII: working with London Ambulance Service, helping evacuate children. Working for aid to Russia. Reelection to Parliament, c.1945. Her husband's death. Traveling to Eastern Europe; describing postwar devastation. Public speaking in U.S. Being chair of Women's Movement against War. Leading women's delegation to Soviet Union; describing economic problems and conditions in 1920s; the Russian Revolution. Becoming factory personnel manager. Working for family planning. Discussing her frustration at not having changed the world; her desire to retain some optimism; the severity of current social problems.

In this informally written memoir Manning looks back over a life of service. She expresses feelings of failure, yet seems to retain an optimism characteristic of her dedication to her many causes. Her political analyses and detailed discussions of social conditions facilitate an understanding of the period marked by tumultuous change between the two world wars.

625 MANNING, Rosemary (Sarah Davys, pseud.). 1911–1988. *A Corridor of Mirrors*. The Women's Press, 1987. 234 pp. BLC 1986–87 13:95.

Born in Weymouth, Dorset. Father: Thomas Davys Manning, physician. Mother: Mary Ann Coles. 3 brothers. Single. Wrote *Look, Stranger* (1960), *The Chinese Garden* (1962). Novelist; feminist; children's author; lesbian; socialist; teacher; shop assistant; secretary; school founder; school administrator; physician's daughter. Middle class.

Searching and poignant memories of a continuing quest for sexual and personal identity within the confines of societal and personal expectations, interspersed with literary and political opinions, covering c.1911–1980s. Author's being a tomboy; enjoying play with her brothers. Mother's platonic friendships with women and her restlessness at being a "mere" wife. Being brought up to believe that men should have the lion's share of everything. Attending day school. Father's resigning his Weymouth practice because of a romantic indiscretion. Growing dissension in parents' marriage. Author's feelings of isolation at boarding school. Finding consolation in writing and producing plays. Her first lesbian encounter, with a housemistress; initial feelings of confusion and betrayal; being disturbed about her sexual identity; attempting suicide. Attending Royal Holloway College. Working as shop assistant and secretary; relating her unhappiness in this work to her socialist leanings. Her unhappiness and frustration with her life culminating in nervous breakdown, then an unsatisfying experience with psychoanalysis. Teaching in a provincial grammar school. Having a brief love affair with a female art teacher. Starting a day school. Taking over a preparatory school in London. Her ill-fated affair with a married woman. Starting a new affair with an editor; editor's ending affair; author's serious suicide attempt. Writing *A Time and a Time* as therapy, publishing it under pseudonym. Having an affair with "Kay"; being unable to adjust to Kay's working-class origins. Embarking on writing career. Publishing *Remaining a Stranger* to good reviews. Writing children's books. Entering into happy relationship with "Jan"; Jan's leaving; author's loneliness and inability to adjust; feeling abandoned. Differences in attitude toward lesbians and homosexuals in her youth and in modern times; prejudices against lesbians. Supporting anti-nuclear position. Her views on the need to oppose all abuse and cruelty.

Manning takes the reader on an intellectual journey in which literary allusions and citations serve as extensions of her feelings. Her writing is philosophic and introspective, frequently suffused with melancholy; she appears to have been most creative in response to the grief of being abandoned by lovers. In **626** *A Time and a Time* (1971), she seems unemotional as she discusses her depression and suicide attempts, using humor to distance herself from past tragedies and confusions. She discusses her lesbianism matter-of-factly.

627 MARKHAM, Beryl. 1902–1986. *West with the Night*. Boston: Houghton Mifflin, 1942. 294 pp. BLC to 1975 211:401. (other ed.: San Francisco: North Point Press, 1983.)

Born in Leicestershire. Father not named, horse racer and breeder, farmer. Mother not named. Married Raoul Schumacher; other marriages. Wrote *The Splendid Outcast: Beryl Markham's African Stories* (1987). Knew pioneer pilot Denys Finch-Hatton and Baron von Blixen (husband of Baroness Karen Blixen, Isak Dinesen, pseud.). Aviator; horse trainer; horse breeder; horsewoman; short storyist; foreign resident (Kenya). Upper middle class.

Childhood in Kenya and experiences as pioneer freelance pilot in East Africa leading to her transatlantic flight, covering c.1906–37. Father's emigration to East Africa when author was age 4. Life on horse breeding farm. Neighbor Lady Delamere's serving as author's "adopted mother." Incident in which a "tame" lion attacked author. Sneaking away from lessons to hunt with Nandi tribe. Her aggressive hunting dog; a boar hunt. Lifelong friendship with a Nandi boy who became her servant. Effects of WWI on East Africa. Taming a breeding stallion for father; delivering a colt foal. At age 17, being given choice of staying in Africa or going with father to Peru to train horses; deciding to remain; getting a racehorse trainer's license. A race won by a filly she trained. First meeting pilot Tom Black; taking flying lessons from him; getting her pilot's license. Friendship with Denys Finch-Hatton, pioneer African aviator.

Freelance flying in East Africa; scouting game by air; taking Baron von Blixen on dangerous air safari. Delivering oxygen by night to a mining camp, 1935. Flying with von Blixen from Nairobi to London, 1936. Her transatlantic flight in September 1936. After taking up residence in America, returning to Africa to visit father.

With its warm, poetic, and richly sensitive style, this book compares to Isak Dinesen's *Out of Africa* and Antoine de Saint-Exupèry's *Night Flight*. When the book was first published, however, some reviewers were scandalized that the author's persona was so unlike the Beryl Markham everyone knew. Some attributed the book to her husband Raoul Schumacher. Markham comes across as nerveless when facing danger, but very sensitive to beauty.

628 MARKHAM, Violet Rosa. 1872–1959. *Return Passage: The Autobiography of Violet R. Markham*, C.H. Oxford University Press, 1953. 260 pp.; front. port.; illus.; apps.; letters; index. BLC to 1975 211:415.

Born in Derbyshire. Father: Charles Markham, engineer, industrialist. Mother: Rosa Paxton. 3 brothers; 1 sister. Married 1915, James Carruthers, soldier on governor-general's staff, South Africa, d.1936. Widow. Wrote *South Africa: Past and Present, A Woman's Watch on the Rhine, Romanesque France,* others. Biographer; travel writer; novelist; political writer; social historian; school administrator; antisuffragist; suffragist; politician (mayor); WWI volunteer; WWII volunteer. Upper middle class.

Personal, professional, and travel reminiscences set within a larger treatment of social and political problems, spanning the 1870s to 1950. Paternal family history. Being an unexpected child, but loved by her family. Deaths of her father and her brother Ernest. Studying with governesses. Being interested in living conditions of working classes. Suffering a bout with illness; traveling to South Africa as convalescent, 1899. Political, racial, and social ramifications of Boer War. Serving as school manager to Chesterfield School Board. Starting settlement house. Traveling across Canada, 1905; negative first impressions of Canada and the U.S. Recalling Edwardian prosperity for some; the unequal distribution of wealth. Initial opposition to women's suffrage, based on her strong view that the vote for women was insufficient without social changes to benefit all women, especially poor women. Undertaking antisuffrage activities with Mrs. Humphry Ward; revising her view to support the advantages of votes for women. Traveling to Russia and China, 1913; discussing the Chinese character and social customs. Touring Japan and Java. Her interest in local government in England. WWI: working on National Relief Fund. Being elected mayor of Chesterfield, 1915. Marriage. Accompanying husband to Germany, 1919. Visiting Switzerland and Greece. Joining Unemployment Assistance Board.

Husband's death. WWII: serving on advisory committee for organizing shelters. Her analysis of social problems faced by the English poor. Perceiving a deterioration in human relations consequent upon technological "progress." Her views on developing the welfare state.

Markham's style is semiformal and her tone is detached; she seems to take her subjects so seriously as to avoid any hint of lightness or warmth. She writes in depth about British social and political issues and attitudes, from the Victorian era to the atomic age, making the book provocative. In **629** *Friendship's Harvest* (1956), she presents biographical sketches of many of the prominent friends who influenced her during more than eight decades, interspersing the account with further personal memories and travel experiences. The book is valuable for its expression of her own and others' social attitudes and her descriptions of principally Victorian and Edwardian luminaries.

MARLBOROUGH, Duchess of. [*See* SPENCER-CHURCHILL, Frances Laura.]

630 MARSDEN, Kate. 1859–1931. *On Sledge and Horseback to Outcast Siberian Lepers*. The Record Press, Ltd., 1891. 243 pp.; front.; preface; map; app. NUC pre56 363:336.

Born in England. Parents not named. Single. Missionary (Russia); health reformer; nurse; foreign resident (Russia). Middle class.

Fascinating in-depth account of intrepid nursing-missionary efforts in Russia and encounters with Russian nobility and bureaucracy, 1885–91. Problem of leprosy in Russia during Russo-Turkish War. Journeying to Siberia. Visiting the prison at Ekaterinberg; her missionary/health care work with convicts and ex-convicts in Tukalinsk. Visiting towns of Tjumen, Omsk, Krasnoyarsk, Kransk, and Irkutsk. Securing permission to visit lepers of Viluisk Circuit. Organizing committee to help lepers; recruiting other missionary women, including convent sisters at Tomsk. Returning to Moscow and St. Petersburg to interest Russians in leprosy problem; securing Countess Alexandrine Tolstoi's financial support; interesting the press in her project. Visiting modern leper colony in Baltic provinces. Organizing Sunday collection in churches all over Russia to benefit lepers. Observing Russian royalty, nobility, and people of other social classes. Offering a vivid description of difficulties of sledge traveling. Peasants' interest in her missionary work. History of lepers and their treatment in Yakutsk province and Viluisk Circuit, 1827–91. Connecting native customs, religious practices, people's attitude toward lepers. Living conditions of lepers in isolation. Plans for more leper colonies. Testimonials and charitable contributions of Russian nobility, medical and other officials to her cause.

In an elevated and moral tone, Marsden focuses on her efforts to bring aid to Russian lepers, and credits the success of her enterprise to her unwavering religious faith. The book offers an excellent account of late-19th-century Russian towns and villages, as seen by an apparently strong-minded, determined, and compassionate Englishwoman.

631 MARSH, Edith Ngaio. 1899–1982. *Black Beech and Honeydew: An Autobiography*. Auckland: William Collins Publishers, Ltd., 1981. 315 pp.; illus. BLC to 1975 212:241. (1st pub. 1965.)

Born in Christchurch, New Zealand. Father: H. E. Marsh, New Zealand Bank manager. Mother: Rose Elizabeth Seager. Single. Wrote *Artists in Crime, Clutch of Constables, Photo-Finish*, others. Novelist; playwright; theatrical producer; theatrical director; actress (stage); travel writer; traveler (South Africa, Europe). Upper middle class.

Unconventional and frank recollections of a creative life in the arts, spanning author's childhood to late middle age. Her early interest in reading. Childhood companions. Attending school; studying with governess at home. Attending St. Margaret's College. Studying art. Performing in amateur theatricals. Traveling through New Zealand with her mother. Writing her first play, *The Medallion*. Acting with Alan Wilkie's Shakespeare company and the company of Rosemary Rees. Mother's psychic experiences; their effect on author. Writing travel articles for New Zealand press. Travel to England, 1928. Visiting in Capetown. Describing Durban, Zulu customs and traditions. Beginning to take an interest in mystery writing. Mother's death. Returning to New Zealand to keep house for father. Collaborating on *The Nursing Home Murder* with Dr. Henry Jellet; dramatizing the novel. Directing repertory societies in New Zealand during WWII. Touring throughout New Zealand. Her father's death. Being producer for Commonwealth Players company in Australia. Opening in Auckland. Traveling to Spain, Rome, Florence. Evaluating Florentine art. Researching detective fiction. Meeting Agatha Christie. Becoming Grand Master of Mystery Writers of America. Extensive discussion of producing Shakespearean plays. Differences between English and New Zealand people; racial friction in New Zealand. Surveying modern theatre companies in New Zealand.

Marsh's style is informal, her tone conversational as she documents her long career as a mystery writer and theatrical director. Frequent literary allusions and citations illustrate the author's most profound and intimate feelings about life. Her principal aim in writing this memoir seems to be to show the tenacity and daring in her approach to various branches of the arts, qualities she insists have contributed to her success. The book's technical information on producing plays, especially Shakespearean plays, charts four decades of changing theatrical traditions.

632 MARSHALL, Mary Paley. 1850–1944. *What I Remember.* Cambridge: Cambridge University Press, 1947. Ed. by C. W. Guilleband (author's nephew). 54 pp.; front.; intro. by Professor George M. Trevelyan; illus.; app. NUC pre56 363:616.

Born in Northamptonshire. Father: Thomas Paley, rector. Mother: Judith Wormald. 2 brothers; 1 sister. Married 1877, Alfred Marshall, Oxford professor of economics. Coauthor with husband of *Economics of Industry* (1879). Knew Henry and Eleanor Sidgwick, Elizabeth Wordsworth, Anne Jemima Clough. Academic; educator; economist; education activist; librarian; philanthropist; academic's spouse; clergyman's daughter. Upper middle class.

Groundbreaking education activist's recollections of change in women's higher education, 1850s–1924. Receiving home education from father: pleasant, lasting memories of his reading aloud to her and siblings; studying Latin, Hebrew, Euclid, and religion with him; his pleasure in her scholarship; her resenting his burning her and her sister's dolls out of evangelical prejudice against frivolity. Pastimes with her younger brother. Studying with German governess. Attending school for young ladies. Being one of first five women accepted at Cambridge; living there with Anne Clough; Clough's accomplishments in education and later tenure as principal of Newnham College. Being one of first two women to attempt Moral Sciences Tripos exam; earning certificate. Lecturing and tutoring in economics at Newnham after graduation; teaching correspondence courses on political economy. Marriage. Husband's becoming an Oxford don. Author's teaching parallel economics courses for women at Oxford. Her friendship with Elizabeth Wordsworth, first head of Lady Margaret Hall, Oxford; social acquaintance with Oxford and Cambridge dons and their wives. Inviting poor people selected by Women's Settlement to stay in her home. Participating in Social Discussion Society. Meeting Octavia Hill, Emma Cons, and Mary Clifford. Becoming member of Ladies' Dining Society. Author's views of women's colleges at Oxford.

Marshall focuses on the dramatic changes at the dawn of formal higher education for women, yet she also presents delightful glimpses of everyday middle-class activity in academic circles. She is outspoken and forthright in this book, which is informed by her apparent dedication to the causes of education and social equality. After her famous husband's death, she spent twenty years as a librarian in the library to which his professional books were given.

MARSHALL, Sybil. [*See* EDWARDS, Kate Mary.]

633 MARSTON, Muriel. c.1900–? *Who Loves a Garden.* Methuen, 1936. 241 pp.; illus.; index. BLC to 1975 212:367.

Probably born in County Donegal, Ireland. Parents, siblings not mentioned. Married, husband not named, Irish. Gardener. Middle class.

One year in the life of a home gardener in Stratford-on-Avon, 1935. Residence with husband. Cultivating shrubs and flowers. Criteria for hiring gardeners and the local mason. Depicting local wildlife: birds, weasels, squirrels. The influence of Gertrude Jekyll on author's garden design. Gains and losses in her garden the previous year. Reading 17th- and 18th-century gardening books and cookbooks. Visiting Cornwall to buy daffodils. Visiting Ireland; traveling by automobile with her husband; visiting their relatives and old haunts in Dublin and County Donegal. Returning to England.

Organizing her book by the cycle of seasons, Marston shares with readers her knowledge of and rewards from creative gardening. Her writing is often poetically descriptive, quoting authorities on horticulture and using Latin taxonomic names even for familiar plants. The author acknowledges Gertrude Jekyll as the authority of an earlier generation; she draws on the history of English gardening in general and in particular to inspire expansion of the gardening avocation and lifestyle.

634 MARTINDALE, Hilda. 1875–1952. *From One Generation to Another,* 1839–1944. George Allen & Unwin Ltd., 1944. 208 pp.; front. port.; index. NUC pre56 365:104.

Born in London. Father: William Martindale, fellow of the Royal Geographical Society, businessman. Mother: Louisa Spicer, philanthropist, feminist, missionary. 1 sister (physician Louisa Martindale); 2 stepbrothers; 2 stepsisters. Single. Factory inspector; civil servant; public speaker; feminist; social reformer; government administrator; child welfare activist. Middle class.

A detailed discussion of a social reformer's working life in her various careers, and observations on pressing societal issues, spanning her childhood to 1944. Mother's family and personal history; influence on author of mother's career and accomplishments. The medical career of author's sister. Author's attending Royal Holloway College. Her interest in social work for children and civil service work. Accompanying her mother and sister on world tour. Employed by government as Inspector of Factories. Working in Ireland. Reviewing extensive anonymous letters of complaint from workers regarding harsh working conditions, their employers' abuses, their fear of employers. Assessing permanent damage to health of workers. Giving public lectures on industrial problems. Working as senior lady inspector for the Midlands. Being promoted to deputy chief inspector for England and Scotland. Becoming director of Women's Establishments at Her Majesty's Treasury. Serving on Banking Trade Board, Rubber Manufacturing Board, and Civil Service Commission after retirement. Becoming member of the Council of

Froebel Educational Institute. Examining problems of children in labor force, c.1901. Consulting on health risks in factories; children's being pressed into labor force by their parents or guardians. Describing social conditions under which married women seek work. How "truck" and "credit" systems are financial traps for workers. Viewing WWI as a stimulant to enterprise. Discussing need for women to apply for higher government positions; job opportunities for women workers in early 20th century.

The lengthy first sections of the book treat the accomplishments in social welfare of the author's mother, Louisa Spicer Martindale, and the medical career of Louisa Martindale, the author's sister (see *A Woman Surgeon*). In the sections about her own career as inspector of factories, Hilda Martindale writes matter-of-factly and unemotionally, but appears to have been genuinely committed to improving the life of all workers, women and children in particular. She charts the progress made in legislative labor protection during her lifetime. Eliciting her unbridled enthusiasm are higher education and improved employment status for women, and she urges women to pursue government careers.

635 MARTINDALE, L[ouisa]. C.B.E. 1873–1966. *A Woman Surgeon*. Victor Gollancz, Ltd., 1951. 253 pp.; front. port.; index. BLC to 1975 213:153.

Born in England. Father: William Martindale, fellow of the Royal Geographical Society, businessman. Mother: Louisa Spicer, philanthropist, feminist, missionary. 1 sister (Hilda Martindale); 2 stepbrothers; 2 stepsisters. Single. Physician; suffragist; justice of the peace; public speaker; WWI volunteer; social reformer; organizer (political); health administrator. Middle class.

Medical trailblazer's recollections of a life of career accomplishments and social service, covering author's childhood to aftermath of WWII. Death of her father. Mother's decision to move family to Germany. Returning to England; studying with governesses. Attending Royal Holloway College. Studying medicine at mother's insistence. Supporting women's suffrage. Attending London School of Medicine for Women. Practicing medicine in Hull. Taking world tour: visiting hospitals in Austria, Italy, India, Australia, New Zealand; unfavorable opinion of hospital conditions in Chicago. Her impressions of American social reformer Jane Addams. Praising hospitals in Boston. Returning to her Hull practice. Starting a Women's Suffrage Society group and a branch of National Council of Women. Moving practice to Brighton. Being appointed honorary secretary of the British Medical Association. Serving on National Union of Women's Suffrage Societies. Her interest in prostitution's social and medical consequences for women. Serving on staff of Islingwood Dispensary for Women and Children, c.1910. Significance to her of doctor-patient relationship. Death of her mother. WWI: working in Royaumont Hospital in France. Opening consulting practice in London, c.1919. Being president of British National Association (later Medical Women's Federation). Becoming justice of the peace for Brighton. Having strong interest in prison reform. Earning Commander of British Empire award for her medical accomplishments. Becoming fellow of Royal College of Obstetricians and Gynecologists. Discussing history of women in the medical profession. Retiring from active practice, 1947.

Martindale's autobiography focuses on her pioneering efforts as a woman physician and advocate of women's political and professional causes. Although some of this book deals with the more technical aspects of the author's medical practice, her catalogue of women's and medical organizations, and her descriptions of her roles in these, have great historical value.

636 MARTINEAU, Alice (née Williams). 1866–1956. *Reminiscences of Hunting and Horses*. Ernest Benn Ltd., 1930. 148 pp.; illus. NUC pre56 365:116.

Born in England. Father: surname Williams. Mother not named. 1 brother. Married Philip Martineau. 3 sons. Society woman; artist (painter); horse breeder; horsewoman; hunter. Upper class.

Personal reminiscences and opinions on changes in the English avocation of hunting, covering the late Victorian era to 1930. Horses author knew in childhood; her pony, Fanny. Studying painting. Her growing interest in riding and hunting. Friendships with fellow equine artists. Creating paintings of dogs. Accepting invitation from her brother to hunt in Ireland. Attending London hunt breakfasts. H.R.H. Prince Christian of Denmark's interest in hunting; her acquaintance with him. Her mare's extraordinary intelligence. Attending Ascot races. Technical aspects of hunting, hunting equipment, differences between fox and stag hunting. Hunting during visit to America. Her favorable impression of how horses are treated in America. Participating in the Hackney Society. Attempting enterprise of horse breeding; its difficulties. Rationalizing the need for fox hunting. Irish love of horses; London horse dealers. Changes in riding in Rotten Row, 1890s–1930; riding customs' being altered by advent of motor car. The French government's place for horse breeding. Importance of children's learning to ride. Rise in prices of horses during the last two generations.

Martineau's memoir explores the author's lifelong passion for horses, hunting, and riding and discusses the changes in these pastimes between the Victorian era and the early years of the 20th century. Defensive concerning the aristocratic flavor of fox hunting and its reputation for cruelty, she attempts to justify this sport. Her book gives an excellent picture of the cultural events surrounding horse racing and breeding in England, as well as showing the huge financial enterprise this aristocratic pastime has generated.

637 MARTINEAU, Harriet. 1802–1876. *Harriet Martineau's Autobiography*. Ed. by Maria Weston Chapman. Virago Press, 1983. 2 vols. Vol. 1: 441 pp.; front. port.; intro. by Gaby Weiner; author's intro.; illus.; app. Vol. 2: 510 pp.; front. port.; apps. NUC 1983–1987 name index microfiche #0219. (1st pub. Smith & Elder, 1877.)

Born in Norwich, Norfolk. Father: Thomas Martineau, cloth manufacturer. Mother: Elizabeth Rankin. 3 sisters; 4 brothers. Single. Wrote *Principle and Practice* (1827), *Illustrations of Taxation* (1834), *Illustrations of Political Economy* (1834). Knew Elizabeth Barrett, Mary Somerville, Fanny Kemble, Thomas and Jane Carlyle. Social reformer; journalist; abolitionist; essayist; economist; feminist; public speaker. Middle class.

In-depth, leisurely walk through personal memories, emphasizing author's religious and political opinions, set against the dramatic social changes of the first half of the 19th century. Vol. 1: Family history. Her imaginary night terrors, nervousness, strong religiosity in childhood. Planning suicide so she could go to heaven. Her passion for justice; its lack in her home. Having little self-respect. Attending day school. Battling partial deafness. Yearning for mother's love and approval. Attending boarding school. Explaining Unitarian vs. more orthodox Christian belief. Illness and death of father, financial stress on family. Becoming engaged; fiancé's mysterious illness and death. Feeling herself suited to single life. Becoming an advocate of political economy, and writing fictional didactic stories about political economy; publishing by subscription. Discussing population control; her friendship with Malthus. Supporting proposed Poor Law of 1834. Writing a series of stories supporting the New Poor Law. Her antimonopoly views. Writing *Illustrations of Taxation*. Having her advice sought by parliamentary reformers. Socializing in London literary and political circles, 1832–34. Believing self-reliance is essential for any advancement. Discussing the absurdity of women's being able to be financially responsible yet unable to vote. Vol. 2: Journey to America. Her opposition to slavery; publishing antislavery articles. Supporting U.S. women's suffrage movement after 1848. Socializing with American politicians, literati: Ralph Waldo Emerson, Daniel Webster, Henry Clay. Writing lead articles for the London *Daily News*. Refusing pension offered by Lord Melbourne for fear of compromising her political principles. Her obsession with illness and death. Being helped by mesmerism. Writing *Forest and Game Law Tales,* stories about the Irish potato famine. Lecturing to children and working-class adults. Writing about the political situation in Europe. Investigating workhouse and factory conditions; opposing factory legislation. Contributing to Dickens's *Household Words*. Promoting wider employment of women. Having a bout with serious illness. Relying on her brother, Rev. James Martineau, for support, advice, and encouragement. Her optimism for the future; her faith in humanity's basic morality.

In a formal and somewhat didactic style, Martineau presents a life of literary and social reform accomplishments. Her introspection and speculations, particularly about religion, are highly self-revelatory. By incorporating the minutiae of the sociopolitical externals of her world into her narrative, she presents painstaking portrait, both real and ideal, of 19th-century English middle-class and rural laboring-class life. For a brief overview of the author's youthful professional interests and political concerns, see **638** "Some Autobiographical Particulars of Miss Harriet Martineau," in *Monthly Repository of Theology and General Literature*, 7:612–615, 1833.

639 MARTIN-NICHOLSON, Mary Eliza, Sister (née Gripper). c.1885–?. *My Experiences on Three Fronts*. George Allen & Unwin, 1916. 288 pp.; intro. NUC pre56 365:67.

Born in England. Parents not named. Single. Nurse (WWI); WWI volunteer; Red Cross worker. Middle class.

Commentary comparing the character of troops of various nationalities, with high praise for the British "Tommies," covering 1914–16. Public reaction in London to impending war. British lack of preparedness. Traveling to Belgium with nursing sisters; advantage of author's fluency in French. Being cut off from France and Belgium by advancing Germans. Being assigned to ambulance duty by city of Brussels for Belgian wounded. German oppression of civilians. Participating in secret civilian network for transmitting news; Germans' execution of her news source. Traveling in disguise to Louvain to witness aftermath of German destruction. Returning to Brussels; offering her services at a Belgian convent receiving Belgian wounded. Takeover of convent by Germans for their wounded; under house arrest, being forced to stay on as nurse to 1,000 German troops, the only woman there. Her near-rape by a German officer. Criticizing Germans' "kultur." Deportation by Germans; arrival in Copenhagen. Traveling with other nurses to assist Red Cross on Russian front. Working in Petrograd hospital. Character of Russian soldiers. Traveling to Warsaw; service in military hospital. Returning to England. Attempting to return to French front; encountering opposition from British nursing authorities. Traveling to France to treat typhoid patients. Complaints about conditions of nursing: low pay, long hours, major personal sacrifices. Serving in British military hospital in France. Busy, intense work among wounded at clearing station for soldiers from trenches. Becoming ill with septic poisoning; eventual return to England.

Both dramatic and novelistic in style, Martin-Nicholson's memoir uses much dialogue. Wartime patriotism strongly affects the author's viewpoint; she consistently praises British soldiers and gives many details on German atrocities. Her autobiography serves as an important source on troops of different nations and on nursing service in WWI.

640 MASSEY, Gertrude (née Seth). 1868–d.a.1934. *Kings, Commoners and Me*. Blackie & Son, 1934. 200 pp.; front. port.; illus.; app. NUC pre56 368:328.

Born in England. Father not named, merchant. Mother not named. 5 siblings. Married 1890, Henry Massey, painter. 1 daughter. Artist (painter); teacher (art); artist's spouse. Middle class.

Author's progression from painting and drawing in childhood to painting miniatures for royalty, 1884–1934. Father's death, which leaves family penniless. Author's supporting siblings after his death. Studying art under future husband. Obtaining Art Teacher's Certificate at age 16. Studying art in France. Painting portraits of the daughter of the Marchioness of Landowne and the Prince of Wales's dog. Her work's being displayed at the Institute of Painters, 1900. Painting the dogs of Prince and Princess Charles of Denmark. Creating miniatures of Prince Edward, Prince Albert, Princess Mary, and Prince Henry. Painting Queen Victoria's portrait from a photograph. Painting a portrait of Queen Alexandra, 1907. Receiving commissions from patrons sent by King Edward VII. Painting miniatures of the King and Queen of Norway and Prince Olaf, the daughters of Lady Mary Wentworth Fitzwilliam and other notables. Husband's acquisition of Heatherlys Art School, which he modernized, c.1920s. Author and husband's working as art teachers; using nude models at their school despite convention forbidding women to paint nudes; admitting pupils of all nationalities. History and tradition of art in England.

Silent about her personal feelings, Massey reveals only her modesty about her artistic abilities. She chooses to relate in a conversational style anecdotes of royalty, aristocratic and other patrons, the history of English art, and her own art training and teaching.

641 MATTHEWS, Caroline, M.D. 1879–?. *Experiences of a Woman Doctor in Serbia*. Mills & Boon, 1916. 247 pp.; front. port.; foreword; prologue; illus.; epilogue. NUC pre56 369:652.

Probably born in Scotland. Parents not named. Physician; WWI volunteer; foreign resident (Serbia). Probably single. Middle class.

Colorful account of author's service with the Scottish Women's Hospital Unit and personal adventures in Serbia, 1915. Joining Scottish Women's Medical Unit. Memories of Malta; introduction to "roughing it." Her first impression of the Balkans: lack of hygiene's increasing opportunity for disease; many prisoners of war. Socializing with international colleagues. German invasion of Serbia. Her preference for difficult, rather than easy, life. Working in military hospital at Uzsitsi. Receiving evacuation order. Staying behind to care for wounded. Recalling Serbian attendants. Discussing Serbian history, customs, food shortages, patients at hospital. Cholera outbreak; setting up stringent precautions. Venturing to attend wounded women in the hills. Noting hard living conditions for peasants. Diphtheria outbreak; contracting it herself. Her room's being ransacked by order of the commanding medical officer; her deteriorating relations with him. Being charged with espionage; being treated badly by Serbs as a possible spy. Arduous journey, as prisoner, through various small towns. British authorities' threatening her with firing squad; her eventual release. Traveling though Switzerland; being followed by Swiss or German agent trying to prevent her leaving the country. Outwitting attempts to detain her. War's devastation beyond battlefield. Reasons for Britain's participation in WWI. Differences in Balkan and English characters.

Matthews's informal style and calm tone belie her dramatic and often heroic exploits. Her descriptive anecdotes about military and civilian personnel range from the melancholy to the humorous, adding a human touch to her war memories. The author's behind-the-scenes look at how prisoners of war were treated and at the Serbian role in the war is of considerable documentary worth.

642 MAYO, Isabella Fyvie (Edward Garrett, pseud.). 1843–1914. *Recollections of What I Saw, What I Lived Through, and What I Learned during More than Fifty Years of Social and Literary Experience*. John Murray, 1910. 441 pp.; front. port.; foreword; illus.; biblio.; index. BLC to 1975 118:94.

Born in London. Father: George Fyvie, Scottish, bakery owner. Mother: Margaret Thomson. 7 siblings. Married 1870, John Mayo, solicitor, d.1877. Widow. Wrote *Gold and Dross* (1874), *Mrs. Raven's Temptation* (1882), *The Mystery of Allenbrale* (1885), many others. Novelist; journalist; editor; copyist; businesswoman; translator; antivivisectionist; animal welfare activist. Middle class.

Memories of writer's childhood, education, and career, and the emergence of her self-reliance, arranged by topic and set against a social history of the City of London, 1840s–1910. Ch. 1: Father's family history. His emigrating to London, working in and ultimately buying bakery. Author's rejecting Scottish Episcopalianism, attributing her nonsectarianism to father's influence. Ch. 2: Scenes from childhood home above bakery. Being accomplished reader by age 4. Preferring her "beloved cats" to dolls. Remembering old black family servant, escapee from American slavery. Her favorite sister's death at 18, author's age 12; mother's grief. Describing London, c.1850s–1860s: foreign immigrants, aristocratic deadbeats, prostitutes, chimney sweeps, shops, the Lord Mayor's Procession. Dying father's confiding to author, age 8, his youthful refusal to marry while still in debt. Ch. 3: Teaching Sunday school for working-class girls. Praising dame schools; damning as useless other female schooling before establishment of women's high schools and colleges, 1860s. Attending coeducational day school; excelling over students of both sexes. Before age 14, being removed from school upon family physician's recommending not overstraining the female brain. Ch. 4: Mother's poor business sense; resulting failure of bakery; author's resolving to pay off large family debt. Unsuccessfully submitting her writing to magazines. Burgeoning women's employment agencies. Being hired as temporary copyist, 1860. Having stories, articles accepted for pay. Becoming law copyist; starting her own agency. Rejecting many women as unqualified to work for her; preferring to hire men. In 1867, being commissioned to write serialized novel for £300. Paying off family debt; marrying family attorney, 1870. Ch. 5: Trekking from publisher to publisher with her work. Mrs. S. C. Hall becoming her lifelong mentor. *St. James's Magazine's* accepting her poems; editor's giving her pseudonym and lucrative commissions to write serials. Husband's death, 1877; author's desolation and recovery. Evaluating popular writers and artists, 1860s–1870s. Sketching her favorite editors, notably Rev. Thomas Guthrie, who shared her ideals: "the brotherhood of all races of men, the cause of international peace, and the recognition of the rights of animals." Ch. 6: Anecdotes of contemporaries: politicians, writers, artists and eccentric friends. Ch. 7: Changes in Anglican worship, 1850–1910. Varying attitudes of clergy toward poor. Social history of London churches. Ch. 8: Author's 1870 and 1890 visits to Canada; noting encroaching deforestation and urbanization. At age 25, traveling to Scotland; eventually residing there. Traveling in Holy Land, Egypt, and Greece; criticizing European condescension toward non-Westerners. Remarking on gentleness of Eastern children, in contrast to bullying English ones. Ch. 9: Praising housework's role in developing female character. Regretting growing working-class scorn for domestic service. Urging modern wives to simplify their homes, obviating need for servants. Ch. 10: Legends of London crimes; public executions. In middle age, author's preaching on Sundays at a women's prison. Speculating on failure of penal system to reform or deter criminals. Ch. 11: Anecdotes of her own and others' occult experiences. Ch. 12: Working with Scottish Society for the Prevention of Vivisection; editing its publication, *Our Fellow Mortals*. Pondering life's essentials: discharging one's duty in God's eyes, developing the mind, and putting one's values into perspective.

Dedicating this volume to her deceased husband, Mayo resurrects the sights and sounds of the City of London during their life together. She also comments on capitalism's ouster of gentler feudal ways. Yet she asserts that earlier times were not necessarily better, citing women's increasing intelligence and self-reliance as signals of commendable social progress. She omits much of her own career, notably her work as English translator for Tolstoy. Her own representation of her life also differs from some biographical references to Mayo, especially in chronology. Although she writes that her memories "are in no sense an autobiography," Mayo inadvertently creates a complex self-portrait. In **643** *Premiums Paid to Experience: Incidents in My Business Life* (1872), published under Mayo's masculine pseudonym Edward Garrett, the narrator uses fictionalized people and locales in the business world to illustrate the role that Christian morality and religious values should play in business practices.

644 McCALL, Cicely. c.1910–?. *"They Always Come Back."* Methuen, 1938. 258 pp.; foreword by E.M. Delafield; prelude. NUC pre56 348:633.

Probably born in England. Parents not named. Social worker; teacher; prison officer; librarian. Probably middle class.

Social worker's service as teacher and counselor to young women prison inmates, covering adult life, 1932–38. Her first visit to Holloway Prison, 1932. Returning two years later as an officer in the Prison Service. Teaching Borstal girls at Aylesbury school for six months. Working as Aylesbury librarian. Serving in Holloway chaplain's office. Teaching handicrafts to prisoners. Taking employment as assistant housemistress at Holloway and at Aylesbury. Counseling prisoners. Teaching history and recreation at Borstal. Enjoying her work. Discussing lesbianism in prison; the system of graded privileges among prisoners.

Although McCall's focus is primarily on women's prisons and their inmates rather than on herself, she includes many personal anecdotes that convey the impression that she was conscientious and enjoyed her work. She effectively demonstrates that women in prison are by and large similar to those in the general population. The book is organized topically and presented matter-of-factly. McCall assigns fictitious names to subordinate officers, women prisoners, and Borstal girls.

645 McCARTHY, Lillah, Lady Keeble (O.B.E.). 1875–1960. *Myself and My Friends*. Thornton Butterworth Ltd., 1933. 320 pp.; preface, "An Aside by Bernard Shaw"; illus.; facsimiles of letters from George Bernard Shaw, Lord Asquith, Thomas Hardy; indices. NUC pre56 349:71.

Born in Cheltenham, Hertfordshire. Father: Jonadab McCarthy, furniture broker, Fellow of Royal Astronomical Society. Mother: Emma Price. 5 brothers; 2 sisters. Married 1906, Harley Granville-Barker, producer; divorced 1918. Married 1920, Sir Frederick Keeble, horticulturist, professor, d.1952. Knew George Bernard Shaw, Sir Philip Ben Greet, Wilson Barrett, Herbert Beerbohm Tree, John Masefield, Thomas Hardy, H. G. Wells, Lord Asquith (P.M.). Actress (stage); theatrical producer; theatre manager; academic's spouse. Middle class; married into upper class.

Actress's apprenticeship, close friendship with George Bernard Shaw, and truncated career after divorce, covering her childhood to 1932. Unhappiness at school, age 8; father's teaching her literature and elocution at home; sharing his wide intellectual interests. Their move to London for her elocution lessons, age 18, on advice of actor-manager Sir Frank Benson. Describing discipline required for acting, including physical fitness, self-control, strict schedule. Shaw's favorable review of her amateur Shakespearean acting. Life in repertory company; tours in England, America, South Africa, Australia. Her initial roles in tragedies; switching to comedies. Appealing to Shaw for leading roles; joining the Court Theatre, age 29; acting in original productions of Shaw's plays. Shaw's writing *The Doctor's Dilemma* for her. Shaw's personal and professional influence on her. How and why she became a producer. Describing reformation of the arts in the early 1900s. Her life as an Oxford professor's wife; her virtual retirement after her second marriage. Continuing to give performances reciting poetry.

McCarthy's stated intent in writing is best summed up in her own words: "Let us now praise famous men in general and Shaw in particular." Her style is somewhat formal. Her ex-husband forbade her to mention him in these pages; together they had managed the Savoy and St. James's Theatres and had produced many plays at these venues. Granville-Barker's abandoning the author, and their divorce, ruined her chances of becoming a famous actress; she was forced to turn away from the theatre, eventually moving with her second husband to a locale near Oxford.

646 McCARTHY, Margaret. 1907–s.l.1957. *Generation in Revolt*. William Heinemann, 1953. 276 pp.; intro. NUC pre56 349:71.

Born in England. Father not named, socialist. Mother: née Catlows, mill worker. 2 siblings. Organizer (labor, political); Communist; anticommunist; political activist; weaver; foreign resident (Russia). Working class.

Political odyssey from active membership in Communist Party to disillusionment with communism, covering author's childhood to middle age. Parents' relationship and work for socialist cause. Mother's rebellious spirit, keen interest in politics, Chartist ancestors. Author's distress over father's death, c.1912. Mother's work in Lancashire cotton mills; horrible working conditions of these mills; mother's remarriage, 1915. Author's schooling from ages 3 to 15. Living with relatives in New Bedford, Massachusetts, as a teenager; her anger at not being able to remain in the U.S. Returning to England. Enrolling in National Council of Labour Colleges, 1926. Joining Youth Guild of International Labour Party at brother's instigation. Supporting coal miners in General Strike of 1926. Being elected to local executive body of Weavers' Association. Leaving International Labour Party. Organizing, publicizing, and speaking for Young Communist League. Publishing letters in *Northern Voice*

(1926) and *Young Worker* (1928). Attending Fifth International Youth Communist League Conference in Moscow, 1928; living in USSR until 1932. Visiting Berlin; feeling horror at fascist political climate. Leaving Communist Party because of her disillusionment with Stalin; subsequently visiting Poland, 1946, which confirmed her decision. Reading that influenced her political views: Engels's *Conditions of the British Worker* and *Origin of the Family*, Fedor Glakov's *Cement*, books by Maxim Gorky, Upton Sinclair, Sinclair Lewis, Jack London, and John Reed.

This book is a political *bildungsroman,* focused on McCarthy's early conversion to communism and on her subsequent disillusionment. Although she changed her political stance, her autobiography indicates that her sense of mission on behalf of working class people remained constant throughout her life.

647 McCLUNG, Nellie Letitia (née Mooney). 1873–1951. *The Stream Runs Fast: My Own Story*. Toronto: Thomas Allen & Son, 1945. 316 pp.; intro. NUC pre56 349:251.

Born in Ontario, Canada. Father: John Mooney, farmer. Mother: Letitia McCurdy. 5 siblings. Married 1896, Robert Wesley McClung, pharmacist. 4 sons; 1 daughter. Wrote *Painted Fires,* others. Feminist; short storyist; novelist; journalist; teacher; political appointee; suffrage leader; politician; farm child; temperance activist; public speaker; philanthropist. Rural farming class.

A farmer-feminist's spirited reminiscences and discussion of a changing Canadian society, spanning 1896–1943. Living conditions, social activities in Manitou, c.1890s. Joining the Women's Christian Temperance Union. Coping with her three toddlers. Joining Dickens Fellowship. Disliking Canadian men's being recruited for Boer War; her growing reluctance to support European war-making. Mother-in-law's encouraging author's writing career. Publishing *Sowing Seeds in Danny*. Raising money for WCTU's Home for Friendless Girls. Seeing women and children as victims of liquor traffic; socioeconomic ramifications. Moving to Winnipeg. Her interest in women's suffrage; hearing Emmeline Pankhurst. Inspecting factory conditions for women workers. Presenting case for women's suffrage at Liberal Party convention. WWI: strongly questioning need for Canadians' involvement; her son Jack's enlisting. Moving to Edmonton. Speaking on behalf of Red Cross. Belonging to Legislative Assembly. Being delegate to General Council of Methodist Church. Her discomfiture at signs of race prejudice at Methodist religious meeting. Noting problems among Presbyterians, United Methodists, and Congregationalists. Describing tradition of Covenanters. Traveling to France and subsequently to U.S. and Mexico. Serving as delegate to League of Nations. Author's views on overt and covert imperialism. Working on behalf of those made homeless by WWII. Her belief in women's obligation to change adverse conditions. Assessing child-rearing and the need for education. Her increasing admiration and affection for church's role in promoting truth and freedom. Discussing the Oxford group, its spiritual beliefs. Recalling social advances in Alberta province. Legal history of women in British Empire. Seeing poverty as a curse in a world of abundance. Concluding that death is a door to the next world, not the end of existence.

Employing an informal style, McClung writes generously about herself, covering a wide array of topics. She seems to have been a woman who took immense delight in helping others. Her work interweaves a discussion of profound social and religious issues with humorous and poignant anecdotes about individuals she met in the course of her spiritual and social reform activities. In an earlier autobiography, **648** *Clearing in the West* (1935), McClung discusses her childhood, education, the formation of her temperance and social reform opinions on the Manitoba frontier, and her support of Louis David Riel's Indian rights rebellion.

649 McHUGH, Mary Frances. c.1900–?. *Thalassa: A Story of Childhood by the Western Wave*. Macmillan, 1931. 218 pp.; illus. NUC pre56 351:423.

Born in rural western Ireland. Parents not named. 2 sisters. Local historian. Middle class.

Sentimental personal and familial memories and experiences, set within vivid description of Irish rural life, covering author's childhood and adolescence. Detailed family history. Her birth in the country; living most of her first five years in Dublin. Family's move to western Irish coast when author was 5. Her strong sense of Irish identity. Discussing domestic servants. Playing on the beach. Going fishing with her father. Describing the Tullys (family servants); landscape; weather; fishermen's temperament. Acquiring early knowledge through reading. Family Christmases, Roman Catholic practices. Discussing rural people's preserving Gaelic language within the home but speaking English in public. Being sent to convent boarding school, 1916; having difficulty making friends during six-year attendance. Problems of girls' forming sentimental attachments to nuns, other girls; enduring teasing by schoolmates, nuns' wrath. Friendship with Marie, who purposely caught colds to avoid school; Marie's subsequent death; author's grief.

McHugh wrote this book to recapture the lost world of her childhood. Her style is informal, and she strongly evokes the spirit of Ireland's west coast in the early 20th century.

650 McLAREN Christabel Mary Melville, Baroness Aberconway (née Macnaghten). 1890–d.a.1966. *A Wiser Woman? A Book of Memories*. Hutchinson, 1966. 176 pp.; illus.; prologue; index. NUC 1963–1967 1:96.

Born in London. Father: Sir Melville Leslie Macnaghten, chief of Criminal Investigation Department, Scotland Yard. Mother not named. 1 sister; 2 brothers. Married 1910, Henry Duncan McLaren, 2nd Baron Aberconway, d.1953. 2 daughters; 3 sons. Wrote *The Divine Gift, A Dictionary of Cat Lovers*. Knew George Bernard Shaw, H. G. Wells, Somerset Maugham, Virginia Woolf, others. Society woman; miscellaneous writer; WWI volunteer; WWII volunteer. Upper class; married into aristocracy.

Anecdotes of society life and changes in English manners during author's lifetime, covering 1890–1945. Family history. Parents' characters. Her birth and infancy. Summer holidays at Rottingdean. Parents' reaction to Boer War. Wide reading in childhood; parents' horrified reaction to her innocent reading of pornography. Home education by governess. Her childhood belief in her own magical powers and premonitions. Being the only girl at a small school for boys; studying violin and ballet. Her father's fostering her interest in theatre; her dreaming of a stage career. Presentation at Court; marriage; giving up her dream of a career. Friendships with Shaw, Wells, Maugham, the Sitwells. Her friendship with Virginia Woolf. Children's births. Meetings with King George V. Her interest in literature, painting, tapestries, music. Eccentric people she knew: Gerald Berners, Lord Alfred Douglas. Reflections on anti-Semitism. Traveling to Egypt. Memories of WWI; husband's work organizing munitions production; her volunteer work. During WWII, opening family's North Wales farm to Liverpool residents evacuated to country. Sons' wartime service. Working in British Museum reading room during blitz. Beneficial changes in ordinary Englishwomen's lives through modern domestic technology.

In this associatively written memoir Lady Aberconway records impressions and anecdotes in no particular order, remembering herself in connection with the legendary figures of her time. Her tone is light and chatty; she discusses her friendships and cultural interests and reveals aspects of changing social patterns and attitudes.

651 MELBA, Dame Nellie (pseud.; née Mitchell; later Nellie Porter Armstrong). 1861–1931. *Melodies and Memories*. Thornton Butterworth, 1925. 335 pp.; front. port.; illus.; index. NUC pre56 374:356.

Born in Melbourne, Australia. Father: David Mitchell, businessman. Mother not named. 1 sister. Married c.1883, Charles Nesbitt Armstrong, plantation manager; separated c.1884. 1 son. Singer (opera); traveler (world). Upper middle class.

Generally lighthearted memories of professional and travel experiences, set within descriptions of artistic and aristocratic circles in Britain and

America, spanning author's childhood to 1925. Father's struggle for financial success. Her singing debut, age 6. Studying the organ, age 12. Attending school. Death of her mother and sister in close succession. Marriage. Hating life in bush country with husband; separating. Finding Presbyterianism gloomy; avoiding church. Her first visit to London, 1886; being poorly received by London singing masters. Going to Paris to study voice under Madame Mathilde Marchesi, devoted to author. Encountering difficulties in supporting herself and her child. Opera debut in Brussels. Achieving eventual success in Europe and England. Meeting Charles Gounod, Paderewski, Ellen Terry, Arthur Sullivan, Oscar Wilde, Puccini, Verdi. Giving a command performance before Queen Victoria. Touring in St. Petersburg, Italy, Sweden, New York. Adopting stage name Melba. Having difficulties in performing Wagner. Performing in *Barber of Seville* in San Francisco. Further touring in Europe, Ireland. Friendships with the Duchess of Devonshire, Alfred de Rothschild, Queen Alexandra, John Jacob Astor, Alice Roosevelt Longworth. Returning to Australia; touring outback. Fantastic rumors' circulating in Australia about author's social life in Europe and the U.S. Touring in New Zealand. Escoffier's creation of the pêche melba dessert for her at the Savoy Hotel; objecting to celebrities' names being attached to commercial products. Singing opera for Hammerstein in America, 1906. Feeling power and triumph at musical success. Making gramophone recordings. WWI. Changes in postwar England. Visiting India. Returning to Australia, 1923. Assessing musical conservatism of England.

Despite her informal style and accessible, personal tone, Melba seems deliberately vague about her early life in Australia. She is forthright and far from modest in speaking of her professional successes as she reflects at length on her music and career. Melba often provides a "who's who" of significant names from the arts and other spheres of influence.

652 MEREDITH, Anne (pseud.; Lucy Beatrice Malleson; other pseud.: Anthony Gilbert). 1897–1973. *Three-a-Penny.* Faber & Faber, 1940. 296 pp. NUC pre56 357:474.

Raised in Upper Norwood, Greater London. Father not named, worked in Stock Exchange. Mother: née Wood. 1 brother; 1 sister. Single. Wrote novels *The Tragedy at Freyne* (1926), *Portrait of a Murderer* (1933), *The Coward* (1934), others. Knew Dorothy Sayers. Novelist; secretary; social worker. Middle class.

Meredith's successful progress toward a writing career; overcoming parental opposition; observations on contemporary society and social problems; covering author's childhood to mid-1930s. Her confusion about the nature of God. Writing stories in childhood; mother's criticizing them. Mother's giving author false information about procreation.

Dame school attendance. Moving to London, age 12; attending St. Bride's School; deficiencies of education at this school, its Anglocentric outlook. At age 16, feeling confusion over choice of vocation; parents' deciding she should prepare for career rather than for marriage; father's forbidding her to write professionally. Attending secretarial college; employment as secretary for Red Cross and in government offices, beginning in 1916. Widespread unemployment in England after WWI. Interviewing desperate applicants for government jobs; feeling sympathy for the job-seekers. Publishing her first novel under male pseudonym, Anthony Gilbert; wearing male disguise for jacket photo. Writing full-time after 1926 while caring for ailing mother. Working as a district visitor. Mother's death. Interviewing pensioners in Stepney; describing social and economic conditions in London's East End. Joining the Hiawatha Club, a women's lecture club. At Dorothy Sayers's invitation, joining the Detection Club for detective fiction writers. Researching unemployment in London, 1933. Traveling in Europe, 1933–34. Discussing the novelist's dilemma in choosing to write for love or money.

Narrating the events of her childhood in the third person, Meredith gives a humorous and light-hearted account of her early years, changing to first-person narration when she reaches her schooldays. Through perceptive and compassionate observations she displays a keen interest in analyzing social and economic conditions and problems.

MEYENDORFF, Baroness. [*See* ARBENINA, Stella Zoe.]

653 MEYNELL, Dame Alix (née Kilroy). 1903–s.l.1988. *Public Servant, Private Woman: An Autobiography*. Victor Gollancz, 1988. 282 pp.; front. port.; illus.; index. BNB 1988 2:2112.

Born in Upper Broughton, Nottinghamshire. Father: Lancelot Kilroy, navy physician. Mother: Hester Dowson, nurse. 4 sisters; 1 brother. Married 1946, Francis Meynell, poet, cofounder of the Nonesuch Press. 2 stepchildren. Knew Evelyn Sharp, Thelma Cazalet-Keir. Political activist; feminist; civil servant; government administrator; political appointee; utilities administrator; bisexual. Middle class.

Feminist civil servant's intertwined public and personal lives, 1903–86. Influence of mother's family: maternal grandmother as Liberal Party activist, antivivisectionist and suffragist; mother's nursing experience in India. Father's family; his long absences on voyages. Her Catholic upbringing and later skeptical religious outlook. Home education by mother and later by governesses. Outbreak of WWI. Receiving inadequate sex education from mother, who encouraged daughters to have careers. Author's unexplained expulsion from Malvern Girls' College, 1920. Admission on second try to Somerville College, Oxford, 1921. Friendship with Evelyn Sharp, beginning at Oxford; Sharp's later career in civil service paralleling author's; Sharp's later triangular sexual relationship with author and author's husband, Francis Meynell. Graduation, 1925. Passing civil service exam; being one of the first women appointed to the Board of Trade, 1932. Drafting tariff and merchant marine policies. Reflecting on compatibility of personal and public life. Residence with sister; closeness to siblings. First sexual relationship, age 26; thoughts on free love and contraception; lover's death in plane crash. Promotion to rank of principal in Board of Trade, 1932. Attitudes toward women's promotions; trade agreement negotiations. Sexual relationship with future husband; keeping appearances of respectability. Activities on Council of Women Civil Servants on issues of women's wages and promotions and married women's opportunity, 1934–49. Working in WWII production and rationing programs. Forming discussion group to help general war effort. Parents' deaths. Buying and renovating Suffolk mill house with future husband, 1945. Marriage; being husband's third wife. Details of his second divorce case; suicide of his second wife. Postwar clothing rationing leading to British women's protest against ample "New Look" Paris fashions. Britain's "quiet" socialist revolution. Author's receipt of D.B.E., 1949. Being secretary of Monopolies Commission, 1949–52; being comptroller of companies, 1952–55. Retirement, 1955. Serving for thirteen years in South Eastern Gas Board after retirement. Unsuccessful campaign, as founding member of the Social Democratic Party, for Suffolk County Council seat, age 83.

Writing in an expository, educated style, Meynell adheres to chronology. She found while writing this book that because who she was had a great deal to do with what she did, she needed to tell the story of her private life and her public career. She discusses her sexual liaisons matter-of-factly, omitting details except for those of her first love affair. This autobiography is a fountain of information about women in the civil service and about social changes in Britain since the 1920s.

654 MEYNELL, Esther (née Moorhouse). c.1887–1955. *A Woman Talking*. Chapman & Hall, 1940. 218 pp. NUC pre56 381:212.

Born in Yorkshire. Father: Samuel Moorhouse, Leeds mill owner. Mother not named. 1 sister mentioned. Married 1911, Gerard Tuke Meynell, wealthy Quaker, Leeds mill owner. 2 daughters. Wrote nine novels, and books on Pepys, Wordsworth, Nelson, others. Knew husband's relative Alice Meynell, Dr. Albert Schweitzer, Edward and Constance Garnett, Ellen Terry. Historian; biographer; novelist; literary critic. Upper middle class.

Memories of author's childhood, writing career, favorite books, and country scenes, covering her life to 1940. Her severe illness, ages 8–9, resulting in her never attending school, a circumstance she considers fortunate. Self-education in history and literature. Moving to Brighton. Friendships with four daughters of a Brighton architect; through them, meeting Edward and Constance Garnett. Residing with Mrs. Browne of

Hove, widow of Dickens illustrator Hablot K. Browne. Socialist intellectual influences on author's family circle: William Morris, Edward Carpenter, John Ruskin, and Kate Greenaway. Studying piano and voice at Brighton School of Music; her love of Bach; meeting Dr. Albert Schweitzer. Writing novels on musical subjects; her reviews (under a male persona) of books on naval subjects for the *Naval Chronicle;* being assigned other subjects after her editor learned she was female. Her marriage and implied reduced financial circumstances. Friendship with the controversial Admiral of the Fleet, Lord Fisher of Kilverstone. Friendship with Bishop Gore; her later conversion to Catholicism. Discussing books she enjoyed; loving Wordsworth's poetry and Thomas Hardy's novels. Affection for country customs and towns; her collection of old farm implements; describing rural communities and people.

Meynell divides her book by three topics: "Persons," "Books," and "Country Things." The last of these is particularly nostalgic in its study of a vanishing rural way of life. However, the book avoids introspection. Of documentary interest are the author's accounts of her friendships, particularly with the Admiral of the Fleet, and her detailed observations on naval subjects.

655 MEYRICK, Kate. 1866–1933. *Secrets of the 43: Reminiscences of Mrs. Meyrick*. John Long, 1933. 281 pp.; front. port.; illus.; foreword by author's children. NUC pre56 381:241.

Raised in Ireland. Parents not named. 1 sister. Married Richard Holmes Meyrick, physician; separated. At least 3 children. Nightclub owner; businesswoman; prison inmate; clairvoyant/psychic; physician's spouse. Middle class.

Fast-paced, gossipy personal and occupational recollections, set amid vivid descriptions of night life on both sides of the law, covering author's childhood to 1933. Her psychic tendencies in childhood. Attending Alexandra College in Dublin. Author's sexual ignorance in youth. Seeing herself as a "mean little beast" for taking up and dropping boys. Marriage. Moving to England. Complaining that she lived in "dull respectability." Craving excitement. Separating from, then returning to husband. Entering nightclub business to fund daughter's medical education. Alluding to extramarital affair. Final separation from husband. Managing Dalton's Club: gangsters and others in its clientele. Experiencing police raid; feeling persecuted, no longer caring whether she operates within the law. Opening establishment, the "43 Club," 1920. Memories of clients Lord Loughborough, Joseph Conrad, J. B. Priestley. American gangsters, millionaires' frequenting club. Managing bootleggers. Describing London's criminal element, 1920s. Being raided. Opening another club. Seeing gambling dens as more iniquitous than nightclubs. Imprisonment in Holloway Prison. Opening club in Paris. Being repulsed by drug element. Opening clubs in London.

Further raids; another prison sentence. Losing all assets in stock market crash. Being charged with bribing a sergeant in the "Goddard Case"; suffering emotional trauma, considering suicide as a result. Being sentenced to 15 months' hard labor. Further prison sentences. Unemployment. Working as Fun Fair proprietress. Maintaining respect and love of her children through difficulties. Wanting to win back her fortune.

Writing in an informal style, her tone chatty, Meyrick charts her life in the nightclub business. Strongly independent and unconventional, she managed to take a bumpy and questionable road to financial success. Although her account is sparse in personal information, it offers an abundance of eyewitness detail about the exciting and dangerous milieu she inhabited.

656 MILLIN, Sarah Gertrude (née Liebson). 1889–1968. *The Measure of My Days*. Faber & Faber, 1955. 394 pp. NUC pre56 384:044.

Born in Beaconsfield, near Kimberley, South Africa. Father not named, diamond miner. Mother not named. 6 brothers. Married Philip Millin, lawyer, Supreme Court of South Africa judge, d.1952. Widow. Wrote *The South Africans* (1926), *Cecil Rhodes* (1933), *The Dark Gods* (1941), *The Burning Man* (1952), others. Knew General Jan Smuts, John Galsworthy, Winifred Holtby, Katherine Mansfield. Novelist; biographer; essayist; playwright; diarist; political advisor; Jewish activist; political writer. Middle class.

Detailed discussion of author's formative years, involvement in South African politics, husband's career and marriage, covering 1890s–1955. Her childhood in a diamond-mining family. Her pride in her Jewish heritage. Voracious reading, beginning at age 5. Schooling in Kimberley. Boer War experience: father's Boer sympathies' causing him to be detained by the British for a few weeks. Author's courtship and marriage. Husband's life story. Eldest brother's death in WWI, 1918; her parents' response; post-WWI influenza epidemic. Traveling to England; beginnings of her literary career; literary friendships with Katherine Mansfield, Winifred Holtby, John Galsworthy, others. Insomnia as a significant medical condition in her life; her husband's irritation at her sleeplessness; their frequent separations. Lecture tour of U.S., 1929; conversations with Theodore Dreiser and Franklin and Eleanor Roosevelt. Friendship with Transvaal administrator Jan Hofmeyr. Writing biography of Cecil Rhodes. Traveling to Palestine in 1933 and 1949. Friendship with General Jan Smuts in 1930s; discussing international Jewish, Zionist situation with him; writing biography of Smuts; husband's dislike of her absorption in that work. 1935–36 political struggle between Smuts and Herzog over votes for blacks. Traveling to England and the USSR, 1936; Lady Muriel Paget's intelligence activities while in USSR. Discussing the Quota Act, 1936, which limited Jewish immigration to South Africa; growing anti-Semitism in South Africa; resulting postponement of husband's receiving judgeship. Researching and writing paper on Nazi activity in South Africa; showing it to South African and English officials. Discovery of husband's heart disease. Outbreak of WWII; writing war diaries. Mother's death, c.1940. Serving as Smuts's informal political advisor. Traveling with husband to U.S. and England, 1946. Attending 1948 Nuremburg war crimes trial. Husband's overwork on South African bench. Defeat of Smuts in 1948 election; her attempts to comfort him after Hofmeyr's death. Her 1949 travel to Israel. Smuts's death, 1950. Travels with husband to London and Rome; his worsening health; his death. Her feelings of grief, guilt, anger. Meditations on death.

This book began as a sequel to **657** *The Night Is Long* (1941), but after her husband's death Millin devoted it to their life together; it covers the same period as the previous book but includes much more information about her marriage, her friendship with General Jan Smuts, her involvement in South African politics, and her interest in Jewish issues. Millin writes in a novelistic style, often using dialogue. Frequently she meditates on death and on what she might have done to prolong her husband's life.

658 MILLS, Lady Dorothy Rachel Melissa (née Walpole). 1889–1959. *A Different Drummer*. Duckworth, 1930. 223 pp.; front. port. NUC pre56 385:14.

Possibly born in London. Father: Robert Horace Walpole, 5th Earl of Orford. Mother: Louise Melissa Corbin, American. Married 1916, Capt. Arthur Hobart Mills, in Duke of Cornwall's Light Infantry, novelist; divorced c.1923. Wrote novels *Phoenix, Master!* and *Jungle!* and five travel books, including *The Road to Timbuktu* (1924), *The Country of the Orinoco* (1931).. Novelist; travel writer; explorer; traveler (world). Aristocracy; married into middle class.

Aristocrat's upbringing, courtship, unhappy marriage, and travels in Africa after divorce, c.1890–1930. Her social debut at age 18. Marriage; being cast out by her parents. Husband's WWI service in the Palestine campaign; author's feelings of uselessness and of being untrained as a wife; husband's return to England. His writing career. Author's beginning her first novel. Her illness in 1919. Three-month journey to Timbuktu via Algiers, Biskra, the Sahara; being first Englishwoman to visit Timbuktu. Her love for travel; difficulties in traveling alone and the treatment of unescorted women. Reflections on African traditions, including magic, love potions, polygamy, religious gatherings. Stories of Arabia. Famous French colonial explorers who fought the sand and tried to find water in Africa: Paul Imbert, André Citroën, René Cailbu, Père de Fouquot. Receiving two marriage proposals from Arabs; discussing low status of Arab women; relating story of a white woman intending to marry a sheikh but absconded upon learning of his other wives. Different Christmases abroad: in Africa, New Zealand, Corsica, Australia. Author's adventures with men; the different ways men declared their love to her during her travels. The legionnaires and missionaries she met; discussion of Good, Evil, and the relativity of the concept of sin. Traveling to Haiti; Haitian people and white magic. Her friends all over the world: a German highness, a queen of Liberia, a journalist in Timbuktu. Author's serious illness, c.1930. Stating her philosophy of life; how the fear of death teaches one to appreciate life.

Lady Dorothy was clearly well educated and fascinated by male-female relations and the exotic customs of non-European cultures. Written with a popular audience in mind, her book employs romantic stereotypes of people she saw in Africa and exploits popular notions of women travelers, such as their supposed erotic allure for nonwhite men. Her divorce, which enabled her to travel, is not mentioned at all. Mills's other travel books are less personally revealing. In the *Country of the Orinoco*, 1931, she goes where no white woman had been before, and unfavorably compares the South American Indians with the Africans she had encountered on previous journeys.

659 MILNER, Violet Georgina, Viscountess Milner (née Maxse). 1872–1958. *My Picture Gallery*, 1886–1901. John Murray, 1951. 250 pp.; preface; illus.; index. NUC 385:196.

Born in England. Father: Frederick Augustus Maxse. Mother: née Steel. 2 brothers; 2 sisters. Married 1894, Lord Edward Cecil, soldier, d.1918. Married 1921, Alfred Milner, 1st Viscount Milner, statesman, d.1925. Widow. 1 son. Society woman; journalist; editor; military spouse; Boer War volunteer; foreign resident (Gibraltar). Upper class; married into aristocracy.

Wistful personal, familial, and travel memories, interwoven with portraits of individuals and details of upper-class Victorian society, covering 1886–1901. Family history; parents' whirlwind courtship; their complete incompatibility, its effect on home. Parents' separation at author's age 5; her great distress. Living with mother in London. Fond memories of her nurse. Mother's friendship with Oscar Wilde, James McNeil Whistler, Sir Edward Burne-Jones. Mother taking her to salons, theatres, concerts. Living in Paris with her father. Studying drawing. Meeting Degas. Studying with governesses. Working for her brother Leo's publication, *The National Review*. Residing in Dublin. Engagement to marry; father's disapproval of her fiancé. Marriage. Traveling to French Riviera with husband. Friendships with Clemenceau and George Meredith. Husband's joining Egyptian and Abyssinian military campaigns. Traveling in Egypt. Being stationed at Gibraltar. Husband's involvement in Conservative politics. Friendship with Sir Alfred Milner. Author's favorable views of British imperialism. Boer War: traveling to South

Africa, relief work among war refugees. Diary entries commenting on events, progress of war. Death of Queen Victoria. Lamenting disappearance of people and life of fifty years ago, especially the degeneration of English language and the passing of the feminine ideal.

In an effort to recall a now-vanished world, Lady Milner presents a formal yet loosely connected collection of portraits, people, and places. An air of wistfulness pervades her work as she tacitly compares the structured civility of Victorianism with the crudeness and harshness of modernity. Although her fierce patriotism is more class-oriented than nationalistic, Lady Milner nonetheless seems a strong-minded and independent woman, capable of compassion for all British people.

MINTO, Countess of. [*See* ELLIOT, Mary Caroline.]

660 MITCHELL, Hannah Maria (née Webster). 1871–1956. *The Hard Way Up: The Autobiography of Hannah Mitchell, Suffragette and Rebel.* Ed. by Geoffrey Mitchell (author's grandson). Faber & Faber, 1968. 260 pp.; preface by George Ewart Evans; intro. by ed.; app.; index. BLC to 1975 223:169. (other ed: Virago, 1977.)

Born in rural Derbyshire. Father not named, tenant farmer. Mother not named. 3 brothers; 2 sisters. Married c.1895, Gibbon Mitchell, shopkeeper. 1 son. Feminist; suffragist, militant; Poor Law guardian; government administrator; magistrate; socialist; public speaker; philanthropist; social reformer; dressmaker; domestic servant; farm child; prison inmate. Rural laboring class. Working class.

Well-known feminist's many political and social reform involvements along with insightful observations on social inequalities, spanning author's childhood to 1946. Doing farm work as a child. Home education by father and uncle. Her brief formal education; being largely self-educated. Mother's violent temper. Attending rural "love feasts" and hiring fairs. Leaving home at age 14. Entering domestic service. Working as a dressmaker. Courtship, marriage; subsequent poverty. Attending "Labour Church." Struggling toward self-improvement. Husband's employment as tailor. Her interest in socialism; working for Independent Labour Party. Lecturing on political topics. Serving as Poor Law Guardian, 1904. Her militant suffrage activities in Manchester; joining Women's Social and Political Union (WSPU). Assisting the Pankhursts, Annie Kenney, Emmeline Pethick-Lawrence. Seeing married life as self-abnegation for women; feeling herself incapable of necessary "double-edged" devotion; feeling she should not have married. Her belief in socialist idea of marriage as comradeship. Assessing birth control as simplest, best way for poor to help themselves. Rejecting idea of male intellectual superiority. Assessing strength of suffragettes; difference between them and the "clinging vine" image of women. Her imprisonment for suffrage activities. Nervous breakdown,

1907. Joining Women's Freedom League in Scotland. Her views on child-rearing. Effects of WWI on society. Writing sketches in Lancashire dialect. Serving as city councillor and magistrate in Manchester. Participating on relief committees, 1926–46. Commenting on social reform from feminist viewpoint.

Mitchell's account centers on her economic, social, and political struggle to improve her personal condition and the lives of many like her. Rather than offering mere theory, she presents her views on many contemporary social ills from the perspective of personal experience.

661 MITCHISON, Naomi Margaret (née Haldane). 1897–s.l.1991. *All Change Here: Childhood and Marriage* (1975). The Bodley Head, 1975. 159 pp.; family tree; illus. BLC to 1975 223:214.

Born in Edinburgh, Scotland. Father: John Scott Haldane, physiologist. Mother: Kathleen Louise Trotter. 1 brother (J. B. S. Haldane, Cambridge professor, leftist, Darwinian geneticist). Married 1916, Richard Mitchison, lawyer, M.P., d.1970. Widow. 6 children. Wrote *The Moral Basis of Politics* (1938), *The Young Alexander the Great* (1960), many others. Knew W. H. Auden, Wyndham Lewis, Aldous Huxley, Dylan Thomas. Novelist; poet; playwright; children's author; journalist; political writer; feminist; socialist; WWI volunteer; WWII volunteer; traveler (world). Upper class.

Growth of a visionary writer from childhood to marriage, and from dependency to freedom of lifestyle and opinion, 1907–1918. Noting that a writer must accurately record memories; using her diaries religiously. From age 10, living at Oxford where her father did research. At age 12, being ignorant of menstruation; after its onset during school hours, mother's shaming author and removing her from the school. Suffering long-term trauma due to mother's silence and embarrassment about female functions. After leaving school, having a governess. Being made to share her mother's bedroom; later believing mother arranged this to avoid sex with father. Enjoying adult cultural activities with her parents, but having her needs babied; not being allowed to grow up. Starting to grow away from her mother's class and racial prejudices. Adoring her older brother; learning to help him in his science laboratory; gaining expertise in botany and zoology. Becoming jealous of brother's romances; discovering jealousy's poisonous quality; ever after, guarding herself against personal or professional jealousy. Disliking plays or stories with jealousy as a theme; preferring issues of social class. Having pro-Jewish sympathies because of Jewish ancestry; noting mother's wish to forget this. At age 17, coming out; courting with her future husband. Beginning to write plays; also writing attacks on harsh sexual morés, c.1915, that kept young people abysmally ignorant about sexuality. Many friends' dying in WWI; author's volunteering as nurse's aid.

Marrying, 1916; because of wartime austerity, refusing to have a formal wedding or wedding dress. Husband's serving in France; receiving head wounds; recovering "miraculously" under author's care; returning to duty. Having difficult childbirth with her first son, 1918, due to twisted pelvis. As a young mother, keenly feeling loss of personal freedom; feeling isolated with her staff officer husband away in Italy. Arranging to meet him in Italy, despite opposition from parents and in-laws over "neglecting" her maternal duties. Their having a marvelous time together; author's finally feeling free of her parents and independent. Enjoying a long-overdue honeymoon in Paris when Armistice was signed.

This volume continues the study of her own mental development that Mitchison began in **662** *Small Talk...Memories of an Edwardian Childhood* (1973). While both volumes trace the origins of her feminine and socialist principles, they cover events that precede her ascendency in the London literary world of the 1920s–1930s. Mitchison grew up in the celebrated Haldane family whose members included scientific pioneers, Lord Chancellors, and noted female autobiographers. Herself a pioneer in the literary field, Mitchison was the first English writer to revise mythology and history from a woman's perspective, with her works predating current interest in that field by fifty years. Her best-known work of comparative mythology is *The Corn King and the Spring Queen* (1931). In her crititical biography of Mitchison, Jill Benton notes that Mitchison's 1935 political novel *We Have Been Warned* is the first work to use fiction to study the inconsistencies plaguing the liberal middle-class blend of feminism, socialism, and communism. Mitchison was also the first popular female science fiction writer, and her work, although little-read today, anticipates the explorations of androgyny and alternate societies that have earned fame for novelist Ursula Le Guin. In the autobiographical sequel to this book, **663** *You May Well Ask* (1979), Mitchison examines her sexuality (both inside and outside of marriage) and follows the growth of her early socialist and feminist views, as well as tracing her intense involvement in the intellectual development of her four children. **664** *Mucking Around—Five Continents over Fifty Years* (1981) covers her world travels, her adoption of an African tribe as her "sons," her multiracial views (which got her into hot water in apartheid Rhodesia), her rejection of authoritarian religion as mentally unhealthy, her enjoyment of practicing "field botany," and her ideological support for the USSR in the face of conventional, conservative criticism. Still writing actively into her 90s, Mitchison has been the subject of BBC specials dedicated to her achievements and has received numerous honorary doctorates from British universities as well as an O.B.E.

665 MITFORD, [the Hon.] Jessica. 1917–1996. *Daughters and Rebels: The Autobiography of Jessica Mitford*. Boston: Houghton Mifflin,

1960. 284 pp.; prologue; illus. BLC to 1975 223:220. (other ed.: Victor Gollancz, 1960, as *Hons and Rebels*.)

Raised in the Cotswolds, Oxfordshire. Father: the Rt. Hon. David Bertram Ogilvy Freeman-Mitford, 1st Baron Redesdale, member of the House of Lords. Mother: Sydney Bowles, Conservative Party supporter. 5 sisters (including novelist Nancy Mitford); 1 brother. Married c.1936, Esmond Remilley, leftist organizer, d.1941. Married c.1942, Robert Treuhaft, lawyer and journalist, American. 2 daughters; 2 sons. Wrote *The American Way of Death* (1963); *Kind and Usual Punishment: The Prison Business* (1974), *Poison Penmanship: The Gentle Art of Muckraking* (1980). Political writer; journalist; emigrant (U.S.); socialist; pacifist; foreign resident (France); saleswoman; restaurant worker; political activist. Aristocracy. American upper middle class.

Witty, satirical account of unconventional childhood and political rebellion of premier investigative journalist, 1926–c.1940. Family's social isolation at Swinbrook House due to father's intransigence, ignorance, and mistrust of outsiders. Her sisters, Unity and Debo, as her sole companions; their secret language, unconventional pastimes. Home education by mother to age 9; being taught by governesses thereafter; tormenting governesses, except for one who taught the children shoplifting. Mother's canvassing for Conservative Party. Family's agitation over General Strike of 1926. Father's tenure in House of Lords; his belief in peerage's divine rights. Eccentric uncles and aunts. Publication of sister Nancy's novels caricaturing father; Nancy's aesthete friends; their influence on author. Author's friendship with Evelyn Waugh. Pen pal friendship with a working-class London girl, author's age 13. Brief school attendance; thwarted friendships with schoolmates of lower social classes, due to mother's rigid ideas about class divisions. Author's early adherence to pacifist and socialist ideas. Her sister Unity's attraction to Nazism; author's being repelled by fascism and beginning to study communism. Unity's travels to Germany; her friendship with Hitler and other Nazi leaders; other family members' supporting Nazis; sister Diana's marrying British fascist Sir Oswald Mosley. Traveling to Paris; being taken to a brothel by a male companion. Future husband Esmond Remilley's leftist, pacifist activities while in public school. Her social debut. Rebelling against mother; bitterness toward Unity. Running away with Remilley to Spain to aid in Spanish Civil War; their shared class rebellion; their eventual marriage; brief residence in France; returning to London. Working as a market researcher; daughter's birth and death, 1938. After Munich crisis, moving to New York City. Working as a saleswoman. Brief residence in Washington, D.C.; her impressions of New Deal liberals. Moving to Miami, Florida; working with husband in restaurant. News of Unity's unsuccessful suicide attempt. Husband's enlistment in Canadian army at outbreak of WWII, 1940; detailed analysis of his character and their rebellion against their inherited class. Plans for her employment in America. Remilley's departure; never seeing him again, as he was killed in action.

A journalist and novelist who resided in America from WWII until her death, Mitford writes in a polished, educated style, with a good deal of humor and irony. This book is a source on generational conflict between the pre- and post-WWI generations and on communist and fascist activity in England between the wars. In her second volume of autobiography, *A Fine Old Conflict* (1977), Mitford discusses her first husband's death, her second husband and his Jewish immigrant background, her civil rights work with him in Oakland, California, and their careers as muckraking journalists.

666 MITFORD, Mary Russell. 1787–1855. *Recollections of a Literary Life; or, Books, Places, and People*. New York: Harper & Bros., 1852. 558 pp.; preface. BLC to 1975 223:225.

Born at Alresford, Hampshire. Father: George Mitford, physician. Mother: Mary Russell, heiress. Single. Wrote *Miscellaneous Poems* (1810), country life sketches *Our Village* (1819), novels *Belford Regis* (1835), *Atherton* (1854), plays *Julian* (1823), *Foscari: A Tragedy* (1826), others. Knew Elizabeth Barrett Browning, John Ruskin, Joanna Baillie, Walter Savage Landor. Novelist; poet; literary critic; playwright; essayist; social historian; physician's daughter. Upper middle class.

Sophisticated and educated examination of friends and endeavors within literary circles, interspersed with personal and familial memories, covering author's childhood to 1851. Parents' courtship. Father a physician; his tendency to alienate prospective patients through zealous Whig politics in his Hampshire election campaign; abandoning practice early on; his becoming an unlucky gambler; his spoiling of author by indulging her childhood whims. Learning to read, age 4. Family's move to Berkshire. Father's financial losses: his gambling, bad investments; his alienation of wife's rich cousin. Family's move to Lyme Regis. Father's attempts to force musical accomplishment on author, beginning at her age 5. Father's loss of all money and property. Family's move to London at author's age 9. Buying lottery ticket with father on her tenth birthday; winning £20,000. Education, ages 10–15, at London private school; French expatriates at this school. Father's further attempts to force author to learn piano, harp; being shut up in school library to practice music, but reading Molière instead. Traveling with parents to Southampton, c.1806. After lottery winnings evaporating from extensive gambling and profligacy, life in poverty, c.1817. Author's friendship with poet John Kenyon and his wife, who encouraged her writing talent. Friendship with Elizabeth Barrett Browning. Residence in cottage near Aberleigh, 1821–51. Advising young women poets brought to her as prodigies. Visiting places with literary associations at Bath and Bristol, 1843; visiting old Berkshire Catholic homes. Residence beside Thames,

1848. Discussing the English countryside: Cromwellian battlefields, ruined castles, abbeys. Visiting Great Exhibition in London, 1851. Leaving her old cottage for a new one.

In her preface the author describes her book as a mixture of literary essays and autobiography; the autobiographical sections are long digressions within Mitford's discussions of various writers and places and their significance for her. Her educated style makes her wide reading apparent. Associative rather than chronological, this book is particularly useful for its glimpses of "lost" women writers and of contemporary attitudes toward women writing professionally.

667 MONTAGU, Lily Helen (O.B.E.). 1873–1963. *The Faith of a Jewish Woman*. George Allen & Unwin, 1943. 70 pp.; illus. NUC pre56 391:389.

Raised in London. Father: Montagu Samuel-Montagu, M.P., 1st Baron Swaythling, businessman. Mother: Ellen Cohen. 5 sisters; 4 brothers. Single. Wrote *The Bible for Home Reading* (1907). Religionist (Jewish); philanthropist; social reformer; Jewish activist; religious/spiritual writer; charitable volunteer; organizer (religious); organizer of societies (women's clubs). Upper middle class.

Author's career in social service and her central position in the establishment of Liberal Judaism in England, covering her childhood to early 1940s. Her strict Orthodox upbringing; home education in Hebrew; Jewish customs and observances. Attending secular school to age 15; self-education thereafter. Her social service in East End London; leading children's services at New West End Synagogue, ages 17–18; doing social work at club for young working Jewish women. First meeting Claude G. Montefiore, a major influence on her, c.1907; his teaching her that authority rests with conscience, not with literal words of the Bible. Working with Montefiore in the Jewish Religious Union for the Advancement of Liberal Judaism; establishing Liberal congregations in London. Discussing menstrual taboos in Jewish law; women's place in institutional Judaism. Her reasons for converting from Orthodoxy to Liberalism; declaring "the teaching of Liberal Judaism had set me free"; her parents' grief and disapproval. Preaching and reading Scripture in services. Her travels to America; receiving honorary doctorate. Serving in philanthropic organizations for working women; cofounding the National Organisation (later Council) of Girls' Clubs. Commenting on current issues in Judaism; her personal statement of faith.

Although Montagu acknowledges her central role in Liberal Judaism, she does not emphasize it; she sees Montefiore as the major figure who drew Orthodox fire for Liberal reforms in doctrine and practice. She writes formally, indirectly proselytizing as she promotes understanding of her sect, and provides few details about her private life. In **668** *My*

Club and I: The Story of the West Central Jewish Club, c.1954, she addresses such topics as her East End social work, her conflict with her family over founding and devoting herself to the club, her father's rejection of her Liberal Judaism. Montagu gives full details of the club's operations, including its expansion to the U.S. In particular, she discusses the club's offering classes, religious services, and social activities, and its members' social class situations. To appreciate the full magnitude of Montagu's role in the founding of Liberal Judaism in England and the uniqueness of a woman's playing that role, see Ellen Umansky's biography *Lily Montagu and the Advancement of Liberal Judaism* (1983), as well as Umansky's anthology of Montagu's writings (1985).

669 MONTGOMERY, Lucy Maud (Mrs. Ewan MacDonald). 1874–1942. *The Alpine Path: The Story of My Career*. Don Mills, Ontario, Canada: Fitzhenry & Whiteside, 1974. 96 pp.; preface. NUC 1973–1977 78:383. (1st pub. in *Woman's World*, 1917.)

Born in Clifton, Prince Edward Island, Canada. Father: Hugh John Montgomery. Mother: Clara Woolner Macneill. Stepmother not named. Married 1912, Rev. Ewan MacDonald. 2 sons. Wrote *Anne of Green Gables* series, *The Story Girl,* the *Emily* series, *Chronicles of Avonlea, Magic for Marigold,* and *The Blue Castle*. Children's author; teacher; novelist; journalist; clergyman's spouse. Middle class.

Wistful memories of congenial childhood milieu to 1912, eventual professional endeavors, emphasizing author's career in children's literature, covering her childhood to 1912. Ancestry and family history; her ancestors' emigration from Scotland to Canada. Mother's death; being raised by grandparents. Contracting typhoid fever. Education, beginning age 6, at Cavendish school. History and description of the Cavendish seashore; her love of nature as source for her later novels. Reading "few novels but lots of poetry"; writing poetry from age 9 and stories from age 12. High school attendance in Prince Albert, Saskatchewan. Publishing her verse, for the first time, in a newspaper. Obtaining teacher's certificate from Prince of Wales College, 1893. Teaching school for one year at Bideford. Publishing more verse; being paid for it for the first time. Employment on staff of *Daily Echo* in Halifax, 1901. Returning to Cavendish, 1902; writing *Anne of Green Gables*; novel's relation to people and places in Cavendish. After five publishers' rejections, novel's publication in 1908. Her honeymoon trip through the British Isles, 1912. Her delight in her personal literary success.

First published in 1917 in six serial installments in the Toronto magazine *Everywoman's World,* this autobiography was intended to "encourage some other toiler along the weary pathway I once followed." Montgomery's approach is lighthearted and sentimental as she uses herself to show that intense desire was an important ingredient on her way to success. Occasionally she includes verbatim excerpts from her journals. The book deals as much with the author's nostalgia for her childhood and surroundings as it does with her skill as a writer. Her novels *Anne of Green Gables* and *Chronicles of Avonlea* remain popular with young readers and, in the form of an often-repeated television series, hold the interest of adults as well.

670 MOODIE, Susannah (née Strickland). 1803–1885. *Roughing It in the Bush; or, Forest Life in Canada*. Toronto: McClelland & Stewart, 1923. 506 pp.; intro.; poems; illus. NUC pre56 392:668. (1st pub. Richard Bentley, 1852; other ed.: Virago, 1986, with intro. by Margaret Atwood.)

Born in Bungay, Suffolk. Father: Thomas Strickland, gentleman. Mother: Elizabeth Homer. 1 brother; 2 sisters. Married John Wedder-burn Dunbar Moodie, sheriff of Hastings County, Upper Canada. 3 sons; 3 daughters. Wrote *Enthusiasm and Other Poems* (1831), novel *Flora Lyndsay* (1853), others; founded *Victoria Magazine* with husband. Knew ex-slave Mary Prince. Emigrant (Canada); novelist; poet; pioneer; farmer; cultural historian. Rural gentry.

Frontier life in Canada, 1832–c.1840. Arrival in Quebec with husband. Homesickness. Being struck by "barbarity" of Irish immigrants. Cholera epidemics in Quebec and Montreal. Their purchasing a farm. Irritation at neighbors' constant borrowing. Social tension between American and British settlers; "Yankee" neighbors' contempt for the Moodies for their supposed pride and literary pretensions, jealousy of their Irish servant's faithfulness. Author's great fear of wild beasts; fearing even cows. Local charivari customs. Having emigrated because of their reduced circumstances back in England. Insubordination of most emigrant servants infected with Yankee spirit of equality. Characteristics of Canadian women. Negative commentary on American woman who lets white servants—but not black ones—eat with her family. Working-class emigrants' greater opportunity for prosperity. Moving household into backwoods; brief residence near her sister Catherine and her brother Samuel; the sisters' contrasting attitudes toward frontier life. Her conflicting ideas about local Indians, finding them brave and honest, yet ugly and dirty. Unprincipled settlers' cheating Indians. Indian religious practices and medicines. Loss of Moodies' house in a fire. Crop failure; struggling to feed family during winter of 1836. Husband's departure for Toronto, 1837, to assist loyalists in Upper Canada rebellion. Author's attempting to write for literary journals. Successfully appealing to Canada's governor for husband's continuance in militia post. Helping neighbors. Moving to town. Suggesting poor gentlemen not come to the Canadian frontier.

Although she later learned to love Canada, Moodie at first disliked the wilderness and was at a disadvantage due to her family's unfamiliarity with hard labor. She writes in a literary and poetic style and gives detailed descriptions of emigration, Indians, and social leveling on the frontier, but wilderness life was for her anything but romantic. The text includes many poems by Moodie and her husband. A valuable autobiographical sequel is her **671** *Life in the Clearings* (modern edition published 1959), which contains observations on Canadian society and social institutions: churches, volunteer fire departments, schools, prisons, and asylums. These institutions are discussed in the context of the formation of a national Canadian identity. She also includes details about emigration, slavery, social class, and Victorian mourning customs. Before her emigration Moodie had lived in London, where she had served as an amanuensis to ex-slave Mary Prince.

672 MOORE, [Lilian] Decima, C.B.E. 1871–1964 and Maj. F. G. Guggisberg, C.M.G., R.E., d. 1930. *We Two in West Africa*. William Heinemann, 1909. 368 pp.; preface; illus.; index; map of Gold Coast. NUC pre56 222:241.

Born in Brighton, Sussex. Father: Edward Moore. Mother not named. 1 brother; 9 sisters (including actress Eva Moore). Married 1905, Maj. Frederick Gordon Guggisberg, C.M.G., R.E. Colonialist (Africa); travel writer; social historian; traveler (Africa); musical actress; military spouse; founder WEC. Middle class.

Travelogue by the wife of a British colonial officer, covering their experiences on Africa's Gold Coast, 1905–06. First impressions of West Africa. Memories of the Haussa people, their adherence to Islam. Daily diet at Accra. Drought conditions. Polo and other recreations in Accra; cricket's popularity with the native people. Touring with husband. Describing rail journey, dense forest, how railroad was built. Impressions of Tarkwa: rubber plantations, tobacco cultivation, other flora. Memories of Dunkwa and Obuasi, the Wangara people. Viewing *omahnin's* (king's) procession. Assisting husband in astronomical observations. Description of bush camp. Observing conference of various chiefs. Touring cocoa plantation. Recalling Tafo and Kokorantumi. Discussing social and political ramifications of gold boom. Commenting on degrading practice of exporting slaves. Dignity of West African customs, clothing, religion, role of king, medicine, daily activities. Noting trading customs; native attitude toward buying and selling wives. Bush farming. History and economic ramifications of gold mining in West Africa; technical aspects of gold mining. Differences between Ashanti and Gold Coast natives. Advent of greed in native peoples' lives with arrival of Europeans: their need to adopt Western economy, customs. Feelings of regret on leaving Africa.

In her rendition of living and traveling in Africa, Moore provides little intimate information about her husband or herself. However, her more sensitive comments about native peoples offer insights into her own character. In an apparent effort to appear objective, she discusses some of the disadvantages European "civilization" brought to Africa. By including a collection of native folktales that bear European influences, she provides an excellent illustration of the African cultural symbiosis. Her detailed descriptions of West African peoples and daily life make this an informative guide to the colonial experience. Later in life, during WWI, Moore originated and founded the Women's Emergency Corps and served as honorary secretary of the British Army and Navy Leave Club in Paris. Aspects of her life and career are discussed in her sister Eva's autobiography, *Exits and Entrances*.

673 MOORE, Eva. 1870–1955. *Exits and Entrances*. New York: Frederick Stokes, 1923. 259 pp.; front. port.; illus.; apps.; index. NUC pre56 393:198.

Born in Brighton, Sussex. Father: Edward Moore. Mother not named. 1 brother; 9 sisters (including Decima Moore). Married 1891, Harry Vernon Esmond, actor, playwright. 1 son; 1 daughter. Actress (stage); theatre manager; teacher (dance); feminist; suffragist; WWI volunteer. Middle class.

Generally lighthearted personal and professional recollections, focusing on theatrical friends and acquaintances, covering author's childhood to the 1920s. Family life in Brighton, 1870s. Father's discipline of children. Leaving school, age 14, to earn her own living; teaching dancing and gymnastics in Liverpool. Father's wrath at her decision to go on stage; his eventual acceptance; sister Jessie's decision to become an actress; sister Decima's singing and acting career. Acting in London. Discouraging would-be suitors. Being attacked and robbed in the street. First meeting her future husband, age 17. Plays in which she appeared. Impressions of theatre people. Marriage. Husband's requesting her not to show her legs on stage. Discussion of producers and agents. Trying theatre management with husband, 1894. Acting in Ireland. Friendships with the Brough and Terry theatre families. Birth of son; continuing her career. Father's death, c.1908. Going on a brief American tour, c.1913. Her experiences in the suffrage movement; her activity in Actresses' Franchise League; appearing as defense witness during Christabel Pankhurst's trial. Another American tour, 1914. WWI: enrolling women in Women's Emergency Corps founded by her sister Decima; helping raise £50,000 for British Women's Hospital. Visiting morgue to identify victim of *Lusitania* disaster. Visiting Belgian trenches, 1918. Receiving the Order de la Reine Elizabeth. Anecdotes of Ellen Terry, George Bernard Shaw, Madge Kendal, W. S. Gilbert. Canadian tour, 1920. Berlin engagements, 1921. Her ideas on letters and letter-writing. Husband's character and talents.

Moore wrote these recollections for her children, believing that they might also interest and amuse other people's children as well. The narrative is in chronological order for about the first seventy pages; thereafter the author recapitulates events of her life in further detail, providing a collection of disconnected humorous anecdotes about the many prominent and obscure theatre people she knew, and also sketching a detailed portrait of her husband.

674 MORDAUNT, Elinor (pseud.; née Evelyn May Clowes). 1872–1941. *Sinabada*. Michael Joseph Ltd., 1937. 352 pp.; foreword. NUC pre56 394:171.

Born in Cotgrave, near Nottingham, Nottinghamshire. Father: surname Clowes, farm manager. Mother not named. 6 brothers; 1 sister. Married twice, husbands not named; first husband a sugar planter. 1 son. Wrote *Royals Free, The Family*. Novelist; journalist; horticulture writer; garden designer; governess; domestic servant; short storyist; foreign resident (Mauritius, Australia); dressmaker; traveler (world); planter's spouse. Middle class.

Fast-paced account of globe-trotting adventures and misadventures, set within observations on societies and human nature, spanning author's childhood to the 1920s. Pastimes with siblings. Everyday life in Nottingham. Her great love for her father. Family's move to Cheltenham. Her love of reading. Her devotion to her Aunt Anne. Studying painting in London. Late Victorian social customs. First infatuation with "Bill"; her grief at his death in Africa. Accepting invitation to Mauritius. Marriage to sugar planter. Suffering severe bout with malaria. Having two miscarriages; their emotional effect on her; her strong desire for children. Separating from husband; returning to England. Deciding to go to Australia. Birth of son in Melbourne. Experiencing economic difficulties; sewing to earn living. Acknowledging the generosity of poor people. Writing for a woman's magazine. Publishing *The Garden of Contentment* to critical acclaim. Losing her job, feeling devastated. Working as garden designer. Keeping house for Horticultural College principal; his falling in love with her; her economic privations after leaving post. Suffering various illnesses. Noting differences in attitudes of English, Australian, and American businessmen toward women workers. Writing short stories. Returning to London. Publishing *A Ship of Solace*. Friendship with publisher William Heinemann. Writing first novel, *The Cost of It*. Researching new novel in industrial town. Going to Perugia as governess. Writing *Simpson;* rift with Heinemann; giving novel to Cassell's. Touring Albania. Her London house's being bombed during WWII. Awakening after serious surgery; feeling anger at having to face life afresh. Death of Heinemann. Anecdotes of working people in London. Taking trip to Tangier; observing Moorish customs. Securing assignments with *Daily News* about Tahiti. Impressions of Tahiti: native peoples, spoilage of environment by dissolute Europeans. Writing serial on racing for American newspaper. Touring Samoan Islands. Suffering new bout with malaria. Joining her son in Kenya to assist him in medical work with natives. Describing Nandi people, their customs. Traveling to America. Her view of Prohibition. Visiting Cuba: discussing Cuban attitudes and customs. Traveling through Central America. Spending time in Hollywood. Writing *Mrs. Van Kleek;* Metro-Goldwyn-Mayer's purchasing book. Returning to Africa to be with her son for birth of her second grandchild.

A feeling of 18th-century adventurism suffuses Mordaunt's book. She comes across as an intrepid individual, fearless in the face of adversity, blessed with an uncanny ability to extricate herself from difficult situations and possessed of advanced social views. Much of the work reads like a travelogue, but there is a wealth of personal and other information in the text.

675 MORGAN, Sydney, Lady (née Owenson). c.1783–1859. *Lady Morgan's Memoirs: Autobiography, Diaries and Correspondence*. 2 vols. Ed. by W. Hepworth Dixon. New York: AMS Press, 1975. Vol. 1: 532 pp.; author's preface; ed.'s preface; front. port.; index. Vol. 2: 559 pp.; front.; index. BMC 177:624. (1st pub. William H. Allen, 1862.)

Born in Dublin, Ireland. Father: Robert Owenson, composer and theatrical songwriter, relative of Oliver Goldsmith. Mother: Jenny Hill. 2 sisters. Married 1812, Sir Charles Morgan, physician. Wrote *The Wild Irish Girl* (1801), *Woman and Her Master* (1840), others. Knew poet Leigh Hunt. Novelist; social historian (women); poet; governess; political activist. Middle class; married into upper class.

Young poet's close relationship with her cultured theatrical father, education, and the beginnings of her literary career, c.1783–1801. Celebrations on the night of her birth; her christening. Her paternal ancestry; father's life story; Oliver Goldsmith's influence on father's early theatre career. Mother's life story; her disapproval of both Catholics and the theatre. In author's early childhood, family's moving into lodgings inside the National Theatre Music Hall in Dublin, which father managed. Failure of this theatre due to father's losing government patent for legitimate drama. Father's miscellaneous business ventures. Parents' Protestantism. Author's sporadic education by occasional tutors at home; her imitation of people she saw around her. Father's many musician friends; few female visitors to home; his sponsorship of poet Thomas Dermody, the "Poor Scholar," who taught author and siblings to read and write. Mother's discipline of children; her sponsorship of home meetings to discuss religious controversies; mother's death before author was age 9. Moving to Drumcondra. Attending a private Huguenot school in Ireland for three years; attending finishing school, age 13. Irish servants' restoring the prefixes "O" and "Mac" to their surnames after passage of Catholic Emancipation Bill. Taking summer holiday at Kilkenny; father's building new theatre there; author's residence with his patron, the Duchess of Ormond. Publishing her *Poems by a Young Lady between the Age of Twelve and Fourteen,* edited by her father. Bankruptcy proceedings against father. Taking a position as governess-companion to the daughters of Mrs. Featherstonehaugh of Bracklin Castle, Dublin, against father's wishes. Her desire to assist father by writing words to his songs; her secret efforts to find a publisher for her first novel, *St. Clair*.

The earliest scenes of Lady Morgan's childhood are presented in third-person narration; she displays her education and literary gifts in her abundant use of dialogue and in her dramatic presentations of herself and other characters. The dictated portion, which constitutes the autobiographical narrative, ends with p. 190 of vol. 1; the rest of vol. 1 and all of vol. 2 consist of letters, diary entries, and editorial interpolations. Lady Morgan freely acknowledges in her preface that she was a figure of controversy, as a novelist who advocated civil and religious liberty in Ireland, France, and Italy; she was often violently attacked in the Tory press. She and her husband worked for Catholic political emancipation in Ireland. She also gathered material for an extensive social history of women from antiquity to her own time, but most of that material was never published.

676 MORIARTY, Dorothy (née Bishop). 1889–s.l.1989. *Dorothy: The Memoirs of a Nurse 1889–1989*. Transworld/Corgi, 1991. 190 pp.; foreword by Edwina Currie, M.P.; illus.; afterword. BNB 1990 2:1541. (1st pub. Sidgwick & Jackson, 1989.)

Born in Kensington, London. Father: Bernard Bishop, stockbroker. Mother: Alice Maule. 3 brothers. Married c.1921, Oliver Moriarty, WWI veteran, barrister, Irish. 2 sons. Wrote *The Shadow of the Pyramid* (1928). Nurse; novelist; scriptwriter; clerk. Middle class.

Centenarian author's sheltered upbringing and career as a nurse before marriage, 1889–c.1921, with brief sketch of her later life. Family life in childhood; her nanny; home education by mother. Family's move to Wimbledon, author's age 7. Mother's growing infatuation with the literary talent of her doctor, Richard Austin Freeman; her collaboration in writing detective novels for which he became famous; gossip and scandal surrounding their relationship. Family's move to Gravesend; Freeman's moving his and author's families under one roof, providing free tutoring and medical care in exchange for mother's literary attentions. Attending the Catholic Church; author's making her First Communion, age 11. Her first menstruation; her awakening sexual feeling. Family's descent into genteel poverty; author's lack of further schooling; her writing poems and painting watercolors, age 16. Not knowing what to do with her life; various relatives' failed attempts to launch her socially. Visiting Florence, Italy, where a family friend attempted to seduce her. Her first romance, with a Presbyterian engineer; his inability to accept her Catholicism. Being hospitalized with appendicitis; being fascinated by hospital routine. Deciding to become a nurse at outbreak of WWI; planning to be a VAD, but realizing that full nursing training was necessary for a career. Training in University College Hospital in London; while training, being almost entirely removed from knowledge of the war and of the women's suffrage movement; working in the men's ward, and in the tuberculosis ward, night duty, the casualty ward, the women's medical ward; seeing a child die in the diphtheria ward when a doctor, attempting to perform a tracheotomy, accidentally severed her jugular vein. Author's coping with her distress at patient deaths; her increasing dedication to her nursing work. Student nurses' discussing the need for better working conditions: eight-hour rather than fourteen-hour days and better pay. Zeppelin raids; one bomb's narrowly missing the hospital. Receiving her final certificate of training at end of WWI. Working briefly as a private nurse in a nursing home; being uncomfortable with the worldliness of the staff after her spartan training; quitting after her lesbian roommate attempted to crawl into her bed. Living with her mother, 1918–20. Hearing of nursing work near Cairo from her brother, who was stationed there; training as a midwife, a prerequisite to winning the job; traveling to Cairo. Meeting her future husband, a patient in the hospital where she worked; courtship; meeting his former mistress; her wedding. Synopsizing her later life: leaving Cairo, 1926; living in Ireland thirty years; coping with her husband's alcoholism; raising two sons; writing a novel; returning to nursing part-time; working as a clerk in the Irish Sweepstakes offices; broadcasting her own radio script during WWII; running an unofficial nursing home for the elderly; having two mastectomies.

Moriarty often looks at her life in terms of late-20th-century feminism, which she embraced in her old age; she apologizes that she was not more involved with women's issues in her youth. By choosing nursing as a career she acquired the self-reliance she ultimately needed to cope with her husband's alcoholism by working outside the home. She writes with a great deal of humor and paints vivid, realistic pictures of the rigors of her nursing training. At 98, Moriarty wrote part of a booklet for the very old, *Take Care of Yourself* (1988).

677 MORRELL, Lady Ottoline Violet Anne (née Cavendish-Bentinck). 1873–1938. *Ottoline: The Early Memoirs of Lady Ottoline Morrell*. Ed. by Robert Gathorne-Hardy. Faber & Faber, 1963. 308 pp.; front. port.; preface; illus.; intro. by ed. NUC 1963–1967 37:498.

Born outside London. Father: Maj.-Gen. Arthur Cavendish-Bentinck, heir to a dukedom, d. 1877. Mother: Augusta Mary Elizabeth Brown, later Baroness Bolsover in her own right. 2 brothers; 1 half-brother

(William John Cavendish-Bentinck, made Duke of Portland in 1879; in 1880, his half-siblings were raised to status of duke's children). Married 1902, Philip Morrell, solicitor, M.P. 1 son; 1 daughter. Knew Augustus John, Bertrand Russell, Lytton Strachey, Leonard and Virginia Woolf, Robert Graves, Aldous Huxley, D. H. Lawrence, Lord Asquith, Ramsay MacDonald. Society woman; literary salon hostess; politician's spouse; political activist; pacifist; art patron. Aristocracy.

Development of author's cultural and political interests, Bloomsbury and other literary, artistic friendships, 1870s–1914. Parents. Father's death, author's age 4. Moving to Welbeck. Her melancholy childhood. Attending dancing classes in London. Being passionately devoted to her mother; mother's death, author's age 19. Teaching Bible class at Welbeck Manor. Attending St. Andrews, Edinburgh. Taking her first Continental tour. Attending Somerville College, Oxford, 1900. Suffering ill health; withdrawing from Somerville. Marriage to Morrell "happy and companionable." Her political canvassing for her husband. Her passionate love of religion, commitment to good works. Feeling overwhelmed by pregnancy; birth of twins; death of infant son. Philosophical thoughts on love and sex. Interest in politics leading to connection with Beatrice and Sidney Webb. Doing political work for the Liberal League. Husband's tenure as M.P. for South Oxfordshire, 1906–10. Moving to Bedford Square, London, 1906. Cultivating and supporting young artists and writers, including Desmond MacCarthy, Virginia Stephen (Woolf), Roger Fry, Vanessa Stephen, Clive Bell, Lytton Strachey, and Duncan Grant. Forming close friendships with women. Lifestyles of her literary friends. Moving to Garsington Manor, 1913; her literary salons.

The editor's preface reveals that much of the narrative was compiled from journal entries. Lady Ottoline was viciously caricatured in writings by her friends Huxley, Lawrence, and Strachey for her unconventional dress, lifestyle, and behavior, all the while that she helped support the English cultural and intellectual scene with her money and her friendship. This memoir was cut to one-fourth its original length for publication, omitting commentary about many living people to spare their feelings; what remains is always sympathetic. Lady Ottoline became a formidable figure not only because of her social skills and connections, but also because of her broad knowledge of world cuture past and present. Her sequel, **678** *Ottoline at Garsington* (1974), covers the war years 1915–18 with particular attention to her and her husband's activity supporting pacifism and conscientious objectors; she also discusses the political and personal activities of literary friends including Desmond MacCarthy, Vernon Lee, Maynard Keynes, John Middleton Murry, Katherine Mansfield, Siegfried Sassoon, and Virginia Woolf.

679 MORTIMER, Elizabeth (née Ritchie). 1754–1835. *Memoirs of Mrs. Elizabeth Mortimer, with Selections from Her Correspondence*. Ed. by Agnes Bulmer. New York: T. Mason & G. Lane, 1836. 287 pp.; front. port.; intro. by ed. NUC pre56 84:103.

Born at Otley, Yorkshire. Father: John Ritchie, surgeon. Mother: Beatrice Robinson. 1 elder brother. Married 1801, Henry Walklake Mortimer, Esq., d.1819. Widow. 2 sons; 2 daughters. Knew John Wesley. Physician's daughter; religionist (Methodist); preacher. Middle class.

Adolescent's internal debate about the pleasures of worldliness and the merits of spirituality, leading to her Methodist conversion, spanning author's first eighteen years. Father's career as naval surgeon; his Christianity and hospitality to Methodist ministers. Author's strict religious education in childhood; fearing to grieve relatives and friends, or to miss prayers; sense of unreadiness to meet day of judgment. At age 12, accompanying father on visit to Mrs. H., of a family that had formerly been his patients; Mrs. H.'s growing so fond of author that she insisted the child remain; author's enduring Mrs. H.'s strict discipline for the sake of flattery and luxury. Mrs. H.'s prejudice against Methodists; author's resulting shame about parents' Methodism. Accompanying Mrs. H. to York; indulging in plays, cards, and company, while still thinking herself a good Christian. Mrs. H.'s decision that author should not accompany her to London, 1770; author's spending this time with her parents. Meeting John Wesley, hearing Methodist doctrine preached; at first resisting applying it to herself. Accepting Methodist doctrine; her conviction of sin; deciding to renounce worldliness represented by Mrs. H. and her friends. Conversion experience. At age 18, 1771, beginning a private spiritual diary.

This brief conversion narrative serves as a preface to a diary Mortimer kept from 1771–93; only this portion, which was written at her husband's request, is annotated here. The rest of the book (pp. 35–287) consists entirely of biographical commentary, diary extracts, and letters. In the 1780s the author traveled as a lay preacher with John Wesley, visiting towns throughout England.

680 MORTIMER, Penelope (née Fletcher; Ann Temple, pseud). 1918–?. *About Time: An Aspect of Autobiography*. Allen Lane, 1979. 190 pp. BLC 1976–1982 31:215. [cat. under Dimont.]

Born in Rhyl, North Wales. Father: Arthur Fletcher, military chaplain, clergyman. Mother: Amy Maggs. 1 brother. Married 1937, Charles Dimont; divorced 1949. Married 1949, John Clifford Mortimer, playwright, lawyer; divorced 1972. 5 daughters; 1 son. Novelist; journalist; playwright; secretary; advice writer; clergyman's daughter. Middle class.

Riveting account of childhood and adolescent emotional and sexual abuse, received at the hands of unbalanced parents, covering author's first two decades. Family history. Her father's accepting a living in Oxfordshire; his increased agnosticism, questionable conduct toward her (including possibly exposing himself). Not being taught religion. Father's falling in love with author's governess. Mother's interest in Theosophy; telling author to be civil to ghosts. Father's attempts at incest with author. Her mixed feelings of sorrow and anger at his pain and guilt. Being considered a difficult child. Her profound feelings of shyness and insecurity. Attending boarding school; liking routine. Family's move to Derbyshire. Father's continuing veiled physical and mental assaults on her. Running away from school. Having semi-dalliance with older man; disliking it. Father's suggestion that author's mother was lesbian due to her friendship with another woman; author's resulting jealousy of the woman. Father's writing romantic poetry to author. Her desire to be a writer. Attending journalism school. Her first serious affair. Renewing positive relationship with brother. Joining Left Book Club. Making sexual advance to father, possibly as revenge; his attempting to rape her. Taking job as secretary. Taking room in boarding house that turns out to be a brothel. Marriage. Husband's work as journalist. Visiting Vienna after Hitler's invasion. Political situation in Europe in pre-WWII days.

Mortimer's highly intellectual, bitter account never loses its sharp-edged sadness. Despite her best efforts to appear detached, the author seems to seethe with self-loathing. If, on some level, she acknowledges herself as a "textbook case," she chafes at the definition, and she does not appear to know how to extricate herself from the morass of negativity that constituted her childhood and youth. In 1936, under the pseudonym Ann Temple, she began writing a lonelyhearts column, "The Human Casebook," for the *Daily Mail;* in her book **681** *Good or Bad—It's Life* (1944), which she published under her pseudonym, she gives only general autobiographical information about herself.

682 MUMFORD, Edith Emily (née Read). 1869–d.a.1950. *Through Rose-Coloured Spectacles: The Story of a Life.* Leicester: Edgar Backus, 1952. 109 pp.; front. port.; illus. NUC pre56 401:173.

Born in Essex. Father: surname Read, physician. Mother not named. 1 sister. Married surname Mumford, physician. 3 sons; 2 daughters. Wrote *The Dawn of Character in the Mind of the Child, The Dawn of Religion, How We Can Help Our Children to Pray*. Religious/spiritual writer; public speaker; educator; child welfare activist; physician's daughter; physician's spouse. Middle class.

Personal experiences and professional achievements within larger discussion of various aspects of Victorian society, covering author's childhood to old age. Pastimes; happy atmosphere in home. Father's belief that daughters should be schooled in London; his building medical practice there. Attending dame school and a boys' private school, where she was accepted as a favor to her father. Attending North London Collegiate School for Girls; discipline there by headmistress Frances Mary Buss; Buss's dislike of "feminine weakness"; author's positive attitude toward being pushed to have a career after finishing school. Starting debating society. Influence on author of political ideas of teacher, Mrs. Bryant. Attending Girton College on scholarship. College life. Studying mathematics; working with tutor; his harsh criticism of her. Her high academic standing; earning designation of Wrangler. Her interest in psychology. Working as clerk for Royal Labour commission. Attending Social Democratic meetings. Working as academic coach at Girton. Her views of marriage, motherhood, grandchildren. Lecturing on children's education. Death of her husband. Her opinion of American psychologist Homer Long and his theories on reform of difficult children. Changes in London and in servants' attitudes, 1870s–1950.

Writing in an informal style, Mumford indicates affection for her Victorian past. This does not, however, diminish her objectivity in recording the problems and advances of women in higher education, particularly regarding their being accepted into the teaching profession. Mumford displays an acute intellect and expresses special interest in child welfare and psychology.

683 MUNDAY, Luta. c.1887–?. *A Mounty's Wife: Being the Life Story of One Attached to the Force, But Not of It*. Sheldon Press, 1930. 217 pp.; front. port.; illus.; foreword. NUC pre56 401:262.

Born in Canada; raised in Toronto. Father not named, physician, outdoorsman. Mother not named. Married 1905, Walter Munday, Northwest Mounted Police officer. Pioneer; WWI volunteer; Canadian Mounty's spouse. Middle class.

Saga of author's courtship and marriage to Royal Canadian Mounted Policeman and their peregrinations to every part of Canada, 1905–c.1927. Her childhood love of animals; life story of her father, an English emigrant to Canada. Unspecified schooling. Courtship; mother's opposition to engagement, then consent. After marriage, having private lessons at home; learning cooking. Life with husband at northern post at Cumberland House, Alberta, 1906–13, as only white people among the Indians. Describing drunkenness of local Indians; helping husband arrest some of the violent ones; having prisoners chained to her kitchen stove, as there was no jail. Traveling by dog train; sleeping outdoors in forty-to-fifty-degree-below-zero weather; going on 100-mile treks to visit nearest neighbors; appreciating sled dogs. Gardening.

Suffering from mosquitoes in summer. Adjusting to her isolated life; feeling discomfort with city life on return visit to Toronto. Taking two visits to England for her health, 1912–13. Discomforts of life at post in southern Alberta on the Montana border. Husband's arresting German and Austrian emigrants trying to reach Europe via the U.S. (neutral until 1917) during WWI. Husband's enlistment in army. Her WWI volunteer work in Coutts, Alberta, and as VAD nurse during flu epidemic. Formation of Royal Canadian Mounted Police, 1920, superseding the Dominion police. Living in Niagara Falls for two years, then at Arctic post on Hudson Bay; sympathetic observations on Eskimos. Husband's promotion to inspector. Returning to Toronto. Husband's posting at Regina and Winnipeg. Her anxiety for husband's welfare during his long absences, her preference for frontier over city life, her getting used to isolation in remote posts.

Munday's narrative strings together anecdotes and incidents of her married years, and interestingly shows the impact of WWI on the Canadian population. Despite the hardships of her chosen path, the author evidently grew so accustomed to frontier living that she came to prefer it to urban life. Munday expresses ambivalent attitudes toward the Eskimos, regarding them with both pity and impatience.

684 MUNDAY, Madeleine C. c.1910–?. *Rice Bowl Broken*. Hutchinson, c.1945. 139 pp.; illus. NUC pre56 401:262.

Born in England. 1 sister. Single. Wrote *The Coast Road, Gypsy Heart, The Ravelled Sleave, Far East*. Travel writer; journalist; teacher; foreign resident (China); foreign correspondent. Middle class.

Chronicle of Far Eastern politics, focusing on the social disintegration of Shanghai during the Japanese occupation, interspersed with personal, professional, and travel experiences, spanning 1936–40. Author's employment as teacher in Shanghai's International Government, c.1932–36. Her fluent knowledge of Chinese. 1936 travels: via Trans-Siberian railroad to Moscow; to Berlin and London; to Capri, Canada, San Francisco, Hawaii. Returning to Shanghai, 1937. Discussing Chinese reaction to Japanese occupation; battles in China. Writing articles for publication in England. Observing contrast between Chinese and Japanese treatment of women. Describing child sellers in Shanghai. Law enforcement during occupation. Traveling to Philippines, Ceylon, Korea, 1940. Speculating on what will become of China when Japan is defeated in WWII. Returning to Shanghai. Experiencing near-arrest by Japanese for taking photo. Departure for Sydney.

In a conversational and expository style, Munday shows herself an experienced journalist as she reports the deleterious social and political effects of the Japanese occupation of Shanghai and the perils she faced there as a foreigner. She incorporates material from articles she first published in the Yorkshire *Evening Post* and from talks she gave under the auspices of the Australian Broadcasting Commission.

MUNSTER, Countess of. [*See* FITZ-CLARENCE, Wilhelmina.]

685 MURRAY, the Hon. Amelia Mathilda. 1795–1884. *Recollections from 1803 to 1837*. With a Conclusion in 1868. Longmans, Green, 1868. 90 pp. NUC pre56 402:333.

Raised in Weymouth, Dorsetshire. Father: Lord George Murray, Bishop of St. David's, director of telegraph at the Admiralty. Mother: Annie Grant, lady-in-waiting to two of George III's daughters. 9 siblings. Married, husband not named. Wrote *Letters from the United States* (1856). Lady-in-waiting; abolitionist (American slavery); child welfare activist. Aristocracy.

Gossip and anecdotes from author's memories of her family's close ties to King George III's family and Court, covering her birth to 1860. Ancestry and family history. Father's death, 1803. Boarding school attendance. Living with elder brother while caring for younger brother. Her social debut. Meeting George III and the royal family, 1805, when mother was appointed lady-in-waiting; living next door to King George, Queen Charlotte, and their family. Discussing the flogging of the king's two eldest sons. Anecdotes about the royal family and royalty and nobility in general. Tidbits of gossip. King's alleged madness; author's impression that he was of sound mind. Receiving a gown from the queen. Author's social relationship, friendship with Princess Charlotte; her belief that the princess was starved to death.

An original member of the Children's Friend Society in 1830, Murray was chosen a maid of honour to Queen Victoria in 1837, and was also one of the most intimate friends of Lady Byron. After touring Cuba, Canada, and the U.S. in 1854, she became a zealous advocate for the abolition of slavery, and resigned her post two years later so that she could publish her ideas. This book, written in her 60s, recounts her youthful memories of the royal family and aristocracy, but does not offer any real personal insight into herself or others. It reads conversationally, as if Murray were telling stories to an audience.

686 MURRAY, Helen. c.1850–d.a.1916. *The Joy of Service*. Marshall, Morgan & Scott, 1934. 88 pp; foreword by F. J. Berning Malan. BLC to 1975 230:360.

Born in Graff-Reinet parsonage, South Africa. Father: surname Murray, Scottish, Dutch Reformed Church minister. Mother not named, French, Dutch, German descent. 8 brothers; 7 sisters. Single. Teacher; teacher (Sunday school); religionist (Huguenot); clergyman's daughter; education activist. Middle class.

Personal, familial, and professional memories, emphasizing the importance of teaching, accompanied by observations on changes in South African society, covering author's childhood to 1916. Influence of parents' gentle, religious characters on her. Having an emotional religious experience, age 14, after reading Angell James's *Anxious Inquirer;* beginning of author's personal quest for holiness. Taking trip to Cape Town with father; happiness at being with him. Father's death, 1866; her great grief. Continuing closeness with mother. Experiencing renewed revelation of religious truth, 1870s. Attending Huguenot seminary in Wellington. Teaching in a girls' school in Graff, 1876; describing her teaching duties, activities. Teaching Sunday school. Working with Christian Endeavour Society, 1891, and with Student Christian Association Movement, 1896. Her interest in establishing a Mount Holyoke Seminary in South Africa to train teachers. Believing that influence of teacher is more profound than that of minister; seeing teaching as holy vocation. Wanting to promote education, especially for the poor. Encouraging those who "have much" to share. Finding great satisfaction in her life's work. Retirement, 1916. Continuing to support work and new movements in the church.

Combining her individual religious convictions with the details of her lifelong commitment to education, Murray intersperses her observations on the significance of the teaching profession with warm memories of her large family and her South African childhood. In this text, which is free from preachiness, she seems to take genuine satisfaction in her years of service, and she encourages others to be generous as well.

687 MURRAY, Margaret Alice. 1863–1963. *My First Hundred Years.* William Kimber, 1963. 208 pp.; intro.; illus. NUC 1963–1967 38:277.

Born in Calcutta, India. Father: James Murray, merchant. Mother: Margaret Carr, missionary, relief worker. 1 sister. Single. Knew archaeologist Sir Flinders Petrie. Wrote many books on Egyptian archaeology, language, and myth, including *Excavations in Malta* (1925), *Egyptian Sculpture* (1930), *The Splendour that Was Egypt* (1949), and *The Genesis of Religion* (1963). Nurse; archaeologist; Egyptologist; academic; mythologist; cultural historian; feminist activist; suffragist; birth control activist. Middle class.

Brisk and entertaining walk through professional experiences and achievements, accompanied by observations on academic life and women's role in it, covering 1863–1963. Family history. Before mother's marriage, her charity work in Bristol slums with Mary Carpenter and in India, 1875, 1880; mother's social work among Indian *zenana* women. Mother's unorthodox system of home education. Numerous Indian servants. Life in Calcutta; anecdotes of survivors of 1857 Mutiny. Extensive travel within India during author's childhood. Family's holiday visits to England, 1867, 1870. Residence with Uncle John, an archaeologist, in Lambourn, Berkshire; education by governesses. School attendance in London, 1877–79. Returning to India. At age 20, becoming the only woman probationary nurse in India. Social stigma attached by English to hospital work for women. Father's opposition to her earning her own income. Living in England after 1886. Attempting career as sculptor. Uncle's encouragement of her archaeological interests. Father's death, 1891. Attending Egyptology program of University College, London, 1894–98. Being mentored by Sir Flinders Petrie. Fighting for Women Students' Union. Advancing from senior lecturer (1899) to fellow and assistant professor. Her attempts to help remove University College's discriminatory social practices toward women. Life in excavation camps in Egypt, 1902–03. Contacts with native laborers. Further excavations in Egypt, Malta, Minorca, Palestine, and Jordan. Being elected to presidency of Folk Lore Society. Supporting suffragette movement and Marie Stopes's birth control campaign. Doing administrative work for years at University College during Petrie's absence. Resting in Glastonbury after unnamed illness during WWI. Appreciation for her students' contributions to archaeology. Writing books on ancient Egyptian religion and history. Her scientific interest in the occult. Traveling to Soviet Union, 1926. Retirement from teaching, 1935. Her personal belief in an impersonal divine creator. Continuing to participate in excavations after retirement.

Although Murray writes in a level-headed manner, her tongue-in-cheek sense of humor nonetheless comes through in this informally written memoir. The book consists of anecdotes and does not follow a strict chronology. The author does not analyze her experiences, but focuses entirely on her professional career, revealing little of her personal feelings except in regard to the students she trained. Murray conveys her belief that women are superior organizers. Although she does not discuss her reasons for remaining single, she implies pride in her independence. She also strongly implies that women in the British Empire would benefit from studying native cultures and anthropology.

688 MURRY, Mary Middleton. 1900–s.l.1957. *To Keep Faith*. Constable, 1959. 190 pp.; front.; illus.; foreword. BLC to 1975 230:432.

Born in Lincoln, Lincolnshire. Father not named, J. P., churchwarden. Mother not named. 1 sister mentioned. Married 1954, John Middleton Murry, well-known writer and literary critic, d.1957. Widow. Knew Gordon and Beatrice Campbell (Lord and Lady Glenavy), Frieda Lawrence, George Orwell, others. Pacifist. Middle class.

Author's worshipful tribute to her well-known literary critic husband and her account of her life as his mistress and wife, covering 1932–57. Being raised in a "conventional Cathedral town." Attending boarding school. Father's character. Mother's death. Romantic friendship with "Val," a woman friend. Author's activities in Peace Pledge Union. Meeting John Middleton Murry, 1932; his activities in the Adelphi Centre and his publishing the *Adelphi* magazine; his unhappy second marriage; his love for his children. Author's becoming sexually involved with John, 1939. Influence of D. H. Lawrence and of John's deceased first wife, Katherine Mansfield, on John's life and work. Separating for a time. Reuniting; cohabiting with John from 1941 on. Wanting to bear his child. Incorporating his children into the household. Their buying a farm in East Anglia. John's illness; his undergoing surgery, 1945. Moving to London; moving again to Suffolk. Their traveling to Geneva and to Ireland. Author's performing in amateur theatricals. Death of John's second wife. Marriage. Having been bothered very little by fear of censure about their cohabitation. Resuming church attendance. John's progressive disease; his death.

Extremely romantic in tone, Murry's book expresses the author's hero-worship of her husband; she frequently quotes from his diary entries and from his love letters to her in this informally written, conversational memoir. She refers to his second wife only as "the younger children's mother." Murry includes little information about her own life outside of her relationship with her spouse.

689 NAPIER, Elma (née Gordon-Cumming; Elizabeth Garner, pseud.). 1892–pre-1975. *Youth Is a Blunder*. Jonathan Cape, 1948. 224 pp.; foreword; app. NUC pre56 405:54.

Born in Scotland. Father: Sir William Gordon-Cumming. Mother: Florence Josephine Garner, American. 3 brothers; 1 sister. Married 1912, Maurice Gibbs, mining and shipping worker; divorced 1923. Married c.1923, Lennox Pelham Napier, businessman, died c.1940. Widow. 2 sons; 2 daughters. Wrote *Nothing So Blue* (1927), *Duet in Discord* (1936, under pseud.), *A Flying Fish Whispered* (1938). Knew singer Dame Nellie Melba. Novelist; foreign resident (Australia). Upper class.

Author's difficult relations with both parents, particularly her mother, 1896–1912, with references to events before her birth and after her first marriage. Parents' marriage the day after father lost his libel suit against those who accused him of cheating at cards, 1891; his subsequent social ostracism; long-term effects of scandal on family. His rudeness and swaggering; his womanizing; mother's unhappiness. Parents' departure for Italy after author's birth, "to recover from the shock of my being a girl," leaving author with a nurse who gave her gin to quiet her crying; her resulting infantile liver disease. Author's being considered too sickly for

Scottish winters; family's winter travels to Italy, Algeria, Switzerland. Their Scottish residences. Feeling constantly criticized by mother; desiring but being unable to obtain her affection. Studying with a governess. Her unhappiness at boarding school near Wimbledon, age 9. Coming home; studying with a German governess. Attending boarding school in West Malvern, 1904–05; receiving encouragement from teacher to continue her creative writing. Summer holidays at German spas. Her love of plants; learning much botanical lore, beginning at age 14. Mother's constant remodeling and redecorating; as an heiress, mother's holding the family purse strings; her generosity. Author's eccentric aunts, including famous traveler Constance Federica Gordon Cumming. Family's move to Devonshire after reduction of mother's family fortune. Continuing tensions within family. Arts and humanities having been left out of the children's educations because mother felt "these things pandered to the emotions [and] the emotions led to sex." Attending convent boarding school in Teignmouth, 1905–08, enjoying having a room of her own there. Living in Wales with mother; mother's ambivalence about author's growing independence. Attending acting school in Covent Garden for one year; being abruptly removed from school to prepare for her social debut. Secretly admiring the militant suffragettes. Traveling to U.S. with mother; visiting mother's family. Falling in love with a married man, 1910; rumors and gossip about them; their parting; mother's blaming author for the attachment. Mother's arranging courtship with Maurice Gibbs; author's feeling helplessly subject to mother's will. Mutual antipathy between families of author and husband-to-be. Marriage, 1912. Alluding to marriage's later failure; partly blaming herself for the divorce in 1923.

The author attributes many of her difficulties in adult life to her fraught relationships with her father, whom she portrays as irresponsible, and her mother, whom she describes as domineering. In this book she records details of late Victorian and Edwardian life mainly for their significance in her own life. Her sequel, **690** *Winter Is in July* (1949), discusses her marriage and residence with her first husband in England and Australia, 1912–28. She notes that in Australia she found a freedom unavailable to her in England, began her writing career, and initiated an important friendship with singer Nellie Melba. Napier ends her autobiographies without discussing her second marriage or children or life in the West Indies, where she became the first woman to be elected to a West Indian legislative coucil.

691 NAPIER, Priscilla (née Hayter; Eve Stewart, pseud.; Penelope Hunt, pseud.). 1908–s.l.1973. *A Late Beginner*. Michael Joseph, 1966. 261 pp.; intro.; photos. BLC to 1975 232:50.

Born in Oxford. Father: William Hayter, civil administrator in Egypt. Mother: Althea Slessor. 1 brother; 1 sister. Married 1931, Trevelyan

Napier, Royal Navy commander, d.1940. 1 son; 2 daughters. Wrote family history *A Difficult Country: Napiers in Scotland* (1972), others; under pseud. Eve Stewart, wrote poems *Sheet Anchor* (1943); contributed to *Punch* under pseud. Penelope Hunt. Foreign resident (Egypt); family historian; poet; military spouse. Middle class.

A brisk rendition of personal and familial memories, focusing on British colonial life in Egypt, spanning author's first twelve years. Family history. Living half her young life in England, half in Egypt. Envy of her Anglo-Indian cousins' adventures in India. At age 2 1/2, learning to read from eavesdropping on brother's lessons with mother. Memories of Egypt: English nanny, neighbors, playmates, servants, school. Contrasting nanny's hygienic principles with dirt of "heathen" Egyptians. Father's letters to mother from Egypt while family spent summers in England. Contrast between beggars of Egypt and of England. WWI: returning to Egypt, December 1914; Australian soldiers in Egypt. Returning to England. Reflecting on effects of war in France, England, and Egypt; British troops stationed in Egypt, 1917. Remaining in Egypt 1917–19 due to government's forbidding women and children from crossing the Mediterranean. Nanny's discipline. Egyptians' friendly attitude toward the British. Church services, summer holidays on Nile delta. Nanny's departure. Playing pranks on Egyptians; feeling remorse afterward. Remembering the 1919 uprising against the British army of occupation. Author's rebellion against new nanny. Father's returning £4 million from Cotton Commission to Egyptian people, refusing his 10 percent cut. Returning to England. Father's receiving a knighthood. Returning to Egypt, 1920. Observing cultural change as Muslim women adopted Western dress. Author's schooling experience in Egypt. Her resisting responsibility. Difficulties of Egyptian independence; commenting on Egypt's political future. Final departure from Egypt, age 12.

Napier writes in a novelistic style, seeking to recapture a child's viewpoint but inserting her adult reflections on politics and the process of her development to maturity. She provides much information on the Egyptians' attitudes toward the British during WWI and immediately afterward, during the period when native nationalism was growing as Egypt moved toward becoming a parliamentary kingdom under British domination.

692 NEAVE, Dorina Lockhart, Lady (née Clifton). c.1880–1955. *Twenty-Six Years on the Bosporus*. Grayson & Grayson, 1933. 256 pp.; front. port.; illus.; index. NUC pre56 409:80.

Father: George H. Clifton, in consular service. Mother not named, English consul's daughter. 2 brothers; 2 sisters; 1 half-brother; 1 half-sister. Married 1908, Sir Thomas Neave, 5th baronet, d.1940. Foreign resident (Turkey); philanthropist; WWI volunteer; diplomat's daughter. Upper class.

Recollections of British colonial life in Turkey, accompanied by personal memories of family life, covering author's childhood to 1916. Father's violent temper and intolerance of ordinary natives. Family's difficulty in keeping English nurses and governesses. Author's Greek nurse. Describing the Bosporus. Turkish society, customs, politics, religion. Decline of British prestige in Turkey. Celebrating Easter holidays. Consular social life. Various disasters and discomforts: fire in family house; earthquake of 1894; vermin. Commenting on Turkish massacre of the Armenians; her family's actively sheltering Armenians, 1896. Arrival of British Mediterranean fleet. Making return trips to England, 1893, 1904. Permanently returning to England, 1907. Marriage, 1908. Residing in Anglesey. Raising funds for Turkish relief during Balkan War; starting a fund for British refugees from Turkey in WWI.

In this largely chronological account, Lady Neave describes her early years in Turkey and her continuing interest in that country, although after her 1907 departure she never returned. The detailed information she provides on the intricacies of Turkish society in the early 20th century is of considerable documentary value. The author's role as an eyewitness to the Turkish persecution of Armenians is perhaps the most significant aspect of this autobiography, for the historical controversy over the veracity of massacres such as she describes continues to this day.

693 NEISH, Rosalie, Lady (née Galsworthy). c.1890–?. *My Scottish Husband: Making Cheerful Fun of One of Scotland's Best.* New York: E.P. Dutton & Co., 1941. 254 pp.; plates. NUC pre56 410:3.

Born in England. Father: surname Galsworthy. Mother not named. Stepmother not named. 1 sister; 1 brother. Married c.1910, Lord Neish. Widow. WWI volunteer; philanthropist; society woman; pacifist. Upper class.

Humorous and poignant personal experiences, with reference to the author's pacifism, c.1910–35. Marriage; honeymoon in Scotland. Returning to London. Visiting Scotland frequently. Always referring to her husband as "Authority"; his stern moral character; his selling her love letters for waste paper. Anecdotes illustrating her ability to circumvent his apparent inflexibility; his essential kindness. Observing the importance of a sense of humor in getting along with a Scottish husband. Feeling stinginess is unjustly imputed to Scots. Scottish foods, customs, role of religion in everyday life. Memories of Prime Minister Ramsay Macdonald, Dame Madge Kendal. Her interest in birth control. Memories of her cousin, novelist John Galsworthy. Friendship with Canon Wilberforce. Outbreak of WWI: author's fears of invasion; aiding Rumanian refugees; working in a hospital; caring for a bombardier's daughter and convalescents in her home. Commenting favorably on pacifism; calling war a violation of divine laws. Writing article for the *Daily Express*, "What Mothers Felt Ten Years after the War." Impressed by Erich Maria Remarque's *All Quiet on the Western Front* (1929). Sudden death of her husband; her grief; desire to stay in home they shared in England. Purchasing a small house in Broadstairs. Making visits to the Victoria Home for Convalescent Children. Fearing advent of new war. Praising patriotism of royal family and government.

Lady Neish's tone is generally light and witty in this delightful presentation of her life with her outwardly stern Scottish husband, but with the advent of WWI her tone darkens. She offers her views on some of life's profoundest issues, particularly war and the folly of human arrogance. WWI provided her first direct experience with the grim results of military conflict. She effectively communicates how facing challenges presented by the war helped her gain moral strength and character.

694 NEVILL, Lady Dorothy Fanny (née Walpole). 1826–1913. *The Reminiscences of Lady Dorothy Nevill*. Edward Arnold, 1907. Ed. by Ralph Nevill (author's son). 336 pp.; preface; front. port.; index. BLC to 1975 234:361.

Born in Mayfair, London. Father: Horatio Walpole, 3rd Earl of Orford, landowner. Mother: Mary Fawkener. At least 2 brothers, 1 sister. Married 1847, Reginald Nevill. 1 son; 1 daughter. Knew the Rothschilds, Lord Randolph Churchill, Thomas Hardy, Benjamin Disraeli, Kate Greenaway, Ellen Terry, Charles Darwin, others. Society woman; art collector; diarist; antisuffragist. Aristocracy.

Anecdotes illustrating family life, social connections, and conservative opinions of aristocratic society woman, covering her childhood to early adulthood. Family's London home. Ancestry and family history. Family's Norfolk home; its ghosts; family's Dorset home, Islington Hall. Father's character; his racehorses. Her governess. Eldest brother's political career, forced upon him by father. Family's extended European travel, 1840s. Father's losing London home to gambling debts. Author's social debut. Her marriage. Biographical sketch of husband. Moving to Hampshire; her experiments with gardening and sericulture. Her Hampshire social circle. Lamenting the demise of "Society." Friendships with Rothschilds, Lord Dufferin, and conservative politicians, including Disraeli. Her interest in art and antique collecting. Her friendships with theatrical celebrities. Literary acquaintances. Friendship with Lord Randolph Churchill. Being a founding member of the Ladies' Grand Council of the conservative Primrose League. Collecting autographs. Her opinion that education of young ladies in the past allowed better development of individuality. Extracts from her 1840s diary; letters of friends and ancestors; extracts from diary of her ancestor, Sophia Churchill. Her criticism of women's suffrage and of Lady Warwick's socialist activity.

Lady Dorothy's three autobiographies constitute a major example of the "life and times" type of memoir. She takes a nostalgic look at the upper-class society she knew in her youth, offering many anecdotes and extracts from correspondence. Her style indicates a literary and artistic education as well as a politically conservative perspective. Her other autobiographical writings focus more on the changing life of high society than on herself: **695** *Under Five Reigns* (1910) is a nostalgic look at Victorian child-rearing, travel, religious groups, social entertaining, and the arts in contrast with those of Edwardian times; **696** *My Own Times* (1912) continues in this vein, covering changes in modern conveniences, transportation, and attitudes toward wealth and leisure.

697 NEVINSON, Margaret Wynne (née Jones). 1857–1932. *Life's Fitful Fever: A Volume of Memories*. A. & C. Black, Ltd., 1926. 293 pp.; index. NUC pre56 412:155.

Born in Leicester. Father: Rev. Timothy Jones. Mother not named. 5 brothers. Married 1884, H. W. Nevinson, Esq., writer, journalist. 1 son (painter Christopher Wynne Nevinson); 1 daughter. Wrote *Workhouse Characters, Fragments from a Life*. Justice of the peace; Poor Law guardian; political writer; short storyist; journalist; feminist; suffragist; public speaker; WWI volunteer; teacher; governess; clergyman's daughter. Middle class.

Assorted recollections and professional experiences, set within a detailed look at English society, with particular emphasis on the underclasses, covering author's childhood to the mid-1920s. Her close, loving relationship with her father. Commenting on Catholic Revival, 1874; High Church movement. Living in poorer quarter of town. Childhood interest in prison reform. Recalling unemployment, social problems in Leicester. Father's interest in her education. Discovering her ability for second sight. Attending Oxford convent school. Wanting to be a nun. Homesickness. Attending school in France. Father's illness and death; her overwhelming grief. Family's financial reverses. Likening marriages of convenience to legalized prostitution. Working as governess. Teaching English in Germany. Seeing teaching as the only profession open to women of her generation. Teaching high school in London. Meeting important women in education. Having prophetic dreams. Seeing dreams as central to psychoanalysis; disagreeing with some Freudian interpretations. Her interest in spiritualism. Marriage. Traveling in Germany with husband; hearing Franz Liszt perform. Returning to London. Working with St. Jude's Girls' Club. Rent-collecting in East End; various social problems of area. Meeting Olive Schreiner. Description of Whitechapel inhabitants and problems. Teaching English evening classes. Serving as school board manager. Her mother's death; being greatly affected. Recalling Jack the Ripper murders in Whitechapel, 1888. Responsibilities of motherhood;

society's not acknowledging motherhood as a serious vocation. Meeting George Meredith, H. G. Wells. Her interest in Fabian Society, Women Writers' Suffrage League. Her election to Board of Guardians for Kilburn. History of English public education. Excerpts of cases before Board of Guardians. Describing significance of English Poor Law. Participating in women's suffrage activities and protests. Recalling split in Women's Social and Political Union (WSPU); formation of Women's Freedom League, Tax Resistance League. Public speaking at Freedom League meetings. Standing for Parliament. Old Age Pensions Act, 1908. Political chicanery against poor. WSPU's civil disobedience tactics, 1911. Author's exhaustion; taking a rest holiday. WWI: volunteering as masseuse, working in hospital. Appointment as justice of the peace. Believing married women should work. Traveling in U.S.; commenting on probation system, women's relative freedom there. Disapproving of Prohibition. Noting continued prejudice against women in Parliament. Enjoying speaking on peace issue.

In a style adorned with literary citations and allusions, Nevinson presents a life of commendable public service; she comes across as well-informed and compassionate. Rather than presenting a purely personal autobiography, she tends to catalogue social problems and her roles in working to solve these. She provides a wealth of data on the sociology of East End London at the close of the 19th century.

698 NEWBERY, Esylt. c.1881–d.a.1949. *Parson's Daughter: An Autobiography*. Leicester: Ulverscroft, 1958. 244 pp. BLC to 1975 235:312.

Born at Llandrindod Wells, Radnorshire, Wales. Father not named, Anglican curate. Mother: Elizabeth Thomas. 8 siblings. Single. Teacher; foreign resident (China); broadcaster; public speaker; paid companion; clergyman's daughter; organizer of societies (social). Middle class.

Independent single woman's upbringing, travels, and teaching, mainly in China, covering 1880s–c.1949, with major gaps after 1930. Her father's never praising the children; his savage and cruel punishments. Getting her first taste of upper-class life visiting the Gaybourne family at their neighboring estate. Attending a girls' boarding school on North Wales coast. Becoming a companion-governess to a British consul's wife; voyage to China: seasickness, quarreling with her employer, losing her job. Boarding with a British couple in Malaya; substitute teaching in a mission school. Leaving Malaya; three months' residence in China with a British family; weathering a typhoon. Departing for Shanghai; teaching a Shanghai boys' choir. Visiting Japan and Russia. Returning to Shanghai via St. Petersburg, c.1910. Outbreak of WWI; returning home. Her father's attempt to make all his children teachers; her mother's increased possessiveness of children. Author's return to Shanghai. Changes since WWI: understaffing at school; students' being of all European nationalities. Organizing a branch of the Overseas Club. The Armistice, 1918. Author's final departure from Shanghai, 1919. Her parents' deaths. Broadcasting from the BBC Cardiff Studios, lecturing on the Far East, 1926–29. Visiting Albania, 1935; lecturing on Albania in London to Near East Association. Continuing her career of traveling to collect material for lectures: going to Nuremberg, Vienna, Budapest, Prague, Romania. Outbreak of WWII; lecturing on foreign countries for Forces Education; the bombing of London. Postwar travels to Sweden, Norway, Denmark. Staying single because eventually every admirer reminded her of her father.

Newbery writes with supreme self-confidence; her tone is breezy. The book consists largely of anecdotes, many of them humorous. Chatty and sometimes coy, the author often passes over major family problems; her narrative is thus somewhat disjointed. However, every time she mentions her father she writes the word FATHER in full capitals, expressing her awe and terror of him. She describes in detail the social customs and landmarks of each country she visited. In **699** *Parson's Daughter Again* (1960), she discusses her childhood fantasies of death, provides further details of her schooling at home and in London and Wales, and includes six life stories of foreigners residing in Shanghai who were interned by the Japanese during WWII.

700 NEWTON, Frances Emily (Dame of Justice of the Venerable Order of St. John of Jerusalem; F.R.G.S.). 1872–d.a.1948. *Fifty Years in Palestine*. Wrotham: Coldharbour Press, 1948. 328 pp. NUC pre56 417:446.

Born at Mickleover Manor, Derbyshire. Father: Charles Edward Newton, banker. Mother: Mary Henrietta Moore, Irish. Maternal grandmother: evangelical children's author Mrs. Favell Lee Mortimer. 3 sisters; 5 stepsiblings. Single. Knew Constance Maynard. Missionary; teacher; foreign resident (Palestine); policewoman; teacher supervisor; WWI volunteer; philanthropist; social reformer; organizer of societies (women's clubs). Middle class.

Social activist missionary's upbringing, teaching, and pro-Arab activity in Palestine, 1872–1948. Ancestry and family history. Author's maternal grandmother as strong influence on children's strict upbringing. Author's incomplete education with Protestant governess, studying little except languages. Family Bible lessons; charity visiting with mother. Father's interest in farming; his teaching author about trees and how to use tools. At age 16, persuading father to let her attend college but failing entrance exam. Running a social service club for village boys at Mickleover. Visiting Palestine, 1889, with stepsister Edith of the Christian Missionary Society (CMS); residence and CMS work with Edith and with stepsister Constance, a Mildmay deaconess in Jaffa. Visiting biblical archaeological sites. After mother's death, doing full-time CMS work. Summer holidays in England, 1889–93. Training in district nursing and social work in Birmingham, age 22. Returning to Palestine, 1895; learning Arabic. Returning to England; studying theology at Westfield College under Constance Maynard, 1903–05. Returning to Palestine; teaching at four schools in Nazareth and in nearby villages; supervising teachers; making souvenirs with Biblical associations for sale in tourist gift shop. Transferring to Haifa; seeking supervisory control over the Haifa division; building schools there; resigning from the CMS after London headquarters decided only male missionaries should have supervisory control, 1914. Discussing German pre-WWI political influence in Palestine. Returning to London; WWI work in Women's Police Patrols. Discussing child rape and murder, prostitution. WWI relief fund work for Syria and Palestine; her honors from the Order of St. John of Jerusalem. Giving British intelligence her photos and maps of the Hedjaz Railway. Returning to Palestine, 1919; its post-WWI British military government. Helping to suppress traffic in illegal antiquities and to establish welfare inspections for women and girls working in Palestine. Founding Newton House, 1932, hostel for young Arab women. How British pro-Zionist policies fanned racial hatred; postwar social conditions of Arab women; cross-cultural tensions between Arabs, Jews, and British. Arab educational and civic organizations. Proposed British remedies to Palestinian situation, 1920s–1930s. British repression following Arab riots of the 1930s. Situation of Zionism following 1945 San Francisco conference. Her assumption that the British government will honor its promise that no Jewish state will be created in Palestine; her support for a Palestinian state democratically governed by Arabs, including Christian Arabs and Jews.

In this book Newton studies in detail the British administration of Palestine. Written from a pro-Arab point of view, her account is composed of two parts: a description of her personal experience in Palestine as a missionary and philanthropist, and an analysis of the social, economic, and political repression of Arabs in Palestine under British rule. Her book appeared just before the creation of Israel in 1948 and is prophetic in assessing the sources of future problems there. She gives many anecdotes about Arab culture in Palestine.

701 NICHOL, Frances. 1889–d.a.1974. *The Life and Times of Francie Nichol of South Shields*. Ed. by Joe Robinson (possibly author's grandson). George Allen & Unwin, 1975. 176 pp.; intro.; epilogue. BLC to 1975 236:151. [cat. under Robinson.]

Born in South Shields, near Newcastle. Father: James Nichol, bricklayer. Mother: Elizabeth Billclough, factory worker. 5 sisters. Married 1909, John Robinson, boxer, died c.1913. Married 1916, Jack O'Callahan;

separated c.1930. 5 sons; 1 daughter. Shopkeeper; landlady; charwoman. Working class.

Unsentimental personal and occupational memories, emphasizing the difficulties of lower-class life, covering author's childhood to WWII. Father's drunkenness and abuse of family; mother's removing family from him. Mother's factory and housework. Author's leaving school at age 12. Scrounging for coal, food, other necessities. Mother's death. Having difficulty living with father, then with sister; their demands for food and money. Courtship and unplanned pregnancy. Attempting a self-induced abortion. Marriage. Conversion to Roman Catholicism, her husband's religion. Opposing his boxing career. Giving birth alone, without a midwife, for each of her six children. Mother-in-law's superior social attitude; author's managing lodging house for mother-in-law. Husband's death from pneumonia. Caring for sister's illegitimate children while sister resided in workhouse. Being forced to give up management of both lodging house and bake shop. Courtship by second husband, her first husband's old sparring partner; marriage. His drunkenness, demands for money, physical abuse; his sexual advances toward author's niece. Having physical fights (wearing boxing gloves) with husband. Managing fish and chips shop; giving up job in 1929 due to husband's drinking. Working as charwoman. Final separation from husband. Sons' defense of author from neighbors' gossip. Father's death, 1932. Moving to council housing. Managing grocery shop. Son's death in WWII. Effects of rationing on author as shopkeeper. At age 85, reflecting that although life has become easier, "men don't need to work any more. Women forget their place. And bairns are spoiled."

Nichol's riveting tale is told in colloquial speech and slang. Making no attempt to present herself as an object of sympathy, she expresses pride in her hard work and in her ability to survive. The long passages of remembered dialogue make the book read at times like an oral history (worth comparing to Mary Hewins's *Mary, After the Queen*). The editor, presumably a descendant of the author, does not describe his role in organizing the text.

702 NICHOLSON, Phyllis. c.1918–?. *Cornish Cream*. John Murray, 1942. 162 pp.; illus. by Katherine Tozer. NUC pre56 418:289.

Raised in rural Oxfordshire. Father not named, Oxford tutor, farmer. Mother: Lucy. 1 brother; 2 sisters. Married "Nick," army colonel. 2 daughters. Military spouse; farmer; WWII volunteer; foreign resident (India, Far East); farm child; family historian; academic's daughter. Middle class.

Sensitive exploration of personal and familial experiences, set within analysis of wartime military and civilian attitudes, covering the summer of 1941. Taking holiday in Cornwall. Exploring shops, attractions in village of Pollyon. Seeing common interest in mutual ailments as characteristic of small-town life. Differences between wartime and peacetime visitors to Cornwall. Cornish residents. British army; psychological aspects of soldiering. Memories of local canteen. Government's commandeering hotel in which author and family reside. Housing privations. Tutoring her daughters. Working in canteen; its parrot, Daisy. Attending a wartime wedding; meditations on marriage. Arrival of evacuated London children. Criticizing some mothers' indifference toward their children. Raising funds for clothing for evacuees. Describing differences between civilian and army wives. Her belief in women's eternal need for marriage and family. Emotional strain of being separated from husband and home. Hospital patients. Patriotism of Cornishmen. Wartime's bringing incongruous and strengthened desire for survival, concerns about future. Emotional, psychological, and physical strains of living through air raids. Her feelings on learning of deaths of many men she served in canteen.

Nicholson presents an extended catalogue of wartime emotions, running the gamut from patriotism to fear, in an effort to recreate civilian life during WWII. Blending descriptions of her personal feelings with details of everyday tasks, she renders a complete, albeit small, picture of wartime England. She portrays a younger self who is supportive of the war effort, but for whom the deaths of many young acquaintances ultimately bring a realization of war as devastation and irreparable loss. In an earlier work, **703** *Norney Rough* (1941), Nicholson employs a breezy style to discuss the serious topic of the impact of WWII on English rural life in the conflict's early years. **704** *Family Album* (1943), covering her childhood to the WWII era, offers memories about the author's tranquil—and now vanished—childhood world of rural Oxfordshire, as well as her experiences of colonial life with her husband in India and the Far East. Elaborating on the aftereffects of WWII in **705** *Country Bouquet* (1947), she presents a metaphorical year of her life, dividing it by the months and characterizing each by seasonal occupations.

706 NICOLL, Catherine Robertson, Lady (née Pollard). 1870–1960. Bells of Memory. Privately printed, 1934. 191 pp.; front.; illus.; apps.; index. BLC to 1975 236:350.

Born in High Down, Hertfordshire. Father: Joseph Pollard, botanist. Mother: Palacia Fenn Howes. 2 brothers; 5 sisters. Married 1897, William Robertson Nicoll, journalist, writer, Anglican canon, knighted 1909. 1 daughter. Literary salon hostess; WWI volunteer; clergyman's spouse. Middle class.

Sometimes sentimental personal and familial memories, interspersed with observations on rural society and class divisions, covering 1870–97. Pastimes with siblings. Home education by governesses. Tending her own garden "à la Gertrude Jekyll." Attending church. Daily country life: holidays, neighbors, social events, domestic servants, shops, popular reading materials. Neighbors' temperance activities. Mother's supporting idea of career for daughters; father's opposition. Family history. Father's activities in his youth with Elizabeth Fry and Quakers. Women's fashions, c.1880s. Author and sister's desire to help poor; saving money to give to poor people in village. Visiting relatives. Traveling in Europe and the British Isles. Taking a trip to Egypt with father, 1892. Meeting future husband while illustrating father's book on Egypt. Marriage to Nicoll, a widower.

Often quoting poetry or proverbs, Lady Nicoll's first autobiography reflects her evident nostalgia for the vanished world of her childhood. She combines anecdotes about people from various social classes with myriad details about middle- and upper-class family life, giving an expanded picture of Victorian country society. In a subsequent book, **707** *Under the Bay Tree: A Record 1897–1923* (1934), Lady Nicoll focuses almost exclusively on her husband's career as editor of the *British Weekly* and on her auxiliary role as hostess as they socialized with literary figures and other significant members of English society.

708 NOAKES, Daisy (née Hook). 1908–? *The Town Beehive: A Young Girl's Lot, Brighton 1910–1934.* Brighton: QueenSpark Books, 1980. 87 pp.; intro.; illus.; port.; drawings by author. Whitaker's Cum. Book List 1980, p.692. (1st pub. 1975).

Born in Brighton, Sussex. Father not named, milk roundsman, factory packer. Mother not named. 5 brothers; 4 sisters. Married 1934, George Noakes, chauffeur, gardener, handyman. 1 daughter; 1 son. Domestic servant. Working class.

Working-class childhood and life as domestic servant before marriage, 1908–34. Early memories of family life: mother's being awarded a willow-patterned tray by *News of the World* for bearing 10 children; prizes as incentives for married women to have many children to make up for WWI's loss of manpower. Mother's strict discipline; her reluctance to ask for charity. Describing streets of Brighton. Mother's pregnancies and use of midwives, not doctors. Bathing and family hygiene. Attending school. Attending Anglican services and Salvation Army meetings; joining Girl Guides. Author's childhood asthma and its treatment. Mother's loss of an eye. Elder siblings' domestic service. Author's domestic service in school dormitory, 1922, with a titled family, 1923, and at an Anglican seminary. Courtship; marriage to George, a shepherd's son. Further domestic service in another aristocratic household. Discussion of her siblings' livelihoods; pride in family sense of industry.

Noakes's style is conversational and associative, showing no conscious attempt to be literary; the loose and casual connections between successive recorded incidents make it appear that the author's main concern was getting her life story down on paper. She did not originally intend to publish this memoir. She seems to have been happy with her early life and the memories she describes are almost all fond ones. In **709** *Faded Rainbow: Our Married Years* (1980), Noakes writes of her struggle to care for her disabled husband while raising children and working at poorly paid jobs, 1934–c.1980. She provides many details about her life and does not ramble as much as in her first book. The major concern she describes is her struggle to cope with her husband's worsening multiple sclerosis and the burden the illness placed on her family; she also comments on the welfare system.

710 NOBLE, Margery Durham, Lady (née Campbell). 1828–d.a.1922. *A Long Life*. Newcastle-on-Tyne: Andrew Reid, 1925 (privately printed). 111 pp.; illus. BLC to 1975 237:358.

Born in Quebec, Canada. Father: surname Campbell, His Majesty's Notary for Lower Canada. Mother: Agnes George. 3 brothers; 3 sisters. Married 1854, Sir Andrew Noble, secretary of Royal Artillery Institution. 3 sons; 3 daughters. Society woman. Upper class.

Entertaining appraisal of growing up in Quebec, followed by details of socializing within distinguished circles in Victorian England, spanning 1828–1922. Family history. Home education. Taking walks with father; his promoting music as pastime in Quebec. Daily life in Quebec. Meeting Lord Durham, the governor-general of British North America. Potato famine in Ireland, 1847, as cause for major emigration to Canada; typhus fever epidemic and subsequent deaths of many emigrants. Meeting future husband. Courtship and marriage. Returning to live in England at Woolwich, 1860. Husband's work with the British Association. Socializing with prominent neighbors: Egyptologist Sir William Flinders Petrie and Captain and Mrs. Edward Bruce. Visiting Canada, 1861. Being rescued from wreck on an iceberg on return trip to England. Living in Newcastle. Entertaining prominent visitors: Professor Sylvester, Sir Henry Lefroy, the son of the Khedive of Egypt and Antonio Garcia, naval attaché to the Spanish embassy. Boer War: receiving visits from Rudyard Kipling, Lord Ridley, Mrs. Humphry Ward. Wishing she had spoken out more during her life in favor of things that are "pure and of good report." Taking great pride in presenting her granddaughter at Court, 1922.

Writing informally and associatively, Lady Noble reviews with pleasure her long life in this account, which is liberally sprinkled with memories of the great and near-great. As she recalls her Canadian childhood and later experiences raising her own children in England, she creates the image of herself as a woman dedicated to family life, compassionate toward suffering and benevolently interested in her numerous friends and associates.

711 NORTH, Marianne. 1830–1890. *Recollections of a Happy Life, Being the Autobiography of Marianne North*. Macmillan & Co., 1892. Ed. by Mrs. John Addington Symonds (author's sister Catherine). 2 vols. Vol. 1: 351 pp.; front. port.; preface by ed.; illus. Vol. 2: 337 pp.; front. port.; end note by ed. BLC to 1975 238:280. (other ed: Charlottesville: University of Virginia, 1993.)

Born in Hastings, Sussex. Father: Frederick North, member of Parliament. Mother: Catherine Marjoribanks Shuttleworth. 1 brother; 1 sister; 1 half-sister. Single. Artist (painter); traveler (world); amateur botanist; diarist. Upper class.

Exploration of landscapes and cultures encountered in intrepid globe-trotting, with much information about flora and fauna of various countries, covering 1830–85. Vol. 1: Family history. Author's great love and admiration for her father. Family's moves between its three country homes and London. Marriage of her half-sister. Having governesses, but mainly educating herself. Briefly attending school in Norwich, c.1846. Family's travels through Germany, Austria, and Hungary, 1847; author's studying music in various cities. Taking flower-painting lessons in London. Meeting artists, including William Hunt and Edward Lear. Her mother's death, 1855; mother's making author promise never to leave her father. Frequently visiting the Royal Botanical Gardens at Kew. Traveling abroad in the autumns with her father and sister, 1859–64. Marriage of her sister to John Addington Symonds. Frequent travels abroad with her father, 1864–69. Father's death, 1869. Traveling to the U.S. with Mrs. S., 1871. Traveling across Canada and U.S. by train; painting Niagara Falls; visiting father's former servants in the Midwest; dining with President Grant. Traveling alone to Jamaica; continually painting plants; discussing edible fruits and local society. Returning to England. Traveling in Brazil, 1872–73; painting Brazilian flora and fauna; being entranced by insects, birds, and plants; describing slaves there, during the gradual shift toward emancipation, as lazy and much "petted"; traveling alone into the highlands. Returning to England. Learning to etch on copper, 1874. Visiting the Canary Islands. Traveling to California; painting sequoia trees; visiting mining towns. Traveling to Japan; living and painting in Kyoto; finding the Japanese "like little children"; visiting Kobe; suffering from rheumatic fever. Traveling to Hong Kong, Saigon, Singapore; painting fruits and flowers new to her. Visiting the Rajah and Rani of Sarawak; traveling to the interior. Traveling to Java; exploring the countryside and Javanese culture. Visiting Ceylon. Returning to England. Being asked to lend her paintings to the Kensington Museum; making a catalogue of the 500 studies she lent them. Traveling to India, 1877–79; Indian towns, plants, landscape, society. Vol. 2: Exploring Indian culture and customs. Returning to England via Italy. Contributing paintings to Kew Gardens; requesting that gallery be built to house them. Meeting Charles Darwin. Traveling to Australia; painting flora and fauna. Sailing to Honolulu and San Francisco. Traveling across the U.S. by rail. Exhibiting her Australian paintings at a party in New York. Journeying to Africa. Visiting Cape Town, Maritzburg. Describing African peoples and customs. Visiting Seychelles Islands; painting seascapes. Return visit to South America and Jamaica.

In her introduction to the 1993 edition of *Recollections,* editor Susan Morgan points out that despite her decidedly unconventional and independent-spirited lifestyle and her distaste for many upper-class customs, North was very much a creature of her time and place in that she upheld British Imperialist attitudes, finding it right and proper that whites "civilize" the natives of tropical lands. North perpetually compares other cultures to her own, finding none that measure up to the standards set by England; small wonder that the first edition of this book won glowing reviews in her homeland. North also reveals a pronounced sensitivity to beauty, particularly the beauty of plants and animals; she seems to take continual delight in encountering new species, and is credited with several botanical discoveries of her own. In the 1880s she funded the building of a gallery in Kew Gardens to house her botanical paintings. Published after her death, *Recollections* sold so well that Macmillan issued **712** *Some Further Recollections of a Happy Life: Selected from the Journals of Marianne North, Chiefly Between the Years 1859 and 1869* (1893), which describes North's early travels with her father around Europe and to the Middle East.

NORWICH, Viscountess. [*See* COOPER, Diana Olivia Winifred Maud.]

713 NYE, Nora Mabel (née Cardinal). 1885–1973. "The Story of My Life," pp. 275–280 in *Destiny Obscure: Autobiographies of Childhood, Education and Family from the 1820s to the 1920s*. Ed. by John Burnett. Allen Lane, 1982. 345 pp. BLC 1982–1985 7:413.

Born in Tendering, Essex. Father not named, lord of the manor of the Tendering hundred. Mother, stepmother not named. 3 sisters; 3 brothers (including Alan, later governor of Falkland Islands); 1 stepsister. Married 1912, Charles Nye. 3 sons; 1 daughter. Emigrant (Australia); farmer. Rural gentry; married into middle class.

Highly personal family recollections, covering author's childhood through the 1920s. Her peaceful early life; her love for horses; studying with a governess. Mother's death at author's age 14. Being sent with her sisters to convent school in Belgium; being brought back four years later. Father's remarriage; mutual dislike between children and stepmother; stepmother's foiled attempts to sell family heirlooms. Father's dying before signing his will; stepmother's taking everything. Author's renting a cottage with her sisters Lilian and Vera. Courtship with Charles, a solicitor's son; marriage. Births of her sons. Frequent moves from farm to farm; educating her sons by governess. Emigrating to Australia, 1920s; making a home; gardening. Birth of her daughter.

This very short extract from an unpublished autobiography is of interest mainly because Nye's vivid narrative can draw readers into a compassionate understanding of one woman's motivations for emigration, moving from her privileged birth to her near-subsistence farming in Australia. In the 1930s Nye and her husband returned to England and farmed in Sussex.

714 OAKE, Mary Elisabeth. c.1910–?. *No Place for a White Woman: A Personal Experience.* Lovat Dickson, 1933. 192 pp. NUC pre56 425:314.

Born in England. Married c.1930, Robert, government servant in West Africa. Colonialist (Africa); foreign resident (France, Switzerland); civil servant's spouse. Middle class.

Discomfort and loneliness of a colonial wife in Africa, 1930–33. Lure of expedition to Cameroon as influence on her decision to marry. Husband's attempt to discourage her from accompanying him. Recalling her earlier university education and residence in French Pyrenees and Switzerland. Arrival in Africa; sense of isolation among so many single men. Suffering from physical and intellectual inactivity. Husband's work as native teacher trainer. Author's failed efforts to teach sewing to African women. Regretting that she allowed herself to be pedagogical and feel superior to her pupils. Poor diet and diseased milk causing decline in husband's health. Native servants; describing marriage from a native perspective. Believing that European education has only a superficial effect on native beliefs and superstitions. Doubting wisdom of decision to come to Africa. Feeling relief upon returning to England.

Clearly unhappy with her African surroundings, Oake frequently complains that she is accomplishing nothing. She comments at length on native life and customs, at times employing dialogue in African pidgin dialect. Although she often alludes to literature, especially French literature, Oake apologizes for this book's literary failings; her "disjointed" paragraphs, she says, mirror the disjointed conditions of her life in Africa. She also expresses shame that she allowed herself to act like the superior being the Africans thought she was. The book's title reflects the tone of depression that prevails in this memoir.

715 OAKELEY, Hilda. 1867–d.a.1931. *My Adventures in Education.* Williams & Norgate, 1939. 215 pp.; front. port.; preface; prologue; reminiscences by Sir Henry Evelyn Oakeley (author's father); index. NUC pre56 425:317.

Raised in Durham and Manchester. Father: Sir Herbert Oakeley, government inspector of schools. Mother: Caroline Howley. 1 brother; 1 sister. Single. Wrote *History and Progress, Greek Ethical Thought, The False*

State, others. Knew Sir Alfred Lyall, Eleanor Rathbone, Beatrice Webb. Educator; academic; philosopher; suffragist, militant; foreign resident (Canada). Upper middle class.

Pioneering achievements in academia and in developing higher education for women, spanning 1870s–1931. Brief discussion of author's childhood home. Being among the first women admitted to Oxford. Receiving scholarship to do research in the London School of Economics. Accepting job as principal of McGill University, Montreal, 1899; working there until 1905. Visiting U.S. colleges; analyzing American education and American attitudes toward blacks. Returning to England. Marching in suffrage parades organized by Millicent Garrett Fawcett and in joint procession of the National Union of Women's Suffrage Societies and Emmeline Pankhurst's Women's Social and Political Union. Briefly tutoring at Manchester University. Becoming vice-principal of Kings College, women's department, 1907; becoming warden of the college, 1910. Working for the inclusion of "domestic science" in women's education curricula and for coeducational institutions. Retiring from warden position but continuing to lecture on ancient philosophy. Being first woman warden of Passmore Edwards Settlement House. Taking full-time philosophy post at King's College; becoming acting head of the philosophy department. Retiring, 1931. Discussing ways in which philosophy may influence the future.

In a style reflecting her immersion in philosophical thought, Oakeley discusses her many accomplishments in the sphere of higher education for women and describes her support for the suffrage movement. This book conveys the author's lifelong commitment to securing greater social and political opportunity for women.

716 O'BRIEN, Kate. 1897–1974. *Presentation Parlour.* Heinemann, 1963. 138 pp.; intro. NUC 1963–1967 40:430.

Born in Limerick, Ireland. Father: Thomas O'Brien, horse breeder. Mother: Catherine Thornhill. 3 sisters; 5 brothers. Married 1923, Gustaaf Renier, Dutch journalist; divorced 1924. Wrote nine novels, two travelogues. Knew Fay Compton. Novelist; playwright; travel writer. Upper middle class.

Retrospective analysis of childhood experiences with author's aunts, including frequent visits to two aunts in convent, and discussion of their personalities, social attitudes, and cultural milieu, c.1900–53. Mother's death, 1902; life story of mother. Five aunts who raised author and her siblings; aunts' closeness to each other, emotional temperaments, narrow outlook, different personalities. Memories, age 7, of maternal grandmother. Father's family history; parents' courtship and married life. Father's support of Charles Parnell. Childhood visits to aunts Fan and Mary, nuns in Presentation House convent in

Limerick; long conversations with them in parlor. Impressions of nuns at convent. Author's adolescent self-consciousness about her clothes and blemished skin. Entertaining the nuns, reciting poetry. Attending convent school, 1902–16; winning prizes awarded by Intermediate Board of Education. Father's pride in her. Staying, in her late teens and early twenties, with Aunt Annie; teasing aunt for reading sentimental novels; going to melodramatic films with her. Visiting Auntie Mick, who liked author; aunt's discussion of George Eliot novels with author; reading Milton and Pope under her direction; observing aunt's duties as Poor Law guardian. Father's death, 1916. Attending University College, Dublin, 1916–18. Auntie Mick's death, 1918. Deaths of two brothers in India. Residence with Aunt Hickey, 1920 and 1922. Aunt Hickey's resistance to the Black-and-Tan soldiers in Ireland. Deaths of Aunt Mary, 1926, and Aunt Hickey, 1929. Aunt Fan's old age; her reading author's first novel with some pages pinned shut by author's sister to hide the parts that would upset her. Aunt Fan's death, 1953, age 85.

O'Brien writes in an educated and literary style, with an ironic, affectionate, and humorous tone. The focus is on her aunts' collective function as substitute mother, with insightful comments on their characters and social milieu. O'Brien's earlier autobiographical work, *My Ireland* (1962), discusses her childhood. More information about O'Brien is provided in the study by Adele M. Dalsimer, *Kate O'Brien* (Boston: Twayne, 1990).

717 OGILVIE, Mary I. 1859–d.a.1952. *A Scottish Childhood and What Happened After.* Oxford: George Ronald, 1952. 79 pp.; preface; foreword. NUC pre56 427:620.

Born in Dundee, Scotland. Father not named, solicitor. Mother: Ann, philanthropist. 8 siblings. Single. Philanthropist; school trustee; traveler (Europe, South America, South Africa, Australia). Upper middle class.

Cheerful account of personal, travel, and philanthropic experiences and observations on society, 1859–1952. Family history. Attending East of Scotland Institution for Young Ladies; its educational methods. Her strong Presbyterian upbringing. Attending Miss Brown's boarding school in Edinburgh. Studying for Edinburgh Higher Local examination. Traveling to Switzerland; studying at the Montreux école Supèrieur. Evaluating the education she received in these different schools. Visiting her sister in Arequipa, Peru; author's criticism of Roman Catholic practices there. Death of her sister; assuming responsibility for sister's children. Author's rationale for remaining single. Discussing difficulty of living as a committed Presbyterian in England. Her membership in governing body for Clifton High School. Working with the Charity Organisation Society of Bristol. Criticizing charities organized by well-meaning, but inexperienced, people. Traveling to South Africa in 1913 and to Australia in 1920. Meditation on aging, written at age 91.

Ogilvie's informal style and punctilious attention to detail provide a lively portrait of upper-middle-class life in late Victorian and early-20th-century Scotland. Only with the advent of the author's old age does the text lose its note of cheeriness, yet Ogilvie appears to hold fast to her steadfast faith that life's questions can and will be answered by Christianity. Her descriptions of individuals, places, and events, particularly in Scotland, make the book useful to social and philanthropic historians.

718 OGILVY, Mabell Frances Elizabeth, Countess of Airlie (née Gore). 1866–1956. *Thatched with Gold: The Memoirs of Mabell, Countess of Airlie.* Ed. by Jennifer Ellis. Hutchinson, 1962. 248 pp.; front. port.; illus.; index. BLC to 1984 240:448.

Born in London. Father: Arthur Saunders Gore, 5th Earl of Arran, 1st Baron Sudley. Mother: the Hon. Edith Jocelyn. 1 brother; 2 sisters. Married 1886, David William Stanley Ogilvy, 9th Earl of Airlie, d.1900. Widow. 3 sons; 3 daughters. Wrote pamphlet, "The Real Rights of Women," historical studies *Whig Society, Lady Palmerston and Her Times, The History of the Red Cross in Angus* (1950). Knew Queen Mary, many society figures. Lady-in-waiting; historian; military spouse; philanthropist; society woman; pamphleteer; feminist; WWII volunteer. Aristocracy.

Childhood, marriage, and widowhood of aristocrat who was lady-in-waiting to Queen Mary for over fifty years, covering 1866–1956. Mother's death, 1870; author's joyless childhood with stern and melancholy grandmother. Describing Victorian mourning customs. Childhood visits to Princess Mary, Duchess of Teck; friendship with her daughter (the future Queen Mary). Philanthropic character of author's uncle, Lord Shaftesbury. Describing social prejudice against schooling for girls and "deplorable" education offered by governesses; later ensuring a sound academic education for her own daughters with the help of her relative Lady Stanley of Alderly, founder of Girton College. Grandmother's death; growing closer to father; his succession as Earl of Arran, 1883. Moving to Castle Gore, County Mayo, Ireland. Learning social poise; being presented at court. Courtship and marriage. Life with mother-in-law at husband's Scottish estate. His service with the 10th Hussars; her sense of being an outsider; her interest in cavalry tactics. Her difficult pregnancy; her dread of bearing children. Social life. Experiencing marital friction, caused by immaturity of author and husband. Writing pamphlet favoring professions for women; Lady Stanley's helping circulate it in high schools. Feeling that her six children immobilize her. Husband's death in Boer War, 1900. Becoming lady of the bedchamber to Princess of Wales. Characters of prince and princess; their domestic life. Author's preoccupation with her children. Returning to full-time service with princess, now Queen Mary; interesting her in Army Nursing Board.

Author's own interest in WWI Red Cross activities and the VAD selection process. Visiting troops in France with queen, 1917. Deaths of son and daughter. Accompanying king and queen to opening of Ulster Parliament, 1921. Performing East End district visiting. Discussing unemployment in England. Traveling to Egypt and Palestine. Commenting on the 1926 General Strike. Noting the queen's responses to George V's death, Edward VIII abdication crisis and George VI's coronation. Author's fondness for Princess Elizabeth, later Elizabeth II. Developing WWII nursing organizations; her friendship with Winston Churchill. Queen's aging. Author's grandchildren. Deaths of George VI and Queen Mary. Receiving honors from Elizabeth II.

Sections from Lady Airlie's unfinished memoirs and her letters are linked together by the editor's biographical commentary. Lady Airlie is frank in her opinions and relates many anecdotes and details of her residence in the royal household. This is an important source on the English monarchy and also contains much information on the English conduct of the Boer War.

719 OLIPHANT, Margaret Oliphant (née Wilson). 1828–1897. *The Autobiography and Letters of Mrs. MOW Oliphant.* Edinburgh and London: William Blackwood, 1899. 3rd ed. Ed. by Mrs. Harry Coghill (author's cousin). 360 pp.; front. port.; illus.; preface by ed.; letters. NUC pre56 429:415. (other ed.: Oxford University Press, 1990.)

Born in Wallyford, Scotland; raised in Lasswade. Father: Francis Wilson, custom-house officer. Mother: Margaret Oliphant. 2 brothers. Married 1852, Frank Oliphant, her cousin, artist, d.1860. Widow. 2 daughters; 2 sons; 2 adopted daughters. Wrote nearly 100 novels, including *The Rector and the Doctor's Wife* (1863), *Miss Marjoribanks* (1866), *Phoebe Junior* (1876); also wrote *The Makers of Florence* (1876), *Sheridan* (1887), *The Victorian Age of English Literature* (1892), *Historical Characters of the Reign of Queen Anne* (1894). Knew John Carlyle (brother of Thomas), Annie Thackeray (later Ritchie), Leslie Stephen, others. Novelist; historian; biographer; literary critic. Middle class.

Episodic insights into domestic life and career of prolific novelist who was a major influence on subsequent women writers, covering her childhood to 1894. Her closeness to her brother Frank. Father's emotional distance from family; mother's hard work running household. Beginning to write, age 17; putting herself and her mother into her fictional characters. Success of her first novel. Family's constantly interrupting her work; feeling her family didn't take her writing seriously enough. Experiencing domestic happiness during eight years of marriage. Mother's death, 1854. Anecdotes of London literary and artistic circles. Traveling in Italy for husband's health, 1859–60; his death;

mourning him. Returning to England; friendship with Blackwood and Blackett publishers. Supporting her family through writing; considering herself "small beer" as a writer. Returning to Italy, 1863; death of her eldest daughter in Rome, 1864. Moving to Eton for her son's education. Financial burden of supporting her brother's family as well as her own. Taking pride in her hard work yet resenting being complimented on her industriousness as a writer. Pride in her nephew and sons' educational achievements; disappointment in her son Cyril. Admiration, envy of George Eliot; identification with her; comparing her own abilities with those of Eliot, Trollope, and Carlyle. Overwhelming grief at her youngest son's death, 1894.

The text is not in chronological order; the editor begins the book with a portion of Oliphant's journal written in 1864, at the time of her daughter's death, and completes her life after 1894 with letters, some of which have apparently been censored. Oliphant's own organization is associative rather than chronological, and her style is informal and unpolished; some of the text was written in fragments at different times. The author is very well read but says little about her education; she often uses French phrases. She expresses self-pity, doubts about her abilities as a writer, and doubt about whether readers would care to know details of her domestic life, but her tone is not maudlin. Rhetorical questions, to or about herself, and exclamations of grief interrupt the text. Toward the end this grief finally succeeds in breaking off the narrative, with the death of Oliphant's youngest son.

720 OMAN, Carola (Mary Anima; afterwards Lady Lenanton). 1897–1978. *An Oxford Childhood.* Hodder & Stoughton, 1976. 192 pp.; illus.; family genealogical tables; index. BLC 1976–1982 33:416.

Born in Oxford. Father: Sir Charles Oman, professor, historian. Mother: Mary Mabel Maclagan. 1 sister; 1 brother. Married 1922, Sir Gerald Lenanton, businessman. Wrote *The Empress* (1932), *Britain against Napoleon* (1942), *Nelson* (1946), others. Biographer; historian; nurse (WWI); academic's daughter. Upper middle class.

Personal experiences and reminiscences of daily life in Oxford, as recalled by daughter of a prominent don, covering her childhood and adolescence. Family history. Her father's career at Oxford; his beginning *The History of the Peninsular War;* her admiration for him. Pastimes and mischiefs with siblings. Studying French with a French governess. Studying music, literature at home. Attending day school. Mark Twain's visiting her family. Her interest in photography. Visiting London, attending the theatre; being fascinated by Shakespeare. Being encouraged by her parents in literary endeavors. Visiting France, Italy, and Germany with her parents. Taking riding lessons. Performing in amateur theatricals. Preparing for confirmation. Popular entertainments at Oxford. Girls' and women's clothing styles. Outbreak of WWI: working as probationer in Leopold Ward at Radcliffe Infirmary.

Providing a fairly detailed family history, with particular emphasis on her father's Oxford career, Oman supplies few emotional details about her own life aside from her immense pride in her rather inaccessible father. She offers vivid recollections of the trappings of life for academic families and general appraisals of the customs and practices of Edwardian life for her privileged economic class.

721 OMAN, Elsie (née Dutton). 1904–?. *Salford Stepping Stones.* Swinton: Neil Richardson, 1983. 84 pp.; illus. BLC 1982–1985 18:98.

Born in Salford, Greater Manchester. Father: surname Dutton, seaman. Mother: Edith, factory worker. 1 brother. Married 1928, Ernest Oman, painter, decorator. Domestic servant; entrepreneur; hotel worker; factory worker. Working class.

Hard-hitting tale of privations of working-class life, accompanied by thoughtful observations on the role of the underclass in society, covering author's childhood to 1928. Mother's death at author's age 7. Going to live with her Aunt Betty. Remembering excitement surrounding father's coming home on leave. Attending school. Visiting Aunt Frances in the country; favorable impression of cleanliness in her home. Helping Aunt Betty with laundry she took in. Squalid living conditions of author's neighborhood; sights and smells of poverty; observing how poverty caused people to lose self-respect. Father's personal history; his visits and letters. Catalogue of expenses and responsibilities: rent, doctor, clothing, food; challenge of making do with little. Father's arranging for author to be reunited with her brother at Aunt Lucy's house; aunt's harsh temper; author's helping her with washing and cleaning. Being visited by a "cruelty inspector"; nothing being said about aunt's striking author; aunt's rage about the visit. Author's unsuccessful attempts at running away to her other aunts. WWI: war's providing opportunities for working women. Her first factory job in a sugar mill, age 13. Returning to live with Aunt Betty. Entering domestic service in Scarborough. Suitors. Illness. Taking job as ward maid at Ladywell Sanatorium: working conditions, patients and treatments. Resurfacing of general financial difficulties in England, 1923; pawnshops' booming business. Illness; being bedridden for six weeks; her continual fear of contracting disease while working at hospital. Taking job as chamber maid; her extremely heavy responsibilities. Taking job in hotel; being promoted to cook. Enjoying higher salary. Meeting future husband. Courtship and marriage. Renting a shop with living accommodations. Opening a cookshop. Celebrating her good fortune in having a home.

Oman's narrative often takes sharp turns in thought; even within paragraphs she jumps from one subject to another as her memories press in. An insightful look at the problems faced by the lower classes in the early decades of this century, Oman's account also expresses the author's optimism and pleasure as she embarks on her marriage and new life. This is a detailed source on WWI conditions in the Manchester area.

722 O'NEILL, Ellen. 1833–?. *Extraordinary Confessions of a Female Pickpocket...Her Serious Charge against the Factory Overlookers of Manchester.* Preston: J. Drummond, 1850. fifty-page pamphlet. BLC to 1975 242:33.

Born in Stockport, Ireland. Father not named, shoemaker. Mother not named. 3 brothers. Married John O'Neill, pickpocket. Thief; mill worker; domestic servant; prison inmate; convicted transportee. Working class.

Lively and frank portrayal of descent into criminality, accompanied by observations on contemporary society, covering author's first seventeen years. Describing parents as sober, industrious, but poor. Author's attending Roman Catholic school for three years. Working in mill for spinner, ages 10–12. Spinner's giving some girls time off to go thieving. Mill conditions. Being intimidated by supervisors. Working as domestic servant, ages 12–14. Learning cap-making. Learning pickpocketing from brother, age 15. Younger brother's conviction for pickpocketing; author's beating up witness who testified against him; her arrest and one-week jail sentence. Upon release, continuing to steal. Visiting Sheffield; getting reacquainted with John O'Neill, her brother's friend. Refusing to live with him without marriage. Staying with eldest brother in Hull; his pickpocketing; his beating her for straying from the house. Running away to Leeds. Encountering O'Neill again. Marriage. Learning finer points of pickpocketing from husband. Being arrested in Sheffield. Pickpocketing with husband in Manchester; his drinking, her paying for his habit. Pickpocketing in Preston Market; being arrested. Receiving sentence of transportation to a penal colony abroad.

This book is an official report of an interview conducted in the presence of a prison chaplain while O'Neill awaited transportation to a penal colony. Quotes are directly from O'Neill, whose life story provides details of how the experience of poverty can pave the way to criminal pursuits. The prisoner's language, recorded in the detailed descriptions of her activities, lends credence and authenticity to the account.

723 ONIONS, Maude. c.1890–?. *A Woman at War: Being Experiences of an Army Signaller in France, 1917–1919.* C. W. Daniel, 1928. 63

pp.; foreword by Canon Charles E. Raven; preface. NUC pre56 430:652.

Probably raised in Liverpool. Parents not named. Single. WWI worker; pacifist. Middle class.

Author's analysis of pacifism in a Christian context, interspersed with account of her personal wartime activities and observations on the causes and effects of WWI, 1914–18. Outbreak of WWI; British responses to war. Author's departure with other women signallers for Boulogne. Conversations with soldiers; her perceiving a conflict between war and Christianity. Soldiers' violations of army "code of honour" despite their heavy church attendance; war's demoralizing effects on faith of both soldiers and chaplains. Talking with a soldier who was a burglar in civilian life and is continuing his profession as a burglar in the army. Playing the piano in a soldiers' canteen. Her defense of conscientious objectors in conversations with soldiers. Talking with a soldier who would rather be killed than kill. Visiting a dying soldier from Liverpool in camp hospital. Consolidation of British offices into one vulnerable building in Boulogne; destruction of building. Her conversation with a German prisoner; discussing Germans' view of war. Describing German offensive of spring, 1918; author's giving water to exhausted British soldiers. British counteroffensive and domination of Germans; the ruse that saved the Channel ports. Responding to Armistice by laying flowers on a German soldier's grave. Suicides of English soldiers convinced life will be worse when they return home. Playing organ for military services at the English Chapel in Boulogne; her implied opinion that British prayers after the war should be offered for forgiveness, not in thanksgiving.

Strongly pacifist in tone and Christian in outlook, this book expresses the author's horror of war primarily through the accounts of her conversations with soldiers about war's brutalizing effects. Personal detail is minimal. Onions's stated purpose in writing is to make English readers reconsider their justification of war, particularly in light of how the Christian principles of charity and honor were inexorably violated as WWI proceeded. She wrote this book about 10 years after the war's end, knowing that immediately after WWI the British public had tried its best to forget the horrors of battle, and books on the subject were then unpopular.

724 ORMEROD, Eleanor Anne. 1828–1901. *Eleanor Ormerod, LL.D., Economic Entomologist: Autobiography and Correspondence.* Ed. by Robert Wallace. New York: E. P. Dutton, 1904. 348 pp.; front. port.; illus.; preface by ed.; biog. chapters; index; app. NUC pre56 433:106.

Born at Sedbury Park, West Gloucestershire. Father: George Ormerod, Esq. D.C.L., U.D., F.R.S., F.S.A. Mother: Sarah Latham. 7 brothers; 2

sisters. Single. Wrote *A Text Book of Agricultural Entomology* (1892), *Handbook of Insects Injurious to Orchard and Bush Fruits, with Means of Prevention and Remedy* (1898). Knew Sir Joseph Hooker, Thomas Henry Huxley, Robert Wallace, others. Scientist; entomologist; scientific writer. Upper middle class.

Factual presentation of pioneering efforts and achievements in science, interspersed with English historical and geographical details, covering author's childhood to 1900. Home education by mother. Collecting flowers and insects as a child; siblings' nature collections. History of local Anglican church; history, geography, and natural history of the Severn-Wye confluence. Describing the advent of rail travel. Recounting history of the Chartist uprising in Monmouthshire, 1839. Memories of her sister Georgiana. In 1852, beginning serious self-education in entomology, using a book with no illustrations, glossary, or convenient abstracts. Sending specimens of harmful insects to Royal Horticultural Society for display at 1868 Paris Exhibition. Publishing annual pamphlets on injurious insects, 1877–1900. Residing at Torquay, Spring Grove, Isleworth, and St. Albans. Holding post of consulting entomologist to the Royal Agricultural Society, 1882–92. Lecturing on economic entomology at Royal Agricultural College and elsewhere. Giving expert testimony at a trial concerning insect infestation of flour. Suffering lameness caused by accident. Making meteorological observations. Receiving medals for her work. Describing the British campaign against house sparrows as pests. Being the first woman to receive an honorary LL.D. from University of Edinburgh, 1900.

The editor has compiled writings by and about Ormerod, including three chapters by her friends and colleagues, extensive correspondence and Ormerod's autobiographical narrative. Ormerod writes with a minimum of personal detail, chiefly analyzing the progress of her research. She apparently remained an amateur all her life, having inherited an independent income. In discussing her field, she concentrates on crop, rather than stock, pests because the latter were considered too unpleasant for women to discuss. Acknowledging the assistance of male colleagues and especially her sister Georgiana, Ormerod disavows any intention to score feminist points through her work.

OXFORD AND ASQUITH, Duchess of. [See ASQUITH, Margot.]

725 PACKER, Joy, Lady (née Petersen). 1905–1977. *Pack and Follow: One Person's Adventures in Four Different Worlds.* Eyre & Spottiswoode, 1950. 428 pp.; illus. NUC pre56 437:101.

Born in Cape Town, South Africa. Father: Julius Petersen, physician, of Danish-German descent. Mother: Ellen Marais, of French Huguenot, English-Irish descent. 2 brothers; 1 sister. Married 1925, Herbert A. Packer, British naval officer. 1 son. Knew Noel Coward. Military spouse;

journalist; ghostwriter; broadcaster; propaganda writer; physician's daughter. Upper middle class.

Military wife's South African childhood and later travels to Southeast Asia and Turkey, 1905–39. Her childhood home in Cape Town. Parents' family histories, courtship. Seeing native servants as part of the family. Regretting that she never learned Afrikaans. Attending convent school, age 13. Visiting uncle's vast tract of farmland. Taking 1920 summer holiday at Nationalist politician's farm near Bloemfontein in Orange Free State; accompanying politician on campaign tour; her first encounter with Boer hatred of British rule. Traveling with parents to London and continental Europe, 1921. Attending University of Cape Town. Meeting future husband. Parents' opposition to engagement until fiancé's promotion. Marriage in England. Perceiving husband's ship as her rival for his affections. Living in Southsea. Pregnancy. Husband's assignment to Malta; her return to South Africa to give birth. Reunion with husband in Malta, leaving baby with her parents. Residing in Germany with husband while he studied German, 1927. Discussing German youth, their vulnerability to Hitler's manipulation. Returning to South Africa with her son; deciding to leave him there and rejoin her husband in Malta. Living with husband in France while he studied French. Returning to London, 1931; writing news stories from a woman's angle for the *Daily Express.* Living in China; following husband's ship to Chinese ports. Meeting "Tinko" Pawley; ghostwriting story of Pawley's kidnapping ordeal, *My Bandit Hosts.* Taking an airplane trip from England to Cape Town and from Cape Town to Singapore, 1934. Traveling with husband in Southeast Asia. His posting to Athens; describing social life there. Visiting Turkey. Discussing Kemal Ataturk's forced Westernization of Turkey. Returning to London during 1938 Munich crisis. Outbreak of WWII.

Packer states that she wrote this book during WWII to distract herself from the war. The style is educated and poetic, using extensive anecdotes. The book provides insight into South African politics after the Boer War and into military and diplomatic family life between the world wars. In **726** *Grey Mistress* (1949) Packer discusses her WWII experience: her life in England while her husband was at sea, her BBC propaganda broadcasts with a South African angle, and her return to South Africa, where she maneuvered herself into propaganda-writing jobs in Cairo and Rome so that she could be near her husband.

727 PALMER, Bessie. 1831–d.a.1904. *Musical Recollections.* Walter Scott, 1904. 314 pp.; front. port.; illus.; index. NUC pre56 438:676.

Born in London. Father not named, printer. Mother not named, amateur singer. 3 brothers; 1 sister. Single. Knew singers Clara Novello and

Jenny Lind, impresario Charles Durand, novelist Sir Arthur Helps, others. Singer (concerts, opera); philanthropist. Middle class.

Passionate, detailed personal and professional recollections, accompanied by shrewd observations on contemporary society and the music world, spanning author's childhood to 1904. Displaying musical talent, age 3. Mother's talent for singing; grandfather's not permitting mother to study voice. Author's loathing medical practice of bleeding, as done to mother. Taking piano lessons; describing her ability to read music and mentally hear the notes. Attending opera with her father, beginning in 1840. Friendships with concert violinist Bernhard Molique and his family. Father's printing work for Clowes; after eighteen years, his starting his own printing office, publishing the *Illustrated London News.* Author's studying at Miss Penson's school. Beginning her singing career; her debut in the *Messiah,* 1854. Father's supporting author's musical career. Performing at Her Majesty's State Concert at Buckingham Palace, 1858. Entering Royal Academy of Music. Signor Crivelli's attempt to elevate her contralto range to soprano, damaging her voice and forcing her to leave Academy; correcting damage through working with Manuel Garcia. Singing English opera, 1870. Her constant engagements for oratorios, concerts in London and large towns in British Isles. Singing in opera companies of Charles Durand and Henry Walsham. Diary entries about visiting La Scala and touring eastern U.S., 1891. At age 72, her singing engagements at philanthropic church and cultural organizations.

Writing in an anecdotal style, Palmer recalls the events of her life with the emotion and verve of the operas in which she performed. Her autobiography reflects her lifelong love affair with music, a passion that increased with time. In describing her professional experiences as her career advanced and her friendships with prominent artists of her time, she provides a vivid portrait of the musical world of the mid- and late-19th century.

728 PANKHURST, Dame Christabel. 1880–1958. "Confessions of Christabel." Series. London Weekly *Dispatch,* April 3, 1921 to June 19, 1921. Part 1: "Why I Never Married," April 3, 1921, pp. 1, 7; Part 2: "My War Chest," April 10, 1921, p. 7; Part 3: "Politicians I Have Met," April 17, 1921, p. 7; Part 4: "What I Think of Lloyd George," April 24, 1921, p. 7; Part 5: "'Cat and Mouse' Days," May 1, 1921, p. 7; Part 6: "My Escape to Paris," May 8, 1921, p. 5; Part 7: "Young Jurywomen and Unsavoury Cases," May 15, 1921, p. 5; Part 8: "Turning the Vote to Good Account," May 22, 1921, p. 5; Part 9: "How I Held Audiences," May 29, 1921, p. 7; Part 10: "Why the Modern Girl Is Flighty," June 5, 1921, p. 5; Part 11: "Have We Done Any Good?" June 12,

1921, p. 7; Part 12: "Revolution of Mothers Coming," June 19, 1921, p. 5. BLC of the Newspaper Library 1:871.

Born in Manchester. Father: Richard Marsden Pankhurst, barrister. Mother: Emmeline Goulden, suffragist, social reformer. 2 sisters (including suffrage leader Sylvia); 2 brothers. Single. Wrote *The Militant Methods of the NWSPU* (1908), *Plain Facts about a Great Evil* (1913; published in England the same year as *The Great Scourge and How to End It*), others; edited *The Suffragette* newsletter; contributed to *Votes for Women* newsletter. Knew Esther Roper, Eva Gore-Booth, Annie Kenney, Flora Drummond, Emmeline Pethick-Lawrence, Lady Constance Lytton, politicians Henry H. Asquith, David Lloyd George. Suffrage leader; suffragist, militant; feminist activist; lawyer; political activist; editor; social reformer; public speaker; WWI volunteer; organizer of societies (political). Upper middle class.

Detailed essays on author's involvement in militant suffrage movement, c.1910–21, with her opinions on the expected effect of the movement's victory. Part 1: Choosing activist career over marriage. Describing early days in the suffrage movement. Parents' support and encouragement. Author's maternal feelings toward her female followers. Writing a series of articles (the basis for her later book, *Plain Facts about a Great Evil,* also published in England as *The Great Scourge*) promoting the idea that men must become as chaste as women to eradicate the epidemics of gonorrhea and syphilis. Denying that suffragettes hate men. Part 2: How the Women's Social and Political Union (WSPU) raised money. Financial sacrifices of WSPU members. Legal and other expenses. Refuting accusations that her family made a fortune through the WSPU. Part 3: Resolving not to socialize with politicians. Intransigence of Prime Minister Asquith. Blaming Sir Edward Grey for the Liberal Party's war on the suffragettes. Praise for Bonar Law and the Australian William Morris Hughes. Part 4: Blaming Lloyd George for making the militant campaign necessary. Lloyd George's superiority to Asquith as a strategist; her warm praise for his WWI leadership. Meeting him in Paris during the war; denial that the granting of the vote to women was a quid pro quo arrangement for their war work. Part 5: General mutual respect between suffragettes and the police; some policemen's sympathy for the women's cause; nonetheless experiencing police raids upon WSPU offices. Women as bodyguards to suffrage leaders. Part 6: Dramatic details of Pankhurst's escape abroad. Part 7: Women's need to be politically active without necessarily being career politicians. Believing women should sit on juries for cases involving women and children. Contrasting what she believes to be men's and women's nature. Part 8: The need for wealthy, socially influential women to continue supporting economic justice for all women. Part 9: Her career as a public speaker. Part 10: Claiming that men and popular culture in general encourage young women to be irresponsible and selfish. Necessity for employers to be better moral influences. Part 11: Assessing potential influence of women's vote. Negative social consequences from women's long exclusion from politics. Part 12: Discussing validity of women's claims to share in their husbands' incomes. Unfairness of child-support laws. Housewives as a potentially revolutionary force in the nation's budgeting and redistribution of wealth.

In these articles, Pankhurst looks back on her suffrage career. Some of the articles are directly autobiographical; others express her opinions on social issues relating to women. The author's high regard for women, her determination and her tactical brilliance are striking; she evidently wrote these pieces from a desire to help the public understand the suffragettes' political strategy. Her implicit faith in "woman's nature" (which she defines as encompassing maternal instinct, constancy, compassion, bigness of spirit, and loyalty), leads her to conclude that votes for women will soon usher in a political and economic utopia, made possible through modern science. Pankhurst also seems to have taken for granted the concept that feminism would be a force in upholding the moral ideals for which she fought.

729 PANKHURST, Dame Christabel. 1880–1958. *Unshackled: The Story of How We Won the Vote.* Hutchinson & Co., 1959. Ed. by The Right Honourable Lord Pethick-Lawrence of Peaslake. 312 pp.; preface; illus.; postscript; index. BLC to 1975 246:209.

Biographical: See "Confessions of Christabel."

Prominent feminist's account of the crucial years of the suffragette movement, c.1905–14, with limited discussion of her own family history. Extraordinary influence on author of parents' enlightened political views and teachings: father's championing of the working classes and international peace, mother's involvement in public service. Parents' joining the Labour movement. Formation of the Women's Social and Political Union. Explanation of movement's militancy as destruction of property without injury to persons. Government's response to militancy, including imprisonment and force-feeding. Author's taking a law degree. Going on lecture tours. Moral Purity crusade. Ceasing her militant suffrage activity during WWI so she could aid in the war effort. Winning the vote; subsequent dissolution of the WSPU by author and her mother. After WWI, author's desire for a quiet life.

Pankhurst states that she wrote this memoir to provide a personal narrative of the struggle for women's suffrage. She writes in a straightforward manner, giving a chronological account of that struggle. The manuscript of this book was found, untitled, in a box given to a friend of Pankhurst's; it was written c.1938, just before she moved to California. The editor, who states that he felt that Pankhurst intended this material to be published after her death, did not change the text, although he did add notes and rearrange some chapters. Throughout the book, Pankhurst attacks the gendered social and political inequities of early 20th-century British society, particularly the double standard for sexual behavior.

730 PANKHURST, Emmeline (née Goulden). 1858–1928. *My Own Story*. Eveleigh Nash, 1914. 364 pp.; illus.; foreword. BLC to 1975 246:209. (other ed.: New York: Source Book Press, 1971.)

Born in Manchester. Father: Robert Goulden, textile works owner. Mother: Sophia Jane Craine. 1 brother; 1 sister. Married 1879, Richard Marsden Pankhurst, lawyer. 3 daughters (including suffrage leaders Christabel and Sylvia); 2 sons. Feminist activist; suffragist, militant; suffrage leader; public speaker; social reformer; organizer of societies (political); Poor Law guardian; school trustee; prison inmate; political conspirator. Middle class.

Fiery personal memories mingled with observations on the development of women's suffrage, covering 1884 to the onset of WWI. Author's lifelong response to others' heroic sacrifice and desire to repair ravages of war. Believing herself always to have been an "unconscious suffragette." Studying in Paris. Marriage. History of Women's Liberal Federation. Working with Annie Besant to help striking women workers. Discussing English Poor Law. Becoming a Poor Law guardian. Becoming a school board member. Helping organize Women's Social and Political Union, 1903. Describing campaign strategies for "Votes for Women," 1905. Her friendship with Annie Kenney. Being injured in political demonstration, 1905. Creating permanent suffrage headquarters. Presiding over meeting of "Women's Parliament," 1907. Being sent to Holloway Prison for the first time, 1908 for disrupting Parliament. Engaging in civil disobedience. Evading police. Being tried for conspiracy; being defended by daughter Christabel, who had earned LL.B. but as a woman was not allowed to practice law. Leading suffrage deputation to House of Commons. Extracts from suffragettes' prison experiences; describing force-feeding, other abuses. Lecturing in America. Outlining history of Conciliation Bill. Case histories of poor women prisoners (not suffrage supporters). The Insurance Bill; its political ramifications for women. Being tried for conspiracy to commit damage; receiving nine-month sentence. Conducting hunger strike in prison. Breaking with the Pethick-Lawrences and moderates. Her renewed dedication to militancy. Being tried for inciting to commit a felony (an attempt to blow up Lloyd George's house); receiving three-year sentence. Suffering illness. Undergoing house arrest. Describing long-term effects of hunger strikes on her health. Participating in demonstrations in England, Scotland, and Ireland.

Pankhurst's style is straightforward, her tone faintly didactic, as she describes the suffragette movement and her essential role in its development. Only once does she mention—in a footnote—the contributions of her daughter Sylvia, but she includes detailed, glowing accounts of her other activist daughter, Christabel (whose perspective on feminist issues more closely resembled Emmeline's own, being less global in scope than Sylvia's; moreover, Sylvia's pacifism regarding both war and suffragist tactics was violently opposed by Emmeline and Christabel). Emmeline's book suggests a theatricality lurking behind her courage, giving this account of her contributions to women's issues a hint of self-promotion.

731 PANKHURST, E. Sylvia. 1882–1960. *The Home Front: A Mirror to Life in England during the World War.* Hutchinson, 1932. 460 pp.; front. port.; illus.; index. NUC pre56 440:120.

Born in Manchester. Father: Richard Pankhurst, lawyer. Mother: Emmeline Goulden, suffrage leader (see *My Own Story*). 2 sisters (including suffrage leader Christabel); 2 brothers. Single. Wrote *The History of the Women's Suffrage Movement* (1911), *Life of Emmeline Pankhurst,* others. Suffrage leader; suffragist, militant; feminist activist; social reformer; pacifist; biographer; journalist; historian; public speaker; socialist; traveler (Europe, U.S., Canada); entrepreneur; organizer (political); organizer of societies (political); prison inmate; artist (painter). Upper middle class.

Personal and philanthropic activities and political views set within a finely etched sociopolitical history of WWI in England. Outbreak of WWI. Setting up toy factory staffed by women workers. Author's demanding stipends for military dependents. Forming League of Rights for Soldiers and Sailors' Wives and Relatives. British suffragettes' support of war effort and government. Serving in Women's International League in Britain. Discussing the No Conscription Fellowship and passage of Conscription Act. Organizing protest against wage scales. Working on peace demonstrations and peace commissions. Describing in detail the economic privations of war and its abrogation of civil liberties for men and women. Formation of and her membership in new constitutional Society for Women's Suffrage. Describing hardships and dangers of munitions work. Her anger at upper-class munitionettes' viewing war work as "sport." Recalling looting, rioting against Anglo-German citizens. British government's order to cease feeding needy children during the war. Discussing the 1916 Irish rebellion; political ramifications and consequences of its occurring during WWI. Explaining how workers were forced to use injurious substances during their war work. Denouncing excessive punishments meted out by British army to soldiers at the front. Demonstrating that pursuing the idea of "being prepared" for war generally is a prelude to war.

In this formal yet eminently readable book focusing on her activities as a peace campaigner, Pankhurst provides numerous anecdotes and correspondence demonstrating the economic and emotional plights of the poor during WWI. Written with the passion and pathos of antiwar fiction, these tragic personal accounts of exploitation and loss are heightened by a series of stark photographs showing the consequences of war on the "home front." Expressing outrage about a war fought for "materialistic ends," Pankhurst gives names and faces to the faceless enterprise of war.

732 PANKHURST, E. Sylvia. 1882–1960. "Sylvia Pankhurst," pp. 259–312 in *Myself When Young, By Famous Women of Today*. Ed. by Margot Asquith. Frederick Muller, 1938. BLC to 1975 12:477.

Biographical: See *The Home Front: A Mirror to Life in England during the World War*.

Account of a youthful life dedicated to social reform, set within observations on contemporary society and personal and familial activism, spanning author's childhood to c.1918. Her intellectual, socialist, politically committed parents. Influence of Dickens's novels on her social ideals. Family's moving to London. Wishing she had received a formal education. Mother's political activities, trade unionism, Fabian Socialism, founding of Women's Franchise League to guard married women's property rights. Family's moving to Manchester for father's health; author's disliking attending high school there. Assisting mother in feeding unemployed during mother's tenure as Poor Law guardian. Father's losing 1895 parliamentary election as socialist candidate. Mother's arrest and near-imprisonment. Attending art school in London, 1898. Family's grief over father's death. Winning scholarship to study art in Venice, 1902. Returning home to find mother and sister Christabel absorbed in women's suffrage. Mother's founding Women's Social and Political Union (WSPU); split between WSPU and Independent Labour Party supporters. Receiving scholarship to the Royal College of Art. Beginning of militant suffrage tactics. Becoming WSPU honorary secretary. Having difficulty finding work as an artist after graduation; deciding to work harder in favor of the suffrage cause. Being imprisoned after House of Commons protest; encountering sordid prison conditions. Making paintings about the oppressive life and conditions of women workers in northern England and Scotland. Lobbying with mother for Women's Enfranchisement Bill, 1905. Second imprisonment, 1907. Major events of suffrage campaign: organized heckling of government candidates, delegations attempting to present suffrage petitions to Parliament. Disagreeing with her mother over Conciliation Bill. Traveling to U.S., Canada, 1911; political lecturing. Mother's trial; visiting Christabel in Paris. Opposing militant destruction of property; favoring mass arrests for civil disobedience. Her third imprisonment and forcible feeding. Agitation against Cat and Mouse Act. Living in East End slums. Separation of WSPU from author's East London Federation of Suffragettes, 1914. Writing secretly in prison for *Workers' Dreadnought* paper. Twice escaping abroad in disguise.

Pankhurst's fiery commitment to social justice and feminist causes informs this essay, which also clarifies her differences of opinion with her activist mother and sister and her regret at having abandoned her art career. Her incisive work regarding her formidable contribution to women's rights, **733** *The Suffragette Movement: An Intimate Account of Persons and Ideals* (1931), interweaves her personal experiences with a painstaking chronicle of how British women won the vote. Demonstrating the historical reasons why suffrage advocates became polarized into mutually antagonistic factions—and never forgetting her fundamental interest in the cause of universal social justice—she focuses on the participants' attitudes and their separate long-range visions of women's role in the overall political scheme.

734 PAPENDIEK, Charlotte Louise Henrietta (née Albert). 1765–1839. *Court and Private Life in the Time of Queen Charlotte: Being the Journals of Mrs. Papendiek, Assistant Keeper of the Wardrobe and Reader to Her Majesty.* Ed. by Mrs. Vernon Delves Broughton (author's granddaughter). Richard Bentley, 1887. 2 vols. Vol. 1: 331 pp.; ed.'s preface; illus. Vol. 2: 325 pp.; illus.; index. BLC to 1975 246:332.

Born in London. Father: Frederick Albert of Saxe-Teschen, attached to the court of Queen Charlotte in London, German. Mother not named. 2 brothers; 2 sisters. Married 1783, Mr. Papendiek, court musician to the queen. 3 daughters; 2 sons. Knew George III and Queen Charlotte, Dr. Samuel Johnson, Mrs. Hester Lynch Thrale Piozzi, Fanny Burney, Johann Christian Bach (son of J.S. Bach), Sir Joshua Reynolds, Franz Joseph Haydn, others. Court lady. Upper class.

Hanoverian court life and intrigue as seen by courtier's daughter, with details on her education, difficult marriage, and acquaintance with 18th-century artists, from before her birth to 1792. Vol. 1: Ancestry and family history. Father's service to royal family. First episode of George III's mental illness; subsequent court intrigue. Author's birth. Death of author's infant brother, 1767; her great sorrow. Author, other court members' receiving smallpox inoculations. Births of sister and brother. Father's promotion to court position at Kew, 1772. Gossip and anecdotes about courtiers, family friends, and neighbors. Attending private day school at Streatham, 1773; analysis of rise of governess system's popularity and decline of girls' private schools; behavior and discipline problems in girls' schools. Sister's death from smallpox. Playing with children in the Royal nursery; attending Royal christenings and birthday parties. Author's severe eye inflammation, followed by smallpox; recuperating and feeling idle at home; taking music lessons; returning to school. Her acquaintance with the family of writer Sarah Trimmer, who established Sunday schools for the poor. Royal family parties and concerts; court painters. Visiting Samuel Johnson and Mrs. Thrale at

Streatham; meeting Joshua Reynolds and other painters. Describing the Gordon Riots in London, 1780. Father's continuing financial worries due to breakdown in royal patronage system; his distress over king's rumored infidelities. Receiving Papendiek's marriage proposal; marrying him for economic security only; father's reluctant acceptance. Their life after marriage; their debts. Pregnancy; birth of daughter. Resenting husband's demand for absolute obedience. Anecdotes of Mrs. Siddons and the Duchess of Devonshire. Living with husband only for short periods. Second daughter's birth. Noting high prices of clothing and other necessities. Anecdotes of the astronomer Herschel and his daughter. Birth of author's first son; inoculation of her children. Courtiers as fashion setters. Her daughter Charlotte's education. Birth of second son. Vol. 2: Political crisis, intrigue following king's severe attack of mental illness; public celebrations of his recovery. Husband's disappointment at the loss of his allowances. Sir Thomas Lawrence as a court painter; his painting of the author. Anecdotes of the Bridgetowers, black concert musicians. Outbreak of French Revolution. Constant visiting between author's children and children of Royal family. Leaving house at Windsor; moving to Dean's Yard. Public unrest and riots incited by radicals in the wake of the French Revolution; riots in Birmingham; perceiving Thomas Paine's writings to be a pernicious stimulus on the riots. Discussion of her own education, female education in general, and women's household duties.

Written for Papendiek's children, this book is a very detailed picture of court life in the late 18th century. It is full of anecdotes and gossip, related intimately and conversationally. At least some of the text, although not in journal form, appears to have been made into a continuous narrative by the editor's use of journal entries. The author often interpolates comments from Fanny Burney's diary for a different viewpoint on the same people and events. In the final chapter the editor discusses later events in the author's life, including her service to the queen as Assistant Keeper of the Wardrobe and as Reader.

735 PARKS, Fanny (née Frances Susannah Archer). 1794–1875. *Wanderings of a Pilgrim in Search of the Picturesque.* Oxford University Press, 1975. 2 vols. Vol. 1: 493 pp.; intro. by Esther Chawner; illus.; glossary of Indian words; notes. Vol. 2: 529 pp.; illus.; app.; notes; index. BLC to 1975 248:81. (1st pub. Pelham Richardson, 1850.)

Born in Conway, Wales. Father: Capt. William Archer, 16th Lancers. Mother: Anne. Married Charles Crawford Parks, writer for East India Company. Colonialist (India); farmer; feminist. Middle class.

A lively and unique slant on India, Indian people and customs, and British colonial policy as recalled by a colonial, covering 1822–45. Vol. 1: Attending colonial social activities in Calcutta. Learning Hindustani.

Traveling on the Ganges. Farming at Allahbad. Taking a trip to Taj Mahal. Discussing Indian domestic servants, justice system, religious ceremonies, social customs. Describing Muslim customs. Providing history of Hindu theology. Noting presence of Methodism in higher native social classes. Influence of European women upon European men in India. Observing Europeans' lack of respect for Indian culture. Outlining history of colonial occupation of India. Vol. 2: Famine in Kanauj. Traveling to Simla from Landowr over mountains. Author's illness and return to England. Criticizing unfair laws governing married women in England. Perceiving women as possessing inherent strength. Returning to India. Describing Delhi; natural beauty of Indian scenery. Benares: snake charmers, temples, sugar mills. Outbreak of famine in northwestern provinces, 1838. Describing Afghani people and their customs. Husband's securing furlough to England; sailing home.

Parks's lively and detailed autobiography provides an unusual slant on India, its customs, and its people during three decades of the early 19th century. Her commentary on changes in Britain's governing of India, the economic ramifications of these policies, and India's domestic social problems reveals her independence of mind. As a woman who preferred riding, exploring, and taxidermy to more conventionally feminine pursuits, she demonstrates a faint disdain for women more traditional than herself. Her descriptions of India express her admiration and high esteem for the richness of Indian culture, and she includes a glossary of terms and an impressive collection of translated Indian proverbs.

736 PARSLOE, Muriel (née Jardine). c.1884–d.a.1931. *A Parson's Daughter.* Faber & Faber, 1935. 296 pp.; preface. NUC pre56 443:252.

Born in Ireland. Father: Charles Jardine, Anglican vicar. Mother not named. 3 brothers; 1 sister. Married 1916, Stanley Parsloe, farmer, gamekeeper, d.1931. Widow. 1 son; 1 daughter. Farmer; horse trainer; cross-dresser; male impersonator; hunter; foreign resident (Canada); clergyman's daughter. Middle class.

Nearly fifty years in the life of a rural woman who was remarkably unconstrained by social or gender considerations, 1888–c.1931. Her wild, free childhood on a tiny rural island; tagging along with her older brothers in games, pranks, and riding horses. Being nurtured by the old groom who taught her to ride, train horses, and box. Failure of attempts to school her at home; author's conspiring with her brother John to harass their shared tutors and have them dismissed, one by one. Mother's giving up on author's home schooling, sending her to a private day school, where she excelled at cricket and football. At age 15, author's becoming companion to her elderly Aunt Helen in Dumfries, Scotland; aunt's putting together a wardrobe for a "nice little girl"; author's having always worn boys' clothes before then.

Sneaking out of aunt's house to attend parties, flirt, and drink beer. Returning to her family; playing pranks on her brother Joe's girlfriends. At age 16, receiving a proposal from the best man at her sister's wedding; discovering he was married; taking an "oath that I would make all men suffer as I had been made to suffer." Acquiring the belief that long hair caused headaches, age 17; cutting her hair off and selling it for £5. Posing as her brother, taking a farm job in Ireland that he had refused; switching identities while on the train; kissing a girl while posing as a boy. One farmhand's discovering her gender and proposing to her; refusing him. Returning to live with her parents, who moved to the south of England to comfort author's newly widowed sister. Breaking her arm while horseback riding; recounting her four serious riding accidents. Moving frequently around rural England with parents as father accepted different parishes. In Essex, finding work as a horsebreaker; having to give it up when father was transferred to Stansted. Finding another job training polo ponies in Norfolk. Outbreak of WWI: training horses for export to Canada. Moving to Wiltshire with parents; meeting Stanley Parsloe. His cousin's housekeeper's despising author as a "man-woman." Marrying Parsloe, 1916; their joining a caravan to Wales; poaching game and giving birth to a daughter along the way. Her parents' sudden deaths, 1919–20. With father-in-law and husband, visiting husband's sister at Australian sheep station, 1922. Returning to England; their finding work on a colonel's estate, where their son was born. Their visiting Canada and briefly farming there; returning to England and setting up a lodging house in Plymouth. Briefly holding a series of shared positions with her husband: caretaking at an animal sanctuary in Hatfield Forest; gamekeeping for a succession of squires; serving as estate bailiff. Husband's death from pneumonia in 1931; her maintaining his gamekeeper position; succumbing to overwork; being hospitalized; having a vision of heaven during her illness. Accepting parish charity; using it as her sole means of support while writing this book.

One of the more whimsical features of Parsloe's book is her chosen title, for the author's life certainly deviated from any parsonish pattern. In documenting the social liberty she enjoyed within rural culture, Parsloe serves as a wonderfully useful reminder that what we are pleased to call Victorian conventions were hardly universal. While scholars in gender studies will have a field day with this book, trying to ascertain where the role-play she enjoyed empowered her socially and where it touched upon other, perhaps sexual, aspects of her psyche, Parsloe herself ignores such subtleties, recreating instead the simple intensity with which she lived.

737 PAWLEY, Tinko (née Edith Muriel Phillips). 1913–?. *My Bandit Hosts*. Ed. by Joy Packer. Stanley Paul, 1935. 288 pp.; front.

port.; intro. & commentary by ed.; illus.; index. BLC to 1975 249:409.

Born in Newchang, Manchuria. Father: Dr. Phillips, physician. Mother not named. 1 brother. Married 1931, Kenneth Pawley. Foreign resident (China); physician's daughter; kidnap victim. Middle class.

Vivid recounting of adventures of kidnapping survivor, accompanied by observations on Chinese society, focused on two months of 1932. Recollections of her earlier life: childhood in rural Manchuria; 1920 visit to England; attending Devon boarding school; engagement and marriage in Newchang. Author and her friend Charles Corkran's being kidnapped for ransom by Manchurian bandits in September, 1932; enduring forced marches through rural Manchuria. Character of bandits; bandits' falling ill; author and Corkran's doctoring them. Chinese customs. Exchange of letters and packages from parents; author's writing letters for the bandits demanding ransom; parents' search efforts. Author's contempt for her smelly and insulting kidnappers. Author and Corkran's being released to the Japanese after ransom payment. Returning home.

Informal, even casual—despite the danger of the circumstances described—Pauley's account reflects her youth, particularly in the use of colloquial speech and expressions such as "beastly awful." Between sections, editor Joy Packer includes her own commentary, indicating that it was she who gave coherence and chronology to the narrative; Packer states her belief that Pawley's extreme naiveté and limited imagination helped her survive her ordeal (see Packer's autobiography, *Pack and Follow,* for further details). Many of the photos, obviously posed, depict reenactments of events that Pawley relates as having occurred during the kidnapping.

738 PEARL, Cora (pseud.; Emma Elizabeth Crouch). 1842–1886. *The Memoirs of Cora Pearl, the English Beauty of the French Empire.* Vickers, 1880. 188 pp.; letters; epilogue. NUC pre56 128:166. (other ed.: 1886.)

Born in Plymouth, Devonshire. Father not named, composer, died c.1847. Mother not named, singer. Stepfather not named. 15 siblings (sisters were singers). Single. Courtesan; adventuress; foreign resident (France). Middle class.

Courtesan's youth and entrée into Continental high life, with selective details about her lovers and candid comments on her disdain for men, 1840s–1880. Childhood memories of family and music rehearsals. Death of father, author's age 5. Residence eight years at a Boulogne boarding school. Returning to London; living with her grandmother. Mother's remarriage. Author's hatred of stepfather. Seduction at age 15 by a stranger; her horror; hating men because of this experience. Living in London with dance-room proprietor; traveling to Paris as his wife; taking the name of Cora Pearl; remaining behind in Paris. Gambling at Baden-Baden and other resorts. Losing enormous sums. Liaisons with various wealthy and titled Frenchmen; their expensive presents. Blackmail paid to her by her married lovers to keep her quiet about their liaisons. Her residence and profligate life in Vichy. Extended liaison with Prince Jerome Bonaparte, cousin of Napoleon III (not named in book); his love letters; traveling with him to London. Lovers' fighting a duel over her. Expulsion from France as a result of the Duval Case (Alexandre Duval spent family fortune on her, then attempted suicide). Subsequent expulsion from Monaco and other European resorts; being forced to live incognito. Lacking knowledge of her relatives in England. Being snubbed in England because of her reputation. Being protected from falling in love by her hatred of men. Describing her "favourite lover"; platonic lovers. Actors she has known. Not being recognized or compensated by French government for her help in Franco-Prussian War (she had turned her Paris house into a hospital for wounded officers). Valuing her personal independence.

A rare example of an autobiography by a woman seduced as a young girl, most of this book consists of Pearl's anecdotes about her lovers, although all names have been changed. The author often uses exclamations and rhetorical questions; her tone is sentimental when she recalls happy times, but occasionally she turns angry, as when she discusses her hatred of men. She leaves much unsaid or only implied in regard to her conduct. Although she suffered in her initial seduction, she says she suffered worse in her treatment as a courtesan. Pearl's only moralizing in this book, which was apparently written for money, lies in her condemnation of what she sees as the hypocrisy of a society that branded her as notorious.

739 PEARSON, Jane (née Sibson). c.1735–1816. *Memoir of the Life and Religious Experiences of Jane Pearson, Extracted from Her Own Memorandums.* York: William Alexander & Co., 1839. 3rd ed. 96 pp.; intro.; conclusion. NUC pre56 446:595.

Born at Newtown, near Carlisle, Cumberland. Father: Jonathan Sibson. Mother: Jane. Married John Pearson. Widow. 3 sons; 4 daughters. Religionist (Quaker); preacher. Lower middle class.

Moving account of a personal religious quest, personal tragedy, and devotion to Quakerism, covering author's entire life. Father's death; her youthful fear of death. Being tutored by schoolmaster. Being tormented by her inability to speak in Quaker meetings; discovering her ability to do so. Marriage. Births of her children. Husband's early death; feeling unconsolable pain at his loss; feeling God had taken husband because author had not fulfilled her religious duties. Deaths of a son, a daughter, and author's mother. Deaths of two more daughters. Experiencing dread about praying in public assemblies. Visiting meetings throughout England. Likening solemn silence of meetings to silence of heaven. Experiencing a vision of God. Her last surviving daughter's bout with cancer; her death. Author's praising and adoring God for granting her the emotional strength to survive her agony. Her spiritual power and commitment's growing as her physical feebleness increases. Exalting God's mercy as the source of consolation.

Centering her narrative on her unwavering faith and conveying her belief that Quakerism is the only path to truth, Pearson employs the traditional Christian metaphor of life as a constant journey of the soul. She follows in the literary path of Bunyan and other spiritual autobiographers in asserting that her experience of a transformative event in this journey—her vision of God—marked the point at which, in both mind and body, she commenced turning away from the material world and toward the heavenly next life.

740 PEARSON, Kay (née O'Loughlin). 1896–s.l.1977. *Life in Hull: From Then till Now.* Hull: Bradley Publications, 1979. 192 pp.; illus. BLC 1976–1982 34:522.

Born in Hull, Yorkshire. Father: C. E. O'Loughlin, seaman. Mother: H. O'Loughlin. 3 brothers; 2 sisters. Married 1915, S. Pearson, railway policeman, d.1949. Widow. 1 son; 3 daughters. Musician (pianist); teacher (music, dance); domestic servant; WWI volunteer. Working class; married into lower middle class.

Entertaining details of growing up—and old—in Hull, including varied aspects of author's musical interests, covering her childhood to 1977. Attending Catholic school. Mother's taking in washing; remembering the stench of washing butchers' coats at home; helping mother arrange clothes for ironing. Family diet. Family pastimes. Mother's buying second-hand piano. Studying music. Father's long absences; mother's assuming role of both parents. Author's playing piano at dances, age 13. Assisting her mother in preparing meals for farmers and auctioneers on market days. Briefly entering into domestic service, age 14: scrubbing, sweeping, kitchen work; earning extremely low wages. Mother's removing author from job. Running errands to earn money. Returning to her musical studies. Her thwarted attempt to join a musical troupe; mother's anger; author's abject apology; this incident's offering her an opportunity to find closeness with mother. Teaching piano, age 16. WWI: her volunteer work entertaining soldiers. Meeting future husband. Marriage. Domestic duties. Teaching music. Husband's being wounded in WWI; his permanent return home. Husband's suffering morning sickness with each of author's pregnancies. Experiencing financial difficulties after arrival of their third child; lacking time to teach. Health and housekeeping problems and solutions. Her strong commitment to family life.

Resuming teaching, 1929. Arranging to play matinées to benefit clothing fund. Finding satisfaction in her successful dealings with social superiors. Working as accompanist for dancing school. Teaching ballroom dancing. Her health problems. Deaths of mother, one daughter, and husband during 1948–49; author's grief. Resuming work as dance pianist. Taking brief job caring for elderly ladies. Resuming music teaching, 1958. Finding satisfaction in a life of varied occupations.

In this loquacious, humorous account, Pearson paints a self-portrait of a decidedly independent woman who harnessed her musical talent to improve her family's finances and her own self-esteem. Buoyant, even in old age, the author speaks of her accomplishments with pride and expresses optimism for the future.

741 PECK, Winifred Frances, Lady (née Knox). 1882–1962. *A Little Learning; or, a Victorian Childhood.* Faber & Faber, 1952. 192 pp. NUC pre56 447.103.

Born in Oxford. Father: Edmund Arbuthnott Knox, Oxford Fellow, Anglican clergyman. Mother: Ellen Penelope French. Stepmother: Ethel Newton. 5 brothers; 1 sister. Married 1911, Sir James Peck, Scottish Education Secretary. 3 sons. Wrote *There Is a Fortress, A Clear Dawn.* Novelist; clergyman's daughter. Middle class; married into upper class.

Personal experiences and reflections on religious, educational, and social aspects of late Victorian and Edwardian society, spanning author's childhood to young adulthood. Family history, Quaker ancestry. Experiencing harmony in her family home. Death of her mother. Attending Miss Quill's Academy: strict school discipline, poor education. Attending Ladies' College, school at Wycombe Abbey; praising its relatively liberal atmosphere and progressive education. Her interest in Anglo-Catholicism. Attending St. Leonard's School; subsequently attending Oxford (but not graduating). Remembering Elizabeth Wordsworth. Discussing Victorian views of "female" education; interpreting Victorian views of Protestantism and Catholicism. Considering conflicts between science and religion. Assessing advantages of a "Victorian upbringing." Commenting on drawbacks in 1940s–1950s primary and secondary education.

Frequent literary allusions and citations help enhance the book's formal presentation and Victorian flavor. Peck writes directly about her concern for the future of education, promoting reforms to foster learning without the inflexibility and prejudices she finds inherent in Victorian methods. Her assessments of pioneer women educators and the first generation of women students at Oxford make the book very useful. Peck offers a detailed look at her early years and milieu in **742** *Home for the Holidays* (1955), which conveys her devotion to family and records the dramatic changes in family life between the Victorian era and later times.

PEEL, Baroness. [*See* LILLIE, Beatrice.]

743 PEEL, Dorothy Constance (née Bayliff; O.B.E.). 1872–1934. *Life's Enchanted Cup: An Autobiography (1872–1933).* John Lane, The Bodley Head, 1933. 297 pp.; front. port.; illus.; poem by Edward Sanford Martin; index. NUC pre56 90:147.

Born near London. Father: Paito Bayliff, Adjutant of the Monmouthshire Volunteers. Mother: née Lane. Maternal grandfather: T. T. Lane, clergyman. At least 3 brothers. Married c.1895, Charles Peel, author's second cousin, electrical engineer. 3 children. Knew Arnold Bennett. Wrote novels *The Hat Shop* (1914), *Tony Sant* (1921), social histories *A Hundred Wonderful Years: Social and Domestic Life of a Century, 1820–1920* (1926), *The Stream of Time: Social and Domestic Life in England, 1805–1861* (1932), cookbook *Meatless Cookery Made Easy* (1911), others. Social historian; novelist; culinary author. Upper class.

Brisk recollections of changing attitudes and ideas in British society, particularly as they affected the upper class, spanning author's childhood to 1932. Family life in childhood: church, education, servants. Queen Victoria. Commenting on the British nobility; perceiving a decline of the aristocracy of birth and wealth in favor of an aristocracy of brains and personality. Remembering the naughty nineties; Beardsley's "Yellow Book" group. Discussing Victorian and Edwardian customs. WWI: assassination of Archduke Ferdinand; bombings; food shortages; wounded soldiers. Discussing unemployment. Recollections of Lady Randolph Churchill. Changes in social attitudes; changing fashions, including motoring caps, bonnets, dust cloaks. Noting status of women and women's suffrage. Memories of Lloyd George. The change from gold to paper money. Author's presentation at the court of King George V. Describing the sexual underworld; the trial of Oscar Wilde. Prison reform. English gardens. National food distribution and common kitchens. Discussing the condition of the working class, especially women. Temperance. Traveling to continental Europe by boat. Playing bridge. Author's writing, mainly on food and fashion. Discussing housework. Her illnesses: influenza, asthma, diabetes, angina.

In this wide-ranging memoir, Peel presents herself as an observer as well as a participant in the events she discusses. Her sense of wonder at life's surprises is tangible as she comments on a plethora of topics, from the notorious Yellow Book collaborators to the characters of prime ministers, from votes for women to prison reform. Collectively, her observations form an absorbing record of a half-century of change in British and European social, political and economic life.

744 PENN, Margaret (pseud.; Hilda Winstanley Huntley). 1896–1981. *Manchester, Fourteen Miles.* Firle, Sussex: Caliban Books, 1979. 241

pp.; intro. by John Burnett; illus. NUC pre56 448:396. (1st pub. Jonathan Cape, 1947.)

Born at Hollins Green, Lancashire. Father: surname Farrington, younger son of country gentry. Mother: Maggie Stringer, nursemaid. Stepfather: George Huntley, laborer. Foster father: Joseph Winstanley, farm laborer, road worker. Foster mother: Elizabeth Ann Winstanley, née Buckley. Illegitimate child. 1 foster sister; 2 foster brothers. Married c.1914, Frank Burton (possible pseud.), journalist, army captain. 1 son; 1 daughter. Domestic servant; dressmaker; secretary. Rural laboring class; married into middle class.

Social milieu of Lancashire farm village and close and loving extended foster family, mingled with author's aspirations for broader experiences, covering her birth to age 14. Attending village school. Self-education through reading. Attending Methodist chapel. Becoming aware of social class distinctions. Discovery, age 10, that her mother had been a nursemaid who was made pregnant by one of the gentry, then married a farm laborer before dying while giving birth to author; learning that her stepfather had emigrated to Canada after her mother's death. Her extended foster family; their wages and employment; description of household. Receiving financial support from her birth mother's mother. Social mores of village; local attitudes toward illegitimacy, drunkenness, gossip. Funeral of Grandma Winstanley, her foster grandmother. Village shops, children's games, seasonal holidays, social events. Her primary school, teachers, and friends. Describing dress and home decoration. Belonging to Band of Hope youth temperance society. Writing and delivering research paper on spiders to Mutual Improvement Society, age 12. Working as assistant to vicar's housekeeper. Foster father's rise in social status as a road ganger. Working as an unpaid apprentice dressmaker. Employment, age 13, as dressmaker's workroom errand girl in Manchester. Feeling shame at her rough, rural background; aspiring to educate herself above the class of her foster family. Discovering that her Aunt Mildred, a relation of her real father, was to bring her to live in London; her excited departure for London.

Penn, who elsewhere has identified herself as the Hilda Winstanley of this book, here presents her childhood in entirely convincing detail. She writes with a novelist's touch, expressing her warm affection for her early home. As in her other autobiographies, she uses third-person narration, disguises characters' names, and employs an ironic tone. Burnett's introduction provides details of the social milieu of Hollins Green, a village unchanged by the industrial influence of nearby Manchester. In **745** *The Foolish Virgin* (1951), Penn describes her adolescence in London, 1910–14, and the middle-class snobbery of her urban relatives; she retrospectively views herself as a foolish virgin with romantic dreams. In **746** *The Young Mrs. Burton* (1954), Penn examines her life from c.1916–25, including her marriage to an injured WWI veteran, his alcoholism, and their family's degradation, which led to her giving up her children for adoption. This tragic story may leave the reader unsatisfied, for what ultimately becomes of the author, her husband, and children is never revealed. Penn seems to have acquired her literary skill through wide reading and through conversation with her husband. Here, her self-portrait appears more critically detached and yet more sympathetic toward herself than in *The Foolish Virgin.* By book's end her illusions about her husband are gone yet she stays with him, she informs the reader, more for the pleasure of his company than from religious duty or family loyalty.

747 PERHAM, Dame Margery Freda. 1895–1982. *African Apprenticeship: An Autobiographical Journey in Southern Africa in 1929.* Faber & Faber, 1974. 268 pp.; front. port.; prologue; illus.; maps; index. NUC 1973–1977 90:435.

Raised in Harrogate, North Yorkshire. Father not named, businessman. Mother: née Needell. 5 brothers; 2 sisters. Single. Wrote *Africans and British Rule* (1934), *East African Journey* (1976), others. Foreign resident (Africa); travel writer; political writer; journalist; teacher. Upper middle class.

Thoughtful and balanced views of Africa and the British colonial presence there, emphasizing political and economic conditions for natives and colonists, covering 1919–1930s. Her childhood dream of going to Africa. Attending Christian boarding schools. Attending Oxford. Taking up teaching career after WWI; parents' disapproval. Sister's career as African missionary and marriage to African explorer; author's being inspired by sister's example to fulfill her own dream of going to Africa. Memories of her first journey to Africa: Hargeisa, Somalia, 1924. Traveling to South Africa, 1929, to study subcontinental affairs. Receiving Rhodes trust grant. Discussing South African history and political situation. Socializing with Capetown society. Discussing occupational opportunities for natives. Lecturing to colonists about Oxford University. Her views of African attitudes toward the continuing European presence. History of Basutoland. Tribal customs, beliefs, diet. Bushmen's customs. Leprosy as a widespread problem in Basutoland. Traveling through Transvaal. Political significance of Russian money being funneled to natives. Status of South African Party in 1930s. South Africa's economic dependence on mining. Describing rise of slums; unspeakable living conditions for natives. Visiting native court, reporting various cases. Europeans' views of natives, 1929. Noting lack of equal justice for natives. Arrival in Zululand. African natives' political agitation, resentment against colonialism. Working in movement for South African unity. Visiting the Congo, 1930. Writing articles for *The Times,* 1933–34. Beginning study of Britain's three eastern dependencies.

Dialogue and in-depth interviews animate Perham's informally written narrative, which purports to present an objective view of contemporary South Africa from both colonial and native perspectives. Although she appears to represent and approve of British imperialism, the author candidly notes the serious economic and cultural problems created for the natives by Europeanization, particularly in the imposed industrialized economy.

748 PETHICK-LAWRENCE, Emmeline. 1867–1954. *My Part in a Changing World.* Victor Gollancz, 1938. 367 pp.; front. port.; preface; index. NUC pre56 453:109.

Born in Weston-super-Mare, Somerset. Father: Harry Pethick, businessman. Mother: née Collen. 12 siblings. Married 1901, Frederick Lawrence (later Pethick-Lawrence), Fellow of Trinity college, editor, lawyer, d.1961. Feminist; suffragist; suffrage leader; social reformer; journalist; editor; publisher; businesswoman; philanthropist; prison inmate; academic's spouse; dressmaker; organizer of societies (political). Upper middle class.

Detailed and moving assessment of the women's "revolution" as a whole, the suffragist movement in particular, and author's pivotal role in both, covering her childhood to mid-1930s. Family history. Her early questioning of religious doctrine. Influence on her of her father's passion for justice; her own awakening social conscience. Attending Quaker school; subsequently attending a finishing school. Undertaking further studies in France and Germany. Her discomfort at her economic dependence on her father; her growing determination to earn her own living. Not wanting to marry; basing her attitude on her insecurity about being able to attract a mate. Going to London to assist at Working Girls' Club. Her increasing desire to see the working class benefit from its labor. Establishing West London Social Guild. Serving on School Management Committee. Noting difficulties, unsanitary conditions faced by teachers in poor areas. Starting a dressmaking establishment in London. Meeting Fred Lawrence; his personal history and purchase of the *Echo* newspaper. Joining council on *Echo*'s policies. Courtship and marriage. Serving as president of Esperance Social Guild, 1895. Closing the *Echo.* Touring South Africa; friendship with Olive Schreiner and family. Supporting Labour Party's claim to secure enfranchisement of women. Meeting Mrs. Pankhurst and Annie Kenney. Forming Central London Committee of the Women's Social and Political Union (WSPU). Forming delegation to call on Prime Minister Henry Campbell Bannerman and Mr. Asquith, Chancellor of the Exchequer. Organizing protest at House of Commons; being arrested and sent to Holloway Prison. Growing division between militant and moderate sections of movement; split into Women's Freedom League and WSPU. The League's new forms of campaigning and expanded goals to secure social, economic, and political equality for women. Author's launching *Votes for Women* paper with husband. Participating in educational campaign throughout the country. Increasing influence of suffrage movement on by-elections. Author's rearrest in demonstration. Describing prison clothing, food; suffragettes' hunger strikes in prison; their suffering and resistance to force-feeding. Being tried, with her husband, for suffrage activities; receiving nine-month sentence. Dissension with Pankhursts over protest methods; being turned out of the WSPU. Outbreak of WWI: caring for Belgian refugees; joining women's Emergency Corps Committee. Forming Women's International League of Great Britain to promote idea that peace and negotiation alone could ensure a stable Europe. Adopting constitution for Women's International League; being elected its president. Limited suffrage's being extended to women. Reflecting on social change in her lifetime in regard to women, children, education, and poverty.

Writing in a compelling style, Pethick-Lawrence provides a detailed political analysis of the suffrage movement and describes its internal dissensions. Although the author might have cause for bitterness over the manner in which she was ejected from the WSPU, she continues to praise Mrs. Pankhurst and expresses enthusiasm for the work of suffrage leaders in Britain and the U.S. Her descriptions of suffrage supporters and opponents provide a cogent framework for her call for social equity.

749 PETRE, Maude Dominica Mary. 1863–1942. *My Way of Faith.* J. M. Dent, 1937. 342 pp.; foreword; intro. NUC pre56 453:372.

Born at Coptford Hall, Essex. Father: the Hon. Arthur Charles Augustus Petre, 4th son of the 11th Baron. Mother: Lady Katherine Howard, daughter of the 4th Earl of Wicklow. 5 brothers; 5 sisters. Single. Wrote *Modernism: Its Failure and Its Fruits* (1918), *Life of George Tyrrell from 1884 to 1909* (1912), *The Ninth Lord Petre* (1928), others. Knew English theologian George Tyrrell, Baron Friedrich von Hugel, Henri Bremond. Religionist (Roman Catholic); biographer; religious/spiritual writer; philosopher; nun (Roman Catholic). Upper class.

Intellectual and spiritual formation of a Catholic theological modernist, with details on her defense of and companionship with theologian George Tyrrell, 1860s–1937. Parents' spiritual lives: father as born Catholic, mother as convert; parents as author's moral teachers. Author's mixed tendencies toward religion and paganism. Memories of nursery life and nursemaid. Noting children's pleasure in "inferior" art. Analyzing her early education. Making her first visit to London. One sister's establishing austere rules for the schoolroom: no feminine amusements, no care for personal deportment; author's going along with these rules. Governesses. Describing Catholicism as "the right religion for children" because it is a life of the heart, rather than the head. Analyzing her intellectual ambition and spiritual aspirations. Being plagued by moral scruples. Her childhood fear of the doctrine of eternal punishment. Not feeling devoted to the Virgin Mary. Character of her sex education. Being attracted to men. Believing that feminism has condoned sexual licentiousness for the modern woman. Discussing the role of passion and the senses in art. Deaths of parents and two brothers, 1882–84. Developing a Catholic sense of religious vocation. Studying scholastic philosophy in Rome, age 22. Her entry into a religious community, c.1885; becoming a Superior in an Order in which she was the youngest member; staying with the order for ten years. Raising her sister's sons. Living in Mulberry House, a mission in Storrington. Her religious beliefs' being increasingly undermined by collective influences of social Darwinism, 19th-century modern historical biblical criticism and the prevailing social distrust of authoritarianism; publishing articles reflecting her changing views. Discussing internal and external problems of modernism. Concluding that Catholic religious catechism should contend with the assumptions of modern science and history; believing that by condemning modernism the Church made science and faith into antagonistic domains. Her close friendships with Catholic modernist theologians Baron Friedrich von Hugel and George Tyrrell. Personal enemies' criticism's forcing her separation from Tyrrell, 1904. Her refusal to let him be reconciled to the Church on his deathbed, 1909. Preparing his work for posthumous publication. Her sense of closeness to Tyrrell even after his death. Her war work in France, 1915–16. Continuing her explorations of spiritual issues.

Petre has written a subtle intellectual and spiritual autobiography, although she would not label it as such. She focuses on gradual changes in her experience and understanding of her faith, following a topical order that is also generally chronological. Sparing of dialogue and discursive, her style reflects her advanced education and study in theology, philosophy, and literature. She felt an intimate connection with Tyrrell and defended his theology even after Pope Pius X condemned modernism in the 1907 encyclical *Pascendi.* Her book stands among the best primary sources on the Catholic modernist movement.

750 PHILLIPS, Catherine (née Payton). 1727–1794. *Memoirs of the Life of Catherine Phillips, to Which Are Added Some of Her Epistles.* James Phillips & Son, 1797. 382 pp.; app. NUC pre56 456:40.

Born in Dudley, Worcestershire. Father: Henry Payton, Quaker minister. Mother: née Fowler. 1 sister; 2 brothers. Married 1772, William Phillips, businessman, investor. Widow. 2 stepchildren. Religionist (Quaker); preacher; clergyman's daughter. Middle class.

Spiritual, personal, and travel experiences of Quaker minister, covering all seven decades of her life. Author's closeness to her father; her mother's religious devotion and affection toward children. Author's early religious instruction and education at boarding school. Her entrance into ministry, age 22. Preaching in Wales, Ireland, Scotland. Traveling to America, 1753. Visiting Friends' communities in South Carolina, North Carolina, Virginia, Maryland, Pennsylvania, and Massachusetts. Experiencing health problems. Commenting on censuring of Friends' Christian testimony during French and Indian War. Marriage. Her continuing bouts of illness. Death of her husband. Discussing vice of alcoholism, its social and moral consequences. The moral dilemma of Friends' keeping slaves. Describing the behavior required of single women in ministry toward single men in ministry. Discussing gender equality in Friends' community and ministry. Differences between religious observances of Friends and other Christian sects. Presence of vanity in other Christian observances.

Phillips demonstrates her devotion to Quakerism, describing the many arduous land and sea journeys she undertook despite travel dangers and discomforts and her own chronic poor health. Although she describes a loving relationship with her parents, an undertone of bitterness runs through her autobiography; even as she praises her sister's devotion to their mother, Phillips's text seems to imply her resentment at what she perceives as her mother's favoritism toward this sister. Nevertheless, her mother's letters to the author, included in the text, reveal a seemingly genuine tenderness and affection for Phillips.

751 PICKERING, Anna Maria Wilhelmina (née Spencer-Stanhope). 1824–1901. *Memoirs of Anna Maria Wilhelmina Pickering. Together with Extracts from the Journals of Her Father, John Spencer Stanhope, Describing His Travels on the Continent and His Imprisonment under Napoleon.* Ed. by Spencer Pickering (author's son). Hodder & Stoughton, 1902. 2 vols. Vol. 1: 474 pp.; index. Vol. 2: 464 pp.; index. NUC pre56 457:252.

Born in Doncaster, South Yorkshire. Father: John Spencer Stanhope, scholar, magistrate. Mother: Elizabeth Wilhelmina Coke. 3 sisters; 2 brothers. Married 1853, Percival Andree Pickering. 2 daughters; 2 sons. Society woman. Rural gentry.

Account of a life in aristocratic society, together with the author's upper-class perspective on contemporary issues, spanning the whole of the Victorian era. Vol. 1: Extensive family history and genealogy. Memories of living in rural Yorkshire. Studying with governesses. Her father's being a classical scholar, archaeologist, magistrate, and gentleman farmer; his classical mind, his devotion to his children's education, his reading history and poetry with them; during his absences, his corresponding with author about history. Gardening with her mother. Becoming lame; recovering with use of a special shoe. Studying French, dancing, fencing. Touring Continent with her family. Her social debut. Vol. 2: Death of her grandfather, Lord Leicester, longtime M.P.; grandmother's remarriage. Attending queen's fancy dress ball. Her father's friendship with Prince Leopold of Belgium. Memories of Queen Victoria, Sir Richard Neave, Jenny Lind. Being guest at Welsh castle. Recalling Marie Gresholtz (Madame Tussaud) and her friendships with Voltaire, Rousseau, Franklin, Mirabeau, and Lafayette. Discussing Reform Bill and resulting unrest. Country Christmas customs. Women's fashions; ladies' making their own shoes, c.1820s. Domestic servants' knowing their employers' secrets. The destruction of the Bastille and the aftermath of the French Revolution. Discussing the rise of Chartism and its political ramifications. Her devotion to her religious faith.

In a formal style that distinctly echoes the 18th century, Pickering traces her life in privileged Victorian society. Although the existence she describes sometimes appears to be an endless social whirl, she also writes informatively on social customs, political movements, and major 18th- and 19th-century figures. In addition, she describes, with evident love, members of her distinguished family. In his commentary her son (who edited her memoir) indicates that Pickering taught her children by her father's method, and that she handwrote her own history of England for them to use in their lessons.

752 PICTON-TURBERVILL, Edith (O.B.E.). 1872–1960. *Life Is Good: An Autobiography.* Frederick Muller, 1939. 319 pp.; front. port.; illus.; app.; index. NUC pre56 604:433.

Born in England. Father: Colonel John Picton-Warlow, later Picton-Turbervill, East India Company ensign. Mother: Eleanor Temple. 8 brothers; 2 sisters; 1 half-brother; 1 half-sister. Single. Wrote *The Musings of a Lay Woman* (1918); with Canon Streeter, *Christ and Woman's Power* (1919); others. Knew Ellen Terry, Lady Kinnaird, Ethel Smyth, Agnes Maude Royden, Ramsay MacDonald, many other leaders and politicians. Missionary (India); religious/spiritual writer; public speaker; organizer of societies (women's clubs); philanthropist; politician; member of Parliament; social reformer; factory inspector; religionist (Anglican); religionist (Evangelical); feminist. Middle class.

Recollections of family life, missionary work, service with YWCA, and career in Parliament, covering author's birth to c.1938. Family history. Parents' living in India before author's birth; their later travels, leaving children with relatives. Life in Brighton household with aunt and siblings. Death of her baby brother after another brother, age 3 1/2, set fire to him, 1880. Attending day school with her twin sister. Visits to aunts in Germany. After father's retirement from army, 1883, moving to Bruges to economize; twins' truancy from Bruges school. Feeling emotional distance from mother; father's role as storyteller, gentle disciplinarian. Moving to Wales, 1884; local entertainments; her interest in sport. Mother's death, 1887. Engaging avidly in studies at Royal School, Bath.

Father's remarriage to affectionate stepmother. Her self-education after age 18. Moving to Ewenny Priory, Wales, 1893, after father inherited the estate. Family's financial security, 1893–1914. Describing 1890s social conventions. Stepmother's Band of Hope activity. Author's playing church organ, teaching Sunday school. Theatre-going in London; friendship with Ellen Terry. Experiencing religious conversion; beginning public speaking on Evangelical Christianity. Her work with Lady Kinnaird (YWCA founder). Taking Evangelical Bible classes; converting her brothers and sisters. Attending Mildmay missionaries' training school; working with YWCA and Settlement for University Women in India, 1900–08. Returning to England. Heading YWCA's Foreign Department; her resulting membership in the British National Council; suffrage debate in council; her support for constitutionalist suffrage leader Millicent Garrett Fawcett over the Women's Social and Political Union militants. Describing her failed attempts to persuade Mrs. Humphry Ward to support women's suffrage and Emmeline Pankhurst to abandon militant methods. Legislative activity in YWCA; her service on committee to pass Criminal Law Amendment Bill increasing penalties for "procurers and persons living on the earnings of prostitution," 1912. Traveling to Palestine with her sister, to Egypt to help establish a YWCA hostel in Cairo, and to Ireland. WWI service and deaths of two of her brothers. With Margaret Bondfield, working during WWI to improve conditions for women munitions workers; inspecting munitions factories in England and Scotland; making speeches for war effort. Receiving the O.B.E., 1917. With Agnes Maude Royden, leading movement for women's ordination in the Church of England. Lecturing in America, 1918, on war and munition work; visiting American philanthropists. Returning to England. Writing books. Beginning her political career, 1919; her Labour Party activities. Her father's death, 1924. Political campaigns; her election as M.P., 1929. Describing women colleagues in Parliament; necessity of their working harder than men. Labour and Liberal members' being in the underdog position and under great pressure. Sponsoring bill protecting pregnant women from execution, 1931. Listing and commenting on legislation beneficial to women. Describing how the press magnified trivial incidents because of her sex. Parliamentary crisis of the coalition government. Losing her seat in the 1931 general election. Traveling in Soviet Union, 1932, and East Africa, 1933; visiting Turkey for a suffrage conference, 1935; investigating child servitude in Hong Kong and Malaya, 1936. Praising her older women friends.

The author gives a serious and detailed account of her life and public career, demonstrating a businesslike, optimistic attitude toward social service. The book is especially useful as a source on women in Parliament, in the Church of England, and in social service work; Picton-Turbervill had a number of close friendships with influential, politically and socially active women of her time. In **753** her contribution to Margot Asquith's anthology *Myself When Young* (1938), Picton-Turbervill provides personal recollections of her childhood, family life, and religious work.

754 PILKINGTON, Laetitia (née Van Lewen). c.1706–1750. *Memoirs of Mrs. Laetitia Pilkington, Written By Herself.* New York: Dodd, Mead, 1928. 3 vols. 487 pp.; front. port.; intro. by Iris Barry; illus.; apps. NUC pre56 458:403. (1st pub. Dublin: privately printed, 1748–54; other ed.: Albion Press, 1804.)

Born in Dublin. Father: John Van Lewen, obstetrician. Mother: née Meade, Anglo-Irish. 1 sister. Married 1725, Matthew Pilkington, Anglican curate; divorced 1738. 4 children. Knew Jonathan Swift, Samuel Richardson, others. Wrote *The Statues, or the Trial of Constancy* (1739). Poet; pamphleteer; secretary; playwright; prison inmate; physician's daughter. Upper middle class.

Often-dramatic personal and literary adventures and misadventures, offering insights into 18th-century thinking, spanning author's childhood to 1750. Her strong childhood interest in literature. Admiring father's eminence as physician, his progressive views toward women, his training women in midwifery. Marriage. Friendship with Jonathan Swift; his aid to her husband's career in England. Traveling to London to be with her husband, 1733. Husband's attempts to advance himself by encouraging her to form sexual liaisons with important men; his temporary incarceration in London for publishing Swift's poetry under his own name. Death of her father in unexplained stabbing accident. Husband's disappointment that she was disinherited by her family; his turning her out of doors. Moving to London. Friendship with poet Colley Cibber. Writing poetry for various clients. Working as secretary to Lord Galway. Her unfavorable impression of Sir Hans Sloane. Being imprisoned for debt. Samuel Richardson's helping her purchase a pamphlet shop. Her views on women writers of the time: Madame Dancier, Catherine Philips, Mrs. Grierson. Lamenting lack of constructive occupations for women and men's ulterior motives for being charitable to women. Authorities' accusing her of writing anticlerical pamphlets; being target of satirical pamphlet *A Parallel between Mrs. Pilkington and Mrs. Philips, Written by an Oxford Scholar.* Returning to Ireland with her son, John. Son's account of her final illness.

In many ways Pilkington's fascinating work reads like fiction; it includes a rich mix of commentary and reporting as well as gossip about numerous 18th-century notables. Evidently victimized by a panderer-husband, the author found herself running a gauntlet of mishaps in order to forge her independent way in the world. Partly as a result of her own circumstances, she shows a strong interest in women's legal rights and education.

755 PINKHAM, Mrs. William Cyprian (née Drever). 1849–?. "Selections from the Unpublished Recollections of Mrs. W. C. Pinkham, an Early Manitoban." *Manitoba Pageant,* 1974. 12 pp.; illus. Part 1: 19(2):21–23; Part 2: 19(3):19–22; Part 3: 20(1):11–17. Ulrich's International Periodicals Dictionary, 1975–1976, p. 687.

Born in Manitoba, Canada. Father: William Drever, Hudson's Bay Company employee, farmer. Mother: Helen Rothnie. 2 brothers; 3 sisters. Married 1868, Rev. William Cyprian Pinkham, later Anglican Bishop of Saskatchewan and Calgary. 2 sons; 4 daughters. Pioneer; teacher (Sunday school); philanthropist; clergyman's spouse. Middle class.

Exciting adventures of daily life on the Canadian frontier, including observations on political and religious aspects of European and American Indian societies, spanning author's first four decades. Part 1: Parents' histories; their separate emigrations to Canada. Family's early privations. Father's working for Hudson's Bay Company; his later farming land granted by company. Moving to Upper Fort, Manitoba, 1851. Scottish Presbyterian parents' joining Anglican church because it was the only church available. Indian and half-breed midwives' aiding at births of author's sisters. Part 2: Father's building their house. Mother's instructing half-breed servants in religion. Father's friendship with local Indians; author's perceiving them as always being well-behaved, even when drunk. After massacre of settlers in Minnesota, 1862, settlers' fearing Santee Sioux perpetrators who fled to Upper Fort wearing scalps at their belts. Indians' stalking settlers, including author and her sisters. Part 3: Father's moving family into town. Marriage; moving to cabin on Assiniboine River; living on an annual income of $750; adjusting to duties of a rural clergyman's wife. Outbreak of the Riel Rebellion, 1870. Loyalist stand of father and brother William; their hiding fleeing Loyalists; author's being threatened by drunken Irish rebels; father's imprisonment by Riel's men. Her sister's marriage to Colonel MacLeod, a major figure in Western Canadian history. Husband's appointment to Board of Education for Manitoba, 1871; his serving as its superintendent, 1871–83. His appointment as Secretary of Anglican diocese, 1881, then as Archdeacon, 1883. Author's serving on Women's Auxiliary, becoming President of Women's Hospital Aid Society to the General Hospital. Family's moving to Calgary, Alberta, 1889.

Pinkham's clear and colorful text vividly describes 19th-century Canadian frontier communities. Although her loyalty to the British government and its institutions (such as the Hudson's Bay Company) is strongly implied, her sense of Canadian identity also emerges as she depicts her deep connections to her local community.

756 PINNEGAR, Eira Gwynneth. c.1910–?. *The Great Awakening.* Newport, Monmouthshire: R.H. John, 1948. 175 pp.; intro. NUC pre56 459:132.

Born in Cardiff, Wales. Married 1940, "Mr. E." Singer (concerts, popular); religionist (Methodist); spiritualist. Middle class.

Passionate, highly personal memories and professional experiences, emphasizing spiritual and artistic influences and activities, spanning author's childhood to the 1940s. Youthful experiences with religion and spirituality. Mother's praying for author because of her frequent illness. Recognizing her gift for fortunetelling with cards. Attending Calvinistic Methodist chapel; discovering her singing talent. Deciding to follow a singing career. Joining Clara Novello Davies's choir. Her first performance before Royal Command, 1928. Working as a variety singer; taking Eira Gwynne as stage name. Her opposition to drinking and smoking. Describing her relationships with men, including "Mr. E.," who was married. Having a life crisis in 1933: needing to give up singing because of poor health and difficult love affair with Mr. E. Declaring that her personal awakening in 1933 occurred when the spirit of Edwardian author Marie Corelli came to her as a "spirit agent" to help her write this book. Having a 1933 dream vision of Christ, who told her how to amend her life and use her spiritual powers. Subsequent closer friendship with Mr. E.; marriage after his divorce. Her dream vision of Christ's crucifixion in 1935; interpreting it as a prophecy of WWII; predicting a world disorder caused by Jews and Arabs. Experiencing visions and automatic writing. Giving spiritual and religious advice to readership.

Displaying a faith which blends Christianity with spiritualism, and frequently quoting inspirational verse, Pinnegar dedicates her book in remembrance of her great awakening through the "Christ Consciousness." In her introduction she explains that her account was written to benefit the general public, whom she addresses urgently and earnestly.

757 PIOZZI, Hester Lynch (née Salusbury; formerly Mrs. Thrale). 1741–1821. *Autobiography, Letters, and Literary Remains of Mrs. Piozzi (Thrale).* Ed. by A. Hayward. Longman, Green, Longman & Roberts, 1861. 2 vols. Vol. 1: front.; ed.'s intro., pp. 1–243; autobiography, pp. 245–307; notes. Vol. 2: 407 pp.; intro. & notes by ed.; illus.; fragmentary writings collected by ed.; index. BLC to 1975 325:385.

Born at Bodvel, Caernarvonshire, Wales. Father: John Salusbury. Mother: Hester Maria Cotton. Married 1763, Henry Thrale, brewery owner, d.1781. Married 1784, Gabriel Piozzi, musician, Italian, d.1809. Widow. 12 children, 8 of whom died during childhood. Wrote *Anecdotes of the Late Samuel Johnson, LL.D., During the Last Twenty Years of His Life, A*

Series of Letters on Courtship and Marriage (c.1797), *Retrospection; or, Review of the Most Striking and Important Events, Characters, Situations, and Their Consequences Which the Last Eighteen Hundred Years Have Presented to the View of Mankind* (1801). Knew Samuel Johnson, James Boswell, Fanny Burney, Elizabeth Montagu, Anne Finch, and the Bluestockings. Biographer; historian; poet. Upper middle class.

Selective, nonchronological account of a woman intellectual's formative experiences, financial hard luck, and triumph over marital and societal victimization, touching upon events from childhood to age 60. Knowing her Welsh ancestry back to the Norman Conquest. Her mother's love-match to a dashing cousin who wasted her fortune; their impoverished life in Wales; their teaching author, their only child, to read and think in French until she was "half a prodigy." Their hoping mother's rich childless brother would leave author his fortune; his agreement; his sudden death without writing a new will in author's favor. Disappointed parents' pinning new hope on author's other childless uncle, Thomas, who brought family to live on his great estate. Author's growing to age 19 there; having a private Latin tutor; both father and uncle's adoring her; uncle's parading her before eligible suitors; father's resenting her wooers. In 1762, uncle's deciding she should marry Thrale, a wealthy London brewer; father's objecting violently. Thrale's wooing author's mother to ensure maternal support for the match. At wedding, author's feeling sacrificed to a man who didn't love her. Resenting Mr. Thrale's restricting her to a life of pregnancy and domesticity. Uncle's eventually marrying an attractive widow and disinheriting author. Author's becoming acquainted with Samuel Johnson, 1764; his stimulating her intellectually; his covertly helping to counter her husband's bad business management. Disastrous brewery losses' forcing the Thrales into heavy debt. In Brighton, 1780, author's encountering Mr. Piozzi; his refusing her request to tutor her daughter in music; his following her home to beg her pardon when he discovered who she was. The infatuated Piozzi's clinging to author's side in England, despite the demands of his illustrious Continental singing career. Alluding briefly to husband's 1781 death. "Mr. Thrale's" daughters persecuting their mother because of her Italian Catholic suitor; societal criticism of the alliance forcing Piozzi's departure; author's falling dangerously ill; wise doctor's curing her by persuading Piozzi to return; their marriage in 1784. Their living five years on Continent until debts in England had been paid. In Italy, living with aristocratic patron of Piozzi in Milan; author's enchanting many Italian men, who could not understand her marital fidelity. Enduring attacks in "public print" due to her marriage to Piozzi. Publishing two books on the life and letters of Samuel Johnson as well as a travel book on France, Italy, and Germany. After returning to England, 1789, being triumphantly welcomed by many who had previously attacked her. Author and Piozzi's retiring to live in Wales; his building Italian villa there; his illness and death; her being his sole legal heir but giving much of the estate away to needy relatives, thus reducing her own circumstances. Giving a retrospective account of her first husband's death from a series of strokes compounded by gluttony, followed by her heroic efforts, assisted by Dr. Johnson, to redeem his brewery business and sell it for profit. Another fragmentary account of the humiliation she suffered from her first husband's infatuation with a young woman, Sophia Streathfield.

Although formerly famed as a literary hostess in the circle of Samuel Johnson, Piozzi is increasingly regarded as a noteworthy 18th-century writer of divergent genres, her letters being especially brilliant. A scant sixty-two pages of this two-volume collection is devoted to Piozzi's autobiography. Written late in life, this memoir represents her fourth attempt at self-documentation, although its evident play for sympathy to her addressee (friend and physician Sir James Fellowes) makes it more biased, fragmentary, and self-ennobling than her other accounts, which thus are necessary for comparison. From the time of her marriage, encouraged by Dr. Johnson and her own early-established writing habits, she kept an ongoing diary of both personal and public events. As her children were born she enlarged her habit of documentation to include their lives, establishing her "Children's Book" covering the intimate life of which her salon guests were largely unaware. Somewhat later, her first husband presented her with six large, bound blank volumes labeled "Thraliana," which she was inspired by Johnson to fill; the stream-of-consciousness mixture of public and private commentary recorded in *Thraliana* (1942; ed. by K. C. Balderson) is the chief record of the author's creative life. However, her characteristically fragmentary writings are most usefully read in tandem with an outside biography, such as William MacCarthy's *Hester Thrale Piozzi: Portrait of a Literary Woman* (1985).

758 PITT, Frances (J.P., F.L.S., M.B.O.) 1888–1964. *Country Years: Being a Naturalist's Memories of Life in the English Countryside and Elsewhere.* George Allen & Unwin, Ltd. 1961. 240 pp.; foreword; poems; index. NUC 1956–1967 90:530.

Born in Bridgnorth, Shropshire. Father: William James Pitt, solicitor, farmer. Mother: Frances Jean Harvey. 1 brother. Single. Wrote *Animal Mind, Woodland Creatures, The Intelligence of Animals, My Squirrels, Friends in Fur and Feather, Birds in Britain.* Naturalist; nature writer; horsewoman; journalist; photographer; justice of the peace; animal welfare activist; hunter. Upper middle class.

Rural reminiscences and personal reflections, spanning seven decades of author's life. Paternal and maternal family history. Author's early interest in creative writing. Teaching herself photography. Noting grimness of domestic servants' lives. Her childhood interest in Anderson's and

Grimm's fairy tales; later reading Walter Scott's novels; her lifelong interest in history and natural history. Joining Zoological Photographic Club. Her early liking for riding and hunting. Keeping various pets. Being influenced by writers Ernest Thompson Seton and Gilbert White. Reacting to her mother's Unitarian beliefs. Accepting Darwin's theories. Contributing articles to *Country Life, London Evening News,* the *National Review.* Traveling to Africa; her views on the future of African wildlife. Traveling to Scotland, Norway, Holland, Finland, and Greece. Serving on committee for "Inquiry into Cruel Sports." Extracts from her hunting diary. Participating in her father's farming business. Becoming justice of the peace. Death of her mother, 1949. Sharing her home with friend Sylvia Trevor; being nervous about how other friends might react; friends' having anticipated it.

In this meditative work Pitt views herself and her past life in relation to natural history and to her lifelong enthusiasm for horses. She also wrote **759** *Hounds, Horses, and Hunting* (1945), a detailed discussion of what every horsewoman should know. Both books are emotionally sparse and devoid of personal disclosure, displaying a reserve that, for the author, appears to be an established principle. In harmony with this practice, she does not enlighten the reader on the nature of her relationship with Sylvia Trevor. Instead, her memoirs train their attention outward, richly evoking the natural living world and her embrace of it.

760 PLESS, Daisy, Princess of (née Mary Theresa Olivia Cornwallis-West). 1873–1943. *Daisy, Princess of Pless. By Herself.* Ed. by Major Desmond Chapman-Huston. New York: E. P. Dutton, 1929. 529 pp.; intro.; illus.; index. NUC pre56 461:557. (1st pub. John Murray, 1928.)

Raised in Newlands, Hampshire. Father: Col. William Cornwallis Cornwallis-West. Mother: Mary Fitzpatrick. 1 brother; 1 sister. Married 1891, Hans Heinrich XV, Prince of Pless; divorced 1922. 3 sons. Princess; nurse (WWI); foreign resident (Germany). Upper class; married into royalty.

Personal and familial memories intertwined with observations on important people and places in upper-class British and Continental society, covering 1870s to WWI's end. Paternal family history. Author's childhood fear of being ugly. Her great love for her father. Mother's coldness to her children. Meeting Prince Henry of Pless; accepting his proposal; feeling unprepared for marriage. Recalling Christmases at Furstenstein. Visiting sick people. Traveling to Russia. Her concern for the unsanitary state of towns and villages in Silesia. Being criticized by German friends for disciplining her children in English fashion. Father-in-law's death; author and her husband's acquiring new duties upon husband's accession to title. Rebelling against Emperor's orders forbidding her to organize a charity concert. Friendship with Empress Eugènie. Her views on

Anglo-German relations. Buying property in south of France. WWI: nursing in hospital, attempting to help British POWs over objections from her mother-in-law. Being told to leave Berlin; refusing; being spied on; being forced to give up hospital work. Feeling herself the object of hatred and jealousy for her suspected divided loyalties. Traveling to Serbia to help and collect wounded. Experiencing constant anxiety over her son Lexel's health. Missing England; longing to speak to an Englishman. Considering German culture to be primitive. Assessing German blindness to inevitable American participation in the war. Discussing the difficulty of educating children in Germany during WWI.

In a formal and educated style, often enlivened by French and German phrases, Pless discusses the personal frictions she experienced as an English member, by marriage, of the German aristocracy. She also describes her views on the various social, political, and economic factors which culminated in WWI, and gives details of her charitable endeavors, particularly her WWI volunteer work. Although a sizable portion of the book is devoted to her social activities with contemporary luminaries, Princess Daisy also offers an unusual perspective on the war, candidly confronting her personal divided loyalties. She continues her reminiscences in **761** *From My Private Diary* (1931), which includes her childhood memories but mainly focuses on her daily life in aristocratic circles, 1890s–1931. Only the first 50 pages of this book are narrative autobiography; the rest consists of diary entries.

762 PLEYDELL-BOUVERIE, Helen Matilda, Countess of Radnor (née Chaplin). 1846–1929. *From a Great-Grandmother's Armchair.* Marshall Press, 1927. 362 pp.; illus.; index. NUC pre56 479:47.

Born in Rutland, near Stamford, Lincolnshire. Father: Henry Chaplin, vicar of Rydell. Mother: née Ellice. Maternal grandfather: Alexander Ellice. 1 sister; 3 brothers. Married 1866, William Pleydell-Bouverie, Viscount Folkstone, later 5th Earl of Radnor, Conservative M.P., d.1900. Widow. 2 daughters; 2 sons. Wrote monograph for the British Israel Association, catalogue raisonné of the Longford Castle pictures. Knew Queen Victoria, Sarah Bernhardt, Ellen Terry, Henry Irving, Gilbert and Sullivan, Edward Elgar, Ralph Vaughan Williams. Singer (concerts); composer; organizer (musical); politician's spouse; anti-suffragist; clergyman's daughter. Middle class; married into aristocracy.

Reminiscences of musician and political wife, spanning eight decades of her life. Father's death in author's infancy. Studying music with her mother. Her mother's death, 1858; her desolation at becoming an orphan. Continuing her musical studies. Her ties to the royal family. Marriage to William Pleydell-Bouverie, a love match, over her father-in-law's objections; not getting on with her in-laws. Traveling to Scotland and to Germany, France, Switzerland, and Italy. Her children's births.

Having good relationships with her daughters. Composing music; singing; conducting church choirs; forming her own orchestra, "The Ladies' String Band." Her daughter Helen's death; her immense grief. Giving charity benefit concerts. Campaigning for her husband in his Parliamentary bid. Identifying with Conservative policies, political figures; opposing Women's Suffrage Bill. Her love of horses; her interest in hunting. Studying spiritualism; having various psychic experiences. Her husband's death; grappling with widowhood. Creating a stained glass window in memory of her husband for Salisbury Cathedral. Musing on "forwardness" of girls in modern times. Outbreak of WWI: political, social ramifications of war.

Lady Radnor states that she composed this memoir for her descendants. Written in a cultured Victorian tone, her book offers detailed accounts of various aspects of Victorian society. Despite her Conservative politics and strongly antifeminist feelings, Lady Radnor pursued a lifelong interest in women's participation in music, thus admirably combining a career—albeit an amateur one—with her domestic responsibilities. She was friendly with many of the most significant composers and performers of her day. Her book serves as a modest "Who's Who" of the musical world of Victorian England.

763 PLUNKETT, Elizabeth Mary Margaret, Countess of Fingall (née Burke). 1866–1944. *Seventy Years Young: Memories of Elizabeth, Countess of Fingall, as Told to Pamela Hinkson.* Collins, 1937. 441 pp.; illus. NUC pre56 172:528. (other ed.: New York: E.P. Dutton, 1939.)

Born in Connemara, Connacht, Ireland. Father: George Burke, Esq., J.P. Mother: Daisy. 4 siblings. Married 1883, Arthur James Plunkett, Earl of Fingall. 2 sons; 2 daughters. Society woman; feminist. Upper class; married into aristocracy.

Detailed personal and family memories, recalled within the context of Irish local and national events and personalities, spanning author's childhood to 1937. Family history; early Irish ancestors. Author's love of reading. Acting scenes of Irish history in tableaux with Ireland's Chief Secretary Gerald Balfour and his wife. Visiting father's Magistrate's Room in County Galway, 1870s; recollections of Irish dialects of witnesses. Her strong feelings of Irish identity and patriotism. Traveling with her family to Lourdes, where father sought cure for cataract. Her interest in dancing, riding, and hunting. Home education; attending convent school in France; attending St. Leonard's in Ireland. Social season; description of her first ball gown; seeing clothing fashions as reflecting the psychology of the time. During ball season, wondering how long poor people would tolerate the rich flaunting their finery. Friendship with Hermoine Leinster, secretary to George Balfour. Having great admiration for Charles Stuart Parnell; his initial suspicions about why a woman of her class would admire him. Meeting 24-year-old Earl of Fingall; courtship; his poor education and silence, but beautiful manners. Plunkett family history. Her parents' initial disapproval of engagement, their feelings that she was too young, had too little money for an earl. Marriage, age 17. Children. Husband's losing money in Australian goldmining scheme. Admiring Constance Lytton's suffragette activities and the suffrage movement in general.

A loosely chronological collection of anecdotes about friends, family, and associates forms the fabric of Lady Fingall's narrative. In this book the personalities of others appear more distinctive than the author's own; she muses that the person who did the things she describes is no longer herself, and thus she feels detached from the material she is recording. Although written in 1937, her subjective impressions anticipate the now-current critical insight of the autobiographical subject being necessarily split in the act of writing between the "I" who experiences events and the "I" who observes and records those experiences. A strong Irish flavor pervades this work despite its absence of political concern; in this regard, the memoir merits comparison with *Seventy Years: Being the Autobiography of Lady Gregory,* a book whose sense of Irishness is indissoluble from its author's political engagement.

764 POLLOCK, Alice (née Wykeham-Martin). 1868–d.a.1970. *Portrait of My Victorian Youth.* Johnson, 1971. 192 pp.; front. port.; intro. by Lady Farrer; illus.; apps. BLC to 1975 262:126.

Born in Purton, Wiltshire. Father: Cornwallis Wykeham-Martin, former naval officer, magistrate, workhouse inspector. Mother: Ann Katherine Rolls. 2 brothers; 5 sisters. Married 1898, Hugh Pollock, barrister, d.1945. Widow. 1 son; 1 daughter. Clairvoyant/psychic. Upper middle class.

Centenarian's detailed recounting of domestic life in childhood and early marriage, with focus on her psychic abilities, covering 1868–1957 and highlighting her life up to WWII. Part 1: Biographical sketch of father; his abandoning naval career to marry. Mother's being cousin to co-founder of Rolls Royce, Ltd. Mother's psychic experiences. Describing family servants; their superstitions. Mother's charity-visiting at workhouse; her organizing a cottage hospital. Building of local railway; 1880s rail travel. Remembering family life in childhood. Governesses. Parents' sincere Broad Church Anglicanism. Idealistic father's rescuing destitute man; father's distress at vicar's keeping a mistress. Holidays, recreations with siblings. Her sister's losing consciousness while having a convulsion after nursemaid shut her in a closet. Recalling smallpox epidemic in Purton; remedies. Author's childhood introduction to the occult: tea leaves; palm, dream, and card readings; Ouija board. Her preference for a crystal ball. Her first incidents of telepathy and clairvoyance. Friendship with local gypsies. Marriage; moving to London; London street scenes and social life. Household finances. Queen Victoria's funeral, 1901. Caring for baby son. Her children's schooling. WWI Zeppelin raids. Part 2: Using her psychic senses to analyze a house considered haunted, 1910. Describing what she "saw" at haunted Leeds Castle. Attending séances sponsored by Sir Arthur Conan Doyle; expressing skepticism about séances and automatic writing. Using crystal ball to inquire into health of absent family members. While visiting friends on the Isle of Wight, psychically identifying ancient burial sites. Analyzing her psychic abilities; expressing desire not to profit financially from them. Husband's death, 1945. Doing charity work with Women's Institute while living with her widowed daughter, 1950s.

Writing at the age of 102, Pollock recreates from memory a remarkably detailed image of everyday Victorian upper-middle-class life. The book is divided topically into two parts, the first focusing on the domestic details of her childhood and early married life, and the second giving extensive details of her psychic abilities. Her discussion of her post-WWII life is not very thorough, with the years after her husband's 1945 death being telescoped into a short section at book's end.

765 POTTER, Louisa. c.1800–?. *Lancashire Memories.* Macmillan, 1879. 200 pp.; illus. NUC pre56 467:613.

Raised near Riverton, Lancashire. Parents not named. Pupil. Middle class.

Author's recollections of her education among extended family in Lancashire and her later attendance at a genteel ladies' school in London, c.1810–25. Childhood holidays in town of Riverton "in the age before railroads"; being visited by cousins who lived ten miles away and traveled by packet boat on the canal to visit family. At age 7, visiting working-class handloom weavers near grandparents' home in rural Lancashire manufacturing district; weavers' customs and religion. Describing a period of working-class unrest. Her youthful impressions of the character of local country gentry. Her cousins' home and family; boys' attending grammar school until age 16; girls' being mostly self-taught. Her grandmother's clear memories of the 1745 Rebellion resulting from the Scottish Pretender's claims to the British throne. Female education in grandmother's youth having been confined to reading, writing, cooking, and needlework; grandmother's habitual mourning attire. Author's attending a ladies' school in Russell Square with five pupils; tuition's being £200 per annum; curriculum's including French, Italian, deportment, music, and drawing. Clergyman friend of author's father's making inquiry about the school; his being told it was "insincere." Author's assessment of education at school; describing teachers and tutors; pupils' supporting "Mrs. Ruleit," the headmistress, when the school was in financial trouble due to criticism of curriculum from "Mrs. Horseman," a woman intellectual.

In this memoir Potter organizes her thoughts by topic rather than by chronology. She disguises the identities of other people with whimsical, satirical names, such as the neighboring squire "Lofty Highway, Esq." or the headmistress "Mrs. Ruleit." Although Potter seems nostalgic about the rural surroundings and relationships of her youth, she also conveys much gritty detail about social realities at the beginning of the 19th century: the disparity between boys' and girls' educations, the phenomenon of cottage industry workers, the onset of labor unrest, and the rigidity of contemporary class distinctions.

766 POWELL, Margaret (née Langley). 1907–1984. *Below Stairs.* Peter Davies, 1968. 177 pp. BLC to 1975 264:189.

Born in Hove, Sussex. Father: Harry Langley, painter, decorator. Mother not named, domestic servant. 2 brothers; 2 sisters. Married Albert Powell, milkman, furniture mover. 3 sons. Wrote *The Treasure Upstairs, The Margaret Powell Cookery Book, Margaret Powell in America, Margaret Powell's Common Market, Albert, My Consort,* others. Domestic servant; culinary author. Working class.

Detailed account of everyday life of a domestic servant, with discussion of her childhood and later life, primarily focused on c.1921–45. Tending her younger siblings. Parents' agnosticism. Acquiring class consciousness; observing wealthy children's being forbidden to play with poor ones. Winning scholarship, age 14, but leaving school due to family's need for her earning power. Mother's telling her to enter domestic service, helping her to find a job as a kitchen maid. Noting differences in food served to employers and to servants; often going hungry. Describing friction between nannies and cooks. Employers' demeaning treatment of servants; servants' discussing it with each other; discussing pregnancy as grounds for dismissal; upper servants' knowing more gossip. Envying her employer, who could take for granted advantages author lacked. Finding a new job as a cook; having several cooking failures; taking cooking lessons. Employers' strictness about job references; their treating servants as if they were invisible. Marriage; leaving domestic service; having first home of her own in Chelsea; children. Being hired to serve at occasional dinner parties. Having to work as a domestic during WWII. Taking classes to reach her sons' level of education. Believing that domestic service has given her insight and perhaps inspiration for a better life.

Powell's in-depth discussion of a domestic servant's daily existence highlights class differences, servants' attitudes toward each other, and demeaning treatment by employers. The many amusing anecdotes (often involving sexual situations) of her various domestic service jobs are delivered in an ironic tone, their effect heightened by humorous use of slang. In **767** *Climbing the Stairs* (1969), Powell discusses her marriage, family life, and desire for education; in **768** *The Treasure Upstairs* (1970), she describes the various households she worked in during WWII and after; in **769** *My Mother and I* (1972), her relationship with her mother is examined; and in **770** *My Children and I* (1977), she describes raising her sons during WWII. Powell became quite successful as a writer and social commentator.

771 PRAED, Rosa Caroline (née Murray-Prior). 1851–1935. *My Australian Girlhood, Sketches and Impressions of Bush Life.* T. F. Unwin, 1902. 270 pp. NUC pre56 469:41.

Born near Ipswich, Queensland, Australia. Father: Thomas Murray-Prior, leader of Conservative Party of upper house of Queensland Colonial Parliament. Mother: Matilda Harpur. 10 siblings. Married 1872, Arthur Campbell Praed, squatter; separated c.1895. 4 children. Wrote *An Australian Heroine* (1880), *Nyria* (1904), *Sister Sorrow: A Story of Australian Life* (1916), *Outlaw and Lawmaker* (1988), many others. Novelist; spiritualist; religious/spiritual writer. Upper class.

Personal reflections and observations on race relations in Victorian Australia, covering author's childhood to young adulthood. Memories of her aborigine nurse, Billabong Jenny, who introduced the children to aboriginal ways; learning early about "common humanity" of people of different races. Absorbing anti-Roman Catholic ideas from first governess. Being affected by deaths of aborigines and their dispossession from land; her awareness of the practice of killing aborigines for sport. Recalling guerrilla warfare between whites and aborigines. Discussing demoralizing effect of alcoholism on detribalized aborigines. Having sensation of dual personality (induced by dose of opium given by doctor), which enabled her to piece together childhood experiences. Beginning to write as a child; having her work published in the family's magazine, *Marroon Magazine.* Memories of domestic servants. Recalling Ringo, a half-caste aborigine boy; her youthful romance with him. Her predilection for reading Bible stories and works of Dickens, Bulwer-Lytton, and the Brontës. Being influenced by writing and speeches of Sir George Bowen, first governor of Queensland. Death of her mother; author's assuming household duties. Her continuing concern about treatment of aborigines; favoring liberal and humanitarian attitudes toward them. Marriage; her first marital home; finding its physical condition harsh and inhospitable. Implying that romance is a "vanity."

Although Praed led a fascinating life, only a partial account of that life is included in this autobiography. For further information about her, Colin Roderick's biography, *In Mortal Bondage: The Strange Life of Rosa Praed* (1948), is invaluable. The prime interest of *My Australian Girlhood* lies in its treatment of racial conflict. Praed asserts that aborigines have been misrepresented historically, and she recognizes the legitimacy of aboriginal claims against colonizing whites, yet her opinions are influenced by 19th-century racial assumptions and language. To her, male aborigine servants are "blackboys," the aborigines are being "domesticated" from their native "barbarism," and "civilization" is the sole property of European culture. In this regard, despite being compassionate, humanitarian, and angered by the victimization of native Australians, Praed serves as an illustration of the inherent difficulty experienced by a well-intentioned individual in trying to overcome her own culturally reinforced prejudices and beliefs. She also wrote an earlier memoir concerned with racial issues, *Australian Life: Black and White* (1885), and more than forty novels, many of them concerned with occult subjects.

772 PRIESTLEY, Eliza, Lady (née Chambers). c.1837–?. *The Story of a Lifetime.* Kegan Paul, Trench, Trubner, 1908. 334 pp.; front. port.; illus.; index. BLC to 1975 265:379.

Born in Edinburgh, Scotland. Father: Robert Chambers, LL.D., writer, publisher, historian, geologist. Mother not named. 4 sisters; 1 brother. Married 1856, Sir William Overend Priestley, LL.D., physician, M.P. for Edinburgh, d.1900. Widow. 2 daughters; 2 sons. Knew Charles Dickens, Louis Pasteur, the Comtesse de Paris, James Pierpont Morgan, others. Physician's spouse. Upper class.

Author's life among noteworthy literary and medical figures, 1840s–1900. Father's literary friends, including Sir Walter Scott. Father's life and ideas; his taking his children "geologizing" among ruins; his writing the controversial *The Vestiges of Creation,* 1944. Attending day school; being punished by teachers for her slow learning. Family friendships with writers Thomas De Quincey, George Henry Lewes, and W. M. Thackeray, artists Noel Paton and Dicky Doyle. Author's admiration for ideas of emigration proponent Caroline Chisholm. Edinburgh social life; daughters' giving balls, mothers' giving dinner parties. Engagement to Dr. Priestley, at author's age 17; marriage and honeymoon two years later. Setting up house in London; husband's appointment at London dispensary for women and children; his later appointment as lecturer at Grosvenor Place School of Medicine. Social life; their acquaintance with Dickens, Thackeray, Wilkie Collins. Their returning to Edinburgh to see students' commencement at Edinburgh University; author's being given an honorary M.D. degree by the chancellor, a former colleague of her husband. Birth of their son. Fear of debt despite husband's advancing career. Death of their young daughter, 1863. Moving to Mayfair. Diphtheria's striking family; her traveling to Paris with convalescing husband to consult physicians; her father and sister's also being seriously ill; returning to England as twin sister was dying. Husband's resuming his career; author's resuming hospital duties treating children. Father's broken health. Appalling sanitary conditions in hospitals, 1860s; significance of Louis Pasteur's discoveries. Traveling with husband to Denmark and Russia; visiting a Russian children's hospital. Traveling to Scandinavia, 1884. Her husband's correspondence with Pasteur; his work spreading word of Pasteur's discoveries to national governments. Application of Pasteur's discoveries in European hospitals. Traveling to Paris to assist Pasteur in his correspondence as consultant on Australian rabbit overpopulation, 1888. Travels to eastern U.S. and Canada, visiting social and literary elite. Husband's knighthood, 1893; his election as M.P.; his death.

This book is of interest to Victorianists for its firsthand anecdotes of Dickens and other literary figures. It is also a significant contribution to the study of the history of medicine, especially with regard to Pasteur and his work's resonant effects in England. Lady Priestley, who took a strong interest in all facets of her husband's profession, writes with much anecdote and digression and includes many letters from prominent friends of her father and her husband.

773 PRINCE, Mary. c.1788–d.a.1833. *The History of Mary Prince, a West Indian Slave, Written By Herself.* Ed. by Moira Ferguson. Pandora, 1987. 124 pp.; intro. by ed.; preface by Ziggi Alexander; map; second preface by Thomas Pringle; apps. BLC to 1975 265:458. (1st pub. 1831.)

Born at Brackish Pond farm, Devonshire Parish, Bermuda. Father: surname Prince, slave, sawyer. Mother not named, household slave. 2 brothers; 4 sisters. Married 1826, Daniel James, free black carpenter, cooper. Knew Susannah Strickland (later Moodie). Slave; domestic servant; charwoman.

Narrative of West Indian slave's abuse by several masters and her escape while in England, c.1788–1830. Her happy childhood under two successive masters. Her subsequent sale to an unnamed captain; his cruelty to slaves; her escape to her parents; mother's wanting to hide her; father's telling her to go back; returning to her owner; being punished harshly every day for five years. Being sold and taken to a remote island for ten years; being sexually abused and forced to labor at salt ponds. Returning with master to Bermuda, c.1810; protecting master's daughter from his physical abuse; refusing to bathe him. Escaping from him; finding work as a laundress and sending her earnings to her master. Asking a Mr. Wood to buy her; his removing her to Antigua; developing rheumatism; being overworked doing laundry. Saving money toward buying freedom, c.1825. Attending her first Methodist prayer meeting. Converting to Moravian church; secretly attending church; learning to read and spell at church. Her marriage in Moravian church, despite the Church of England's at this time forbidding slaves to marry; her owners' anger. Being taken to England by the Woods; being forced to do heavy laundry, despite her rheumatism; being aided by English washerwomen who pity her. Escaping to Moravians; her appeal to the Anti-Slavery Society to help her win freedom. Working as charwoman and domestic servant;

permanent domestic service with the Pringle family in London. Anti-Slavery Society's unsuccessful attempts to force Mr. Wood, since departed for the West Indies, to free Mary; his prevarications; extracts of his letters to the Anti-Slavery Society accusing Mary of sexual immorality. Missing her husband and friends, still in Antigua; continuing to correspond with her husband.

In her introduction, Ferguson indicates that Prince's narrative was written with a slant acceptable to promoters of the abolition of slavery. Because abolitionists promoted female slaves as pure and free of moral corruption, Prince has, in Ferguson's words, employed "strategies for encoding the truth and inviting interpretations beyond the surface message," particularly with regard to her sexual victimization. This book is therefore useful for studies of both slavery and the attitudes of abolitionists toward slaves. In 1831 the future Canadian frontier autobiographer Susannah Moodie (née Strickland) was Prince's amanuensis in London.

774 PROCTER, Zoe. 1867–c.1959. *Life and Yesterday.* Ed. by George Baker. Kensington: The Favil Press, 1960. 171 pp.; illus. BLC to 1975 266:170.

Born at Royal Bareilly, India. Father: Lt. Montagu Procter, 31st Native Infantry. Mother: Anne Forrest. 3 sisters; 1 brother. Single. Knew Agnes Maude Royden. Feminist; suffragist, militant; teacher (Sunday school); editor; secretary; prison inmate. Middle class.

Personal experiences and reflections on feminist political activism and religious reform, spanning author's Victorian childhood to old age. Living in the Indian countryside; Indian social customs and industries. Family's returning to London, 1871. Her father's appointment as governor of County Gaol at Bury St. Edmunds. Her childhood in Governor's House. Her paternal grandparents' entertaining Dickens, Lamb, Edmund Kean, Hazlitt, Browning, others. Attending Alspham High School. Incipient feminism of author and her sisters. Parents' taking family back to India; her father's retiring from the Army; returning to England; father's death. Teaching Sunday school (Church of England) in London. Author's sister's doing charity work with East End girls. Working as secretary for Pearl Craigie; editing book of Craigie's writings. Memories of Mrs. Pankhurst and Millicent Garrett Fawcett. Entering the women's suffrage movement as militant, 1911. Being arrested at demonstration: serving six-week sentence. Outbreak of WWI. Working for Women's Freedom League and the Church League for Women's Suffrage. Memories of Maude Royden. Working for Fellowship Guild and with Guildhouse Players. Outbreak of WWII: spending war years in Cornwall with her sisters. Sharing cottage with friend, Dorothea Rock, 1952. Noting history of Women's Social and Political Union and National Union of Women's Suffrage Societies. Changes in relationship between the sexes, marriage, 1871–1952.

In an informal, conversational style Procter relates the details of Victorian family life in India and England, and of the friendships that her paternal grandparents enjoyed with many of London's 19th-century literati and artists. However, the author identifies the main focus of the book as her increasing interest in political activism on behalf of women, a concern which induced her to join both the suffrage movement and the movement promoting women's ordination as priests in the Church of England. Inspired in her youth by an older sister's charity work, Procter turned to activism herself in indignation over the plight and living conditions of poor women.

775 RABER, Jessie (née Browne). c.1888–?. *Pioneering in Alberta.* New York: Exposition Press, 1951. 171 pp. NUC pre56 478:221.

Born in Shrewsbury, Shropshire. Father: surname Browne. Mother: Rosa. 4 sisters; 5 brothers. Married Carl Raber. Emigrant (Canada); pioneer; farmer; paid companion; clerk; hotel worker. Middle class.

Detailed account of family life within a Canadian farming community, covering c.1894–1902. Parents' decision to leave England; auctioning their household goods. Family's sailing to Canada, then traveling through Quebec, Ottawa, and Winnipeg. Author's memories of Calgary; seeing American Indians for the first time. Father's building house at Lacombe. Their celebrating Dominion Day and Christmas. Local pastimes. Family's fencing their farm, acquiring chickens and cows. Experiencing severity of Canadian winter. Studying at home with her mother. Being given a pony. Recollecting their English and Scottish neighbors; their helping each other. Attending school and church. Taking a temporary job as companion to neighbor woman. Community's building Methodist church. Author's being confirmed. Father's taking job in town as a bookkeeper. Author's creating "Literary Society." Going berrypicking. Studying music on an organ bought by father. Working in drugstore, then at town hotel purchased by father.

Raber's memories of her life on a Canadian farm at the turn of the century are charming, if perhaps idealized. The gentle home atmosphere she depicts is defined by her hard-working parents, put forward by the author as the models for her own strong sense of personal responsibility. Of particular interest is Raber's description of the profound harmony among immigrants, who are shown in the process of forming their Canadian identity.

RADNOR, Countess of. [*See* PLEYDELL-BOUVERIE, Helen Matilda.]

RAGLAN, Baroness. [*See* SOMERSET, Ethel Jemima.]

776 RAINE, Kathleen. 1908–s.l.1995. *The Land Unknown.* New York: George Braziller, 1975. 207 pp.; intro. BLC 1976–1982 37:187.

Born in Ilford, Essex, near London. Father: George Raine, schoolmaster. Mother: Jessie Wilkie, teacher, Scottish. Married Hugh Sykes Davies, Cambridge don; divorced. Married Charles Madge, poet, professor; divorced. 1 daughter; 1 son. Wrote *Stone and Flower* (1943), *The Pythoness* (1949), *The Lost Country* (1971), and other volumes of poetry, criticism *Blake and Tradition* (1962); translated works of 19th-century French literature. Knew critic Jacob Bronowski, William Empson, Helen Sutherland, Gavin Maxwell, others. Poet; literary critic; editor; translator; academic; academic's spouse. Middle class.

Evolution of poet's literary ideas and spiritual beliefs, alongside changes in her personal circumstances, c.1926–49. Studying science; winning a scholarship to Girton College, Cambridge. Virginia Woolf's visiting Girton to read *A Room of One's Own*. Being happy at Girton in a dreamlike way. Until she left Cambridge, not questioning the prevalent opinion that "a literature of the temporal" was of greater value than a literature that celebrates "eternal" values. Her scientific studies' holding more poetry for her than the work of poets she met at Cambridge. Joining "The Heretics," a Cambridge intellectual clique. Marrying Hugh Sykes Davies "without love, without sexual attraction, without any good reason at all" except their mutual rejection of all old values, good and bad. Her husband's friendship with Malcolm Lowry. Being "rescued" from her first marriage by writer and Marxist Charles Madge, her eventual second husband. Being neurotic and unhappy. Her and Charles's both writing poetry influenced by the French surrealists. Lacking Charles's strong faith in communism. Leaving Charles over a new lover who awakened her passion. Alluding to the "daimons" that govern her poetry as if they are independent entities. Outbreak of WWII: her lover's being posted abroad. Author's taking refuge, with her two children, with writer friends in Penrith; later renting a vicarage. Earning money through writing book reviews. Mystically perceiving the unity of all life. Writing a few poems; being happy. Regretting later that she had hidden her inner life from her children. Being befriended by arts patron Helen Christian Sutherland. In her early 30s, leaving her children with Sutherland when she moved to London, then realizing she had made a mistake. Being miserable and alienated from her poetic vision in London. Holding unnamed government jobs. Floundering in the London literary world. Finally having her first book, *Stone and Flower,* published. Becoming acquainted with Antonia White and Graham Greene. Wandering into and out of Catholicism; eventually adopting Platonic philosophy. End of WWII: writing for pay, teaching night classes. Briefly working for the Publications Department of the British Council. Feeling her second book of poems, *Living in Time* (1946), was inferior to her first. Visiting British Museum daily to study Blake's poetry, as Yeats had done. Not writing poems for many years, but acknowledging her need to do so.

In this contemplative autobiography, Raine voices regret about what she sees as the damage she did to her second husband and her inadequate mothering of her children. She also expresses pride in independently pursuing her poetic vision. In an earlier autobiography, **777** *Farewell Happy Fields* (1973), she describes how her childhood experiences in the Northumbrian moors had a lifelong influence on her, and charts the rupture of her relationship with her stern Wesleyan father and her more free-thinking mother, both of whom objected to her engagement (at age 13) to a former student of her father's. In her final volume of autobiography, **778** *The Lion's Mouth* (1977), Raine analyzes her friendship with naturalist Gavin Maxwell, her love of nature rooted in her childhood experiences, and her intellectual studies of Blake and religion.

779 RATCLIFFE, Dorothy Una. 1891–1967. *Delightsome Land*. Eyre & Spotiswoode, 1945. 182 pp.; illus. by Fred Lawson; glossary. NUC pre56 481:692.

Raised in Sussex and Yorkshire. Parents not named. Sisters. Married Charles Ratcliffe, businessman. Married again, second husband not named. Wrote travel books *To the Blue Canadian Hills, South African Summer, Swallow of the Sea, Icelandic Spring*, Yorkshire local history *What Do They Know of Yorkshire?* and *From All the Airts; Poems*. Travel writer; local historian; folklorist; poet; traveler (Europe, New Zealand, South America). Upper middle class.

Author's early, close attachment to the family nursemaid and her love for Yorkshire as key to her sense of identity and perspective on her family history, covering unspecified period 1890s–1914, with allusions to her later life. Grandfather's estate in Upper Yorladale, Yorkshire; the anti-Catholic attitudes and Nonconformist beliefs author encountered there. Being told by her nurse, Hannah, that she resembles her late grandmother. Great-aunt Ellen's telling family legends; Hannah's having "deep affection for the Northern Dales" and recounting local customs, beliefs, and folklore. Describing physician and other local characters. Exploring grandfather's library. Having ongoing dialogues with Hannah about birds, fairies, songs, and verses. As a child, author's visiting gypsy caravan, stealing a gypsy baby which she had to return. Hannah's telling gypsy stories. Author's love for her pet pony. As adult, visiting Cannes; meeting a university professor there who gave her English lessons. Meeting a blind organist who taught her to play piano. Recalling school days: studying geography, memorizing poetry. Believing she saw her grandmother's ghost and rambled with it in the dales. Briefly discussing adult holidays after 1914 to Copenhagen, Panama, and New Zealand.

Ratcliffe's primary focus is on her childhood nursemaid Hannah, whom she characterizes in long passages of quoted dialect. Setting also plays a major part in this memoir, as the author recreates the Yorkshire Dales and the rural characters she knew as a child. The nurse becomes a mother figure who opens Ratcliffe to the past and assists in making her late grandmother vivid. Significantly, Ratcliffe ends her book when the identification between herself, her nurse, and her grandmother is complete, and the present merges psychologically with the past for her. Her references to her later travels around the world do not break the spell; she alludes to them only as a trigger for strong childhood memories. In the 1920s and 1930s Ratcliffe achieved modest fame as a travel writer and prolific author of books about Yorkshire.

780 RAVENHILL, Alice. 1859–1954. *Alice Ravenhill: The Memoirs of an Educational Pioneer*. Toronto & Vancouver: J. M. Dent, 1951. 241 pp.; front. port.; preface; foreword by Norman MacKenzie; apps. NUC pre56 482:458.

Born at Snaresbrook, Essex. Father: John Ravenhill, naval architect, marine engineer. Mother not named. 4 brothers; 2 sisters. Single. Wrote *School Training for Home Duties of Women* (1907), *Eugenics Education for Women and Girls* (1908), *The Native Tribes of British Columbia* (1938), others. Educator; public speaker; social reformer; sanitary inspector; emigrant (Canada); education issues writer; cultural historian; teacher; organizer of societies (professional). Middle class.

Life history of an educational and social reformer in England and Canada, 1859–1950. Describing family history, background. Recalling her early years and education: lessons with governess; curriculum, religious instruction, strictures on behavior. Sister's invalidism from spinal curvature. Family's moving to London, 1871. Attending private school for five years; analyzing its curriculum; feeling shocked when father's sudden financial loss forced her to leave, 1875. Girlhood and social life, 1876–92; self-education at home. Receiving physical therapy for her own spinal curvature. Breaking engagement due to fiancé's financial troubles. Enduring ongoing poor health. Yearning for further education; telling her impoverished father she would support herself. Deciding to train to be a sanitary inspector, 1875 public health reforms' having opened training to women. Being offered appointment as sanitary inspector, 1893; refusing it because she felt other appointees were more suited to the job. Lecturing on hygiene to villagers for County Council of West Riding, 1893–94; obtaining information on local conditions, including those of women working in the Grimsby fish-curing industry. Employment as secretary to Royal British Nurses Association, 1894–97; describing internal controversy over length of nurses' training. Her father's death, her own illness; resigning her paid position. Taking secretarial courses in business school. Becoming a close friend of physician Mary Scharlieb. Being appointed by National Health Society as lecturer on Sanitary Law for the Women's Cooperative Guild. Helping to found the Association of National Health Workers, 1898. Working on the staff of the West Riding County Council, 1899–1904; devising thirty classes on public sanitation for the Council. Being asked by the secretary of the Board of Education to examine American methods of teaching home economics; making her official visit to the U.S. in 1901. Being elected the first woman fellow of the Royal Sanitary Institute, 1903. After her mother's 1903 death, moving in with her sister Edith; their visiting Holland to study domestic servants' training programs. Founding a degree course in social and household science at the University of London. Working often as a lecturer. Touring European physical training colleges for women with Scharlieb. Her pioneer work in securing training for personnel at children's day nurseries. Emigrating to British Columbia, 1910, with sister, brother, and nephew; finding that Canada was less progressive than she had anticipated. Lecturing in U.S. and Canada on home management, 1911–17. Working as director of home economics at Utah State College in Logan, 1917–19. Suffering severe illness; ending her lecturing career; returning to British Columbia. Donating many of her books to the new University of British Columbia library. Promoting interest in culture of British Columbian coastal Indians by founding the Society for the Furtherance of B.C. Indian Arts and Crafts, 1940. Receiving honorary Doctor of Science degree from the University of British Columbia, 1948. Living in the Victoria Home for Aged Women, age 92.

Despite her precarious health, Ravenhill filled a lifetime with constant teaching and work on behalf of public health, social welfare, and educational reform. She was a pioneer in training for day care, elementary school, and home economics courses. She was also one of the first to awaken public interest in British Columbia native tribal art. Her style is educated and formal, her narrative full of details.

RAVENSDALE, Baroness. [*See* CURZON, Mary Irene.]

781 RAVERAT, Gwen (née Gwendolyn Mary Darwin). 1885–1957. *Period Piece: A Cambridge Childhood.* Faber & Faber, 1952. 282 pp.; illus.; genealogical tables. NUC pre56 482:496.

Born in Cambridge. Father: George Darwin, astronomy and experimental philosophy professor. Mother: Maud Du Puy, American. Paternal grandfather: Charles Darwin, author of *On the Origin of Species*. 2 brothers; 1 sister. Married 1911, Jacques Raverat, d.1925. Artist (painter, engraver); family historian; academic's daughter. Upper middle class.

Lighthearted family and personal memories and general observations on late Victorian society, emphasizing its inconsistencies, covering author's childhood and adolescence. Family history. Parents' life in Cambridge before author's birth. Father's chronic ill health; noting that hypochondria and ill health are Darwin family traits. Mother's encouraging children's independence. Mother's theories about food; her imposing austere diet on household. Author's opinion that parents generally are criticized by their children, regardless of how children are raised. Engaging in small mischiefs. Studying with Scottish governesses; disliking them; believing they offered poor quality instruction. Longing to go to school. Her lifelong love of art and poetry. Learning French and Latin with her brother; going to Hanover with him to study German. Attending boarding school in England, age 16; feeling homesick. Description of school; telling lies to emulate deceitful schoolmates; being thought strange because of her seriousness. Defining "ladies" as women who never do things for themselves; vowing never to become a "lady." Recalling Cambridge life and customs. At mother's request, chaperoning young couples visiting family home. Recounting hypocrisies of Victorian rules of propriety. Disliking her "proper" clothing styles. Believing she would have a better chance at a career in art if she were a man. Having difficulty reconciling her own values with the Victorian moral code of conduct. Harboring doubts about Christianity; flirting with agnosticism. Being interested in sports and exploring. Memories of family friends Ralph Vaughn Williams and E. M. Forster. Celebrating her old age: being herself and not minding what others think.

Writing with irreverence and wit about the cloistered Cambridge world of her upbringing, Raverat stresses the comedic side of its transition from the Victorian proprieties to the greater openness of the 20th century. Many of the changes she notes are of considerable interest; for example, the 1878 passage of the Revised Statutes allowing college Fellows to marry, which resulted in the appearance of ever-greater numbers of Fellows' families (including her own). With self-deprecating humor she chafes at herself for her youthful inability to rebel openly against the hypocrisies and injustices of her era, particularly the code of conduct imposed upon women. After the time period covered by this autobiography, Raverat became an artist much noted, in particular, for her wood engravings. She was a founding member of the Society of Wood Engravers, and created illustrations for *The Cambridge Book of Poetry for Children* (1932), edited by Kenneth Grahame.

READING, Marchioness of. [*See* ISAACS, Eva Violet.]

782 RENNIE, Jean. 1906–s.l.1977. *Every Other Sunday: The Autobiography of a Kitchen Maid*. Arthur Barker, 1955. 231 pp. NUC 1978 12:877. (other ed: Seven Oaks: Cornet, 1977.)

Born in Greenock, Strathclyde, Scotland. Father not named, fireman on Vanderbilt yacht. Mother not named. 1 sister. Married 1950, Max Mukerji. Domestic servant; cook; dance hostess; singer (concerts, popular); actress (film). Working class.

Money-pinched childhood and working woes of a domestic servant ultimately turned actress, covering c.1910–1950s. Her father's alcoholism;

its effect on family. Being a weak and anemic child. Liking school. Having a beautiful singing voice; longing for a singing career. Reacting to growing financial and emotional problems of parents and conflict between them. Being unable to pursue her education. Briefly working in a woolen mill. Her financial problems during the economic Depression. Working as a housemaid. Feeling herself an object of ridicule to fellow servants. Describing ways in which employers test honesty of domestic servants—for instance, "hiding" money in plain sight. Being dismissed for refusing to treat the gentry as superiors. Her fear of being branded a rebel. Moving to England and taking a housemaid job; her duties; the nearly impossible working conditions. Attending Church of England services; characterizing that institution as hypocritical. Comparing Church of England with United Presbyterian Church. Her growing anger, bitterness at the attitudes of the upper classes; her disgust at their use of religion to justify the existence of different social classes. Recalling backbiting among fellow servants. Being promoted to kitchen maid. Being injured at work; receiving no time off to recover. Describing Christmas preparations in employer's household. Concluding that chefs were cruel because they were "trained by the whip." Her increased responsibilities; difficulties in fulfilling them during the "London Season." Moving to a new position in London. Taking singing lessons. Her first post as a cook. Meeting Bill on a visit home; falling in love with him. Winning fourth place in a singing contest. Publishing a short story. Taking a job as a nightclub dance hostess. Reveling in being out of domestic service. Returning to Scotland. Becoming cook-housekeeper in a ladies' club in Edinburgh. WWII: her infatuation with a younger soldier; his death. Alluding to her changed circumstances and to her work as a singer and film actress. Marriage.

Recalling her life as a working woman during the Depression Era, Rennie dishes the dirt on what being in domestic service was like. If anything comes through with breathtaking clarity in this autobiography, it is the grinding, backbreaking quality of the labor that servants routinely endured. Interestingly, Rennie seems to have seen herself as belonging to a different category of people than her fellow servants, for she had a high school education, but economic circumstances dumped her into domestic drudgery anyway. Much of the rancor she expresses against her employers and her coworkers seems to stem from the conviction that her education gave her the right to a better life and a fuller measure of social respect than she was granted.

783 REPINGTON, Mary (née North). 1868–d.a.1925. *Thanks for the Memory*. Constable, 1938. 316 pp.; front. port.; illus. NUC pre56 489:39.

Born in Earl's Court, London. Father: Charles Augustus North, employed in the City of London. Mother: Rachel Elizabeth Grant, daughter of Sir Francis Grant, artist, president of the Royal Academy. Stepmother: Elizabeth Hayward. 2 brothers; 1 sister. Married 1888, Sir William Garstin, civil engineer; divorced 1901. 2 daughters; 1 son. Knew Margot (Tennant) Asquith, H. G. Wells, Max Beerbohm, Lord Haldane, others. Foreign resident (Egypt); mistress; secretary; artist's grandchild. Upper class.

Emotional recollections of romance and scandal surrounding author's long-term liaison with an army officer, with details on her education, marriage, and eventual divorce, covering her late Victorian childhood to 1925. Characters of her parents. Mother's death, c.1873. Father's remarriage to cousin, 1874; stepmother's employing new governess for author and sister. Death of stepmother, 1878. Sisters' attending a London girls' school, 1879–80, then Val d'Arno School, Streatham, 1881. Author's wanting to go on to Lady Margaret Hall, Oxford; headmistress of Val d'Arno discouraging this, saying that author knew "a great deal too much already." Flirtation and broken engagement, age 17. After leaving school, 1886, traveling to Paris and Egypt; Cairo society woman's introducing her to future husband, twenty years her senior, 1888. Being sexually ignorant; wanting to break engagement because she did not love fiancé; father's calling her reluctance "maidenly fears." Marriage; believing husband had married her to advance his career. Living in Cairo for thirteen years; marital unhappiness; births of two children. Converting to Catholicism; husband's rage at this; further dissension in their marriage. Meeting Col. Charles à Court and his wife; falling in love with him. Returning to England; starting adulterous liaison with à Court; being happy with him; knowledge of affair leaking to relatives on both sides. Author's confessing affair to Father Sebastian Bowden of Brompton Oratory; his refusing to absolve her unless she broke off affair. Husband's discovering affair; his apologizing tearfully for treating her cruelly; his relapsing quickly to old habits. Families' conspiring to break liaison. Being socially stigmatized for affair. Departure of à Court for the Boer War. Returning to her husband, but being indifferent to him. Death of author's daughter, 1900; meeting à Court again; his threatening suicide if she returned to her husband. Refusal of à Court's wife to divorce him; scandalous articles in newspapers; his being forced to resign from the Army; her husband's divorcing her, 1901. With loss of financial support, taking job as a typist. Inheritance by à Court requiring him to adopt surname of Repington; author's taking name also. Ex-husband's refusal to let her see her son; son's death in WWI. Implying that she and à Court had an illegitimate daughter. His later infidelity to her; her forgiving him. His writing and behind-the-scenes military activities. His death, 1925.

Throughout her memoir—a memorial and tribute to her lover—Repington defends her conduct, placing the value of love over that of family. Behind her story lies an unspoken background of changing divorce and property laws which enabled her to pursue a public long-term liaison that, twenty years earlier, would have brought her to ruin. Her book is interesting for its rejection of Victorian mores, its testimony to the growing social phenomenon of divorce, and its record of the degree of social acceptance that she and à Court regained despite her abandonment of her children and the stigma of divorce surrounding them.

784 REYNOLDS, Mrs. Herbert (Margaretta Catherine). c.1835–d.a.1883. *At Home in India; or, Taza-be-Taza*. Henry J. Drane, c.1903. 352 pp.; preface; diary entries. NUC pre56 491:269.

Born in rural England. Parents not named. 2 sisters mentioned. Married 1856, Herbert Reynolds, civil servant in India. 4 daughters; 6 sons. Memsahib; foreign resident (India); civil servant's spouse. Middle class.

Memsahib's struggle for stable family life in India despite frequent moves, family illnesses, and husband's absences, covering 1856–63, with diary entries to 1889. Immediately after marriage, author and husband's departing for India on assignment expected to last ten years. Arriving in Calcutta; traveling to husband's duty station in Mymensing, Bengal. Their being caught in 1857 Indian Sepoy Mutiny; escaping on an elephant. Expressing her pity for "misguided" mutinous native sepoys in British army. Giving birth to her first child, 1858. Husband's being appointed assistant to revenue survey officer in Dacca; moving there with him; accompanying him on surveys. Author's living briefly with children in China, 1860, while husband remained in India. Returning to Dacca; author's sister's coming from England to live with them, 1862. Deaths of her two children and sister from cholera, 1863. Author and husband's returning to England on furlough, 1864. Their return to India, 1865. Being the sole woman at Midnapur station. Deaths of two more children causing her poor health and emotional stupor, 1869; family's returning to England with remaining daughters. Their coming back to India, 1871; author and husband's being stricken with dengue fever; her being sent to recuperate in Shillong mountains. Attempting to cultivate English fruits and vegetables in Mymensing; organizing a horticultural show. Seeing a native wedding. Writing poetry as a hobby. Witnessing Behar famine, 1874. Their moving to Calcutta, 1874. Visiting Darjeeling. Another sister's visiting author, being taken ill, 1876. Author's deciding to take surviving children home to England, 1877; husband's visiting them on furlough. Returning to India. Their living in Calcutta, 1879–81; diary entries from her life there; sister and brother-in-law's living with them after 1882. Husband's being appointed vice-chancellor of Calcutta University, 1883; his supporting female education in India. More diary excerpts.

This account of the author's life in India serves less to document the experiences of an Englishwoman abroad than to record the progress of a marriage; we see in Reynolds a woman whose attention was absorbed by her devotion to husband and family. For Reynolds, the dramatic political events serving as a backdrop to her story were apparently less important than her need to establish stability in her domestic arrangements. This author serves to exemplify the many women in Britain's far-flung colonial domains who maintained their ties to England through a determined preservation of British culture.

785 RHODES, Elizabeth. 1759–d.a.1827. *Memoir of Mrs. Elizabeth Rhodes, Widow of the Late Rev. Benjamin Rhodes, Who was an Itinerant Preacher in the Wesleyan Connexion for Upwards of Forty Years.* J. Mason, 1829. 215 pp.; apps.; hymns and poems by Rev. Benjamin Rhodes. NUC pre56 491:669. [bound with *Memoirs of the Life of Richard Burdsall* (Thetford: Rogers, 1823); cat. under Burdsall.]

Born in Scotland. Father not named, officer in the Queen's regiment of dragoons. Mother not named, English. 3 half-siblings. Married c.1786, Rev. Benjamin Rhodes, Methodist minister, d.1815. Widow. 1 son; 3 daughters. Knew John Wesley. Religionist (Methodist convert); clergyman's spouse; paid companion; domestic servant. Lower middle class.

Author's difficult childhood, adult personal struggles, and religious conversion, covering 1759–1827. Parents' courtship; mother's education and Anglican upbringing. After author's birth, father's resigning his Army commission and returning to York. Father's irresponsibility, implied drunkenness; his eloping with a family maidservant when author was age 6. Author's education at home by mother. Mother's prejudices against Methodists; her overcoming them by attending their services; her joining Methodists, c.1769. At age 13, author's living in Manchester with uncle, a cotton trader; taking refuge with neighbors from her scolding aunt; attending Methodist chapel; her employment one year, possibly in domestic service. Returning to her mother in York. Being curious about her father; finding him in a Surrey village with a married woman (who had deserted her husband and children) and their three children, the author's half-siblings. Being employed as a cook by a respectable local gentleman; feeling shame at what father had done; fearing that local people would identify her as his daughter. Becoming a lady's companion near Windsor; describing her temptations upon being exposed to persons of rank; developing worldly attitudes. Securing a position as companion to two young ladies in London. Describing the Gordon Riots, 1780. Returning to York to visit ailing mother; traveling to Scotland with an earl as housekeeper to him and his mistress; her determination not to become his next mistress. Mother's death. Moving to Bury, Lancashire, for post as housekeeper to an unmarried baronet. Attending Wesleyan Bible classes; having a vision of an angel; undergoing conversion to Methodism. Observing how Methodists were persecuted by Anglicans. Congregation's struggling to build local chapel; John Wesley's sending Rev. Rhodes to them; author's marriage to Rhodes. Keeping a spiritual diary about herself, her family, and the needs of the many circuits in which her husband preached. Doing charity work in Bristol, 1787; witnessing an exorcism there. Family's moving to Redruth, Cornwall; John Wesley's visiting their converts. Diary entries: accompanying husband on his circuit riding, 1788– 92; son's death, 1790. Her visiting and preaching to Methodist congregations in Cornwall. Their moving to Birmingham, 1794, then Essex, 1797. Residing 1802–04 in London, then in Gloucestershire, then in Margate, Kent, where daughter Hannah died in a fire, 1812. Husband's death, 1815. Author's illness, 1827; her recovery after dreaming of Jesus. Commenting on effects of religious revivals on young people, the growth of Wesleyan Methodism, and God's goodness to her, especially in times of persecution.

Rhodes states that she wrote this memoir for her surviving daughters. A straightforward account, the book contains many details of 18th-century social and domestic life in provincial England. Rhodes pays as much attention to her economic and social condition as to her life of faith; her emphasis is very much on the circumstances by which God made His presence known to her. She frequently quotes the Bible and hymns, including hymns written by her husband. The book is historically important for its many details of Wesleyan chapel activities.

RHONDDA, Viscountess of. [*See* MACKWORTH, Margaret Haig.]

786 RHYS, Jean (pseud.; Ella Gwendolen Rees Williams). 1890–1979. *Smile Please: An Unfinished Autobiography.* Ed. by Diana Athill. New York: Harper & Row, 1979. 151 pp.; ed.'s foreword; illus.; chronology; biblio. BLC 1976–1982 38:117.

Born in Dominica, West Indies. Father: Dr. William Rees Williams, physician. Mother: Minna Rees Lockhart, of an old Dominican slave-owning family. 2 brothers; 2 sisters. Married 1919, Jean Lenglet, songwriter, journalist; divorced 1927. Married 1932, Leslie Tilden Smith, publisher's reader, d.1945. Married 1947, Max Hamer, d.1964. Widow. 1 son; 1 daughter. Wrote novels and sketches *The Left Bank* (1927), *Postures (Quartet)* (1928), *Voyage in the Dark* (1934), *Wide Sargasso Sea* (1966), others. Knew Ford Madox Ford. Novelist; chorus girl; governess; WWI volunteer; foreign resident (Holland). Middle class.

Melancholy, disillusioned reflections on novelist's West Indian upbringing, failed love affairs, and writing career, covering her childhood to c.1975. Her distant relationship with both parents. Father's estates in Dominica. Characters of father's sister Clarice and mother's twin Brenda. Voracious childhood reading. Wishing she were a beautiful black baby because her mother thought black babies were prettier than white ones. Being terrified of a black nursemaid; nursemaid's obeah beliefs. Mother's family history; mother's character. Author's destroying her own toys, being disobedient. Describing Protestant-Catholic riots in Dominica, c.1902. Race relations; feeling hated by coloreds. Attending convent school. Dreading maturity and marriage. Visiting St. Lucia. Loving poetry. Her sexual ignorance. Describing father's character. Experiencing conflict between her attraction to Catholicism and family's Anglicanism. Her misguided efforts at charity toward servants. Traveling to England, 1907. Attending the Perse School for Girls, Cambridge, and the Royal Academy of Dramatic Art. Working as a chorus girl in music halls. Having a love affair; becoming pregnant; getting an abortion. Living in poverty in London, on funds provided by her ex-lover. Doing canteen work during WWI. First marriage; living in Paris; being employed as a governess. First husband's atheism. Death of their infant son. First husband's brief employment as secretary to a Japanese officer of the Interallied Commission. Writing novels; her literary association with Ford Madox Ford. Living in Amsterdam with her second husband. Revisiting Dominica, 1930s. Not writing for a long time. Third marriage. Extracts from her 1947 diary. Living with her husband in Devon.

This is not an autobiography in the conventional sense; "Smile Please" (part 1) is an account of Rhys's childhood; the second part, which Athill has titled "It Began to Grow Cold," consists of rough drafts and sketches by Rhys of her life after coming to England at age 16. Athill, who edited two of Rhys's novels, comments that "Smile Please" was a nearly finished work at Rhys's death, while the second part required minor rearrangements, omissions, and alterations in style. Rhys's style is literary, using much dialogue. In the diary extract she stages a mock trial of her values and goals. Her tone is generally reflective and melancholy; she says of herself: "I haven't got what the English call 'guts.'" She omits mentioning her turbulent love affair with Ford Madox Ford.

787 RICHARDSON, Eliza Smith. c.1820–?. *Personal Experience of Roman Catholicism with Incidents of Convent Life.* Morgan & Chase, n.d. 174 pp.; intro.; front. NUC pre56 493:162. (1st pub. 1851; other ed.: Philadelphia: J. B. Lippincott, 1869.)

Probably born in Worcester. Parents not named. 1 brother; 2 sisters. Single. Wrote *The Veil Lifted, Clarendon: A Tale of Recent Times.* Knew Rev. William Henry Havergal. Religionist (Roman Catholic convert; anti-Catholic); religious/spiritual writer. Middle class.

Ambivalent, intensely personal assessment of author's experience in and out of Evangelical Protestantism and Roman Catholicism, set amid theological and social observations on Roman Catholicism and emphasizing differences between English and non-English Church, spanning c.1840–45. Being raised a "pure and strict" Evangelical Protestant. Searching for religious truth after deaths of her brother and sister. Being introduced to Catholicism by a friend; undergoing conversion;

her family's consequent distress. Spending five years in a convent abroad. Writing Catholic tracts. Commenting on Catholics' worship of Mary; her choosing not to do litanies to Mary. Wanting to fulfill the obligations of her order but being unable to comply. Her growing scruples concerning confession; becoming overwrought with dread of sacrilege. Her reservations about Catholicism: perceiving it as idolatrous and superstitious; disapproving of priests' supposedly inducing young ladies to entertain indecent thoughts in confessional. Seeing profound differences between English and foreign Catholicism. Somewhat regretfully leaving the convent. Returning to England. Warning readers against what she sees as the spiritual thralldom of Catholicism.

Although Richardson's tone is sharply critical in this conventionally Protestant attack upon Catholicism, she seems nevertheless to regret her inability to remain within the Roman Catholic Church. Her criticism of the Church's tenets apparently has social as well as spiritual roots; part of her shock is due to the cultural differences between Catholicism as practiced on the Continent and in England.

788 RICHARDSON, Ethel M. (née Stronge). 1867–d.a.1930. *Remembrance Wakes*. Heath Cranton, Ltd., 1934. 210 pp.; index. BLC to 1975 275:253.

Born in Tynan Abbey, County Armagh, Ireland. Father: Edmond Robert Francis Stronge, 4th son of 2nd baronet. Mother: Charlotte Newman Henderson. 2 brothers; 1 sister. Married 1887 Capt. Arthur Percy Richardson, formerly of the Royal Irish Rifles. 3 sons. Wrote *The Story of Purton, The Lion and the Rose, The Parting of the Way, Next-Door Neighbours, Long Forgotten Days*. Novelist; WWI volunteer; nurse (WWI); Red Cross worker. Upper class.

Novelist's memories of WWI's impact on the lives and fates of her family, her nation, and herself. Political conditions and events preceding the war: labor strikes, Irish and Indian unrest, fear of German invasion. Outbreak of war, 1914. All three of author's sons' enlisting in military service; husband's volunteering to be Army adjutant. Public effect of pro-war propaganda. Canada's joining allies; Belgian refugees' arriving in England. Author's work in caring for children whose parents were in danger zones. Details of spies in England, ambulance activities, Red Cross working parties. Receiving letters from youngest son; his description of "truce" between British and German soldiers on Christmas Day, 1914; his being wounded, 1915. Accounts of hard-fought battles; brief visits from sons on leave; their returning to war. Emotional hardships felt by mothers with sons at the front. Author's journeying to France to visit hospitalized youngest son; describing field hospital. Noting sinking of *Lusitania* by Germans, 1915. Describing zeppelin raids on London; bravery of British civilians. Author's sister's working in Army canteen in France. British evacuations of Anzac and Sula Bay. Death of youngest son on French front, winter 1915. Author's volunteering as hospital nurse; camaraderie of nursing personnel. Evaluating women's wartime contributions in industry and agriculture. Remembering entrance of the U.S. into the war, 1916; accelerating air raids over England; food shortages, 1917; menace of submarine attacks, 1918. Evaluating Britain's "Great Push" of military force, March 1918. Author's continuing to work at a military medical hospital; her own illness and convalescence. Describing the role of airplanes in warfare. Author's middle son's befriending German prisoner of war. Increased British losses just before the Armistice, 1918. Evaluating the political and economic aftermath of war. Family's erecting memorial for lost youngest son; author's comments on lives sacrificed to war.

Richardson's memoir of the WWI years conveys an immediacy beyond its considerable historical relevance. Although much of her account is written in retrospect and consequently benefits from her later observations of postwar societal changes, she intersperses these memories and reflections with letters from her sons written as battles were being waged and with her own diary entries recorded at moments of uncertainty and dread. Of particular interest is the struggle evident between the author's wartime patriotism and her later antiwar sentiments, developed as a direct result of her personal experiences.

789 RICHARDSON, Mary Raleigh. c.1890–?. *Laugh a Defiance*. George Weidenfeld & Nicholson, 1953. 194 pp.; index. NUC 493:250.

Born in Canada. Parents not named. Feminist activist; suffragist, militant; political activist; journalist. Middle class.

Firsthand testimony on the civil disobedience and other political activities of the militant wing of Britain's women's suffrage movement, covering the author's childhood to the onset of WWI. Author and mother's living with author's beloved grandfather in Canada; author's moving to England after his death. Meeting Christabel Pankhurst; becoming involved with the women's suffrage movement; writing article on the movement for Toronto newspaper. Hearing Emmeline Pankhurst speak. Being arrested for destruction of property; giving details of her jail experience. With other suffragists, staging demonstrations at restaurants; obtaining political support of Bishop of London. Facing antisuffrage mob in Hyde Park. Defacing property at the Home Office; receiving six-month jail term; enduring force-feeding. Being arrested again; escaping with aid of fellow suffragists. Helping to plant a bomb in Birmingham. Gate-crashing official receptions. Authorities' viewing her as unstable and dangerous; their attempting, with government psychiatrists, to have her committed to an insane asylum. Her personal protest: trying to deface Velázquez's *Venus* in National Gallery. Participating in arson protest plot; being arrested again. Amnesty's being granted to suffragettes just prior to WWI. Evaluating the antisuffragist movement; grassroots support of poor women; inequalities of justice system; prison sentences, goals of suffrage movement; hunger strikes as protest strategy.

In an informal and readable style, Richardson documents the militant actions of herself and others in service to the suffrage movement, including explicit details of her own bold attempts to secure support for suffrage from people in high places. As her writing shows, Richardson took the confident long view that women's securing the right to vote would be their first step toward achieving complete social equality with men.

790 RIDDELL, Florence. c.1896–?. *I Go Wandering: A Travel Biography.* J. B. Lippincott, 1935. 315 pp.; front. port.; illus. NUC pre56 494:208.

Raised in Hampshire. Parents not named. Sisters. Married c.1915, "G," civil servant, import-export businessman, Scottish, died c.1922. Widow. 1 son. Wrote *Kismet in Kenya, What Women Fear, Wives Win,* others. Teacher (art, dance); foreign resident (India, Kenya); governess; headmistress; landlady; novelist. Middle class.

Adventure-seeker's life in India and Africa, covering her childhood to c.1935. Feeling wanderlust, beginning age 10, from reading adventure books. At age 17, answering advertisement for a governess to a Parsee family; obtaining father's reluctant consent to accept position. Traveling to India with employers; her near-seduction by ship's doctor. Living in Bombay. Describing her life as a governess; friendships with other governesses. Teaching drawing at day school for sons of Eurasians and rich natives. Marriage; residence with husband in Calcutta. Childbirth and child-rearing. Difficulties of raising a sickly, delicate child. Describing servants. Running a boarding house for Europeans in Bombay during WWI; refusing to house a Eurasian woman with black children. Discussing her dislike of races' intermixing. Cholera epidemic in Bombay; deciding to leave India. Residence, life, and work in Kenya, c.1918–22; feeling Kenya is unlucky, "not a white man's country." Husband's struggling import-export business; author's teaching dance classes to help make ends meet. Becoming headmistress of "The Hill" School, Nairobi; not allowing white pupils to converse with the native servants. Author's returning to England with her son, to further his schooling. Husband's death in Kenya one year later. Writing about her Kenya experiences in novels. Describing difficulties of writer's trade. Traveling around Europe, North Africa, and U.S.

Riddell's conversationally written memoirs reveal her disdain for people of color; she deplores any social intercourse between whites and nonwhites. She also finds novels with white heroines and "coloured" heroes objectionable. Although a decidedly independent woman, she declares that she would be happier if she were a "clinger," someone "blond, little, and helpless," because then men would cater to her every whim. Yet she seems happy with the life she led, and she evidently dotes on her son.

791 RING, Elizabeth (Nerissa Scott, pseud.). 1912–s.l.1986. *Up the Cockneys*. Paul Elek, 1975. 166 pp.; foreword. BLC to 1975 275:327.

Born in London. Father: Herbert Scott, clerk. Mother: Susan Yull, domestic servant. 1 half brother. Married 1937, William Ring, librarian. 1 daughter. Bookkeeper; clerk; journalist. Lower middle class.

Slightly racy memories of an adolescence and young adulthood spent in a London working-class district, covering 1920s–30s. Author's sense of being a proper Cockney, born within sound of "the Bow Bells." Describing living conditions in London's Islington district: pastimes, housing, eccentricities of neighbors. Her childhood contempt for wealth; feeling above such things. Her mother's premarital pregnancies with author and brother; frequent occurrence of this circumstance in author's social class. Mother's history: leaving the comparative shelter of a middle-class Norfolk home to marry and become a domestic servant in London. Author's father's being well-read but shiftless, a WWI deserter earning tips as a billiard marker. Mother's determination to shed Norfolk country accent but to avoid adopting Cockney working-class tones; her attempts to prevent author from speaking in Cockney accent. Father's socialism, sexual infidelities, unemployment, obsession with gambling. Family's moving to cheaper lodgings. Grandmother's rustic home in Norfolk; mother's sisters' entering domestic service. Attending junior school; learning swear words; acquiring love of reading and writing. Despite poverty, taking advantage of London's cultural activities. Advancing to coeducational school; dating boys; experimenting sexually with her cousin James. Becoming enthralled with Finsbury Public Library. Living near Sadler's Wells; acquiring enthusiasm for ballet. Recalling visit with her aunt, who cooked for Baroness Orczy, author of *The Scarlet Pimpernel*. In later adolescence, having naive ideas about contraception. Working as a verse-writer for a greeting card company, then as a junior clerk. London's depression era: her neighbors' Labourite opinions; economic woes; hungry and homeless people's being visible everywhere. In 1930s, studying fine arts, attending Open Air Theatre, discovering advantages of having grown up in a working-class borough. Helping her mother financially. Describing public anxieties over threat of coming European war. Courtship; becoming engaged; marrying; moving with husband to nearby borough of Hornsey; their lively sex life. Outbreak of WWII: husband's enlisting in Army; author's taking bookkeeping job; giving birth to a daughter. Motherhood's inspiring her renewed enthusiasm for writing. Publishing article evaluating rural holidays for children. Rating the compensations of being a working woman.

Writing in her 60s, and calling herself "another old girl looking back," Ring nevertheless declares that she "will never admit to being old." According to friends, she derived occasional income from posing as a 17-year-old when writing letters to magazines which promised payment; this facility for thinking herself back into adolescence is evident in her fresh, immediate memoir. At the time of this book's publication the author's mother was still living, and omissions of relevant names and dates may have been for reasons of privacy. Nonetheless, Ring offers a valuable historical portrait of working-class London between the world wars.

792 RIPLEY, Dorothy. 1767–?. *The Extraordinary Conversion and Religious Experience of Dorothy Ripley, with Her First Voyage and Travels in America.* New York: G. & R. Waite, 1810. 168 pp.; preface; "Address to the Mayor and Corporation of New York." NUC pre56 96:114.

Born in Whitby, Yorkshire. Father: William Ripley, Wesleyan preacher. Mother not named. 1 brother; at least 2 sisters. Single. Abolitionist; social reformer; religionist (Quaker convert); preacher; traveler (U.S.). Lower middle class.

Itinerant preacher's intensely personal account of her spiritual call, ministry, and labors to promote abolition and education for slaves in the U.S., covering her childhood to 1810. From age 3, hearing audible commands of God and feeling conviction of sin. Fasting, age 12, until near death. Having vision of the Crucifixion. After recovery, visiting deathbeds to warn sinners. Feeling she cannot tell her parents of her guilt as a sinner; thinking of suicide, 1783. Her conversion to Quakerism. Father's death, 1784. Author's becoming consumptive after nursing her dying sister. Mother's losing property in a natural disaster, 1788. Author's deciding to remain single. Experiencing divine call to preach in America; having visions of God and Christ. Studying Bible intently; hearing the "voice of Jesus" preaching to her; being considered insane by some. Living solely upon bread and water. Departing from England, 1801. Believing that divine intervention grounded her ship at Rhode Island in order to fulfill God's command for her to meet with Quakers there. At Philadelphia Yearly Meeting, meeting with Ann Mifflin, Quaker abolitionist. Receiving a divine order for her to meet with President Jefferson in Washington. Meeting with President, 1802; securing his approval for her plan to teach and preach to black slaves; his pessimism about the educability of blacks in contrast to Indians. Describing her plans to establish a school for sixty black women in Washington. Traveling in Virginia, Maryland, Delaware, and New York; staying with Quakers; their kindness and hospitality. Preaching to slaves and slaveowners in Virginia; witnessing cruelty; aftermath of slave revolt in Richmond. Some Quakers' calling her base and wicked for her activities; others' supporting her. Premonitions and then news of her mother's death. Encountering opposition to her plan for a black school in Washington. Meeting with Methodists and preaching at their meetings; meeting with black Methodist clergy in Philadelphia, 1803. Heeding a divine call to return to England; quieting English Quakers' fears that she had turned Methodist; being reunited with her sisters in Whitby. Returning to Philadelphia, 1809. Protesting 1810 law prohibiting the preaching of the Gospel in a New York park.

Constantly quoting and alluding to Scripture, Ripley compares herself to prophets and other biblical figures. The book is a valuable source on Quaker abolitionist activity in early America, giving evidence of the differences of opinion among various Quaker sects and the contrast between Quakers in America and Britain. As an interesting sidelight, this memoir also suggests Thomas Jefferson's pessimism regarding the educability of blacks.

793 RITCHIE, Anne Isabella, Lady (née Thackeray). 1837–1919. *Chapters from Some Unwritten Memoirs.* Macmillan & Co., 1894. 215 pp. NUC pre56 496:288.

Born in Hyde Park, London. Father: William Makepeace Thackeray, novelist. Mother: Isabella Shawe. 2 sisters. Married 1877, Sir Richmond T. W. Ritchie. 2 children. Wrote *The Village on the Cliff* (1867), *Old Kensington* (1873), others. Knew Margaret Oliphant, Count D'Orsay, Leigh Hunt, Edward Trelawny, Charles Dickens, Charlotte Brontë, Thomas Carlyle, Elizabeth Barrett Browning, Fanny Kemble. Literary critic; novelist; essayist; novelist's daughter. Upper middle class; married into upper class.

Introspective memories of writer's experiences in her father's mid-Victorian literary circle, together with her youthful travels and residence on the Continent, c.1840–60. Childhood after age 8 in London: attending school in South Audley Street; reciting French poetry, loving French literature, visiting grandparents in Paris. Earlier memories of attending school in Paris and playing near Arc de Triomphe while living with her grandparents; adoring Chopin's music and hearing him play. With her sisters and cousin Amy, attending "fitful and backward" lectures by a Frenchwoman whom she calls "my Professor of History." Her personal memories of illustrious French and English writers. Her father's taking her to theatre and opera. Reading *Jane Eyre;* visiting Charlotte Brontë's home. Friendship with Charles Dickens and his family. Being taken to visit artists, including Landseer and G. F. Watts. At age 13, making Grand Tour of Europe with sister and father; traveling with Charles Kingsley. From ages 14–26, serving as father's amanuensis. Attending her father's lecture series on English Humorists; father's departing for lecture tour of America, author's age 17. Author's touring Switzerland, visiting French countryside with grandparents and seeing Rome, age 19.

Father's long-term friendship with Kemble family; author's affectionate and respectful portrait of Fanny Kemble's character.

Looking backward from her maturity, Lady Ritchie seems less concerned with historical documentation than with creating a subjective record of her emotional growth. Instead of ordering the text chronologically, she organizes it into sections featuring images and figures important in the formation of her early sense of identity. For example, the first four divisions are named after "My Poet"—a versifier named Jasmin whose work she recited in French lessons; "My Musician"—Chopin;" My Triumphal Arch"—the scene of her childhood fancies; and "My Professor of History." Her famous father's literary friends are mentioned not for their own sakes but for the role that knowing them played in the development of Lady Ritchie's mind; her later marriage and motherhood are mentioned only peripherally, and she omits entirely her own mature writing career. She is silent also on the issue of her mother's commitment to an asylum for the mentally ill, because of which the author spent her early years with her grandparents in Paris. The external documention of Lady Ritchie's life available in Winifred Gerin's 1981 biography of her is a useful adjunct to this more private memoir.

794 ROBERTSON, Hannah. 1724–c.1800. *The Life of Mrs. Robertson, Grand-Daughter of Charles II. Written by Herself.* Derby: J. Drewry, 1791. 37 pp.; "Subscribers names"; "To the Most Noble Marchioness of Stafford." NUC pre56 498:103.

Born in Glasgow, Scotland. Father: took surname Swan, businessman, proprietor. Mother: Anna Huntington. Stepfather not named. 5 siblings; 12 half-siblings. Married 1749, surname Robertson, businessman. Widow. 5 children. Shopkeeper; tavern manager; prison inmate; society woman. Upper middle class.

Emotional and dramatic narrative of the fluctuating fortunes and romantic misfortunes of a member of the illegitimate side of Britain's royal family, 1720s–1790s. Father's personal history as a natural son of Charles II; his marriages to his first wife and to author's mother; his death; author's grief. Being conceited as a child from the sense of her royal kinship. Refusing to go to school. Disliking her mother's second husband; his penchant for "revelry" with other women. Learning that unrequited love for her had possibly caused a young male cousin's suicide; her consequent lifelong guilt. Commenting on widespread violence of the Scottish Rebellion of 1745–46. Mourning death of her fiancé Captain B. in Flanders; feeling increased grief at the report of the death at sea of her second fiancé, Captain J. On eve of wedding to Mr. Robertson, discovering Captain J. was still alive; going through with marriage to Robertson; feeling desolation over her decision and over husband's subsequent friendship with J.; J.'s remaining single his entire life. Immersing herself in caring for her children. Husband's undergoing chronic illness, financial reverses and imprisonment for debt; plummeting of their social status. Author's managing tavern in Aberdeen for the Freemasons. Being turned out with her children by tavern owners, who claimed she owed them money. Failing in her attempts to teach school and do millinery work. Being imprisoned for debt; describing sordid prison conditions. Husband's freezing to death after losing his way in snow. Eldest daughter Anna's husband's becoming dissipated after receiving an inheritance; his forcing Anna into dissolute life; Anna's being kidnapped by husband's friend. Author's moving to York; working in boarding school there; suffering asthma. One son's securing an apprenticeship to an architect. Her younger son's painting shawls and handkerchiefs to support family. Death of author's mother; receiving no inheritance because the merchant who handled stepfather's estate declared bankruptcy. Finding daughter Anna after seven years; moving with her to London; their opening shop for fancy-work (embroidery, lacework, etc.). Author's being indicted for debt by English judicial system; referring to Bishop's Court as "English Inquisition." Deaths of her two elder daughters, younger son, and granddaughter in close succession. Losing contact with eldest son after his departure for France.

Robertson's book, composed as a plea for friendship and financial assistance from the Marchioness of Stafford, vividly portrays the tragic events of her life and her descent from affluence to virtual destitution. Her account of her trials and tribulations permits the reader a long look at 18th-century institutions and attitudes, particularly as these concern women and the economically disadvantaged.

795 ROBINSON, Mary (née Darby; "Perdita"; Anne Frances Randall, pseud.). 1758–1800. *Memoirs of the Late Mrs. Robinson, Written by Herself.* Ed. by Mary Elizabeth Robinson (author's daughter). Cobden-Sanderson, 1930. 197 pp.; front. NUC pre56 498:621. (1st pub. Wilks & Taylor, 1801, 4 vols.)

Born in Bristol, Avon. Father: John Darby, whaling captain, American. Mother: Mary Seys. 3 brothers; 1 sister. Married 1774, Thomas Robinson, articled clerk. 2 daughters. Mistress of George IV 1779–80. Wrote Angelina (1795), *Hubert de Sevrac* (anti-Catholic novel, 1796), *The Widow, Thoughts on the Condition of Women* (1799, under pseud.), others. Knew David Garrick, Richard Brinsley Sheridan, the Duchess of Devonshire. Actress (stage); novelist; poet; pamphleteer; women's issues author; mistress; feminist; religionist (anti-Catholic); disabled woman; prison inmate. Middle class.

Stage and literary career of 18th-century actress, poet, and novelist, with emphasis on her love affairs and intellectual friendships, from childhood to c.1785. Family history. Parents' characters. Father's financial ruin by rash scheme to establish a whale fishery off the Labrador Coast; his Canadian mistress; his return to England and eventual return to

America. Author's education at boarding school in Chelsea under the sisters of Hannah More, 1768. Attending Oxford House, Marylebone; being encouraged by dancing master there to try acting. Marriage to an unfaithful spendthrift; birth of child. Beginning writing while in debtors' prison with family. Publishing first volume of poems, 1775. Her stage career; receiving support from David Garrick and Richard Brinsley Sheridan. Infatuating George IV during her role as "Perdita" in *The Winter's Tale;* becoming his mistress, 1779–80; his leaving her before giving her a promised £20,000. Receiving financial support from other lovers and from the Duchess of Devonshire. Suffering a miscarriage; becoming paralyzed from the waist down as a result, c.1783. Writing pamphlets and novels to support herself.

This autobiography was completed by the author's daughter, who added material covering Robinson's life from 1785 to her death. Apparently Robinson believed that she ought to have received a useful rather than an elegant education, yet she expresses the belief that mental occupations fatigue the brain and injure the health. She supported the French Revolution while condemning its tyranny and applied its principles of liberty to women, although she continued to portray sentimental heroines in her fiction.

796 ROBINSON, Sarah. 1834–d.a.1914. *"My Book," A Personal Narrative.* S. W. Partridge, 1914. 265 pp.; preface; illus.; poems. NUC pre56 498:666.

Born in Blackheath, Greater London. Father not named, businessman, farmer. Mother not named, invalid. 2 brothers; 1 sister. Single. Temperance activist; philanthropist; social reformer; religionist (Evangelical Protestant); disabled woman; publisher; pamphleteer; public speaker. Middle class.

Christian commitment of temperance worker and her social reform activities among soldiers and sailors, covering her youth to old age. Father's opinion that she should have been male, for "she would make a good man of business." Enjoying lessons at home with "Coz," possibly a relative; disliking boarding school she attended later. Detesting babies; disliking dolls and fancy clothes; wishing she were a boy. Suffering from acute spinal curvature as a schoolgirl; spending a year in London undergoing treatment; having recurring spinal problems throughout her life. Converting to Evangelical Protestantism, 1851. Signing temperance pledge, c.1860; working for temperance movement. Discussing interconnection between criminal activities and alcoholism. Seeing her life's work as bringing Jesus and teetotalism to soldiers and sailors. Describing appalling living conditions in Victorian Portsmouth for poor and working classes. Persevering despite encountering opposition to her plan to establish the Portsmouth Soldiers' Institute; fundraising for the institute; living and working there, 1874–91. Feeling proud of her work with soldiers and sailors, although some people considered this work not "respectable." Happily noting that "during my reign, over eighty of our maidservants married soldiers or sailors." Undertaking a 1,000-mile speaking tour of England for National Temperance League, 1889; conducting a longer tour of Scotland, 1891. Discussing Boer War, Crimean War, Indian Mutiny. Writing and publishing *Ready,* a newspaper; writing Christian and temperance tracts. Living with a woman friend in old age.

Having written one book, *The Soldier's Friend: A Pioneer's Record* (c.1913), "to suit the Publisher," Robinson states in the preface to this autobiography, "I thought I would write a second to please myself; embodying what had been omitted." Her tone in this conversational memoir is cheerful and no-nonsense, occasionally a bit self-righteous, as she describes her dedication to advancing the causes of temperance and Christianity among military men.

797 ROBY, Marguerite. c.1875–?. *My Adventures in the Congo.* Edward Arnold, 1911. 312 pp.; front. port.; illus.; map; index. NUC pre56 499:133.

Born in England. Parents not named. Unmarried at time of journey; may have been a widow. Traveler (Africa, China, U.S., South Pacific Islands). Middle class.

Travels of an Englishwoman, focusing on her independent expedition by bicycle from South Africa up through Rhodesia and into the Congo, 1909–10. Departing from England under alias "Henderson," as maid to a titled lady. While on board ship, deciding to travel into Rhodesia and the Congo the following June. Briefly mentioning her visiting Australia and Samoa. Traveling on to Durban, South Africa, 1910. Visiting Johannesburg. Contracting fever at Victoria Falls. Employing Thomas, a black mission boy, as her servant. Going on a shooting expedition. Traveling with a trader and his black wife into interior of the Congo; author's riding a bicycle and frequently falling off. Her intention of photographing any evidence she might encounter of atrocities. Being deserted by Thomas; deciding to trust him upon his return. Quarreling with the trader; his departure. Suffering sleeping sickness. Continuing her journey alone, except for Thomas and the porters; failing to find evidence of reported Belgian atrocities. Observing an attack on a cannibal village; noting the Belgian custom of shooting into the air rather than at the natives. Commenting favorably on Catholic missions. Suffering recurring fevers; taking large doses of quinine. Hunting on Lake Tanganyika. Seeing harsher treatment of natives in German colony at Ujiji east of Lake Tanganyika than in Belgian territory. Threatening the porters to keep them from deserting; perceiving that they feared no punishment from a woman; having them whipped. Desertion of some of the porters. Shooting birds on Lake Albert Edward. Her continuing illness; being treated by an incompetent doctor. Upon reaching Fort

Portal, the District Commissioner's sending police to bring in the mutineers. Arriving in Kampala; saying farewell to Thomas, "one of the whitest black men I shall ever meet." Taking a steamer across Lake Victoria; arriving blinded in Mombasa; being given cocaine for her headache. Returning to England.

Roby's travels took place only a few years after the major colonial powers had finished carving up the largely uncharted wilds of Africa into separate territories in 1902. In 1903, with the rubber trade in full swing in the Congo, allegations of forced labor and atrocities committed by white men against natives were confirmed in an official report by Roger Casement, a British official, resulting in the formation of the Congo Reform Association in Britain and international political maneuvering to change conditions in central Africa. By 1910, the time of Roby's journey into Africa, conditions were improving. This memoir ends with an essay, "The Congo and Its Critics," written to shatter some of the popular concepts about the horrors of Belgian rule. Interesting as a document on Belgian and German colonialism, *My Adventures* also offers insight into the kind of medical treatment available to early travelers in Africa, as well as the gendered attitudes of both white and black men toward a woman traveling alone. Prior to 1909 Roby had also visited Manchuria, the western U.S., and Tahiti, journeys only briefly mentioned in this book.

798 ROGERS, Clara Kathleen (née Barnett; Clara Doria, stage name). 1844–1931. *Memories of a Musical Career*. Boston: Little, Brown, 1919. 503 pp.; front. port.; foreword; prelude; illus.; index. NUC pre56 501:131. (other ed. Norwood, MA: Plimpton Press, 1932.)

Born in Cheltenham, Gloucestershire. Father: John Barnett, opera composer. Mother: Eliza Lindley. 4 brothers; 1 sister; 9 other siblings died in childhood. Married 1878, Henry Munroe Rogers, Boston lawyer. Wrote *The Philosophy of Singing, My Voice and I, The Voice in Speech,* and *English Diction in Song and Speech*. Knew Julia Ward Howe, William Randolph Hearst, John Singer Sargent, Edward MacDowell, Madge Kendal, Eliza Lynn Linton, William James, Nellie Melba, Amy Lowell, others. Singer (concerts, opera); teacher (music); musicianship writer; foreign resident (Italy, U.S.). Middle class.

Author's career as an opera and concert singer in Europe and U.S., from childhood to marriage. Parental history: father's musical career, mother's limited musical ability. Family homes in Cheltenham; father's unusual friends; her mother's erratic, hysterical behavior being seen as due to frequent pregnancy. Father's high standards for children's educations. Governesses, home tutors. Author's learning piano; her precocity as a singer. Family's bout with typhoid: author's contracting it; brother's dying from it. Younger brother's mental retardation. With sister, briefly attending private school. Moving with mother and siblings, c.1856, to

Leipzig, Germany, for children's musical education. Studying at the Leipzig Conservatory of Music, age 12. Moving to Berlin, age 15, for further voice study. Learning opera and Italian in Milan. Author and sister's both taking the stage name "Doria." Author's anxieties about the quality of her voice and about retaining a respectable reputation. Making her opera debut in Turin, age 17; performing opera tours in Italy with sister. Family's returning to England because of mother's fear that her sons would learn Italian manners. Author's debut in Dublin; her father's writing an opportunistic letter to a London impresario, ruining her chance of a London opera career. Author's turning to concert singing but feeling it was artistically demoralizing. Being introduced to London society by aristocratic friends; making concert tours of England. Embarking on a singing career in U.S. after 1871; performing church solos in Brooklyn and Boston; describing her social life and travels in U.S. Visiting her family in England annually. Her friendship with Longfellow. Befriending Henry Munroe Rogers; their courtship and marriage, 1878.

Rogers humorously describes her musical training and discusses the musical tastes of English, American, and European audiences in this chronological narrative. With **799** *The Story of Two Lives: Home, Friends, and Travels* (1932), she describes her charity and teaching work in Boston, 1878–1918. Her style is conversational, exclamatory, and full of anecdotes. The book includes a memoir written by Rogers's husband when he was 92, focusing on his memories of Clara and bringing the book up to 1931, the year of her death. This autobiography is most valuable for its accounts of the author's interaction with people she met in artistic circles.

800 ROGERS, Rose Annie. c.1902–?. *The Lonely Island*. George Allen & Unwin Ltd., 1926. 223 pp.; front.; In Memoriam, Henry Martyn Rogers; preface; illus.; apps. NUC pre56 501:267.

Born in England. Parents not named. Married Henry Martyn Rogers, curate, Church of England, d.1926. Widow. 2 children. Missionary (Tristan da Cunha); teacher; clergyman's spouse. Lower middle class.

Teaching activities, hardships, and cultural reactions of a missionary's wife on a small South Atlantic island, 1922–25. Tristan da Cunha's history and geography; its earlier missionaries, including Rev. E. Dodgson, Lewis Carroll's brother. Husband's deciding to serve as a missionary there after reading an appeal in the *Times* about islanders' need for education and religious ministration. Their arriving in Tristan da Cunha, April 1922, with a year's provisions. Her fearing "coloured races"; natives' first frightening her, then evoking her pity. Living in mission house for one month while their own house was built. Suffering food shortages; sharing provisions with natives. Their starting day school, young men's night school, church services, and a boy scout troop. Doing her own housework when native girls proved unsuitable domestic servants. Describing the various dangers she and husband faced "on sea and land." Her son Edward's being the first English baby born on the island. Spending first Christmas on island; different ethnic groups there; living conditions, agricultural economy; husband's trying to grow English crops. Being isolated from civilization; reckoning time by visits from ships provisioning the island rather than by calendar. Her daily schedule of teaching infants and girls' classes. Their building a church, stocking stores, and distributing mail on island. Island weddings and cultural customs, festivities, importance of birthdays; islanders' helping celebrate her son's first birthday. Working at potato harvesting. Husband's exploring surrounding islands, doing meteorological studies. Diary extracts, 1924–25, calling this her "period of greatest stress": her son's illness; lack of ships and failure of the dairy causing food shortages; increased sickness among islanders. Their being visited by islanders with grievances; their serving as the informal local government. Daily longing to see a ship; one finally arriving to take them home, February 1925. Exchanging gifts and tearful farewells with islanders.

Although Rogers's preface states that her book's primary goal is "to describe in familiar terms the daily life of the quaintest and most isolated community in the British Empire," this aim is overshadowed by the publisher's announcement that "the proceeds . . . will go to the Henry Martyn Rogers Memorial Fund for the benefit of the widow . . . left in care of their two small children." Certainly Rogers furthers the latter goal in her treatment of their three-year mission, which reads more like a hard-luck tale than a picturesque island scapbook, while her chosen title exposes her private opinion of their experiences. Mindful of her role as a missionary, she strikes a benevolent tone, but this is frequently overwhelmed by tales of the family's problems or her own prejudices about the natives. Perhaps the greatest worth of Rogers's book lies in the insight it gives to the ambivalent impulses that can be inherent in the historical role of missionary.

801 ROSS, Janet Anne (née Duff-Gordon). 1842–1927. *Early Days Recalled*. Chapman & Hall, 1891. 203 pp.; front. port. NUC pre56 505:128.

Born in London. Father: Sir Alexander Cornewall Duff-Gordon, Commissioner of Inland Revenue, baronet. Mother: Lucy Austin, translator. 1 brother; 1 sister. Married 1860, Henry James Ross. 1 son. Niece: writer Lina Waterfield. Wrote *Italian Sketches* (1888), *Three Generations of English Women* (1888); translated Von Sybel's *Crusades* (c.1862). Knew William Thackeray, Charles Dickens, Nassau Senior, George Meredith, Thomas Carlyle, others. Journalist; translator; travel writer; foreign resident (Egypt); foreign correspondent; family historian. Upper class.

Author's childhood and youth among her parents' literary circle, closing with her early married years in Egypt, 1842–c.1872. Her first memories: adults' excitement over Corn Law Debates, 1846; her father's illness from cholera. Paternal grandmother's individualism and friendship with the Misses Berry, 18th-century society writers. Touring France with her maternal grandparents, 1846. After age 6, loving to read; receiving books from Dickens and Thackeray, both friends of her mother. Remembering the many artists and authors present at her birthday parties. During 1848 revolution in Europe, family's harboring Duchess of Orleans; England's undergoing Chartist unrest. Father's idolizing the Duke of Wellington, understating political disturbance, insisting "the duke will see to it." Author's parents sending her to France and Germany to learn languages. Author's mother and grandmother's being active in predominantly male literary and political circles which included writers A. W. Kinglake, Thomas Carlyle, historian George Grote and others. Recalling being taken to the Great Exhibition, 1851. Family's moving to rural estate in Esher. Naming her new pony "Eothen" after one of Kinglake's characters. Death of the Duke of Wellington, 1852; its effect on her father. Father's being appointed to serve the chancellor of the exchequer, 1854; after 1856, his serving as commissioner of inland revenue until his death in 1872. Author's working as *Times* Egypt correspondent, 1857–63. Marrying, 1860; author and husband's living in Egypt. Witnessing building of Suez Canal. Returning to England for birth of her child. Mother's visiting them in Egypt; mother's death, 1864.

This account of Ross's youthful memories closes with her reminiscences of traveling with a desert caravan during the last year of her mother's life, as if the death of her mother, who was Ross's link to mid-Victorian luminaries, signaled the end of the era she wishes to document. Focusing chiefly on the literary and intellectual figures she met through her parents' connections, Ross tells her story in a succession of associative anecdotes narrated against a backdrop of larger historical events. Her style is informal and charming, her tone affectionate; her extensive familiarity with English, French, and German literature is evident. Ross also published **802** *The Fourth Generation: Reminiscences of Janet Ross* (1912), which links her life story with those of her literary mother, grandmother, and great-grandmother.

803 ROYDEN, Agnes Maude (C.H., D.D.). 1876–1956. *A Threefold Cord.* Victor Gollancz, 1947. 125 pp.; foreword; illus. BLC to 1975 283:250.

Born at Mossley Hill, Frankby, Lancashire. Father: Tommy Royden, Liverpool shipowner, Conservative M.P. Mother: Alice Dowdall. 2 brothers; 5 sisters. Married 1944, Rev. George William Hudson Shaw, Anglican minister, d.1944. Widow. 1 adopted daughter. Wrote *The Great*

Adventure: The Way to Peace (1915), *The Church and Woman* (1924), others. Knew Millicent Garrett Fawcett, Edith Picton-Turbervill, Albert Schweitzer, others. Feminist; preacher; suffragist; religionist (Anglican); public speaker; political activist; organizer (religious); religious/spiritual writer; pacifist; clergyman's spouse. Middle class.

Anglican lay preacher's account of the long-term close relationship between herself, an Anglican minister, and his second wife, 1901–44. Attending Lady Margaret Hall, Oxford; being attracted to the ritual beauty of Roman Catholicism. First meeting Rev. Shaw through her service at Liverpool Settlement House, c.1901–03; feeling instantly drawn to him; being unaware the attraction was romantic. Assisting Shaw as an unpaid curate in his South Luffenham parish. Meeting his wife, Effie; being instantly drawn to her also. Effie's fearing childbearing after perilous birth of son; her unstable mental condition; the Shaws' consequent celibate marriage; Effie's lack of jealousy at author's closeness to her husband. Author's believing she and Shaw could never have kept their love a secret; implying that it was spoken but not consummated. Her living with the Shaws at Alderley and London. Touring England to speak on behalf of women's suffrage and employment. Her support for women's ordination. Shaw's work and ministry habits; his support for the League of Nations, women's ordination, and the work of Albert Schweitzer. Preaching from Shaw's pulpit at Good Friday services one year, both of them defying the Anglican Bishop's refusal to let a woman preach at a specially sacred service. Outbreak of WWI; death of the Shaws' son; Effie's collapse. Author's receiving Companionate of Honour. Shaw's retiring; their moving to Kent; author's moving into a house next door to them. Death of Effie Shaw, 1944; author's marrying Shaw shortly afterwards; her realizing that he was dying; his death eight weeks after wedding. Denying any physical involvement with Shaw during Effie's lifetime; explaining why it was unthinkable to both of them.

The biography of a relationship rather than of an individual, this book keeps a balanced focus between the three principals, using the image of the threefold cord to place their three-way friendship in a spiritual context. However, the reader is tempted to wonder what Effie Shaw might say, given the opportunity. The text is illustrated with four of Effie Shaw's satiric drawings. Information of a more self-reflective nature on Royden's personal faith and attraction to the sacramental life is included in **804** her contribution to the 1938 anthology *Myself When Young,* edited by Margot Asquith. A thorough biography of Royden's life and career is Sheila Fletcher's *Maude Royden: A Life* (1989).

805 ROYDEN, Agnes Maude (C.H., D.D.). 1876–1956. "Maude Royden Shaw, C.H., D.D.," pp. 147–159 in *If I Had My Time Again: An Anthology Contributed by Twenty Distinguished Men and*

Women. Ed. by Sir James Marchant. Odhams Press, 1950. 256 pp.; intro. by Lord Horder. NUC pre56 361:16.

Biographical: See *A Threefold Cord*.

Author's early life and subsequent career as an Anglican lay preacher and pacifist, covering c.1890–1950. Speculating on who else she might have wanted to be: Sarah Bernhardt or St. Teresa of Avila. Being unable to act professionally because lame; when young, enjoying acting with Chipping Campden Guild of Craftsmen. Regretting nothing in her life; accepting celibacy as her fate. Not wanting to be a man. Tallying the good life choices she made: to leave parents' overcrowded home in Frankby, to live as an unpaid Anglican curate for a rural parish, and later to accept lowest-level Oxford University Extension lectureship. Evaluating Elizabeth Wordsworth, principal of Lady Margaret Hall, as uninterested in the cause of women's education. As a lecturer, encountering employers' concern for her supposed feelings of womanly modesty. Accepting restriction against women speaking in cathedrals as not worth fighting. Writing and speaking for National Women's Suffrage Societies, 1908. Working politically in ecclesiastical circles to promote women's ordination. Believing that her sense of vocation to the priesthood prevented her ordination in a Nonconformist denomination, which would have welcomed her. Becoming a pacifist at outbreak of WWI; writing a peace pamphlet, "The Great Adventure." Congregationalists' inviting her to preach at the City Temple, 1917–20. Founding Fellowship Services at the Guildhouse, Eccleston Square, London, with Dr. Percy Dearmer, 1921. Preaching in U.S. and Canada under Guildhouse auspices. Touring world for the Guildhouse, 1928. Taking year of rest, 1929. Working for ideals of League of Nations covenant; feeling uneasy with absolute pacifism. Proposing concept of a Peace Army to League in Shanghai, 1932. Resigning from Guildhouse ministry due to increased pacifist commitment, 1938. Briefly joining Peace Pledge Union; disagreeing with its absolute pacifism. Leaving peace movement at outbreak of WWII; being denounced by pacifists, including Mahatma Gandhi; wishing she had left sooner. Desiring only that she had prayed more in her lifetime.

This essay, solicited by the anthology's editor, covers the theme of what Royden might have done differently or better could she live her life over again. More than in her other writings, she uses this forum to spotlight her public career. Although brief, this text is informative both on social attitudes toward women preachers in the Church of England and on the 20th-century pacifist movement.

806 RUCK, Amy Roberta. 1878–1978. *A Story-Teller Tells the Truth: Reminiscences and Notes*. Hutchinson, 1935. 303 pp.; front. port.; author's note; index. BLC to 1975 283:383.

Born in Murree, India. Father: Col. Arthur Ruck, ensign in 8th King's Liverpool Regiment. Mother: Elizabeth West D'Arcy. 4 brothers; 3 sisters. Married 1909, Oliver Onions, writer. 2 sons. Wrote short story collection *Wanted on the Voyage*, 15 novels including *His Official Fiancée*, *The Lad with Wings*, *The Unkissed Bride* (1928). Knew Marjorie Bowen, Vita Sackville-West, Rebecca West, Virginia Woolf, others. Novelist; short storyist. Middle class.

Author's Welsh background, literary career, and friendships, c.1880–1935. Her childhood in India. Developing a strong sense of Welsh identity. Attending school in Wales; being an avid reader. Living in both England and Wales, then in Germany. Returning to England; training at the Lambert School of Art and the Slade School in London. Visiting an art school in Paris. Beginning her writing career. Meeting and marrying another writer; becoming pregnant immediately. Forming good relationship with her Yorkshire in-laws. Discussing the inspiration and financial aspects of her writing career. Outbreak of WWI. Commenting on activities of the Women's Land Army in Wales. Author's making a book tour of U.S.; receiving fan mail. Meeting celebrities; meeting Virginia Woolf after Woolf by chance used the name "Berta Ruck" in *Jacob's Room*. Explaining her methods of working as a writer; giving advice to beginning writers. Describing her dreams and methods of dream interpretation. Her interests in aviation and in psychic phenomena. Commenting on the experience of facing death.

Primarily an account of Ruck's career as a writer, this autobiography is most interesting for its evocation of her family life in India, her love of Wales, and the books she read as a child. Her breezy style—she laughs at highbrow critics who called it "sprightly"—befits a novelist experienced in writing for a mass audience.

807 RUDKIN, Mabel S. (née Medd). c.1890–?. *Inside Dover 1914–1918: A Woman's Impressions*. Elliot Stock, 1933. 216 pp.; intro. BLC to 1975 283:425.

Born in England. 1 brother. Married 1914, Rev. Ernest Horace Rudkin, Anglican curate. Wrote Seeing Sussex. Clergyman's spouse; social historian; WWI volunteer; organizer (youth). Middle class.

Entertaining recollections of daily life in besieged Dover during WWI, accompanied by more serious reflections on war and wartime society, covering 1914–18. Calm before the storm of 1914. Depicting anti-German sentiment before WWI in England. Author and husband's living in Sussex; moving to Dover, 1914. Their social engagements. Her work as a district visitor. Responses to WWI among Dover citizenry; their horror of receiving WWI wounded. Author's support for League of Nations. Rumor's spreading that Germans had landed at Dover. Discussing the role of the church and individual clergymen during war. Giving

Temperance Teas for soldiers. Remembering an anonymous book which cited sexual laxity in Women's Land Army. Criticizing immorality of flappers. Helping found Girls' Patriotic Club; arranging social events for soldiers' wives; participating in amateur theatricals. Britain's holding National Day of Prayer, 1915. Doing missionary support work. Discussing the range of people's responses to air raids. Dover's being bombed; her husband's conducting services in cliffside caves designated as air raid shelters. Commenting on women's contributions to the war effort, the collapse of social barriers in war work, and food shortages. Modern politicians' being ignorant of history and its lessons. Armistice Day. Praising the brave people of Dover who stayed in the city during the bombing.

Rudkin writes from a mildly ironic perspective, focusing on the lighter side of wartime life in Dover. A fountain of information on the social changes occasioned by the war, her book also testifies to war's grimness and its toll on the civilian population. Rudkin's earlier work, *Heard at the Vicarage* (1928), is a humorous look at her role as a vicar's wife. It includes nostalgic reminiscences of Sussex village life and of the author's WWI volunteer work in Dover.

808 RUSSELL, Dora Winifred, Countess Russell (née Black, M.B.E.). 1894–1986. *The Tamarisk Tree*. Elek/Pemberton, 1975. 3 vols. Vol. 1: 304 pp.; preface; illus.; index. Vol. 2: 218 pp.; preface; index. Vol. 3: 372 pp.; preface; illus.; apps.; index. NUC 1982 17:951.

Born in London. Father: Sir Frederick Black, member of Civil Service. Mother: Sarah Davisson. 1 brother; 2 sisters. Married 1921, Bertrand Russell, 3rd Earl Russell; divorced 1935. Married 1940, Pat Grace, d.1949. Widow. 2 sons; 2 daughters. Wrote *Hypatia, or Woman of Knowledge* (1925), *The Right to Be Happy* (1927), *In Defence of Children* (1932). Political writer; journalist; academic; socialist; feminist; educator; civil servant; political activist; WWII volunteer; foreign resident (China); academic's spouse; child welfare activist; birth control activist; public speaker; traveler (Russia). Upper class; married into aristocracy.

Ethical, political, and career development of a feminist educator, set in the larger context of her turbulent marriage to philosopher Bertrand Russell, covering her childhood to mid-1930s. Her family history and closeness to her father. Her youthful interest in feminism. Joining Children's League of Pity. Attending Church of England and Salvation Army meetings. Attending high school, then finishing school in Germany. Receiving a scholarship to Girton. At Cambridge, joining Heretics' Society; meeting Bertrand. WWI: befriending Belgian refugees; accompanying father on war-related business to U.S. Bertrand's being persecuted under Defense of the Realm Act for his support of the No Conscription Fellowship. Author's being appointed junior don at Cambridge. Becoming interested in socialism and the problems of the working class. Joining 1917 Club and delegation to Russia. Accompanying Bertrand to his teaching appointment in Peking; fellow Europeans' being harshly criticized in China. Daily life, customs, culture in China. Nursing Bertrand during his bout with illness. Returning to England. Memories of noted guests: W. B. Yeats, T. S. Eliot, Leonard Woolf. Anecdotes of birth control pioneers Margaret Sanger and Marie Stopes; Britain's first birth control clinic. Forming workers' birth control group. Visiting Welsh mining towns. Writing for Spanish paper *El Sol*. Attending conferences of World League for Sex Reform. Practicing open marriage with Bertrand: having an affair with a man in London; Bertrand's starting an affair with their children's governess. Author's founding experimental school; lecturing in America on education. Becoming sexually involved with American journalist Griffin Barry; accompanying him to Soviet Union. Having daughter with Barry; Bertrand's acceptance. Having another child, not knowing if father is Bertrand or Barry. Bertrand's leaving her for another woman; going through bitter divorce trial and custody battle for children; feeling betrayed; her health lapsing. Becoming friends with future husband Pat Grace. Defining feminism's goals. Seeing love as the factor most lacking in the modern world. Men's having created political system based on their sexual self-image.

Lady Russell continues her life story in two more volumes. In **809** *Vol. 2: My School and the Years of War* (1980), covering 1935–47, she describes founding and directing her experimental school, which was based on the principles of progressive education; she also offers insightful observations on British society and its changing values in the postwar years. In **810** *Vol. 3: Challenge to the Cold War* (1985), Russell focuses on her many activities, particularly her work in women's rights and other political organizations, 1947–80. Her extended travel experiences and political observations, especially on Soviet-British relations, are interwoven with the personal and relational aspects of her narrative, concluding with a strong emphasis on the need for love between individuals and nations. Consciously dedicated to the concepts of open marriage and free love, she candidly discusses her many lovers without an apparent sense that her feeling of betrayal over Bertrand Russell's marital conduct had a sexual basis. Her unconventional views and strong will inform her ruthlessly open portrait of her first husband.

811 RUSSELL, Philippa Augusta Maria (Mrs. Frank). c.1855–d.a.1920. *Fragments of Auld Lang Syne*. Hutchinson, 1925. 324 pp.; illus.; index. NUC to 1975 284:424.

Born in London. Father: Henry Baillie, M.P. Mother: née Strangford. Stepmother: "Mrs. Rush." Married 1889, Maj.-Gen. F. S. Russell, military attaché, M.P. Widow. Society woman; lady-in-waiting; foreign resident (France, Germany). Upper class.

Personal reminiscences and reflections on changing Scottish and English societies, with emphasis on exploits of author's celebrated family, spanning 1850s–1920s. Extended, detailed family history. Visiting English country houses. Being presented at court. Friendship with Lady Augusta Stanley and Empress Eugènie. Traveling to the Continent: visiting Naples; living at Cannes with her father. Describing Cannes society, c.1880s. Being appointed lady-in-waiting to the Duchess of Albany. Marriage. Husband's appointment as military attaché in Berlin; his attending Emperor William; his election as M.P.; his early death. Berlin society, c.1880s. Taking over management of her son's estates. Feeling blessed about her good life. Noting degeneration in society's attitude toward duty to parents, mid-19th century to c.1920. Discussing Scottish customs, superstitions, religious history. Berlin Society, 1890s. German social customs, mistaken stereotypes of German women. Changes in customs for balls and parties. Perceiving a general decline of religious commitment in society. Her perspective on the secret of the British empire's power. Speculating on whether passage of women's suffrage will benefit the British nation.

In this account Russell focuses on the people and rituals that held together the social fabric of upper-class society, attempting to recreate the gentler, pre-WWI years whose passing she clearly regrets. Her attention to the myriad details of Victorian life, as well as her anecdotes about some of the most important English and Scottish families of the 18th and 19th centuries, make the book a valuable biographical resource.

812 RUTHERFORD, Dame Margaret. 1892–1972. *Margaret Rutherford: An Autobiography, as told to Gwen Robyns*. W. H. Allen, 1972. 230 pp.; photos. BLC to 1975 286:42.

Born in Balham. Father: née Benn, changed his name to Rutherford, writer. Mother not named. Orphan. Married 1945, Stringer Davis, actor. Knew Esme Church, Ivor Novello, John Gielgud, Sir Lawrence Olivier, Charlie Chaplin, Dame Edith Evans, Agatha Christie, others. Actress (stage, film); teacher (music); philanthropist. Middle class.

Childhood and later professional career of notable stage and screen actress, covering 1892–1972, with emphasis on her adult years. Her father's working as a commercial traveler in India. Author's being sent to England to be raised by her Aunt Bessie following her mother's death, c.1895; death of her father. Aunt Bessie's being "conventional but unusually emancipated" for her time. Throughout childhood, author's acting in amateur theatrical productions with her cousins. Loving poetry, bicycling, long walks; disliking her personal physical appearance. Teaching music lessons to supplement her scanty acting income. Aunt Bessie's death, 1925, providing a small legacy which freed author to concentrate solely on acting. Enrolling at the Old Vic School for acting training. Playing her first speaking role, 1925; lacking acting work for two subsequent years; resuming teaching music. In later years, preferring the stage to the screen. Attributing her late marriage to her shy temperament. Her husband's being devoted to his mother. With husband, funding many charities; being devoted to a home for delinquent boys and a women's prison. Touring the U.S., Australia, Ireland, and Italy with husband. Listing plays and films in which she acted, characters she portrayed, writers, actors, producers, and directors, and her most important parts; admitting she can't remember them all. Being indifferent to playing Miss Marple, Agatha Christie's detective, but needing the income to pay a tax debt. Mentioning her four nervous breakdowns; these being common in the theatre world because actors "live in a mixed world of fantasy and reality." Author and husband's "adopting" adult children, including one young man who proved to be transsexual and became Dawn Pepita Simmons; author and husband's being astonished but accepting. One friend's calling author "the original flower child"; author's agreeing with characterization.

Rutherford was 80 years old when she undertook this autobiography during recuperation from her second broken hip, and the book's tone carries intimations of her own mortality. She dictated her narrative to Gwen Robyns; the result is a chatty, frank, and informative review of the author's life, aimed at providing a record of her career for younger actors.

813 SACKVILLE-WEST, The Hon. Victoria Mary ("Vita"). 1892–1962. Part 1 (pp. 3–42) and Part 3 (pp. 103–132) of *Portrait of a Marriage*. Ed. by Nigel Nicolson (author's son). New York: Atheneum, 1973. 249 pp.; front. port.; preface; illus.; chronology; index. BLC 1976–1982 39:223. [cat. under Nicolson.]

Born near Sevenoaks, Kent. Father: Lionel Edward Sackville-West, 3rd Baron Sackville. Mother: Victoria Sackville-West (Lionel's first cousin). Married 1913 the Hon. Harold Nicolson, diplomat, writer, statesman. 2 sons. Wrote *Poems of West and East* (1917), *Passenger to Teheran* (1926), *Knole and the Sackvilles* (1922), *The Edwardians* (1930), *All Passion Spent* (1931), others. Knew Rudyard Kipling, Violet Trefusis, Virginia and Leonard Woolf. Novelist; poet; biographer; feminist; bisexual; cross-dresser; male impersonator; diplomat's spouse. Aristocracy.

Introspective reconstruction of author's aristocratic and impulsive youth, including the turmoil caused by her dual sexual nature, from childhood to age 28. Loving her "dada" and her cranky grandfather, Lord Sackville; loving but fearing her charming, imperious, manipulative mother. Growing up on ancient family estate of Knole as an only child; being secretive, intellectual, and a tomboy. Envying males their freedom and their trousers. Terrorizing playmates. At age 12, beginning to write turgid historical novels. Being sent to day school in London; besting all the other students. Making friends with schoolmate Violet Keppel. Until age 16, being constantly with Violet. Meeting future husband at theatre party, age 18; getting to know him better in Monte Carlo; feeling a strong intellectual affinity with him despite initial lack of sexual attraction. Harold's leaving on diplomatic business; author's falling into sexual intimacy with visiting schoolmate Rosamund Grosvenor. Coming to understand that her love for Harold is deep, her liaison with Rosamund superficial. Returning to England; willingly accepting Harold's marriage proposal; his departing on diplomatic business. Author's resuming her affair with Rosamund. Retrospectively justifying her behavior by separating her loves into two halves: Harold her pure love, Rosamund the love of her "perverted" nature. Marriage, 1913; experiencing happiness as a diplomat's wife for the next five years; believing her attraction to women would not revive. Giving birth to two sons. Violet's reentering author's life and declaring passion for her during Harold's absence, 1918. Entering into wild affair with Violet; feeling urge to dominate her. Violet's marrying when author refuses to leave her family for her. Author's pursuing Violet to Paris; living there with her incognito; cross-dressing and being called "Julian" by Violet; writing a novel with Julian as protagonist and Violet as his lover "Eve." Returning to England; lapsing into suicidal depression over the suffering she had caused Harold and the public scandal her liaison had occasioned. Quarreling endlessly with Violet and Violet's husband, Denys Trefusis; leaving Violet and then pursuing her, back and forth through England and France; contrasting her serene, loving relationship with Harold and her violent, deceit-ridden one with Violet. Thinking that she may never see Violet again, and that although she herself escaped from the affair relatively unscathed, Violet might yet commit suicide.

In this autobiographical narrative (contained in parts 1 and 3 of the book), written in 1920, the author is closely concerned with illuminating secret corners of her own mind, and appears uninterested in details or people outside her own emotional concerns. In her own autobiography, *Don't Look Round,* Violet Keppel Trefusis writes of her attachment to the author but skirts any discussion of its homoerotic element. Sackville-West clearly states her intention never to publish this memoir, a wish violated by her son, who continues the story and provides commentary on the remaining forty-one years of his parents' marriage. In parts 2, 4, and 5, Nigel Nicholson balances his mother's viewpoint with particulars about his father's reactions to abandonment and with details about his distinguished career; unlike his mother, Nigel also discusses Harold's bisexuality. In **814** an autobiographical essay published in *Little Innocents* (Cobden-Sanderson, 1932, ed. by Alan Pryce-Jones), Sackville-West is explicit about her cruelty to other children in her childhood.

ST. HELIER, Baroness. [*See* JEUNE, Susan Mary Elizabeth.]

815 SALMOND, The Hon. Monica Margaret, Lady (née Grenfell). 1893–1983. *Bright Armour: Memories of Four Years of War*. Faber & Faber, 1935. 251 pp. NUC pre56 516:503.

Raised in Taplow, Buckinghamshire. Father: William Henry Grenfell, later 1st Baron Desborough, M.P., K.C.V.O. Mother: Ethel Anne Priscilla Fane, lady-in-waiting to queen. 3 brothers; 1 sister. Married 1924, Sir John Maitland Salmond, Marshall of the RAF. 2 children. Nurse (WWI); foreign resident (France); masseuse; x-ray technician. Aristocracy.

Close look at the experiences and life changes of a volunteer nurse during WWI, including her observations on society's attitudes on the homefront, 1914–18. Leading a sheltered childhood. Discussing the great social changes brought about by WWI. Noting the irony of having to be accompanied by a chaperone while seeking probationary nursing work in London, as young ladies could not go out alone. Being hired by London Hospital to serve first in Royal Ward, then in Cambridge Ward; describing her duties and the physicians, nurses, and wounded French war prisoners; noting progress of war during her stint there. Transferring to British hospital in France in December, 1914. Finding relief from tedium of ward service through her enjoyment of other women's companionship. Two of her brothers' dying in the war, summer of 1915. Being transferred to a hospital in Calais; serving there, 1915–16. Returning to London; experiencing its ongoing air raids. Undertaking instruction in therapeutic massage, 1916; having to study *Gray's Anatomy* in preparing for certification. Being licensed as a masseuse. Studying medical electricity and x-ray techniques.

Dividing her account into four chronological sections, Lady Salmond gives substantive details of problems faced by medical personnel—particularly nurses—in dealing with the wounded during WWI. Her book is also a record of the transformations occasioned in a privileged and protected life when the war disrupted traditional gender barriers. Like many other upper-class young women, Lady Salmond found that the need for women's wartime services made the leisured life of a socialite only one of the options open to her. Her book documents how her voluntary war service led her to become a woman of greater social independence.

816 SALT, Annie Gwendoline (née Harding). 1887–d.a.1930. *My Lot—A Pillar of Salt*. Ilfracombe: Arthur Stockwell, 1946. 288 pp. BLC to 1975 288:328.

Born in London. Father: Alfred Bennick Harding, popular scientific lecturer. Mother, stepmother not named. 4 brothers; 1 sister. Married 1906 Selwyn Salt, later Anglican vicar. 2 sons; 4 daughters. Colonialist (New Zealand); clergyman's spouse; charitable volunteer. Middle class.

Late Victorian childhood and peripatetic married life of a vicar's wife in both England and New Zealand, with her observations on colonial society, 1890s–1930s. Reflecting on contrast between turbulent 1930s and "comparative quiet" of 1890s. At age 6, being hospitalized for one year for unexplained illness; eagerly awaiting parents' visits. Recalling her family's closeness, diversified pastimes, reading novels aloud. Father's being fellow of the Physical Society, gifted speaker on popular science and a "Mr. Micawber optimist." Deaths of mother and sister, author's age 18. At 19, being courted by brother's friend Selwyn Salt, local clergyman's son; their marrying shortly after her father's remarriage. Selwyn's initial indecisiveness about following his father's profession. Living in Weston, then Oxford, while Selwyn attended Evangelical school and studied for arts degree; ill health's slowing his progress. Her father's death, 1908. Having three daughters, 1908–10. During WWI, coping with servant shortage. Giving birth to son, 1915. Selwyn's spending a year at Wycliffe Hall Theological College, 1918, his accepting vicarage in New Zealand, 1921. Their seven-week voyage aboard cargo ship; describing New Zealand cities and the reversal of the seasons. Premature birth of author's new baby. Selwyn's taking over parish of Mangere, eight miles from Auckland. Her tending house and churning butter, with children's help; her visiting assorted parishioners. Musing on why Chinese immigrants seem to prosper there. Noting New Zealand history, including Maori customs and culture. Her second son's birth, 1926. With all five children, their making a 1,000-mile automobile tour of New Zealand's north island. Husband's transfer to parish in Paparoa; their liking its primitive surroundings; finding local people prejudiced against Oxford-educated English; winning them over; refurbishing their vicarage, with children's help. Observing prejudices among colonists: farmers vs. British newcomers; upper-class settlers vs. farmers; Irish vs. English immigrants. Making parish visits with Selwyn; giving parties at vicarage; being visited by Archbishop. Selwyn's being given the Auckland diocese, 1930. Starting a Mothers' Union in Auckland for new mothers. Despite their hard work, Selwyn's career's failing from his lack of wealthy sponsors to bring money into church. Their being returned to England and assigned a parish living in Nottinghamshire, 1931. Her finding the new rectory ghastly and the village "practically feudal"; attempting to cope by joining women's organizations. Family's suffering from England's cold climate and their miserable housing. Two children's catching scarlet fever; younger son's dying from diphtheria. Family's eventually gaining more comfortable quarters in Gamston parish. Commenting on the ingratitude of many parishioners for whom she did charity work, in contrast to communities in New Zealand. Resenting Church of England's lack of appreciation for her husband's self-sacrificing labors in New Zealand and later in England.

The chronological progression of this account highlights the contrast between the author's idealized memories of her English childhood and the disappointments she experienced through her husband's lack of career rewards; the book charts Salt's increasing pessimism as circumstances repeatedly forced her to rebuild her family's life from scratch. Although valuable for its record of a colonial parish's everyday life and its connection with the Church in England, Salt's autobiography is more informative about family matters than it is about public affairs. As her punning title implies, her husband's career effectively defined her fate, which she apparently sees as being analogous to that of the biblical Lot's wife.

817 SALUSBURY, Hilda Ann (née Wood). 1906–s.l.1988. *Only My Dreams: An English Girlhood.* Chicago: Academy Chicago, 1990. Ed. by Anita Miller. 271 pp.; illus. by Kathy Blankley; ed.'s note. Books in Print 1991–1992 3:5685.

Born in Great Yarmouth, Norfolk. Father: Richard Wood, marine engineer, draughtsman. Mother: Ada. 1 brother; 2 sisters. Married 1934, David Salusbury, Air Ministry maintenance engineer, d.1984. Widow. 1 son; 1 daughter. Nurse (maternity); midwife; teacher; governess. Lower middle class.

Record of a young woman's struggle against her father's domination in her quest for self-esteem and self-determination, focused on c.1910–34. Recalling Great Yarmouth. Family's moving to Gorleston-on-Sea at author's age 7. WWI: father's long work hours, neglect of family; mother's "entertaining" soldiers at home; relatives' telling father; mother's deserting family, 1918; author's blaming herself. Father's destroying all traces of mother and ordering children never to utter her name. At age 12, author's assuming maternal duties and becoming household drudge. Winning a singing competition at age 13; having her desire for a singing career and teaching certificate frustrated by her father, who required her to leave school to bear full-time household responsibility. Mother's visiting children, wanting to come home for their sake; father's refusing to forgive her but being willing to allow her to return as a housekeeper; mother's rejecting idea of returning under such conditions. Father's demanding perfect housekeeping; his knocking author unconscious over her failure to meet his expectations; her blaming herself for failing to soothe him adequately. Colluding with her grandmother to write letters to her mother; father's banishing grandmother. Author's taking a temporary waitress job. Returning to being father's drudge. Blaming her mother for abandoning her. Father's allowing grandmother's return; her assisting author's courtship with Fred; father's discovering romance and ending it. Father's sending grandmother away permanently because her worsening bronchitis needed care. Upon adulthood of author's sisters, father's partially loosening his grip on author; her finding refuge in playing tennis. Escaping home by attending pregnant cousin in Huntingdon; father's ultimately telling her not to return home but to start supporting herself. Resolving not to go into domestic service. With no training, finding a governess position in Nottinghamshire for eighteen months, then serving as secretary for a blind man. Suffering another romantic disappointment. Enrolling in nurses' training program in London. Taking maternity training; delivering babies in hospital and in East End slums; passing nursing exams; returning to Norfolk. Finding her grandmother dying in poverty, attended by author's mother. Lodging with a Methodist preacher; as district nurse, attending maternity cases and providing family care. With sister's marriage, father's demanding that author return to take care of him. Giving up her career; coming home; her father's lapsing into his old pattern of controlling and abusing her. Deciding she will no longer be a victim; advising her father to hire a housekeeper; departing.

A brief postscript covers the remainder of Salusbury's life, from her 1934 marriage through her fifty-odd years of international living with her Air Ministry husband. The body of her book addresses a single theme—personal freedom gained—in relation to multiple issues of gender and family power structures. Although Salusbury was born in 1906 her family seems characteristic of an earlier era, for her father stands out as a patriarchal oppressor of biblical proportions, and her mother's wretched fate as a reviled and cast-out adultress mirrors that of Isabel in the legendary 1847 novel of adultery, *East Lynne*. By book's end, however, the author has caught up with modern times to revel in a personal liberation. Her book documents a type of rigid family hierarchy which by the 1900s was waning in affluent, urban circles, but which determined the course of her own maturation in less prosperous, provincial surroundings.

818 SANDES, Elise. 1851–1934. *Enlisted; or, My Story. Incidents of Life and Work among Soldiers*. S. W. Partridge & Co., 1915. Ed. by M. T. Schofield. 277 pp.; front. port.; preface; illus. BLC to 1975 289:274. (1st pub. Cork: Office of "Forward," Sandes Soldiers' Home, 1896.)

Born in Ireland. Parents not named. 2 brothers; 6 sisters. Single. Organizer of societies (philanthropic); missionary (India); philanthropist; religionist (evangelical). Lower middle class.

Success story of author's project establishing Soldiers' Homes throughout Ireland and India, set within framework of her personal commitment to evangelical Christianity, spanning 1850s–1914. In childhood, believing in greatness of eternity. Because of her delicate health, being freed from lessons; living with aunt rather than with parents and siblings. Adoring her father; his religious devotion; her fear of losing him;

tending him during his illness; his death. Becoming friends with Marie Fry, who devoted herself to Christian work for various Irish regiments; upon Fry's illness and death, author's making Fry's cause her own. Doing Christian missionary work with soldiers from 65th Regiment. Attending soldiers' prayer meetings in Cork; remembering the first donation she received toward Soldiers' Home; opening first Soldiers' Home there. Remembering death of Mary Stokes, another colleague in the cause. Corresponding with soldiers fighting in Afghanistan, c.1879–80. Seeing Soldiers' Homes as necessary because of civilians' unwillingness to take soldiers into their private homes. Going to London to raise funds from philanthropists; being rejected by most of them; ultimately raising £4,000 for new Soldiers' Home. In London, interesting several prosperous women philanthropists in the cause of soldiers' Christian redemption. After taking a holiday for her own health, renewing her fundraising efforts to build a Soldiers' Home in Belfast. Remembering individual soldiers she helped to overcome drink. Opening more Homes throughout Ireland. Outbreak of South African War, c.1895. Sending coworkers to work with Council of the Soldiers' Christian Association in South Africa. Establishing Homes in India; sending workers to staff them. Soldiers' expressions of gratitude for Homes. Discussing how good women serve as positive influences for fighting men. Describing how confidence schemes and other exploitations are perpetrated on soldiers on leave. Her pride in the goodheartedness of British soldiers; feeling the need to help prepare them to die should their country call them. Expressing her belief in the urgent need to save souls.

Sandes's work may have been written with fundraising for her Soldiers' Homes operation as one of its primary aims; a plea for money, accompanied by various letters of recommendation, concludes the book. She demonstrates a flair for combining religious, charitable, and dramatic elements in her writing, and portrays herself as a tenacious and determined organizer. The anecdotes she presents about the religious commitments and personal problems of military men, as well as her stories about the philanthropists who helped underwrite Soldiers' Homes, make the book a valuable source on the Victorian and Edwardian eras.

819 SANDES, Flora. 1876–1956. *Autobiography of a Woman Soldier: A Brief Record of Adventure with the Serbian Army 1916–1919*. H. F. & G. Witherby, 1927. 222 pp.; illus. NUC pre56 519:140.

Born in England. Single. Soldier; nurse (WWI); public speaker. Middle class.

Detailed portrait of unconventional military service, set against backdrop of the Serbian-Bulgar conflict in WWI. Praying as a child that she would awaken to find she had become a boy. WWI: joining Mme Grovitch's unit in Serbia as a volunteer nurse. Feeling nursing a "hopelessly" feminine occupation. Returning to England after three months to raise money for Serbian Red Cross. Returning to Serbia. Working in Valjevo as nurse and dresser for 2nd Infantry Regiment. Living conditions: sleeping on hay and in overcrowded rooms. Recounting history of peasant women's occasionally fighting with Serbian army. Her ability to ride and shoot being vital in her joining 2nd Infantry Regiment as a private. Being accepted by fellow soldiers, who hoped she represented England's future aid to them. Graphic description of wartime conditions: freezing or scorching weather, exhaustion. Fighting the Bulgars; daily life in the trenches with comrades. Being promoted to sergeant. Overcoming difficulties in transporting the wounded; being wounded in the leg herself; convalescing in Serbian hospital and French naval hospital. Returning to active duty. Details of Serbian internal rebellion, 1916. Serving with the shock troops. Having recurring problems with her wounded leg; returning to hospital. On sick leave, raising money in England and France for Serbian cause. Rejoining unit in Serbia. Serbs' talents for mountain warfare; their habits, including looting. Contracting Spanish flu; returning to Serbian hospital, where privations were evident. Doing nursing work during her convalescence. Rejoining her regiment; going to Belgrade with them, 1918; describing postwar civilian life there. Being promoted to lieutenant in 3rd Battalion; duties of Serbian officers. Drilling her company. Dealing with personal problems of her men. Describing Serbian culture, customs. Taking 18-month leave, 1920; returning to Serbian unit, 1921. Being promoted to captain. Commenting on changes in Serbian peacetime army. Dealing with Russian soldiers under her command. Receiving orders to demobilize, 1922. Enumerating her difficulties and discomforts in readjusting to life as a civilian woman.

A thorough and vivid portrait of WWI in the Balkans, Sandes's account also provides clearheaded documentation of the valuable role the author carved for herself in a national army structure operating outside the gender constraints of British society. Sandes joins many other British writers in re-creating the ghastly conditions of WWI trench life, but her litany of hardships does not include any obstacles occasioned by gender prejudice. She notes her childhood wish to have been born male, but her account stands as testimony to her success in having rethought what it means to be female.

SARAWAK, First Ranee of. [*See* BROOKE, Margaret Alice Lilly.]

SARAWAK, Second Ranee of. [*See* BROOKE, Sylvia Leonora.]

820 SAXBY, Mary (née Holloway). 1738–d.a.1794. *Memoirs of a Female Vagrant*. Dunstable, 1806. Ed. by Samuel Greatheed. 68 pp. NUC pre56 522:545.

Born in London. Father: John Holloway, silk weaver, soldier. Mother: Susanna. Stepmother not named. 2 half-brothers. Married 1771 John Saxby, "common traveller," soldier, d.1782. Widow. 6 daughters; 2 sons. Transient; farm laborer; religionist (Methodist convert); preacher. Working class.

Roguish but repentant memoirs of rebellious child, migrant field worker, and Methodist convert, 1738–94. Mother's death during childbirth in author's early childhood. Because of her ungovernable temper, author's being moved from home of one relative to another during father's trips abroad. Briefly being sent to Methodist school and Methodist services by strict, pious aunt; rebelling against aunt's chastisement; being rescued and spoiled by father. After father's remarriage, running away from home several times, 1749; being chained and whipped by father to punish her acts of willful destruction and disobedience. Running away for good into the country; wandering from town to town; joining a gypsy band. Cohabiting one year with a gypsy man; leaving him rather than accept role as servant-wife to woman he loved more. Thieving with another gypsy band. Hiring on as a field worker. Suffering a swollen arm from blood poisoning; returning to her father's London home; recuperating in hospital. Running away again; taking up field work in Kent and Essex. Being arrested along with a friend for prostitution. Reuniting with her gypsy lover; being rescued by Saxby (whom she had met in Kent) and given shelter with his mother and sisters. Despite moral resolutions, getting pregnant by Saxby; his deserting her for the army; her singing ballads at local markets to support herself. Their reunion; her bearing three children by him before their marriage in 1771; refusal of many clergy to marry "travellers." Their living as migrant harvesters, constantly on the move. Saxby's frequent drunkenness; his beating her while she was pregnant, once nearly strangling her; resulting loss of most of her hearing. Deaths of her twin children. Their working the hay harvest near London. Her praying for more twins; having pangs of conscience over her habits of obscenity and swearing; seriously wishing to amend her life. Praising God for directing her to books and moral companions. Heeding Methodist preaching. Bearing twins again; undergoing religious conversion during her difficult pregnancy; death of one twin. Traveling and preaching with Methodist companions; praying for husband's conversion. Her favorite son's death. Husband's illness and fatal decline; his converting to Methodism before death, 1782. Paying husband's debts. Recovering from her illness among Methodist friends. Moving to Olney, 1791. Her grief over her eldest son's death, 1794.

Showing its antecedents both in the picaresque memoir and in the Protestant conversion narrative, Saxby's account is an uncommon fusion of the two. Looking back on her hard and often profane life, Saxby frequently exhorts the reader to avoid pitfalls similar to those that entrapped her. The editor, however, appears to have in mind a thoroughly Christianized audience, for the tone of his footnotes is more restrained as he makes edifying comments on Saxby's experiences and on the insights her account can yield to preachers in evangelizing other vagrants. At times Saxby allows her emotional and spiritual state to be dictated by passages of scripture that come randomly to mind, taking these as direct messages from God and answers to prayer. Much is also implied about informal social arrangements among England's migrant population.

821 SAYERS, Peig. 1873–1958. *An Old Woman's Reflections: The Life of a Blasket Island Storyteller*. Trans. from Gaelic by Seamus Ennis. Oxford: Oxford University Press, 1962. 133 pp.; front. port.; intro. by W. R. Rodgers; map. BLC to 1975 291:227. (1st pub. Dublin, 1939, as *Machtnamh Seana Mhna*.)

Born in Dunquin parish, Dingle peninsula, County Kerry, Ireland. Father: Tom Sayers, fisherman, master storyteller. Mother: Peig Brosnan. 2 brothers. Married Patrick (Padraig) O'Gaoithin. Widow. 2 sons; 1 daughter. Storyteller. Rural laboring class.

Stories of people author knew in Dingle town and on Great Blasket Island, from her childhood to c.1917, with references to 1917–39. Regretting that the storytelling tradition is dying out; lamenting her lost youth. Recalling the wreck of a local fishing boat in which all on board drowned, author's age 6. At age 26, making a pilgrimage to honor St. Kathleen's day; while there, meeting an old woman storyteller who shared stories from her own locale. Cutting peat turf with her brother's wife. Recounting tales of passion and marriage among young folk. An itinerant tailor's visiting the family home, telling a story about a larcenous woman. Recalling a childhood visit with her father to visit kin in Flagstone Hollow. Describing the folk custom of using a snail to divine the identity of a girl's future husband. Father's description of a perilous storm at sea when he and comrades were shipping a load of peat; how he rescued a fellow crewman from drowning. Relations between laborers and the local gentlewoman for whom they worked. Women's making a pilgrimage to Wethers' Well; the pious legend surrounding that place. Author's first and only ride on a train. Her marriage; first meeting her husband the day of the wedding; their loving relationship. Stories of local quarrels between neighbors, in-laws, and sweethearts. When associating with people of Dingle, the island people's sense of shame at their scanty knowledge of English. Arrival of an Irishman born in Mexico; his tale of how his parents emigrated yet still kept up the Gaelic language and customs. Correctly predicting her father's death when, at 98, he forgot one of his stories. The 1916 Easter Rebellion; invasion of the island by Black and Tans. Visiting Dunquin in an unsuccessful attempt to get her widow's pension. Taking her first ride in a motorcar. Meditating on death and on her trust in God. Praising her island home.

One of the great female Irish storytellers (to one folklore collector she dictated 375 tales and 44 songs), Sayers originally dictated these episodic reflections to her son Michael. The rather literal translation from the Gaelic captures the poetry of her speech. Most of the book's biographical information is to be found in the introduction, which includes her responses to the deaths of her father and her son.

822 SCANNELL, Dorothy. 1911–s.l.1979. *Mother Knew Best.* New York: Macmillan, 1974. 182 pp. NUC 1973–1977 102:429.

Born in London. Father: Walter Chegwidden, plumber. Mother: Leah Mitchard. 4 sisters; 5 brothers. Married 1933 Charles Scannell, insurance agent, grocer. 1 son; 1 daughter. Businesswoman; shopkeeper; insurance agent; clerk; secretary; teacher (Sunday school). Working class.

Reminiscences of growing up in a large family in London's East End, covering author's childhood to her marriage at age 22. Father's origins in Cornwall; his being a wonderful craftsman. Mother's quick-mindedness. Parents' unspoken discontent with their lot in life. Recalling East End as a lovely place to live. Outbreak of WWI: her father and brothers' joining military. Moving to Grove Villas. Memories of school activities and schoolmates. Enjoying writing; winning composition contest; being offered scholarship to coeducational school but mother's forbidding her to go, saying it was improper for girls. Joining Girl Guides. Her father's being a "red-hot socialist" who made her aware of inequities limiting the working class. Commenting on unusualness of mother's having raised 10 children; commonness of miscarriages and infant mortalities in other families. Describing how joining the public library opened up her mind. The parish church's being the center of all the family's social activities. Teaching Sunday school to kindergarten class. Buying a hat for a "stylish garden party"; enjoying having an occasion to shop with the gentry. Noting social problems of living through the General Strike, 1926; listening to her father rant; acknowledging that the working class's grievances were widespread. Tackling a series of short-lived office jobs. Accepting ride on a motorbike; her mother's displeasure at author's unladylike display; her mother's social attitudes being generally conservative. Enjoying dating; looking for "Mr. Right." Working for London Orphans' School. Meeting her future husband; describing his character and various occupations. Finding work in office of a large food firm. Making preparations for wedding; being amused by her mother's evasive attitude toward sex. Taking honeymoon trip to Isle of Wight; finding the first three weeks of marriage a nightmare; seeing unpleasant aspects of her new husband's character.

In this autobiography the author resurrects her loving and large family which, although working class, raised her to have genteel pretentions. Perhaps because Scannell was the delicate child in the family, her mother looms as the most influential and loving figure in her life, who both protected her and limited her ambitions with a generous poultice of gender stereotype and feminine self-doubt. Scannell is sometimes quite funny and vivid in her accounts of her family but seems—as her title indicates—to have accepted her affectionate mother's ideas despite their limiting effect. In **823** *Dolly's War* (1975), Scannell touches upon a wide range of emotions in her stories of daily life on the English homefront during WWII. She continues her story in **824** *Dolly's Mixture* (1977), covering 1953–71, in which she narrates a series of amusing vignettes on her assorted experiences as a grocer and relates vivid anecdotes about friends and neighbors.

825 SCHARLIEB, Mary Ann (née Bird; C.B.E.). 1844–1930. *Reminiscences*. Williams & Norgate, 1924. 239 pp.; front. port.; prayer; intro. NUC pre56 524:199.

Born in London. Father: William Chandler Bird, merchant. Mother not named. 3 half-sisters; 1 half-brother. Married 1865, William Scharlieb, barrister, civil servant abroad, d.1890. Widow. 2 sons; 1 daughter. Wrote *A Woman's Words to Women* (1890), *The Care of the Expectant Mother* (1917), others. Physician; academic; women's issues author; health issues writer; feminist; WWI volunteer; foreign resident (India). Upper middle class.

Inception and growth of the medical career of a pioneer female surgeon and medical academic, c.1850–1920s. As a child, being cared for by her grandmother. Attending boarding schools in Manchester and London. At age 21, traveling to India with her civil servant husband; recording her first impressions of Madras; helping husband produce two law journals there. Upon observing the lack of health care for Indian women, becoming interested in studying medicine; studying midwifery. Working under doctor's auspices at lying-in hospital in Madras. Meeting resistance from male doctors during her course at Women's Hospital. Describing the customary life of medical students. Receiving title of Licentiate of Medicine. Returning to England for further medical studies. Meeting Florence Nightingale; galvanizing her interest in Eastern women and author's own work. Studying in Royal Free Hospital in England; earning Bachelor of Surgery degree. Interning at lying-in hospital in Vienna. Attending Queen Victoria at Windsor; expressing her favorable views of queen. Returning to her work in Madras hospital; lecturing at medical college to women students. Returning to England for her health. Lecturing on medical jurisprudence at School of Medicine for Women. Becoming increasingly interested in mental health. Taking a Harley Street house for her practice. Raising funds to build New Hospital for Women. Being appointed school lecturer and clinical assistant to Mrs. Garrett Anderson, physician, at New Hospital. Being made president of University of London Women Graduates' Association. Earning M.D., the first one granted to a woman in London. Her husband's short illness and death. Being appointed gynecologist to Royal Free Hospital, 1902. Earning Master of Surgery degree. WWI: chairing Midwifery Committee for Council of War Relief for Professional Classes. Discussing food rationing; problems faced by women and children in England; women's running hospital during WWI. Her interest in forming Women's Medical Service in India. Writing articles on mental illness. Receiving the C.B.E. Serving as president of Women's Section of Royal Institute of Public Health. Serving on Commission on National Birth-Rate; describing its findings on abortion and birth control. Her views on the usefulness of women doctors in India: noting men's resistance but Indian women's preference for female physicians. Discussing changes for women doctors brought about by WWI. Affirming her strong religious convictions.

Stating that her medical career was inspired by the lack of health care available to women in India, Scharlieb describes in detail her unconventional and ambitious professional life. Her account contains a wealth of historical information about the introduction of medical education for women into Great Britain, using the author's own training experiences as a paradigm for that process. Despite her distinguished achievements Scharlieb is also, plainly, a product of her imperialistic culture, and although her strong humanitarian impulses suffuse the text, they are juxtaposed with her tendency to be dismissive toward Indian customs and religions. Ironically, the anecdotes she relates about her male Indian and subsequent European patients show that they shared the prevailing distrust of women physicians and sometimes treated her with less respect than they would give her male counterparts.

826 SCHIMMELPENNICK, Mary Anne (née Galton). 1778–1856. *The Life of Mary Anne SchimmelPennick*. Ed. by Christiana C. Hankin. Longman, Brown, Green, Longmans & Roberts, 1858. 2 vols. Vol. 1: 345 pp.; front. port. Vol. 2: 275 pp. NUC pre56 526:74.

Born in Birmingham, West Midlands. Father: Samuel Galton, businessman, amateur naturalist, cousin to the Darwins. Mother: Lucy Barclay. Several siblings. Married 1806, Lambert SchimmelPennick, of Dutch descent. Wrote *The Principles of Beauty, Essays on the Temperaments, Abolition*. Essayist; religious/spiritual writer; pamphleteer; poet; abolitionist; political writer; physically handicapped woman. Upper class.

Meditative, Christian-oriented perspective on a child's coming to maturity amid the political and spiritual upheaval of late 18th-century history, 1778–92. Her father's telling stories from the *Iliad* and the *Odyssey;* her mother's encouraging her intellectual curiosity, having spiritual "talkings" with her on Sundays. Parents' giving her devotional literature and classics to read; their forbidding fairy tales. Her Quaker parents' teaching her their principles: nonviolence, compassion, dislike of ostentation and frivolity, antagonism to slavery. Family's moving to Staffordshire. Author's increasing love for animals. Her father's practicing botany and astronomy. Visiting grandfather's mill and absorbing his knowledge of birds and natural history. When still young, being left in household run by governess while ill mother was absent; living in Bath during mother's convalescence; worrying over mother's ongoing decline. Meeting the noted Dr. Joseph Priestley. Being sent to stay with aunt, Lady Watson; condemning the Fielding and Smollett she read there as frivolous and devoid of Christian feeling. Family's moving to Seagrove, then to Barr. Studying with tutor; resuming her Sunday "talkings" with mother. Mother's being attended by Dr. Erasmus Darwin; author's hearing his medical views; being repelled by his agnosticism and excessive eating. Becoming increasingly religious; seeking out the "spark of the divine" in everyone; attending Friends meetings. Her growing interest in antislavery cause; slave trade as a popular topic of discussion, c.1788. Giving anecdotes of several Quaker friends and relatives. Author's suffering spinal problems; enduring treatment by many doctors; being unable to play with other children because confined to a spinal brace. Yearning to please her father; reading Voltaire, Moliere, and Swift to that end. At age 12, pitying French royal family as French Revolution advanced; wishing she were a man so she might fight against the revolutionaries. Discussing early Revolution's challenge to political and class structures; pondering its ramifications for the rest of Europe. With the Revolution, her mother's decline and her own chronic pain, beginning to doubt the existence of God; struggling to reconcile God's holiness and mercy with her distressing experience. On family trip to Liverpool, noticing black slaves in homes of West Indian merchants. Being presented with a tropical coconut; giving it away to a slave to relieve his homesickness. Progressing in her academic studies. Perceiving true art as reflecting divine essence as well as material beauty; temporal things being transitory in nature.

SchimmelPennick's careful exploration of her emotional, spiritual, and intellectual growth is both informative and entertaining as she resurrects the 1780s. While her account invites readers to reevaluate the attitudes of that era toward education, government, and human and animal rights, in reaching back sixty years to highlight a time of violent political shifts, SchimmelPennick's work also mirrors the inner doubts and upheavals that took the author's gentle soul from Quakerism to agnosticism and back. Such questioning would later lead her to the Methodist and ultimately to the Moravian Church. Her descriptions illuminate many otherwise obscure features of the time, particularly the multiple roles of women.

827 SCOTT, Ellen (J. P.). c.1870–d.a.1925. "A Felt Hat Worker," pp. 81–101 in *Life as We Have Known It by Cooperative Working Women*. Ed. by Margaret Llewelyn Davies. New York: W. W. Norton & Co., 1975. 141 pp.; ed.'s note; intro. letter by Virginia Woolf. BLC to 1975 78:2. (1st pub. Hogarth Press, 1931.)

Born in Stockport, Greater Manchester. Father not named, linen draper. Mother not named. Married Mr. Scott. Milliner; political activist; social reformer; organizer (labor); trade unionist; magistrate; suffragist; feminist; pacifist. Working class.

Thoughtful account of journey from factory worker to magistrate, emphasizing author's work in labor and women's organizations, spanning 1870s–c.1925. Her parents' being politically involved; their following socialist ideas of Charles Bradlaugh, Annie Besant, John Ruskin, and William Morris. Family's opening a draper's shop, author's age 7; author's having to collect customers' past-due bills. Mother's being both a staunch Congregationalist and a progressive thinker; uncle's enthusing over social Darwinism. At age 10, becoming fascinated with designing beautiful cities to replace sordid factory towns. Going to work in a hat shop, age 12. At age 14, working in a different hat shop, an unheated, unventilated warehouse; realizing that her coworkers were prostitutes; teaching them history and geography. Living with her uncle, who brought back new books and periodicals from sales trips to America, c.1888. Working in several more hat shops; enduring fourteen-hour workdays and damp workrooms. Joining the Stockport Clarion Fellowship and Ruskin Hall Settlement. Meeting her future husband; their marrying with £20 to their names. Remaining childless; preferring not to have a child that would have to do factory work. Joining and campaigning for Felt Hatters' Trade Union; fighting to bring other women hat trimmers into the union; staging strikes. In 1907, being made secretary of Stockport's new Women's Cooperative Guild; over next fifteen years, working for its successful expansion. Being first woman delegate to Co-operative Wholesale Society; standing for its Management Committee; receiving threatening letters from those who thought a woman should not seek office. Quitting hatmaking to superintend Derbyshire center for feeding children, 1911–14. Working as a sickness visitor for County of Derbyshire, 1915–21. Valuing her position as a local magistrate, c.1925. Reflecting on her national executive work for the Labour Church; feeling that although church failed, its views successfully permeated other movements, e.g. women's suffrage and internationalism. Confidently assessing brighter future for working women worldwide through the guild's expanding influence.

From an early age, Scott was committed to politics and social reform. She calmly states that her family might have been comfortable had her father been willing to oblige his employers by turning Conservative and

Anglican Church. Although his principles may have impeded family finances, they informed his daughter's mind; Scott's text suggests she received a wide-reaching education in her family's active and free-thinking intellectual environment, an education that stood her in good stead in her later political activities.

828 SCOTT, Ina. pre1900–?. "The Land," pp. 46–66 in *Women War Workers: Accounts Contributed by Representative Workers of the Work Done by Women in the More Important Branches of the War*. Ed. by Gilbert Stone. George Harrap, 1917. 320 pp.; foreword by Lady Jellicoe; ed.'s preface. NUC pre56 571:165.

Probably born in England. WWI volunteer; lady gardener; feminist. Rural middle class.

Recollections and activities of WWI market gardener. Growing vegetables for her London household. Volunteering to do market gardening for war effort, 1915. Her wages; fellow workers. Working conditions on an estate; kinds of tools used for gardening; planting potatoes; camaraderie with neighboring workers. Food shortages. Observing need for women to enter all phases of work force. Attitudes of local men and women toward "lady gardeners." Having to give up potato planting before crop was ready; satisfaction gained from partially completed work.

Emphasizing the idea that women can undertake work usually performed by men and are capable of working hard, Scott conveys her belief that the most important element in volunteer work is the contribution one makes to the overall war effort, whether or not one likes the tasks to be performed.

829 SCOTT, Mary (née Clarke). 1888–s.l.1966. *Days That Have Been*. Auckland: Blackwood & Janet Paul, 1966. 207 pp.; foreword; illus. BLC to 1975 296:234.

Born in Waitmate North, New Zealand. Father: Marsden Clarke, farmer, landowner. Mother: née Craig. 1 brother; 1 sister. Married 1914 Walter Scott, d.1960. Widow. 3 daughters; 1 son. Wrote novels *It's Perfectly Easy*, *Dinner Doesn't Matter*, *The White Elephant*, others. Novelist; journalist; librarian; postal worker; farmer; teacher. Middle class.

Adult adventures amid the hardships of farming on New Zealand's west coast, with a brief discussion of author's life before marriage, covering 1890s–1960. After father's death, mother's moving family to Napier when author was very young. Mother's supporting family by teaching piano. Author's boarding school and grammar school experiences; her fondness for literature. Graduating from Auckland University College; receiving a scholarship to work toward master's degree in English and French. After completing degree, teaching high school briefly in Christchurch and Auckland; quitting teaching to care for her invalid mother. Meeting and marrying Walter Scott. With husband, acquiring farm in the backblocks on the west coast of New Zealand's north island, near her sister's family. Bearing four children there; enduring primitive conditions for twelve years; delivering mail with her sister. Moving closer to small town and school. Receiving a small inheritance, 1930; being financially able to send her two eldest children to boarding school. Publishing a newspaper article, c.1930, marking the beginning of her career as a writer. Noting that it was considered unladylike for a woman to earn money by writing for a newspaper; independent-minded author's ignoring community opinion. Working as a librarian. Writing numerous articles for various newspapers. Sister's death, 1954. Her career as a novelist: writing a novel a year; her desire to write "significant" works; her acceptance of her tendency to facile production of amusing stories about life and the people in the backblocks. Husband's death, 1960.

Scott's humorous writing style attracted a very loyal following of readers, and this success led her to give up her dreams of being a "serious" writer. She states that she wrote this autobiography at the urging of her publisher; the book includes many humorous anecdotes of farm life and rural New Zealand people.

830 SEACOLE, Mary (née Grant). 1805–1881. *Wonderful Adventures of Mrs. Seacole in Many Lands*. New York and Oxford: Oxford University Press, 1988. The Schomburg Library of Nineteenth Century Black Women Writers, General Editor, Henry Louis Gates, Jr. 199 pp.; front.; intro. by William L. Andrews; foreword by Henry Louis Gates, Jr.; "A Note from the Schomburg Center," by Howard Dodson; preface by W. H. Russell, Esq., *Times* correspondent in the Crimea. BLC to 1975 296:470. (1st pub. Blackwood, 1857.)

Born in Kingston, Jamaica. Father not named, soldier, of Scottish ancestry. Mother not named, boarding house proprietor, Creole. 1 brother. Married 1836 Edwin Horatio Seacole, d. soon after marriage. Widow. Knew Florence Nightingale. Nurse (Crimean War); hotel administrator; shopkeeper; miner. Lower middle class.

Journeys and travails of a self-taught nurse, accompanied by her experiences with racial issues and prejudice, covering c.1805–57. Her early yearning for medical knowledge; being taken in by an old woman doctor; practicing medicine on her doll, dogs, cats, and herself. Visiting England; encountering racism even though her skin was "only a little brown." Back in Kingston, marrying; husband's death soon after the wedding; her grief. Death of her mother, followed by loss of their house in great Kingston fire, 1843. Resisting other suitors; preserving her self-reliance. Commencing her nursing career by caring for British soldiers encamped in Jamaica. Visiting her brother in Panama; cholera's erupting during her stay; nursing cholera victims in Cruces, then opening a hotel there catering to Americans. Being glad to see blacks in Panama fight Americans; expressing her sentiments against American slavery. Moving briefly back to Kingston; returning to Panama. Opening a store in Colon. Mining gold at Escribanos. Feeling unneeded; wanting to witness and serve firsthand in any war. Traveling to England; seeking but failing to obtain nursing position in Crimea during war; traveling to Turkey to meet with Florence Nightingale; winning her consent to nursing assignment. Giving dramatic details of battles during Crimean War. Managing a store at Balaclava and operating the British Hotel in the Crimea, interspersed with periods of nursing, until 1855. Returning to England.

Focused primarily on Seacole's experiences during the Crimean War, this account takes its tenor from the author's independent-minded determination to rely on no one but herself, even in the Panamanian jungle. Racism, although peripheral to her saga, keeps cropping up; outside Britain, Seacole reports, she was taken on her own merits, but when in Britain she confronted an atmosphere of exclusion. In addition to vividly depicting the blood-and-battle arena of the Crimean War and documenting Seacole's remarkable nursing career, this story illuminates the geographic boundaries that governed the effects of Victorian prejudices.

831 SELDON, Marjorie (née Audrey Marjorie Willett). 1919–?. *Poppies and Roses: A Story of Courage*. Sevenoaks, Kent: Economic and Literary Books, 1985. 199 pp.; family tree chart; author's note; foreword by Richard Cobb; afterword by Jonathan Smith; illus. NUC 1983–87 microfiche #0311.

Born at Matfield, Kent. Father: Wilfred Leslie Willett, nature writer, journalist, churchwarden, communist. Mother: Eileen Estelle Josephine Stenhouse. 1 brother; 1 sister. Married 1940 Rex Perrott; separated 1942, d. in WWII. Married 1948 Arthur Seldon, academic economist. 3 children. Publisher's assistant; academic's spouse. Upper middle class.

Author's loving tribute to her father, with glances at her own education, from before her birth to her father's death, 1913–61. Parents' secret courtship and marriage; their moving to "The Rosery" in Kent; father's paralysis from WWI wounds. Births of the children. Nanny's lending a stabilizing influence to family. Father's being intensely Christian and patriotic; his thwarted dream of a medical career; his engaging in scientific study of birds; his serving also as churchwarden to local vicar. Brother's attending boarding school; father's educating Marjorie at home. Father's anticommunist opinions being undermined by family money crisis and 1926 General Strike. At age 7, author's beginning school in Tunbridge Wells; being switched by grandmother to St. Clair's, a private school more suited to a gentleman's daughter; resulting financial hardship's making parents dismiss nanny, devastating author. At age 9, becoming her father's constant companion. Father's beginning to write about birds, becoming a vegetarian, trying to publish a novel; his supervising author's reading. Father's becoming disillusioned over Church's failure either to help poor or oppose munitions makers, c.1930; his suffering depression, reading Lenin, converting to Leninism. Although still a churchwarden and Christian, father's preaching Leninism to vicar as the means to achieve peace. Father's joining the Communist Party; his organizing local branch of National Union of Agricultural Workers. Father's selling the *Daily Worker* in the streets of Tunbridge Wells and writing nature articles for it; author's pride in him, despite not sharing his political beliefs. Author's leaving school, age 18; reflecting on the lack of expectation that St. Clair girls would go to university. Her working for *Harper's Bazaar*. Visiting cousins in South Africa; having to return to England suddenly, 1939, with outbreak of WWII. Marrying; separating from husband two years later; his death in WWII. Marrying again, 1948. Having two children. In later years, sensing her father's unspoken disillusionment with communism. Deaths of both her parents, 1961.

Seldon's beloved father gained some prominence in his later life; in 1942 his chief work, the twelve-volume *British Birds,* commenced publication, and he continued with his political journalism as well. In her memoir, Seldon draws upon two other books in telling the story of her parents: *Wilfred and Eileen,* a 1976 novel by Jonathan Smith which reconstructs her parents' early life, and Richard Cobb's *Still Life,* which evokes the Tunbridge Wells of the 1920s and 1930s. Information about Seldon's own youth is interwoven into the text; as to her later life, she only briefly refers to her two marriages in the book's last pages.

832 SELLAR, Eleanor Mary (née Dennistoun). 1829–d.a.1890. *Recollections and Impressions*. Blackwood & Sons, 1907. 335 pp.; note; illus. BLC to 1975 297:451.

Born in Normandy, France; raised in Germiston, Scotland. Father: Alexander Dennistoun, industrialist, banker, M.P. Mother: Eleanor Jane Thomson. 5 brothers; 2 sisters. Married 1852 William Sellar, academic, writer, d.1890. Widow. 4 sons; 5 daughters. Society woman; traveler (Europe). Upper class.

Warm personal and travel memories, emphasizing positive aspects of family life, spanning author's childhood to 1890. Deaths of four siblings in close succession; mother's grief and her untimely death; author's shock and grief. Her subsequently quiet childhood: being encouraged to amuse herself; studying with a governess; taking dancing lessons. Her love of literature. Her great affection and admiration for her father. Meeting her future husband. Marriage. Living in St. Andrews, then in Edinburgh. Suffering chronic headaches. Traveling extensively in

Europe with husband and children; living abroad for several months at a time. Commenting on the Indian Mutiny of 1857; praising the heroism of the English soldiers. Friendships with Alfred, Lord Tennyson, Sir Alexander Grant, Dr. John Brown, Robert Louis Stevenson. George Eliot's marriage to author's cousin. Her first-born son's scarlet fever; his death, 1872; her profound anguish. Nursing her dying mother-in-law. Husband's occasional maladies; their spending more time in Europe for his health; his death.

Quoting many conversations and vividly recreating scenes from her life, Sellar laments the passing of the gentler aspects of her childhood. Her overall attitude, however, is positive; indeed, she seems to have been content with her roles as devoted daughter, wife, and mother. She states that she wrote this chronological narrative to provide her grandchildren with information about her life and a bygone era.

833 SENNETT, Maud Arncliffe (née Mary Kingsley). 1861–1936. *The Child*. C. W. Daniel, c.1936. 336 pp.; front.; foreword by H. Arncliffe Sennett (author's husband); intro.; illus.; obit. BLC to 1975 298:176.

Born in England. Father not named, Italian. Mother not named, English or Welsh. 1 sister. Married 1906 H. Arncliffe Sennett. Wrote political pamphlets, *The State and the Woman, Make Way for the Prime Minister*. Suffragist, militant; political activist; suffrage leader; pamphleteer; antivivisectionist; animal welfare activist; organizer (political); prison inmate; feminist activist; actress (stage); businesswoman. Middle class.

Record of the political activism and opinions of an actress, militant suffragist, and antivivisectionist, covering 1906–18. Commencing political work as a suffrage activist after marrying and giving up her prior career as a well-known Shakespearean actress. In 1911, owning a London manufacturing business, run by her mother; resenting her male employees' having the vote while she did not. Describing her suffrage protests: breaking a newspaper window, going to prison; being imprisoned four times in her life; male political prisoners' being treated as gentlemen, while women protesters were treated as common criminals. Expressing solidarity with other women in prison, the streetwalkers. Writing an article, 1917, "Ruined! By Order of the Court," condemning law permitting widows to be evicted from their homes. Looking backward to origins of her suffrage involvement, 1906: reading letter in *Times* by Millicent Garrett Fawcett. From 1907, organizing marches; working in the Actresses' Franchise League. Organizing a suffrage march from Edinburgh to London. Bringing a suffrage deputation from the town councils of Glasgow and Edinburgh to Prime Minister Asquith; citing Asquith's "betrayal" of the Reform Bill, 1913. Being allies with Emily Davidson and Mrs. Cavendish-Bentinck. Refusing to endorse WWI cause, 1914. Organizing and presiding over the Northern Men's

Federation for Women's Suffrage. Defying her husband's wishes by working for suffrage; declaring that despite mutual love, "a married woman under coverture can never be a free agent to develop mentally." Sketching characters of Lloyd George, Lord Balfour of Burleigh, and other members of House of Lords Committee considering Electoral Reform Bill, and recording each one's stance on female suffrage. Reflecting on the aftermath of women's enfranchisement, the conflict and split between suffragists over militant vs. constitutional tactics; resulting formation of Women's Freedom League. Lamenting her poor education from attending inferior schools and leaving school at age 12. Founding Midhurst-Haslemere Anti-Vivisection Society, affiliated with the Animal Defence and Anti-Vivisection Society, of which she was vice president. Declaring her considered opinions on motherhood, women, and the state.

In the introduction to this associatively organized book Sennett sharply criticizes those Edwardian women's autobiographies which she considers egotistical, and in her own memoir she avoids recounting family history or even the story of her acting career. She explains that she entitled this autobiography *The Child* because she had no children of her body; this book is a child of her spirit. She treats her suffrage activity in considerably greater detail than her antivivisection activity. Edited and published posthumously, the book is only a fragment of a projected longer work on 6,000 years of women's oppression.

834 SEVERN, Merlyn. c.1900–?. *Double Exposure: A Photographer's Recollections*. Faber & Faber, 1956. 219 pp.; foreword by Tom Hopkinson; illus.; postscript. BLC to 1975 299:10.

Born in England. Parents, siblings not named. Single. Published photo-essays *Ballet in Action, Sadler's Wells Ballet at Covent Garden, Congo Pilgrim.* Knew Margot Fonteyn. Photographer; artist (sculptor); journalist; foreign resident (Africa); WWII enlistee. Middle class.

Author's career as a professional photographer, stressing her intuitive approach to her subjects, covering 1935–52. Lacking any formal training in sculpture or photography. Being an unsuccessful sculptor in Cheltenham, 1935; beginning her photography career by photographing her sculpture. Reading books on photography; developing her own prints. Her work's being published in the Manchester *Guardian, Amateur Photographer,* and *Home Photographer*. Discussing states of mind necessary for good photography: self-forgetfulness, intuition. Moving to London in response to an inner voice, 1936. Desperately searching for work; being inspired to photograph ballet dancers in action; this work's becoming part of her book, *Ballet in Action*. Mounting her own photo exhibition. Being offered columns in photography magazines. Describing principles of shooting and developing. Publishing second book of ballet photos. Being frustrated in her plans to visit Java by outbreak of WWII, 1939; volunteering as photographer for the WAAF; discovering that the military term "photographer" really meant radar technician. Being interned on Isle of Guernsey during German occupation; working for Guernsey dairy farmer. At war's end, 1945, joining staff of the *Picture Post;* contrasting socialist opinions of colleagues with her Tory background; enjoying her assignments. Publishing another photographic ballet study, inspired by dancer Margot Fonteyn. Leaving *Picture Post* staff, 1950. Traveling to Africa to photograph tribes in the Belgian Congo. Reading Olive Schreiner's *Story of an African Farm* as background. In Cape Town, discovering the magazine she worked for wanted only whites in its photos; commenting on status of South African "coloureds," 1955, and on African race relations. Photographing African big game and tribal dancers; selling these photos to the *Picture Post.* Refusing to take certain assignments from *Picture Post* and other periodicals for fear of South African government's disapproval. Opting to move to Rhodesia; joining staff of *Central African News Review,* 1950. Publishing written account of her tour of Rwanda in *Congo Pilgrim.* Returning to England, 1952.

Although Severn's account charts the progress and range of her photographic career, she also frequently delves into technical elements of photography and provides analyses of the relative aesthetic merits of photos she has taken. Her meditations on the photographer's mindset, coupled with her remarks on heeding an "inner voice" in following her vocation, illustrate her reliance on intuition as well as on technical skill, while her observations on South African apartheid during the 1950s augment the documentary value of her camera work.

835 SEWELL, Elizabeth Missing. 1815–1906. *The Autobiography of Elizabeth M. Sewell.* Ed. by Eleanor L. Sewell (author's niece). Longmans, Green & Co., 1907. 253 pp.; biblio.; front. port.; preface by ed.; intro. by A. Llewelyn Roberts; letters; journal extracts; index. NUC pre56 540:102.

Born at Newport, Isle of Wight. Father: Thomas Sewell, solicitor and land agent. Mother: Jane Edwardes. 6 brothers; 4 sisters. Single. Wrote *Experience of Life* (1853), *Katherine Ashton* (1854), *Principles of Education* (1865), others. Novelist; educator; religious/spiritual writer; historian; school founder. Middle class.

Growth and working career of a novelist and women's educator, among the mid-Victorian influences of strong paternalism and the Oxford movement's religious upheaval, c.1820–1900. Her mother's kind nature, family history, and literary interests; her entertaining people of all ranks; mother's belief that girls should be educated; her desire to win education for her husband's tenant farmers. Author's father's coldness; her fearing him. Studying history, geography, and the Bible; suffering from harsh discipline and living conditions at her boarding school. With her bad temper and desire to be the center of attention, feeling herself the family black sheep. Being sent next to a school at Bath with inferior teaching. Forming a book club among fellow students. Being confirmed despite entertaining skepticism on religious doctrine. Author and sister Ellen's collaborating to teach their younger sisters. Teaching herself Spanish; reading Scott and Byron. Discussing the Reform Bill, 1832. Her brother William's being ordained. Meeting Cardinal Newman at a dinner party; being impressed by his reverence despite her bias against Catholicism. Anonymously publishing *Studies on the Lord's Prayer*. Family's having economic hard times; father's illness and death. Family's moving to Bonchurch. Writing her first novel, *Amy Herbert*. Being distressed over the Oxford Movement and the many people it was luring into Catholicism. With death of her sister-in-law Lucy, assuming responsibility for Lucy's children. Being shy about discussing her writing; beginning to keep a journal. Writing *Laneton Parsonage,* 1846. Caring for her mother through failing health and death. Extracts from her 1848 journal on social doings, church concerns, and memories of Algernon Swinburne. Writing *The Experience of Life,* 1853, her positive treatment of the single life for a woman; its becoming her most popular book. With sister Ellen, starting a successful girls' school in their Bonchurch home. Journal entries from 1845–49 indicating her antagonism to Roman Catholicism. Writing *Katherine Ashton,* 1854. *Cleve Hall*'s representing her first attempt to write a mainstream novel. Journal extracts, 1850–60, on reading Ruskin and hearing Jenny Lind perform. Praising Charlotte Brontë's novel, *Jane Eyre*. Giving history of Radley College, Oxford, founded by her brother William. 1864–85 journal extracts commenting on her travel experiences, religion, and 70th birthday. Writing *The Notebook of an Elderly Lady;* its discussion of new educational system for girls and her experiences with St. Boniface School. Outbreak of the Franco-German War. Giving up the directorship of her school.

Sewell's aversive awareness of the Oxford movement owes much to her family's ties to Oxford University, as two of her elder brothers were Oxford professors and Anglican clerics. The *Feminist Companion to Literature in English* indicates that in Sewell's family female inferiority was implicitly assumed, and that her own education, while not neglected, was of secondary importance in the "male-dominated household." In her account the author forbears to give some of the more salient details of the family paternalism toward her, such as her brother William's taking it upon himself to "edit" her first four novels. Not surprisingly, her later fiction frequently deals with issues both of paternalism and women's right to be educated, something she alludes to here in her discussion of writing *The Experience of Life;* in that novel, the protagonist (like the author) succeeds as the director of her own school.

836 SHANNON, Kitty. c.1889–?. *For My Children.* Hutchinson, 1933. 288 pp.; front.; illus.; index. NUC pre56 541:587.

Born in England. Father: Sir James Jebusa Shannon, artist, Irish. Mother not named. Married 1912 "Tina," Australian, undergraduate at Cambridge. 1 daughter; 1 son. Artist (painter); artist's daughter; foreign resident (France, Holland, Australia). Upper class.

The connected lives of an artist and her artist father, at the center of the London art world, covering author's childhood to 1929. Father's life story. Her earliest memory being of a tiny house in Chelsea. Family's moving to a larger house in Kensington. Mother's sister as author's primary caretaker. Father's art studio; childhood memories of posing for him; his character; his being her greatest inspiration. Accompanying parents to Holland to visit an art exhibition. Experiencing Dutch culture; meeting other artists. Discussing father's Impressionist art, his having designed and built their Kensington house. Having the artist Frederick Leighton as their neighbor. Parents' immersion in London's fashionable society life and artists' circles. Commenting that her own adult artwork shows pre-Raphaelite influence. Family's friendship with the artist Edward Ward. Author's knowing Philip Burne-Jones. Memories of celebratory Boer War parades, 1899. Father's reading aloud to her. Author's spending all her spare time drawing. Father's prosperity as an artist; his famous sitters: Sir Henry Irving, Ellen Terry, James Whistler, Oscar Wilde, others. Author's attending Westminster Art School. Family's visiting grandparents in America; attending lavish New York parties; father's painting the Rockefellers and the Mellons. Visiting Germany and Italy. Studying at King's College Art School. Meeting future husband while hiking in the Pyrenees. Marrying, 1912, and moving to Australia. After birth of son, returning to England; her distress at finding father ill and unable to walk. WWI: husband's being commissioned to 12th Wales unit; their moving frequently during the war. Author's holding English exhibition of her many historical illustrations, 1919. Father's receiving a knighthood for his service to the Royal Academy, 1922; his final illness and death, 1923. Birth of author's daughter. With onset of the worldwide economic Depression, 1929, husband's family money from Australia being cut off; their becoming members of the "new poor." Final elegaic remembrances of her father.

Shannon's book serves to commemorate not only her own life, but the life and career of her illustrious father, who served for many years as the president of the Royal Academy of Art. Her text is illustrated with her vivid, drawing-like watercolor portraits. As her title indicates, she wrote this memoir for the benefit of her children, whom she often addresses in an intimate tone. Her myriad anecdotes, particularly about artists and art circles on both sides of the Atlantic, mingle with her personal impressionistic memories to create a vivid and chronologically accurate picture of the late-19th- and early-20th-century artistic milieu.

837 SHEARS, Sarah. c.1910–?. *Tapioca for Tea: Memories of a Kentish Childhood*. Elek, 1971. 187 pp.; intro. by R. F. Delderfield. BLC to 1975 300:299.

Born in Kent. Father: Edward, sergeant major. Mother: née Prior. 2 brothers; 1 sister. Single. Domestic servant. Working class.

Author's emotional and physical problems and her difficult relationship with her mother during childhood, ages 5–14. Attending school, beginning at age 5. WWI's leaving only women and children in the village. Mother's character: hardy, courageous, frugal, rigidly self-disciplining; author's both fearing and adoring her mother. Mother's being determined that children respect their absent father. Author's feeling shame at wearing homemade clothing. Loving language and nature. Beginning to stutter out of fear of her harsh teacher; faking illness to avoid school; continuing to stutter throughout childhood. Being incensed that mother is lenient toward author's brothers but rigidly disciplines author. Children's pleading to join Methodist chapel; mother's relenting, but wondering what the Anglican vicar will say. Father's returning from India and the Middle East; author's adoration of him; his craving "fresh fields to conquer." Beginning of author's sleepwalking; father's departure for Baghdad after mother's refusal to bring family to join him; his dying abroad one year later. Author's taking his death hard, turning restless and rebellious. Family's taking in a lodger who acts as a surrogate father. Author's outgrowing her stuttering and sleepwalking, but suffering from painful, protruding stomach. Wondering, at age 13, why her breasts have not developed. Attending Girl Guides and Band of Hope meetings. Her anguish at learning the truth about Santa Claus. Hop-picking season's bringing gypsies and London Cockneys to village; village children's feeling superior to Cockneys. Leaving school, age 14, to work as vicar's domestic servant; other servants' considering her haughty for thinking herself better than them. Wishing she were a boy. Being hospitalized for her increasing stomach pains; believing her failure to attain puberty is tied to her stomach disorder. Undergoing abdominal surgery; being told by doctors and medical students that she has made medical history; appearance of her photograph in the Kent *Messenger*. Being sent to London for third operation; losing weight dramatically; being homesick for trees of her native Kent; being made happy by doctors' letting her sit in the hospital garden. Associating this small pleasure with hearing a Grieg concerto on her way to be x-rayed "a few days ago"; implying that her medical problems persist throughout her life.

This book illustrates, rather than analyzes, the conditions of Shears's life. The tone is rather ironic, indirectly revealing the adult narrator, yet the child's point-of-view predominates to the extent that Shears never reveals the exact nature of her stomach condition. Although rigidly disciplined by her mother, the author implies strong affection for her, even though her chosen title refers directly to one incident in which her mother forced her to eat cold leftover tapioca at teatime or go hungry.

838 SHEPHERD, Dolly. 1886–d.a.1982. *When the 'Chute Went Up...The Adventures of an Edwardian Lady Parachutist*. Written with Peter Hearn, in collaboration with Molly Sedgwick (author's daughter). Robert Hale, 1984. 171 pp.; illus.; preface. NUC 1983–87 microfiche #0315.

Born in Potters Bar, Hertfordshire. Father not named, police detective. Mother not named. 1 brother; 1 sister. Married c.1919, husband not named, London district valuer. Widow. 1 daughter. Parachutist; WWI military officer, waitress, charitable volunteer; WWII volunteer. Middle class.

Author's career as an amateur parachute jumper, 1903–12, with a summary of her later life as a military officer and volunteer welfare officer from WWI to 1974. Working as a waitress. Meeting French parachutist and balloonist Auguste Gaudron and American Wild West entertainer Samuel Franklin Cody, 1903. After working in Cody's sharpshooting display, being invited by Gaudron to parachute jump from a balloon. Outlining history of ballooning, aviation, and parachuting prior to 1903. Learning skills of parachuting from Gaudron; details of balloons' construction and operation. Character of her aunt, proprietor of ostrich feather business in Holborn; aunt's tacit disapproval of author's career; father's approval. Accidents and deaths among members of Gaudron's parachuting team. Her parachuting mishaps: free fall from 5,000 feet; failures of balloon cords; 15,000-foot ascent with balloon after chute failed to separate; injuries suffered during landings. Her daring, close-fitting knickerbocker suit. Being accorded celebrity treatment; mingling with crowds; meeting working-class people. Between jumps, working for her aunt in the ostrich feather trade. In 1908, rescuing a coworker in mid-air during a jump, resulting in the first recorded double descent on the same parachute; resulting injury to author; her long recuperation. Mother's substituting for author without her knowledge in a jump. Being accepted into the fraternity of pioneer aviators; foreseeing parachuting's future military application; realizing that the days of parachuting as spectacular entertainment are numbered. Performing WAAC service during WWI in France. Marrying a veteran. Doing volunteer welfare work in 1930s. During WWII, performing volunteer work as a shelter welfare officer. Husband's death. Summarizing history of parachuting since WWI. In 1974, being honored for her lifetime contributions to parachuting by an invitation to fly with RAF parachute team.

Shepherd's lively autobiography places her as a pioneer in aviation at a time when she, and everyone else, considered parachute jumping from balloons to be mere entertainment. The text and the accompanying photographs capture the charm of the Edwardian era. At age 96, Shepherd was persuaded by her daughter to record her adventures for posterity. Her daughter and Peter Hearn have included passages concerning the history of air flight and parachuting, which are valuable in placing Shepherd's achievements in context.

839 SHERIDAN, Clare Consuelo (née Frewen). 1885–1970. *Naked Truth (or Nuda Veritas)*. New York: Harper & Bros., 1928. 383 pp.; front. BLC to 1975 301:31. (1st pub. Thornton Butterworth, 1927.)

Born in London. Father: Morton Frewen, economist, Irish. Mother: Clare Jerome (Jennie Churchill's sister), American. 2 brothers. Married 1910 Wilfred Sheridan, stockbroker. Widow. 2 daughters; 1 son. Wrote *Russian Portraits* (1921), *A Turkish Kaleidoscope* (1926), *The Substitute Bride* (1931), *Offspring* (1936), many others. Artist (sculptor); journalist; travel writer; novelist; traveler (Europe, Middle East, Mexico, U.S.); communist sympathizer; religionist (Roman Catholic convert). Upper class.

Multifaceted career growth and extraordinary international experiences of a journalist, travel writer, and artist, covering author's childhood to 1927. Spending her early childhood in London and the Rhineland with family; being schooled by governesses. Family's moving to Ireland, father's birthplace. Spending summers with her aunt, Lady Randolph Churchill, who enabled author's social debut in London society. At age 18, believing herself a social failure. Beginning to write and to meet writers in England and Europe. Marriage, 1910. Reacting to her daughter's death, 1912, with a burgeoning interest in Catholicism. Outbreak of WWI: husband's death in war; deciding not to remarry but to tackle a sculpting career. Teaching herself sculpting; becoming known through exhibiting her work in New York and London; meeting famous artists and Bolsheviks. Traveling to Russia, 1920, with Russian Trade Delegation; sculpting busts of Lenin and Trotsky; publishing extracts of her travel diary in *London Times* and *New York Times*. On returning from Russia, being mobbed by reporters; being disowned by some family members for her pro-Soviet politics. Going on lecture tour of U.S.; halting the lecturing; taking up sculpting in New York. With son Richard, traveling to Mexico; meeting Mexican generals and living in the wilderness. Traveling to San Francisco and Hollywood; meeting celebrities in Hollywood; sculpting and camping with Charlie Chaplin. Struggling to support her family alone; becoming determined to write professionally. Becoming roving correspondent for New York *World* in postwar Europe: interviewing Irish revolutionaries; attending League of Nations; interviewing Eastern European dignitaries; traveling to Italy to interview

Mussolini. Frequently traveling to the U.S., Spain, and Germany; living in Berlin. Revisiting Moscow; becoming disillusioned with the Soviet Union's government. Writing her second novel in Constantinople. Traveling to Algeria; deciding to live there.

Writing at age 43, roughly the midpoint of her life, Sheridan shows herself traveling unescorted as a woman and journalist into dangerous and distant world regions. Pressed by constant emotional and financial setbacks, Sheridan confronted them by adopting new interests and more daring ways to support her family, including—shortly after *Naked Truth*'s publication—bounding back from the death of her only son by taking up a new artistic challenge, wood sculpture, which earned her lasting fame. Her fame as an artist, her eminence as a writer, and her predilection for espousing controversial political positions gave her wide journalistic access to the rich and powerful, yet Sheridan wastes little time or reverence on them in her memoir. Her other autobiographical works include *Mayfair to Moscow—Clare Sheridan's Diary* (1921), which focuses on her Russian travel and sculpting experiences and political assessments, 1920–21; *West and East* (1923), in which she offers further travel reminiscences and compares politics and society in Eastern and Western European nations; and **840** *Redskin Interlude* (1938), a thoughtful account of her sojourn among various American Indian tribes, principally the Blackfoot, accompanied by clear-eyed and sensitive commentary on historical and contemporary Indian affairs in the U.S. In *My Crowded Sanctuary* (1945) Sheridan describes how the horrors of WWII inspired her to renew her lifelong spiritual quest. In **841** *To the Four Winds* (1957), which covers her childhood to the end of WWII, she maintains a light tone as she records her associations with celebrated Victorians and Edwardians, but the tone becomes somber and introspective when Sheridan describes the spiritual journey that culminated in her conversion to Roman Catholicism.

842 SHERIDAN, Lisa. 1893–1966. *From Cabbages to Kings: The Autobiography of Lisa Sheridan*. Odhams Press Ltd., 1955. 190 pp.; front. port.; illus.; index. NUC pre56 543:261.

Born in Kew, Surrey. Father: Walter, writer, artist. Mother not named. 1 brother. Married c.1915 James Sheridan, bank clerk, photographer. 2 daughters. Photographer; traveler (Russia); foreign resident (France). Upper middle class.

Photographer's good-humored reminiscences, including details of her personal encounters with the royal family, spanning her childhood to the early 1950s. Unconventional father's taking family on many jaunts to Europe. Briefly adhering to father's socialism; experiencing patriotic feelings while observing the funeral procession of King Edward VII; converting to a firm belief in the sanctity of the royal family and the British class system. During a domestic upheaval between parents, being sent alone at age 10 to St. Petersburg, Russia, to live with her aunt; studying with a governess, then being sent back to England to attend school; returning to Russia between terms. Meeting her future husband at a dance class in Berlin, age 11. Meeting Tolstoi and finding him insensitive; seeing the czar. Hearing about Rasputin's influence on the Russian court; seeing him briefly. Becoming close friends with her future husband aboard a ship returning to England, 1914. Marriage. WWI: husband's military service; author's living in Paris; husband's receiving discharge due to serious war wounds; their returning to England. Birth of their daughter. Losing their income from family investments in Russia after the Bolshevik Revolution. Renting a cottage in Hampstead Garden suburb; husband's finding ill-paid work in a chemists' firm. Author and husband's renewed interest in photography. Birth of their second daughter. Moving to Broadstairs; husband's employment as a bank clerk. Author and husband's resolving to give up photography, but later setting up a darkroom in their basement. Author's winning newspaper "amateur snap" contest. Gaining commissions from Fleet Street newspapers; photographing food, women, and children. Becoming a full-time photographer; husband's resigning his bank job to help with the business. Moving to larger quarters in Welwyn Garden City, a "planned city" in Hertfordshire. Gaining good professional reputations; winning upper-class clients; being invited to photograph Princesses Elizabeth and Margaret, 1936. Describing the royal family with respect and affection. Upon the Duke of York's accession to the throne as King George VI, believing that their royal assignments were over; moving from photographing kings back to cabbages. WWII: photographing servicemen and their families. Photographing the royal family again, 1940; continuing to do so throughout the war. Being visited by eccentric and possibly criminal would-be clients. Working with children and other models. Creating an illustrated book about Princess Elizabeth. Death of George VI. Photographing new Queen Elizabeth and her children at Balmoral Castle, Scotland. Publishing *The Queen and Her Children* just before the 1953 coronation. Photographing the Duke and Duchess of Gloucester and their children, George Bernard Shaw, John Masefield, A. A. Milne, H. G. Wells, the Archbishop of Canterbury, C. Day Lewis.

Nearly half of this memoir is occupied by Sheridan's recollections of photographing the royal family, embellished with anecdotes about King George VI, Queen Elizabeth II, and their relatives—revelations made more interesting in light of the author's self-proclaimed refusal to violate royal privacy by telling reporters anything about the sessions. Sheridan ultimately published thirteen photographic books about the royals. This autobiography describes many aspects of the author's career, along with technical information about how certain photographic effects were achieved. Most of the autobiographical facts are crowded into the first thirty-three pages. Some of the stories should perhaps be taken with a grain of salt, in light of Sheridan's claim to an acquaintanceship with photographer Julia Cameron—who died in 1879, fourteen years before the author's birth.

843 SHERWOOD, Mary Martha (née Butt). 1775–1851. *The Life and Times of Mrs. Sherwood (1775–1851) from the Diaries of Captain and Mrs. Sherwood*. Ed. by F. J. Harvey Darton. Wells Gardner, Darton & Co., 1910. 519 pp.; front. port.; intro.; illus.; apps.; index. NUC pre56 543:483. (1st pub. Darton & Co., 1854.)

Born in Stanford, Worcestershire. Father: Dr. George Butt, chaplain to George III, county rector. Mother: Martha Sherwood. 1 brother; 1 sister (children's author Lucy Lyttleton Cameron). Married 1803 her cousin Henry Sherwood, infantry captain. 3 daughters; 2 sons; 2 adopted children. Wrote over 350 novels, children's books, and works of pious instruction, including *Susan Gray* (1802), *The Indian Pilgrim* (1815), and *The Fairchild Family* (1847). Novelist; children's author; religious/spiritual writer; school founder; teacher; colonialist (India); military spouse; memsahib. Middle class.

Happy childhood and adult labors of a prolific 19th-century writer and teacher in India and England, c.1780–1854. Butt family history. Father's education and career. Author's being an imaginative child. Remembering innumerable acts of parental kindness, including mother's writing down six-year-old author's invented stories. Reflecting on differences between 1770s and 1850s in fashion and manners. Being a happy child despite plain diet and having to wear an "iron collar" to correct her spine, ages 6–13. Father's being made chaplain to George III; anecdotes of court ladies. Family's moving to Kidderminster, c.1788. At age 13, author's writing and staging plays for her parents; studying French with a tutor. Memories of pastimes, local scandal, and her cousin and future husband, Henry. Recalling father's taking her to Oxford and Reading. Attending St. Quint's ladies' school in Reading, ages 15–18; acting in school plays; father's predicting she would turn out to be a genius. French nobles' fleeing French Revolution and taking refuge in England, 1790–93; anecdotes of refugees in Reading. Writing *The Traditions*. Being horrified at thought of being a "literary lady." Father's dying, 1795; family's retiring from society; difficulties adjusting to life without father, 1796. Recalling English fears of a French invasion, 1798. Author's interest in Hannah More's writings to instruct the poor in religion, morals, and practicalities. Author's recognizing her family's privations as small compared to those of the poor. Publishing *Susan Gray,* 1802; calling book "the first narrative with refined sentiments ever prepared for the poor, with religion as its object." Marrying Henry Sherwood, 1803. His being stationed in remote Sunderland, Northumberland with regiment; her life "following the camp." Leaving her baby daughter with her mother and sailing to India to join husband, 1805; settling in Madras. Finding Indian "heathen superstitions" dark and corrupt; feeling mixed compassion and horror toward Indian women; expressing dual need to respect native peoples and bring them out of their superstitions. Working on a new book, *Lucy Clare*. Giving her impressions of India: native life and servants, clothing, entertainers, human depravity, European residents' social life. Birth of a son. Grieving over deaths of her son and daughter; experiencing deepening of her spiritual convictions, 1808. Teaching school in Madras. Adopting two European children. Becoming pregnant; doctor's telling her to leave India to raise child. India's being prey to rising hostility of Sikhs, c.1808. Explaining value of English rule in India. Noting Muslim influences, beliefs. Working on story "The Child's Manual," which became *The Fairchild Family*. Starting native school in Meerut, 1813. Returning to England, 1816; delighting in reunion with family. Mother's death; author's grief. Assuming duties as head of family. Editing Sarah Fielding's *The Governess*. Opening school in her home, 1819. Persisting in her prodigious literary work; giving up her pupils. Working at dictionary of Hebrew emblems used in prophetic books. Lamenting death of her husband. Explaining her highly personal religious views.

Sherwood's account concludes with a final note by her daughter Sophia Kelly (the autobiography's original editor) describing the author's continuing literary labors, her final illness and death, and her great love for her children. Sherwood's antagonism toward Indian religion and her enthusiasm for British colonial rule are not remarkable for the early 19th century, but her astonishingly prolific writing career would make her notable in any era. Her strength of character is indicated by her self-appointed teaching mission in India and her shouldering the burden of family support upon her return to England. Sherwood is best remembered today for her writings for young children and for her opus *The Fairchild Family,* begun in India but completed in England, 1818–47.

844 SHUTE, Nerina. 1908–s.l.1995. *We Mixed Our Drinks; The Story of a Generation*. Jarrolds, c.1945. 152 pp.; preface; front. port. BLC to 1975 301:422.

Born in Northumberland. Father: Cameron Shute. Mother: "Renie," novelist. 4 stepfathers. 1 brother; 1 stepbrother. Married c.1936, Howard Marshall, Fleet Street journalist; divorced. Married 1944 "John," radio commentator, public relations executive. Wrote novels *Another Man's Poison* (1931), *Malady of Love,* others; one play; many biographies of literary figures. Knew Aimée and Philip Stuart, Paul Robeson, others. Journalist; biographer; literary critic; novelist; advertising executive; playwright; secretary; charitable volunteer; foreign resident (U.S.). Upper class.

Bohemian life and early London working years of a rising journalist and novelist, including the 1930s growth of her political consciousness, covering 1928–43. Briefly working as typist at *Times Book Club,* 1928; leaving to take cram course in shorthand, typing, and bookkeeping. Living in a residence hotel. Moving in with playwright friends Aimée and Philip Stuart while job-hunting. From influence of reading Aldous Huxley and D. H. Lawrence, talking glibly of sexual liberation despite her own sexual inexperience. Yearning to be a bohemian, age 19. Taking job as reporter for *Film Weekly;* editor's encouraging her to write impertinent articles about celebrities. Perceiving people in the early film industry as being much like Victorians in seeking wealth as their moral duty; absorbing the idea that success must be ruthlessly pursued. Courtship with "Charles"; being attracted by love, not sex, but resolving not to marry or sleep with him. Losing her early faith in socialism partly due to Minister of Labour Margaret Bondfield's refusal to negotiate with unemployed workers. Quitting *Film Weekly* job and writing a novel; its 1931 publication. Being offered a column at Sunday *Graphic,* in which to view the world as a "modern girl"; wanting to write instead about modern girls' lack of religion. Having disappointing sex with Charles; nevertheless living with him without marriage in Liverpool. Writing another novel; its sentimentality winning high praise from the conservative newspaper magnate, Lord Beaverbrook. Being increasingly dismayed with the sexual preoccupation of the 1930s when political events were so ominous. In 1933, reading Vera Brittain's *Testament of Youth* about the earlier generation's upsurge of social commitment during WWI. Visiting Russia, 1934; noting lax sexual morals there; losing enthusiasm for Russia. Interviewing H. G. Wells, 1935. At age 28, marrying a Fleet Street journalist who wanted her to give up her career. Writing publicity for Max Factor cosmetics. Having her play produced at Kew Theatre, 1937. Separating from husband, 1938. With outbreak of WWII, 1939, driving a London ambulance. Working on hospital staff of a lunatic asylum; despite low wages, finding the job rewarding. Describing the blitzkrieg bombing of London. Starting a new love affair. Wartime's being the happiest time of her life; war's teaching her to believe in God. Affirming her sense of renewed political idealism, 1943; rejecting her personal prewar decadence.

Finished when Shute was only 34, this account documents the turning point she had reached in her social and political thinking during WWII. She later published a historical novel about Fanny Burney and critical biographies of Percy Bysshe Shelley and Dante Gabriel Rossetti, as well as a biography of her mother. Forty years after *We Mixed Our Drinks* she published another autobiographical work, *The Escapist Generations: My London Story* (1973), which covers her life from childhood to the late 1960s, including several adolescent years in California, her early career and first marriage, her troubled second marriage, her unsatisfied longing for a child, her novel writing, her secretarial jobs, her increasing appreciation for her mother, her attempts to reform her mother's alcoholic sixth husband, and her voluntary social service work with other alcoholics.

845 SIBBALD, Susan (née Mein). 1783–1866. *The Memoirs of Susan Sibbald, 1783–1812*. Ed. by Francis Pagett Hett (author's nephew). John Lane, the Bodley Head, 1926. 339 pp.; illus.; index. BLC to 1975 301:452.

Born in Fowey, Cornwall. Father: Dr. Thomas Mein, Royal Navy. Mother: Margaret Ellis. 2 brothers; 7 sisters. Married 1807 Lt. Col. William Sibbald. 9 children. Military spouse. Upper middle class.

Childhood and early married life of a woman born and married into military families, set against the backdrop of Britain's involvement in the French Revolutionary and Napolconic Wars, covering her birth to 1812. Describing Cornish town on Channel coast where she grew up; memories of mother and sisters. At author's age 10, outbreak of war with France; father's being appointed inspector of naval ships at Devonport. Family's acquaintance with notable naval officers; meeting Adm. Sidney Smith, who later defeated Napoleon's navy in Egypt. Being sent to Sophia Lee's boarding school in Bath; discipline and studies there. Noting contemporary modes of medical treatment, dress, and travel. Withdrawing from school to join family in London at father's insistence, age 17; entering society; describing prevailing social customs, c.1800. Attending wedding in Newcastle, age 18; observing differences in dress, especially for lower-class women, between south and north of England. Making several visits to military acquaintances in Scotland; giving her impressions of Edinburgh and of Scottish servants. Remarking that spinning was one of the few livelihoods open to women. Recalling her grandmother's memories of the 1745 Scottish Rebellion. In Melrose, Scotland, socializing with notable political and military figures, including the Sibbald family. Remarking on changes in education between beginning and middle of 19th century. Returning to London; reencountering Lt. Col. William Sibbald; marrying him, 1807. Their rejoining his regiment in Yorkshire; describing Yorkshire way of life and regimental social activities. Having two babies, 1808 and 1809; living in lodging houses in several Yorkshire coastal towns. Moving to Jersey upon husband's transfer there because of Napoleon's threatened invasion of the Channel Islands; remembering austere conditions, women friends, and cultural activities in Jersey. Explaining difference in character of the various regiments.

With its firsthand anecdotes about people and social customs in upper-class military circles, this book is an excellent resource for a behind-the-scenes look at late-18th and early-19th-century Britain. The twenty years of war in which Britain was engaged with France governed the motions of Sibbald's own peripatetic life with her husband. Although the autobiography ends with Sibbald's 29th year, the introduction supplies further details regarding her life between 1812 and 1866. Extracts from her letters, appended to the text, provide a contemporary perspective on the Crimean War, the Fenian Raids in Canada, and the American Civil War.

846 SIDDONS, Sarah (née Kemble). 1755–1831. *The Reminiscences of Sarah Kemble Siddons*. Ed. by William Van Lennep. Cambridge, Mass.: Harvard College Widener Library, 1942. 33 pp.; foreword by ed. NUC pre56 545:234.

Born in Breconshire, Wales. Father: Roger Kemble, theatre manager. Mother not named. 1 brother (actor John Philip Kemble). Married 1773 William Siddons, actor. 1 son; at least 1 other child. Knew Samuel Johnson, Richard Brinsley Sheridan, others. Actress (stage). Upper middle class.

Author's early acting career, 1773–84. Marrying, age 19. With husband, first being engaged to act at Cheltenham in father's theatre company. Winning favorable notice for her role in *The Fair Penitent;* being invited by David Garrick to join his Drury Lane acting company. Acting role of Portia at Drury Lane, 1775. Touring in provincial theatres during the summer; expecting to return to her Drury Lane position in autumn but being suddenly discharged by Garrick; feeling devastated at losing her means of supporting her children. Traveling nightly between different acting jobs in Bristol and Bath. Earning a good acting reputation while performing in the provinces for three years. Playing Beatrice in *Much Ado about Nothing*. Receiving an invitation to return to Drury Lane. Returning to London, 1782. Triumphing as Isabella in Garrick's adaptation of Southerne's *Fatal Marriage*. Winning enormous success as a tragic actress. Being welcomed into close ties with members of the royal family; giving dramatic readings at Buckingham Palace and Windsor Castle. Being befriended by the ailing Dr. Samuel Johnson. Sitting for Sir Joshua Reynolds for his most celebrated portrait, *Mrs. Siddons as the Tragic Muse*. As part of her acting discipline, avoiding social events which interfered with the tranquility and rest she required.

Siddons wrote her brief memoir at age 75, during the last year of her life. Numerous conversations between the author and assorted celebrities of her day are re-created in these pages. After 1803 Siddons acted with her brother at Covent Garden and made her reputation as Lady Macbeth, a role she last played in 1812. This memoir, which is written in a style which reflects good humor, education, and taste, was rediscovered for publication in 1940, more than a century after it was written.

847 SIMPSON, Alyse. c.1900–?. *The Land That Never Was*. Lincoln: University of Nebraska, 1985. 271 pp.; foreword by Dane

Kennedy; preface. BLC to 1975 303:164. (1st pub. Selwyn & Blount, 1937.)

Born in England. Parents not named. Married "John," possibly a pseud. 1 daughter. Farmer; colonialist (Africa). Middle class.

Disillusioning experiences in author's attempt, with husband, at homestead farming in Kenya, 1930s. Moving to Kenya with husband to get away from their parents' interference and to stake out a new life. On shipboard, overhearing conversations foreshadowing their failure to prosper in Kenya; other colonials' disparaging author about her city of origin in the British midlands. Author's advising husband to forget farming and open a shop; her taking a job assisting a female boarding-house keeper. Husband's buying a 1,000-acre farm thirty miles from the nearest train station. In city of "Nymba," observing attempts by colonial women of various social classes to preserve their British ideals of appearances and class differences. Suffering fever. Concealing her pregnancy from husband. Criticizing Irish priest for wasting his dedication to God on Africa and the natives. Husband's being determined to farm even though author acquires more evidence that farming in Kenya will not make money. Their setting up housekeeping on farm; birth of daughter; author's postpartum illness. Raising scrawny pigs. Together with natives, being vaccinated against smallpox. Baby's catching dysentery. Husband's seeking a loan to continue farming; author's questioning why they ever came to Kenya. With husband absent, being threatened by a white man demanding drink; his being driven away by the black cook. Their livestock's dying; her child's suffering eye disease; a deadly snake's invading her bedroom. Husband's buying sixty fowl, which die within three months. Locusts' devouring their maize and vegetables. Taking in a mother and her two sons, who prove to be bad boarders. Author's increasing misery; wishing she were dead. Receiving an offer on their farm; eagerly accepting it. Returning to England. Being harshly judged by their elders for failing to make their fortunes and come back happy.

The author's preface, written in the 1930s, asserts her intent to inform the public of the darker side of life in Kenya as an antidote to other books which extoll Kenya's delights. In the Depression years when Simpson and her husband made their venture, grim economic conditions caused English working people to be particularly susceptible to rosy government-sponsored images of instant prosperity available in the colonies. Simpson's witty and satirical book shows her bitterness at the fact that she and her husband, in attempting to improve the conditions of what she calls the first "five dreary years" of their life together, were lured into colonial homesteading. She has used pseudonyms for the names of the main characters and has disguised place names both in Africa and in England.

848 SIMPSON, Evelyn Mary (née Spearing). 1885–1963. *From Cambridge to Camiers under the Red Cross*. Cambridge: W. Heffner & Sons, 1927. 87 pp.; preface. NUC pre56 547:295.

Probably born in England. Married, husband surname Simpson. Wrote *A Study of the Prose Works of John Donne* (1924). WWI volunteer; nurse (WWI); literary critic. Middle class.

Professional and personal memories of a VAD nurse in England and France, 1914–18. Describing Cambridge university life before the war. Opening of First Borough Red Cross hospital in Cambridge; Christmas celebration there for the first British wounded to arrive. Setting up entertainment for men to honor a newly decorated soldier. Moving to a camp hospital in France; its harsh winter weather. Liking her fellow VADs. Contrasting "France she used to know" with France's wartime reality. Barriers between juniors and seniors' breaking down in congenial camp life. Her daily routine. On front, British wounded's being less cheerful than those she nursed in England. Noting war's personal impact on many VADs through loved ones' fighting at the front. Moving to a new hospital in a large French town. Describing sicknesses she treated, in addition to wounds; nursing ailing locals. Difficulties in tending dying men. Being sent to a hospital in northern France. Using reading, particularly poetry, to help console men; popularity of Rupert Brooke's poetry; recalling his having been her fellow student at Cambridge. Feeling compassion for gravely wounded men. Being moved by the extreme youth of some soldiers. Recalling the men's attempts at letter writing. Returning to Cambridge. Believing value of military discipline is more appreciated in France than in England. Feeling grateful patriotism toward English fighting men.

A Cambridge University academic whose VAD service represented a hiatus in her career, Simpson vividly re-creates the immediacy of her wartime experiences and appears nostalgic over the camaraderie at army hospitals. Her anecdotes showing humorous aspects of the soldiers' characters give war a human face. However, despite her evident compassion, Simpson remains a firm British patriot convinced of war's usefulness, and she assesses the sacrifices of the British "Tommies" as being properly justified by the "much" their country has given them. Her first-hand reporting and her many recollections about Belgian, Northern Irish, and English soldiers make the book both useful and interesting.

849 SIMPSON, Mary Charlotte Mair (née Senior). c.1825–d.a.1899. *Many Memories of Many People*. Edward Arnold, 1898. 334 pp.; preface; index. NUC pre56 547:357.

Born in England. Father: Nassau William Senior, political economist, academic, social reformer. Mother: Mary Mair. 1 brother. Married 1865, Charles Simpson, barrister. Children. Wrote *Letters and Recollections of*

Julius and Mary Mohl and Reminiscences of a Regicide. Biographer; historian; editor. Upper middle class.

Childhood and adult memories of life and travels in political and intellectual social circles of author's father, covering c.1825–65. Family home at Hyde Park; summers at seaside. Her friendship with the family of Count Mierjejewski. Travels to Germany and Italy. Visiting Paris, 1847, in the last days of the July monarchy. Memories of Alexis and Madame de Tocqueville. Visiting Jenny Lind. Outbreak of Crimean War. Remembering visiting William Thackeray; first publication of *Vanity Fair,* 1847. Visiting country houses in Ireland and England. Meeting prime ministers: Lord Melbourne, Gladstone, Lord Russell. Describing her father's work with the Royal Commission for Education. Visiting Parisian intellectual circles; befriending Russian exiles in Paris. Remembering the noted philologist, Ernest Renan. Describing the Great Exhibition in London, 1862. Her father's illness and death, 1864. Recalling her father's friends in England: Duke of Sussex, John Stuart Mill, Malthus, the Carlyle family; in France: Guizot, Prosper Mérimée, Michel Chevalier; in America: Daniel Webster, George Sumner. Her father's interest in the living conditions of the poor and in legal reform; his journal, 1855–56; his political and religious opinions.

For many years Simpson served as her father's literary editor and helped to shape his political and economic texts; after his death she established a reputation as a historian in her own right. She gives substantial space in this memoir to her father's private journal, with its wealth of information about contemporary British and European politics and politicians, and ends her book with his death. Serving as a coda both to her father's notable career and her own, Simpson's formally written book resurrects the individuals who shaped mid-Victorian literary and societal trends. The book also provides occasional commentary on the political situation in England, Europe, and Russia in the 1840s and 1850s.

850 SITWELL, Constance (née Talbot). 1886–s.l.1972. *Bright Morning*. Jonathan Cape, 1942. 132 pp. NUC pre56 548:371.

Born in Ceylon. Father: Gustavus Talbot, Member of the legislative council in Ceylon, later member of Parliament. Mother: Susan Elwes. 3 brothers; 1 sister. Married 1912 Colonel William Sitwell, acting chief of staff for the Southern Army, Madras, India. 1 daughter; 2 sons. Wrote five novels and a book on Ceylon, *Flowers and Elephants* (1927). Knew G. K. Chesterton, Edith and Osbert Sitwell, Ben Nicolson, Henry H. Asquith, Violet Asquith Bonham-Carter, others. Military spouse; novelist; foreign resident (Ceylon, India); colonialist (India). Upper class.

Reflective, nostalgic explorations of memories of Ceylon, England, and India, covering author's childhood to 1915. Living in Ceylon with parents until age 8. Family's return to England; her father's having no money; their living in Harpenden, Hertfordshire. Remembering her grandfather Talbot, son of the 2nd earl. Childhood memories of Queen Victoria's Diamond Jubilee, 1897; the Boer War, 1898; Queen Victoria's death, 1901. Keeping a diary to record 1902 events, including King Edward's coronation and the end of the Boer War. Family's giving annual summer fête for workhouse inmates. Being taken to visit her father's cousins, Countesses Brownlow and Pembroke; visiting other Talbot cousins in London; visiting Sir George Sitwell's family and his children Edith, Osbert, and Sacheverell. Social events in London. Her presentation at court. Returning to Ceylon; living with her brother on his tea plantation. Visiting Scotland; recalling being taken as a child to annual autumn shooting parties at the Gladstones' estate in Scotland. Her sister's marriage to Sir Hugh Gladstone. Her impressions of various visits to Egypt and India. Against her family's wishes, sailing out alone to India to marry a military officer she did not know well; never regretting it. Her husband's being acting chief of staff for the Southern Army; their attending balls at Government House in Madras. Traveling in arid northwestern India; remembering travels in lush, green England. Birth of her daughter, 1913. Moving to Baluchistan, where husband commanded a brigade. Their being sent back to England after the outbreak of WWI. Battle death of her brother on the Ypres front. Reflections on war.

Written during WWII, Sitwell's disjointed, impressionistic memoir seems to grow out of her associative reflections on the earlier world war which brought her youth to a close. She does not mention her mother until after the first third of her narrative, and does not describe the war years after 1915 or her husband's wartime role, assuming that her audience, like herself, has memories of the conflict "engraved" on their minds. Sitwell speculates on the nature of memory, wondering why some impressions remain distinct in the mind out of all proportion to their importance; the reader might also speculate on the accuracy of the author's memory, since at least one of her recollections (visiting Egypt before General Gordon's 1885 death at Khartoum) would have had to occur before her 1886 birth. Sitwell later wrote two other autobiographical works: **851** *Frolic Youth* (1964), a lighthearted account of her life from age 19 to her marriage, and **852** *Bounteous Days* (1976), which describes her social life and travels c.1913–25.

853 SITWELL, Dame Edith Louisa (D.B.E.). 1887–1964. *Taken Care Of: The Autobiography of Edith Sitwell*. Hutchinson, 1965. 239 pp.; front. port.; preface; illus.; poems; index; postscript. NUC 1963–1967 50:146.

Born in Scarborough, Yorkshire. Father: Sir George Reresby Sitwell, 4th baronet. Mother: Lady Ida Denison. 2 brothers (writers Osbert and Sacheverell). Single. Wrote poetry *Bucolic Comedies* (1923), *Selected*

Poems: With an Essay on Her Own Poetry (1936), biography *Alexander Pope* (1930), literary criticism *Aspects of Modern Poetry* (1934), novel *I Live under a Black Sun* (1937), others. Poet; biographer; literary critic; novelist; anthologist; foreign resident (U.S.); physically handicapped woman. Upper class.

Innovative poet's settling of scores with her enemies and examination of her work's evolution, covering her lifetime. Growing up at Renishaw, family estate in Derbyshire. Being unpopular with her parents from birth, "in disgrace for being female" and able to think. Mother's rages and mindless reading; father's insipidity and meanness. Author's happiness when not being bullied. Learning to read before age 4. Running away at age 5, but being caught. Being exposed to "middle-class grinders" in schoolroom, age 11, and to "grinders of upper-class mentality" when older; never being mastered by them. Parents' submitting her curved spine and weak ankles to the mercies of an orthopaedic surgeon; being imprisoned in metal braces like a "bastille of steel," which gave her permanent back and leg afflictions. Enduring two years of punishment for refusing to memorize "The Boy Stood on the Burning Deck." Noting how the physical world influenced her life and writing. Influence upon her of Arthur Rimbaud, Alexander Pope, Igor Stravinsky. Being forced into art school despite having no artistic talent. WWI: author's escaping with her governess to London and working in the Chelsea Pensions Office. With her brothers, launching the anthology *Wheels*. Having her portrait painted by Roger Fry. Remembering Nina Hamnett's generosity toward her. Avoiding acquaintance with occultist Aleister Crowley. Admiring Virginia Woolf. Memories of painters Walter Sickert and Percy Wyndham Lewis. Anecdotes of her friends Aldous and Maria Huxley, Sir Edmund and Lady Gosse, others. Composer William Walton's setting her experimental *Facade* poems to music; this work's hostile reception at its London performance, 1923. Author's disentangling differing versions of Wilfrid Owen's war poems. Moving to Paris; getting to know Gertrude Stein and painter Pavel Tchelitchew. Defending modernist poets. Returning to England before WWII. Giving readings with Osbert and with Dylan Thomas. Making a reading tour of U.S. with Osbert, 1948. Living in Hollywood; lunching with George Cukor; discussing Rudolph Steiner with Marilyn Monroe. Observing and pitying the homeless on Skid Row. Returning to England. Intimations of her approaching death.

Exceedingly witty despite its frequently dark subject matter, this posthumously published autobiography has been used by its author as an opportunity to slay various enemies in print, beginning with her parents and progressing through literary critics she considers dull-witted. Interspersing acidic sketches with comments on modern poetry—particularly her own—Sitwell makes her personality palpable on every page.

854 SITWELL, Georgiana Caroline. 1824–1900. "The Dew, It Lyes on the Wood," pp. 1–145 in *Two Generations*. Ed. by Osbert Sitwell (author's great-nephew). Macmillan, 1940. 308 pp.; ed.'s preface; "Vestals and Vestries, being the Journal of Miss Florence Alice Sitwell," pp. 147–308; illus. BLC to 1975 319:22.

Born at Renishaw, near Sheffield, Derbyshire. Father: Sir George Sitwell, 2nd baronet. Mother: Susan Tait. 4 brothers; 4 sisters. Married 1856 Archibald Campbell Swinton. Artist. Upper class.

Memories of author's close-knit family, home, travels, and acquaintances, covering the first three decades of her life. Remembering the Anglican parish church in Eckington and its family monuments. Describing family estate, Renishaw. Her love for her childhood nurse. From age 6, being schooled by governesses; studying eight hours a day. Fondly admiring her two elder sisters; noting closeness of siblings. Her father's dabbling in natural science, his friendship with botanist Sir William Hooker. Mother's Scottish background, intellectual interests, charity to local children. Memories of mother's sister Charlotte, Lady Wake, and brother Archibald, later Archbishop of Canterbury. Spending summers and autumns in Scotland, winters and springs at Renishaw. Death of her younger brother. Remembering the 1830s construction of a railroad through Renishaw's park; trains' adversely affecting old roads and hostelries. Suffering from scarlet fever, 1844. Author and sisters' editing a schoolroom newspaper, the *Renishaw Comet,* 1846; parodying famous poets. Newspapers subscribed to by her father; author and sisters' being forbidden to hear more than the occasional political or historical article. Dickens's novels being greeted with enthusiasm by young people, headshaking by their elders. Feeling that "a much warmer feeling" existed between the classes in her youth than in the 1880s. Father's incurring large debts from his "want of business habits"; forced reduction of family expenses from £12,000 to £700/year, 1846. Family's traveling to Wiesbaden, 1847; living circumscribed life in German Court presided over by the Grand Duchess. Commenting pejoratively on German character; being sustained by her love of drawing from nature. Traveling to French Riviera and Italy, 1847. Auction of Renishaw's furniture and art after failure of Sheffield Bank. Her father's death, 1853. Spending one last winter at Renishaw, 1853; never living there again. Making drawings of the rooms as she remembered them.

Luminous descriptions of landscapes and individuals bring these early-19th-century memories to life. Great-aunt of the poet Edith Sitwell, Georgiana Sitwell demonstrates a capacity for felicitous phrasing as she recalls her childhood at the family estate, Renishaw, which to her seems to symbolize an entire historical era and vanished way of life. Several of her drawings are reproduced in this book.

855 SLADE, Madeleine (a.k.a. Mirabehn). 1892–1982. The *Spirit's Pilgrimage*. New York: Coward-McCann, 1960. 318 pp.; foreword by Vincent Sheean; illus.; app. BLC to 1975 222:458.

Raised at Milton Heath, near Dorking, Surrey. Father not named, British naval admiral. Mother not named. Grandfather: General Sir John Slade. 1 sister. Single. Knew Mohandas Gandhi. Political activist; social reformer; foreign resident (India); religionist (Buddhist convert); teacher (crafts). Upper class.

Chronicle of how author's spiritual development led her to devote her life and work to Mohandas Gandhi, covering 1892–1958. Becoming fascinated with the idea of the unknowable and of eternity, age 5. Being happy to be taught at home by governess; having horror of the regimentation and crowds of children at school. At author's age 11, family's moving to Greenwich, where father was captain of the Royal Naval College. Acquiring a passion for Beethoven's music. Moving to India for two years when father was appointed commander-in-chief of East Indies Station. After returning to England, being courted by naval officer, 1911; refusing him; his death in WWI. During WWI, appointing herself agent for married concert pianist; facing up to her growing passion for him; seeking solace in prayer. When war ended, visiting Bonn and Vienna to see Beethoven's birthplace and grave. Traveling to Paris; learning French to meet Romain Rolland, author of a biographical novel about Beethoven; being inspired to join Gandhi through reading Rolland's biography of him. Moving to Gandhi's ashram, 1925; adoring Gandhi and calling him "father." Taking part in India's Congress Open Session. Adopting Indian name Mirabehn; suppressing her aversion to schooling to embrace communal life; taking vow of celibacy. Gandhi's suggesting that author adopted wearing of the sari too hastily; his wanting her to be "perfect" but remain herself. Teaching spinning and weaving in rural India. Taking part with Gandhi in numerous civil disobedience demonstrations. Serving Gandhi as maid and housekeeper on his political tours. Attending Round Table Conference in London with Gandhi, 1931. Being arrested and imprisoned twice for promoting Gandhi's Congress Party. Traveling to London and America to gain working-class support for Gandhi's movement. Gandhi's encouraging her to marry Prithvi Singh, a Punjab revolutionary; her refusing; falling into a deep depression; recovering through meditation and prayer. Being arrested again after passage of the Quit India Resolution, 1941. Nursing Gandhi during his fasts. Gandhi's assassination, 1948; author's continuing his political and social programs after his death. Founding a cooperative village cattle-raising venture. Returning to Austria; renewing her devotion to Beethoven's spirit, 1958.

Slade pursued charismatic figures (Beethoven, Gandhi) to whose work she could utterly devote herself. She states that her inner tensions increased as she progressively crushed her independent nature in order to serve Gandhi better; interestingly, although she had taken a vow of celibacy to devote her life to Gandhi, he not only suggested she marry but picked out the bridegroom. Her refusal and subsequent depression suggest her resentment at her hero's gentle attempt to provide some focus to her life other than himself. Until the end of her life Slade was faithful to Gandhi's ideals. Just before her death she was awarded India's second highest civilian medal of honor, the Padma Vibhushan.

856 SLATER, Lilian. 1907–s.l.1984. *"Think on!" said Mam: A Childhood in Bradford, Manchester 1911–1919*. Swinton: Neil Richardson, 1984. 66 pp.; illus. BLC 1982–1985 22:288.

Born in Manchester. Father: Alfred Ernest Barrington, grocer. Mother: Eliza Murray, grocer, Scottish. 1 brother; 1 sister. Lower middle class.

Warm memories of a happy urban childhood, covering author's fourth through eleventh years. Parental history. Believing herself her father's favorite. Admiring her mother for her beauty, style, devotion; mother's having natural singing talent. Describing family living quarters over shop. Mother's having favorite expression: "Think on" (meaning "beware, take care"). Parents' working hard in shop; shop's inventory; author's helping in grocery. Attending infant school, age 5. Mother's generosity and kindness: remembering her arriving in school yard with cocoa on a cold day. Anecdotes about neighbors' friendliness. Pastimes. Adults' using deaths of local children as examples to nurture compassion in neighborhood children. Taking seaside holiday with mother. Attending Sunday school. Family's participating in religious celebrations; church's fostering a sense of belonging. Mother's taking an interest in Christian Science. Author's great admiration for her father; their closeness; his encouraging and believing in her.

Focusing on her "no-nonsense" but loving mother and her accepting, supportive father, Slater re-creates the gentler aspects of her early years. The nurturing atmosphere which she remembers is all the more remarkable for its having been achieved in the midst of Britain's WWI privations, which seem to have cast no shadow on the author's childhood.

857 SMEDLEY, Constance (Mrs. Maxwell Armfield). 1881–1941. *Crusaders: The Reminiscences of Constance Smedley*. Duckworth, 1929. 265 pp.; front. port.; illus.; biblio.; apps. BLC to 1975 305:51.

Born in Birmingham, West Midlands. Father: William Thomas Smedley, accountant, director of corporations. Mother: Anne Elizabeth Duckworth. 1 sister. Married Maxwell Armfield, painter, musician. Wrote *An April Princess, The Unholy Experiment* (1925). Organizer of societies (women's clubs); organizer (theatrical); novelist; journalist; playwright; literary representative; suffragist; costume designer. Upper middle class.

Early artistic ambitions and later promotional success of a women's club founder and professional organizer, covering 1880s–1927. Being proud of Birmingham, a city "associated with many sturdy Crusaders." Prizing parents who turned ideas into reality: mother's hosting an intellectual salon, father's founding "beautiful and dignified" communal homes for the poor. Parents' encouraging her to excel. In high school, receiving wonderful reply to letter she had sent to Robert Browning; attributing her later boldness in seeking out the famous to this experience. Attending art school, taught by colleagues of William Morris and dedicated to pre-Raphaelite "dreamworld" of beauty. First using her knack for organizing by writing and producing a Christmas play for fellow art students; her father's showing script to a dramatic critic, who praised it highly. Plunging into playwriting; having her one-act play, "Mrs. Jordan," bought by Mrs. Patrick Campbell as a star vehicle for herself. Moving to London; joining Bohemian 1890s literary circles; her family's distrust of her new rebel values. Writing a novel, *An April Princess,* based on her unconventional friends; its success. Following book's publication, her artistic circle's breaking up due to emigration, divorce, abandonment, and death. Author's feeling lost; meeting self-supporting girls for the first time through the Writers' Club; embracing this "entirely new concept of femininity"; publishing novel *Conflicts* with a modern business girl as heroine. Entering into journalism. Living at Writers' Club, 1902; describing its shabbiness; recognizing how lacking a respectable place for business meetings endangered single women's reputations. Ambitiously organizing Lyceum Club, first women's club to enter Piccadilly; successfully seeking paying members; her father's encouragement and help. Being chosen honorary secretary of Lyceum; her hectic schedule's leaving her no time to pursue her literary career. Journeying to Holland and Germany to open Lyceum Clubs. Becoming active in women's suffrage movement; writing a book, *Women: A Few Shrieks,* on male opposition to women's success. Becoming European representative for American publications *Everybody's* magazine and *The Delineator*. Meeting Kenneth Grahame; helping him find a publisher for *The Wind in the Willows*. Interviewing George Bernard Shaw. Beginning Lyceum Club in Italy. Becoming engaged to artist Maxwell Armfield; his career and family history. After wedding, their moving to Gloucestershire. Joining Liberal Party. Helping found Sesame Bookshop in Stroud. Organizing the Cotswold Players. Noting social conditions for working class in rural areas, poor living conditions for women workers, c.1909. Outbreak of WWI. Visiting New York in 1916; admiring American culture. Meeting novelist William Dean Howells. Touring the U.S. and teaching drama course in New York and California. Opening Greenleaf Theatre Studio in London, 1927; designing costumes for Greenleaf Players. Commenting on the state of the theatre and on socialism.

Centered on Smedley's organization of the first Lyceum Club for women in London, this autobiography describes how the writer's organizing efforts superseded her own creative career. Smedley's work to promote the arts acquainted her with many prominent members of Edwardian artistic and social circles. Although celebrating these social connections sometimes seems to overshadow the author's project of creating cultural outlets, her anecdotes about many historical figures—as well as the actual lists she includes of committee members, club subscribers, and attendees at historical events—make her book a fund of factual information. The "crusaders" of the title are those idealists whom the author considers "crusaders for sincerer art," a group to which she implies she belongs.

858 SMITH, Dodie (Dorothy Gladys; C. L. Anthony, Charles Henry Percy, pseuds.). 1896–1990. *Look Back with Love: A Manchester Childhood*. William Heinemann, 1974. 181 pp.; illus. NUC 1980 305:251.

Born in Lancashire. Father: Ernest Smith, bank manager. Mother: Ella Furber. Stepfather not named. Married Alec Beesley. Wrote novels *I Capture the Castle, A Tale of Two Families*, plays *Autumn Crocus, Dear Octopus, Amateur Means Lover,* and children's book *The Hundred and One Dalmatians*. Novelist; playwright; children's author; WWI volunteer; foreign resident (U.S.). Upper middle class.

Whimsical account of author's emotional and intellectual growth in a large, intergenerational family, covering her first fourteen years. Family history. Father's early death. Moving with mother to Manchester to be with mother's family. Being mother's confidante. Influence on author of her unconventional, writer/musician maternal grandmother. Stories about her aunts and uncles; author's trying to be their center of attention. Unfavorably comparing her Manchester home with Darley, her mother's rural childhood home. Attending Sunday school, pantomimes, and other entertainments. Having a violent temper; throwing frequent crying fits over personal injuries, injustice, and the deaths of small animals and insects; suffering from the bullying teasing of her uncles. Being bridesmaid at two weddings; luxuriating in the beautiful dresses and cakes. Taking immense pleasure in attending several plays in London. Visiting Southampton to meet her paternal grandfather, an architect and photographer; in his house, feeling the personality of her dead father; being given her father's trains and books when she left. Mother's acquiring a new fiancé; author's enrolling in Mrs. North's Girls' School. At age 10, beginning to write "long and dreary" plays. Family's moving to new home in Thorncliffe. Embarking on maturity by putting aside toys and sitting down to write stories. Taking elocution lessons. Disliking study of Scriptures. Staging plays at school. Receiving her first kiss from a "caveman" boy. Feeling emotional wrench at permanent departure from childhood home and friends. Living in Whalley Range, attending local high school, and being gratified by her election as school prefect. Waxing enthusiastic over the plays of George Bernard Shaw. Performing with Amateur Dramatic Society. Suddenly maturing physically. At age 12, witnessing ceremony of King Edward's funeral. Mother's remarriage at author's age 14. Mingled feelings of regret and anticipation about moving to London.

Greatly enlivened by a gentle, occasionally self-deprecating sense of humor, Smith's narrative traces the growth of her creative imagination through the events of her childhood. Her anecdotes about her eccentric family members and her analysis of her younger self set the stage for her later studies of her mature life as an author and intellectual. In **859** *Look Back with Mixed Feelings* (1978) she continues her personal reminiscences, discussing the theatrical aspirations and disappointments of her young adulthood. **860** *Look Back with Astonishment* (1979) offers the author's introspective speculations about her increasing success as a playwright, spanning the 1920s to the eve of WWII. The concluding work, **861** *Look Back with Gratitude* (1985), combines reflections on Smith's life in America and postwar England. Anecdotes illustrating her lifelong love of animals are prominently featured in these books. Smith relates the small pleasures of everyday life with as much intensity as she discusses her stage triumphs.

862 SMITH, Lady Eleanor Furneaux. 1902–1945. *Life's a Circus*. New York: Doubleday, Doran & Co., 1939. 339 pp.; front.; illus. BLC to 1975 305:275.

Born in Birkenhead, Cheshire. Father: Frederick Edwin Smith, later 1st Earl of Birkenhead, Oxford scholar, M.P., Lord Chancellor. Mother: Margaret Eleanor Furneaux. 1 brother; 1 sister. Single. Wrote *Flamenco* (1931), *Satan's Circus* (1934), *The Spanish House* (1938), others. Novelist; journalist; film critic; traveler (Europe, U.S.). Aristocracy.

Imaginatively remembered growth and adventures of an unconventional writer, from her childhood to the 1930s. Maternal grandmother's disapproval of mother's marriage. Circumstances surrounding author's birth: baby's mistakenly being pronounced dead before first breath. After father's election as M.P., 1906, family's moving to Eccleston Square, London; recalling the indulgent home atmosphere. Remembering a thrilling visit to Madame Tussaud's Chamber of Horrors. Imagining herself accompanied by a "ghost dog," Gyp; her parents' trying to banish him by giving her a live dog. Being expelled from kindergarten; being schooled at home by a French governess; later being sent to day school in Westminster. Hating schools of all kinds. Adoring Anna Pavlova upon first attending a ballet, age 10. Outbreak of WWI: her father's commission to France; air raids in London. Spending summers at Blenheim Palace, home of her father's close friend, Winston Churchill. Parents' sending her to boarding school; author's begging to be released. Parents' yielding, sending her to school in France; her later schooling in Belgium. Becoming engaged briefly but breaking it off; having other romances. After returning to England, writing a first novel, 1925. Getting her first job, writing for "Women's Gossip" page in weekly newspaper; being promoted to film critic for another weekly. Meeting Frederick Martin, manager of the Carmo Circus; resolving to tour England with circus and learn circus horseback riding; writing about her experiences. Meeting dancers Diaghileff and Pavlova. Publication of her novel, *Red Wagon*. Traveling to America with her father; her great admiration for him; his dislike of feminists; his friendships with King George VI, Churchill, and Lloyd George; his death, 1930. Traveling to Spain to study gypsies and flamenco music; basing her published novel *Flamenco* on this experience. Her memories of Togare, the wild animal trainer, and their secret romance. Meeting the American gangster, "Kid Spider"; his proposing marriage to her; his eventually being sentenced to Devil's Island by French authorities. Traveling among the gypsies of Rumania and Bosnia to study folklore; being arrested by the authorities. Touring with production company of a play based on her book, *Ballerina*. Adoring bullfighting and the gypsy poetry of Spain. Depicting the Spanish Civil War and Spanish refugees in Portugal.

Smith's vivid work, painted in all the colors of romance, may serve better as a barometer of her exotic imagination than it does as a historical document. For the purposes of research it should be read in tandem with *Lady Eleanor Smith, A Memoir* (1953), the posthumous remembrance of her written by her brother, Lord Birkenhead. He methodically examines her autobiography, remarking on which parts may be trusted and which spring from—as he puts it—her tendency "to regard mundane questions in the terms of her own fantasy." In the end, however, although he applies the cooling hand of an outside perspective to his sister's memories, Birkenhead reinforces Smith's own image of herself as daring, tenderhearted, and wildly original.

863 SMITH, Eliza. c.1810–?. *Memoir of Eliza Smith Who was Transported for Shoplifting, written by herself, with some introductory remarks.* Dublin: Hardy & Walker, 1839. 14 pp.; intro. by Mary John Knott. BLC to 1975 305:277.

Born in Galway, Ireland. Parents not named. 3 siblings. Married, husband not named, shop worker; separated 1835. 3 children. Thief; convicted transportee; prison inmate; domestic servant; seamstress. Working class.

Plain-spoken account of being saved by spiritual conversion from a lifetime of personal adversity, despair, and criminal activity, covering author's childhood to 1839. Finding the opportunity for self-examination in prison's solitude. Her good prison conduct's bringing scorn from other inmates. Being helped by divine grace to defeat her sinful nature. Laboring to reform fellow convicts. Describing her prior history: being born to a well-off family with an extravagant father; his dying without making financial provision for them. Mother's supporting family with help from friends. Author's living with her sister, a devout Methodist. Hearing the Gospel preached but being skeptical; joining Methodist Society anyway and pretending to believe. Returning to live with her mother; working as a needlewoman to contribute income. Continuing to wear the outward garb of a Methodist; expressing shame over having been a sinner disguised as a Christian. Feeling disgraced by her mother's drinking. Yearning for a respectable job; finding position as governess in aristocratic, religious household; losing job when domestic staff was reduced. Marrying young man of respectable family; his falling into bad company and squandering income on drink. Childbirth; staying with husband nine years despite his abuse. Leaving husband to take work, 1835; his taking up with landlady in her absence. Leaving her children with him; despairingly taking to drink. Working one job after another; being hospitalized; accepting charity. Having illegitimate child which died. Husband's rejecting her attempted reconciliation with him. Meeting a woman who earned her livelihood by shoplifting; learning the trade and joining her. Being arrested; receiving a six-month prison sentence. Being corrupted in prison; deciding to return to life of crime, motivated by her continuing need for drink. Returning to shoplifting; being arrested again; receiving sentence of transportation to a penal colony abroad; accepting this as a just punishment. Acquiring conviction of sin; praying for repentance; experiencing conversion. Praising great kindness of women prison visitors. Being transported; repenting her earlier religious doubts; on shipboard resolving to devote the remainder of her life to God.

Employing a traditional conversion narrative, the author uses prison memories to create a testimonial to the worth of the British penal system and to make an appeal to other convicts to find their own spiritual renewal. Although the nominal author of this brief account is Eliza Smith, Mary John Knott's introduction—setting Smith's words into a calculated context of spiritual understanding—indicates Knott's targeting of a convict readership; both the praise of prison's effects on the incarcerated and the story of how one of their own kind found salvation seem designed to work moral change in prisoners' outlooks. Knott was the author of many penitent reform tracts which were largely propaganda in the form of fictional tales; among her titles are *The Life of Anne* ________, *A Penitent Female,* and *The Life of a Thief.*

864 SMITH, Ellen (née Wootton). 1909–s.l.1982. *Memories of a Country Girlhood: A Trilogy—Part 1.* Wymeswold, Loughborough, Leicestershire: privately printed, 1983. 128 pp.; front. port.; foreword; illus. by Susan Jalland; epilogue. BLC 1982–1985 22:332.

Born in Wymeswold, Leicestershire. Father: Thomas Warner Wootton, farmer, master builder. Mother: Mary Hardy. 3 brothers; 3 sisters. Married c.1931 John Sidney Smith, farmer. 4 sons; 1 daughter. Farmer; dressmaker; businesswoman; factory worker. Rural farming class.

Author's early family life, factory work, and marriage to a farmer, accompanied by a description of the effects of WWII on traditional farm life, 1910–45. Describing village of Wymeswold. Family history; her memories of paternal grandparents. Her childhood home's lacking indoor plumbing. Attending village school. Childhood games and escapades. Family Christmases. Loving to read. Acquiring an early interest in fabric and dressmaking. Describing contemporary girls' frocks and rural fairs. Remembering a royal hunt held nearby, at which her brothers saw the Prince of Wales (Edward VIII) urinate from his horse. Farm animals; her pet ferrets; her father's horses. Being curious about sex. WWI food shortages. Taking piano lessons, age 11. Mother's refusing to let author take exam for Loughborough High School; leaving school at age 13. Working in a factory making boxes for perfume. Taking her first seaside holiday, age 15. Playing piano at local dances. Being apprenticed to a local dressmaker, age 16; aunt's helping her set up her own business. At age 18, courting with future husband; their early married years. Her difficult first childbirth and second pregnancy. Their taking over his parents' farm, 1934, when parents retired. Haymaking; birthing calves. Buying a car. WWII: introduction of sugar beet farming for war effort, rationing, experiencing difficulties renting to evacuees. Describing village theatricals.

This autobiography was typed and hand-illustrated by the author's friend and workmate Susan Jalland, and the author's signature is written in ink on her portrait. Smith's feelings are expressed clearly and she gives many details of farm life. The epilogue summarizes her life to 1982. The author states that she wrote this book to please and to educate her fourteen grandchildren. She continued her trilogy with **865** *Seven Pennies in My Hand* (1984), an account of her experience of farm life c.1934–45; in this book she discusses cattle-raising, changes in farm technology, and her role in leading a delegation of farm women against an egg packer who was cheating them. The third volume of her trilogy, *Many Fingers in the Pie* (1985), was not available for use in this project.

866 SMITH, Lesley N. 1891–?. *Four Years Out of Life*. New York: Minton, Balch & Co., 1931. 302 pp.; front.; illus. by the author. NUC pre56 551:579. (1st edition, Glasgow: University Press, 1931.)

Born in Scotland. Parents not named. 1 sister. Nurse (WWI); WWI volunteer. Upper class.

Disillusioning experiences of a WWI VAD nurse in France, covering 1914–18. Enjoying calm prosperity of her family's social life: tennis, garden parties, balls; at age 23, being annoyed when WWI broke out because a family yachting trip must be postponed. For several months, war's seeming remote and unimportant; author's suddenly recognizing war's reality from reading newspaper casualty lists; finding among the dead the names of six sons of neighbors. Despite having no training, volunteering as a nurse. Most trained nurses' being in France, October 1915; hospitals desperately needing new trainees. Author's spending four months in intensive ward training: scrubbing, preparing dressings, learning sepsis precautions, 1914–15. Reporting with fifty other VADs to the London War Office in November, 1915; being shipped to Boulogne, then assigned to a field hospital. Arriving at her hospital, 129 General; discovering it was a tent camp. Hospital's command structure: one matron's supervising many nursing Sisters; each Sister supervising numerous VADs. Nurses falling into a routine of preassigned duties to handle incoming convoys of wounded. Describing endless rounds of tending, lifting, bathing, and bandaging the wounded. Feeling nausea at watching a medical officer jam tubing through a rotten shoulder; realizing her sensitivity was useless in war conditions. Being changed to night duty; describing its eerie isolation. After two weeks, being reassigned to a "head ward" of brain injury victims; reassuring them in their constant hallucinatory babbling for two months. In September 1916, receiving new assignment as an "extra," working daily in the ward with the worst emergencies; dreading changing dressings and looking at the wounds beneath. Nursing through a winter in the tent camp: steel knives and forks' freezing to fingers, patients dying of cold. Treasuring one patient, a pickpocket, who stole coal from main supply for her patients; concealing him when the supply corporal came to arrest him. Being granted leave; returning to her family in Scotland; being infuriated by their denial of the war's real atrocities. After returning to France, being sent to a different hospital, 111 General; joining its surgical ward. Describing twenty-four-hour routine there: cutting down stinking bandages, tending patients with multiple amputations. Discussing the "unspeakably personal" aspect of face wounds; packing gauze in empty eye sockets; feeding gruel to a soldier whose jaw was blown away. Covering patients' eyes to prevent their nausea at seeing their own wounds. Describing uncontrollable deaths from abscess. Helping haul corpses to the mortuary, making room for new incoming wounded. Accepting transfer to a medical ward; tending dying patients with pneumonia, nephritis, and tetanus. During autumn of 1917, storms threatening the tent camps. Tentmate's suggesting they escape their tent by attending evening chapel; after the service, discovering all the tents (including theirs) destroyed by gales. Helping rescue nurses and patients trapped under the canvas; moving the hospital into newly built huts. In spring 1918, author's getting new assignment to hospital 50 General near Rouen; Allied retreat's beginning soon after her transfer. Retreating troops and medical staff's streaming through Rouen. Feeling ashamed to treat the lightly wounded, returning them to the front; everyone's believing the Allied cause was lost. Attending Easter services in the hospital chapel; rejecting sermon on the righteousness of the Allied cause as futile. Suddenly discovering France to be full of Americans determined to save the day. Hospital 50's being flooded with Americans; author's resenting their loud "pep" and cheeriness. Gas attacks increasing as weather warmed; medical staff's tending influx of gas victims with blinded eyes and corrosive burns. Receiving another home leave, September 1918; in Scotland, angering neighbors by contradicting platitudes about happy soldiers with marvelous morale. Being relieved to return to her field hospital, November 1918; with other nurses, being shocked to learn of the Armistice. Amid civilian rejoicing, nurses' worrying about readjustment to the trivialities of civilian life after seeing the evil beneath life's civilized veneer.

In this WWI memoir, solicited by Glasgow University Press as part of a series of historical nursing experiences, Smith rejects patriotic euphemism in favor of hard, often ugly facts about the war. Using a fictional name for herself, "Nurse Kay," Smith traces the one-way journey of WWI nurses from civilian innocence to war-induced cynicism. She suggests that these women, having had to confront war's random atrocities, could never afterwards return to society's comforting beliefs about the essential goodness of humanity or the benevolence of God. As a result, they were barred from emotionally rejoining civilian society, which wanted to hear only platitudes about constant British "pluck" and to deny information about either the real nature of war wounds or the real confusion and despair dominating the Allied front. After the war Smith did not return to her family's social milieu, but became a book illustrator. In addition to the woodcuts she has provided in this memoir, her work may be seen in Lorna Rea's *The Happy Prisoner* (1932) and in many children's books published during the next few decades.

867 SMITH, Mary. 1822–1899. *The Autobiography of Mary Smith, Schoolmistress and Nonconformist, A Fragment of a Life*. Bemrose & Son, 1892. 2 vols. Vol. 1: 327 pp.; letters from Jane Carlyle and Thomas Carlyle. Vol. 2: 245 pp., poems. NUC pre56 551:634.

Born in Cropredy, Oxfordshire. Father: William Smith, shoemaker. Mother: Ann Pride. Stepmother not named. Sisters; 2 half-brothers. Single. Wrote *Progress and Other Poems*. Teacher; schoolmistress; governess; suffragist; poet; journalist; clerk; religionist (Nonconformist); school founder; public speaker; temperance activist. Lower middle class.

Intellectual maturation and adult work of a feminist educator, with her reflections on women's education, rights, and spirituality, 1820s–c.1880. Her mother's character. At age 8, being discouraged from reading by mother, who thought it idle; father's taking her part. Mother's death. Father's remarriage to housekeeper. His adoption of Nonconformism; author's doing likewise; her esteem for Nonconformists like her father, who led morally consistent lives and displayed "greater knowledge and thought" than average people. At dame school, enduring disapproval because her father did not attend Anglican services. Attending grade school where education for girls was mostly needlework. Father's buying old books to gratify author's love of reading. Working in family grocery shop. At age 20, moving to Brough, Cumberland with family of Mr. Osborn, a Baptist preacher who believed "all"—including women—should use their gifts. His insisting that both she and his wife testify in church; author's learning public speaking. Discovering spiritual life to be the source of intellectual vigor. Teaching in a girls' school; experiencing her pupils' respect for her mind; resolving never to return to village life, which had "neither help nor hope for a person of intellectual aspirations." Rejecting marriage in favor of the intellectual life. Moving to Carlisle with Osborn family; teaching as Mr. Osborn's assistant in a coeducational school. Publishing verse in the Carlisle *Journal* and *The People's Journal*. Looking for work teaching young women; finding that employers wanted teachers of French and music, not of history, science, and literature. Accepting governess position in Bristol. Returning to Carlisle; starting her own girls' school teaching serious subjects. Writing articles for Carlisle *Examiner*. Becoming interested in Women's Suffrage Society. Lecturing on temperance to women; discussing alcohol-related problems of working-class families. Seeing that women's education requires improvement. Disapproving of loose behavior and of women's conceding to be sex objects for men. Discussing social customs of English middle class. Noting Church of England clergy's frequent detachment from their parishioners' problems. Examining and explaining aspects of English legal system. Discussing cotton famine, American Civil War, and Crimean War. Approving of gender equality within Quaker tradition. Her views on God.

An early supporter of the women's suffrage movement, Smith asserts the principle that gender inequality creates special hardships for poor women. Her egalitarian sentiments also lead her to denounce war and other political expediencies which exploit the poor. She depicts herself as committed to a religion of deed as well as word and to educational reform. Her detailed descriptions of political and religious movements and the many social problems confronted by small-town working-class people provide a valuable look at these aspects of 19th-century life.

868 SMITHSON, Annie Mary Patricia. 1873–1948. *Myself—And Others: An Autobiography*. Dublin: Talbot Press, 1944. 293 pp. NUC pre56 552:450.

Born in Sandymount, Dublin, Ireland. Father: Samuel Smithson, attorney. Mother: née Carpenter. Stepfather: Peter Longshaw, chemical factory owner. Second stepfather not named. 3 half-sisters; 1 half-brother. Single. Wrote 19 novels. Nurse; novelist; religionist (Roman Catholic convert); Irish nationalist. Middle class.

Sensitive exploration of author's increasing Irish nationalism, emphasizing her conversion to Roman Catholicism, covering her childhood to c.1942. Describing her childhood home; ancestry and family history. Her close attachment to her maternal grandfather. Catholic-Protestant intermarriage among her relatives. Father's early death. Mother's remarriage; author's disliking her stepfather and the necessity of leaving Ireland to be near his factory in Warrington, Lancashire. Attending boarding school near Liverpool, age 9; home education by grandmother's sister. Births of half-siblings; mother's ignorance of proper infant feeding methods. Living in poverty in Rathmines after stepfather's business failed; resenting being deprived of further education. Mother's unrealistic scheme for starting a private school. Author's going to meetings of Plymouth Brethren. Moving to Bray, outside London; being relatively happy at day school there. Stepfather's death; family's removal to Dublin, then to Dalkey, 1890s. At age 21, inheriting £600, all but £30 of which was spent by her mother. Leaving home to seek advice of relatives. Shelving her journalistic aspirations and beginning nursing career on advice of her aunt Susan Carpenter, a well-known journalist and suffrage activist. Working at the Chelsea Hospital for Women, then at Queen Victoria's Jubilee Institute in London. Moving to Edinburgh, 1898; training at the Royal Infirmary. Returning to Dublin, 1900, to be a queen's nurse. Taking a post in Portadown, Ulster; witnessing Protestant violence against Catholics there. Working as district nurse in County Down, 1901; leaving to escape her infatuation with a married doctor; taking further training in Edinburgh and Glasgow. Attending a Catholic Redemptionist Mission and deciding to convert to Roman Catholicism. Mixed reactions of relatives; Aunt Susan's never speaking to her again. Changing her baptismal name from Margaret Anne Jane to Anne Mary Patricia. Returning to Ireland; nursing in various regional hospitals, being transferred to Dublin as tuberculosis nurse. After lapse of many years, revisiting her mother. Nursing in County Mayo when the 1916 Easter Rebellion erupted; discovering police had listed her as a Sinn Fein sympathizer. Writing a novel on the 1916 uprising; discussing publication and Irish themes of this and subsequent books. Working for Sinn Fein political candidates in 1918 General Election; this causing trouble with her employers; resigning her post. Taking work as queen's nurse in Waterford, with employers who shared her politics. Discussing

Sinn Fein, Black and Tan raids in local towns, occupation by British militia. Visiting Belfast; making a quick escape because of Protestants' attacks on Catholics. In Dublin, teaching first aid in Cumann na mBan, the women's arm of Sinn Fein, during 1921 Irish civil war; being captured but released by a Free State officer. Becoming friends with Eamon de Valera's secretary, Kathleen O'Connell. Working as Child Welfare nurse, 1922–30. Being made secretary of the Irish Nurses' Union, 1929. Devoting herself solely to writing fiction after resigning from secretary's chair in 1942.

Smithson's autobiography gives a lively account of the author's nursing career and of the development of her twin religions, Irish nationalism and Catholicism. When discussing her childhood and children in general, she is often sentimental, recalling happy times with nostalgia. She conveys an insider's knowledge of Sinn Fein and a deep love for Ireland.

869 SMYTH, Dame Ethel. 1858–1944. *Impressions That Remained*. New York: Alfred Knopf, 1946. 509 pp.; front. port.; intro. by Ernest Newman; preface; illus.; app.; index. NUC pre56 552:598. (1st. pub. Longmans, Green, 1919.)

Born in Footscray, Kent. Father: John Hall Smyth, member of horse artillery in India, commander of artillery brigade in England, magistrate, chairman of County Conservative Union. Mother: Emma Struth. 5 sisters; 2 brothers. Single. Wrote operas *The Wreckers* (1906), *The Boatswain's Mate* (1916), *Fête Gallante* (1923); wrote travel book *A Three-Legged Tour in Greece* (1927). Knew Emmeline Pankhurst, Empress Eugènie, Virginia Woolf, Pyotr Ilich Tchaikovsky, Gustave Mahler, Clara Schumann, others. Composer; theatrical producer; feminist; suffragist, militant; foreign resident (Germany); travel writer; singer (concerts). Upper middle class.

Childhood, burgeoning musical destiny, and public career of a noted female composer, against the backdrop of her illustrious friendships in musical and social circles, covering 1858–95. Family history. Memories of her brother and sisters; their characters; their sibling quarrels. Her father's financial reversals; his having made his fortune in India; his conservatism and dislike of her artistic temperament. Mother's having gift for languages and music; her mourning death of author's brother. Family's moving to Farnborough, author's age 9. Her childhood interest in music and composing. Making her first public singing appearance, age 11. Composing chants and hymns. Studying music with composer Alexander Ewing despite father's disapproval of her musical ambition. Hearing Brahms play for the first time. Moving to Leipzig to study music; attending Conservatorium there; giving poor rating to its teaching; associating with circle of successful Leipzig musicians. Attending Gewandhaus concerts; hearing Clara Schumann play. Commenting on life for single women in Leipzig, c.1870s; describing rigid class distinctions. Germans' attitude toward English people; Germany's role in the Boer War. Forming a special friendship with Lisl (Elizabeth von Herzogenberg); her musical talent. Studying with Lisl's husband and joining performance group Bach Verein at his invitation. Having a nervous breakdown; being nursed by Lisl; returning to England. Her father's belatedly accepting her career choice. Memories of Brahms, Grieg, Clara Schumann, others. Touring Italy. Lisl's illness; deterioration of their friendship due to author's romantic association with Henry Brewster, husband of Lisl's sister. Commenting on probable impossibility of perfect relation between a man and a woman, her own need to put her work first, and how women are more understanding than men. Memories of Mahler and Tchaikovsky. Continuing to work on orchestral compositions on advice of Tchaikovsky, 1888. Commenting on her disbelief in God. Having her compositions "Serenade" and "Overture to Anthony and Cleopatra" accepted for performance in London. Meeting Sir Arthur Sullivan, 1890. Composing *Mass in D*; its London performance, 1893. Death of her mother. Touring Adriatic coast in Empress Eugènie's yacht. Lisl's death, 1892; author's painful reflections about Lisl's "unfeelingness." Elaborating on reasons why artists die young.

Interspersed with Smyth's remembrances of the high points of her career are numerous anecdotes concerning her acquaintance with aristocrats, wealthy patrons, and others of lofty name in late-19th-century social circles. She also includes letters from friends and relatives pertaining to time periods and events she describes. Her reminiscences about many celebrated 19th-century musicians provide insights into their lives and characters and help define cultural trends of her time. With **870** *Female Pipings in Eden* (1934), Smyth comments wryly on difficulties and rejections she faced as an independent-minded woman composer; she also gives many details of her suffrage activities. This book is the last in a series of collected sketches that began with **871** *Streaks of Life* (1921) and *A Final Burning of Boats* (1928), all on similar autobiographical themes combined with social criticism and descriptions of the author's involvement in feminism and the struggle for suffrage. In her later autobiographies, **872** *As Time Went On...* (1936) and **873** *What Happened Next* (1940), Smyth elaborates on her extensive career in orchestral and opera composing and includes anecdotes about musical luminaries and titled friends.

874 SOLDENE, Emily. 1840–1912. *My Theatrical and Musical Recollections*. Downey & Co., Ltd., 1897. 315 pp.; intro.; ports.; index. NUC pre56 555:344.

Born in Islington, London. Father not named, lawyer. Mother not named. 1 sister. Married surname Powell. Wrote *Young Mrs. Staples*. Singer (opera); theatrical director; theatrical producer; biographer. Middle class.

Account of the career progress of a noted operatic singer and producer, from her early adulthood to the 1890s. Showing early enthusiasm for music. Being apprenticed, 1864, to Howard Glover, musician and music critic of *Morning Post*. Making her debut concert at St. James's Hall, 1864 and at Drury Lane Theatre, 1865; battling stage fright. Attending premiere performance in London of Gounod's "Ave Maria." Recounting anecdotes of contemporary musical performers and directors. Describing music venues in which she performed throughout London and southeast England. Singing in Offenbach's *Grand Duchess* and *Barbe Bleu*. Commenting on difficulties touring company members faced in collecting their salaries; women's ballet costumes, c.1867; the Lyceum Theatre. Touring in Liverpool, Newcastle, and Glasgow. Directing *Geneviève de Brabant,* 1871; Prince of Wales's attending one performance. Touring Dublin with *Geneviève*. Forming Soldene Opera Bouffe Company; explaining her responsibilities as producer. Touring throughout the U.S., 1870s; remembering Soldene fashion "fads" sweeping U.S. after her New York debut. Encountering racial tensions in American South; meeting Sitting Bull in Chicago. Assessing American women's fashions, social customs, 1874–96; comparing American and British tastes in music; noting differences between English and American ballet companies. Touring in Australia and New Zealand; performing in Sydney, Melbourne, and Adelaide. Returning to England, 1878; producing *Carmen* at Theatre Royal in Leicester. Making return tour of Western U.S., 1880–81. Meeting P. T. Barnum; noting popularity of Barnum's "showmanship" in U.S. Returning to England. Commenting on similarities between Jack the Ripper scare, 1888, and furor over anarchists in Chicago, 1887. Assessing changes in English music halls and general theatrical landscape between 1864 and the end of the century.

By her own admission, Soldene undertook this book to preserve a record of her career, an understandable need in an era before any mechanical means of musical recording. Her account, which includes both anecdotes about noted British and American 19th-century performers and detailed accounts of the venues in which they worked, gives firsthand witness to musical trends and methods of production during the late 1800s.

875 SOMERSET, Ethel Jemima, Baroness Raglan (née Ponsonby). 1857-pre1946. *Memories of Three Reigns*. Ed. by Erica Beale. Eveleigh Nash & Grayson, 1928. 256 pp.; front. port.; illus.; index. BLC to 1975 307:377.

Born at Canford, Dorsetshire. Father: Rev. Walter Ponsonby, 7th Earl of Bessborough. Mother: Louisa Susan Cornwallis. 7 siblings. Married 1883, the Hon. George FitzRoy Somerset, later 3rd Baron Raglan, d.1921. Widow. At least 4 children. Society woman; philanthropist; civil servant's spouse. Aristocracy.

In-depth look at aristocratic Victorian and Edwardian societies via personal and family memories, emphasizing manners and customs in a changing world, from before author's birth to death of her husband, 1921. Anecdotes of family history and high society, c.1802–14. Her parents' youth. Her father's instructing her in religion. At age 4, first encountering her future husband. Life with her affectionately close family in their country estate; enjoying her affluent childhood. Taking her first railway journey, age 7. Being schooled by governesses in languages and sciences and by "masters" in music and painting. Visiting her grandfather, Lord St. Germans. Attending dancing class, age 14. Making her social debut, age 17; enjoying her debutante days. Refuting modern misconceptions about Victorian social morés; declaring life was just as exciting and rowdy then as in the 1920s. Becoming engaged; husband's background; their wedding and honeymoon in India. Attending court functions and royal garden parties. Describing fashions and manners of 1880s–1890s. Husband's War Office service; his appointment as governor of the Isle of Man, 1902; their living there 17 years until failing health forced his retirement. Her charity work; taking over some of husband's duties as his health failed; his resignation, 1919, and death, 1921. Declaring that "modern girls" should not be chastized, for each generation produces them; the older generation should support the younger one, rather than criticizing. Anecdotes of royalty past and present.

In this associatively organized book, Lady Raglan portrays late-Victorian society as less stodgy and more natural than she apparently fears her readers will believe. In her heyday, she states, "We were happy. We were natural. Those were not the days where you psychoanalyzed your feelings and your dreams. . . . We knew how to extract the essence and poetry out of life." But Lady Raglan also acknowledges that society faced practical and psychological difficulties when she describes the many social changes affecting the upper classes during the late 19th and early 20th centuries. She is especially sympathetic to modern women who desired to take advantage of new freedoms only to find that much gender stereotyping continued, stubbornly, to prevail.

876 SOMERVILLE, Edith OEnone, and Martin Ross. 1858–1949 (Somerville). *Wheel-Tracks*. Longmans, Green & Co., 1923. 283 pp.; front. port.; prelude; illus.; apps. NUC pre56 556:82.

Born in Corfu, Greece; raised in Ireland. Father: Col. Somerville. Mother: née Coghill. 1 sister; 5 brothers. Single. Wrote *Some Experiences of an Irish R.M., The Real Charlotte, Irish Memories,* others. Novelist; social historian; feminist; hunter; suffragist. Upper middle class.

Fond memories of rural Irish society and life within its upper echelons, from author's childhood to the end of WWI. With her mother, living at Drishane, her grandfather's country house in Cork, while her father was stationed in Corfu, Greece. Being her grandparents' "pet." Recalling village of Castle Townshend, its inhabitants, popularity of spiritualism there. Studying with governesses. Studying music. Her adventurous nature; exploring countryside with brothers and boy cousins. Learning to ride; being given her own pony. Soldiers' arriving at her house during Irish Rebellion, giving her brother a ride on a horse but ignoring her; her resulting strong feelings against gender stereotyping. Her liking for working people she knew in her childhood. Memories of strolling musicians; their disappearance. Her love of hunting. Serving as master of Foxhounds for twelve years. Defending fox hunting on grounds that country people complain of foxes' stealing their domestic fowl. Visiting Lismore; staying with suffrage speaker Fanny Currey. Supporting women's suffrage. Visiting Kerry with Violet Martin, her cousin (who co-authored this book under pseud. Martin Ross). Describing aspects of Victorian discipline: need for children to be seen and not heard. Discussing 19th-century Irish history and the role of the Fenians in the 20th century. Her views on Home Rule and the Sinn Fein movement.

Somerville's informally written memoir, full of anecdotes ranging from the sentimental to the humorous, shows an Irish-flavored passion for land, family, and good storytelling. Devoting many pages to accounts of fox hunting and depicting her own hunting experiences in elaborate detail, she is quick to rationalize the need for this sport, which drew considerable public protest in the late 19th century.

877 SOMERVILLE, Mary (née Fairfax). 1780–1872. *Personal Recollections, from Early Life to Old Age of Mary Somerville*. Ed. by Martha Somerville (author's daughter). John Murray, 1874. 377 pp.; front. port. NUC pre56 556:88.

Born in Jedburgh, Scotland. Father: Adm. Sir William George Fairfax. Mother: Margaret Charters. 2 brothers. Married 1804, Samuel Greig, British Consul for Russia, d.1807. Later married Dr. William Somerville, Army Medical Board member. Widow. 2 sons; daughters. Wrote *Mechanism of the Heavens* (1831), *On the Connexion of the Physical Sciences* (1834), *Molecular and Microscopic Science* (1869), others. Knew Sir John Herschel, Joanna Baillie. Astronomer; scientist; geographer; scientific writer; feminist; social reformer; antivivisectionist; animal welfare activist; foreign resident (Italy). Upper class.

Astronomer-geographer's enduring victory over the gender-based educational restrictions of her childhood, spanning her nine decades in the Georgian and Victorian ages. Her Calvinist mother's using Bible to teach her to read. Being a lonely child, fond of wild birds. At age 10, being sent to boarding school; doing lessons while confined in an uncomfortable posture corset; lessons' consisting of memorizing and reciting a page from Johnson's dictionary. After a year of this, being unable to compose or spell; her mother's reproaching her for wasting the tuition money. Being sent to day school to learn needlework; at night secretly studying the stars. Receiving a set of Euclid and an algebra text from her brother's tutor; reading them nightly by candlelight until servants told her mother; thereafter being deprived of candles at bedtime. Continuing to learn algebra by evoking the text from memory. Father's telling mother "we must put a stop to this," for girls who pored over studies were liable to go mad. Studying writing and music; teaching herself Latin. Meeting her uncle, Dr. Somerville; his approving of her desire for learning; contrasting life at her uncle's house and at her home. Describing English pro-French Revolution sentiments, c.1790. Marrying Samuel Greig, 1904; his sharing her parents' restrictive gender views. Their moving to London; his death after three years; author's continuing her studies, despite family disapproval. Returning to Edinburgh; marrying her cousin William Somerville, 1812; his encouraging her to expand her studies. Writing monograph for the *Quarterly Review* anticipating 1835 return of Halley's Comet. Seeing Napoleon I's reign, 1804–15, as greatest period of French physical astronomy. Teaching her daughters by her own methods; mourning death of her oldest girl. Becoming interested in geology. Extracts of letters: from Sir John Herschel on astronomical principles; from Professor Peacock praising her work. Being honored by having a bust of herself placed in the Hall of the Royal Society; receiving a pension granted by King George IV. Publishing *Mechanism of the Heavens*. Moving to Paris; writing *On the Connexion of the Physical Sciences* (1834). Befriending Italian astronomer Padre Vico; touring Italy. Being elected associate of the College of Risurgenti in Rome and honorary member of the Italian Royal Academy. Spending Christmas with Herschel's family. Becoming friends with Michael Faraday. Publishing *Physical Geography* (1848). Discussing Italian politics, war between Austria and Italy, alliance between Napoleon and Italian king. Sudden death of her husband, 1860. Studying volcanic activity of Mt. Vesuvius. Deciding to remain in Italy; seeing British laws as unfair to women, and American ones as worse. Noting John Stuart Mill's work on behalf of women's equality; her own lifelong desire for such equality. Joining in petition to Senate of London University, urging that women be granted degrees. Receiving first gold medal ever awarded by Geographical Society of Florence. Grieving over death of her pet bird; condemning the cruelty to animals she witnessed in Italy; working to change Italian animal protection laws; recalling her long friendship with animal activist Frances Power Cobbe. Continuing her scientific researches, even in old age. Preparing for death. Thanking God for innumerable blessings.

Somerville's memoir reconstructs the social barriers she faced as an 18th-century oddity, a woman with a scientific mind. In recording her efforts to win respect as an astronomer and physicist, she discusses contemporary prejudices against women intellectuals and her tactics for surmounting them. It is of interest that she led, rather than followed, the pack of feminist theorists; by the time she could read John Stuart Mill's supportive *Subjection of Women* in 1869, she had long since fought her solitary way to scientific preeminence. After her death, her achievements were granted permanent recognition in the foundation of Somerville Hall, a new women's college at Oxford University.

878 SOOTHILL, Lucy (née Farrar). 1858–1931. *A Passport to China, Being the Tale of Her Long and Friendly Sojourning amongst a Strangely Interesting People*. Hodder & Stoughton, 1931. 339 pp.; front. port.; foreword, intro., epilogue by Dorothea Hosie (author's daughter); illus. BLC to 1975 308:27.

Raised in Yorkshire. Father: Charles Farrar, farmer. Mother not named. 5 brothers. Married 1884, husband not named (referred to as "Sing Su"), clerk in English Foreign Service, later university president. 1 daughter; 1 son. Knew Sir Robert Hart, inspector-general of Customs in China, Times Peking correspondent Dr. Morrison, Grace Stott. Foreign resident (China); diplomat's spouse; school founder. Rural farming class; married into upper middle class.

Entertaining and culturally balanced look at the Chinese and China, accompanied by author's personal experiences in that country, covering 1884–c.1910. Traveling out to Shanghai to marry. Husband's holding religious services for Chinese Christians in his house. Describing 1884 riots in Shanghai; situation of foreigners there. Bobbing her hair and burning her bustle; enjoying less restrictive Chinese dress and hairstyle. Sympathizing with the tough job of British consuls; forming friendships with them. Author and husband's attending a church in Shanghai; promoting Protestantism among Chinese. Adjusting to poor sanitation and Chinese food; recounting her efforts to learn Cantonese. Having two babies while in Shanghai. Evaluating Westerners and Christianity from a Chinese perspective; giving details of how Chinese Christian converts were persecuted. Husband and author's return visit to England, 1892; readopting English dress and hairstyle while in England. Recalling history of her native district of Yorkshire. Returning to China. Founding a girls' school in China although her own children attended school in England. Firmly opposing footbinding. Visiting Peking and the Great Wall. Commenting on the 1900 Boxer Rebellion. Her husband's accepting presidency of Shansi Imperial University in North China.

In her introduction, Hosie recalls her mother as "a lady with white hair, luminous hazel eyes under arching eyebrows, and an expression of taking vivid interest in everything she saw." She learned to speak Cantonese fluently and worked tirelessly to assist both her Chinese women friends and the girls she taught. Soothill's style has a self-conscious quaintness, as if she were trying to import the use of Chinese idiom into her English; she invariably calls Shanghai the "City-of-the-South," her husband "Sing Su," and her son "Sea-borne" because he was born on a ship.

Soothill and her husband ended their stay in China and returned to London before WWI.

879 SOSKICE, Juliet M. (née Hueffer). 1880–1943. *Chapters from Childhood: Reminiscences of an Artist's Granddaughter*. New York: Harcourt Brace & Co., 1922. 239 pp.; foreword by A. G. Gardiner; illus. NUC pre56 557:81. (1st pub. Selwyn & Blount, 1921; other ed.: G. Prior, 1973.)

Probably born in London. Father: Francis Hueffer, physician. Mother: Catherine Madox Brown. Grandfather: Ford Madox Brown, artist. 2 brothers (including Ford Madox Hueffer, later Ford Madox Ford). Married c.1900 David Soskice, Russian barrister, d.1941. 3 sons. Wrote novel *The Stronger Sex,* others. Translated *Poems* by Nicholas Nekrasov, others. Knew Prince Pyotr Kropotkin. Novelist; translator; artist's granddaughter. Upper middle class.

Childhood and adolescence spent among artists in the pre-Raphaelite circle and later in convent school, featuring author's successive enthusiasms for the ideals she encountered, covering c.1889–97. At age 9, being sent to live with her aunt and uncle, Lucy Madox Rossetti and artist/poet W. M. Rossetti, after her father's death. Acquiring their interest in social reform and the anarchist movement; with her cousins, writing and printing the *Torch*, an anarchist paper; propagandizing for socialism with cousins in Hyde Park. Visiting her aunt, poet Christina Rossetti; Christina's strange appearance and religiosity. Remembering visit of artisan/poet/publisher William Morris to the Rossetti household. Memories of her maternal grandfather, painter Ford Madox Brown: his storytelling gift, his egalitarian socialist ideals, his teaching author to draw and paint. Her maternal grandmother's turning her drawing room into a soup kitchen for the needy. Grandfather's grieving at his wife's death; his own death, 1893. Being sent to convent school; Mother Superior's successfully converting author to Roman Catholicism; defending anarchists against Mother Superior's verbal attacks. Taking her first Communion; feeling disenchanted at her lack of religious rapture; leaving the convent at the Reverend Mother's request. Traveling to Germany; memories of a small town on the Rhine river, German friends there, church festivals, local shrine and its miracle seekers. Attending another convent school; describing the Reverend Mother, convent priest, and strictness of school's policy; suffering from homesickness. Returning to England to live with her mother; details of her mother's character and art. Attending spiritualist meetings; describing trance-channelers, spiritualist beliefs, and procedures to contact spirits. Meeting Prince Pyotr Kropotkin; describing his views on religion.

Soskice's esteem for her pre-Raphaelite grandfather is reflected in her lucid re-creation of his personality, principles, and the noted figures in his circle of friends. The author's early ardor for the socialist ethos to which she was exposed anticipates some of her later concerns and experiences; in 1900 she married a Russian barrister exiled by the czarist regime, and her home became a meeting place for artistic and political figures, including Kropotkin and others central to the Russian revolutionary movement. Soskice became skilled in Russian and won praise for her translations of Russian poetry and other writings.

880 SPEED, Maude (née Maturin). c.1860–d.a.1929. *Snapshots on Life's Highway*. Longmans, Green, 1929. 176 pp.; preface; illus. NUC pre56 561:155.

Born in Lymington, Hampshire. Father: Mr. Maturin, Anglican canon. Mother not named. 2 brothers; 2 sisters; 1 half-brother. Married 1883 Henry Speed. Wrote *A Yachtswoman's Cruises, Through Central France to the Pyrenees, More Cruises*. Travel writer; sailor; clergyman's daughter. Upper middle class.

Observations on changing social attitudes and innovations from the late 19th century through 1929, connected to memories of the author's Victorian upbringing and peripatetic married life. Depicting her childhood home, pets, and large family. Praising lifetime loyalty of her family's servants, c.1860–70; remarking on social and attitudinal changes among the middle classes as they adjusted to getting along with fewer servants. Being schooled at home by both parents in poetry of Pope, Tennyson, and Shakespeare, as well as in history and needlecraft; playing many outdoor sports; contrasting her mother's personal care of her with the comparative indifference of many early-20th-century mothers. Being sent to a rigid London finishing school which restricted girls' exercise, 1870s. Pleading to attend a more relaxed, intellectual, and sports-oriented school; parents' assenting. Noting the marked changes in girls' education since then; commenting that the phenomenon of modern women displacing men in business springs from women's higher education. Family holiday in Ireland; discussing Irish origins of Maturin family. On Isle of Wight, her parents' being friends with Tennyson, photographer Julia Margaret Cameron, and poet Coventry Patmore. Commenting on how the clergy had to protect their church buildings from the suffragettes. Acquiring an interest in great historical naval battles. In her teens, enjoying the social life at the seaside resorts of Brighton and Weymouth. Marrying, 1883; author and husband's sailing and traveling in the Near East together. Commenting on fashions of the 1880s in the theatre; seeing Lily Langtry and Mrs. Cornwallis-West perform. In the 1880s, author and husband's bicycling together; their purchasing their first car, 1904. Commenting on vast advances in modern technology and transportation. Onset of WWI. Author's traveling to France to observe war's aftermath, 1919; embarking on her travel-writing career by trying to sell the story of her journey; publisher's turning it down, telling her the public wanted to forget the war.

As its title acknowledges, Speed's book is a subjective collection of miscellaneous observations, or "snapshots," that primarily documents shifting social attitudes, 1900–29. Speed's anecdotal memoir seems to assume a readership contemporary with herself that is intimate with the social phenomena she critiques. Her book's illustrations are by her brother-in-law Lancelot Speed, an illustrator for *Punch.*

881 SPENCE, Catherine Helen. 1825–1910. *Catherine Helen Spence: An Autobiography*. Ed. by Jeanne F. Young. Adelaide: Libraries Board of South Australia, 1975. 101 pp.; front.; intro. by ed. NUC pre56 561:252. (1st pub. Adelaide: W. K. Thomas, 1910.)

Born in Melrose, Scotland. Father: David Spence, tenant farmer. Mother: Helen Brodie. 3 brothers; 4 sisters. Single. Wrote novels *Clara Morison: A Tale of South Australia during the Gold Fever* (1854), *Tender and True* (1856), *An Agnostic's Progress,* others. Knew Charlotte Perkins Stetson (later Gilman), William Lloyd Garrison, Jr., Julia Ward Howe, Helen Keller, others. Social reformer; child welfare activist; political writer; novelist; speaker; emigrant (Australia); politician; journalist; preacher; governess; religionist (Unitarian); feminist; suffragist. Rural farming class.

Scottish childhood and Australian career of multifaceted social reformer and writer, from the 1830s through 1887. Boys and girls' receiving different qualities of education in her childhood; her brothers' attending one of the best schools in Scotland. Her mother, born 1791, having received an inferior education at a finishing school; her only real learning deriving from author's grandfather's purchase of *The Encyclopedia Britannica* and *Johnson's Dictionary,* from which she practiced the Greek letters. Author's attending a religious Protestant day school, where gloomy Calvinism was "the only cloud on my young life." Two sisters' dying of consumption, author's age 12; author's developing consumptive symptoms, later cured by Australian climate. Maternal grandfather, owner of three farms growing native grain, having been influential in Parliament's vote to maintain the Corn Laws, 1837; father's losses from speculating in foreign wheat in the belief the Corn Laws outlawing its importation would be repealed. Maternal grandmother's giving author's ruined father £500 to start over in South Australia. Family's emigration to Australia, 1839. In Adelaide, author's teaching music and beginning to publish verses in local paper, age 15. At age 17, working as a governess. Opening a school with her mother and sister, age 20. Refusing to marry and have children, out of Calvinist-inspired fear that so few souls found salvation. Contributing stories to the *Adelaide Observer*. Becoming Adelaide correspondent for the *Melbourne Argus;* with her brother, editing the *Argus* for three months. Writing her first two novels anonymously; finding the work lucrative; giving up teaching, age 25. Shaking off the "shackles" of Calvinist Presbyterianism by converting to Unitarianism.

Publishing third novel in her own name; discussing its British reception. Selling article to the London periodical *Cornhill,* 1865. Revisiting Scotland and England, 1865–69. Meeting George Eliot. Becoming acquainted with John Stuart Mill; praising his *Subjection of Women,* but remarking that Mary Wollstonecraft was the first to champion women's rights. Noting that general electoral reform had helped women more than suffrage; supporting suffrage herself only after the movement had gained great momentum. Returning to Australia. Publishing her fourth novel. Analyzing motives for prejudice against women as public speakers. Committing herself to child welfare work; publishing newspaper articles on the need for reform of Australian state child care, education, taxation, and electoral system. Also promoting spiritual education; becoming a Unitarian preacher. Becoming a regular contributor to several newspapers. Serving on Advisory Board for Education Department. Infusing her fifth and sixth novels with unconventional spiritual and social ideas; using fictional form to reject doctrine of innate human depravity and to challenge traditional marriage. Breaking off her memoir with the memory of her mother's 1887 death, at age 96; feeling too grief-stricken to continue.

Originally published in 1910, this memoir was later revised and extended by editor Jeanne Young, who ghostwrote a first-person account of Spence's life from 1887–c.1900. Young's contribution, although lengthy enough to expand Spence's original by half, contributes a complacent catalogue of travels, achievements, and famous acquaintances that jars with the meditative private autobiography. Spence attributes her autobiographical impulse to her reading of the *Autobiography* of Margaret Oliphant, with whom she intensely identified. Both she and Oliphant led lives of transition, being Scottish by birth, Calvinist by upbringing, freethinking by inclination, and self-made as women writers in "a man's world"; of primary importance, Spence remarks, "like her I had an admirable mother, but she lost hers at the age of 60, while I kept mine till she was nearly 97." Spence breaks off her account with the death of her mother, whose passing configures a significant closing in her own life.

882 SPENCER-CHURCHILL, Frances Laura, Duchess of Marlborough (née Charteris). 1915–1990. *Laughter From a Cloud.* Weidenfeld & Nicolson, 1980. 260 pp.; illus.; index. NUC 1982 466:472. [cat. under Marlborough, Laura Spencer-Churchill, Duchess of.]

Born in Westminster, London. Father: the Hon. Guy Charteris, son of the 11th Earl of Wemyss and March. Mother: Frances Tennant. 2 sisters; 1 brother. Married 1933, David Long, 2nd Viscount Long; divorced 1942. Married 1943, Eric Ward, 3rd earl of Dudley; divorced 1954. Married 1959, Michael Canfield, businessman, d.1969. Married 1972,

John Albert Spencer-Churchill, 10th Duke of Marlborough, d.1972. Widow. 1 daughter. Knew the Duke and Duchess of Windsor, Randolph Churchill, Lady Diana Cooper. Society woman; businesswoman; horsewoman; foreign resident (New Zealand); nurse (WWII). Aristocracy.

Colorful adventures of a much-married member of the aristocracy, focused on her love affairs and her socializing in affluent circles, c.1925–75. Genealogy of the Wemysses, Charterises, and Tennants. Assorted childhood memories; at age 10, suffering death of her adored mother; spending remainder of her childhood with various relatives. Father's being distant and self-absorbed. Marrying David Long, age 18; trying to cancel wedding; father's saying it was too late to cancel. With new husband, sailing immediately to New Zealand, unhappy and pregnant; birth of her only child nine months later. Separating from husband. Describing her life as a single parent: living with her father, working mornings, partying afternoons, conducting love affairs. Having premonition of coming war. Traveling through Europe, 1939. Commencing affair with Eric Ward, Earl of Dudley; divorcing her first husband. Entering nursing school; outbreak of war; describing her WWII nursing experiences and war death of her ex-husband. Marrying Eric, 1943. Indulging her love of horses and riding. Their social circle's including Randolph Churchill and the Duke and Duchess of Windsor. Having ongoing love affairs; leaving Eric because of their stormy relationship; divorcing him, 1954. Launching a career at Christian Dior. Tallying her numerous lovers, particularly Gerry Koch do Gooreynd and artist Anthony Pelissier. Opening her own boutique with money she inherited from Gerry, 1956. Anthony's leaving her, 1958; author's marrying Michael Canfield, 1959. Their traveling in Europe and U.S. during 1960s; picnicking with President Kennedy's family, 1963; experimenting with marijuana and LSD. Worsening of Michael's drinking problem; his sudden death, 1969, followed by Eric's death six days later. Mourning these losses. In 1972, marrying the Duke of Marlborough; his falling suddenly ill a few days after the wedding and dying six weeks later. Hating having to live at Blenheim Palace; her depression and suicide attempt. Recuperating in a nursing home. Becoming estranged from her daughter and sister, her only remaining family.

In her chatty memoir, the Duchess frequently changes the subject and drops names without explanation, calmly assuming a readership already familiar with the personages and events involved. She mentions many men who "adored" or "admired" her, and she seems preoccupied with clothing, jewelry, and furnishings. Her tone is one of self-absorption and status-consciousness; she also seems to ask for the reader's sympathy as she describes her ups and downs. Her obituary in the *Times* describes her as being "widely known for her spirited demeanour and her numerous marriages to English noblemen." This tell-all autobiography was controversial when it first appeared.

883 SPENCER-KNOTT, Justina. c.1910–?. *Fools Rush In*. Hammond, Hammond & Co., 1949. 244 pp.; note; foreword by F. M. W. King; illus. by Eric King. NUC pre56 561:419.

Probably born in England. Parents not named. 1 brother; 1 sister. Earlier marriages implied; married c.1938 Harold Knott, civil servant in Africa, farmer. 2 sons; 1 daughter. Wrote articles for *Farmer and Stock-Breeder, Farmer's Weekly, Home Farmer*. Farmer; journalist; foreign resident (Sierra Leone, South Africa); civil servant's spouse. Middle class.

Humorous account of experiences with farm life in Africa and England by a transplanted urbanite, c.1938–47. Author and husband's refurbishing farm in Devon and moving in with their three children, 1946, despite having only cursory farming experience in Africa. Flattering herself she knew farming, having kept chickens in Sierre Leone before WWII and having published articles on farming in agricultural periodicals. In Devonshire, their deciding to go in for dairy production; recounting experiences with buying expensive Guernseys, having them tested for tuberculosis, performing artificial insemination on cows. Also raising turkeys, ducks, and pigs. Anecdotes of refractory hired help and farm machinery. Memories of her whirlwind courtship and marriage; being a "much-married matron" before she met Harold; his giving her a wedding ring in 1938, a week after they met, and taking her to Sierra Leone with him a week later. Their farming briefly in Natal, South Africa, 1941; during WWII, working for Freetown Secret Branch in Sierra Leone, where Harold was stationed. After the war, their returning to England; restoring "Luckett Farm" in Knowstone Parish, Devonshire. History of the surrounding village and local school; author's application to teach there being rejected. Having problems with the lack of public roads, the need for ongoing maintenance of farm roads and gates, telephone and telegraph inconveniences. Attending Women's Institute meetings. Wishing she had a close woman friend. Being pitied as a poor relation by well-meaning relatives back in Africa; their sending cast-off clothing. Describing the ritual of Market Day in nearby Tiverton. Her negative view of WWII Women's Land Army workers; finding them stuck-up. Noting that, as she writes, they have lived on the farm a full year. Advising farmers on how to choose their wives.

Spencer-Knott's opinion of those who want to begin farming with little previous experience, as she and her husband did, is implied by the book's title; she freely offers advice to like-minded "fools." The author represents one of several urban women, including Enid Barraud and Margaret Leigh, who adopted farm life in the 1930s and 1940s; her work also merits comparison with the rural recollections of Phyllis Nicholson.

884 SPRING, Marion Ursula (née Pye). 1890–d.a.1965. *Frontispiece: A Childhood Portrait*. Collins, 1969. 127 pp.; foreword by Derek Tangye; intro. BLC to 1975 310:273.

Born in Hampstead, Middlesex. Father not named, cotton merchant. Mother: Ellen Lamb, concert singer, teacher, French/Dutch Huguenot. 2 brothers. Married 1920 (Robert) Howard Spring, novelist, journalist, d.1965. 2 sons. Wrote *Howard* (1966), biography of her husband. Secretary; advertising agent; biographer; garden designer. Middle class.

Meditative look at the carefree childhood and early career choices of a worker for the Manchester *Guardian,* from her late Victorian birth to her marriage. Family's moving to London suburb of Harlesden, author's age 3. Her hardworking father's having made good as a London cotton merchant; memories of father's employee, future theatre star Edward Compton, and his little daughter Fay. Her mother's giving up a concert-singing career when she married. Mother's dressing author in Kate Greenaway attire. Attending deportment classes, age 4. At age 7, turning tomboy. Author and brothers' attending different schools, but receiving the same "good basic education." Acquiring an early love of gardens; remembering family's garden. Retrospectively contrasting her modest childhood treehouse with the unrealistically costly children's playhouses recommended by Gertrude Jekyll in her 1908 *Children and Gardens*. Mother's strategically placing book on facts of life in author's dress-up trunk during her teen years. In earlier childhood, being taken on holidays to Cornwall and allowed to run free with local children; later choosing Cornwall for her honeymoon. Remembering public rites of her childhood: the Boer War Procession, 1898, Queen Victoria's Funeral, 1901. Being exposed to the world of commerce through her father's City of London business; seeing tie factories and silk weavers; learning to take inventory. Being transferred from dame school to a private girls' school, age 14. Working toward an art teacher's certificate from the Royal Drawing Society, age 18. Mother's dying just after author left school, age 19; author's feeling compelled to keep house for her father instead of teaching. After father's remarriage, resolving to earn her own living to escape from conflict with father and stepmother. Taking secretarial training at Kensington College. Working abroad as an English tutor for a family in Brittany; after returning to London, finding work at the firm of Radium, Ltd.; her advertising work there leading to a new job with the London advertising department of the *Manchester Guardian*. With outbreak of WWI, August 1914, most of paper's staff being let go; author's continuing to work there without pay. Taking offer from a former *Guardian* editor to work in the Foreign Office; being unhappy and returning to the *Guardian*. Gradually moving to the editorial side by taking reporters' dictated stories over the telephone in the evening; after the 1918 Armistice, working only on the editorial side, as secretary to the London editor. Howard Spring's coming to work in the *Guardian*'s London office, 1919; falling in love at first sight; their wedding the following spring.

Although this is Spring's second published autobiography, the title she chose for this associatively organized memoir defines it as the opening piece in her ongoing chronicle of her life. Moved by the death of her husband to conduct a retrospective, she concludes this volume with their union, marking the onset of a new and different phase in her life. The nature of the change brought about by her marriage is suggested in an earlier autobiography, **885** *Memories and Gardens* (1964), in which a tacit shift in persona is evident as Spring surrenders her habits of self-support and self-determined career choice in order to let her husband take the initiative. In this book, she focuses primarily on her lifelong interest in gardening, homes, and pets, her husband's success as a novelist, and her WWII Red Cross activities.

886 SQUIRE, Rose Elizabeth (O.B.E.). 1861–1938. *Thirty Years in the Public Service: An Industrial Retrospect*. Nisbet & Co., 1927. 238 pp.; foreword by Sir Edward Troup; preface; index. NUC pre56 563:236.

Raised in London. Father: William Squire, physician. Mother not named. Single. Factory inspector; sanitary inspector; social reformer. Upper class.

Professional experiences of a woman factory inspector and social reformer, covering her adult life from 1893–1926. Depicting her privileged upbringing, in which women had "no lack of occupation" due to their entertaining and parish activities. Unexplained necessity of her having to seek a career, age 32. Avoiding the traditional, poorly paid livelihoods of teacher, governess, or woman's companion. Dismay and outrage of her family and the public at her appointment as one of the first women sanitary (later factory) inspectors, 1893. Working in the North Kensington district, 1893–96; recalling working conditions for laundresses there. Passing exams designed for male inspectors. Seeing her suggestions to improve conditions incorporated into the 1895 Factory Act. Being appointed one of the first four women factory inspectors, 1896. Recounting the history of factory inspection in England, including the saga of the women's branch from its inception to its 1921 disbanding. Describing principles and major concerns of factory health inspection. Gathering undercover evidence in northwest Ireland that workers were being paid with goods rather than wages, 1899. Remembering passage of legislation for the sixty-hour workweek, 1901. Being transferred to Royal Commission on Poor Law, 1906. Her successive appointments: special investigator of factory conditions; senior lady inspector for the northern counties, 1908; deputy principal lady inspector of factories, 1912. Training women inspectors under her supervision; discussing problems of women within the male hierarchy. Evaluating textile mill conditions. Being transferred during WWI to the Welfare Department of the Ministry of Munitions. Receiving O.B.E., 1918. Discussing summary dismissal of women workers after the Armistice. Being director of Women's Training Branch, 1918–20. Being principal in Factory Department of Home Office, 1921–26. Retiring, 1926.

Concentrating on what she observed of the abuses of workers in manufacturing, Squire describes how industrial and social conditions for these workers advanced during her thirty-three years of employment. Despite her advocacy for workers' rights, she apparently accepts the dismissal of women workers after WWI as natural, and downplays the gender prejudice she encountered in her own career—including the unwritten rule that women could not combine marriage with employment. The text is at its liveliest when Squire describes her undercover work and on-site inspections, aspects of her job that she clearly enjoyed.

887 SQUIRRELL, Mary Elizabeth. 1838–?. *The Autobiography of Elizabeth Squirrell of Shottisham, and Selections from Her Writings: Together with an Examination and Defence of her Statements Relative to Her Sufferings, Blindness, Deafness, Entire Abstinence from Food and Drink during Twenty-Five Weeks, and Other Extraordinary Phenomena: Also Facts and Opinions Illustrative and Suggestive: By One of Her Watchers*. Anonymous ed. Simpkin, Marshall, 1853. 300 pp.; intro., commentary by ed.; other miscellaneous pieces by Squirrell; index. NUC pre56 563:251.

Born at Shottisham, Suffolk. Father not named, small tradesman. Mother not named. 2 brothers. Single. Clairvoyant/psychic; physically handicapped woman. Lower middle class.

Adolescent girl's controversial account of fasting and communicating with a guardian angel, covering her birth to 1853, supplemented by editor's discussion of her treatment by hypnosis. Becoming blind in one eye from a cataract, age 2, and suffering near-fatal illness, age 3. At age 4, reading children's books; being able to read the Bible, age 5. Attending infant school and Sabbath school, age 6. Meditating on death; imagining, from reading Fox's *Book of Martyrs,* details of the Christian afterlife of a dead schoolmate. At age 7, being sent briefly to an advanced school; leaving because of serious illness; thereafter, expanding her vocabulary by reading the dictionary. At age 10, conscientiously tutoring her younger brother; having enthusiasm for spiritual subjects, including angels and the nature of the resurrection. Studying natural history, age 11. Returning to school; learning shorthand. In concern over the state of her soul, beginning to do works of charity until stricken with paralysis and "nervous hysteria"; suffering convulsions and locked jaws; after twelve weeks, permanently losing sight, hearing, and taste; being unable to eat for twenty-one weeks; praising her mother's constant attendance. Finally opening her mouth again; taking liquid nourishment. Learning sign language; experiencing sensitized powers of touch; declaring that she could read with her fingertips. Writing in shorthand, although blind. Being unable to explain her survival, but denying that she ever said it was a miracle, although local people accuse her of this claim and of attention-seeking; their animosity and "calumnies" about her causing her father's loss of trade, necessitating family's move to Ipswich. At age 14, attributing ringing sounds from a glass water tumbler by her bedside to messages from her guardian angel; recounting the glass's responses to other people's questions and prayers. Because of her supernatural claims, being interviewed and tested by skeptics. Undergoing mesmeric treatment, 1853; hearing predictions of her recovery by the supernatural "beings" surrounding her; demonstrating an apparent ability to see through shut eyes. Protesting that she is neither a fraud nor deluded.

Diary entries, letters to friends and family, and religious poetry by Squirrell flesh out the last seventy-odd pages of her volume; collectively these suggest the precocity of her intellect coupled with the morbid nature of her preoccupations. As for the elaborate medical complaints she describes, separating their origins into physical and emotional components is tricky. Some of her symptoms resemble those of tetanus. Hysteria also seems a component of her condition, especially because hypnosis seemed to help her. Elements of the paranormal also appear to be present, but—unlike the self-proclaimed spiritualists of a later generation—Squirrell is vague about mediumistic communication. The anonymous editor, a rationalist, urges that her case be studied scientifically.

888 STACK, Prunella. 1914–s.l.1988. *Movement Is Life: The Autobiography of Prunella Stack*. Collins & Harvill Press, 1973. 256 pp.; foreword; illus.; index. NUC 1973–1977 111:144.

Born in Lansdown, India. Father: Hugh Bagot Stack, army lieutenant. Mother: Mary Meta Bagot Stack, educator, suffragist. Married 1938, David Douglas-Hamilton, physical fitness teacher, d. in WWII. Married 1950, Alfred Albers, d.1951. Widow. 2 sons. Wrote *Movement Is Life: The Intimate History of the Founder of the Women's League of Health and Beauty* (1937, with her aunt Norah Cruickshank) and *Zest for Life: Mary Bagot Stack and the League of Health and Beauty* (1988). Teacher (physical fitness); organizer of societies (women's clubs); biographer; foreign resident (South Africa); women's issues author; feminist; editor. Middle class.

Author's lifelong involvement in Women's League of Health and Beauty, accompanied by extended family history, covering her first six decades. Her mother's activities: crusading for national fitness during WWI; later promoting peace through health for women; founding magazines *Beauty* and *Mother and Daughter*. Mother's taking training in physical therapy; her divorcing her first husband to marry author's father; their moving to India; mother's campaigning for women's suffrage there. Death of author's father in WWI. Author's growing up among extended family of female relatives; practicing dance and her mother's exercises; attending mother's lectures and demonstrations as her publicity vehicle. Retrospectively feeling deprived of emotional privacy and independence. Attending day school. Being one of the first pupils at the Bagot Stack Health School after its founding by her mother, 1925; from ages 13–16, taking teacher training there. Describing her mother's original regimen of dance and exercise. Receiving only a spotty academic education from a woman undergraduate student hired as her tutor. Rebelling, age 16; telling her mother she wanted a more conventional education and mother; mother's sending her to boarding school; author's hating it. Mother's founding the Women's League of Health and Beauty, 1930, her death five years later. Author's continuing the League with her Aunt Norah. Studying physical education in Germany and Czechoslovakia. Serving on the National Fitness Council, 1937; describing growth of league in England. Marrying another physical fitness teacher, 1938. Returning to Europe; noting contrasts between the league and the Nazi physical culture system. With outbreak of WWII, the league's existence and operations being severely restricted. Becoming editor of the league's magazine. Giving birth to two sons, 1940 and 1941. Her husband's serving abroad in the war; his death. Marrying a second time, 1950. Author and second husband's living in South Africa; his death in a hiking accident; her grief leading to renewal of her Christian faith. Forming League Centres in South Africa. Holding exercise classes for coloured (mixed-race) girls. Recounting public anger at presence of coloured girls on the South African team she brought to Queen Elizabeth's 1953 coronation. Deciding to move to Scotland for her sons' education. Developing girls' activities for Outward Bound. One son's becoming a zoologist, studying elephants in Kenya. Touring the world, visiting League Centres in Canada, South Africa, and New Zealand, 1970s.

Stack's autobiography is a major contribution to the history of physical education in Britain and the Empire. In this book, and in her biographies of her mother, she traces the league's growth from her mother's pacifist and eugenicist ideas to an international means for promoting women's health. Stack writes reflectively of the major persons and places in her life and enthusiastically of the league as a resource for women.

889 STANNARD, M. c.1830–d.a.1873. *Memoirs of a Professional Lady Nurse*. Simpkin, Marshall & Co., 1873. 239 pp.; preface; illus. NUC pre56 564:588.

Born at Laxfield, Suffolk. Parents not named. Married, husband not named, miner, builder, stationery business proprietor, operator of temperance tea and coffee house, d.1863. Widow. Nurse; midwife; shopkeeper; foreign resident (Australia); paid companion; traveler (Canada, U.S.); laundry worker; seamstress; governess; dairymaid; teacher (Sunday school); hospital administrator. Middle class.

Colorful life of nurse and traveler, covering her childhood to 1873. Being a much-loved only child. Attending day school and boarding school. Her mother's dying during author's absence at finishing school. Father's remarriage; soon afterward, author's becoming Sunday school teacher at Laxfield Chapel, where she had been a pupil. Working briefly as child-minder, shop assistant, and dairymaid; later assuming duties as bailiff and storekeeper. Marriage. Floundering of husband's building business; their moving to Framlingham to run stationery business and Temperance tea and coffee house; prospering of these establishments. Their settling in Ipswich. Moving with husband to London. Doing nursing work at Bethlehem Royal Hospital for the Insane; taking midwife training. Husband's deciding to emigrate to the Australian gold fields; their embarking for Australia, 1853. Author's aiding the ship's doctor on the voyage out; five children's dying on the way, but five babies' being born, with author assisting as midwife. Taking in washing and ornamenting ladies' sidesaddles to support herself while husband was absent in the gold fields. Packing her goods to join her husband; describing rough and ready camp life. Nursing miners and their families; nursing husband through typhus. Organizing church services in the camps. Traveling from camp to camp; noting high prices of food; describing making her own yeast for bread. Foiling a robbery with her husband's pistol. Rescuing a man and a boy from drowning. Their tent's being attacked by strangers. Engaging a Chinese cook, whom she taught to read and write English. Husband's helping to build town of St. Arnaud. Collecting specimens of birds, snakes, insects. Encountering tribes of bushmen. Her husband's being brutally murdered; author's being robbed by his partner. Leaving gold fields for Melbourne; being hired as head nurse for a Melbourne hospital. Returning to England, 1863. Taking several voyages from England to America and back, working as a lady's companion; having trouble finding lodgings in New York due to locals' suspicion (during Civil War) that she was an English spy; wanting to travel to American South to nurse Civil War soldiers but being barred from doing so. Describing her longest voyage, to Vancouver Island; commenting on Indians and their customs; being glad that God made her English and not Indian. Traveling to San Francisco, then down the Pacific coast to South America. Ultimately returning to England and settling in Manchester; serving as matron in a Midlands hospital after 1872.

Writing with humor and a great deal of piety, Stannard often quotes poems and hymns, exhorting readers to trust in God and to teach the Gospel informally, as she did. She emphasizes adventure and travel more than her nursing work. Despite her good intentions, her Eurocentric prejudices are evident, as in her remark about Australian natives being "black as niggers," or in her statement about how she found it "extremely amusing" to see the dignity with which the Chinook medicine man approached his patients. She supplements her narrative with an extensive glossary of words and phrases in the Chinook Jargon trade language of the Pacific Northwest Indians.

890 STARK, Dame Freya. 1893–1993. *Beyond Euphrates: Autobiography 1928–1933*. John Murray, 1951. Vol. 2 of 4. 341 pp.; map; foreword; illus.; letters; index. NUC pre56 128:459.

Born in Paris, France. Father: Robert Stark, artist, landowner, farmer. Mother: Flora, amateur artist, carpet factory manager. 1 sister. Married 1947 Stewart Perowne, writer. Wrote *The Valleys of the Assassins* (1934), *The Southern Gates of Arabia* (1936), many others. Journalist; travel writer; foreign resident (India, Middle East); photographer; intelligence agent; feminist. Upper middle class.

Memories of exploring and beginning to write about the Middle East, 1928–1933, interspersed with contemporary diary entries and private letters. At age 35, crossing Atlantic Ocean to Quebec, then spending four months with her aging father in British Columbia, Canada. Returning to Scotland via Niagara Falls and New York City; contrasting charm of Scotland's antiquity to the "go-ahead west." Lured by its exoticism, journeying through the near East: Lebanon and Syria, Babylon and Kish. Settling in Baghdad; boarding with a shoemaker's family, then renting a house in Baghdad's native quarter. Living with Arabs, wearing native attire, and speaking Arabic; being considered eccentric and disreputable by the English bureaucrats stationed in Baghdad; being suspected of being a Russian spy. Commenting on Iraq's desire for independence and for entry into the League of Nations; hearing rumors about Kurdish and Assyrian discontent. Reflecting that her former differences with her mother had been largely resolved through putting thousands of miles between them. Embarking on her writing career; beginning in 1929, publishing travel articles in *The Cornhill, Baghdad Times, Spectator, Contemporary Review*. Accepting a job with the *Baghdad Times*, 1932; her editor's giving her a free hand in choosing her subject matter. Traveling to Persian Khurdistan, summer of 1932; her travel companion's suddenly begging her to run away with him to Samarkand; author's refusing, later expressing conflicting attitudes about singleness, marriage, and men. After obtaining an old treasure map, following its leads through Persia (without success). Receiving a Back Grant from the Royal Geographic Society and a Burton Medal from the Royal Asiatic

Society. Traveling through Jordan, Amman, and Petra, 1933; writing what would become *The Valley of the Assassins*. Adjusting to the slow place of Middle Eastern servants and guides. Being stricken with malaria and dysentery; writing that she must not die before her father, for the emotional blow would destroy him. Receiving news of her father's death; gaining her inheritance; still having meager finances, despite inheritance and the income brought in by her writing. Attending League of Nations Disarmament Conference in Geneva, 1933. Visiting Jerusalem en route to her home in the Piedmont Alps of Italy.

Freya Stark is now a legend for her intrepid one-woman travels through the Middle East and her open-minded response to the cultures she encountered. A 1993 biography of her by Molly Izzard, profiting from personal interviews with Stark, discloses that the travel writer served for a time as a British intelligence agent in the Middle East. Izzard also describes other aspects of Stark's life which the author left out of her autobiographies—for instance, her apparently disastrous marriage. Stark's autobiography appeared in four chronological volumes, of which *Beyond Euphrates* is volume 2. In volume 1, **891** *Traveller's Prelude: Autobiography 1893–1927* (1950), she describes coming of age, her early self-doubts and frailties, and the beginnings of her rugged individualism. Volume 3, **892** *The Coast of Incense: Autobiography 1934–1938* (1953), records the travels of the peripatetic author throughout Europe and the Middle East, and renders her evolving assessments of the cultural and political situations she encountered, along with her ideas about the relationship between men and women, and women's need for independence. The final volume, **893** *Dust in the Lion's Paw: Autobiography 1939–1946* (1961), gives Stark's seasoned opinions of the social and political changes in the world during and immediately after WWII, emphasizing the rights and integrity of the peoples in the Arab nations. Stark's books are rich in the firsthand background information necessary to understanding the complex origins of current Middle East conflict.

894 STARKIE, Enid. 1897–1970. *A Lady's Child*. Faber & Faber, 1941. 341 pp.; front port.; preface; illus. NUC pre56 565:144.

Born in Killiney, County Dublin, Ireland. Father: the Right Hon. William J. M. Starkie, last Resident Commissioner of Education for Ireland under British rule, classical scholar. Mother: May. 2 brothers; 3 sisters. Single. Wrote *Baudelaire* (1933), *Arthur Rimbaud* (1938), *From Gautier to Eliot* (1960), *Flaubert* (1967). Academic; biographer; literary critic; academic's daughter. Upper class.

Intellectual's privileged upbringing in Ireland before the establishment of the Irish Free State, 1897–1918. Feeling uncomfortably aware of her status as an Anglo-Irish "lady's child"; sensing that she was being raised for idle "ladyhood" herself. Learning to read, age 4, from brother's governess. Both parents' remoteness; their restricting contact with their children to official drawing room visits; author's aching for "simple maternal love." Father's having been the most distinguished classical scholar of his generation; his serving as professor at Trinity and president of Queen's College before his 1899 appointment as Ireland's education commissioner; his being invited by Queen to serve on Privy Council; his refusing a knighthood. Father's being the example author secretly aspired to emulate. Author's being brought up by a series of governesses; being taught entirely in French by a Frenchwoman who beat the children, but nonetheless whetted author's hunger for French culture, language, and literature. Author's having tried to kill herself over harsh discipline from "Madame"; citing this as evidence of her own passionate temperament. Being raised Catholic. Adoring the family cook, who gave author love. Becoming sensitive to unfair gender perceptions, age 10. Family's moving from Killiney to a suburb of Dublin. Attending Royal Academy of Music in Dublin, beginning at age 10. Enjoying a close relationship with one brother. Clashing with her mother during adolescence. Attending Alexandra School in Dublin, a preparatory school her mother had attended. At age 15, reading a copy of André Gide's *Les Nouritures terrestres;* finding in Gide's passionate addresses to a person of his own sex "the explanation of my adolescent malaise, the justification of my desires of rebellion." Winning a scholarship to Alexandra College, 1913; enjoying its adult freedoms; earning reputation for brilliance. During her last year at college, 1915, finding outlet for her turbulent feelings in classical music. Father's wishing that Ireland would participate in her own right in WWI; author's being much more interested in the 1916 Easter Rebellion than in Ireland's WWI role. Being torn between her desire to study music and literature, 1916; deciding on literary study at Somerville College, Oxford to win her father's approval and love. During her university years, family's undergoing financial crisis. Alluding briefly to both her student days in Paris and her later career as an academic lecturer.

Starkie takes the phrase "lady's child" from the notice announcing her birth in the *Irish Times*. In her biography, *Enid Starkie* (1973), critic Joanna Richardson alludes repeatedly to Starkie's childhood attraction to both male and female friends as having been the factor which made her feel like a misfit. While her passion for French literature started early—Starkie states that she could read French before she could read English—the French authors whom she chose for closer contemplation tended to share an interest in unconventional sexuality. Richardson observes that Starkie was always more of a biographer than a literary critic. Starkie's distinguished academic career as lecturer, professor, and don was concluded at Oxford, where she spent the last forty years of her life.

895 STAWELL, Mary F.(rances) E.(lizabeth), Lady (née Greene). 1830–d.a.1889. *My Recollections*. Richard Clay, 1911 (privately printed). 264 pp. BLC to 1975 312:33.

Born in London. Father: surname Greene, naval officer. Mother: Anne Griffith. 6 brothers. Married 1856 Sir William Foster Stawell, attorney general of Melbourne, lt. governor of Victoria, knighted 1858, d.1889. Widow. 6 sons; 4 daughters. Colonialist (Australia); politician's spouse; emigrant (Australia). Upper class.

Personal and familial memories of emigration to Australia and colonial life there, covering author's childhood to c.1889. growing up in London; being schooled by a governess, Miss Ormsby. Father's ill health and doctor's recommendation as determinants in family's emigration to Australia, c.1842. Family's preparing to emigrate; urging relatives to come with them. Emigration Party's consisting of Greene family members, author's distant cousin (and future husband) William Stawell, and many specialized household servants and craftsmen. Excerpts from family letters expressing anticipation, speculations about their new country, and details of the voyage. Miss Ormsby's looking for romance on shipboard. Family's landing at Port Phillips Bay, near Melbourne; their building a country home, "Woodlands." Excerpts from her parents' letters home regarding availability of supplies and servants, environment, cheapness of goods in Australia. Attending Sunday school taught by Miss Ormsby. Miss Ormsby's restlessness and turning "strange and wild"; father's shipping her home to Ireland. Being taught by a new governess, then a male tutor; later attending boarding schools. More letter extracts discussing expediencies in their remote area: exchange of clothing among growing boys, having one servant act as nurse/physician, financial business of running the estate. Author's positive impressions of the cultures and customs of native tribes. Father's death. Admiring her mother's strength in carrying on and managing the estate. Arrivals of relatives and friends from Ireland and England, and emigrants from Tasmania, California, and elsewhere. Discussing Australian gold fever. Recalling British policy regarding convicts; discussing free settlers vs. freed convicts. Becoming reacquainted with William Stawell, 1848; their courtship; marriage, 1856. Husband's political career; his becoming chief justice in Melbourne, 1857; his traveling the legal circuit, sending author descriptions of judicial situations he encountered. Mother's death, 1865. Visiting England, 1873; leaving sons in school while author and husband visit Paris. Author's remaining in England for several years while the boys attend school; enduring separation from husband, who must return to Australia. Including a selection of his letters to her. Taking pride in her children's education and accomplishments; daughter Melian's becoming classical lecturer at Newnham College, Cambridge. Returning to Australia, 1877; remarking on changes effected during her absence.

Distinguishing between mere politicians and ministers, both in England and Australia. Her husband's retirement; extracts from the official notice of his death and accomplishments. Extracts of tributes she received valorizing him for his public service.

As the wife of a barrister who rose to positions of great public responsibility during Australia's period of expansion, Stawell is unusually able to record many of the inner workings of the colonial legal system. Generous excerpts from her husband's correspondence are included in this book, along with the author's commentary. Stawell also vividly recalls the particulars of her domestic life in Australia, ranging from her childhood responsibilities to her later conscientiousness in raising a large family. Her informally written memoir provides a clear and extended picture of customary social and domestic activities, particularly in upper-class circles, in 19th-century Australia.

806 STEEL, Flora Annie (née Webster). 1847–1929. *The Garden of Fidelity: Being the Autobiography of Flora Annie Steel*. Macmillan, 1929. 293 pp.; front. port.; preface; illus.; final chapter by Mabel Helen Webster (author's daughter). BLC to 1975 312:103.

Born in Harrow, Middlesex. Father: George Webster, Scottish parliamentary agent and sheriff-clerk of Forfar, Scotland. Mother: Isabella McCallum, heiress of Jamaican sugar planter. 7 brothers; 3 sisters. Married 1867, Henry William Steel, colonial official in India. Widow. 1 daughter. Wrote *Wide Awake Stories* (1884), *On the Face of the Waters* (1896), *In the Permanent Way* (1897), *Mistress of Men* (1917), many others. Novelist; short storyist; colonialist (India); memsahib; philanthropist; social reformer; suffragist; civil servant's spouse; school founder; WWI volunteer. Upper class.

Feminist-oriented views of late-19th-century India from a civil servant's spouse, within the context of her family life and writing career, 1850s–1929. Remembering her father as charming and kind despite his violent temper. Her mother's being a great heiress who "ought to have had control over her own money"; parents' ceasing marital relations in anger over money disputes; author's championing female financial independence. Mother's writing plays and stories for her children; her educating them according to her own theories. Her brothers' attending Harrow until father's financial failure; family's moving to Scotland upon father's appointment as parliamentary agent, 1858. Father's friendships with William Thackeray and George Cruickshank. Author's attending school in Brussels for six months, age 13; this being her "only real schooling." Getting married, 1867; not knowing why she married; doubting either partner had been in love; being wholly sexually ignorant. Author and husband's sailing to India. Spending most of her life in India, where she "stifled regrets with duty" rather than be homesick. Depicting Madras; settling in Ludhiana. Nursing Indian women and children. Her first pregnancy's ending in a miscarriage. Beginning to write. Directing local singing and theatricals. At age 23, giving birth to a daughter. Discussing philosophy with Hindus; mulling over the religious insights of Indian Muslims. Having been baptized Presbyterian in childhood, but having converted, age 16, to the Church of England. Improving English language instruction in an Indian school. Beginning eight schools, four Hindu and four Moslem, for Indian girls. Native Indian rulers' coming to respect her peacemaking abilities and asking her to become a "Begum," ruler of a private fief; being tempted to do so. Contributing articles to the Lahore newspaper to help preserve the native Indian arts. Family's moving frequently in India because of husband's many Civil Service posts. Publishing her first book, Wide Awake Stories. Publishing an Indian-themed story in Macmillan's Magazine. Working for the editor of the Indian Public Opinion. Family's leaving India for good, 1889; author's publishing many more stories and a history, *India through the Ages*. Struggling to write novel, *On the Face of the Waters* (about 1857 Indian Mutiny). Writing story "The Permanent Way" based on a psychic vision. In London, promoting charity to help women in Delhi. Returning alone to visit India, 1894. Commenting on attitudes of Hindu and Moslem women; discussing Indian folk tales, domestic servants, female infanticide. Praising the open cultural attitudes of African traveler and writer Mary Kingsley; recommending ways to stop the practice of "purdah," involuntary seclusion of women. Noting causes of Indian civil unrest; condemning racism; supporting Indian nationalism. Reflecting on her old age, her initial opposition to her daughter's marriage, her grandson, her residence in Wales. Being interested in metaphysics, the concept of God having both male and female aspects. Supporting women's suffrage. Continuing to write. Reflecting on humanity's victimization by sex and the mutual jealousy between men and women.

Steel carefully weeds through her "garden of fidelity," cultivating particular memories and leaving out many names and dates that might contextualize events. Although reticent about family matters, she speaks frankly about her own distaste for the "sensual side" of life. This memoir serves primarily as a vehicle for the author's opinions on the treatment of both British and Indian women under the British colonial system; she expresses outrage about the Indian people's lack of educational and medical facilities, and describes how she worked actively to make these services available.

897 STEEN, Marguerite (Jane Nicholson, pseud.). 1894–1975. *Looking Glass: An Autobiography*. Longmans, Green, 1966. 231 pp.; illus.; index. BLC to 1975 312:137.

Born in Liverpool. Father: George Conolly Benson, infantry captain. Mother: Margaret Ratcliffe (stage name), actress. Adoptive father:

Joseph Steen, gardener. Adoptive mother: Margaret Moore. Single. Wrote novels *The Reluctant Madonna* (1929), *Matador* (1934), *The Marriage Will Not Take Place* (1938), others; biographies *The Lost One: A Biography of Mary (Perdita) Robinson* (1937), *William Nicholson* (1941), *A Pride of Terrys* (1962); plays *French for Love,* others. Novelist; biographer; short storyist; playwright; actress (stage); teacher; teacher (dance); foreign resident (France, Spain). Middle class.

Unconventional writer's literary, theatrical, and travel experiences, c.1894–1939. Her birth mother's being indifferent to her. After her father's death in West Africa, being adopted by the Steens; her happy childhood with them. Moving from Liverpool to the Lake District. As a young girl, idolizing Ellen Terry. Attending Moorhurst school for the "daughters of gentlemen"; being ridiculed as a gardener's daughter. Attending Kendal High School. Attending a teaching college in Sheffield at adoptive mother's insistence; wanting a more creative career. Teaching in a Hertfordshire boarding school. Visiting her birth mother in London. Outbreak of WWI: playing piano to entertain troops. Writing and burning her first novels. Meeting Ellen Terry and forming a lifelong friendship with her. Leaving her teaching job, 1918. Studying dance in Stratford-upon-Avon; teaching dance classes in the West Riding and further north. Briefly joining Mrs. Patrick Campbell's theatrical company at Blackpool; leaving rather than waiting to be sacked for inadvertently mimicking the leading lady in rehearsal; returning to teaching dance. Seeing Isadora Duncan and Eleanora Duse perform. Joining theatrical company of Julia Neilson and Fred Terry, Ellen's brother; having a love affair with a married man; leaving company and lover after three years. Becoming friends with Maud Ffoulkes. Going to Paris; meeting Sorbonne students, wandering the streets alone, seeing a woman murdered in a café, trying cocaine. Returning to England to find her first novel accepted by Geoffrey Bles; using earnings to build a house for her adoptive parents. Accepting writing assignments; teaching theatre to children; writing three more novels and many stories in three years. Having a breakdown from overwork; recovering. Returning often to Paris. Forming friendship with Hugh Walpole. Visiting Spain, 1933; researching flamenco music; afterwards writing her novel *Matador*. Living in Spain intermittently for three years; writing more novels set there. Meeting and falling in love with English artist William Nicholson; returning to live with him in England. Their being harassed by former lovers and suitors; Nicholson's second wife's refusing to divorce him. Their traveling to Segovia: witnessing the burning of churches, monasteries, and convents during the preliminaries of the Spanish Civil War; author's expressing her pro-Franco views; distinguishing between Spanish and German fascism. Returning to England. Working on dramatization of Matador, for which Nicholson created set designs. Death of her adoptive father; her sense of emptiness and loss; death of her adoptive mother one week later. Doing research in Brighton for novels about the slave trade. Meeting novelist Violet Hunt; contrasting Hunt's frustrated desire to become the wife of Ford Madox Ford with author's own insouciance about being Nicholson's "unmarried wife." Death of her birth mother. Living in France with Nicholson, 1938–39; with outbreak of WWII, their proclaiming "To hell with Schickelgrüber" (Hitler) and continuing to work.

Filled with anecdotes about the author and her eminent intimates, this autobiography strongly evokes the theatrical world of early-20th-century London and conveys a sense of what life in Spain was like for expatriate writers and artists before the Spanish Civil War. In the last third of the book Steen's relationship with painter William Nicholson takes center-stage. Her sequel, **898** *Pier Glass* (1968), covers 1939–1960s, giving further details of her life with Nicholson until his 1949 death, the social and political realities of WWII and its aftermath in England and in Europe, and Steen's travels to the U.S., Tenerife, Holland, and elsewhere.

899 STENHOUSE, Fanny. 1829–d.a.1872. *An Englishwoman in Utah: The Story of a Life's Experience in Mormonism.* Sampson Low, Marston, Searle & Rivington, 1880. 404 pp.; front. port.; illus.; preface by Harriet Beecher Stowe; author's preface; postscript. NUC pre56 567:375. (1st pub. as Tell It All, Hartford, Conn.: Worthington, 1874.)

Born in St. Heliers, Jersey, Channel Islands. Parents not named. Siblings. Married 1850 Thomas B. H. Stenhouse, Mormon missionary and elder. 6 children. Knew Brigham Young. Religionist (Mormon convert, anti-Mormon); missionary; teacher; governess; emigrant (U.S.). Lower middle class.

Firsthand exposé of the Mormon belief system, author's exploitation by it and ultimate rejection of it, highlighting the 19th-century scandal over the polygamy doctrine, covering her childhood to 1872. Joining parents' Baptist church in Jersey, age 14. Because of large family, resolving to support herself early; finding work teaching English and needlework at convent school in France; having to leave because she refused to convert to Catholicism. Mother Superior's finding author a job as governess for a wealthy French family. Becoming engaged to employer's brother; being unsure about marrying a French Catholic. Returning home to consult parents; discovering they had moved to Southhampton and converted to Mormonism, 1849. Hearing reports that Mormonism was evil but finding it, at that time, little different from other evangelical, charismatic, millenialist denominations in England. Hearing her future husband preach; feeling her antipathy to Mormonism melting away. Converting; being required to marry a

Mormon; breaking engagement to Frenchman in belief that his French Catholicism was sinful. Marrying Stenhouse; their attending a Mormon conference in London, 1850; meeting American "Apostle" who avowed having a revelation that Stenhouse must join him as a missionary in Italy. Being subject to tithing despite their poverty. Author's suffering during pregnancy and illness. Hearing rumors of polygamy; denial of rumors by visiting American "Apostles" who, author later learns, already have plural wives in Utah. Birth of her daughter. Joining her husband as a missionary in Geneva; as a woman, being forbidden to speak during services. Undergoing poverty and illness in Switzerland; giving birth to her second child; husband's returning to England to raise money; author's living in home of converts in Lausanne. Upon publication of polygamy doctrine, author's feelings of outrage; her being commanded by elders to teach polygamy doctrine to Swiss women; women's resulting fury. Returning to England, 1854; being rebaptized for her rebelliousness, having her fourth child. Family's being ordered to emigrate to America. Living in New York City, 1856–57; husband's working on Mormon newspaper. Arrival of floods of immigrants expecting to cross the plains using only handcarts. Husband's losing his job in Panic of 1857. Family's being ordered to move to Salt Lake City. Discussing Mormon marriage doctrines: "spiritual" wives for eternity and "proxy" wives for this lifetime; each man's being free to have several wives of each type; jealousy among the wives; Mormon heaven's being stratified by class. Meeting Brigham Young and his wives; feeling Young had lost all sense of right and wrong. Opening millinery shop; making bonnets for Young's wives; finding her fees were withheld as tithes. Going through "endowment" marriage ceremony with husband to make their marriage binding. Providing examples of friends author saw as being ruined by polygamy. Describing Mormon doctrines and policies: political intimidation, indiscriminate marriages, church's use of secret blood revenge. Author and husband's ultimately succumbing to polygamy pressure after five years. Husband's second and third marriages. Husband's founding *Telegraph* newspaper. Her eldest daughter's marriage to Brigham Young's son. Author's discovering proof that Young, Joseph Smith, and others practiced polygamy before, not after, the "Revelation on Celestial Marriage" in 1843. Young's coercing author's husband to move to Ogden and publish his paper there; Young's divorcing his daughter from author's husband. Author's finally deciding to leave the church. Husband's being disfellowshipped for his silence on political matters, c.1869; author and husband's having filth squirted on them by Mormons. Husband's selling his newspaper. Young's beginning his monopoly of merchandise sold through the Zion Cooperative Mercantile Institution; resulting financial failure of many. Author's avowing her purpose of rallying her Mormon sisters against polygamy.

Stenhouse's detailed and indignant catalogue of Mormon abuses coincided with the early 1880s British media furor over Mormonism. Like Stenhouse, many people in England had family members who had converted because of Mormon proselytizing, and there was a public scare—because Mormons in England coerced emigration and concealed their social and marital practices—that elements of white slavery were involved. Stenhouse's book is of great use when read in conjunction with articles published in the New York *Times* and London *Times* during this period; this is a valuable, although far from objective, source on the history of the Mormon church in Europe and America, c.1850–80.

900 STERN, Gladys Bertha Bronwyn. 1890–1973. *Monogram*. New York: Macmillan, 1936. 293 pp.; front. NUC pre56 568:84.

Born in London. Father: Albert Stern. Mother: Elizabeth Rakonitz, Viennese. 1 sister. Married 1919 Geoffrey Lisle Holdsworth. 1 child. Wrote 40 novels, including *Twos and Threes* (1916), *A Deputy Was King* (1926), *Mosaic* (1930), and play *The Man Who Pays the Piper*. Knew Sheila Kaye-Smith. Novelist; playwright; screenwriter; feminist. Upper middle class.

Kaleidoscopic presentation of experiences in the development and early career of a versatile writer, interspersed with assertive opinions on literary topics and contemporary society, spanning author's childhood to age 45. Being a dreamy, imaginative child; being cared for by nannies and governesses. Enjoying children's books, history, and Jane Austen's novels. Seeing her mother as harsh and aloof. Father's financial reverses; author's going to live with her sister. Outbreak of the Boer War. Attending day school. Becoming interested in pantomime, performing in school plays, and writing. Discussing history of pantomime in England. Temporarily attending school in Germany. Her youthful interest in jazz; studying piano. Becoming friends with playwrights John van Druten and Noel Coward; portraying Coward; their encouraging her writing career. Becoming engaged to a German; her father's opposing the match. Feeling that she was only "half-educated." Experiencing zeppelin raids in WWI. Expressing her views of contemporary theatre, c.1920s. Noting differences between American and English theatrical presentations and audiences. Explaining official reasons for censorship in the arts. Working on her writing career; suffering mild nervous breakdown from overwork. Analyzing at length English authors and literary works that have influenced her: Shakespeare, Marlowe, Austen, Dickens, Zola, Dorothy Parker. Discussing difficulties faced by women breadwinners under the patriarchal assumption of men as the providers. Questioning advantages of "ruthless efficiency" of life in the modern age. Finding it difficult not to be self-conscious; feeling that all the "best people" prefer solitude.

Stating that she is disinclined to write a "proper autobiography," Stern eschews chronological and thematic order of any kind, a practice which is disconcerting as she juxtaposes tidbits about Peter Pan (whom she sees as a shirker of responsibility), modern women's having become too chivalrous, the ugliness of sea urchins, hermits as exhibitionists, and many other amusing subjects to more weighty matters. Replete with literary and historical allusions and citations, this book also contains many analyses of other authors. **901** *Another Part of the Forest* (1941) expresses nostalgia for Stern's prewar residence in Europe, further airs her literary opinions, and recounts her illnesses. In **902** *Trumpet Voluntary* (1944), Stern reconstructs her memories of WWII within a framework of introspection and self-analysis, providing wry opinions on cultural and political topics and on the general changes war brings to society. In her last autobiography, **903** *Benefits Forgot* (1949), the author recalls the 1940s, interspersing her professional experiences, including her work with the Hollywood film industry, with keen observations and speculations on the human condition and its myths. Stern's articulate literary analyses form the centerpieces of these autobiographical accounts.

904 STEWART-MURRAY, Katharine Marjorie, Duchess of Atholl (née Ramsay). 1874–1960. *Working Partnership: Being the Lives of John George, 8th Duke of Atholl (K.T., G.C.V.O., C.B., D.S.O.) and of his Wife Katharine Marjory Ramsay (D.B.E., Hon. D.C.L., Hon. LL.D., F.R.C.M.)*. Arthur Barker, 1958. 256 pp.; front. port.; illus.; index. NUC 1942–1962 8:440.

Born in Banff, Perthshire, Scotland. Father: Sir James Ramsay, historian. Mother: Charlotte Fanning. 2 brothers; 2 sisters; 3 half-sisters. Married 1899 John George Stewart-Murray, Marquess of Tullibardine, afterward 8th Duke of Atholl, M.P., d.1940. Widow. Wrote *Women and Politics* (1929), *The Conscription of a People* (1931), *Searchlight on Spain* (1938). Knew Sir Hubert Parry, Elizabeth Haldane, Lloyd George, Stanley Baldwin, Dame Maude Lawrence, Eleanor Rathbone. Politician; member of Parliament; feminist activist; anti-Nazi activist; anticommunist activist; public speaker; child welfare activist; philanthropist. Upper class; married into aristocracy.

Many-faceted public career of the first Scottish woman elected to Parliament, accompanied by memories of her husband's career as statesman and their political partnership, covering her childhood to 1952. Family history. Her early years in Scotland. Being schooled at home by her half-sisters. Attending Wimbledon High School for Girls. Being offered a scholarship to a women's college at Oxford, but opting instead to enroll at the Royal College of Music, 1891; studying under composer Sir Hubert Parry. Making her social debut, 1892; being presented at court, 1893. Being dissuaded from a musical career by her great-aunt; leaving the Royal College, 1895. First meeting her future husband; his fearing she would turn out a "bluestocking," like her sister. Their engagement and speedy marriage, 1897, knowing he would be sent to the Sudan. His return; his 1898 departure for Boer War service. Author's traveling to South Africa to be with him. Discussing the Boer War. After their return to Scotland, author's editing book on Perthshire military history. Husband's losing campaign as Unionist parliamentary candidate for East Perthshire, 1905; his successful campaign to represent West Perthshire, 1907; his reelection, 1910. Author's finding her own roles in public service: president of Perthshire VADs, president of Church of Scotland Fellow Workers' Union, head of committee investigating medical services in rural areas. Husband's sitting in Parliament until onset of WWI; his returning to military service in Gallipoli; author's traveling to Egypt to join him. Their returning to Scotland. With his father's death, husband's inheriting title and family castle; their turning part of Blair Castle into a hospital. Author's investigating tinkers' living conditions; her committee's recommendations being shelved. Visiting France to inspect war factories. Being created a D.B.E., 1917; winning election to school board in Highland District, along with Elizabeth Haldane; their becoming friends. Serving on the Scottish Board of Health. Lloyd George's suggesting to her that she stand for Parliament; her election to West Perthshire seat, making her Scotland's first woman M.P., 1923. Husband's being appointed Lord Chamberlain; their working together politically; believing that women should not be submissive, but rather comrades and partners with men. Supporting child welfare, education, and suffrage's being expanded to include women aged 21–30. Opposing the creation of a women's political party as too divisive. Being appointed parliamentary secretary to the Board of Education, a cabinet-level post. Visiting Northern Ireland, 1925, three years after its partitioning. Being delegate to League of Nations meeting in Paris. Making political tours of Canada, 1926; later visiting Jamaica and New York. Selling property and possessions to economize. Becoming active in several education and youth organizations. Losing her position on the Board of Education with accession of Labour government, 1929; writing *Women and Politics*. Participating in movement to suppress female circumcision in Kenya. Making broadcasts, speaking publicly on Soviet forced labor and political repression; writing book on this subject, *The Conscription of a People* (1931). Being president of Christian Protest Movement, publicizing Soviet religious persecution. Giving anti-Hitler lectures in Paris; being dropped from Christian Protest Movement presidency after exposing Nazi persecution of Christians. Visiting Yugoslavia; expressing support for Yugoslavia, Romania, and Czechoslavakia against Hitler. Setting up Spanish Relief Committee, 1936; writing anti-fascist book, *Searchlight on Spain* (1938). Visiting U.S. and Canada on behalf of Spanish Children's Fund; meeting Franklin Delano Roosevelt; sensing his lack of commitment to the Spanish cause and his insensibility to the dangers of Hitler. Losing parliamentary seat because she championed military defense, 1938. Outbreak of WWII. Husband's suffering a stroke; his death, 1940. Working with counter-invasion planners. Assisting refugees following the war. Helping to found British Free Russia movement, 1951. Declaring her hopes for the freedom of the Soviet Bloc countries, 1952.

Although this memoir constitutes a public record of the joint career forged by Lord and Lady Atholl, its confinement to external events limits its ability to illuminate Lady Atholl's personality. It is noteworthy that, although both she and her husband were selfless in their public labors and committed to preventing Nazi and Communist takeovers of weaker countries, they were also both Unionists who opposed Irish home rule and cheerfully defended Britain's right to occupy Northern Ireland. Historically, Lady Atholl's book has great worth for its knowledgeable, firsthand testimony to nearly fifty years of British national politics, diplomacy, and governmental workings.

905 STIRLING, Anna Maria Diana Wilhelmina (née Pickering; Percival Pickering, pseud.). 1865–1965. *Life's Little Day: Some Tales and Other Reminiscences*. Thornton Butterworth, 1924. 388 pp.; foreword; front. port.; illus.; index. NUC pre56 570:58.

Born in London. Father: Perceval Andree Pickering, queen's counsellor, county attorney general. Mother: Anna Maria Wilhelmina Spencer-Stanhope. 1 sister (Pre-Raphaelite painter Evelyn De Morgan); 2 brothers. Married 1901 Charles G. Stirling. Wrote *Coke of Norfolk and his Friends* (1908), *William DeMorgan and His Wife* (1922), *Victorian Sidelights* (1954), others; wrote (under pseud.) novels *A Life Awry* (1893), *The Spirit Is Willing* (1898), others. Biographer; historian; novelist; children's author; teacher (Sunday school). Upper class.

Progressive development of upper-class writer strongly interested in psychic phenomena, accompanied by observations on topical issues, covering author's childhood to the end of WWI. Ancestry and family history. Her lonely childhood as the youngest; being a "distinct afterthought" in her family. Mother's being well educated; her teaching the children at home and telling them stories of her youth in high society. Maternal grandmother's being an eloquent orator, but referring to servants as "inferiors": author's becoming friends with her nursemaid and ultimately dedicating this book to her. Beginning to write creatively in childhood. Family's living in Germany for one year, author's age 8. After return to England, beginning to have psychic experiences; relating several paranormal events, including one concerning her father's death. Becoming sickly; living with her great-aunts in Yorkshire to recover her health; disliking their rigid household regime and tyranny by their servants. Having lessons in music, German, math, and reading, taught by family members and hired tutors. Publication of her children's book, *The Adventures of Prince Almero; A Tale of the Wind Spirit*. Remembering her

Stanhope uncles. Teaching Sunday school. Taking her first visit to London, for health reasons; being introduced by her famous sister, artist Evelyn De Morgan, to theatre and parties; discovering "How I do *love* the World, the Flesh and the Devil!" Traveling to Florence to visit uncle Roddam Spencer-Stanhope; anecdotes about his prodigal social life. Being presented to Queen Victoria. Resenting her social life's limitations due to her lack of a chaperone; increasingly venturing out alone, using hansoms and the omnibus; noting how the "New Woman" was being labeled a monstrosity. Citing her friend Lady Harberton as an advocate of women's dress reform; discussing how women's bicycling lessened prejudice against comfortable clothing; having been friends with Constance Wilde, another advocate of dress reform, before her husband Oscar's 1895 trial and imprisonment. The 1890s spiritualist movement's reinforcing her belief in the metaphysical world. Enjoying her artistic uncle and sister despite social opinion that their transgressive behavior made them outcasts. Forming friendships among novelists, journalists, and artists, including the Japanese enclave in London; feeling the Japanese "make Europeans appear clumsy and gauche by contrast." WWI's causing "a sudden obliteration of all petty social landmarks." Deaths of her brother-in-law and her sister Evelyn. Realizing she had pro-czar feelings during the troubled reign of Czar Nicholas; likening the massacre of the Romanov family to the butchery of the French Revolution, but with none of the public interest.

In gaining social freedom, Stirling benefited from her sister's status as an established artist. As she moved to the Chelsea district of London to join Evelyn, Stirling entered a venue in which independent female effort and a loosening of gender constraints had been accepted for some time. Stirling's account of forging an independent life in London, 1890s–1920, sets her within the matrix of many contemporary issues and phenomena, including New Womanhood, increased female mobility, dress liberation, the Chelsea art colony, and London's incipient multiculturalism.

906 STOBART, M. A. St. Clair (née Mabel Annie Boulton). 1862–1954. *Miracles and Adventures: An Autobiography*. Rider & Co., 1935. 383 pp.; front.; illus.; app. BLC to 1975 314:98.

Born in England. Father: Sir Samuel Boulton, deputy lieutenant of the county, J. P. Mother not named. 4 sisters; 2 brothers. Married surname St. Clair Stobart, Irish landlord. Married 1911 J. S. Greenhalgh, barrister, judge in Burma. 2 sons. Wrote *The Flaming Sword in Serbia and Elsewhere, Ancient Lights, The Either-Or of Spiritualism, Psychic Bible Stories*. Knew Sir Arthur Conan Doyle. Religious/spiritual writer; spiritualist; organizer of societies (women's clubs); philanthropist; farmer; WWI volunteer; foreign resident (Africa); Balkan War volunteer; Red Cross worker; public speaker. Upper class.

International peregrinations and diverse ventures of a writer, farmer, hospital commander, and spiritualist, glancing briefly at her childhood, covering 1862–1934. Childhood memories: studying with a German governess and tutors; being catechized in the Church of England; acquiring early interest in spiritualism. Writing for the *St. James Gazette*. After marriage, living in Falmouth with her husband and two sons. Organizing a club for factory girls. Family's moving to London. Working with Girls' Clubs in East End. With husband's financial reverses, their accepting land settlement in Transvaal at close of Boer War. Farming in the High Veldt; opening a general store. Translating the Bible into Zulu to bring religion to the natives. Discussing African peoples and customs; criticizing European attitudes toward natives. At her father's request, returning to England. Working with Women's First Aid Nursing Yeomanry. Marrying a second time, 1911. Going to Bulgaria to serve the British Red Cross in the First Balkan War, 1912; setting up a hospital. Losing election as a Progressive candidate for London County Council. Supporting women's suffrage but insisting women also must prove themselves intellectually. Commenting on women's exclusion from Church of England clergy. Touring U.S.; describing New York, Montreal, and American ranch life. Outbreak of WWI: forming Women's Units to relieve suffering and wounded; setting up unit in Brussels; confronting German officers who suspected her of spying; being imprisoned and threatened with execution. Upon release, working at hospitals in Antwerp, Cherbourg, and Serbia; being appointed field hospital unit commander at Bulgarian front. Describing the Serbian army's retreat; hardships of evacuating with army. Returning to England. Writing *The Flaming Sword in Serbia and Elsewhere;* speaking publicly on her Serbian experiences in England, Ireland, and the U.S. Researching psychic phenomena. Both her sons' dying in WWI. Serving as chair of the British College of Psychic Science. Collaborating with Sir Arthur Conan Doyle to advance spiritualism. Discussing the need to incorporate spiritualism into organized religion; asserting that spiritualism's authenticity is confirmed by established religion. Serving as chair of The World Fellowship of Faiths. Joining Women's Honourable Fraternity of Ancient Masonry.

Stobart describes herself as a feminist, in contrast to her first husband (whom she terms a "masculinist"). She welcomed but did not join the suffrage movement, believing that when women had proven their intellectual worth they would receive the vote. Although she omits some facts with personal relevance, such as the fate of her first husband and the origins of her nursing qualifications, the historical testimony which she includes on turn-of-the century South African colonialism, the Balkan battlefront, and the inner circle and workings of the spiritualist movement gives her memoir value for a wide range of historians.

907 STOCKS, Mary, Baroness (née Brinton). 1891–1975. *My Commonplace Book*. Peter Davies, 1970. 246 pp.; prologue; illus.; index. NUC 1968–1972 90:387.

Born in London. Father: Roland Danvers Brinton, physician. Mother: Constance Rendel. 1 brother; 1 sister. Married 1913 John Stocks, professor of philosophy, university vice chancellor, d.1937. Widow. 1 son; 2 daughters. Wrote *Fifty Years in Every Street, A Hundred Years of District Nursing, Unread Best-Seller,* others. Knew Eleanor Rathbone, Beatrice Webb, Octavia Hill, Millicent Garrett Fawcett, Gilbert Murray, Marie Stopes. Academic; academic's spouse; school administrator; politician; member of Parliament; suffragist; philanthropist; social historian; economist; social service administrator; birth control activist; social reformer; broadcaster; justice of the peace. Upper middle class; awarded life peerage, 1966.

Memories of a long and multifaceted career in academia, social reform, and broadcasting, covering 1891–c.1970. Author's comfortable childhood and extended family; their friendship with the family of Sir Richard and Lady Strachey. Discussing doctor-patient relationships in the 1890s, inequities in health care and education for different social classes, patterns of girls' and boys' education. Attending girls' day school to age 17. Describing social activism of her mother's side of the family. Author's becoming honorary secretary of the Saffron Hill Elementary School Care Committee. Being involved in the National Union of Women's Suffrage Societies, 1907–18. Entering the London School of Economics, age 19; courtship with fellow student John Stocks; being introduced to his circle at Oxford. After marriage, lecturing at the London School of Economics; aiding the Workers' Educational Association. WWI: husband's military service; her pension work for servicemen's wives. Having her first child. Noting postwar changes at Oxford. Their moving to Manchester, 1924; husband's academic teaching; author's work as a tutor; her appointment as justice of the peace. Opening a birth control clinic, 1925. Serving on various government committees and commissions. Family's moving to Liverpool; recounting husband's tenure as university vice-chancellor and his 1937 death. Beginning work as a BBC broadcaster, 1936. Returning to London; doing social service administration; serving as principal of Westfield College, 1939–51. Traveling to the USSR, Cyprus, and the Middle East. After being awarded life peerage, serving as Labour member in the House of Lords, 1966. Discussing Liberal Party social legislation, the birth of the welfare state, Octavia Hill's housing reform, women's dress reform, the militant suffrage movement, national health insurance, and the political situation in Cyprus.

In her meticulous account of her academic, philanthropic, and political involvements, Lady Stocks also provides a history of social welfare movements in England since c.1900. For every social movement and every significant figure that she encountered, she gives a capsule summary or biography. Although not wholly chronological, her account includes abundant topics, closely analyzed. Much that was cut from this book at her publisher's insistence appears in her sequel, **908** *Still More Commonplace* (1973), and concerns the Webbs, her friendship with Marie Stopes, her civil service and college administration work, her love of the theatre, her broadcasting work and review of the BBC's charter, and 1890–1970 student activism in English universities. Lady Stocks became well known as a radio broadcaster.

909 STODDART, Jane T. 1863–d.a.1933. *My Harvest of the Years*. Hodder & Stoughton, 1938. 285 pp.; index. NUC pre56 570:465.

Born in Kelso, Roxburghshire, Scotland. Father not named, Presbyterian evangelist. Mother not named. 4 siblings. Single. Wrote *A Door of Hope* (1886), *Woman at Home* (1897), *The Girlhood of Mary Queen of Scots* (1908), *The Christian Year in Human History* (1919), *The New Socialism* (1926), *Great Lives Divinely Planned* (1930), others. Knew Rev. William Robertson Nicoll. Journalist; religious/spiritual writer; biographer; editor; political writer; translator; pupil-teacher; teacher. Middle class.

Detailed presentation of writer's development and journalistic immersion in social and political issues, covering c.1869–1933. Describing Kelso and surrounding Cheviot Hills; churches in the town. Her early schooling in Kelso, ages 6–14. Her father's work as a Presbyterian evangelist; his teaching her Shakespeare. At age 14, meeting Rev. William Robertson Nicoll, pastor of Free Church of Kelso until 1885. Working as pupil-teacher at Edinburgh boarding school, 1879–81. During one year's study in Germany, 1881, earning certificate to teach German. Returning to Scotland; translating German literature for Nicoll. Moving to west of England; teaching at Clifton private school, 1883–86; while there, attending Anglican instead of Presbyterian services; writing articles on these services at Nicoll's request for his monthly, *The Contemporary Pulpit*. Becoming engrossed in Liberal politics. Writing two novels. Contributing articles to the *British Weekly,* under Nicoll's editorship, beginning in 1887. Passing Cambridge Higher Local Exam for high school teaching; teaching for five terms at Maida Vale High School. Writing series on monastery life that provoked enormous interest. Nicoll's inviting her to join the *British Weekly* staff, 1890. Moving to rooming house in Hampstead. Describing the thick black fogs in 1890s London. Watching Liberal Party's fortunes throughout the decade; discussing the Charles Stewart Parnell scandal and politics of other Irish leaders. Beginning to interview public figures for a new magazine in the *Weekly,* "Sunday at Home"; interviewing women social reformers and authors; making the magazine a success. Becoming the *Weekly*'s assistant editor; being enormously busy; moving into central London, 1893, to be closer to the paper. Witnessing Victoria's Diamond Jubilee; discussing Queen's politics toward South Africa; writing weekly Boer War diary for the newspaper, 1899. Interviewing many Americans on various topics. Nicoll's supporting the Liberal Party because its ideals benefited Nonconformist Churches; Liberals' winning the 1906 general election; author's believing the parliamentary outlook to be the brightest since 1880. Being the *Weekly*'s political writer during France's Disestablishment Crisis, 1906. Interviewing many preachers; writing *Great Lives Divinely Planned.* Discussing political antecedents of WWI. Because of the *British Weekly*'s Liberal politics, its preserving a policy of neutrality in print. Describing air raids over England. Believing that Free Churchmen were responsible for keeping the League of Nations alive by holding regular meetings between Anglican and Nonconformist clergy. Describing strikes of police, railroad workers, and miners. After Nicoll's death, 1923, Rev. William Ross's becoming editor of the *British Weekly;* his death soon after. Conservative Party's winning the 1924 general election. Memories of the Depression of 1929. Publishing *A Book of the Golden Rule* just before her 70th birthday.

One might call Stoddart the Barbara Walters of her era; her interviews with the famous and sometimes with the virtuous were a well-known institution in the *British Weekly*. This newspaper itself was a curious media vehicle; under the baton of Rev. W. R. Nicoll, it successfully combined Nonconformist morality with political analysis, much as did the Liberal prime minister, Gladstone, whom the *Weekly* championed. Stoddart retired from the paper in 1937, forty-four years after assuming an editor's chair; to a considerable degree, her book is as much a biography of the *Weekly* as of herself. Because her work brought her into direct dialogue with the world movers of her era, her memoir constitutes an eagle's-eye view of the British political and international scene in the years before WWI.

910 STOKES, Agnes. 1867–?. *A Girl at Government House: An English Girl's Reminiscences "Below Stairs" in Colonial Australia*. Ed. by Helen Vellacott. South Yarra, Victoria, Australia: John Currey, O'Neil, 1982. 145 pp.; foreword by ed.; illus. Australia National Bibliography 1982 p. 446. [cat. under Vellacott, Helen.] (1st pub. anon. as *Autobiography of a Cook*, 1932.)

Born in Richmond, Surrey. Father not named, sailor. Mother not named, domestic servant. 1 brother. Single. Domestic servant; emigrant (Australia). Working class.

Hard-luck childhood and work-related travels of an adventurous domestic servant, highlighting the workings of Australia's powerful Government House from a servant's-eye perspective, 1867–1900. Anecdotes of author's childhood penchant for stealing; her father's death, author's age 7. Mother's working as a domestic servant, leaving children home alone. After mother's death, author's being taken in by one aunt, brother's being farmed out to another. Leaving aunt's house due to friction; being hired as kitchen help by mother's former employer, then dismissed. Finding new job as kitchen maid and nursemaid. Seeing advertisement for well-paid domestic jobs in Australia and applying; sailing for Australia, 1886; describing voyage and arrival in Brisbane. Being housemaid to a bishop; disliking compulsory chapel attendance. Relishing her freedom from the advice of relatives back in England. Leaving bishop's household upon reduction of staff; sailing to Sydney; finding domestic work on a nearby estate. Witnessing celebrations of Sydney's Centenary Year. Being courted by a fellow servant; their informal engagement; his mother's opposing the marriage. After death of Sydney estate's owner, moving to Melbourne; describing city in the 1880s; finding job as kitchen maid in Government House, residence of Sir Henry Loch, the governor. Depicting house's opulence and the waste of food in its kitchen. Being taken with household staff to visit Mount Macedon, the governor's country estate. Resenting sexual advances of another household servant; knocking him out cold when he persisted. At Mount Macedon, the caretaker's wife's beseeching author to protect her young sister back at Government House from the sexual attentions of the governor's valet; author's dumping a jug of water on the governor after mistaking him for his valet. Domestic staff's trying spiritualist experiments among themselves; author's giving up spiritualism in fright after prophecies came true. Being promoted to under-still-room maid by new governor, Lord Hopetoun; his being esteemed by Australian public for his egalitarian principles. His instituting strict standards of sexual conduct for servants; their nevertheless knowing how to sneak out at night. Visiting the Melbourne Centenary Exhibition, 1888. Resisting being sent back to Macedon House; sailing to England, 1890; describing visiting ports en route: Ceylon, Malta, Naples, and Pompeii. Visiting ex-employer; reuniting with her brother. Rejecting an unwelcome suitor. Finding the English much stiffer about the proprieties of courtship than the Australians. Wanting to return to Australia, where domestics could earn more than £15 a year. Returning to Sydney; her employment in a number of households, including a brief stint back in Government House. Planning to marry a dead friend's husband, but being told by a fortuneteller it wouldn't come to pass; dreading the approaching marriage because of his jealousy. Resolving the issue by departing for America; on shipboard, encountering a "Mr. Moss of Brisbane" and wondering if he might be the "Mr. M" the fortune-teller foretold she would marry.

Sections of Stokes's 1932 *Autobiography of a Cook* are reprinted here, with interpolated commentary from editor Helen Vellacott; Stokes's identity was unknown until discovered by the editor. The author's simple style, phonetic spelling, and inconsistent grammar display her lack of formal education, but she seems to have turned her domestic talents to the greatest possible advantage. Contained in the chronicle of her international adventures is much topical commentary on the lifestyle discrepancies of the different classes, and her picture of the prodigal waste in late-19th-century upper-class households is a needed complement to reminiscences from upper-class women themselves. Much as middle-class women of her time were increasingly rejecting marriage in favor of a career, Stokes ultimately rebuffed every suitor who threatened to interfere with her self-direction. Her life story also provides a fascinating look at the behind-the-scenes lives of the Australian governors and their households, c.1880–1900.

911 STOPES, Marie Charlotte Carmichael. 1880–1958. "Dr. Marie Stopes," pp. 82–92 in *If I Had My Time Again: An Anthology Contributed by Twenty Distinguished Men and Women*. Ed. by Sir James Marchant. Odhams Press, 1950. 256 pp.; intro. by Lord Horder. NUC pre56 361:16.

Born in Edinburgh, Scotland. Father: Henry Stopes, Quaker, archaeologist, skilled brewer, architect. Mother: Charlotte Carmichael, Calvinist, Shakespearean scholar. 1 sister. Married 1914, Reginald Ruggles Gates, botanist, Canadian; marriage annulled 1916. Married 1918, Humphrey Verdon Roe, airplane manufacturer. Wrote *Ancient Plants* (1910), *Married Love* (1918), *Radiant Motherhood* (1920), *Enduring Passion* (1928), others. Knew David Lloyd George, Lady Constance Lytton, Edward Carpenter, Arnold Bennett, others. Birth control activist; scientist; women's issues author; social reformer; scientific writer; poet; public speaker. Middle class.

Meditations of a noted birth control activist on her intellectual formation, family planning evangelism, humanitarian ambitions, and inner life, covering her childhood to 1950. Family's moving to London when author was age 1. Her mother's being learned, a Calvinist, and a stern disciplinarian; her father's Quakerism and prehistoric tool collecting; their mutual love for her; their support for women's suffrage. Parents' traveling on archaeological digs during mother's pregnancy with her; author's suggesting she absorbed her paleontological interest prenatally. Writing poetry in adolescence; her adored biology teacher's making her tear it up as a waste of time; not publishing her poems until years later, after teacher's death. While author was at London University, father's losing all his money and dying prematurely; author's having to learn to economize. Loving science; discovering preserved cells of extinct species; determining the four ingredients in banded coal. Doing further fossil research in Japan. Being happier in adulthood than in childhood; at age 11, having felt responsible for the whole world; never entirely losing this burden; suffering for "the millions of pitiful lives" she could have eased if couples had known of her birth control methods. After publishing *Married Love* (1918), receiving many grateful reader responses, but having hospitals turn against her because of the book's notoriety. With her second husband, opening the first Mother's Clinic, 1921, to dispense free information on all aspects of sex; not understanding why their efforts were opposed. Goals of the birth control crusade: healthy babies and mothers, wanted babies, birth spacing. Giving public lectures on birth control, at Lloyd George's suggestion; these meeting with great success, but exposing her to criminal charges. Wishing she had a fortune to spread her birth control gospel to the world. Retrospectively wishing she had been harder on her opponents, knowing of their death threats against her, theft of her ideas, and exploitation of her name as a contraceptive trademark. Using poetry and contemplation to counterbalance the grinding practical side of her work. Opposing the rigid Church of England laws concerning marriage and divorce; desiring to "Christianize the Church," to put back its compassion for humanity.

In this brief essay Stopes sifts her life and studies its contrasts, frequently quoting her own poetry. She omits mentioning that her interest in birth control was instigated by the shock of discovering the facts of sexuality only after her first marriage; the marriage was in fact annulled for non-consummation. While giving an excellent condensed look at Stopes's own ambitions for the birth control movement, this essay is best read in concert with more fact-oriented sources, such as Aylmer Maude's *Authorized Life* (1924), which is largely from Stopes's direct dictation, and Ruth Hall's well-researched *Passionate Crusader* (1977), the most recent critical biography.

912 STORIE, Elizabeth. 1818–?. *The Autobiography of Elizabeth Storie, a Native of Glasgow, Who Was Subjected to Much Injustice at the Hands of Some Members of the Medical, Legal, and Clerical Professions.* Glasgow: Richard Stobbs, 1859. 159 pp.; list of subscribers; app. BLC to 1975 314:450.

Born in Glasgow, Scotland. Father: John Storie, small tradesman. Mother not named. 2 brothers; 2 sisters. Single. Physically handicapped woman; dressmaker; milliner. Lower middle class.

Grim, detailed recollections of medical malpractice and legal injustice, including a perceptive look at early-19th-century society, spanning author's childhood to 1859. Suffering common childhood complaint, "nettle rush," age 4; being given powders containing mercury and "aquafortis" (nitric acid) by Dr. Falconer, son of her father's friend; acid's eating away part of her jaw, tongue, and teeth. Falconer's prescribing another drug, withheld by author's father, later found to be a fatal dose of arsenic; her parents' believing that the doctor prescribed a fatal dose to murder her and conceal his bungling. Growth of her jaw into a solid mass, resulting in her impaired speech and inability to eat solid food. Having more than twenty operations throughout her lifetime to enlarge her jaw opening. Father's winning lawsuit against doctor for £1,000, 1823; doctor's absconding. Father's death, 1833. Author's lacking the strength to support herself through dressmaking and millinery. Having her attempts to collect from the doctor thwarted by her unscrupulous former attorney. Attending Bible classes, joining Presbyterian church in Glasgow, 1840–49. Persisting in her unsuccessful attempts to collect from doctor; again being thwarted by her former attorney. Being dealt a crushing blow by her mother's death, 1849. Discovering the original documents in her case had been lost; unsuccessfully petitioning to recover them. Believing there is collusion among the lawyers; resolving to become her own attorney. Her former attorney's being found liable for £1,000, but refusing to pay; his expressing personal animosity toward author. Appealing without success to her church for aid in her cause; her name's being removed from communion rolls; minister's believing her insane. Unsuccessfully petitioning Presbytery and Synod for assistance. Threatening to publish all documents in the case after leaving local church, 1858. Having her appeal to the Supreme Court of Scotland denied. Having another operation, resulting in her greater ease in breathing, speaking, and eating. Believing she would have received justice had she been of a higher class. Considering that Falconer might have been experimenting with her rather than trying to ruin her life. Finding consolation in the hope of happiness in the world to come.

Publishing this book was apparently Storie's last resort in her relentless, almost obsessive pursuit of justice, which seems to have become more all-consuming the more her appeals were rejected. Storie's account characterizes—although in an extreme way—the discrepancies of power between 19th-century physicians and their patients, particularly if those patients were female and/or poor. The author's style reveals self-education, particularly in technical aspects of the law, and her tone is pleading as she presents her endless battle with the legal and medical professions.

913 STORY, Janet L. (née Maughan). 1828–?. *Early Reminiscences*. Glasgow: James Maclehose & Sons, 1911. 341 pp.; front. port.; illus. NUC pre56 571:568.

Born in India. Father: Philip Maughan, employed by East India Company. Mother: Elizabeth Arnott. 3 brothers; 2 half-brothers. Married 1858 the Rev. R. Herbert Story, principal and vice chancellor of Glasgow University. Daughters. Wrote *Charley Nugent,* others. Novelist; teacher (Sunday school); clergyman's spouse. Upper middle class.

Memories of generally peaceful and contented life in Scotland, as well as observations on Scottish society, covering author's childhood to 1862. Moving to Edinburgh. Maternal family history. Father's financial reverses; their effect on family. Attending boarding school, acquiring "suitable" education, wanting to be head girl in English class. Her interest in singing. Keeping a diary. Recalling Prince Albert and Queen Victoria's first visit to Scotland, 1838. Attending school in Hampstead. Mother's ill health and subsequent death. Keeping house for her father; fearing he might remarry; attending concerts with him. Meeting Jenny Lind; singing for her. Attending opening of Great Exhibition in London, 1851. Taking trip to English Lake District with father. Socializing with Glasgow society. Her father's belonging to Episcopalian church. Diary extracts about social events, other current events. Celebrating the end of the Crimean War, 1856; discussing attitudes in Scotland toward the losses of the war. Memories of Florence Nightingale's accomplishments. Social ramifications of the Indian Mutiny, 1857, for Europeans in India. Attending a ball at the Lunatic Asylum in Morningside; dancing with a patient whom she mistook for a guest. Writing *Charley Nugent,* sending manuscript to Thackeray; his encouraging her. Father's serious illness. Attending General Assembly of Church of Scotland; meeting her future husband. Marriage. Living in Roseneath with husband; meeting villagers; teaching Sunday school. Describing her happy married life. Commenting on etiquette for children at parties. Noting changes in music between her youth and the present.

Story's book is a collection of gentle, wistful vignettes of her early years as an admired, although untitled, member of Edinburgh society. This autobiography features extensive descriptions of daily life in the upper echelons of Scottish society and of Story's personal encounters with luminaries in the arts. In the book's only real flash of intimacy, the author acknowledges that, having reached the age of 30, she had given up all hopes of marriage when she met and wed the Rev. Story. The author's **914** *Later Reminiscences* (1913) continues her recollections in a framework of upper-middle-class Scottish life, and covers the mid-Victorian era to the end of the Edwardian period. In this sequel, Story concentrates on her husband's achievements and her participatory sense of fulfillment through them.

915 STOTT, Grace. c.1845–d.a.1897. *Twenty-Six Years of Missionary Work in China*. New York: American Tract Society, 1897. 366 pp.; front. port.; preface by J. Hudson Taylor; illus. NUC pre56 571:659.

Born in Glasgow, Scotland. Parents not named. Married 1870 George Stott, missionary, d.1889. Widow. Knew Lucy Soothill, Hudson Taylor. Missionary; religionist (nondenominational); foreign resident (China); school founder; preacher; charitable volunteer; organizer (philanthropic). Middle class.

Progress of the author's evangelism from her conversion through three decades of missionary work in China, 1865–97. Being a tract distributor and Sunday school teacher. Dating her conversion to missionary ideals to meeting J. Hudson Taylor of the Overseas Mission Society (OMS), 1865. His planning a missionary crusade to China's interior, newly opened to the West; author's asking if she could join; his consenting. Traveling to OMS headquarters in London; meeting other missionaries, including her future husband, an Aberdeen schoolmaster with only one leg. His departing for China, autumn 1865, with the first group of volunteers in the China Inland Mission. Author's staying behind because she was ill; believing this a sign God was calling her elsewhere; preaching the gospel and visiting the Glasgow poor, 1867–70. Describing Mr. Stott's missionary work during this time; agreeing to marry him; leaving for China to share his mission, 1870. Their marriage; living in Wenchow. Chinese natives' being steeped in anti-foreign propaganda following 1870 Tientsin riots; their shouting at and cursing the missionaries. Describing Chinese idol worship. Lamenting Chinese indifference to the Gospel. Converting a Buddhist priest, an opium grower, and others, but commenting on backsliding converts. Deciding to start a girls' boarding school, so young male converts could have Christian wives. Fighting the practice of footbinding. Citing growth of her girls' school, 1875–97; conversions of pupils. Taking a furlough to England, 1877; returning to China, 1878. Opening a home for girl graduates of her mission school; husband's raising funds in Ireland for this purpose. Teaching a weekly Bible class. Women converts' forming a Missionary Band to convert other Chinese. Author's departing for rest in Shanghai; outbreak of 1884 anti-foreign riots in Wenchow after French bombarded Foochow; the Soothills' Methodist church and the Stotts' church and schools being destroyed. Their rebuilding church; receiving reparations for losses. Depicting persecution of Christian converts through malicious lawsuits. Their turning over their work to three newly arrived missionaries from England; returning to England. Death of her husband, 1889. Author's returning to China. Beginning homes for blind men and old widows. Attending Shanghai Missionary Conference, 1890. Diary extracts and letters from women doing mission work. Establishing a sanitorium for missionaries; her own health's failing. Exerpts from testimonials by pastors at her 50th birthday party. Noting the riots against foreign missionaries, beginning in 1895. With onset of cholera epidemic in Wenchow, author's sailing for England; receiving news that some of her friends have died in the epidemic.

Stott's book is one of the few by a woman missionary in the nondenominational China Inland Mission, founded by the legendary Hudson Taylor. Taylor, unlike other mission sponsors, encouraged the participation of young women. In his six-volume work, *Hudson Taylor and China's Open Century* (1981–88), historian A. J. Broomhall writes, "if Chinese girls and women were to have an equal chance to hear the gospel, Christian women must go to them, beyond the walls of institutions. . . .

Quiet work in Chinese homes could be as effective as overt evangelism among men." With the 20th-century opening of China to the West, the China Inland Mission has attracted new historical interest.

916 STOTT, Charlotte Mary (née Waddington). 1907–s.l. 1992. *Forgetting's No Excuse: The Autobiography of Mary Stott, Journalist, Campaigner, and Feminist.* Virago, 1989. 203 pp.; port.; foreword. BLC 1976–1982 43:195. (1st pub. Faber & Faber, 1973.)

Born in Leicester, Leicestershire. Father: Robert Guy Waddington, newspaper owner. Mother: Amalie Maria Christina Bates, newspaper columnist. 2 brothers. Married 1937 Kenneth Stott, journalist, d.1967. Widow. 1 daughter. Journalist; editor; feminist; pacifist. Middle class.

Journalist's career, feminism, and thoughts on widowhood, covering 1907–73. Her emotional development: being aware she looked plain; her early closeness to her mother changing to aversion; having close schoolgirl friendships; later evaluating such ties as not lesbian, but preparation for heterosexual love. Her closest relationship with a man being marriage; its liberating her from fear of inadequacy. Opposing feminist condemnations of marriage; citing women's need of mutually committed marriage. Having relied on her husband's parents for two years after the 1943 birth of her daughter; providing similar support for her own daughter after birth of her grandchild. Her political development: until adolescence, copying her father's enthusiasm for the Liberal Party; later supporting Labour. Discussing class distinctions between political parties. Witnessing effects of 1930s depression in Bolton and Manchester. Discussing her work for co-operative movements in Britain. Taking part in pacifist work, notably Canon Richard Sheppard's Peace Army. Fascism's growth; its devastating European co-operative movements in the 1930s; remembering attending a parade in which both Hitler and Mussolini rode; wondering if she would have been capable of assassination. Condemning the increasing violence of political protests; looking back at her own youthful idealism and at social gains through legislation. Her career development: finding her first newspaper job at the Leicester *Mail,* age 17; working as a reporter there for six years. Taking a job at the Bolton *Evening News,* 1931. Editing women's and children's publications for the Co-operative Press in Manchester. Working as a sub-editor for the Manchester *Evening News,* 1945–50; enjoying a job usually closed to women; leaving when men she had trained were promoted over her. Editing the women's page of the Manchester *Guardian,* 1957–71; discussing how the need for a liberal-minded paper transformed the *Guardian* from regional to national. Being proud of the many grassroots women's activist groups spawned by the women's page. Evaluating why some papers succeed and others fail; her journalist husband's having been devastated by the 1960 failure of his home newspaper, the *News Chronicle*. Believing the future of the press lies with small-circulation newspapers. Applauding the erosion of sexual taboos in media language; noting that the Victorian concept of ladies' asexual "purity," upheld by class barriers and prostitution, was successfully debunked by the frank speech of feminist Josephine Butler and newspaper editor W. T. Stead. Blaming the contemporary media for equating love with sex; believing publishers should discourage pornography by self-censorship. Commenting on the feminist movement in Britain and America, 1960s–70s. With her husband's death, 1967, retrospectively analyzing the grieving process; gaining heightened awareness of widows' economic plight; having more time for feminist activism. Defending both abortion and euthanasia for the "worn-out old."

In an afterword to this account, written for a later edition, Stott notes that she joined the newly founded Social Democratic Party in 1981, won a seat on its national committee in 1982, and ultimately withdrew from political activity when the SDP merged with the Liberal Party, 1987. Since the sections of this memoir are not chronological, it is likely that the whole is a collection of topical essays on her life and work. Her observations on wide-ranging social phenomena—the feminist movement, sexual liberation, the rise and fall of different types of media predominance—are subjective, but written from an unusually good vantage point as both feminist and journalist. Stott also wrote *Before I Go* (1985), a sequel to this autobiography.

917 STRACHEY, Jane Maria, Lady (née Grant). 1840–1928. "Some Recollections of a Long Life," in *Nation and Athenaeum* 34–35: Jan. 5, 1924, pp. 514–15; Feb. 25, 1924, pp. 730–31; July 12, 1924, pp. 473–74; Aug. 30, 1924, pp. 664–65.

Born aboard East India Company ship, en route from India to England. Father: Sir John Peter Grant, secretary to British Government in Bengal. Mother not named. 1 brother; 2 sisters. Married 1859 Sir Richard Strachey, engineer, scientist, geographer, d.1908. Widow. 13 children (including feminist Philippa; Pernel, principal of Newnham College; Lytton, critic and biographer; and James, editor of Freud's writings). Feminist activist; suffragist; philanthropist. Upper class.

Brief, entertaining glimpses of Indian colonial life and Victorian worthies in India and England, with historical memories of the Women's Cause and the author's contributions to it, covering her childhood to 1917. Part 1: Being born at sea, during mother's voyage back to England from India. Mother's returning to India with her three daughters, 1851, despite family opposition; their arrival in Calcutta, 1852, beginning the most important epoch in author's life, liberating her from suppression. Father's character. Part 2: Author's second visit to Calcutta, this time with her brother, 1858. Her third visit to India, 1862. Her social life at Simla with her husband. Being friends with the Viceroy of India, Lord

Lytton, 1878; depicting the characters of Lord Lytton and his wife; discussing how he and Sir Alfred Lyall responded to the late 1870s crisis in Afghanistan. Part 3: Social life in London. Having close friendships with Thomas Henry Huxley and Thomas and Jane Carlyle. Meeting Robert Browning in England, c.1863; remembering crowd of American women fawning over him. Discussing going to plays and concerts with her close friend George Eliot; Eliot's lover, critic G. H. Lewes, telling author she had been the model for the character Dorothea Brooke in *Middlemarch*. Part 4: Meeting Tennyson socially several times; meeting the tragic actor Salvini. Discussing French comedy actors she saw perform in 1857. Expressing her interest in women's rights; advocating John Stuart Mill's ideas in *On Liberty* after reading this book at age 19. Contributing part of her husband's salary to the founding of Girton College for women. Signing first parliamentary petition for women's suffrage, 1867. Being friends with suffrage leader Millicent Garrett Fawcett. Author's being present, on her 77th birthday, at the great Albert Hall meeting granting women the vote, 1917.

Concerning this autobiography, Virginia Woolf wrote (in *Moments of Being*) that Lady Strachey waited to write her memoirs until she was too old and had forgotten too much, and thus these installments are very brief. They are, however, part of a longer unpublished typescript in the Strachey Trust Papers. Lady Strachey's memoirs read like scattered notes in no particular chronological order, skipping many years and alluding only briefly to many major experiences.

918 STRANGE, Kathleen R.[edman]. 1896–1968. *With the West in Her Eyes: The Story of a Modern Pioneer*. New York: Dodge, 1937. 292 pp.; foreword. NUC pre56 572:328. (other ed.: Toronto: Macmillan, 1945.)

Born in London. Parents not named. Married 1918, Harry Strange, WWI veteran. 1 daughter; 1 son; 3 stepsons. Emigrant (Canada); farmer; pioneer; WWI administrator; journalist. Middle class.

Complex portrait of an urban emigrant's farm life in Canada, charting her shift from urban to rural values, 1914–36. Husband's life before marriage. WWI: author's leaving school to work in War Department, competing with men and gaining self-reliance. Meeting Harry, 1917; marrying one year later. Leaving to take up farming in Hawaii, 1919; husband's falling ill en route; doctor's recommending a more bracing climate. Their buying and renovating a farm in Fenn, Alberta, Canada; bringing husband's mother and three young sons from Hawaii to live with them. Author's feeling unfit for farm life; not knowing how to cook; learning from mother-in-law. Neighbors' being hostile to her urban origins. Discussing the difficulty of keeping frontier schoolteachers from marrying and leaving; husband's efforts to do so as chairman of the school board. Community's initial furor over author's wearing riding breeches. Mother-in-law's departure for England. Describing her arduous household work and farm chores. Hiring, then firing, a socialist farmhand who believed himself entitled to a share of their hay. Seasonal harvesters' migrating annually to the western prairies for the wheat harvest. Contrasting mechanized wheat farming with traditional English harvest methods. Noting diversity of community's ethnic origins: British, northern and central European, Chinese. Community life's centering around local branch of United Farmers of Alberta; author's participating in its United Farm Women subsidiary. Her first pregnancy. Death of her 8-year-old stepson from heart defect; praising country doctors. Hospital death of her newborn daughter from birth injuries, 1921. Raising pedigreed chickens and purebred hogs; feeling an aversion to eating any animal she had raised. Author and husband's winning World's Grand Championship for wheat sample at the Chicago International Show, 1923; husband's consequently being elected national president of Canadian Seed Growers' Association. Being proud of her achievement in running the farm. Being inspired by attending Canadian Women's Press Club to write a story about her early farm days; its acceptance by the *Grain Growers' Guide* at time of her new daughter's birth, 1924. Selling stories about prairie life to publications all over Canada, the U.S., and England; creating her own newspaper syndicate: becoming news correspondent for two local papers. Birth of author's third child, 1926; series of farm disasters beginning one year later: drought, fire, tornado. Returning to London to visit her ill mother; discovering she preferred farm life to the urban social whirl. Returning to Fenn. 1929 stock market crash's producing farm failures and collapse of Alberta oil boom; moving to Winnipeg, 1930, when Seed Growers Association invited husband to start his own research lab. With loss of farm, author's lacking inspiration despite having more time to write; contrasting city life unfavorably with farm life; losing, with regret, her sense of partnership with her husband.

Strange's autobiography is one of several from urban British women who ventured back to the soil in the early 20th century. Its closest comparison might be with Justina Spencer-Knott's *Fools Rush In* (1945). Strange's detailed picture of western Canadian farm life illuminates women's lives on the prairie, farm women's organizations, and the many types of agricultural labor indigenous to the region. Her comments contrasting rural and urban life indicate that, for her, farm existence came to represent "the *only real way of life*."

919 STRETTON, Emily Bell. c.1860–1923. *Things Were Different: Compiled from the Diary of Emily Bell Stretton*. Constable, 1927. Ed.

by Elisabeth Fagan (author's niece). 297 pp.; front. port.; illus.; ed.'s note. NUC pre56 165:472.

Born in the Midlands. Father: Rev. Richard Stretton, Anglican rector. Mother: Susan Bell. 2 brothers; 1 sister. Single. Traveler (India); WWI volunteer; secretary; suffragist. Middle class.

Author's sheltered upbringing and spinster lifestyle, highlighting her stormy long-term friendship with the woman who stole the man she loved, c.1860–c.1920. Ancestry and family history. Father's death in author's infancy. Mother's dying, author's age 6, from long-term gynecological illness; her refusing from "ineradicable modesty" to confide in a male doctor until too late. Living with her aunt; attending day school; looking for sex information in the Bible. Emulating behavior she had read in novels by flirting at school, age 13; consequently being sent to a "College for Gentlemen's Daughters." At age 16, meeting Mollie Parker; describing Mollie's "love affairs." Author's refusing her own first marriage proposal. Mollie's marrying her physician father's Eurasian assistant and leaving for India; author's contrasting this to her own singleness and loneliness in old age. Inheriting an independent income; becoming companion-secretary to a married friend; accompanying a colonial wife and family to India as the children's companion. Being courted by an English major, Jack Mansol. Mollie's joining them; author's employer's expressing horror at Mollie's interracial marriage. Major Mansol's flirting with Mollie. Mollie's husband's beating her; Mollie's killing him and being tried for murder; transcript of trial testimony; Mollie's acquittal. Mollie's marrying author's beau, the major; author's taking post as companion to a senile old lady in Bombay. The major's dying after Mollie broke his heart; author's wearing a bag of earth from his grave around her neck for the rest of her life. Visiting Burma with her friend, feminist and suffragette Susan Lawson. Sailing back to England with Mollie, c.1901, but refusing to live with her. Becoming secretary to the "Ladies' Green Room Club" for actresses; joining the Actresses' Franchise League. Unsuccessfully urging Mollie to join her in a suffrage march. Mollie's embroiling herself in a series of intrigues with married men, then going abroad to escape scandal. Years later, author's encountering Mollie in France while doing WWI hospital liaison work. Mollie's nursing a young Italian soldier; her marrying his wealthy 80-year-old father. Postscript: after a long interval, Mollie's being widowed again. Author's never quite overcoming her bitterness at being robbed of the man she loved; alluding to Mollie as being like the wicked in the Bible who "flourish like a green bay tree."

Although the editor had a hand in transforming the text from diary entries to narrative, the details are entirely Stretton's. Her account documents the repeated impact on her life of Victorian gender role restrictions: the death of her mother from the taboo against ladies' discussing sexual matters with men, even male doctors; the author's own prolonged sexual ignorance; the limitations on her schooling. However, the greatest negative impact she experienced was from being victimized by a friend trapped in another Victorian female role, that of the beautiful woman who finds her identity in being a sexual adjunct to men. Stretton's own life took another turn: at first filling the traditional spinster roles as companion and governess, she found her feminist feet after becoming involved with the Actresses' Franchise League, accurately if belatedly critiquing her friend Mollie as the "coaxing, cuddling, parasitic type of woman, against whom the fighters among us [feminists] were always inveighing."

920 STRIDE, Louie. 1907–?. *Memories of a Street Urchin*. Ed. by Graham Davis. Bath: Bath University Press, 1984. 46 pp.; ed.'s preface; intro.; illus. BNB 1985 2:2942.

Born in Bath, Avon. Father: Arthur Burton, navvy, Welsh. Mother: surname Stride, charwoman, prostitute. Stepfather not named. Illegitimate child. Married 1957, husband not named, Irish. Domestic servant; telephone operator; waitress; factory worker; hotel worker. Working class.

Difficulties of an illegitimate, impoverished member of the working class, 1907–1960s. Discussing class attitudes toward illegitimacy; hating, being ashamed of her father. Author's and mother's being evicted; explaining poor people's "moonlight flit" maneuver of absconding to avoid paying rent. Mother's doing char work and selling the furniture for rent money. Author's attending infants' school. Mother's becoming a prostitute. Author's feeling constant hunger; stealing bread from fellow students; scavenging for food. Having her hair cropped because of lice. Being a lonely, shunned child; befriending cats to save her own sanity. Envying characters in books. WWI: Increase in mother's "business"; author's learning to disappear discreetly; mother's marrying an alcoholic Canadian soldier and deteriorating mentally. Author's surviving through escaping into fantasy life. Going hungry due to mother's improvidence with money; eating snails off the pavement. Suffering wartime food shortages. Noting the 1918 beginnings of the welfare state and aid to new mothers. At age 13, suffering molestation attempt by male welfare worker. Attending Band of Hope meetings. Having tonsillectomy; remembering only the good food and clean surroundings of the sanitarium, not wanting to go home. Mother's being committed to an asylum; her dying of consumption fifteen years later. Author's working as a babysitter and charwoman. Trying to keep house for her alcoholic stepfather. Taking temporary domestic service jobs in large homes. Working as a chambermaid in a hotel spa. Buying a small cottage with accumulated savings. Waitressing during summer hotel seasons, c. age 30. WWII: Losing cottage in Bath blitz; working as a flour sack scraper; describing dangers of job; being fired for leaving a few minutes early.

Being unable to get a government post without a legitimate birth certificate; eventually finding work as a telephone operator. Marrying an Irish widower. Retiring and moving to Ireland, 1966.

In this unsentimental memoir, Stride's obsession with the continual hunger in her early life illustrates the extent to which an individual's world can be circumscribed by this most basic of human needs. At a time in the early 20th century when middle-class and upper-class women could focus on the larger picture of politics, war, social reform, and the progress of women's equality, Stride's empty stomach restricted her outlook to meeting her own requirements. Her illegitimacy raised further hurdles in her path in the form of social opprobrium and occupational difficulties, but her self-portrait suggests that she successfully transcended these hurdles to create a more satisfying life for herself.

921 STRINGER, Mabel E. c.1870–d.a.1924. *Golfing Reminiscences.* Mills & Boon, 1924. 254 pp., front. port., illus., preface, index. NUC pre56 573:463.

Raised in Littlestone, Kent. Parents not named. Single. Golfer; sportswriter; editor; paid companion. Middle class.

Entertaining look at British women's golf and author's various professional enterprises in connection with the sport, spanning c.1879–1924. Her athletic, outdoor pursuits in childhood. After completing unspecified schooling, playing golf enthusiastically at the Littlestone Club, formed in 1887. Serving as captain of the Littlestone Ladies' Club for its first five years, 1891–96; observing inferior facilities and second-class treatment of women golfers. Winning match with Issette Pearson, unaware that Pearson was the women's champion; their forming lifelong friendship; their planning county clubs for women and interclub competition; Pearson's developing universal handicapping system. Joining the Ladies' Golf Union (LGU) at its 1893 founding. Noting 1890s dress regulations that hampered movement in women golfers; describing improvements since then. Overcoming resistance of men golfers to organized amateur women's golf. Memories of competing in Women's Open Championships, 1893–1900. Participating in county golf since 1899. Unspecified crisis's forcing her to earn her own living after 1901; trying to earn her living as a lady's companion. Being sidelined by lung ailment, 1902; having corrective surgery, 1903. Working since 1904 as a golf journalist. Returning to competition, 1906; playing in her last Open Championship, 1907. Becoming editor of woman's page of *Golfing*, 1910. National County Golf Alliance's breaking away from the LGU, 1910, in dispute over basis for forming clubs. Attending and covering regional championships in Ireland, Scotland, and Wales; serving as Southerndown Club's assistant secretary, 1909–13. Death of author's father, 1912, while she was editor of monthly *Ladies' Golf*. Author's having phlebitis, 1912–13; experiencing recurrences to 1920. National

Alliance's being taken over by the LGU, 1914. Suspension of the Opens during WWI; railway strike's causing cancellation of 1919 Open; the 1920 Open's being held in Ireland during the British/Irish war over Home Rule; families' forbidding many would-be players to attend. Author's instituting championships for girls under age 20 and women over age 50. Discussing team golf and how it is scored. Writing comic verses on golf. Itemizing formation of various women's golfing associations since 1911. Noting periodicals that covered and/or sponsored women's golfing events. Depicting many women's golfing pioneers and her close friends in the sport; discussing her golfing "nieces," younger golfers who called her "Auntie Mabel."

Closely associated with the history of British women's golf as a player, organizer, and journalist, Stringer includes a wealth of detail on the sport's development, established competitions, and famous players. She never comments on the potential for women to play golf professionally; if the opportunity had been available, she would undoubtedly have benefited, for a combination of financial pressures and health troubles forced her to give up competition in middle age. As she reconstructs particular matches in loving detail, Stringer's nostalgia for her own competitive years becomes increasingly evident.

922 STUART-WORTLEY, Violet Hunter (née Guthrie). 1866–d.a.1946. *Life Without Theory: An Autobiography*. Hutchinson, 1946. 158 pp.; foreword by Tahu Hole; illus. NUC pre56 574:315.

Born in London. Father: James Alexander Guthrie, a director of the Bank of England. Mother: née Stirling. Stepfather: Forster Fitzgerald Arbuthnot, retired Indian official. 3 brothers; 5 sisters. Married 1891, Maj. Edward James Montagu Stuart-Wortley, raised to rank of earl's son, 1900. 1 son; 2 daughters. Knew Louisa, Marchioness of Waterford, Olive Maxse, Dame Nellie Melba, others. Military spouse; traveler (Egypt, Middle East, Russia, Europe); foreign resident (Gibraltar, France); philanthropist. Upper middle class; married into aristocracy.

Family life, social life, and travels of the wife of an upper-echelon army officer, highlighting her husband's military service and political figures author knew personally, 1866–1946. Her mother's Scottish background; her father's Bank of England directorship; his dying, author's age 5. Attending Anglican Sunday school. Her stepfather's being agnostic, interested in Eastern religions. Remembering her affluent family's distress at East End plight pictured in General Booth's 1890 *In Darkest London;* author and sister's "adopting" a slum area. Having been "haphazardly" schooled in Brussels and London. Meeting future husband on a trip to Egypt; his recent experiences in unsuccessful expedition to relieve General Gordon at Khartoum, 1885; her social debut that same year. Their marriage, 1891, and honeymoon in England. Husband's early military career, told in his own words. Their living on Malta for three years; returning to England. Births of their children. Husband's serving in Battle of Omdurman, 1898, and Boer War, 1899–1901; his being promoted to colonel and made a military attaché in Paris. Author's being spat upon by anti-British crowds in Paris. Remembering visit to Paris of the newly crowned Edward VII, 1902. Visiting her sister in Rome; spending summer near brother's home on Island of Mull, 1904. Remembering 1899 death of husband's uncle, the Earl of Wharncliffe; his life story. Royals of many nations visiting their home, including Kaiser Wilhelm II; her picture of his character. Author's remembering 1908–14 as calm years: family visits to Italy, daughter's coming out, son's entering Oxford. Returning to England at outbreak of WWI. Husband's heading battalion in France; author's volunteering at YMCA and doing policing. Noting that Englishwomen were granted suffrage to reward them for their war work. Visiting Italy in 1920 and 1932; discussing Italian politics and rise of Mussolini. Visiting family and friends in Budapest and Teheran; Turkish ambassador's discussing with her the travels of her husband's ancestor, Lady Mary Wortley-Montagu. Returning home via Russia; commenting that its Church had regained lost ground; crediting Stalin with Russia's rebirth. Visiting Athens and Egypt, 1927–30; touring King Tut's tomb. Spending two winters in Constantinople with her daughter and son-in-law; discussing Kemal Ataturk. Taking a motor tour of Salzburg, Prague, Dresden, and Weimar, 1939; noting Nazi youth groups; discussing her own failure to start youth organizations in England. Italian and Papal politics in 1939. Outbreak of WWII. Criticizing the Vatican for its silence on the invasions of Abyssinia and Poland. Discussing the remainder of WWII: Dunkirk, the Italian surrender in Abyssinia, Churchill's speeches, the Battle of Britain, D-Day.

Taking her book's title from a quotation by Disraeli: "Read no history; nothing but biography, for that is life without theory," Stuart-Wortley shows no reserve about creating a history of her life that, while mostly travelogue, includes some worthwhile commentary on political figures with whom she became acquainted through her marriage. She records one unusual venture of her own: in WWI, she and two women from New Zealand and Australia patrolled the London streets at night, seeking to get young soldiers into shelters and out of the clutches of prostitute "harpies." She expresses frustration at the inability of European leaders to stem the tide of 1930s fascism.

923 STURGE, Elizabeth. 1849–d.a.1927. *Reminiscences of My Life and Some Account of the Children of William and Charlotte Sturge and of the Sturge Family of Bristol*. Bristol: Printed for private circulation, 1928. 202 pp.; front. ports.; foreword; illus.; genealogical tables. BLC to 1975 316:312.

Born in Bristol, Avon. Father: William Sturge, surveyor, land agent. Mother: Charlotte Allen. 6 sisters; 4 brothers. Single. Charitable volunteer; feminist; suffragist; WWI volunteer; prison service officer; organizer of societies (women's clubs). Upper middle class.

Author's Quaker upbringing, socially committed life work, and friendships among reformers and activists, c.1850s–1927. Being schooled at home by governess. Her father's belonging to the Society of Friends; family's adhering to Quaker principles and plain dress. Attending school in Weston-super-Mare; depicting education for girls, c.1850s. Mourning the death of her brother Charlie, 1862. Teaching her younger siblings. Attending lectures for ladies, part of the early movement toward higher education for women. Managing Red Lodge Reformatory for Girls; remembering reformer and Red Lodge founder Mary Carpenter. Being friends with Mary Talbot; recalling her social work and support for women's suffrage. Working for Octavia Hill; learning Hill's system of managing working-class property. George Eliot and George Macdonald's paying visits to Miss Hill's. Living with her sisters in Bloomsbury. Death of her mother, 1891. Returning home to Bristol, at her father's request; sharing responsibilities of running family home with her sister Helen. Discussing careers of her father, her sisters Emily (school board member and suffragist) and Caroline (physician), her brothers Clement (educator) and William (physician). Working with Charity Organisation Society. Recounting Josephine Butler's moral crusade to repeal the contagious Diseases Act, 1869, which subjected prostitutes to arrest and imprisonment. Visiting Egypt. Father's death, 1905. Supporting women's suffrage. Distinguishing between the strategies of the "old guard" and the Pankhursts in the women's suffrage movement. WWI: Helping train women police; organizing clubs for wives of soldiers in Bristol.

Born into a generation immediately preceding the founding of colleges for women, Sturge had to content herself with attending "ladies' lectures" and later working to improve educational and political opportunities for women. A strong supporter of suffrage, she viewed the new work opportunities for women as the only positive aspect of WWI. She devotes a substantial part of her book to discussing the social contributions of immediate family members and to general Sturge family history, which she traces back to the 18th century.

STURGE, Mary Charlotte. [*See* Anonymous.]

924 SUMMERSKILL, the Rt. Hon. Edith, Baroness Summerskill, MRCP. 1901–1980. *A Woman's World*. Heinemann, 1967. 258 pp.; index. BLC to 1975 317:194.

Born in Bloomsbury, London. Father: William Summerskill, physician. Mother: Edith. 1 sister. Married 1925, E. Jeffrey Samuel, physician. 1

son; 1 daughter. Physician; social reformer; politician; government administrator; member of Parliament; feminist; political activist; physician's daughter. Upper middle class; awarded life peerage.

Paternal influences in childhood, adult medical practice, parliamentary career, and strong progressive opinions of a noted stateswoman and physician, 1905–66. Earliest memories: being doctored by her father for bronchitis; going on medical rounds with him. Considering his commentary on these visits "the strongest single influence in my life." Father's working to improve health of the poor; his indicting lax midwifery standards for high birth mortality; his showing author the physical defects produced by malnutrition; his being an ardent feminist; his demanding achievement from his daughter. Author's entering King's College medical school when male WWI absences lowered barriers to women; their being raised again after the 1918 Armistice. Qualifying as physician, 1924; marrying a former fellow medical student a year later. Author and husband's settling in North London; her opening family practice, 1925. Giving birth to two children under "twilight sleep," 1926 and 1931; working to promote use of anesthesia in childbirth. In 1933, being invited to join Wood Green Council's all-male Maternity and Child Welfare Committee; discussing the vitriolic sexism of some male members; her acceptance's marking her entry into politics. Both author and physician husband's being confirmed Labourites; their campaigning jointly at public meetings for Labour family welfare agenda. Standing for Conservative-held council seat in her district, 1934; canvassing door to door with her women patients, promoting preventive health care for families; winning easily. Contesting Conservative-held parliamentary seat in her district, the same year; losing narrowly. Working with Dr. Marie Stopes in public campaign for birth control and family planning; earning hatred of Catholic Church; priests' trying unsuccessfully to swing parishioners' votes against her. Winning entry to House of Commons, 1938, as Labour member for West Fulham; overcoming challenge to her taking seat in her maiden name. Lengthy discussion of her personal understanding of women's child care needs. Allying with other women M.P.s Mavis Tate, Ellen Wilkinson, and Katherine Stewart-Murray against gender discrimination. Using her experience with refractory patients to handle senior M.P.s. Making her maiden speech on the Cancer Bill, 1938, opposing its denial of free treatment to nonworking women. Raising parliamentary issues of equal pay for the sexes, the bar against married women's serving in the military, and discriminatory prosecution of female conscientious objectors. Urging Commons to approve free early treatment of tuberculosis by National Health Service, 1939; promoting inspections to end tubercular contamination of milk. WWII: Husband's joining Royal Marines; author's evacuating her children from London bombing; cofounding Women's Home Defence group that trained women to fight in the event of German invasion.

Labour's winning massive victory in 1945 General Election with Clement Atlee as new prime minister; his appointing author minister of food; author's supervising rationing and monitoring purity of national food supply. Being received by George VI as a new Privy Councillor. Becoming minister of National Insurance and Industrial Injuries, 1950; losing this post with the Conservative sweep in the 1951 general election. Serving from 1951–61 as opposition spokesperson on health; twice failing to secure passage of a Women's Disabilities Bill establishing money as equal marital property. Being named minister of National Insurance, 1960. Extolling the Married Women's Association and the National Health Service. In 1961, being granted a Life Peerage for her contributions to public health. Continuing her parliamentary career in the House of Lords.

Clear and assertive in her opinions about preventive health care and politics, Summerskill uses the story of her own medical and political activism to chart Britain's legislative progress toward securing working-class health, normal childhood development, and women's economic empowerment. Vivid in its re-creation of the ideology and ambitions of the early-20th-century Labour Party, Summerskill's book is especially noteworthy for its meticulous picture of 1930s political gender discrimination and her female colleagues' reaction to it. In one incident, she recounts that Winston Churchill angrily told a female M.P. that her entry into Commons meant her entry into his private bathroom, and that he had no bath sponge to defend himself; the woman member retorted that Churchill was far too ugly to have to worry about being attacked. Summerskill debated actively in the House of Lords until her 1977 retirement.

925 SWAN, Annie S. (Annie S. Smith; Mrs. Burnett Smith; David Lyall, pseud.). 1859–1943. *My Life: An Autobiography*. Ivor Nicholson & Watson, 1934. 318 pp.; foreword; illus.; index. NUC pre56 550:401. [cat. under Smith, Annie S.]

Born in Berwickshire, Scotland. Father: Edward Swan, farmer, potato merchant. Mother not named. Stepmother: Barbara. 4 sisters; 2 brothers. Married 1883, James Burnett Smith, schoolmaster, physician, d.1927. 1 son; 1 daughter. Wrote more than 250 novels, including *Thankful Rest* (1899), *The Outsiders* (1905), *The Pendulum* (c.1927), others. Knew Frances Balfour, Sir James Barrie, Margaret Oliphant. Novelist; journalist; advice writer; short storyist; publisher; religious/spiritual writer; politician; public speaker; farm child. Rural farming class; married into middle class.

Early years and career of prolific novelist and journalist, covering 1860s–1920s. Growing up on a Berwickshire farm. Comparing her stern but passionate father with her gentle, reserved mother. Family's moving to Edinburgh. Paternal grandmother's moving in with them; grandmother's being bad-tempered but clever; author's being her favorite grandchild. Attending dame school and Queen Street Ladies' College. Moving to Midlothian farm after grandmother's death. Her later novels' being much influenced by her rural upbringing. Father's rejecting Calvinism; his practicing Morisonian Christianity; his joining the Evangelical Union Church at Leith. Mother's passing on to author her love of reading, especially Shakespeare; family's forming a Shakespeare reading circle in which members acted various parts. Writing stories from childhood on; selling her first story; winning second prize in a story competition, thus beginning her long connection with publisher John Long & Co. Author's moving to London to pursue her writing career, despite parents' opinion that writing was not real work. Publishing her first novel; modeling her second novel, *Aldersyde,* on Margaret Oliphant's *Border Stories;* being wounded by Oliphant's critical attacks. Author's being ignorant of "physical side" of marriage before her own, 1883. By 1885, author's having income from two more novels. Husband's fulfilling his dreams of attending medical school. Author's father's accusing him of unmanliness in letting a woman pay for his education. Itemizing her fiction written over the next eight years, her extensive reading, and family's several moves, concluding in London. Having two children, 1893 and 1895. Attending annual Women Writers' dinner in London, 1897. Writing Boer War stories for the *British Weekly* under pseudonym, David Lyall. Beginning *Woman at Home* magazine. Writing a correspondence advice column. Presiding over the Women Journalists' Society. Family's moving to Hertford. Writing books for the Salvation Army. Investigating spiritualist contact after her son's accidental death, 1910. WWI: Chairing the Hertford committee on Belgian refugees. Lecturing on wartime food conservation in America, 1918. Standing as Liberal parliamentary candidate for Maryhill division of Glasgow, 1922. Death of her husband, 1927. Evaluating the rewards of authorship.

Throughout this book Swan states that her domestic duties always took precedence over her writing career, yet her literary output was prodigious and her documentation of it is elaborate. A later autobiographical work, **926** *We Travel Home* (1935), uses her reflections on social and literary influences in her youth to advise mothers of the next generation. Topics include contrasts between Victorian and later modern child-rearing, encouragement of children's imaginations, boarding schools, courtship and marriage, domestic life and servants, health care and health fads, as well as social class and the social order.

927 SWANWICK, Helena Maria Lucy (née Sickert). 1864–c.1938. *I Have Been Young*. Victor Gollancz Ltd., 1935. 512 pp.; front. port.; intro. by Lord Ponsonby; preface; index. BLC to 1975 318:158.

Born in Munich, Germany. Father: Oswald Adalbert Sickert, artist, cartoonist, naturalized British citizen. Mother: Eleanor, dancer. 5 brothers (including artist Walter Sickert). Married 1888, Frederick Swanwick, lecturer in mathematics. Widow. Wrote *The Future of the Women's Movement* (1913), *Women in the Socialist State*. Suffragist; feminist activist; academic; political writer; journalist; editor; political activist; public speaker; pacifist; atheist; academic's spouse. Middle class.

Restricted upbringing, intellectual rebellion, and mature political activism of a dedicated international feminist and pacifist, including her questioning of prevailing gender attitudes and politics, c.1860s–1935. Parents' ignoring social norm by not having nursemaid; caring for their children themselves. Their emigrating to England, author's age 4. Suffering neglect from mother's frequent absences; fearing her father's authoritarianism. Being sent to unsatisfactory girls' school in Neuville, Germany; in four years, learning only to discard her religiosity; returning home an atheist, age 12. Forming alliance with one brother against father's gender-specific discipline; feeling enraged when brother also showed sexism. Sharing her brothers' activities, contrary to her mother's feminine ideals; mother's forcing her to sew. Writing a serial story for sharing with school friends; mother and governess's declaring it immoral, informing author "bedroom scenes" were unsuitable for little girls. Loving intellectual stimulus of Notting Hill High School, age 14. Meeting Oscar Wilde during a holiday; being enchanted by his recitation of his own poetry. Delighting in John Stuart Mill's *On Liberty;* identifying with his feminism. Resolving to study economics at Girton College, Cambridge; being coached for entrance exams, 1880, by unqualified women students. Noting the struggles of women educators to make their curriculum conform to the established boy's curriculum. Her mother's endorsing higher education for women (but not for her daughter), yet disapproving of the Married Women's Property Bill. During the 1880s, meeting actress Ellen Terry, seeing Henry Irving perform, discussing art with Edward Burne-Jones, being friends with William Morris's daughters and visiting Kelmscott Press, meeting Bernard Shaw. Attending Girton College, c.1882, with godmother's money after parents refused support. Resisting mother's tearful attempts to compel her to return home; relishing her liberation from "incessant" parental interruptions of her privacy. Being appointed lecturer at Westfield College. Visiting her artist brother Walter in Dieppe, France; meeting James Whistler there. Mother's being shattered by father's death; her struggling to reconcile with author. Marrying a university lecturer, 1883; finding the obligation to surrender her teaching appointment because of marriage "preposterous." Author and husband's settling in Manchester, 1885. Author's being among the earliest women to adopt bicycling, 1891; its giving her a means of independent transportation. Joining Women's Trade Union Council. Addressing meetings of Women's Co-operative Guild. Applying to the Manchester *Guardian* for reviewing work; being assigned to write articles on domestic subjects; being horrified at being assigned hundreds of male-authored books, all uttering platitudes about women's inferiority. Celebrating news of suffragists' disrupting Liberal political meetings, 1905, but disapproving of many militant suffrage strategies; deciding to work for the moderate suffrage wing under Emmeline Pethick-Lawrence. Joining North of England Society; discussing its affiliation with the National Union of Women's Suffrage Societies. Reporting on suffrage for the *Guardian*. Addressing pro-suffrage meetings in England and Scotland. Writing inaugural essay for National Union's weekly paper, the *Common Cause,* 1912. Writing *The Future of the Women's Movement*. WWI: Refusing to endorse accusation of Germany's unilateral guilt; chairing the Women's International League (WIL); visiting Ireland on behalf of Suffrage Society under dangerous wartime conditions, 1916. Being moved emotionally by the Zurich Peace conference; deciding to establish WIL headquarters in Zurich. Working on her book, *Women in the Socialist State*. Close-spaced deaths of her mother and brothers; being devastated by death of her journalist brother Oswald. Becoming substitute delegate to Fifth Assembly of the League of Nations; lamenting the League's probable futility; realizing how men's public influence surpasses women's. Attending committee meetings of League of Nations, 1931. Working extensively for British Labour and in international pacifist and feminist organizations. Mourning death of her husband; retreating to a flat outside London and abandoning public life. Waxing increasingly cynical about politicians; indicting Christianity for endorsing war; prophesying calamity in future European air warfare. Wondering cynically whether being ill or growing old are obligatory.

Swanwick vividly depicts her fight to escape the home of her well-intentioned but traditional parents. Part of the difficulty she faced arose from the fact that when her parents came to England, they had no acquaintance with its longstanding tradition of women's independence, which extended well back into the 18th century. By the 1890s women's roles had become a popular subject for public debate, and the topic of the employed, educated "New Woman" of the middle and higher classes was prominently featured in the periodical press. Swanwick's chronicle of the background of suffragism stands in contrast to accounts by militant suffragettes such as Christabel Pankhurst, who conveys a different perspective in *Unshackled: The Story of How We Won the Vote*. Swanwick's record more fairly and inclusively covers contemporary critical reactions to the tactics of the WSPU.

928 SYRETT, Netta (Janet). c.1865–1943. *The Sheltering Tree*. Geoffrey Bles, 1939. 286 pp.; preface. NUC pre56 580:330.

Born in West Country of England. Parents not named. 4 brothers; 5 sisters. Single. Wrote 15 novels, including *The God of Chance, Julian Carroll,*

Strange Marriage, Portrait of a Rebel, others. Knew Aubrey Beardsley, Frances Mary Buss, Mary Vivian Hughes, William Somerset Maugham, May Sinclair. Teacher; novelist; playwright; feminist; school founder; foreign resident (France); organizer (theatrical). Middle class.

Education and literary acquaintances of innovative teacher, novelist, and 1890s "New Woman," c.1876–c.1939. Receiving a sketchy education from governesses to age 11, then attending North London Collegiate School for Girls with her younger sister, as boarders in the private home of its headmistress, Frances Mary Buss. Disagreeing with benevolent representations of Buss written by other pupils; condemning Buss's methods of teaching and discipline; her sister's being afraid of Buss; author's blaming Buss in part for her sister's death from tuberculosis. Later publishing fictional depictions of Miss Buss and school incidents in her novel, *The Victorians.* Leaving this school, age 15. Despite antipathy, seeking Buss's help in starting her teaching career, age 19. Studying for Cambridge Higher Local exam; attending Training College for Women Teachers at Cambridge; later describing this college in her novel, *The God of Chance.* Discussing her friendship with writer Grant Allen and his wife, her relatives by marriage; his frank discussions of sex and his literary influence on her; his introducing her to novelist George Meredith. Discussing the women's movement of the 1880s and 1890s. Working for a teaching certificate at Swansea High School; noting its edicts against women students' socializing with men or riding bicycles. Allen's helping her to publish her first short story. Author and four sisters' moving to London and renting a flat; being regarded as daring for living without chaperonage. Teaching at Polytechnic School for Girls. Through Aubrey Beardsley's sister (one of her students), becoming familiar with the *Yellow Book* set; discussing their experimental publishing ideas and *fin-de-siècle* decadence; using the *Yellow Book* set in her later novel, *Strange Marriage.* Beardsley's creating the cover for her first published novel, *Nobody's Fault.* Discussing Beardsley's deathbed conversion to Catholicism, 1897, and similar last-minute conversions of Wilde and Harland. Being friends with writers Ella D'Arcy and May Sinclair. Beginning an unorthodox private school for children; writing plays for her pupils; winning contest to have her play *The Finding of Nancy* (1898) produced by Herbert Beerbohm Tree and George Alexander. Becoming friends with Somerset Maugham. Visiting Paris; meeting artist Gerald Kelly through Maugham. Moving in London artistic and literary circles; meeting novelists G. K. Chesterton and Thomas Hardy. Moving to Soho; beginning a Children's Theatre, 1913. Spending duration of WWI writing novels. Discussing reviews of her novels; young writers of 1939; the decline in quality of education and child-rearing; her sleepwalking and psychical interests.

Particularly interested in the genre of autobiography, before writing her own Syrett consulted many memoirs by women whose place of education and time of young adulthood coincide with hers. Her negative estimate of both Miss Buss and the education provided by the North London Collegiate School fleshes out the unfavorable picture given by Mary Vivian Hughes's *A London Girl of the Eighties* (which Hughes and Syrett discussed in 1936) and explicitly challenges the praise of Buss in Sara Annie Burstall's *Retrospect and Prospect*. Syrett's book is also an enjoyable source on Aubrey Beardsley, the *Yellow Book* set, and the pre-WWI London theatre.

929 TALBOT, Mary Anne (John Taylor, pseud.). 1778–1808. "The Intrepid Female: or, Surprising Life and Adventures of Mary Anne Talbot, Otherwise John Taylor," pp. 160–225 in *Kirby's Wonderful and Eccentric Museum,* Vol. 2. R. S. Kirby, 1820. NUC pre56 582:85.

Father: Lord William Talbot, Steward of king's household, Colonel of Glamorganshire. Mother not named. Illegitimate child. 15 siblings. Single. Cross-dresser; male impersonator; sailor; prison inmate; actress (stage); seamstress; domestic servant; jeweler's assistant. Aristocracy.

Colorful and dramatic exploits, particularly in the military while posing as a man, with caustic commentary on contemporary British society, covering three decades of author's life. Being the youngest of sixteen natural children of her father. Mother's death at author's birth. Attending boarding school in Chester. Being befriended by her only surviving married sister; after this sister's death, author's realizing she will have to be self-reliant. Mr. Shuker's becoming her guardian. Accompanying Capt. Bowen, a presumed friend of Shuker, to London; his taking advantage of her. Disguising herself as a foot boy, John Taylor, to accompany Bowen to the West Indies. Enduring extreme hardships aboard ship. Learning to be a drummer boy. Describing siege of Valenciennes, France; Bowen's death in battle. Being forcibly conscribed by crew of a French ship; her distress at having to wage war against her countrymen. Being able to rejoin English ship after English victory. Being severely wounded in a siege; recuperating in a Gosport hospital. Sailing on another British ship. Being taken prisoner by the French. Taking a job as a cabin steward on a cargo ship bound for New York. Accompanying ship's captain to Rhode Island; his niece's falling in love with author; author's revealing her sex; being discharged. Drinking excessively. Returning to England. Experiencing difficulties from an old wound. Working for a jeweler; devising a machine for the manufacture of gold wire; losing position. Confronting Shuker about his scheme to defraud her; his sudden death. Filing suit for assault after being victimized by a merchant in a case of mistaken identity. Taking on the responsibility of caring for an orphaned child; child's death in a drowning accident. Being robbed of all her possessions. Working in theatres, performing in plays. Being arrested for debt to her landlady; finding convivial friends in prison on both the men's side (which she visits dressed as a man) and on the women's side. Working as a washerwoman and seamstress after leaving prison; suing her new employer for nonpayment of wages. Again being in arrears on rent; having her goods confiscated. Wishing she had been brought up in the humblest of tranquil circumstances.

Talbot's literate tale is riveting reading; her melodramatic life unfolds chapter by chapter. Yet despite its engaging elements, this account is readily recognizable as belonging to the 18th-century genre of sensational memoirs. Because this popular category contained both real and fictional examples, the status of Talbot's book as a legitimate autobiography must be considered problematic. On the one hand, the testimony of the picaresque protagonist who rises above an improbable series of adversities was the stuff of engaging literary characters from Moll Flanders to Roderick Ransom. On the other hand, such fictional treatment mirrored the memoirs of genuine historical figures who were moved to write, precisely because their unusual life circumstances had potential popular appeal. Consequently, whether Talbot's account represents a particular life or is an exaggeration, it is representative of an 18th-century social issue: by what means might a woman—bereft of traditional male protection—prosper and thrive in a man's world? In this light, Talbot's record profits from comparison with another autobiography in this collection, *A Narrative of the Life of Mrs. Charlotte Charke, Daughter of Colley Cibber*. Charke also discovered that passing as a man facilitated her progress in the world. In both books, depiction of the implications of cross-dressing shed light on gender issues specific to the time.

930 TAYLER, Henrietta. 1869–1951. *A Scottish Nurse at Work: Being a Record of What One Semi-Trained Nurse Has Been Privileged to See and Do During Four and a Half Years of War*. John Lane, 1920. 157 pp.; illus. OCLC #22378956.

Born in Scotland. Parents not named. Nurse (WWI); Red Cross worker. Middle class.

WWI nurse's memories of her professional relationship with military and civilian patients and personnel, spanning 1914–18. Her sense of being stigmatized as a semi-trained nurse. Working with the Red Cross in Scotland. Organizing and running a VAD hospital for Belgian wounded in the south of England. Organizing a Red Cross hospital in Scotland. Discussing wounded soldiers' alcohol consumption; attitudes of the wounded; feelings of competition among the regiments. Working for the British Red Cross in (free) Belgium. Working in surgical ward of hospital at La Panne; treatment of wounds; abdominal cases. Feeling glad to be useful. Being treated for a serious bout of pneumonia; learning firsthand to appreciate the kindness of the nursing staff. Discussing Allied plans for capturing Belgian coast. Treating patients suffering from the aftereffects of poison gas. Serving refugee children at Adinkerke; describing living and working conditions there, children's illnesses and problems. Being reassigned to a hospital in France. Ministering to sick, starving civilians. Describing the unglamorous, unromantic nature of war nursing. Working for the Italian Red Cross in Florence; describing living conditions, scarcity, and expensiveness of food. Discussing the difference in discipline between Italian and English hospitals. Dealing with Eastern European wounded soldiers; their pride in teaching her various languages; their wanting to go home, not be great warriors. Austrian soldier's asking for last rites, having difficulty communicating his need to author. Noting lack of camaraderie between soldiers and officers in Italian army. Socializing with British Sisters. Combatting outbreak of Spanish influenza. Evacuation of her unit after signing of Italo-Austrian Armistice. Moving to new quarters near Monte Pasubio. Being greatly moved by deaths of many patients. Italian patients' rejoicing over Austrian debacle. Forming close friendships with other nurses. Being transferred to a French hospital. Warlike conditions' continuing even after the Armistice. Recalling Christmas in Italy, 1918. Working conditions in French unit; bureaucratic aspects of French military field hospital. History of Gorizia during WWI. Speculating on German and Yugoslav rule of Adriatic provinces. Recalling other Balkan wars. Significance of inscriptions in many languages in Gorizia cemetery. Her last post in an Italian hospital. Feeling pride in having helped in the long struggle.

Tayler's memoir describes in detail the author's many duties in WWI field hospitals, providing a vivid portrait of wartime conditions in Belgium, Italy, and France. Tayler presents herself as desiring only to be of use to the many patients of various nationalities who came under her care. Although her text preserves a carefully unemotional tone, the author's compassionate response to the devastation of war colors some of her narrative, including her portrayal of soldiers' deathbed scenes. Tayler's memoir provides an interesting contrast to Lesley Smith's *Four Years Out of Life*, which also records the eyewitness reactions of a Scottish nurse to battlefield injuries. Unlike Tayler, however, Smith strongly expresses the political cynicism she acquired through her experiences.

931 TAYLOR, H. M. (pseud.; possibly Anne Grainger). c.1880–?. *No One to Blame*. Jonathan Cape, 1939. 208 pp.; intro. by Elizabeth Bowen. BLC to 1975 321:380.

Born in Lancashire. Father not named, weaver, grocer, news agent. Mother not named. 7 siblings. Married surname Wilson, insurance agent. Mill worker; teacher; news agent; socialist; cook; physically handicapped woman. Lower middle class.

Obstacles and disappointments in the author's upbringing, the vicissitudes of her vocational attempts, and her relationship with her mother, retrospectively analyzed from a psychological perspective, covering her late Victorian childhood to middle age. Reading psychoanalytical theory, such as G. Groddeck's *The Unconscious Self*; writing autobiography to explore the importance of psychoanalysis and the damage done by ignorance of human psychology. Being an unwanted child; its lifelong effect on her. Father's predilection for religious books and magazines; his teaching Methodist Sunday school; his impracticality and dreaminess. Author's working halftime at a mill. Her deafness and chronic bronchitis. Death of her brother; rejoicing that she would have mother's love all to herself. Her feelings of feminine inferiority. Learning to weave cotton. Mother's unsuccessful attempts to open a business; her great anger at burdens of pregnancy. Birth of another brother. Author's fearing adverse opinions about herself. Mother's materialistic rationale for sending author to work. Suffering with double pleurisy; its lifelong effects on her; speculating on whether her physical disease might be caused by unconscious rebellion against her circumstances. Going to work in a different mill. Teaching school briefly; losing job due to her physical disabilities. Always desiring her mother's approval; never being appreciated by her. Being permanently maimed through a tonsillectomy. Her father's interest in hydropathic treatment; author's taking the waters cure at Scarborough. Enjoying attending Methodist Sunday school; disliking evangelistic meetings; becoming a Sunday school supervisor. Falling in love with a young ministry student; her love's being unrequited. Her father's generous nature; her mother's vigilance over that generosity. Preparing to become a missionary to China with the China Inland Missionary Society; facing her mother's objections; being forestalled by her father's death. Continuing father's news agency business. Going to London to attempt to join Dr. Stephenson's Institute of Deaconesses; being rejected; the other deaconesses' ridiculing her. Joining Portchester Evangelical Mission as an evangelist; being disappointed by her inability to find other people to work with her; blaming the autocratic and unspiritual nature of the leader. Working as a confectioner. Joining Spiritualist Church because of her enmity toward Methodist church leaders. Attending séances. Being unsure of spiritualist ideas; leaving the church. Becoming interested in socialism; reading *The Fabian Essays,* other books; seeing socialist leaders as weak. Marrying Mr. Wilson, a socialist millworker. Husband's role as a leader in the local socialist movement; being visited often by enthusiastic comrades until author brought her crippled mother to live with them. Caring for her mother for twelve years; discussing psychological causes of her mother's ailment; mother's death. Husband's taking insurance job in a resort area; author's enjoying her life there; their pursuing "various cultural pursuits and progressive movements" in their new home. Discussing theory of fetus's ability to take revenge against mother; most women's lacking knowledge about birth control; the human mind's ability to deceive itself; the similarities and vested interests of all modern organized religions; problems and humiliations faced by deaf people; the need to explore psychic causes of disease.

Presenting what she believes are the hidden psychological motives for her own actions and experiences, Taylor expresses particular interest in the idea that psychological factors influence physical disease and in the role of the unconscious in decision-making. Although she acknowledges having felt bitter over her rejection by various religious foundations, she retrospectively suggests that since she had neither the background nor the education to allow her to succeed in such roles, she was unconsciously punishing herself for perceived faults by targeting herself for failure. Although Taylor's account is deliberately introspective rather than historical, the author does include her opinions on family planning, the failings of organized religion, and the need for greater education.

932 TEAL, Gladys. 1913–s.l.1976. *Grasp the Nettle: An Autobiography*. Leeds: Arthur Wigley & Sons Ltd., n.d. 122 pp.; illus. BLC 1976–1982 44:278.

Born near Yorkshire Dales. Father not named, gardener, caretaker. Mother not named, cleaning woman, caretaker. 2 brothers; 1 sister; 1 stepbrother. Married, husband not named, nurse. 1 son. Paid companion; laundry manager; news agent; restaurant manager. Working class.

Varied occupational history and personal memories of a working-class woman, 1913–76. Country living and customs. Admiring her mother's strength; mother's working as a cleaning woman and laundress. Recalling a zeppelin raid in WWI. Helping her parents in their duties as caretakers of the Conservative Club. Attending Young Conservatives (earlier known as the Primrose Buds). Attending a local board school; not mixing well with other children. Visiting her aunt, housekeeper to an ivory merchant in London. Joining the St. John ambulance cadets. Winning scholarship to Prince Henry's Grammar School; enjoying her studies; enduring the resentment of some paying students. Looking after her mother during mother's illness. Working for news agencies. Her aunt's working as a palmist and phrenologist; listening to aunt's "readings." Meeting her future husband; marriage. Outbreak of WWII: Living conditions in wartime. Birth of her son. Working in a hospital canteen after WWII. Death of her mother and eldest brother. Being misdiagnosed as having cancer; undergoing painful surgery and treatment. Managing a dry cleaning business. Taking holidays in Italy and Switzerland. Serving as a paid companion to an elderly lady. Working as a manager of a coffee bar. Cruising to Greece and Holy Land with her husband for their silver wedding anniversary. Taking boat trips to Spain and North Africa; later voyaging to Scandinavia and Russia. Attending

Oberammergau Passion Play. Looking after her grandchildren. Having difficulties in her restaurant cashier job after the decimalization of money; resigning. Caring for elderly people and children at intervals. Returning to cashier job. Considering loneliness the greatest scourge of society.

A rather disjointed amalgam of the bits and pieces of Teal's life, this autobiography conveys a sense of its author as disarmingly honest and forthright, without claim to intellectual pretension. Teal presents the minutiae of her life with the same seriousness she gives significant personal events; the cumulative picture created by these details helps to identify changes in working-class existence wrought by war and economic fluctuations in the 20th century.

933 TENNENT, Madge (née Madeline Grace Cook). 1889–1972. Autobiography of an Unarrived Artist. New York: Columbia University Press, 1949. 180 pp.; foreword by Ernest Field; preface; illus.; "Notebook of an Unarrived Artist." NUC pre56 586:365.

Born in Dulwich, Greater London. Father: Arthur Cook, housebuilder, maker of jewelry. Mother: Agnes Caroline, suffragist, magazine publisher. 1 sister. Married 1915, Hugh Cowper Tennent, soldier, later government treasurer in British Samoa. 2 sons. Artist (painter); headmistress; foreign resident (South Africa, New Zealand, Samoa, Hawaii, U.S.); school founder; anticommunist; teacher (art); organizer (artistic). Upper middle class.

Growth and international development of an artist's career, accompanied by her impressions of native peoples, filtered through the lens of Western aesthetics, spanning author's childhood to 1949. Parents' settling in rural South Africa, author's age 5. Mother's ardent suffragism; publishing her own women's magazine, *South African Women in Council.* Family's returning to England for two years, author's age 10. Attending a boarding school in Kent for a few months. Parents' considering younger sister the pretty one, author the clever one in the family; their encouraging author in her wish to have an art career. Author's attending Cape Town School of Art. Studying art in Paris, ages 13–16. Exhibiting art in South Africa. Becoming the director of a government school of art in Johannesberg; serving as art headmistress in several South African girls' schools. Seeing Africans as law-abiding but childlike. Working as a commercial artist. Starting her own art school in Cape Town, age 24. Marrying a New Zealand soldier during WWI, age 26. Living with in-laws in New Zealand while husband fought in France; author's starting her own studio; being appointed head instructor at Government School of Art in Invercargill, New Zealand. Births of her sons, 1916 and 1918. After WWI, living with husband in British Samoa, then moving permanently to Hawaii, 1923. Believing in reincarnation but never losing her Christian beliefs. Acquiring fame for painting Hawaiians after manner of Gauguin and Cézanne. Exhibiting in Hawaii, mainland U.S., London, Paris. Receiving awards from Cleveland Museum and from IBM in New York. Establishing Madge Tennent Gallery of Modern Art in Hawaii, 1934. Forming "Seven," a group of seven women artists; later helping found the Hawaiian Mural Guild. Exhibiting in first show sponsored by Association of Honolulu Artists, 1939. WWII: Painting murals for U.S. Navy and Army. Retiring after the war. Becoming a U.S. citizen. Holding patriotic, anticommunist opinions. Discussing modern art and art criticism, as well as her lack of critical success. Commenting on and comparing the various countries she has called home. Describing her own religious beliefs; being a formal member of the Episcopal church but open to other churches' teachings. Feeling that the "so-called animal urge of motherhood" will always prevent women from matching men as artists. Commenting on Gauguin, Cassatt, Velazquez, other painters.

The three distinct parts of this book are the author's autobiography, her mother's memories of the author as a child, and the "Notebook of an Unarrived Artist," in which Tennent juxtaposes evaluative opinions from other artists with her own. Tennent's subjective views of the peoples native to the regions she lived in frequently seem Eurocentric; hence, the Africans employed by her father are "grown-up children" and the Hawaiians she painted are "beautifully primitive." In addition to its narrative of Tennent's life story, the book contains a miscellany of her aesthetic ideas and experiences, enhanced by many family photographs and reproductions of her paintings.

934 TERRISS, Ellaline, Lady Hicks (née Lewin). 1871–1971. *Ellaline Terriss by Herself and with Others*. Cassell, 1928. 300 pp.; front. port.; illus.; foreword by Dame Madge Kendal. BLC to 1975 323:40.

Born at Stanley, Falkland Islands. Father: William Charles James Lewin (William Terriss, stage name), actor. Mother: Isabel Lewis. 2 brothers. Married 1893, Seymour Hicks, actor, producer, playwright. 1 son; 1 adopted daughter; 1 daughter. Knew Sir Henry Irving, Ellen Terry, Charles Wyndham, others. Actress (comic, stage); philanthropist. Middle class.

Anecdotal recollections of childhood and career of musical comedy actress, covering her birth to 1928. Author's birth in the Falkland Islands. Her father's history: his wanderlust, silvermining in Colorado, and sheepfarming in Australia; his establishing himself in a stage career in London. Attending a private school; living on a Newbury farm; going to live with her parents in Bedford Park, age 12. Childhood memories of

Sir Henry Irving and Ellen Terry. Author's first role, age 15; having the support of Irving and her father as she began her stage career. Defending the stage as a career; arguing against the view that acting spells ruin for young women. Acting in Charles Wyndham's company at the Criterion Theatre, 1889–91. First meeting Seymour Hicks, 1893; marrying without father's permission; father's eventual fondness for Hicks. Converting to Roman Catholicism, Hicks's religion. Her success as a pantomime Cinderella in London and New York. Acting at the Gaiety Theatre; actor-manager George Edwardes's inventing the genre of musical comedy. W. S. Gilbert's writing a part for her in a comic opera. Quarreling with her husband over money. Anecdotes of Lily Langtry. Author and husband's giving a command performance before the Prince of Wales. Deaths of her infant son, father, and mother, 1897. Adopting a daughter, 1897, after doctors told her she could never again become pregnant. Leaving musical comedy to act in a team with her husband; their acting in children's plays; their success in long-running productions; enjoying a generally happy marriage. Discovering she was pregnant; birth of daughter, c.1903. Author and husband's biggest mistake: building Hicks Theatre, 1907, in addition to two other theatres; losing approximately £47,000 and owing £14,000 more at beginning of WWI; recouping money through husband's writing and through performing frequently in the provinces. Naming and evaluating her chief rival actresses. WWI: Deciding, with husband, to form a company to entertain British troops in France. Discussing changes wrought in the theatre by WWI: Less cultured audiences, higher expenses and profits, replacement of old generation of actor-managers by new mercenary administrators, declining standards of taste. Touring Australia, 1923; tours of New Zealand and Canada; urging further emigration to Canada. Death of Ellen Terry, 1928.

Terriss begins her memoir by saying that this is not altogether the story of her own life, but a sort of clothesline on which to hang anecdotes and memories. She includes a wealth of detail on personalities, business practices, and financial dealings in the theatre during the first three decades of the century. She frankly discusses the mistakes she and her husband made in their management venture, which they embarked upon with insufficient knowledge about profit-and-loss calculations. In her autobiographical sequel, **935** *Just a Little Bit of String* (1955), Terriss describes how this naiveté drove her and Hicks to bankruptcy, leaving them to start life over again, at the outset of WWI, "on a ten-pound note." More cohesively organized than her first autobiography, this sequel expands upon the material of the earlier book and adds new information about the author's life from 1928–55.

936 TERRY, Dame Ellen. 1847–1928. *The Story of My Life.* Hutchinson, 1908. 2nd ed. 381 pp.; front. port.; intro.; illus.;

index. NUC pre56 587:360. (other ed.: New York: Schocken Books, 1982.)

Born in Coventry, Warwickshire. Father: Benjamin Terry, actor. Mother: Sarah Ballard, actress. 3 sisters; 5 brothers. Married 1864, George Frederick Watts, artist; divorced 1865. Married 1876, Charles Kelly (stage name; Charles Wardell), actor; separated 1881; d.1885. Married 1907, James Carew, actor, American; divorced 1909. 1 daughter (actress, suffragist Edith Craig); 1 son. Wrote *The Russian Ballet* (1913). Knew Sir Henry Irving, George Bernard Shaw, many others. Actress (stage); theatrical producer; theatrical writer. Middle class.

Famous actress's dedication to her theatrical career, covering her childhood to 1908. Being on tour in Glasgow with her parents; receiving early training in elocution from them. Her first performance, 1856, with Charles Kean's company in *The Winter's Tale;* continuing to act with the company until 1859. Performing with her parents and her sister Kate in farces at Ryde during the summers; touring with them, 1859–61. Performing at the Royal Soho Theatre in London; acting in a Bristol stock company, 1862–63. At age 16, marrying George Frederick Watts; temporarily retiring from the stage. Meeting Tennyson, Gladstone, Disraeli, Browning, Julia Cameron. Separating from husband due to incompatibility, age 17; returning to the stage, but not being happy there. At age 20, acting with Henry Irving for the first time; describing his woodenness as a young actor. Deciding to leave the stage; quietly disappearing into the countryside; authorities' discovering a corpse that resembled author; father's misidentifying the body as author. After reading in the newspapers that she had been found dead, author's returning to London to prove she was alive. Living in a Hertfordshire cottage, 1868–74; anecdotes about her two children. For financial reasons, returning to the stage in *The Wandering Heir,* at invitation of Charles Reade; being surprised at her warm reception. Playing the part of Portia in *The Merchant of Venice* under the Bancrofts at the Prince of Wales Theatre. Her friendship with playwright Thomas Taylor; his being more of a father to her than her own father. Memories of James Whistler and Oscar Wilde; their audaciousness. Marrying actor Charles Kelly, 1876. Playing Ophelia to Irving's *Hamlet* after he took over the Lyceum Theatre, 1878; conducting research for her part in a lunatic asylum. Irving's vast improvement as an actor; commencing her quarter-century onstage association with him. Touring with Kelly in the summers until 1880. Analyzing Irving; comparing their very different personal and acting styles. Noting qualities important to actors and actresses. Appearing in *Much Ado about Nothing, Twelfth Night, Othello, Faust,* many other plays. Receiving both critical acclaim and negative reviews for her Shakespearean performances. Anecdotes about many actors, including William Terriss. Touring America seven times with Irving, beginning in 1883; her fondness for the U.S.; her positive impressions of American audiences and critics; her impressions of black servants in Washington; her friendship with Mrs. Henry Ward Beecher. Comparing American and British cultures and institutions. Last days at the Lyceum. Corresponding with George Bernard Shaw; agreeing to appear in his play, *Captain Brassbound's Conversion*, written with her in mind; meeting Shaw; finding him a "good, kind, gentle creature" and "not a man of convictions." Playing in matinées at the Lyceum and in *The Merry Wives of Windsor* at His Majesty's Theatre. Irving's weak health, 1898 on; end of her collaboration with him, 1902. Deciding to venture into producing plays with her son; having a financially unprofitable season at the Imperial Theatre; going on tour. Irving's death, 1905; his burial in Westminster Abbey. Celebrating her stage jubilee, 1906. Her last American tour, and marriage to an American, 1907. Memories of old friends: Lewis Carroll, sculptor Albert Gilbert, others.

Claiming that she has had little life outside the theatre, Terry declines to tell much at all about her nonprofessional involvements, omitting information about any personal disappointments and scandal and mentioning little about her family life. In her declaration at the autobiography's outset that this book is intended for "the good, living public which has been considerate and faithful to me for so many years," she implicitly acknowledges the limitations on what a public woman of her time could say. For this reason, her omissions concerning architect Edward William Godwin, their living together unwed, 1868–74, and his fathering of her children, are as historically significant as the theatrical material she includes. Rich in anecdotes about the late-19th-century theatre in England and the U.S., this memoir describes in great detail Terry's views and theories on acting, rates the stagecraft of her contemporary theatrical colleagues, and offers insights into the character of Sir Henry Irving. Christopher St. John (pseud.; Christabel Marshall) assisted anonymously in the writing of this autobiography, and served as official editor, with assistance from Terry's daughter, in annotating *Ellen Terry's Memoirs* (1932), an expanded version of *The Story of My Life*. One particularly well-informed and recent biography of Terry is Nina Auerbach's *Ellen Terry: Player in Her Time* (1987).

937 THOMAS, Helen (née Noble). 1877–1967. *World without End*. New York: Harper & Bros., 1931. 218 pp. NUC pre56 590:692–693. (1st pub. partially as *As It Was*, by H. T., 1926.)

Probably born in Liverpool. Father: James Ashcroft Noble, essayist, critic. Mother: Helen. 2 sisters; 1 brother. Married (Philip) Edward Thomas, poet, essayist, biographer, critic, d.1914. Widow. 1 son; 2 daughters. Knew W. H. Davies, Eleanor Farjeon, Robert Frost, D. H. Lawrence. Governess; poet's spouse. Middle class.

Introspective recollections of childhood, courtship, marriage, and economic struggles, covering author's adolescence to 1914. Part 1: Family's moving from Liverpool to London. Describing her progressive upbringing; parents' interest in new movements. Feeling close to her father. Hating school. Her future husband's visiting her home; her father's encouraging Edward's interest in pursuing a writing career. Describing her strong attraction to Edward; awareness of her own sensuality, but ignorance of sexual love. Her mother's antagonism to author's developing love for Edward. Father's death. Leaving home for employment as a governess. Edward's plans of working for the civil service. His publishing a book on nature. Their first sexual experience in a country garden environment. His winning an Oxford scholarship. Author's understudying Edward's education in poetry and art. His melancholy moods. Their bohemian friends in London. Discovering she is pregnant; her happiness. Friends' urging them to marry; breaking news of marriage to their families. Compelling description of her labor and childbirth experience, which she considers a "dark mystery" and had looked forward to with expectant "ecstasy"; not having anticipated pain and suffering. Part 2: Edward's returning to Oxford for his last term. Author's happiness in motherhood. Edward's absorption in his university work and his immersion in writing; his moodiness, depression, emotional instability, increasing emotional distance from family. Living in poverty. Publication of Edward's first volume of essays. Moving from London slums to a country house in Kent. Author's growing self-confidence when meeting Edward's intellectual friends. His receiving an advance commission for his book; their increased financial security. Birth of their daughter. Moving to farmhouse in the Weald of Kent, then one in Hampshire. Her love of housework, gardening, physical exercise, and untraditional lifestyle. Enduring her husband's frequent absences to London. Staff at son's school in Hampshire showing intolerance toward family's bohemianism. Speaking at local suffrage meetings; her distaste for anti-male attitudes. Worrying about Edward's depressions. Amusements and discipline of her children. Disliking Edward's close acquaintance with other women during his absences. Suffering difficult childbirth of second daughter. Having financial difficulties; Edward's refusing work procured for him by his father; author's babysitting for extended periods to support family. Outbreak of WWI: Husband's enlistment in the Artists' Rifles; military life's relieving his melancholy. Author's moving to be near his regiment; their last Christmas together; Edward's departure for the front; her strong foreboding of his death.

In the first part of this poetic, sensuous autobiography, Thomas dwells on her sensitive reactions to falling in love and to the beauties of nature, melded with her idealization of Edward. Her explicit descriptions of her pleasure in physical eroticism are unusual for a woman autobiographer of this period. In the second section, she vividly depicts her sense of loss as Edward becomes obsessively absorbed in his writing, and she perceives a growing distance between them. She masks the identity of the principal figures in her life, and is deliberately vague about dates. Excerpts from this book were first published in a different form in the *Adelphi* magazine, edited by John Middleton Murry. Complete biographical information about the author is given in 938 *Under Storm's Wing* (1988), edited by her daughter, Myfanwy Thomas.

939 THOMAS, Helen Elizabeth Myfanwy. 1910–?. *One of These Fine Days: Memoirs*. Manchester: Carcanet New Press, 1982. 164 pp.; front. port.; illus. BLC 1982–1985 24:118.

Born near Steep, Hampshire. Father: (Philip) Edward Thomas, poet, essayist, biographer, critic. Mother: Helen Noble. 1 brother; 1 sister. Marriage implied. Knew Eleanor Farjeon. Poet's daughter; editor; secretary. Middle class.

Emotional relationships with parents and siblings and their effect on author's search for a positive self-image, focused on her birth to age 17. Portraying family history and relatives. Describing her childhood home; her siblings' education at a progressive coeducational boarding school. Her childhood dependency on her mother. Admiring her father's carpentry as well as his poetry. Her friendship with Eleanor Farjeon. Taking nature walks with father. Believing herself to be ugly. Sensing that her father did not care for her; at age 70, reading his letters to Robert Frost and discovering that her father had indeed cared for her. Author's mother's teaching English to diverse foreign women who periodically lived in the family home. Recalling the last family Christmas with father; his death in WWI; family's deciding to avoid discussing him after his death. Her early schooling. Moving with her mother to Otford, Kent. Feeling curious about church and Christianity; expecting church services to be entertaining. Attending Wesleyan chapel school mainly to receive prizes for perfect attendance. Summer holidays. Being miserable at a girls' school in Sevenoaks, Kent; attending a school "for the daughters of gentlefolk" which her mother could not afford. Suffering scarlet fever. Moving to Tonbridge to live with her aunt and uncle; attending a county school. Becoming closer to siblings; their breaking silence about father's death; their shock at reading, in their mother's autobiography, about tensions between their parents. Mother's depression and nervous illness; her medical treatment while residing with Mrs. C. E. M. Joad; her recovery. Belonging to Girl Guides. Author's envying her older sister's boyfriends; being introduced to London social life by older siblings. At age 13, being encouraged by a teacher to read her father's poetry; recognizing the image of herself in his poems. Leaving school despite passing School Certificate exam because she lacked desire to be a nurse or a teacher, the occupations girls were expected to pursue. Taking a motor tour through France and Switzerland with her uncle; being happy at last with the feeling she was valued. Planning to work as a secretary in uncle's London engineering firm.

The early part of this autobiography is a tribute to Thomas's father; in the manner of Dorothy Wordsworth, who in her *Journals* discusses her brother William's poetry, Thomas tells how her father's nature poems came to be written, and how she came to appear in them. The book is most interesting for the comparisons that can be drawn between her version of her childhood and that given in her mother's writings, *As It Was* and *World without End*. Perhaps Thomas waited so long to write this account of her childhood so that she could be free to tell her version without hurting the feelings of her mother, who died fifteen years before this book's publication.

940 THOMPSON, Flora Jane (née Timms). 1876–1947. *Lark Rise to Candleford: A Trilogy*. Harmondsworth, Middlesex: Penguin, 1973. 537 pp.; intro. by H. J. Massingham. BLC to 1975 325:4. (1st pub. Oxford University Press, 1945.)

Born at Juniper Hill, Oxfordshire. Father: Albert Timms, stonemason, carpenter. Mother: Emma, nurse before marriage. 5 siblings. Married John Thompson, postmaster. 3 children. Wrote book of poetry *Bog Myrtle and Peat*. Teacher; poet; essayist; postal worker. Rural laboring class.

Detailed, multifaceted remembrance of life in rural Victorian England, emphasizing local social order, from 1876–1900. Her native hamlet; cottagers' large families, diet, clothing, rustic housing, and plumbing. Author and siblings' learning that their poverty barred them from attending nearby Oxford University. Mother's having been taught in her childhood by local vicar. Author's brief home schooling by father; teaching herself to read. Describing nearby Fordlow village: dialect, farm laborers, village pub as center of social conversation about politics, folk beliefs, popular songs. Sketches of elderly residents of Lark Rise; memories of her maternal grandparents. Effects of poverty on her grandparents' and parents' generations as the self-sufficiency possible for the earlier yeoman farm class was taken away by expanding industrialization, land enclosures, and imposition of wage labor. Discussing lifestyles of local women and their standards of sexual conduct. Recalling vendors, gypsies, beggars, traveling entertainers. Community's negative attitudes toward both birth control and illegitimacy. Children's games and amusements. Commenting on employment of adolescent girls as domestic servants; their parents' pushing them into the job market as soon as possible. Attending Fordlow National School, early 1880s; children's teasing the new schoolmistress; egalitarian ideas communicated by new teachers. Local squire's providing entertainments for children. Describing Anglican church; local prejudice against Catholics; author's attending Sunday evening Methodist services. Christmas and seasonal celebrations; Queen Victoria's Golden Jubilee, 1887. Visiting wealthier relatives in Candleford, nearby market town; comparing her narrow prospects with her cousins' educational aspirations. Describing the bicycling craze. Lark Rise's still being unaffected by industrialization. Her cousin's having an illegitimate daughter; discussing lack of information given to children about sex. Meeting her future employer, Dorcas Lane, postmistress at Candleford Green; Lane's unusual position as a single, employed woman; her managing the old family forge business. Moving to Candleford Green, age 14, to work as post office assistant. Contrasting more urban village life with hamlet life. Sketches of coworkers; village life and social order; getting to know residents of all social classes; starting to make rounds as a postal carrier. Petty crimes and scandals. New villas' making the village more suburban; author's views on the worldly suburbanites.

Thompson's book is in effect a comprehensive history of social transition for rural England from an agrarian-based economy and lifestyle to the more impersonal industrial system. Vividly depicting the dynamics of socioeconomic change, she laments the loss by rural England of its traditional, more interdependent relationships. In this account she writes of herself in the third person, calling herself "Laura." Thompson's sequel, **941** *Still Glides the Stream* (1948), expands upon her youthful memories and adventures, using the village stream as a metaphor for the current of human life. The author also wrote nature essays for the *Daily News,* the *Catholic Fireside,* and other publications.

942 THOMPSON, Jemima (afterward Mrs. Luke). 1813–1906. *Early Years of My Life. By the Author of "I Think when I Read that Sweet Story of Old."* Hodder & Stoughton, 1900. NUC pre56 325:32. [also cat. under Luke.]

Born in England. Father: Thomas Thompson, creator of Home Missionary Society. Mother not named. Stepmother: the Hon. Charlotte Margaretta Welman. Siblings. Married surname Luke. Wrote *The Child's Desire, Missionary Stories.* Religionist (evangelical); religious/spiritual writer; missionary (India); children's author; songwriter; editor; teacher; organizer of societies (professional). Middle class.

Missionary's varied domestic and foreign activities, covering her childhood to c.1860. Discussing social and economic changes from her childhood to mid-1800s. Her younger brother's being bled with leeches, leading to his death; author's sorrow; mother's blaming herself although still having faith in current medical beliefs and treatments. Recalling the great love between father and children. Father's pioneering efforts in missionary work; his originating the Home Missionary Society for sending ministers to destitute English villages. Mother's invalidism; her teaching author to read and recite; author's later studying with a family friend, who used a rote-memorizing system to teach geography, English history, genealogy of kings, arithmetic, French grammar, map drawing, and the Bible; author's love for this teacher. Telling a lie, age 10; father's use of silence as punishment; her deep remorse; marking this as the turning point in her life; making a commitment to higher impulses. Traveling with her parents to Yorkshire, the Lake District, Lincolnshire. Moving to Kent for mother's health; reading her father's old books and new magazines. Publishing a poem in magazine *The Juvenile Friend*, age 13. Living with an aunt for a year so she could study with teacher-writer Caroline Fry. Moving with family to London, 1829. Mother's initiating evening religious services in their home. Author's studying with various teachers. Caring for her younger siblings during mother's illness. Formation of Society for Promoting Female Education in the East, to establish female missionary agency abroad; organization's aim of combatting prejudices and difficulties encountered by women missionaries. Author's attending meetings, working to support this idea with Quaker Anna Braithwaite. Her mother's death, 1837. Finding solace in Christian work. Believing strongly that Christian women, especially single ones, should enter missionary life. Being freed from domestic duties by father's remarriage. Going to India with missionaries Mr. and Mrs. Crisp, with father's approval; enduring criticism from other family members. Teaching in Mrs. Crisp's school for Indian women of all ages. Returning to England. Studying teaching methods for children. Ill health's preventing her from accepting a formal missionary appointment in India. Beginning to write hymns for her personal pleasure; father's hearing one of her hymns, sending it to *Teacher's Magazine;* its being published. Editing *The Missionary Repository,* a magazine for children. Writing books to encourage children's participation in the missionary effort.

Thompson's principal claim to fame is the hymn listed in her book's subtitle. She states that she is an unimportant person whose only reason for writing a memoir is to satisfy public curiosity about the hymn's creator. In portraying her own life as one devoted to helping others, particularly women and children, Thompson conveys her belief in the need to export Christian missionary service, and in the importance of harnessing women's capabilities to this end. Her steady commitment to these ideas both facilitated her resistance to prevailing prejudice against women missionaries abroad and motivated her didactic writing.

943 THORP, Margery Ellen (pseud.; Margery Ellen Robertson). 1906–s.l.1977. *Quiet Skies of Salween*. Jonathan Cape, 1945. 115 pp. BLC to 1975 325:320.

Born in Rangoon, Burma. Father not named, principal at a British-run school for tribal chiefs' sons. Mother not named. 1 brother; 2 sisters. Wrote novel *Swelling of Jordan* (1950), history *Ladder of Bones* (1956), stories *Ibrahim the Teacher, and Other Stories* (1960). Historian; short storyist; novelist; foreign resident (Burma). Upper middle class.

Warm personal and familial reminiscences, accompanied by vivid recollections of Burmese colonial and native societies, covering author's first sixteen years. Family's moving to Taunggyi in author's infancy. Family pets: dogs, cats, rabbits, baby leopard, baby bear. Playing with siblings. Reading Victorian nursery tales and Hindu folk tales. Remembering earthquakes and monsoons. Studying with an English governess for seven years; father's subsequently teaching girls Latin and other subjects. Family's having seven servants; one servant's special ability to cure arthritis and headaches through walking on the sufferer's spine; her dismissal due to her gambling addiction, a common problem among the Burmese. Food: bad meat, good fruits, vegetables, and dairy products; bakeries in individual homes. Father's collection of knives and guns; children's acceptance of weapons as a part of daily life. Native art, costumes, craftsmen. Mountain caves; ruby mines, including one owned by father. Family's agriculture: rice, nuts, fruits, flowers, tea. Pastimes: cycling, picnics, cricket, baseball, school and church plays. Traveling by oxcart. Burmese history, geography, holidays, architecture, gardens, music, diseases. Author's tolerance of surrounding religions: Buddhism, Anglicanism, Catholicism, American Baptist. General culture shock upon introduction of automobile into Burmese society. Family's return to England, 1922.

Written when Thorp was 39, this memoir of her first 16 years in Burma seems isolated from the remainder of her life. "Returning" to England meant that she became exposed to English customs and religion for the first time as an adolescent, when she left her own "native" culture of Burma behind. This cultural dislocation shows in the author's outspoken acceptance of a diversity of Eastern and Western religions and ideas. She followed the publication of this memoir with a novel based on Christian missionary activities abroad, a collection of short stories, and a history of the political formation of Nigeria.

THRALE, Mrs. Hester. [*See* PIOZZI, Hester Lynch.]

944 TIBBLE, Anne (née Northgrave). 1905–1980. *Greenhorn: A Twentieth-Century Childhood*. Routledge & Kegan Paul, 1973. 126 pp.; illus. by Karen Heywood. BLC to 1975 326:34.

Born at Rounton Grange, Yorkshire. Father: Fred Northgrave, coachman for steel magnate Sir Isaac Lowthian Bell. Mother: Elizabeth. 2 sisters. Married 1930, J. W. Tibble, English and Latin professor, d.1972. 1 son; 1 daughter. Wrote (under Anne Northgrave) novel *The Apple Reddens* (1951), biography *Gertrude Bell* (1958), poetry *Labyrinth* (1972); with J. W. Tibble, *John Clare: A Life* (1932), others. Knew traveler Gertrude Bell. Biographer; poet; novelist; academic's spouse. Rural laboring class; married into middle class.

Memories of a rural upbringing governed by traditional ties between the gentry and servants, contrasting with author's growing intellectual ambitions and sophistication, covering her childhood to age 16. Her parents' characters; father's mistrust of schooling. Remarking on country people and their changeless way of life. Father's family history in his own words, using Yorkshire dialect; the family standard of living; television's arrival in rural Britain decades earlier than indoor bathrooms. Describing family's rural cottage; playing in the woods, loving nature. At age 7, author's submitting to sex with a farmer's adolescent son; feeling bewildered at mother's anger when author told her; her continuing sexual ignorance despite the incident. Engaging in sex play with neighbor children; observing animals mating. Remembering father's generosity to tramps and mother's contrasting frugality; father's sometimes raging against mother. Parents' having lost infant son before author's birth; father's wish that author were male; his teaching her to have "guts"; her strong desire to excel at everything to please him. Memories of father's training horses for his wealthy employer; foxhunts; noting that gentry, not the working class, introduced socialist ideas into her community. Scorning William Morris and Virginia Woolf's characterizations of the working class as brutish and unthinking. Attending dreary Church Board School; contrasting school's brutal educational methods with her father's encouragement of observation. Learning poetry and singing from Lady Bell, wife of her father's employer. Visiting her aunt, who lived in drab, ugly, bathroomless charity housing in Teeside; realizing that those who built this housing, rich philanthropists such as her father's employer, were not really "kind and enlightened." Feeling torn between her desire to read and the obligation to do housework. Resolving not to lead a life of servitude as her father did. Attending coeducational grammar school, ages 12–17. Determining to win a scholarship and earn her living as a children's writer. Coming to realize she must live in cities as an exile from the country.

This earliest of three autobiographies from Tibble depicts the class attitudes and barriers she faced in progressing from her rustic, lower-class background to a life of intellect and education. She recreates her father as a perceptive, intelligent man whose livelihood as a rural squire's coachman was a living remnant of the feudal system; through this portrait, Tibble debunks upper-class notions of the lower or rural classes as vulgar and unthinking. Nevertheless, in concluding that she must escape to the cities to elude the subordination her father experienced, she implies her awareness that such class prejudices govern an individual's social chances. Taking up the author's story where the first volume ends, **945** *One Woman's Story: An Autobiography* (1976) spans Tibble's adolescence to middle age, discussing her college experience and stressing the need for education for all social classes. In this book Tibble discusses her courtship and marriage, but stresses her relationship with her children.

946 *Alone* (1979) focuses on Tibble's dialogue with her recently deceased husband, and provides a platform for her reflections on the vicissitudes of aging and the negative changes afflicting modern society.

947 TODD, Marjory (née Black?). c.1900–s.l.1960. *Snakes and Ladders: An Autobiography*. Longmans, Green, 1960. 204 pp. NUC 1942–1962 134:231.

Born in England. Father: Andy, sailor, boilermaker. Mother: Laurie, schoolmistress and governess before marriage. 2 brothers; 2 sisters. Married twice, husbands not named. 1 son. Knew Cyril E. M. Joad, C. K. Ogden, Nina Hamnett, Philippa Fawcett, Lady Ottoline Morrell. Civil servant; prison service officer; domestic servant; tutor; secretary. Working class.

Recollections of a difficult working-class childhood and adolescence, followed by occupational success, spanning c.1900–1950s. Book's opening in 1943; author's working for BBC near Birmingham; enduring separation from her son, who was evacuated to countryside to escape WWII bombing; her resulting depression. Learning news of her father's death; its jolting her memories. Remembering her father's pennypinching; his often being away at sea in author's childhood; his drinking and stubbornness; his physical punishment of the children. Recounting how her parents met and married in South Africa, 1902. Reading books with her mother; wearing glasses to overcome poor vision. Attending local school, beginning age 5; winning scholarship to grammar school; feeling alienated from father due to educational differences. Mother's death, 1918. Father's swindling children's Christmas money from them. Father's hiring servants to replace mother's domestic management; one's stealing from the family; another's refusing to provide author with clean clothes. Author's consequently being shamed at school; lying and being accused of theft there. Her privacy's being invaded at home. At age 15, selling newspapers and living with her aunt in Kent; commenting on what work means to her. Persuading father to fire servant; taking over housework herself. Gaining powers of self-expression and intellectual discipline through attending Workers' Educational Association history and economics classes. Joining the Independent Labour Party. Taking job as a nursemaid; traveling to Switzerland with her employers. Being evicted from home by father; finding work as a housemaid. Passing the Civil Service exam. Working in East End employment office during the General Strike of 1926; joining the 1917 Club endorsing principles of the workers' revolution. Attending University College of Hull. Finding employment as a tutor in France and as secretary for author Vilhjalmur Stefansson. Marriage to "E." Birth of her son. Author and first husband's working in different cities. Moving to Evesham, near Birmingham, 1940; working in BBC Monitoring Office. Death of her father, 1943. Alluding briefly to a second marriage and her employment as a probation officer.

Reflecting on having waited a long time (until age 60) to put her autobiography on paper.

The chosen title of Todd's circular autobiography refers to the children's board game Snakes and Ladders, in which, after a series of contorted and seemingly random moves, the player ends up where she began. Todd uses her narrative to address the problems, both individual and class-related, that plagued her attempts to escape the traditional subordinate woman's role in the working class and to win success in the business world. Both efforts caused friction with—and alienation from—her resolutely working-class father, yet her intense regrets over his death prove her ties to him to be unabated. While Todd's rise in the world of commerce characterizes Britain's increasing 20th-century class mobility, her narrative shows the consequences of such a transition on personal family relationships.

948 TONNA, Charlotte Elizabeth (née Browne). 1790–1846. *Personal Recollections by Charlotte Elizabeth*. New York: Scribner's, 1858. 396 pp.; app. on life of author's brother, by Dr. Southey; concluding remarks by L. H. J. Tonna (author's husband). NUC pre56 597:282. (1st pub. Seeley, Burnside & Seeley, 1841.)

Born in Norwich, Norfolk. Father: Michael Browne, Anglican rector. Mother not named. 1 brother. Married 1813, George Phelan, British army officer, d.1837. Married 1841, Lewis Hippolytus Joseph Tonna, religious/spiritual writer. Wrote *The Deserter* (1837), *Helen Fleetwood* (1841), and other novels, *Perils of the Nation* (1843), essays and sketches *The Wrongs of Women* (1844), *Kindness to Animals*, books for children, others. Religious/spiritual writer; novelist; religionist (anti-Catholic); religionist (evangelical); children's author; social reformer; animal welfare activist; poet; clergyman's daughter. Middle class.

Intellectual and moral formation of an evangelical Protestant and later polemical novelist, from birth to her 1836 founding of *Christian Lady's Magazine*. Being a precocious reader; going temporarily blind studying French grammar, age 5. Beloved brother's reading to her. Her grandmother's claiming Scottish Calvinist ancestry and delivering diatribes against "Papists." Her father's telling her stories about Catholic Queen Mary: his giving her *Foxe's Book of Martyrs* to study. Author's wanting to be martyred for Protestantism; her father's saying she would be, if Catholics ever won political power in England. Being educated in her father's study; his Tory friends' discussing political issues there. Teaching herself to write, age 7. Becoming intoxicated with romantic literature; feeling sensually lured to music until dosing with mercury made her permanently deaf, age 10. Family's moving to a rural parish for her health. Benefitting from open air life; later condemning the confined upbringing suffered by "that oppressed class called young ladies." Her father's parenting policies against tight corsets freeing her from headaches and other "lady-like maladies." Father's fearing that passage of Catholic Emancipation in England might provoke a French invasion; his condemning repeal of the Test Act which had barred Catholics from holding parliamentary office. Author's turning to a career in writing to compensate for her deafness; composing political squibs for father's Tory friends. Father's death's leaving family without income; author's resolving to write fiction for pay, until saved from this "profane snare" by marrying an army officer. Living with husband in Halifax, Nova Scotia, 1818–20. Moving with husband to Ireland; author's prejudice against the "discontented and malignant" Irish being reversed by personal experience. Husband's abandoning her in Kilkenny, 1821; his moving to Dublin and entertaining other women. Her becoming convinced of her own sinfulness; believing she could be saved by serving God through writing tracts; their publication by the Dublin Tract Society. Reading the Catholic prophecy that Protestants would be slain in Ireland in 1825. Receiving death threats; murders of Protestants in her neighborhood by militants. Author's teaching deaf and dumb residents in a convent, converting them to Protestantism; adopting a deaf-mute boy. Returning to England without husband, 1824. Becoming friends with Religious Tract Society founder, Hannah More. Choosing to write under pseudonym "Charlotte Elizabeth" to thwart estranged husband's claim on her earnings. Being proud that the Catholic Church put her writings on their list of forbidden books. Reacting to the Catholic Emancipation Act, 1829; exhorting her women readers to influence public events and policies through praying, lobbying men to take anti-Catholic action, and circulating petitions and other writings. While mourning the deaths of her brother and adopted son, working to found an Irish Episcopal Church in Norwich and continuing her polemical writing. Moving to London. Collecting funds for Irish famine relief, 1830. Helping found the short-lived *Protestant Magazine*. Beginning *Christian Lady's Magazine*, 1836.

In 1836 Tonna changed from tract-writing to what we know as the social problem novel. Coinciding with a national economic depression, 1839–41, Tonna's polemic novel *Helen Fleetwood* was designed to arouse public indignation over the evils of child and female labor, the latter of which she addressed more extensively in her later anthology of stories, *The Wrongs of Women*, written in the context of the contemporary evangelical solution to social ills: a national call to moral revival, and a resurrection of the pre-industrial sense of brotherhood and human obligation between employer and worker. For this perspective, she grounded her fiction in rigorous study of the governmental "Blue Books": Parliament's publication of official reports on its inquiries into socioeconomic questions. In his epilogue, Tonna's husband indicates that, after the Chartist Riots of 1842, the author was requested by the Christian Influence

Society to write a nonfiction book addressing *The Perils of the Nation*. It remains her most farseeing and influential book (despite anonymous publication), unflinchingly confronting industrial accidents, unsanitary filth, and robbery of workers through employer fraud, while pleading for wholesale reform. *Perils* is said to have influenced many later parliamentary reforms addressing these specific issues. Mr. Tonna further asserts that Charlotte Elizabeth wrote this autobiography to avoid having a future biographer distort her life and work.

949 TOPHAM, Anne. c.1880–?. *Chronicles of the Prussian Court.* Hutchinson, c.1926. 255 pp.; front.; illus.; index. NUC pre56 597:382.

Born in Derbyshire. Parents not named. Single. Wrote *Memories of the Fatherland* (1916). Knew Kaiser Wilhelm II of Germany and his family. Governess; foreign resident (Germany); social historian. Middle class.

Firsthand testimony on both the private and the political dealings of the Prussian court, including activities of Kaiser Wilhelm, written during WWI from an English perspective, covering 1902–14. Joining the Prussian court as governess to Princess Victoria Louise, 1902. Noting German envy and rivalry with the British Empire; the rise of German imperial power; German contempt for England's conduct of the Boer War. First meeting the kaiser; discussing his character. Anecdotes of the kaiser and his mother, the late Empress Frederick, daughter of Queen Victoria. Returning with the court from Hamburg to the New Palace near Potsdam. Finding her place in the kaiser's enormous household staff; her concern for the princess's maturing character as well as for her academic education; infighting among doctors, tutors, and governesses of the prince and princess. Observing other governesses' authoritarian methods with the princess. Rivalry among nobility attached to the court. Earning more respect from the Germans through demonstrating her knowledge of first aid than through her intellect. Spending holidays at Cadinen, the summer palace in Poland. Patiently overcoming princess's refusal to converse in French. With princess, visiting empress's sister in Denmark; discussing Danish-German politics. Traveling in imperial entourage throughout the German Empire. Kaiser's character: his vanity and refusal to hear contrary opinions; his ambivalence toward England and glorification of warfare. Marriage of the Crown Prince, 1904. Noting German aversion to modern simplicity in home furnishings and their perpetuating the discomforts of royal residences. Discussing Prussian political struggles: socialist opposition to kaiser; Prussian attitudes toward foreign powers. During court visit to England, 1907, kaiser's sending anti-English telegram to ex-President Kruger of South Africa, who had led the Boer War against the British. German people's voicing outrage that kaiser had tried to send military aid to the Boers. King Edward VII's paying official visit to government in Berlin, 1909.

Discussion at court of impending war with France, 1912. Visiting Berlin for marriage of the princess; the princess's move to Brunswick as the Duchess of Brunswick. Outbreak of WWI, 1914.

The historical value of Topham's memoir may be enhanced by comparative reading with Edith Keen's somewhat later account, *Seven Years at the Prussian Court*. Keen served as governess to the daughter of Emperor Friedrich (whose marriage during his tenure as Crown Prince is recorded by Topham); her book, published at the height of WWI, is single-mindedly anti-German. In contrast, Topham shows greater objective balance. While she conscientiously assesses both German character in general and that of the Kaiser in particular, the events and attitudes to which she attributes significance appear colored by her hindsight about contributory causes of WWI. She fleshes out her analysis of the Prussian court with dialogue and anecdotes.

950 TOTTENHAM, Edith Leonora. 1876–?. *Highnesses of Hindostan*. Grayson & Grayson, 1934. 331 pp.; front.; foreword; illus.; index. NUC pre56 598:357.

Born in England. Parents not named. Single. Tutor; secretary; foreign resident (India). Middle class.

Author's personal experiences in British colonial India as a tutor to the ruling family of Baroda, highlighting the character and influence of the Maharani (queen), 1911–20. Meeting the Maharani at a social event in England; being invited to India by a former college friend, Frances West, now secretary and tutor to the Maharani. Thrilling at the voyage to India, exoticism of its foreign culture, and luxury of the royal lifestyle. Being presented to palace dignitaries, British governmental wives, and the Maharani herself. King Edward VII's visiting country for his coronation as Emperor of India. Illustrating cultural differences: the Maharajah's innocently causing a scandal by turning his back on King Edward during a formal presentation. Touring Nagpur, Calcutta, and Darjeeling. Frances's returning to England; author's becoming the Maharani's English tutor and secretary. Contrasting her own conservatism with the liberal political ideas of the Maharani. Giving the Maharani tennis, bridge, and piano lessons. Being installed in the Maharani's palace quarters and given eight servants. Teaching English language and customs to the Maharani's new daughter-in-law and to other young household brides. Accompanying the royal family to Europe, 1914; WWI's outbreak stranding them in Austria. Returning to Baroda via England. Evaluating *The Commandments of a Chaste Wife*, a Hindu treatise for wives; deciding the "chaste wife" described is a "negative creature," dependent upon "he who held the purse." Discussing the rise of the new Indian middle class and prospects for the future of Indian government. The Maharani's reading Indian history, noting 7th-century Indian women's opportunities in education and politics; her wishing early-20th-century Indian women could be stirred by the "right spirit." Discussing weaknesses in the prevailing method for teaching English in India; the Indian educational system. Traveling in the Maharani's retinue; visiting Khyber Pass with an English couple. Planning to open an adult school for ladies in Baroda; the Maharani's strong support of this plan. Author's first pupil's being a dignitary's wife; rapidly acquiring more students. Visit of the English Viceroy to Baroda.

As Tottenham's title indicates, her account is first and foremost a profile of the Maharani and of her enlightened quest for female equality and Indian social progress. A fascinating figure whose intellectual force Tottenham successfully conveys, the Maharani is a reminder that the women politicians who are the progressive power in late-20th-century India have notable earlier antecedents. Deeply influenced by her royal employer, who remarked upon hearing of Tottenham's conservatism, "I am sorry! You ought to be liberal," Tottenham comes to sound increasingly protofeminist in the later pages of her memoir, which address the establishment of her ladies' school. Tottenham declares herself enchanted to be in India, a land she regards as the quintessence of romance. She utilizes much dialogue and scene-setting to create a vivid anecdotal portrait of early-20th-century life in Baroda, and to compare and contrast how Indian men and women viewed their changing world.

951 TOWNLEY, Lady Susan Mary Keppel. 1868–1953. *Indiscretions of Lady Susan*. New York: D. Appleton & Co., 1922. 314 pp.; front. port.; illus.; index. BLC to 1975 328:252.

Born in England. Father: William Coutts Keppel, P.C., K.C.M.G., M.P., 7th Earl of Albemarle. Mother: Sophia Macnab, Canadian Prime Minister's daughter. 8 siblings. Married 1896, Walter Beaupré Townley, later Sir Walter, K.G.M.G., of the Foreign Office. 1 son. Foreign resident (China, Turkey, U.S.); diplomat's spouse; society woman; WWI volunteer; traveler (world); Red Cross worker; cultural historian. Aristocracy.

Memories of various cultures by an undiplomatic diplomat's wife, including her unconventional observations on society, covering author's childhood to 1918. Remembering her paternal grandfather's telling her stories; playing with paints in her father's study. Her parents' enforcing strict discipline. Her brothers' playing pranks on governesses. Her social debut. Meeting the Prince and Princess of Wales. Marriage, 1896; accompanying her husband on his diplomatic appointments to Lisbon, and later Berlin. Memories of Empress Frederick. Enjoying the sights of Berlin. Explaining diplomatic etiquette in Germany. Boer War's creating pro-Boer, pro-English camps in Germany. Dining with Cecil Rhodes. Her husband's accepting post in Rome. Memories of Queen Elena; assassination of Italy's King Humbert. Engaging in popular pastimes in

Roman society. Attending private audience with Pope Leo XIII. Moving to China upon husband's appointment as Secretary of the Legation at Peking, 1901. Attending audience given by the Dowager Empress on her return from exile after Boxer uprising. Being granted a personal audience with the Empress; her secret sympathies with the Boxer movement; their increasing friendship. Memories of Viceroy of Chihli and his pro-Western views. Discussing Chinese burial customs, cleanliness, and practice of footbinding. Accompanying husband to his new post as Secretary of the Embassy at Constantinople, 1903. Recounting the reign of Caliph Abdul Hamid, recently passed away; observing a religious procession presided over by his deputy. Noting Turkish women's unhappiness that they could not aspire to Western customs. Publicly expressing frank, sometimes negative, opinions about non-Western cultures. Visiting the Holy Land; riding to Samaria, Cana, and Nazareth; describing Damascus. Husband's promotion to councillor of embassy in Washington. Traveling across the U.S. on inspection tour. Visiting Palm Beach, Florida; touring the Bowery in New York. Memories of Teddy Roosevelt; attending official White House receptions. Being attacked by the press for her social ambition. Living in Argentina during husband's tenure as Envoy Extraordinaire, 1906–11. Discussing European nature of Buenos Aires. Taking riding trips throughout Argentina. Residing in Bucharest, 1911–12, during husband's envoyship. Memories of Queen Elizabeth of Romania, her interest in social causes. Following husband's reassignment as Envoy to Persia, meeting young Shah after his father's assassination. Visiting Russia. WWI: husband's assignment at the Hague; author's working with Belgian Red Cross. Opening branches of Needlework Guild in Holland after the war. Vising Ghent after the German evacuation; hearing rumors of prospective German revolution. Memories of Queen Wilhelmina of Holland; their sharing a love of children. Her husband's being informed that her "indiscretions" have made further advancement in the diplomatic corps impossible for him; his decision to resign; her resulting feelings of bitterness. Their retirement to the country.

Focusing on her life in the social sphere of the official British Diplomatic Corps, Townley rates the ruling elite in both Western and non-Western countries. Between the lines of this book a vengeful spirit emerges; Townley wrote this memoir after her behavior toward American officials (offending local dignitaries, upsetting traditional hierarchy, upstaging visiting VIPs) resulted in her husband's being recalled from the diplomatic service in 1919. Her more restrained earlier work, **952** *My Chinese Notebook* (1904), which recalls her 1901–03 stay in China, is more objective in its examination of that country's culture and history. Although filtered through a colonial lens, this semi-pedagogical work provides substantial information on turn-of-the-century China and on Townley's personal reactions to that country's cultural problems and complexities.

953 TOWNSHEND, Zoe. c.1889–c.1930. *An Officer's Wife*. Country Life, 1932. 130 pp.; foreword by Col. Sir Francis N.E. Dalrymple; illus. NUC pre56 599:231.

Raised in Derbyshire. Parents not named. 2 sisters; 3 brothers. Married c.1912, Tony Townshend, British Army officer. 2 sons. Military spouse. Middle class.

Recollections of an emotionally uncomfortable childhood and later life as the wife of an army officer posted to India, France, Russia, and Ireland, c.1889–c.1925. Mother's beauty; her dislike of children and men (including her husband). Author's yearning for love from mother and others in childhood; her devotion to her sister Noll. Sisters' being beaten by their cruel nanny; after her removal, their being taught by a much-liked governess. Attending a Westbourne boarding school with Noll for four years; their being transferred to a "perfectly hateful" school by parents. Commenting on the bad effects of neglect and ill treatment of children; implying that she was often filled with terror and remorse for breaking rules. Traveling with parents to Channel Islands. Receiving further lessons at home with tutors. Social debut; attending dances; discussing her social life in teenage years; courtships, age 19. Traveling to Egypt with her parents. Noll's marriage to a cavalry officer in India. Author's traveling to Algiers and India with her mother; meeting her future husband in India, age 24. Social life and courtship in India. Marrying Tony in England, c.1912. Returning to India in a troopship with husband. Having a difficult childbirth in India. Returning to England at outbreak of WWI. Husband's WWI service; author's being fearful for his safety; visiting him in France; her praise for the British Army and empire. Wounded husband's return to England; living with him at different stations in England. Rejecting sexual advances of other officers. Second son's birth. After the Armistice, husband's being ordered to Russia to fight the Bolsheviks. Author's domestic life with her children. Moving with husband and sons to Curragh, Ireland, c.1921; describing dangers to officers and their families due to anti-British Sinn Fein activity. Gardening, dances, sports, and amusements in Ireland. Traveling with husband to French Riviera, c.1922. Refusing the advances of another man while Tony was in Belfast. Living with husband in Bangor, County Down, and Belfast. Husband's refusal to proceed to India to join his regiment at a frontier station where no women were allowed; his resigning from Army and declaring his intention to run a hotel. Their returning to Belfast.

In failing health when she wrote this book, Townshend died before it was published. Useful for its documentation of the life of an army officer's family in WWI and in early-1920s Ireland, Townshend's account covers some of the same ground as the anonymous autobiography entitled *Experiences of an Officer's Wife in Ireland* (1921). Both authors were in

Ireland because Britain's occupying army was working to suppress the Irish nationalist rebellion, and both women view the native Irish—especially members of Sinn Fein—as savages threatening the safety of the civilized British. For this reason, their accounts gain perspective from comparison with Annie Mary Smithson's *Myself and Others—An Autobiography* (1944), in which nurse/novelist Smithson discusses her own 1921 work for Sinn Fein.

954 TREFUSIS, Violet (née Keppel). 1894–1972. *Don't Look Round: Her Reminiscences*. Hutchinson, 1952. 240 pp.; front. port.; preface; illus.; family tree chart; "The Tail," by Sonia Keppel (author's sister); index. BLC to 1975 329:76.

Born in London. Father: Lt.-Col. The Hon. George Keppel, 3rd son of the 7th Duke of Albemarle, Lord Advocate of Scotland, Mayor of Tower of London. Mother: Alice Edmonstone, daughter of 4th Baronet Edmonstone. Aunt: Lady Susan Keppel Townley. 1 sister (Sonia Keppel). Married 1919, Denys Trefusis, d.1929. Widow. Wrote novels *Sortie de Secours* (1929), *Echo* (1931), others. Knew Vita Sackville-West, Harold Nicolson, the Sitwells, Rebecca West, Virginia Woolf, Lady Diana Cooper, Anna de Noailles, Eugène Girardoux, Colette. Foreign resident (France); novelist; essayist; broadcaster; bisexual. Upper class.

Lively, humorous account of author's passions for France, art, and culture, 1890s–1952. Aesthetics, history, and social milieu of aunts' and uncles' estates in Scotland. First visiting Paris, age 10; experiencing "love at first sight" upon seeing city; resolving to live there when she grew up. Meeting Vita Sackville-West; competing with her in learning languages; their becoming best friends. Mother's bribing author to study foreign languages with travel as a reward. Traveling to France with Vita; being piqued that Vita's French was better than author's. Continuing with Vita to Italy; Vita's becoming infatuated with the country; both girls' learning German to show their mothers they could. Touring Spain. Describing living in wealthy part of London. Attending a private girls' school. Traveling to Ceylon with her mother and younger sister, 1910–11; belatedly growing close to her sister. Being sent with sister to school in Munich. Meeting Vita again after several years; newly perceiving her as a "beauty." Author's flirting with a young man; Vita's being amusedly condescending about this. Vita's marrying Harold Nicolson six months later without author's knowledge, 1913. Becoming godmother to Vita's eldest son one year later. Outbreak of WWI; the decimation of brilliant young men. Attending Slade Art School, London. Meeting her future husband, 1918; courtship and marriage, 1919. Author and husband's both having violent tempers and knowledge of several languages. Living with him in Paris. Commenting on differences between English and French marriages. Traveling to Poland, Greece, America, and Cuba with husband. His traveling with a friend to Russia, 1928; this marking the onset of his declining health; his death, 1929. Living in a French country house. Rejecting a proposal from Max Jacob. Writing novels and travel essays. Recalling Roman Catholic legends and customs of rural France. Interviewing Mussolini in Rome, 1936. Recalling the war scare in France during the 1938 Munich conference. Working for the French Red Cross; attempting to return to England with parents, 1940. Giving BBC broadcasts to France on literary subjects, 1944. German occupation of her French country house. Returning to France, 1946. Briefly living near Cremona, Italy with Guido, an Italian friend who thought she might suit him as a wife; feeling ill at ease in his home. Deaths of her parents. Commenting on life after age 60, her love of France and French culture, contrasts between English and French society.

An intense Francophile, Trefusis gilds her lighthanded treatment of fact with French phrases. She tells her readers that "I have not lied, I have merely omitted, bypassed the truth, whenever unpalatable"; thus, she skates over her sundry relations with men and entirely avoids mention of her ardent affair with Vita Sackville-West, begun in their mutual adolescence and renewed after Vita had been happily married five years. Vita treats this ongoing romance frankly in her own account, which forms part of Nigel Nicolson's biography of his parents, *Portrait of a Marriage*. Trefusis, however, romantically fictionalizes the affair with Vita in her novel *Broderie Anglaise* (1935), in which Vita's character is incarnated as a young man. Although acknowledging her mother's hand in giving her a broad, multilingual education, Trefusis admits that both parents spoiled her dreadfully. In her essay collection **955** *Prelude to Misadventure* (1941), Trefusis discusses her travels, her French friends, and historical episodes that interested her.

956 TREMAYNE, Mrs. L. c.1880–?. *Experiences of a Psychometrist and Medium*. A. M. Stockwell, 1922. 48 pp. BLC to 1975 329:109.

Born in England. Father: first name Henry, lay worker for the Baptist preacher Charles Spurgeon of London's Metropolitan Tabernacle. Mother not named, also lay worker for Spurgeon. Married surname Tremayne. 4 sons; 4 daughters. Clairvoyant/psychic; spiritualist; shopkeeper. Lower middle class.

Author's sixteen-year involvement in spiritualism and her passionate defense of its practice and worth, with backward glances at her Christian upbringing, c.1880–c.1921. Prophets and fortunetellers' enduring scorn; a medium's being "a person to be shunned by all respectable members of the community." Fortunetelling's being punishable by British law. WWI's fueling spiritualism through people's efforts to contact dead loved ones; their believing their own mediumistic experiences. Author's rejecting Christian "fall of man" and consequent state of sin; declaring babies not sinful but gifts from God. Both parents' being Christian workers yet deeply interested in spiritualism; author's inheriting from them her thirst for spiritual knowledge. Both seeing and hearing future events; fearing to speak out because of scorn, but finding some things must be said, for keeping silent provokes headaches. Joining the Spiritualist movement, c.1905. Giving examples of her visionary messages. Beginning active work as clairvoyant, 1917; noting that gift fades if not regularly developed. Father's having died, author's age 19; his appearing to her in dreams when she needed advice. His warning her against marrying her future husband, saying he had abandoned a wife and eight children in the north. Marrying anyway; being left by her husband, c.1921; realizing the abandoned wife in her father's warning was herself. Early in their marriage, her husband's needing a new means of income; author's dreaming of a locale with the right house and shop; going to the place she dreamed of and finding the house and shop to let. Their business's becoming valuable, but husband's not maintaining it well. WWI: Having visions during air raids; predicting zeppelin attacks; predicting the signing of the peace treaty. Pleading for readers to take spiritualists seriously.

Along with writer Mabel Stobart, professional psychic Gladys Leonard, Sir Arthur Conan Doyle, and others, Tremayne became caught up in the tide of British spiritualism, named "The Great Awakening" by its early-20th-century proponents. As Tremayne notes, the movement's greatest impetus came from the massive WWI deaths that disrupted families, leaving the survivors psychologically disposed to believe in life after death, since belief offered hope of renewed contact. With WWI, the disrepute which psychics had long endured began to dissipate. A worthy historical account from someone within the movement's ranks, Tremayne's record also illustrates technical terms of spiritualist practice such as "clairaudience," the ability to hear as well as see future events, and "psychometry," the power to know an object's history and human associations merely from touching it. Tremayne asserts that she herself wielded both of these psychic faculties.

957 TREMLETT, Mrs. Horace. c.1890–?. *With the Tin Gods*. John Lane, 1915. 308 pp.; illus. BLC to 1975 329:121.

Probably born in England. Parents not named. Married Horace Tremlett, mining engineer. 1 son. Wrote novel *Curing Christopher*. Colonialist (Africa); novelist; miner's spouse. Middle class.

Humorous observations by mining engineer's wife on the situation of white women in colonial Nigeria, c.1914. Husband's planning to go to Nigeria as a tin prospector. Author's deciding to accompany him. Depicting husband as a decisive sort who cannot abide delays, animal commotions, or breaches of conduct; referring to him throughout as "the P.M." (Primitive Man); his having visited Nigeria previously without her. Their different ideas about supplies necessary for the trip. Feeling guilty and torn about leaving her small son with her mother in London.

Traveling to Nigeria. Visiting government officials; their preferring to chat about current events in England rather than their own African adventures. Confiding her thoughts about why the men are not permitted to bring their wives to Nigeria; her low opinion of men's desire for isolation and freedom from women. Her sense of being in Nigeria on sufferance and of men's conscious chivalrous superiority. Her fear of being infected with diseases carried by insects. Experiencing fever and delirium during a dinner party; feeling enormous fatigue. Wishing she could wear pajamas in the heat, but not having the figure or the nerve to do so; knowing she would have to secure the P.M. in a straitjacket first. Her relief at occasionally wearing pretty frocks. Modestly crediting herself with making her husband dress up for a jungle luncheon party. Contrasting the lives of native and white women in Nigeria. Noting her husband's self-dramatizing tendency: "His adventures that never happen are almost as exciting as those that do." Her contempt for missionaries; feeling they make other whites in Africa look ridiculous. Her loneliness and lack of female companions. Husband's severe fever. Returning to England; being happily reunited with son; husband's poor health for several months after their return.

An independent personality imbued with a strong sense of irony emerges in this witty account. Tremlett's commentary is consistently informed by her generally low opinion of men, including her husband, and she often expresses a superior attitude toward them. This is a good source on white women's attitudes toward life in colonial Africa and the stress that colonial life put on their marriages. Like Mary Gaunt, Tremlett expresses a somewhat cynical awareness of white men's reasons for keeping white women out of Africa.

958 TRENEER, Anne. 1891–?. *School House in the Wind*. Jonathan Cape, 1950. 221 pp. NUC pre56 600:625. (1st pub. 1944.)

Born in Gorran, South Cornwall. Father: Joseph Treneer, headmaster. Mother: Susan Nott. 1 sister; 4 brothers; 1 half-sister. Single. Wrote *The Sea in English Literature from Beowulf to Donne* (1926), *Charles M. Doughty: A Study of His Prose and Verse* (1935), poems *This World's Bliss* (1942), stories *Happy Button, and Other Stories* (1950), *The Mercurial Chemist: A Life of Sir Humphrey Davy* (1963). Literary critic; short storyist; biographer; poet; teacher. Middle class.

Young girl's personal experiences in turn-of-the-century Cornish society, covering family history before her birth to author's age 14. Describing the Gorran schoolhouse and the South Cornish landscape. Father's growing up in a farming family; his becoming a schoolteacher because lameness made farming impossible for him. Parents' family history and early married life. Likening Cornish landscape's bareness and enchantment to the qualities of the Arabian Desert remarked on by T. E. Lawrence and Near East travel writer Charles Doughty. Being spoiled, despite not being "a greatly desired baby"; opposing birth control, because under scientific schemes of family planning, as the youngest child in a large family she would "never have been." Associating the Cornish wind with the Holy Spirit. Learning to ride a bicycle; being nearly knocked off by an early motorist. Author and brother's using strong Cornish dialect in order to have a laugh at tourists' expense. Her father's admiring Charles Doughty's book *Travels in Arabia Desarta;* sharing Doughty's type of Christianity, which loved beauty but rationalized away any belief in hell. Author's ideas of hell and wrath being influenced by her later reading of T. S. Eliot, G. M. Hopkins, and the 17th-century metaphysical poets. Extended memories of siblings; their collecting bird eggs, celebrating holidays, playing on the seashore at Hemmick, Mevagissey, Gorran Haven. Author's likening sights in Cornwall to descriptions from the 17th-century diary, *Through England on a Side-Saddle in the Time of William and Mary*. Describing Anglican festivals and hay harvesting. Author's wanting to preserve the Cornish dialect. Disliking school; learning to read at home; eventually attending father's school in Gorran. Moving to Caerhays, age 10; attending father's new school there. Comparing her experiences in Chapel and Quaker meetings to Church of England services; disliking sermons that pushed modern, relatavistic religious ideas like those of philosopher C. E. M. Joad. Failing an exam for a minor scholarship to St. Austell School; passing the second time. Being confirmed, age 14; beginning school at St. Austell.

This volume constitutes Treneer's retrospective on the pre-WWI innocence and beauty of her Cornish upbringing. Although it covers her childhood, it is her second book of autobiography. In the first, **959** *Cornish Years* (1949), the author reconstructs the intellectual progress of her life, from Cornish schoolgirl through her higher education in English literature and teaching experiences, to her eventual academic career. After creating this overview of her life, she returned to the memories of her childhood and reconstructed them in more detail in *School House in the Wind*. In *A Stranger in the Midlands* (1952) she describes her school teaching career, 1931–45, including eloquent details of school life and her myriad excursions through the English countryside.

960 TURNER, Joanna (née Cook). 1732–1785. *Memoir of Mrs. Joanna Turner, as Exemplified in Her Life, Death, and Spiritual Experience*. Ed. by Mary Wells. New York: J. C. Totten, 1827. 256 pp.; "Recommendations" by Thomas McAuley et al.; preface by Rev. David Bogue. NUC pre56 655:418. (1st pub. Nisbet, 1820.)

Born at Trowbridge, Wiltshire. Father: John Cook, clothier. Mother: née Shrapnell. Stepmother not named. 2 brothers. Married 1766, Thomas Turner. Religionist (Methodist); preacher. Lower middle class.

Worldly and spiritual influences upon Methodist cottage preacher in her youth, 1730s–c.1750. Experiencing an unhappy childhood, "through my proud passionate disposition." Being disciplined by her mother's brother, who told mother that the child would suffer from lack of discipline. Receiving religious instruction from mother; sensing mother's concern for her soul. Mother's death, author's age 8. Enduring spiritual anxiety; praying seven times a day to improve her conduct. Doing much spiritual reading, but retaining materialistic love of fine clothes. Gradually reducing her prayers to two a day. Aunt's persuading author's father to let her, age 12, accompany a cousin to genteel boarding school "too high for my station." School's bad moral influence; author's ceasing to pray and read the Bible; reading and trying to write romances, novels, and plays. Stealing a shilling from her roommate. Gambling at cards with other girls. Looking back at this time and praising God that she eventually obtained free grace. Returning home shortly after father's remarriage. Stepmother's dislike and severe discipline of author. Father's death, author's age 17; her being greatly affected; attending church more frequently. Living with a devout Methodist family. Reading more Christian works; burning her romances; becoming deeply convinced of personal sin; repenting her past sins. Doing works of charity and mercy; giving away her spare money. Her conversion experience. Writing out and signing a covenant with God. Realizing she has not fully lived up to this covenant, but trusting in God's grace and rejoicing that she gave herself entirely to him.

Only the first seventeen pages of this book are autobiography; the rest consists of letters and journal entries strung together with biographical commentary by the editor, Mary Wells, who compiled this memoir after Turner's death. Turner was a Methodist cottage preacher of the kind described in Barbara Taylor's *Eve and the New Jerusalem*. Her 18th-century conversion narrative, while conventional in its picture of the early sin from which she was saved, suggests a more individual family problem in the background; she never mentions her father when recounting her early life, and the reader may think he is dead until suddenly his name appears in connection with her schooling and his remarriage. In its brevity, Turner's memoir contains as much between the lines as in them.

961 TWEEDIE, Ethel Brilliana (née Harley). 1866–1940. *My Tablecloths, A Few Reminiscences*. New York: George H. Doran Co., 1917. 320 pp.; front.; illus.; index of figures in arts, sciences, and military who have signed her tablecloths. NUC pre56 605:596–97. (1st pub. Hutchinson & Co., 1916.)

Born in London. Father: George Harley, physician. Mother: Emma Muspratt. 1 brother; 1 sister. Married 1887 Maj. Alec Tweedie, investment broker, d.1896. Widow. 2 sons. Wrote *Mexico as I Saw It, George Harley, F.R.S.,* others. Society woman; travel writer; biographer; feminist; charitable volunteer; physician's daughter. Upper class.

Memories of fifty years of London life, reconstructed from the material of author's friendships with the era's significant figures, 1867–1916. Being raised by her parents in Harley Street, London; their home's being cultured and interesting. Marrying, age 21. Establishing tradition of having important guests sign her tablecloths; noting history of this idea. Discussing anecdotes of guests remembered from their signatures: Marconi, inventor of the radio; Lloyd George, the liberal politician. Death of her husband; resolving to stay solvent by writing professionally; attending dinner of Women Journalists. Entertaining diverse people: a Rabbinical scholar, a judge, and the Maharajah and Maharani of Baroda. Joining committee of notable writers in organizing charity bazaar for University College Hospital. Publishing *Thirteen Years of a Busy Woman's Life*. Anecdotes of hosting King George and Queen Mary, YMCA founder Lord Kinnaird, and illustrator John Tenniel. Artists Sir James Linton and Linley Sambourne's making artistic contributions to her tablecloth. Recalling the personalities and stagecraft of Henry Irving, Ellen Terry, and Sarah Bernhardt. Becoming friends with playwright Sir William Gilbert. Holding luncheons in the Tower of London. Attending a dinner of the Royal Geographical Society soon after it began admitting women. Meeting notable women through social events: novelist Mary Elizabeth Braddon, essayist and poet Alice Meynell. Enjoying the friendship of Royal Academicians Sir Lawrence Alma-Tadema and John Singer Sargent, playwright Arthur Pinero, and Dr. Joseph Lister. Memories of Clara Montalba, one of the first women members of the Watercolour Society; author's own passion for watercolor painting. WWI: Author's training women for diverse jobs. Becoming friends with Sir Hiram Maxim, inventor of the machine gun. Concluding narrative at a significant moment in her destiny: sailing to Ireland on the *Lusitania,* 1916, disembarking, and the ship's continuing across the Atlantic to its destruction by the Germans.

Tweedie seems to enjoy the fact that her signed tablecloth, which is the stimulus behind this character study of an era, brings together the signatures of an extraordinary diversity of distinguished friends. A brilliant hostess, she comes through in her memoir as the Pearl Mesta of her day, whose table served as a convivial magnet for the great. Her own people-oriented character is also on display, as is the sense that she would be great fun at a dinner party with her wit and storytelling talent. Tweedie was the author of eight travel books, assorted biographies, novels, and specialized histories of wars and women's contributions. In the earlier **962** *Behind the Footlights* (1904) she imaginatively tours thirty years of London stage life, sketching stage personalities and explaining techniques from acting to costume design. In **963** *Thirteen Years of a Busy Woman's Life* (1912), she discusses how her husband's death, which left her with two young children and plenty of debt, changed the course of her life, and determined her writing professionally. In **964** *Me and Mine: A Medley of Thoughts and Memories* (1932) and **965** *Tight Corners of My Adventurous Life* (1933), she intersperses memories of her active social life with memories of her equally energetic travel, although many of her comments on non-Western peoples are limited by the class and ethnic prejudices characteristic of her time. Tweedie also served on many charitable and philanthropic committees, and in 1909 she assisted in the collection of 25,000 garments for sufferers in the Sicilian earthquake. Her additional public involvements included service on the councils of the Women's Institute and the Divorce Law Reform League.

TWEEDSMUIR, Baroness. [*See* BUCHAN, Susan Charlotte.]

966 TWINING, Louisa. 1820–1912. *Recollections of Life and Work: Being the Autobiography of Louisa Twining*. Edward Arnold, 1893. 291 pp.; front port.; preface; illus. NUC pre56 605:691.

Born in London. Father: Richard Twining, prominent London merchant. Mother: A. Smythies. 4 sisters; 3 brothers. Single. Wrote *Workhouses and Women's Work* (1858), *Recollections of Workhouse Visiting and Management during 25 Years* (1880), *The Emancipation of Women* (pamphlet), *Workhouses and Pauperism and Women's Work in the Administration of the Poor Law* (1898), others. Social reformer; philanthropist; pamphleteer; journalist; political activist; feminist; Poor Law Guardian; organizer (philanthropic); temperance activist. Upper class.

Social reformer's privileged upbringing and manifold adult efforts to improve conditions for women and the working class, 1820–93. Her mother's providing her first lessons; later having special tutors for each subject. Loving to read. Studying drawing with famous painter Samuel Palmer; winning praise for her talents. Contemplating becoming an artist; attending lectures at the Royal Institution. Describing her mother's industriousness, her father's taste for classical literature and patriotism. Contributing to family periodical, *The Budget*. Attending Queen Victoria's coronation, 1837. Recalling charity schools of her youth; her mother's superintending the Maternity Charity. Family's frequently attending the theatre; memories of celebrated actors of the 1840s. Traveling to Paris to study at the Bibliothèque Imperiale in Paris; painting in the Louvre. Doing research in the British Museum for *The Types of Figures of the Bible*. Publishing her first book, *Symbols and Emblems of Early and Medieval Christian Art,* 1852. Discovering the sufferings of the poor by visiting an old nurse in a workhouse, 1853. Inventing a plan for a system of ladies' workhouse visiting. Visiting charitable institutions in Paris; publishing an account of them in the *Guardian;* starting her lifelong work to improve their conditions. Writing "A Few Words about the Inmates of our Union Workhouses," describing inmates and living conditions in workhouses. Emphasizing that poverty affects women more drastically than men because of social inequities. Founding the

Workhouse Visiting Society. Contributing a series of letters on Poor Law reform to *John Bull.* Stories of individual working-class friends and their fluctuating fortunes. Doing charity work in the parish of St. George the Martyr; eventually moving there. Visiting Poor Law Board at Whitehall. Briefly contemplating a nursing career; studying nursing in the Children's Hospital. Attending Social Science Congress in Glasgow. Meeting feminist Frances Power Cobbe, touring institutions with her. Opening first home for workhouse girls. Coping with cholera victims in the East End. Assisting in night school for boys. Beginning temperance work for parish of St. George the Martyr. Touring Russia; later writing book on Russian workhouse conditions. Helping found the Workhouse Infirmary Nursing Association. Being the second woman in English history to be elected a Poor Law Guardian; serving on the Kensington Board of Guardians. Living in Worthington; investigating social problems there. Seeing Cottage Homes as a means of rescue for poor children. Favoring emigration to alleviate overcrowding in England. Publishing "The Losses and Gains of Fifty Years" in the *Monthly Packet.* Discussing 19th-century progress in both technology and philanthropy. Itemizing popular social reform literature of 1840s–1850s. Endorsing the parliamentary bill separating infirmaries from workhouses as the beginning of positive change. Stressing the need to utilize and train women as the key figures in charity work. Commenting on Florence Nightingale, her career and role in the Crimean War. Suggesting remedies for education problems. Discussing women's higher education movement, 1880s. Observing that county councils need the fresh viewpoints that women members would provide.

As a girl of wealthy background, Twining had no need to work for a living. Artistically gifted, she had been given all the elite training necessary to further her hoped-for career as an artist, when her social conscience intervened. Indignant over the wretched circumstances of women in workhouses, she believed that their lives could be substantially improved if women, not men, became active in workhouse administration. Her wealth and connections helped her considerably in furthering this viewpoint and in gaining a public platform for her recommendations. By making herself into an acknowledged expert in the Poor Law, she was drawn into the women's movement by way of an intellectual group of women relentless in their work for women's higher education; critic Anna Jameson, a member of this enclave, was an influential figure in Twining's life. Twining's memoir is overly modest, and does not fully convey the vital nature of her work. The *Europa Biographical Dictionary of British Women* is more open, remarking that "no woman of her generation did more to raise the standard of Poor Law administration or to reduce the widespread prejudice against women in local government."

967 TYACKE, Mrs. Richard Humphrey. c.1865–?. *How I Shot My Bears; or, Two Years' Tent Life in Kullu and Lahoul.* Sampson Low,

Marston & Co., 1893. 318 pp.; illus.; map; index. NUC pre56 608:88.

Probably born in England. Parents not named. Married Richard Humphrey Tyacke, former military serviceman. Hunter; explorer; traveler (India). Upper middle class.

Two years of author's hunting life with husband in the Himalayas, with details on great quantities of animals killed, 1890–92. Having taken previous hunting trips with husband in Kashmir and Albania. Beginning of present excursion in Kullu, central Himalayas, November 1890. Describing Kullu's geography, game, forests, crops. Discussing native superstitions; finding native people and villages filthy and their marriage customs immoral; noting oppression of the Kullu women. Venting indignation over natives' destruction of small game; her suggestions for better game management. Attacks by panthers on the Tyackes' dogs, killing three of the four; panther attacks on natives and livestock; methods of hunting and trapping the wildcats. Finding the native game beaters they hired to be disorganized and undisciplined, "a degenerate race of Hindoos." Camping on the Himalayan snow line, April 1891. Going bearhunting with husband; deciding to dispense with their native guides; traveling over narrow and dangerous roads; finding shepherds and sheep "a great bother," as they kept the bears away. Surviving avalanches. Killing fourteen bears and three musk deer in two months; curing the skins themselves. Spending the summer without hunting in Nugger; visiting the castle there. Ascending Rotang Pass; arriving in Lahoul, Sept. 1891. Shooting game birds. Seeing the Kullu natives as cowardly because they were afraid of the proposed military draft. Describing forest, gorges, bridges; noting dearth of European doctors and dentists in Kullu. Wintering on the estate of a British colonel at Bajaora. Describing funeral customs of local rajahs. Returning to Kullu hunting grounds, April 1892. After resorting to native methods of divination to discover which native servant killed their cow, disbelieving the answer and firing a different servant. Finding scarcity of bears to shoot due to hot weather. Discussing habits of native postal officials; thievery among their native porters. Exploring remote valleys; firing their thieving cook. Enduring a plague of locusts. Outbreak of a cholera epidemic. Returning to Lahoul, May 1892. Being surprised by the strength and endurance of young native women coolies, who shouldered harder work than the men. Author's urging the British Raj to build sleeping shelters for European travelers' native porters. Visiting a Moravian mission near Kailing. Describing Lahouli villages; natives' beliefs and polyandry; efforts by a local missionary to convert them to Christianity. Hearing news of a smallpox epidemic in Kullu; seeing native superstition as a contributing factor in poor sanitation, epidemics. Their difficulties shooting snow leopards. Discussing native superstitions against killing certain animals. Describing Tibetan traders. Attending an annual lama dance at Kailing. Acquiring a pet snow leopard cub; its becoming ferocious as it matured. Marching to Bara-Lacha Pass, August 1892; visiting a castle. Commenting on agricultural mismanagement by natives and their "ingratitude." Continuing travels until arrival at Lahoul; departing for England.

In her travelogue, Tyacke shows herself to be the type of male-acculturated woman whom 19th-century feminists feared might develop if women adopted the ideology of the male patriarchy. It is notable that she expresses her husband's views constantly, and they seem always to coincide with her own. Their shared view of the animals they shoot is both sentimentally unrealistic and predatory, and is remarkably parallel to their view of the "thieving natives," who are perceived to be good only when they fulfill their function of serving the white traveler. Tyacke's discussion of how the natives have killed all the small game is telling. She is irate not over the wanton slaughter, but because the natives have been greedy; they were supposed to have left the animals for her husband and herself to shoot. In her 1987 critical study, *The Animal Estate: The English and Other Creatures in the Victorian Age,* Harriet Ritvo examines the similarities between the twin 19th-century enthusiasms for hunting and colonial domination. Tyacke's account, written by a proponent of both, has its greatest usefulness in clearly illustrating how these two schools of thought arose from the same mindset.

968 TYNAN, Katharine (Mrs. H. A. Hinkson). 1861–1931. *Twenty-Five Years: Reminiscences*. New York: The Devin-Adair Company, 1913. 405 pp.; front. port.; illus.; index. NUC pre56 246:663.

Born in Dublin, Ireland. Father: Andrew Tynan, army cattle supplier. Mother: Elizabeth O'Reilly. 10 siblings. Married 1893, Henry Albert Hinkson, barrister, English. 2 sons; 3 daughters. Wrote *Louise de la Vallière, and Other Poems* (1885), other books of poetry; more than 100 novels, including *Her Ladyship, Mary Gray, Men and Maids*. Poet; novelist; journalist; Irish nationalist; foreign resident (Germany). Middle class.

Poet/novelist's literary development and evolution of her Irish nationalism, 1866–91. Family history. Her great love for her father; his fearlessness and humor. Her placid mother's scarcely influencing author's life; their arguments about what books author could read; author's reading widely anyway. Vaguely remembering the Fenian uprising, 1867, and the resulting harshness of British rule; Catholic Church's feeling social repercussions from the puritanical ideology of the Protestant British population. Attending day school in London; attending convent school, 1872; praising the nuns but refusing their request that she sign a pledge forswearing reading novels. Explaining the Irish notion of "spirit of place." Holding strong Catholic convictions. Writing her first poem, c.1878; her father's encouraging her writing. Publishing poems in the *Graphic and The Spectator*. The rise of Charles Stuart Parnell in the 1870s; his political championing of Home Rule and the resulting nationalist unrest. Joining the Ladies' Land League, 1881; memories of Anna Parnell (Charles's sister), her political views and work with the League. Becoming friends with Fr. Matthew Russell, who published her poems in the *Irish Monthly*. Meeting writers through publishing circles: Sarah Atkinson, poet Rosa Mulholland, the Irish nationalist poet Esperanza Wilde (mother of Oscar). Memories of Oscar Wilde. Publishing her first book, *Louise de la Vallière,* 1885, to favorable reviews. Meeting Yeats; extracts of letters from him; his role in the new Irish poetry. Visiting London; getting to know artists and writers living in Chelsea, such as William and Christina Rossetti; meeting novelist Bulwer Lytton, who expressed interest in her poetry. Also befriending Frances Wynne, the Canadian poet. Theosophy's being introduced in Dublin. Attending a spiritualist séance but not believing in it. Making the acquaintance of "A. E." (George Russell, who in 1930 edited her collected poems). Writing for the New York–based *Catholic World* magazine. Spending summer at Oxford; attending social and literary events. Meeting Cardinal Manning, instigator of the Oxford Movement in which many Anglicans converted to Catholicism. Discussing middle-class conventions in Dublin and the Irish political situation, c.1890s. Joining the National League; its continuing loyalty to Charles Stuart Parnell despite his sexual scandal; struggling to conciliate her own staunch Catholicism with being Parnell's follower; losing many Catholic friends by supporting him in his divorce case. Parnell's dying suddenly in 1891; attending his state funeral.

Although a minor author, Tynan was undeniably prolific, especially in her novel writing. She produced some work addressing social concerns, such as articles for *The Irish Statemen* on working conditions for shop girls. Nevertheless, poetry was her forté and won favor for her during the Irish Renaissance of the late 19th and early 20th centuries. In this autobiography Tynan develops a portrait of herself as religiously and patriotically Irish. After her 1893 marriage, however, she and her husband lived in England until 1911, and Tynan's name consequently figures in several other memoirs from this period by English artists and writers. She continues her life story in **969** *The Middle Years* (1916). In **970** *The Years of the Shadow* (1919), Tynan's account of her later life and writings is set against the backdrop of the Irish political ferment over terrorism and the deferral of Home Rule, 1912–18, while in **971** *The Wandering Years* (1922) she focuses on the continuing Irish social and political struggles in the aftermath of WWI, emphasizing her loyalty to her native land and to the Roman Catholic Church. Concluding her autobiographical accounts with **972** *Life in the Occupied Area* (1925), she gives a firsthand account of the aftermath of WWI in Germany, emphasizing the social and economic disorder she observed during her 1918–23 stay in that country.

973 TYRRELL, Minnie (née Baxter). c.1880–?. *My Husband Still: A Working Woman's Story*. Ed. by Helen Hamilton. G. Bell & Sons, 1914. 303 pp.; note by ed.; foreword by John Galsworthy. BLC to 1975 138:385. [cat. under Hamilton.]

Raised in Chilford. Parents not named. At least 1 brother, 1 sister. Married c.1895, Jim Tyrrell, cart driver. 2 sons. Abused wife; domestic servant. Working class.

Grim exposition on wife abuse issues, implicitly emphasizing the general need for divorce law reform, covering c.1894–c.1905. Working as a domestic servant in London, age 14. Distrusting church and clergymen. Courtship with Jim. Mother's disapproving of author's job and fiancé. Finding employment as a waitress in a hotel, age 15. Eloping with Jim to Rochester. Having fears and doubts about this marriage. Jim's relatives regarding her with hostility and suspicions. Working as a bookkeeper when Jim couldn't find work; his unreasonable jealousy of other men. Their returning to Chilford. Births of their sons. Jim's infidelity; his drinking and physically abusing author upon her confronting him. Suffering confused feelings of resentment, anger, fear, and pride toward her husband. Jim's managing his father's carting business; its threatened financial failure. Author's beating Jim and his mistress after catching them together; in retaliation, Jim's beating author and driving her and their children from home. Supporting herself and their children through needlework. Husband's return; her implying that he raped her. His imprisonment for beating his brother; her feeling pity for him; his broken promises to do better.x Becoming inured to his infidelity. Persevering in supporting her family through needlework; resisting employer's advice that she sue her husband for child support. Resenting both church's treatment of poor and attitudes of the wealthy toward the working class; being softhearted herself toward beggars and tramps. Becoming a cook-housekeeper for a ladies' school. Taking Jim back on advice of clergyman; Jim's selling all her furniture for money. Falling in love with another man; Jim's jealousy; author's discovering divorce to be unobtainable. Jim's imprisonment for housebreaking; his release and continued abuse of author. Telling her lover of her willingness to emigrate to Canada and commit bigamy with him; lover's unwillingness to commit bigamy; his despair over impossibility of her divorce; his committing suicide.

Although the text is based on interviews or material supplied by Tyrrell, Hamilton seems to have played a large role in creating this memoir; much literary skill is employed in telling the story through dialogue. Tyrell's conflicts with her husband are foreshadowed with literary sophistication, although she is depicted in clichéd situations, such as when she discovers her husband with his mistress. Galsworthy's foreword indicates that this book was published as a plea for more easily obtainable divorces, yet Tyrrell barely mentions her desire for divorce. It seems that Hamilton and Galsworthy were using Tyrrell's experience as propaganda for their cause.

974 TYTLER, Harriet (née Earle). 1828–1907. *An Englishwoman in India: The Memoirs of Harriet Tytler 1828–1858*. Ed. by Anthony Sattin. Oxford University Press, 1986. 229 pp.; illus.; intro. by Philip Mason; ed.'s note & afterword; app.; notes; glossary; index. Whitaker's Books in Print 1989 4:7931.

Born in Oudh province, India. Father: John Lucas Earle, army captain. Mother not named. 3 brothers; 2 sisters. Married 1848, Robert Tytler, army captain, d.1870. 10 children; 2 stepchildren. Memsahib; military spouse; foreign resident (India); artist (painter); teacher (art). Middle class.

Memories of colonial India from a woman born and married into British Army families, highlighting her presence at the 1857 siege of Delhi, covering 1828–58. Military family's moving frequently within India during author's childhood. Father's parsimony, due to meager Army pay; author's longing for a doll. Giving examples of the cruelty of the caste system and Hindu religious beliefs. Remembering prices' being lower and servants more faithful in the 1830s, as compared to the 1850s. Describing cities where father was stationed. Being raised on stories about native thieves and thuggery. Accompanying her siblings to England, 1840, to attend school there; living temporarily in London with their family lawyer; moving to Birmingham to live with an aunt who was cruel to the children. Departing for India, age 17; learning en route of her father's death; discovering her mother was returning to England with the younger children only, since author would lose her father's death pension if she left India. Undertaking a 900-mile journey alone, age 18, with native bearers, to reside with an uncle in northwest India. Courtships; receiving and rejecting marriage proposals; describing British marriage customs in India. Discussing the inequity in the military between those who could afford to stay home and purchase their commissions, and those in India who were the queen's officers and unable to guarantee pensions for their wives; falling in love with an Irishman in the latter situation. Attending a native king's breakfast in Lucknow; witnessing staged fights between bullocks, tigers, bears, elephants, donkeys, and hyenas; declaring the terrified natives to be the most entertaining part of the spectacle. The British governor-general's threatening to annex the king of Oudh's domain because of his poor rulership. Author's marrying Captain Tytler, a widower and young father, out of pity, age 19; failing in her struggle to teach her stepchildren. Lawlessness of the king of Oudh's soldiers; his harem of 300 wives. Birth of her first son. Birth and death of her second son; grieving; blaming his death on the regimental doctor's callous treatment. Describing a Hindu feast involving child sacrifice; praising the missionaries who rescue these children. To distract her from her sorrow, her husband's bringing her paints and canvas; author's taking up painting. High-caste sepoys in her husband's regiment refusing order to ship out to Burma; British officers' angrily ordering them to walk to Dacca instead. Author's becoming ill at Dacca; family's enduring rough voyage to England three weeks after birth of her third son. Visiting relatives in the British Isles; birth of her daughter in London. Returning to politically turbulent India. Moving from Cawnpore to Oudh, now annexed to British rule. Warning signs of mutiny in her husband's regiment. Being separated from husband in early hours of mutiny, May 11, 1857; evacuating with other military families to the Flag Staff Tower. Describing secondhand experience of the Mutiny in Delhi. Reuniting with husband; anecdotes of rebels' atrocities against British women and children; their fleeing with other families; living with refugees in British encampment above Delhi. Birth of author's son during siege; having great difficulty caring for baby and sick children because of heat, insects, poor sanitation, lack of food and clean water. Rebels' attacking their encampment. Miraculous escape of one British woman, who played dead while her children were murdered around her. Successful British counterattack on Delhi. Declaring that the British soldiers should have been allowed to loot the city freely, in retribution for sepoy atrocities. Capture of the king and his family. Author's painting the royal palace before its destruction by the British.

Writing in the last years of Queen Victoria's reign, Tytler intended this dramatization of life in India for publication. She became famous for having borne a child during the Siege of Delhi, which was the opening attack of the 1857 Sepoy Rebellion. Protected from seeing most of the fighting, Tytler nonetheless brings this crisis, and much else, to life. In her lack of awareness concerning the political resentments behind the mutiny, Tytler is highly representative of the ideas and attitudes held by middle-class Englishwomen of her time about the natives and about the legitimacy of British colonial rule. She retrospectively dramatizes every incident of native unwillingness, such as the sepoys' refusal to set sail for Burma, as if they were foreshadowings of the mutiny to come. In the afterword, the editor notes that Tytler and her husband stayed in India until 1860. In 1862 he was posted as superintendent of the penal colony in the Andaman Islands. In 1866 the author raised funds in England to found the Himalayan Christian Orphanage in Simla; her husband died in 1870, and she remained in India for the rest of her life, painting and giving art lessons.

975 UTTLEY, Alison (née Alice Jane Taylor). 1884–1976. *Country Things*. Faber & Faber, 1946. 148 pp.; illus. by C. F. Tunnicliffe. NUC pre56 627:32.

Born near Cromford, Derbyshire. Father: Henry Taylor, farmer. Mother: Hannah Dickens, former lady's maid. 1 brother mentioned. Married 1911 James Uttley, d.1930. 1 son. Wrote *The Country Child* (1931), *The Farm on the Hill* (1941), *Carts and Candlesticks* (1973), others. Children's author; novelist; suffragist; teacher; farm child; social historian. Rural farming class.

Depiction of the author's late-Victorian childhood in rural England, c.1884–1900. Family and neighbors' holding regular ritual of telling folktales; tales' becoming traditional within the group through repetition; their being based on older people's memories, historical legends, social events, and crimes. Children's learning rural history through listening to stories. Remembering her childhood Christmas celebrations via scrapbook of old Christmas cards; connecting each one to a past event. Playing and studying in the farmhouse's attic; its holding special associations for her with the growth of her imagination and intellect. In later life, buying a 17th-century vicarage because of its similar attic; this being the same house Elizabeth Gaskell described in her novel *Cranford,* with an attic full of secrets. Sealing friendships by lending books; remarking "we were a reading family." Mother's reading to children; author's learning to read early. At age 12, traveling by train to school in nearby market town; school's providing books new to her. Remembering children's inventing games with tops, marbles, and hoops. Posing with her hoop for a Royal Academy artist. Depicting her village school; schoolmaster's importance to village life. Discusing education given by country schools, late 1890s, including gardening, field geology, sewing, and play acting. Associating houses of her childhood with miniature houses seen as an adult. Recalling folk remedies for children's ailments that she later found cited in old English literature. Author's nursemaid's being a "born healer": a reputed wise woman. Recounting rural beliefs about lucky omens, animals' behavior, weather changes, and plant signs. Old roads' signifying events in local history later embellished by personal memory.

Evoking historical rural culture and traditions now being dissipated by the workings of modernization in the 20th century, Uttley writes from a childhood perspective, enriched by her adult infusion of closer detail and interpretation. This book is the centerpiece of a triptych of these memoirs: **976** *Country Hoard* (1943) widens Uttley's focus beyond her family and self, describing farmcraft, the rural economy, and the changes looming with the onset of WWI. **977** *Ambush of Young Days* (1974) focuses narrowly on Uttley's childhood: her family poverty, her faith in the Bible, her closeness to her father, and local hero worship of professional cricket players. The author eventually took a degree in physics in 1906 from Manchester University, worked as a teacher, went on suffrage marches, and was a friend of future Prime Minister Ramsay MacDonald. Uttley's husband committed suicide in 1930, and her only son did likewise in 1978—events she excluded from her autobiographies, which address only her youth.

978 VANBRUGH, Dame Irene (stage name; née Barnes; C. B. E.). 1872–1949. *To Tell My Story*. Hutchinson & Co., 1948. 218 pp.; illus.; index. BLC to 1975 336:351.

Born in Heavitree, near Exeter, Devonshire. Father: Reginald Barnes, vicar. Mother: Fanny Nation. 3 sisters; 2 brothers. Married 1901 Dion Boucicault, actor, producer, d.1929. Widow. Wrote *Hints on the Art of Acting* (1951). Actress (stage); suffragist; philanthropist; clergyman's daughter; theatrical writer; broadcaster. Middle class.

Author's professional stage career, from birth to 1948. Remembering the disciplined household, rural environment, and rigid formal schooling of her childhood. Her father's influencing her strongly; his admiring contemporary theatre and being friends with actors Edmund and Charles Kean. Author and her elder sister Violet's pursuing acting careers, adopting stage names, auditioning for plays in London, appearing in plays together. Lewis Carroll's arranging author's first professional London engagement. Touring Australia with the Toole Acting Company, 1891. In London, being given her first opportunity to create an original part in J. M. Barrie's *Ibsen's Ghost*. Becoming a success; being constantly employed. Working professionally with actor Herbert Beerbohm Tree and writer/producer George Alexander; playing the role of Cecily in Oscar Wilde's *The Importance of Being Earnest*. Playing her first leading role in *Trelawny of the Wells,* produced by her future husband Dion Boucicault and Arthur Chudleigh. Courtship and marriage. Arthur Pinero's writing role for her in *The Gay Lord Quex;* the play's success; its American tour, 1902. Attending the coronation of Edward VII, 1901; describing the Edwardian social scene; conveying gossip about the theatrical world. Discussing the importance of the National Theatre and its production of plays specifically for children. Joining the Actresses' Franchise League, 1913, although she disapproved of militant suffrage methods. Evaluating impact of WWI on theatres. Expounding her acting theories; admiring Sarah Bernhardt's stagecraft. Discussing difficulties women encounter in the acting profession. Making stage tour of South Africa and Australia. Suffering loneliness after her husband's death; thinking about retiring from the stage; being encouraged to do so by her doctor. Making her comeback at a charity performance for King George V's jubilee, 1938. Receiving title of Dame of the British Empire, 1941. After WWII, broadcasting on the BBC. Giving a speech at Shakespeare's birthday celebration in Stratford-upon-Avon, 1947. Appreciating Sir Barry Jackson's adulation of her as an actress.

Vanbrugh's narrative describes her public life in minute detail, concentrating on her sixty years in the theatre and the independence required of a woman to succeed in this field. In **979**, an autobiographical essay published in Margot Asquith's *Myself When Young* anthology (1938), she looks back romantically at her early career, her happy childhood, and some of the stage luminaries with whom she worked. She is remembered today not only as an actress, but as a crucial figure, along with colleagues such as Dame Sybil Thorndike and Gerald Du Maurier, in persuading the London City Councillors officially to recognize acting as one of the fine arts, putting the theatre on the same level as painting, music, and sculpture. She also raised funds for the Elizabeth Garrett Anderson Hospital and the Children's Aid Society.

980 VANBRUGH, Violet (stage name; née Barnes). 1867–1942. *Dare to Be Wise*. Hodder & Stoughton, 1925. 160 pp.; front. port. BLC to 1975 336:356.

Raised in Exeter, Devonshire. Father: Reginald Barnes, vicar. Mother: Fanny Nation. 3 sisters; 2 brothers. Married c.1892, Arthur Bourchier, theatre manager, divorced 1917. Knew Gen. Charles Gordon, Madge Kendal, Ada Rehan, Ellen Terry, Henry Irving, Sarah Thorne. Actress (stage); clergyman's daughter. Middle class.

Author's stage career and impressions of leading theatre people, c.1877–c.1907. Father's telling children frankly that all would have to earn their own livings in adulthood. Mother's coaching author for private theatricals. Father's objecting to her desire for an acting career but consenting reluctantly. His giving author her £50 inheritance with warning that he could provide no other money. Seeking theatrical work in 1880s London; running out of money; being invited to stay with Ellen Terry for several months; Terry's giving author her first chance at a walk-on part in a burlesque. Author's persuading manager Sarah Thorne to hire her for Thorne's regional company, 1886; playing Shakespearean roles. Substituting for the leading lady of the Kendal company on its 1889 American tour; praising Madge Kendal as a stage manager and mentor. Father's death. Returning to London, 1891; playing role of Anne Boleyn in Henry Irving's production of *Henry VIII*; describing Irving. Comparing the acting styles of Terry, Kendal, Ada Rehan, Sarah Bernhardt, Eleanora Duse, and Rejane. Her husband's becoming manager of the Garrick Theatre. Commenting on how actors perform despite illness. Playing Catherine of Aragon in Herbert Tree's revival of Henry VIII; impressions of Tree, manager George Alexander, and actor Sir Charles Wyndham. Offering advice to young women seeking acting careers regarding personal habits, manners, marriage, the importance of religious faith, and sexual self-control.

Stating that she wrote her life story to illustrate how she chose her profession and prospered in it, Vanbrugh devotes nearly half of the book to advising young women in search of a career. While her own writing style expresses the values of tact and pleasant manners, her many anecdotes sketch some of the leading theatre people of late Victorian times. Vanbrugh plays up the "breaks" she was given and downplays her own fortitude and determination.

981 VANE-TEMPEST-STEWART, Edith Helen, Marchioness of Londonderry (née Chaplin). 1879–1959. *Retrospect*. Frederick Muller, 1938. 259 pp.; front.; illus.; index. NUC pre56 340:19.

Possibly born in Scotland. Father: Rt. Hon. Henry Chaplin, later Viscount, M.P., first minister for agriculture in Lord Salisbury's Cabinet. Mother: Lady Florence Sutherland Leveson Gower. 1 brother; 1 sister. Married 1899 Charles Stewart Henry Vane-Tempest-Stewart, Viscount Castlereigh, later 7th Marquess of Londonderry, M.P. 3 daughters; 1 son. Knew King Edward VII and Queen Alexandra, King George V, Lloyd George, Ramsay MacDonald, Queen Mary, Queen Victoria. Society woman; WWI administrator; suffragist; feminist; politician's spouse; traveler (India, Japan). Aristocracy.

Personal and political experiences in Scotland, England, Ireland, India, Japan, and Spain, covering author's childhood to 1931. After mother's death, author's age 3, being raised by maternal grandparents in Scotland and London. Narrating incidents in which she dared to ride horses astride instead of sidesaddle, defying convention. Learning to ride a bicycle, age 14; seeing the advent of the bicycle as a factor in women's emancipation. Marrying eldest son of a marquess, 1899. Recounting husband's travels in Australia and the Near East, and his presence at the Olympic Games, 1900. Their traveling in India, 1903–04. Remarking on the beauty of the Maharani (queen) of Jodhpur; assessing English education to be unsuitable for the restricted lives of high-caste women. Discussing attitudes toward women in the Edwardian era. Riding and foxhunting with her husband. Visiting Japan during the Russo-Japanese War; asserting that adoption of Western clothing and customs makes Japanese appear ridiculous; finding Japanese women beautiful, Japanese men ugly. Growing increasingly interested in women's suffrage and tariff reform; discussing contemporary prejudices about women's social roles and newer notions of female equality. Husband's winning election as Conservative M.P., 1905. Discussing the anarchist attack on Spanish royalty during her visit to Spain, 1906. Working for the suffrage campaign, despite her family's opposition. Working during WWI as colonel-in-chief of the Women's Volunteer Reserve. Noting WWI's effects on leadership in women's organizations and on women's employment. Husband's serving as under-secretary for the Air Corps, 1920–21; their living in Ireland at that time; husband's being appointed minister of education for Ulster, 1921. Outbreak of civil war in Ulster, 1921. Condemning Home Rule, Sinn Fein, and IRA terrorism; asserting that the Black and Tans' police regime was necessary to restore order. Sympathizing with the Protestant Unionists who wanted to keep British rule. Giving details of her social life, 1915–31. Lamenting the postwar decline in social graces resulting from the adoption of American manners and dress; regretting the upper-class loss of the sense of noblesse oblige, which placed social duty above self-interest.

Illustrating her account with anecdotes, the marchioness describes pre-WWI society and the changes wrought by the war in upper-class people's lives. The tenor of her commentary indicates her desire for a revival of the prewar way of life, including the *status quo ante* of the British Empire. Although radical in her thinking concerning women's emancipation, she evaluates people of other cultures from a conventional, Anglocentric perspective; she describes Japanese men as "frightfully ugly, more like apes than human beings," and calls Chinese she encountered "none too trustworthy." In the same year this memoir was published, Lady Londonderry contributed an autobiographical essay, **982**, to Margot Asquith's *Myself When Young* anthology. She devotes it to memories of her childhood, depicting the eccentric living arrangements that her newly-widowed father imposed on his children, farming them out to relatives and visiting them only to take them riding and hunting.

983 VIDAL, Lois. 1889–?. *Magpie: The Autobiography of a Nymph Errant.* Faber & Faber, 1934. 493 pp. NUC pre56 656:306.

Born in England. Father: R. W. Vidal, vicar. Mother: "C. E. V." 4 brothers; 3 sisters. Married 1933 "Jolly Jack the Sailor." Clerk; domestic servant; journalist; mental patient; transient; clergyman's daughter; WWI volunteer; charitable volunteer; hotel worker; governess. Middle class.

Author's inheritance of the family manic-depressive illness and its powerful impact on her life, covering her childhood to 1933. Growing up in a seemingly healthy, athletic family and an Eden-like country vicarage; until age 9 being ignorant of "the family skeleton." Deaths of youngest brother and 19-year-old sister, 1898, draining father's nerves and finances, sparking his manic cycles. His becoming unfit to manage a parish. Siblings making jam, weaving hammocks to raise money for college. Family's moving to Oxford after committing father to Bedlam, 1901. Siblings Peter and Bridget's also developing mania, being hospitalized; author's taking over Bridget's work as day-governess, age 16. Feeling deficient in French; teaching English at a Paris lycée in exchange for French lessons; boarding in Paris with mother and sister Dorothy. After returning to England, becoming manic herself, age 18: feeling powerful and creative; staying awake for days at a time; feeling privileged to share "the journey to the other side" already taken by her father, brother, and sister. Gardening school therapy making her mania worse; eventually signing herself into Bedlam to join her sorely missed father. Finding hospital mental treatment well-meaning but ineffectual. Returning to Oxford; becoming engaged to a young pianist; concealing her mental illness from him. Believing love had cured her; lapsing into depression when he married another. At new family home outside Oxford, entering new manic cycle; writing exaltedly day and night; believing fame to be imminent. Father's dying suddenly in Bedlam, 1911. Bridget's emigrating to Canada, hoping to train as a missionary; her committing suicide, 1912. Outbreak of WWI: Author, mother, and sister Dorothy's doing volunteer work, but needing paid jobs; mother and Dorothy's finding work in London; author's being hired as clerk by British Intelligence. Transferring to the Paris office; moving there with mother and Dorothy. Suddenly believing the job overstrained her nerves; quitting to work for the YMCA; Dorothy's working there also. Quitting abruptly again; stating Dorothy persuaded her that her work was useless. Finding job in London war office; being offered a permanent secretarial career there; refusing offer because Dorothy, now working in Women's Land Army, insisted that author take job as her assistant. Their jobs vanishing with the Armistice, 1918. Working many brief secretarial jobs in France and England, 1919–21. Abruptly collapsing with depression; being shipped home. Begging to be committed to Bedlam; family's refusing, seeing her illness as mere self-dramatization. Running away, committing bizarre acts; eventually recuperating in Bedlam, 1921–23. Deciding to be a journalist; applying for many positions; being hired by the Sheffield *Daily Telegraph* as assistant. Writing daily column for four weeks, then coming down with a "neurosis" that crippled her writing hand. Being fired; family's declaring she was a failure; author's going on a reactionary manic jag to France; spending her savings; having sex with strangers. Finding herself penniless in London. Suddenly believing she must leave England; persuading London family with castle on Corsica to hire her as a parlormaid. Experiencing mania again; taking over cooking at the castle; talking nonstop; staying up writing all night; being sacked after four weeks. Going from job to job; collapsing when new depression intervened; sailing back to England. Finding clerical work and library work at Oxford, 1927–28. Her cycles worsening; escaping to France. Traveling to Canada to seek work; scandalizing her fellow passengers by her promiscuity aboard ship; failing to find work and returning to England. Tramping in English countryside; living in cheap London lodgings; living on the hospitality of friends and strangers in Winchester, Southampton, and Bournemouth. Working briefly as domestic help in various seaside hotels; struggling to save money. Living in a suburban London Salvation Army Hostel and in an Anglican convent. Mother's death. Working again as a cook and parlormaid. Feeling her spirits revive; commencing to write again; selling a few articles. Renting a cottage at Tintagel to write in; suddenly meeting and marrying a sailor.

Vidal's retrospective on the ups and downs of her life shows how profoundly her illness governed her life. In describing one incident of being fired, she confesses, "I am utterly and incorrigibly unemployable . . . this inner thing that is me leaps up and hits [my employers] in the eye, and they begin to fabricate reasons for ceasing to employ me." Because the control of manic depression through lithium salts was unknown until the 1940s, the sanitariums which treated her could offer little real aid. Although Vidal's descriptions of treatments are fragmentary, she does relate the use of talk therapy at Bedlam, as well as more experimental treatments using relaxation, physical training, and guided positive thinking, none of which worked for long. Although manic depression was identified in the 19th century, Vidal remarks (writing in 1928) that she abhors the current popularity of Freudian terminology for it; she wields instead a highly individual vocabulary of euphemism to describe her condition. This book shows signs of being written over a period of years, during which the cycling of her illness markedly affected the clarity and tenor of her writing.

984 VIGERS, Edith M. 1893–?. *Notebook Cavalcade*. Hodder & Stoughton, Ltd., 1942. 208 pp. NUC pre56 637:174.

Born in England. Father not named, sea captain. Mother not named. Single. Journalist; fashion designer; WWI volunteer; nurse (WWI); traveler (world). Upper middle class.

The world travel experiences and international celebrity acquaintances of a journalist specializing in shipboard interviews, as well as her WWI volunteer activities, covering the first four decades of the 20th century. Accompanying her mother to meet her father's ship in English and Dutch ports. Learning to sail proficiently; sailing up the Norwegian coast. As a child, being unsociable; liking to paint and draw better than to write. Growing increasingly interested in travel. Working as a fashion artist; making friends with fashion designer Bessie Ascough. Outbreak of WWI: drawing anti-German caricatures and reproducing them on postcards; donating proceeds to Belgian Relief Fund; volunteering as a VAD nurse. Being hired as a reporter to cover Southampton ship arrivals; describing various illustrious contemporary ships: the *Aquitania,* the *Majestic,* the *Mauritania*. Recounting anecdotes of interviewing Mary Pickford, Douglas Fairbanks, Sr., Charlie Chaplin, John Galsworthy, Anna Pavlova, Noel Coward, many others. Relating gossip about celebrities' amorous affairs. Meeting Elsa Schiaparelli, founder of the famous Paris fashion house; attending Paris fashion shows. Attending elite social events: royal performances at Covent Garden, the Ascot racing season, presentations at the Royal Court. Taking part in the jubilee of King George and Queen Mary, 1935. Describing traveling in Italy; scenes of life in Venice. Recounting her experiences in Saudi Arabia; Arab customs and dress. Trekking through Spain, Morocco, Turkey; being distressed at these countries' dirtiness. Remembering her first experiences of New York City: social events, American generosity and hospitality, the excellence of Southern cuisine. Remembering meeting Franklin and Eleanor Roosevelt, their characters and daily routine.

In this sprightly memoir Vigers dramatizes the blossoming of her early love of sea travel into a career as a reporter interviewing maritime travelers. Initially awed by the celebrities she interviewed, Vigers eventually saw them as individuals, separate from their glamorous auras of fame and affluence. Nonetheless, the lively esteem she retained for British royalty and aristocracy fuels her focus, making her book a lively and worthwhile representation of the upper class social scene in the years before WWII.

985 WAKE, Charlotte Murdoch, Lady (née Tait). 1800–1888. *The Reminiscences of Charlotte, Lady Wake*. William Blackwood & Sons, 1909. Ed. by Lucy Wake. 326 pp.; front. port.; preface; illus. NUC pre56 645:159.

Born in Edinburgh, Scotland. Father: Craufurd Tait of Harviestoun, landowner, Scottish. Mother: Susan Campbell. 7 brothers (including Archibald, Archbishop of Canterbury); 2 sisters. Married 1822, Charles Wake (after 1847 Sir Charles Wake), d.1864. Widow. 7 daughters; 6 sons. Domestic manager for Archbishop of Canterbury; foreign resident (France). Upper class.

Family biography emphasizing its members' interconnections with 19th-century historical events, and highlighting author's ties with her brother Archie, who rose to become Archbishop of Canterbury, covering 1800–87. Tait family history. Father's inheriting family estate, 1800; family's summering there, wintering in Edinburgh. Being schooled by governess, but hearing Scottish history firsthand from grandparents. Witnessing George III's 50-year Jubilee celebrations, 1810. Her mother's performing charitable works in the midst of family tragedies: one baby's paralysis; another, Archibald's, club feet. Recounting rural Scottish belief in witches; removal of author's birthmark through folk medicine. After mother's sudden death, 1814, father's sending children to live with paternal grandfather. Grandfather's having permanent houseguests, including Charles Wake, who later married author, and author's sister. Sister's marriage, 1818. Author's accompanying couple on Highland honeymoon; residing with them in London. Worrying about sister's childbirth prospects; remembering Princess Charlotte's death in childbirth, 1817. Stating that unorthodox medical treatments cured Archie's club feet. After author's first London season, returning to father's Edinburgh home. Extracts from family letters concerning sister's childbirth, death of paralyzed brother, and George IV's coronation, 1821. Author's marriage, 1822. Brother Thomas's Army career in India;

Archie's Oxford matriculation. Author and ailing husband's moving to sea climate of Dieppe, France. Father's death, 1832. Archie's rise at Oxford: his classics degree, fellowship, tutorship, and Anglican ordination, 1836. Author's family and Archie's touring Continent, 1839–40; his burning a Geneva Library copy of Matthew Lewis's *The Monk* as indecent; his being acquainted with Cardinal Newman and condemning the Oxford Movement, 1841. Archie's succeeding Thomas Arnold as Rugby's headmaster, 1842; author's sons attending Rugby. Illness forcing Archie's retirement from Rugby and appointment as Dean of Carlisle, 1841. Deaths of five of author's daughters in 1855 scarlet fever epidemic. Recounting Archie's appointment as Bishop of London, 1856. Extracts from letters concerning heroism of author's son Herwald, magistrate in India during 1857 Mutiny. Griefs' plaguing family: deaths of husband and one son, 1863–64; author's helping another son recover from shattered health, 1865–72; third son's being court-martialed for destroying his ship during the Haitian Rebellion. Archie's becoming Archbishop of Canterbury, 1868; his falling ill a year later, receiving Queen Victoria's permission to recuperate in France with his wife; author's joining them. Author's discussing his domestic life and his wife's death; author's assuming official domestic duties for him at Lambeth Palace. His final illness and death, 1882; author's being personally consoled by Queen Victoria, who corresponded with author for three years.

Lady Wake's account demonstrates the seemingly matter-of-fact acceptance of death in the 19th century, with even the most prosperous of families being vulnerable to decimation by disease, before the advent of modern medicine. Ironically, her later life vocation as domestic manager for her brother, the archbishop, came about only because the deaths of his wife and her entire family made such an arrangement necessary for both. Having this connection, Lady Wake's account is both a first-hand record of political and religious events affecting 19th-century England and a character study of her brother Archibald Tait, of whom the *Dictionary of National Biography* records that "no archbishop since the Reformation had so much weight in Parliament or in the country generally."

986 W[ALKER], B[eatrice] M[ary] and H[enrietta] and J[osephine]. Beatrice's life dates: 1854–d.a.1930. *Recollections: Sixty Years Ago and Onwards*. Leeds: Richard Jackson, 1930. 96 pp.; preface; list of subscribers. BLC to 1975 343:478.

Born at Adel, near Leeds, Yorkshire (Beatrice). Father: James Walker, cloth manufacturer, iron mine owner, railway board member. Mother: née Cole. 4 brothers; 2 sisters. Occupations for Beatrice: governess; tutor; paid companion; foreign resident (Canada, Holland). Middle class.

Memories of three sisters' family life, jointly written but told from Beatrice's viewpoint, covering 1854–1914 and alluding to later events. Birth of sister at Beatrice's age 4. Father's moving family to nearby Levisham in order to mine for iron. Mother's teaching Sunday school and giving needlework lessons. Beatrice and brother's attending coeducational school in Leeds for six months and staying with her grandfather, deacon of a Baptist chapel; remembering his Sunday services. Hearing parents' discussing current events: Lincoln's assassination, Leeds bank failures, Lancashire cotton famine due to American Civil War. Recounting father's service on the planning committee for the 1851 Great Exhibition. Village life in the 1860s: old residents with historical tales, regional dialect, Methodist chapel, and revival meetings. Family's attending Anglican services at Lockton. Death of Prince Albert, marriage of Prince of Wales, 1863. Sisters' attending boarding school, 1863. Father's shutting down iron mine to avoid repair costs, 1866. Mother's death, 1867; author and siblings' accompanying father to live in Nova Scotia for one year, c.1868. Returning to England; sisters' attending day school. Discussing Salvation Army work in Leeds and London; revival visits by American evangelists. Noting flurry over Phoenix Park murders, 1882, and consequent arrest of Charles Stuart Parnell. During 1880s visit to Scotland and London, observing social changes: expressing amazement at seeing women riding bicycles and traveling on upper levels of tramcars. Describing later advent of automobiles and airships. Contrasting moorland village of 1860s with suburban Leeds of 1870s–1880s. Attending lectures of the Leed's Philosophical and Literary Society. Alluding to the women's movement; noting the new trend for women to seek careers. Beatrice's being hired as junior governess in a school, but feeling poorly qualified; commenting on contemporary ridicule of colleges for women. Beatrice, as Liberal-Unionist, opposing the push for Irish Home Rule. Her traveling to Alsace to live with a friend; attending state school there and teaching English. Traveling to Holland, 1902; finding work there as child's companion, and later as English and French tutor. Describing Dutch history, life, and customs. Traveling to France, 1907. Noting the transformations wrought in England by WWI, but visiting Levisham and finding village life unchanged.

Perhaps because of its shared authorship, this text contains many digressions which interrupt its chronological progression. Written for the authors' great-nieces as a record of mid-Victorian life, the account dwells briefly on many contemporary issues, such as the evolving women's movement and the British struggle over Ireland's fight for independence, without discussing most of them in detail. Although the book does not illuminate the characters of Beatrice Walker and her sisters, it does illustrate their desire to sentimentalize the past and idealize village life while also revealing discomfort in their awareness of the limitations on female aspirations imposed by rural thinking.

987 WALKER, Laura Maple (née Dewsnap). 1896–s.l.1971. *Heart to Heart: Being the True Life Story of a Retired Nurse and Midwife*. Sherwood, Nottingham: Duprint Service, 1971. 96 pp.; foreword; prologue; illus. BLC to 1975 344:22.

Born near Chesterfield, in Derbyshire. Father: Frederick James Dewsnap, watchmaker, jeweler. Mother not named, shop assistant, sweetshop owner. 3 brothers; 4 sisters. Married, husband not named. Widow. Nurse; midwife; charitable volunteer; nursemaid. Lower middle class.

Cheerful reminiscences by a nurse about family affections and personal advancement, emphasizing her Christian spirituality, from childhood to 1971. Describing her family's devoutness and Christian education of its children; her father's character and methods of discipline. Deaths of father and brother, author's age 13; author's having to leave school. Mother's opening sweetshop to support the family; author's finding work as nursemaid, age 14. Recounting her Anglican confirmation. Holding successive nursemaid positions with gentry families; wanting higher wages. Helping deliver employer's baby; discussing her awakening desire to be a nurse; mother's opposing her ambitions. Continuing to work as nursemaid until mother's death. After working for a wealthy family in Leeds, resolving to train as a nurse; winning her first nursing job with County Council and Nursing Association, c.1940. Being employed as District Nurse for thirteen years. Alluding to life with her husband. Retiring from nursing after becoming bedridden; becoming active in the Anglican Church and the Women's Institute. Taking holidays with husband; their moving to Nottingham; husband's illness and death. Noting the sorrows of widowhood; rendering a tribute to her husband. Moving to Skegness; becoming active in its Old Age Pensioners' Centre. Writing loving tributes to her elderly friends. Stressing how firm adherence to Christian beliefs and values had supported her throughout life.

Walker intersperses her narrative with original essays and poems, scriptural citations, and poetry by others. Avoiding direct reference either to her married life or to her husband's extended illness, she highlights those parts of her life which seem, in her own mind, to have been signs that Providence was guiding her. Although the life she describes was a modest one, her record is useful in illuminating vocational aspects of nursing in the mid-20th century and its availability to ambitious young women of modest means.

988 WALLAS, Ada (née Radford). 1859–1934. *Daguerreotypes*. New York: Macmillan, 1930. 118 pp.; foreword. NUC pre56 646:448.

Raised in Devonshire. Father: George David Radford, draper. Mother: Agnes Kentispeare. 2 brothers; 3 sisters. Married 1897, Graham Wallas, writer, political psychologist, Fabian socialist, d.1932. 1 daughter. Wrote *Before the Bluestockings* (1929). Political writer; academic's spouse; feminist. Middle class.

Ironic retrospective on the family and religious and educational attitudes influencing author's antifeminist ideas in her youth, covering her childhood to adolescence. Attending Bible class given by her father to her brothers. Extensively discussing her maternal grandfather: his condemning works of fiction; her mixed pity and admiration for grandfather's strict Protestant principles. Father's fearing the French Catholic Emperor Bonaparte and all other Catholic influences; his believing Garibaldi was the man raised up by God to defy "the anti-Christ," i.e. the Pope. Attending dame school at age 7; receiving equal education with boys. Commenting on the family ideal of women as not "strong-minded" but silent; remembering family's opposition to women's rights advocates such as Lydia Becker; these women's also being ridiculed in her schoolroom. Author's mother's softening her stance after meeting one of these women. Being taught by antifeminist governess, author's age 9, who feared education would rob girls of feminine modesty; author's resenting governess's desire to turn them all into "Little Miss Hannah Mores" who devoted their lives to moralizing. Being afraid that her parents would send her to a girls' boarding school. Parents' deciding, author's age 12, to send her to new high school for girls. Taking pleasure in education but resisting confining methods in teaching. Coping with conflict between her own talent and family ideology of female limitations by adopting a provisional belief that only exceptional women are entitled to display their attainments.

Wallas's narrative indicates the extent to which her early opinions were influenced by family and environment, even as she caricatures many of those influences, such as her father's Napoleon-phobia. Clearly, some of the images she recalls offer conflicting messages, such as her own evident enjoyment of unrestricted education coupled with her mother's enthusiasm for restricting women's rights. The narrative functions as a snapshot of her mental confusion at that time, remaining resolutely within a child's perspective and never resolving inconsistencies. However, it is suggestive that, at the time of writing this memoir, Wallas had worked professionally for over forty years with her husband, political psychologist Graham Wallas, who specialized in analyzing the origins of political beliefs. In his book *The Great Society* (1914), he emphasizes the role of irrational forces in determining both opinions and attitudes.

989 WALSH, Jane. 1905–?. *Not Like This*. Lawrence & Wishart, 1953. 144 pp.; illus. by Paul Hogarth. NUC pre56 647:81.

Raised in Oldham, Lancashire. Father not named, iron-dresser. Mother not named. 2 brothers; 3 sisters. Married c.1924, Charlie Walsh, factory worker, d.1945. Widow. 3 daughters. Journalist; mill worker. Working class.

Clear-eyed narrative of the poverty-induced hardships in one working-class family's life, with the author's insights on class differences, from her childhood to 1953. Parents' poverty and drinking. Describing effects of their violent fights on the children. Family's being frequently evicted, malnourished; 1909–12 being the worst years. Author's facing temptations to steal. Finally getting a house of their own, though "the poorest of the poor." Attending Catholic school; being whipped every Monday for missing Sunday Mass; her absences actually resulting from having nothing to wear, because mother made the children wash their only set of clothes on Sundays. Author's preferring whipping to confessing the truth. When seeing the country for the first time on a class picnic, being filled with ecstasy and also with fury that experiencing nature's beauty was denied to poor, urban children. Working in a cotton mill, age 13; feeling uneducated, except for her reading. Playing hopscotch with other young mill workers; losing job when the cotton boom ended, but making a lifelong friend in fellow worker Nora Smith. Nora's father's belonging to Salvation Army; his introducing author to Salvation Army outings; author's being grateful that Salvation Army accepted her despite ragged clothes and poverty. Marrying "Charlie," author's age 19; seeing marriage as chance for financial independence. Nora's father's offering the couple his house to live in. Being sexually ignorant; not knowing how to distinguish working-class prudery about lust from the passion of two people in love. Their scraping by on 25 shillings weekly; buying a house on credit. Losing their savings when author came down with appendicitis; being unable to draw sick pay; recuperating in Catholic Friendly Holiday Home where sick benefit patients were barely "tolerated." Giving up their house; rooming with Nora's family to save money. Persuading Charlie to let her have a child, age 27; having difficult birth. Husband's losing job during daughter's infancy; their going hungry. Returning to work herself; concealing earnings from means test inspectors who would dock husband's dole. Giving birth to second daughter, 1937. Husband's getting high-paying steel-mill job in Coventry; their moving to Coventry only a few months before WWII. Describing German bombing of Coventry. Unsuccessfully attempting to abort her unplanned third child; changing her mind; welcoming third daughter's birth. Beginning to write for newspaper; hiding job so neighbors would not think her "queer." Corresponding with the paper's women's features writer, Carey Smith. Mourning her husband's sudden death, 1944; being supported by Nora and Carey until his pension came through. Carey's finding house for her in London. Polio's afflicting author's youngest daughter; family's having to leave home and take family assistance. By 1952, family's rallying again: youngest daughter's getting surgery to repair polio damage; oldest daughter's studying at training college. Author's declaring her pride in her girls.

Walsh gives an unsentimental account of her economic struggle. While valuable for its documentation of Lancashire working-class conditions, replete with monetary details, her account also reveals a consistent, protective social mechanism among working-class women: their formation of an active female alliance to mitigate the repeated blows of job loss, illness, and poverty. Walsh tacitly shows that the ties between women friends were often more effective in keeping marriages and families afloat than were the ties between wife and husband. Accordingly, her account merits closer attention.

990 WARBURTON, Katherine Anne Egerton. 1840–d.a.1912. *Old Soho Days and Other Memories*. A. R. Mowbray, 1906. 216 pp.; preface by Stewart D. Headlam. NUC pre56 648:90.

Born in Cheshire. Father not named, Anglican village parson. Mother not named. 1 brother. Single. Religionist (Anglican); nun (Anglican sister); teacher; clergyman's daughter; charitable volunteer; organizer (philanthropic). Upper middle class.

Experiences of an Anglican sister among working classes in East End London, 1858–1906. Teaching and working with the poor at Soho's House of Charity; depicting neighborhood's degradation and poverty. Describing her young colleagues and their compassionate idealism. Explaining routine of parish visiting. Thieving as a way of life for slum boys. Soho's suffering from lack of sanitation and no hospitals or playgrounds. Author's telling stories to the children. Helping found the Guild of St. Michael and All Angels for girls and young women, 1863. Distinguishing between facilities for the working poor and for the homeless. Opening facility for "ragged boys," 1864; asserting that such boys need rough discipline. Local slaughterhouse's being converted to homeless refuge. Author's expanding facilities by opening women's shelter. Taking temporary charge of women's ward in Newport Market Mission, 1865–66. Being transferred to St. Saviour's Priory amidst the appalling poverty of Haggerston. Sisters' establishing country hostels as retreats for London working class, 1880s. Describing deaths of young children; death and funeral of a boardinghouse resident, 1905. Memories of funerals of sisters she knew at St. Margaret's in East Grinstead. Her dogs' being the emotional support she relied on; anecdotes of their relationship. Beginning tradition of teas for working men at St. Saviour's. Recording eulogies for fellow sisters and for a lifelong (unnamed) friend and colleague.

Having commenced her religious career among the poor at age 18, Warburton spent a half-century working to improve their lives. An unpracticed writer, she often sounds excessive in her descriptions, but her emotional expression reveals her refusal to become hardened to the conditions she viewed daily. The Anglican vicar Stuart Headlam, who contributed Warburton's preface, was a friend of George Bernard Shaw and a Fabian socialist who was also intensely committed to ameliorating the plight of the poor. In 1912, Warburton anonymously published **991** *Memories of a Sister of St. Saviour's Priory*, which gives an account of her childhood in Cheshire, her father's participation in the Oxford Movement, her convent education and her sympathies with radical socialism.

992 WARD, Annie Wadsworth. 1819–?. *My Mother; or, Home Scenes in Yorkshire*. E. Marlborough, 1866. BLC to 1975 345:19.

Born in West Riding, Yorkshire. Parents not named. 2 brothers; 2 sisters. Nurse; mental health worker; nursemaid; farm child. Middle class.

The rural upbringing, affectionate family bond, and later working experiences of a nurse in a mental asylum, from 1827 to the 1850s. Remembering party for her eighth birthday, 1827, as typifying Yorkshire celebrations. Mother's being father's "right hand" and a local "Lady Bountiful," more worldly than the villagers because town-bred. Father's doing farm work; being roughly dressed but "a priceless gem" underneath. Author's describing what "home" symbolizes to her. Another baby's being born, author's age 8; mother's keeping school, taking in sewing from neighbors to make ends meet. Author's taking care of baby brother; learning to do dairy tasks; taking butter to market. Helping in her mother's school by teaching proper diction; being happy in loving, honoring, and serving God and her parents. Studying at night; reading *Pilgrim's Progress* and the like, novels being forbidden. Describing their house and village, c.1833. Longing to see London, age 14; feeling guilty over wish; villagers' thinking all Londoners must be sinful. Backtracking to 1820 memories of schism among local Wesleyans, with the Methodist "New Connexion" leaving the old congregation. Giving history of Wesleyan Sunday school she attended until age 14. Visiting London via steamship from Hull, c.1840; being hired as nursemaid by a London society woman who had been treated for mental illness; author's becoming interested in mental illness. Being helped by employer's physician to become nurse probationer in public asylum for two years. Discussing new mental treatments and new understanding that patients need no restraints: "No longer any fear that the poor maniac will be ill-treated." Pitying her patients; describing individual cases. After a four-year absence, happily visiting her parents in Yorkshire; believing that their lessons of love and responsibility had fortified her life. Returning to work in London as a nurse for the mentally ill.

The reunion between Ward and her parents at the conclusion of her book would be their last, although she had no presentiment that this was the case. Although her work environment differed radically from the surroundings of her upbringing, the faculty for warm relationships forged in her childhood home helped her in professional life. Ward's picture of rural Yorkshire life in the early 19th century is evocative; her commentary on changing modalities of psychological treatment at the beginning of Victoria's reign has potential interest for medical historians.

993 WARD, Mrs. E. M. (née Henrietta Mary Ada Ward). 1832–1924. *Memories of Ninety Years*. Ed. by Isabel G. McAllister. New York: Henry Holt & Co., 1925. 332 pp.; front.; illus.; index. NUC pre56 648:220. (1st pub. Hutchinson, 1924.)

Born in London. Father: George Raphael Ward, member of the Royal Academy. Mother: Mary Webb, artist. Married 1848, Edward Matthew Ward, artist, member of the Royal Academy, d.1879. Widow. 3 sons; 5 daughters. Artist (painter); teacher (art); artist's daughter. Upper middle class.

Childhood, friendships, and working experiences of a portrait painter from a family of notable artists, among a circle of England's most eminent figures, from c.1830s–1920s. Enjoying a lenient upbringing; escaping the trauma of a formal "coming out"; meeting artist friends of her parents; parents' involving themselves deeply in her education. First meeting artist Edward Matthew Ward; his helping her gain skill with painting. Having a painting accepted for exhibit by the Royal Academy, age 14. Secretly marrying Ward, author's age 16, with help of family friend Wilkie Collins. Author and husband's sharing happy life as professional painters; avoiding feelings of professional rivalry; author's enjoying her own studio. Meeting painter J. E. Millais; recalling his scandalous marriage to John Ruskin's former wife. Being close to Lewis Carroll; his sending manuscript of one novel to her for commentary. Establishing friendships with artists Sir Frederic Leighton, Edward Poynter, and Sir Thomas Lawrence. Husband's painting portraits of Queen Victoria and Prince Albert, 1951; author's painting two of their sons. Commenting on Victoria's coronation, Jubilees, and reign. Dining with Charles Dickens and his illustrator George Cruikshank; visiting Paris with Dickens and his wife. Discussing current actors and 1860s enthusiasm for spiritualism. Anecdotes of W. M. Thackeray, the Terry family, Bulwer Lytton, Robert Browning and others. Commenting on the Victorian attitude toward married women painters. Discussing suffrage activities and U.S. lecture tours of Anna Jameson. Noting the profound impact made by *Uncle Tom's Cabin* on Queen Victoria and the rest of Britain's upper echelon. Moving to Windsor for husband's health; deaths of her husband and father in close succession. Author's teaching art to royal family members. Lamenting vanished English customs: May Day, Guy Fawkes Day, elegant Victorian dinner parties. Discussing her ties to the Royal Academy. Remarking on art revolution of 1870s and

Oscar Wilde's aesthetics. Extracts from letters spanning 1858–1910. Noting changes between past and present in science, education, and politics. Conditions for working-class children having worsened in modern era; regretting working-class apathy toward WWI. Remembering her son Leslie; his death in 1922.

Ward juxtaposes memories with the social and cultural history of the Victorian period. Her era-spanning memoir constitutes an impressive resource on the 19th-century artistic, literary, and political milieux. Her earlier work, **994** *Mrs. E. M. Ward's Reminiscences* (1911), also uses the Victorian and Edwardian artistic and aristocratic spheres as backdrop for an account of her personal experiences and professional artistic life.

995 WARD, Mrs. Humphry (née Mary Augusta Arnold). 1851–1920. *A Writer's Recollections*. Harper & Bros., 1918. 2 vols. Vol. 1: 242 pp.; illus. Vol. 2: 259 pp.; illus.; epilogue. NUC 1946 159:411.

Born in Hobart, Tasmania, Australia. Father: Dr. Thomas Arnold, educator. Grandfather: Dr. Thomas Arnold, headmaster of Rugby. Mother: Julia Sorrell. 1 sister; 1 brother. Married 1872, Thomas Humphry Ward, Fellow and Tutor of Brasenose College, Oxford, art critic. 1 son; 2 daughters. Wrote *The Coryston Family, The Marriage of William Ashe, Life of W. T. Arnold,* others. Biographer; novelist; academic's daughter; academic's spouse; antisuffragist; organizer (philanthropic). Upper middle class.

Novelist and antisuffragist's moral retrospective on her upbringing, relationships with significant Victorian figures, and fifty years of British social transformation, from her childhood to 1917. Family's returning to England from Tasmania. Loving French literature; studying on her own. Noting her father's intimacy with his own father, Thomas Arnold of Rugby. Remembering family friend John Henry Newman as Anglican vicar before his Catholic conversion; her father's own Catholic leanings. Recalling her uncle Matthew Arnold: his associations with Newman, views on Catholicism, and scholarly career. Meeting Wordsworth through her grandfather's friendship with him; describing Wordsworth's home at Rydal Mount. Family's moving to Oxford; author's being sent to girls' boarding school offering limited education. Rejoining family at Oxford; describing its academic makeup, 1860s. Meeting George Eliot and George Henry Lewes there; attending lectures by visiting French historian Hippolyte Taine; meeting the poet Algernon Swinburne. Marriage, 1872; author and husband's remaining in Oxford, writing in cooperative partnership. Anecdotes of critic Walter Pater, classicist Benjamin Jowett. Traveling in France, 1874; seeing Sarah Bernhardt perform; visiting philologist Ernest Renan. Writing her novel, *Robert Elsmere;* explaining its anti-Theist premise. Renan's paying visit to the Wards at Oxford. Contributing articles on Spanish lives to the *Dictionary of Christian Biography;* helping establish Spanish language exams at

Oxford. Husband's becoming staff editor at London *Times;* their moving to London, 1881; anecdotes of politician Arthur Balfour, American writers Henry James and James Russell Lowell, and Robert Browning. Death of author's mother and Matthew Arnold, 1888; publication of *Robert Elsmere*. Helping found University Hall Settlement, 1890, to provide the teaching of history and religious philosophy to the working classes. Publishing several novels; *Helbeck of Bannisdale* being praised by George Meredith, J. M. Barrie, and Henry James. WWI: visiting France to research patriotic history of Britain's war effort. War's changing women's traditional roles. Discussing advances in girls' education, 1850s–1917, but believing gifted women have always been able to find outlets for their talents, despite social restrictions. Noting changing intellectual milieu of London, 1880s–1918. Describing "Life and Liberty" movement's attempt to bring disillusioned apostates back to the Church of England; asserting England's need for religious revival.

Ward's 1918 memoir resurrects the personalities of her famous family, as well as major 19th-century spiritual and educational issues. Her familiarity with the Oxford movement through Matthew Arnold and Cardinal Newman stood her in good stead; although she had published several novels prior to *Robert Elsmere,* Ward first achieved fame with this romanticized treatment of the mid-19th-century crisis of religious doubt. Ironically, considering her family's strong ties to boys' education, Ward's only formal education was within traditional female limits. She compensated by educating herself, seizing the opportunity of living in Oxford to study at the Bodleian Library and attend student lectures. Her promotion of women's education features prominently in her memoir, but she omits her equally firm leadership of the Women's National Anti-Suffrage League, founded in 1908.

996 WARD, Maisie (Mary Josephine). 1889–1975. *Unfinished Business.* Sheed & Ward, 1964. 374 pp.; foreword; index. BLC to 1975 345:71.

Born on the Isle of Wight. Father: Wilfrid Ward, editor of *Dublin Review,* biographer. Mother: Josephine Mary Hope, novelist. 3 brothers; 1 sister. Married 1924, Frank Sheed, publisher. 1 daughter; 1 son. Wrote *Insurrection versus Resurrection,* biographies *Gilbert Keith Chesterton, The Wilfrid Wards and the Transition, Saints Who Made History,* WWI history *This Burning Heat,* others. Publisher; biographer; religious/spiritual writer; historian; social reformer; religionist (Roman Catholic); nurse (WWI); preacher; teacher; textbook writer; public speaker; foreign resident (U.S.). Upper middle class.

Childhood, intellectual growth, and public contributions of a Catholic crusader, within a context of contemporary Catholic theological and social issues, from 1890s to 1964. Family's longtime history on Isle of Wight; author's pride that her grandfather, W. G. Ward, was the first

Oxford movement convert. Parents' writings: mother's novel, father's Catholic biographies. Author and siblings' being schooled by mother and governess. Describing personalities of family and Catholic friends, including intellectual Maud Petre and Rev. Charles Maturin, author of *Sebastian Melmoth*. Family's moving to Surrey, 1901. Mother's sending author and sister to convent day school, but instructing them in Catholicism herself. After confirmation, age 16, author's attending York convent school instead of university, because father opposed higher education. Finding settlement house work unsatisfying; reviewing books for the *Dublin Review*, her father's journal; receiving no vocational guidance from her parents. Visiting her brother Herbert at Oxford; meeting his friend G. K. Chesterton, whose biography she was to write. Family's moving nearer London. Discussing Catholic Church's crisis of Modernism, which questioned miracles, Christ's deity, and the transcendence of God; its making her father defensive in editing the *Dublin Review* and writing about Cardinal Newman, author and family's keeping traditional beliefs. Outbreak of WWI; author's doing VAD nursing in Italy, 1915. Family's moving to London after father's death, 1916. As member of Catholic Evidence Guild, author's defending traditional Catholic doctrine by oratory in London parks; meeting Frank Sheed, another Guild orator from Australia; later working with him in Catholic Truth Society (CTS). Author's becoming Secretary of the CTS, 1922. Marrying Frank after his graduation from law school. Author and husband's founding Sheed & Ward publishers, London; being aided by Catholic writers Hilaire Belloc, G. K. Chesterton, and Father Ronald Knox. Falling seriously ill after giving birth to her daughter, 1925; recovering through prayer alone. Family's moving to rural Surrey; opening public chapel there for Catholics. Birth of her son; leaving him with mother-in-law to make lecture tour of U.S. with her husband, 1930. During depression of 1931, their attempting to apply philanthropic economic theories of Belloc and Chesterton by bringing Glasgow slum boys to work farm; bad economic luck's forcing abandonment of the project, 1933. Mother's death. Emulating her mother by instructing her children in Catholicism herself. Author and husband's becoming interested in communism; joining the Catholic Worker Movement in England and the U.S. Befriending Dorothy Day, American founder of *The Catholic Worker;* with her help establishing U.S. branch of Sheed & Ward in New York, 1936–37. During WWII, their moving to Philadelphia with children; author's making lecture tours of U.S. and Canada, 1940–41. Family's moving to New York; author's writing biography of Chesterton there. Discussing Catholic welfare center in Harlem; explaining how the Catholic Church can break down race and class barriers. Family's returning to England, 1946; author's commencing her biography of Newman. Author and husband's touring the world to speak, 1954. Commenting on church's role in social reform, her old age, and unfinished business before death.

In this not-strictly chronological book Ward digresses from her personal narrative into various topics, thoroughly explores them, and then returns to the story of her family life. The wide scope of her lengthy memoir makes it a primary source on 20th-century Catholic intellectual and social activity in England, the U.S., and Europe before the Second Vatican Council.

997 WARRENDER, Lady Ethel Maud (née Ashley-Cooper). 1870–1945. *My First Sixty Years.* Cassell & Co., 1933. 308 pp.; front. port.; illus.; apps.; index. NUC pre56 649:284.

Born in Dorset. Father: Anthony Ashley-Cooper, 8th Earl of Shaftesbury. Mother: Lady Harriet Augusta Chichester. 1 brother; 3 sisters. Married 1894, Capt. Sir George Warrender, 7th Baronet, later Admiral. 2 sons; 1 daughter. Knew Maude Valèrie White. Society woman; singer (concerts); military spouse; colonialist (India); suffragist; philanthropist; WWI volunteer; foreign resident (India); organizer (youth). Aristocracy.

Childhood religious upbringing, adult social contacts, and charity work of a society woman and amateur singer, from 1870s to 1933. Ashley family history. Receiving strict evangelical religious training. Recalling her father's uprightness and her mother's religiosity; author's own dislike of church attendance. Being schooled by governesses before attending high school. Extracts from writings of previous Earls of Shaftesbury, 1672–1867, on ethics and philosophy. Author's marriage, 1894. Being much praised for her voice; singing at Maud White's concerts. Accompanying husband on military trip to China. Being made an attendant to Queen Victoria. Recounting anecdotes of acquaintance with composers Gilbert and Sullivan, noted British statesmen, and King Edward VII. Cruising the Greek Islands with composer Edward Elgar. Accompanying husband on his tour as commander in chief of East India Station. Noting incidents of native terrorism against Europeans. Their living in Jodhpur; hunting big game with the Maharajah. Singing in concert with soprano Rosa Albani at Bombay Town Hall concert. After returning to England, chairing Winchelsea Village Children's Historical Play Society. Endorsing suffrage for women. WWI: singing at hospital concerts, working for the Red Cross Hospital Library. Becoming district commissioner for Girl Guides at Rye. Writing a new marching song for guides. Giving paper on "Social Life in the Village" to Oxford Church Congress. Visiting the U.S., 1927; noting Prohibition's effect. Memories of writers Henry James and Max Beerbohm. Describing her fundraising efforts for charities and her charity concerts for prisoners. Asserting her belief in the importance of instituting national opera in England.

As part of the social establishment in turn-of-the-century London, Lady Maud hobnobbed with policymakers, entertained notable figures in the art world, and did charity work. In general, her account characterizes the lifestyle of upper-class women in her time. The most notable aspect of her life is her family link to the distinguished line of Shaftesburys, and the most substantive portion of her memoir is its inclusion of Shaftesbury history and extracts from the writings of previous earls, especially her grandfather, the 7th Earl and heralded 19th-century philanthropist and social reformer.

WARWICK, Countess of. [*See* GREVILLE, Frances Evelyn.]

998 WATERFIELD, Lina (née Duff Gordon). 1878–d.a.1948. *Castle in Italy: An Autobiography*. New York: Thomas Y. Crowell, 1961. 277 pp.; index. NUC 1942–1962 146:457.

Born at Saint-Germain, France. Father: Maurice Duff Gordon. Mother: Fanny Waterton. Married 1902, Aubrey Waterfield, artist, d.1944. Widow. 3 sons; 1 daughter. Wrote (with husband) *Rome and Its Story*. Journalist; foreign resident (Italy); historian; artist (graphic); foreign correspondent. Upper class.

Author's Victorian childhood, Continental youth, and journalistic career in two world wars, tied together through the image of her aunt's castle in Italy and the profound social changes it endured, 1880s–1940s. Mother's being descended from the 16th-century jurist Sir Thomas More; marrying a Frenchman; after his death in a riding accident, marrying an Englishman. Author's being born in France; spending her childhood in London and Paris; being schooled by French governess and raised a Catholic. Father's inheriting Fyvie Castle in Scotland; family's moving there. Parents' separating due to father's infidelity; author's moving to London with mother. Attending convent schools in Brighton and Paris until her mother's death, 1889. Deciding, age 16, to live in Florence, Italy, with Uncle Henry and Aunt Janet Ross, the noted journalist, in their castle. Father's remarriage. Recounting Aunt Janet's history; her rivalry with novelist "Ouida." Robert Browning and Poet Laureate Alfred Austin's visiting the castle. Author's discussing her friendship with Italian residents John Addington Symonds and his daughters. Writing a history of Perugia with Madge Symonds, 1896. Aunt Janet's introducing her to historian R. C. Trevellyan and art historian Bernard Berenson. On trip to London, author's great-aunts' taking her to meet the painter G. F. Watts. Meeting her future husband at Oxford; their living in London after marriage, 1902; having son a year later. Author and husband's being commissioned to write history of Rome; their returning to Italy and buying Fortress of Aulla to live in, 1903; describing housekeeping happily in their castle. Befriending D. H. and Frieda Lawrence during the Lawrences' Italian stay, 1907–14. WWI: husband's enlisting, author and children's staying with aunt in Italy. Describing Italy's own war involvement and public antiwar sentiment in Italy. Author's creation of patriotic poster winning her a job in office of *Assistenza e Resistenza*. Helping found the British Institute of

Florence, an Anglo-Italian library. Trying to counter German anti-British propaganda in Italy by promoting Anglo-Italian friendship. Rejoining her husband in England; their returning to live in Italy, 1921. Becoming Italian correspondent to the *Observer;* covering the election of Pope Pius XI; interviewing fascists, including Mussolini, and their political opponents; publishing criticism of fascist repression. Fascists' arresting, then releasing author and husband. After death of Aunt Janet, 1927, inheriting her castle; using it to open an art school for girls. School's being spied upon, having its mail opened by fascists. Being compelled to abandon journalism by crippling hip fracture; devoting herself to the art school. Author and husband's bringing their children to England at outbreak of WWII; returning to Italy to run the new British Institute at Palermo; escaping to England to elude fascist arrest. Describing German bombardment of London, 1942; Italy's surrendering in 1943; husband's death, 1944. Author's returning alone to Italy after the war; revisiting her aunt's castle; concluding her book with evaluations of Italy and the Italian character.

Early in Waterfield's memoir, she discusses her friendship with John Addington Symonds, the noted mid-Victorian historian of classical Italy; by the book's end, she is contemplating Italy's future after its fascist regime. Consequently, although Waterfield's discussion covers half a century, it takes in a much broader conceptual span of European intellectual and political history. Many of the individual anecdotes she tells of British expatriates and political movers will also be of value to historians interested in the intersection of politics and culture.

999 WATT, Rachel. c.1864–s.l. 1922. *In the Heart of Savagedom: Reminiscences of Life and Adventure During a Quarter of a Century of Pioneering Missionary Labours in the Wilds of East Equatorial Africa.* Ed. by Stuart Watt (author's husband). Pickering & Inglis, 1922. 422 pp.; front. ports.; preface; foreword; illus.; map. NUC pre56 651:210. (1st pub. Marshall Brothers, 1912.)

Born in County Down, Ireland. Parents not named. Married 1885, Stuart Watt, missionary, d.1914. 4 sons; 3 daughters. Missionary (Africa); religionist (Evangelical). Lower middle class.

Detailed account of delights, duties, and dangers of bringing Western religion and customs to Africa, covering c.1885–1912. Being converted by future husband at author's age 16; his having been converted by the American evangelist, Dwight L. Moody. Their marriage, author's age 21. Family's journeying by steamship to Zanzibar, 1885; traveling inland by donkey; enduring stinging insects, bad water, and disease; death of her young son. Other children survive. Husband's deterring native chief from wife-swapping. Explaining native African customs: polygamy, child-raising, hunting, intertribal warfare. Husband's preventing a human sacrifice. Natives' preferring nudity to the Western clothing she made for them. Depicting the Arab slave trade; her husband's admonishing the traders. Recounting attacks by hostile tribes, including the slaughter of an entire German caravan. Recommending to her British readers that "disobedient" native porters be punished; compassion's being a sign of weakness to the natives, although she declares flogging to be unnecessary. Author and husband's leaving for England; their taking health-restoring voyage to Australia. Author's fearing for family's safety if they return to Africa, but having dream vision of Christ's protecting them. Family's traveling to Kenya, 1893. Discussing history of African exploration by Europeans and present task of missionaries to turn African speech into written language. British authorities' warning husband not to take wife and children into the jungle; their defying advice; setting off carried in hammocks by native porters. Author's calling the Masai "bloodthirsty marauders" and citing their slaughters. On their journey, meeting a tribe that had never before seen a white man. Arriving at Imperial British East India Company fort. Author's alternately describing the natives as "brutal and depraved" and as "children of God." Husband and petty chief's sealing their friendship with blood brotherhood ceremony. Family's dismissing their porters; building mission station. Author's studying the Akamba language; finding the language philosophic despite its speakers' savagery. Their mission's being threatened by warlike tribes after British government established Kenya protectorate; one tribal attack's being aborted, according to author, by God's sending a meteorite "to confound the attackers." Distinguishing between the physical features of the "niggers" of West Africa and these more "handsome" Eastern tribes. Witnessing arrival of U.S. missionaries and their deaths from disease. Husband's suffering from recurrent fevers. Explaining that natives have a belief in a Supreme Being; missionaries' chief hurdle is preparing natives for Christian conversion. Asserting secular education to be irrelevant to making converts; proclaiming that the Gospel should be put first. Enduring a plague of locusts; husband's seizing occasion to make the natives more receptive to the Bible. Sending her children to boarding school in England; family's returning briefly to England before resuming their African ministry. Deaths of her son and husband in Africa, 1913–14. Discussing the spiritual degeneracy of Islamic belief among African natives. Piously reminding her readers that their Briton and Celt ancestors were once savage also. Urging her readers to look to their own spiritual regeneration.

In this exhortatory account, Watt assumes that her readers share her horror of non-European customs and employs a vocabulary equating African customs with "savagery," in opposition to the "civilization" which the missionaries import. While her family's hardships in the African interior—including the deaths of some of her children—are deeply moving, Watt's personal record of her experiences is disturbing. Watt might try to save the souls of the African natives, but she never ceased to believe that they were profoundly inferior, or that her notions of culture must annihilate theirs. Her record contains items of historical interest—notably, the cheerful continuance of the interior slave trade by Arabs ninety years after its international abolition. Her account is most useful as a study in profoundly characteristic colonialist thinking, incorporating ideas of native degeneracy, the white man's burden, and every other nuance of race-based assumption. The first edition of this book, edited by Stuart Watt, was published in 1912; this later edition conveys information about his death through letters from the author's daughter.

1000 WAZAN, Emily, Shareefa of (née Keene). c.1850–d.a.1910. *My Life Story*. Edward Arnold, 1912. Ed. by S. L. Bensusan. 327 pp.; front. port.; illus.; preface by R. B. Cunningham-Graham; note; apps.; index. NUC pre56 651:539.

Possibly born in Newington, Surrey. Father not named, governor of Surrey County Gaol. Mother not named. 1 sister mentioned. Married 1873, the Shareef of Wazan, d.1892. Widow. 2 sons; 4 daughters; 1 stepdaughter; 3 stepsons. Native chieftain's spouse; foreign resident (Morocco). Middle class; married into foreign culture.

Author's life as wife of the Shareef of Wazan, 1873–c.1910. Being determinedly wooed by the Europeanized Shareef while she lived in Tangier; his having divorced his Muslim wives in order to marry a European woman. Author's loving him; accepting his second proposal. Her father's bitterly opposing the union; consenting only to keep his daughter's love. Her parents' attending the wedding in Tangier; father's begging author afterwards to let him help her escape back to England. Being introduced to countless stepchildren by her husband's divorced wives; culture shock's firing her resolve to learn Arabic; discovering many in household opposed Shareef's Europeanization. Being approached by Europeans in Tangier; their accepting her into emigré society. Palace's holding birth festivities for her first son, 1874. Author's accompanying husband on diplomatic missions to Algeria, 1876; describing an attack on town in which she was barricaded. After their return to Tangier, Shareef's building private residence to house author and her child. Giving birth to twins, one stillborn, 1876. Traveling with husband to France, England, Spain, 1877; visiting her home village in Surrey. At that time, her father's being governor of the Surrey County Gaol; Shareef's vowing to reform his country's prisons along similar lines. Back in Tangier, author's hiring an English governess for her children. Describing stepdaughter's elaborate marriage rites, 1882, and the funeral rites after her death in childbirth, 1885. Marital troubles' beginning with husband's ill health; European advisor's whispering to Shareef that author was trying to assassinate him. Author's fending off an anonymous attempt to poison her, 1887. Her husband's behaving erratically: trying to sell her house; sending her away and then refusing to let her leave; distributing false news of his assassination. After sending her away again, his marrying one of his servants. Her returning to Tangier, 1890, after hearing Shareef's health had worsened; his doctor's suspecting that palace retainers were slowly poisoning him. At Shareef's request, author's taking him to Italy for recovery; nursing him through fever and delirium; staying with him for the children's sake. Returning to Tangier with his health improved; his dying mysteriously, 1892, although author suspected poisoning. Winning legal battle at the Fez court against Wazan officials who tried to steal her inheritance. Revisiting England for three months, 1893; sensing tremendous cultural changes since her departure 20 years earlier. Discussing her social status in Tangier as Shareef's widow. After kidnapping of a *Times* correspondent in Angora, her son's successfully exerting political power to have him released. Commenting on her own influence in having kidnap victims released, her function in entertaining visiting royalty, her hopes for the future with the births of grandchildren.

Nothing seems to faze this author, who coped equally well with culture shock and with her husband's bizarre and threatening behavior. Wazan did her best to stay in favor with both Europeans and Muslims in Morocco; those studying 19th-century women's absorption into different cultures will find much useful material in this book and in Morag Abdullah's *My Khyber Marriage*.

1001 WEBB, Beatrice (née Potter). 1858–1943. *My Apprenticeship*. Longmans, Green, 1926. 390 pp.; intro.; apps.; index. NUC pre56 651:665. (other ed.: Cambridge University Press, 1979.)

Born in Standish, Gloucestershire. Father: Richard Potter, Director of Great Western Railway, Grand Trunk Railway, Canada. Mother: Laurencina Heyworth. 8 sisters; 1 brother. Married 1892, Sidney Webb, civil servant, writer, later Baron Passfield. Wrote *History of Trade Unionism* (1894), *Industrial Democracy* (1898), *History of the English Poor Law,* others. Political writer; journalist; socialist; trade unionist; social reformer; historian; philanthropist; antifeminist; feminist; economist; school founder; public speaker. Upper middle class.

Iconoclastic intellectual growth of a radical Fabian reformer, in the context of her socialist-oriented commentary on late-19th-century poverty and capitalism, from childhood to her 1892 marriage. Family's central figure being her father, who held women to be superior to men. Mother's disliking other women in general and author in particular; mother's believing author to be slow-witted. Mother's disapproving author's rejection of the conventional female education-by-governess, as well as author's enthusiasm for Utilitarian economics. Author's being encouraged by family friend, philosopher Herbert Spencer. Restrospectively describing mother's domestic arrangements as "typical mid-Victorian capitalism" dominated by everyone's overriding desire for power. Attending boarding school only one year; thereafter educating herself by reading what she pleased: Herbert Spencer, Goethe. Her readings in Eastern mysticism annihilating belief in Christianity. Avowing that mother's death, author's age 24, revolutionized her life; discussing secret ambition to win intellectual renown. Rebelling against father's demands that she serve as his secretary, be his domestic manager, and remain single to help him. Joining Charity Organisation Society; becoming an inspector of slums. Wondering if poverty was an element necessary to the wealth of a nation. Commenting on laborers, their living conditions. Discussing politics, trade unionism, and male suffrage issues, 1880s. Remembering activities of social reformer Octavia Hill. Negatively assessing the Christian philosophy of charity, asserting that indiscriminate doles exacerbate poverty. Working as rent collector for public housing project. Outlining the career of her mentor, social reformer Charles Booth, who invented the social survey; his concluding that high birth rates, disease, and drunkenness caused poverty, and that charity was irrelevant. Author's serving on the Board of Statistical Research, studying London's poor; being transformed from "society girl" to "brain worker." Managing working-class dwelling in East End. Wanting both a successful marriage and intellectual independence. Studying political economists Adam Smith, Karl Marx, and Alfred Marshall. Describing Sundays in Victorian Park where "odd-minded" reform enthusiasts met. Publishing articles on dock life; attending meetings of dock laborers. Training as a garment worker; slaving in workshops herself; publishing "The Pages of a Workgirl's Diary" in *Nineteenth Century*. Refuting idea that capitalism is the "natural order of things"; her socialism's deriving from her respect for basic human dignity. Becoming known for supporting the antisuffragist Mrs. Humphry Ward, 1889; later attributing this phase to her reaction against her father's overvaluation of women, as well as to her conservative temperament, and her ability to carve out a career for herself. Working with Co-operative movement; believing in the necessity of trade unions; charting the stages of socialist revolution. Describing her first interest in the Fabian Society and its ideas. Meeting and marrying Sidney Webb, one of the Fabian Society's founders.

Webb's clear-eyed critique is an excellent survey of the conflict between the late-19th-century forces of capitalism and labor. In addition, her account of her personal history underscores motivations shared by many wealthy and privileged people who joined the ranks of the Labour or Socialist parties. In the 1890s, however, with socialism yet untroubled by the spectre of several bloody Russian revolutions, its idealism was still strong. Not a book that drops names, Webb's account has its greatest value in illustrating the process by which socialists formed economic theories, and in depicting their tactical and practical strategies.

1002 WEBB, Beatrice (née Potter). 1858–1943. *Our Partnership*. Ed. by Barbara Drake and Margaret I. Cole. Longmans, Green, 1948. 544 pp.; preface; intro.; illus.; index. NUC pre56 651:665.

Biographical: See *My Apprenticeship*.

Further analyses of contemporary issues and social problems from the author's first two decades of political work with her husband, 1892–1912. Recounting the biography of Sidney Webb, including his 1884 cofounding of the Fabian Society, up to their marriage. Their being secretly engaged before her father's death; marrying seven months afterwards. Together, their publishing *The History of Trade Unionism* and *Industrial Democracy* and investigating Dublin trade societies. Describing their home in Westminster. Rendering her impressions of fellow Fabians Graham Wallas and George Bernard Shaw. Discussing Fabian schemes for reforming government at the county level. Author and husband's inaugurating London School of Economics and Political Science; calling it "our child." Extracts from her diary outlining Fabian tactics, negatively assessing some individual socialists, and describing her service in the National Union of Women Workers. Referring to herself as an atheist, but believing in a spiritual force. Memories of Liberal politician R. B. Haldane, his conversion to the Labour Party and influence on her husband's career. Outlining tenets of the Fabian Society and their manifesto; recounting the outbreak of Boer War and Fabian reactions to its political ramifications in England. Becoming friends with Bertrand Russell, c.1900; his being known at that time for his 1896 book *German Social Democracy*. Diary extracts analyzing the policies of contemporary political leaders, c.1900. Describing passage of the London Education Act of 1903; its consequences; extracts from her husband's handbook *London Education*. Discussing the views of their friend H. G. Wells on education. Observing political situation in Russia during the first Communist Revolution, 1905; noting resulting British reaction against Liberalism, Labour, and Poor Law reform. Serving on Royal Commission on the Poor Law and the Relief of Distress. Recanting her earlier anti-women's suffrage position. Noting mutually destructive trilogy of Christian religion, capitalism, and political democracy. Publishing *A Constitution for the Socialist Commonwealth of Great Britain*.

Webb perceives this work as "practically an autobiography with the love affairs left out," and states that she is chiefly interested in recording her life's work, which was inseparable from that of her husband, Sidney. By drawing on extracts from her journal, Webb is able to juxtapose her contemporary views, untarnished by hindsight, with her retrospective analysis. Of much interest here are the shifts in Fabian thinking as the society's members watched the Russian revolutions. Webb's mature memoir is an excellent source of background material on many social movements that galvanized late-19th- and early-20th-century Britain.

1003 WEBLING, Peggy (Arthur Weston, pseud.). c.1870–?. *Peggy: The Story of One Score Years and Ten*. Hutchinson, 1924. 303 pp.; front. port.; illus.; "To the Reader." NUC pre56 652:423.

Born in London. Father: Robert James Webling, jeweler, silversmith. Mother: Maria Webling. 4 sisters (including actress and poet Lucy Webling). Wrote *Blue Jay* (1905), *The Story of Virginia Perfect, A Spirit of Mirth, Verses to Men* (1920). Knew Lewis Carroll, Ellen Terry, Oscar Wilde. Short storyist; novelist; journalist; actress (child, stage); foreign resident (Canada); playwright. Middle class.

Memories of an unusual upbringing as a Victorian child actor, emphasizing the family ties to John Ruskin, together with her adult rejection of the stage and adoption of a writing career, from the 1870s to 1900. Family history. Describing mother's strategies for disciplining a family made up entirely of girls. Having only one week of formal schooling, but plenty of music lessons. Her career as child performer beginning at age 8; mother's organizing public appearances. Acting with sisters; their receiving public notice as child actors. John Ruskin's corresponding by letter with the young Webling sisters; author's remembering reading Maria Edgeworth's novels with the middle-aged Ruskin. Describing close childhood friendship with Ruskin. Reciting poetry on tour; acting with one sister in "Little Lord Fauntleroy." Her dramatic power's waning at age 14. Recalling her family as eccentric; never receiving sexual or religious instruction from her mother. Sisters' visiting aunt and uncle in Canada; author's beginning to write stories with her sister Lucy. Sisters' struggling to earn money; making performance tour of Ontario, western Canada, and later the U.S. Eventually turning her back on her stage career; starting career as journalist for *Mainly about People* and the *Morning Leader* in Canada. Writing Canadian stories under pseudonym Arthur Weston. Closing her memoirs with the death of John Ruskin in 1900, author's age 30.

Although Webling's memoir achieves distance from her younger self by third-person narration, it is unsettling for what it seems to leave unsaid. Written nearly a quarter-century after the close of the events it documents, Webling's account omits the interior growth of the woman she later became. The major interest of this memoir lies in its treatment of her stage childhood, her mother's opportunistic management of her daughters' public images, and the attractions that this family of little girls evidently held for John Ruskin, then in his late fifties. The stage family also caught the attention of Lewis Carroll, who also became a family friend. The twenty pages that Webling devotes to Ruskin deal exclusively with the girls' esteem for him as a benevolent friend, but will interest Ruskin scholars in connection to his documented late-life infatuation with the child Rose la Touche. Webling also wrote a thirty-page sketch of Ruskin published in pamphlet form after his death. After her journalistic ventures, Webling went on to Hollywood; her most notable work is her writing of the original screenplay for the 1931 film *Frankenstein*.

1004 WEBSTER, Nesta Helen (née Bevan). 1876–1960. *Spacious Days: An Autobiography*. Hutchinson & Co. Ltd., 1949. 169 pp.; front. port.; foreword; illus.; index. BLC to 1975 347:10.

Born in Hertfordshire. Father: Robert Cooper Lee Bevan, Welsh. Mother: Frances Shuttleworth, writer. 3 brothers; 4 sisters; 6 half-siblings. Married 1904, Capt. Arthur Webster. 2 daughters. Wrote *The Chevalier de Boufflers* (1916), *The French Revolution, A Study in Democracy* (1919), *The Surrender of an Empire,* others. Historian; miscellaneous writer; novelist; military spouse; traveler (world). Middle class.

Eclectic early interests of a versatile writer, filled with odd religious influences, popular trends, and world travel, covering author's childhood to the beginning of her serious writing career in 1920. Family history. Being powerfully influenced by her father's sister, Favell (Bevan) Mortimer, author of *Peep of Day* and other didactic children's books. Her mother's publishing *The Life of John Wesley* and *The Three Friends of God* and joining the Plymouth Brethren. Author's depicting her mother's religious fervor, strictness, and lack of maternal warmth. Disliking Sunday stringency; accompanying her father to Church of England services instead. Receiving most of her schooling from nurse and tutors; excelling in languages. Disliking the contemporary surge of religious revivalism, c.1880s. Mother's banning children from pursuits intended to be pleasurable, such as playing with toys and reading novels. Editing a nursery periodical, *Auntie's Monthly Magazine,* age 13; gaining an interest in writing. Family's spending each winter in Cannes, France; after father's death, mother's deciding to live abroad; author's suffering misery during "exile" with her mother. Attending a neglectful English school which left her cold, dirty, and hungry; returning to live with mother in Cannes. Commencing study at Westfield College in Hampstead; struggling because she had not attended high school. Becoming interested in 1890s novelists: Oscar Wilde, Robert Hichens, George du Maurier. Also following 1890s popular interests; witnessing psychic phenomena; believing in telepathy and ghosts; stressing need for serious study of psychic phenomena. Deciding on impulse to accompany two friends on world tour: visiting Egypt, India, Ceylon, Burma, Singapore, China, Japan, Australia, U.S., Canada. Describing ironic contrast of rich beauty and horrible squalor in India; Indian folk beliefs, treatment of women, and religions. Becoming interested in Buddhism; discussing link between reincarnation and Christianity. Traveling in Japan, learning Japanese. Disliking squalor and opportunism in New York City. Upon return to London, renting a flat. Meeting her future husband, an Army captain, on her return trip to India; their marrying,

1904. Due to ill health, his retiring on half-pay; their settling in the English countryside. Births of her daughters. Death of her mother, 1909. Successfully publishing novel *The Sheep Track,* 1914. After WWI, believing women needed employment more than the vote; deciding to write. Researching the origins of the French Revolution in Paris; coming to believe the revolution was caused by a Freemason conspiracy; asserting that her two books to that effect, *The Chevalier de Boufflers* and *The French Revolution,* were "killed by silence" on the part of the publisher.

As Webster's account closes, she was just beginning to explore what would become her principal topic in writing: political conspiracies. The year 1920 marked the publication of both her novel and her serious history addressing the secret origins of the French Revolution, even though neither earned public notice. Undismayed, in her next book, *The French Terror and Russian Bolshevism* (1920), she linked the earlier French conspiracy to the Russian Revolution. She published further conspiracy studies in *World Revolution: The Plot against Civilization* (1921), *Secret Societies and Subversive Movements* (1924), and *The Socialist Network* (1926). She also published treatments of figures and forces within the French Revolution. Recently, Webster's writing has undergone a surge of popularity, with many of her works being newly reprinted in the 1990s.

1005 WEETON, Ellen ("Nelly"; later Stock). 1776–1850. *Miss Weeton: Journal of a Governess, 1807–1811; 1811–1825*. Oxford University Press, 1936, 1939. Ed. by Edward Hall. 2 vols. Vol. 1: 351 pp.; foreword & intro. by ed.; maps; letters; journal entries; index. Vol. 2: 422 pp.; foreword by ed.; illus.; letters; journal entries; epilogue; index. NUC pre56 570:178. [cat. under Stock, Mrs. Nelly.]

Born in Lancaster, Lancashire. Father: Thomas Weeton, slave ship captain. Mother: Mary Rawlinson. 1 brother; sisters. Married 1814, Aaron Stock; separated c.1822. 1 daughter. Teacher; governess; paid companion; traveler landlady. Lower middle class.

A highly introspective analysis of personal experiences and misfortunes with observations on Regency society including women's roles and conditions, covering author's childhood to late middle age. Admiring her widowed mother's child-raising methods, despite mother's attempts to prevent author's pursuit of sciences and mathematics, regarding them "inappropriate" for girls. Loving to read, but disdaining books without intellectual appeal. Writing a well-received play, performed at her school, age 11; mother's henceforth forbidding her to write and making author's brother spy on her to ensure obedience. Suffering trauma after mother's death at author's age 21. Becoming sole support of brother and self. Taking over mother's school; taking in boarders to make ends meet. Eventually leaving childhood home, becoming a boarder herself by working as a governess and later as companion. Marriage, age 38; giving birth to a daughter, Mary, the next year, 1815. Problems with a "treacherous" husband. Obtaining a formal decree of separation, c.1822, but contemporary marriage laws' mandating that she forfeit custody of her daughter. Being granted only rare visits with her child. Avoiding depression and illness by walking ten to fifteen miles per day. Proclaiming herself a freethinker, even after attending both church and chapel on the same day. Deriving her main income from a property purchased at age 32. Traveling when her finances permitted; defying the prevalent attitude that women should not travel alone. Commenting on poor treatment of women: lack of respect, physical abuse, discrimination by law. Expressing the feelings of superfluousness, loneliness, fear, and financial hardships endured by single women.

Although Weeton's journals and letters end when she was 49, her 20th-century editor draws from government, church, and court records to describe what is known of her life beyond her own narrative. The prolixity of her letters, as well as her obsessive transcription of each one by hand in order to retain a copy, suggest that into those letters Weeton had poured her frustrated desire to write. "I could have risen to something higher," she confided to one correspondent, "but such pains were taken by my mother to repress my too great ardour for literature, that any talents I then possessed as a child have been nearly extinguished." Collectively, her writings document many instances in which the public prejudice faced by self-supporting women in the Regency period adversely affected her life.

1006 WEIR, Molly. 1920–s.l. 1989. *A Toe on the Ladder*. Hutchinson, 1973. 417 pp. BLC 1976–82 48:506. (Chivers edition, 1979.)

Born in Glasgow, Scotland. Father: Thomas Weir, train engineer. Mother: Jeannie Clark, machine operator, railway charwoman. 2 brothers; 1 sister. Married Alexander Hamilton, shipbroker, R.A.F. in WWII, office worker. Actress (comic, radio); broadcaster; chorus girl; miscellaneous writer; secretary. Working class.

Beginnings of author's acting career, and her advancement in stage and radio productions, c.1936–1946. Having talent in childhood for singing and acting. Studying shorthand in college; doing office work and giving shorthand demonstrations; also taking free tapdancing lessons at the Pantheon Club. Attending tryouts at a drama festival; being hired as chorus girl for musicals such as *Show Boat* and *Desert Song*. Sharing the stage with famous stars. Being seen onstage by BBC scout; BBC's hiring her to do impersonations. Her mother's supporting her emotionally during her career struggles. Holding down an office job by day while acting at night. Having a lucky break when BBC asked her to join the cast of *The McFlannels,* a Glasgow radio show. Doing other radio characters for the BBC, especially male ones because of her husky voice. Marrying a shipbroker; being extremely happy. Performing in Caroll Levi's *Discovery Show,* doing impersonations of the famous; getting her own radio show. Acting in a BBC revue, "Lights Up," which later toured to entertain WWII soldiers. Outbreak of WWII just as author and husband had settled in Glasgow; his joining the military. Producing a government-sponsored documentary film. Coproducing radio broadcast of Henry James's *The Tragic Muse* for the BBC. Working in a typing pool to help the war effort. Reaching a turning point in her acting career when director John Mills offered her a Hollywood film role; refusing role in order to remain near home and family. Losing potential roles because of wartime danger in traveling between London and Scotland. Being told to lose her Scottish accent or go without roles. With her husband at war, risking moving to London without a guaranteed job; finding parts in plays and broadcasts. Husband's coming home in 1945. Author's embarking on her successful, long running London radio show, *It's That Man Again.*

Weir closes her account at the moment of winning the role which made her famous. Playing the radio character Tattie MacIntosh, she became a British household name. As she did in her broadcasts, Weir often employs Scots dialect in her writing. This is the third of her memoirs charting her Glasgow youth and later public career; the first is **1007** *Shoes Were for Sunday*, which affectionately remembers her working-class milieu to age 12. In the second volume, **1008** *Best Foot Forward* (1972), Weir picks up the story of her progress from ages 12–18, describing her secretarial training and work and her studies with a drama coach. In **1009** *Stepping into the Spotlight* (1975), she discusses her success in radio, stage, and television; **1010** *Walking into the Lyons' Den* (1977) covers the peak of her fame in the successful *Life with the Lyons* radio comedy. In **1011** *One Small Footprint* (1980), Weir discusses her Scottish identity, her mother's death, and her attempts to come to terms with the end of her acting career. Ultimately she turned her memories of Scotland into a professional writing career, publishing several more books including *Spinning Like a Peerie* (1983) and *A Gangin' Fit's aye Getting* (1989).

1012 WELLESLEY, Dorothy Violet, Duchess of Wellington (née Ashton). 1889–1956. *Far Have I Travelled.* James Barrie, 1952. 240 pp.; front. port.; illus.; epilogue. BLC to 1975 347:468.

Born in Berkshire. Father: Robert Ashton. Mother: Lucy Cecilia Dunn Gardner. Stepfather: Earl of Scarborough. 1 brother; 1 stepsister. Married 1914, Lord Gerald Wellesley, later 7th Duke of Wellington, secretary in the Diplomatic Service. 1 son; 1 daughter. Wrote ten books of poetry, including *Early Light* (1955), and the biography *Life of Sir George Goldie*. Knew Vita Sackville-West, Virginia Woolf, W. H. Auden, W. B. Yeats, many others. Poet; biographer; lesbian; traveler (Middle East);

foreign resident (Italy); diplomat's spouse. Upper class; married into aristocracy.

Privileged upbringing and free-thinking adulthood of a writer in the Bloomsbury circle, highlighting her extensive travel and its effects on her philosophy, from the 1890s to early 1950s. Father's death when she was age 7; his extraordinary effect on her; both author and father's having similar inability to "fit in." Mother's remarrying; their living on aristocratic stepfather's grand Yorkshire estate. Studying with governesses; reading avidly. Remembering her mother's coldness and dislike of having other women kiss her. Also spending time in Lumley Castle, owned by stepfather's family: its history, lore, and legends. Spending autumns in Scotland, winters on the French Riviera, and springs in Rome. Her only brother's death traumatizing her. Marrying Gerald, 1914; accompanying him to diplomatic post in Constantinople. Settling in Rome at outbreak of WWI; spending duration in Rome with circle of intellectual English friends; dismissing last months of war as "boring." Returning to live on her mother's English estate. Meeting Virginia Woolf. Beginning her thirty-five-year editorship of the *Living Poets* series for Hogarth Press. Settling in country house in Sussex, "Penns," 1928; entertaining society and literary people, including Ethel Smyth, Lady Ottoline Morrell, W. B. Yeats. WWII: taking in refugees at Penns. Death of her mother. Traveling to Egypt and India; expressing her esteem for Gandhi. Exploring Russia and Persia with Vita Sackville-West; trekking off the beaten path; describing Persian history and religion, flora and fauna. Exploring classical ruins in Sicily; while there, being introduced to the ritual magic practices of Aleister Crowley. Continuing her travels through Cyprus and Turkey; commenting on native religious rites. Negatively assessing modern science as a worship of death rather than life; its being a dangerous replacement for ancient beliefs. Having married solely to acquire male help with hardships of travel. Disliking modern poetry.

Wellesley juxtaposes the account of her journeys with those from earlier women travelers, such as Lady Mary Wortley Montagu's travel letters from her stay in Turkey, 1716–18. She also uses travel as a metaphor for the distance she has covered in her life between the modern, Western beliefs of her upbringing and her later attraction to ancient pagan religions. Written to mirror her intellectual growth, Wellesley's book evades both the mundane details of her domestic life and most of her accomplishments as a published poet. Consequently, the reader never hears that she abandoned her husband permanently after a few years, took her children to live with her mother, and shared Penns with her same-sex partner, Hilda Matheson, nor that she formed a long-time publishing alliance with Virginia and Leonard Woolf. At present, no satisfactory biography of Wellesley exists, although she figures peripherally in the biographies of other Bloomsbury figures.

WELLINGTON, Duchess of. [*See* WELLESLEY, Dorothy Violet.]

1013 WEST, Charlotte. c.1770–d.a.1820. *A Ten Years' Residence in France During the Severest Part of the Revolution from the Year 1787 to 1797, Containing Various Anecdotes of Some of the Most Remarkable Personages of that Period.* William Sams & Robert Jennings, 1821. 100 pp. NUC pre56 567:85.

Born in England. Married, husband not named, died c.1796. Widow. Society woman; political hostess; foreign resident (France); loyalist (French Revolution). Upper class.

Upper-class Englishwoman's account of her family's victimization in the French Revolution, emphasizing her active support for the monarchy during the conflict. Author and husband's emigrating to France, 1787, to live more cheaply; taking a country house near Challons in Champagne; socializing with aristocrats. Recalling the events of Bastille Day, July 1791, in Challons. Being harassed by *citoyens* for her aristocratic clothing; recounting murders committed by the revolutionaries. Dining, going to chapel with Louis XVI and Marie Antoinette when they passed through on their unsuccessful escape attempt. Remembering later meetings in England with friends who did escape: the Duchess d'Angoulême, the Duke of Brunswick. After mob attacked their house, family's fleeing to Paris, January 1893; witnessing guillotining of Louis XVI four days later; describing Paris during the Reign of Terror. All English subjects in France being imprisoned; author's family's being imprisoned in Amiens, attempting escape; author's being held in four different prisons; depicting their appalling conditions. Sharing prison with two English supporters of the revolution who "were most cordially detested by the French Revolutionists themselves" for being traitors to their native land. Author's being denounced by one of them, an English colonel, for singing "God Save the King"; being hauled before a tribunal. Author's winning release for herself and ill husband, 1794. Their being trapped in France; author's attempt to get passports in Paris nearly getting her captured by a mob. After husband's death in France, 1796, author's returning to England. Warning English readers that a similar revolution is likely, c.1821; urging loyalty to their king.

Moved by revolutionary mutterings in England in the 1820s, West testifies to the earlier bloody events in France. She has in effect written a companion piece to Edmund Burke's more general survey in his 1796 essay, "Reflections on the French Revolution." West's book provides personal witness that complements Burke's historical commentary, while sharing Burke's conservative, royalist perspective. At this time, liberal proposals for the democratization of the British government were being opposed by angry Tory defenders of the status quo, who increasingly identified reform with revolution. West's account seems intended for a British readership besieged by its own political and class-based problems. Although endorsing Tory political restraints, she emphasizes the human costs of revolution.

1014 WEST, Katharine (née Leaf). 1900–s.l.1971. *Inner and Outer Circles*. Cohen & West, 1958. 184 pp.; front. port. BLC to 1975 348:393.

Born in London. Father: Walter Leaf, banker. Mother: Charlotte Mary Symonds. Grandfather: classicist, historian John Addington Symonds. 1 brother. Married, husband not named. 2 sons. Wrote *Power in the Liberal Party: A Study in Australian Politics* (1966). Biographer; political writer. Upper middle class.

Family analysis and personal memories, spanning author's childhood to early adolescence. Ancestry and family history. Mother's being gifted but neurotic and morbidly apprehensive of the children's health. Expressing "unmixed delight" in her father's company; sharing evenings in the library with him, reading history, mythology, art. Family's having tradition of a reading circle; reading aloud to one another. Being dependent on her beloved nanny; at age 9, having her mind awakened by a governess "who took me from my cage and let me use my wings." Studying music and dance. Loving her pets but detesting dolls. Family's spending summers in Littlehampton. Discussing books from her childhood. Author and brother's playing in the Royal Botanical Gardens at Regent's Park. Discussing her love of horses. Family's socializing with relatives, especially numerous cousins. Remembering family visits to country house of Aunt Katharine (Symonds) Furse, the respected naturalist; admiring this aunt and feeling her "the only grownup who could understand my boyish aspirations" to live an unconfined, outdoors life. Attending funeral procession of Edward VII, age 10; witnessing coronation of George V. Accompanying family to Italy, 1913; explaining her detestation of travel. Attending boarding school. Outbreak of WWI.

West re-creates her childhood topically rather than chronologically, emphasizing the contrasts between her inner circle and the outer ones of her extended family and social milieu. West's grandfather John Addington Symonds, historian of the Italian Renaissance, had settled his family in Italy; thus West's mother grew up in Florence, surrounded by Continental sophistication and art. West's father, on the other hand, grew up as a draper's son. West alludes to this contrast when she remarks, "Mother's early married life must have confirmed her worst doubts about English middle-class conventionality." West's book serves well as a companion piece to the autobiographies of her aunts Katharine Furse *(Hearts and Pomegranates)* and Madge Vaughan *(Out of the Past)*, which also focus on the Symonds family's aestheticism and high culture.

1015 WEST, Dame Rebecca (pseud.; Cicily Isabel Fairfield; C.B.E.). 1892–1983. *Family Memories: An Autobiographical Journey*. Ed. by Faith Evans. New York: Penguin Books, 1989. 255 pp.; intro. by ed.; illus.; app.; notes; ed.'s note. NUC 1988–90 Microfiche #0324.

Born in London. Father: Charles Fairfield, businessman, journalist, Irish, d.1906. Mother: Isabella Mackenzie. 2 sisters. Married 1930, Henry Maxwell Andrews. 1 son (by H. G. Wells before marriage to Andrews). Wrote *Henry James* (1916), *The New Meaning of Treason,* novels *The Thinking Reed, The Fountain Overflows, This Real Night, Cousin Rosamund, Sunflower,* travelogues. Novelist; biographer; political writer; mistress; travel writer. Middle class.

West's bio-historical study of the lives of her parents, and of her own childhood, with fragmentary comments on later life and husband's history, covering c.1892–1983. Extensive history of mother's Scottish family. Noting effects on mother's character encoded by customary Scottish male prerogative; discussing repression of sexual knowledge among women during mother's childhood, 1870s, and its effect on men in her mother's family, 1870s. Discussing male homosexuality as one result. Giving father's family background; discussing parents' relationship before her birth. Recounting fragments of her own childhood memories and the family's poverty. Discussing diverse characteristics of her sisters and herself; her later feeling that they had got the wrong person when she was made a dame, 1959, for her literary achievements. Noting father's infidelity; connecting it to male hostility toward women. Commenting that she herself had experienced being both mistress and wife. Attending Richmond High School; losing her religious belief there; going from there to a boarding school in Bournemouth. Evaluating reactions to her father's death, 1906. Reflecting on how her partial deafness alters her ability to appreciate music. Detailed life story of husband.

West apparently wrote several versions of her autobiography, and the editor has assembled a sequence of fragments from them. Only the editor's introduction discusses West's life in detail, including her love relationship with H. G. Wells as well as their illegitimate son—subjects West does not discuss at all. West often refers cryptically to some key decision or event in her life without identifying it, as when she refers to her refusal to endorse Soviet communism. Her style is highly literary, her tone introspective and sometimes ironic, sometimes angry in discussing and judging family members. From her verbal family portraits she seems to imply insights about herself; a fragmentary portrait of West herself emerges, but her explicit portrayal of her mother is very full.

WESTMINSTER, Duchess of. [*See* GROSVENOR, Loelia Mary.]

1016 WESTON, Agnes Elizabeth. 1840–1918. *My Life Among the Bluejackets*. James Nisbet, 1912. 333 pp.; front. port.; illus. NUC pre56 658:206.

Born in London. Father not named, attorney, Fellow of the Royal Geological and Astronomical Societies. Mother: Agnes Bayly. 3 brothers; 1 sister. Single. Wrote *Jottings from My Log* (1889). Temperance activist; missionary; teacher (Sunday school); social reformer; pamphleteer; organizer (philanthropic, religious); preacher; religionist (Anglican). Middle class.

Childhood, formative experiences, and adult philanthropic ministry of a Christian missionary to British sailors, from the 1840s to 1910. Growing up in Bloomsbury. Father's being a Cambridge-educated amateur scientist; his having lost two sons before author's birth; his becoming her playmate, guide, and teacher. Parents' having affirmed their Christianity before marrying; mother's living her faith through community work. Family's moving to Bath for mother's health, c.1846; death of another son, 1848. Father's taking author on seashore excursions, teaching her natural history. Attending school in Bath, from age 9. Learning of war's hardships through the Crimean War, author's age 14, and military experiences of two cousins in the 1857 Sepoy Mutiny. Experiencing conversion, age 16; taking Anglican confirmation. Teaching Sunday school. From studying fossils and books of geology, doubting biblical version of Creation; renewing her faith by studying astronomy with father and seeing the universe's grand design. Doing community work: conducting prayer services for hospital patients; consoling the dying. Being inspired to charitable work for sailors by reading Miss Marsh's *Work Among the Navvies at the Building of the Crystal Palace.* Discovering her gift for working with strong, rough men; abstaining from alcohol as an example to them. Writing monthly Christian tract for soldiers; teaching Bible at soldiers' coffee bar; corresponding with Christian soldiers and sailors. Acquiring a lifelong working partner, Miss Mintz. With death of her father, 1873, author's hearing divine call to leave home and give her life to bringing navy men to God. With Miss Mintz, settling in Devonport; preaching on shipboard, recruiting for Royal Naval Temperance Society. Establishing a Sailors' Rest temperance house at Devonport, 1876, and at Portsmouth, 1878–80. Miss Mintz's extending author's ministry to London, Manchester, Liverpool, and Scotland. Publishing sailors' newsletter, *Ashore and Afloat*. Receiving royal patronage for the Sailors' Rests, 1895. Helping sailors' needy wives collect pay due them; befriending dead sailors' widows and parents. Feeling honored that sailors called her "mother." Expressing pride in navy's contribution to Boer War, 1899–1901. Remembering death of Queen Victoria, 1901; paying tribute to the royal family's support of her work; the same year, receiving honorary doctor of laws degree from Glasgow University. Visiting American warships. Believing she succeeded in her work by turning a "blind eye" to its opponents, those Christians who disapproved of evangelizing through music and entertainment. Statistically documenting the steady expansion of her sailors' hostels and newsletter. Closing with memories of King George V's coronation review of the navy, 1910.

Weston did not embark on her ministry to the navy until age 33; before then she lived in her parents' home under their spiritual influence. In becoming a surrogate mother and sister to men isolated at sea, she found in the navy new family ties to replace the ones she had lost with the death of her beloved father. Consequently, while her account documents missionary work and social conditions among British sailors, it holds additional historical interest. Like Edmund Gosse's widely read autobiography *Father and Son,* Weston's memoir charts the author's spiritual development in an era of scientific ferment and religious doubt. Both Gosse and Weston, trained in geology by their fathers, confronted the conflict between fossil evidence and biblical creation, but Gosse abandoned Christian belief while Weston preserved it. In its unusual female perspective on this mid-19th-century dilemma, as well as on a type of social work that anticipates later 20th-century efforts, Weston's book merits closer examination.

1017 WETHERED, Joyce, Lady Heathcoat-Amory. 1901–s.l. 1973. *Golfing Memories and Methods*. Hutchinson, 1933. 255 pp.; front. port.; preface; illus. BLC to 1975 349:72.

Born in Brook Corner, Brook, Surrey. Father: Newton Wethered, professional golfer. Mother not named; also a golfer. 1 brother. Married 1937, Sir John Heathcoat-Amory, 3rd Baronet. Golfer. Middle class.

Sports-related memories of a champion golfer, covering her childhood to 1933. Discussing how people's motivations for taking up golf affect their development as players. Golfing in Cornwall during childhood, but abandoning golf and sports during WWI. Brother Roger's return after the war; his golfing enthusiasm's restoring her own. Family's moving to Sutherland, Scotland, into house abutting golf links. Improving her play there; watching her brother golf in Oxford matches; playing against his male friends. Joining the Sutherland county team, 1919; coming in second in the Surrey Championship. Experimenting with theories of the golf swing. Establishing friendship with golfer Molly Griffiths. Entering and unexpectedly winning 1920 English Ladies' Championship, age 19. Author and brother Roger's being defeated by Cecil Leitch and partner in two mixed-foursomes championships, 1921. Winning British Ladies' Open, 1922, but failing to defend her title in 1923. Discussing her brother's golfing career; their never winning titles in the same years. Winning 1924 British Ladies' Open. Depicting ongoing rivalry between herself and Leitch, who defeated her in 1925 British Ladies' Open. Withdrawing from open competitions until 1929; narrowly defeating

Leitch in 1929. Giving sketch of American champion Glenna Collett. Explaining techniques of play and advances in women's golf. With various male partners, winning the Warplesdon mixed-foursomes eight times. Recommending ways to introduce children to golf. Recounting anecdotes of playing golf in Scotland. Playing in matches against French women, 1931, and American women, 1932.

In 1935, two years after the publication of her memoir, Wethered made a golf tour of the U.S. and beat the acclaimed woman golfer Babe Zaharias in both matches they played. The evident pride that Wethered displays in her own accomplishments is more than justified; the *International Dictionary of Women's Biography* notes that she is considered "the finest woman player of all time." Eager to play by the standards of male competitors, she denied there was such a thing as "ladies' golf." Wethered retired from the game in 1948.

1018 WHISH, Violet Evangeline (née O'Donoghue). c.1880–?. *Partners in Friendship*. Privately printed, 1949. 206 pp.; preface. BLC to 1975 349:303.

Probably born in England. Father: Rev. E. G. O'Donoghue, Irish-Cornish. Mother not named, invalid. Stepmother not named. 1 brother; 2 sisters. Married 1906, husband not named, d.1941. Widow. 1 daughter. Wrote children's book *Come-to-Good Farm*. Journalist; columnist; editor; children's author; WWII volunteer. Middle class.

Anecdotal collage of a society columnist's experiences with people and events in upper-class British circles, highlighting her working friendship with Lady Norah Spencer-Churchill, spanning 1918–45. Having previously worked as society reporter for the *Daily Mirror,* 1914–18; with the end of WWI, losing that job and starting her own news agency. Introducing herself to Lady Norah with request that Lady Norah contribute articles on domestic subjects. Excerpt from Lady Norah's writings on Churchill family history. Author's discussing psychic events involving herself; claiming the ability to see ghosts and read teacups; having premonition of her husband's WWII death; seeing a vision of her dead father, who had also been psychic. This ability's countering her childhood memories of feeling inferior to her two "brilliant" sisters. Author's attending weekly séances; confiding her experiences there to Lady Norah. Recounting anecdotes of society ladies garnered in another job as society columnist for the *Daily Express,* c.1920s–1930s; discussing her need to earn her own living, her Fleet Street colleagues, and their shared poverty. Anecdotes of society life between the wars: Ascot race meetings, charity sporting events, other society functions. Discussing her methods of gathering information for her society column. Interviewing theatrefolk: Mrs. Patrick Campbell, Ellen Terry, Dame Nellie Melba. Stating that she was imprisoned in her youth for militant suffrage activity, inspired by Emmeline Pankhurst's oratory to join the movement.

Claiming to have worked for many causes since then, including a stint as WWII Red Cross nurse. Problems of society women: divorce, alcoholism, other scandals. Defying her editor by refusing to report on illicit romances of society ladies. Discussing those romances. Becoming editor of the *Daily Express*'s society section. Leaving the *Daily Express;* returning to literary partnership with Lady Norah. Excerpts by Lady Norah assessing her cousin, Winston Churchill, and describing their family residence, Blenheim Palace. Author's grievances about journalistic work: distress at finding her newspaper columns pirated; poverty of ex-journalists; dislike of journalists' being bribed with food to write flattering stories. Working briefly writing publicity for film actresses; returning to society journalism. Lamenting the passing of grand family estates, as well as the unemployed people and derelicts filling London between the wars. Illness and death of author's husband, 1941; death of Lady Norah, 1945. Author's present life in Cornwall with her grandchildren and her hopes for Britain to regain its lost glory.

This book incorporates four essays by Lady Norah into Whish's own memoirs. There is no chronological and little topical organization; most of the book consists of anecdotes pieced together from her diary. Although all of her memories are lively, some of them—especially regarding her own endeavors—contain problematic details whose accuracy needs to be verified. Whish's anecdotes, although fragmentary, contain many items that help recontruct London society events and relationships during her journalistic tenure.

1019 WHITAKER, Malachi (pseud.; Mary Whitaker; née Taylor). 1895–1975. *And So Did I.* Manchester: Carcanet, 1987. 148 pp. BLC to 1975 349:338. (1st pub. Jonathan Cape, 1939.)

Born in Bradford, Yorkshire. Father not named, bookbinder. Mother not named. 10 siblings. Married 1917, Leonard Whitaker. 1 adopted son; 1 adopted daughter. Wrote *Frost in April* (1929), *Selected Stories* (1949), *The Crystal Fountain and Other Stories* (1984), others. Short storyist; military spouse. Lower middle class.

Fragmentary meditations on the author's childlessness and hopes to adopt, her father, her marriage, and her writing career, held together by family memories, from her childhood to 1930s. Acquiring love of books by reading those her father was commissioned to bind. Loving her mother but resenting her heavy-handed beating of the children; never loving her father. Their household's living in poverty. At age 22, marrying a WWI soldier; catching venereal disease from their first sexual intercourse. Living briefly with him in France during the war, then in England after the Armistice; their staying in tents and borrowed country cottages. Describing their first house. Author's writing her first book there and part of a second; being amazed at her good reviews. For twenty years, author's consulting doctors and trying to bear children; deciding to adopt children. Commenting on the many legal and social hurdles making adoption difficult. After many years, visiting her senile father in hospital; his death. Author's spending much time reading the Bible. Citing scriptural passages that seem to offer consolation, especially in the face of death; endeavoring to analyze her own indifference to their spiritual appeal. Most people's seeming to be helped by religion; remembering her Nonconformist upbringing. Discussing at length her reading of secular books. Recounting the other activities which fill her life: gardening, cooking, going to cinema, family holidays. Analyzing the personalities of various housekeepers whom she employs.

The book's title comes from Coleridge's "Ancient Mariner": "And a thousand thousand slimy things/Lived on; and so did I." The book is not a unified account, but instead consists of brief passages probably taken from a journal. In writing that is frequently humorous, although sensitive and controlled, Whitaker focuses primarily on her present-tense life, with some ongoing narrative and some retrospection. The reference to the "Ancient Mariner" expresses the author's inability to lose the albatross of indifference (to her father and to religion) metaphorically hanging around her neck.

1020 WHITE, Antonia (née Eirene Adeline Botting). 1899–1980. *As Once in May: The Early Autobiography of Antonia White and Other Writings*. Virago Press, 1983. Ed. by Susan Chitty. 340 pp.; front. port.; illus.; intro.; fiction; ephemera; epitaph; biblio. BLC 1982–1985 26:103.

Born in London. Father: Cecil Botting, head of classics, St. Paul's School, London. Mother: Christine White. Married 1921, husband not named; annulled 1924. Married 1924, husband not named; annulled, 1929. Married 1930 Thomas Hopkinson; divorced 1937. 2 daughters. Wrote novels *Frost in May* (1933), *Beyond the Glass* (1954), others. Novelist; journalist; translator; academic's daughter. Upper class.

Author's first ten years in a cultured but repressive Edwardian family, 1899–1909. Recounting father's distinctions as a scholar and boys' educator. His being disappointed that she was a girl; her mother's loving author without offering physical affection. Deriving only real affection from her father's dog, Socrates; consequently loving all dogs. Being given first trip to the countryside by mother's servant, Lizzie. Remembering father's strictness from his teaching her Greek; being overwhelmingly anxious to please him. Mother's having been a governess before marriage; teaching author to read. Describing family home's art and adornments, and mother's ritual "At-Home" days. At ages 4–7, feeling happy with her mother; later becoming embarassed by mother's irresponsibility with money. Depicting enticements available for children in Kensington shops; being given half-sovereign by father's pupil to buy something; suffering trauma when father made her give it back. Remembering father's taking her on educational trip to the British Museum and treating her to tea and cakes. Mother's being frosty to author's paternal grandparents over father's paying their rent; author's taking tea alone with grandparents. Their taking author to meet great-aunt Clara, who told her about God; author's never having religious instruction before. Remembering mother's friend, Louise Edwards, with "advanced" opinions about women's rights. At age 7, author's beginning nine-year romance with Edwards's nephew; their playing together, discussing theology; author's experiencing awakening sexuality. Father's taking her to the Regents Park Zoo; their having an educational lunch with resident zoologists. Grandparents' bringing her to Earls Court Exhibition at night; thrilling at riding the ferris wheel and seeing stars for the first time. Commenting on the unwholesomeness of Victorian attitudes and education regarding sex.

After age 10, White attended Catholic convent school, where she was expelled for writing a novel about love. She enrolled in St. Paul's School for Girls and later attended the Academy of Dramatic Art, subsequently making a short-lived attempt at age 21 to act professionally. Before age 30, she had suffered two marriages annulled for nonconsummation, and then married for a third time. She wrote her first novel at age 34. Her novels—all autobiographical—examine the paternal, religious, and sexual traumas in her life from a Freudian perspective acquired during four years of psychoanalysis. While writing, she also worked at several different careers, teaching and translating for British Intelligence during WWII, as well as being one of the major English translators of the works of Colette and Guy de Maupassant. This early memoir primarily addresses her relations with her reserved father—classicist first, educator second, and father a distant third—a man caught between his natural kindliness and the artificial rigidity imposed by his profession and era.

1021 WHITE, Florence. 1863–d.a.1935. *A Fire in the Kitchen: The Autobiography of a Cook.* J. M. Dent, 1938. 340 pp.; front. port.; foreword; epilogue; postscript. NUC pre56 659:697.

Raised in Peckham, Greater London. Father: Richard White, lace buyer, founder of school for orphans and needy children. Mother: Harriet Jane Thirkell. Stepmother not named. 3 brothers; 1 sister; 6 half-brothers; 2 half-sisters. Single. Wrote *Easy Dressmaking* (c.1890), *Good Things in England: A Practical Cookery Book for Everyday Use* (1932), *Flowers as Food* (1934), *Where Shall We Eat or Put Up?* (1936), others. Knew French mathematician and scientist Henri Poincaré, Labour politician St. Loe Strachey. Cook; journalist; culinary author; teacher; governess; physically handicapped woman; fashion writer; charitable volunteer. Middle class.

Detailed account of a socially active working woman's life, 1866–1935. Commenting on middle-class autobiographies' being important to history; noting need to illuminate the mental attitude of children born before WWI. Discussing her partial blindness; channeling her long-time desire to write a novel into this memoir. Parents' having been Anglican, although father was low church. Having both nursemaid and governess, but learning to cook by observing mother. Being disfigured by childhood accident to her right eye. Father's remarrying after mother's death; stepmother's disliking author. Hating living at home; misbehaving so stepmother would send her to boarding school; stepmother's making her leave school instead, age 14. Father's finances worsening, making work necessary for all the children. Author's being the family's cook and laundress; tutoring to earn money for clothes. Passing College of Preceptors Examinations; longing to attend Girton College. Doing social work and culinary journalism. Being told no one would want to marry her because of her blind eye. Starting a school with her sister; sharing teaching duties with her, ages 19–21. Teaching as governess and as tutor; joining staff of boarding school at Warwick high school, age 27, and becoming full staff mistress. Wanting to abandon teaching for art, but realizing it wouldn't support her. Suffering headaches caused by blind eye; having it removed and replaced with a glass eye. Learning to sew from friends' maids; writing a dressmaking book. Being treated for neuralgic headaches by doctor, who tells her she can't teach anymore. Having emotional breakdown; reevaluating her life. Having no family to depend on; consequently moving to low-income housing. Finding short-lived job as fashion journalist, then as "women's interests" writer for Edinburgh *Evening News,* age 34, which sparked her interest in women's employment. Discussing prejudices against women journalists. Moving to Paris to take teaching job, age 46, although suffering weak heart and other ailments; training at Paris cooking school. Traveling throughout England to research history of English cookery; funding her travel by reporting on events for local papers. Returning to Edinburgh; attending a working girls' suffrage meeting there; doing social work; helping form a Christian reading circle; becoming a matron for the Scottish Girls' Friendly Society. Holding cooking jobs with diverse employers: a Catholic priest, a widow, a girl's school, and a hospital. Teaching cooking at a girls' club. Noting that she found happiness in life through domestic service, love of Christ, and avoiding marriage. Founding English Folk Cookery Association, 1928. Proudly itemizing her cookery publications; evaluating various cookbooks. Experiencing severe heart problems, 1934.

In this autobiography, White discusses at length women's employment opportunities during her lifetime. The hurdles she herself faced were greater than most, since her impaired vision would have made university study a full-time job for her, and thus being incompatible with earning a living. However, by developing her early domestic skills into a specialized journalism career, she found an innovative solution to her vocational problems, the record of which both illuminates the field of cookery during 1900–30 and surveys contemporary writing in that specialty.

1022 WHITE, Maude Valerie. 1855–1937. *Friends and Memories*. Edward Arnold, 1914. 383 pp.; preface; index. NUC pre56 660:204.

Born in Normandy, France, raised in Staffordshire. Father not named, businessman, son of British naval officer who became English consul in Valparaiso, Chile. Mother: née Harrington, b. England, raised in France. 3 brothers; 4 sisters. Single. Translated Axel Munthe's *Letters from a Mourning City*. Knew Lord Alfred Tennyson, Sir John Millais, Alfred Lyttleton, Lady Cowper, Jenny Lind, Dame Nellie Melba, others. Songwriter; composer; translator. Upper middle class.

French, English, and South American childhood, musical studies, and early career of songwriter, c.1855–c.1900. Refusing to tell readers her age. Defending her spinsterhood; ruefully resenting that married people "lord it" over single women. Mother's having lived in France from her infancy. Mother's being Catholic, but father Protestant; children's being raised Protestant. Paternal grandfather's residing in Chile, having earlier been British Consul at Valparaiso. Parents' moving to England during author's infancy; living in Staffordshire. Family's moving to join grandfather in Chile, author's age 8. Being schooled at home by German governess while brothers attended school; governess's providing her first musical education. Mother's dismissing governess because of author's excessive attachment to her; author's thereafter attending boys' day school with younger brother; becoming a tomboy. Being sent to school in Paris; adoring it; studying music there. Having to change to an English day school, age 14, because of ill health; living with a trustee. Loving to attend opera; continuing her music lessons, especially voice. Mother's returning to live in Cheshire; author's living with her, age 16. Beginning to compose songs; attempting to sell her work. Entering the Royal Academy of Music (RAM), age 21, despite mother's objections. Becoming the first woman to win the RAM's Mendelssohn Scholarship, 1879, but being forced by ill health to resign, 1881. Living on her own in London, selling her musical compositions. Converting to Catholicism, age 24. Recounting her extensive travels through Germany, Austria, Hungary, Russia, Italy, Sweden, and Chile, as well as her many vocal musical performances and social gatherings. In 1892, settling in Westminster, among her friends in London's musical circle.

This account of White's early years is rich with anecdotes of musical and literary worthies. From middle age onward, White resided mostly in Taormina, Sicily; in her autobiographical sequel, **1023** *My Indian Summer* (1932), she discusses her close friendship and collaboration with English novelist Robert Hichens in writing songs for a play he wrote.

She also describes her friendships with other English foreign residents (including Gertrude Bell) in the Mediterranean and in North Africa, her concerts and her precarious financial situation as a free-lance songwriter. A few of the 200 songs she wrote are "Absent yet Present," "A Song of the Sahara," and "Leave-Taking." Her ballet, *The Enchanted Heart,* was produced in 1913.

1024 WHITEHOUSE, Mary (née Hutcheson). 1910–s.l.1971. *Who Does She Think She Is?* New English Library, 1971. 189 pp.; foreword by Malcolm Muggeridge; intro.; epilogue; Malcolm Muggeridge's Convention Speech. BLC to 1975 350:73.

Raised in Shrewsbury, Shropshire and Chester, Cheshire. Father: James Hutcheson, farmer. Mother: née Searancke. 1 sister; 2 brothers. Married 1940, Ernest Whitehouse. 3 sons. Wrote *Cleaning-Up TV* (1966). Anti-pornography activist; social reformer; charitable volunteer; teacher (Sunday school), teacher (art). Middle class.

Childhood, teacher's training and career, and anti-pornography crusade of a leading conservative activist, emphasizing her lifelong Christian religious commitment, from c.1914 to 1971. Scottish family history. Family's moving from Shrewsbury to Chester during WWI; father's raising cattlefeed; struggling financially due to one child's medical treatments for polio. Author's going to Chester council school; later attending a good Central school, age 13. Receiving a small grant to train as a teacher, the only career she ever considered. Doing volunteer teaching at St. John's Church School; later training as art teacher in Crewe. Having to spend most of her life teaching in the industrial Midlands, away from the rural areas she loved. At age 25, meeting her future husband through a a young Methodists group; their commitment to putting God first in their marriage. Birth of her first son; becoming pregnant the next year with twins; rejecting abortion despite illness; deaths of the twins shortly after birth. Having two more children, 1941 and 1945; also adopting her infant niece after sister-in-law's death. Moving to rural Wednesfield near Wolverhampton, 1945; teaching art there. Teaching at Madeley Secondary Modern School, 1950s; being assigned to develop a visual human reproduction project; sharing her pupils' embarrassment. Noting church and society's lack of moral leadership; publishing article asserting that moral education should accompany biology, and should come from parents, not school. Believing that advertising's use of women as props lowered the status of motherhood and family. Acting on her outrage over 1963 Profumo sex scandal in government, as well as premarital sex on television, by resigning her teaching post; beginning crusade against BBC and ITA programming policies. Becoming enraged by BBC's biased reporting on her efforts; winning her libel suit against the network. Being endorsed by the Catholic Teachers Federation despite BBC pressure. Her followers' founding the National Viewers and

Listeners Association, c.1965. Writing her book *Cleaning-Up TV*. Conservative intellectual Malcolm Muggeridge's endorsing her crusade. Countering accusations of censorship by accusing BBC of censoring her. Giving interview on ATV, which was edited to make her look foolish; being manipulated by Granada TV into visiting 1970 Copenhagen "Sex Fair" as its guest. Attempting to prosecute BBC for showing full frontal male nudity. Taking part in "teach-in" on censorship at Leicester University, 1971. Discussing her fears about sex education in American elementary schools.

Whitehouse states that her existence was very ordinary until 1965, when she committed her life—and even this book—to her attempts to instill moral responsibility in British television programming. Whitehouse's strongest ally, and her memoir's editor, was the intellectual rebel Malcolm Muggeridge, who repudiated his own youthful licentiousness by resigning his Edinburgh University post, 1968, to protest student promiscuity. Whitehouse's book documents the crucial roles that she and Muggeridge played in the conservative backlash against the sexual liberation movement of the 1960s–70s.

1025 WILKINSON, Ellen Cicely. 1891–1947. "Ellen Wilkinson, M.A., M.P.," pp. 399–416 in *Myself When Young: By Famous Women of To-Day*. Ed. by Margot Asquith (Emma Alice Margaret Asquith; Countess of Oxford and Asquith). Frederick Muller, 1938. 422 pp.; foreword by ed.; illus.; index. BLC to 1975 12:477.

Born in Manchester. Father not named, factory worker. Mother not named. At least 1 brother; 1 sister. Married, husband not named. Wrote novel *Clash* (1929), *Peeps at Politicians* (1930), and *The Town That Was Murdered: The Life Story of Jarrow* (1939). Politician; Member of Parliament; cabinet minister; socialist; political writer; education activist; suffragist; Communist; pupil-teacher. Working class.

Perceptive reflections on the formative upbringing and education of a fiery socialist politician, from the 1890s to 1909. Father's being out of work when author was born, 1891, before existence of public assistance for unemployment or maternity aid; mother's suffering permanent injury during unaided childbirth. Mother's showing advanced thinking; her defying "iron conventions" of working class, such as standards of housekeeping. Father's being author's primary influence; his being an inspired Wesleyan lay preacher despite minimal education; his endorsing trade unionism but not socialism; his insisting he had pulled himself from the gutter and so must others. His sending three children to university on his wages. Author's being sent to state-run infant school, age 6; nearly dying from illnesses caught there. Mother's thereafter teaching her at home. Returning to state school, age 8. Being the brightest pupil but also naughty; hating state education's punitive teaching methods; its stifling of bright students. Attributing her later education activism to personal anger. Winning her first scholarship of many, age 11. Accompanying father to public lectures on philosophy, theology, and evolution, from age 12. Training herself at home in public speaking by emulating father's style of preaching. Reading Haeckel, Huxley, and Darwin, age 14. Entering a Manchester pupil-teacher training program, age 16; loving to invent better educational methods, but hating actual teaching because it necessitated reentering elementary schools, where she had been traumatized; not overcoming her phobia about visiting them until she entered Parliament, many years later. Being introduced to socialism by running as her campus political club's socialist candidate; converting to ardent socialist faith through studying the writings of Robert Blatchford. Joining Independent Labour Party, age 16; attending political meetings that she says bore the fervor of religious revivals. Resenting that, as a woman, she could neither vote nor run for Parliament, 1907, being told by a male socialist friend to "cheer up" and help him get elected instead. Studying for open national scholarship to Manchester University; after taking exam, suddenly having prescient sense that she had won over thousands of other students, this proving true; entering Manchester University, age 18, on scholarship; thriving there.

This essay ends when Wilkinson was only 18, but is filled with pertinent information on working-class cultural, political, and religious points of view. Wilkinson comments sensitively that her father's search for brotherhood through Christianity was identical to the impulse that brought her to socialism, but was expressed in a form conditioned by his era. The yearning that Wilkinson expresses for women's political enfranchisement would be assuaged when women over 30 won the vote in 1918, making possible her own election to Parliament in 1924. Wilkinson's later political activities are discussed in Beverly Parker Stobaugh's *Women and Parliament 1918–1970* (1978). Wilkinson was eventually appointed minister of education by Clement Atlee, in which position she continued her work for educational reform.

1026 WILSON, Harriette (née Dubochet). 1786–1846. *The Game of Hearts: Harriette Wilson's Memoirs, Interspersed with Excerpts from the Confessions of Julia Johnstone, Her Rival.* New York: Simon & Schuster, 1955. Ed. by Lesley Blanch. 532 pp.; intro.; illus.; app.; biographical notes; index. BLC to 1975 352:482. (1st pub. 1825.)

Born in London. Father: John Dubochet, clockmaker. Mother: Amelia Cheney. 15 siblings. Married c.1825, Col. William Henry Rochfort. Wrote novels *Paris Lions and London Tigers* (c.1826), *Clara Gazul* (1830). Knew the Earl of Craven, Duke of Wellington, Lord Byron, Duke of Argyll, Beau Brummell, Duke of Leinster, others. Courtesan; mistress; novelist. Lower middle class.

Saga of a courtesan's progress among the Regency beau monde, with sketches of the author's numerous titled lovers, covering c.1801–c.1825. Becoming mistress to the earl of Craven, age 15; moving directly to his house from her father's. Boldly writing to the Prince of Wales, offering her sexual services to him. Lord Melbourne's inducing her to become mistress to his son, Frederick Lamb. Craven's rejecting her; author's tiring of Lamb and making successful overtures to the Marquis of Lorne. First meeting Julia Johnstone, another courtesan; expressing rivalry toward her. Author's having two sisters, Fanny and Amy, who also adopted the courtesan trade; Amy's becoming mistress to the Duke of Argyll, whom author had desired. Julia, Fanny, and Amy's all having illegitimate children by their lovers. Julia's setting up sexual liaison between Amy and Beau Brummell. Author's dallying with the Duke of Wellington, and with John, later Viscount Ponsonby. Sister Sophia's eloping with Viscount Deerhurst. Author's discussing her mother's illegitimate origins, amiability, 15 offspring, and unceasing concern for her children's welfare despite hard economic conditions. Lord Ponsonby's rejecting author after his wife discovered their liaison. Author's being sidelined by scarlet fever while Julia and author's sisters continued their sexual careers; author's deliberately citing every aristocrat with whom they established connections. Author's moving to Brighton, 1811. Recounting her dalliances with Lord Worcester and Lord Hertford; traveling to Spain to visit Worcester; deducing that he had cheated on her. Attempting to raise funds by blackmailing the Duke of Beaufort. Taking up with Lord Ebrington, then Prince Esterhazy. Meeting Lord Byron; later corresponding with him during his exile on the Continent. After delivering these memoirs to her publisher, being threatened with lawsuits by ex-lovers. Recounting deaths of her sister and mother in quick succession, as well as "death" of Julia Johnstone (although Johnstone was not, in fact, dead).

This last edition of Wilson's memoirs contains the most extensive treatment of her life and times, as well as contemporary illustrations depicting Wilson, Julia Johnstone, and their various lovers. Although the *Dictionary of National Biography* suggests that Wilson's publisher, Stockdale, may have been her ghostwriter, the author's personal voice seems evident in the defensive tone which prevails throughout. However, while telling her life story in the most favorable light, Wilson also seems to have an eye to the sales potential of providing unsparing details. Her sole motive in writing was money, not only from sales, but from those lovers whose liaisons she omitted in return for payment. Julia Johnstone's *Confessions* (1825), published in response to this book and excerpted within this later edition, vilifies Wilson and alleges many lies and evasions, but Johnstone's book is questionable as well. Wilson's most accurate comment is that her memoir provides an interesting addition to the society chronicles of her times; having served her contemporary readers as gossip, it provides her 20th-century ones with a sociocultural document of the actual sexual behavior patterns behind the official legal and moral codes of the Regency.

1027 WILSON, Helen (née Ostler). c.1870–s.l. c.1950. *My First Eighty Years*. Hamilton, New Zealand: Paul's Book Arcade, 1951. 241 pp.; preface; illus.; app. NUC pre56 666:612.

Born at Ben More station, New Zealand. Father: W. H. Ostler, sheep farmer. Mother not named, dancing school teacher. 2 brothers; 1 sister. Married 1893, Charles Kendal Wilson, "bushwhacker," logger. 1 son; 2 daughters. Wrote novel *Moonshine*. Pioneer; politician's spouse; colonialist (New Zealand); teacher; novelist. Middle class.

Origins, youthful years, and married life of a New Zealand homesteader, featuring a detailed account of New Zealand's agricultural, social, and political development, from c.1870–1950. Father's Yorkshire origins; his trying to make his fortune by managing a sheep-farming station, Ben More. His bringing his 18-year-old bride from civilized Melbourne to live in frontier New Zealand. Depicting settlers' life during the station's early boom years. Father's prospering; buying his own isolated station, Ben Ohou; family's moving there. Describing floods, harsh climate, and home education by her mother. Witnessing the ruthless treatment of animals in sheepfarming; loving the farmyard animals; coming to believe they were really people reborn into some form of punishment. Discussing the waste inherent in sheep-raising, as well as New Zealand's boom-or-bust economy. Father's death from heart attack, author's age 9, resulting in forfeiture of Ben Ohou; family's moving to Timaru. Mother's needing to support the family; author's discussing the pitifully few livelihoods open to women, c.1880s. Mother's opening a dancing school. Author's lonely, fantasy-filled secondary school years. Using a sensational local murder as illustration of the passionate jealousies resulting from isolation in frontier society. Discussing fraudulent bankruptcies among local businessmen resulting from a collapse in New Zealand's economy. Mother's sending author's brother to prestigious private school in England, 1886. Author's attending local boarding school for one year; school's upper-class principal's treating lower-class scholarship girls with contempt. Being hired, age 16, to teach in an impoverished Irish settlement. Discussing how emigrant Irish practiced economic independence and thus escaped effects of New Zealand's 1880s economic depression. Author's quitting teaching, age 18; buying homestead with her mother in New Zealand's unsettled north island; winning desirable twenty-acre parcel in land lottery. Building a house. Meeting future husband, a frontier scout, through his helping them get settled. Author and mother's being the first white settlers in this area; other settlers' being Maoris. Depicting local history from Maori tribal days. The Maori and white settlers' establishing an ideal mutual relationship. Describing details of farm management. Author's marrying, 1893; pioneering with husband at Ohau. Hiring a maid after having her first child. Mother's gradually becoming rich from buying and selling land. After six years, author and husband's selling the Ohau farm; raising their growing family in another farm at Levin, 1898–1905; moving to a farm in the King Country, c.1905. After husband won Reform Party parliamentary seat, 1910, author's studying politics closely. Husband's endorsing prohibition of liquor, c.1910–20; author's rejecting suffrage movement and calling suffragettes "disgruntled females and acidulated spinsters." Believing discovery of contraception to be death-knell of British empire, since population pressure had traditionally led to expansion. During WWI, helping found the National Council of Women; noting this group's interior dispute over conscientious objectors. After husband's loss of reelection, their retiring to the King Country farm. Suffering bad times: house's burning down; husband's forced amputation of septic leg. Author's joining a women's mutual aid society, 1925. Noting effects of 1930s depression in King Country. Author's being appointed commissioner, 1932, to report on female unemployment in New Zealand; describing general unemployment in detail. Her suggestions on ameliorating unemployment being put into action, 1933. Death of her husband. Becoming president of the women's division of the Dominion; being awarded a coronation medal and the Order of the British Empire. Discussing her lifetime spiritual development and her anticipations for her old age.

Wilson's story serves as a yardstick measuring eighty years of social changes in New Zealand during its transition from unspoiled wilderness to a culturally developed British dominion. Wilson writes sympathetically of the lives of both English settlers and Maoris. The political engagement of her husband and herself lends a firsthand perspective to the book's picture of New Zealand's political growth. Appended to the text is the farewell speech of lawyer Sir Hubert Ostler, the author's brother, to his New Zealand legal society; it serves as a closer look at the legal preoccupations within New Zealand during its period of expansion.

1028 WINKWORTH, Susanna. 1820–1884. *Memorials of Two Sisters: Susanna and Catherine Winkworth*. Completed and edited by Margaret Josephine Shaen (author's niece). Longmans, Green, 1908. 341 pp.; front. port. of Catherine; preface by ed.; port. of Susanna; biblio.; index. NUC pre56 668:164. [cat. under Shaen.]

Born in London. Father: Henry Winkworth, silk manufacturer. Mother: née Dickenson. Stepmother: Eliza Leyburn. 3 sisters; 2 brothers. Single. Edited and translated *The Life and Letters of Barthold George Niebuhr* (1852) and *The History and Life of the Rev. Dr. John Tauler of Strasbourg* (1857); also translated five works of German Protestant theology. Translator; editor; religionist (Unitarian); biographer. Middle class.

Author's memorial to her sister Catherine, who died in 1880, comprising memories of their joint upbringing and adult literary work, set within the framework of their family friendships with noted early Victorian writers and moralists, c.1825–58. Family histories of both parents. Author and sister's being given scholarly and Unitarian religious education by their parents; both girls' teaching Sunday school, beginning age 12. Being tutored by Rev. William Gaskell, husband of novelist Elizabeth Gaskell. Noting Catherine's advanced intellect in childhood. After mother's death, their acquiring stepmother who furthered the girls' literary interests. Discussing their meeting social reformer Harriet Martineau; commenting on her character and her written *Autobiography;* their being tutored in Latin by Martineau's brother. Their visiting France for two years, author's ages 17–18, and beginning to write; noting Rev. Gaskell's influence on Catherine's literary style. Discussing how differing religious affiliations affected the moral expressions of acquaintances Elizabeth Gaskell, Charlotte Brontë, and Jane Walsh Carlyle; making distinctions between a Unitarian intellect and an Anglican one. Author's making her first attempts at translation. Her translation of the *Life of Niebuhr's* being rejected by two publishers. At age 30, author's moving in with her brother in London, apart from her sisters; living there 1850–61. Traveling in Bonn for two years, 1850–51, to revise her Niebuhr translation; also writing a successful original biography of him. Her translation of the *Deutsche Theologie* being published, 1853. Author and her sisters' avidly reading Martineau, Elizabeth Gaskell, Brontë, and other contemporary authors. Extensive excerpts from their correspondence with the Gaskells and Brontës. Author's translating eighty-four sermons of Rev. Johann Tauler; Catherine's publishing *Lyra Germanica,* a collection of translated German hymns. Author and Catherine's visiting Heidelberg, 1856. Commenting on British trade policy that ruined the national silk industry, 1858, resulting in the financial ruin of their father.

Because of Susanna's death in 1884, her account was left incomplete. The remainder is ghostwritten by the author's niece, who also served as editor, adding commentary on Susanna's attendance at the Congress of Women Workers in Darmstadt, 1872, as well as material on her aunt's work with social reformer Frances Power Cobbe. The text consists mainly of the Winkworth sisters' correspondence, pieced together by linking passages of narrative. Written from within the early-19th-century framework of social and religious concerns, Winkworth's account charts the activism of many Victorian intellectuals outside of their published writings.

1029 WOODWARD, Kathleen. 1896–1961. *Jipping Street: Childhood in a London Slum*. Harper & Bros., 1928. 150 pp.; front. port. BLC to 1975 355:239.

Born in London. Father not named, invalid. Mother not named, laundress. 5 siblings. Social reformer; trade unionist; suffragist; seamstress; public speaker. Working class.

Author's youthful perspectives on growing up in the London slums, together with her personal reactions to its poverty and limitations, from c.1890s to 1911. Father's having married "beneath" him; author's recounting father's parents' anger at mother's inferior status. Childhood memories of pinched family life in slums; hard working conditions; poor people's fixation on money and diet. Recalling eccentric and notable neighbors. To support her family, mother's working several jobs, such as laundress and housecleaner; author's noting mother's strength in the face of exhaustion, but also her lack of concern for her children beyond their physical survival. In adolescence, author's cynically discovering the contrast between how the deaths of "superfluous" members of the working class were viewed by their families and by their social betters. Her learning to view sexually related problems as just part of the general squalor. Author's beginning to work in a sewing factory, age 13; moving from her mother's home to a boardinghouse; depicting working conditions and health problems for the factory's woman workers. Attending Borough Night School. Becoming increasingly interested in reform; beginning to attend Ethical Society meetings; joining the Sons and Daughters of Revolt; discussing their political iconoclasm and atheism. Working for unions and women's suffrage; becoming a street-corner speaker. Describing her growing resentment toward working-class acquiescence and apathy toward protest. Remarking on the tendency of "inventive" working-class individuals to prey on the naiveté of their own class.

Woodward's highly personal narrative makes no attempt to study the historical details of east London at the turn of the 20th century; instead it focuses on her reactions as a typical child caught within the drab monotony and poverty of London slum life. In her own case, anger and resentment led to activism for social reform. Such was not the case, however, for the majority of her working-class cohorts. Her portrait of the early-20th-century socialist reform movement, and the lower class's wholesale apathy toward it, culminates in her conclusion that the poor were effectively their own worst enemies.

1030 WOOLF, Virginia (née Adeline Virginia Stephen). 1882–1941. *Moments of Being: Unpublished Autobiographical Writings*. San Diego: Harcourt Brace Jovanovich, 1985. Ed. by Jeanne Schulkind. 2nd ed. 230 pp.; preface; ed.'s notes; intro.; app.; index. BLC 1976–1982 50:46. (1st pub. Chatto & Windus, 1976.)

Born in Hyde Park Gate, London. Father: Sir Leslie Stephen, literary critic, first editor of *Dictionary of National Biography*. Mother: Julia

Duckworth, née Jackson. 1 sister (artist Vanessa Bell); 2 brothers; 2 half-sisters; 2 half-brothers. Married 1912, Leonard Woolf, writer, publisher. Wrote 11 novels, many literary essays, *Diary* (five vols.), *Letters* (six vols.), biography *Roger Fry*. Knew Lytton Strachey, Desmond and Mary MacCarthy, Maynard Keynes, Katherine Mansfield, Henry James, Lady Ottoline Morrell, Dame Ethel Smyth, Margot (Tennant) Asquith, E. M. Forster, many others. Novelist; diarist; publisher; essayist; feminist; suffragist; bisexual. Upper middle class.

Introspective essays on the author's childhood and the childhood of her sister's children, together with more animated studies of her Bloomsbury days and colleagues, covering 1882–1914 and c.1935–40. Genealogy and history of her family, with sketches of ancestors' characters. Extensively analyzing her parents' lives and temperaments, as well as her ambivalent feelings toward them. Tracing her awakening self-awareness in childhood. Enduring a combination of afflictions, 1895, including her mother's death, "the greatest disaster that could happen," her father's distracted grieving, and ongoing sexual molestation by her half-brothers Gerald and George Duckworth. Relying on her emotional ties to her sister Vanessa to support her within the adverse family environment. Abetting Vanessa's rebellion against their father and his patriarchal social values. Evaluating the character of her half-brother George Duckworth. Commenting on women's inferior social position. Describing the Bloomsbury circle of writers and her intellectual friendships with Bloomsbury men. Recounting her marriage to fellow intellectual Leonard Woolf, 1912. Musing on her emotional and intellectual response to assorted criticism of her writing. Discussing her fascination with aristocracy and her friendships with aristocratic women.

As one of the major modernist writers, Woolf used innovative narrative techniques to trace psychological process. In a similar vein, she uses the essays in this volume to illuminate her own formative mental mechanisms and experiences. This collection's short autobiographical meditations were produced throughout her life; they include "Reminiscences," which reflects on Vanessa Bell's children; "22 Hyde Park Gate," which focuses on her later adolescence; and "Old Bloomsbury" and "Am I a Snob?" which discuss her Bloomsbury peers. This group of essays, ending in 1914, omits reference both to her several emotional breakdowns and suicide attempts and to her most productive years of writing, c.1920–30. "A Sketch of the Past," written c.1940, deals with Woolf's childhood and adolescence more frankly and insightfully than does "Reminiscences." These essays seem written primarily for Woolf's own contemplation, and focus on the influence of impersonal (social, genetic, even cosmic) forces on her life. Although her reflections on her oppressive upbringing are melancholy, the shorter Bloomsbury essays contain humor and wit.

1031 WOOTTON, Barbara, Baroness Wootton of Abinger. 1897–s.l.1960. *In a World I Never Made: Autobiographical Reflections*. George Allen & Unwin, 1967. 283 pp.; front. port.; preface; illus.; epilogue; index. BLC to 1975 355:308.

Born in Cambridge. Father: James Adams, fellow and senior tutor of Emmanuel College. Mother: Adela Marion Kensington, Girton scholar, linguist. 2 brothers. Married 1917, John Wesley Wootton, d.1917. Married George Wright, taxi cab driver, adult education organizer. Wrote short stories *Twos and Threes* (1933), novel *London's Burning*, economics history *The Social Foundations of Wage Policy, Social Science, and Social Pathology* (1959), and *Crime and the Criminal Law: Reflections of a Magistrate and Social Scientist* (1963). Knew Beatrice Webb, H. G. Wells, G. E. M. Jebb. Economist; magistrate; government administrator; feminist; socialist; broadcaster; novelist; short storyist; crime writer; WWI volunteer; academic; academic's daughter; public speaker; traveler (world). Middle class; awarded life peerage.

Intellectually privileged upbringing, academic career, and public service of a distinguished economist, along with the articulation of her feminist, socialist, and egalitarian views, from the 1890s to 1960. Discussing both parents' vocations as classical scholars; their characters and intellectual influence on all their children. Mother's holding conservative views except on women's suffrage. Despite yearning for the freedom of boarding school, author's receiving lessons at home until age 13; reading literature in various languages. Family's suffering crisis with death of her father, c.1907. Attending Perse High School in Cambridge, 1910. Outbreak of WWI: doing volunteer hospital work. At age 17, deciding to study economics rather than classics, much to her mother's displeasure. Becoming engaged to John Wesley Wootton. Entering Girton College, 1915, to study economics. Death in WWI of her brother Arthur. Marriage, 1917; husband's being called up for military service two days later; receiving news of his death in France. Passing Girton exam for economics with highest distinction; resenting university's not granting B.A. degree to women. Immediately being awarded a Research Scholarship at the London School of Economics; eventually leaving school in uncertainty over what to do with her life. Lecturing at Westfield College at University of London. Accepting Girton post of Director of Studies in Economics. Joining the University Labour Club; beginning her social activism. Encountering academic prejudice against a woman's teaching male students; in her dissatisfaction with academic life, turning to socialism as a vocation. Doing research for the Labour Party, age 25. Working for Workers' Educational Association. Being appointed a magistrate, age 28, at a time when women could not vote until age 30; discussing how her judicial experiences gave rise to personal questions of justice. Being made principal of Morley College for

Working Men and Women. As a woman, experiencing second-class treatment at the World Economic Conference, Geneva, 1927. Discussing her fiction writing. Serving as academic director of University of London's economics program, 1927–44. Noting social problems she saw on visits to Chicago and to USSR. Falling in love with taxicab driver George Wright; suffering intense press persecution because of the disparity in their social origins. Rendering an economic summary of the 1930s. Outbreak of WWII. Recounting her activism in Federal Union Movement. Working as reader at Bedford College, 1944–48; serving as professor there, 1948–57. Working as a visiting professor at Barnard College; citing other 1950s visits to U.S. Receiving honorary doctorate from Columbia University. Discussing her global travel and public speaking. Working to help develop United Nation's pension plans. After retiring, age 60, being one of the first four women admitted as Life Peer to the House of Lords; discussing her opinions of that institution as an insider. Being appointed to the BBC Board of Governors, 1950; noting her radio broadcasts from the 1920s on. Commenting on progress in women's economic opportunities, prejudicial media treatment of women, patronizing attitudes toward women and people of color, childcare, equal pay, women's property rights, her own education and modern education generally, and social sciences as an academic discipline.

Lady Wootton's autobiography is a vital document both in the history of liberal economics and in the history of women's belated academic enfranchisement. In this latter light, her education and career run parallel to those of the noted intellectual, Dorothy Sayers. Both women were children of the 1890s, and both grew up in Britain's principal university towns. Because they were also intellectually gifted, both were singularly equipped to take advantage of family university ties, despite women's general academic disqualification. Both—Wootton at Cambridge, Sayers at Oxford—faced the ironic paradox that, despite dominating the academic field in their undergraduate careers, they were barred by their sex from being granted degrees. Both developed into crime writers, although Sayers worked in fiction and Wootton's factual efforts were based on crime's relation to economic deprivation. Lady Wootton's account suggests that the gender barriers she faced also colored her thinking on barriers of class and race, although her most explicitly articulated political views are feminist in nature.

1032 WORDSWORTH, Elizabeth. 1840–1932. *Glimpses of the Past*. A. R. Mowbray, 1913. 235 pp.; front. port. of author's mother; prefatory note; illus.; postscript: memoir of sister Susanna. BLC to 1975 355:365.

Born at Harrow, Middlesex. Father: Christopher Wordsworth, headmaster of Harrow School, later Bishop of Lincoln. Mother: Susanna Hatley Frere. Great-uncle: poet William Wordsworth. 4 sisters; 2 brothers.

Single. Wrote *Onward Steps; or the Incarnation and Its Practical Teaching; Only a Feather;* and, with J. H. Overton, *Life of Christopher Wordsworth, Bishop of Lincoln* (1888). Educator; education activist; headmistress; religious/spiritual writer; biographer. Middle class.

Traditional upbringing and later educational activism of an early women's university head, contrasting her family's eminent literary and academic connections with her own scanty education, from the 1840s to 1913. Growing up at Harrow during her father's tenure as headmaster. Recalling the nationally mourned death of William Wordsworth, 1850; author's family's inheriting Wordsworth's home at Rydal Mount; moving there. Excerpts from family correspondence with Samuel Coleridge; anecdotes of her great-aunt, Dorothy Wordsworth. Moving to Stanford-in-the-Vale, c.1855. Receiving religious instruction from her pious parents; growing up reading New Testament commentaries. Praising moral earnestness and noble spirit of the Victorian age, in contrast to the lax morals of Jane Austen's earlier generation. Bishop Wilberforce's being a family friend. Being sent to a Brighton boarding school, 1857; describing its education as "superficial"; commenting on moral strengths and intellectual weaknesses of her home education; using her brother's cast-off textbooks to teach herself. Doing charity visiting with her mother. Accompanying father to Dresden and Italy, 1862. Extensive diary entries, recording visits to Cambridge University, to Wellington College, and to Berlin with her brother, 1867. Family's moving to Lincoln after father's consecration as Bishop, 1869. Father's receiving honorary degree from Keble College, Oxford at its opening, 1870. Becoming independent by accepting the headship of a new women's college at Oxford, Lady Margaret Hall, in 1878. At Oxford, becoming acquainted with Walter Pater, classicist Benjamin Jowett, and Mr. and Mrs. Humphrey Ward. Citing the various people active in the 1873–74 movement for women's education at Oxford, including John Ruskin; providing complete list of courses offered to women, but noting ridicule of women's education in the media. The Honour Moderations major's being opened to Oxford women, 1884. Deaths of her mother, 1884, and father, 1885. Discussing Lady Margaret Settlement House at Lambeth and the college's other charitable hostels. Author's sister Susan's becoming head of Greyladies School, Blackheath Hill. Retiring as head of Lady Margaret Hall, 1909, at age 70. Commenting that the chief moral to be gleaned from her last forty years' experience is the need for a religious basis in the lives of all educated women.

Much like the novelist Mrs. Humphrey Ward, whom she knew well, Wordsworth seems to have derived her calling as a women's education activist from the rude contrast between her own inadequate female education and the sterling intellectual boys' education that her headmaster father was in the business of providing. Ward, as the daughter of Rugby's headmaster, and Wordsworth, as the daughter of Harrow's head, both saw the value of education and seized every chance to acquire it for themselves. Both sought to make sure that younger women would have the access to academics that they personally had been denied. Although Wordsworth very likely was offered the headship of St. Margaret's Hall because of her family's educational preeminence, she took great advantage of the opportunity, becoming a passionate and effective advocate for women's educational reform. Mrs. Ward's *A Writer's Recollections* is of considerable historical interest when read in tandem with Wordsworth's own account.

1033 WRIGLEY, Mrs. (née Jones). 1858–d.a.1930. "A Plate-Layer's Wife," pp. 56–66 in *Life as We Have Known It by Co-operative Working Women*. Ed. by Margaret Llewelyn Davies. New York: W. W. Norton & Co., 1975. 141 pp.; ed.'s note; intro. letter by Virginia Woolf. BLC to 1975 78:2. (1st pub. Hogarth Press, 1931.)

Born in Cefn Mawr, Wales. Father: surname Jones, shoemaker. Mother not named, seamstress. 4 siblings. Married surname Wrigley, platelayer. Widow. 5 sons. Domestic servant; dairymaid; temperance hotel worker; seamstress. Working class.

Working woman's brief clear-eyed account of personal hardships and her resulting social activism, from childhood through the end of WWI. At age 6, being rescued from drowning by a Sunday school teacher whom her father later rescued in the same place; concluding that humans are divinely intended to help each other. Father's making boots for 12 shillings weekly; mother's earning 1 shilling weekly by sewing. As oldest child, author's tending all the younger children. Carrying coal and water many miles for household use; considering it a treat to join other children at the River Dee doing the laundry. All children's being expected to work for pay as soon as able. At age 9, being hired by the local Anglican vicar as a "child nurse"; leaving because they denied food to the servants. Being hired as nursemaid by a doctor; discovering that the job really involved hard labor and punishment with no wages. Finding job as a well-treated dairymaid; staying until age 12. Holding successive dairymaid jobs, then working as domestic servant at temperance hotel, ages 14–19. Hotel master's discovering her illiteracy; his sending her to night school for two years. Taking further domestic servant positions, ages 19–24. Meeting a handsome platelayer; marrying him, age 26. Discovering her "condition" after five months of marriage; laboring to save money before the baby came. Attributing her postnatal mastitis to overwork; being glad to think modern women are better cared for during pregnancy. Taking food to a neighbor who worked several jobs and went hungry to feed her children; author's revealing she herself often forfeited dinner to feed her sons. Family's low financial point after the birth of their fifth son, with no children working; considerable financial improvement when two boys, ages 14 and under, started earning wages. Author and husband's resolving to make every boy self-supporting; proudly apprenticing them to their chosen trades at age 14. Saving to give them all music lessons; father and the boys' playing "every instrument there was," being a happy musical family until WWI. War death of her eldest son, and her husband's death eleven months later. Thanking God that the four other sons came back safe from the war. Joining the Women's Co-operative Guild during WWI to distract her mind from fear for her boys. Rejoicing that she has contributed to the fight for better conditions for women and children. Working on WWI relief committees. Joining the suffrage movement. Devoting herself to pacificism: "There's no mother or wife in England nor Germany that would give their loved one to be killed. Now we are working for peace." Praising Ellen Wilkinson's fight as M.P. to improve child welfare.

Wrigley's account focuses on poor women's urgent economic needs. She was determined to make the necessary sacrifices for her sons to enjoy trades and a general education, and her success is the high point of her autobiography. In her introductory letter to this volume, Virginia Woolf confesses that she had thought the determination of working-class women such as Wrigley doomed to be frustrated by their lack of the vote, but Woolf happily acknowledges her error. Wrigley's narrative is illuminating both on the monetary details of early-20th-century laboring life and on the motivations that turned women like herself into committed political activists.

1034 WYLIE, Ida Alexa Ross. 1887–1959. *My Life with George: An Unconventional Autobiography*. New York: Random House, 1940. 351 pp.; illus. NUC pre56 676:542.

Born in Melbourne, Australia. Father: Alexander Coghill Wylie. Mother: Ida Millicent Ross. Stepmother: Maud. 1 half-sister; 1 half-brother. Single. Wrote novels *Towards Morning, To the Vanquished, Silver Virgin*, others. Knew Annie and Jessie Kenney and other suffrage leaders. Novelist; short storyist; screenwriter; suffragist, militant; feminist; lesbian; foreign resident (U.S.). Middle class.

Unconventional upbringing and career of a versatile writer, including the life story of her extravagant father and her eventual success as a Hollywood screenwriter, 1890s–1940. Being a "born writer"; owing her creativity to "George" (her personified unconscious mind). Author's being the only person who disliked her charming, unscrupulous father. His spending two years in debtor's prison; his seducing virtuous women into throwing their lives and money away on him. After his first marriage, family friends' daughter Christine's becoming infatuated with him. His eloping to Paris with Christine; wife's filing for divorce. His abandoning Christine and sailing for Australia; his meeting and marrying author's mother on voyage. Author's birth in Australia; her beginning to shoplift and play tough physical sports, age 4. Mother's dying, author's age 5. Returning to England. The still-besotted Christine's becoming the author's unmarried, unpaid, live-in mother. Author's believing she inherited her father's emotional and financial extravagance; her also identifying with traits of her mother's sister Aunt Maimie, who preferred women to men, wore masculine clothes, was athletic, and supported women's suffrage. Being schooled at home by Christine; briefly attending art school, 1890s. Father's vices worsening; his striking Christine. Author's receiving an exorbitant weekly allowance. Starting to write on her father's old typewriter. Father's marrying a third time; author's rejecting new stepmother, Maud, and biting her; Maud's throwing author downstairs and departing permanently. Father's moving a rich widow with three adolescent children into the house. Author's secretly visiting Christine. Being sent with her stepsister to Queen's College School, age 10. Becoming entranced with theatre; seeing every London production, 1895–99; spending her allowance on bouquets for actresses; analyzing her worship of actresses as part of her "mother complex." Being "pitchforked" with stepsister into a Belgian lycée, age 14; father's charming the female teachers into letting him manage the school. Her increasing desire to be a writer being guarded by her masculine unconscious mind, "George." Attending Cheltenham Ladies' College; adoring headmistress Dorothea Beale. Attending German finishing school, age 19. Becoming romantically involved with "another mother figure," Frau Von Vogelweid, who influenced author to become blindly pro-German. Moving in with Vogelweid; receiving her only marriage proposal from a German grenadier; his vanishing after being informed of "the true state of affairs." Sending her short stories to her father; father's denigrating them; their being accepted anyway and earning her a publishing contract, age 21. Sending her father a letter denouncing his belittlement of her talent. Father's death. Returning to England; joining militant suffrage movement; enjoying serving as Pankhursts' bodyguard; being arrested for jumping into royal carriage to give suffrage literature to King George. During WWI, cohabiting with Vogelweid in London; becoming friends with Rachel Barrett, editor of *The Suffragette*. After Vogelweid departed for New York, establishing intimacy with Barrett. Through writing for *The Saturday Evening Post,* learning of American literary opportunities; moving to U.S. with new friend Jessie Kenney, 1918. Being drawn to the flamboyance of Southern California; writing Hollywood screenplays, including the movie *My Four Sons,* which won the Academy Award for Best Picture, 1928. Becoming disillusioned with ethics of Hollywood before WWII; discussing the suppression of her screenplay *Exiles* for Samuel Goldwyn through Nazi political pressure; believing this exposed Hollywood's sell-out of its creative ideals. Touring the U.S. with Barrett and establishing a permanent home with her. Reflecting on her spiritual identification with America. Offering final thoughts on "George," her creative inspiration.

Wylie's allusions to being partners in her writing career with "George," the independent personality of her unconscious, helps to illuminate the masculine side of her psyche. She also discusses matter-of-factly her long series of same-sex liaisons, but does not formally declare her lesbianism, something which, at the book's 1940 publication, might have provoked troublesome controversy. Nevertheless, she does focus on this aspect of her character, psychoanalyzing her attraction to women in terms of her search for a permanent mother figure. Wylie's memoir is useful both for gay studies, in terms of how an early figure thought of same-sex relationships, and for historians of the political climate in the early film industry.

1035 WYNNE, Frances (née Macrory). c.1885–d.a.1946. *Eastward of All.* Dublin: M. H. Gill, 1946. 194 pp.; intro. by W. Malachy Lynch, O Carm.; foreword; illus.; epilogue. NUC pre56 676:641.

Born in Northern Ireland. Father: surname Macrory, president of Unionist Party in Ulster. Mother not named, clergyman's daughter. 3 brothers; 2 sisters. Married c.1906, Richard Wynne, died c.1933. Widow. 1 son. Religionist (Roman Catholic convert); political activist; artist (painter). Middle class.

Parental and spiritual influences leading to author's Catholic conversion, along with an account of her art studies before motherhood, from birth to 1946. Growing up in Ulster country house; mother's being the disciplinarian. Discussing her childhood fears of death. Mother's being artistic and religious; father's being matter-of-fact. Author's briefly sharing tutor with brothers, but driving him away through teasing. Education for author and her sisters' being "perfunctory" and their textbooks' conveying Protestant, anti-Catholic viewpoints; regular Protestant church attendance being mandatory. Author's brothers' attending English schools. Father's debts' preventing formal schooling for the girls; their being secretly delighted and indulging instead in voracious novel reading. From ages 14–16, boarding in England with her mother's cousin, a vicar's wife; taking painting lessons with her. At age 17, traveling with mother and sister to St. Jean de Luz, France to study painting. Despite none of the siblings' attending university, mother's ardently encouraging her daughters' art studies. Moving to London to room with her youngest brother, an engineering student; author's attending Calderon's School of Animal Painting. Author and brother's attending church services of many denominations in London; on first beholding a Catholic church's interior, feeling ill at the "idolatry rampant!" Retrospectively believing that her Protestantism was undermined by her Bohemian existence as an art student. Taking life drawing classes; winning an art scholarship, but being prevented by poor health from using it. Discussing Catholicism with mother; mother's retorting she would rather see her children dead than Papists. Meeting future husband at Calderon's School when he was over 40 and she was 21; marrying; meeting and adoring Welsh in-laws. At this time, starting to be drawn in direction of Catholicism; reading many books of Catholic mysticism. Birth of son, Robert, just before mother's death, 1908. Many family changes occurring after her death: all of author's siblings' marrying; several deaths in husband's family. Author's using Catholic beliefs to console husband's grief. Castigating Modernism in Anglican Church, which repudiated reality of the Resurrection. Sending one of her early paintings to the Royal Academy; family's happiness when it was accepted. Commenting that motherhood had generally ended painting days. Death of father at the outbreak of WWI; commenting on the fusion of religion and patriotism on the homefront. Trying to interpret Bible stories for son in a spiritual sense only, but finding both he and she yearned for a real sense of divinity. Son's attending prep school, c.1920, his later attending Oxford. Her husband's entering his final, lingering illness. After lengthy legal battle, husband's ancestral estate in Conway, Wales, being restored to them; family's moving there, c.1930s. Son's informing her he planned to become a Catholic; taking instruction together from local parish priest. Regretting that ailing husband knew of her conversion. His death, 1933. Concluding her account with her son and herself being received into the Catholic Church, and the start of WWII.

Like Sheila Kaye-Smith's autobiography *Three Ways Home*, this book is largely an exposition of the author's conversion to Catholicism. In its sequel, **1036** *The True Level* (1947), Wynne recounts her political activism, 1930–47, which resulted from her growing awareness of the Catholic faith's role in British history. Her attempts to restore the Catholic church in Wales led her to support Welsh nationalist militants in 1936. She also discusses her pilgrimages to Rome, the Holy Land, France, and Spain, and the further effects of her conversion.

1037 YATES, Agnes (née Rutter). 1859–d.a.1938. *Putting the Clock Back: Reminiscences of Childhood in a Quaker Country Home, During the Middle Years of Last Century*. Allenson & Co., c.1939. 192 pp.; illus.; poems by Elizabeth Rutter, author's sister. NUC pre56 678:154.

Raised at Mere, Wiltshire. Father: John Farley Rutter, lawyer. Mother: Hannah Player, abolitionist, temperance advocate. 4 brothers; 6 sisters. Married, husband not named. Children. Religionist (Quaker); dressmaker; temperance activist; charitable volunteer. Upper middle class.

Author's upbringing and character formation in a mid-19th-century Quaker family, and her efforts at self-education and charity work, from childhood through her 1880 marriage. Growing up in an extended family on a country estate; paternal grandmother who lived in household being an important childhood influence. Children's being introduced early to Friends' meetings; each child's being made to save pennies to sponsor a poor child's schooling. Being sent to dame school, age 3. Father's reading Bible to children each day. Mother's being an ardent abolitionist; her being author's primary moral influence and breaking down spirit of rebellion. Extensively discussing family holiday traditions and imaginative games with favorite brother Clarence. Mother's determinedly breaking her of inventing stories; author's believing her creativity atrophied as a result. Author and favorite sister Elizabeth's wanting to learn carpentry; being forbidden because it was thought unsuitable for girls. Children's having a Quaker governess who remained until author's marriage. Discussing the extensive religious and secular reading of her childhood. Family's having circle of Quaker acquaintances who morally influenced author's upbringing. Author's being sent to stay with a housemaid's family because of ill heath; being cured by robust, unsupervised living. Parents' endorsing the natural cure of illness through homeopathy. At age 14, being sent to Church of England school in Bath; the resulting challenge to her Quaker beliefs making her develop a conscious rationale for defending them. Mother's suffering illness from many childbirths, being treated by repeated courses of mineral baths. Author's fearing to discuss her mother's approaching death frankly with her. After mother's death, author's age 16, author and sister Elizabeth's trying to educate themselves in art history, Greek, cookery, and literature; their reading the Brownings, Longfellow, Shelley, Wordsworth. With father's support, sister's opening temperance coffee room for working men, c.1880, and doing workhouse visiting together. Their opening a dressmaking business to earn money. Author's pride in having been an active figure in local Quaker youth organizations. Author's marriage, age 21.

In this remembrance of her youth and of the moral climate of the mid-19th century, the 79-year-old Yates fleshes out a portrait of the era's social concerns, Quaker homelife, and the stability of Quaker beliefs despite a period of national religious doubt. It is enlightening to consider that the author herself was born in the year that Darwin's *Origin of Species* was published, yet her family's beliefs show no signs of having been affected by its implications. Written at the beginning of World War II, Yates's account serves as a reminder of the clarity of ethical purpose often attributed to Victorian Britain.

1038 YOUMANS, Letitia (née Creighton). 1827–1896. *Campaign Echoes: The Autobiography of Mrs. Letitia Youmans, the Pioneer of the White Ribbon Movement in Canada*. Toronto: William Briggs, 1893. 311 pp.; intro. by Frances E. Willard; preface; front. port.; illus. NUC pre56 679:168.

Born in Baltimore, Ontario, Canada. Father: John Creighton, Methodist minister, Irish. Mother: Annie Bishop, American. 4 brothers; 1 sister.

Married 1850, Arthur Youmans, farmer, d.1882. Widow. 8 stepchildren. Knew Women's Christian Temperance Union founder Frances E. Willard, temperance workers Margaret Bright Lucas and Annie Wittenmyer. Temperance activist; social reformer; school founder; teacher; teacher (Sunday school); philanthropist; clergyman's daughter; farmer; public speaker. Middle class; married into rural farming class.

Canadian temperance activist's crusade, with secondary focus on her youth and married life, c.1820–90. Depicting Canadian frontier life before her birth. Author's being first surviving child in family. Being sent to a rural schoolhouse, age 4, run by a Roman Catholic woman who taught the Anglican catechism. At age 10, being instructed in temperance at school; signing the pledge. Discussing the tragedy of drink on the Canadian frontier; citing childhood memories of alcohol's harm to families. Having to attend a local ladies' academy rather than the prestigious Cobourg Academy she yearned for; having an intense conversion experience at school. Teaching at Cobourg Academy. Taking further teacher training in Hamilton, Ontario, age 20. Teaching school in Burlington, Vermont, then at Picton Ladies' Academy. Describing contemporary camp revival meetings. Deciding to marry a widower with eight small children; cautioning her female readers against marrying merely to acquire a home. As young wife, author's learning domestic work from Catharine Beecher's *Treatise on Domestic Economy*. Expounding on Ontario's butter-making industry and how farmwives might learn how to make better butter. Proving to her neighbors that her booklearning did not preclude domestic ability. Advising farm husbands to make wives' household duties pleasant; noting that her visit to the London, Ontario Insane Asylum revealed that most of its female inmates were farmers' wives, ruined by toil and monotony. Teaching a girls' Bible class, but advocating coeducation; her students' having alcoholic parents; author's inducing students to take the pledge. Working in the Women's National Temperance Association and the Band of Hope. Working to outlaw sale of liquor in Canadian grocery stores. Discussing start of Canadian Women's Christian Temperance Union. Attending WCTU conventions in U.S. Her husband's sharing her temperance sentiments. Author's delivering speech documenting biblical support for abstinence from liquor. Disassociating herself from the women's suffrage campaign; feeling there would be too much opposition to temperance if it were linked to suffrage. Husband's death, 1882. Voting in the 1885 Ontario municipal election (as a widow) when the Ontario government gave unmarried women the municipal vote. Touring the U.S. and Canada on temperance crusades. Serving as delegate to British WCTU meeting, 1883. Serving as Dominion president of WCTU. Conveying women's temperance concerns to President Rutherford B. Hayes. Asthma and rheumatism's forcing her retirement from the temperance crusade, 1888.

Youmans's mid-19th-century account of Canadian living underscores the conflicts between a loose frontier lifestyle and the moral ideals of Victorian England, disseminated in Canada via popular English literature and the influx of British immigrants. Youmans provides a moving picture of her immigrant Methodist father reading the novels of Maria Edgeworth and Mrs. S. C. Hall by lamplight, and of her own struggles, when first married, to persuade her neighbors that she could still run a farm despite being a skilled and scholarly teacher. This account informatively sketches the progress of the North American temperance movement over several decades.

1039 YOUNG, Ella. 1867–1956. *Flowering Dusk: Things Remembered Accurately and Inaccurately*. Longmans, Green, 1945. 356 pp.; front. port.; illus.; index. NUC pre56 679:318.

Born in Ireland. Parents not named. 4 sisters; 1 brother. Single. Wrote *The Rose of Heaven, The Wonder Smith and His Son, The Tangle-Coated Horse and Other Tales: Episodes from the Fionn Saga,* and *The Unicorn with Silver Shoes*. Irish nationalist; Theosophist; public speaker; poet; short storyist; anthologist; organizer of societies (cultural); mythologist; clairvoyant/psychic. Middle class.

Political, occult, and literary preoccupations of an Irish nationalist and poet, from her 1870s childhood to 1945. Being schooled by her father, instructed in Presbyterianism by her mother. Developing early gift for fantasy. Beginning school, age 7. Becoming romantically attached to fellow schoolgirl she calls "Brysanthe"; this inspiring her creation of the school's King Arthur society. Associating local Irish landscape with myths and legends; seeing ghosts in family home. Narrative's jumping ahead to Dublin in the 1890s; attending lecture by Annie Besant on Theosophy; through the Theosophical Society, meeting many poets who shared her Irish cultural and supernatural interests. Beginning to research Irish folk myths in primitive western Ireland. First seeing Maud Gonne and W. B. Yeats together. Attending 1890s Dublin theatre. Hiking in the mountains with sister May, Maud Gonne, and Yeats. Discussing value of Irish cultural revival as a weapon against British oppression. Recounting growth of Irish culture movement and nationalism; noting trend for plays based on Irish myth. All Irish revivalists' being entranced by mythology and New Age visions; their gathering on Samhain Eve, invoking the lost world of Faery to return to Ireland. Having her own visions of ancient gods. Discussing Yeats's occult activities. Maud Gonne's seeing ghosts in author's home outside Dublin; author's secretly storing armaments there for Irish Republican Army (IRA). Outbreak of WWI; remembering accurate 1914 prophecies of the war's outcome and of the 1916 Sinn Fein uprising. Describing the actual uprising during Easter week, 1916. British troops' executing all of the rebel leaders, including Maud Gonne's husband, John MacBride; Irish fury over the massacre. American Congress's resolving to promote Ireland's interests at a planned Dublin peace conference, but British soldiers' stopping Americans and Irish patriots from entering Dublin. Author's publishing a book of nationalist poems. British troops' raiding her house but failing to find the ammunition. Being sent as covert Sinn Fein envoy to IRA in County Kerry. Recounting the 1921 "Betrayal," when Irish delegates signed away Irish sovereignty; further violence's resulting from IRA and Irish President De Valera's repudiation of the treaty. British forces' again unsuccessfully raiding her house; their executing four IRA leaders the same day. Touring America to speak on Irish revival; visiting Irish emigré friends and Theosophical branch societies. Meeting Georgia O'Keeffe and photographer Ansel Adams; staying at the Taos ranch of D. H. Lawrence. Associating native American mysticism with Irish beliefs. Obtaining U.S. citizenship. Having homesick dreams of Ireland. Discussing WWII in mythic terms, 1942. Evaluating her life in old age.

Young's dual roles as Irish cultural revivalist and as Sinn Fein revolutionary make her memoir highly informative about Ireland's developments from the 1890s through 1921. Her angry disillusionment with the political sellout of Ireland, in which the rebel leaders signed a treaty agreeing to defer Irish Home Rule under threat of even more punitive British occupation, seems to have motivated her emigration from the country she loved. It is useful to read Young's highly poetic account in tandem with Annie Mary Smithson's *Myself—And Others: An Autobiography*. Writing at the same time as Young, Smithson looks back on the Irish political turmoil and her own Sinn Fein activities in practical, common-sense terms that help to balance Young's mythic perspective.

1040 YOUNG, Florence S. H. 1856–d.a.1924. *Pearls from the Pacific*. Marshall Brothers, c.1925. 256 pp.; front. port.; foreword by J. Stuart Holden; illus. NUC pre56 679:340.

Born in Motueka, near Nelson, New Zealand. Father: Henry Young, Nonconformist minister. Mother: Catherine Anne Eccles. At least 6 siblings. Single. Religionist (Nondenominational); missionary (Australia, China, the Solomon Islands); clergyman's daughter. Middle class.

Early life in New Zealand and Australia and adult missionary work, covering author's childhood to 1924. Birth in New Zealand; father's moving to England for the children's education, author's age 3, but being forced by business troubles to return to New Zealand. Author and siblings' being schooled by their eldest sister; receiving Bible teaching from their parents. Missing the New Zealand forest when family moved to Australia, author's age 10. At age 15, author's uncle's paying for her schooling in England; her returning to family in 1873. Experiencing religious conversion, age 17. Family's being disrupted by mother's death and siblings' marriages, 1875. Father's taking author and remaining brother to visit England, but his dying there, 1881. Author's returning to Australia to live on her brothers' sugar plantation, c.1882. Feeling need to perform Christian service; opening a boys' Sunday school among the Kanaka plantation workers; winning her first convert, 1885. Organizing missionaries to proselytize at Queensland's other plantations. Traveling to England, 1888, and to India; unexplained mission problems' forcing her return to Australia. In Brisbane, meeting with Rev. Hudson Taylor of the China Inland Mission (CIM); hearing a voice during his sermon telling her to go to China. Joining the CIM; arriving in Shanghai, 1891; like Taylor's other missionaries, adopting Chinese dress. Living in the Yang-Chau training home six months, learning Chinese language and customs. Taylor's sending her to Kuei-k'i for eight months, then to Shang-t'sing, "the headquarters of Taoism—practically devil-worship." Being hampered by the language barrier. Also working in missions at Hö-k'eo and Ien-shan. Returning to Australia to deal with difficulties at its missions, c.1894; communicating excitement of her work in China to Australian missionaries; bringing ten new volunteers back to China with her, 1897. Working at An-ren mission until the Boxer Rebellion, 1900; women missionaries' being evacuated to evade Empress's order to slay all foreigners; many of her colleagues being murdered. Returning briefly to Australia and mission work among the Kanaka; establishing new mission in Solomon Islands, 1904. Kanaka workers in Solomons being angry over their deportation by Australia; their reluctance to sell land to whites, making it hard to build the mission station. Noting spiritual revivals among the Kanaka in Queensland, 1905–06. Author's acquiring yacht to travel between her missions in Australia and the Solomons. Beginning island mission schools with converted native teachers. Starting new mission outposts in Makira and Quadalcanal, 1908. Recounting her impressive conversions of a witch doctor and a cannibal. Anecdotes of converts rescued by missionaries from cannibalism; murders of native teachers after whites retreated from mission outposts. Author's touring the British Isles to raise mission funds. Rendering eulogies of fellow missionaries who gave their lives to their calling; praising her sister, Emily Baring Deck, and her sister's children for aiding her missionary goals.

Young's effusive account documents the organizational side of missionary activity in Australia and the South Seas from the 1890s through the 1920s. For historians of Hudson Taylor's nondenominational China Inland Mission, Young's memoir is a crucial supplement to the earlier account by Grace Stott, *Twenty-Six Years of Missionary Work in China* (1897), and picks up the story of Taylor's missionaries in the perilous years of the Boxer Rebellion. Young's account also sheds light on the dramatic changes wrought in Kanaka culture by the influx of Christianity and Christian values.

Bibliography

Auerbach, Nina. "Feminist Criticism Reviewed." In *Gender and Literary Voice,* Janet Todd, ed. New York: Holmes & Meier, 1980.

Ayers, Pat and Jan Lambertz. "Marriage Relations, Money, and Domestic Violence in Working-Class Liverpool, 1919–1939." In *Labour and Love: Women's Experience of Home and Family, 1850–1940,* Jane Lewis, ed. Oxford and New York: Basil Blackwell Ltd, 1986.

Bailey, Susan F. *Women and the British Empire: An Annotated Guide to Sources.* New York: Garland Publishing, 1983.

Barrow, Margaret. *Women 1870–1928: A Select Guide to Printed and Archival Sources in the United Kingdom.* New York: Garland Publishing, London: Mansell, 1981.

Bell, Susan Groag and Marilyn Yalom, eds. and Intro. *Revealing Lives: Autobiography, Biography, and Gender.* Albany: State University of New York Press, 1990.

Benstock, Shari. *The Private Self: Theory and Practice of Women's Autobiographical Writings.* Chapel Hill: University of North Carolina Press, 1988.

Brodzki, Bella and Celeste Schenke. *Life/Lines: Theorizing Women's Autobiography.* Ithaca: Cornell University Press, 1988.

Buckley, Jerome Hamilton. *The Turning Key: Autobiography and the Subjective Impulse Since 1800.* Cambridge: Harvard University Press, 1984.

Bunkers, Suzanne L. "Self-Reflexivity in Women's Autobiography: A Selected Bibliography." In *a/b: Auto/Biography Studies,* Winter 1988, pp. 57–89.

Burnett, John, ed. *Destiny Obscure: Autobiographies of Childhood, Education and Family from the 1820s to the 1900s.* New York: Penguin Books, Ltd., 1984.

Burnett, John, David Vincent, and David Mayall, eds. *The Autobiography of the Working Class: An Annotated, Critical Bibliography,* vol. 1: 1790–1900. Brighton: Harvester Press, 1984.

Burton, Antoinette. *Burdens of History: British Feminists, Indian Women, and Imperial Culture, 1865–1915.* Chapel Hill: University of North Carolina Press, 1994.

Caine, Barbara. *Victorian Feminists.* Oxford: Oxford University Press, 1992.

Chaudhuri, Nupur and Margaret Strobel. *Western Women and Imperialism: Complicity and Resistance.* Bloomington: Indiana University Press, 1992.

Cobbe, Frances Power. "Wife Torture." In *The Contemporary Review*. Vol. XXXII, July 1878, pp. 55–87.

Cockshut, A.O.J. *The Art of Autobiography: In Nineteenth- and Twentieth-Century England.* New Haven: Yale University Press, 1984.

Colmer, John. *Australian Autobiography: the Personal Quest*. Melbourne and Oxford: Oxford University Press, 1989.

Corbett, Mary Jean. *Representing Femininity: Middle Class Subjectivity in Victorian and Edwardian Women's Autobiographies*. New York: Oxford University Press, 1992.

Culley, Margo, ed. *American Women's Autobiography: Fea(s)ts of Memory*. Madison: University of Wisconsin Press, 1992.

Davidoff, Leonore and Catherine Hall. *Family Fortunes: Men and Women in the English Middle Class 1780–1850*. London: Century Hamilton, 1987.

Davidson, Phebe. *Religious Impulse in Selected Autobiographies of American Women*. Lewiston: E. Mellen Press, 1993.

Davis, Tracy. *Actresses as Working Women: Their Social Identity in Victorian Culture*. London & New York: Routledge & Co., 1991.

Dolan, Marc. *Modern Lives: a Cultural Re-reading of the "Lost Generation."* West Lafayette: Purdue University Press, 1996.

Dyhouse, Carol. *Girls Growing Up in Late Victorian and Edwardian England.* Boston: Routledge and Kegan Paul, 1981.

———. "Mothers and Daughters in the Middle-Class Home, c.1870–1914." In *Labour and Love: Women's Experience of Home and Family, 1850–1940*, Jane Lewis, ed. Oxford and New York: Basil Blackwell Ltd, 1986.

Etter-Lewis, Gwendolyn and Michele Foster, eds. *Unrelated Kin: Race and Gender in Women's Personal Narratives*. New York: Routledge & Co., 1996.

Finney, Brian. *The Inner I: British Literary Autobiography of the Twentieth Century*. New York: Oxford University Press, 1985.

Folkenflik, Robert. *The Culture of Autobiography: Constructions of Self-Representation*. Stanford: Stanford University Press, 1993.

Fowler, Lois J. and David H. Fowler. *Revelations of Self: American Women in Autobiography*. Albany: State University of New York Press, 1990.

Friedman, Susan. "Women's Autobiographical Selves: Theory and Practice." In *The Private Self: Theory and Practice of Women's Autobiographical Writings*, Shari Benstock, ed. Chapel Hill and London: University of North Carolina Press, 1988, pp. 34-62.

Gagnier, Regenia. *Subjectivities: A History of Self-Representation in Britain 1832–1920*. Oxford: Oxford University Press, 1991.

Gilmore, Leigh. *Autobiographics: a Feminist Theory of Women's Self-Representation*. Ithaca: Cornell University Press, 1994.

Gorham, Deborah. *The Victorian Girl and the Feminine Ideal*. London: Croom Helm, 1982.

Goodwin, James. *Autobiography: the Self Made Text.* New York: Twayne Publishers, 1993.

Gusdorf, Georges. "Conditions and Limits of Autobiography." In *Autobiography: Essays Theoretical and Critical,* James Olney, ed. Princeton: Princeton University Press, 1976. pp. 28-48.

Hackett, Nan. *XIX Century British Working Class Autobiographies*. New York: AMS Press, 1985.

Heilbrun, Carolyn. *Writing a Woman's Life*. New York: W.W. Norton and Co., 1988.

Holcombe, Lee. *Victorian Ladies at Work: Middle-Class Working Women in England and Wales 1850–1914*. Hamden: Archon Books, 1973.

Hollis, Patricia. *Ladies Elect: Women in English Local Government 1865–1914*. Oxford: Clarendon Press, 1987.

Holton, Sandra Stanley. Feminism and Democracy: Women's Suffrage and Reform Politics in Britain, 1900–1918. Cambridge: Cambridge University Press, 1986.

Hooton, Joy. *Stories of Herself When Young: Autobiographies of Childhood by Australian Women*. Melbourne and Oxford: Oxford University Press, 1990.

Humm, Maggie. "Feminist Literary Criticism in America and England." In *Women's Writing: A Challenge to Theory*, Moira Monteith, ed. Sussex: Harvester Press, 1986.

Jalland, Pat. *Women, Marriage and Politics (1860–1914)*. Oxford and New York: Oxford University Press, 1988.

Jay, Paul. *Being in the Text: Self-Representation from Wordsworth to Roland Barthes*. Ithaca: Cornell University Press, 1984.

Jelinek, Estelle C., ed. *Women's Autobiography: Essays in Criticism*. Bloomington: Indiana University Press, 1980.

———. *The Tradition of Women's Autobiography: From Antiquity to the Present*. Boston: Twayne Publishers, 1986.

John, Angela, ed. *Unequal Opportunities: Women's Employment in England 1800–1918*. Oxford: Basil Blackwell Ltd., 1986.

Kanner, Barbara, ed. "Introduction" and "Autobiographical Reflections on Being a Woman." In *Women in English Social History 1800–1914: A Guide to Research*, vol. I. New York: Garland Publishing, 1990, pp.1–26, 56–70.

———, ed. "Introduction." In *Women in English Social History, 1800–1914: A Guide to Research,* vol. III. New York: Garland Publishing, 1987, pp. 1–38.

———, ed. "Introduction." In *Women of England: From Anglo-Saxon Times to the Present*. Hamden, Connecticut: Archon Books, 1979, pp. 9–31.

Kent, Susan Kingsley. *Making Peace: The Reconstruction of Gender in Interwar Britain*. Princeton: Princeton University Press, 1993.

Landow, George P., ed. *Approaches to Victorian Autobiography*. Athens, Ohio: Ohio University Press, 1979.

Lejeune, Philippe. *On Autobiography*. Minneapolis: University of Minnesota Press, 1989.

Levine, Philippa. *Victorian Feminism*. London: Hutchinson, 1987.

Levy, Anita. *Other Women: The Writing of Class, Race and Gender 1832–1898*. Princeton: Princeton University Press, 1991.

Lewis, Jane, ed. *Labour and Love: Women's Experience of Home and Family, 1850–1940*. Oxford: Basil Blackwell Ltd., 1986.

———. *Women in England 1870–1950: Sexual Division and Social Change*. Bloomington: Indiana University Press, 1984.

Lionnet, Françoise. *Autobiographical Voices: Race, Gender, Self-Portraiture*. Ithaca: Cornell University Press, 1989.

MacMillan, Margaret. *Women of the Raj*. New York: Thames & Hudson, 1988.

Marcus, Laura. *Autobiographical Discourse: Theory, Criticism, Practice*. Manchester: Manchester University Press, 1994.

Mason, Mary G. "The Other Voice: Autobiographies of Women Writers." In *Autobiography: Essays Theoretical and Critical*, James Olney, ed. Princeton: Princeton University Press, 1980, pp. 207–35.

———. *British Autobiographies: An Annotated Bibliography of British Autobiographies:*

Published or Written Before 1951. Berkeley: University of California Press, 1955. Reprinted Hamden: Shoestring Press, 1968.

Matthews, William. *British Diaries: An Annotated Bibliography of British Diaries Written between 1442 and 1942*. Berkeley: University of California Press, 1950.

Melman, Billie. *Women's Orients: English Women and the Middle East, 1718–1918: Sexuality, Religion and Work*. Ann Arbor: University of Michigan Press, 1992.

Miller, Nancy K. *Getting Personal: Feminist Occasions and other Autobiographical Acts*. New York: Routledge, 1991.

Monteith, Moira, ed. *Women's Writing: A Challenge to Theory*. Sussex: Harvester Press, 1986.

Neuman, Shirley, ed. *Autobiography and Questions of Gender*. London and Portland: F. Cass, 1991.

Nord, Deborah Epstein. *The Apprenticeship of Beatrice Webb*. Amherst: University of Massachusetts, 1985.

Nussbaum, Felicity A. *The Autobiographical Subject: Gender and Ideology in Eighteenth-Century England*. Baltimore: The Johns Hopkins University Press, 1989.

Okely, Judith and Helen Callaway. *Anthropology and Autobiography*. London and New York: Routledge & Co., 1992.

Olney, James. *Metaphors of Self: The Meaning of Autobiography*. Princeton: Princeton University Press, 1972.

———. *Autobiography: Essays Theoretical and Critical*. Princeton: Princeton University Press, 1980.

———. *Studies in Autobiography*. New York: Oxford University Press, 1988.

Personal Narratives Group, eds. *Interpreting Women's Lives: Feminist Theory and Personal Narratives*. Bloomington: Indiana University Press, 1989.

Peterson, Linda H. *Victorian Autobiography: The Tradition of Self-Interpretation*. New Haven: Yale University Press, 1986.

Porter, Bernard. *The Lion's Share: A Short History of British Imperialism, 1850–1970*. London: Longman Group, 1975.

Prochaska, F.K. *Women and Philanthropy in Nineteenth-Century England*. Oxford: Oxford University Press, 1980.

Rendall, Jane, ed. *Equal or Different? Women's Politics 1800–1914*. Oxford: Basil Blackwell Ltd., 1987.

Robe, Margaret. "Conceiving a Self in Autobiography by Women: Virginia Woolf, Violette Leduc, and Anaïs Nin." Ph.D. dissertation. Los Angeles: University of California, 1987.

Romero, Patricia W. *Women's Voices on Africa and Africans: A Century of Travel Writings*. Princeton: Markus Wiener Publications, 1992.

Rosenwald, George C. and Richard L. Ochberg, eds. *Storied Lives: The Cultural Politics of Self-Understanding*. New Haven: Yale University Press, 1992.

Ross, Ellen. "'Fierce Questions and Taunts': Married Life in Working-Class London, 1870–1914." In *Feminist Studies*, Vol. 8, 1982, pp. 575–602.

———. *Love and Toil: Motherhood in Outcast London, 1870–1918*. New York and Oxford: Oxford University Press, 1993.

Rowbotham, Sheila. *Woman's Consciousness, Man's World*. Harmondsworth: Penguin, 1973.

Sanders, Valerie. *The Private Lives of Victorian Women: Autobiography in 19th Century England*. New York: Harvester Wheatsheaf, 1989.

Sturrock, John. *The Language of Autobiography: Studies in the First Person Singular*. Cambridge and New York: Cambridge University Press, 1993.

Smith, Harold L. *British Feminism in the Twentieth Century*. Amherst: University of Massachusetts Press, 1990.

Smith, Sidonie. *A Poetics of Women's Autobiography: Marginality and the Fictions of Self-Representation*. Bloomington: Indiana University Press, 1987.

Smith, Sidonie and Julia Watson, eds. *De/colonizing the Subject: the Politics of Gender in Women's Autobiography*. Minneapolis: University of Minnesota Press, 1992.

———, eds. *Getting a Life: Everyday Uses of Autobiography*. Minneapolis: University of Minnesota Press, 1996.

———. *Subjectivity, Identity, and the Body: Women's Autobiographical Practices in the Twentieth Century*. Bloomington: Indiana University Press, 1993.

Snarey, John R. *How Fathers Care for the Next Generation: a Four-Decade Study*. Cambridge: Harvard University Press, 1993.

Spengemann, William C. *The Forms of Autobiography: Episodes in the History of a Literary Genre*. New Haven: Yale University Press, 1980.

Stanley, Liz. *The Autobiographical I: The Theory and Practice of Feminist Autobiography*. New York: Manchester University Press, 1992.

Stanton, Donna C. and Jeanine Parisier Plottel, eds. *The Female Autograph*. Chicago: University of Chicago Press, 1984.

Steedman, Carolyn. "Biographical Questions; Fictions of the Self." In *Childhood, Culture and Class in Britain: Margaret McMillan, 1860–1931*. New Brunswick: Rutgers University Press, 1990.

Stimpson, Catharine R. "On Feminist Criticism." In *What is Criticism?* Paul Hernadi, ed. Bloomington: Indiana University Press, 1981.

Stone, Gilbert. *Women War Workers: accounts contributed by representative workers of the work done by women in the more important branches of war employment*. London: G.G. Harrap & Co., 1917.

Stull, James N. *Literary Selves: Autobiography and Contemporary American Nonfiction*. Westport, Connecticut: Greenwood Press, 1993.

Turner, Cheryl. *Living by the Pen: Women Writers in the Eighteenth Century*. New York: Routledge, 1992.

Vicinus, Martha, ed. "Introduction: New Trends in the Study of the Victorian Woman." In *A Widening Sphere: Changing Roles of Victorian Women*. Bloomington: Indiana University Press, 1977.

———. *Independent Women: Work and Community for Single Women: 1850–1920*. London: Virago Press, 1985.

Vincent, David. *Bread, Knowledge and Freedom: A Study of Nineteenth-Century Working Class Autobiography*. London: Europa Press, 1981.

Voss, Norine Kay. *Saying the Unsayable: A Study of Selected American Women's Autobiographies*. Bloomington: Indiana University Press, 1983.

Veeser, H. Aram. *Confessions of the Critics: Authors, Readers, and Autobiography*. New York: Routledge & Co., 1996.

Wachter, Phyllis. E. "Bibliography of Works about Life-Writing Which Links the Decades." In *Biography*, Vol. 14(4), Fall 1991, pp. 379–386.

Weeks, Jeffrey. "A Survey of Primary Sources and Archives for the History of Early Twentieth-Century English Women." In *The Women of England: From*

Anglo-Saxon Times to the Present, Barbara Kanner, ed. Hamden, Connecticut: Archon Books, 1979, pp. 318–418.

Wiltsher, Anne. *Most Dangerous Women: Feminist Peace Campaigners of the Great War*. London: Pandora Press, 1985.

Wood, Mary Elene. T*he Writing on the Wall: Women's Autobiography and the Asylum*. Urbana: University of Illinois Press, 1994.

Woolf, Virginia. "Diary: Vol. II." In *Women and Writing*, Michelle Barrett, ed. London: Women's Press, 1979.

Yalom, Marilyn. *Blood Sisters: The French Revolution in Women's Memory*. New York: Basic Books, 1993.

Author Index by Twenty-Year Cohorts

At the end of each author's index entry is a number in boldface that corresponds to her entry number in the text.

I. 1701–1720

Ashbridge, Elizabeth. 1713–1755. Religionist (Quaker convert); teacher; indentured servant; preacher; emigrant (U.S.). Middle class. **44**

Charke, Charlotte. 1713–1760. Actress (stage); playwright; novelist; cross-dresser. Widow. Middle class. **216**

Pilkington, Laetitia. c.1706–1750. Anglo-Irish. Poet; pamphleteer; secretary; prison inmate; physician's daughter. Upper middle class. **754**

II. 1721–1740

Candler, Ann. 1740–1814. Workhouse inmate; poet. Working class. **202**

Hopwood, D. Caroline. c.1725–c.1800. Religionist (Quaker convert); teacher; domestic servant. Lower middle class. **202**

Pearson, Jane. c.1735–1816. Religionist (Quaker); preacher. Lower middle class. **739**

Phillips, Catherine. 1727–1794. Religionist (Quaker); preacher; clergyman's daughter. Widow. Middle class. **750**

Robertson, Hannah. 1724–c.1800. Scottish. Shopkeeper; tavern manager; prison inmate; society woman. Widow. Upper middle class. **794**

Saxby, Mary. 1738–d.a.1794. Transient; farm laborer; religionist (Methodist convert); preacher. Widow. Working class. **820**

Turner, Mrs. Joanna. 1732–1785. Religionist (Methodist); preacher. Lower middle class. **794**

III. 1741–1760

Alexander, Mary. 1760–1809. Religionist (Quaker); preacher; clergywoman's daughter. Single. Lower middle class. **4**

Cappe, Catherine. 1744–1821. Social reformer; clergyman's daughter; clergyman's spouse; religionist (Anglican, Evangelical); teacher (Sunday school); religious/spiritual writer. Widow. Middle class. **204**

IV. 1761–1780

V. 1781–1800

VI. 1801–1820

tionist; diarist; poet; foreign resident (U.S.). Divorcée. Upper middle class. **520**

Kirby, Georgiana. 1818–1887. Social reformer; emigrant (Canada, U.S.); teacher; governess; abolitionist. Middle class. **532**

Kirby, Mary. 1817–1893. Children's author; short storyist; clergyman's spouse. Middle class. **533**

Le Breton, Anna Letitia. 1808–1885. Biographer; publisher's assistant; society woman. Upper middle class. **548**

Lucy, Mary Elizabeth. 1803–1889. Welsh. Family historian. Widow. Upper class. **594**

Martineau, Harriet. 1802–1876. Social reformer; journalist; abolitionist; essayist; economist; feminist; public speaker. Middle class. **637–638**

Moodie, Susanna. 1803–1885. Emigrant (Canada); novelist; poet; pioneer; farmer; cultural historian. Rural gentry. **670–671**

Richardson, Eliza. c.1820–?. Religionist (Roman Catholic convert; anti-Catholic); religious/spiritual writer. Single. Middle class. **787**

Seacole, Mary. 1805–1881. Born in Jamaica. Nurse (Crimean War); hotel administrator; shopkeeper; miner. Widow. Lower middle class. **830**

Sewell, Elizabeth Missing. 1815–1906. Novelist; educator; religious/spiritual writer; historian; school founder. Middle class. **835**

Smith, Eliza. c.1810–?. Irish. Thief; convicted transportee; prison inmate; domestic servant; seamstress. Working class. **863**

Storie, Elizabeth. 1818–?. Scottish. Physically handicapped; dressmaker; milliner. Single. Lower middle class. **912**

Thompson, Jemima. 1813–1906. Religionist (Evangelical); religious/spiritual writer; missionary (India); children's author; songwriter; editor; teacher; organizer of societies (professional). Middle class. **942**

Twining, Louisa. 1820–1912. Social reformer; philanthropist; pamphleteer; journalist; political activist; feminist; Poor Law Guardian; organizer (philanthropic); temperance activist. Single. Upper class. **966**

Ward, Annie Wadsworth. 1819–?. Nurse; mental health worker; nursemaid; farm child. Middle class. **992**

VII. 1821–1840

Anon. (*Up and Down the World, by a Passionate Pilgrim*). c.1840–d.a.1916. Scottish. Foreign resident (Italy, Philippines, China); religionist (Presbyterian). Upper middle class. **16**

Ansell, Evelyn. c.1830–?. Colonialist (Australia, New Zealand); miner; teacher; school administrator. Middle class. **38**

Bancroft, Marie Effie. 1839–1921. Actress (child, stage); theatre manager; singer (popular). Middle class. **68–69**

Barr, Amelia Edith. 1831–1919. Novelist; emigrant (U.S.); journalist; feminist. Widow. Middle class. **76**

Bayley, Emily, Lady. 1830–d.a.1880. Anglo-Indian. Colonialist (India); civil servant's spouse; memsahib. Upper class. **84**

Becher, Augusta. 1830–1909. Born on shipboard. Colonialist (India); military spouse; memsahib. Upper middle class. **85**

Betham-Edwards, Matilda. 1836–1919. Travel writer; novelist; antivivisectionist; foreign resident (France). Rural gentry. **98–104**

Blackwell, Elizabeth, M.D. 1821–1910. Physician; academic; school founder; foreign resident (U.S.); feminist. Middle class. **110**

Bloomfield, Georgiana, Baroness Bloomfield. 1822–1905. Diplomat's spouse; foreign resident (Russia). Aristocracy. **126**

Blunt, Fanny, Lady. 1840–d.a.1901. Born in Turkey. Diplomat's daughter; diplomat's spouse; foreign resident (Turkey, U.S.). Upper class. **127**

India, South Pacific, U.S.); travel writer; artist (painter); biographer; journalist. Single. Upper class. **398**
Haldane, Mary Elizabeth. 1825–1925. Society woman; feminist. Widow. Upper middle class. **430**
Hanbury, Charlotte. 1830–1900. Philanthropist; social reformer; religionist (Quaker, anti-Catholic). Single. Middle class. **440**
Hardy, Emma Lavinia. 1840–1912. Novelist; poet. Middle class. **441**
Heckford, Sarah. 1839–1903. Trader (farm produce); farmer; governess; emigrant (South Africa); physician's spouse. Widow. Middle class. **449**
Holmes, Alice A. 1821–d.a.1888. Emigrant (U.S.); poet; teacher (music); physically handicapped. Lower middle class. **463**
Johnston, Ellen. c.1831–?. Scottish. Factory worker; poet. Single. Working class. **508**
Leonowens, Anna. 1831–1914. Anglo-Indian. Governess; teacher; foreign resident (Siam). Widow. Middle class. **566**
Linton, Eliza Lynn. 1822–1898. Journalist; anti-feminist; novelist; essayist; clergyman's daughter; lesbian. Middle class. **581–582**
Lloyd, Anna. 1837–1925. Philanthropist; feminist; Poor Law Guardian; clergywoman's daughter; charitable volunteer. Single. Middle class. **584**
Lumsden, Dame Louisa. 1840–1935. Scottish. Educator; academic; feminist; suffragist; poet; antivivisectionist; animal welfare activist; editor. Single. Upper class. **595**
Malleson, Elizabeth. 1828–1916. Educator; feminist; teacher; social reformer; publisher; journalist; education issues writer. Middle class. **616**
Nevill, Lady Dorothy Fanny. 1826–1913. Society woman; art collector; diarist; anti-suffragist. Aristocracy. **694–696**
Noble, Margery Durham, Lady. 1828–d.a.1922. Canadian. Society woman; civil servant's spouse. Upper class. **710**
North, Marianne. 1830–1890. Artist (painter); traveler (world); amateur botanist; diarist. Single. Upper class. **711–712**
Oliphant, Margaret. 1828–1897. Scottish. Novelist; historian; biographer; literary critic. Widow. Middle class. **719**
O'Neill, Ellen. 1833–?. Irish. Thief; mill worker; domestic servant; prison inmate; convicted transportee. Working class. **722**
Ormerod, Eleanor Anne. 1828–1901. Scientist; entomologist; scientific writer. Single. Upper middle class. **724**
Palmer, Bessie. 1831–d.a.1904. Singer (concerts, opera); philanthropist. Single. Middle class. **727**
Pickering, Anna Maria Wilhelmina. 1824–1901. Society woman. Rural gentry. **751**
Priestley, Eliza. c.1837–?. Physician's spouse. Widow. Upper class. **772**
Reynolds, Mrs. Herbert. c.1835–d.a.1883. Memsahib; foreign resident (India); civil servant's spouse. Middle class. **784**
Ritchie, Anne Isabella, Lady. 1837–1919. Literary critic; novelist; essayist; novelist's daughter. Upper middle class. **793**
Robinson, Sarah. 1834–d.a.1914. Temperance activist; philanthropist; social reformer; religionist (Evangelical Protestant); physically handicapped; publisher; pamphleteer; public speaker. Single. Middle class. **796**
Sellar, Eleanor. 1829–d.a.1890. Scottish; born in Normandy, France. Society woman; traveler (Europe). Widow. Upper class. **832**
Simpson, Mary Charlotte Mair. c.1825–d.a.1899. Biographer; historian; editor. Upper middle class. **849**
Sitwell, Georgiana Caroline. 1824–1900. Artist. Upper class. **854**
Smith, Mary. 1822–1899. Teacher; schoolmistress; governess; suffragist; poet; journalist; clerk; religionist (Nonconformist); school founder; public speaker; temperance activist. Single. Lower middle class. **867**

Soldene, Emily. 1840–1912. Singer (opera); theatrical director; theatrical producer; biographer. Middle class. **874**

Spence, Catherine Helen. 1825–1910. Scottish. Social reformer; child welfare activist; political writer; novelist; public speaker; emigrant (Australia); politician; journalist; preacher; governess; religionist (Unitarian); feminist; suffragist. Single. Rural farming class. **881**

Squirrell, Mary Elizabeth. 1838–?. Clairvoyant/psychic; physically handicapped. Single. Lower middle class. **887**

Stannard, M. c.1830–d.a.1873. Nurse; midwife; shopkeeper; foreign resident (Australia); paid companion; traveler (Canada, U.S.); laundry worker; seamstress; governess; dairymaid; teacher (Sunday school); hospital administrator. Widow. Middle class. **889**

Stawell, Mary Frances Elizabeth, Lady. 1830–d.a.1889. Colonialist (Australia); politician's spouse; emigrant (Australia). Widow. Upper class. **895**

Stenhouse, Fanny. 1829–d.a.1872. Jerseywoman. Religionist (Mormon convert, anti-Mormon); missionary; teacher; governess; emigrant (U.S.). Lower middle class. **899**

Story, Janet Leith. 1828–?. Anglo-Indian. Novelist; teacher (Sunday school); clergyman's spouse. Upper middle class. **913–914**

Tytler, Harriet. 1828–1907. Anglo-Indian. Memsahib; military spouse; foreign resident (India); artist (painter); teacher (art). Middle class. **974**

Warburton, Katherine Anne. 1840–d.a.1912. Religionist (Anglican); nun (Anglican sister); teacher; clergyman's daughter; charitable volunteer; organizer (philanthropic). Single. Upper middle class. **990–991**

Ward, Mrs. E.M. 1832–1924. Artist (painter); teacher (art); artist's daughter. Widow. Upper middle class. **993–994**

Weston, Agnes Elizabeth. 1840–1918. Temperance activist; missionary; teacher (Sunday school); social reformer; pamphleteer; organizer (philanthropic, religious); preacher; religionist (Anglican). Single. Middle class. **1016**

Winkworth, Susanna. 1820–1884. Translator; editor; religionist (Unitarian); biographer. Single. Middle class. **1028**

Wordsworth, Elizabeth. 1840–1932. Educator; education activist; headmistress; religious/spiritual writer; biographer. Single. Middle class. **1032**

Youmans, Letitia. 1827–1896. Canadian. Temperance activist; social reformer; school founder; teacher; teacher (Sunday school); philanthropist; clergyman's daughter; farmer; public speaker. Widow. Middle class; married into rural farming class. **1038**

VIII. 1841–1860

Allison, Susan Louisa. 1845–1937. Anglo-Indian (Ceylon). Emigrant (Canada); pioneer; farmer; poet. Middle class. **10**

Anon. (Miss M.E.). c.1856–s.l.1918. Religionist (Roman Catholic convert); social reformer; philanthropist; temperance activist; short storyist. Upper middle class. **25**

Anon. (Panton, Jane Ellen). 1848–1923. Gossip writer; columnist; novelist; artist's daughter; artist's model. Upper middle class. **32–35**

Anon. (Sturge, Mary Charlotte). 1860–?. Religionist (Quaker). Single. Middle class. **36**

Balfour, Lady Frances. 1858–1930. Suffragist; social reformer; biographer; feminist activist. Aristocracy. **67**

Barrington, Charlotte, Viscountess Barrington. 1850–1935. Philanthropist; traveler (South Africa, Egypt). Widow. Upper class; married into aristocracy. **79**

Benson, Gertrude, Lady. 1860–1946. Anglo-Indian. Actress (stage); theatrical producer; costume designer; choreographer; WWI volunteer. Upper middle class. **91**

Besant, Annie. 1847–1933. Social reformer; feminist activist; Theosophist; birth control activist; religious/spiritual writer; physician's daughter. Upper middle class. **96–97**

Bond, Jessie Charlotte. 1853–1942. Singer (popular); actress (stage). Widow. Lower middle class; married into middle class. **130**

Brooke, Margaret Alice, 1st Ranee of Sarawak. 1849–1936. Born in France. Ranee (royal colonial wife); society woman; travel writer; feminist; foreign resident (Malaysia). Middle class; married into aristocracy. **158–159**

Brown, Mary Solomon. 1847–1935. Anglo-South African. Philanthropist; temperance activist; political activist; social reformer; editor; Poor Law Guardian; suffragist; teacher (Sunday school). Middle class. **168**

Burrows, Mrs. ?. c.1840–?. Farm laborer; factory worker. Working class. **179**

Burstall, Sarah Annie. 1859–1939. Scottish. Teacher; educator; academic; headmistress; justice of the peace; education issues writer; education activist; religious/spiritual writer. Single. Middle class. **180**

Butler, Elizabeth Southerden, Lady. 1850–1933. Born in Switzerland. Artist (painter); military spouse; society woman. Upper middle class. **183**

Carr, Alice. 1850—s.l.1915. Born in Italy. Costume designer; clergyman's daughter; foreign resident (Italy); miscellaneous writer. Middle class; married into upper class. **207**

Child-Villiers, Margaret, Countess of Jersey. 1849–1945. Society woman; diplomat's spouse; traveler (world). Aristocracy. **223x**

Cholmondeley, Mary. 1859–1925. Novelist; clergyman's daughter. Single. Middle class. **224**

Corkran, Henriette. c.1850–1911. Irish; born in France. Artist (painter). Upper class. **252–253**

Deichmann, Hilda Elizabeth, Baroness. 1848–d.a.1925. Anglo-Prussian. Spiritualist; religious/spiritual writer. Widow. Aristocracy. **289**

Diehl, Alice Georgina. 1844–1912. Musician (pianist, violinist); novelist; journalist; short storyist; teacher (music). Upper middle class. **300–301**

Dixon, Ella Hepworth. 1857–1932. Novelist; journalist; short storyist; playwright; WWI volunteer; artist (painter); editor; feminist. Single. Middle class. **302**

Fane, Lady Augusta Fanny. 1858–1950. Society woman; horsewoman. Aristocracy. **331**

Fawcett, Dame Millicent. 1847–1929. Suffrage leader; political activist; political writer; organizer of societies (social reform); novelist; biographer; magistrate; academic's spouse. Widow. Upper middle class. **336**

Flower, Constance, Baroness Battersea. 1843–1931. Philanthropist; society woman; political activist; Jewish activist; politician's spouse; political hostess; historian. Upper class; married into aristocracy. **347**

Gell, Edith Mary. 1860–d.a.1920. Novelist; philanthropist; Oxford hostess; suffragist. Aristocracy. **379**

Gilmore, Isabella. 1842–1923. Deaconess; religionist (Anglican); nurse. Widow. Middle class. **386**

Glover, Elizabeth Rosetta, Lady. c.1855–1927. Diplomat's spouse; foreign resident (Newfoundland, Antigua, Germany); biographer; women's issues author; traveler (Egypt, U.S., India, Burma, Ceylon). Widow. Upper class. **389**

Gordon, Ishbel Maria, Marchioness of Aberdeen and Temair. 1857–1939. Philanthropist; political hostess; political activist; travel writer; foreign resident (Canada); feminist; organizer of societies (philanthropic); politician's wife. Aristocracy. **393–395**

Mayo, Isabella Fyvie. 1843–1914. Novelist; journalist; editor; copyist; businesswoman; translator; antivivisectionist; animal welfare activist. Widow. Middle class. **642–643**

Menzies, Amy Charlotte. c.1850–d.a.1917. Military spouse; colonialist (India, Egypt); cultural historian; memsahib; society woman. Rural gentry. **27–31**

Murray, Helen. c.1850–d.a.1916. Teacher; teacher (Sunday school); religionist (Huguenot); clergyman's daughter; education activist. Single. Middle class. **686**

Nevinson, Margaret Wynne. 1857–1932. Justice of the peace; Poor Law Guardian; political writer; short storyist; journalist; feminist; suffragist; public speaker; WWI volunteer; teacher; governess; clergyman's daughter. Middle class. **697**

Ogilvie, Mary I. 1859–d.a.1952. Scottish. Philanthropist; school trustee; traveler (Europe, South U.S., South Africa, Australia). Single. Upper middle class. **718**

Pankhurst, Emmeline. 1858–1928. Feminist activist; suffragist, militant; suffrage leader; public speaker; social reformer; organizer of societies (political); Poor Law Guardian; school trustee; prison inmate; political conspirator. Middle class. **730**

Pearl, Cora. 1842–1886. Courtesan; adventuress; foreign resident (France). Single. Middle class. **738**

Pinkham, Mrs. William Cyprian. 1849–?. Canadian. Pioneer; teacher (Sunday school); philanthropist; clergyman's spouse. Middle class. **755**

Pleydell-Bouverie, Helen, Countess of Radnor. 1846–1929. Singer (concerts); composer; organizer (musical); politician's spouse; anti–suffragist; clergyman's daughter. Widow. Middle class; married into aristocracy. **762**

Praed, Rosa Caroline. 1851–1935. Australian. Novelist; spiritualist; religious/spiritual writer. Upper class. **771**

Ravenhill, Alice. 1859–1954. Educator; public speaker; social reformer; sanitary inspector; emigrant (Canada); education issues writer; cultural historian; teacher; organizer of societies (professional). Middle class. **780**

Rogers, Clara Kathleen. 1844–1931. Singer (concerts, opera); teacher (music); musicianship writer; foreign resident (Italy, U.S.). Middle class. **798–799**

Ross, Janet Ann. 1842–1927. Journalist; translator; travel writer; foreign resident (Egypt); foreign correspondent; family historian. Upper class. **801–802**

Russell, Philippa. c.1855–d.a.1920. Society woman; lady-in-waiting; foreign resident (France, Germany). Widow. Upper class. **811**

Sandes, Elise. 1851–1934. Irish. Organizer of societies (philanthropic); missionary (India); philanthropist; religionist (Evangelical). Single. Lower middle class. **818**

Scharlieb, Dr. Mary Ann. 1844–1930. Physician; academic; women's issues author; health issues writer; feminist; WWI volunteer; foreign resident (India). Upper middle class. **825**

Smyth, Dame Ethel. 1858–1944. Composer; theatrical producer; feminist; suffragist, militant; foreign resident (Germany); travel writer; singer (concerts). Single. Upper middle class. **869–873**

Somerset, Ethel Jemima, Baroness Raglan. 1857–pre-1946. Society woman; philanthropist; civil servant's spouse. Widow. Aristocracy. **875**

Somerville, E. 1858–1949. Novelist; social historian; feminist; horsewoman; hunter; suffragist. Single. Upper middle class. **876**

Soothill, Lucy. 1858–1931. Foreign resident (China); diplomat's spouse; missionary; school founder. Rural farming class; married into upper middle class. **878**

Speed, Maude. c.1860–d.a.1929. Travel writer; sailor; clergyman's daughter. Upper middle class. **880**

IX. 1861–1880

Anon. (Haweis, Alethea Olive). c.1873–?. Artist's daughter. Upper middle class. **24**

Anon. ("Martha"). c.1866–?. Domestic servant. Orphan. Single. Working class. **19**

Anon. ("May," Miss). c.1865–?. Cornish. Foreign resident (Poland, Austria, Italy); governess (royal). Middle class. **26**

Anson, Lady Clodagh De La Poer. 1879–?. Philanthropist; WWI volunteer; charitable volunteer. Aristocracy. **39–40**

Aria, Eliza Davis. 1866–1931. Journalist; publisher; editor; artist's daughter; religionist (Jewish). Divorcée. Upper middle class. **43**

Ashby, Lillian Luker. 1876–s.l.1928. Anglo-Indian. Memsahib; civil servant's spouse (India); hotel administrator; restaurant manager; foreign resident (U.S.). Upper middle class. **45**

Ashwell, Lena. 1872–1957. Actress (stage); theatre manager; suffragist; theatrical writer; WWI volunteer; feminist; physician's spouse. Divorcée. Upper middle class. **47**

Asquith, Margot, Duchess of Oxford & Asquith. 1964–1945. Political hostess; society woman; novelist; anthologist; politician's spouse. Upper class; married into aristocracy. **50–54**

Bacon, Gertrude. 1874–1949. Public speaker; scientific writer; balloonist; biographer. Single. Middle class. **57**

Bailey, Alice Ann. 1880–1949. Theosophist; religious/spiritual writer; vegetarian; foreign resident (U.S.). Upper class. **61**

Banks, Emily. c.1867–d.a.1928. Missionary; missionary's spouse (Africa); emigrant (U.S.). Widow. Middle class. **71**

Barry, Alice Frances. 1861–1951. Essayist. Single. Middle class. **80**

Beddington, Frances Ethel. c.1880–?. Society woman; horsewoman. Upper class. **87**

Binnie-Clark, Georgina. 1871–c.1947. Emigrant (Canada); pioneer; farmer; journalist; feminist activist; political activist. Single. Middle class. **106–107**

Blomefield, Mathena. pre-1880–d.a.1944. Farm child; children's author. Rural farming class. **112–114**

Bondfield, Margaret Grace. 1873–1953. Politician; member of Parliament; cabinet minister; trade unionist; feminist activist; suffragist; religionist (Congregationalist). Single. Working class. **131**

Booth, Mary Warburton. 1872–c.1947. Missionary (India); deaconess; religionist (Wesleyan); social reformer. Single. Middle class. **134**

Broad, Lucy. c.1864–?. Cornish. Temperance activist; missionary; religionist (Methodist); traveler (world). Single. Working class. **155**

Bromet, Mary. c.1870–1937. Artist (sculptor); foreign resident (France, Germany, Italy, Switzerland); organizer (artistic). Upper class. **156**

Buchan, Anna. 1877–1948. Scottish. Novelist; WWI volunteer; charitable volunteer. Upper middle class. **173**

Byng, Marie Evelyn, Viscountess Byng. 1870–1949. Society woman; military spouse; novelist; WWI volunteer; foreign resident (South Africa, Canada). Widow. Upper class; married into aristocracy. **187**

Cameron, Agnes Dean. 1863–1912. Canadian. Explorer (Canada); teacher; school trustee. Single. Middle or upper middle class. **192**

Cameron, Charlotte. c.1880–1946. Travel writer; traveler (Africa, U.S., Canada, New Zealand, Australia). Middle class. **193**

Campbell, Beatrice Stella ("Mrs. Pat.") 1865–1940. Actress (stage); theatrical producer; traveler (Europe, U.S.). Upper middle class. **198**

Carbery, Mary. 1867–?. Novelist. Upper middle class. **205**

Carr, Emily. 1871–1945. Canadian. Artist (painter); teacher (art); boarding house owner. Middle class. **209–210**

Keen, Edith. c.1875–?. Governess; paid companion; foreign resident (Germany). Single. Middle class. **517**

Kelly, Ethel Knight. c.1879–?. Canadian. Travel writer; journalist; short storyist; playwright; foreign resident (India); actress (stage); WWI volunteer; society woman. Upper middle class. **519**

Kenney, Annie. 1879–1953. Suffragist, militant; mill worker; organizer (political); public speaker; prison inmate; Theosophist. Rural laboring class. **523**

Kerswell, Kate L. 1871–?. Religionist (Methodist); clergyman's spouse; missionary (Africa); preacher. Middle class. **527**

Keynes, Florence. 1861–1958. Social historian; politician (mayor); feminist; charitable volunteer; academic's spouse; clergyman's daughter. Upper middle class. **528**

Kingston, Gertrude. 1866–1937. Actress (stage); suffragist; playwright; WWI volunteer; nurse (WWI); philanthropist. Widow. Middle class. **531**

Knight, Dame Laura. 1877–1970. Artist (painter); teacher (art). Widow. Middle class; married into upper middle class. **536–537**

La Chard, Therese. 1874–?. Teacher; governess; socialist; political activist; ghostwriter; miscellaneous writer. Middle class. **539**

Larymore, Constance. c.1875–?. Military spouse; colonialist (Nigeria, India). Middle class. **543**

Le Blond, Mrs. Aubrey. 1861–1934. Anglo-Irish. Explorer; mountaineer; travel writer; philanthropist; military spouse; foreign resident (Switzerland); organizer of societies (cultural, women's clubs). Upper class. **547**

Lehmann, Liza. 1862–1918. Composer; singer (concerts); teacher (music); textbook writer. Upper middle class. **555**

Leslie, Mary. 1879–d.a.1967. Health administrator; midwife; feminist; foreign resident (China); philanthropist; clergyman's daughter. Middle class. **572–573**

Lodge, Eleanor Constance. 1869–1936. Educator; academic; historian; feminist; WWI volunteer; governess. Single. Upper middle class. **586**

Lowndes, Marie Adelaide. 1868–1947. Novelist; journalist; biographer; translator. Upper class. **589–592**

Lutyens, Lady Emily. 1874–1964. Theosophist; religious/spiritual writer; journalist; public speaker; feminist; suffragist; political activist; vegetarian; organizer of societies (political, religious); editor; traveler (India). Aristocracy. **597**

Lytton, Lady Constance. 1869–1923. Feminist; suffragist, militant; philanthropist; vegetarian; prison inmate. Single. Aristocracy. **601**

Macartney, Catherine Theodora, Lady. 1877–1949. Scottish. Civil servant's spouse (extended empire); foreign resident (China); traveler (Asia). Middle class; married into upper class. **602**

MacBride, Maud Gonne. 1865–1953. Irish nationalist; political activist; organizer of societies (political); politician; editor; publisher; intelligence agent; actress (stage); public speaker; prison inmate; political conspirator. Upper middle class. **603**

MacDonald Bosvill, Alice Edith, Lady. 1861–d.a.1929. Scottish. Singer (concerts); Scottish chieftain's wife; organizer (musical). Upper class. **605**

MacKay, Helen. 1876–1966. Novelist; short storyist; nurse (WWI); foreign resident (France). Middle class. **608**

Mackirdy, Olive Christian. c.1880–1914. Anglo-Indian. Philanthropist; novelist; journalist; social reformer; public speaker; social issues writer; temperance activist; Salvation Army worker; organizer of societies (philanthropic); actress (stage). Middle class. **612**

Markham, Violet Rosa. 1872–1959. Biographer; travel writer; novelist; political writer; social historian; school administrator; anti-suffragist; suffragist;

Newton, Frances Emily. 1872–d.a.1948. Missionary; teacher; foreign resident (Palestine); policewoman; teacher supervisor; WWI volunteer; philanthropist; social reformer; organizer of societies (women's clubs). Single. Middle class. **700**

Nicoll, Catherine Robertson, Lady. 1870–1960. Society woman; literary salon hostess; WWI volunteer. Middle class; married into upper class. **706–707**

Oakeley, Hilda. 1867–d.a.1931. Educator; academic; philosopher; suffragist, militant; foreign resident (Canada). Upper middle class. **715**

O'Brien, Kate. 1897–1974. Novelist; playwright; travel writer. Divorcée. Upper middle class. **716**

Ogilvy, Mabell Frances, Countess of Airlie. 1866–1956. Lady-in-waiting; historian; military spouse; philanthropist; society woman; pamphleteer; feminist; WWII volunteer. Aristocracy. **718**

Pankhurst, Dame Christabel. 1880–1958. Suffrage leader; suffragist, militant; feminist activist; lawyer; political activist; editor; social reformer; public speaker; WWI volunteer; organizer of societies (political). Upper middle class. **728–729**

Peel, Dorothy Constance. 1872–1934. Social historian; novelist; culinary author. Upper class. **743**

Pethick-Lawrence, Emmeline. 1867–1954. Feminist; suffragist; suffrage leader; social reformer; journalist; editor; publisher; businesswoman; philanthropist; prison inmate; academic's spouse; dressmaker; organizer of societies (political). Upper middle class. **748**

Petre, Maud Dominica Mary. 1863–1942. Religionist (Roman Catholic); biographer; religious/spiritual writer; philosopher; nun (Roman Catholic). Upper class. **749**

Picton-Turbervill, Edith. 1872–1960. Missionary (India); religious/spiritual writer; public speaker; organizer of societies (women's clubs); philanthropist; politician; member of Parliament; social reformer; factory inspector; religionist (Anglican); religionist (Evangelical); feminist. Middle class. **752–753**

Pless, Daisy, Princess of. 1873–1943. Princess; nurse (WWI); foreign resident (Germany). Upper class; married into royalty. **760–761**

Plunkett, Elizabeth, Countess of Fingall. 1866–1944. Irish. Society woman; feminist. Upper class; married into aristocracy. **763**

Pollock, Alice. 1868–d.a.1971. Clairvoyant/psychic. Widow. Upper middle class. **764**

Procter, Zoe. 1867–c.1959. Feminist; suffragist, militant; teacher (Sunday school); editor; secretary; prison inmate. Single. Middle class. **774**

Repington, Mary. 1868–d.a.1925. Foreign resident (Egypt); mistress; secretary; artist's grandchild. Upper class. **783**

Richardson, Ethel M. 1867–d.a.1930. Novelist; WWI volunteer; nurse (WWI); Red Cross worker. Upper class. **788**

Roby, Marguerite. c.1875–?. Traveler (Africa, China, U.S., South Pacific Islands). Middle class. **797**

Royden, Agnes Maude. 1876–1956. Feminist; preacher; suffragist; religionist (Anglican); public speaker; political activist; organizer (religious); religious/spiritual writer; pacifist; clergyman's spouse. Middle class. **803–805**

Ruck, Amy Roberta. 1878–1978. Anglo-Indian. Novelist; short storyist. Middle class. **806**

Sandes, Flora. 1876–1956. Soldier; nurse (WWI); public speaker. Single. Middle class. **819**

Sayers, Peig. 1873–1958. Irish. Storyteller. Widow. Rural laboring class. **821**

Scott, Ellen. c.1870–d.a.1925. Milliner; political activist; social reformer; organizer (labor); trade unionist; Justice of the Peace; suffragist; feminist; pacifist. Working class. **827**

X. 1881–1900

Anon. (Vince, Sydney). 1888–?. WWI factory inspector; foreign resident (U.S.). Single. Upper middle class. **37**

Arbenina, Stella Zoe, Baroness Meyendorff. c.1890–?. Born in Russia. Actress (stage, film); foreign resident (USSR); anti-Communist. Upper class; married into aristocracy. **41**

Asquith, Lady Cynthia. 1887–1960. Society woman; children's author; biographer; anthologist. Aristocracy. **48–49**

Athlone, Alice, Countess of (Princess of Great Britain). 1883–1981. Princess. Royalty. **56**

Baden-Powell, Olave, Lady Robert. 1889–1977. Philanthropist; organizer (Girl Guides); charitable volunteer. Widow. Rural gentry; married into aristocracy. **56**

Bagnold, Enid. 1889–1981. Novelist; playwright; poet; nurse (WWI). Upper middle class; married into upper class. **59–60**

Baillie, Isobel Douglas. 1895–1983. Scottish. Singer (concerts, opera); traveler (world). Working class; married into middle class. **63**

Baker, Daisy Ellen. 1894–s.l.1974. Domestic servant. Widow. Working class. **64**

Baldwin, Monica. c.1891–1975. Religionist (Roman Catholic); nun (Roman Catholic); ex-nun; munitions worker; aircraft designer; librarian; novelist. Upper middle class. **66**

Bankes, Violet. c.1900–s.l.1965. Novelist. Upper class. **70**

Barlow, Amy. 1893.–c.1960. Teacher; schoolmistress; genealogist; family historian. Single. Middle class. **73**

Barnes, Annie. 1887–d.a.1958. Suffragist, militant; political activist; social reformer; pupil-teacher. Widow. Working class. **74**

Bax, Emily. 1882–1943. Secretary; WWI volunteer; emigrant (U.S.). Single. Middle class. **83**

Beckwith, Lady Muriel. 1884–1961. Society woman. Aristocracy. **86**

Bedells, Phyllis. 1893–1985. Dancer; teacher (dance). Middle class. **88**

Bentinck, Lady Norah. 1881–1939. Novelist; philanthropist; society woman; singer (concerts). Widow. Aristocracy. **92**

Bentley, Phyllis. 1894–1977. Novelist; public speaker; feminist; literary critic; teacher. Upper middle class. **93**

Bentwich, Helen Caroline. 1892–1972. Jewish activist; Zionist; organizer (labor); socialist; social reformer; WWI volunteer; political activist; emigrant (Palestine); Zionist. Upper class. **94**

Black, Catherine. c.1883–?. Irish. Nurse. Single. Middle class. **108**

Bloom, Ursula. 1893–1984. Novelist; journalist; advice writer; clergyman's daughter; military spouse; dressmaker. Middle class; married into upper middle class. **115–125**

Bond, Alice. 1896–s.l.1980. Farm child; teacher; photographer. Widow. Rural laboring class. **129**

Booker, Beryl Lee. c.1888–?. Society woman; foreign resident (South Africa, India). Upper middle class. **132**

Booth, Doris Regina. c.1900–?. Australian. Planter's spouse; miner; foreign resident (New Guinea). Middle class. **133**

Bottome, Phyllis. 1882–1963. Novelist; religionist (anti-Catholic); traveler (U.S., Europe); clergyman's daughter. Middle class. **136–138**

Bowen, Elizabeth. 1899–1973. Irish. Novelist. Upper middle class. **140**

Bowen, Stella. c.1893–c.1955. Australian. Artist (painter); art critic. Single. Upper middle class. **141**

Braddock, Elizabeth. 1899–1970. Politician; member of Parliament; social activist; WWII volunteer; Communist; anti-Communist. Working class. **144**

Bradley, Josephine. 1900–1961. Dancer; teacher (dance); broadcaster. Widow. Middle class. **145**

Britnieva, Mary. 1893–1964. Born in Russia. Nurse (WWI); physician's spouse; foreign resident (Russia); translator. Widow. Upper class. **148–149**

Brittain, Vera. 1893–1970. Political activist; feminist; pacifist; public speaker; socialist; novelist; poet; nurse (WWI); WWII volunteer. Upper middle class. **150–153**

Brooke, Gladys, her Highness, the Dayang Muda of Sarawak. 1884–?. Society woman; farmer; shopkeeper. Upper class; married into aristocracy. **157**

Brooke, Sylvia Leonora, 2nd Ranee of Sarawak. 1885–1971. Ranee (royal colonial wife); society woman; novelist; playwright; foreign resident (Malaysia). Widow. Middle class; married into aristocracy. **160–161**

Brooksbank, Mary. 1897–1978. Scottish. Organizer (political); political activist; social reformer; Communist; poet; atheist. Widow. Working class. **162**

Brown, Jean Curtis. c.1900–?. Clergyman's daughter. Middle class. **166**

Brown, Lady Lilian Mabel. 1885–1946. Travel writer; explorer; traveler (Panama). Aristocracy. **167**

Brown, Winifred. 1899–1979. Feminist; aviator; sportswriter; nurse; WWI volunteer; traveler (Europe, Australia, New Zealand, Hawaii, Canada, South U.S.). Divorcée. Middle class. **169**

Bryher (pseud.; Annie Winifred Ellerman). 1894–1983. Poet; novelist; literary critic; travel writer. Upper middle class. **171–172**

Buchan, Susan Charlotte, Baroness Tweedsmuir. 1882–1977. Society woman; philanthropist; foreign resident (Italy, Canada). Aristocracy. **174–176**

Butler, Eliza Marian. 1885–1959. Academic; literary critic; mythologist; biographer. Upper middle class. **182**

Butts, Mary Frances. 1892–1937. Novelist; historian. Middle class. **186**

Byrne, Muriel St. Clare. 1895–1983. Historian; playwright; editor. Single. Upper middle class. **188**

"Caddie." 1900–s.l.1950. Australian. Barmaid; bookie; domestic servant. Working class. **189**

Caldwell, Taylor. 1900–1985. Novelist; foreign resident (U.S.). Divorcée. Middle class. **190**

Cameron, Clare. (pseud.; Winifred Wells). 1896–?. Poet; religionist (Buddhist convert); pacifist; clerk. Working class. **194**

Cameron, Lady Mary (pseud.). 1900–?. Actress (stage); nurse (WWI); secretary; traveler (South Africa, India, China, U.S.); clergyman's daughter. Middle class. **196**

Campbell, Beatrice, Baroness Glenavy. c.1888–d.a.1955. Irish. Artist (painter); teacher (art); artist's model. Lower middle class; married into aristocracy. **197**

Campbell, Margaret (Gabrielle Margaret Vere Campbell). 1886–1952. Novelist; biographer; playwright; children's author. Middle class. **200**

Canziani, Estella. 1887–1964. Artist (painter); teacher (art); social historian; religionist (Quaker convert); artist's daughter; WWI volunteer; travel writer; traveler (Europe, Morocco). Single. Upper middle class. **203**

Cheesman, Lucy Evelyn. 1881–1969. Scientist; entomologist; traveler (South Pacific); scientific writer. Single. Middle class. **219–220**

Chorley, Katharine Campbell, Baroness Chorley. 1897–1986. Miscellaneous writer; editor; political activist. Middle class; married into aristocracy. **225**

Christie, Dame Agatha. 1890–1976. Novelist; short storyist. Divorcée. Upper class. **226**

Clarke, Moma E. c.1882–?. Journalist; theatrical writer; art critic; fashion writer; travel writer; foreign resident (France). Upper middle class. **228**

Le Gallienne, Eva. 1899–1991. Actress (stage); theatrical producer; theatrical director; translator; foreign resident (U.S.); biographer; children's author; poet's daughter. Upper middle class. **553–554**

Leigh, Margaret Mary. 1894–s.l.1952. Academic; historian; farmer. Middle class. **557–559**

Leighton, Clare. 1900–s.l.1941. Artist; social historian; art critic; horticulture writer; novelist's daughter. Upper middle class. **560–561**

Leith-Ross, Sylvia. 1883–1980. Raised in France. Colonial administrator (Nigeria); linguist; cultural historian; WWI volunteer. Upper middle class. **562–563**

Lejeune, Caroline. 1897–1973. Film critic; journalist; playwright; screenwriter. Middle class. **564**

Leonard, Gladys Osborne. 1882–1926. Spiritualist; clairvoyant/psychic; vegetarian. Middle class. **565**

Leslie, Henrietta. 1884–?. Journalist; novelist; travel writer; suffragist, militant; social reformer; pacifist; charitable volunteer; feminist. Upper middle class. **569–571**

Lester, Muriel. 1883–1968. Philanthropist; missionary; religionist (Christian Scientist); teacher (Sunday school); socialist; pacifist; public speaker; WWI volunteer; organizer (religious). Single. Upper middle class. **574**

Lillie, Beatrice, Baroness Peel. 1898–1989. Actress (stage, music hall, radio, comic); broadcaster; cross-dresser. Middle class; married into aristocracy. **579**

Lloyd, Anne Gladys. 1889–?. Journalist; interpreter. Single. Middle class. **584**

Longbottom, Eva H. 1892–?. Singer (concerts); musician (pianist); teacher (music); songwriter; composer; physically handicapped; short storyist; columnist. Single. Middle class. **587**

Lynch, Patricia Nora. 1898–1972. Irish. Poet; short storyist. Lower middle class. **599**

Lyons, Dame Enid Muriel. 1897–1981. Politician's spouse; teacher. Widow. Rural laboring class; married into upper class. **600**

MacCarthy, Mary. 1882–1953. Biographer; novelist. Upper middle class. **604**

Mack, Marjorie. 1887–1982. Novelist; socialist; diarist. Middle class. **607**

Mackenzie, Faith Compton. 1882–1960. Novelist; biographer; short storyist; music critic; actress (stage); WWI volunteer. Upper middle class. **609–611**

Mackworth, Margaret Haig, Viscountess Rhondda. 1883–1958. Publisher; businesswoman; feminist activist; suffragist, militant; journalist; editor; secretary. Aristocracy. **613**

MacManus, Emily. 1886–1978. Hospital administrator; nurse; nurse (WWI); midwife; physician's daughter; foreign resident (Egypt). Single. Middle class. **614**

Malleson, Lady Constance. 1895–1975. Anglo-Irish. Actress (stage); political activist; pacifist; playwright; traveler (Europe, South Africa). Divorcée. Aristocracy. **615**

Mannin, Ethel. 1900–1984. Novelist; travel writer; short storyist; socialist; pacifist; vegetarian; editor; advertising writer; secretary. Middle class. **617–623**

Manning, Leah, Dame Elizabeth. 1886–1977. Academic's spouse; politician; member of Parliament; justice of the peace; political activist; teacher; socialist; factory manager; birth control activist; WWI volunteer; WWII volunteer; organizer (political); pacifist; philanthropist. Widow. Upper middle class. **624**

Marsh, Edith Ngaio. 1899–1982. New Zealander. Novelist; crime writer; playwright; theatrical producer; theatrical director; actress (stage); travel writer; traveler (South Africa, Europe). Single. Upper middle class. **631**

Perham, Dame Margery Freda. 1895–1982. Foreign resident (Africa); travel writer; political writer; journalist; teacher. Single. Upper middle class. **747**

Pitt, Frances. 1888–1964. Naturalist; nature writer; horsewoman; journalist; photographer; justice of the peace; animal welfare activist; hunter. Single. Upper middle class. **758–759**

Raber, Jessie. c.1888–?. Emigrant (Canada); pioneer; farmer; paid companion; clerk; hotel worker. Middle class. **775**

Ratcliffe, Dorothy Una. 1891–1967. Travel writer; local historian; folklorist; poet; traveler (Europe, New Zealand, South U.S.). Upper middle class. **779**

Raverat, Gwen. 1885–1957. Artist (painter, engraver); family historian; academic's daughter. Upper middle class. **781**

Rhys, Jean. 1890–1979. Born in the West Indies. Novelist; chorus girl; governess; WWI volunteer; foreign resident (Holland). Middle class. **786**

Richardson, Mary Raleigh. c.1890–?. Canadian. Feminist activist; suffragist, militant; political activist; journalist. Middle class. **789**

Riddell, Florence. c.1896–?. Teacher (art, dance); foreign resident (Kenya, India); headmistress; governess; landlady; novelist. Middle class. **790**

Rudkin, Mabel S. c.1890–?. Clergyman's spouse; social historian; WWI volunteer; organizer (youth). Middle class. **807**

Russell, Dora Winifred, Countess Russell. 1894–1986. Political writer; journalist; academic; socialist; feminist; educator; civil servant; political activist; WWII volunteer; foreign resident (China); academic's spouse; child welfare activist; birth control activist; public speaker; traveler (Russia). Widow. Upper class; married into aristocracy. **808–810**

Rutherford, Dame Margaret. 1892–1972. Actress (stage, film); teacher (music); philanthropist. Middle class. **812**

Sackville-West, the Hon. Victoria "Vita." 1892–1962. Novelist; poet; biographer; feminist; bisexual; cross-dresser; male impersonator; diplomat's spouse. Aristocracy. **813–814**

Salmond, Lady Monica Margaret. 1893–1983. Nurse (WWI); foreign resident (France); masseuse; x-ray technician. Aristocracy. **815**

Salt, Annie Gwendoline. 1887–s.l.1930. Clergyman's spouse; colonialist (New Zealand); charitable volunteer. Middle class. **816**

Scott, Ina. pre-1900–?. WWI volunteer; gardener; feminist. Class unknown. **828**

Scott, Mary Edith. 1888–s.l.1966. New Zealander. Novelist; journalist; librarian; postal worker; farmer; teacher. Middle class. **829**

Severn, Merlyn. c.1900–?. Photographer; artist (sculptor); journalist; foreign resident (Africa); WWII enlistee. Single. Middle class. **834**

Shannon, Kitty. c.1889–?. Artist's daughter; artist (painter); foreign resident (France, Holland, Australia). Upper class. **836**

Shepherd, Dolly. 1886–d.a.1982. Parachutist; WWI military officer; waitress; charitable volunteer; WWII volunteer. Widow. Middle class. **838**

Sheridan, Clare Consuelo. 1885–1970. Artist (sculptor); journalist; travel writer; novelist; traveler (Europe, Middle East, Mexico, U.S.); Communist sympathizer; religionist (Roman Catholic convert). Widow. Upper class. **839–841**

Sheridan, Lisa. 1893–1966. Photographer; traveler (Russia); foreign resident (France). Upper middle class. **842**

Simpson, Alyse. c.1900–?. Farmer; colonialist (Africa). Middle class. **847**

Simpson, Evelyn Mary. 1885–1963. WWI volunteer; nurse (WWI); literary critic. Middle class. **848**

Sitwell, Constance. 1886–s.l.1972. Military spouse; novelist; foreign resident (Ceylon, India); colonialist (India). Upper class. **850–852**

Sitwell, Dame Edith. 1887–1964. Poet; biographer; literary critic; novelist; anthologist; foreign resident (U.S.); physically handicapped. Single. Upper class. **853**

Slade, Madeline "Mirabehn." 1892–1982. Political activist; social reformer; foreign resident (India); religionist (Buddhist convert); teacher (crafts). Single. Upper class. **855**

Smedley, Constance. 1881–1941. Organizer of societies (women's clubs); organizer (theatrical); novelist; journalist; playwright; literary representative; suffragist; costume designer. Upper middle class. **857**

Smith, Dodie. 1896–1990. Novelist; playwright; children's author; WWI volunteer; foreign resident (U.S.). Upper middle class. **858–861**

Smith, Lesley. 1891–?. Scottish. Nurse (WWI); WWI volunteer. Upper class. **866**

Spring, Marion Ursula. 1890–d.a.1965. Secretary; advertising agent; biographer; garden designer. Middle class. **884–885**

Stark, Freya. 1893–1993. Journalist; travel writer; foreign resident (India, Middle East); photographer; intelligence agent; feminist. Upper middle class. **890–893**

Starkie, Enid. 1897–1970. Anglo-Irish. Academic; biographer; literary critic; academic's daughter. Single. Uppcr class. **894**

Steen, Marguerite. 1894–1975. Novelist; biographer; short storyist; playwright; actress (stage); teacher; teacher (dance); foreign resident (France, Spain). Single. Middle class. **897–898**

Stern, Gladys Bronwyn. 1890–1973. Novelist; playwright; screenwriter; feminist. Upper middle class. **900–903**

Stocks, Mary. 1891–1975. Academic; academic's spouse; school administrator; politician; member of Parliament; suffragist; philanthropist; social historian; economist; social service administrator; birth control activist; social reformer; broadcaster; justice of the peace. Widow. Upper middle class; awarded life peerage. **907–908**

Strange, Kathleen R. 1896–1968. Emigrant (Canada); farmer; pioneer; WWI administrator; journalist. Middle class. **918**

Tennent, Madge. 1889–1972. Artist (painter); headmistress; foreign resident (South Africa, New Zealand, South Pacific, Hawaii, U.S.); school founder; anticommunist; teacher (art); organizer (artistic). Upper middle class. **933**

Townshend, Zoe. c.1889–c.1930. Military spouse. Middle class. **953**

Trefusis, Violet. 1894–1972. Foreign resident (France); novelist; essayist; broadcaster; bisexual. Widow. Upper class. **954–955**

Tremlett, Mrs. Horace. c.1890–?. Colonialist (Africa); novelist; miner's spouse. Middle class. **957**

Treneer, Anne. 1891–?. Cornish. Literary critic; short storyist; biographer; poet; teacher. Single. Middle class. **958–959**

Uttley, Alison. 1884–1976. Children's author; novelist; suffragist; teacher; farm child; social historian. Rural farming class. **975–977**

Vidal, Lois. 1889–?. Clerk; domestic servant; journalist; mental patient; transient; clergyman's daughter; WWI volunteer; charitable volunteer; hotel worker; governess. Middle class. **983**

Vigers, Edith. 1893–?. Journalist; fashion designer; WWI volunteer; nurse (WWI); traveler (world). Single. Upper middle class. **984**

Walker, Laura Maple. 1896–s.l.1971. Nurse; midwife; charitable volunteer; nursemaid. Widow. Lower middle class. **987**

Ward, Maisie. 1889–1975. Publisher; biographer; religious/spiritual writer; historian; social reformer; religionist (Roman Catholic); nurse (WWI); preacher; teacher; textbook writer; public speaker; foreign resident (U.S.). Upper middle class. **996**

Wellesley, Dorothy Violet, Duchess of Wellington. 1889–1956. Poet; biographer; lesbian; traveler (Middle East); foreign resident (Italy); diplomat's spouse. Upper class; married into aristocracy. **1012**

West, Katharine. 1900–s.l.1971. Biographer; political writer. Upper middle class. **1014**

West, Dame Rebecca (pseud.; Cicily Fairfield). 1892–1983. Novelist; biographer; political writer; mistress; travel writer. Middle class. **1015**

Whish, Violet Evangeline. c.1886–?. Journalist; columnist; editor; children's author; WWII volunteer. Widow. Middle class. **1018**

Whitaker, Malachi (pseud.; Mary Whitaker). 1895–1975. Short storyist; military spouse. Lower middle class. **1019**

White, Antonia. 1899–1980. Novelist; journalist; translator; academic's daughter. Middle class. **1020**

Wilkinson, Ellen. 1891–1947. Politician; member of Parliament; cabinet minister; socialist; political writer; education activist; suffragist; Communist; pupil-teacher. Working class. **1025**

Woodward, Kathleen. 1896–1961. Social reformer; trade unionist; suffragist; seamstress; public speaker. Working class. **1029**

Woolf, Virginia. 1882–1941. Novelist; diarist; publisher; essayist; feminist; suffragist; bisexual. Upper middle class. **1030**

Wootton, Barbara, Baroness Wootton of Abinger. 1897–s.l.1960. Economist; magistrate; government administrator; feminist; socialist; broadcaster; novelist; short storyist; crime writer; WWI volunteer; academic; academic's daughter; public speaker; traveler (world). Middle class; awarded life peerage. **1031**

Wylie, Ida Alexa Ross. 1887–1959. Australian. Novelist; short storyist; screenwriter; suffragist, militant; feminist; foreign resident (U.S.); lesbian. Middle class. **1034**

Wynne, France. c.1885–d.a.1946. Irish. Religionist (Roman Catholic convert); political activist; artist (painter). Widow. Middle class. **1035–1036**

XI. 1901–1920

Ackland, Valentine. 1906–1969. Poet; short storyist; religionist (Roman Catholic convert); lesbian; cross-dresser; Communist. Divorcée. Upper middle class. **2**

Ali, Beatrice. c.1916–s.l.1975. Domestic servant; prison inmate. Working class; married person of different race. **5**

Allinson, Francesca. 1902–?. Academic's daughter. Single. Middle class. **9**

Argall, Phyllis. 1910–?. Canadian. Journalist; foreign correspondent; prisoner of war; missionary; foreign resident (Japan). Middle class. **42**

Athill, Diana. 1918–?. Publisher. Single. Upper class. **55**

Bailey, Doris M. 1916–?. Clerk; teacher (Sunday school). Working class. **62**

Balderson, Eileen. 1916–s.l.1982. Domestic servant. Working class. **65**

Barnett, Lady Isobel Morag. 1918–s.l.1973. Scottish. Physician; broadcaster; politician (mayor); politician's spouse; public speaker; physician's daughter. Upper middle class; married into upper class. **75**

Barraud, Enid. c.1908–?. WWII volunteer; farm laborer; clerk. Single. Lower middle class. **77**

Batten, Jean Gardner. 1909–?. New Zealander. Aviator. Single. Middle class. **82**

Beechey, Winifred. c.1911–s.l.1991. Shopkeeper; secretary. Lower middle class. **89**

Bell, Mary Hayley. 1914–s.l.1995. Born in China. Actress (stage); playwright; novelist; foreign resident (China). Middle class. **90**

Bertenshaw, Mary. 1904–s.l.1991. Factory worker. Working class. **95**

Bielenberg, Christabel. 1909–s.l.1971. Foreign resident (Germany); anti-Nazi activist. Upper class; married into foreign culture. **105**

anti-Communist; political activist; weaver; foreign resident (Russia). Working class. **646**
Meynell, Dame Alix. 1903–s.l.1988. Political activist; feminist; civil servant; government administrator; political appointee; utilities administrator; bisexual. Middle class. **653**
Mitford, the Hon. Jessica. 1917–1996. Political writer; journalist; emigrant (U.S.); socialist; pacifist; foreign resident (France); saleswoman; restaurant worker; political activist. Aristocracy. **665**
Mortimer, Penelope. 1918–?. Welsh. Novelist; journalist; playwright; secretary; advice writer; clergyman's daughter. Divorcée. Middle class. **680–681**
Munday, Madeleine C. c.1910–?. Travel writer; journalist; teacher; foreign resident (China); foreign correspondent. Single. Middle class. **684**
Murry, Mary Middleton. 1900–s.l.1957. Pacifist. Widow. Middle class. **688**
Napier, Priscilla. 1908–s.l.1973. Military spouse; foreign resident (Egypt); family historian; poet. Middle class. **691**
Nicholson, Phyllis. c.1918–?. Military spouse; farmer; WWII volunteer; foreign resident (India, Far East); farm child; family historian; academic's daughter. Middle class. **702–705**
Noakes, Daisy. 1908–?. Domestic servant. Working class. **708–709**
Oake, Mary Elisabeth. c.1910–?. Civil servant's spouse; colonialist (Africa); foreign resident (France, Switzerland). Middle class. **714**
Oman, Elsie. 1904–?. Domestic servant; entrepreneur; hotel worker; factory worker. Working class. **721**
Packer, Joy, Lady. 1905–1977. South African. Military spouse; journalist; broadcaster; propaganda writer; physician's daughter. Upper middle class. **725–726**
Pawley, Tinko. 1913–?. Born in China. Physician's daughter; foreign resident (China); kidnap victim. Middle class. **737**
Pinnegar, Eira Gwynneth. c.1910–?. Welsh. Religionist (Methodist); singer (concerts, popular); spiritualist. Middle class. **756**
Powell, Margaret. 1907–1984. Domestic servant; culinary author. Working class. **766–770**
Raine, Kathleen. 1908–s.l.1993. Poet; literary critic; editor; translator; academic; academic's spouse. Divorcée. Middle class. **776–778**
Rennie, Jean. 1906–s.l.1977. Scottish. Domestic servant; cook; dance hostess; singer (concerts, popular); actress (film). Working class. **782**
Ring, Elizabeth. 1912–s.l.1986. Bookkeeper; clerk; journalist. Lower middle class. **791**
Rogers, Rose Annie. c.1902–?. Missionary (Tristan da Cunha); teacher; clergyman's spouse. Widow. Lower middle class. **800**
Salusbury, Hilda Ann. 1906–s.l.1988. Nurse (maternity); midwife; teacher; governess. Widow. Lower middle class. **817**
Scannell, Dorothy. 1911–s.l.1979. Businesswoman; shopkeeper; insurance agent; clerk; secretary; teacher (Sunday school). Working class. **822–824**
Seldon, Marjorie. 1919–?. Publisher's assistant; academic's spouse. Upper middle class. **831**
Shears, Sarah. c.1910–?. Domestic servant. Single. Working class. **837**
Shute, Nerina. 1908–s.l.1995. Journalist; biographer; literary critic; novelist; advertising executive; playwright; secretary; charitable volunteer; foreign resident (U.S.). Divorcée. Upper class. **844**
Slater, Lillian. 1907–s.l.1984. Child. Lower middle class. **856**
Smith, Lady Eleanor Furneaux. 1902–1945. Novelist; journalist; film critic; traveler (Europe, U.S.). Single. Aristocracy. **862**
Smith, Ellen. 1909–s.l.1982. Farmer; dressmaker; businesswoman; factory worker. Rural farming class. **864–865**

Spencer-Churchill, Frances Laura, Duchess of Marlborough. 1915–1990. Society woman; businesswoman; horsewoman; foreign resident (New Zealand); nurse (WWII). Widow. Aristocracy. **882**

Spencer-Knott, Justina. c.1910–?. Farmer; journalist; foreign resident (Sierra Leone, South Africa); civil servant's spouse. Middle class. **883**

Stack, Prunella. 1914–s.l.1988. Anglo-Indian. Teacher (physical fitness); organizer of societies (women's clubs); biographer; foreign resident (South Africa); women's issues author; feminist; editor. Widow. Middle class. **888**

Stott, (Charlotte) Mary. 1907–s.l.1992. Journalist; editor; feminist; pacifist. Widow. Middle class. **916**

Stride, Louie. 1907–?. Domestic servant; telephone operator; waitress; factory worker; hotel worker. Working class. **920**

Summerskill, Edith, Baroness Summerskill. 1901–1980. Physician; social reformer; politician; government administrator; member of Parliament; feminist; political activist; physician's daughter. Upper middle class; awarded life peerage. **924**

Teal, Gladys. 1913–s.l.1976. Paid companion; laundry manager; news agent; restaurant manager. Working class. **932**

Thomas, (Helen Elizabeth) Myfanwy. 1910–?. Poet's daughter; editor; secretary. Middle class. **939**

Thorp, (Margery) Ellen. 1906–s.l.1977. Born in Burma. Historian; short storyist; novelist; foreign resident (Burma). Upper middle class. **943**

Tibble, Anne. 1905–1980. Biographer; poet; novelist; academic's spouse. Rural laboring class; married into upper middle class. **944–946**

Todd, Marjory. c.1900–s.l.1960. Civil servant; prison service officer; domestic servant; tutor; secretary. Working class. **947**

Walsh, Jane. 1905–?. Journalist; mill worker. Widow. Working class. **989**

Weir, Molly. 1920–s.l.1989. Actress (comic, radio); broadcaster; chorus girl; miscellaneous writer; secretary. Working class. **1006–1011**

Wethered, Joyce. 1901–s.l.1973. Golfer. Middle class. **1017**

Whitehouse, Mary. 1910–s.l.1971. Anti-pornography activist; social reformer; charitable volunteer; teacher (Sunday school); teacher (art). Middle class. **1024**

Identification Index

Subject Index

Bracketed numbers refer to the autobiographers' entries.

About the Author and Staff

Barbara Penny Kanner, project director and author, is a continuing research scholar at the UCLA Center for the Study of Women and a Visiting Scholar in the UCLA Department of History. She is also adjunct professor of history at Occidental College. Her publications include the three-volume *Women in English Social History, 1800–1914*; *Women in England from Anglo-Saxon Times to the Present* and "Women of England in a Century of Social Change."

Jane Decker is a doctoral student in the UCLA Department of English. A specialist in Victorian studies, she has published three articles and has taught numerous composition and literature courses at UCLA. She is currently preparing her dissertation on the representation of animals in nineteenth-century British literature.

Penelope Moffet, past senior editor at the UCLA Center for the Study of Women, is a poet and writer whose work has appeared in the Los Angeles*Times, Publishers Weekly,* the *Missouri Review,* and other publications. Her first collection of poetry, *Keeping Still,* was published in 1995.

Anne-Marie Poole is a doctoral candidate in the UCLA Department of History with a major research field in modern France. She is completing her dissertation, "An Impossible Quest for Identity: San Simonian Women and the Rest of Their World(s), Paris 1832–34."

Margaret Robe Summitt earned her doctorate in English literature at UCLA, where she taught in the English writing program. She is working on a book based on her dissertation, "Conceiving a Self in Autobiography by Women: Virginia Woolf, Violette Leduc, and Anaïs Nin."

Rhona Zaid earned her Ph.D. in early modern European history at UCLA, writing a dissertation entitled "Popular Discontent and Unsung Heroes: The Holy Office of the Inquisition in Cuenca, 1550–1590." She has taught courses in history and women's studies at California State University, Los Angeles.